MW01618276

Graphis Inc. is committed to celebrating exceptional work in Design, Advertising, Photography, & Art/Illustration internationally.

Published by **Graphis** | Publisher & Creative Director: **B. Martin Pedersen**

Chief Visionary Officer: **Patti Judd** | Design Director: **Hee Ra Kim** | Senior Designer: **Hie Won Sohn** | Associate Editor: **Colleen Boyd**

Interns: **Haley Pero-Favazzo, Rachel Liza Raphy, Kara Roda, Wen Wang, Sophie Ward**

Account/Production: **Bianca Barnes**

Graphis Design Annual 2024

Published by:
Graphis Inc.
389 Fifth Avenue, Suite 1105
New York, NY 10016
Phone: 212-532-9387
www.graphis.com
help@graphis.com

ISBN 13: 978-1-954632-24-0

We extend our heartfelt thanks to the international contributors who have made it possible to publish a wide spectrum of the best work in Design, Advertising, Photography, and Art/Illustration.
Anyone is welcome to submit work at www.graphis.com.

Printed in China

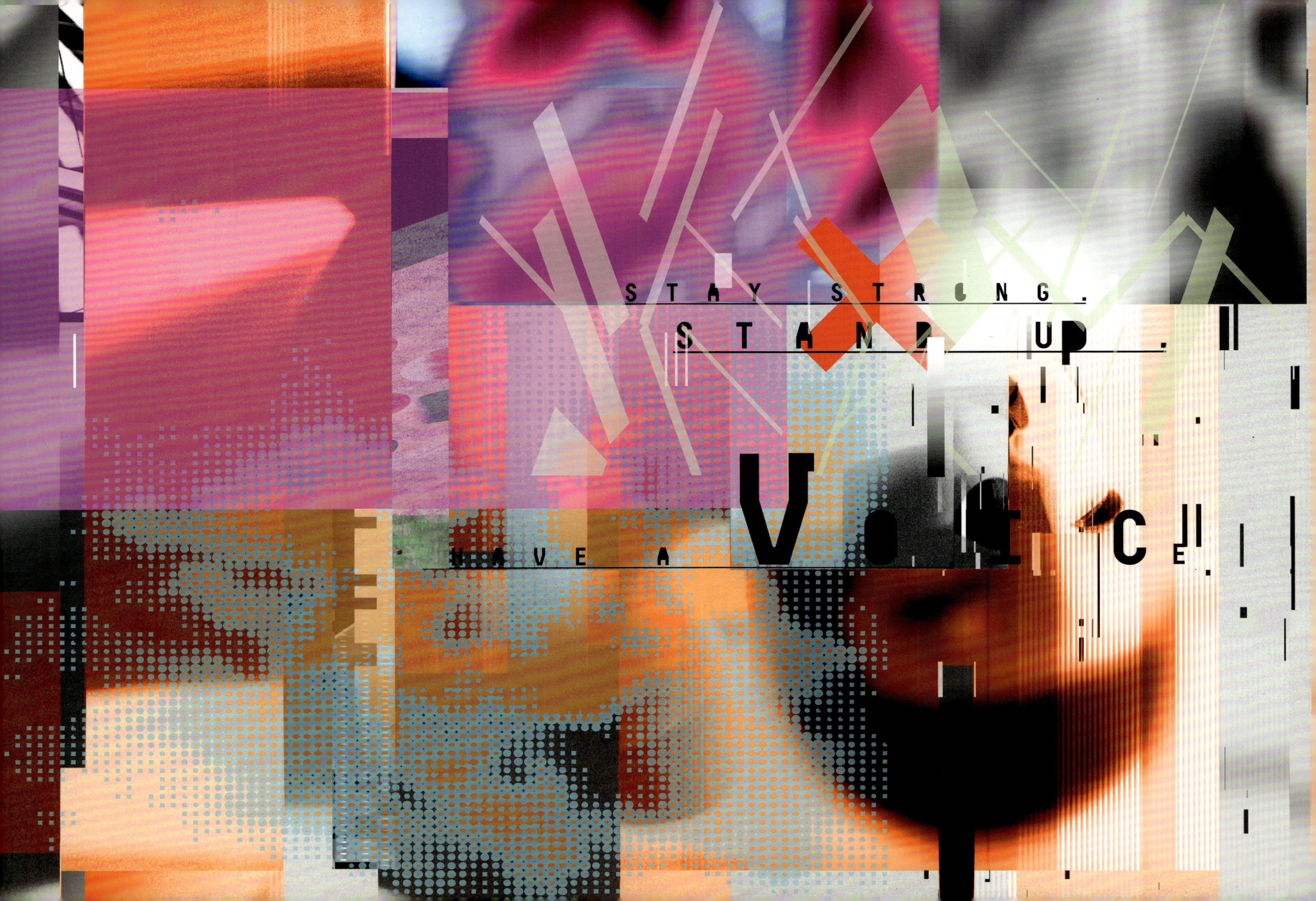
STAY STRONG.
STAND UP.
HAVE A VOICE

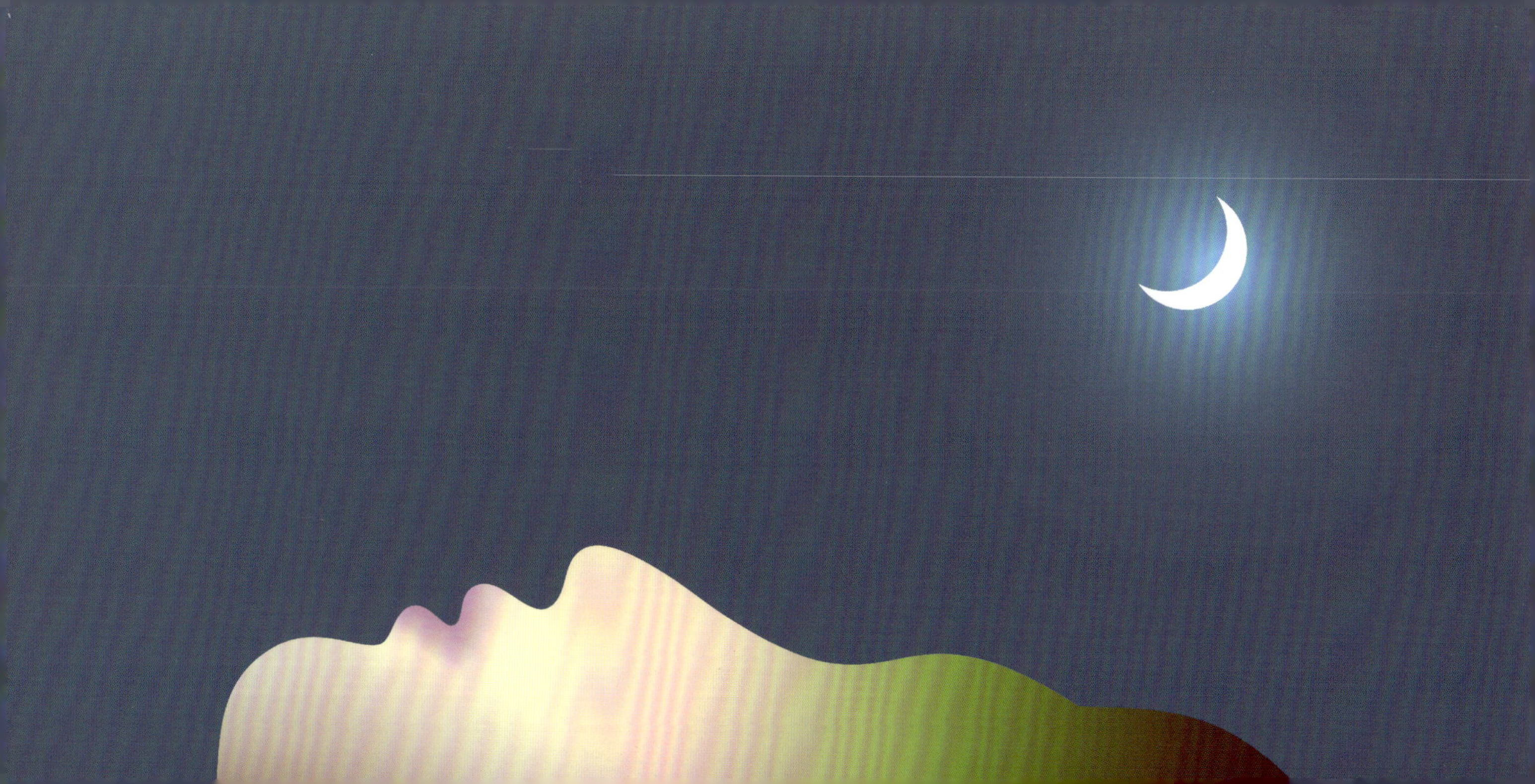

Contents

Page 3: *"Stay Strong, Stand Up, Have a Voice,"* by Studio Eduard Cehovin
Page 4: *"Jeju Evening,"* by May & Co.

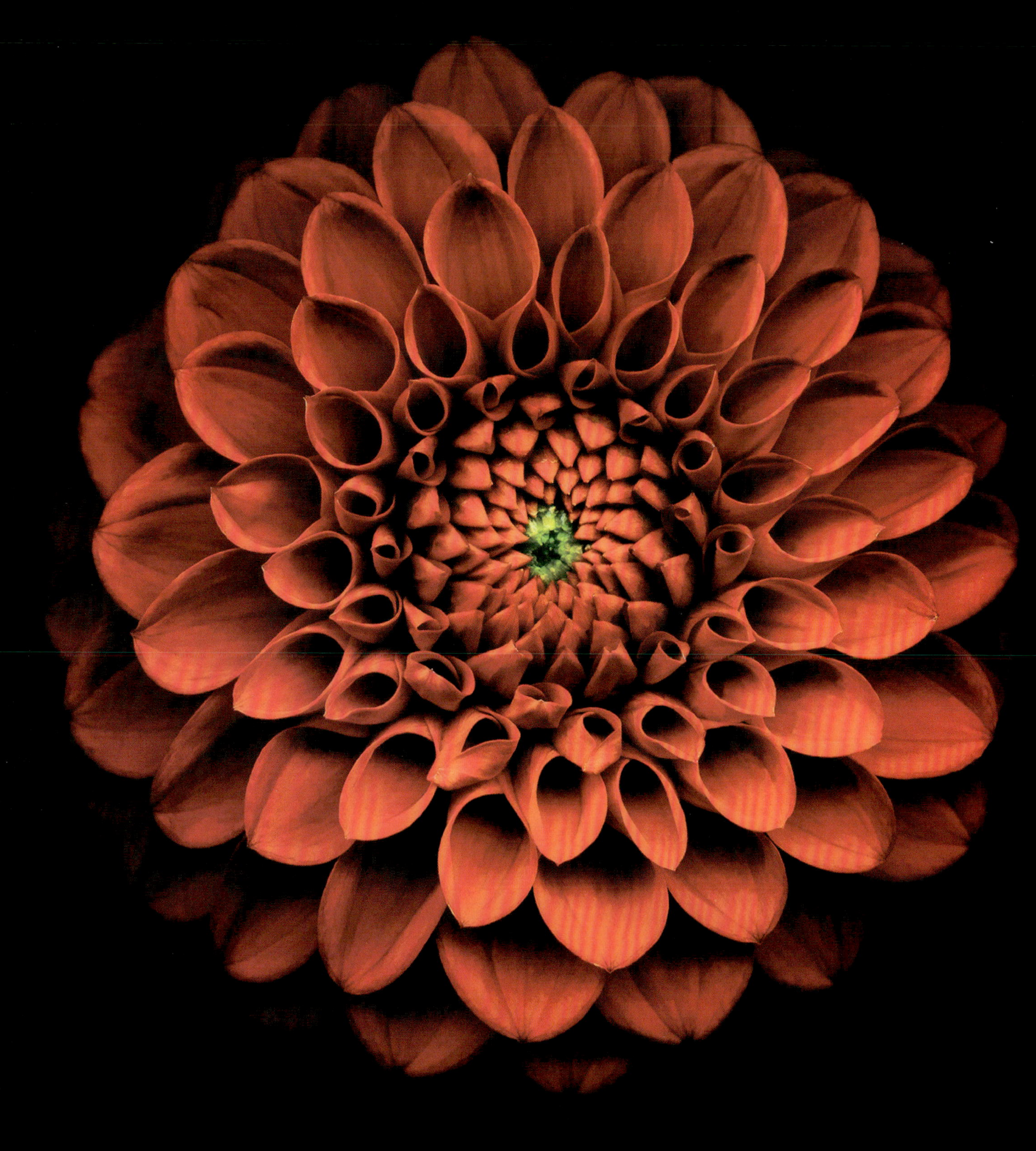

AMERICAS

Byron Barton
American Illustrator & Writer
1930 – 2023

Michael Berlyn
American Video Game Designer & Writer
1949 – 2023

Harry Bentley Bradley
American Car & Toy Car Designer
1939 – 2023

Gordon Bradt
American Art Designer
1924 – 2022

Albert Brenner
American Production Designer
1926 – 2022

Fernando Campana
Brazilian Designer
1961 – 2022

Rolly Crump
American Designer & Animator
1930 – 2023

Alice Estes Davis
American Costume Designer
1929 – 2022

Jane Davis Doggett
American Graphic Designer
1929 – 2023

Tyrone Flint
American Fashion Designer
1966 – 2022

Paul Giambarba
American Graphic Designer & Cartoonist
1928 – 2023

Carin Goldberg
American Graphic Designer
1953 – 2023

Peter Good
American Graphic Designer
1943 – 2023

James "Jim" Howard
American Fashion Illustrator
1931 – 2023

John Iacovelli
American Theater Designer
1959 – 2023

Frank Kozik
American Graphic Designer & Artist
1962 – 2023

Eugene Lee
American Set Designer
1939 – 2023

Alphonse Mattia
American Furniture Designer
1947 – 2023

Bruce McCall
Canadian Illustrator & Author
1935 – 2023

Albert Nipon
American Fashion Designer
1927 – 2022

Robert L. Peters
Canadian Graphic Designer
1954 – 2023

Hedda Kleinfeld Schachter
Austrian-American Wedding Dress Designer & Co-founder of Kleinfeld Bridal
1924 – 2023

Ruth Adler Schnee
German-American Textile & Interior Designer
1923 – 2023

Amparín Serrano
Mexican Graphic Designer
1965 – 2022

Anton Sovetov
Russian-American Graphic Designer
1978 – 2022

Jonathan M. Thompson
American Game Designer
1971 – 2023

Rafael Viñoly
Uruguayan Architect
1944 – 2023

José Vivas
Venezuelan Architect
1928 – 2022

Robin Wagner
American Set Designer
1922 – 2023

Eric Lloyd Wright
American Architect
1929 – 2023

EUROPE & AFRICA

Renato Balestra
Italian Fashion Designer
1924 – 2022

Marc Berthier
French Designer & Architect
1935 – 2022

Erik Rud Brandt
Danish Fashion Designer
1943 – 2023

Edwin Chiloba
Kenyan Fashion Designer
1997 – 2023

Antonio D'Amico
Italian Fashion Designer
1959 – 2022

Ambra Danon
Italian Costume Designer
1948 – 2023

John Godwin
British-Nigerian Architect
1928 – 2023

Rein Jansma
Dutch Architect
1959 – 2023

John Chris Jones
Welsh Design Researcher
1927 – 2022

Tom Karen
Austrian-British Industrial Designer
1926 – 2022

Charles Knode
British Costume Designer
1942 – 2023

Serge Laget
French Board Game Designer
1959 – 2023

Ivan Moscovich
Yugoslav-Dutch Toy & Game Designer
1926 – 2023

Shyqri Nimani
Albanian Graphic Designer
1941 – 2023

Timothy O'Brien
British Theater Designer
1929 – 2022

Kevin O'Neill
British Comic Book Illustrator
1953 – 2022

Valérie Oka
Ivorian Designer & Artist
1967 – 2023

Franc' Pairon
Belgian Fashion Designer
1949 – 2023

Gunilla Palmstierna-Weiss
Swedish Costume Designer
1928 – 2022

Stephan Pelger
Romanian Fashion Designer
1979 – 2023

Claude Perchat
French Graphic Designer & Illustrator
1952 – 2022

Dame Barbara Mary Quant
British Fashion Designer
1930 – 2023

Paco Rabanne
Spanish Fashion Designer
1934 – 2023

Norman Reynolds
British Production Designer
1934 – 2023

Gerald Rose
Chinese-British Illustrator
1935 – 2023

Konstantinos Staikos
Greek Architect & Historian
1943 – 2023

Klaus Teuber
German Board Game Designer
1952 – 2023

Virginia von Fürstenberg
Italian Fashion Designer, Artist, & Poet
1974 – 2023

Dame Vivienne Westwood
British Fashion Designer
1941 – 2022

Valentin Yudashkin
Russian Fashion Designer
1963 – 2023

Vyacheslav Zaitsev
Russian Fashion Designer, Theatrical Costume Designer, Graphic Artist, & Painter
1938 – 2023

ASIA & OCEANIA

B.V. Doshi
Indian Architect
1927 – 2023

Audrey Eagle
New Zealand Botanical Illustrator
1925 – 2022

Christian Espiritu
Filipino Fashion Designer
1934 – 2023

Iraj Etesam
Iranian Architect
1931 – 2022

Kim Jung Gi
South Korean Illustrator & Comics Artist
1975 – 2022

Mubasshar Hussein
Bangladeshi Architect & Activist
1943 – 2023

Arata Isozaki
Japanese Architect & Urban Planner
1931 – 2022

Raymond Jones
Australian Architect
1925 – 2022

William S.W. Lim
Singaporean Architect
1932 – 2023

Edgar Madamba
Filipino Fashion Designer
1950 – 2023

Hanae Mori
Japanese Fashion Designer
1926 – 2022

Peter Muller
Australian Architect
1927 – 2023

Iraj Kalantari Taleghani
Iranian Architect
1937 – 2023

Sir Miles Warren
New Zealand Architect
1929 – 2022

Guan Zhaoye
Chinese Architect
1929 – 2022

Opposite page: *"100th Anniversary KOMORI 2023 Calendar,"* by Toppan Inc.

THE AMERICAS

Bata Shoe Museum
www.batashoemuseum.ca
327 Bloor St. W
Toronto, ON M5S 1W7
Canada
Tel +1 416 979 7799

Brooklyn Museum
www.brooklynmuseum.org
200 E. Parkway
Brooklyn, NY 11238
United States
Tel +1 718 638 5000

Chicago Athenaeum
www.chi-athenaeum.org
601 S. Prospect St.
Galena, IL 61036
United States
Tel +1 815 777 4444

Color Factory
www.colorfactory.co
251 Spring St.
New York, NY 10013
United States
Tel +1 347 378 4071

Contemporary Arts Museum Houston
www.camh.org
5216 Montrose Blvd.
Houston, TX 77006
United States
Tel +1 713 284 8250

Design Museum of Chicago
www.designchicago.org
72 E. Randolph St.
Chicago, IL 60601
United States
Tel +1 312 894 6263

Goldstein Museum of Design
www.design.umn.edu/goldstein-museum-design
241 McNeal Hall, 1985 Buford Ave.
St. Paul, MN 55108
United States
Tel +1 612 624 7434

Grand Rapids Art Museum
www.artmuseumgr.org
101 Monroe Center St. NW
Grand Rapids, MI 49503
United States
Tel +1 616 831 1000

IK Lab
www.sferik.art
Carretera Tulum-Punta Allen KM 5
Zona Hotelera, 77780 Tulum, Q.R.
Mexico
info@sferik.art

Inhotim Institute
www.inhotim.org.br
Rua B, 20 Fazenda Inhotim
Brumadinho - MG 35460-000
Brazil
Tel +55 31 3571 9700

Los Angeles County Museum of Art
www.lacma.org
5905 Wilshire Blvd.
Los Angeles, CA 90036
United States
Tel +1 323 857 6000

MUMEDI
www.mumedi.mx
Av Francisco I. Madero 74
Centro Histórico de la Cdad. de México
Centro, Cuauhtémoc,
06000 Ciudad de México, CDMX
Mexico
Tel +52 55 5510 8609

Museo de Arte Latino Americano de Buenos Aires
www.malba.org.ar
Av. Pres. Figueroa Alcorta 3415
Buenos Aires CABA C1425CLA
Argentina
Tel +54 11 4808 6500

Museo Nacional de Bellas Artes
www.bellasartes.gob.ar
Av. del Libertador 1473
Buenos Aires
Argentina
Tel +54 11 5288 9900

Museu Oscar Niemeyer
www.museuoscarniemeyer.org.br
R. Mal. Hermes, 999 - Centro Cívico
Curitiba - PR 80530-230
Brazil
Tel +55 41 3350-4400

Museum of Arts & Design
www.madmuseum.org
2 Columbus Circle
New York, NY 10023
United States
Tel +1 212 299 7777

Museum of California Design
www.mocad.org
361 N. Orange Dr.
Los Angeles, CA 90036
United States
Tel +1 323 930 2700

Museum of Contemporary Art
www.moca.ca
952 Queen St. W
Toronto, ON M6J 1G8
Canada
Tel +1 416 395 0067

Museum of Latin American Art
www.molaa.org
628 Alamitos Ave.
Long Beach, CA 90802
United States
Tel +1 562 437 1689

Museum of Modern Art
www.moma.org
11 W. 53rd St.
New York, NY 10019
United States
Tel +1 212 708 9400

National Gallery of Canada
www.gallery.ca
380 Sussex Dr.
Ottawa, ON K1N 9N4
Canada
Tel +1 613 990 1985

National Museum of American Illustration
www.americanillustration.org
492 Bellevue Ave.
Newport, RI 02840
United States
Tel +1 401 851 8949

Noguchi Museum
www.noguchi.org
9-01 33rd Road
Long Island City, NY 11106
United States
Tel +1 718 204 7088

Pasadena Museum of California Art
www.pmcaonline.org
490 E. Union St.
Pasadena, CA 91101
United States
Tel +1 626 568 3665

Poster House
www.posterhouse.org
119 W. 23rd St.
New York, NY 10011
United States
Tel +1 917 722 2439

Pinacoteca do Estado de São Paulo
www.pinacoteca.org.br
Praça da Luz, 2 - Luz
São Paulo 01120-010
Brazil
Tel +55 11 3324 1000

Renwick Gallery
www.americanart.si.edu/visit/renwick
Pennsylvania Ave., 17th St. NW
Washington, DC 20006
United States
Tel +1 202 633 7970

Royal Ontario Museum
www.rom.on.ca
100 Queens Park
Toronto, ON M5S 2C6
Canada
Tel +1 416 586 8000

Solomon R. Guggenheim Museum
www.guggenheim.org
1071 5th Ave.
New York, NY 10128
United States
Tel +1 212 423 3500

Telfair Museums
www.telfair.org
207 W. York St.
Savannah, GA 31401
United States
Tel +1 912 790 8800

The Skyscraper Museum
www.skyscraper.org
39 Battery Place
New York, NY 10280
United States
Tel +1 212 968 1961

Whitney Museum of American Art
www.whitney.org
99 Gansevoort St.
New York, NY 10014
United States
Tel +1 212 570 3600

Wolfsonian-FIU
www.wolfsonian.org
1001 Washington Ave.
Miami Beach, FL
United States
Tel +1 305 531 1001

EUROPE AND AFRICA

Amos Rex Art Museum
www.amosrex.fi
Mannerheimintie 22–24
Helsinki 00100
Finland
Tel +358 9 6844 460

Bauhaus Archive Museum of Design
www.bauhaus.de
Klingelhöferstraße 14
Berlin 10785
Germany
Tel +49 30 254 0020

Danish Museum of Art & Design
www.designmuseum.dk
Bredgade 68
1260 Kobenhavn K
Denmark
Tel +33 18 56 56

Designmuseo
www.designmuseum.fi
Korkeavuorenkatu 23
Helsinki 00130
Finland
Tel +358 09 622 0540

Design Museum Gent
www.designmuseumgent.be
Jan Breydelstraat 5
Gent 9000
Belgium
Tel +32 9 267 99 99

Design Museum Helsinki
www.designmuseum.fi
Korkeavuorenkatu 23
Helsinki 00130
Finland
Tel +358 9 6220 540

Fondazione Prada
www.fondazioneprada.org
L.go Isarco, 2
Milano MI 20139
Italy
Tel +39 02 5666 2611

Furniture Museum Vienna
www.moebelmuseumwien.at
Andreasgasse 7
Wien 1070
Austria
Tel +43 1 524 3357

Groninger Museum
www.groningermuseum.nl
Museumeiland 1
Groningen ME 9711
Netherlands
Tel +31 50 3 666 555

Irish Museum of Modern Art
www.imma.ie
Military Road, Kilmainham
Dublin 8
Ireland
Tel +353 1 612 9900

Kunsthaus Zürich
www.kunsthaus.ch
Heim-Platz 1
Zurich 8001
Switzerland
Tel +41 044 253 84 84

Lahti City Museum
www.lahdenmuseot.fi
Urheilukeskus,
Salpausselänkatu 8
Lahti 15110
Finland
Tel +358 50 398 5523

MAK
www.mak.at
Stubenring 5
Wien 1010
Austria
Tel +43 1 711360

Moco Museum
www.mocomuseum.com
Honthorststraat 20
Amsterdam DE 1071
Netherlands
Tel +31 20 370 1997

Moomin Museum
www.muumimuseo.fi
Tampere-talo Oy,
Yliopistonkatu 55
Tampere 33100
Finland
Tel +358 3 2434 111

MUDE
www.mude.pt
R. Augusta 24
Lisboa 1100-053
Portugal
Tel +351 21 817 1892

Musée des Arts Décoratifs
www.madparis.fr
107 Rue de Rivoli
Paris 75001
France
Tel +33 1 44 55 57 50

Musée Tomi Ungerer Center
www.musees.strasbourg.eu/
musee-tomi-ungerer
2 Av. de la Marseillaise
Strasbourg 67000
France
Tel +33 3 68 98 50 00

Museo ABC
www.museo.abc.es
C. de Amaniel, 29
Madrid 28015
Spain
Tel +34 917 588 379

Museum aan de Stroom
www.mas.be
Hanzestedenplaats 1
Antwerpen 2000
Belgium
Tel +32 3 338 44 00

Museum für Gestaltung Zürich
www.museum-gestaltung.ch
Toni-Areal,
Pfingstweidstrasse 96
Zurich 8005
Switzerland
Tel +41 43 446 67 67

Museum of Architecture & Design
www.mao.si
Pot Na Fuzine 2
Ljubljana 1000
Slovenia
Tel +386 01 548 42 70

Museum of Decorative Arts
www.upm.cz
17. Listopadu 2
Josefov 110 00
Czech Republic
Tel +420 778 543 901

Museum of Domestic Design & Architecture
www.moda.mdx.ac.uk
Middlesex University, 9 Blvd. Dr.
Beaufort Park, London NW9 5HF
United Kingdom
Tel +44 20 8411 5244

Museum of the Home
www.museumofthehome.org.uk
136 Kingsland Road
London, E2 8EA
United Kingdom
Tel +44 20 7739 9893

Rijksmuseum
www.rijksmuseum.nl
Jan Luijkenstraat 1
Amsterdam CJ 1071
Netherlands
Tel +31 20 674 7000

Sir John Soane's Museum
www.soane.org
13 Lincoln's Inn Fields
London, WC2A 3BP
United Kingdom
Tel +44 020 7405 2107

Stedelijk Museum Amsterdam
www.stedelijk.nl
Museumplein 10
Amsterdam DJ 1071
Netherlands
Tel +31 20 573 2911

The Design Museum
www.designmuseum.org
224-238 Kensington High St.
London, W8 6AG
United Kingdom
Tel +44 20 3862 5900

The MAXXI Museum
www.maxxi.art
Via Guido Reni 4a
Roma RM 00196
Italy
Tel +39 06 320 1954

Wellcome Collection
www.wellcomecollection.org
183 Euston Road
London, NW1 2BE
United Kingdom
Tel +44 20 7611 2222

Wits Art Museum
www.wits.ac.za
Cnr Jorissen & Bertha St.
Johannesburg 2001
South Africa
Tel +27 11 717 1365

Zeitz Museum of Contemporary Art
www.zeitzmocaa.museum
V&A Waterfront Silo District, S.
Arm Road
Waterfront, Cape Town 8001
South Africa
Tel +27 87 350 4777

ASIA AND OCEANIA

Arte Museum
www.en.artemuseum.com
1503 Eoeum-ri 478 Eorimbi-ro
Aewol-eup, Jeju, Jeju-do
South Korea
Tel +82 064 799 9009

Bunka Gakuen Costume Museum
www.museum.bunka.ac.jp
3 Chome-22 Yoyogi
Shibuya City, Tokyo 151-0053
Japan
Tel +81 3 3299 2387

Dongdaemun Design Plaza
www.ddp.or.kr
281 Eulji-ro
Jung-gu, Seoul
South Korea
Tel +82 2 2153 0000

Elgiz Museum
www.elgizmuseum.org
Maslak Mahallesi,
Maslak Meydan Sk. Beybi Giz
Plaza
Sarıyer 34485
Turkey
Tel +90 212 290 25 25

Ghibli Museum
www.ghibli-museum.jp
1 Chome-1-83 Shimorenjaku
Mitaka, Tokyo 181-0013
Japan
Tel +81 570 055 777

Mori Building Digital Art Museum
www.teamlab.art
1 Chome-3-8 Odaiba Palette
Town 2F
Aomi, Koto City, Tokyo 135-0064
Japan
Tel +81 3 6368 4292

Museum of Contemporary Art Australia
www.mca.com.au
140 George St.
The Rocks, NSW 2000
Australia
Tel +61 2 9245 2400

Museum of Islamic Art
www.mia.org.qa
Al Corniche St.
Doha
Qatar
Tel +974 4422 4444

Museum Meiji-mura
www.meijimura.com
Uchiyama, 1
Aichi, Inuyama 484-0000
Japan
Tel +81 0568 67 0314

National Art Museum of China
www.namoc.org
1 Wusidajie
Dongcheng, Beijing 100875
China
Tel +86 10 6400 1476

National Gallery of Indonesia
www.gni.kemdikbud.go.id
Jl. Medan Merdeka Tim. No.14,
RT.6/RW.1
Gambir, Kecamatan Gambir, Kota
Jakarta Pusat
Daerah Khusus Ibukota Jakarta
10110
Indonesia
Tel +62 21 381 3021

National Gallery of Victoria
www.ngv.vic.gov.au
180 St. Kilda Road
Melbourne, VIC 3006
Australia
Tel +61 3 8620 2222

Powerhouse Museum
www.powerhouse.com.au
500 Harris St.
Ultimo, NSW 2007
Australia
Tel +61 2 9217 0111

ADDITIONAL MUSEUMS:
If you are a museum that collects posters and are not listed above, please contact us for inclusion in our next Annual at help@graphis.com.

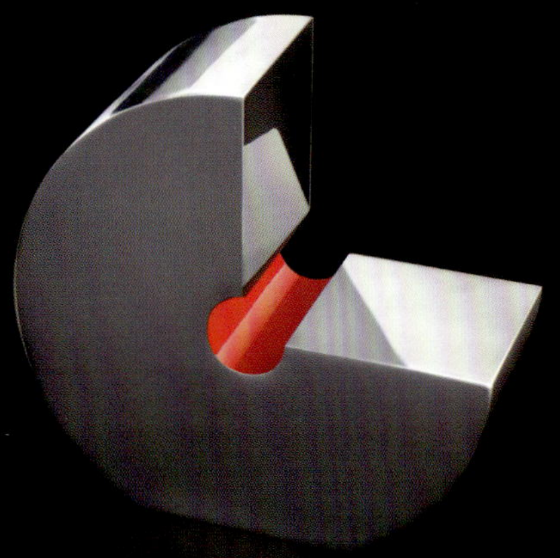

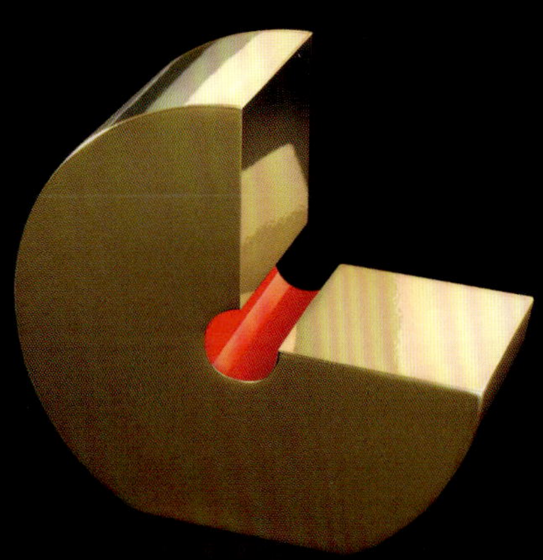

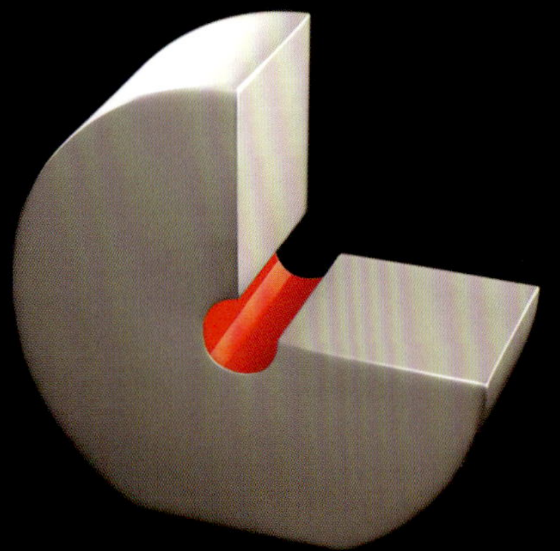

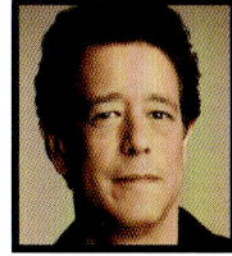

Antonio Alcalá | Studio A | Designer, Art Director, Founder, & Co-owner

Biography: Antonio Alcalá is the founder and co-owner of Studio A, a design practice working with museums and art institutions. He also art directs and designs postage stamps for the United States Postal Service and teaches/lectures at schools such as the Corcoran College of the Arts and Design, SVA, Pratt, and MICA. Alcalá's work and contributions to the field of graphic design were recognized with his selection as a 2008 AIGA Fellow. His designs are represented in the AIGA Design Archives, the National Postal Museum, and the Library of Congress's permanent collection of graphic design. Alcalá graduated from Yale University with a BA in history and from the Yale School of Art with an MFA in graphic design. He lives with his wife in Alexandria, Virginia.

Commentary: What a pleasure (and honor) it was to help judge this year's entries. There are strong, thoughtful, and beautiful works being produced around the globe. Many entries impress with their careful attention to typography, color, composition, and the content of their message. Notable designs with experimental approaches are the minority but stand out with their energy and risk-taking. Overall, the entries demonstrate that quality design can be created for both start-ups and giant corporations, with both small and large budgets, and with social and commercial intentions. The work, as a whole, is inspirational.

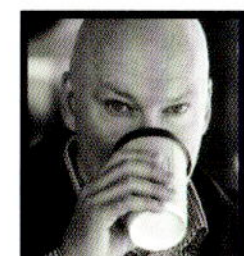

Roger Archbold | Roger Archbold | Designer & Art Director

Biography: Thoughtful and authentic ideas are what Roger lives for. Establishing his own design practice in Melbourne, Australia, over 20 years ago, Roger has created compelling brand solutions for corporate and public sector clients, as well as helping to establish many new not-for-profit brands. After graduating with a distinction in graphic design from La Trobe University, he has worked for over 30 years as a designer and art director. Roger is a professional member of the Australian Graphic Design Association.

Commentary: Graphis remains, as it has been for decades, the preeminent exponent of good design, and it was a privilege to be invited to be on the jury for the 2024 Graphis Design Awards. It was also encouraging to see the very high standard of submissions this year. There were, in particular, many beautiful and thoughtful solutions in the packaging category from both individual designers and larger design firms and departments.

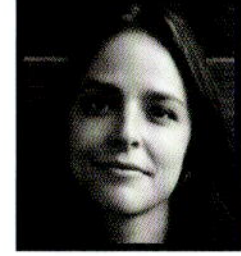

Maria Alma Guede | Ralph Appelbaum Associates | Graphic Designer

Biography: Maria Alma is a graphic designer from Mexico City who is especially interested in using design to translate social issues into unique experiences that inspire change. She currently works for Ralph Appelbaum Associates, where she has contributed to multiple exhibition design projects for national and international clients, including the National Air and Space Museum in Washington, DC, the International African American Museum in South Carolina, and the Obama Presidential Center in Chicago. Maria Alma graduated with honors from Pratt Institute, where she earned a BFA in communications design with minors in art history and museum practices.

Commentary: The projects presented at Graphis are a clear example of how designers leave their hearts in each project they work on. It was very inspiring to take a look at all the entries and be able to appreciate the variety of graphic techniques, color palettes, and typographic treatments that our generation of designers is bringing to the table.

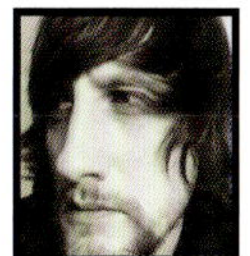

Mike Hughes | Mike Hughes Creative Direction + Design | Creative Director, Art Director, & Designer

Biography: Mike Hughes is a multi-award-winning creative director, art director, and designer with over 25 years of experience. He has lent his creative talents to brands such as Adidas, Converse, MINI, and Fiat. He is also an avid writer and musician who has penned screenplays and launched his own band, Mount Deed. He is a co-founder/executive creative director of the fashion and design magazine *ROTOR*. He is from the US and currently resides in Montreal, Canada.

Commentary: Taking risks is what I love to see above all else in design. This year's entries (from all parts of the world) prove designers are still risk-takers, all the while crafting within the context of the strategies and requirements put in place by clients. I am honored to have judged the 2024 Graphis Design Awards. Beyond being a judge, I was inspired by the typography, use of color, texture, and ideas put forward. The work is simply a catalyst for wanting to do better work myself.

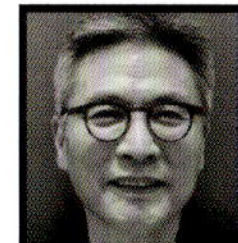

Byoung il Sun | Byoung il Sun | Designer & Professor

Biography: Byoung il-Sun was born in South Korea in 1958. Since 1995, he has been a professor of visual information design at Namseoul University. He has won several international design awards from organizations such as the BIPB Poster Biennale Awards, the Golden Bee, Graphis, the Red Dot Award, Gdie, Ekoplakt, China-Italy Design Innovation Hub, the Virtual Biennial Prague Poster competition, and the Poster for Tomorrow competition. Over the years, he has served on numerous international design juries and as academic chair for groups such as 4th Block, Paper Beauties Orient International, Poster for Tomorrow France, Iran Red Ribbon, China Adack, Asia NEXT, and others in locations such as Poland, Slovakia, Turkey, Ukraine, and more.

Commentary: The Graphis Design Award has been around for a long time, and there were a lot of high-quality designs. The entries showed that the artists had thought deeply about what they wanted to convey with each project and made a lot of effort to find the best ideas and images. It was great to see new and experimental skills in design techniques. I think the designs that show the identity of each designer will be shared and especially liked by many people when the book is published. I am glad that I could participate in the judging process, and it was a great opportunity.

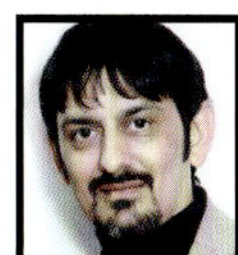

Vishal Vora | Sol Benito | Designer & Founder

Biography: Sol Benito is an award-winning packaging design studio based in Mumbai, India, and headed by founder and designer Vishal Vora. He studied graphic design at I.S. College of Fine Arts and is an intrinsic creative talent with over 20 years of multidisciplinary and multi-sector experience in design direction, management, and implementation in India and overseas. He has worked for various markets in Europe and North America, and has a keen eye for quality design. Vishal's profound experience helps apply graphic principles to produce innovative designs for any media. He would describe his approach to design as emotional, intuitive, and aspirational. His inclination lies in branding, packaging design, product design, and exhibition design.

Commentary: Design is the embodiment of storytelling. Its essence lies in the act of narrating a tale, whether it takes the form of packaging, products, art, or any other expression of design. If the design fails to convey a story, it loses its vitality. Design is a dynamic medium that serves a purpose. Design is a sensory awakening in tangible form. Design is a conversation manifested visually. Design is an emotional catalyst. Design is an uplifting force, enhancing your mood. Design is thought-provoking, inviting contemplation. Design is a wellspring of inspiration. Design is a poetic craft. Design enriches the world, making it more livable. Design is not stagnant; it perpetually evolves and moves forward.

For judges who were also entrants and winners, special care was taken to insure that they did not judge their own work.

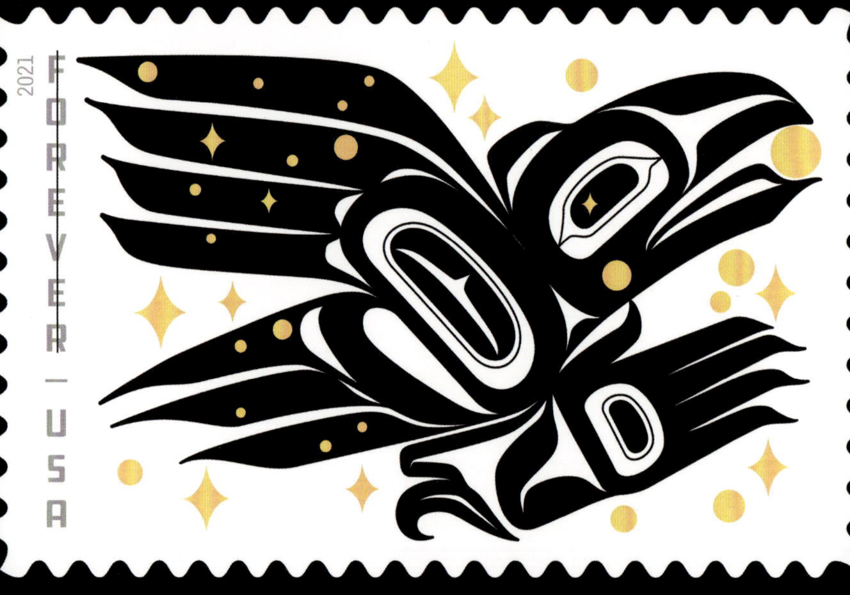

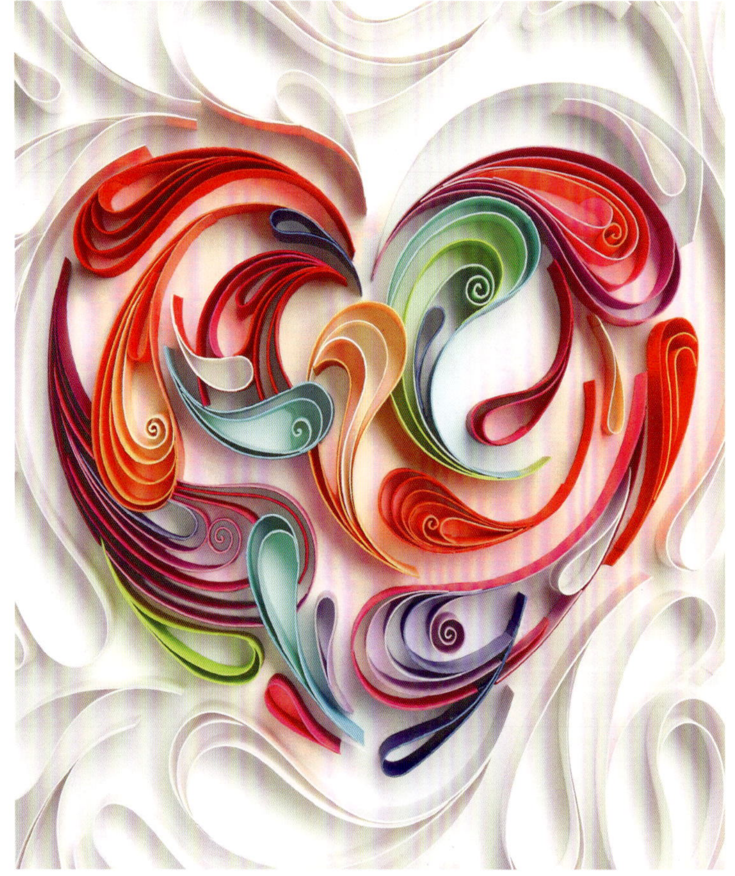

Titles: Raven Story, Quilled Paper Heart | **Client:** United States Postal Service

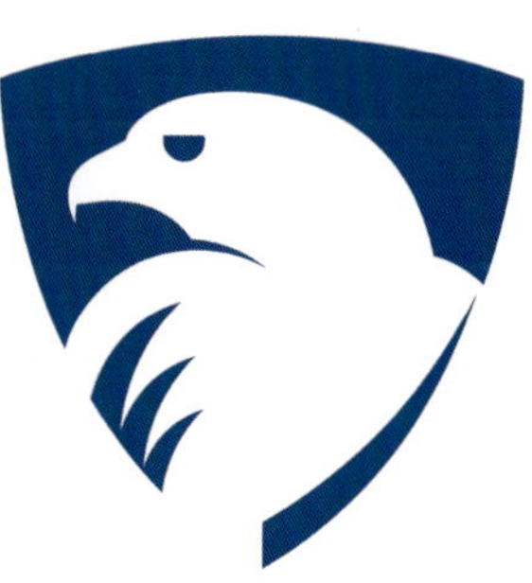

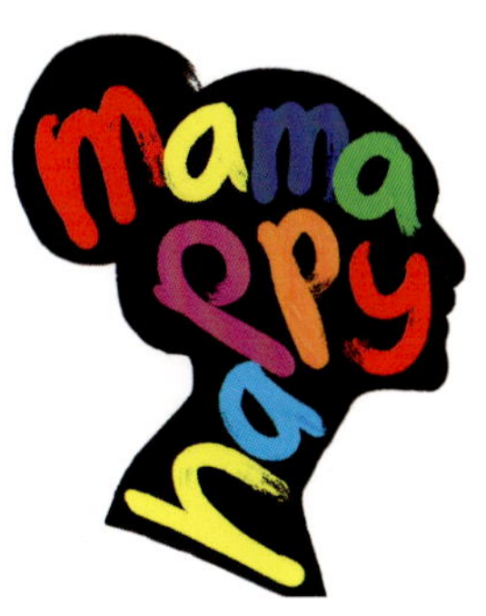

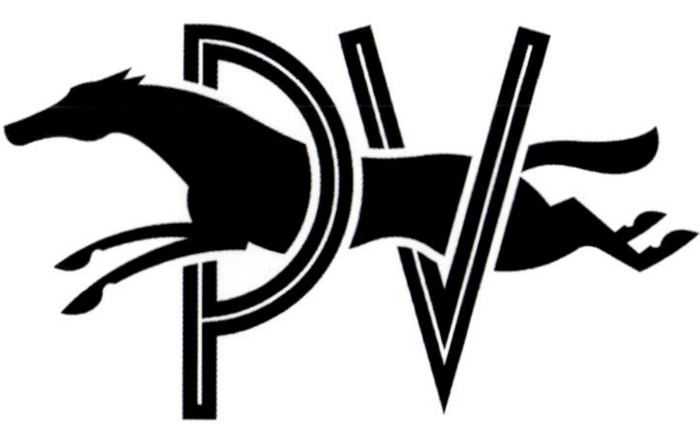

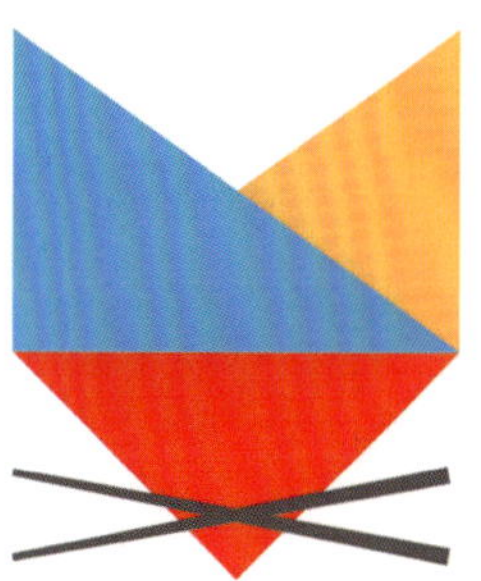

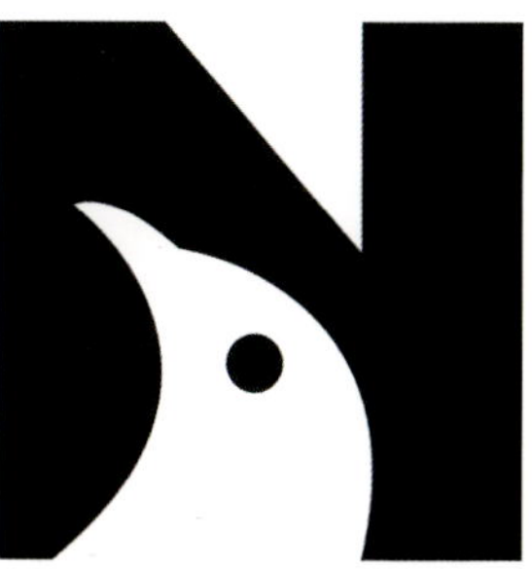

Titles: Eagle HR, Mama Happy, Peter Vogl, The Culinary Fox, Nalini Scarfe Logos
Clients: Eagle HR Consulting, Mama Happy, Peter Vogl, Urban Life, Nalini Scarfe

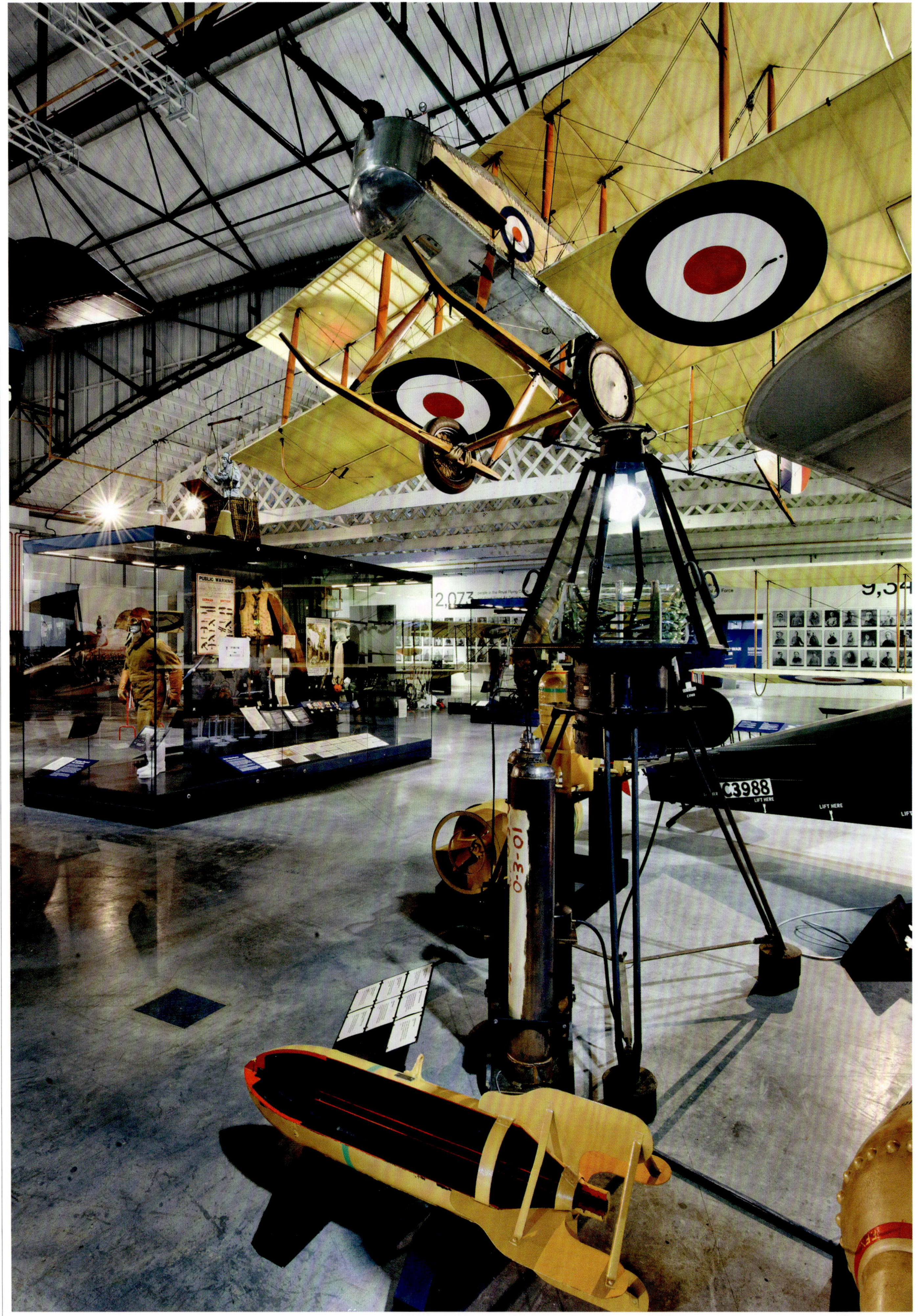

Title: The First World War in the Air | **Client:** The Royal Air Force Museum

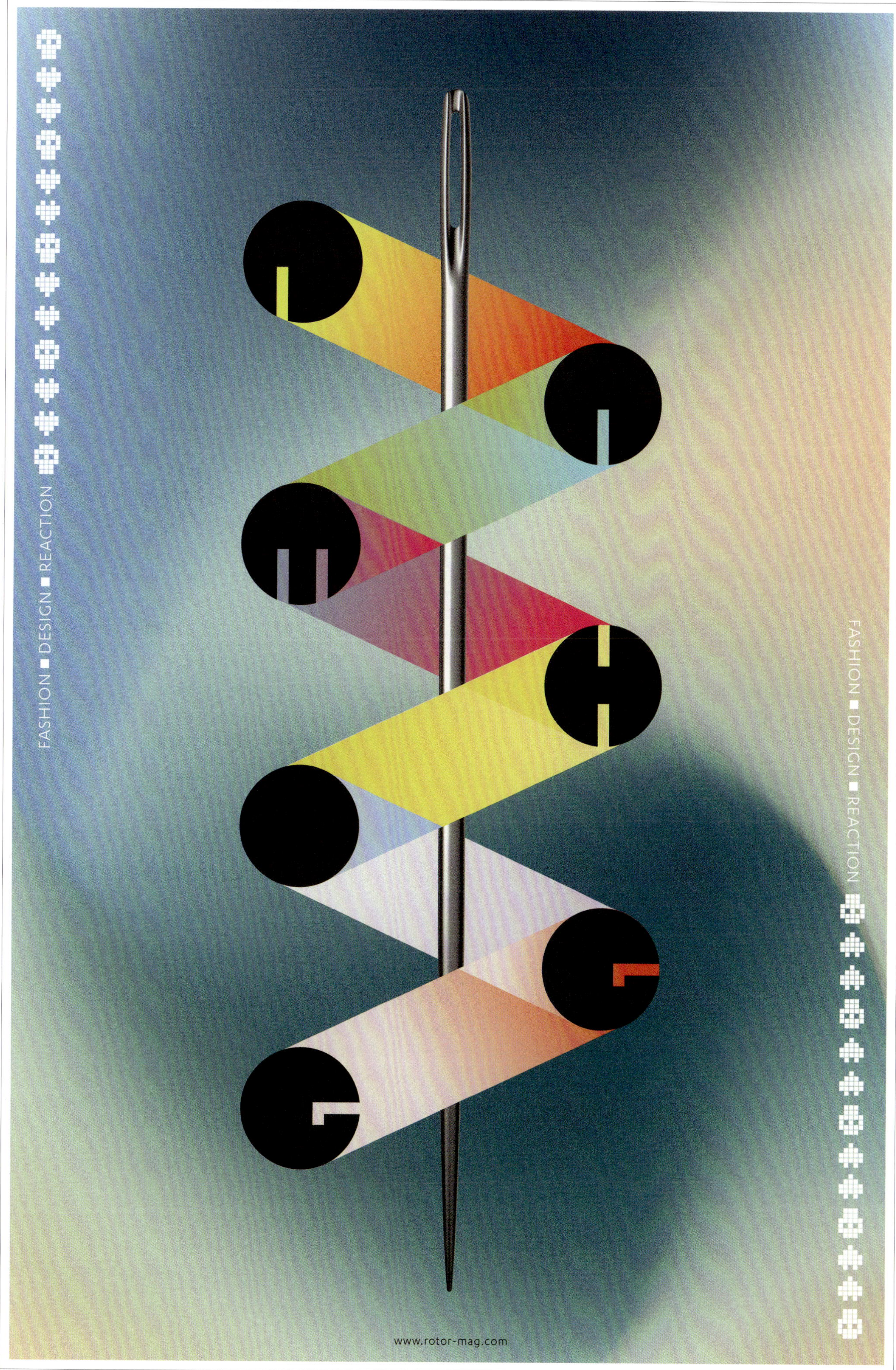

Title: Pam Hogg Poster | **Client:** ROTOR Magazine

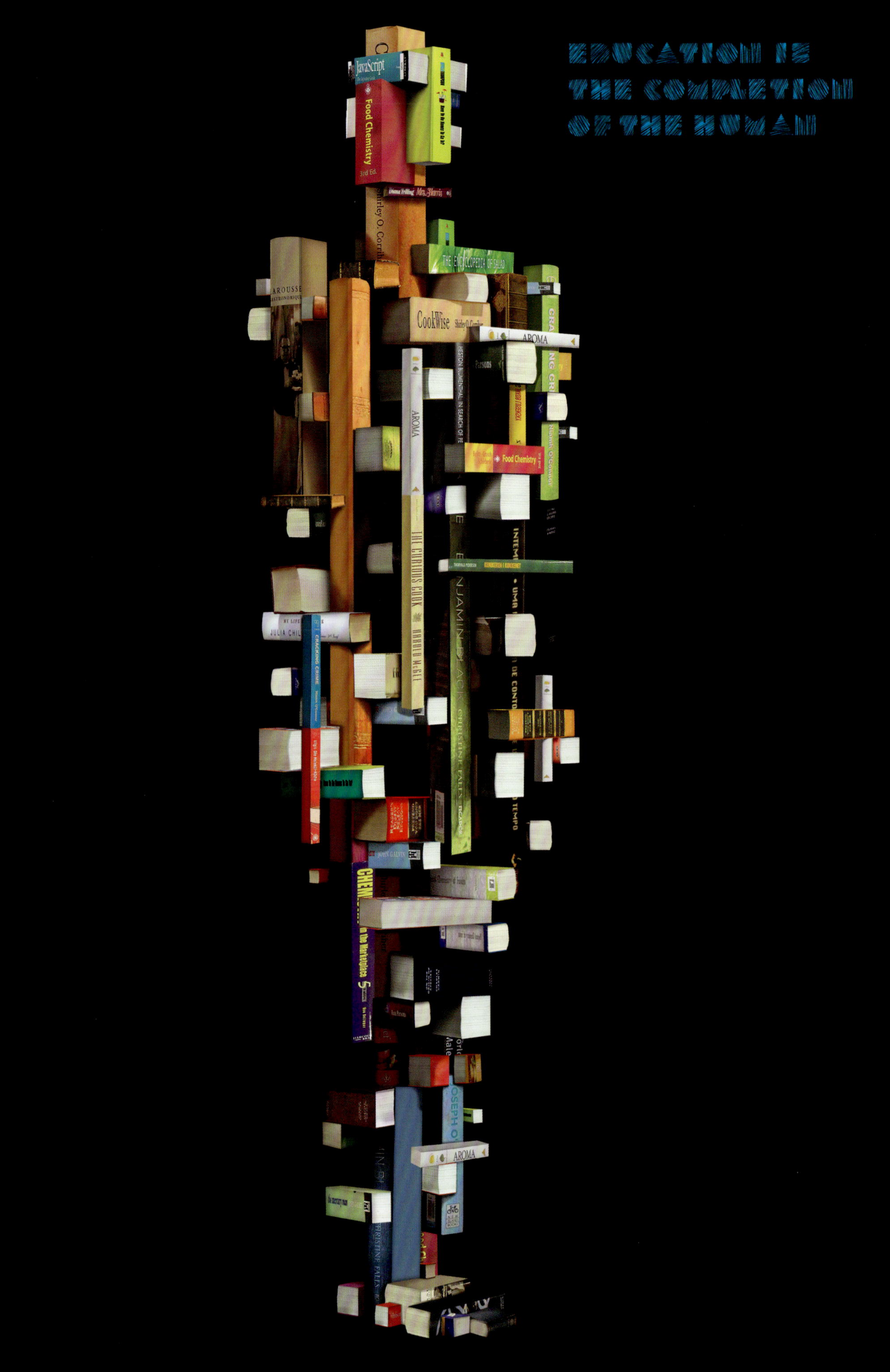

Title: Education is the Completion of the Human | **Client:** Poster for Tomorrow

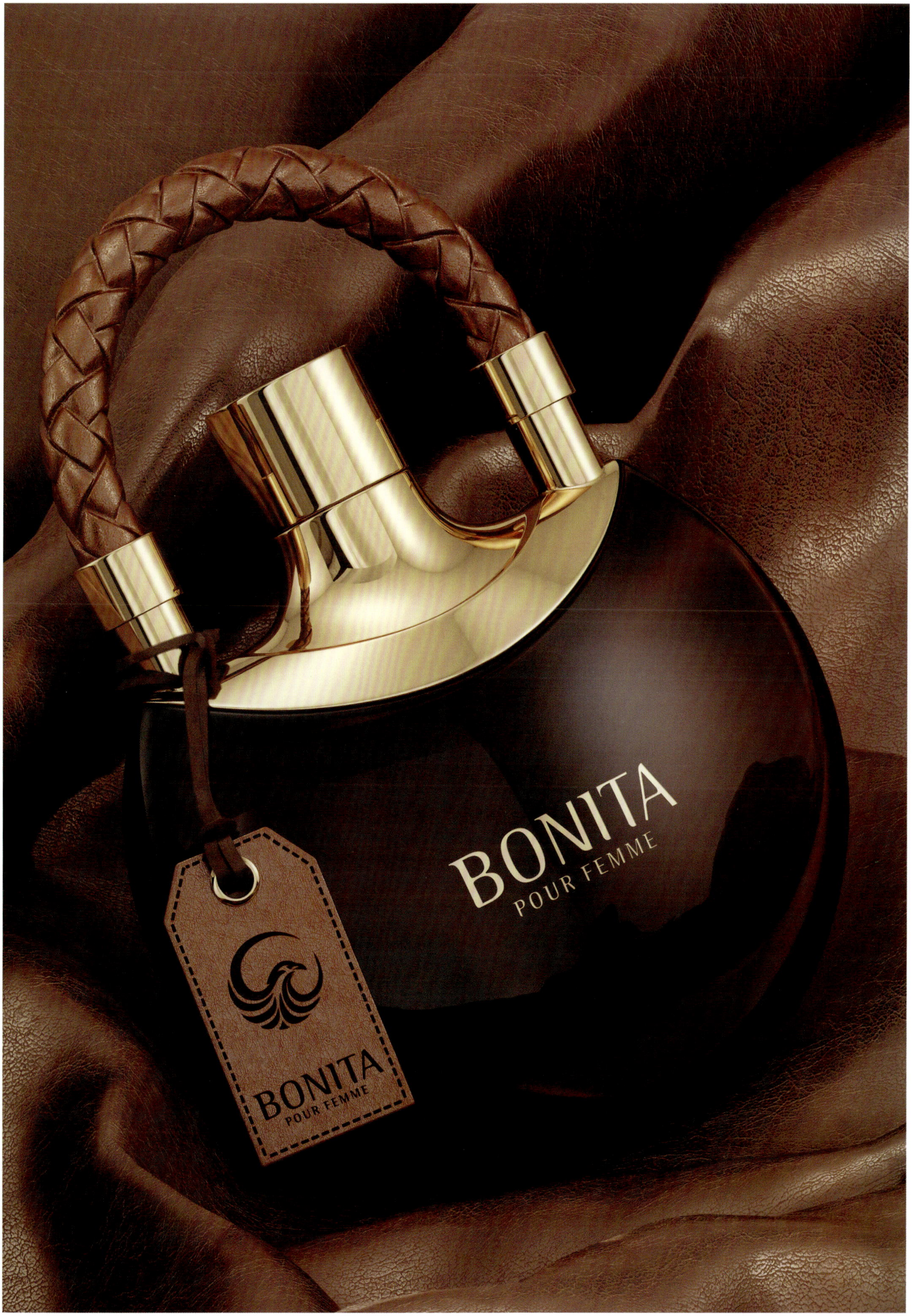

Title: Bonita | **Client:** Elite Brands

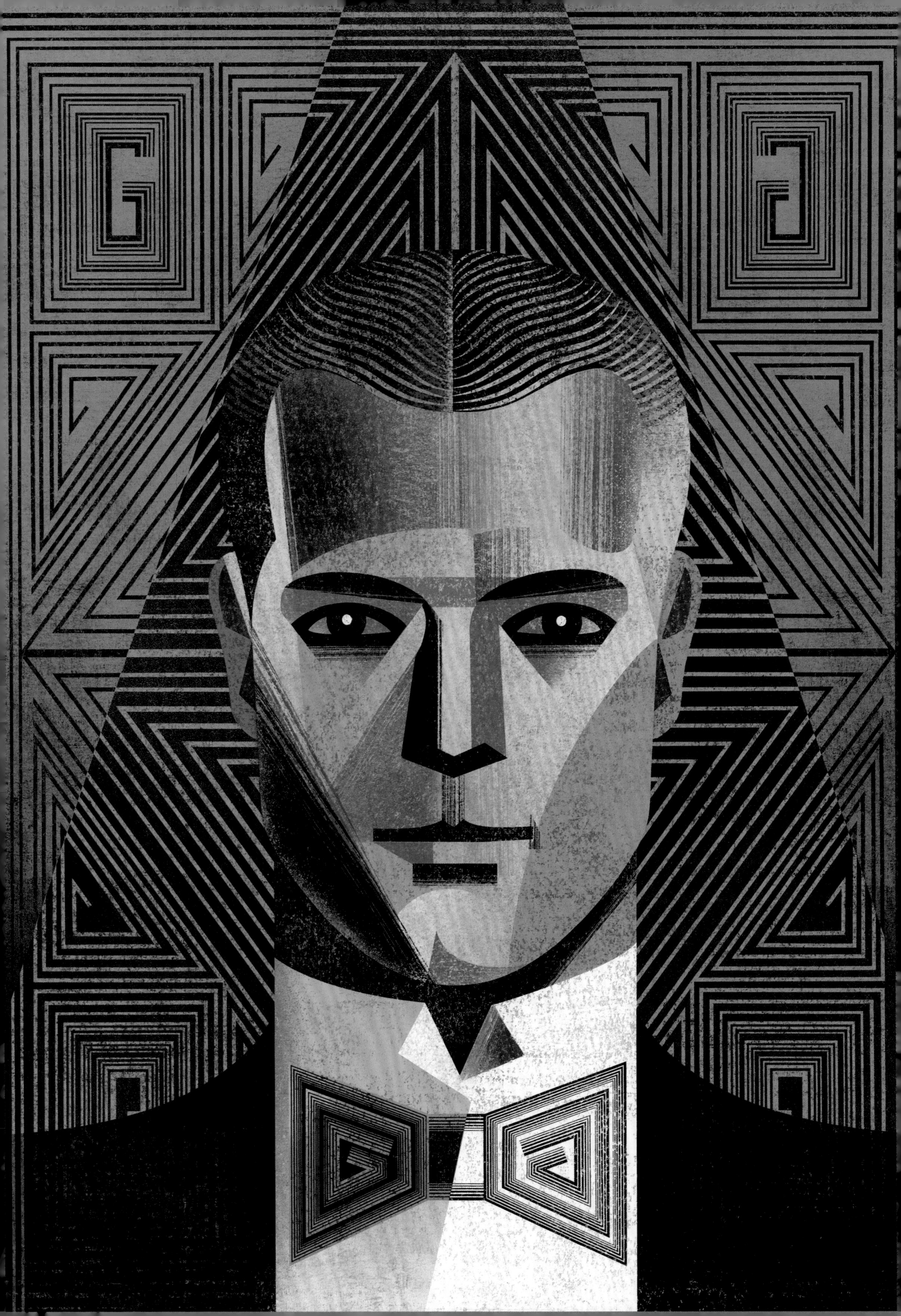

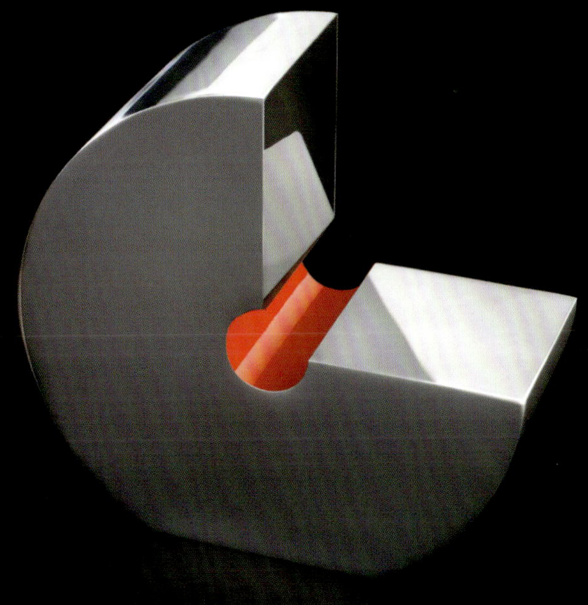

Opposite page: *"The Great Gatsby by F. Scott Fitzgerald Luxury Edition."* by Anna and Elena Balbusso (Balbusso Twins Artist Duo)

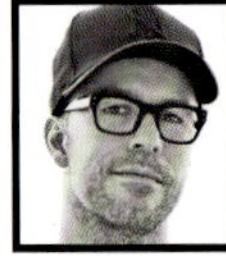

Lyle Owerko | Wonderlust Industries, Inc. | Photographer | Page: 22 | www.lyleowerko.com
Biography: The work of Lyle Owerko has an enduring place in the realms of both pop culture and journalism. He is best known for his *TIME* magazine cover photo of the Sept. 11, 2001 attack on the World Trade Center complex. His recent series, "The Boombox Project," consists of photographs of vintage portable stereos, chronicling the history and influence of the boombox on youth culture. Amongst many accolades, Owerko was awarded the title of Hasselblad Master for his work in Kenya. His photography has been collected by museums such as the Victoria & Albert Museum, and his work has been featured in *The New York Times*, *The Village Voice*, and *NPR*.

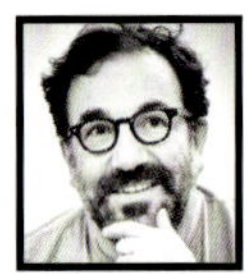

Eduardo Aires | Studio Eduardo Aires | Art Director | Page: 23 | www.eduardoaires.com
Biography: Eduardo Aires lives and works in Porto, Portugal. He studied graphic design at Porto University's Faculty of Fine Arts (FBAUP, 1987), where he is now an associate professor and was awarded his Ph.D. (2006) with a thesis on editorial design. At FBAUP, he would later be the founder of the MA program for graphic design and editorial projects. He is the artistic director of Studio Eduardo Aires, a multidisciplinary design agency focused on visual communication. Among the studio's many internationally recognized projects is the identity of the city of Porto (2014). In addition to commissioned projects, he is dedicated to the creation of unique objects.

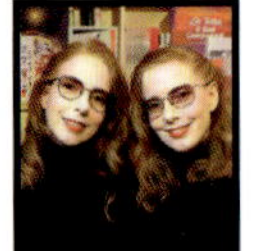

Anna and Elena Balbusso | Balbusso Twins Artist Duo | Artists & Illustrators | Page: 24 | www.balbussotwins.myportfolio.com
Biography: Anna and Elena Balbusso, also known as the Balbusso Twins, are two award-winning Italian sister artists living in Milan, Italy. Their work has been published by major international publishers and companies throughout the world in various forms of media. They've illustrated more than 50 books, including the luxury limited edition of The Great Gatsby for Beehive Books, as well as the deluxe Folio Society editions of The Handmaid's Tale, Pride and Prejudice, and Atlas Shrugged. Some of the many publications that have featured their work include The Economist, The New Yorker, The New York Times, Reader's Digest, Corriere Della Sera, and Le Figaro. They have also been featured in numerous illustration annual books, magazines, and newspaper articles, including the Communication Arts Design Annual 51, issue 21 of 3x3: The Magazine of Contemporary Illustration, and The Atlantic American where they were interviewed by American author and critic Steven Heller. Their artwork has been exhibited internationally, with the Norman Rockwell Museum including them in the Illustrators of the Decade, 2010. Throughout their career, they have received more than 90 international honors and awards, including three gold medals, a silver medal, and the Stevan Dohanos Award from the prestigious Society of Illustrators of New York, two Joseph Morgan Henninger Awards, a silver award from the SILA of Los Angeles, a gold award from 3x3 magazine, the Victoria and Albert Museum Illustration Award for Best Book, a silver award from Graphis' Designers for Peace poster competition, and the Chelsey Award from the Association of Science Fiction and Fantasy Artists (ASFA). Recently, their work has been included in The Power and Influence of Illustration by Alan Male, emeritus professor of Falmouth University, and Editorial Illustration: Context, Content and Creation by Andrew Selby, a professor at Loughborough University. They have been included among 18 great Italian artists in the "Children's Illustration: Italian Excellence" international travel show curated by Bologna Children's Book Fair, and the Italian art historian Paola Pallottino also included the twins in Le Figure per Dirlo, an account of the history of Italian women illustrators.

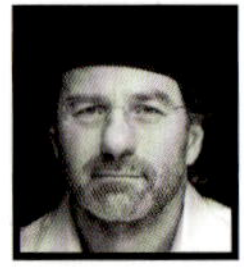

Michael Pantuso | Michael Pantuso Design | Graphic Designer, Artist, & Illustrator | Page: 25 | www.pantusodesign.com
Biography: Michael Pantuso is a Graphis Master in design and also art/illustration and internationally acclaimed graphic designer, artist, and illustrator celebrated for his groundbreaking and intellectually-engaging work. He is known for forging profound connections through his creative fusion of typography, color, imagery, imaginative illustrations, and photography. With multiple platinum and gold awards with Graphis, a shortlisting in the World Illustration Awards for 2023, and recognition as a finalist for the prestigious Lumen Prize, Michael's artistic prowess is widely acknowledged. His artwork has been featured in esteemed publications, galleries, and exhibitions, solidifying his reputation in the art world. Exciting upcoming collaborations, including a summer show with former Journey frontman Robert Fleischman, continue to showcase Michael's visionary work that inspires and resonates with audiences worldwide.

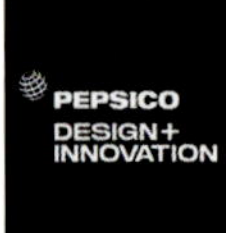

PepsiCo Design & Innovation | Page: 26 | www.design.pepsico.com
Biography: PepsiCo products are enjoyed by consumers more than one billion times a day in more than 200 countries and territories around the world. PepsiCo generated more than $86 billion in net revenue in 2022, driven by a complementary beverage and convenient foods portfolio that includes Lay's, Doritos, Cheetos, Gatorade, Pepsi-Cola, Mountain Dew, Quaker, and SodaStream. PepsiCo's product portfolio includes a wide range of enjoyable foods and beverages, including many iconic brands that generate more than $1 billion each in estimated annual retail sales. Guiding PepsiCo is their vision to be the global leader in beverages and convenient foods by winning with pep+ (PepsiCo Positive). pep+ is their strategic end-to-end transformation that puts sustainability and human capital at the center of how they will create value and growth by operating within planetary boundaries and inspiring positive change for the planet and its people.

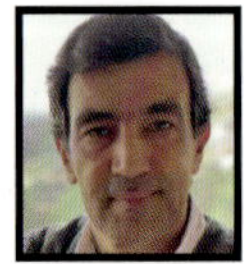

Diogo Gama Rocha | Omdesign | Founder & General Manager | Page: 27 | www.omdesign.pt
Biography: Diogo Gama Rocha was born in 1973 in Oporto into a family of artists from his mother's side and managers from his father's side. This unique heritage, combined with the industrial approach of his secondary studies, bestowed upon him profound know-how and passion for both creativity and the intricacies of the production process, which is constantly innovating and challenging Omdesign's partners to go further. Obsessed with detail, he graduated from ESAD (Portugal) after studying graphic design and received his MBA in marketing and international trade at ESADE (Spain). Passionate about nature, Diogo has been involved in several sustainable projects to inspire and promote an ecologically friendly mindset. Diogo founded Omdesign in 1998, and since then, the creative agency has worked with leading brands in different areas around the world and carries in its DNA the pursuit of excellence, not just as a goal but a way of being and embracing each project as unique, only achievable with great demand and consistency.

21 PLATINUM WINNERS

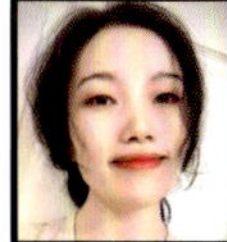

Xian Liyun | Sun Design Production | Design Director | Page: 28
Biography: Xian Liyun was born in 1990 in the Zhejiang province of China. She works as a Chinese national psychological counselor and family education mentor and is currently pursuing a doctoral's degree in design under the tutelage of Professor Byoung Ii Sun of South Korea, a famous graphic designer. Xian also serves as the design director of Sun Design Production in South Korea. She formerly held the position of design director at the headquarters of China's largest stationery enterprise, Deli Group, and also formerly served as the design director at Sina. Xian has been invited multiple times to participate in international poster exhibitions in countries such as the United States, Germany, France, South Korea, Iran, and China.

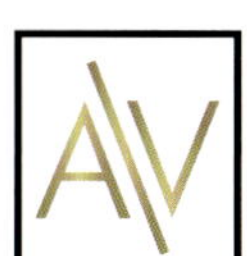

AV Print | Page: 29 | www.avsquad.com
Biography: AV Squad is a creative advertising agency specializing in entertainment marketing. Founded by Chad Miller and Seth Gaven in 2004, AV Squad has grown into one of the leaders in the entertainment marketing space, garnering numerous awards for campaigns that span all genres, audiences, and budgets. Fostering a culture of collaboration, respect, creativity, and diversity, AV Squad's work speaks for itself. In 2019, Peter Stark joined the team, adding a new division, AV Print, to handle all key art, illustration, design, and OOH capabilities. Together these teams continuously collaborate to create outstanding, attention-grabbing campaigns that stand out in the busy media landscape. AV Squad hails independent artistic expression while also embracing audience, client, and creator feedback to build some of the finest and most impactful advertising creatives imaginable. Every client is a creative partner on a shared mission to produce successful marketing campaigns that garner industry acclaim and yield commercial success. AV Squad is proud to employ some of the most talented designers, editors, artists, and illustrators in the industry. It's difficult not to encounter a piece of creativity that this agency has produced. Be it trailers and key art across theaters, billboards around any major city, or the numerous TV and digital spots, AV Squad is proud to help share the delight and excitement of entertainment with the world.

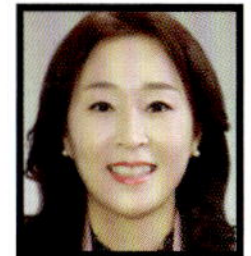

Mi-Jung Lee | Namseoul University | Graphic Designer & Assistant Professor | Page: 30 | www.nsu.ac.kr/en
Biography: Mi-Jung Lee was born in 1975 in South Korea. She received her Ph.D. in design from graduate school at Hongik University. From 2016 to 2021, she worked at Woosuk University, and she is currently an assistant professor in the Department of Visual Information Design at Namseoul University, as well as an invited artist and jury member for the Korea International Design Award. She has won more than 60 international awards from competitions hosted by Red Dot Design, Graphis Annual, the Lahti Poster Triennale, the Trnava Poster Triennale, the Ukraine 4th Block Poster Triennale, the Sofia Poster Triennale, the Mexico Poster Biennale, the Moscow Golden Bee Graphic Biennale, the Lublin Poster Biennale, the Bolivia Poster Biennale, the Peru Design Biennale, the China Poster Biennale, the Tehran Poster Biennale, the Taiwan Design Award, and more. Domestic awards include the Korea International Design Award silver and bronze prizes, among others.

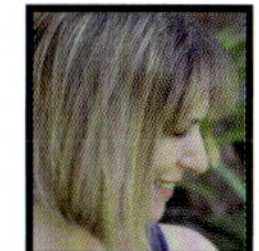

Carmit Makler Haller | Carmit Design Studio | Visual Communications Designer & Owner | Page: 31 | www.carmitdesign.com
Biography: Carmit Haller is a visual communications designer and the owner of Carmit Design Studio. For the past two decades, she has been working as a lead graphic designer in the fields of consumer markets, high-tech startups, and luxury real estate. Her passion lies in poster design and typography. She addresses cultural, social, and political topics in a strong and thought-provoking way. Carmit is the recipient of worldwide, prestigious awards from organizations such as Graphis and Rockport Publishing. She has taken part in international exhibitions such as the Tolerance Poster Show, the What Unites Us Online Poster exhibition, the International Reggae Poster Contest, Graphis' Designers for Peace worldwide poster exhibition, and PosterPoster.org. She has been invited to judge Graphis' New Talent and Poster competitions and has been a Graphis Master since 2023. She has also been a member of AIGA since 2007 and a Mentor since 2020, and is also a member of the China Europe International Design Culture Association (CEIDA) since 2022. Originally from Israel, Carmit holds a BA in social work from Tel Aviv University and a BFA in new media from the Academy of Art University, San Francisco. She currently resides in San Francisco, California.

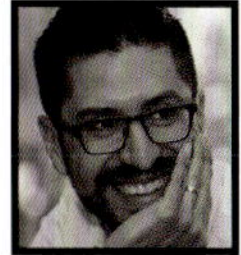

Fidel Pena | Underline Studio | Graphic Designer, Creative Director, & Co-founder | Page: 32 | www.underlinestudio.com
Biography: Fidel Peña is a graphic designer, creative director, and co-founder of Underline Studio. His work has received numerous accolades from across Canada, the US, and Europe, including from D&AD (UK), the ADCC, and the Type Directors Club (NY). Fidel gained his early experience working at top design firms in Canada and the UK, including Concrete Design Communications and Pentagram's London office. Fidel was born in El Salvador and graduated from the graphic design program at George Brown College in Toronto. He has taught editorial design at OCAD University and lectured on design topics in Europe, North America, and Latin America. He has been a guest speaker on panels held by the RGD, and his writings about design have been published by the magazine *Design Edge*. Fidel has been on the board of directors for cultural organizations, regularly serves as a juror for creative awards, and is an industry mentor for students at George Brown College's School of Design. Fidel is the former president of the Advertising and Design Club of Canada.

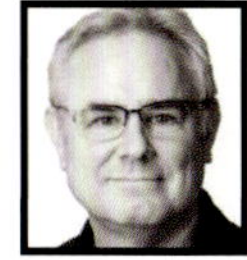

Greg Breeding | Journey Group | Graphic Designer, President, & Co-founder | Page: 33 | www.journeygroup.com
Biography: Greg Breeding studied design and typography at Virginia Commonwealth University, graduating with a BA in fine arts. He began his career by working as a designer for several nonprofits. In 1992, Greg co-founded Journey Group, a design firm where he currently serves as president. He has also taught design courses internationally for nonprofits. Greg has received many industry awards from Print's Regional Design Annual, Communication Arts, the Society of Publication Designers, and the Florida Magazine Association. Greg's first stamp as art director for the US Postal Service was "The War of 1812: USS Constitution." "I'm interested in creating art for the public good," Greg says, "and honoring a person or event on a stamp highlights and celebrates what's positive in our culture." Greg lives in Charlottesville, Virginia, with his wife, Lyndee.

Visit our Credits & Commentary section in the back of the book to read the full assignments, approaches, and results from this year's Platinum Winners.

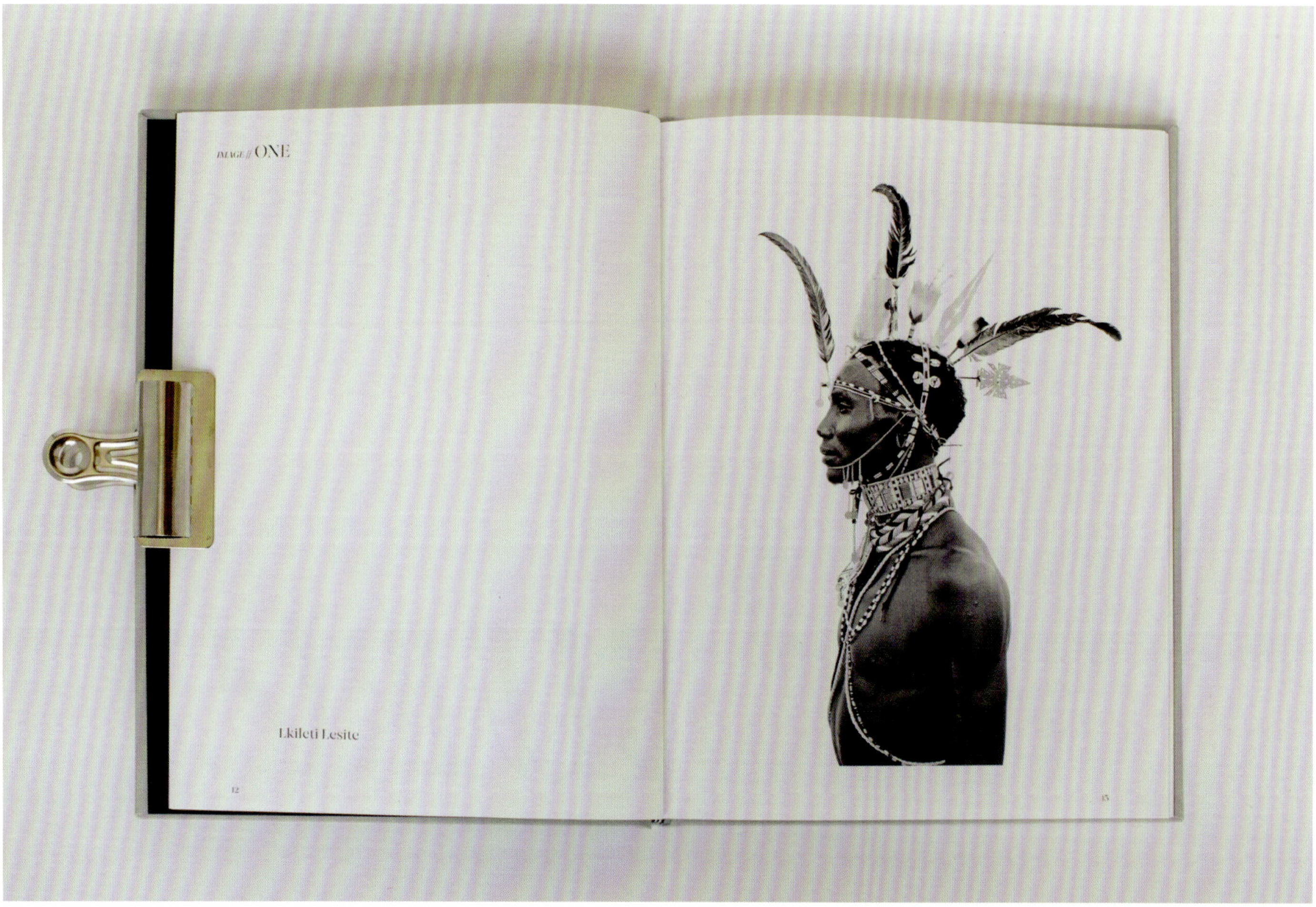

IMAGE // ONE

Lkileti Lesite

12 13

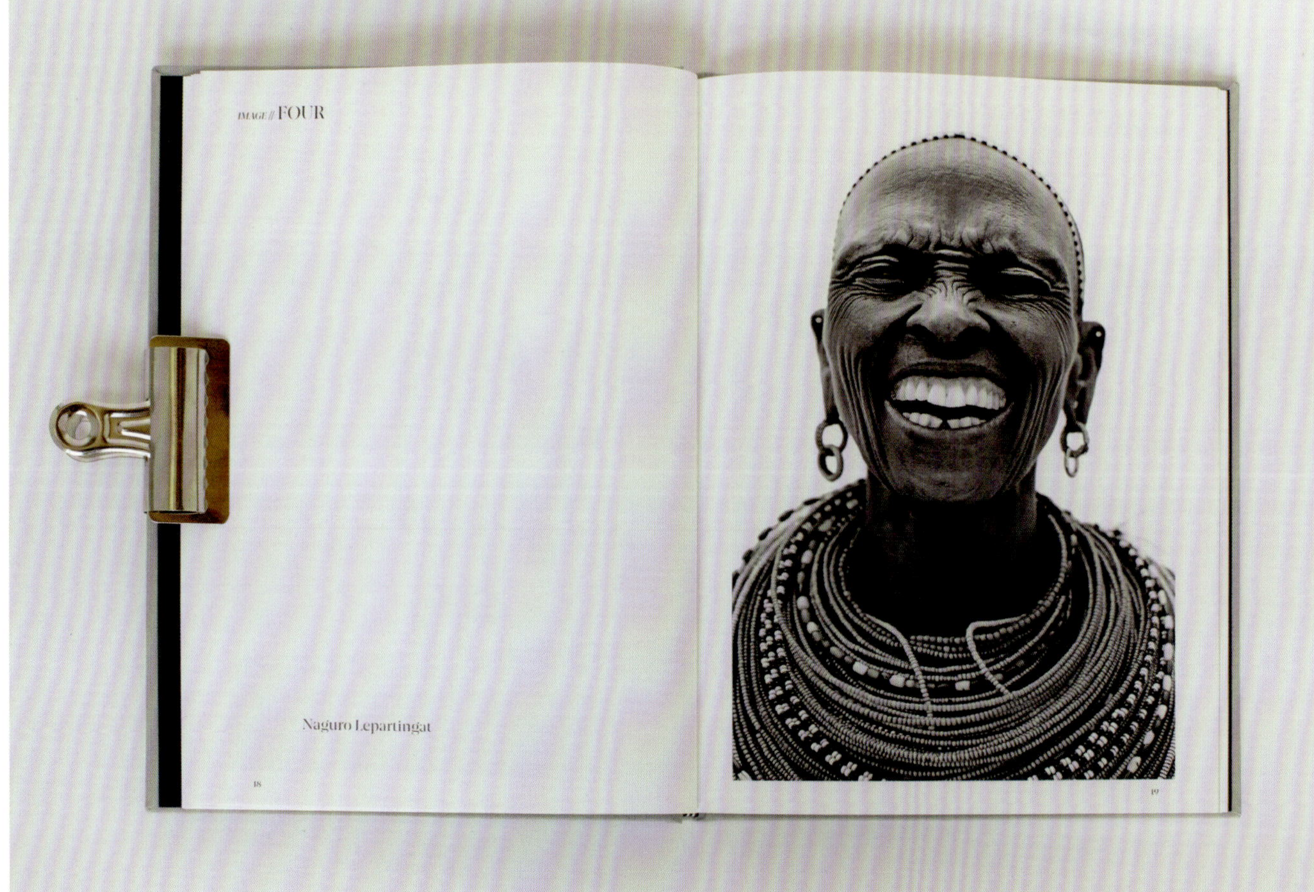

P233: Credit & Commentary **Title:** The Samburu | **Client:** The Thorntree Project | **Design Firm:** Wonderlust Industries, Inc. Images 1, 2 of 7

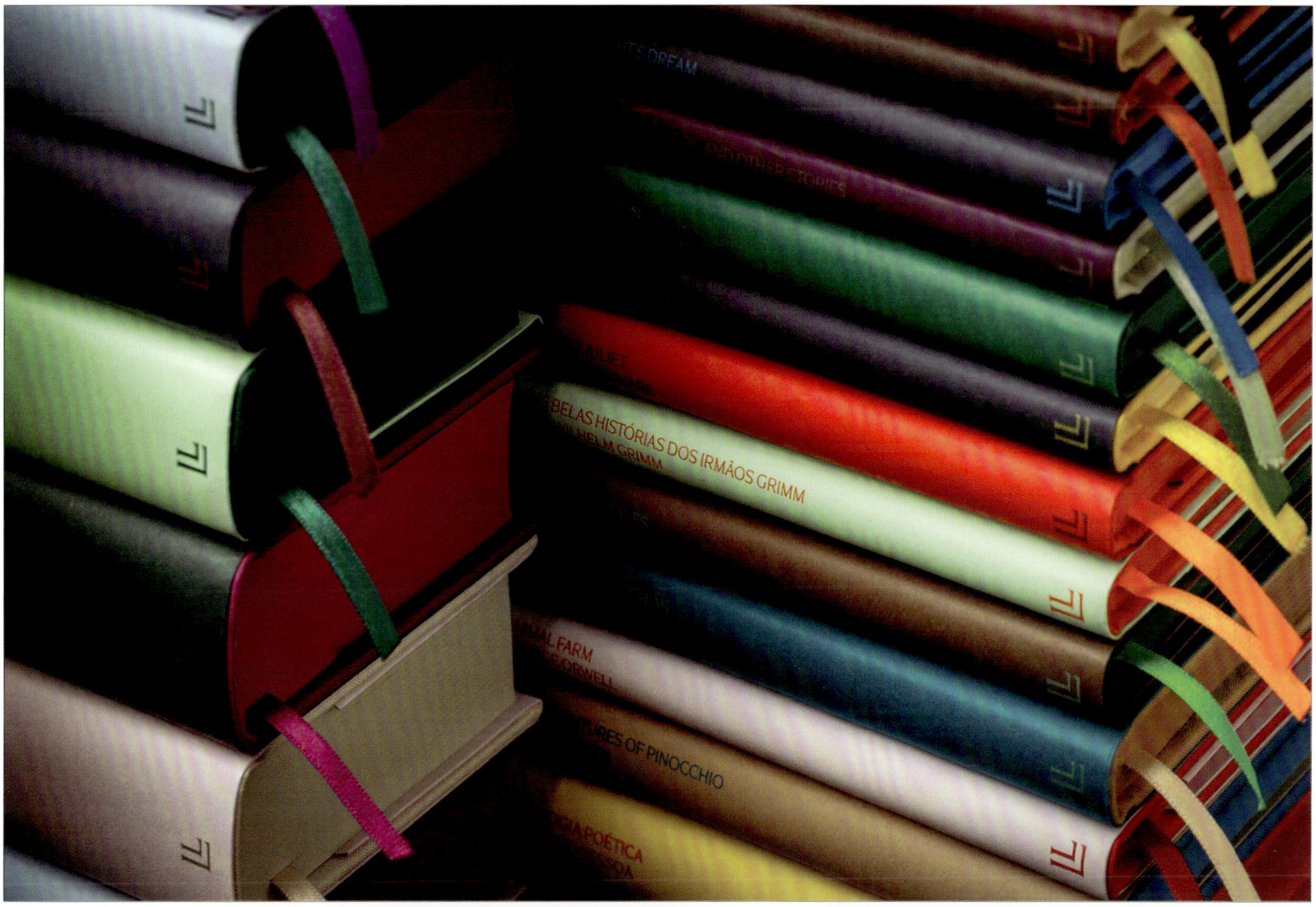

Title: The Pop Collection | **Client:** Livraria Lello | **Design Firm:** Studio Eduardo Aires

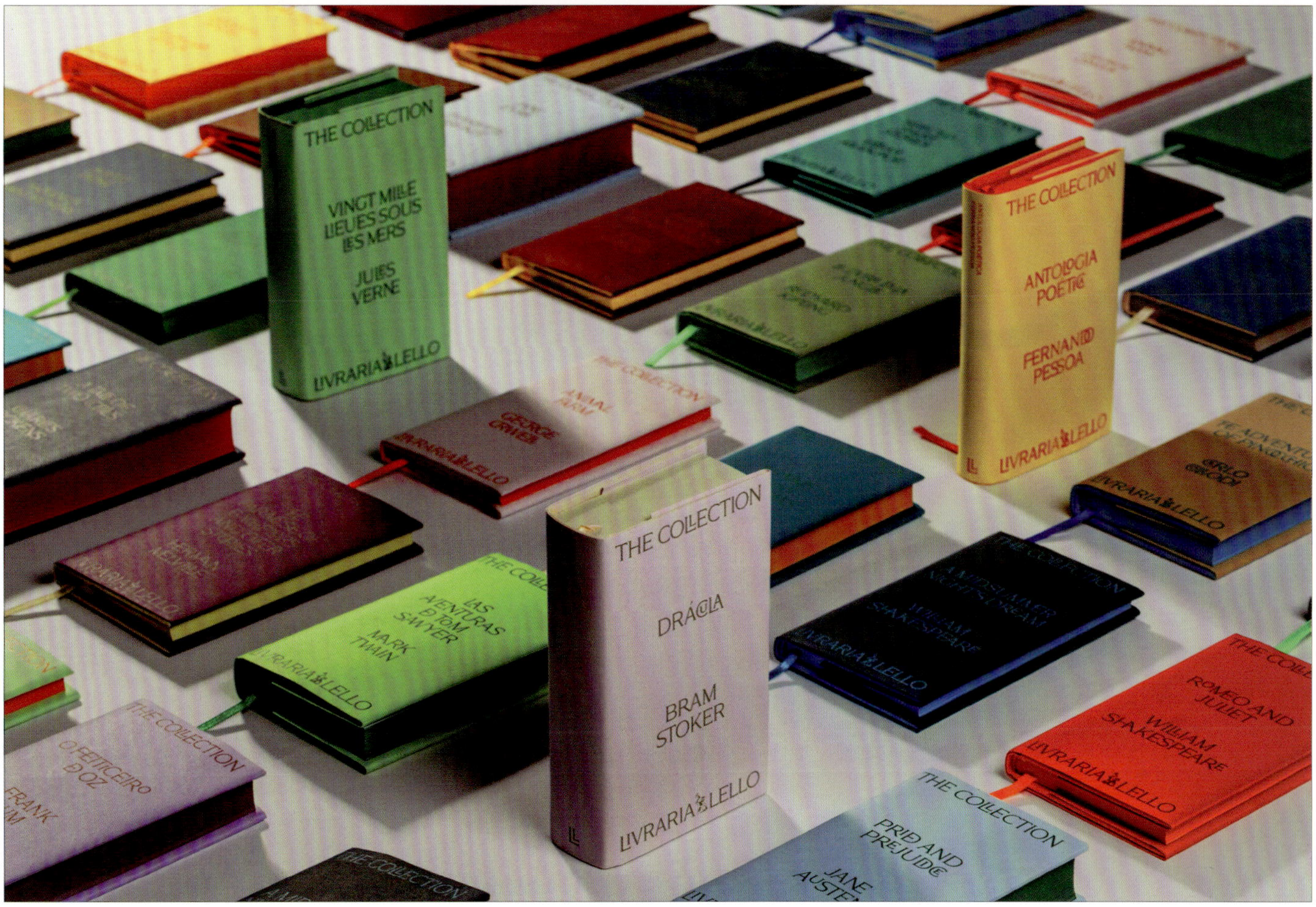

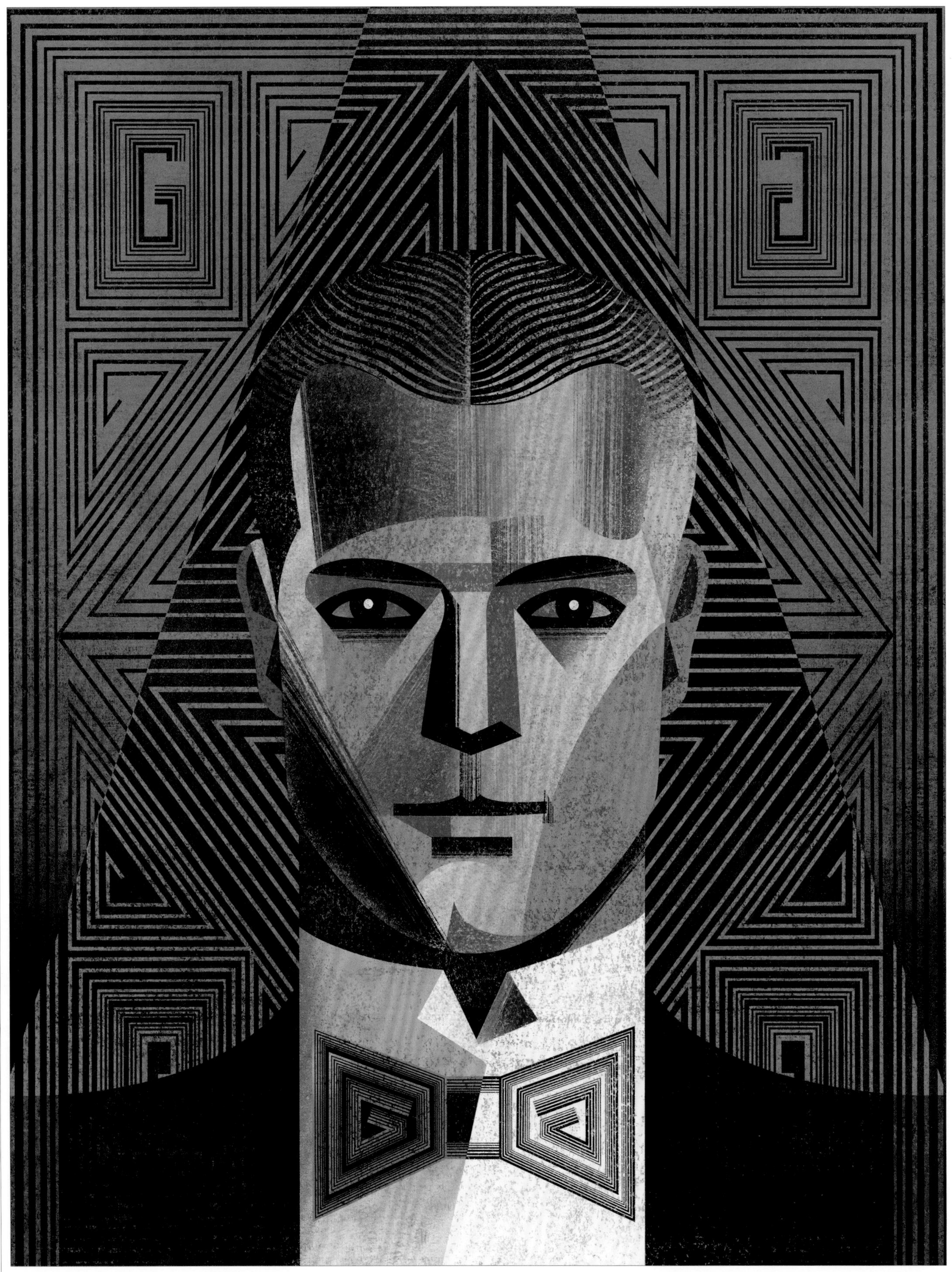

Title: "The Great Gatsby" by F. Scott Fitzgerald Luxury Edition | **Client:** Beehive Books
Design Firm: Anna and Elena Balbusso (Balbusso Twins Artist Duo) | **P233:** Credit & Commentary | Image 1 of 7

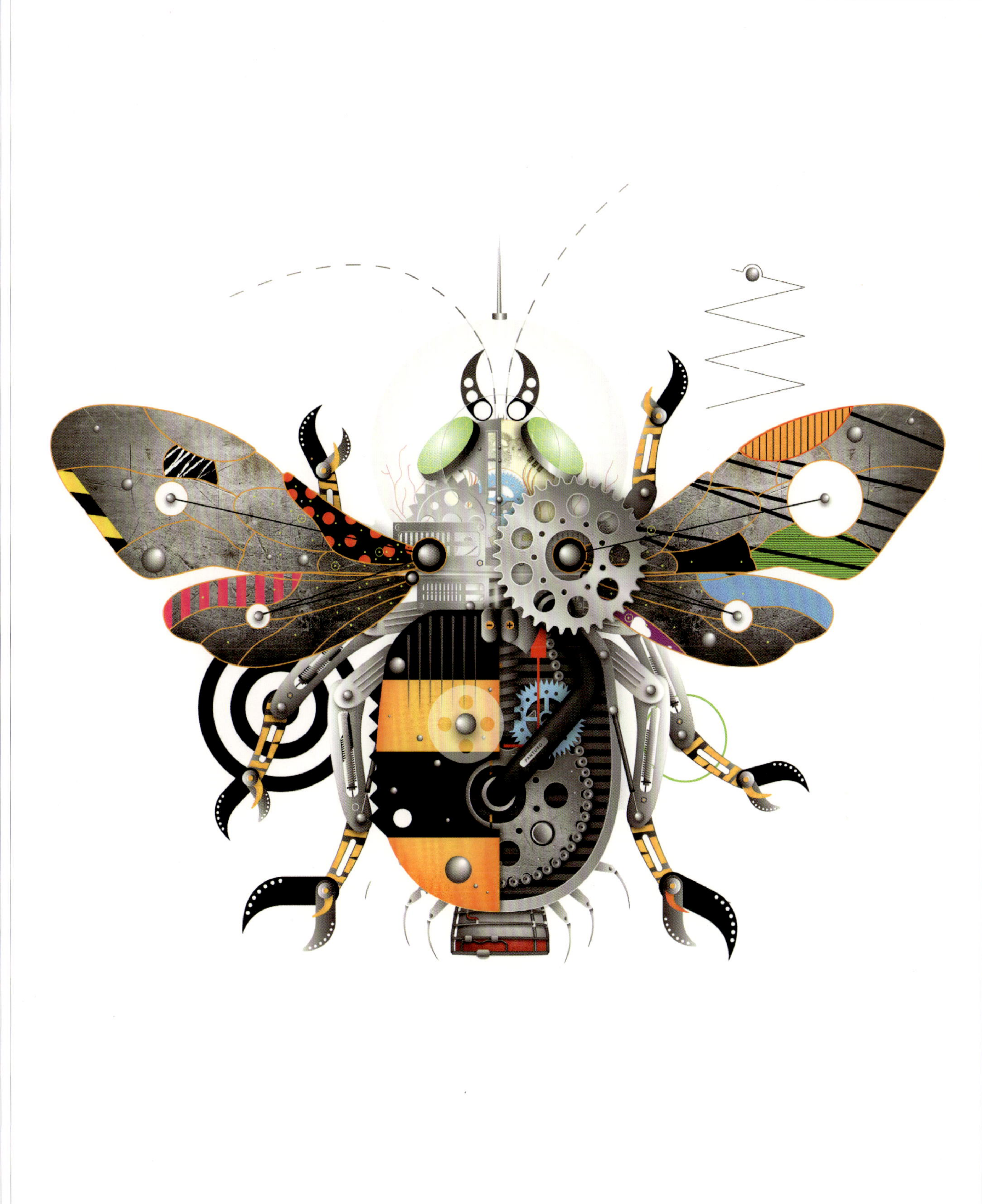

Title: Chelsea Bee | **Client:** Self-initiated
Design Firm: Michael Pantuso Design | **P233:** Credit & Commentary

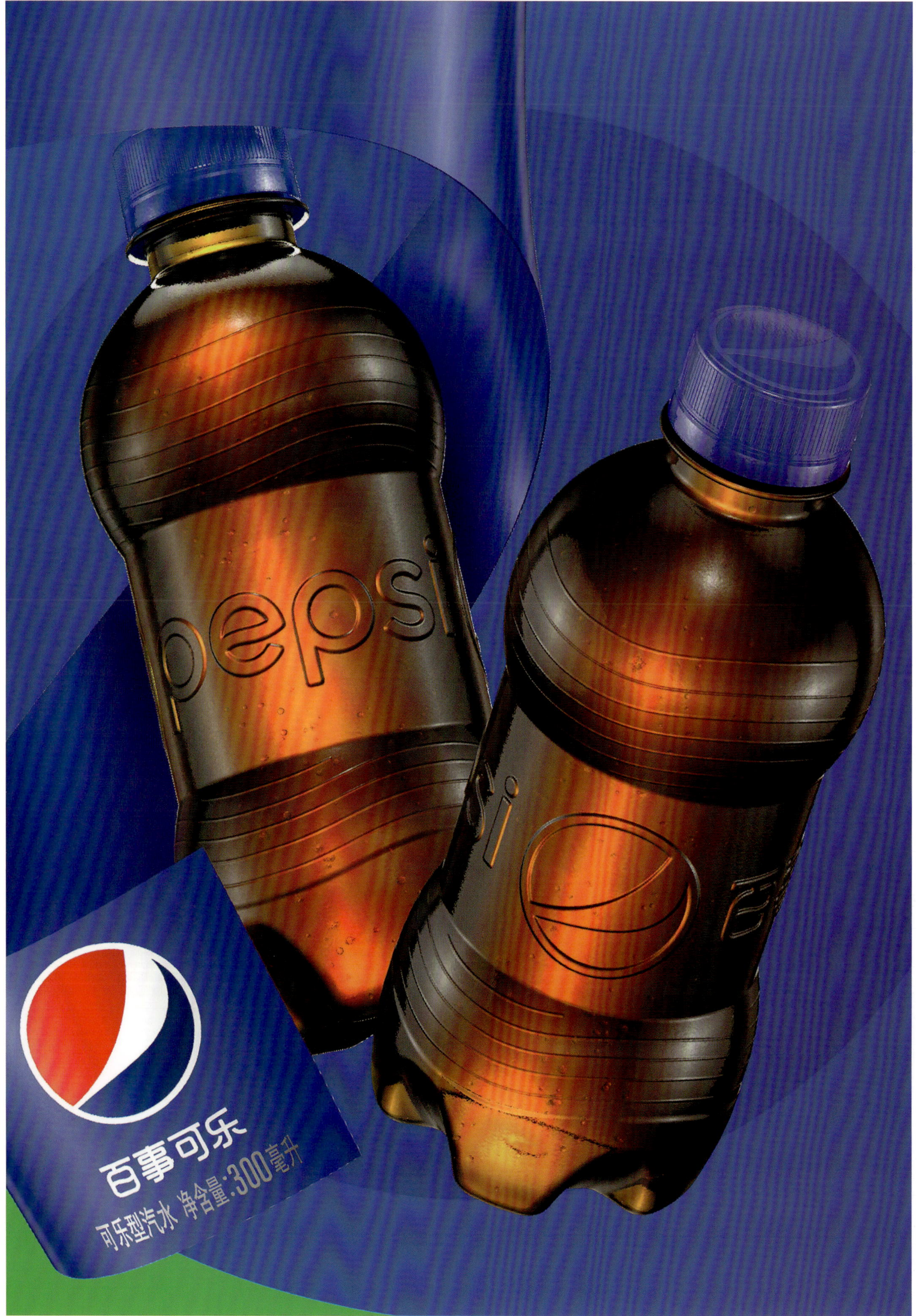

P233: Credit & Commentary **Title:** Pepsi Label-free Multipack | **Client:** Self-initated | **Design Firm:** PepsiCo Design & Innovation Image 1 of 4

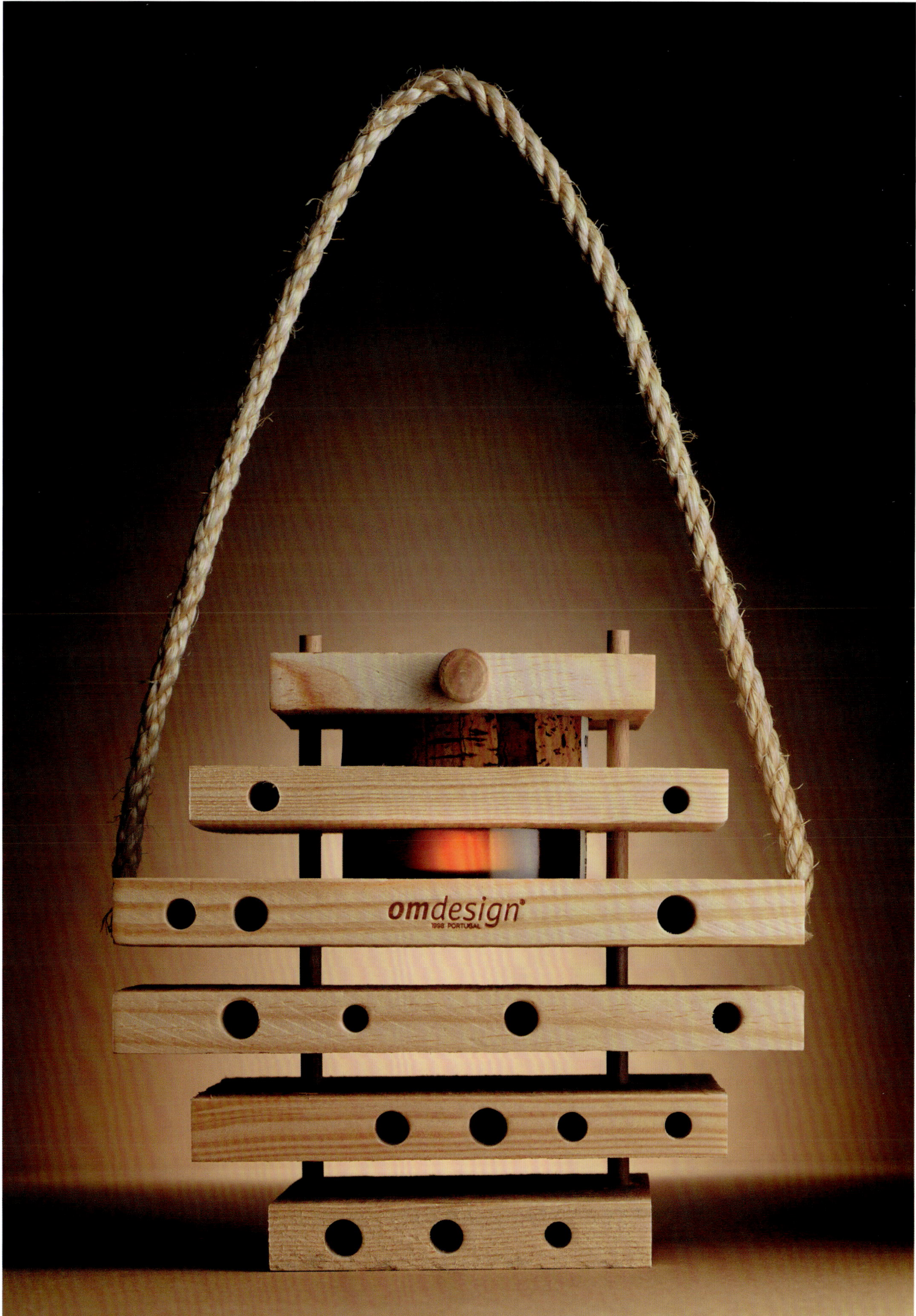

P233: Credit & Commentary

Title: OMel | Client: Self-initiated | Design Firm: Omdesign

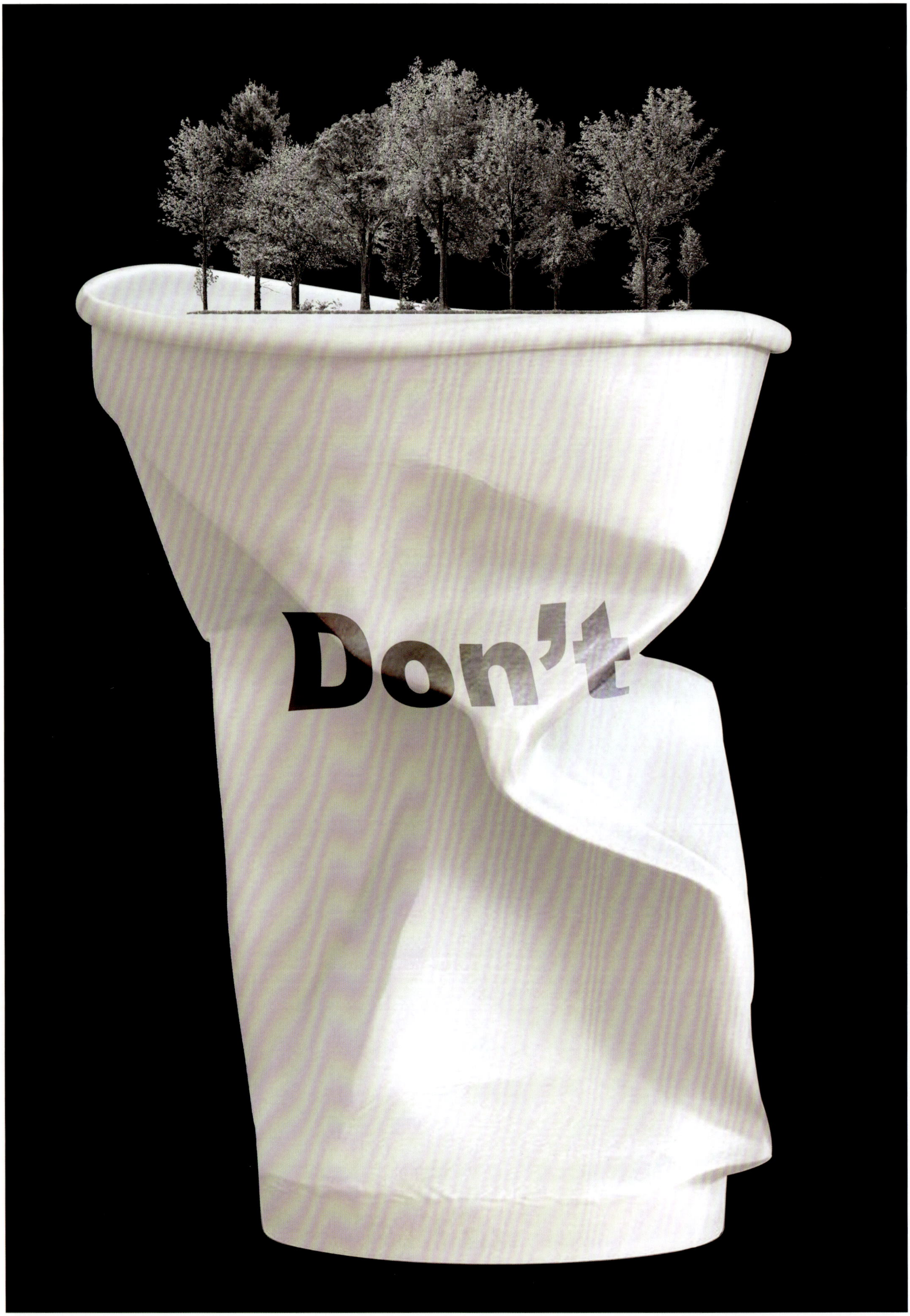

Don't

P233: Credit & Commentary **Title:** Don't | **Client:** Shanghai Municipal Government | **Design Firm:** Sun Design Production

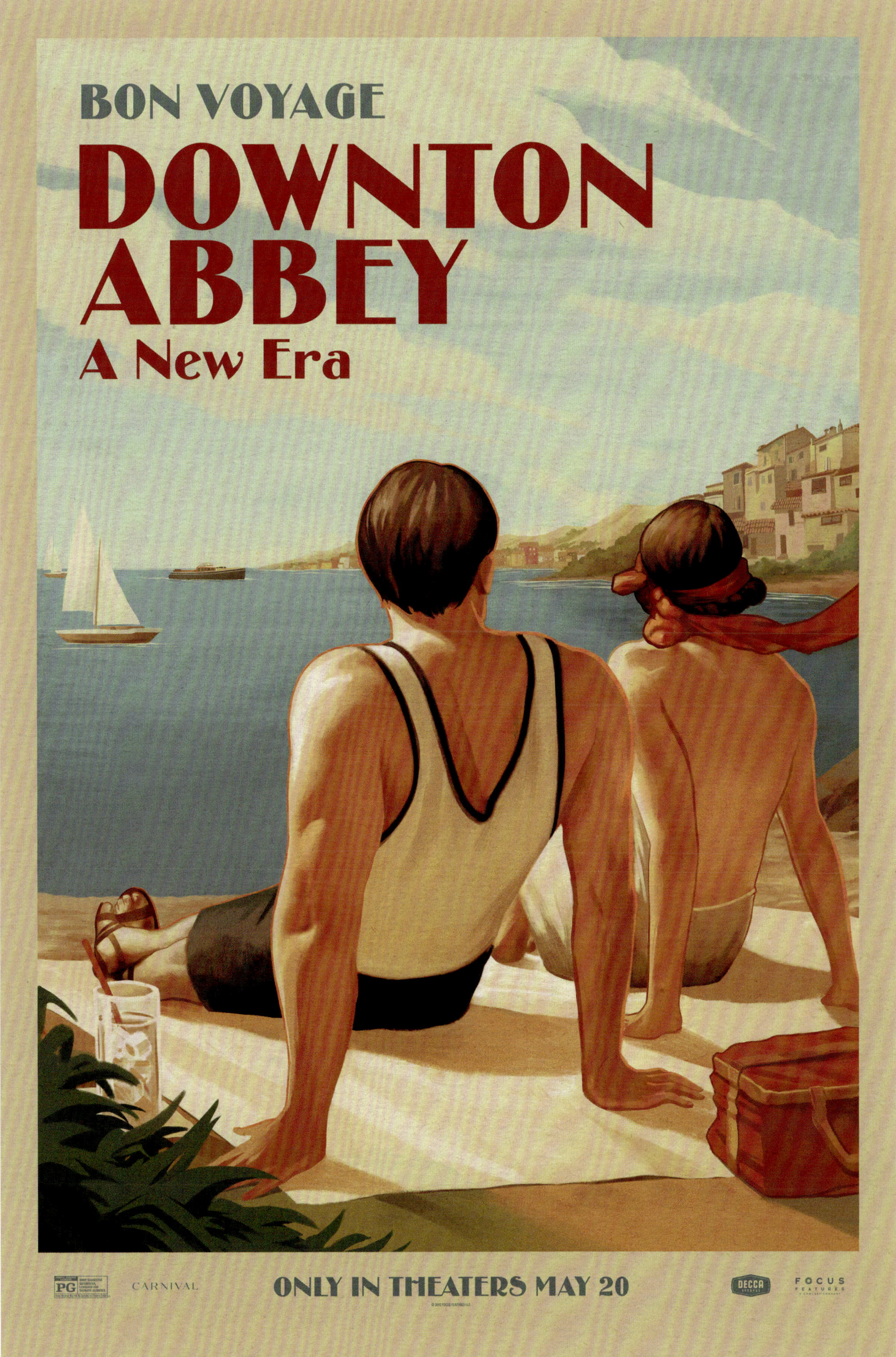

Title: Downton Abbey: A New Era - Illustrated Travel Poster Series | **Client:** Focus Features | **Design Firm:** AV Print
P233: Credit & Commentary | Image 1 of 4

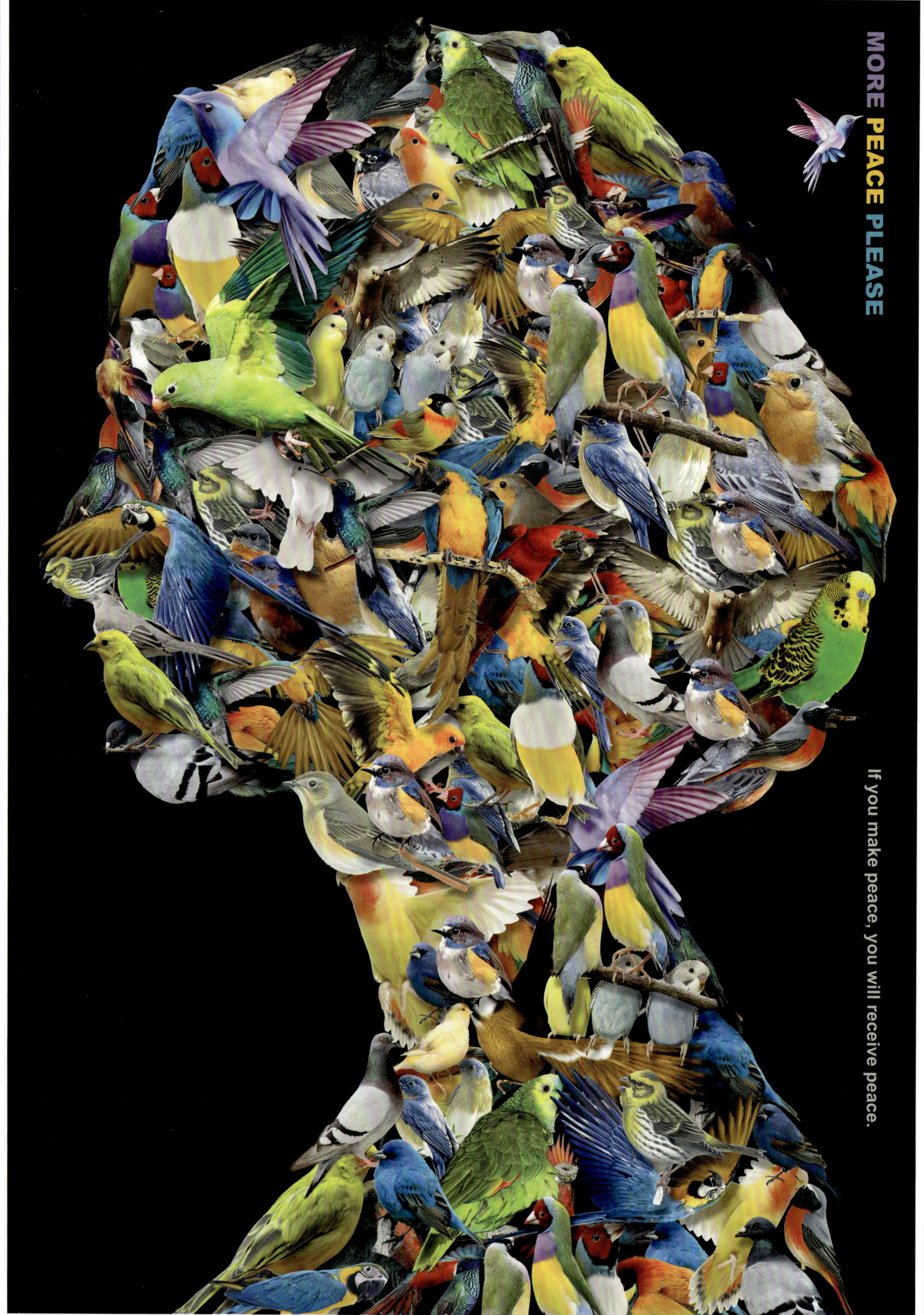

P233: Credit & Commentary **Title:** Peace | **Client:** Ministry of Unification | **Design Firm:** Namseoul University

Title: Fixed | **Client:** Self-initiated | **Design Firm:** Carmit Design Studio

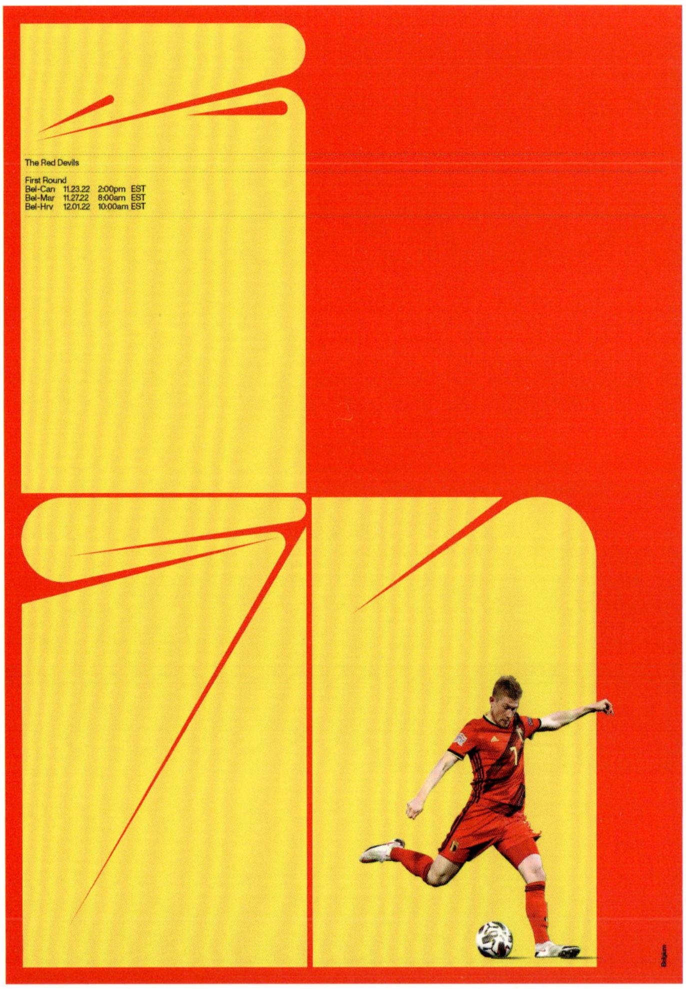

The Red Devils

First Round
Bel-Can 11.23.22 2:00pm EST
Bel-Mar 11.27.22 8:00am EST
Bel-Hrv 12.01.22 10:00am EST

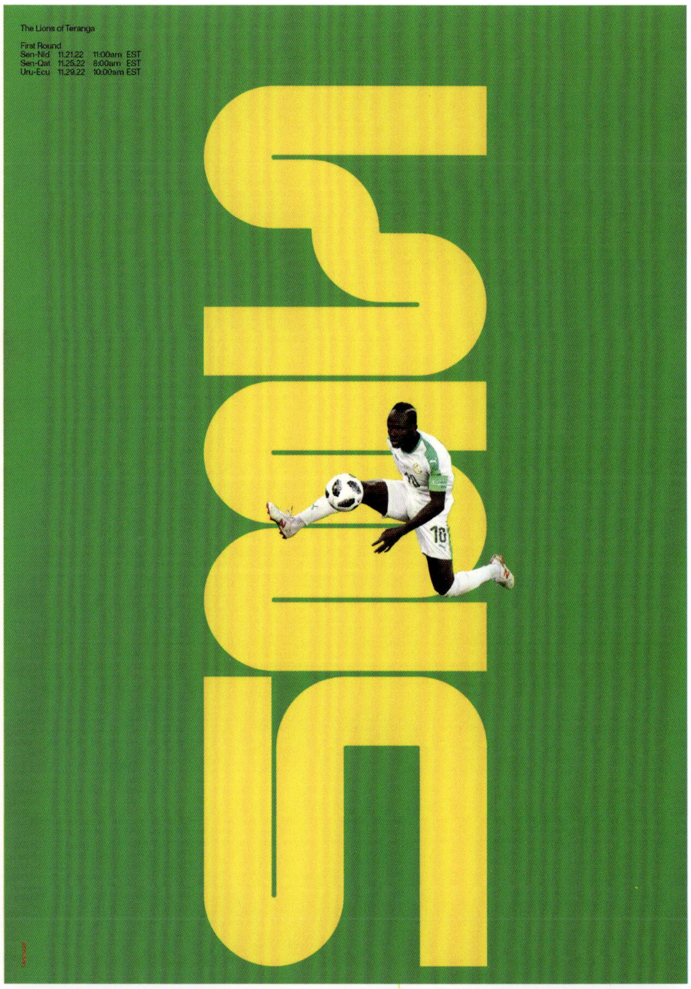

The Lions of Teranga

First Round
Sen-Nld 11.21.22 11:00am EST
Sen-Qat 11.25.22 8:00am EST
Uru-Ecu 11.29.22 10:00am EST

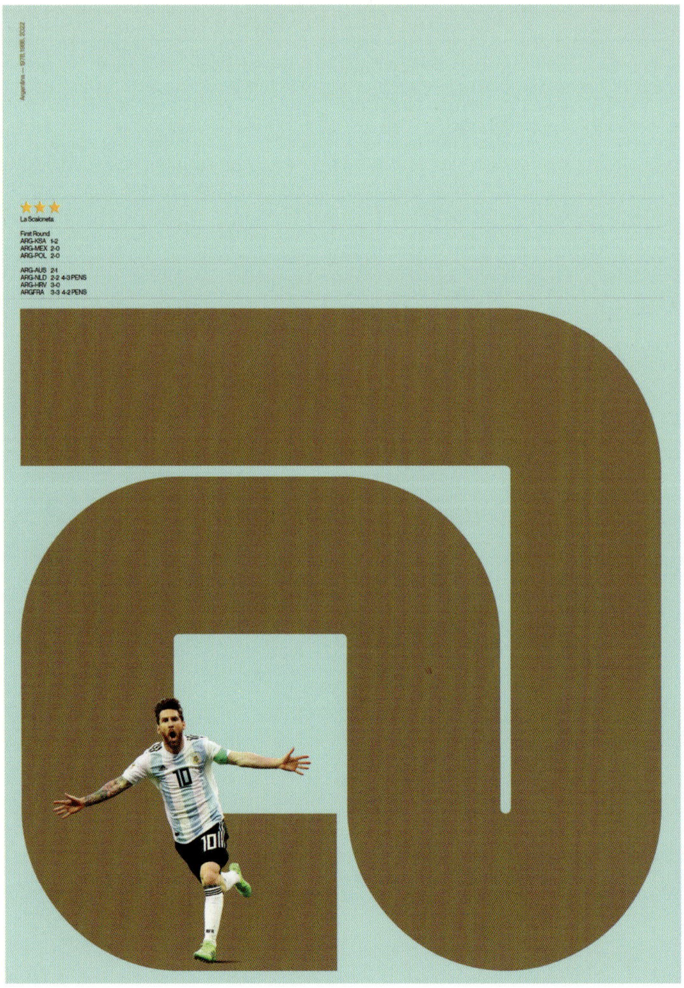

★★★
La Scaloneta

First Round
ARG-KSA 1-2
ARG-MEX 2-0
ARG-POL 2-0

ARG-AUS 2-1
ARG-NLD 2-2 4-3 PENS
ARG-HRV 3-0
ARGFRA 3-3 4-2 PENS

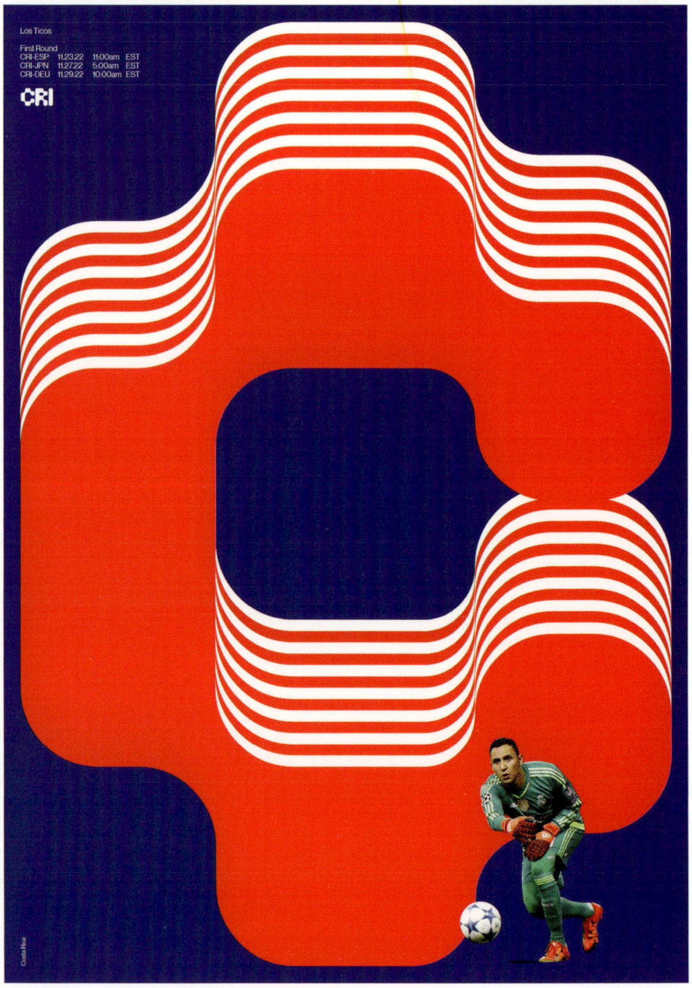

Los Ticos

First Round
CRI-ESP 11.23.22 11:00am EST
CRI-JPN 11.27.22 5:00am EST
CRI-DEU 11.29.22 10:00am EST

CRI

Title: World Cup 2022 Posters | **Client:** George Brown College School of Design
Design Firm: Underline Studio | **P234:** Credit & Commentary | Images 1-4 of 6

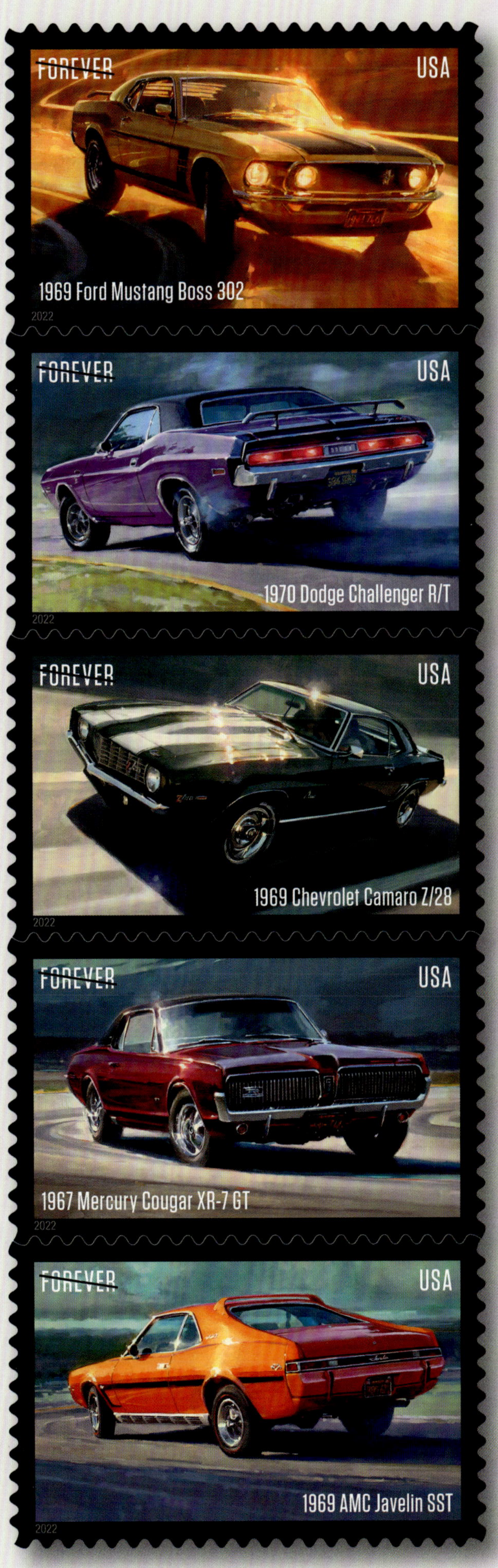

P234: Credit & Commentary **Title:** Pony Cars | **Client:** United States Postal Service | **Design Firm:** Journey Group

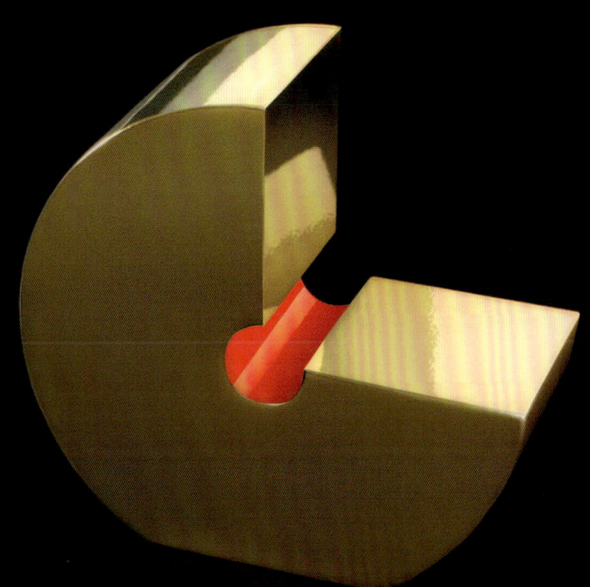

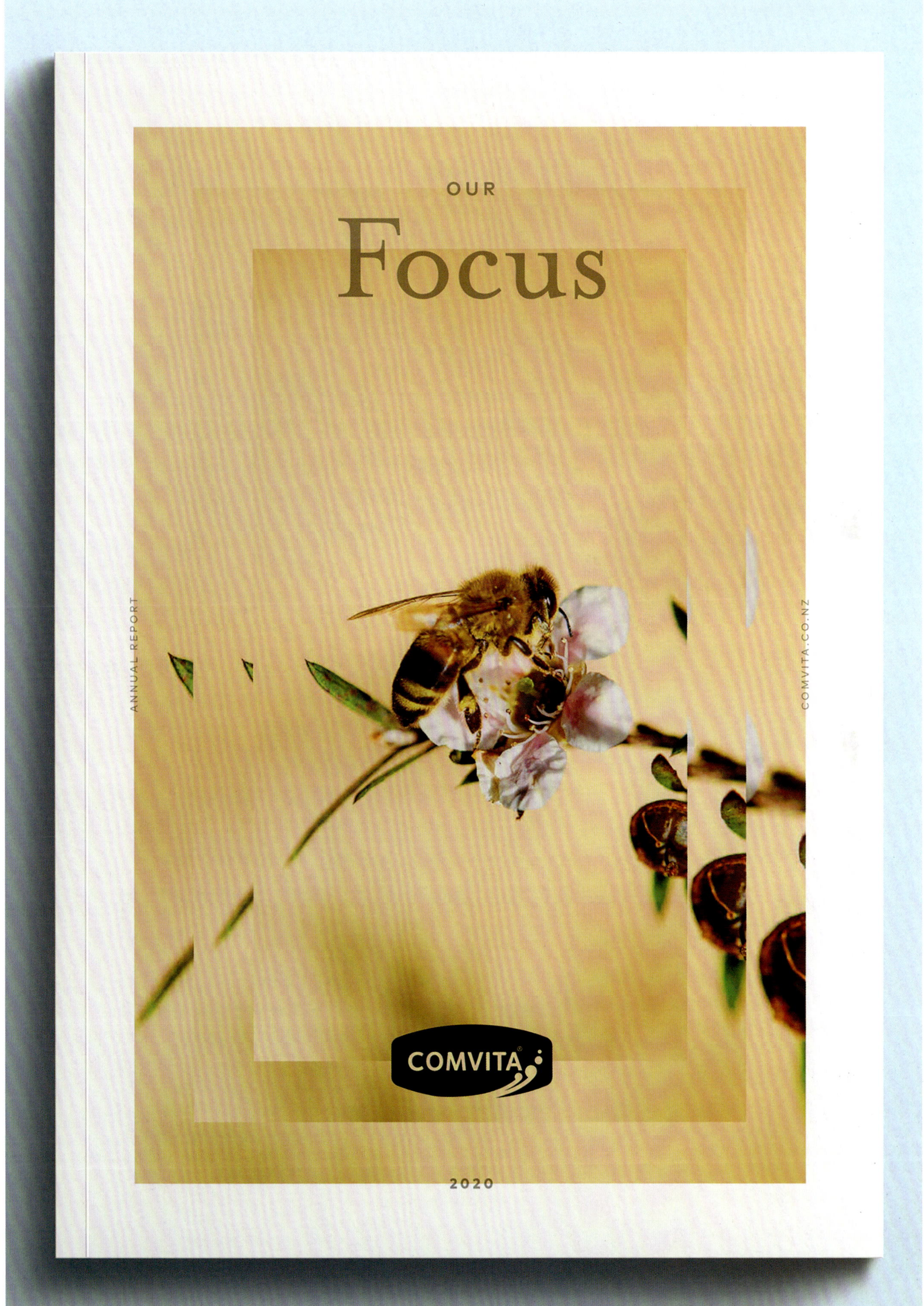

Title: Comvita Annual Report | **Client:** Comvita | **Design Firm:** Insight Creative

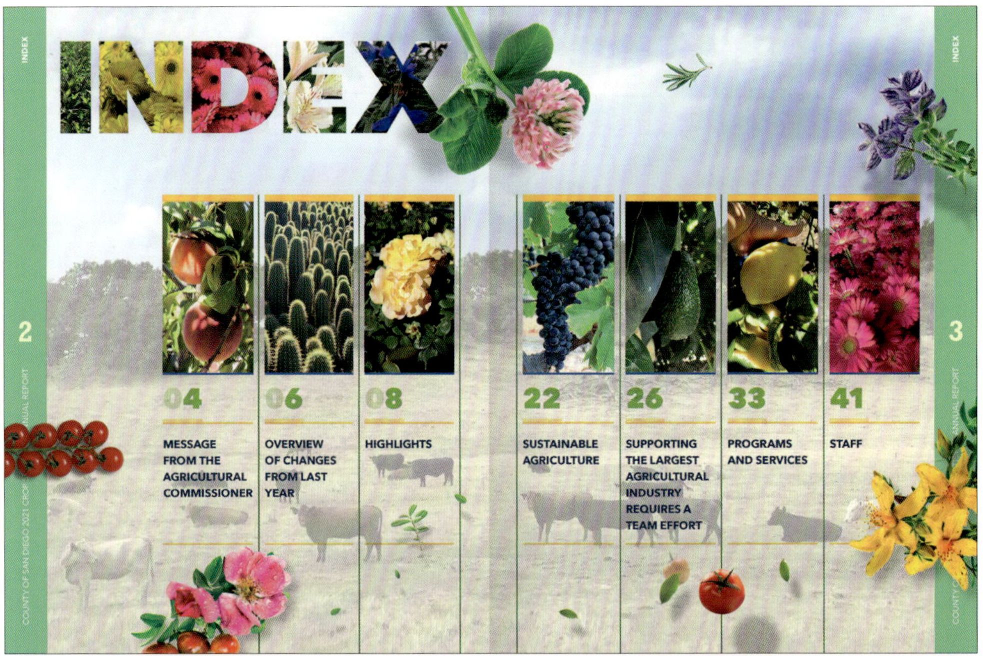

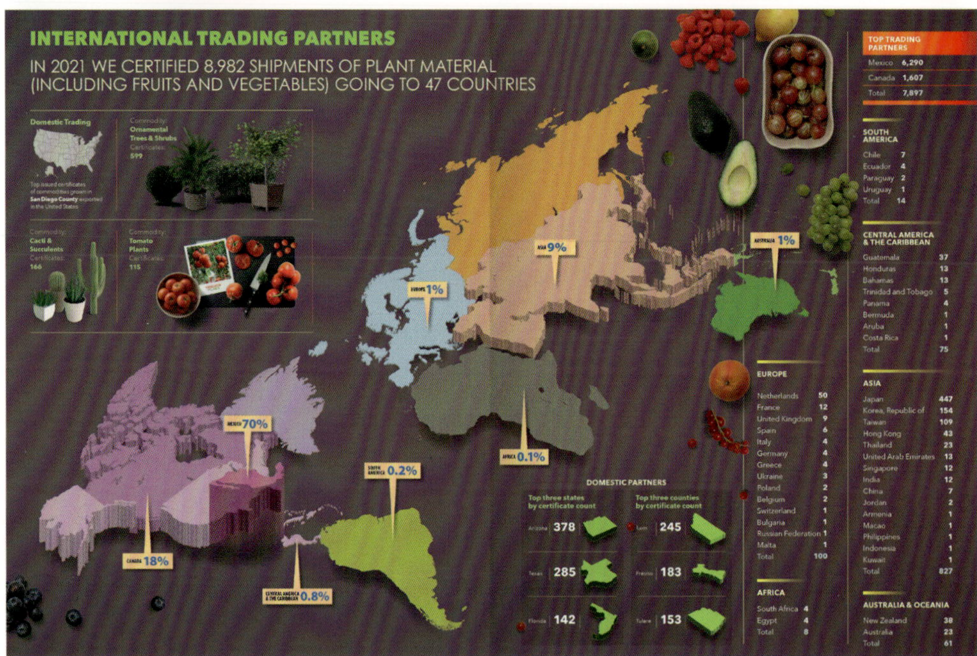

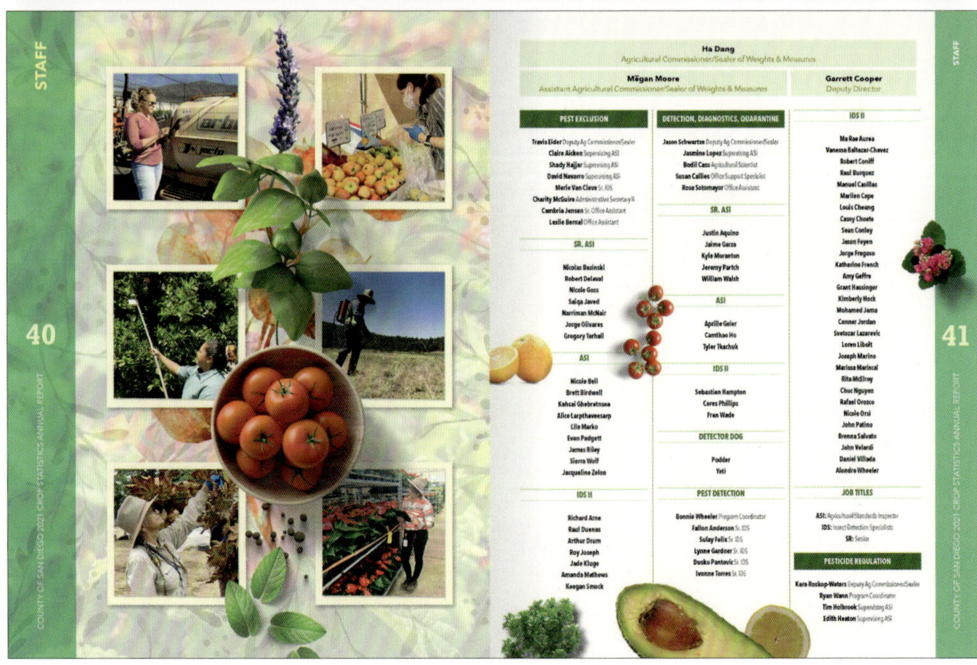

Title: Agricultural Weights and Measures 2021 Crop Report | **Client:** San Diego County Agricultural Weights and Measures
Design Firm: Freaner Creative & Design | **P234:** Credit & Commentary | Images 1-3 of 7

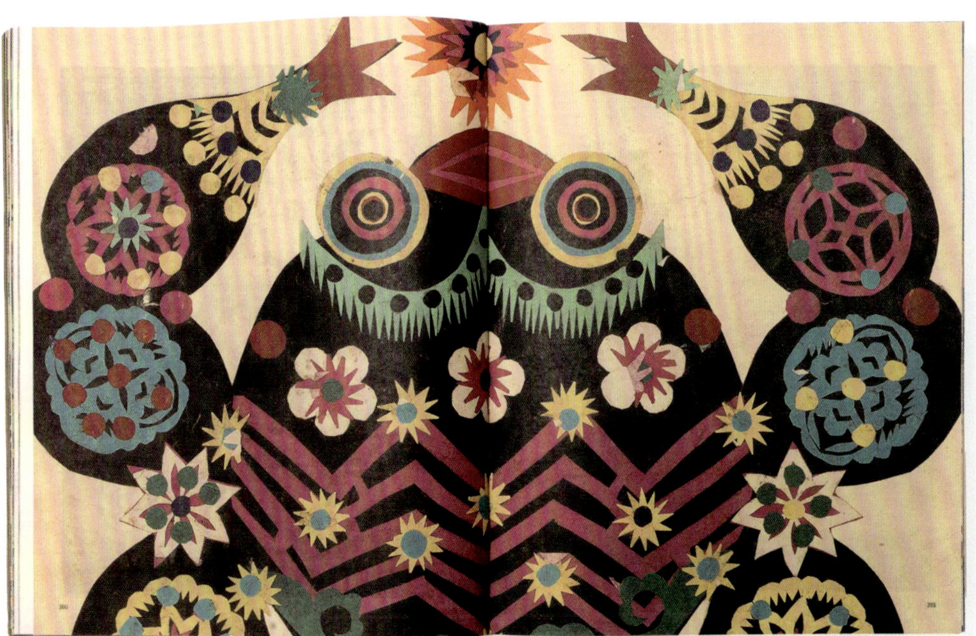

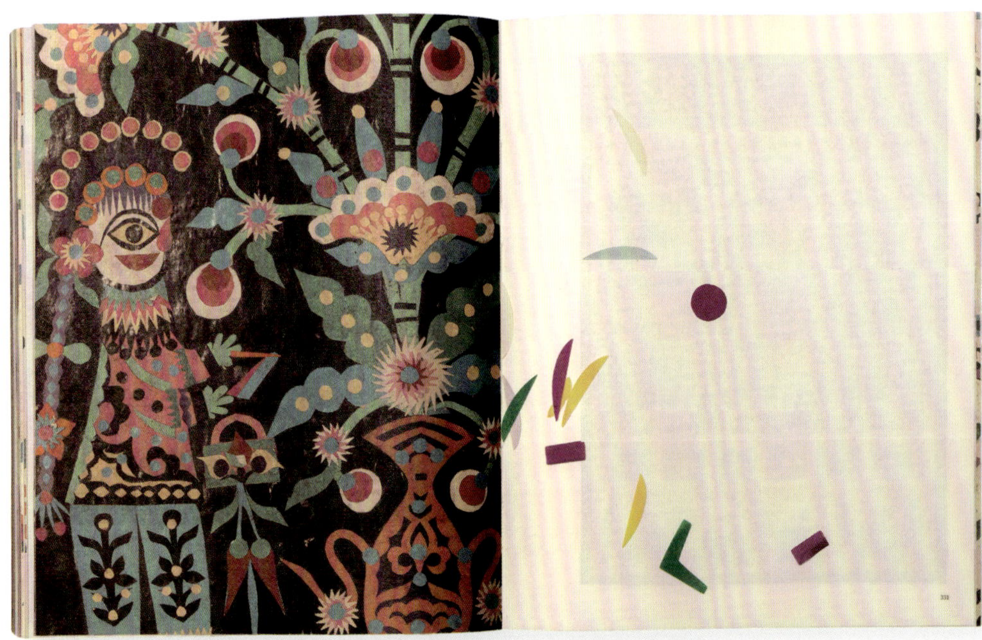

Title: The World Among Flowers - A Research Exhibition of Ku Shulan's Works Collected By the Shaanxi Province Art Museum
Client: Shaanxi Province Art Museum | **Design Firm:** HILLS | **P234:** Credit & Commentary | Images 1-3 of 7

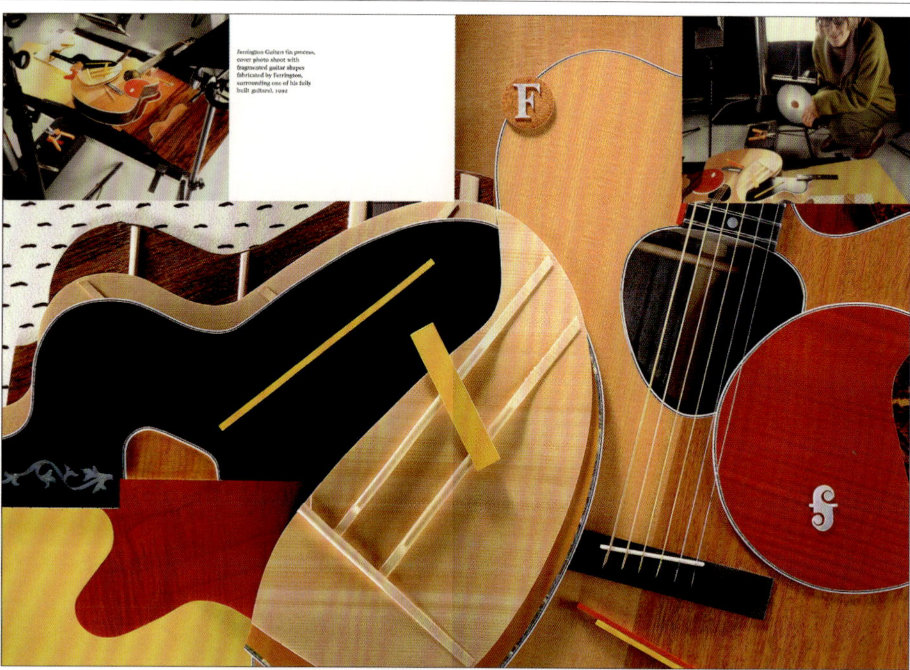

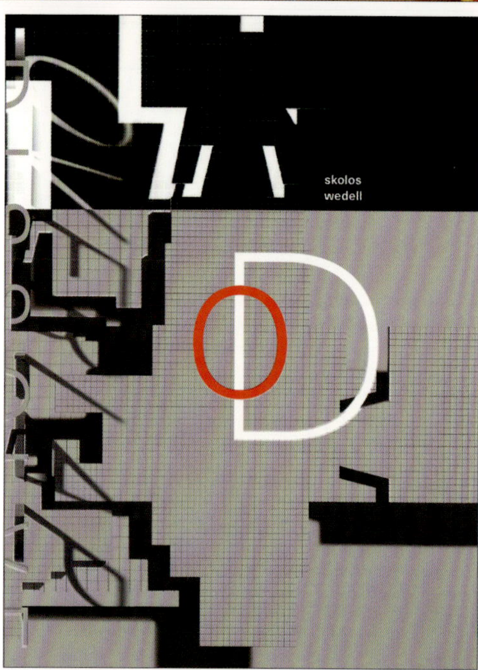

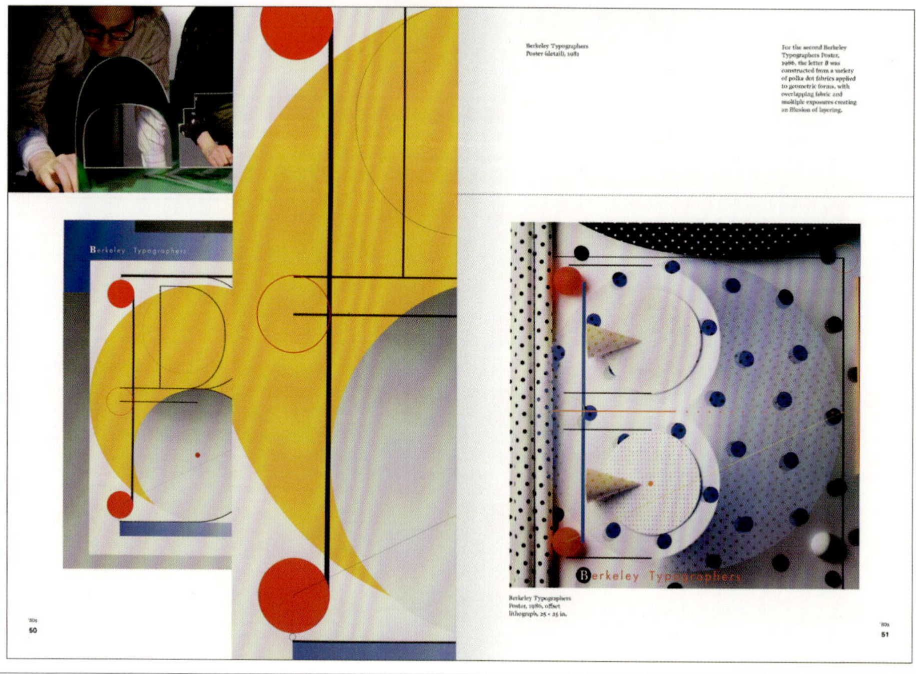

Title: Overlap/Dissolve | **Client:** Self-initiated | **Design Firm:** Skolos-Wedell

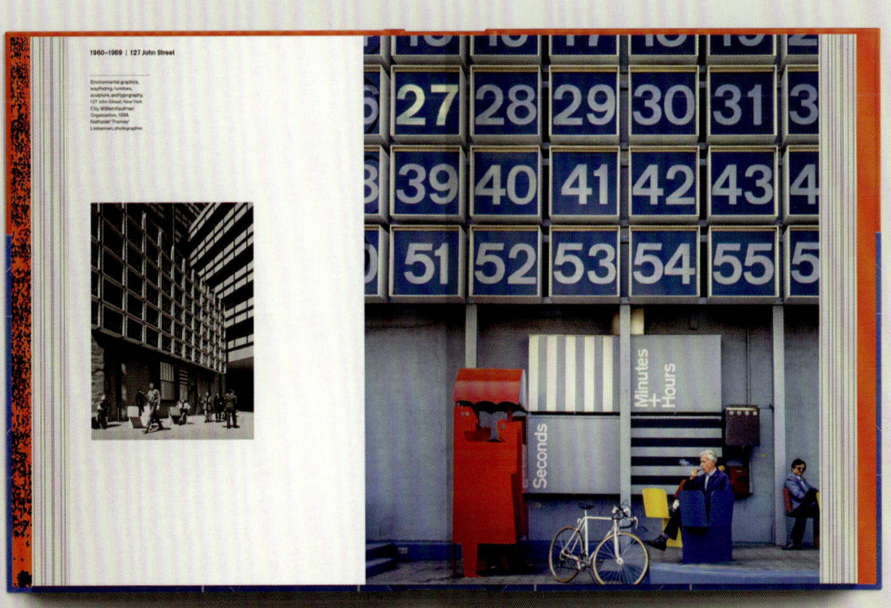

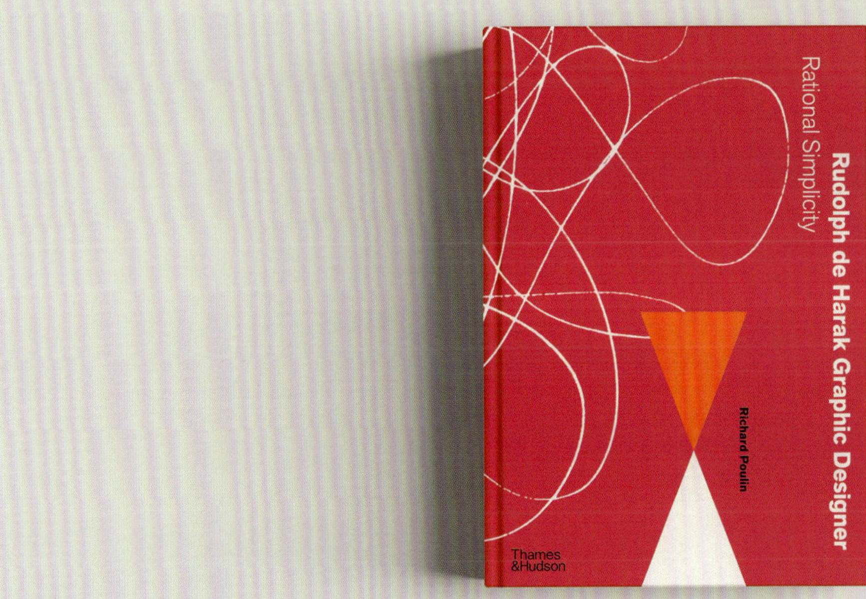

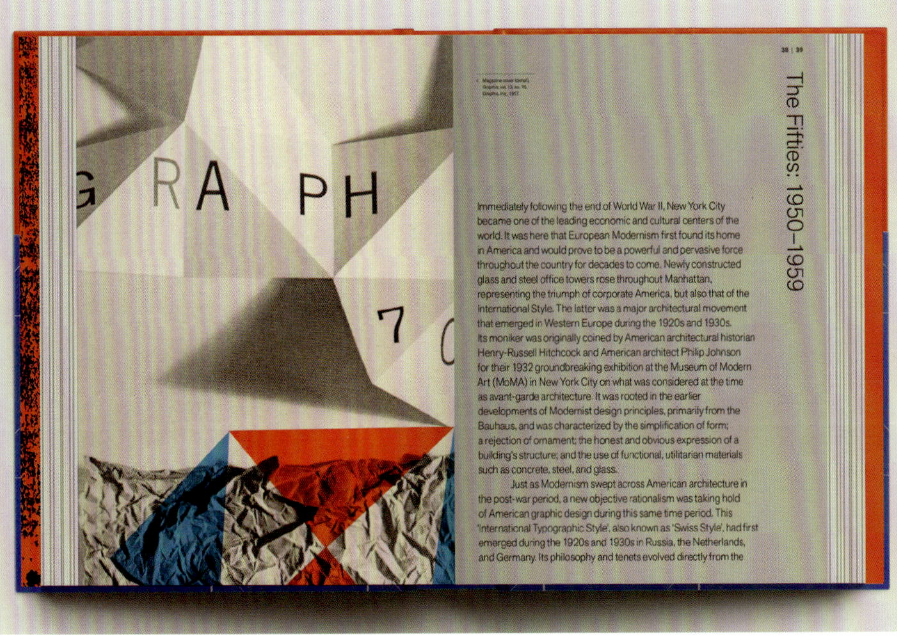

Title: Rational Simplicity: Rudolph de Harak, Graphic Designer | **Client:** Thames & Hudson Ltd.
Design Firm: Poulin + Morris Inc. | **P234:** Credit & Commentary | Images 1-3 of 7

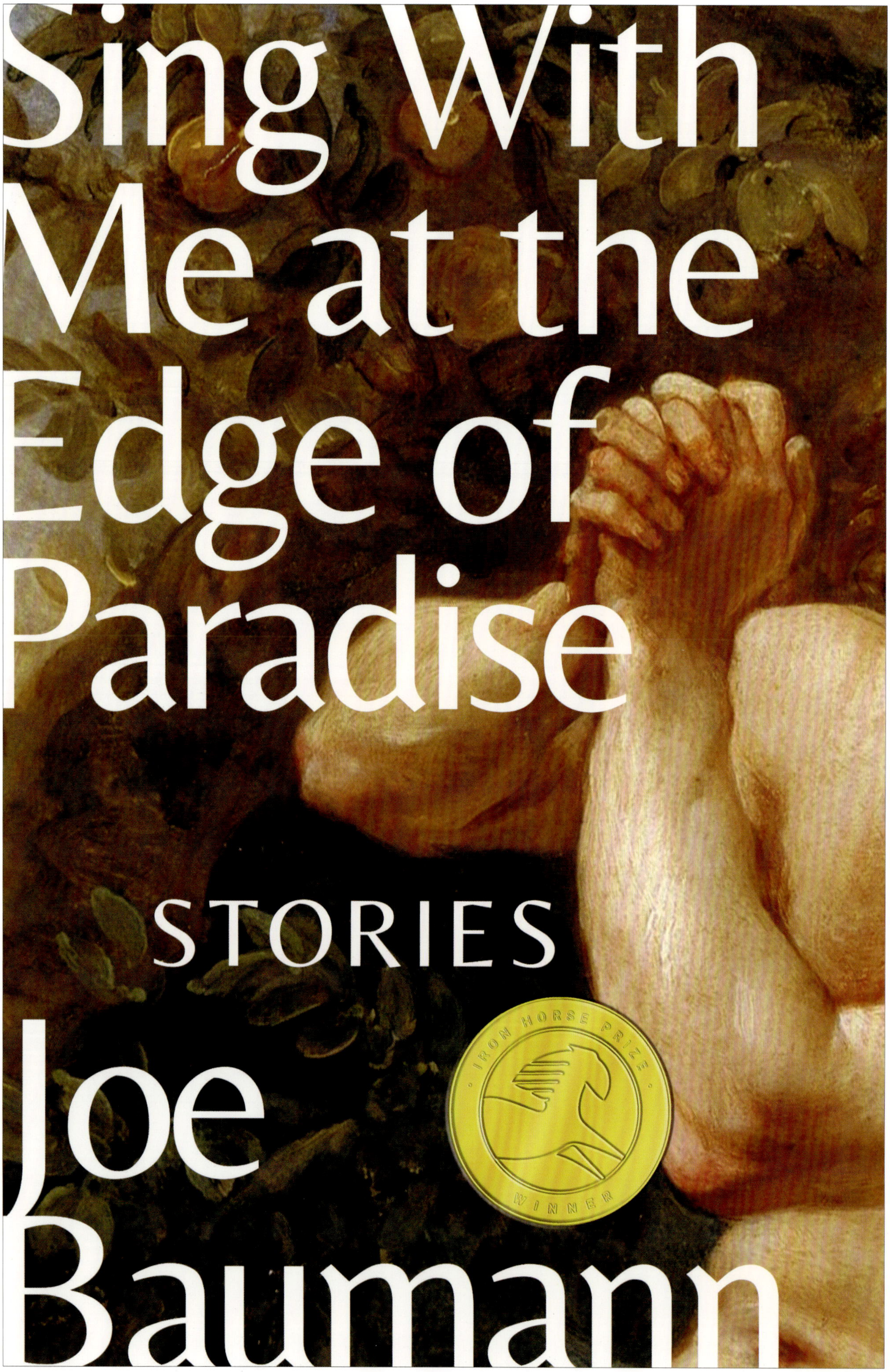

Sing With Me at the Edge of Paradise

STORIES

Joe Baumann

IRON HORSE PRIZE WINNER

Title: Sing With Me at the Edge of Paradise | **Client:** Self-initated
Design Firm: Texas Tech University Press | **P234:** Credit & Commentary

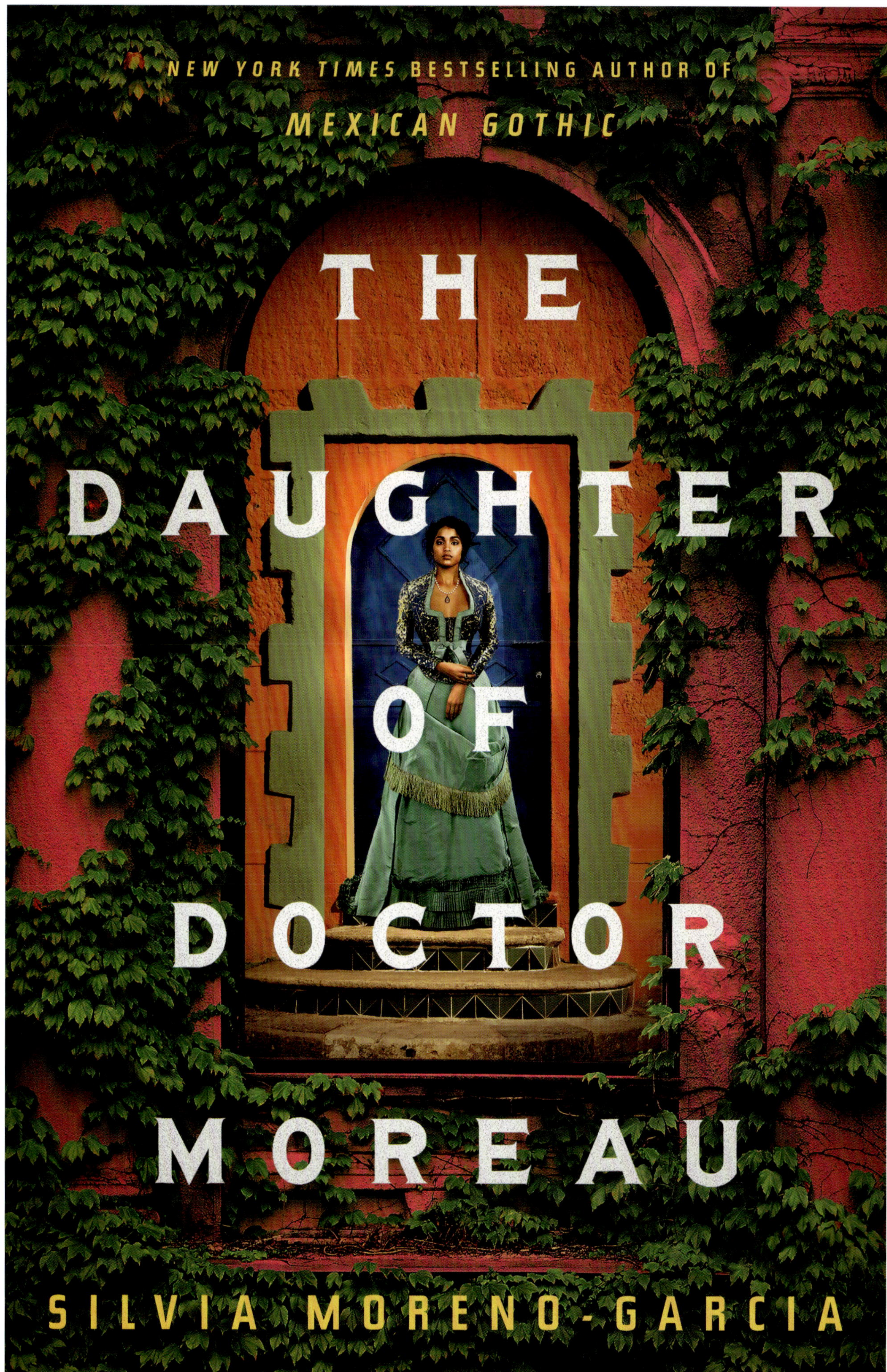

Title: The Daughter of Doctor Moreau | **Clients:** Penguin Random House, Cassie Gonzales
Design Firm: Faceout Studio | **P234:** Credit & Commentary

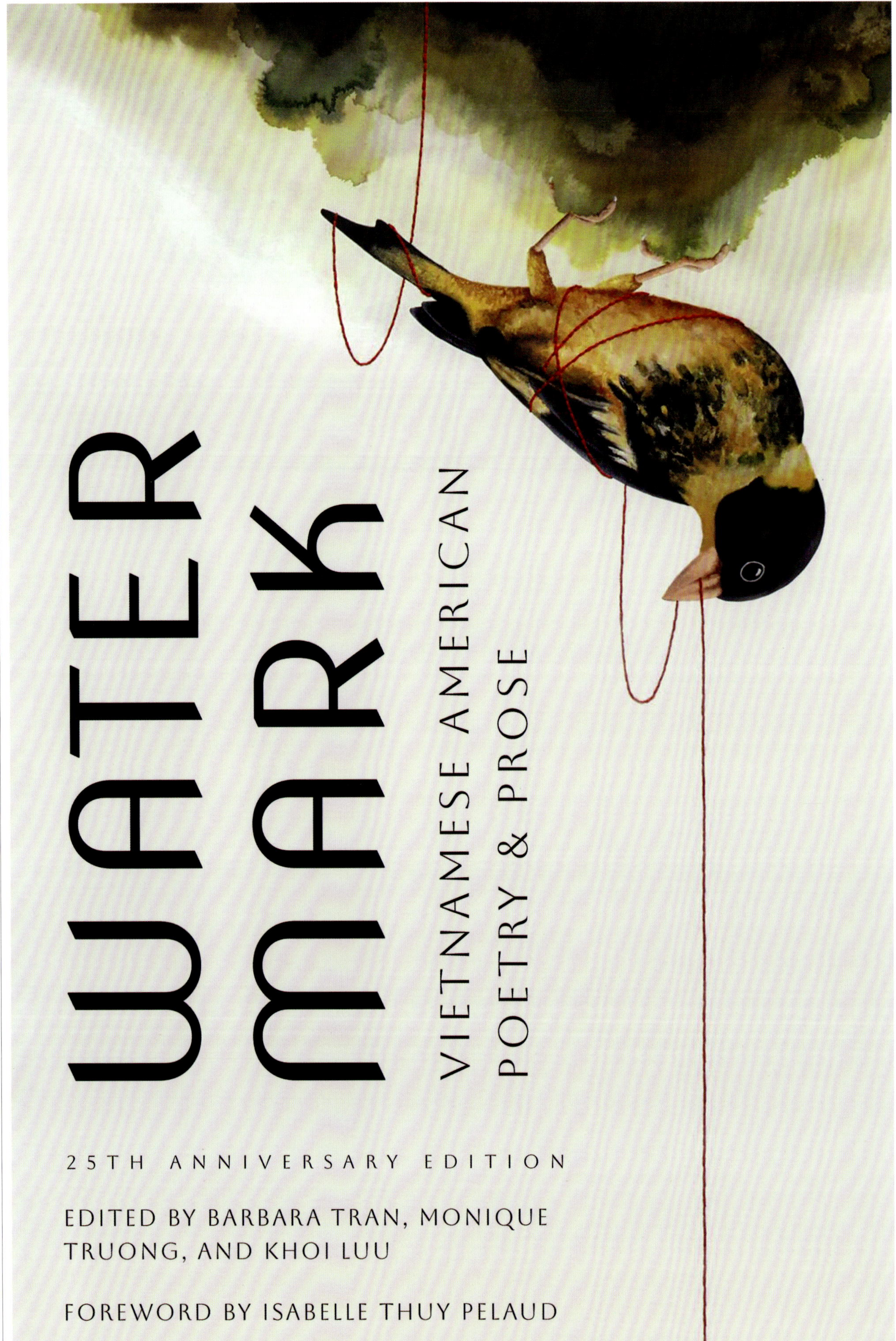

Title: Watermark | **Client:** Self-initated
Design Firm: Texas Tech University Press | **P235:** Credit & Commentary

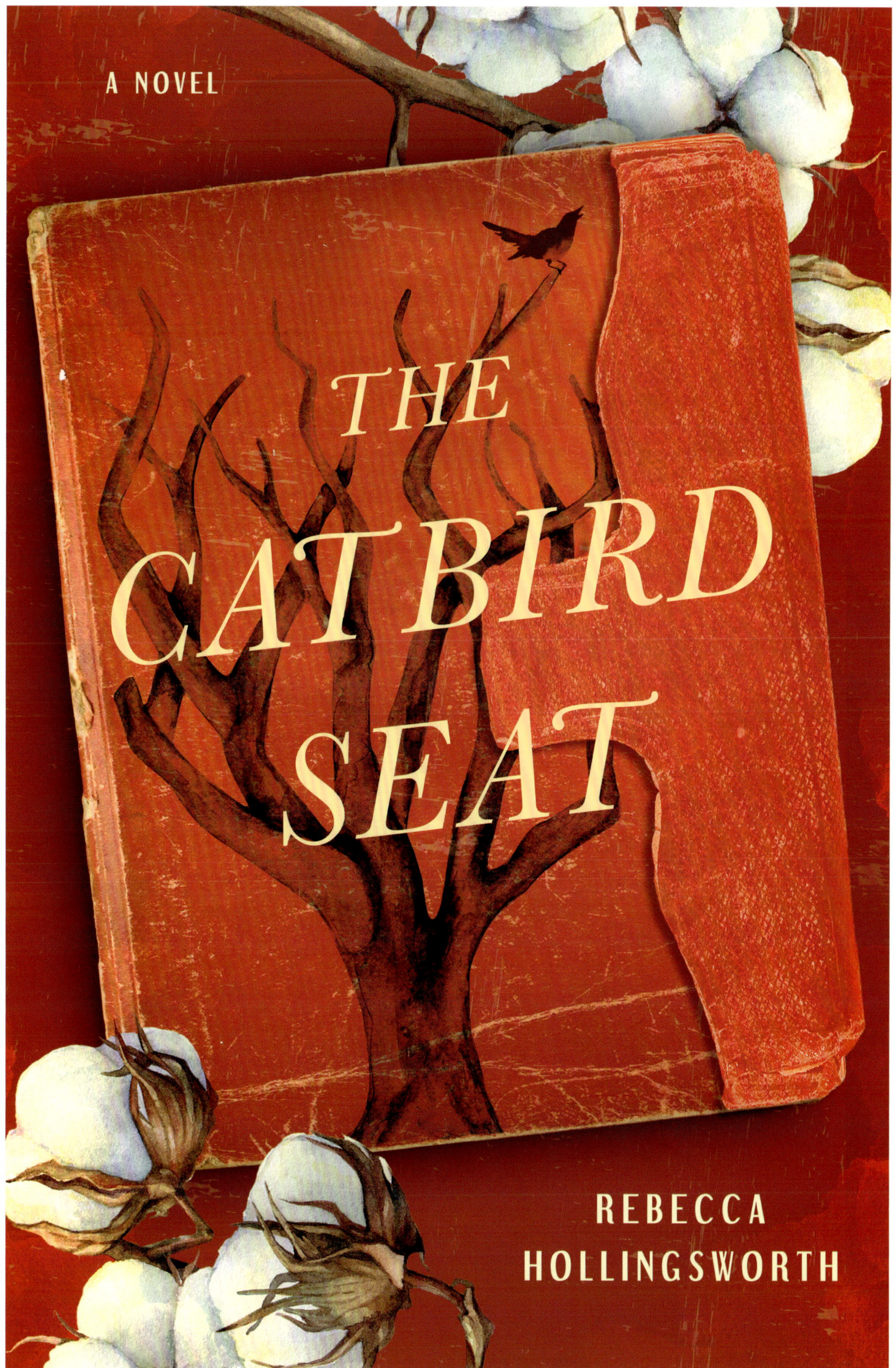

Title: The Catbird Seat | **Client:** Rebecca Hollingsworth
Design Firm: Greenleaf Book Group | **P235:** Credit & Commentary

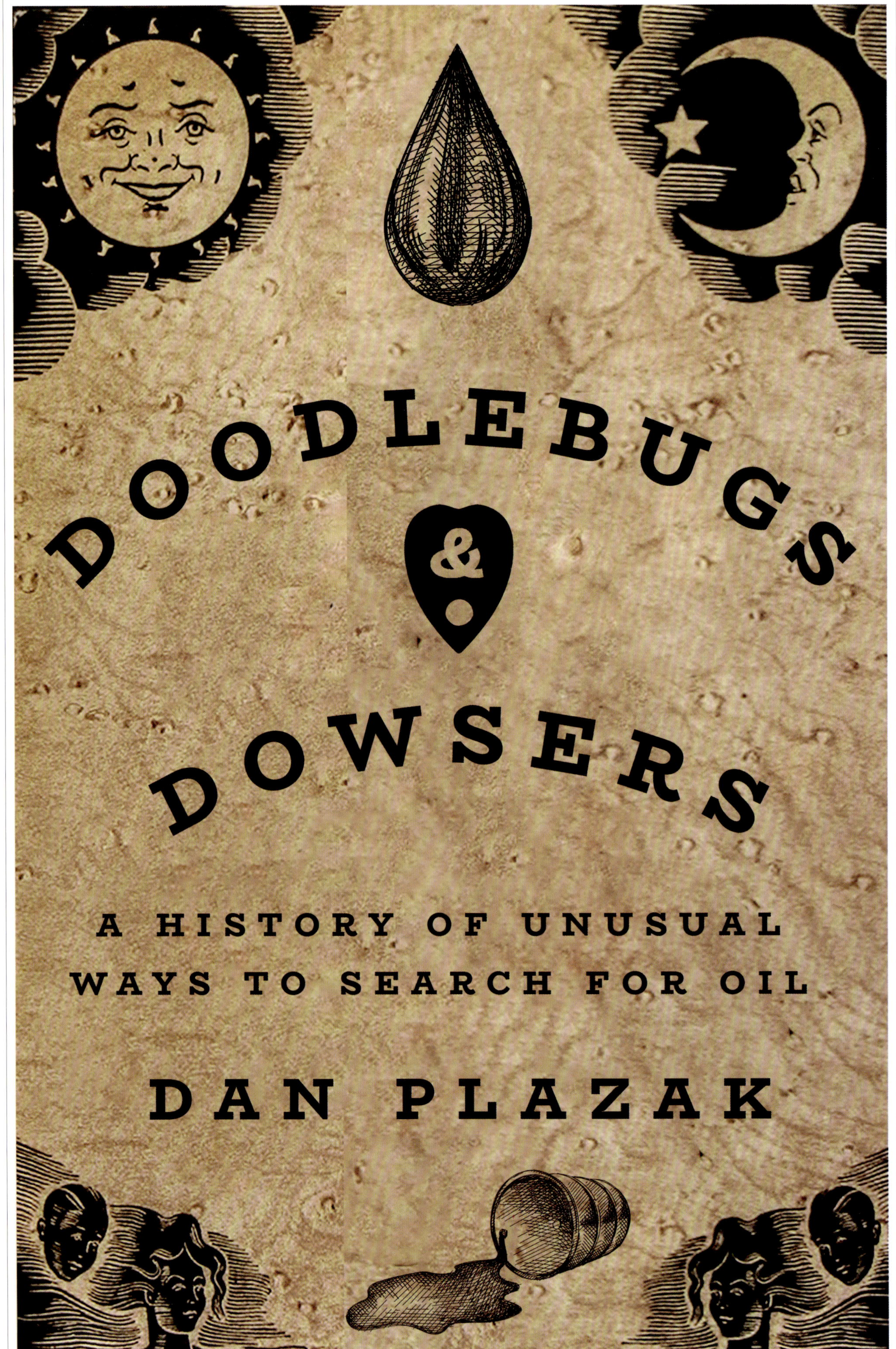

Title: Doodlebugs and Dowsers | **Client:** Self-initated
Design Firm: Texas Tech University Press | **P235:** Credit & Commentary

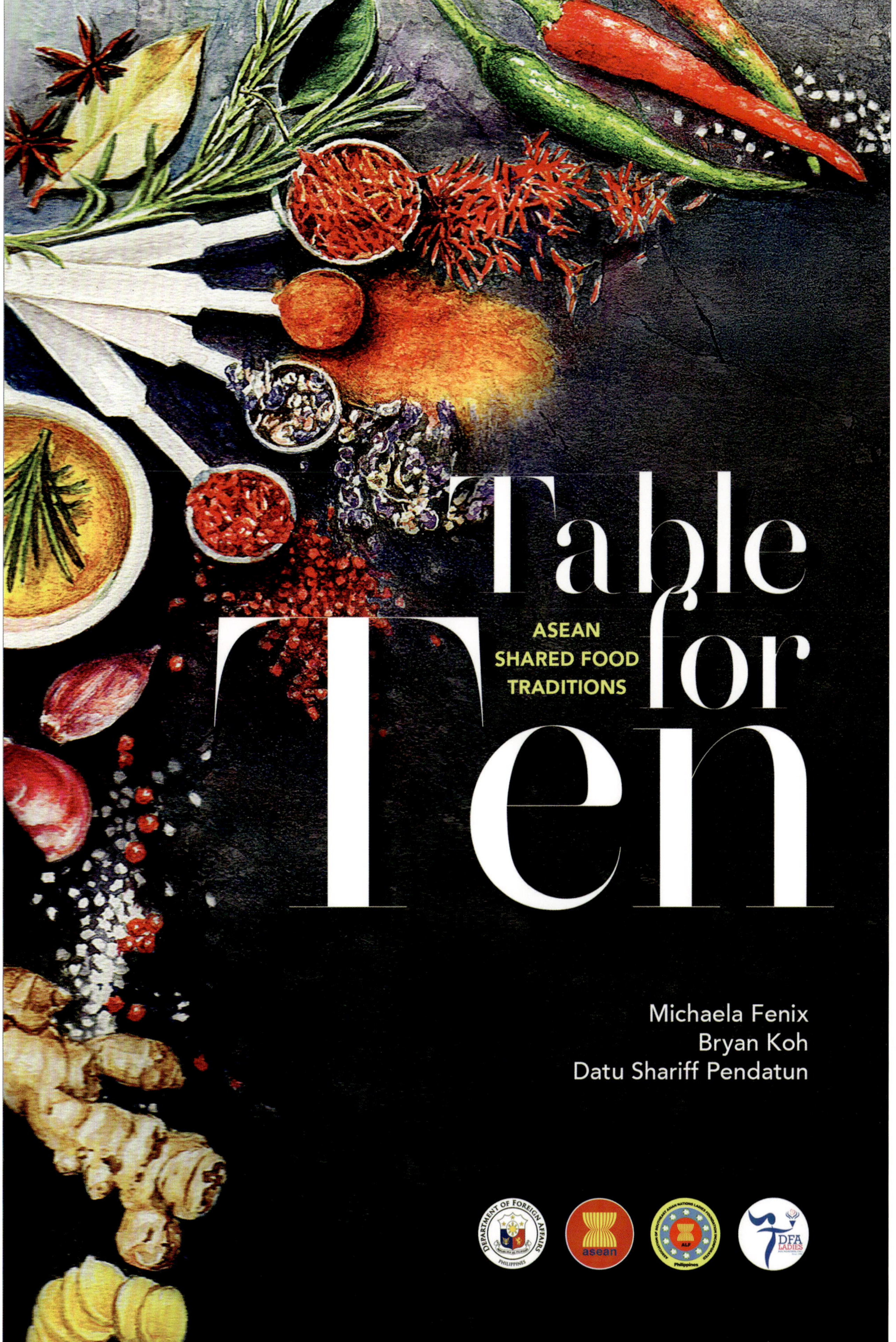

Title: TABLE FOR TEN (ASEAN Shared Food Traditions) | **Clients:** Asean Ladies Foundation, Department of Foreign Affairs, Ma. Luisa Locsin, Cecille Wenceslao | **Design Firm:** Studio 5 Designs Inc. | **P235:** Credit & Commentary | Image 1 of 7

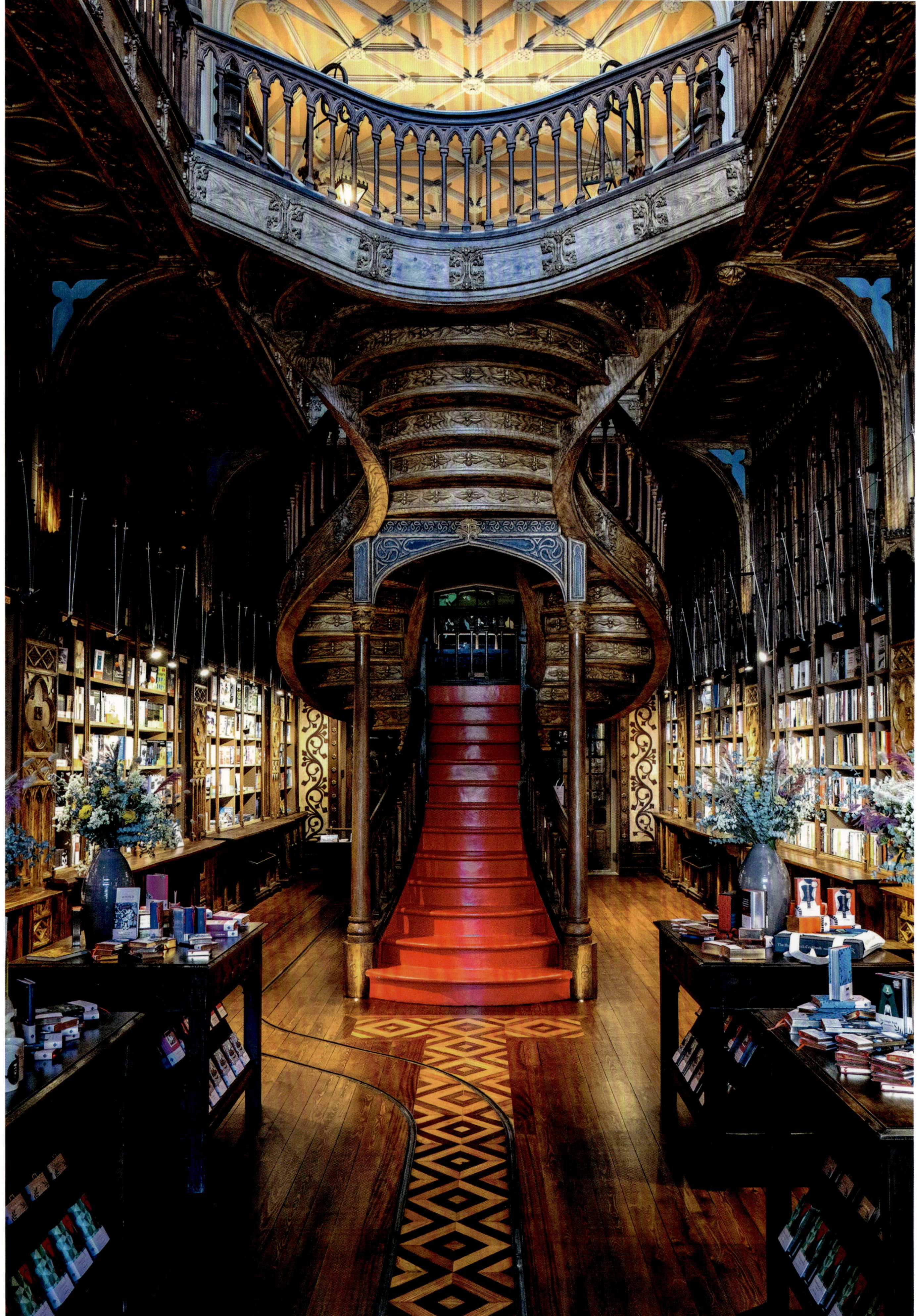

 Title: Livraria Lello Branding | Client: Livraria Lello | Design Firm: Studio Eduardo Aires

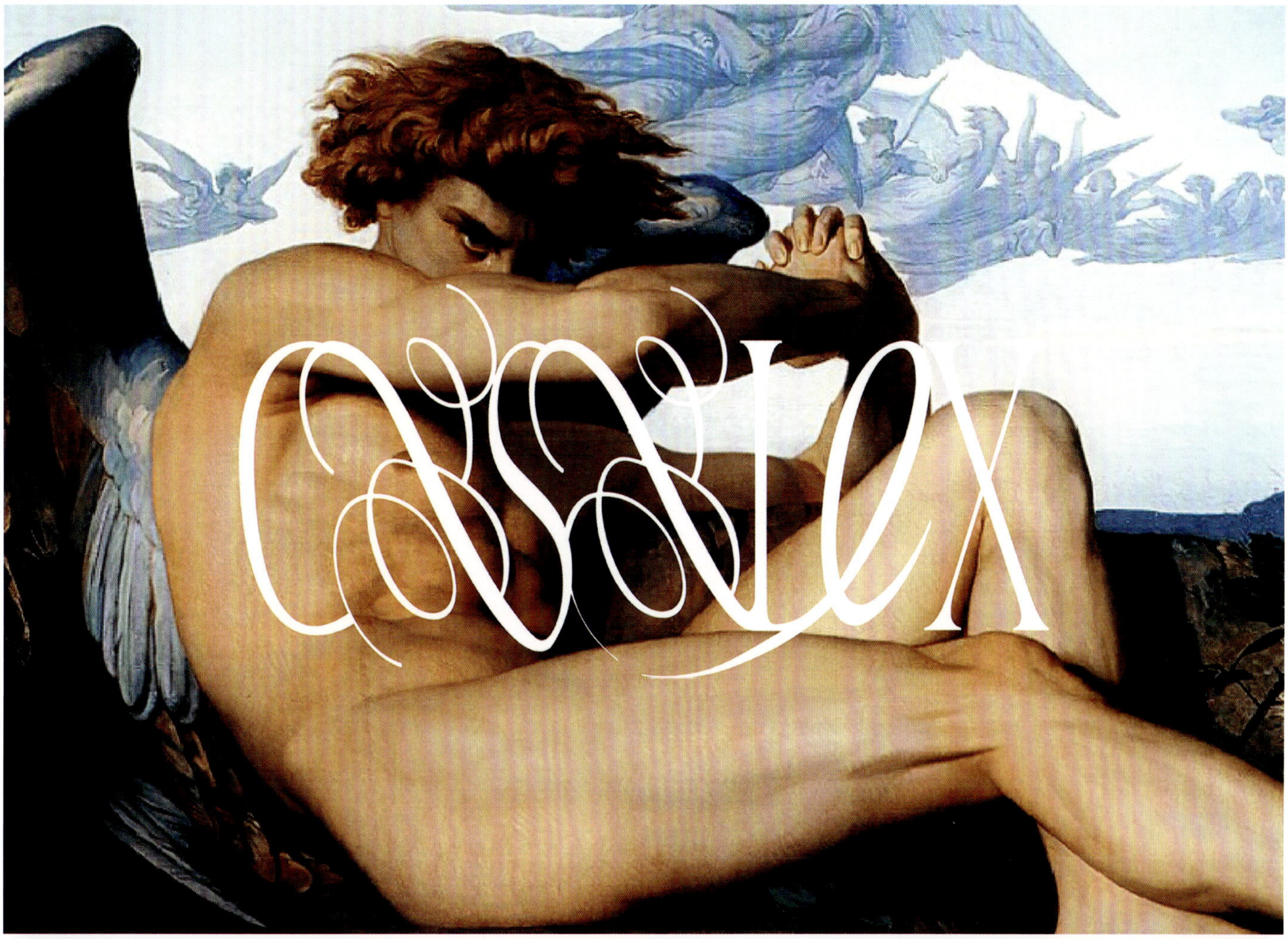

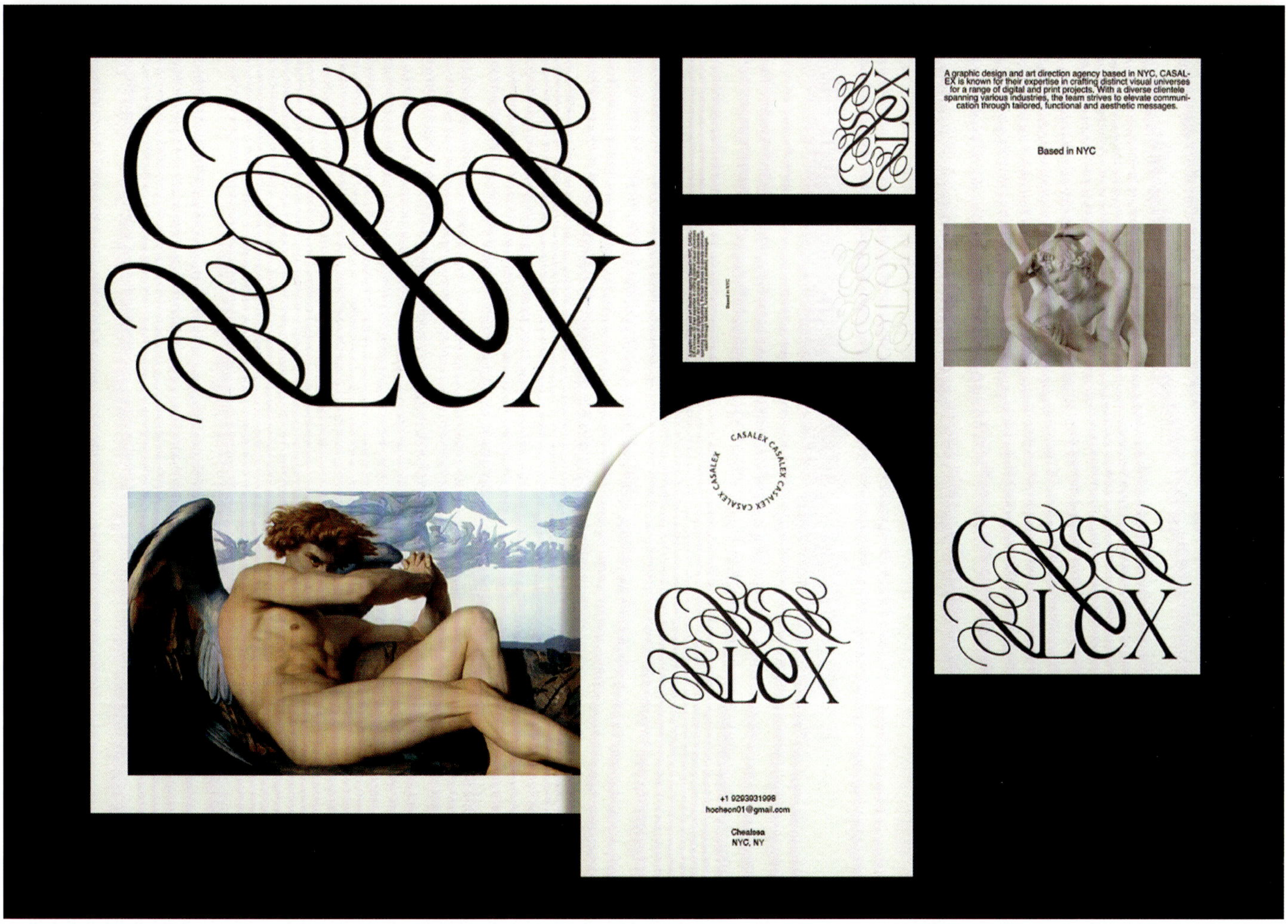

Title: CASALEX | **Client:** Alex Beaufort | **Design Firm:** Haotian Dong

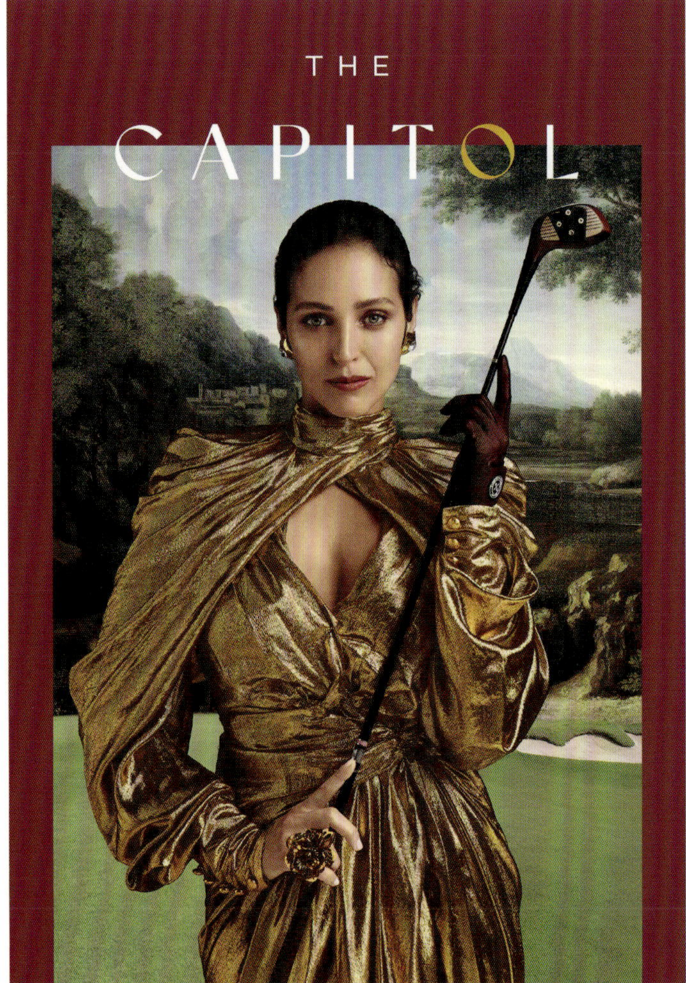

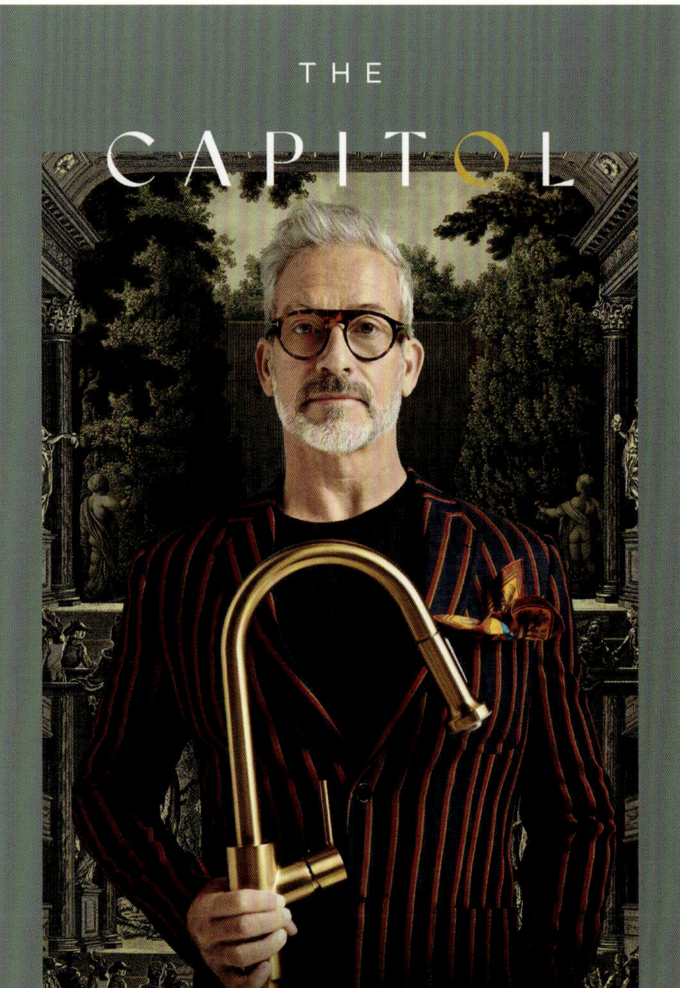

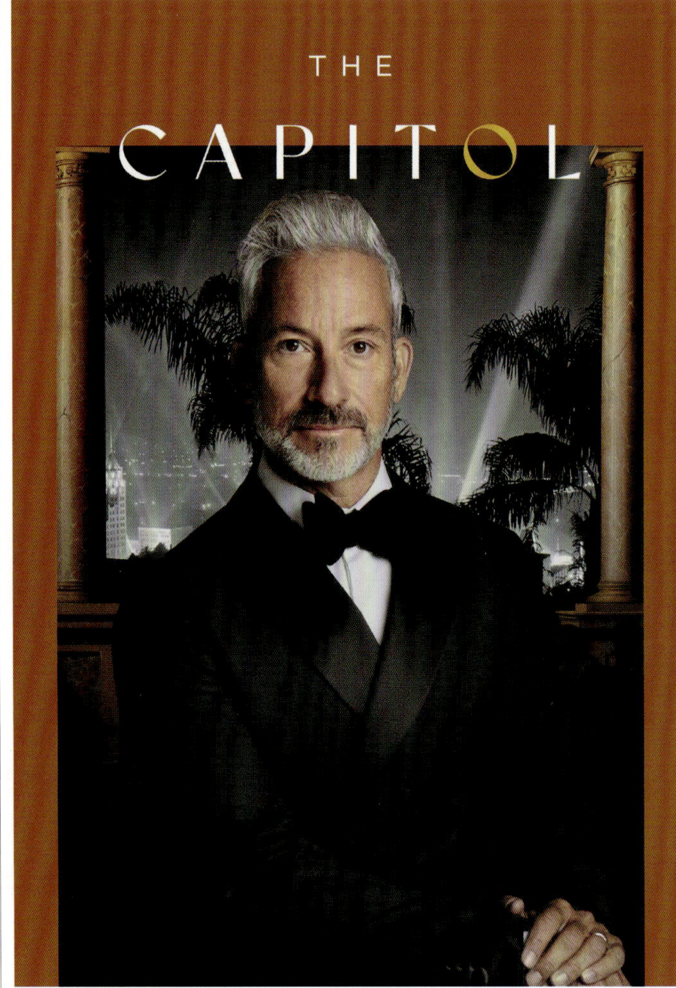

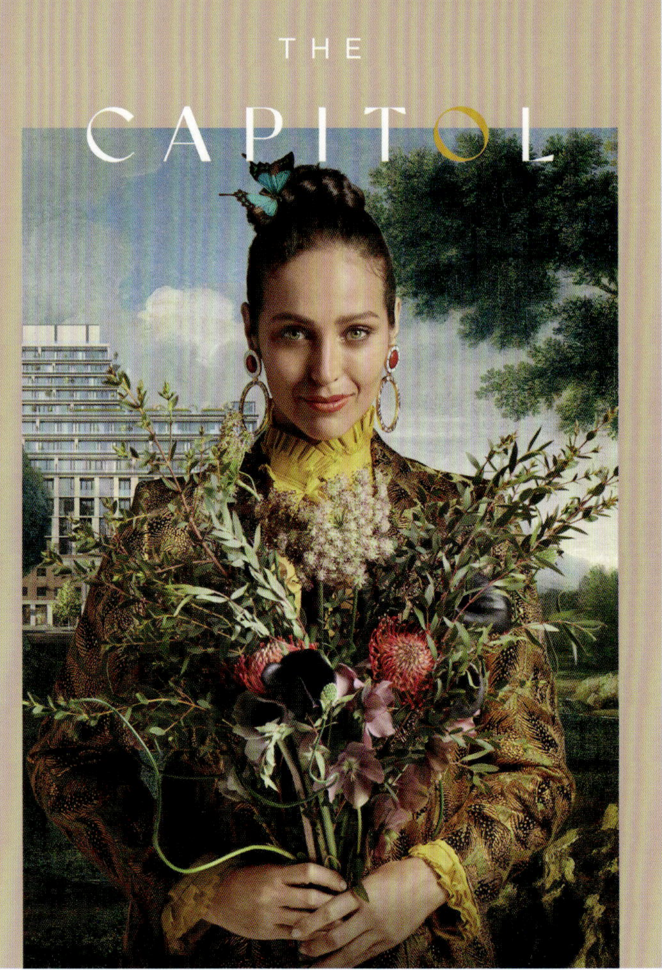

P235: Credit & Commentary **Title:** The Capitol Folder | **Client:** Madison Group | **Design Firm:** IF Studio

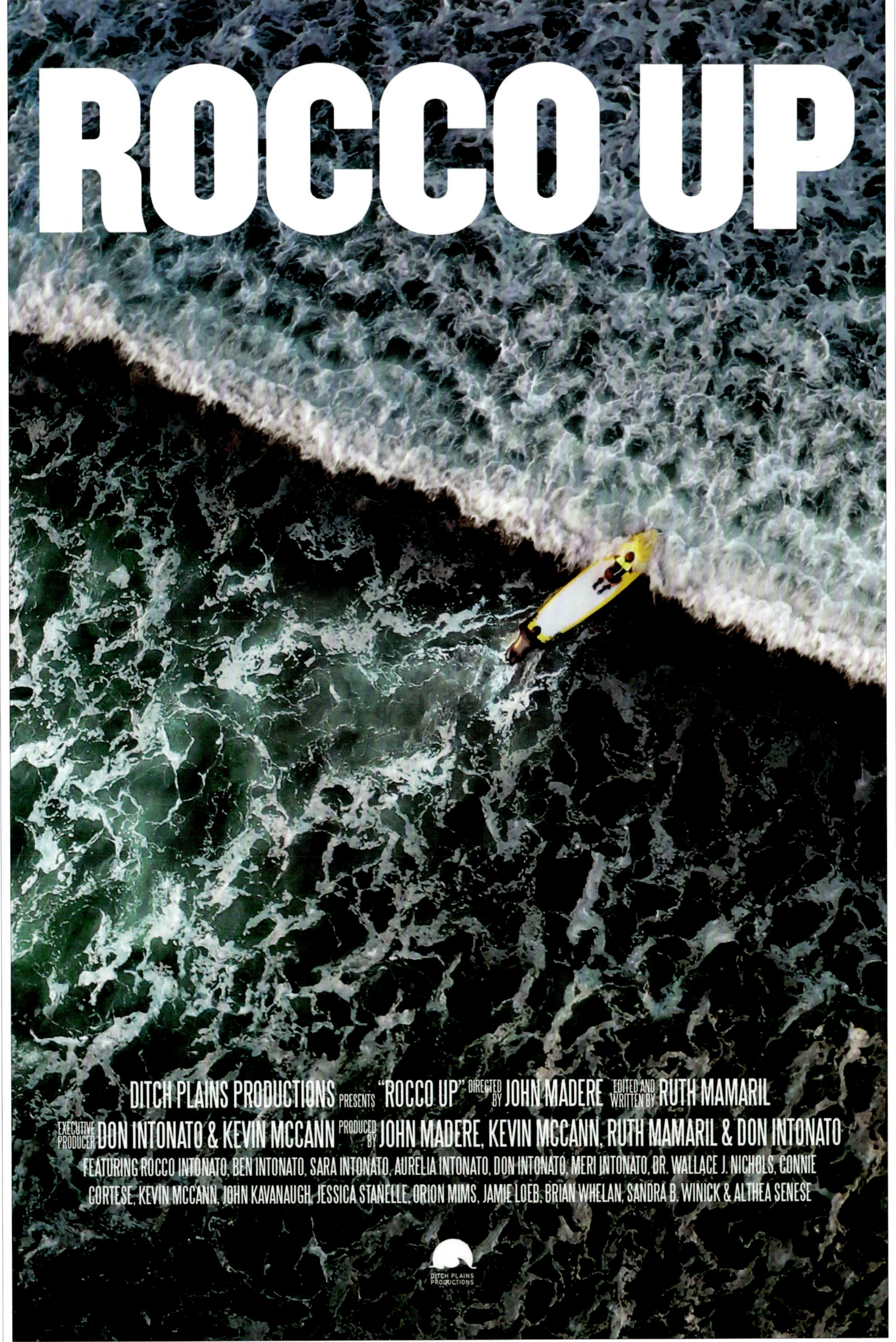

Title: Rocco Up Film Brand Strategy & Design | **Client:** Ditch Plains Productions
Design Firm: Decker Design | **P235:** Credit & Commentary | Image 1 of 7

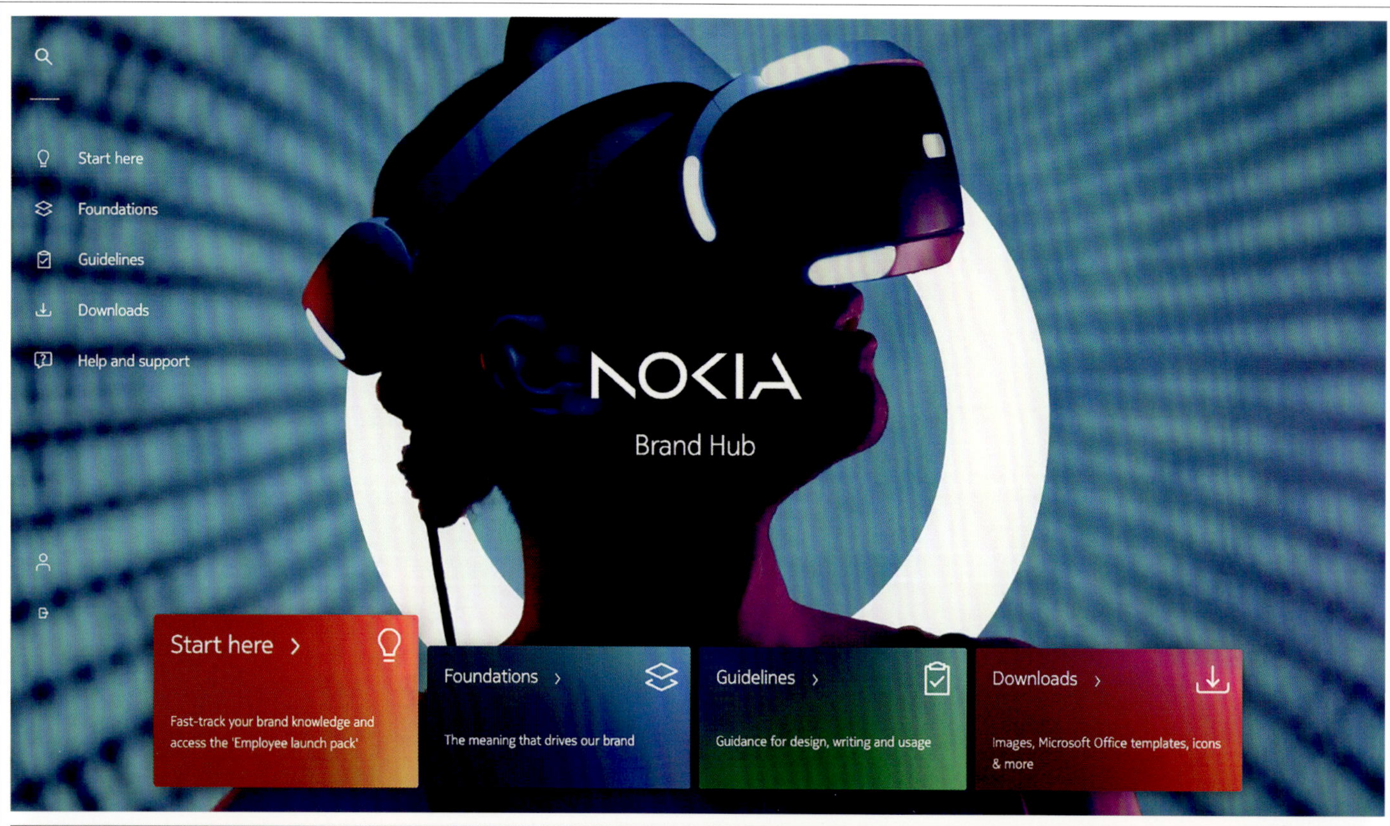

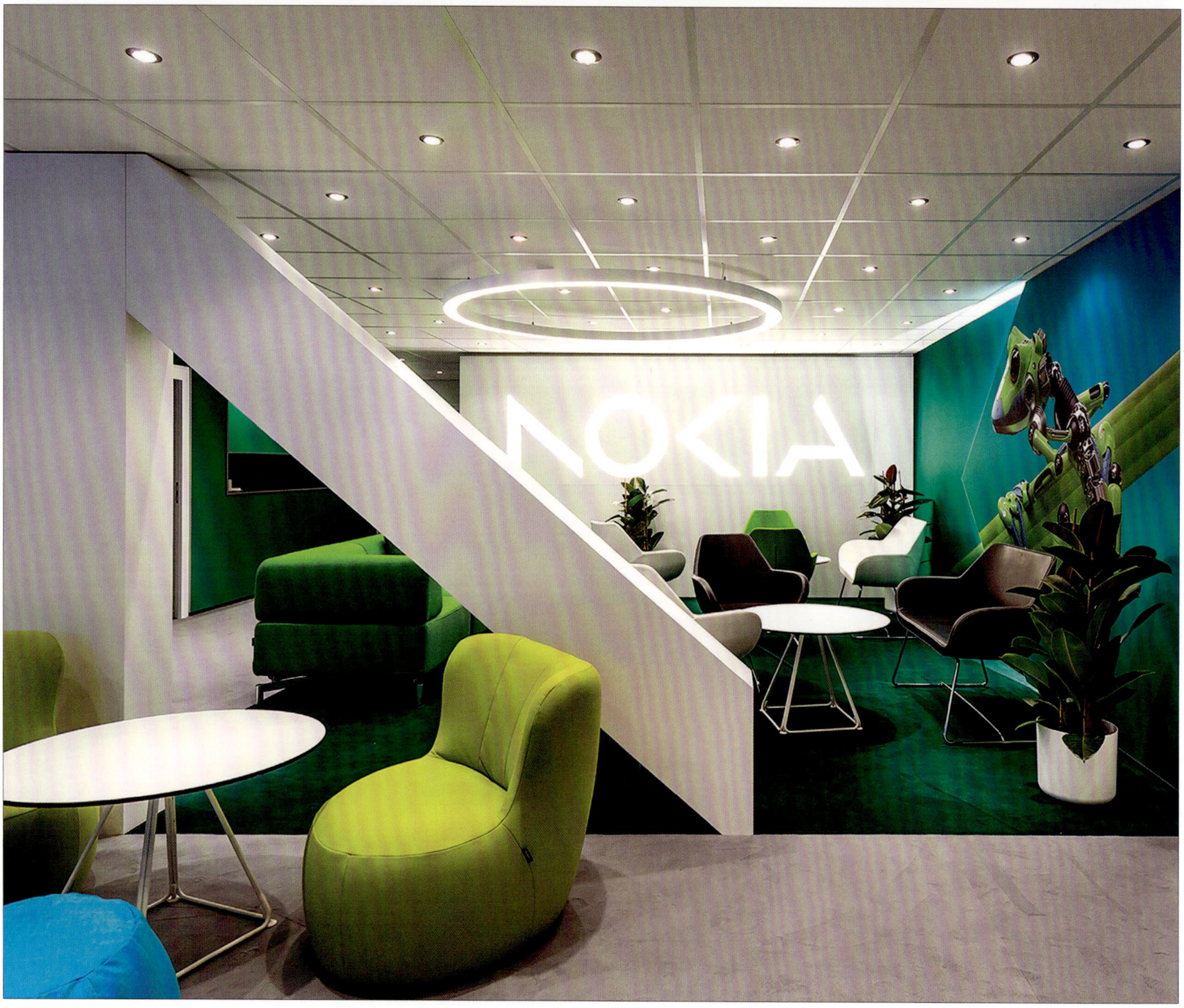

Title: Driving Recognition for Nokia As A B2B Tech Powerhouse | **Client:** Nokia
Design Firm: Lippincott | **P235:** Credit & Commentary | Images 1, 2 of 7

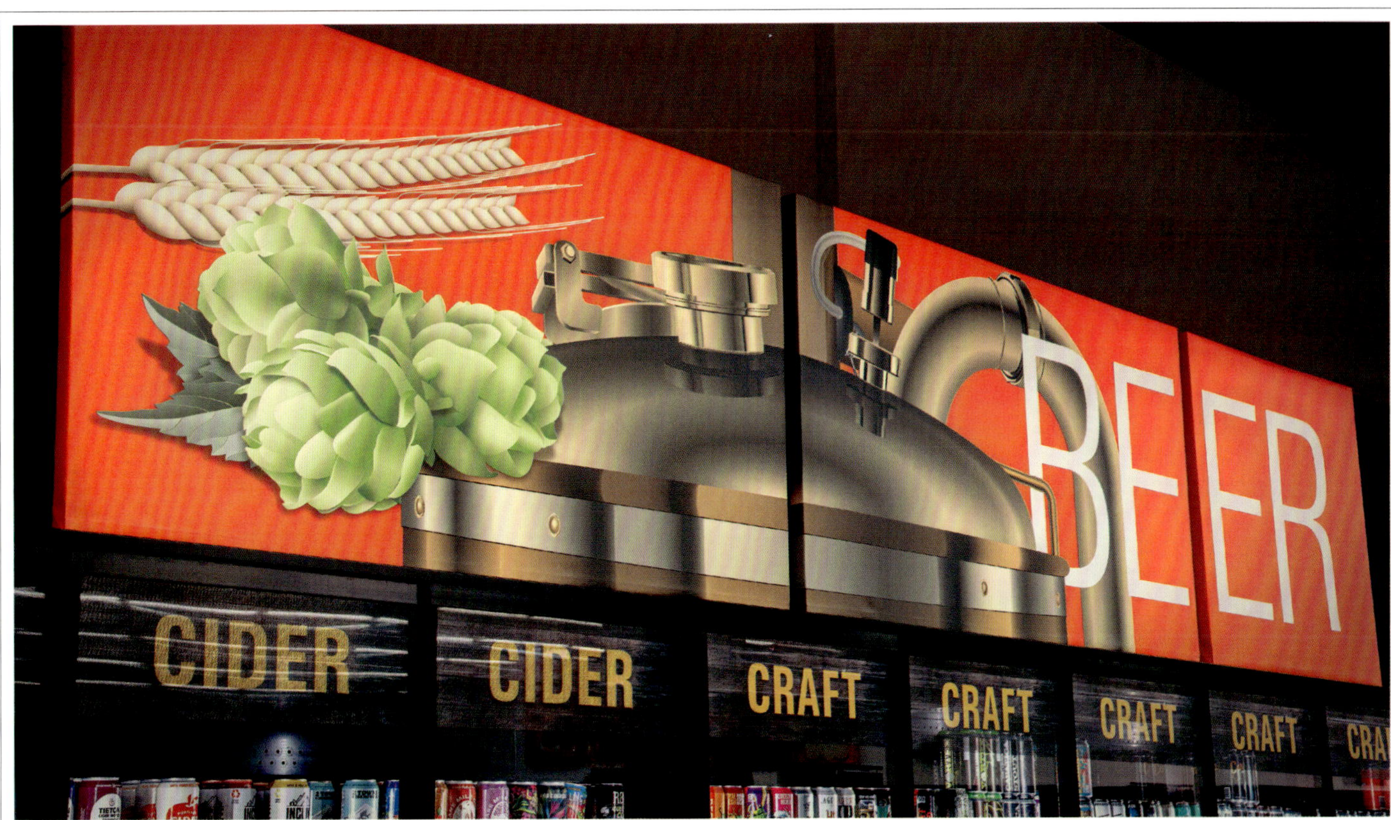

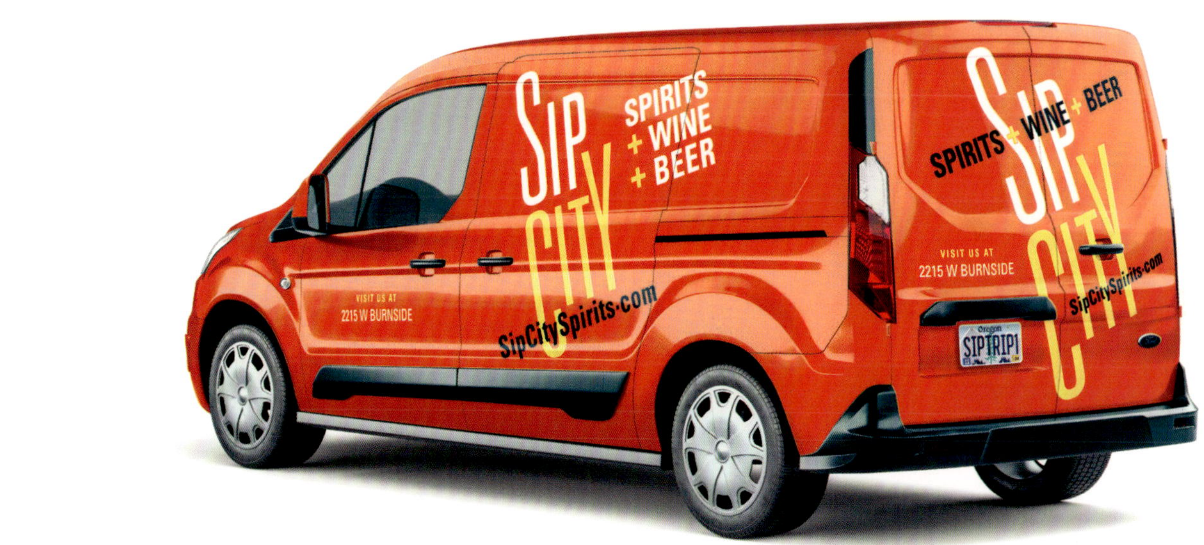

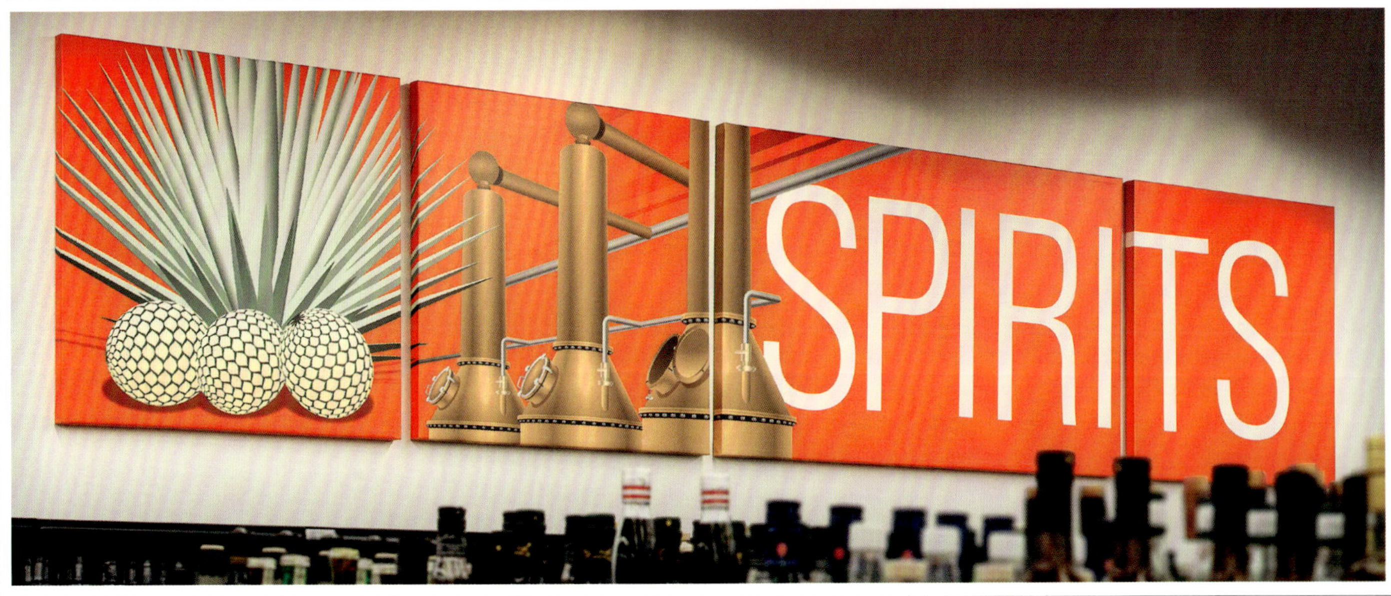

Title: Sip City Spirits, Wine, & Beer Identity Program | **Client:** Randall Family Enterprises Inc.
Design Firm: Ventress Design Works | **P235:** Credit & Commentary | Images 1-3 of 7

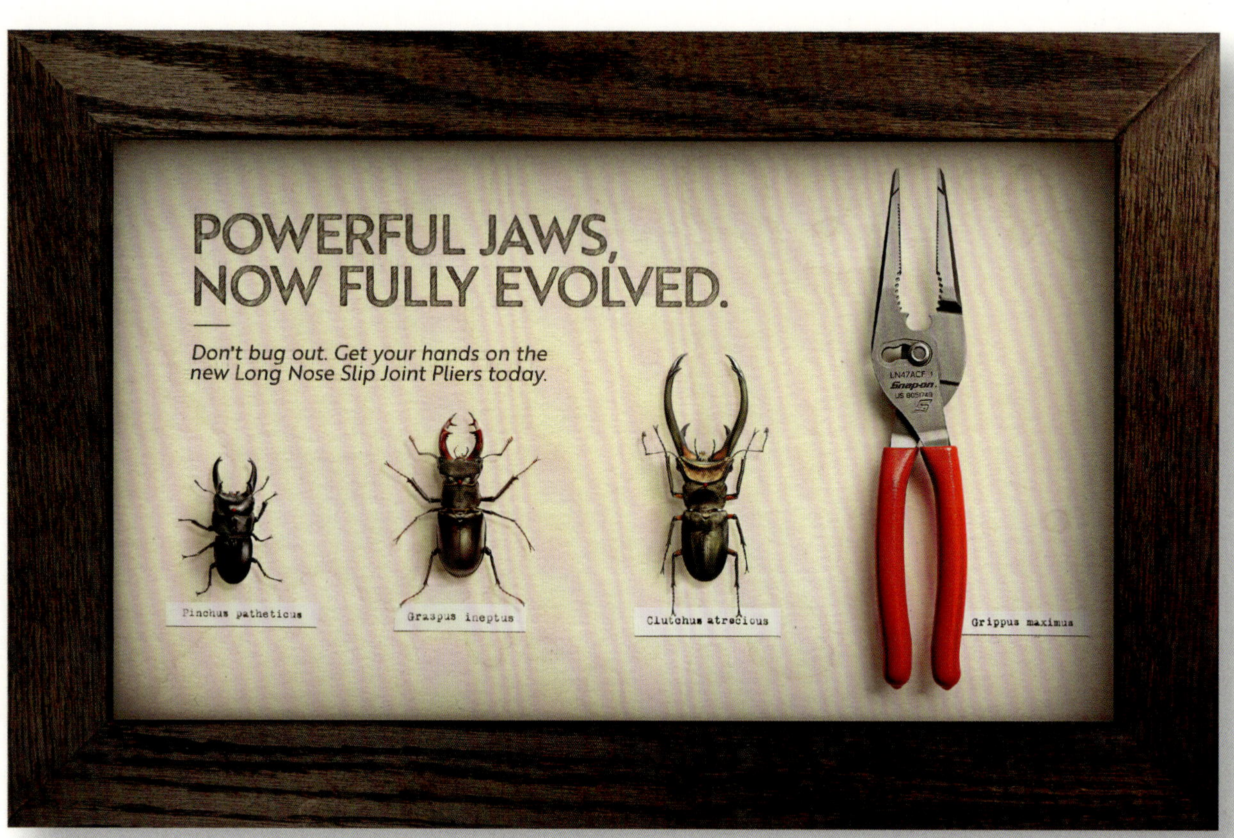
POWERFUL JAWS, NOW FULLY EVOLVED.
Don't bug out. Get your hands on the new Long Nose Slip Joint Pliers today.
Pinchus patheticus
Graspus ineptus
Clutchus atrocious
Grippus maximus

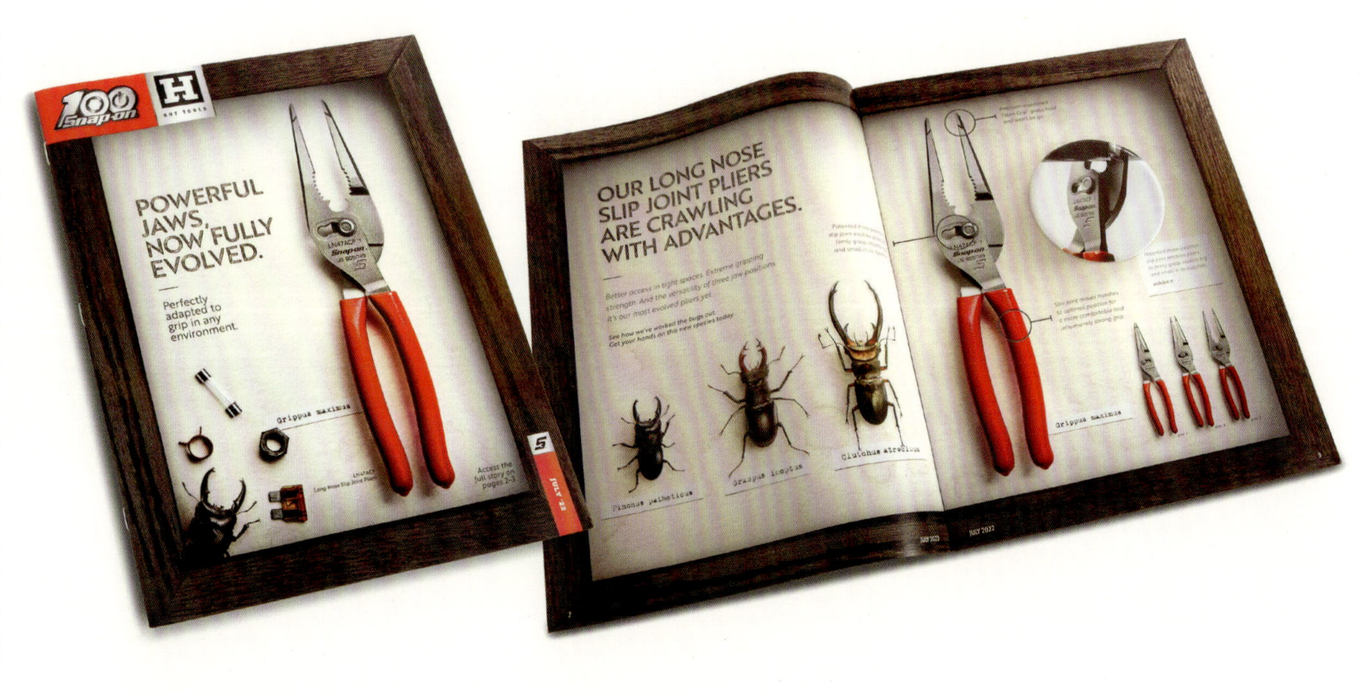
POWERFUL JAWS, NOW FULLY EVOLVED.
Perfectly adapted to grip in any environment.
Grippus maximus
OUR LONG NOSE SLIP JOINT PLIERS ARE CRAWLING WITH ADVANTAGES.
Pinchus patheticus
Graspus ineptus
Clutchus atrocious
Grippus maximus

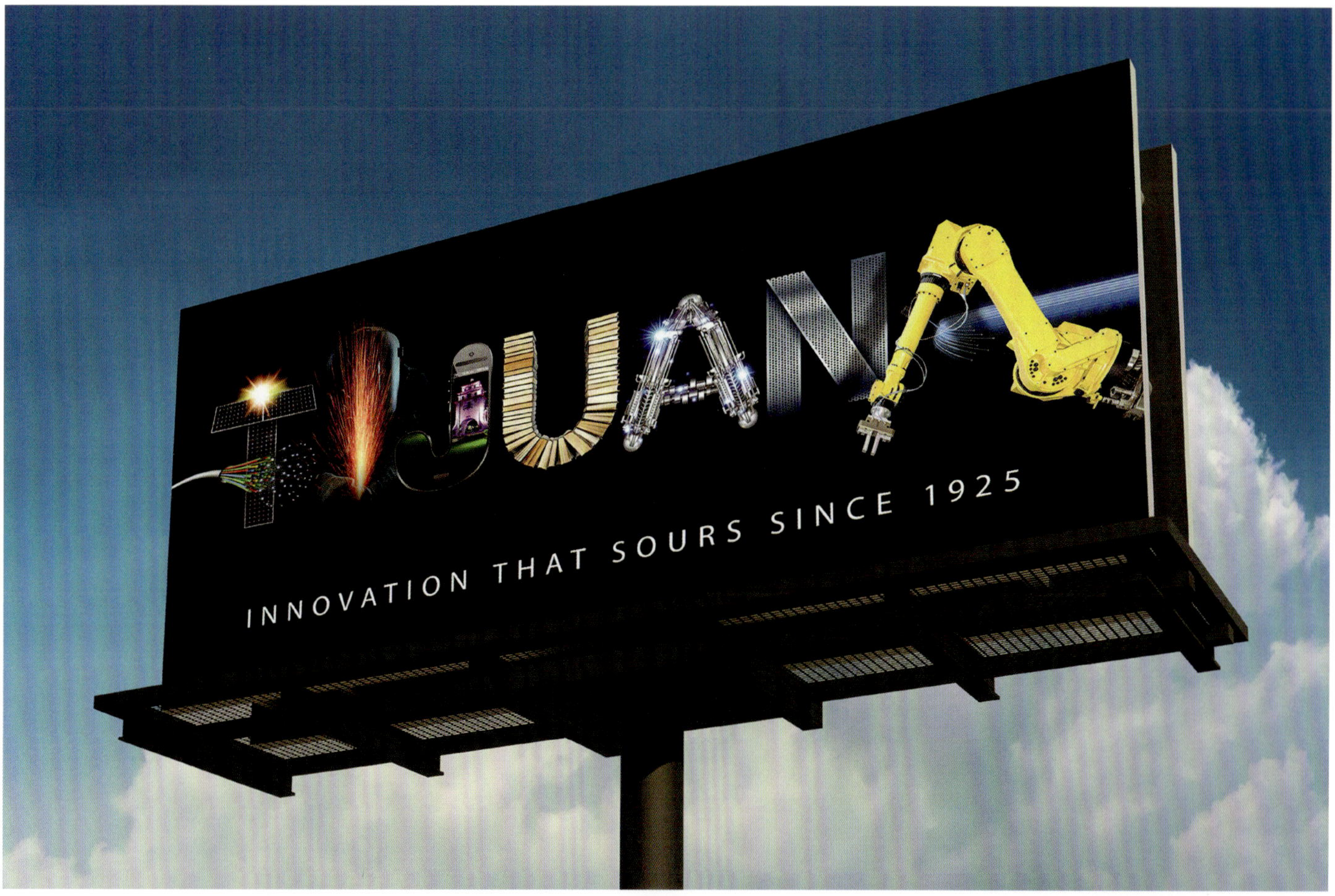

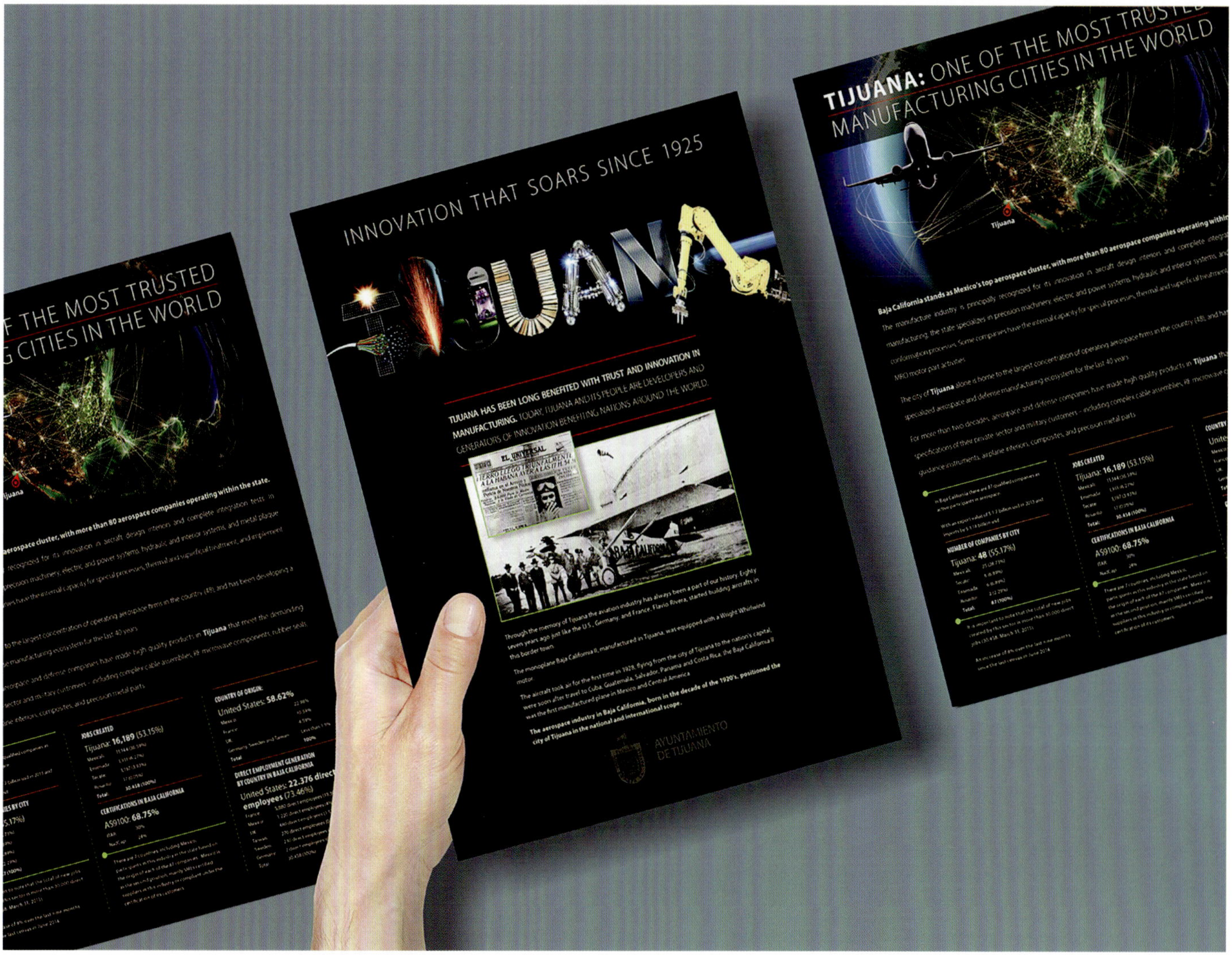

Title: Tijuana City Brand | **Client:** City of Tijuana | **Design Firm:** Freaner Creative & Design

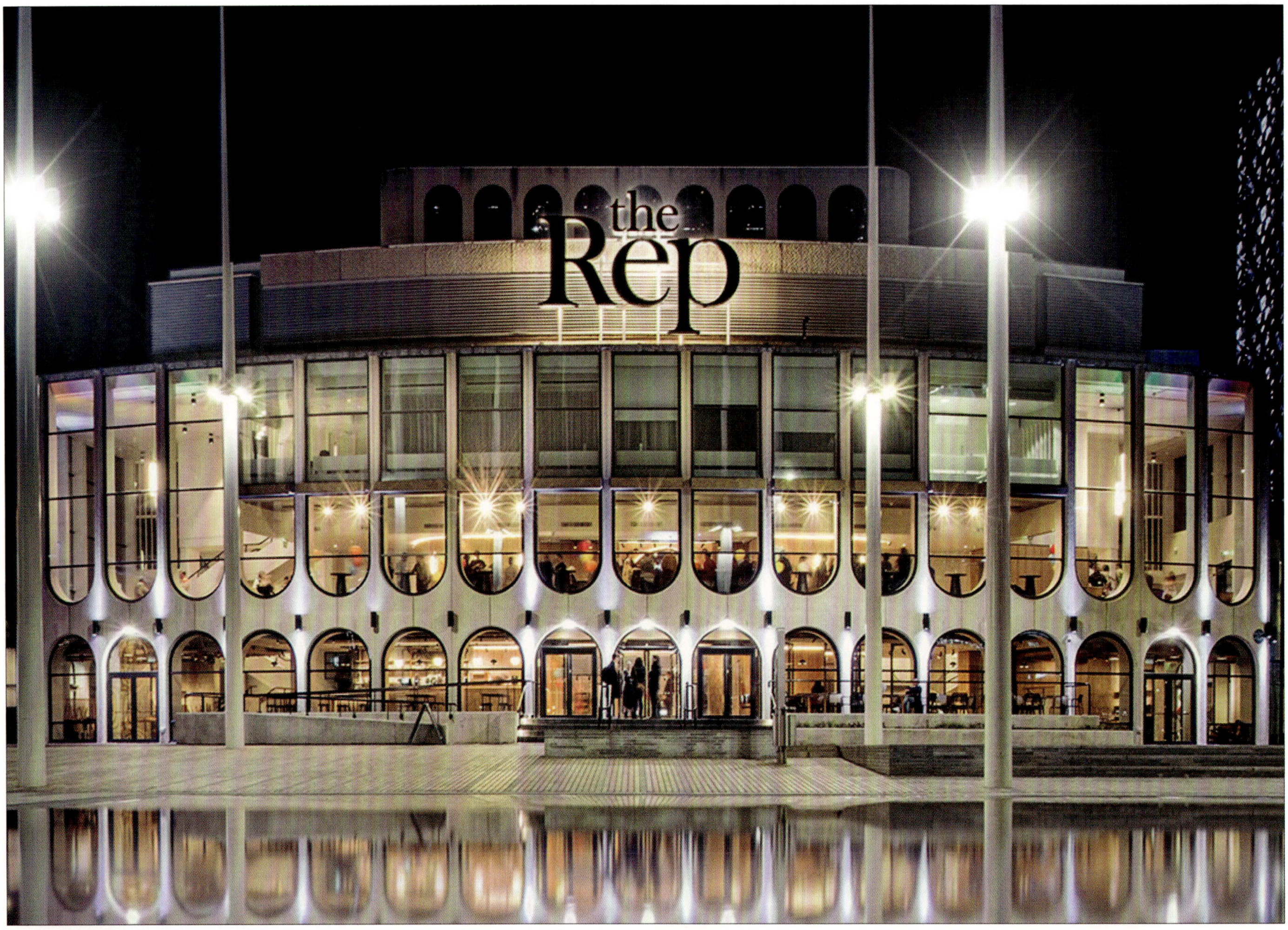

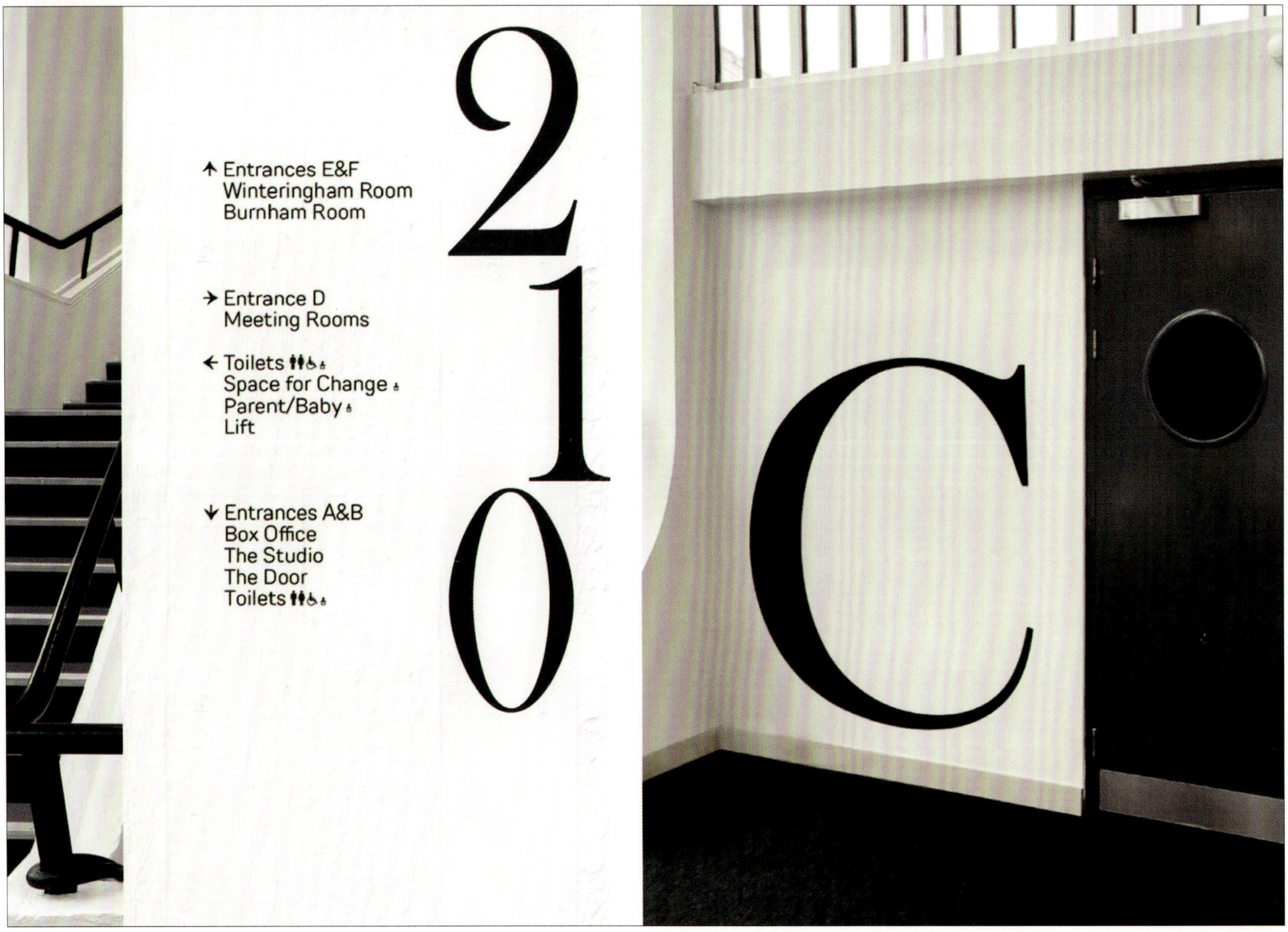

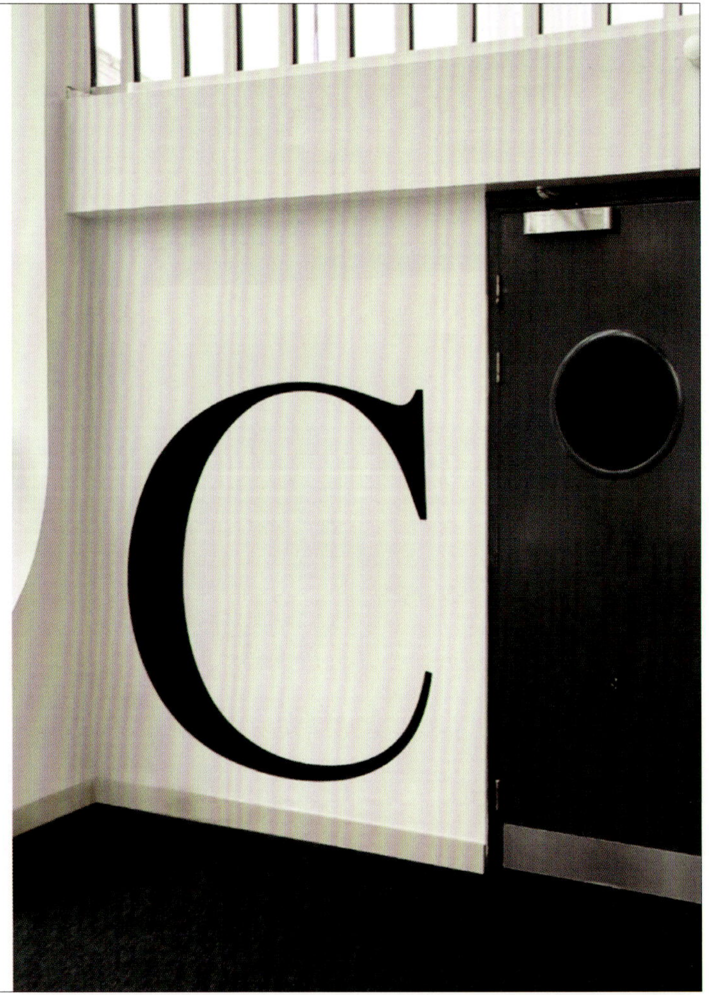

P236: Credit & Commentary **Title:** The Rep Rebrand | **Client:** Birmingham Repertory Theater | **Design Firm:** Rose Images 1, 2 of 7

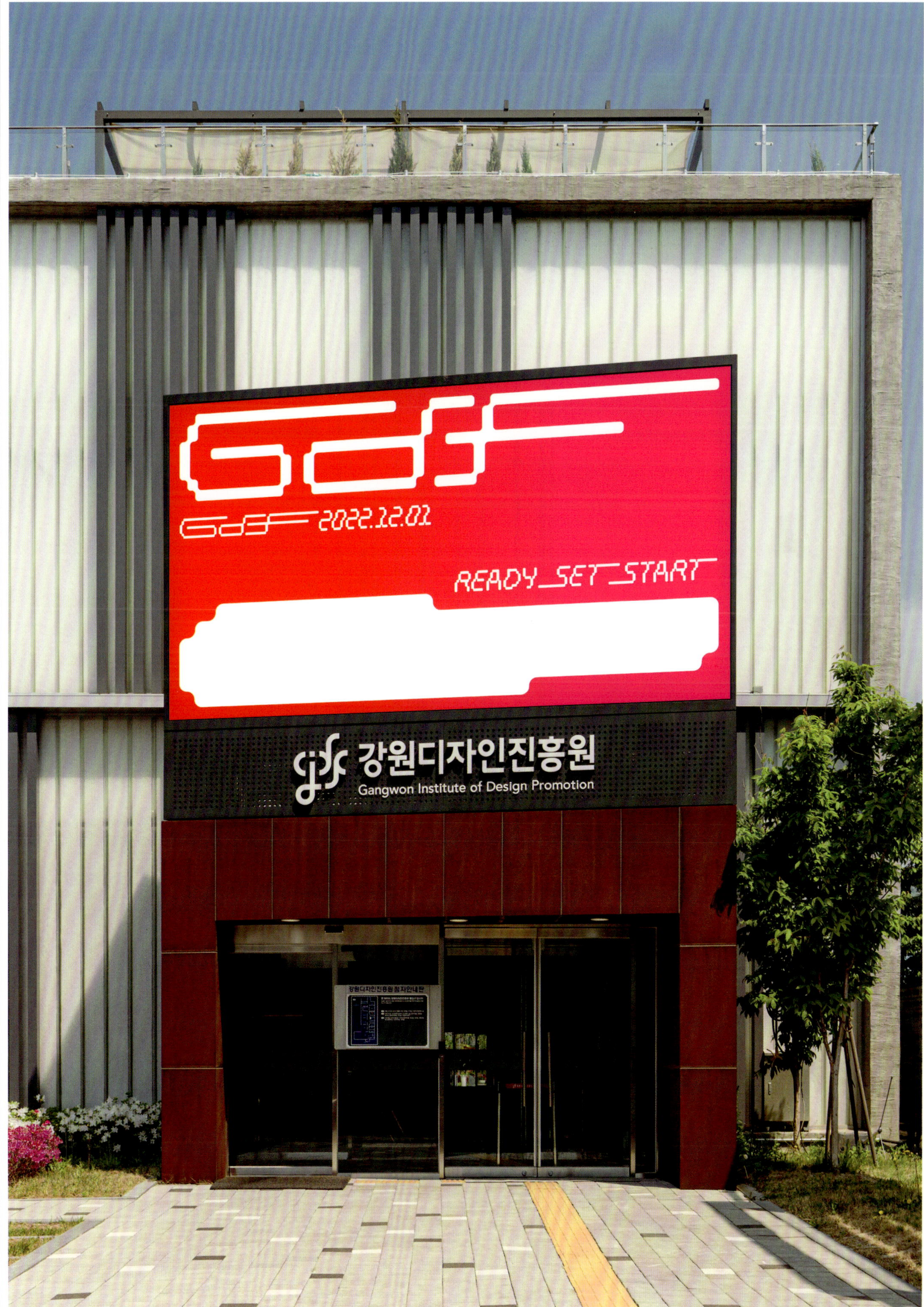

Title: GDF Branding | **Clients:** Gangwon State, Gangwon Institute of Design Promotion (GIDP)
Design Firm: DAEKI and JUN | **P236:** Credit & Commentary | Image 1 of 7

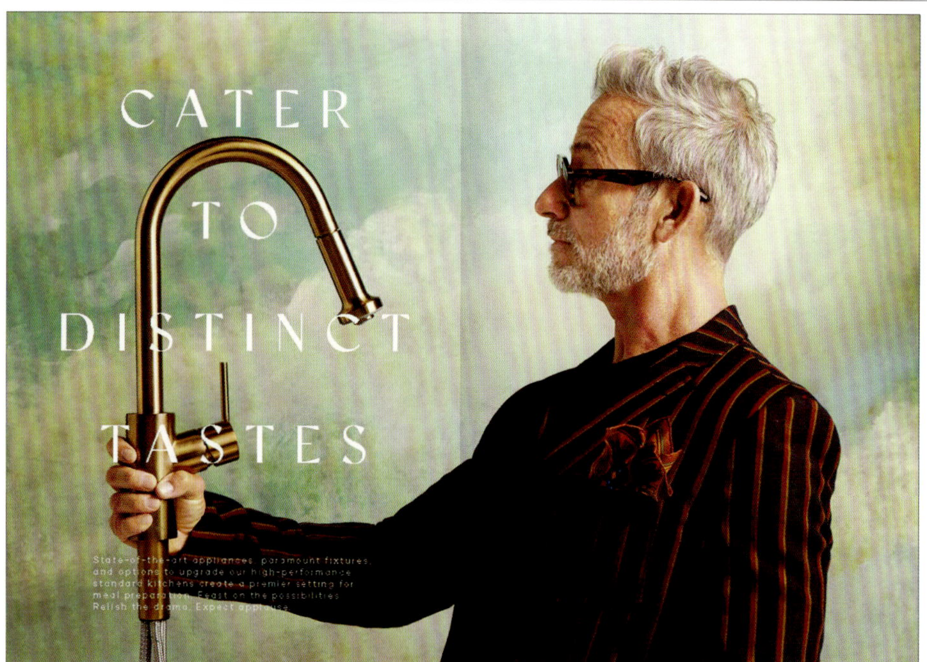

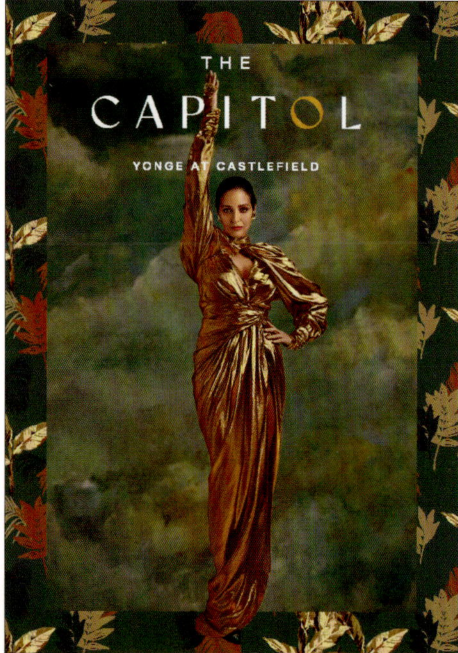

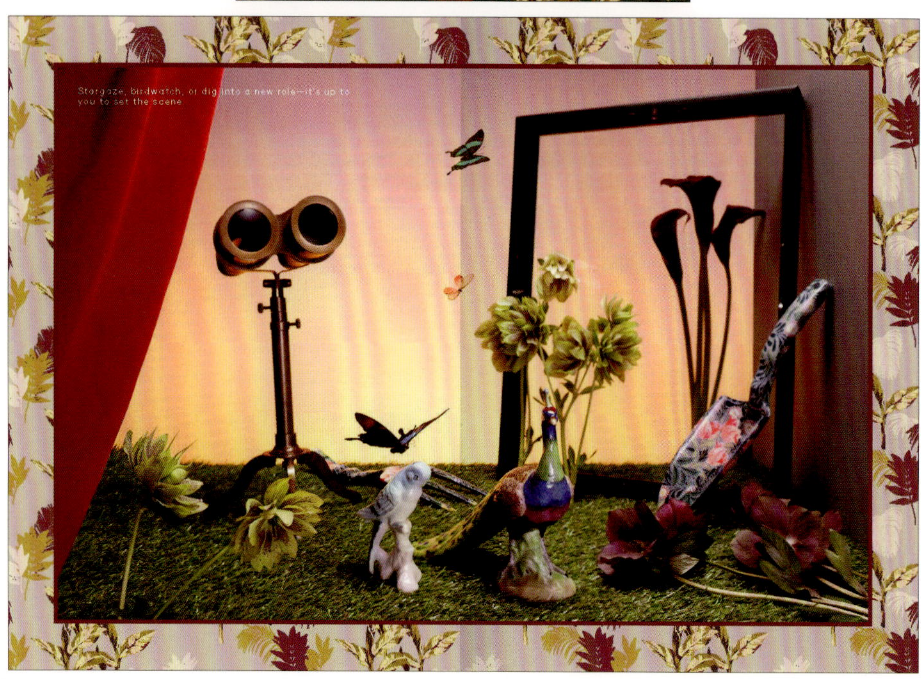

 Title: The Capitol Brochure | **Client:** Madison Group | **Design Firm:** IF Studio

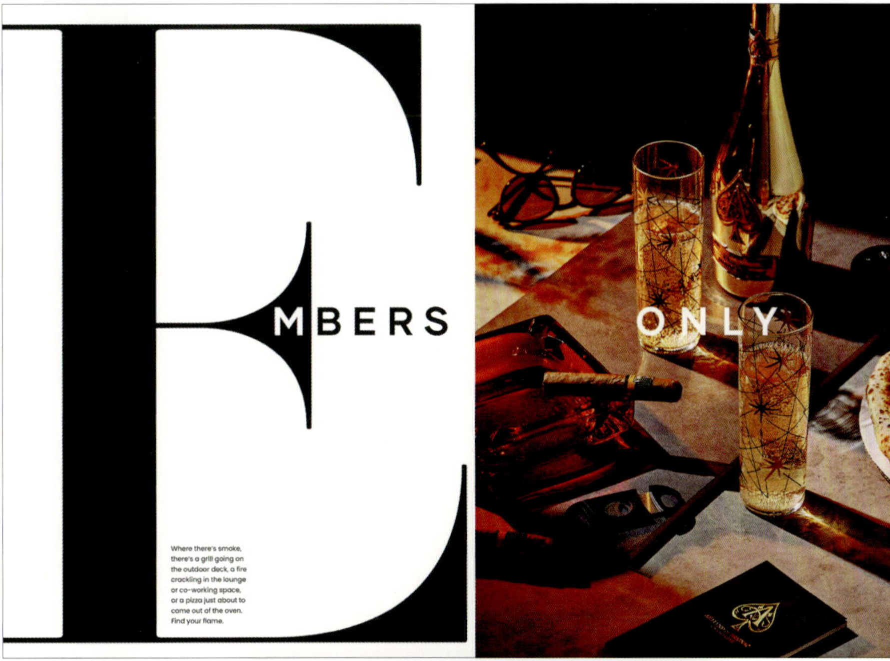

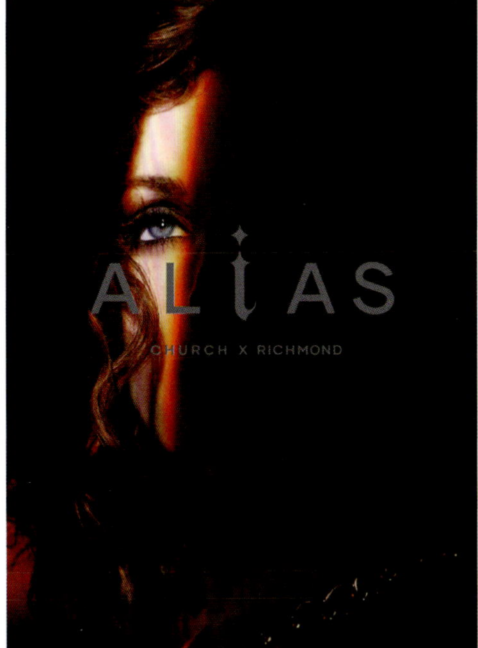

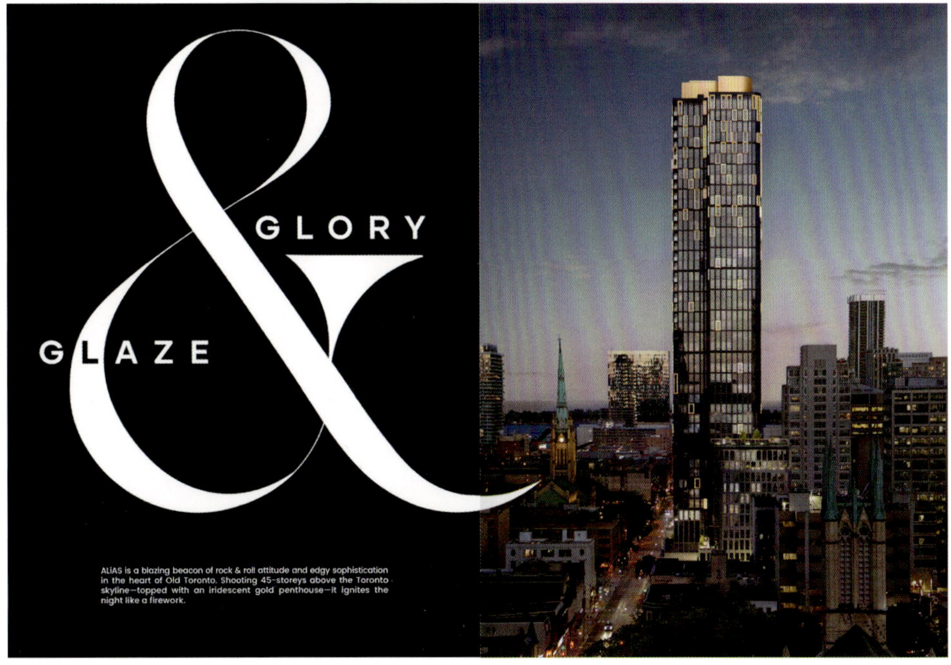

Title: Alias Brochure | **Client:** Madison Group | **Design Firm:** IF Studio

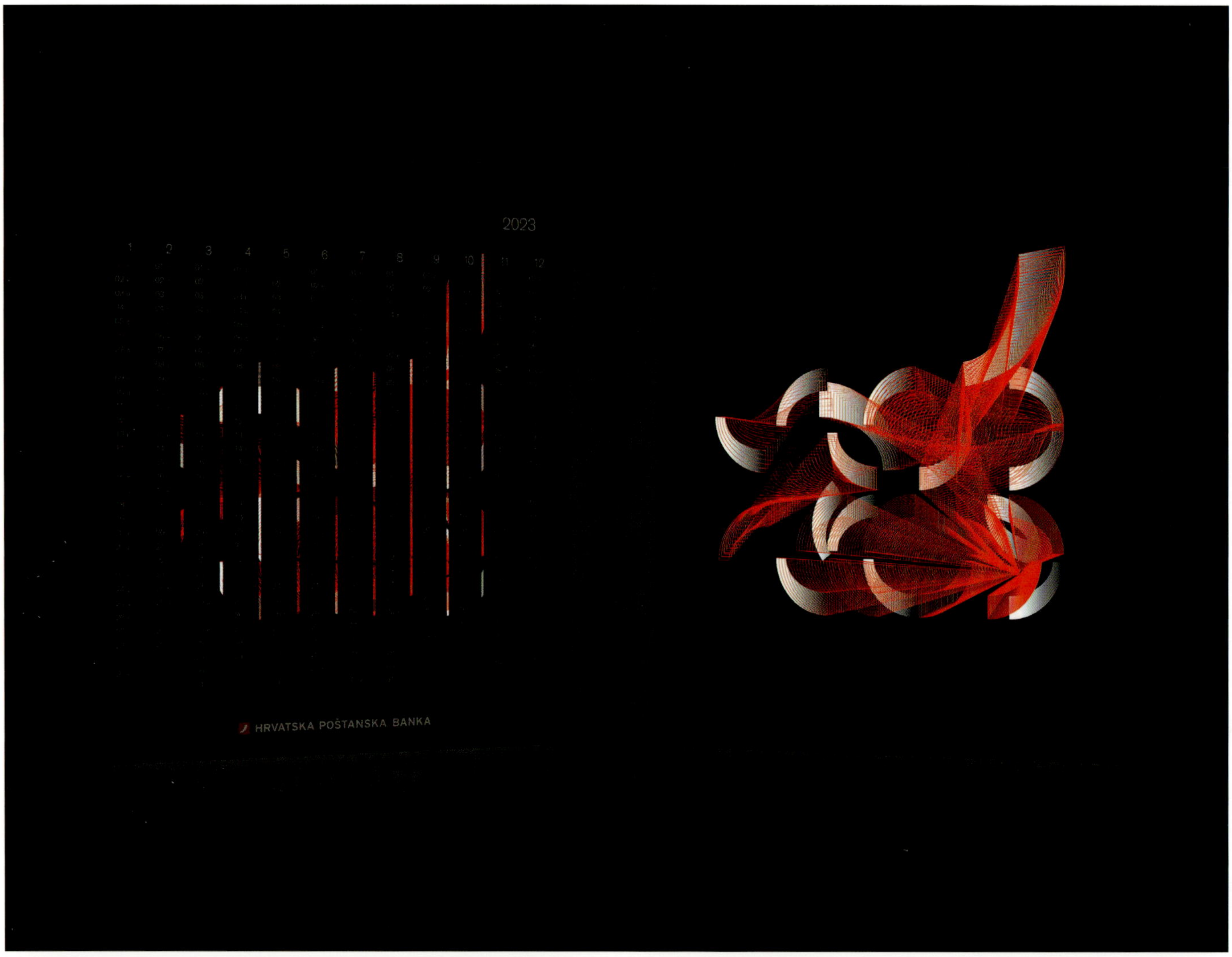

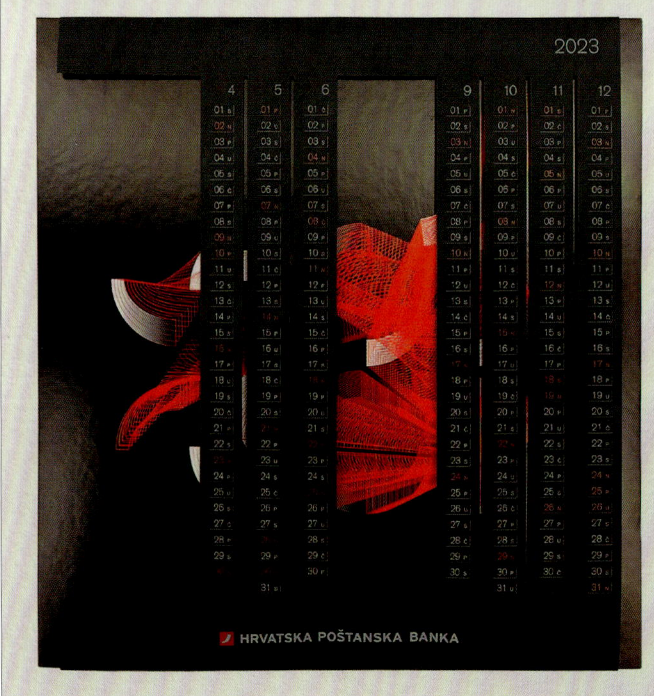

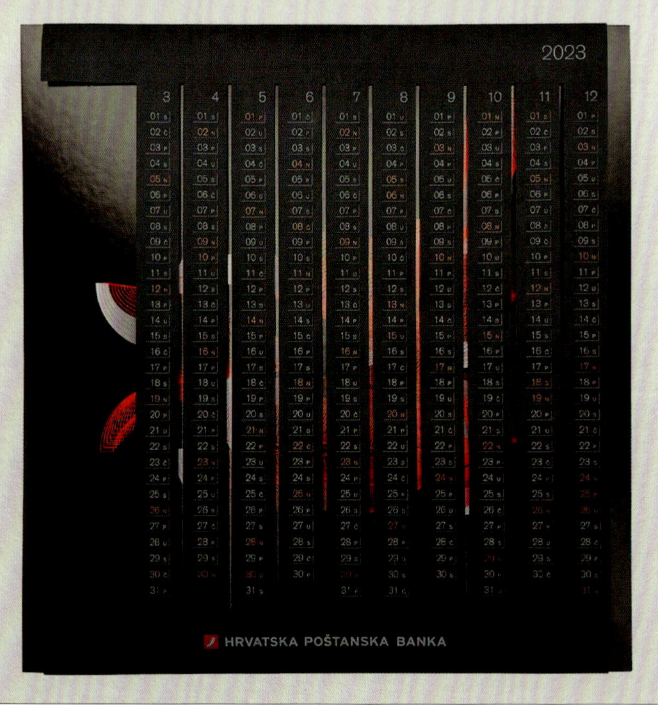

Title: Charm of Financial Matrices | **Client:** HRVATSKA POŠTANSKA BANKA
Design Firm: Bekar Haus D.O.O. | **P236:** Credit & Commentary | Images 1-3 of 7

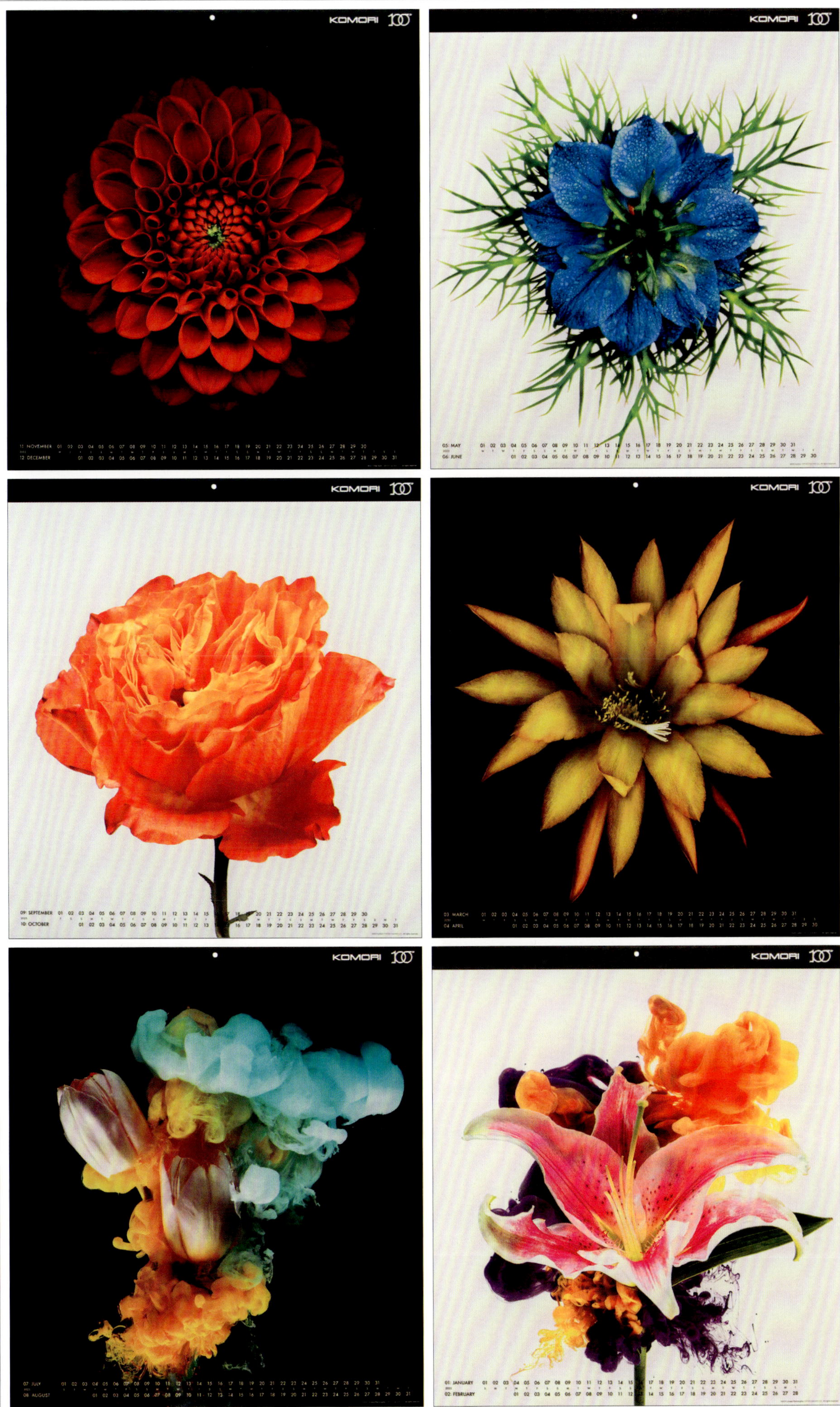

Title: 100th Anniversary Komori 2023 Calendar | **Client:** Komori Corporation
Design Firm: Toppan Inc. | **P236:** Credit & Commentary | Images 1-6 of 7

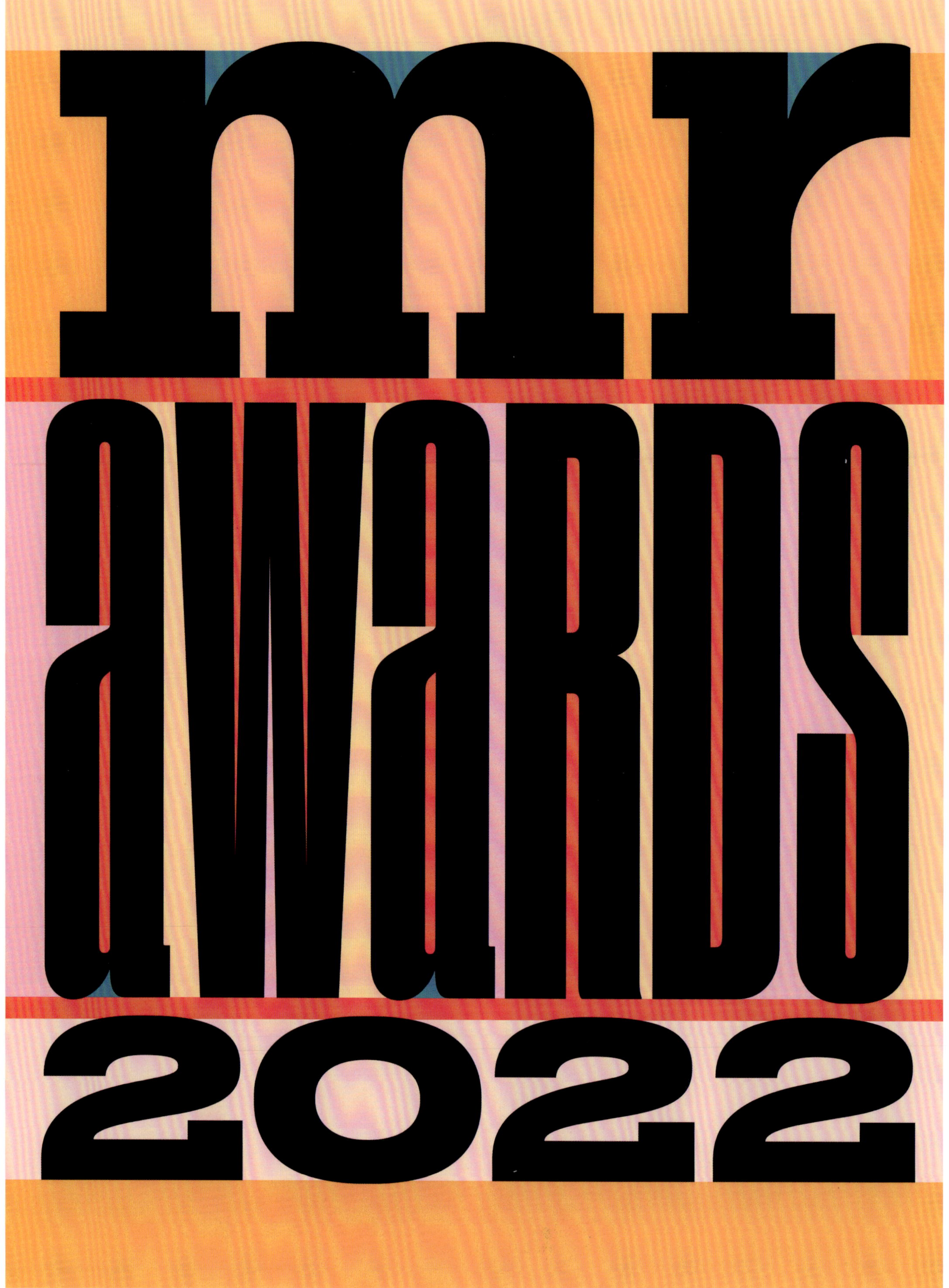

P236: Credit & Commentary **Title:** MR Magazine Awards Cover | **Client:** MR Magazine | **Design Firm:** Wainscot Media

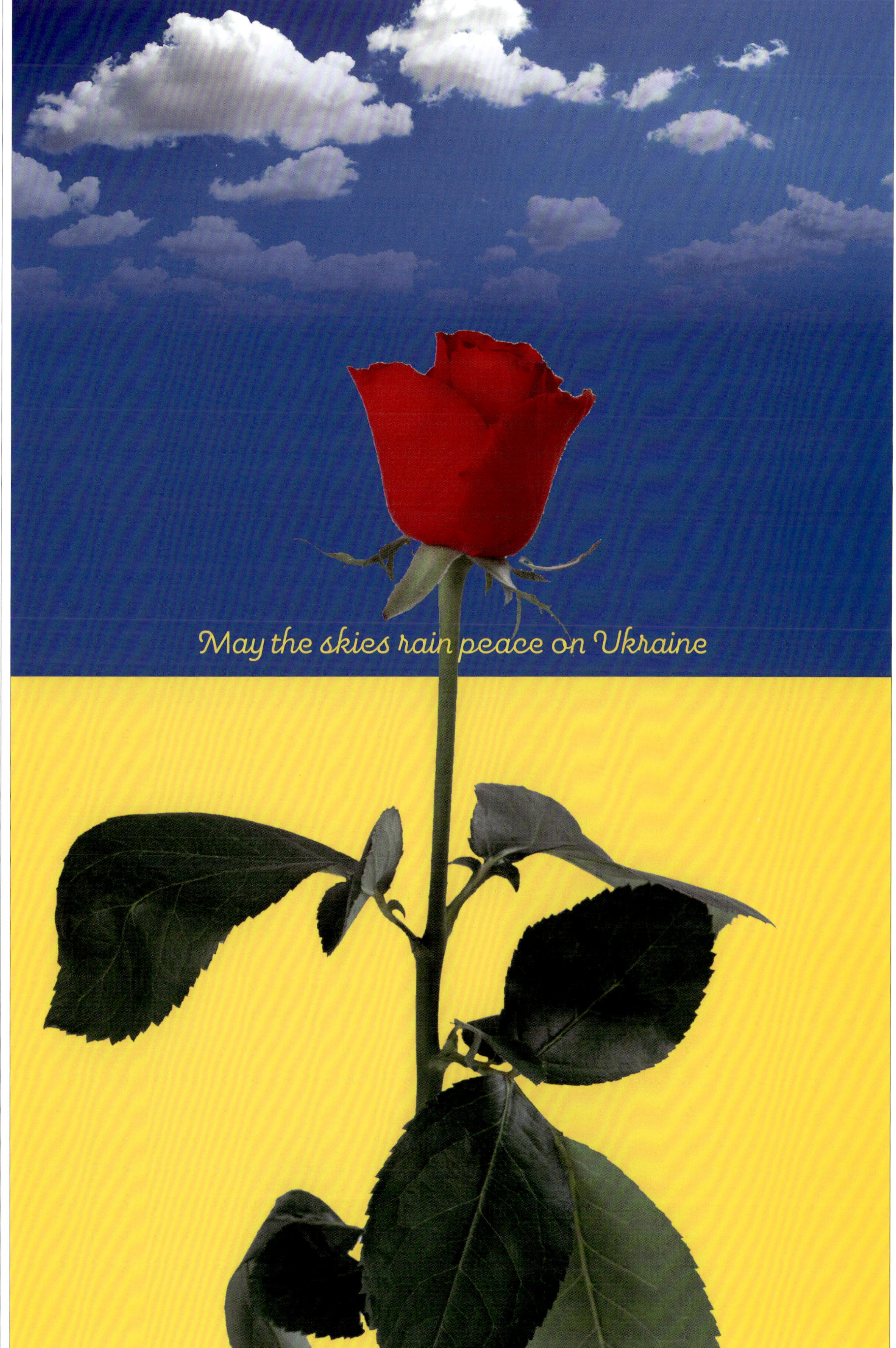

P236: Credit & Commentary **Title:** Rain Peace in Ukraine | **Client:** Self-initiated | **Design Firm:** Randy Clark Graphic Design

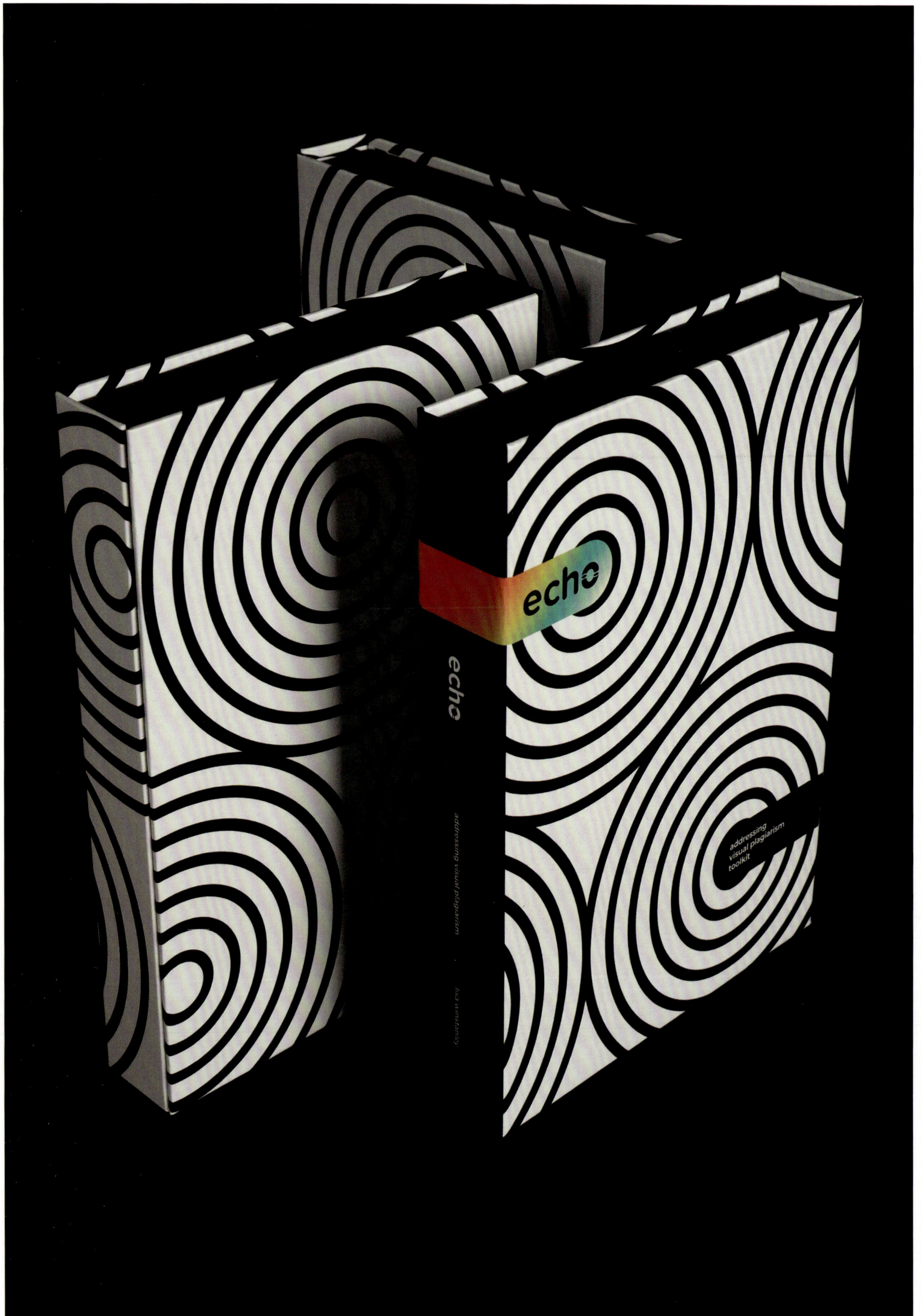

Title: Project Echo | **Client:** Project Echo | **Design Firm:** Lisa Winstanley Design

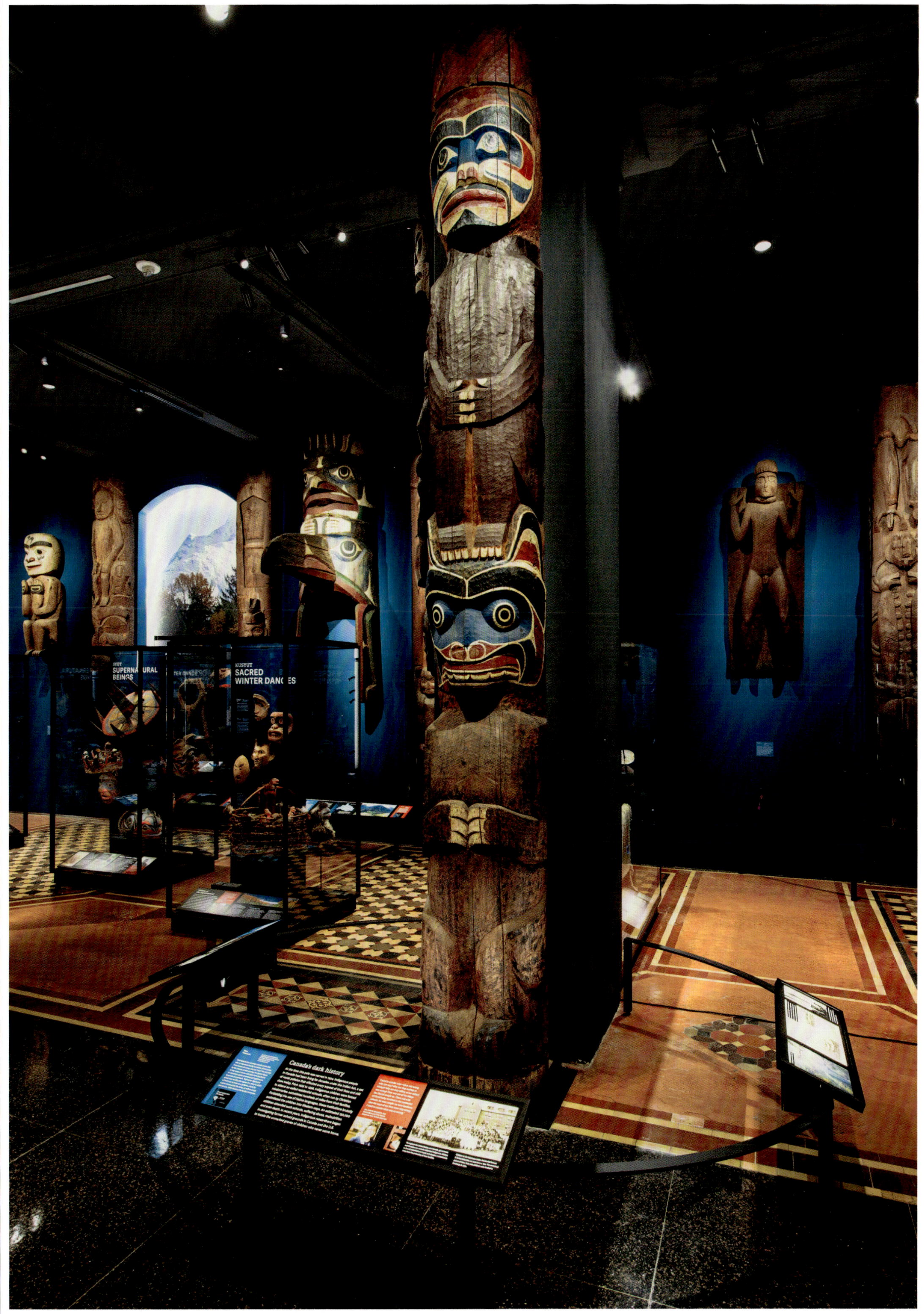

Title: Northwest Coast Hall | **Client:** Self-initiated
Design Firm: American Museum of Natural History (In-House) | **P237:** Credit & Commentary | Image 1 of 6

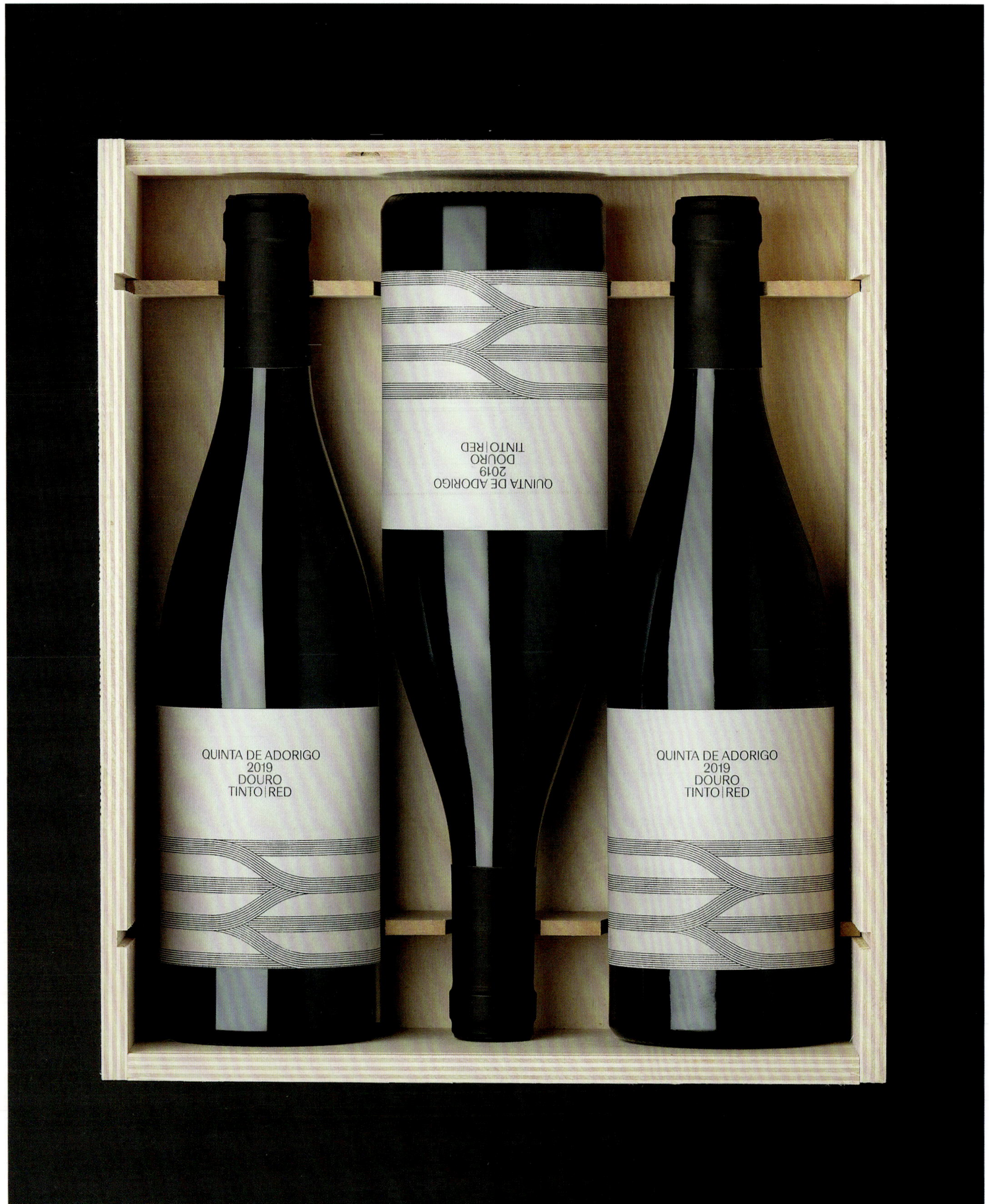

P237: Credit & Commentary **Title:** Quinta de Adorigo | **Client:** Quinta de Adorigo | **Design Firm:** Studio Eduardo Aires Image 1 of 6

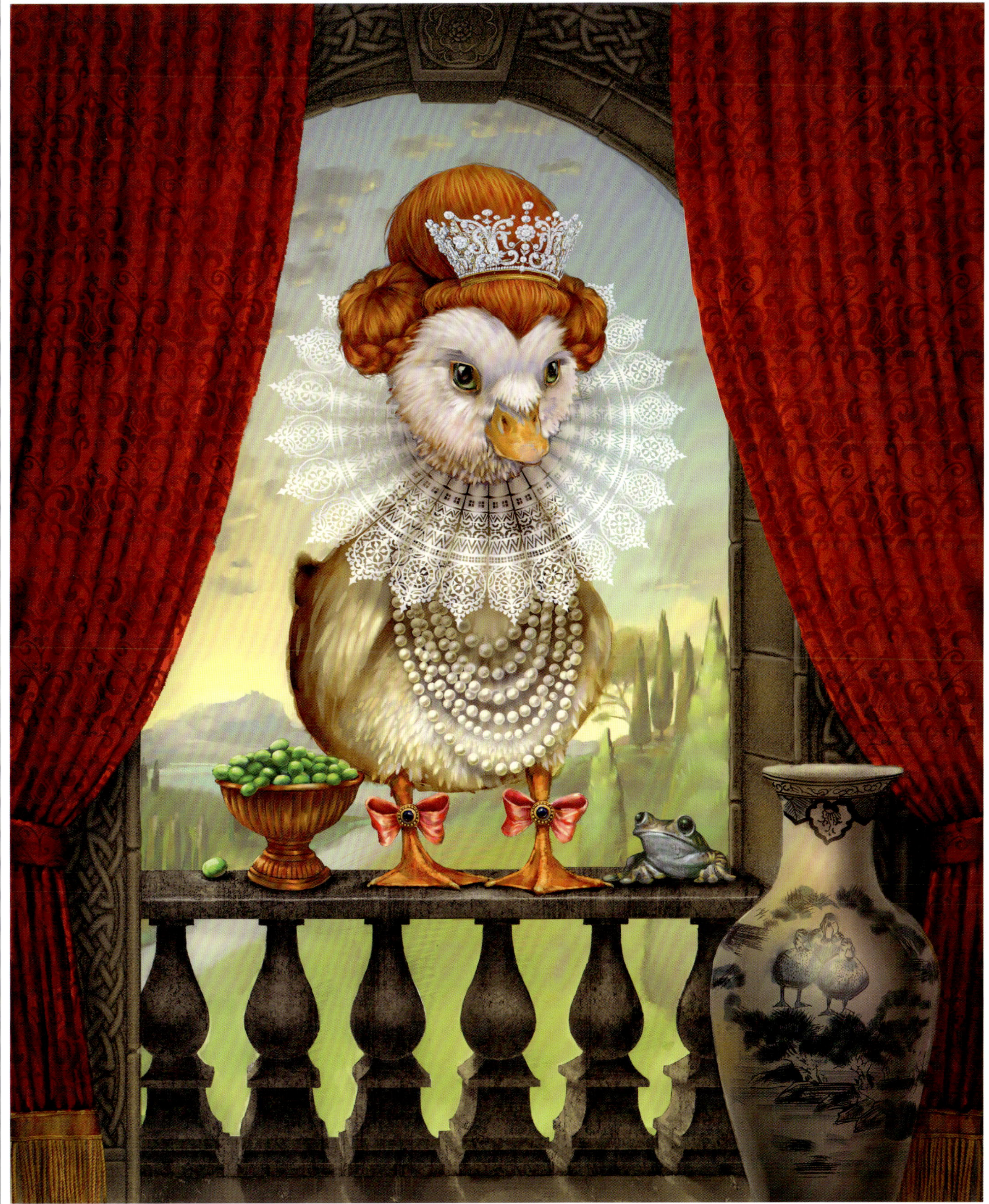

P237: Credit & Commentary **Title:** Lauda Regina | **Client:** Strange Duck Brewery | **Design Firm:** Mark Braught Studios

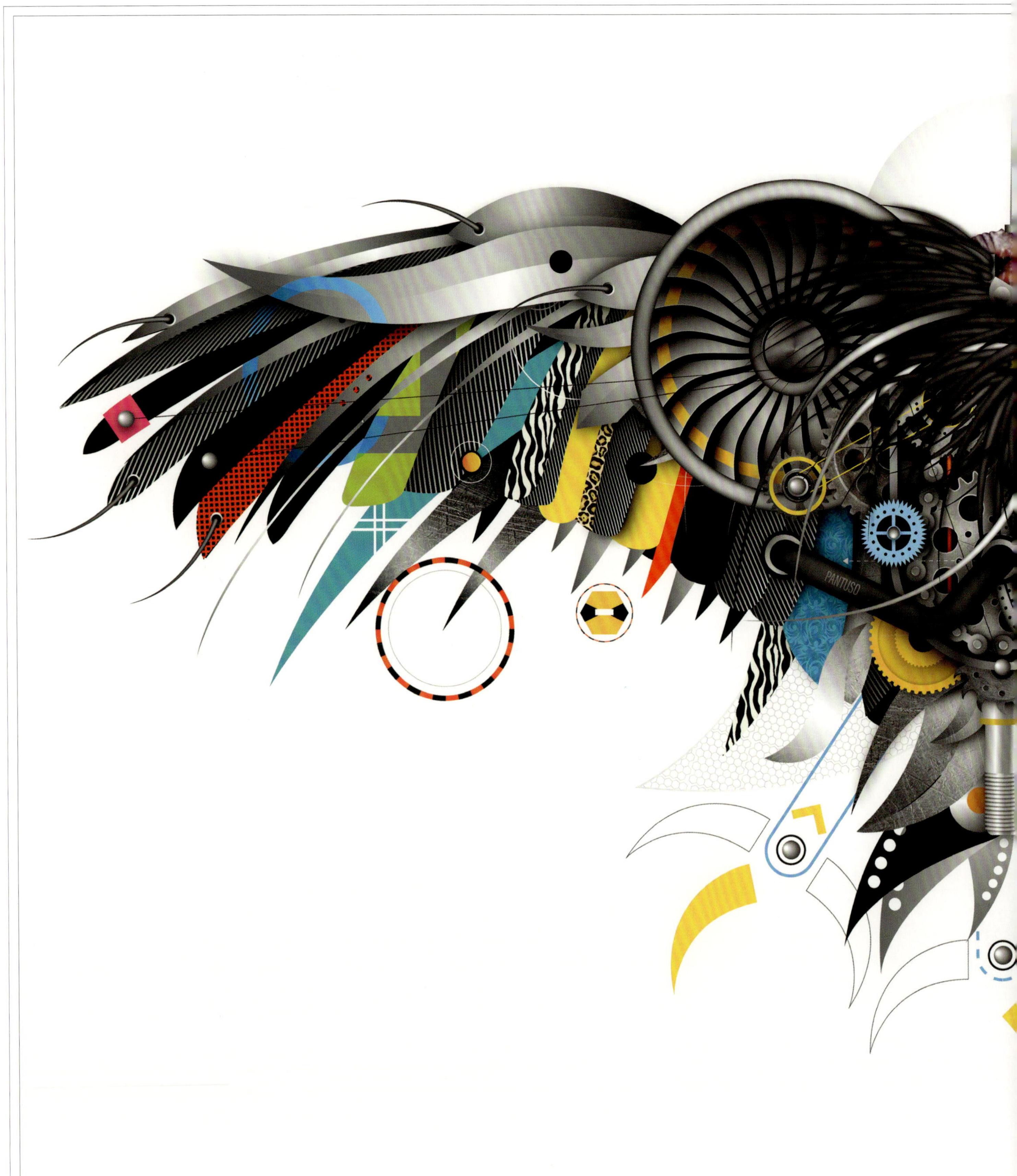

P237: Credit & Commentary

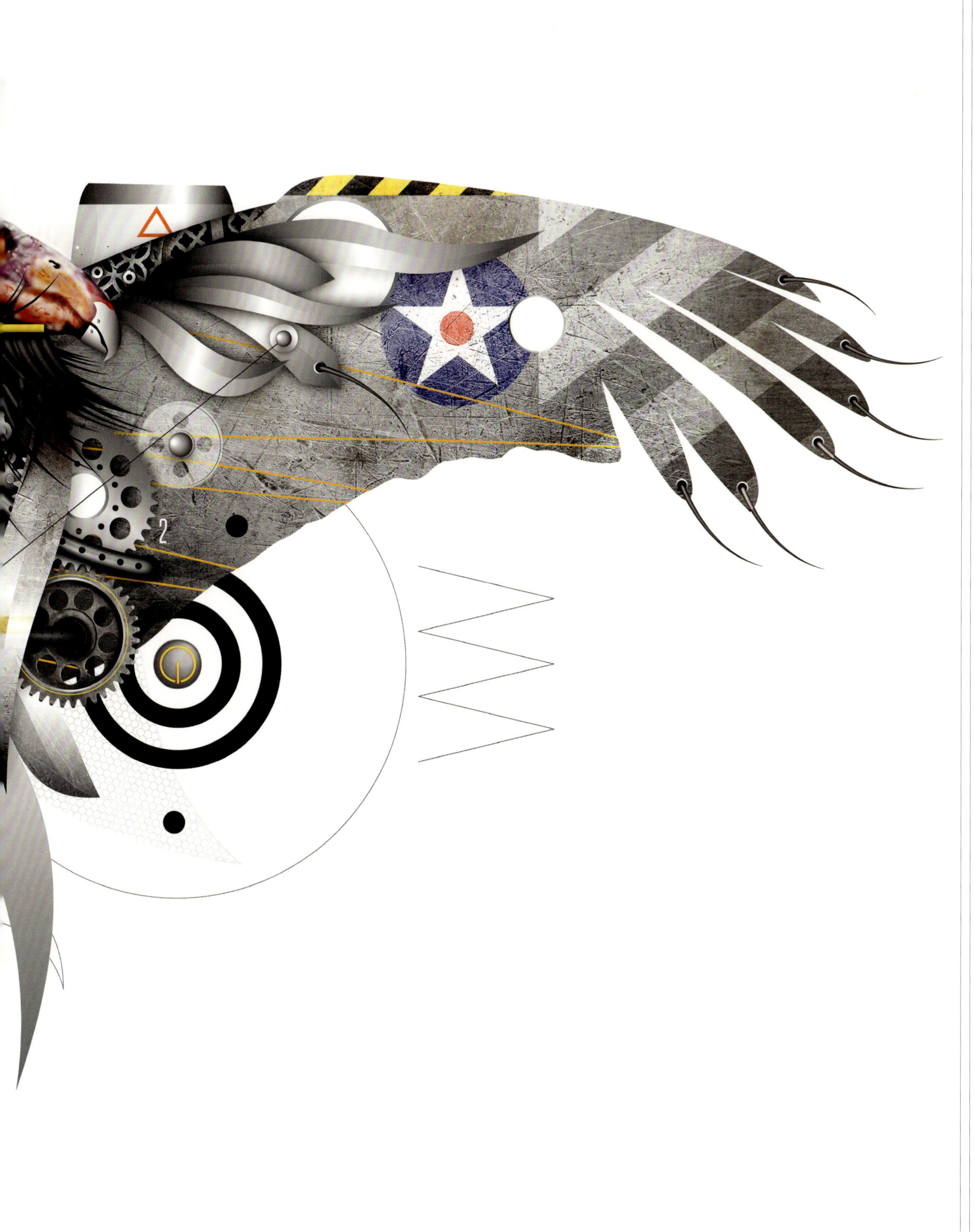

Title: California Condor | **Client:** AOFA Gallery | **Design Firm:** Michael Pantuso Design

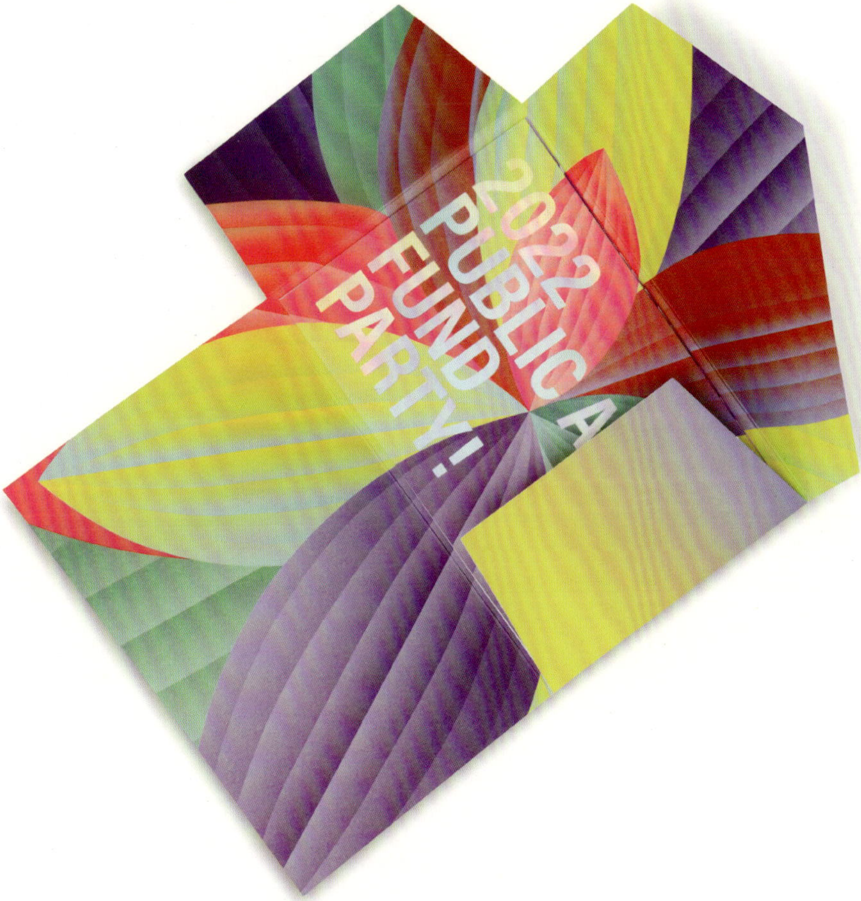

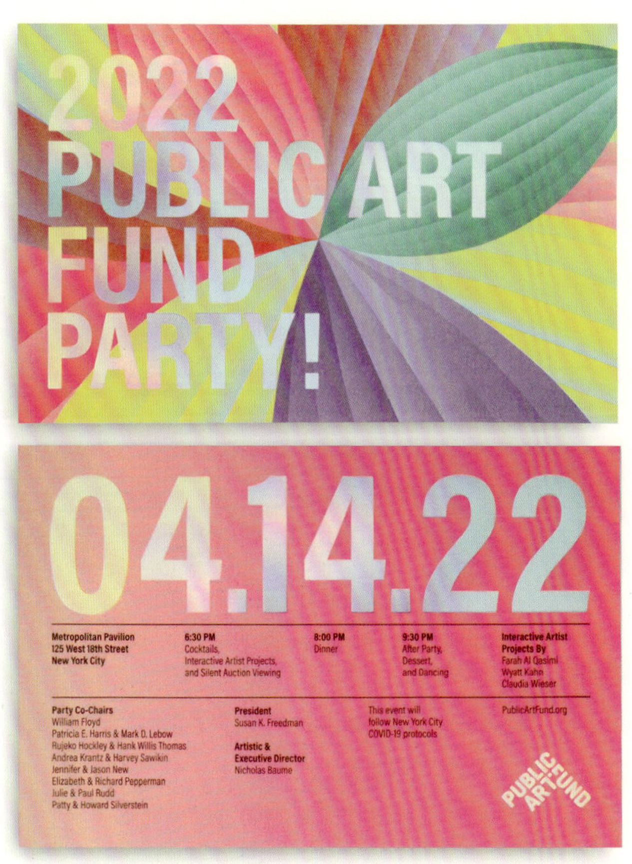

Title: 2022 Public Art Fund Spring Party Invitation | **Client:** Public Art Fund
Design Firm: Ahoy Studios | **P237:** Credit & Commentary | Images 1, 2 of 6

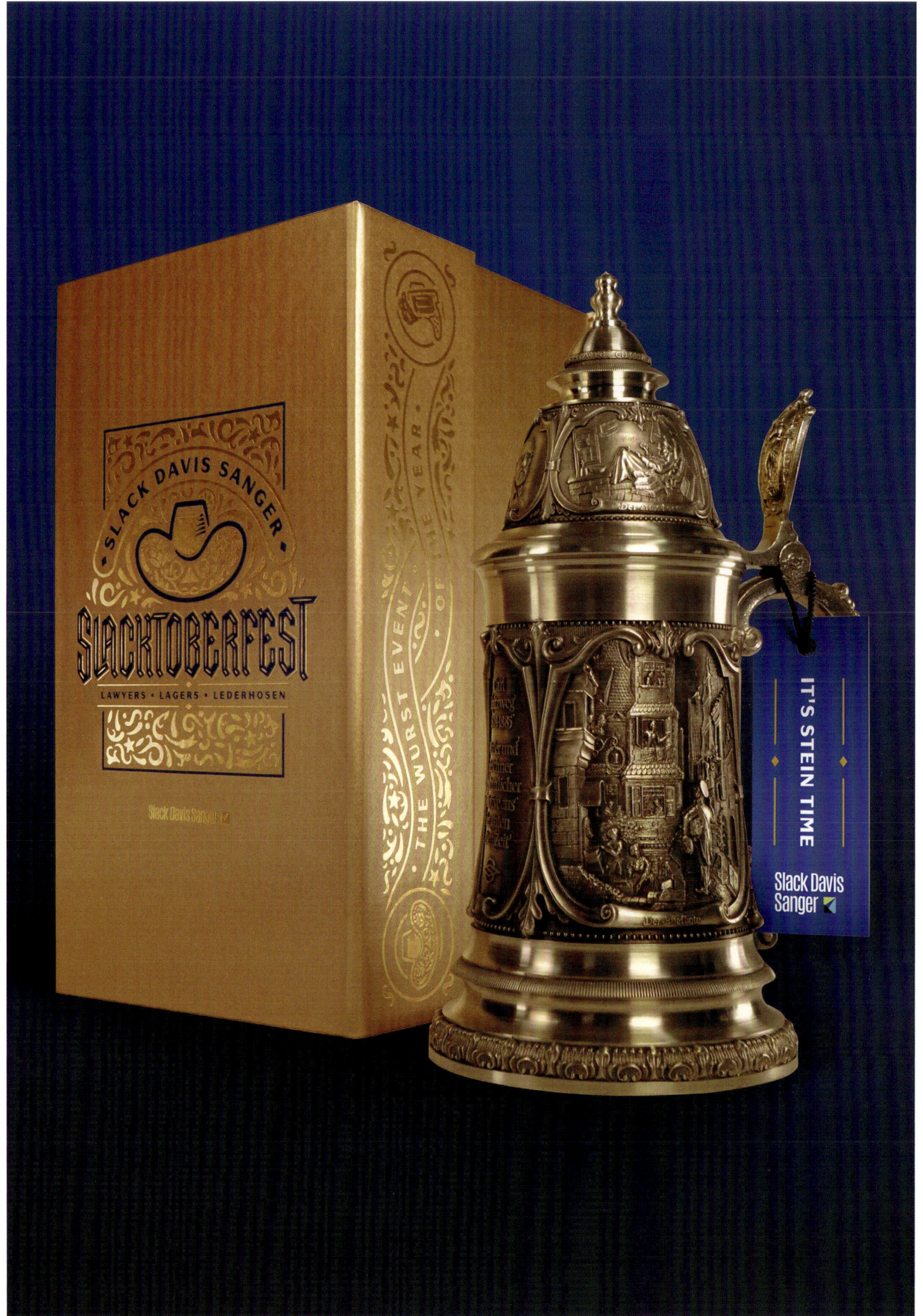

Title: Slacktoberfest Invitation | **Client:** Slack Davis Sanger | **Design Firm:** Spire Agency

RESOURCE BRANDING

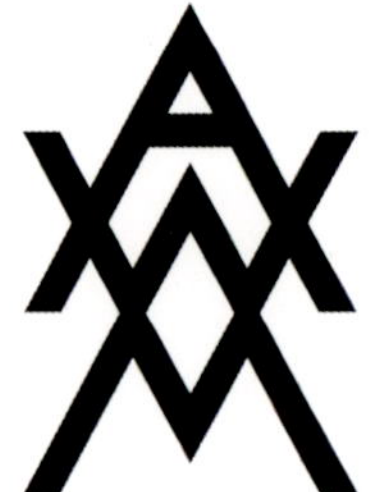

P237: Credit & Commentary   **Title:** Alta West Morehead Logomark | **Client:** Wood Partners | **Design Firm:** Resource Branding

STUDIO 5 DESIGNS INC.

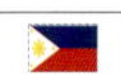

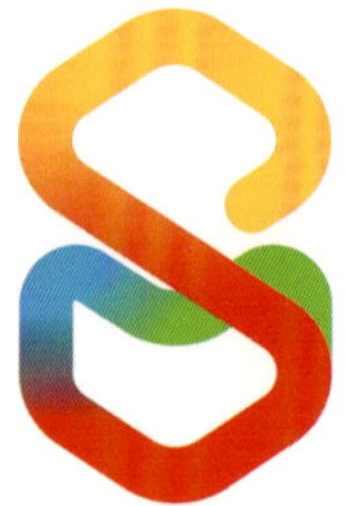

P237: Credit & Commentary   **Title:** SMGP Logo | **Clients:** San Miguel Global Power, Kim de Leon-Morgan | **Design Firm:** Studio 5 Designs Inc.

ROBERT TALARCZYK

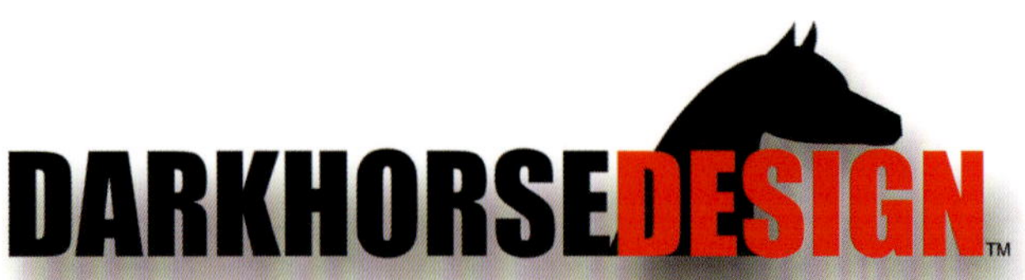

P238: Credit & Commentary   **Title:** Darkhorse Design Logo | **Client:** Self-initiated | **Design Firm:** Darkhorse Design, LLC

KRISTOFER MACÍAS

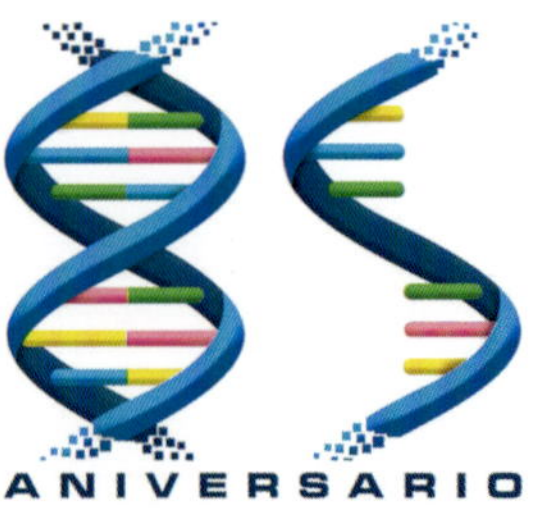

P238: Credit & Commentary   **Title:** 85th Anniversary | **Client:** Laboratorios Liomont | **Design Firm:** Paco Macias Velasco Studio

ROGER SAWHILL

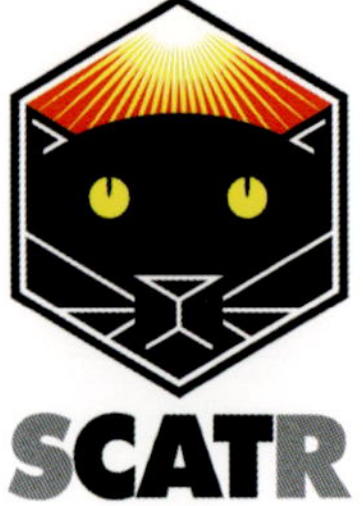

P238: Credit & Commentary   **Title:** Cat Defense System Logos | **Client:** Joanna Sawhill | **Design Firm:** UP-Ideas   Image 1 of 2

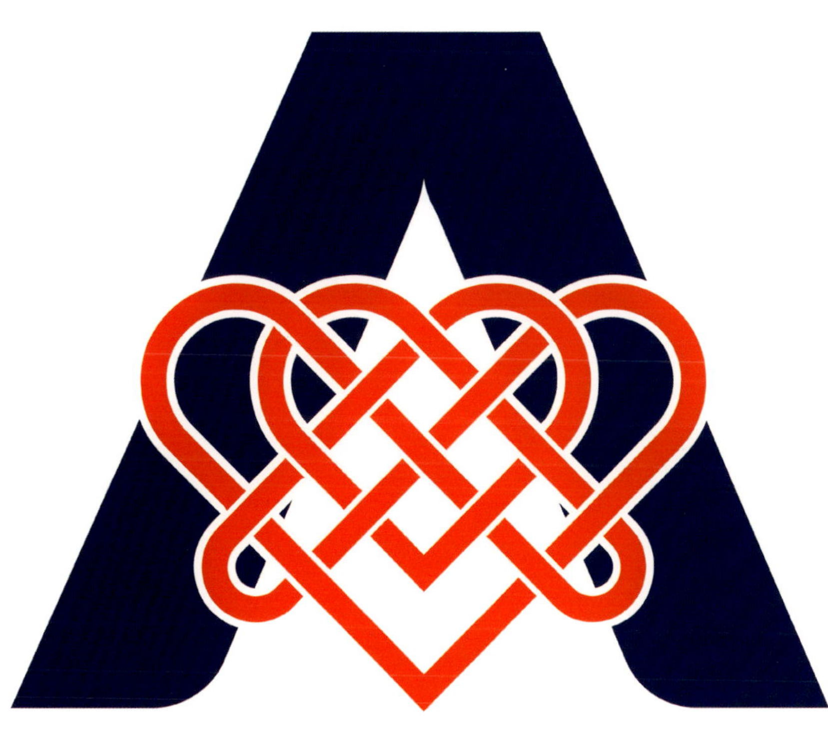

Title: Abyssinian Baptist Church Federal Credit Union Logomark | **Client:** Abyssinian Baptist Church Federal Credit Union
Design Firm: Mermaid, Inc. | **P238:** Credit & Commentary

RYAN BURLINSON, JOHANN A. GÓMEZ, MAT MCINELLY, JESSICA LARKIN, JESSAH HOFKER

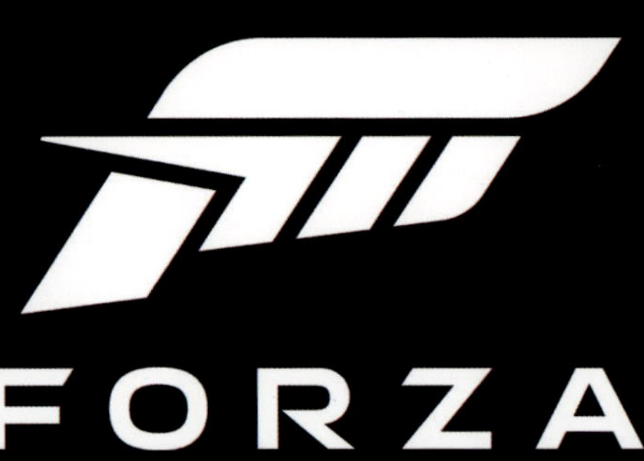

P238: Credit & Commentary **Title:** Forza Motorsport Rebrand | **Clients:** 343 Industries, Ryann Merritt | **Design Firm:** TGD Image 1 of 2

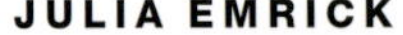

JULIA EMRICK

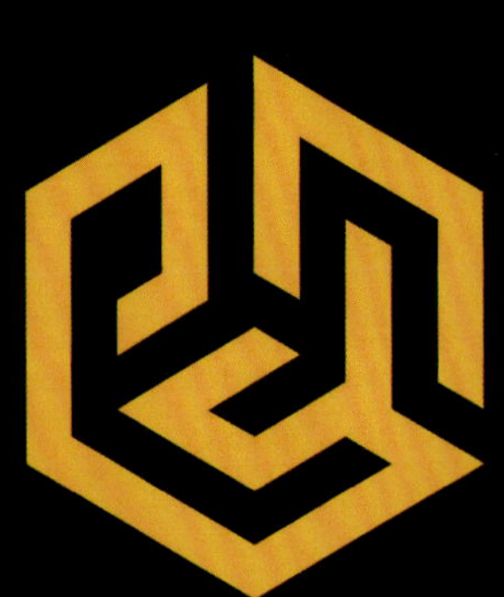

P238: Credit & Comm. **Title:** PTS Contracting | **Client:** Harrison Edwards Integrated Marketing | **Design Firm:** Kate Borman Creative Design Co.

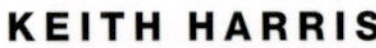

KEITH HARRIS

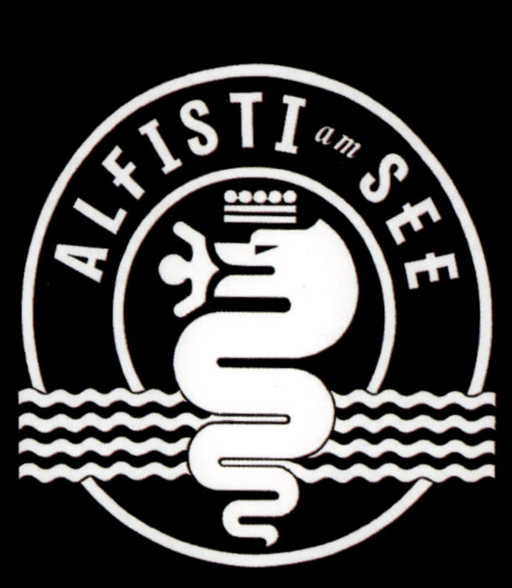

P238: Credit & Commentary **Title:** Alfisti am See Logo | **Client:** Alfisti am See | **Design Firm:** Keith Harris Design

EL PASO, GALERÍA DE COMUNICACIÓN

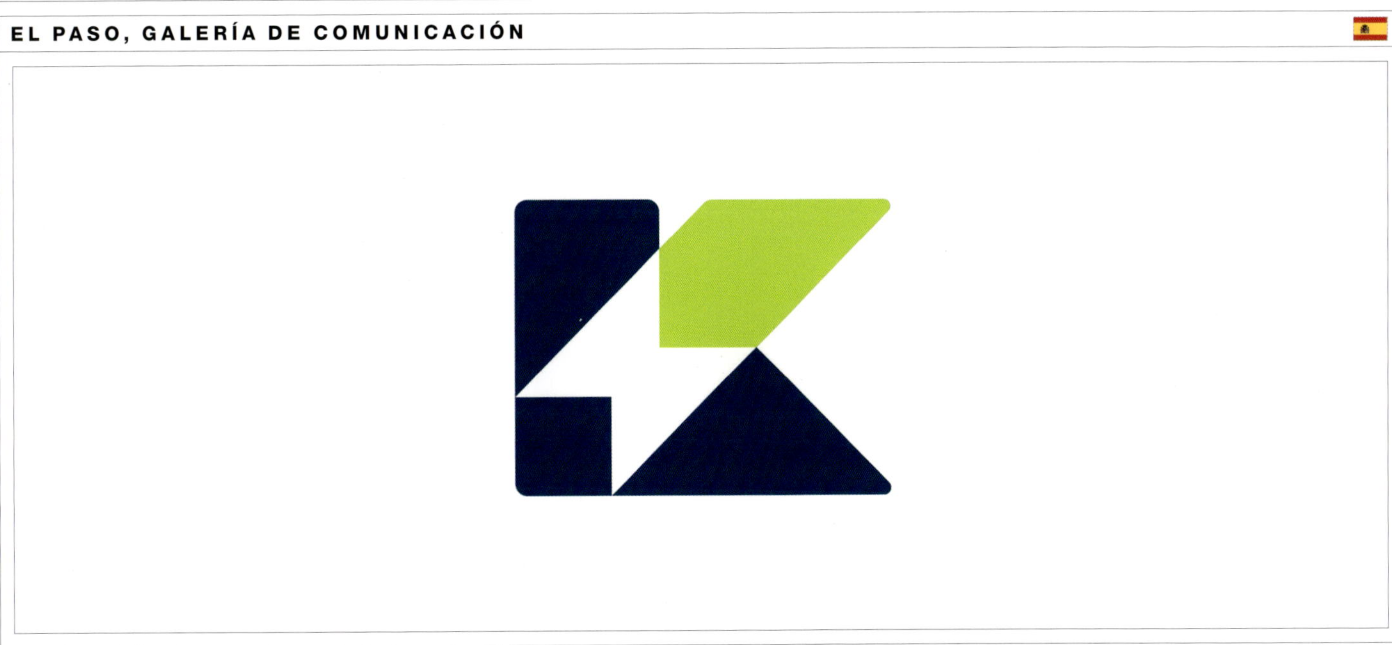

P238: Credit & Commentary Title: Kernova | Client: Kernova | Design Firm: El Paso, Galería de Comunicación

ARIEL FREANER

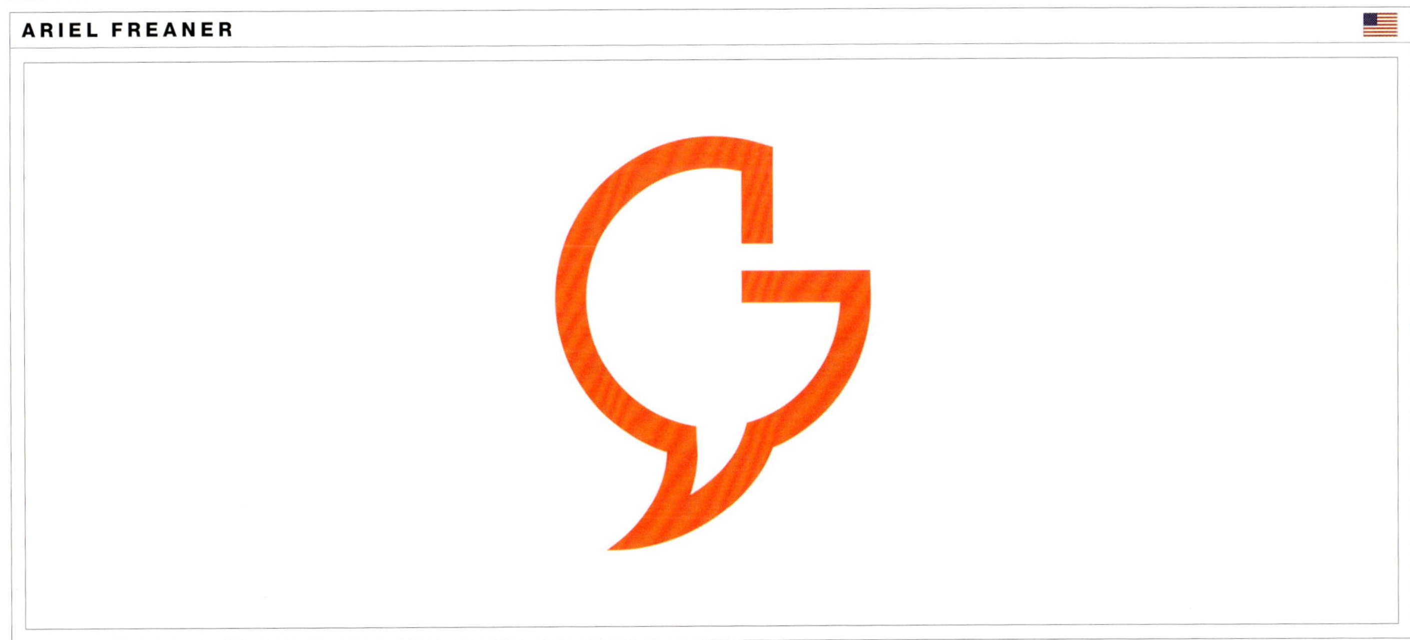

P238: Credit & Commentary Title: Glocal Media News Logo | Client: Glocal Media News | Design Firm: Freaner Creative & Design

EL PASO, GALERÍA DE COMUNICACIÓN

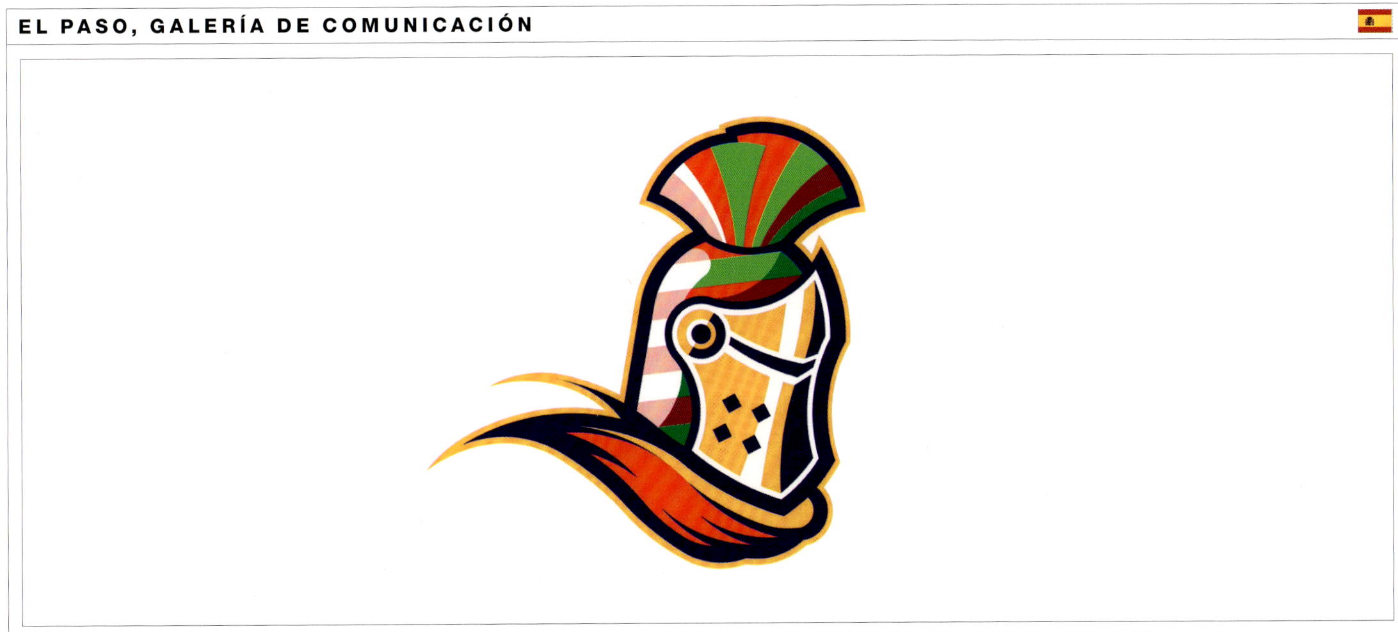

P238: Credit & Commentary Title: Tu Herrero de Caramelo | Client: Iván Domene | Design Firm: El Paso, Galería de Comunicación

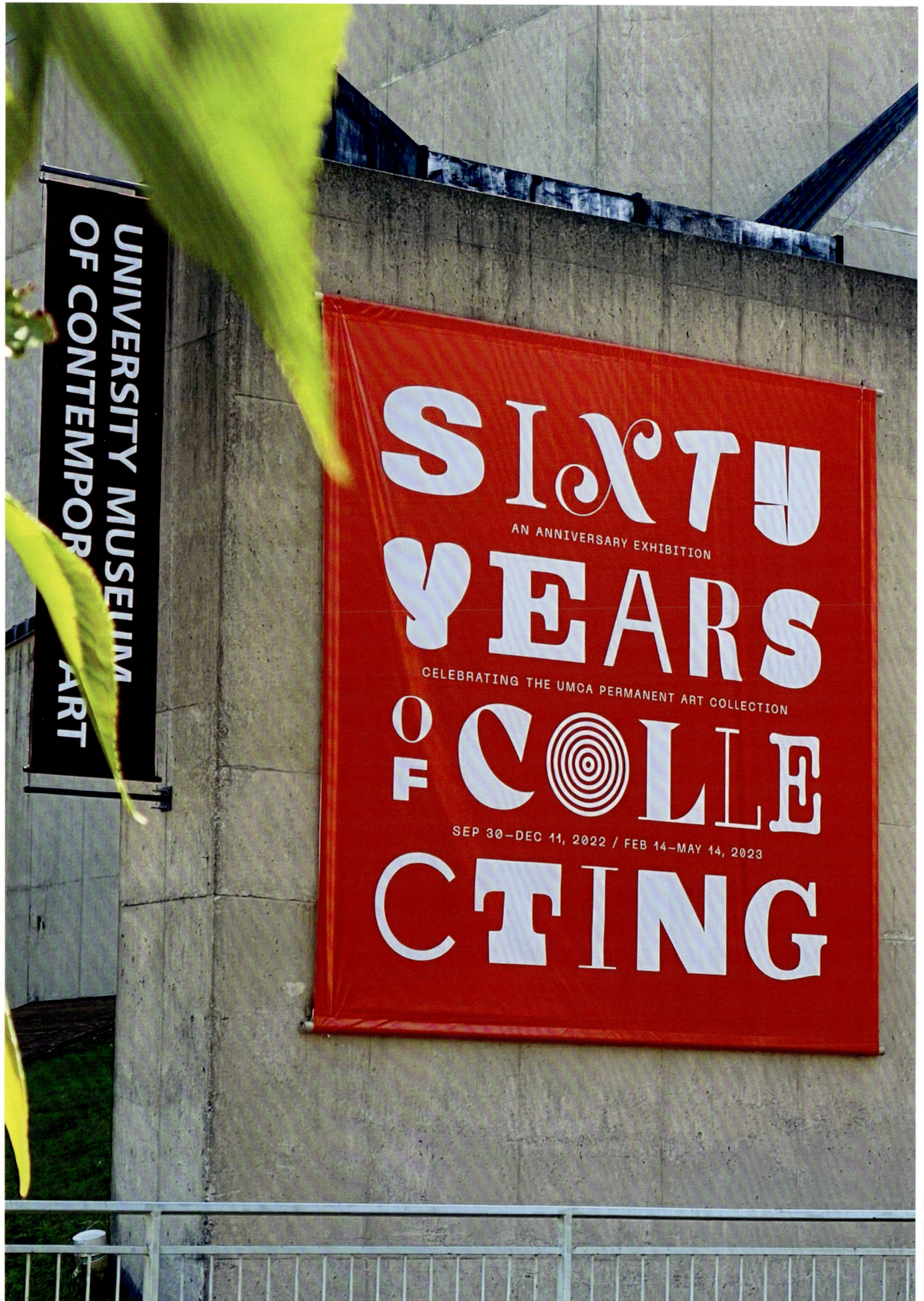

Title: Brand Identity for Anniversary Exhibition "Sixty Years of Collecting" | **Client:** University Museum of Contemporary Art at University of Massachusetts, Amherst | **Design Firm:** Code Switch | **P238:** Credit & Commentary | Image 1 of 6

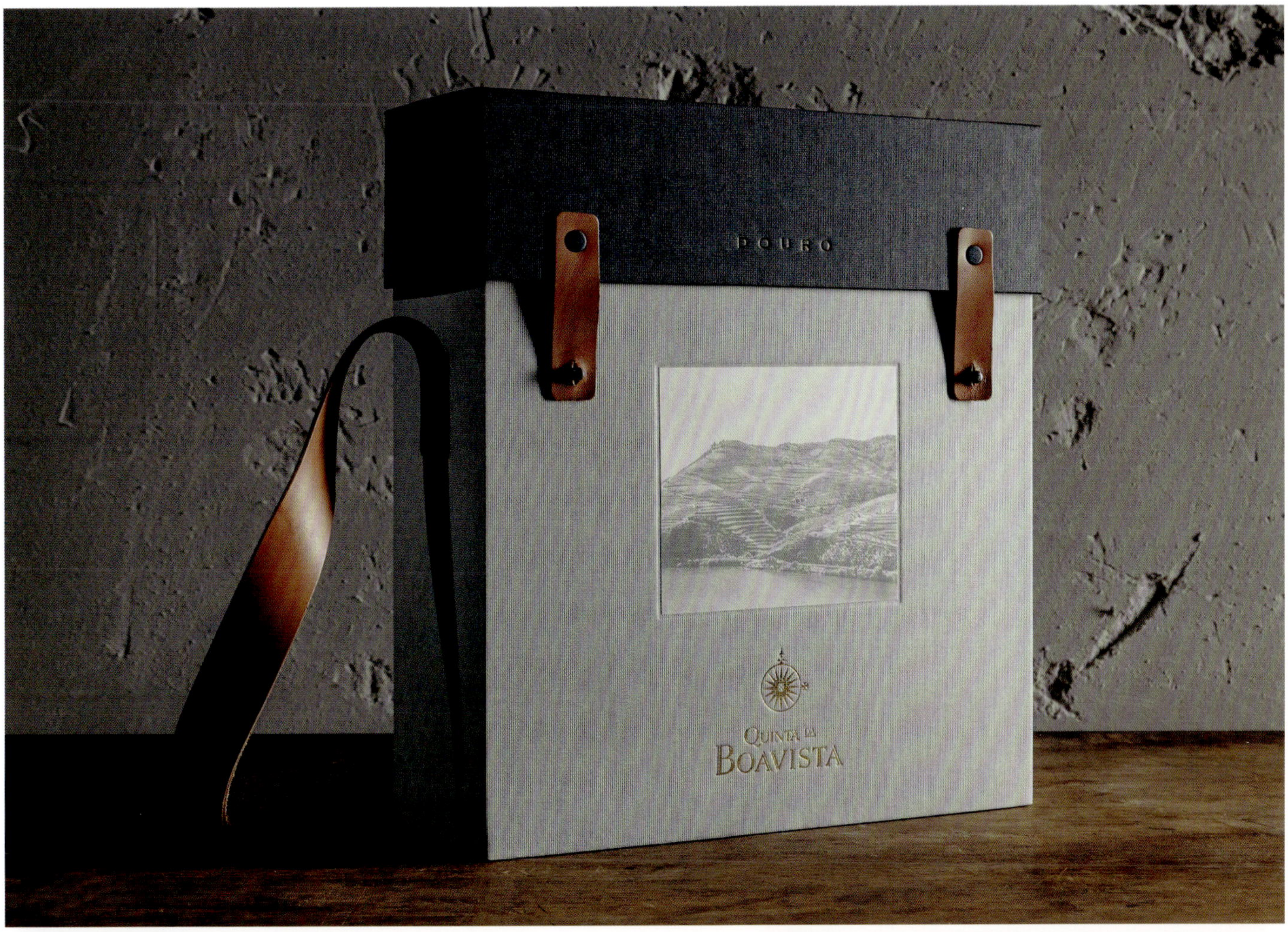

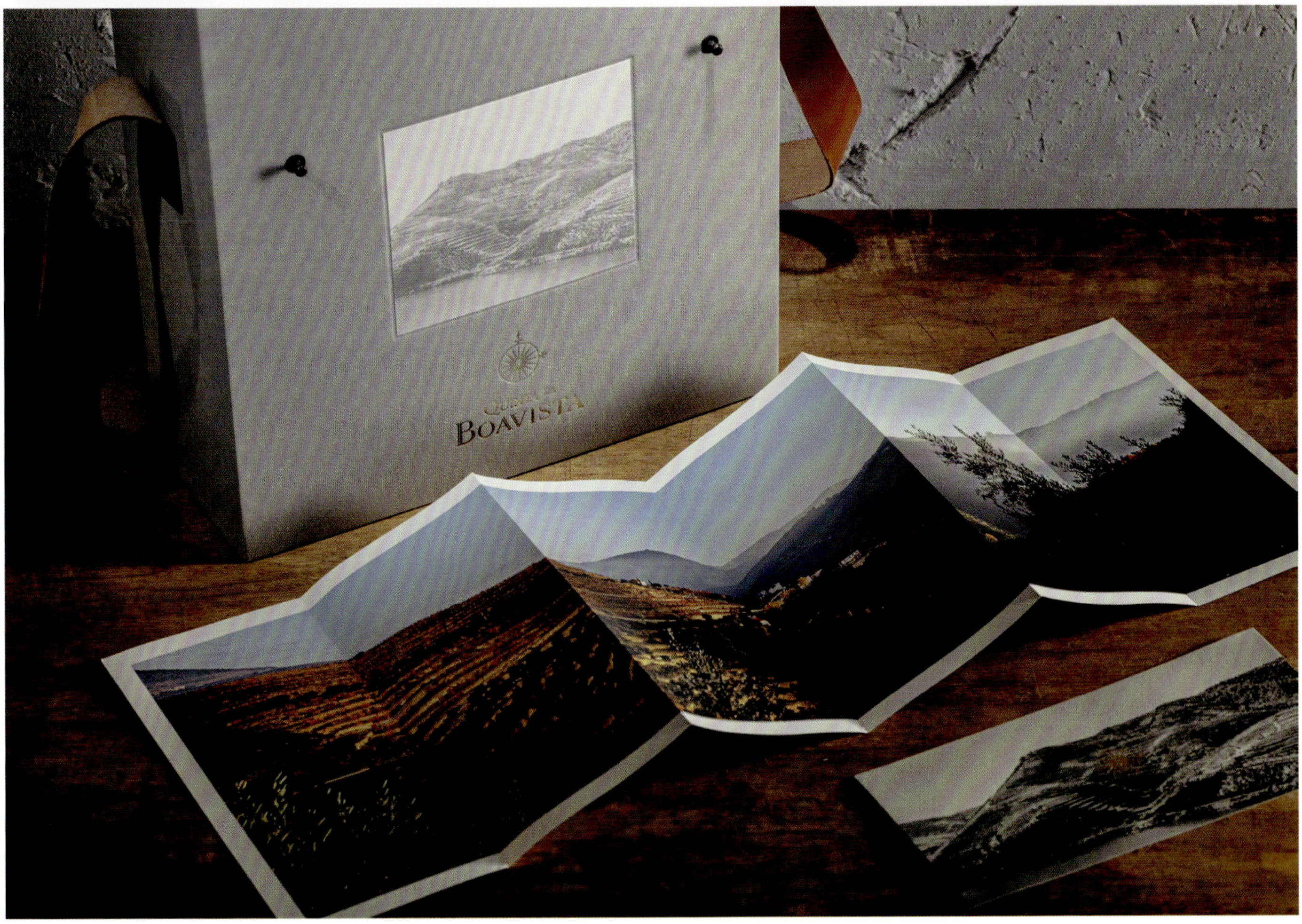

Title: Quinta da Boavista - Michelin Guide | **Client:** Quinta da Boavista - Sogevinus
Design Firm: Another Collective | **P238:** Credit & Commentary | Images 1, 2 of 7

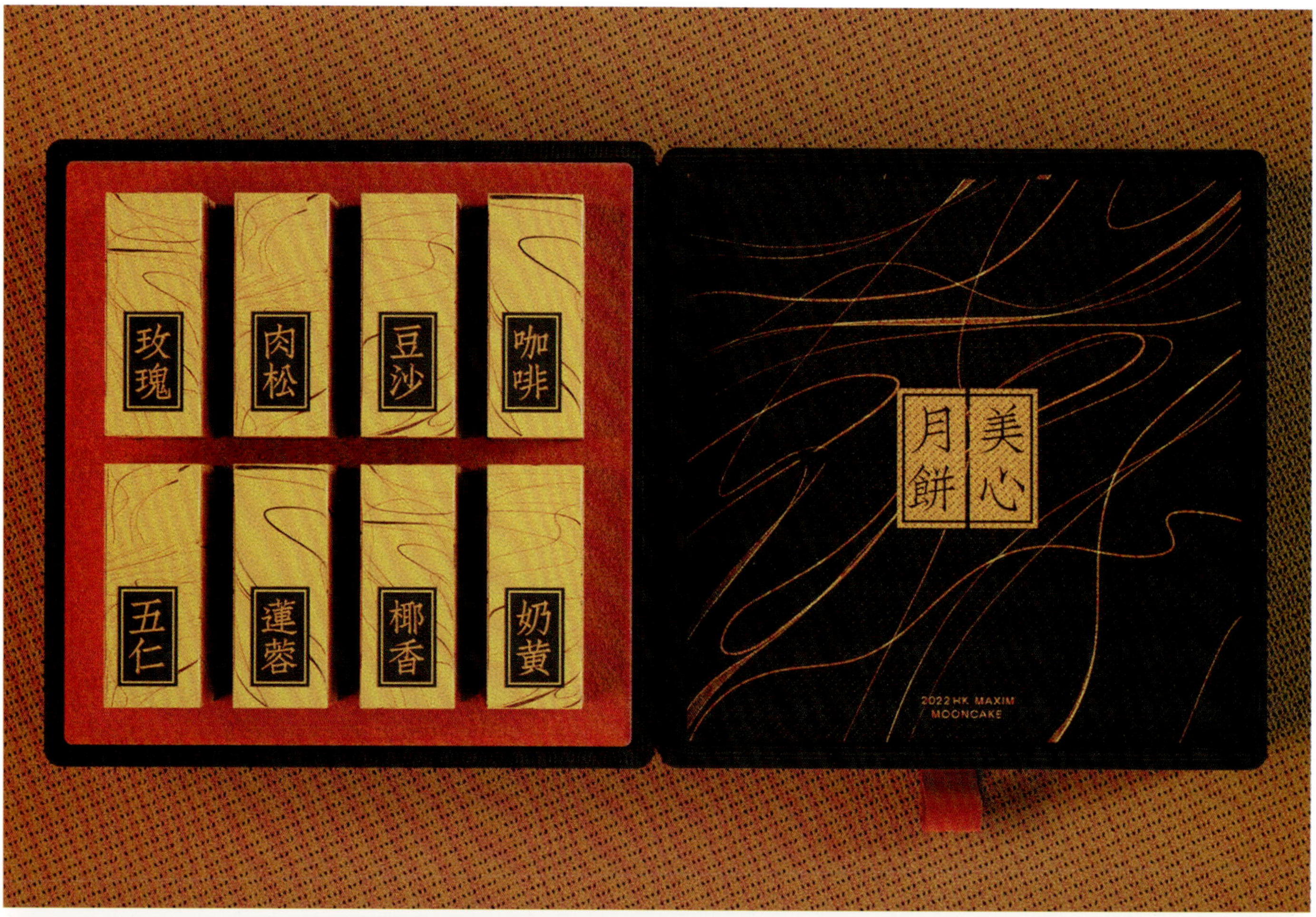

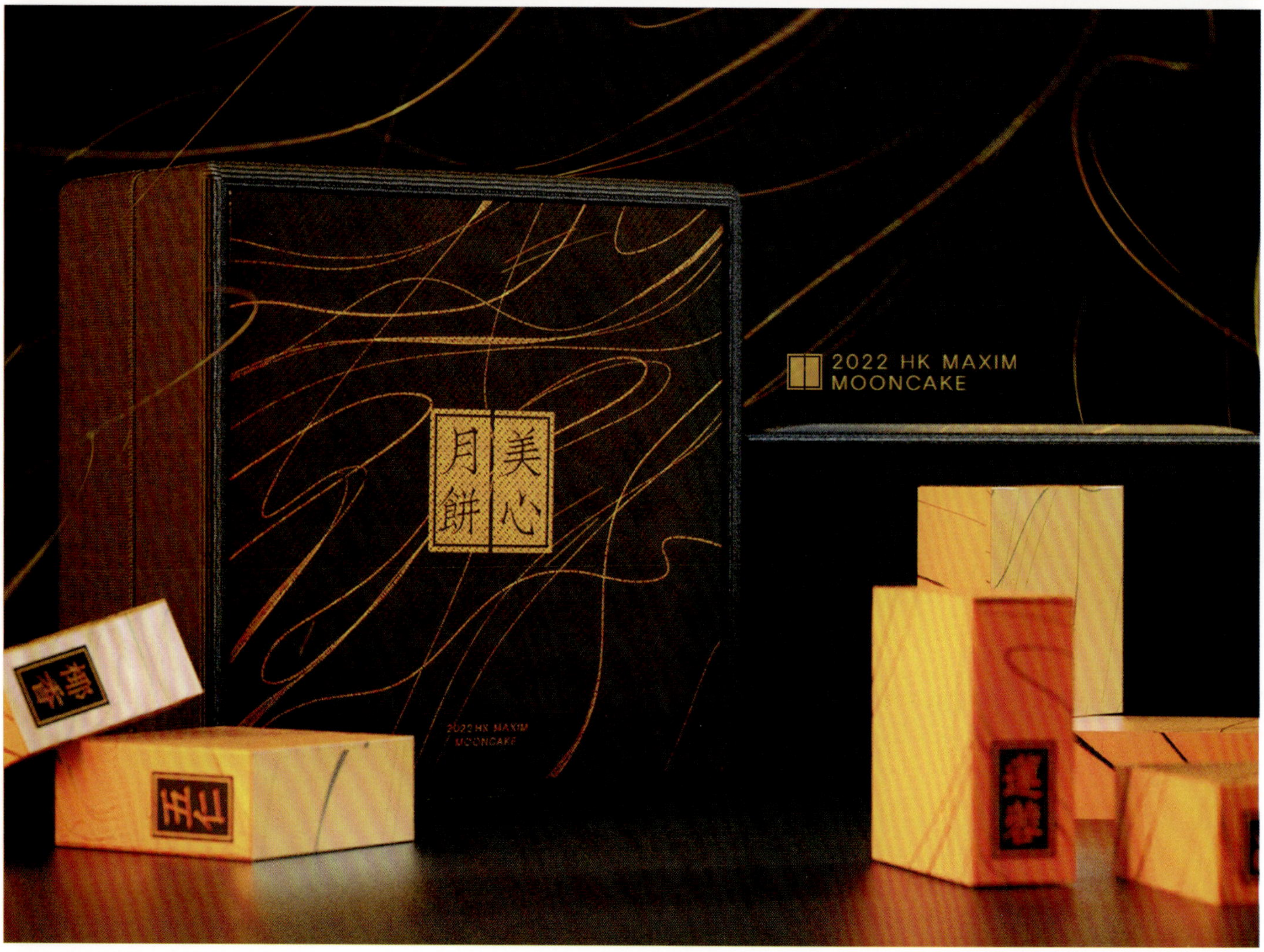

P238: Credit & Commentary

Title: "The Thread" Mooncake Packaging Design | **Client:** Self-initiated | **Design Firm:** Tianyun Jiang

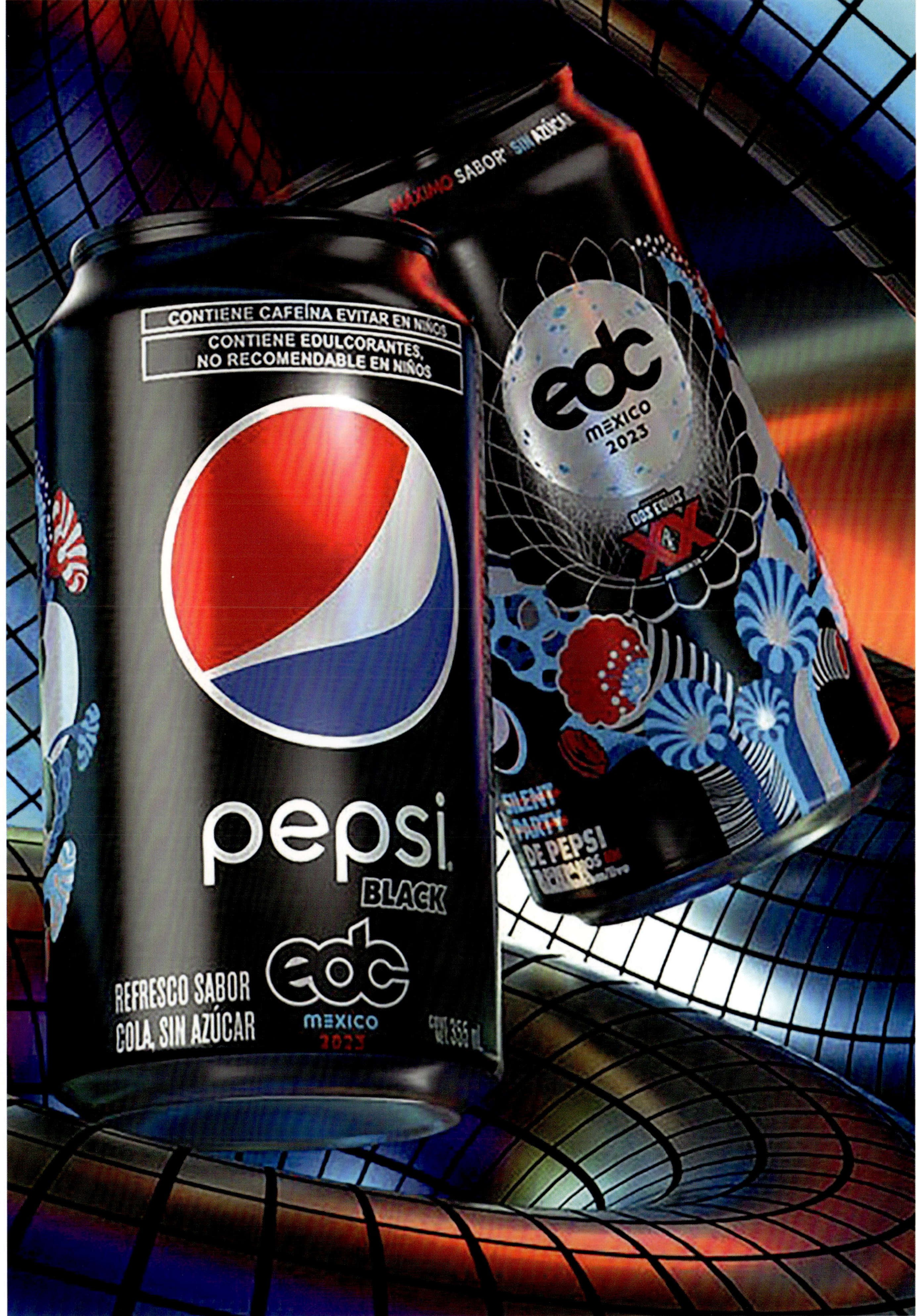

 Title: Pepsi Black EDC Mexico 2023 | **Client:** Self-initated | **Design Firm:** PepsiCo Design & Innovation

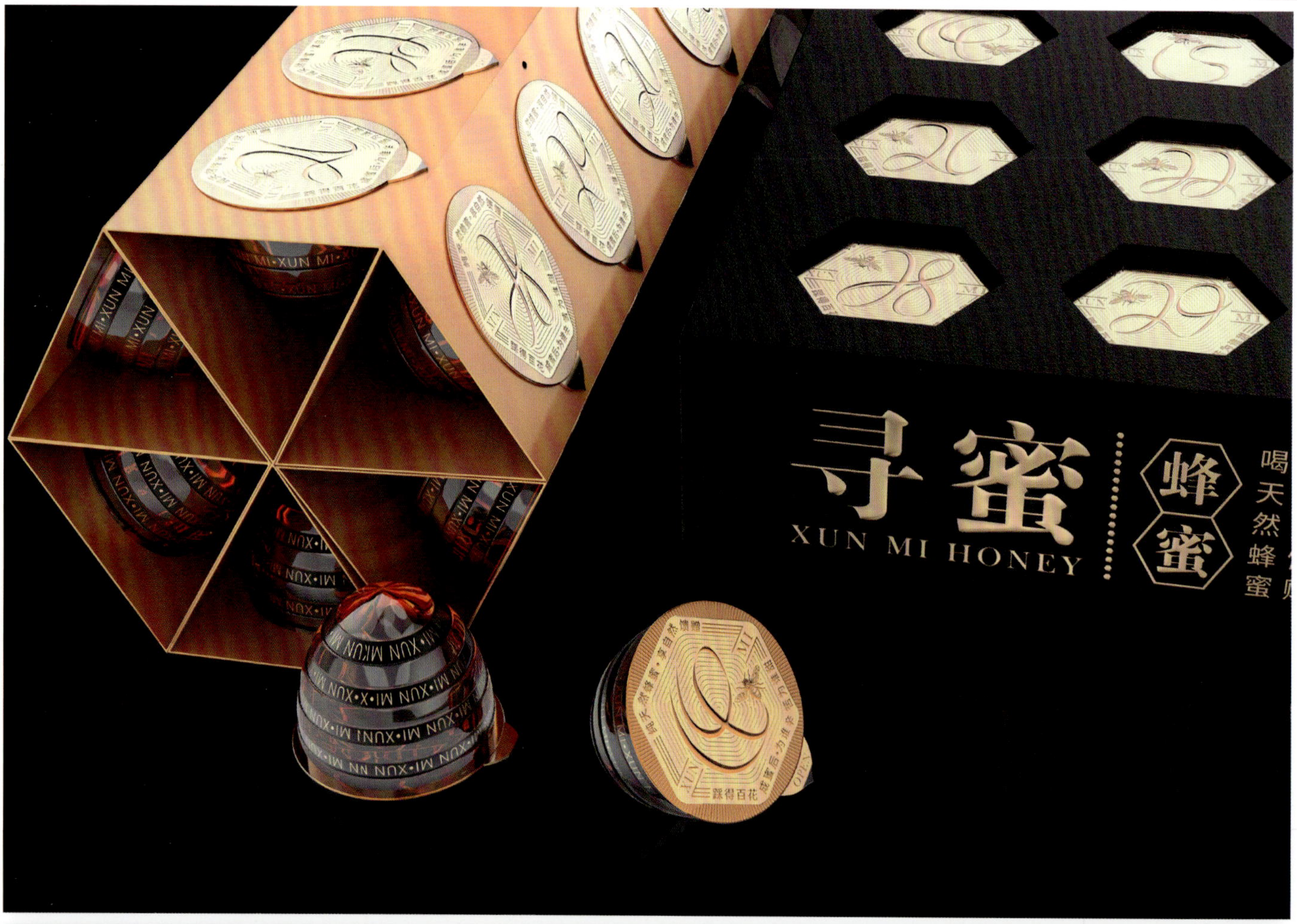

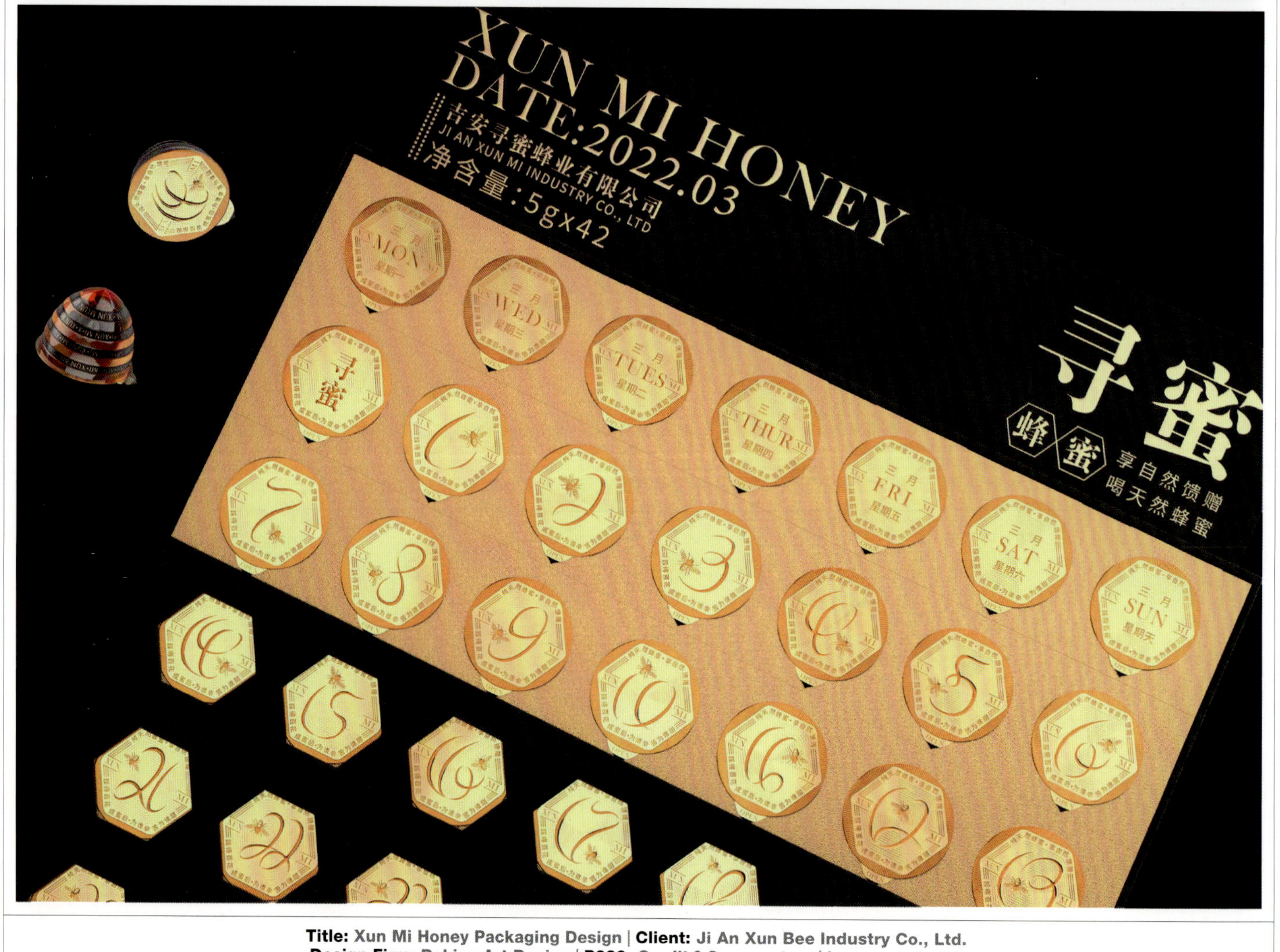

Title: Xun Mi Honey Packaging Design | **Client:** Ji An Xun Bee Industry Co., Ltd.
Design Firm: Roking Art Design | **P239:** Credit & Commentary | Images 1, 2 of 6

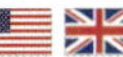

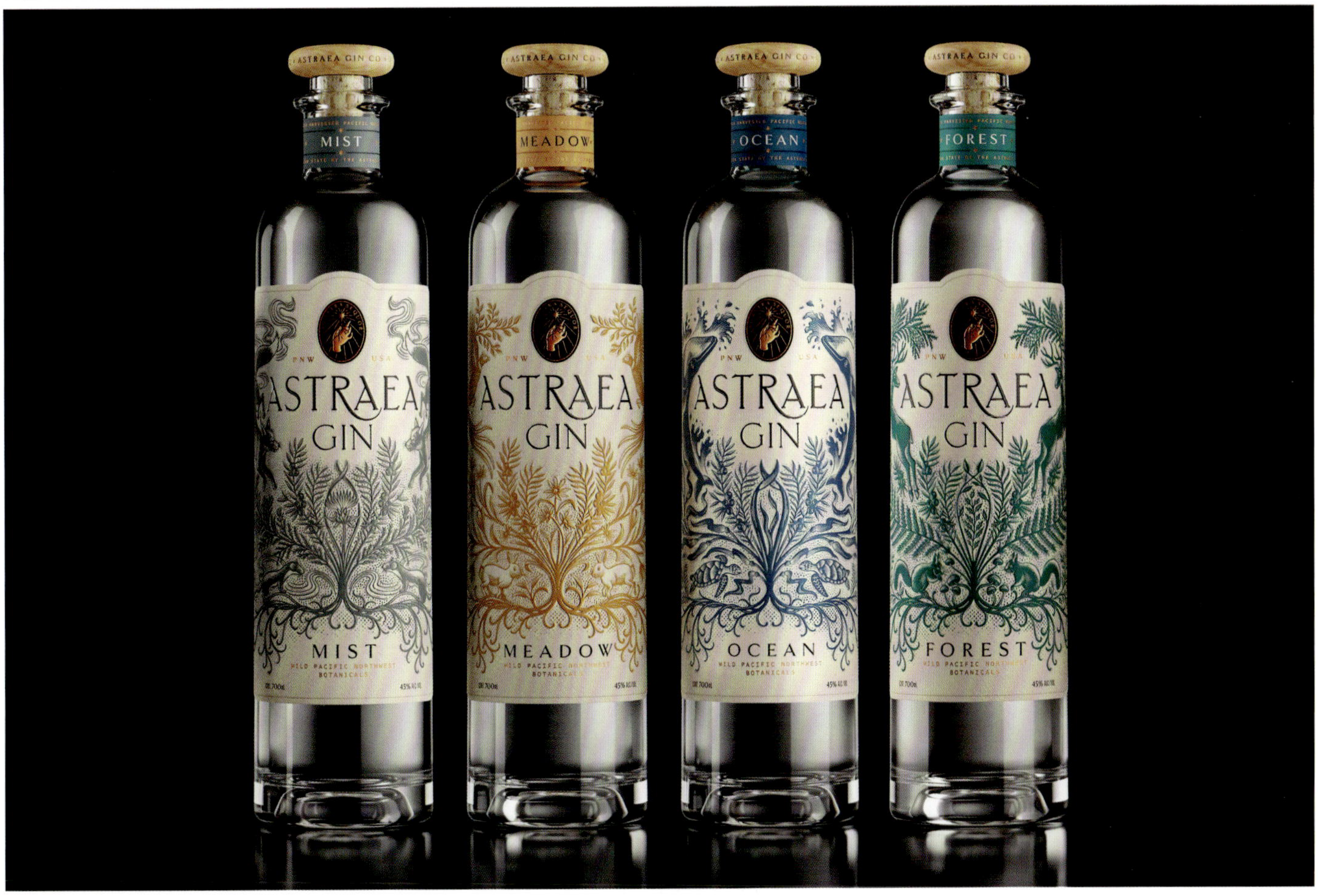

P239: Credit & Commentary

Title: Astraea Gin | **Client:** Astraea LLC | **Design Firm:** Stranger & Stranger

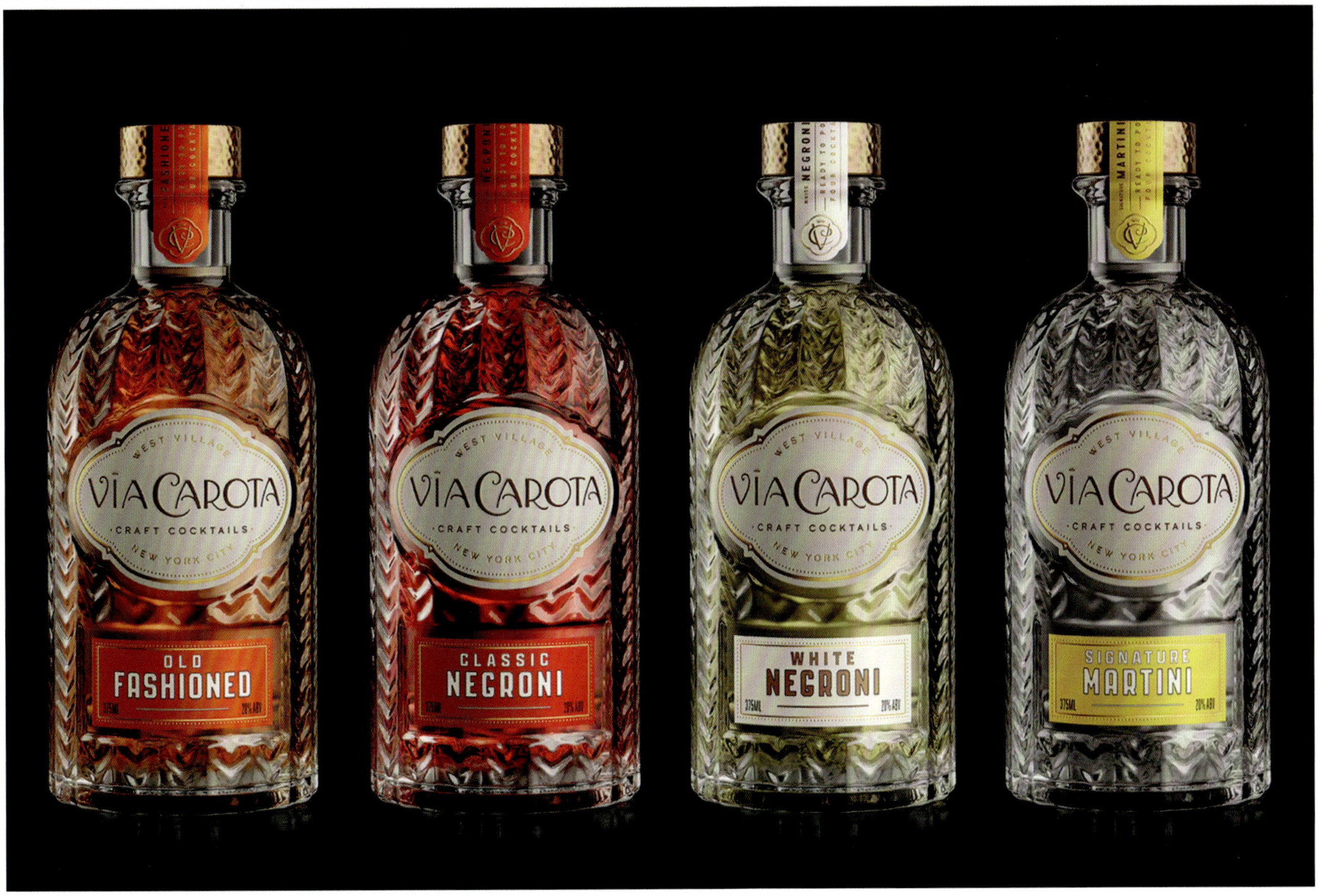

STRANGER & STRANGER GOLD

PACKAGING

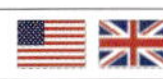

P239: Credit & Commentary

Title: Via Carota Craft Cocktails | **Client:** Via Carota | **Design Firm:** Stranger & Stranger

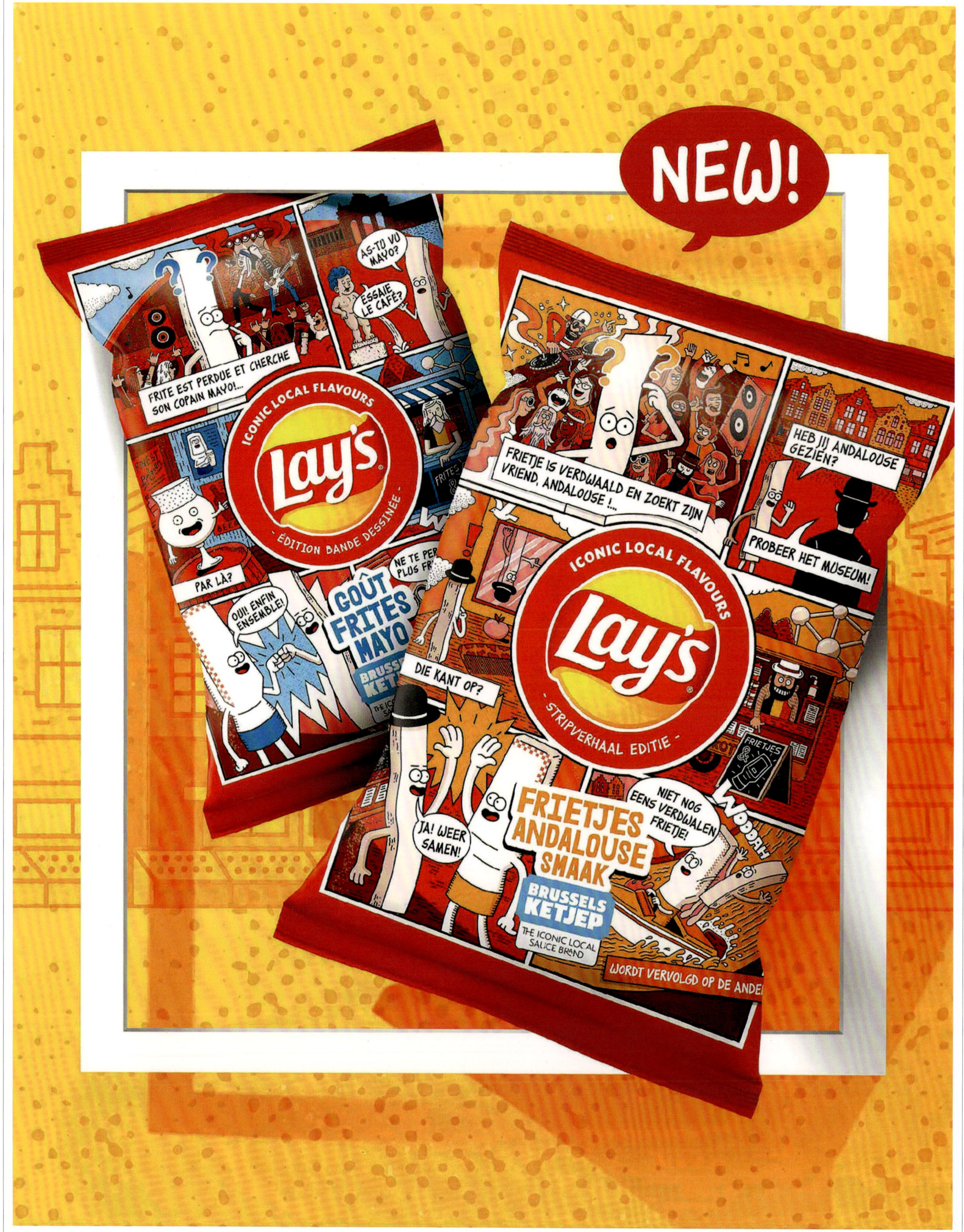

Title: Lay's - More Belgian Really Impossible! | **Client:** Self-initated
Design Firm: PepsiCo Design & Innovation | **P239:** Credit & Commentary | Image 1 of 3

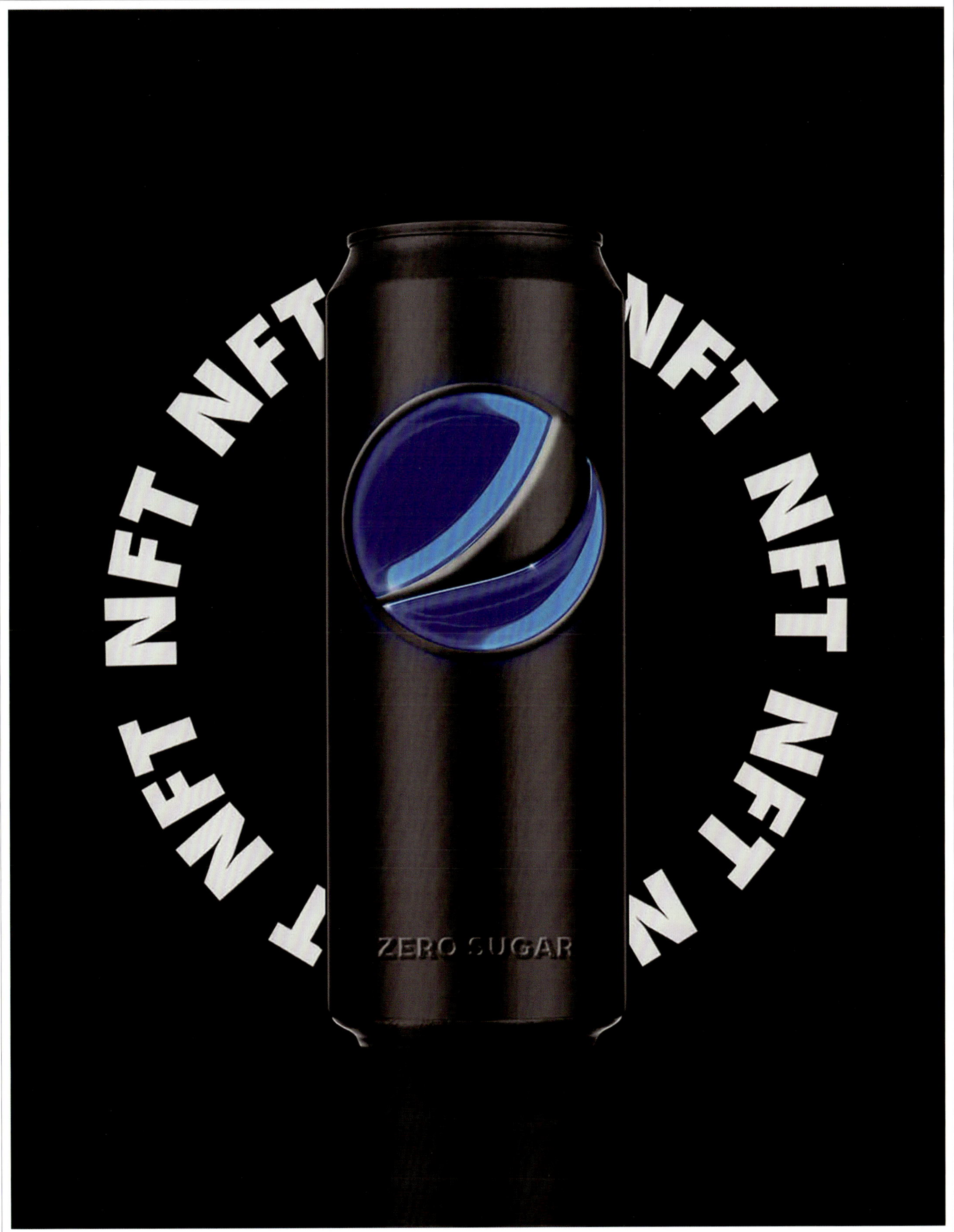

Title: Pepsi Black Zero NFT Collection | **Client:** Self-initated
Design Firm: PepsiCo Design & Innovation | **P239:** Credit & Commentary

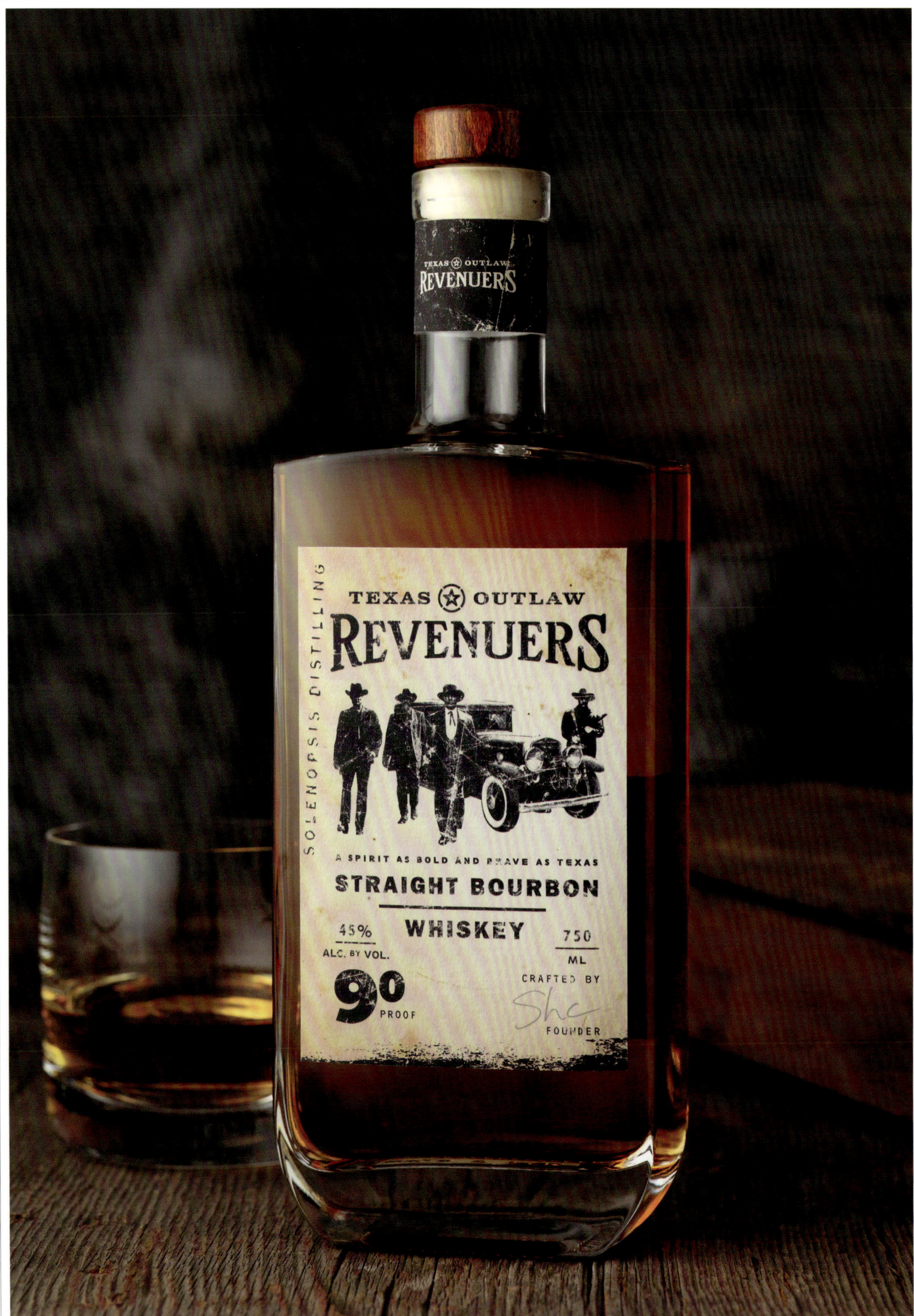

P239: Credit & Commentary **Title:** Texas Outlaw Revenuers | **Client:** Solenopsis Distilling | **Design Firm:** CF Napa Brand Design

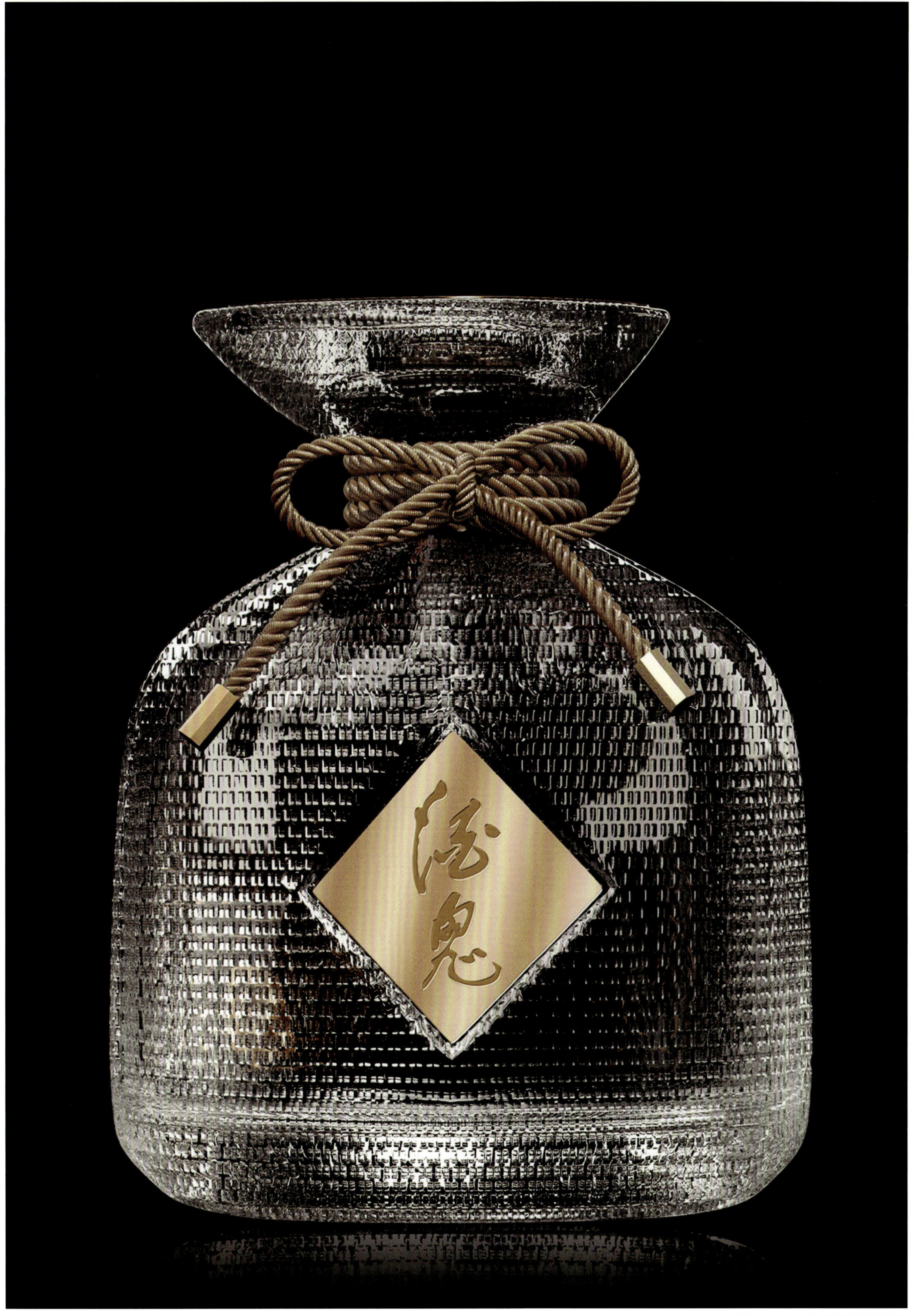

Title: Wanlizoudanji | **Client:** Drunkard Wine Co., Ltd. | **Design Firm:** Sungoo Design

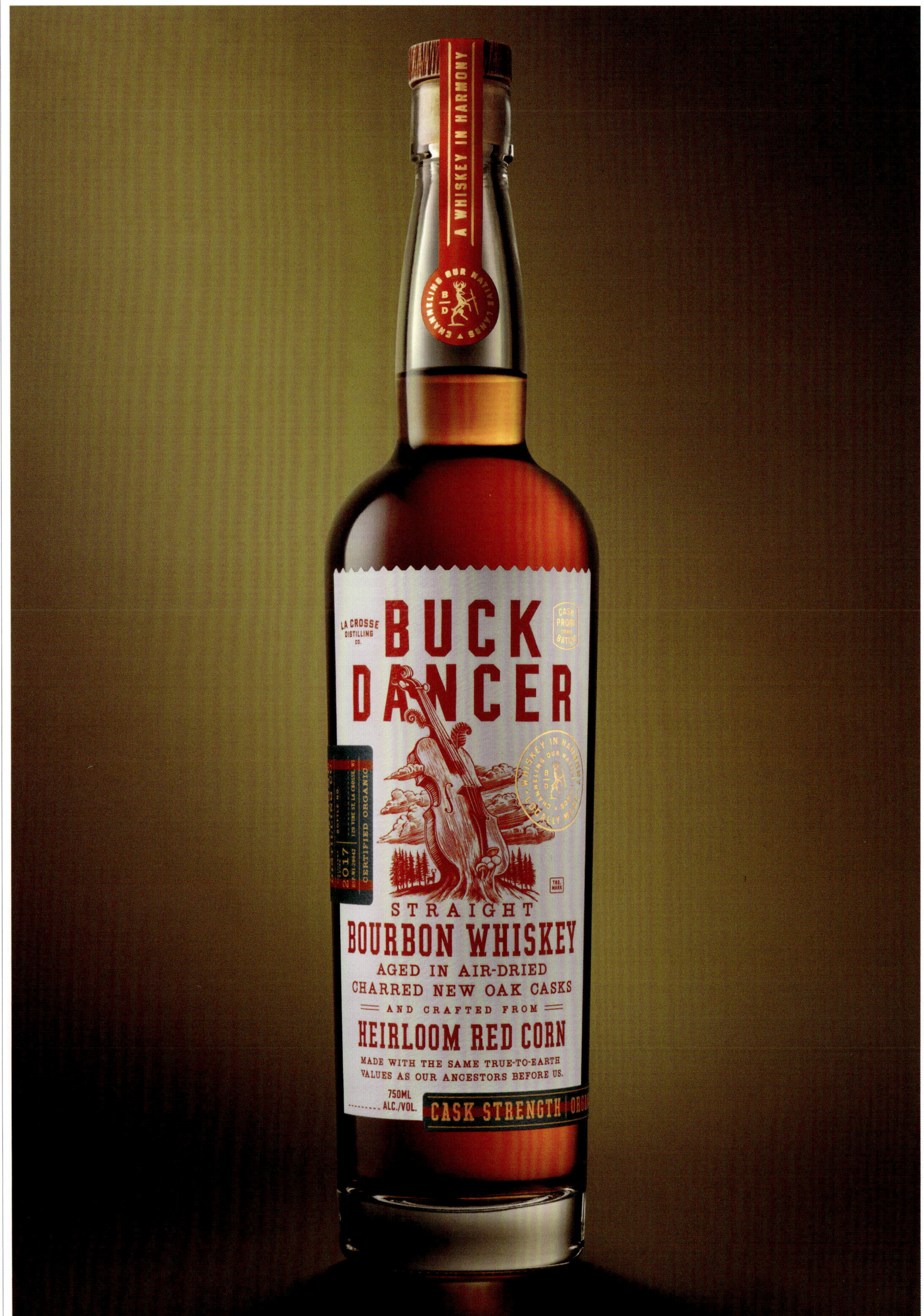

P239: Credit & Commentary **Title:** Buck Dancer Bourbon | **Client:** La Crosse Distilling Co. | **Design Firm:** Chad Michael Studio

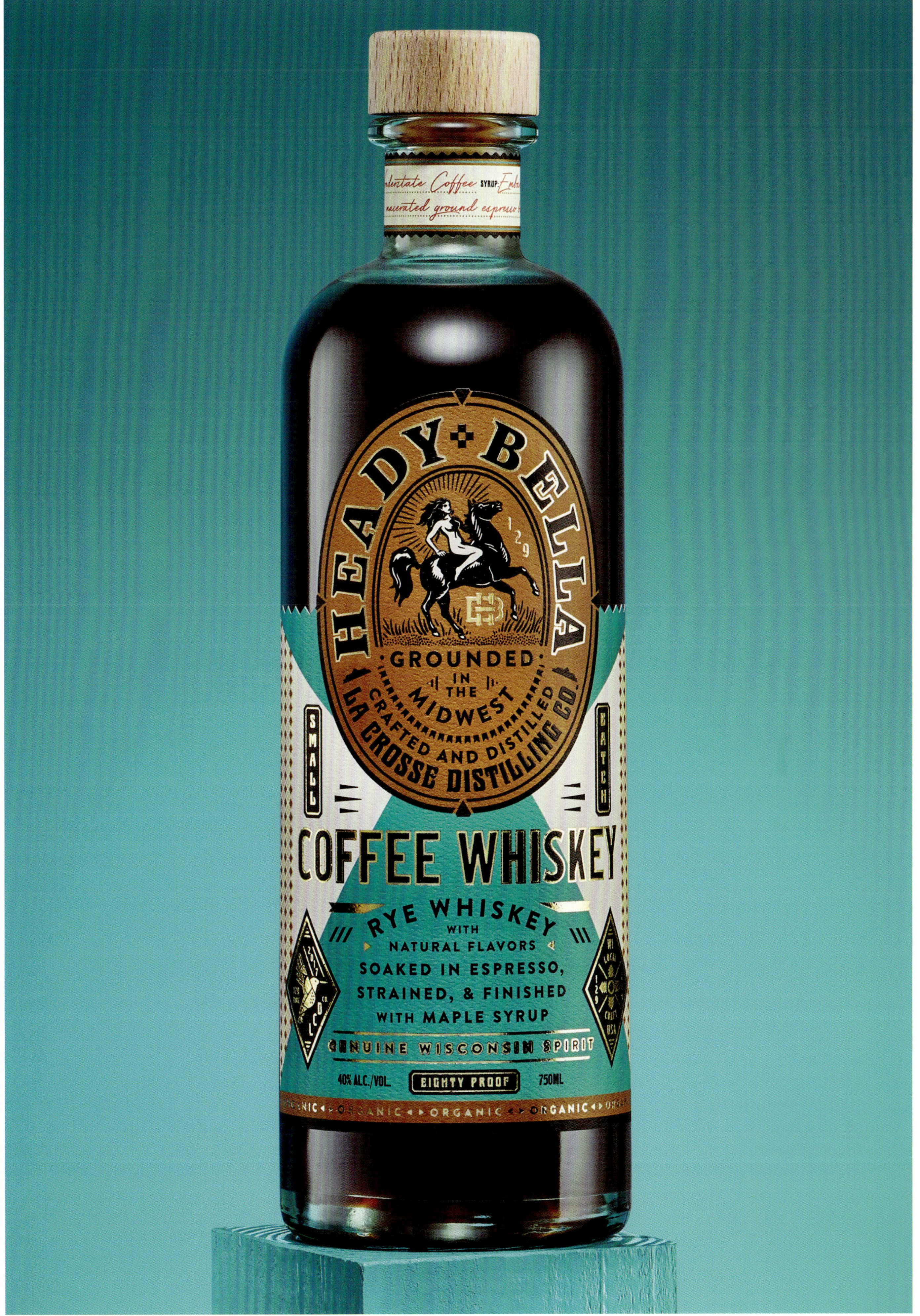

P239: Credit & Commentary **Title:** Heady Bella Coffee Whiskey | **Client:** La Crosse Distilling Co. | **Design Firm:** Chad Michael Studio

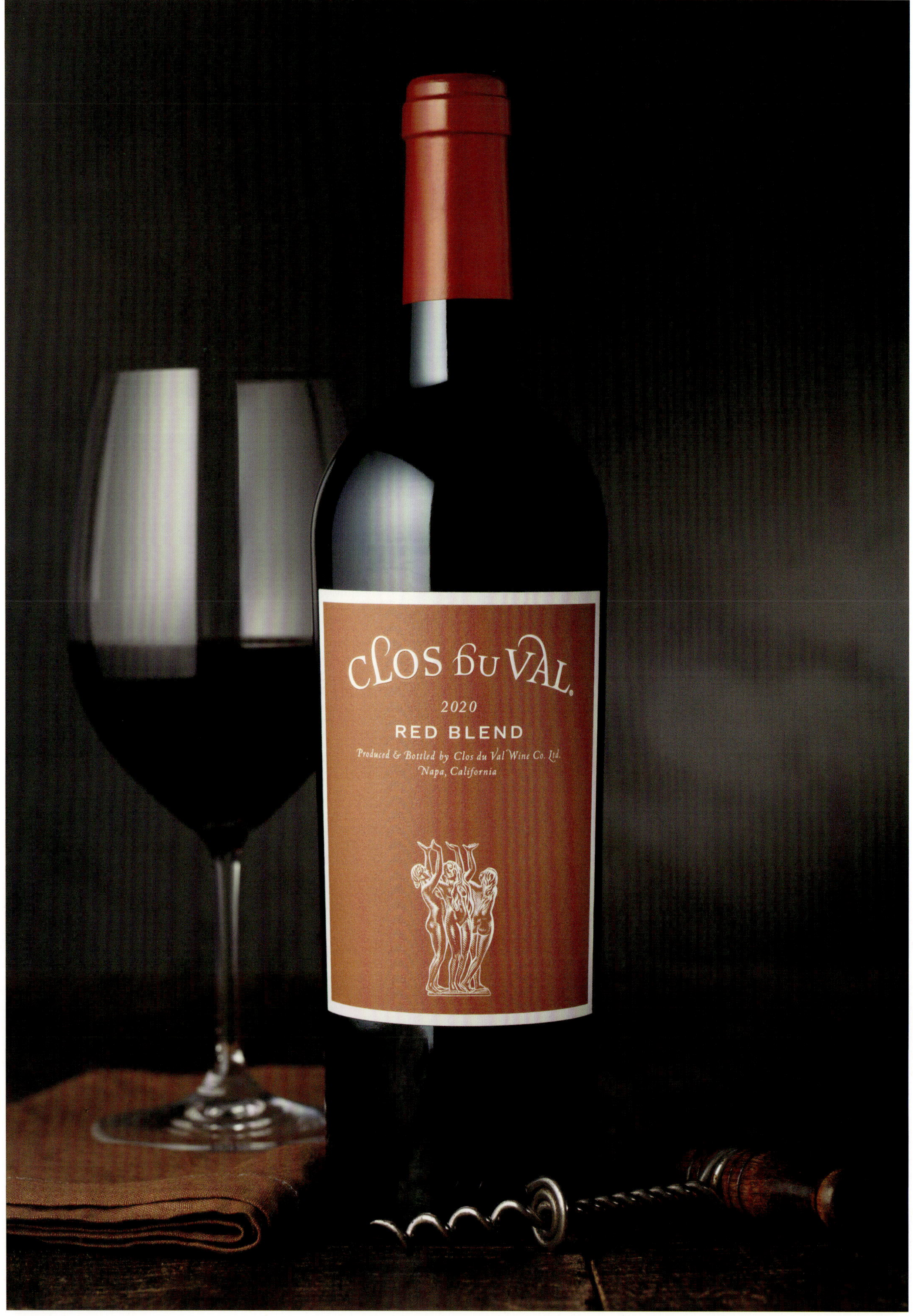

Title: Clos du Val Portfolio | **Client:** Clos du Val | **Design Firm:** CF Napa Brand Design

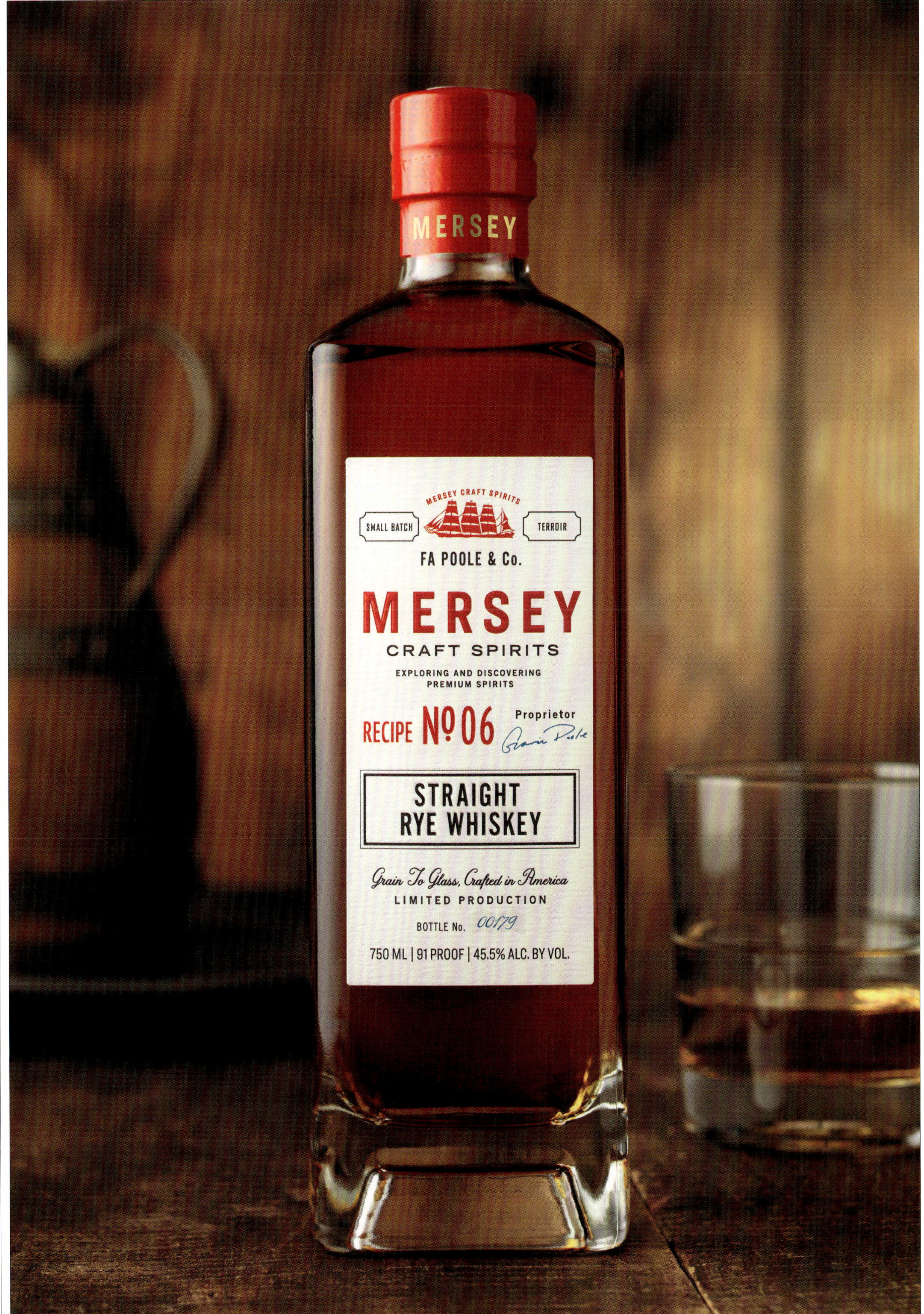

P240: Credit & Commentary **Title:** Mersey Craft Spirits | **Client:** FA Poole & Co. Distillers | **Design Firm:** CF Napa Brand Design

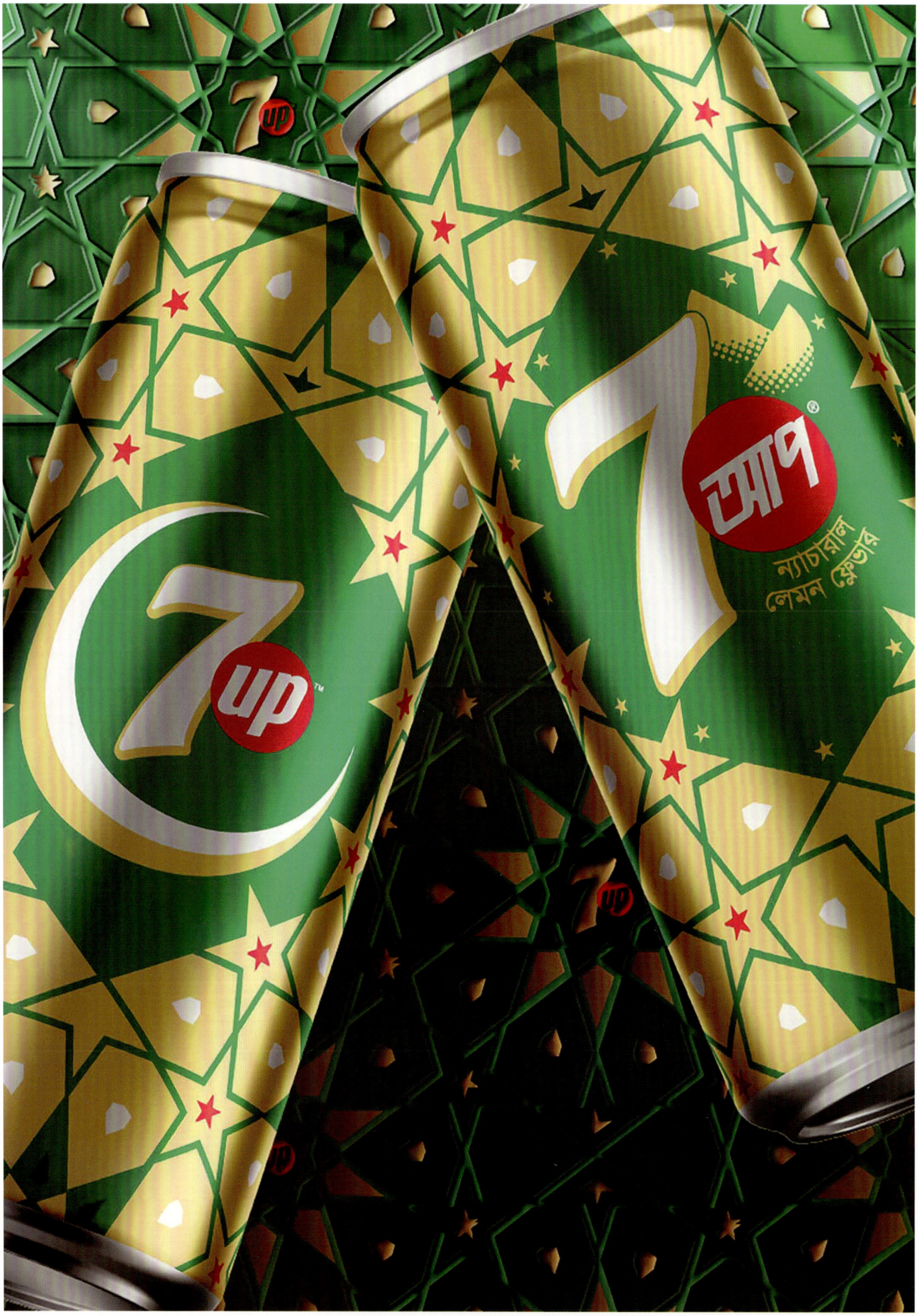

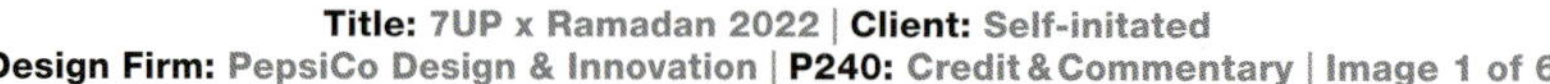

Title: 7UP x Ramadan 2022 | **Client:** Self-initated
Design Firm: PepsiCo Design & Innovation | **P240:** Credit & Commentary | Image 1 of 6

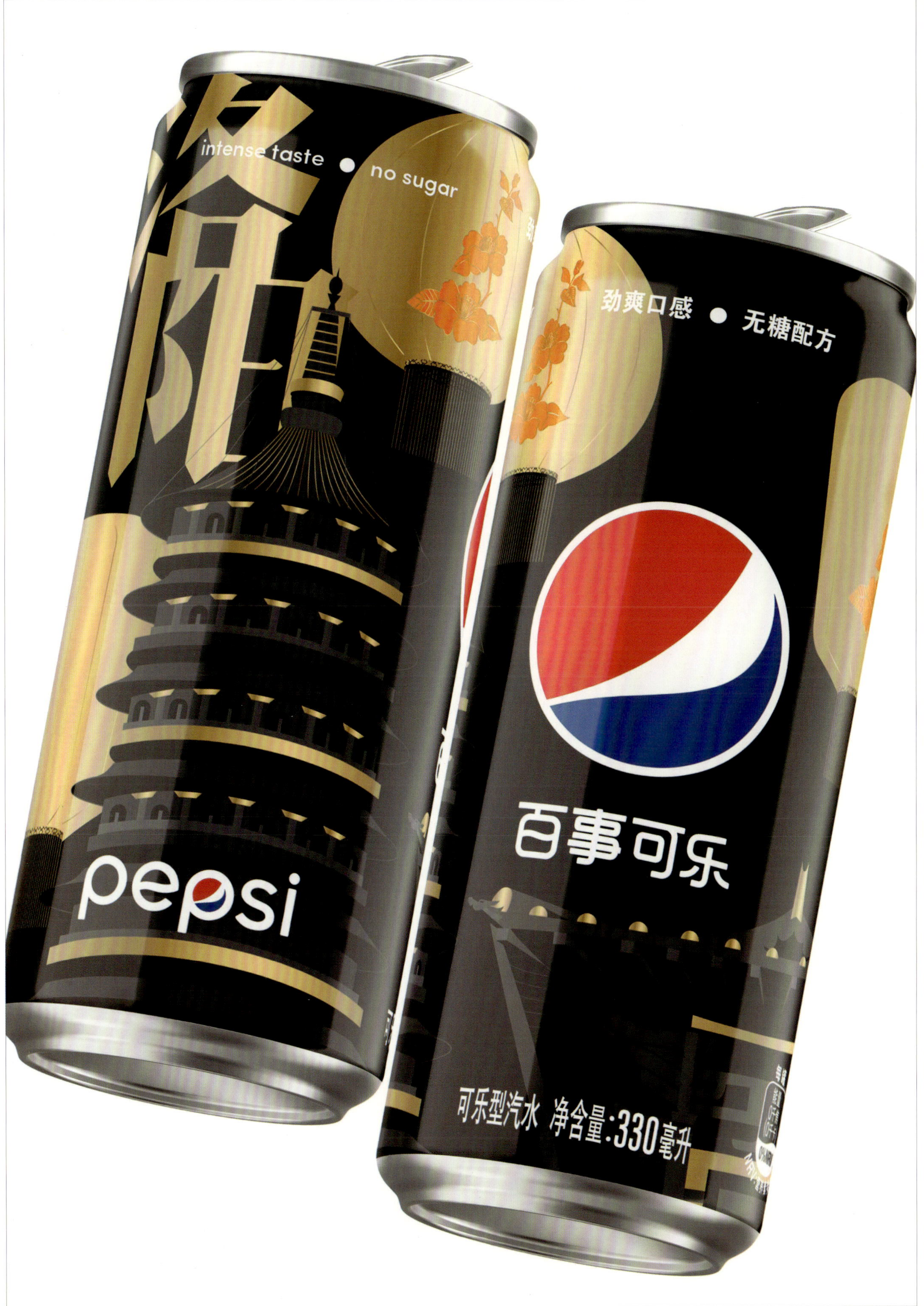

Title: Pepsi Culture Can – China City Edition | **Client:** Self-initated
Design Firm: PepsiCo Design & Innovation | **P240:** Credit & Commentary | Image 1 of 4

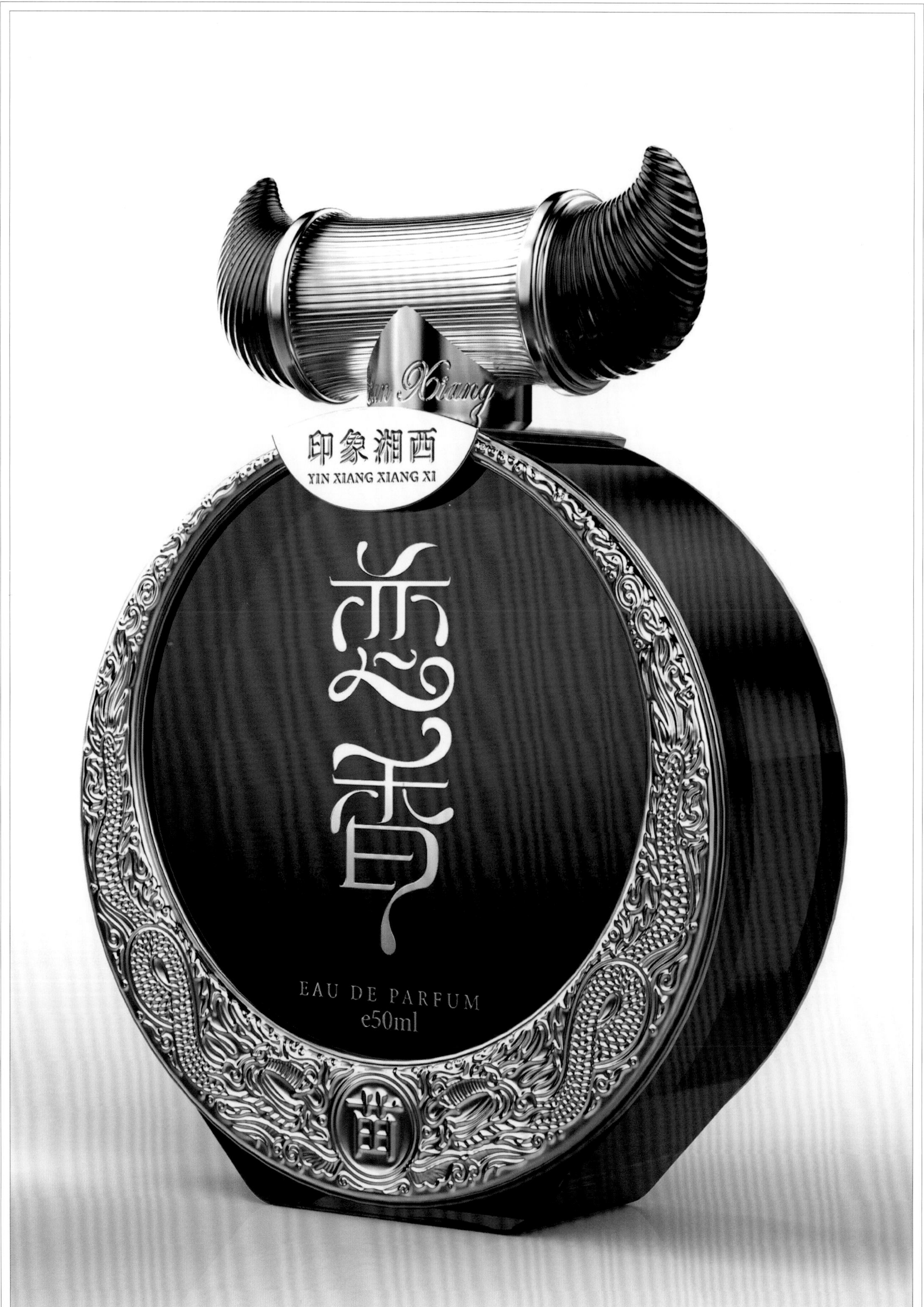

Title: Lian Xiang Perfume Packaging Design | **Client:** Xiangxi Lotus Fragrance Perfume Co., Ltd.
Design Firm: Roking Art Design | **P240:** Credit & Commentary | Image 1 of 6

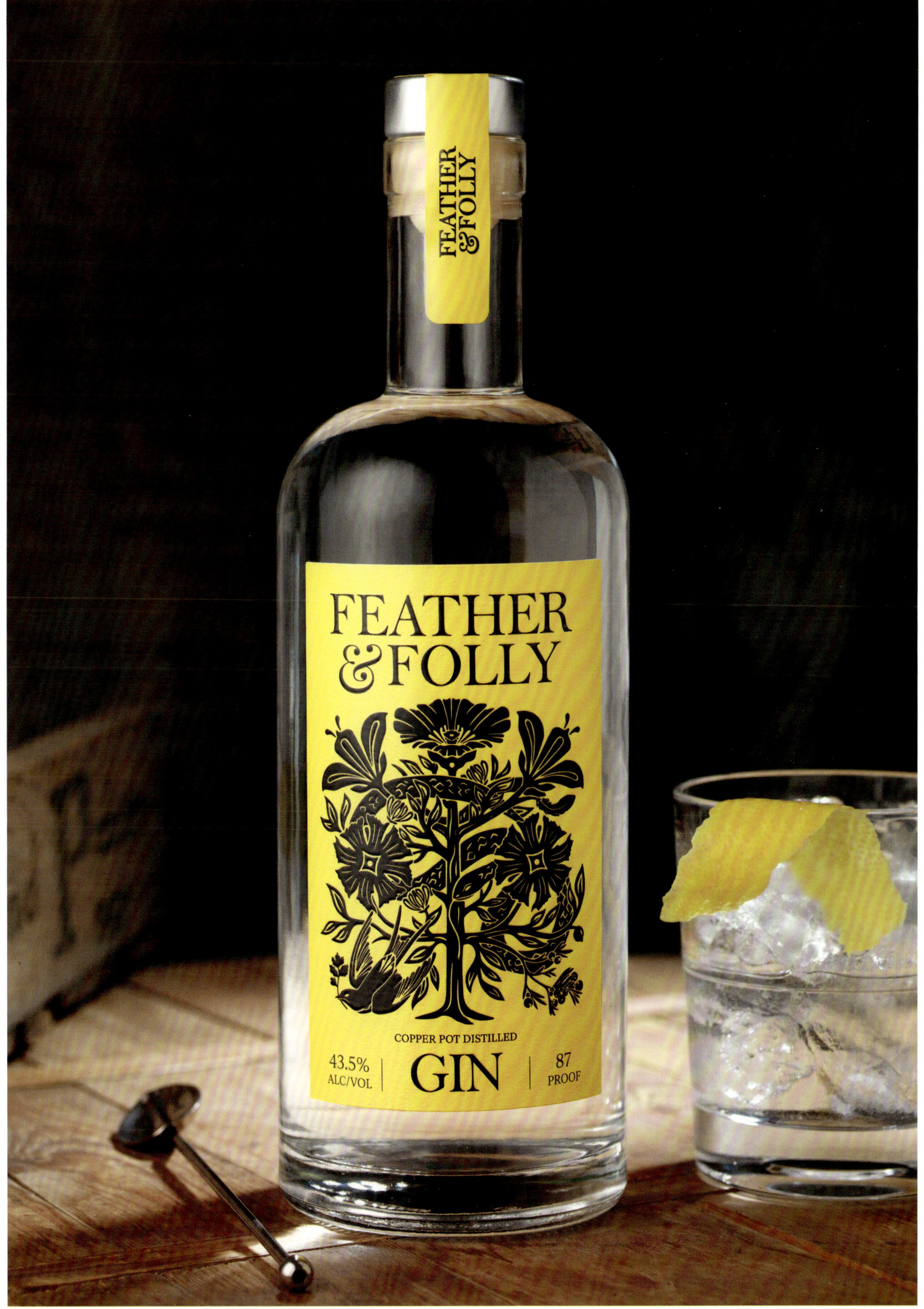

Title: Feather & Folly | **Client:** Goose Ridge Estate Vineyard & Winery
Design Firm: CF Napa Brand Design | **P240:** Credit & Commentary

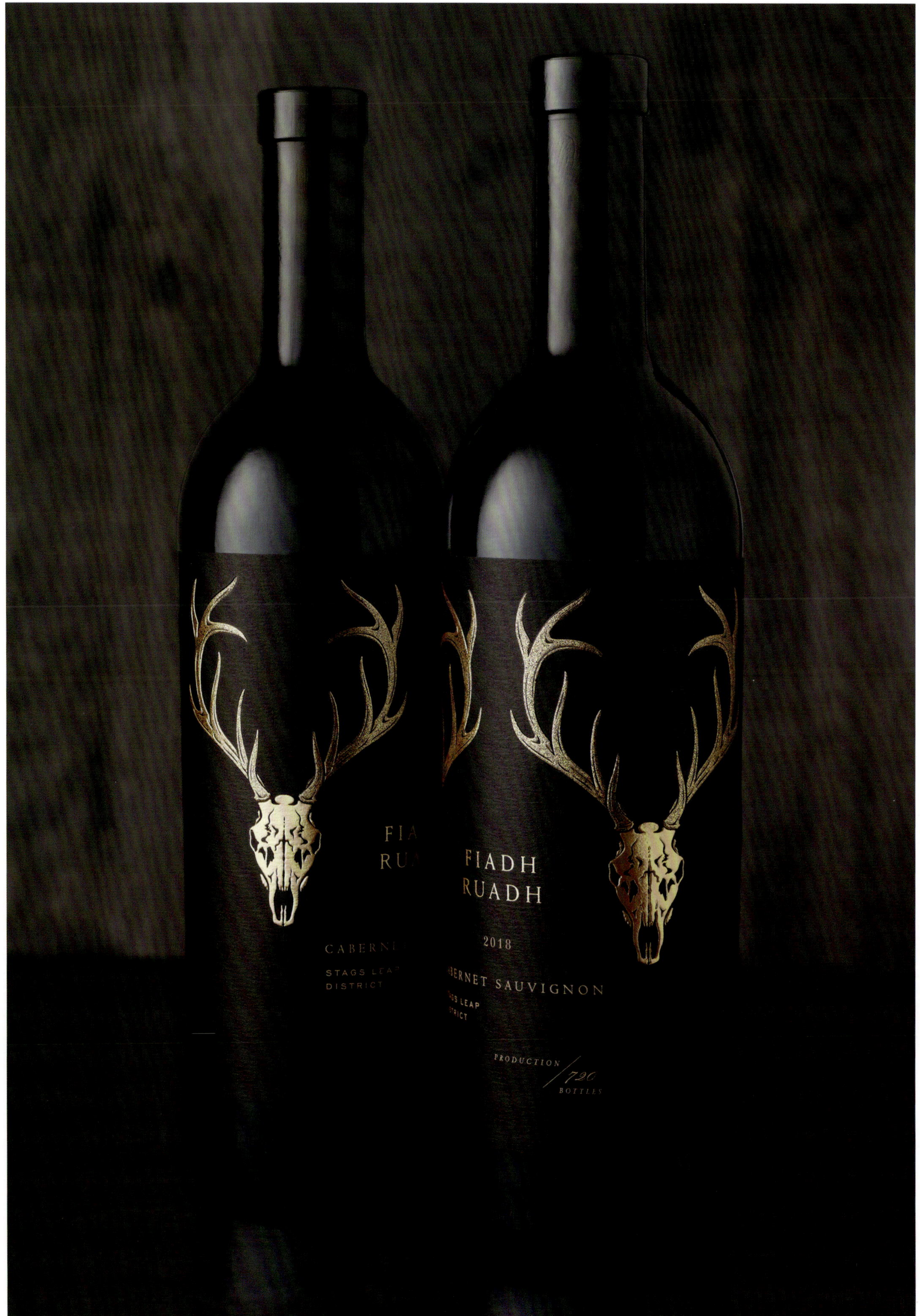

P240: Credit & Commentary **Title:** Fiadh Ruadh | **Client:** Fiadh Ruadh | **Design Firm:** CF Napa Brand Design

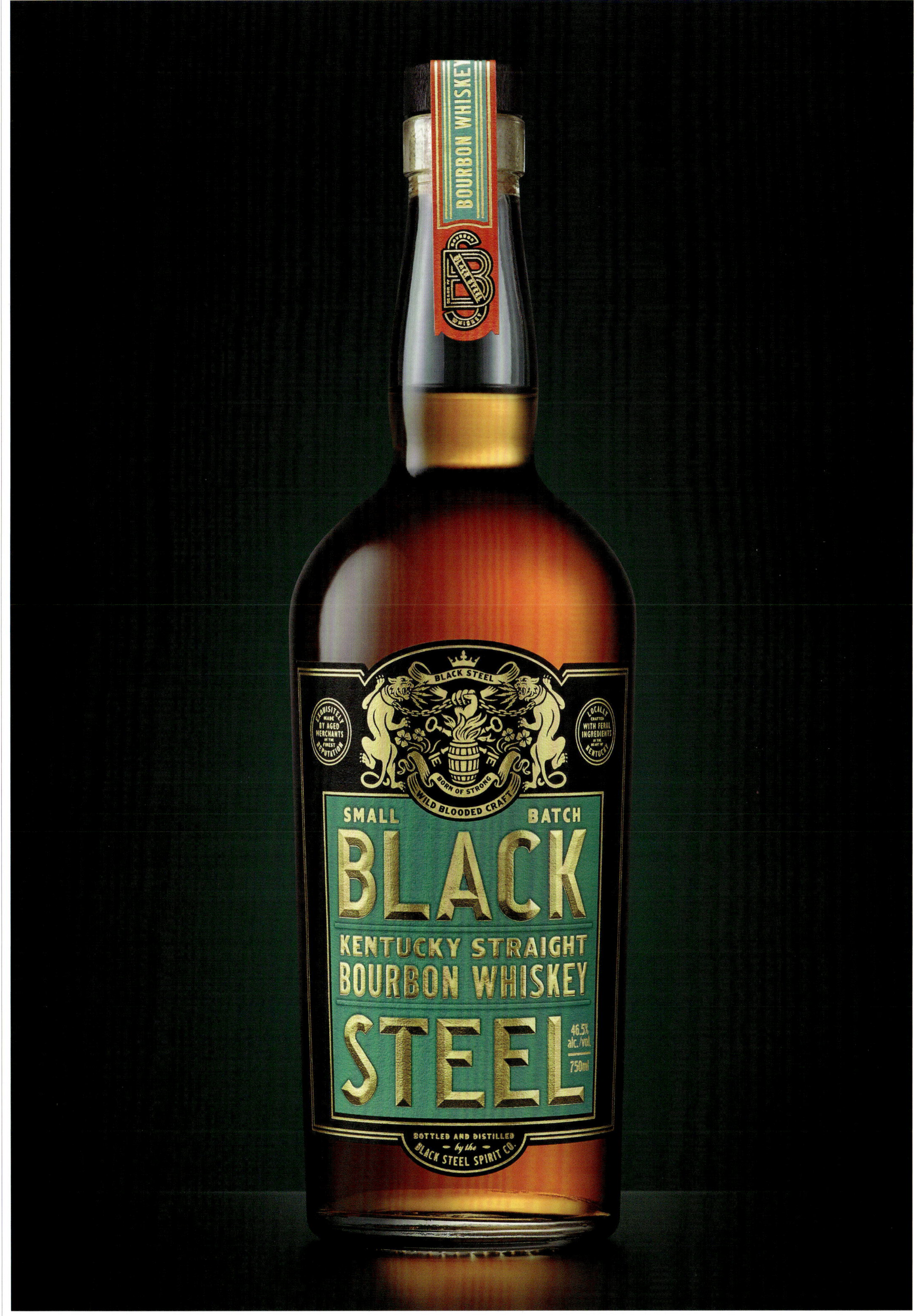

 Title: Black Steel Bourbon | **Client:** Black Steel Spirit Co. | **Design Firm:** Chad Michael Studio

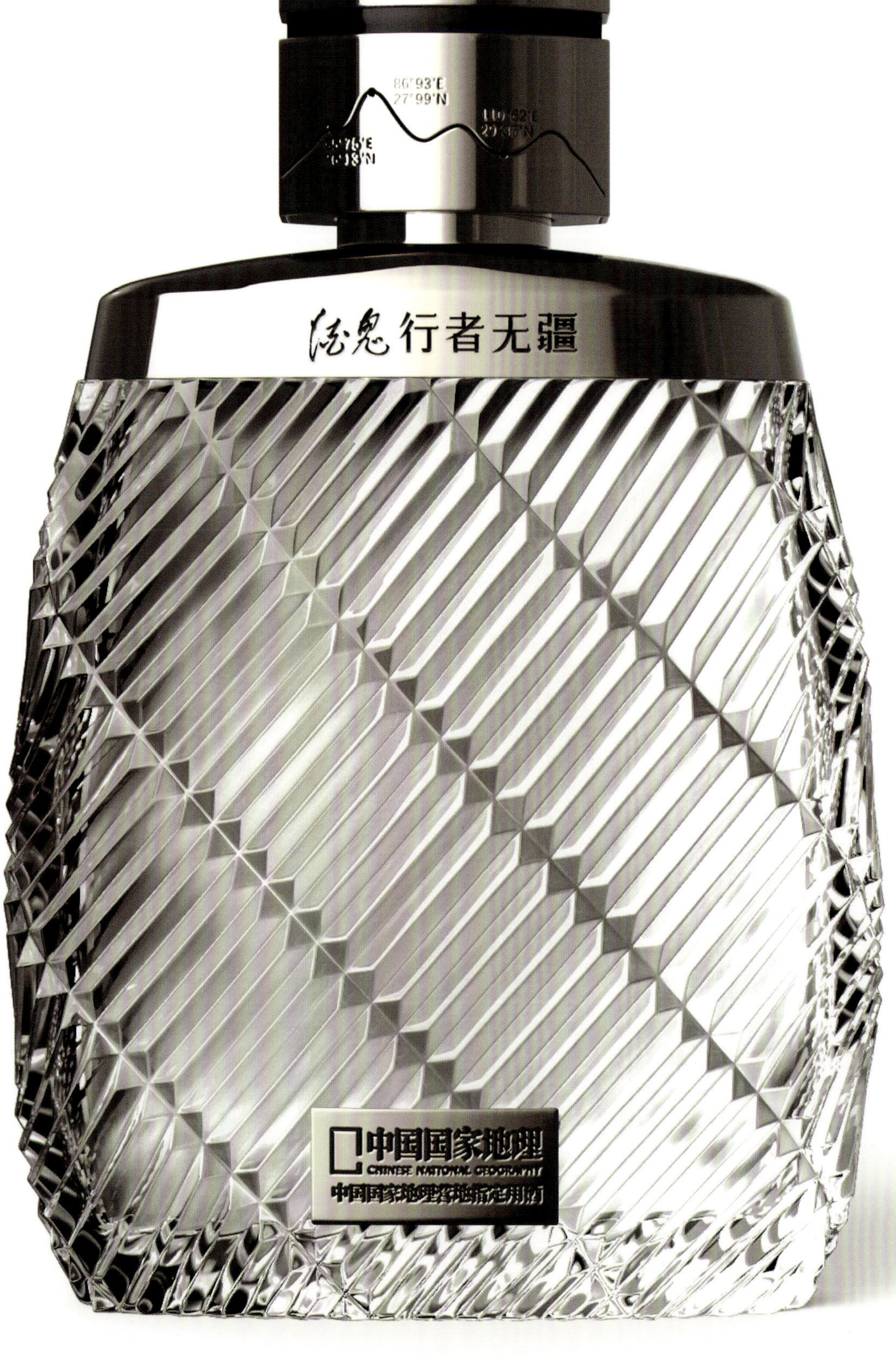

Title: WALKER·BOUNDLESS | **Client:** WALKER
Design Firm: Shenzhen Excel Brand Design Consultant Co., Ltd. | **P241:** Credit & Commentary | Image 1 of 5

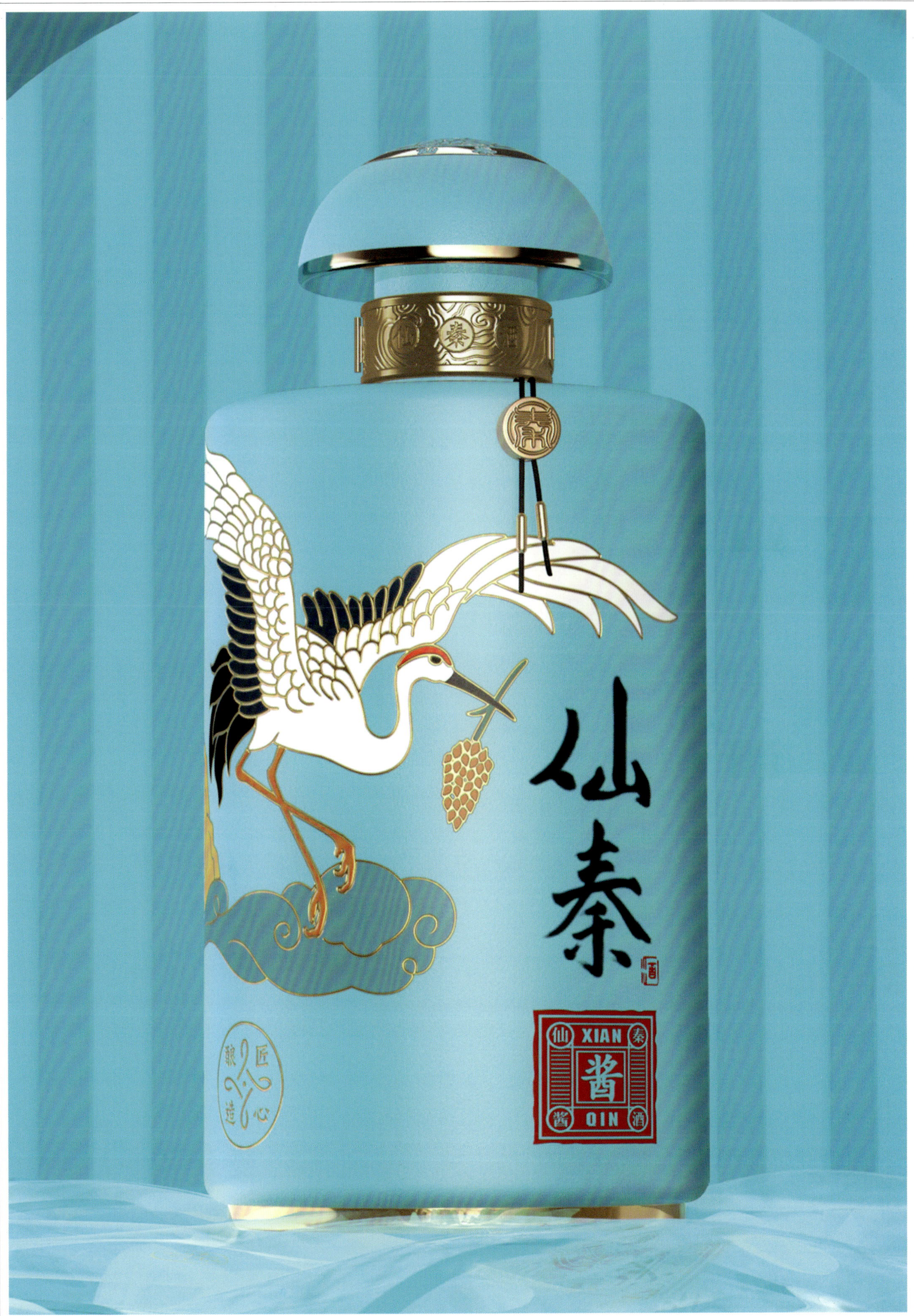

P241: Credit & Commentary Title: Xianqin | Client: Qin Hanzhang Wine Sales Co., Ltd. | Design Firm: Sungoo Design

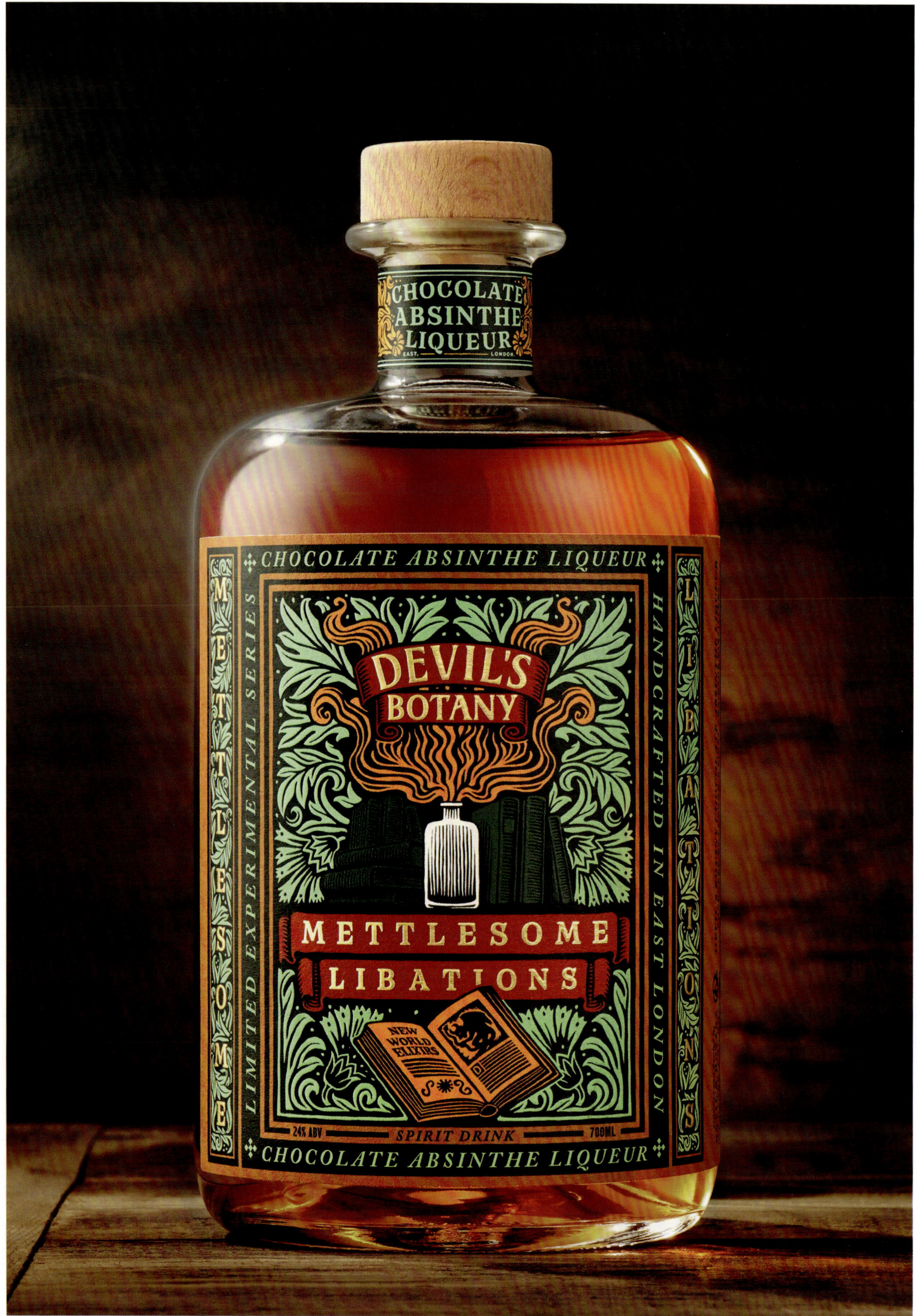

P241: Credit & Commentary **Title:** Devil's Botany Mettlesome Libations | **Client:** Devil's Botany | **Design Firm:** Chad Michael Studio

P241: Credit & Commentary **Title:** Rimfire Whiskey | **Client:** Lightburn Spirits | **Design Firm:** CF Napa Brand Design

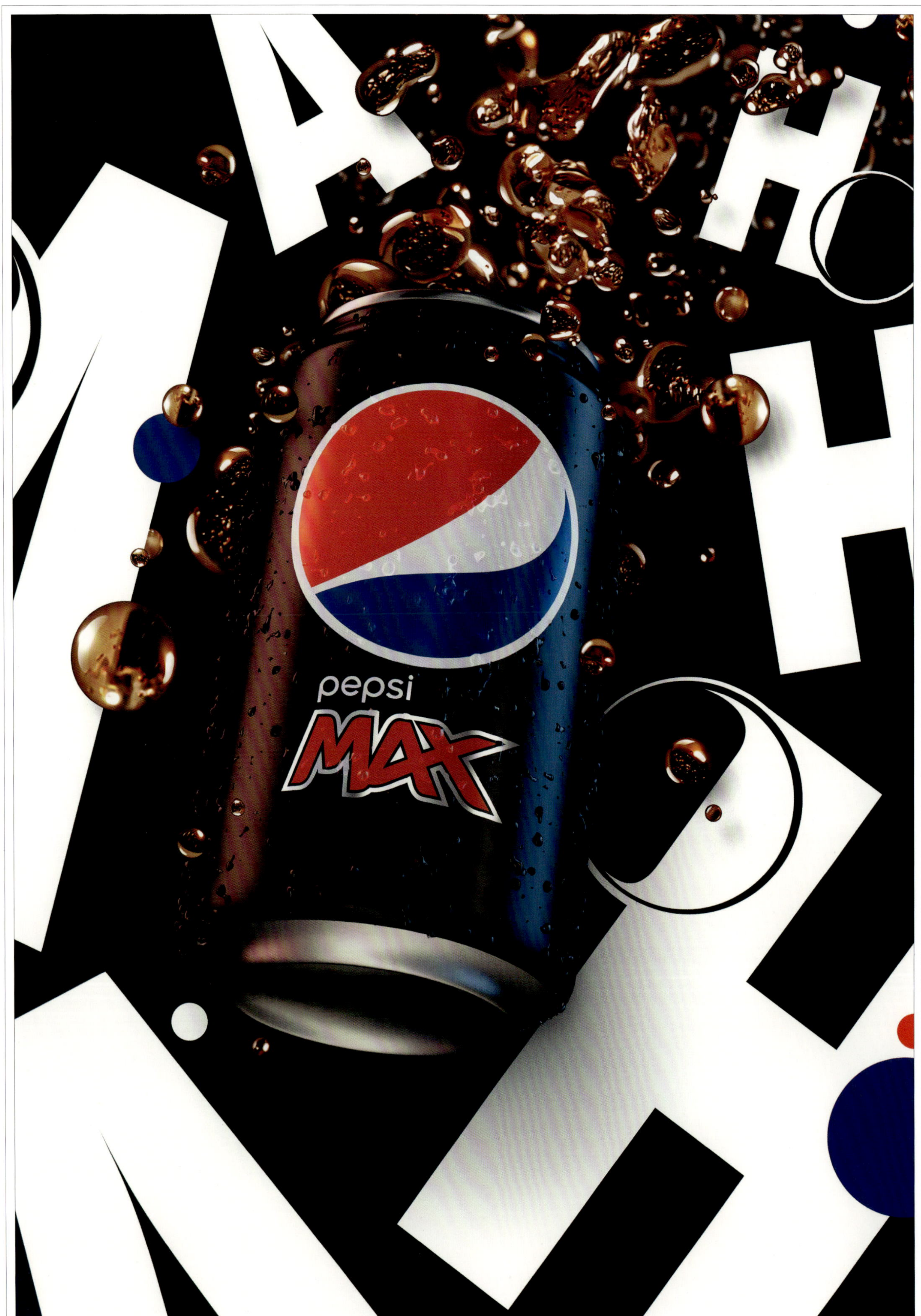

P241: Credit & Commentary Title: PepsiMax PopFizzAhh 2022 | Client: Self-initated | Design Firm: PepsiCo Design & Innovation

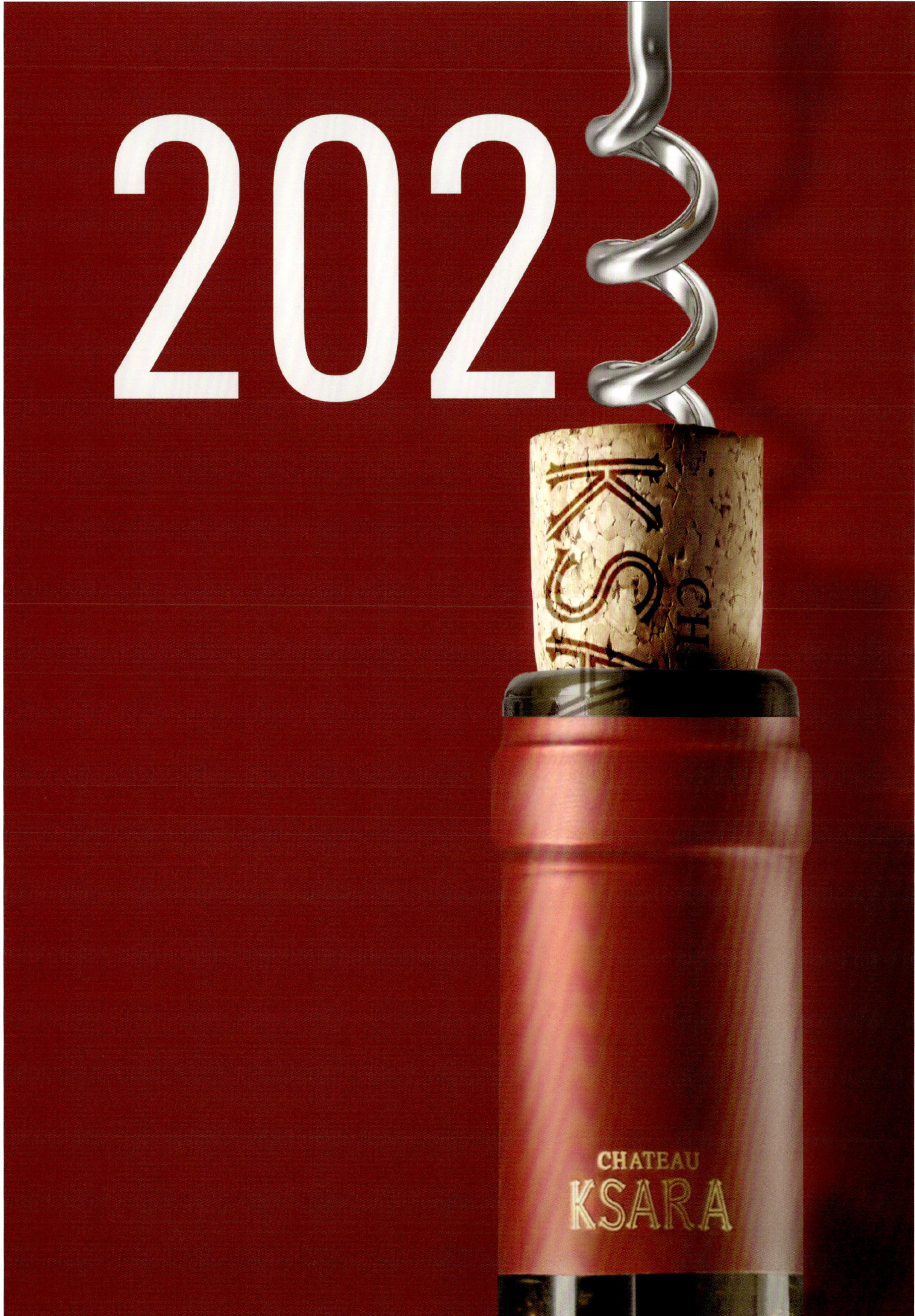

P241: Credit & Commentary

Title: Château Ksara New Year 2023 | **Client:** Château Ksara | **Design Firm:** Mink

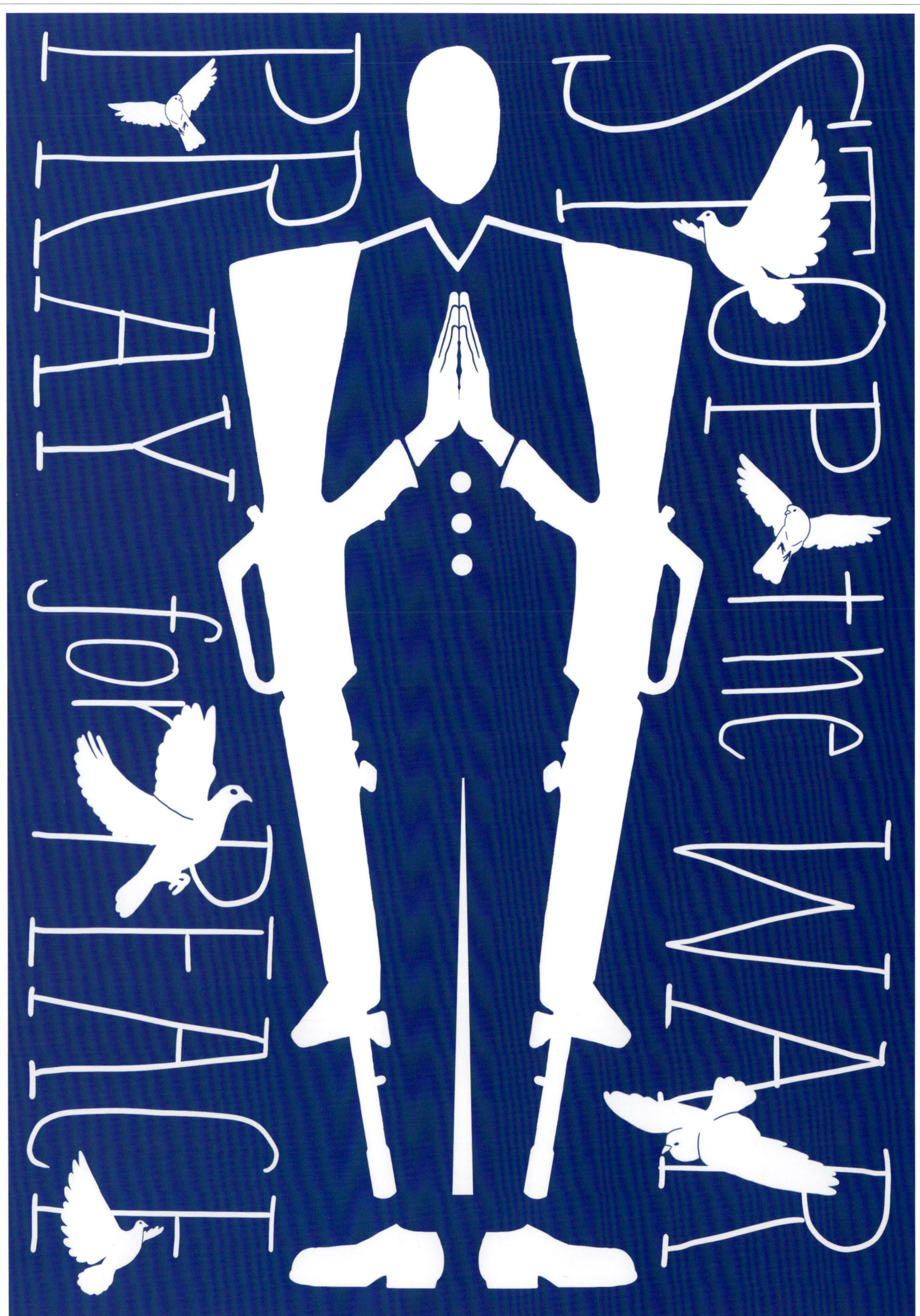

P241: Credit & Commentary

Title: Pray for Peace | **Client:** Self-initiated | **Design Firm:** Jingyi Cai

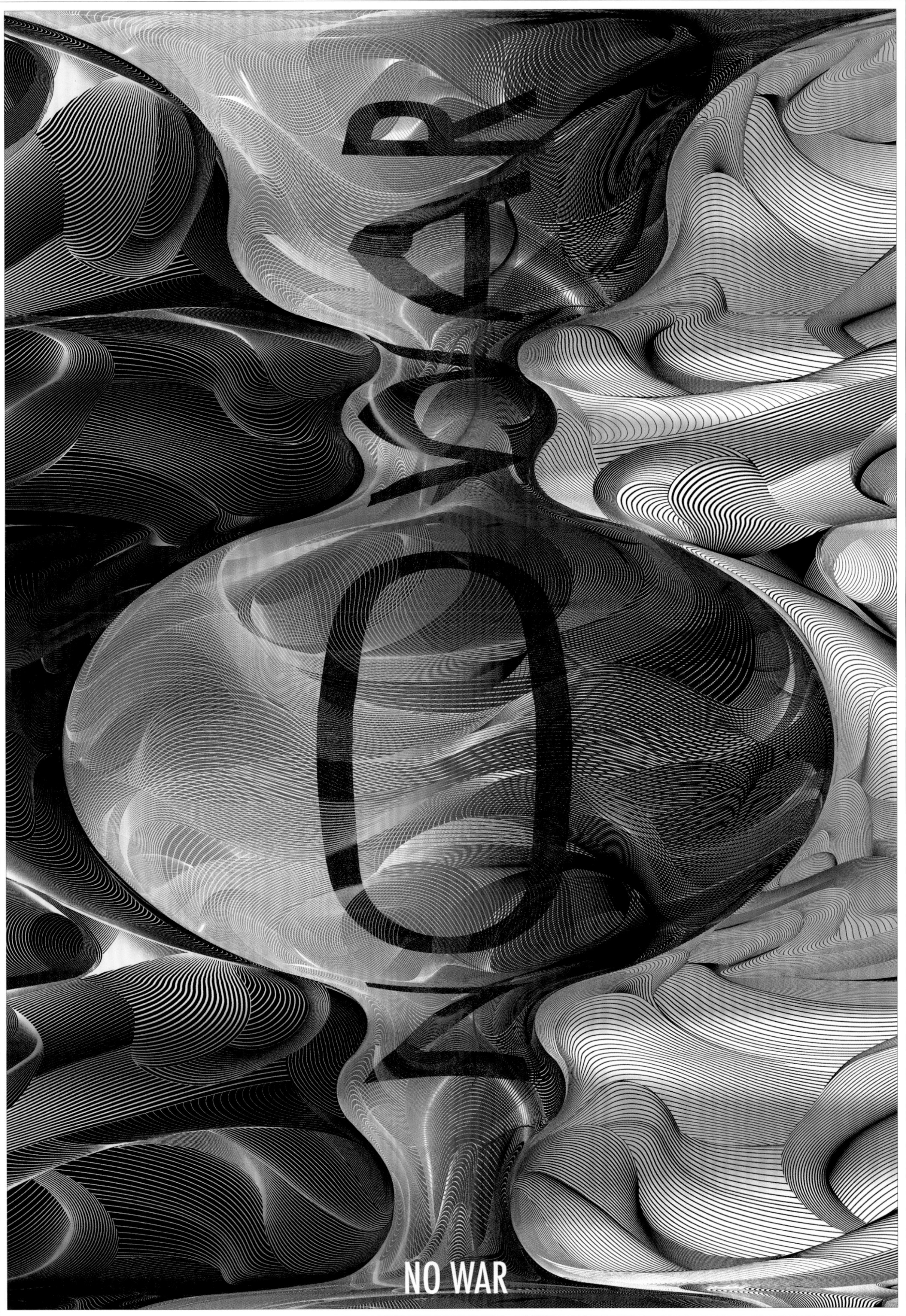

P242: Credit & Commentary **Title:** NO WAR | **Client:** Peace-Loving Innovators of Nations | **Design Firm:** Tsushima Design

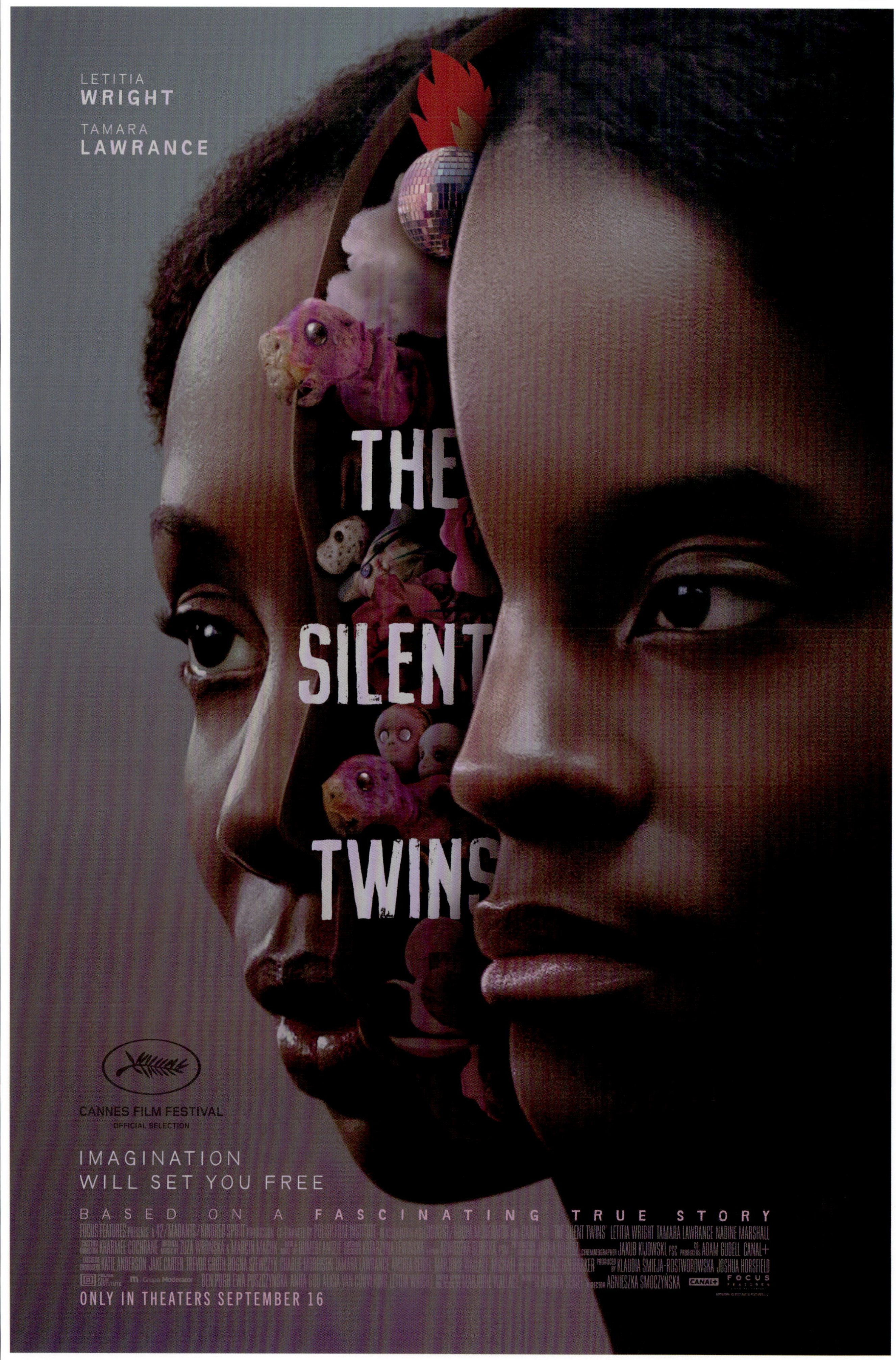

P241: Credit & Commentary **Title:** SILENT TWINS | **Client:** Focus Features | **Design Firm:** ARSONAL

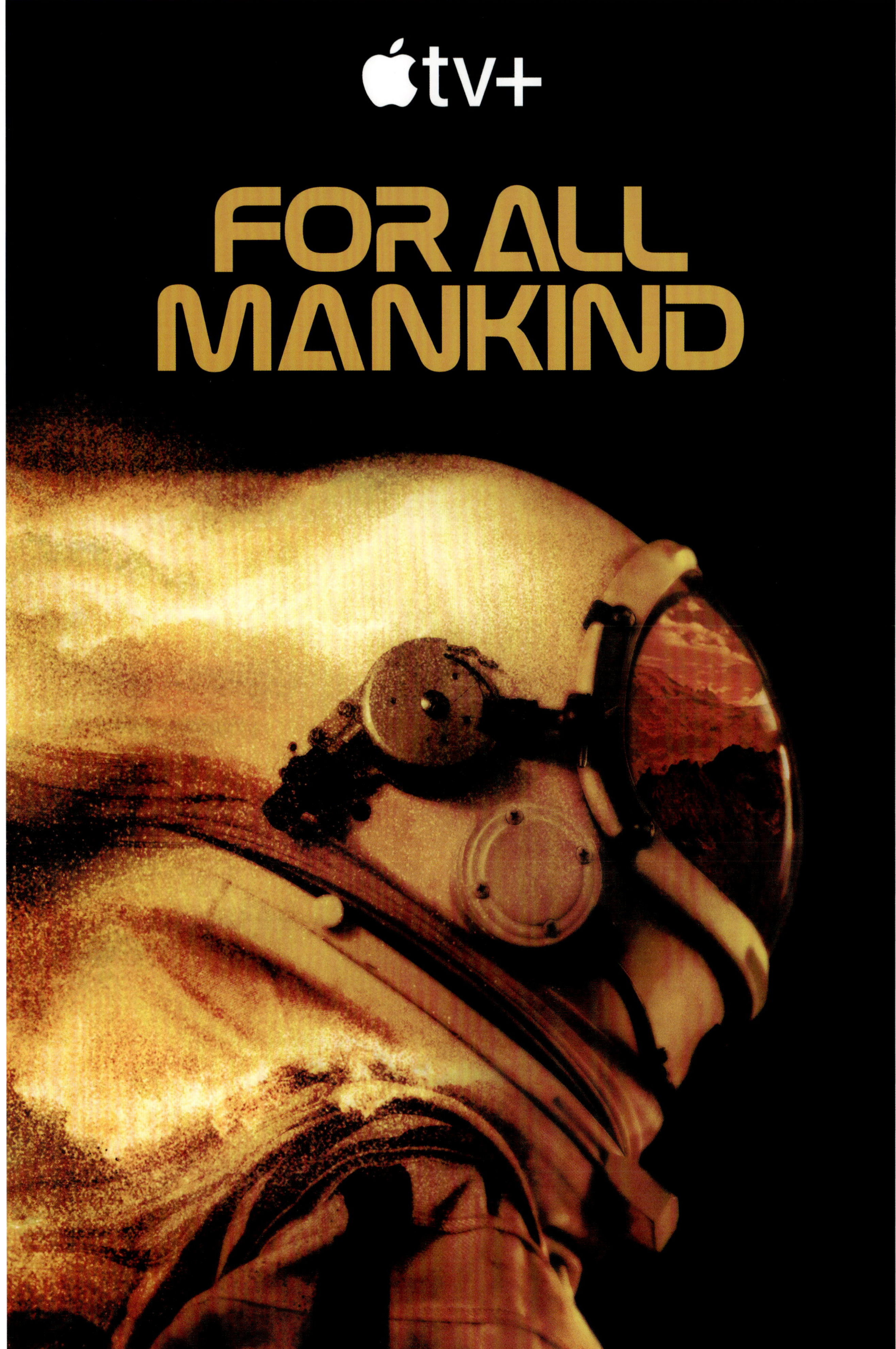

P241: Credit & Commentary Title: For All Mankind S3 | Client: Apple TV+ | Design Firm: ARSONAL

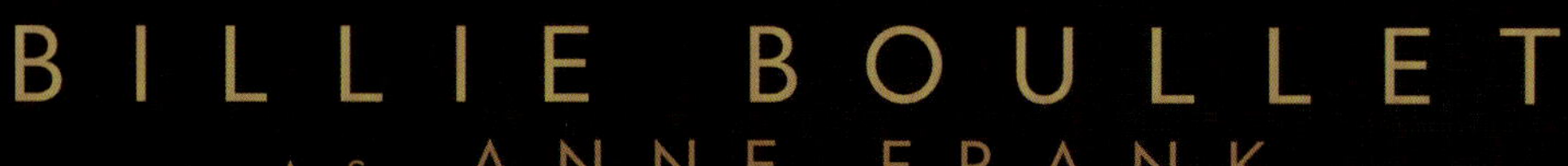

NEW LIMITED SERIES

A SMALL LIGHT

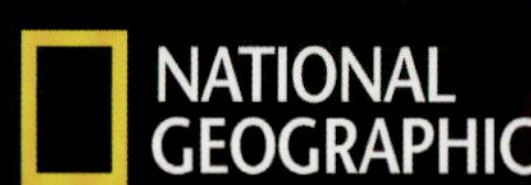

Mon May 1 | 9/8c

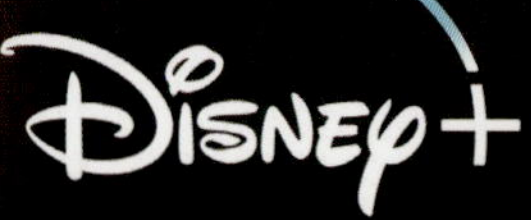

Next Day

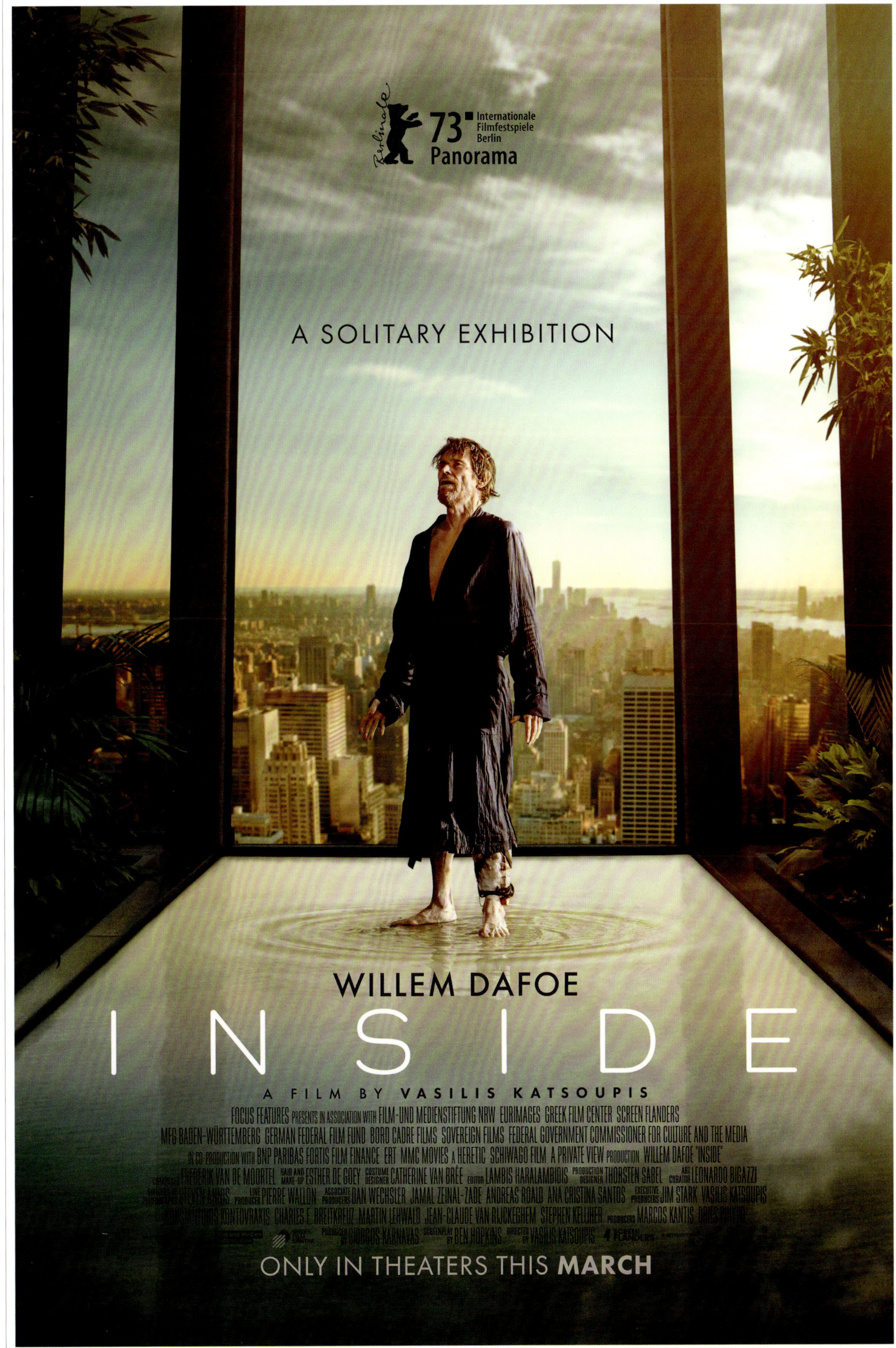
Berlinale
73 Internationale Filmfestspiele Berlin
Panorama
A SOLITARY EXHIBITION
WILLEM DAFOE
INSIDE
A FILM BY VASILIS KATSOUPIS
FOCUS FEATURES PRESENTS IN ASSOCIATION WITH FILM-UND MEDIENSTIFTUNG NRW EURIMAGES GREEK FILM CENTER SCREEN FLANDERS
MFG BADEN-WÜRTTEMBERG GERMAN FEDERAL FILM FUND BORD CADRE FILMS SOVEREIGN FILMS FEDERAL GOVERNMENT COMMISSIONER FOR CULTURE AND THE MEDIA
IN CO-PRODUCTION WITH BNP PARIBAS FORTIS FILM FINANCE ERT MMC MOVIES A HERETIC SCHIWAGO FILM A PRIVATE VIEW PRODUCTION WILLEM DAFOE "INSIDE"
HAIR AND MAKE-UP ESTHER DE GOEY COSTUME DESIGNER CATHERINE VAN BRÉE EDITOR LAMBIS HARALAMBIDIS PRODUCTION DESIGNER THORSTEN SABEL ART CURATOR LEONARDO BIGAZZI
LINE PRODUCER PIERRE WALLON ASSOCIATE PRODUCERS DAN WECHSLER JAMAL ZEINAL-ZADE ANDREAS ROALD ANA CRISTINA SANTOS EXECUTIVE PRODUCERS JIM STARK VASILIS KATSOUPIS
CHARLES E. BREITKREUZ MARTIN LEHWALD JEAN-CLAUDE VAN RIJCKEGHEM STEPHEN KELLIHER PRODUCERS MARCOS KANTIS
SCREENPLAY BY BEN HOPKINS DIRECTED BY VASILIS KATSOUPIS
ONLY IN THEATERS THIS MARCH

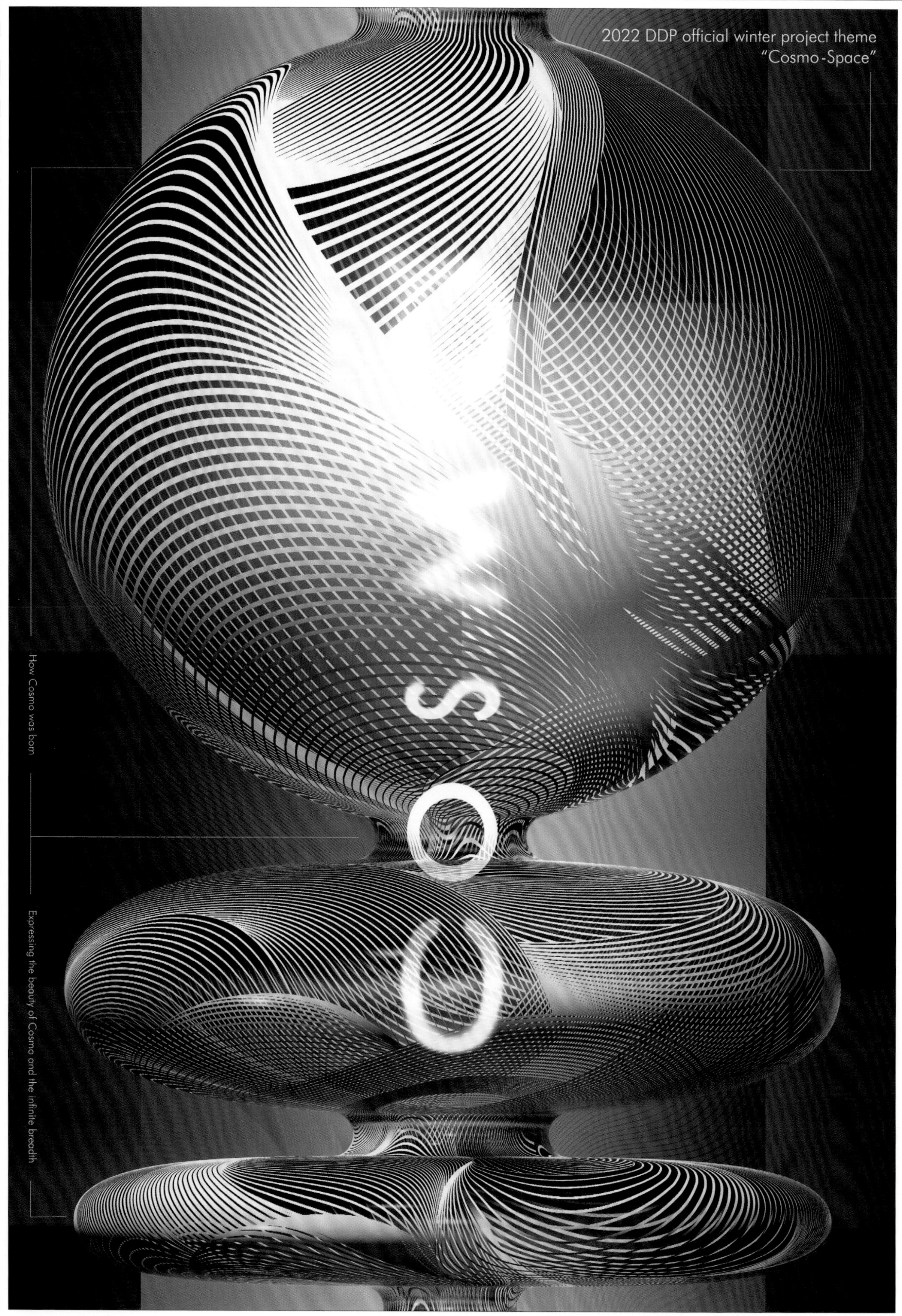

P242: Credit & Commentary **Title:** COSMO | **Client:** Visual Information Design Association of Korea | **Design Firm:** Tsushima Design

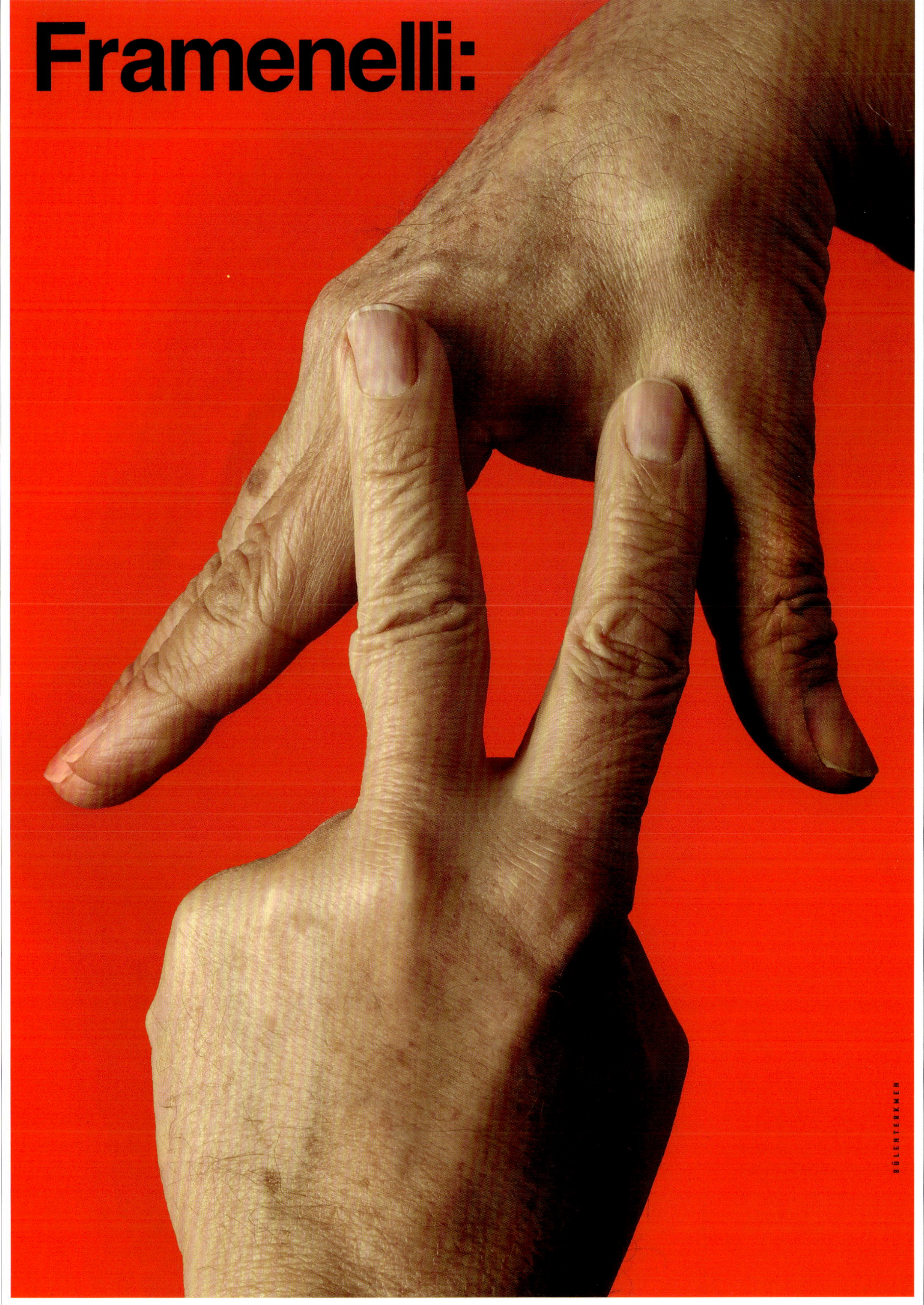

Title: Framenelli | **Clients:** Amijai Benderski, Juan Martín Lusiardo, Santiago Ternande
Design Firm: BEK Design | **P242:** Credit & Commentary

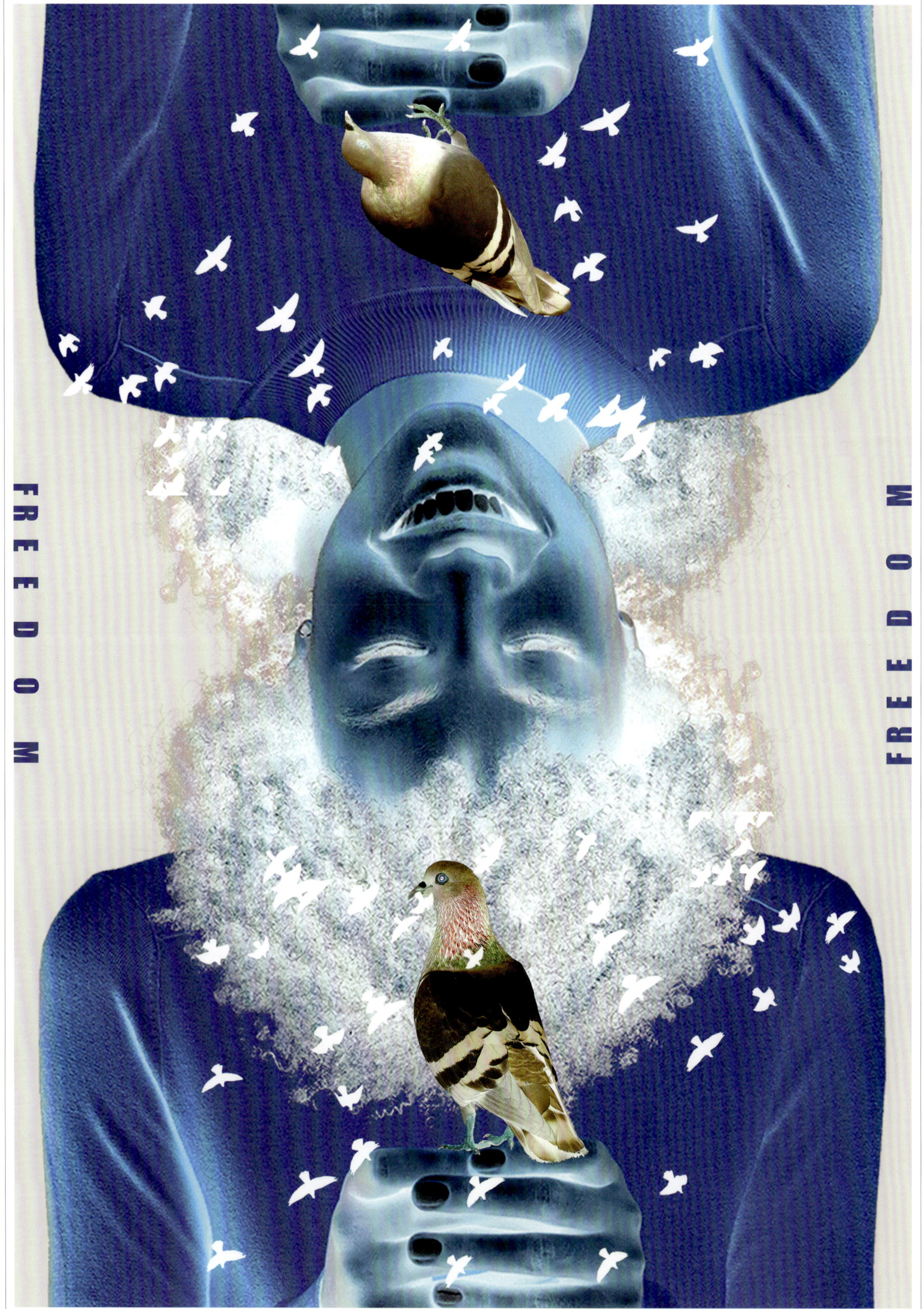

P242: Credit & Commentary Title: Freedom | Client: Shanghai Women's Federation | Design Firm: Sun Design Production

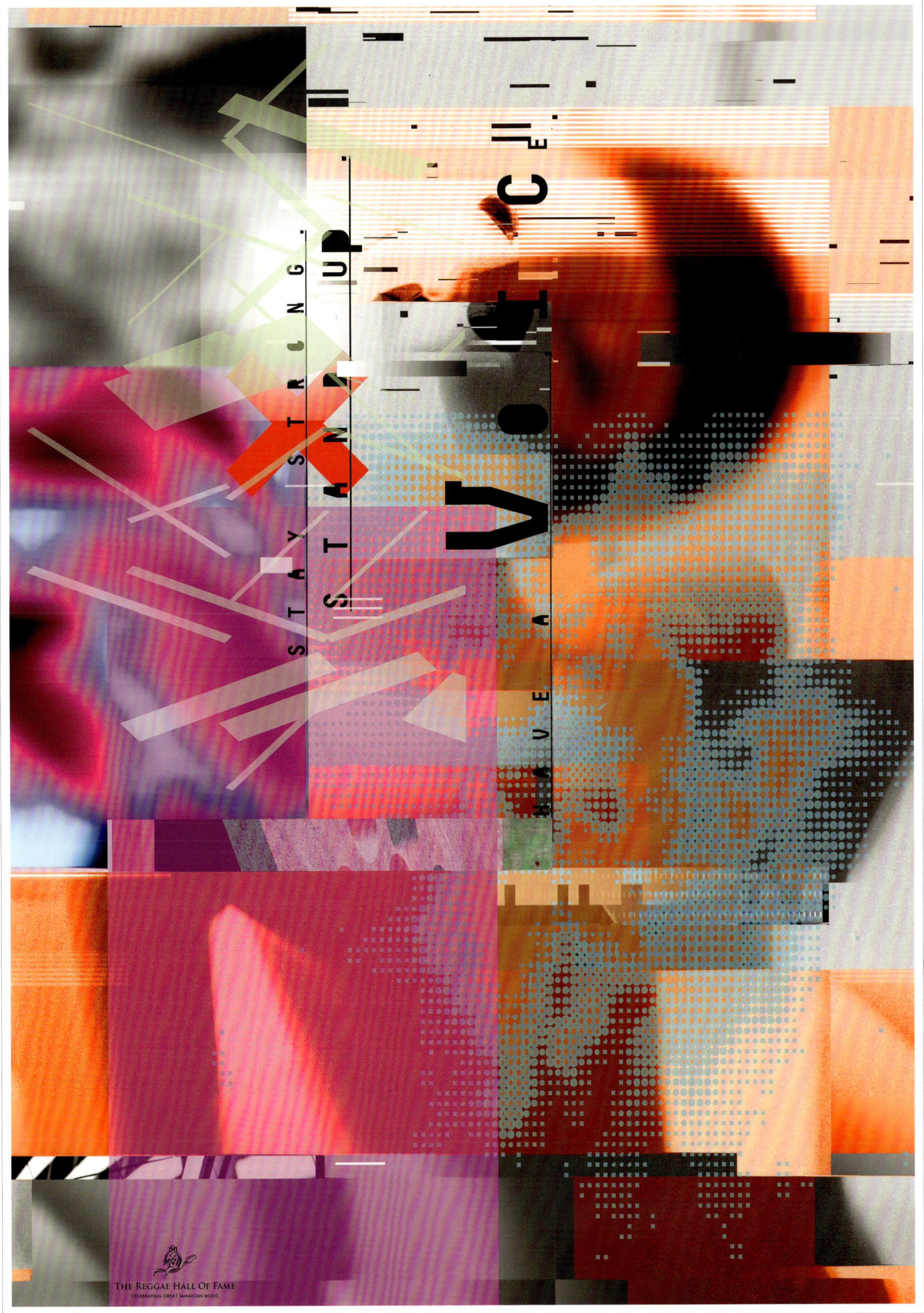

Title: Stay Strong, Stand Up, Have a Voice | **Client:** The International Reggae Poster Contest
Design Firm: Studio Eduard Cehovin | **P242:** Credit & Commentary

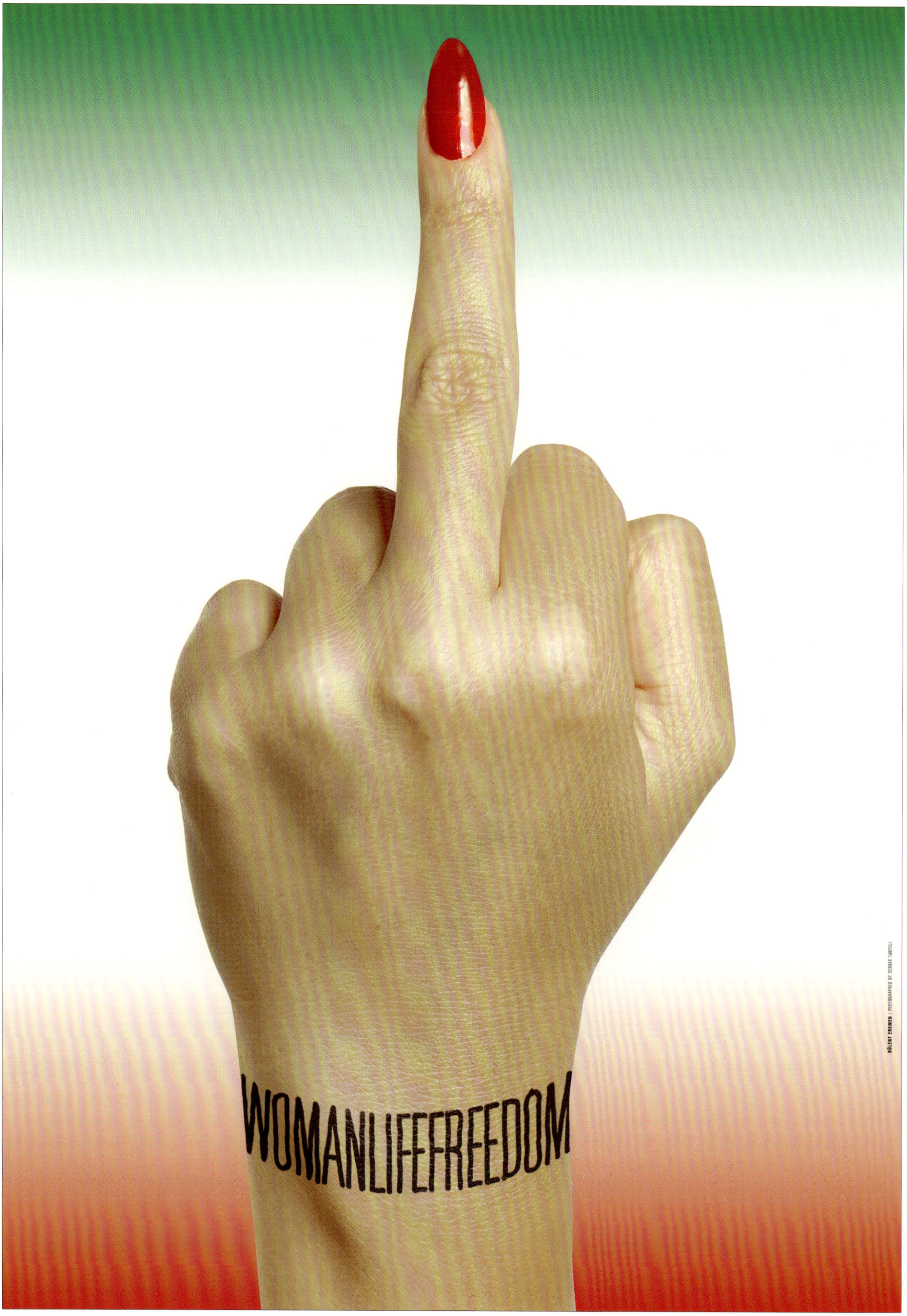

WOMANLIFEFREEDOM

P242: Credit & Commentary **Title:** Woman, Life, Freedom | **Client:** Movement for Women of Iran | **Design Firm:** BEK Design

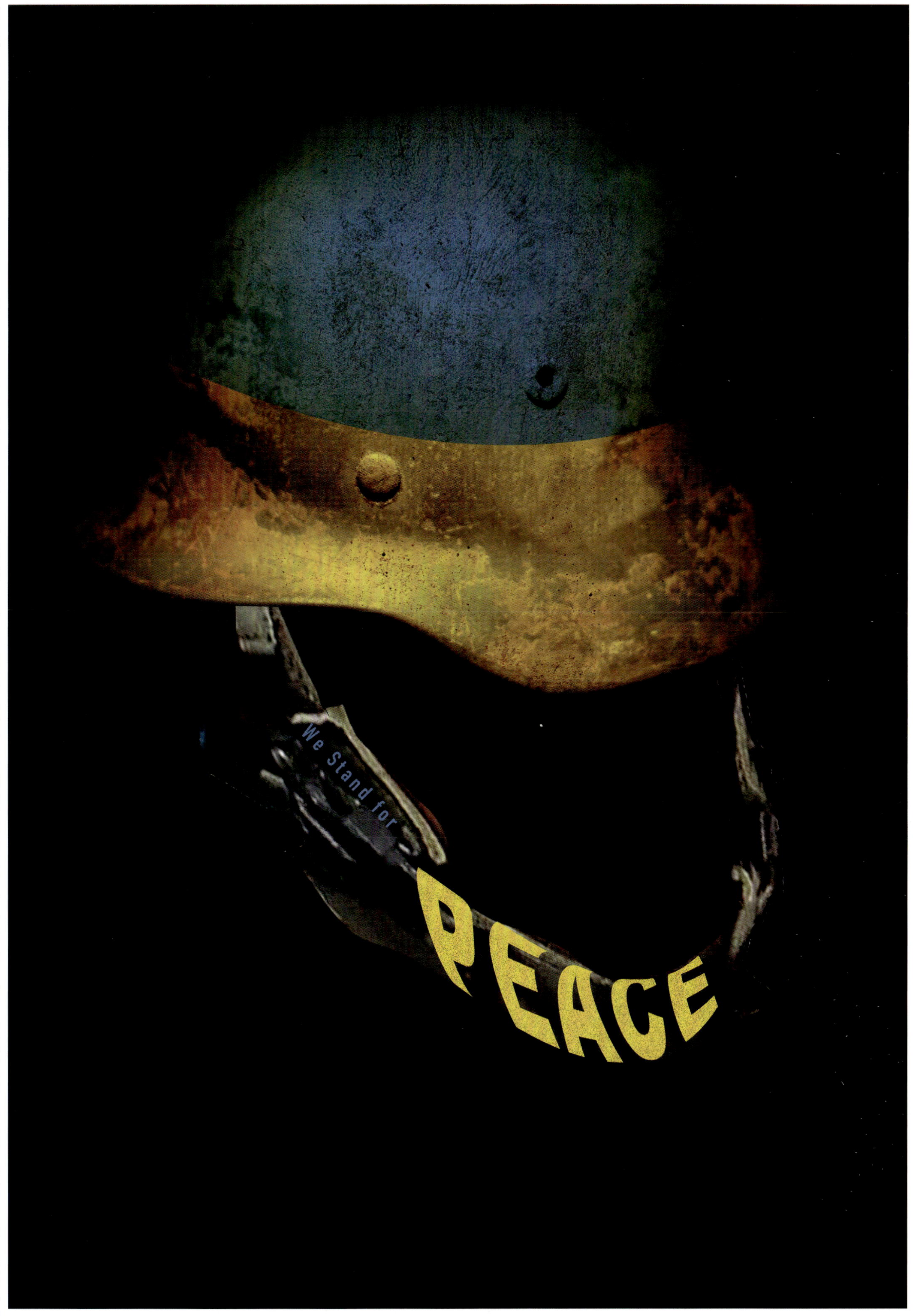

P242: Credit & Commentary **Title:** We Stand for Peace | **Client:** Ogaki Poster Museum in Japan | **Design Firm:** Purdue University

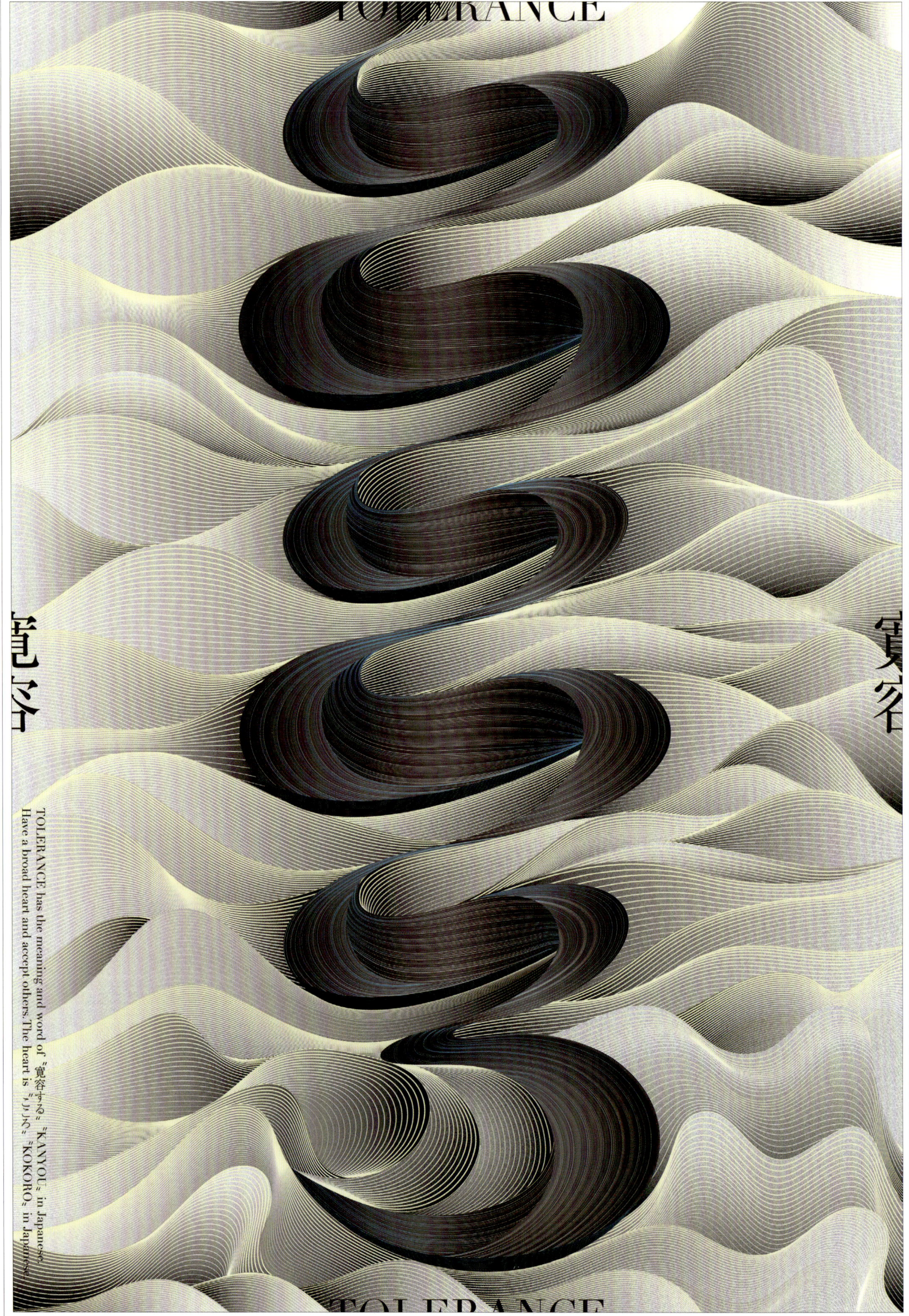

 Title: TOLERANCE | **Client:** Tolerance Poster Show | **Design Firm:** Tsushima Design

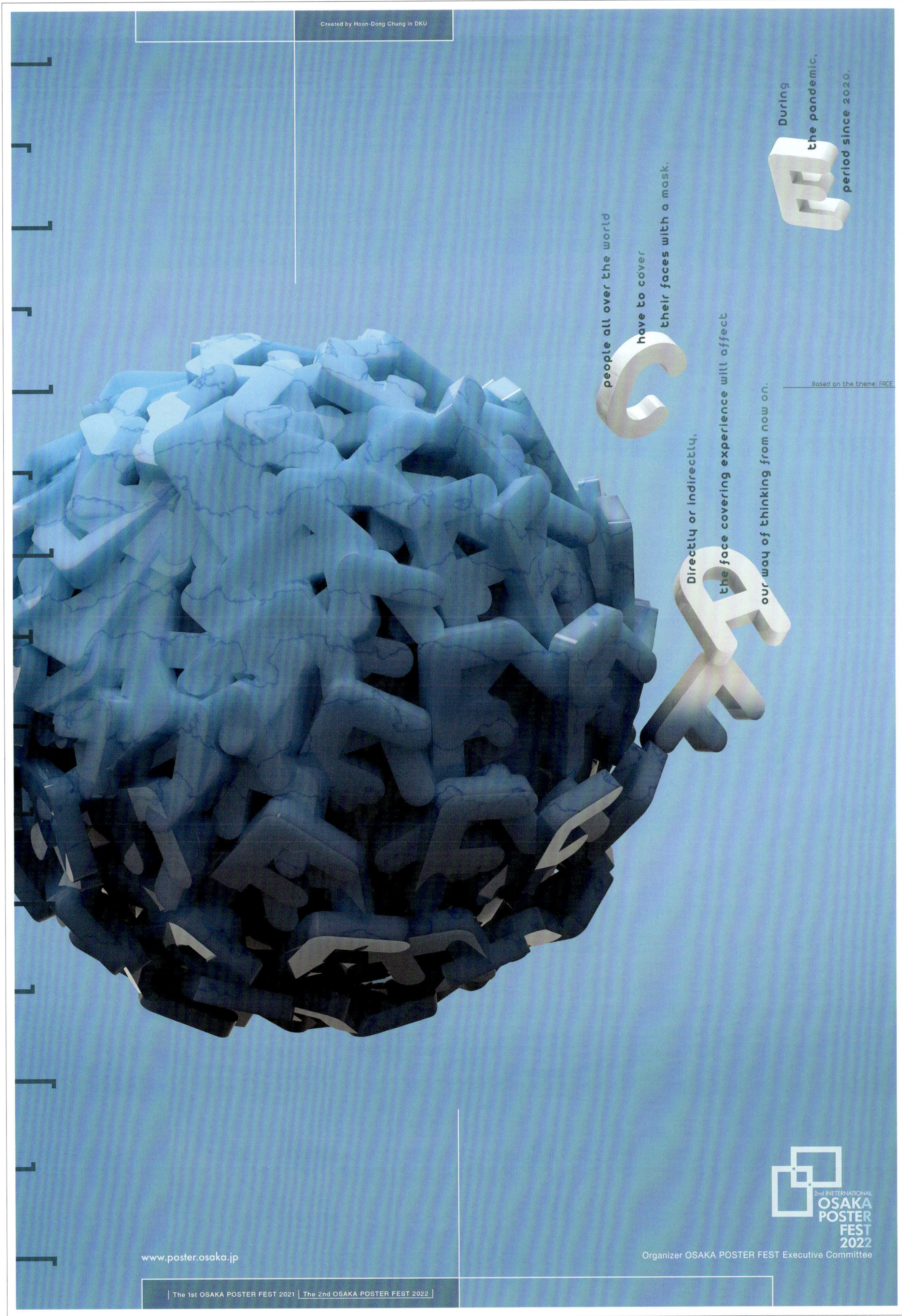

P242: Credit & Commentary **Title:** F for Face | **Client:** Osaka Poster Festival 2022 | **Design Firm:** Dankook University

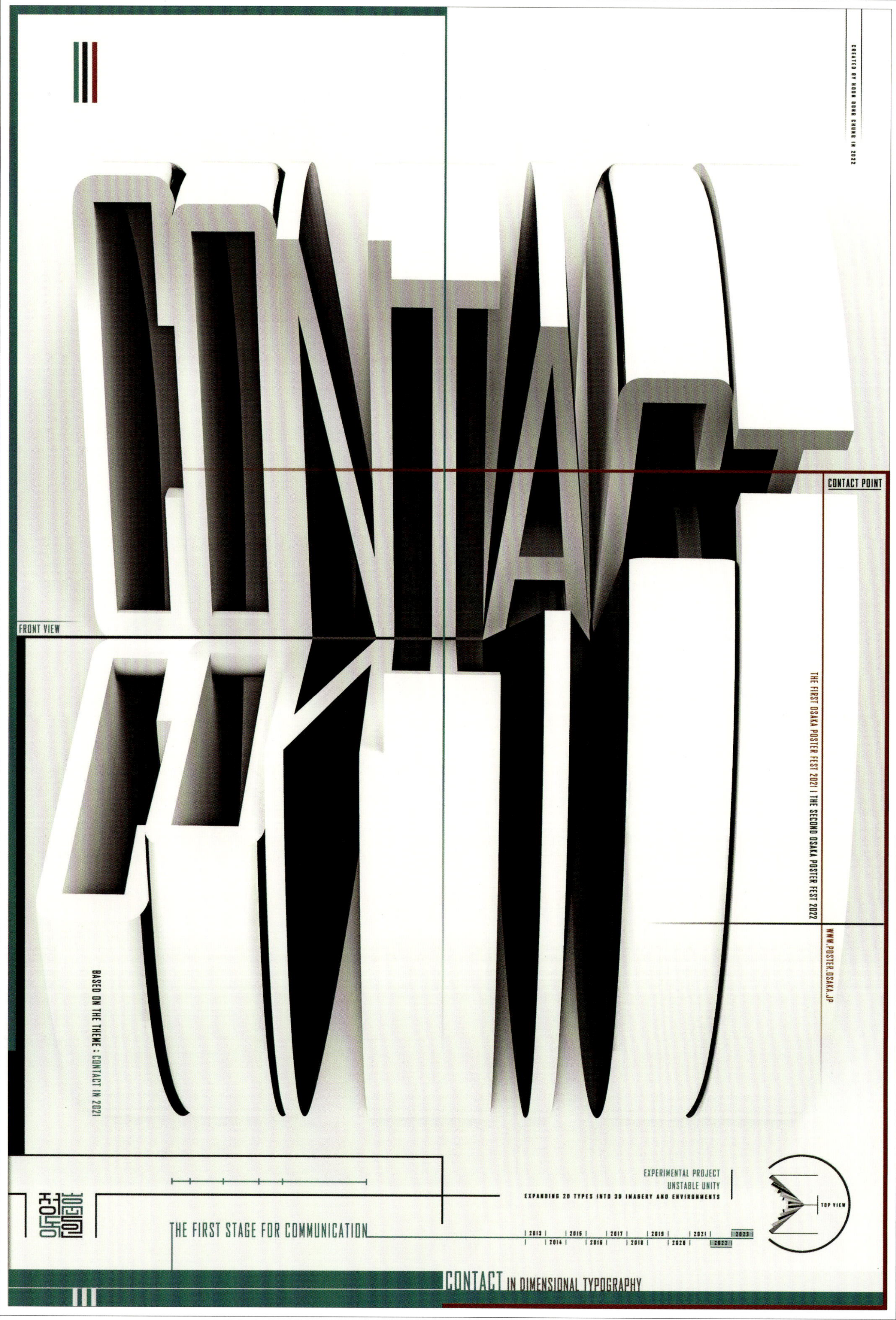

Title: CONTACT | **Client:** Osaka Poster Festival 2022 | **Design Firm:** Dankook University

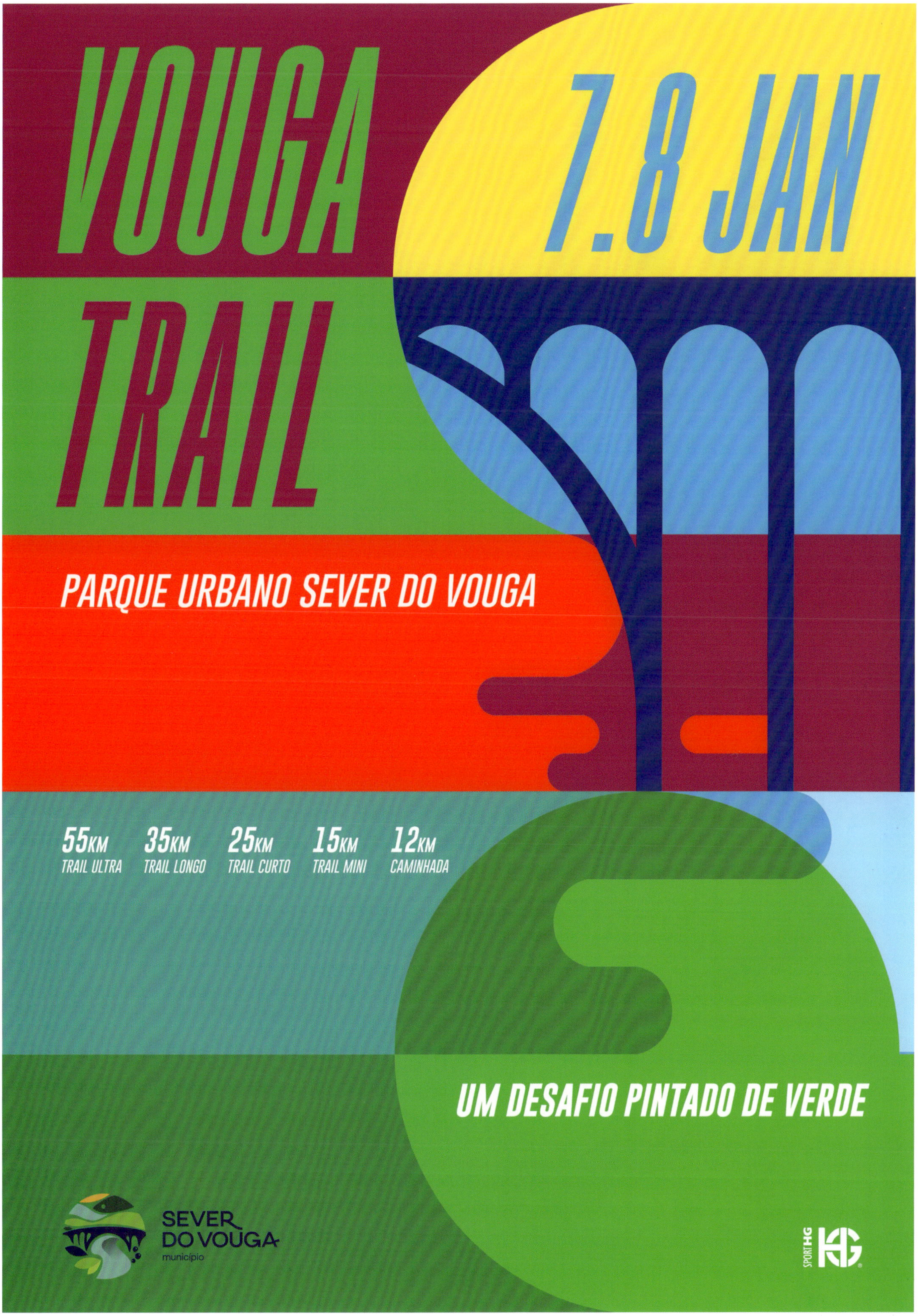

VOUGA TRAIL

7.8 JAN

PARQUE URBANO SEVER DO VOUGA

55KM TRAIL ULTRA
35KM TRAIL LONGO
25KM TRAIL CURTO
15KM TRAIL MINI
12KM CAMINHADA

UM DESAFIO PINTADO DE VERDE

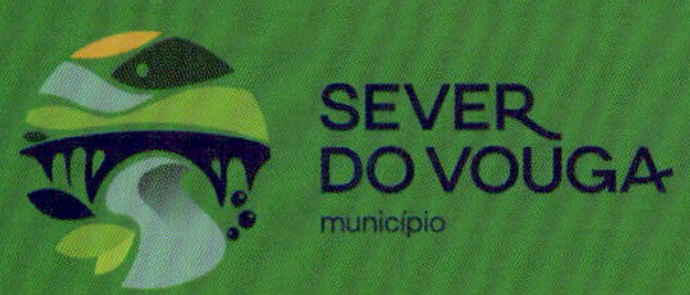

SPORT HG

Title: Vouga Trail National Championship Poster | **Client:** Municipio de Sever do Vouga
Design Firm: Duas Faces Design | **P242:** Credit & Commentary

A rising toll of protesters have been killed by Iranian authorities since demonstrations triggered by the death of Mahsa Jina Amini who was arrested and then later died in police custody.

Women-led protests across Iran have been met with violence. And yet, Iranian women and their allies bravely persist. Support their struggle for freedom by calling for an immediate end to violence.

This is a very important moment for the global community to unequivocally demonstrate their support for women's rights by standing in solidarity with every Iranian women and girl.

Title: Women. Life. Freedom. | **Client:** Self-initiated
Design Firm: Goodall Integrated Design | **P242:** Credit & Commentary

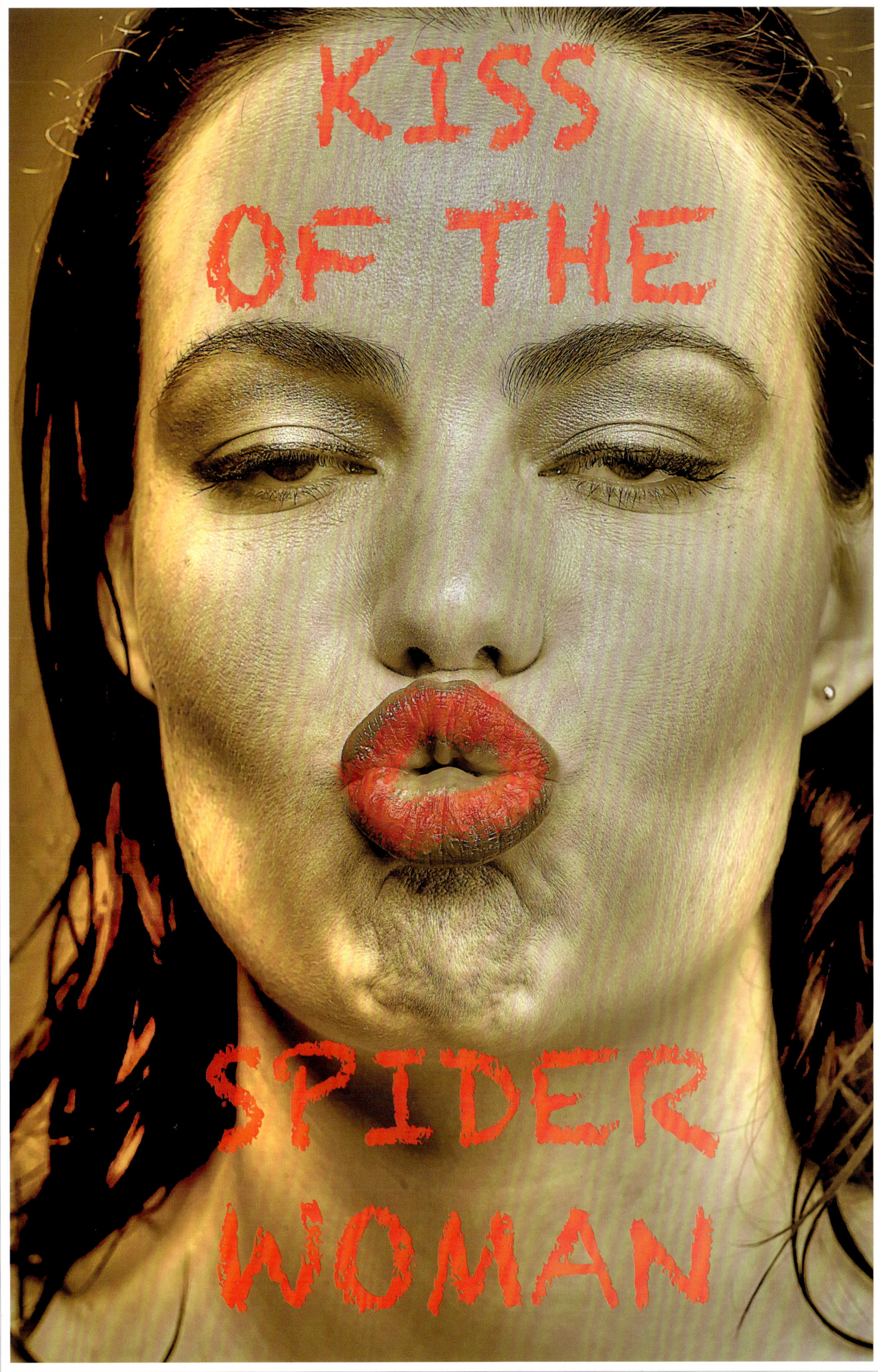

Title: Kiss of the Spider Woman | **Client:** Self-initiated
Design Firm: Paco Macias Velasco Studio | **P242:** Credit & Commentary

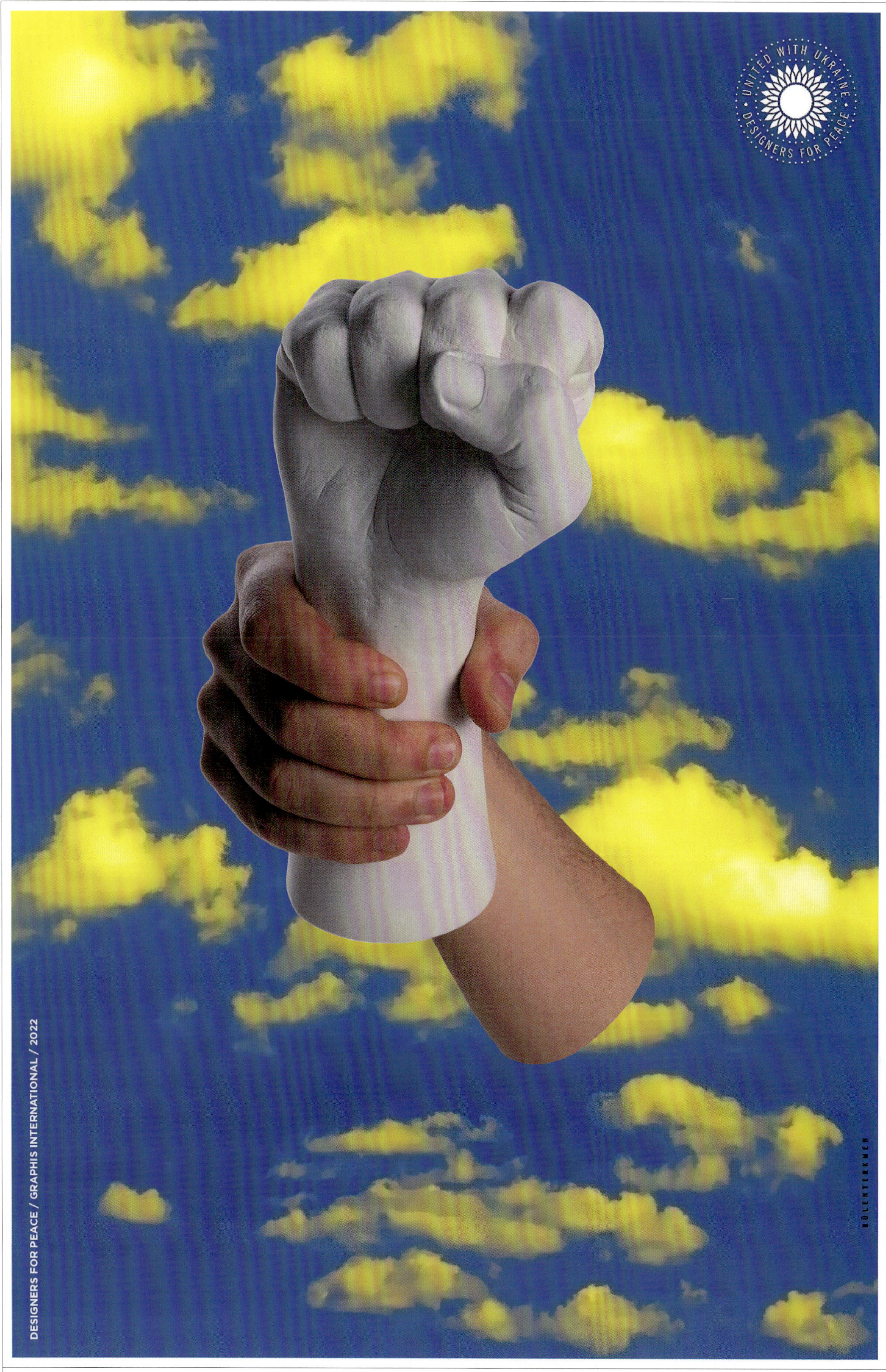

Title: Designer for Peace: United with Ukraine | **Client:** Graphis Designers for Peace Poster Competition
Design Firm: BEK Design | **P243:** Credit & Commentary

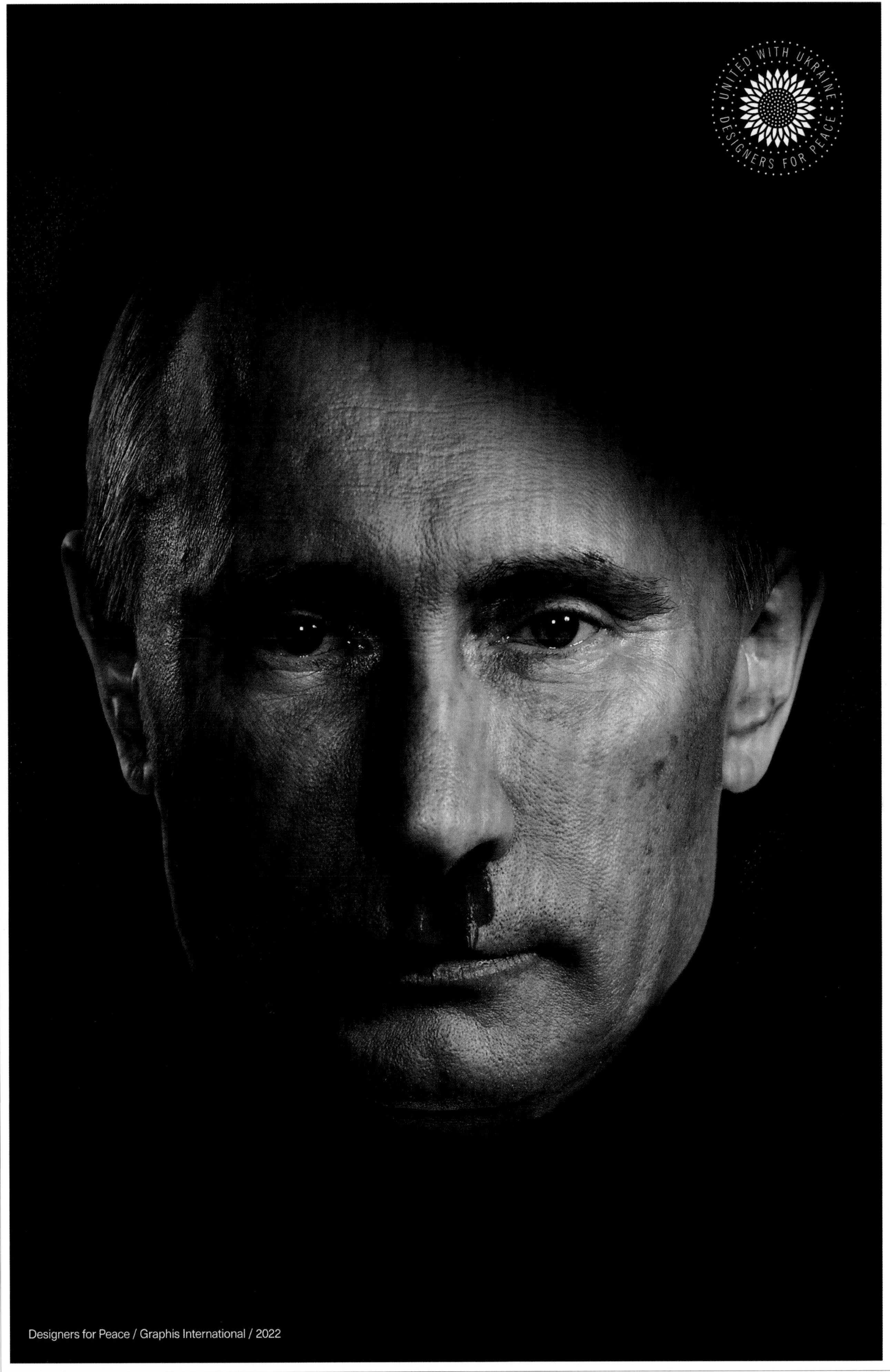

Title: War Criminal | **Client:** Graphis Designers for Peace Poster Competition
Design Firm: Code Switch | **P243:** Credit & Commentary

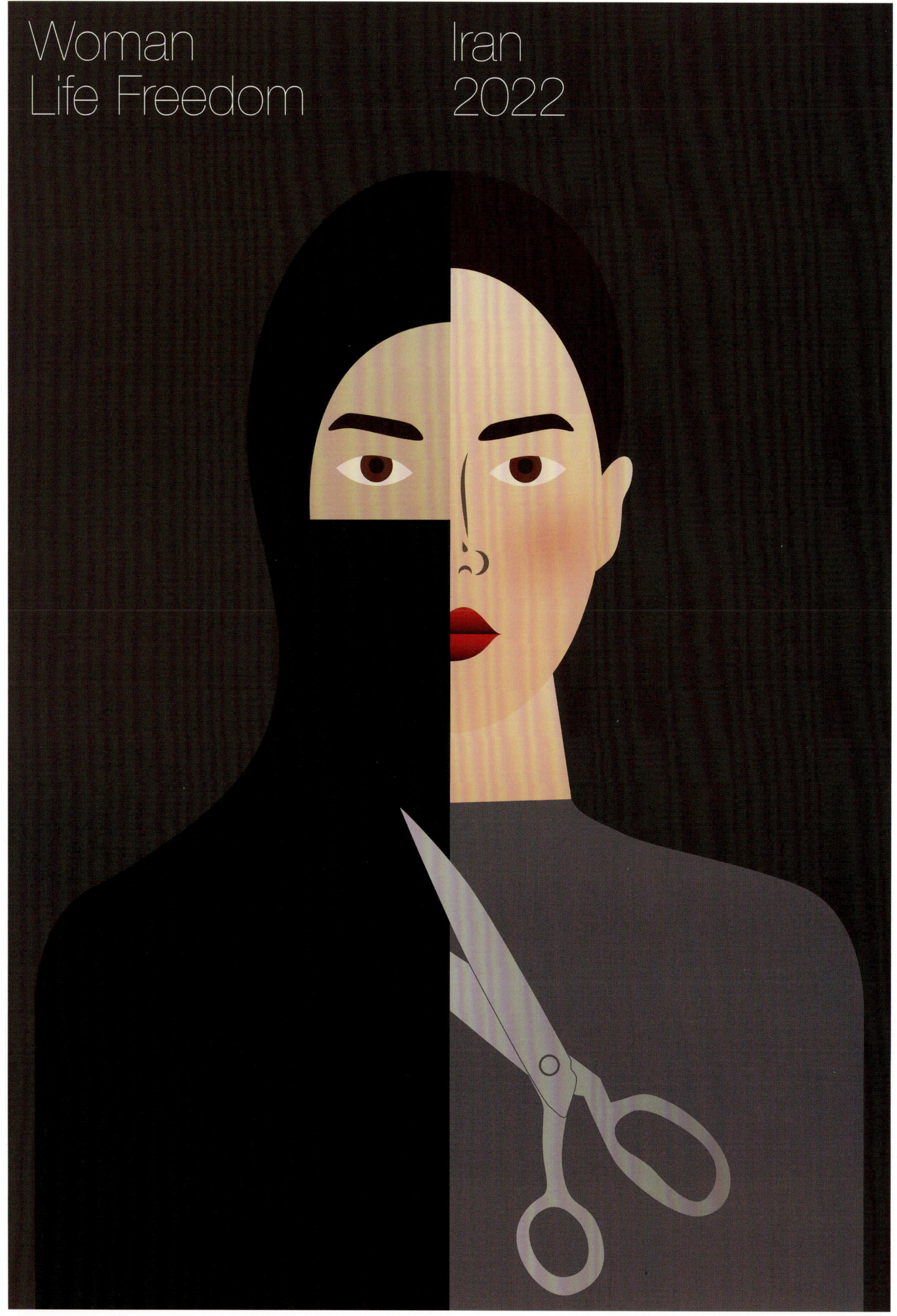

Title: Woman Life Freedom | **Client:** Woman, Life, Freedom Movement
Design Firm: Vanderbyl Design | **P243:** Credit & Commentary

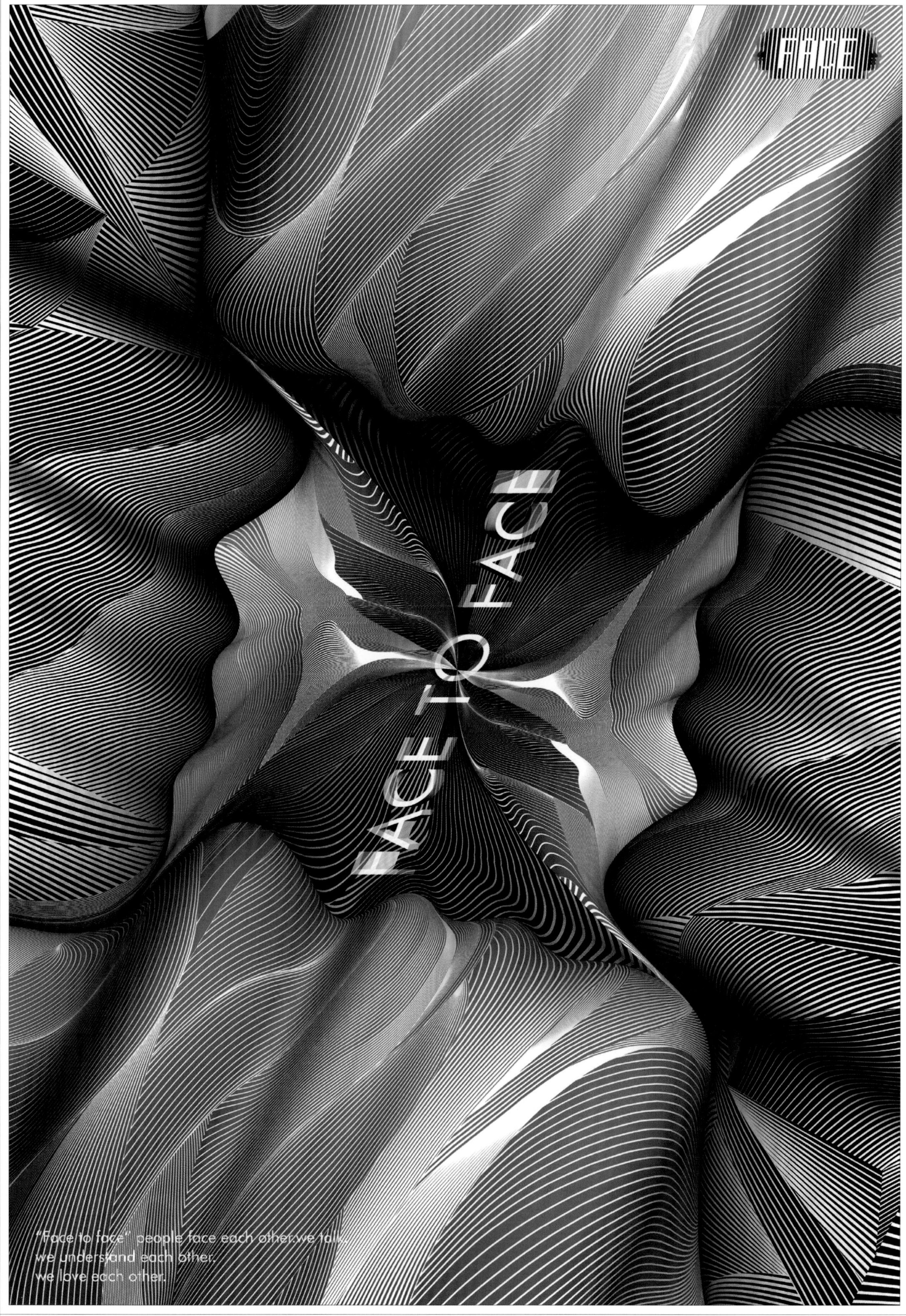

P243: Credit & Commentary **Title:** Face to Face | **Client:** Osaka Poster Festival 2022 | **Design Firm:** Tsushima Design

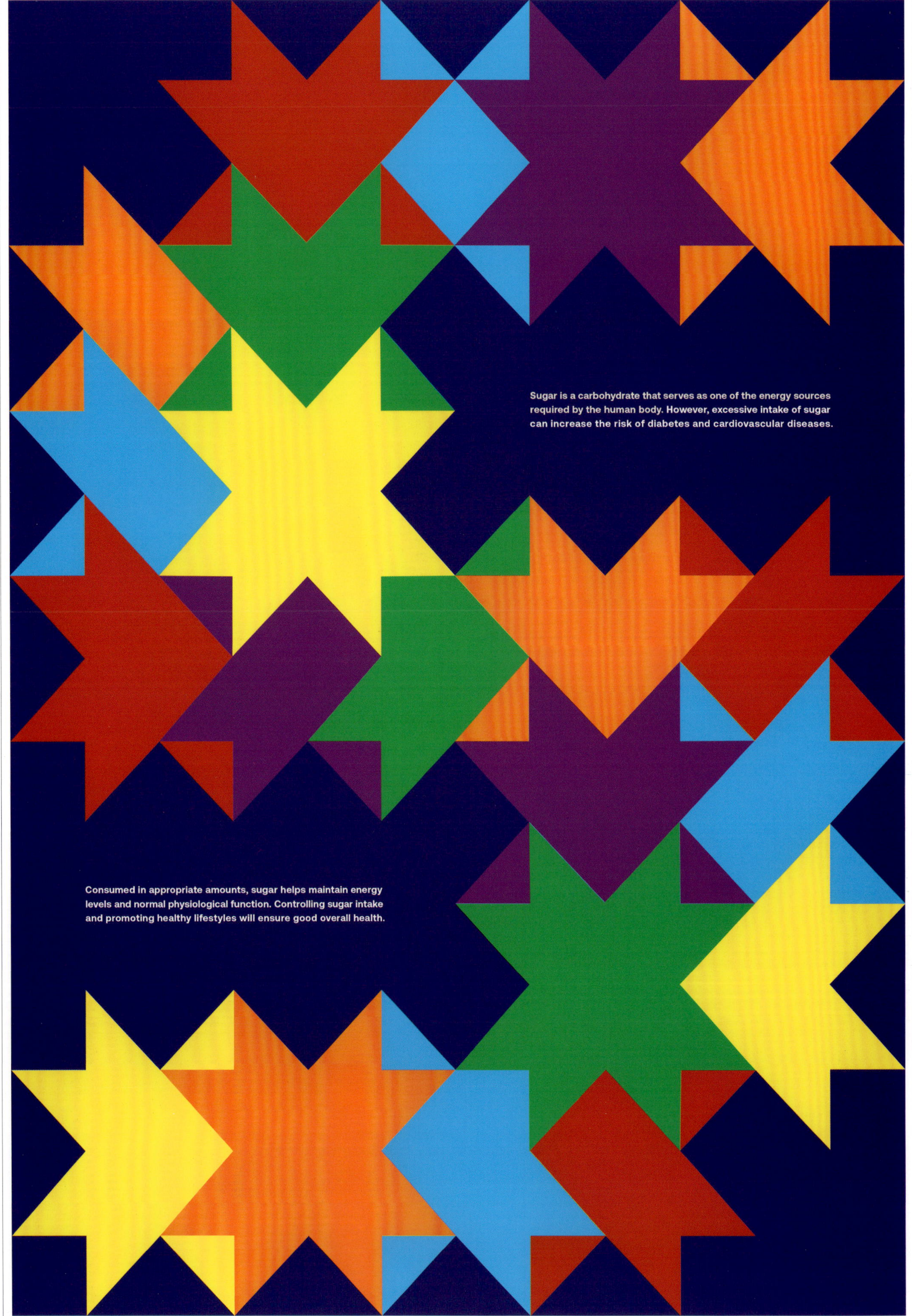

Title: Sugar Energy | **Client:** 2023 Sweet & Health International Poster Design Exhibition
Design Firm: Goodall Integrated Design | **P243:** Credit & Commentary

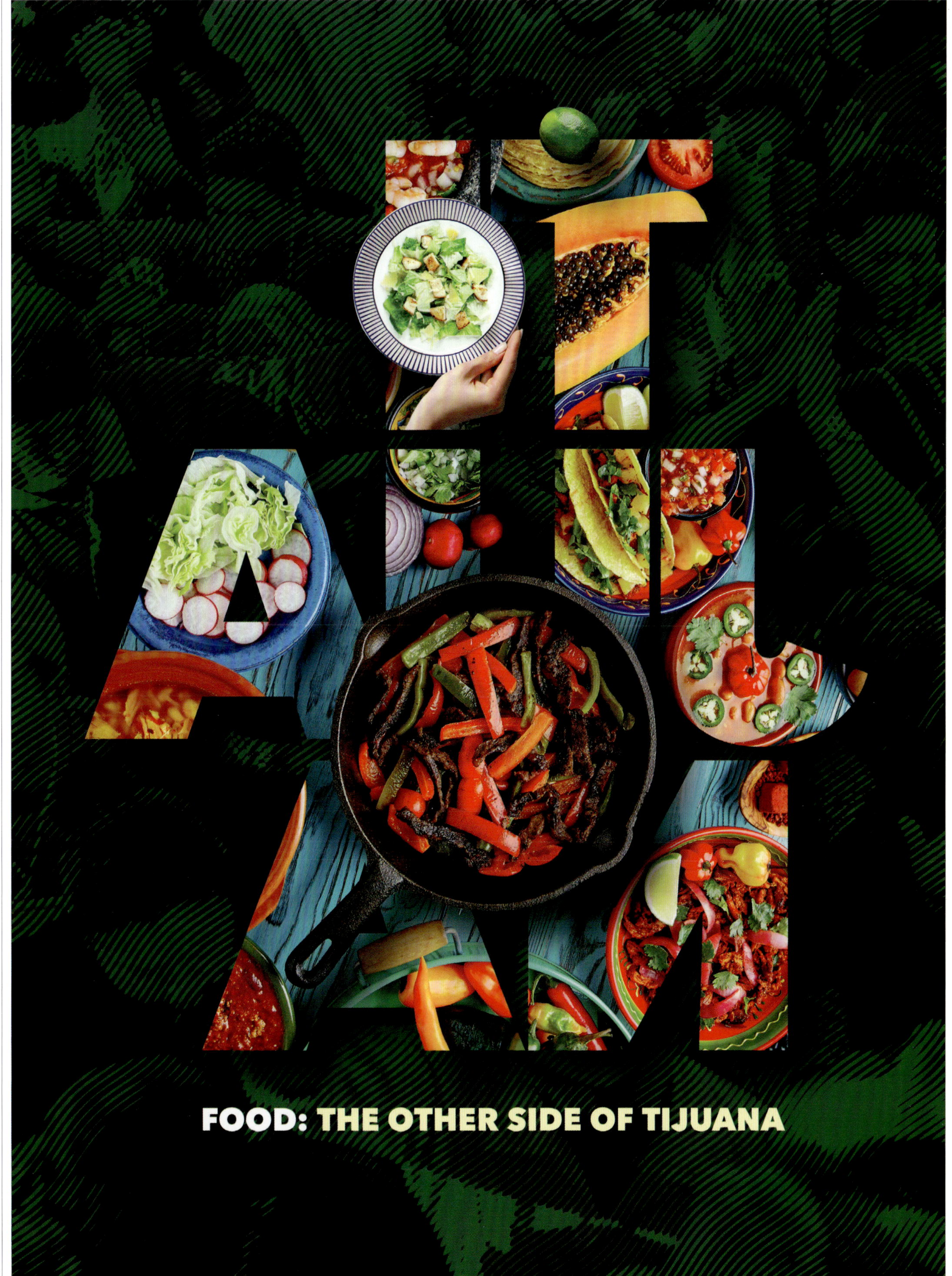

Title: The Other Side of Tijuana | **Clients:** City of Tijuana, Jorge Astiazaran
Design Firm: Freaner Creative & Design | **P243:** Credit & Commentary | Image 1 of 5

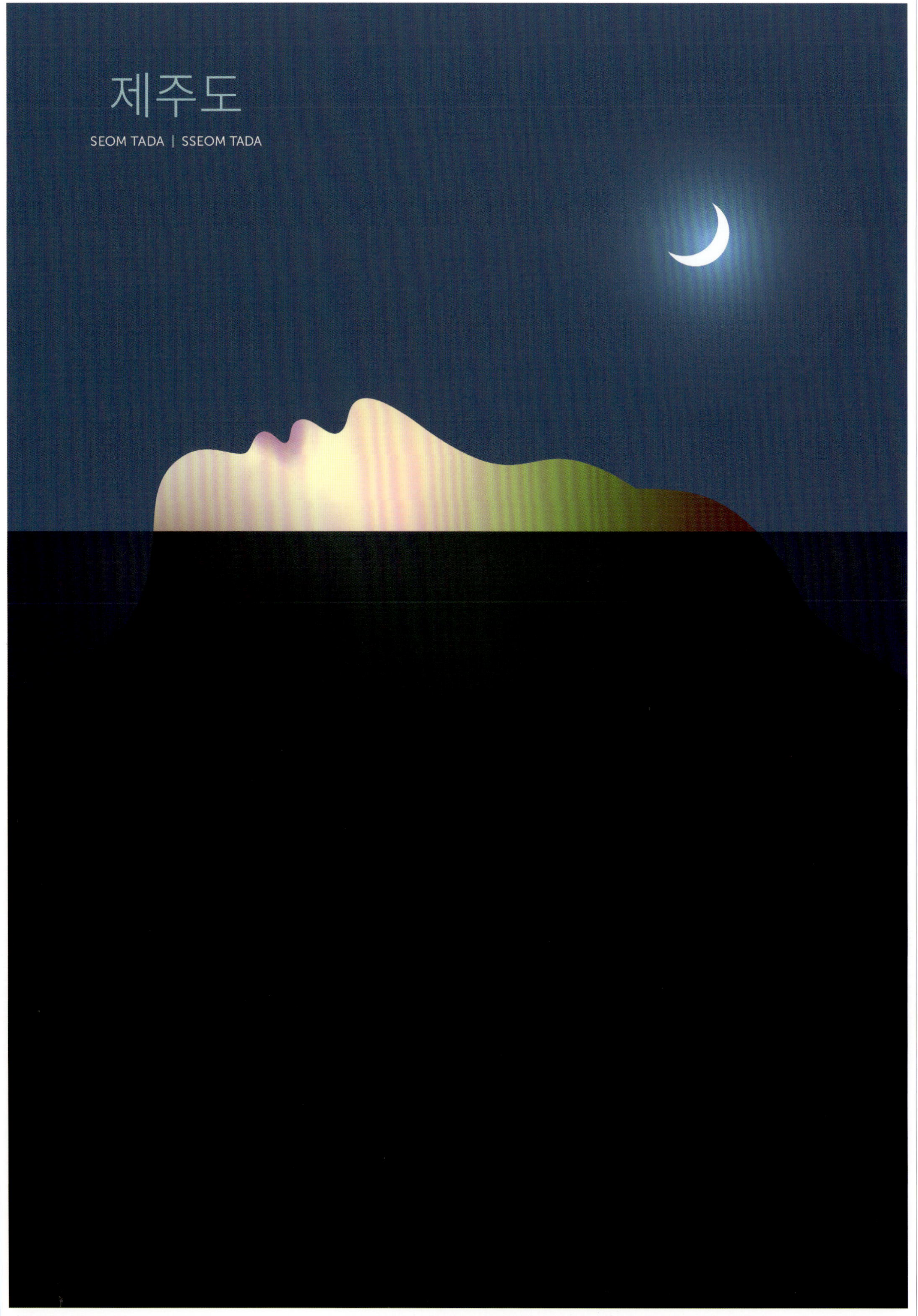

P243: Credit & Commentary **Title:** Jeju Evening | **Client:** Communication Design Association of Korea | **Design Firm:** May & Co.

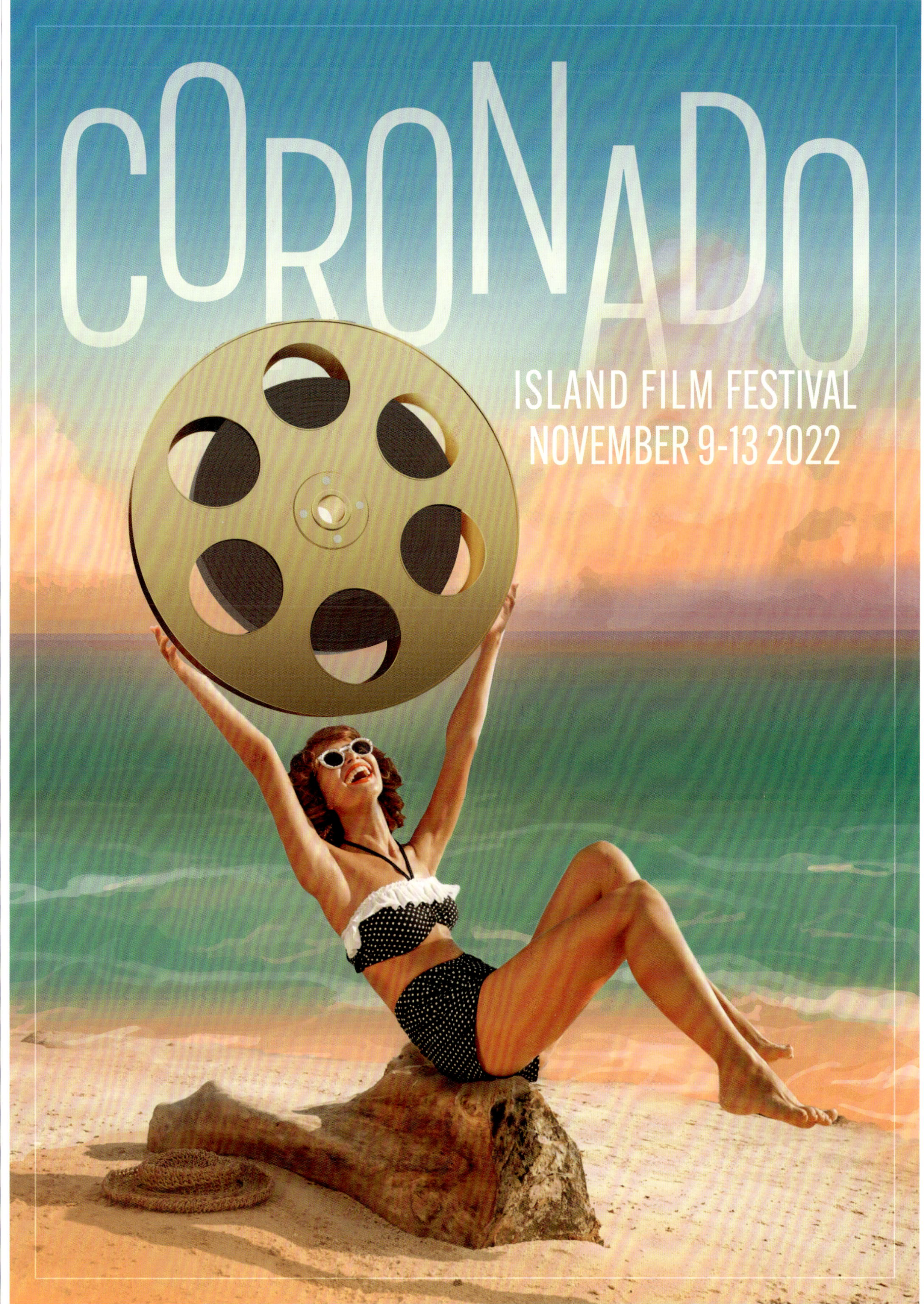

Title: Reel Time | **Client:** Coronado Island Film Festival
Design Firm: Judd Brand Media | **P243:** Credit & Commentary

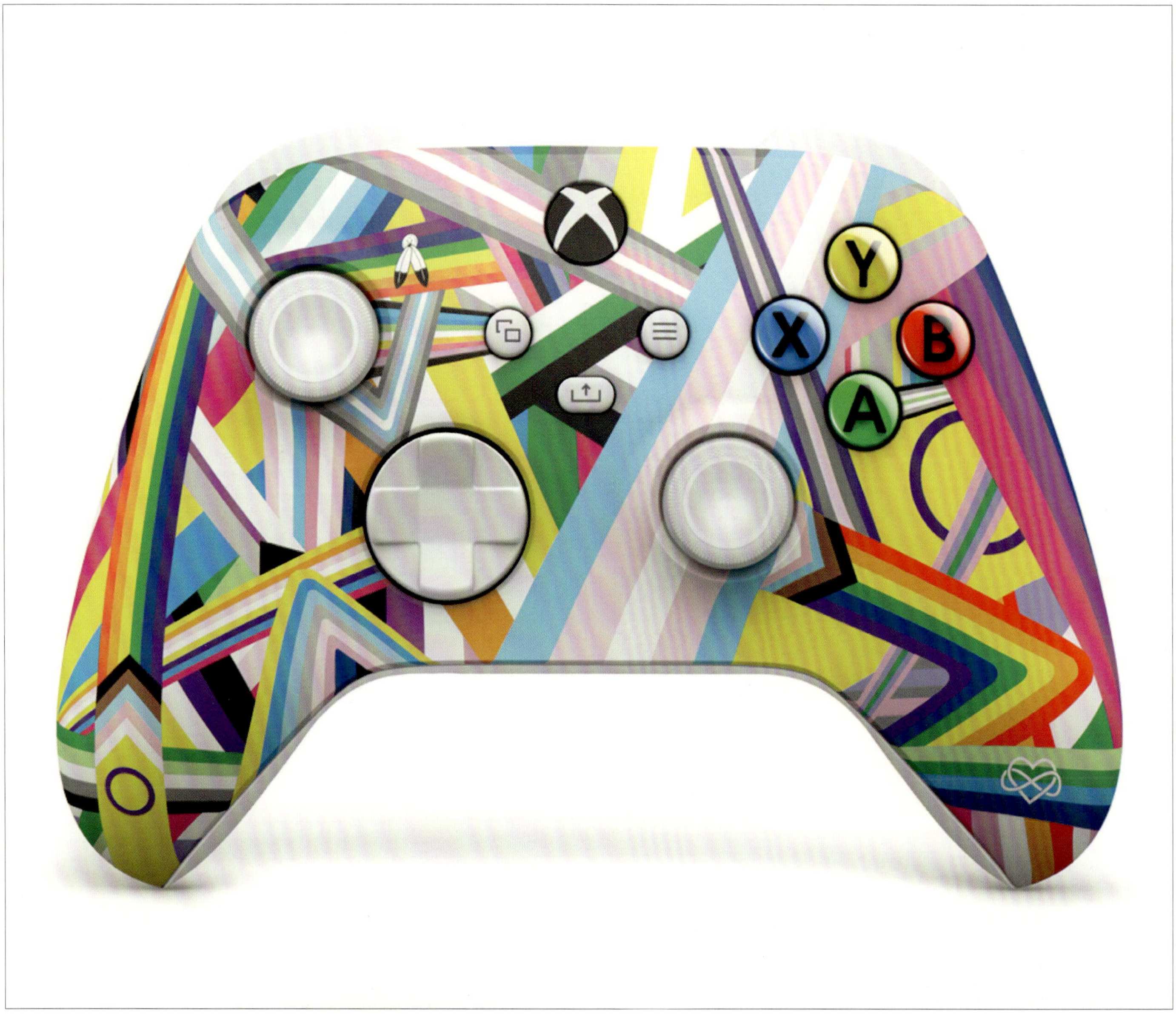

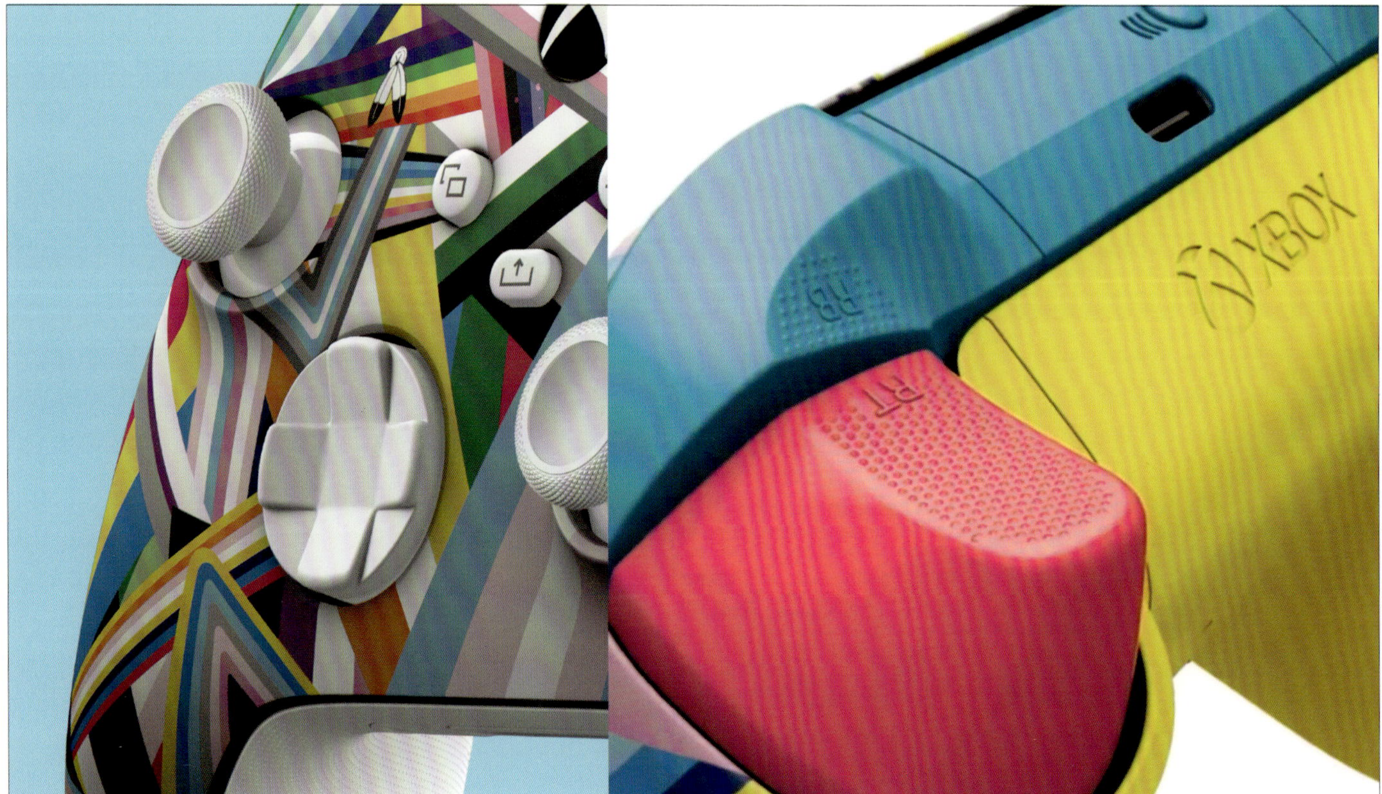
XBOX
RT

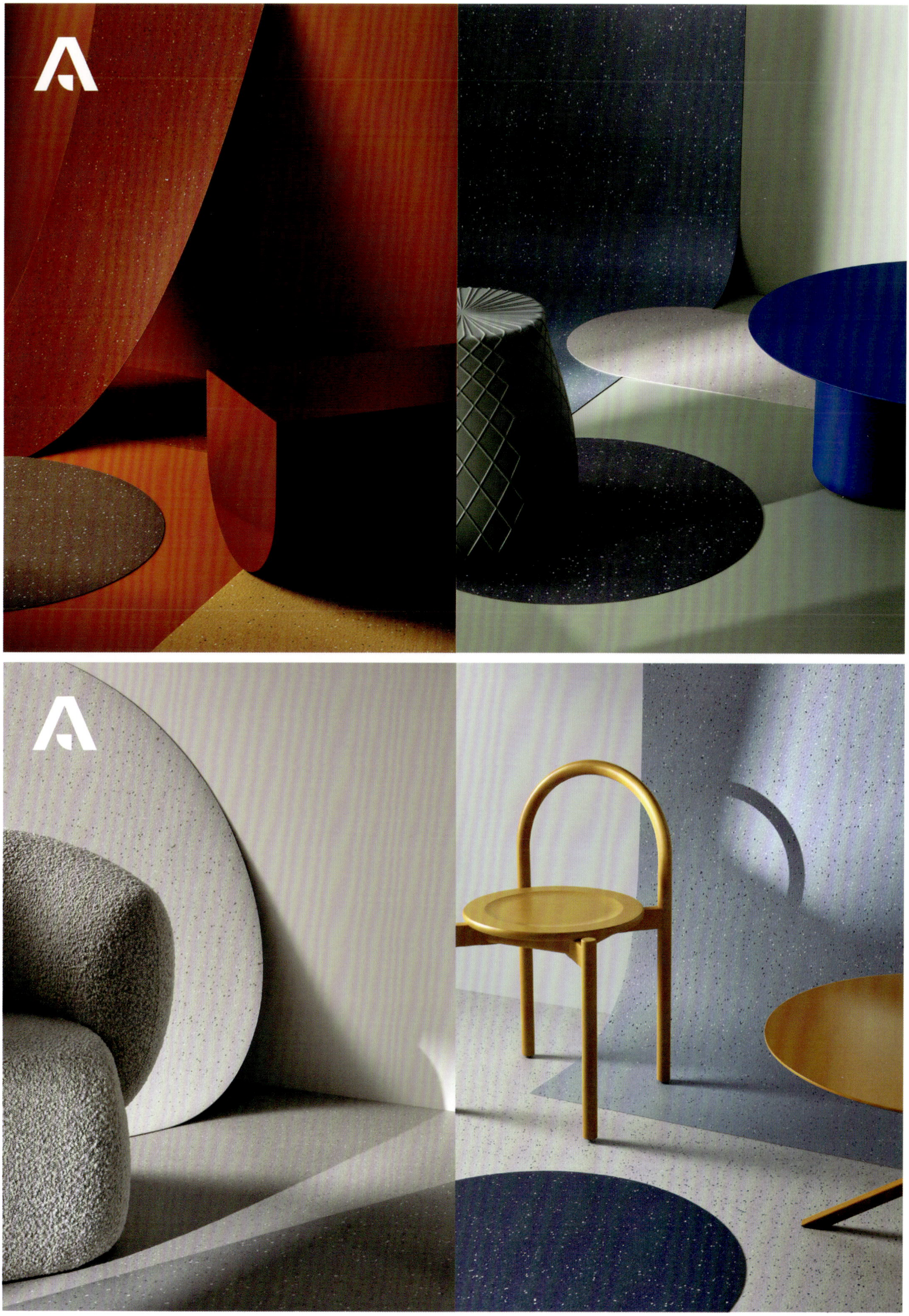

 Title: Natralis™ Product Launch | **Client:** Armstrong Flooring Australia | **Design Firm:** Nexus Designs Images 1, 2 of 7

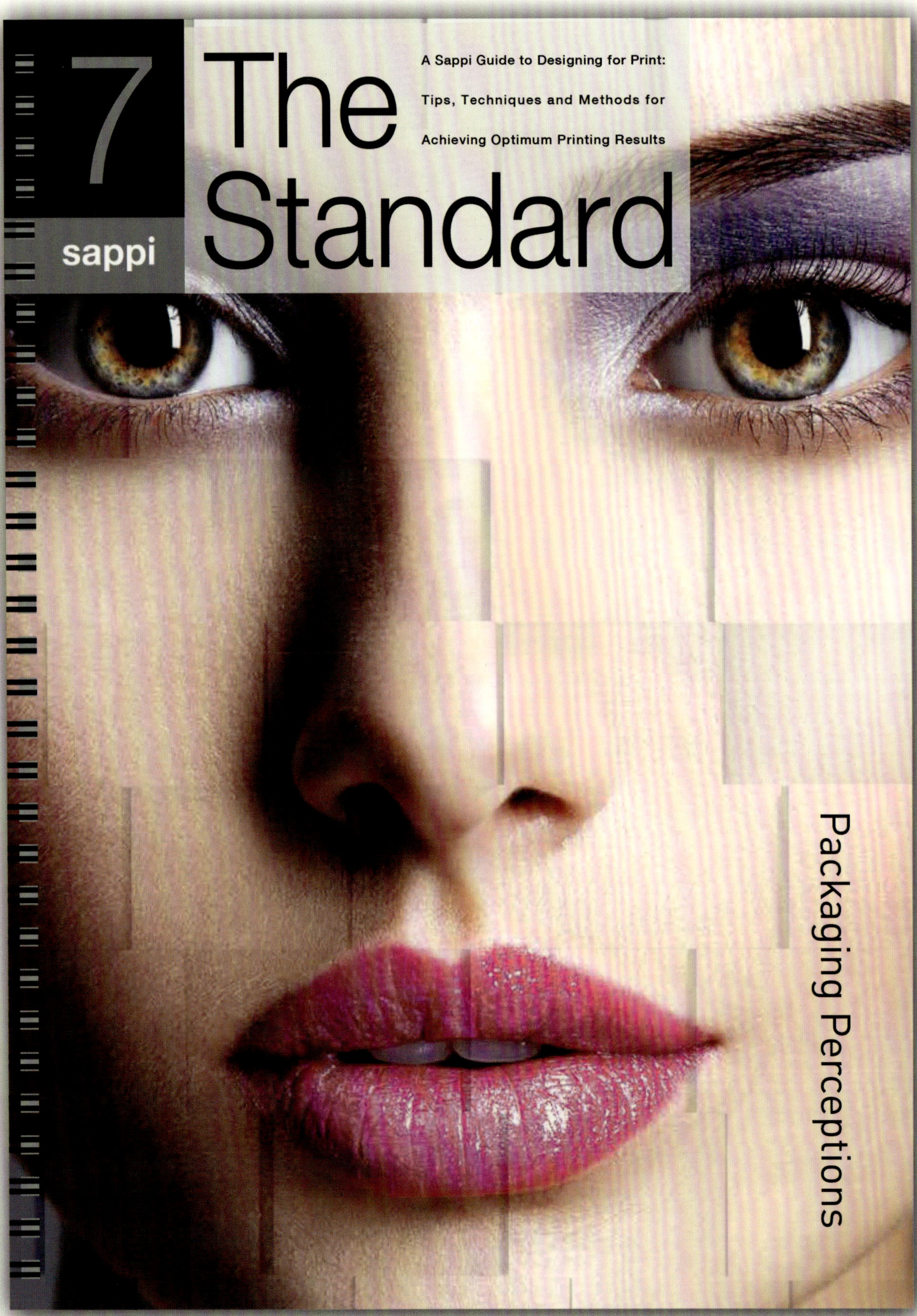

7

sappi

The Standard

A Sappi Guide to Designing for Print: Tips, Techniques and Methods for Achieving Optimum Printing Results

Packaging Perceptions

Title: The Standard 7: Packaging Perceptions | **Client:** Sappi | **Design Firm:** Studio Hinrichs

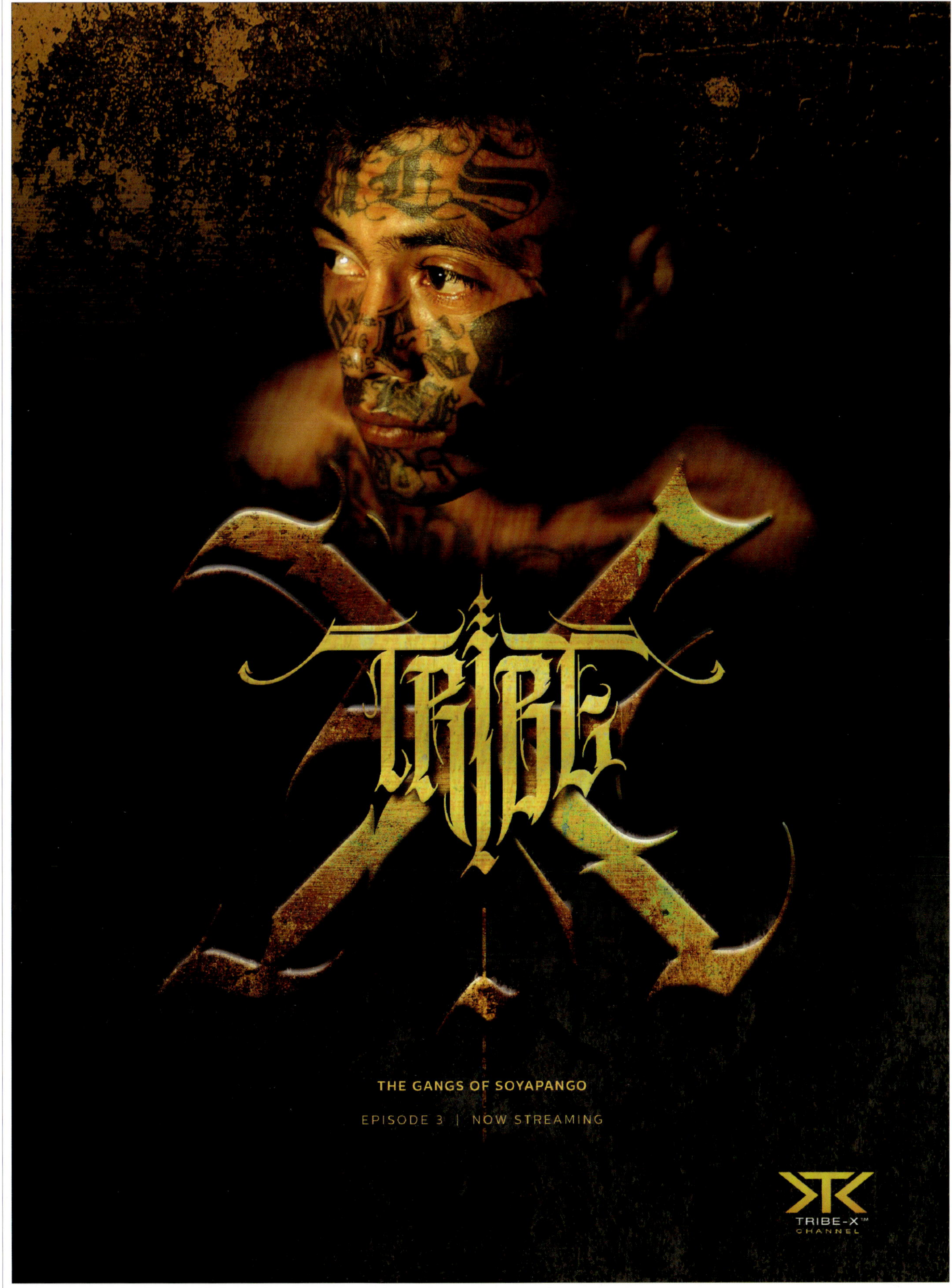

P244: Credit & Commentary **Title:** Tribe-X | **Client:** Creative Projects Group | **Design Firm:** Ron Taft Brand Innovation & Media Arts

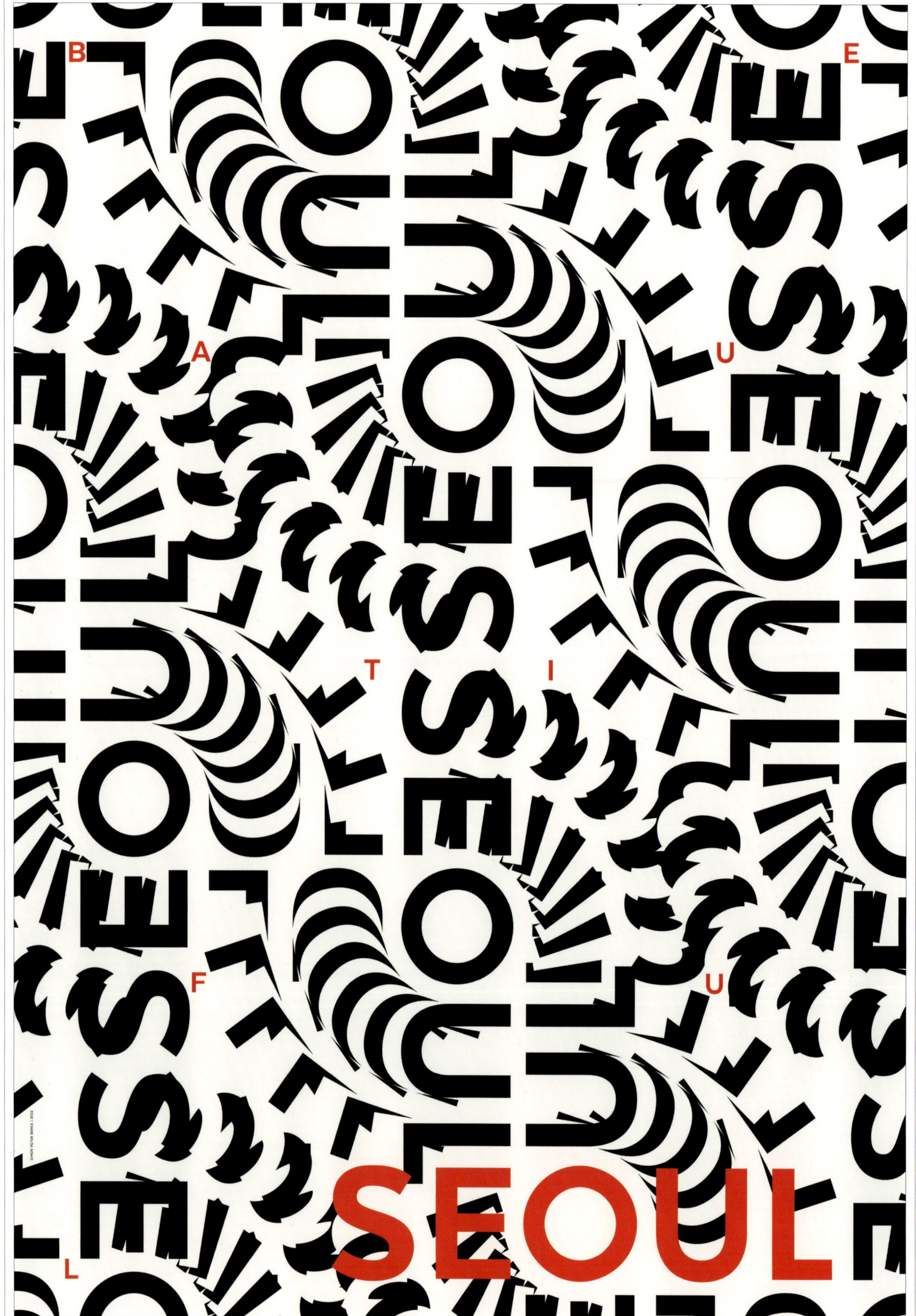

Title: TYPO LANTERNS / Beautiful Seoul | **Client:** KECD (Korea Ensemble of Contemporary Design Association)
Design Firm: Simon Peter Bence | **P244:** Credit & Commentary

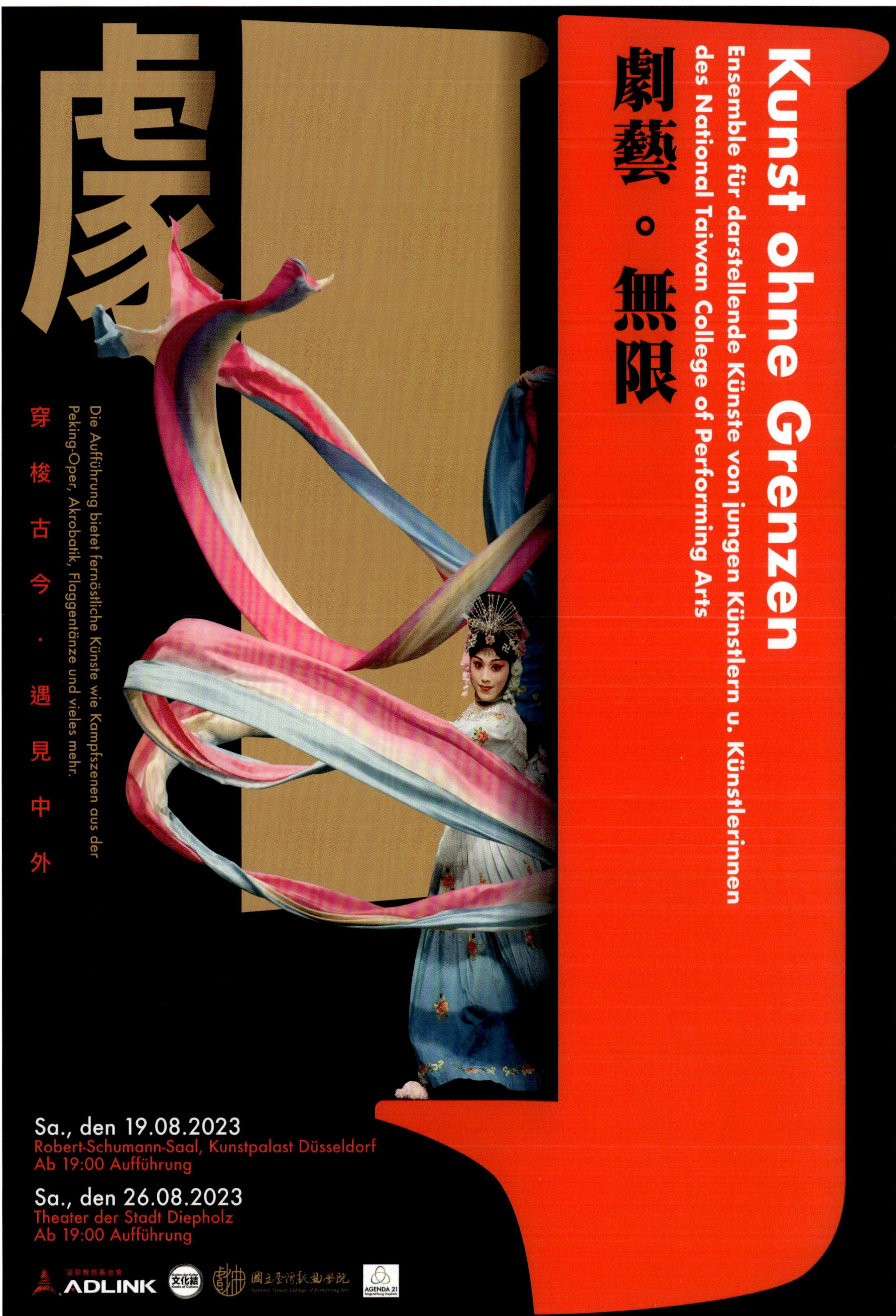
Kunst ohne Grenzen
Ensemble für darstellende Künste von jungen Künstlern u. Künstlerinnen
des National Taiwan College of Performing Arts
劇藝。無限
Die Aufführung bietet fernöstliche Künste wie Kampfszenen aus der
Peking-Oper, Akrobatik, Flaggentänze und vieles mehr.
穿梭古今・遇見中外
Sa., den 19.08.2023
Robert-Schumann-Saal, Kunstpalast Düsseldorf
Ab 19:00 Aufführung
Sa., den 26.08.2023
Theater der Stadt Diepholz
Ab 19:00 Aufführung
ADLINK
國立臺灣戲曲學院
AGENDA 21

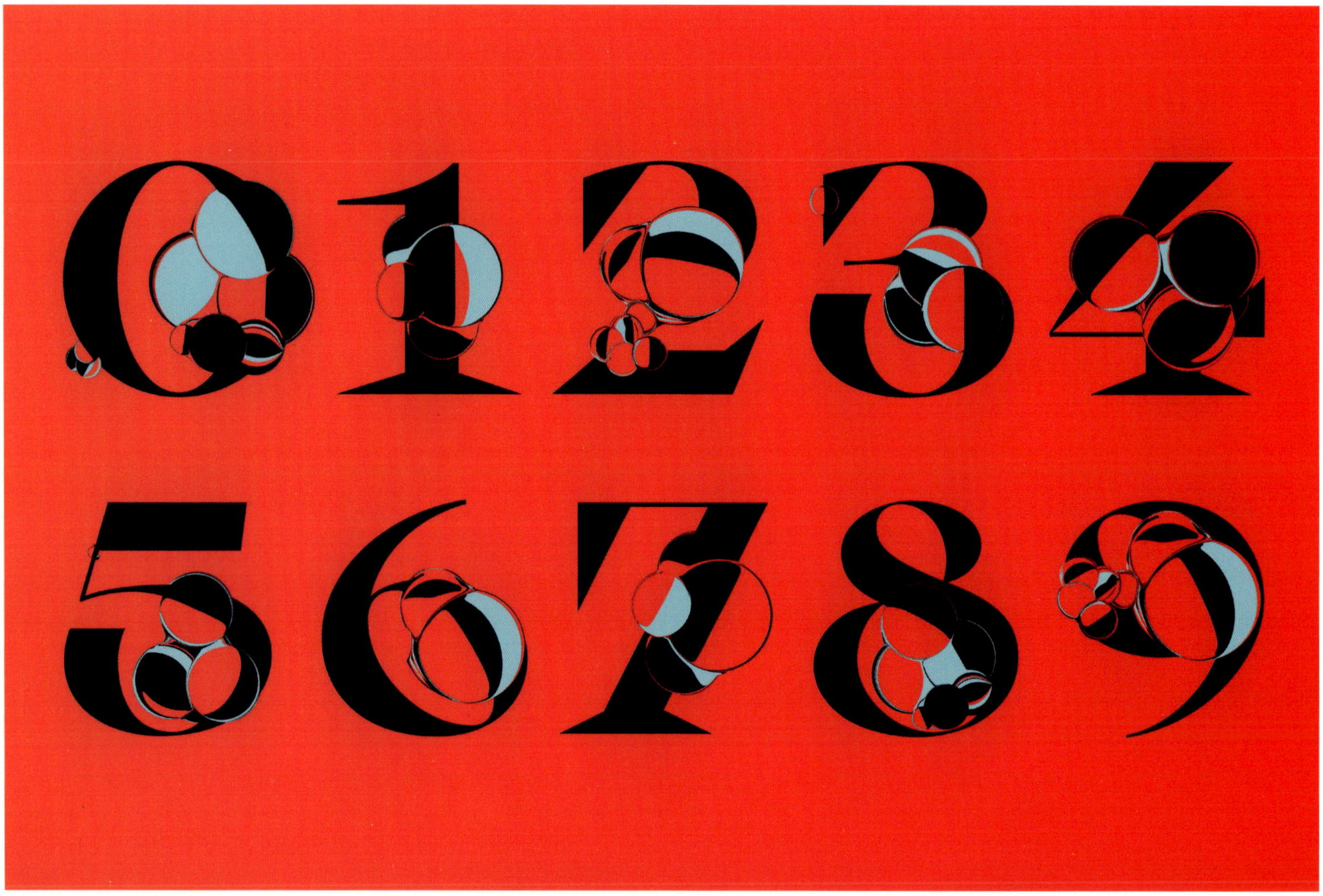

0 1 2 3 4 5 6 7 8 9

P244: Credit & Commentary

Title: YOUTUBE COUNTDOWN | Client: YouTube | Design Firm: Sunday Afternoon

Image 1 of 7

ARIEL FREANER GOLD TYPOGRAPHY

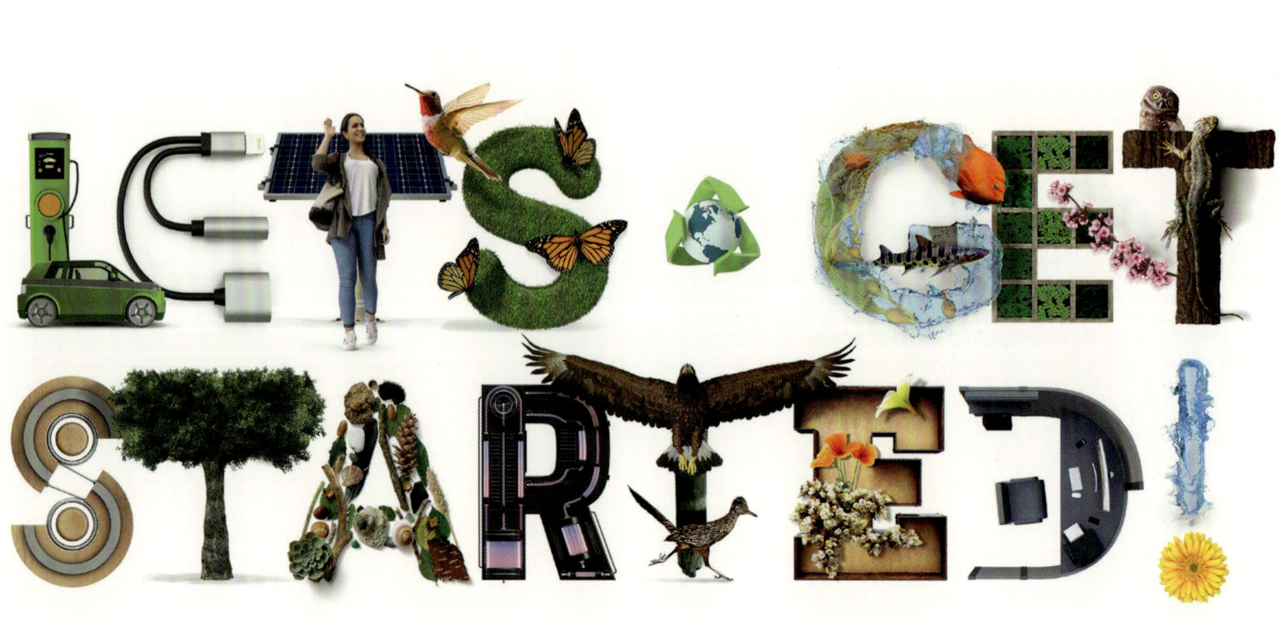

Title: Let's Get There Campaign Logo | Clients: County of San Diego Land Use & Environment, Donna Durckel
Design Firm: Freaner Creative & Design | P244: Credit & Commentary

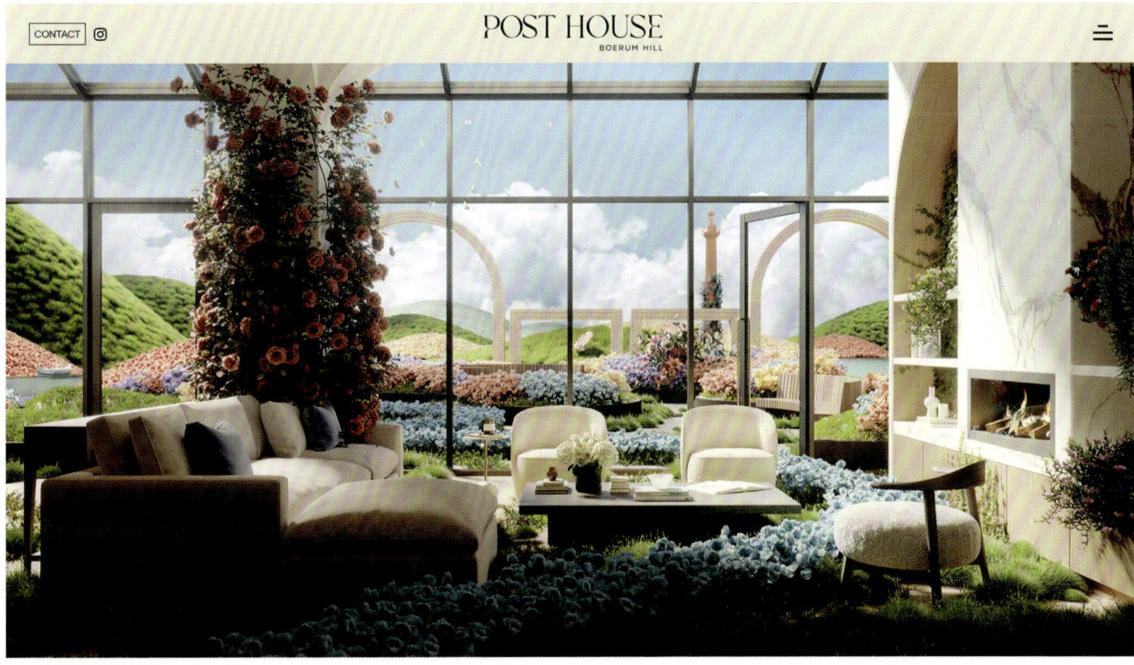

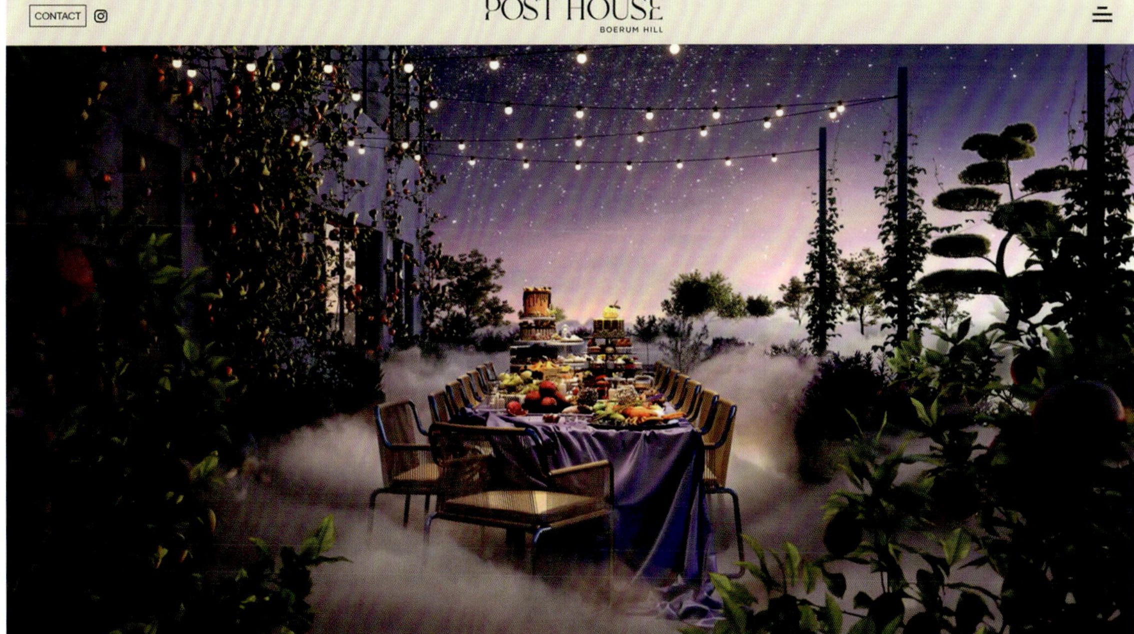

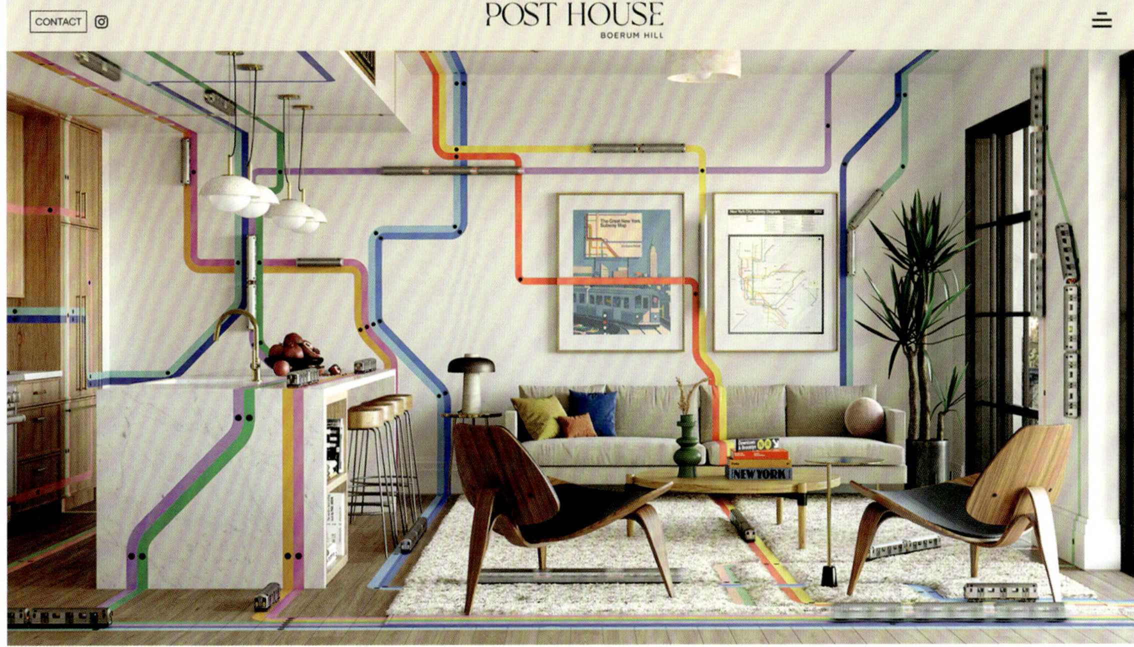

Title: Post House Website | **Client:** Sterling Town Equities | **Design Firm:** IF Studio

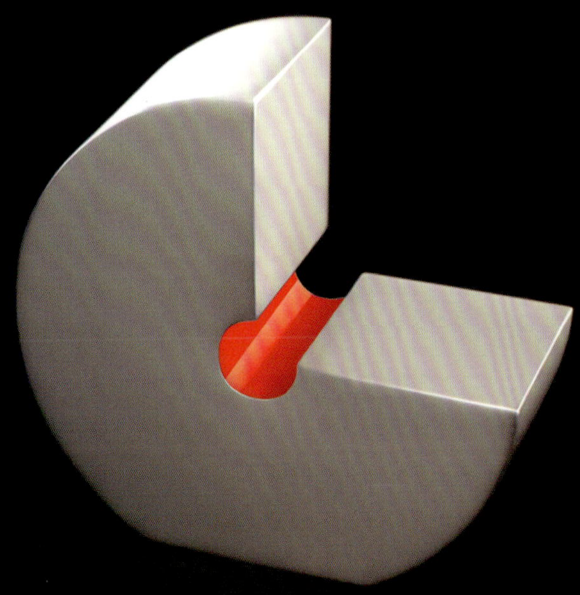

INSIGHT CREATIVE

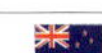

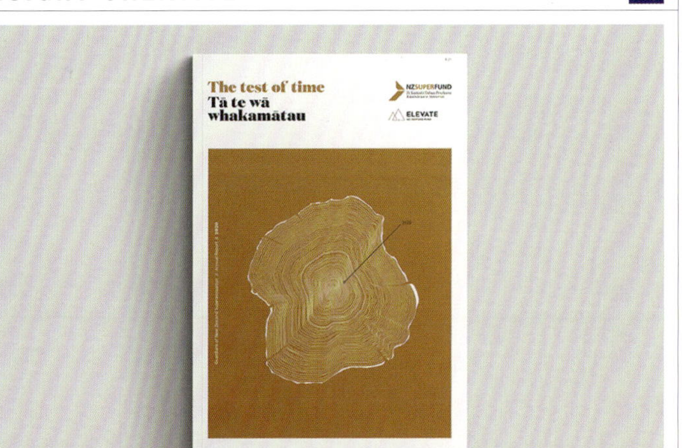

Title: New Zealand Superfund Annual Report
Client: New Zealand Superfund | **Design Firm:** Insight Creative

ATELIER NUNES E PÃ, LDA

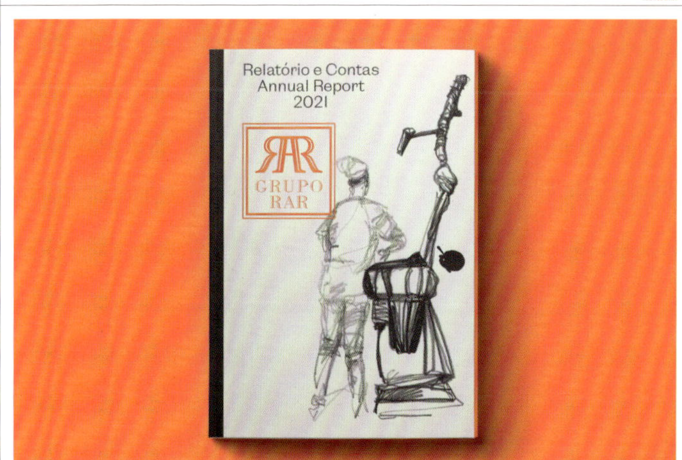

Title: "RAR Seen By"
Client: RAR Holding, S.A. | **Design Firm:** Atelier Nunes e Pã, lda

TYLER FONVILLE

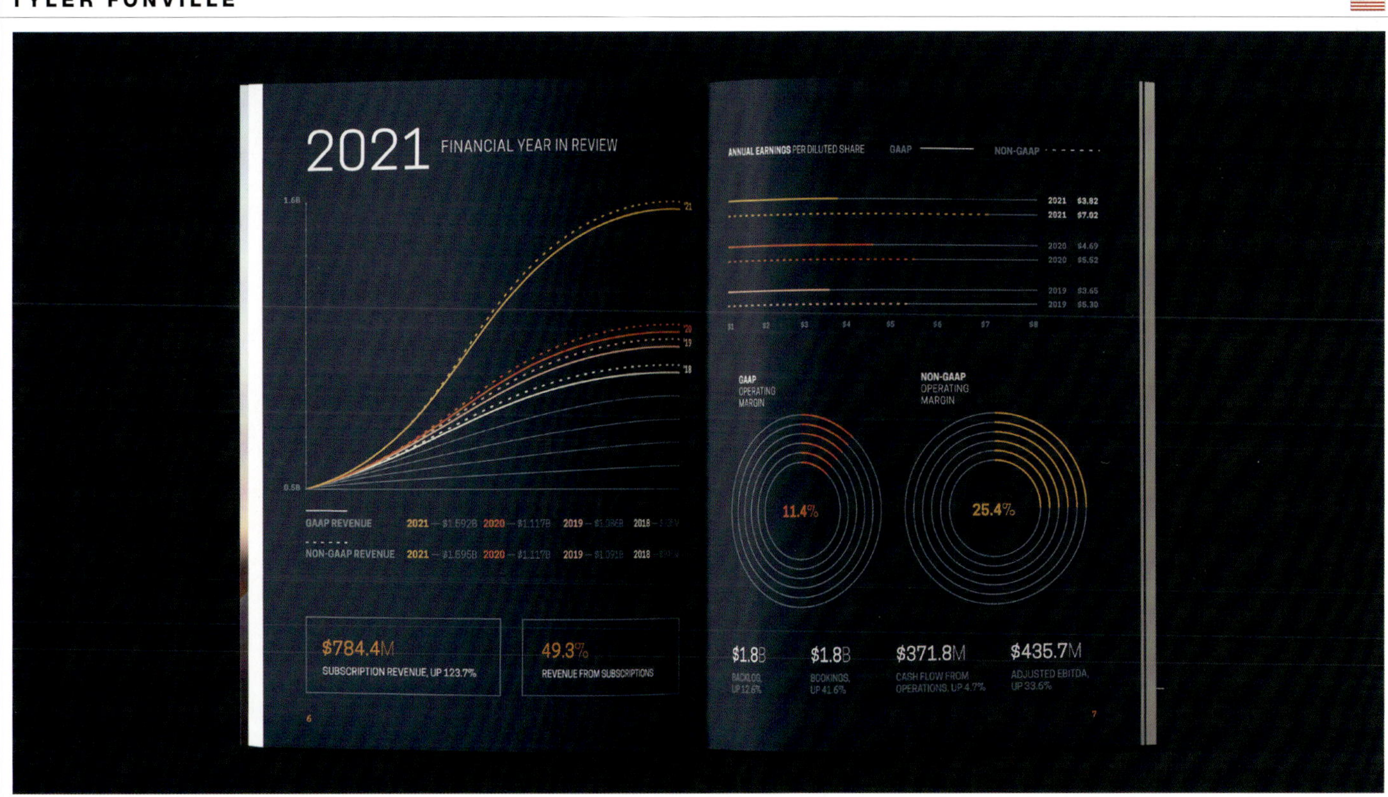

Title: Vision Without Limits - Tyler Technologies 2021 Annual Report | **Client:** Tyler Technologies | **Design Firm:** Spire Agency

NEW YORK PUBLIC RADIO

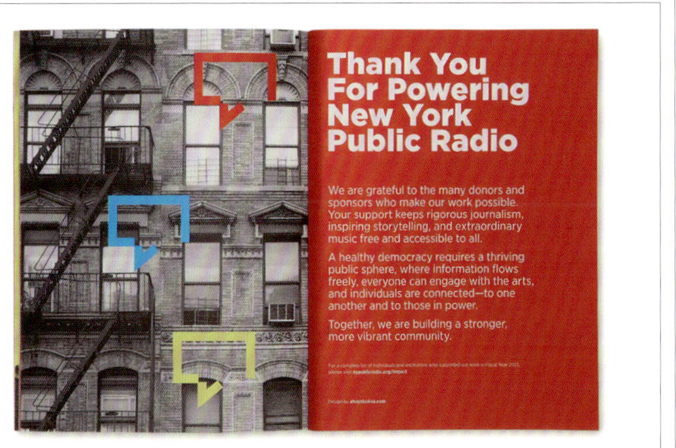

Title: Resilience in Action – New York Public Radio – Annual Report – Fiscal Year 2021
Client: New York Public Radio | **Design Firm:** Ahoy Studios

SILVIA YU, CHRIS CHUNG, CHIEN CHUN FENG (+8)

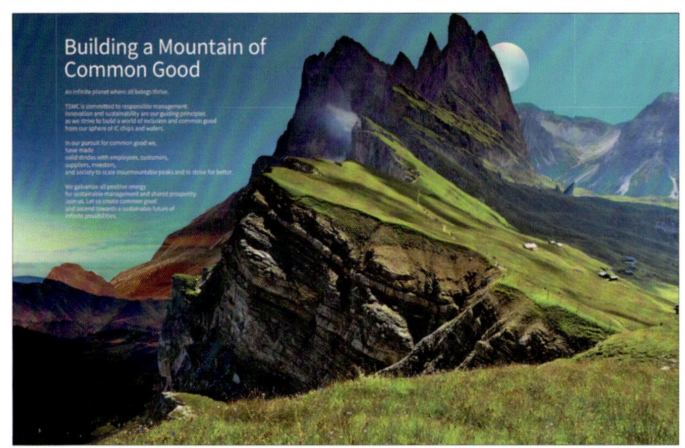

Title: TSMC 2020 CSR Annual Report
Client: Taiwan Semiconductor Manufacturing Company (TSMC)
Design Firm: RedPeak Global

KATHY MUELLER

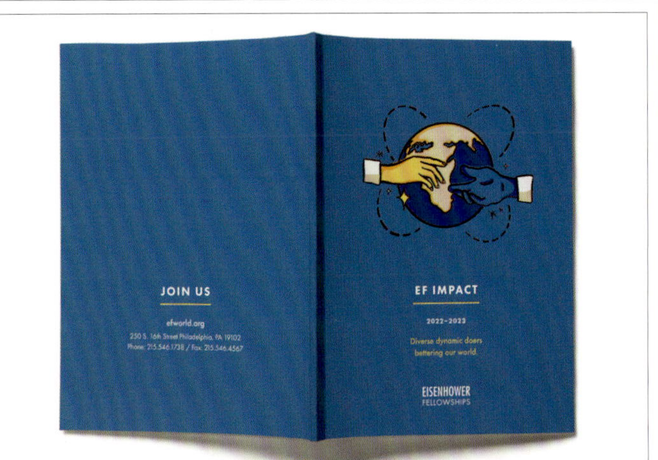

Title: EF Impact Report | **Client:** Eisenhower Fellowships
Design Firm: Kathy Mueller Design, LLC

ANNE M. GIANGIULIO DESIGN

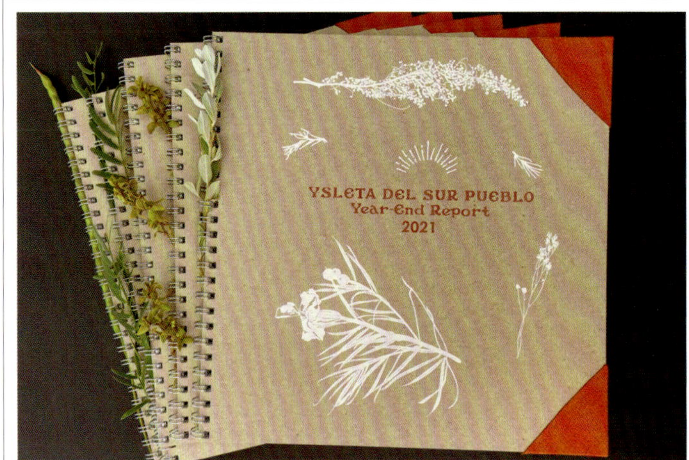

Title: Ysleta del Sur Pueblo 2021 Year-End Report | **Clients:** Ysleta del Sur Pueblo, Helix Solutions | **Design Firm:** Anne M. Giangiulio Design

TOPPAN MERRILL

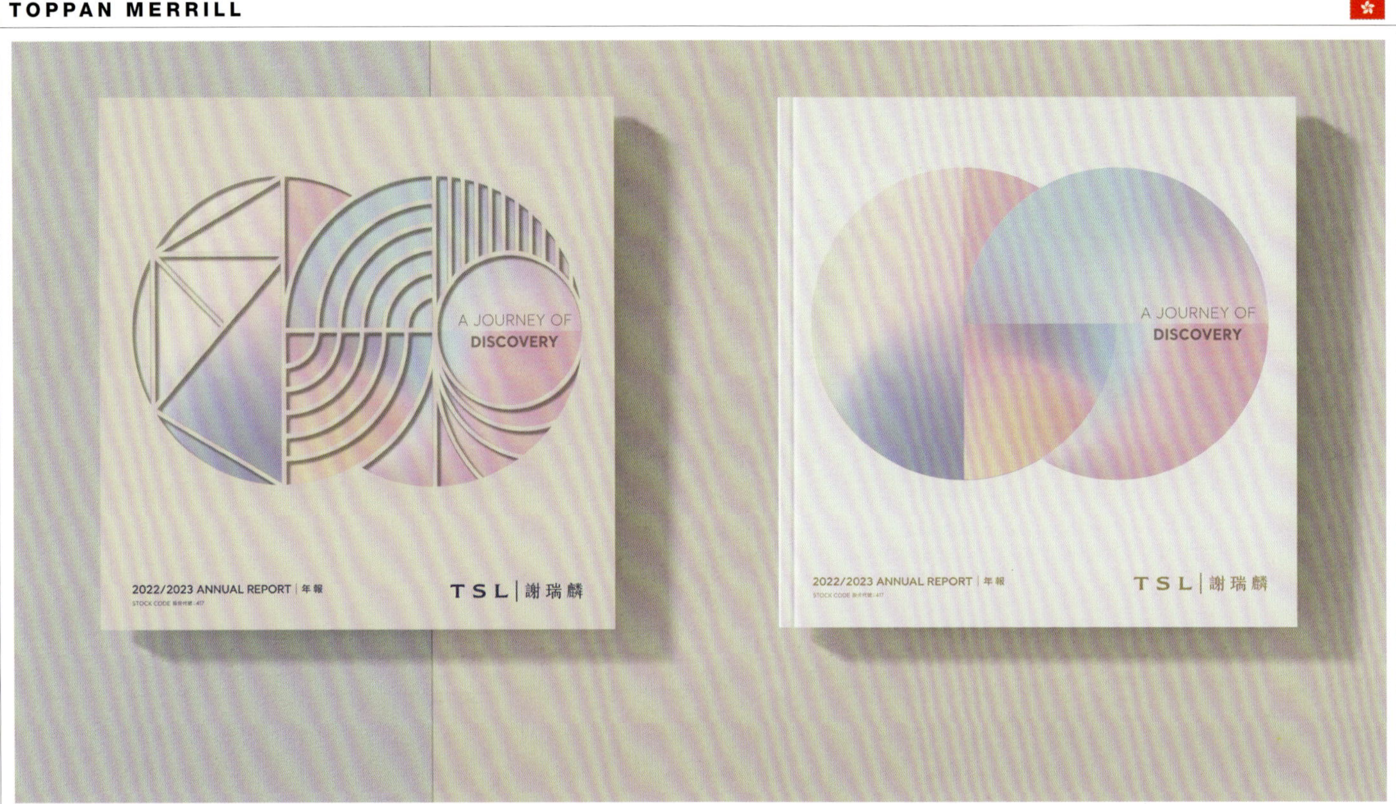

Title: TSL Annual Report 2021/22 | **Client:** Tse Sui Luen Jewellery (International) Limited | **Design Firm:** TSL Group Creative

ARIEL FREANER

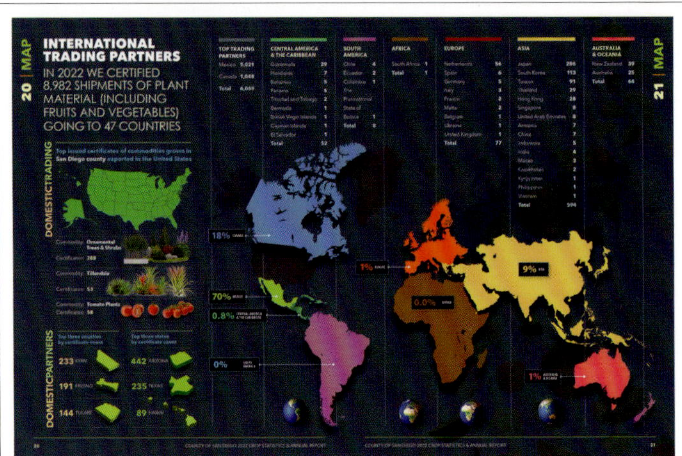

Title: AWM 2022 Crop Report | **Client:** San Diego County Agricultural Weights and Measures | **Design Firm:** Freaner Creative & Design

LISA SIRBAUGH CREATIVE

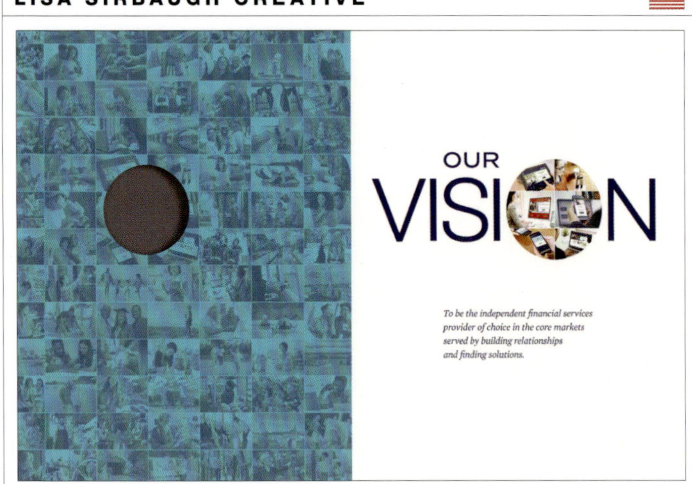

Title: ACNB Corporation 2021 Annual Review
Client: ACNB Corporation | **Design Firm:** Lisa Sirbaugh Creative

M.P. CURTET

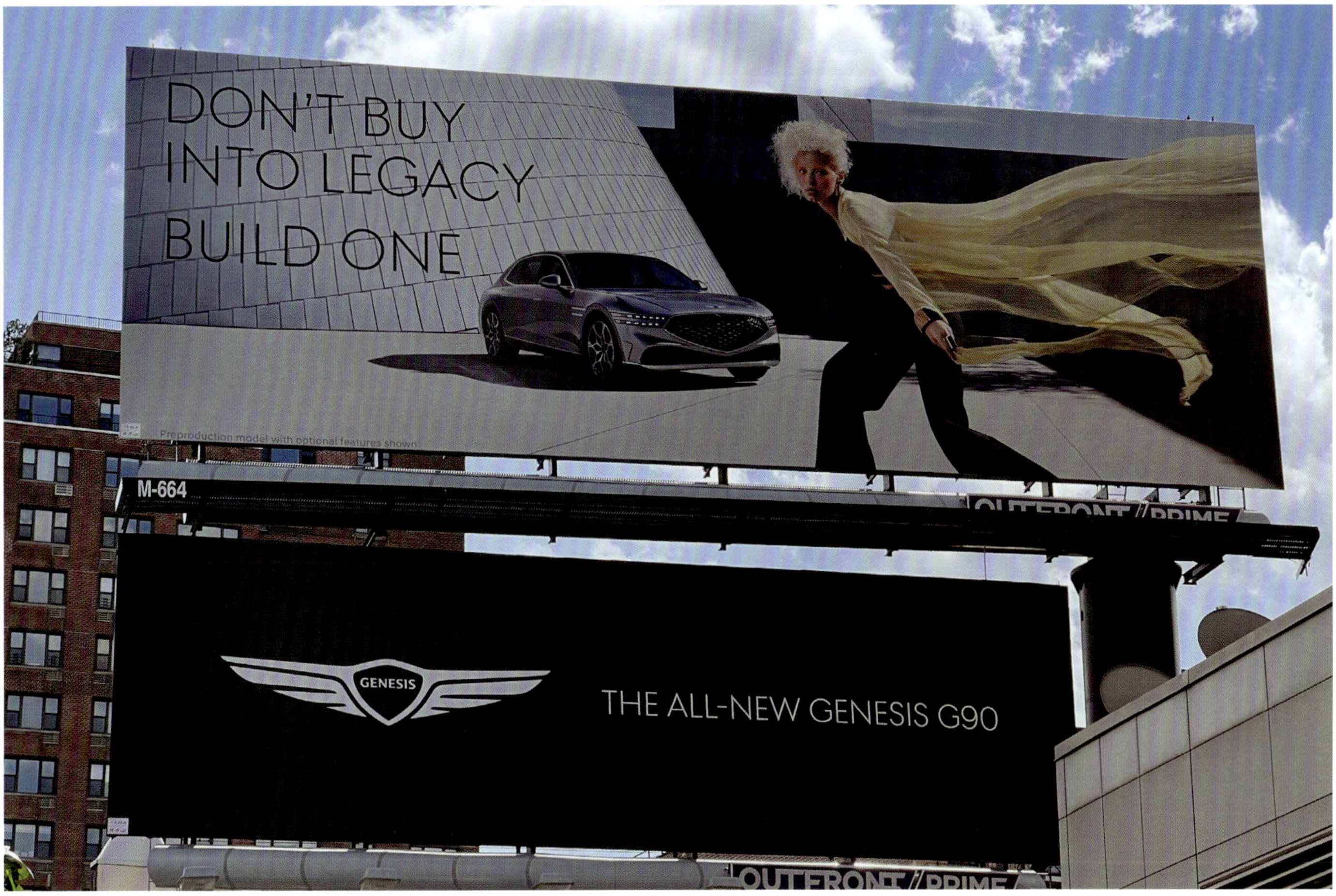

Title: Make Your Mark from Coast to Coast | **Client:** Genesis Motor America | **Design Firm:** INNOCEAN USA

EDWARD CHIQUITUCTO

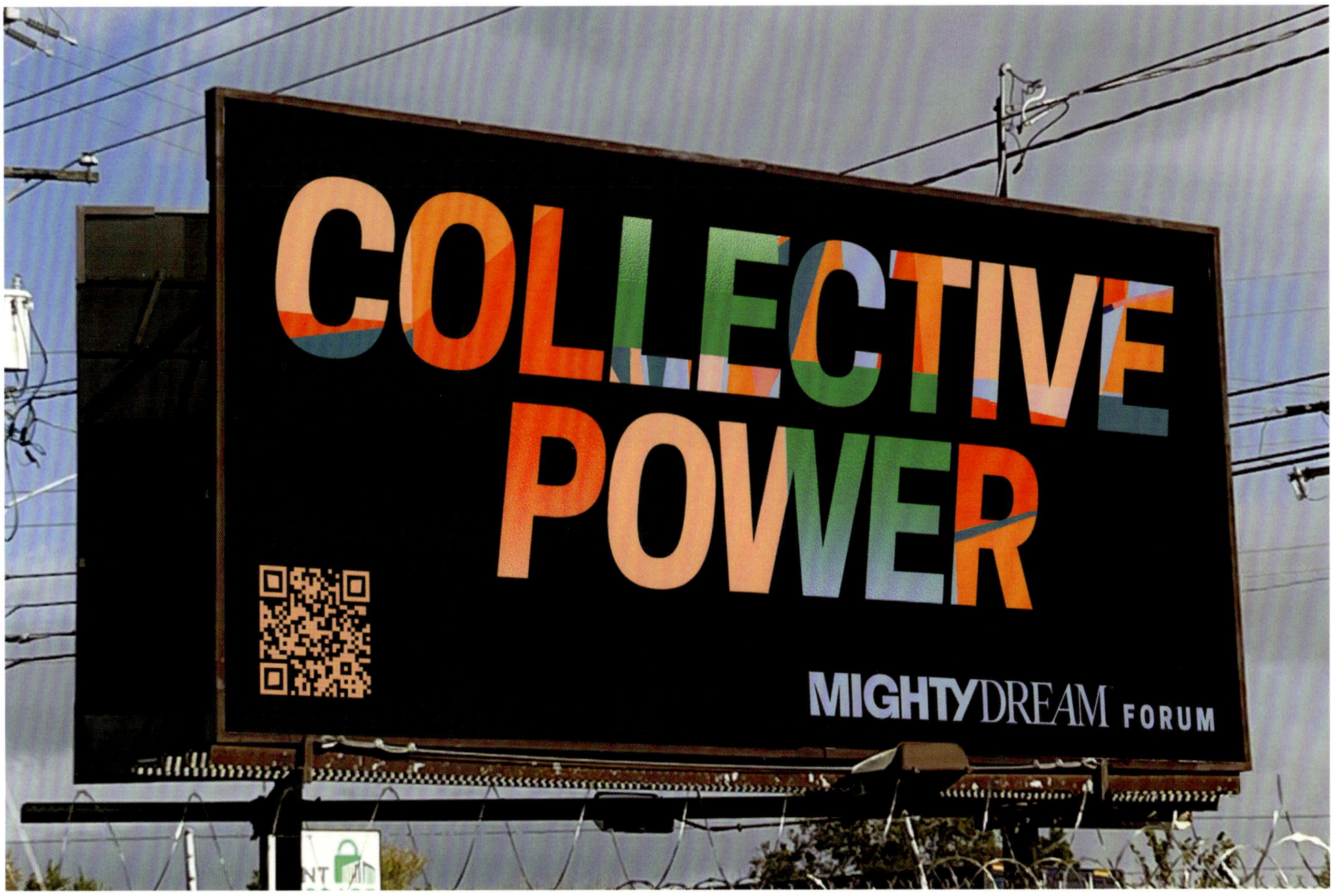

Title: "Mighty Dream Forum" Billboards | **Client:** I Am Other by Pharrell Williams | **Design Firm:** Chiquitucto Group

SIENA SCARFF DESIGN

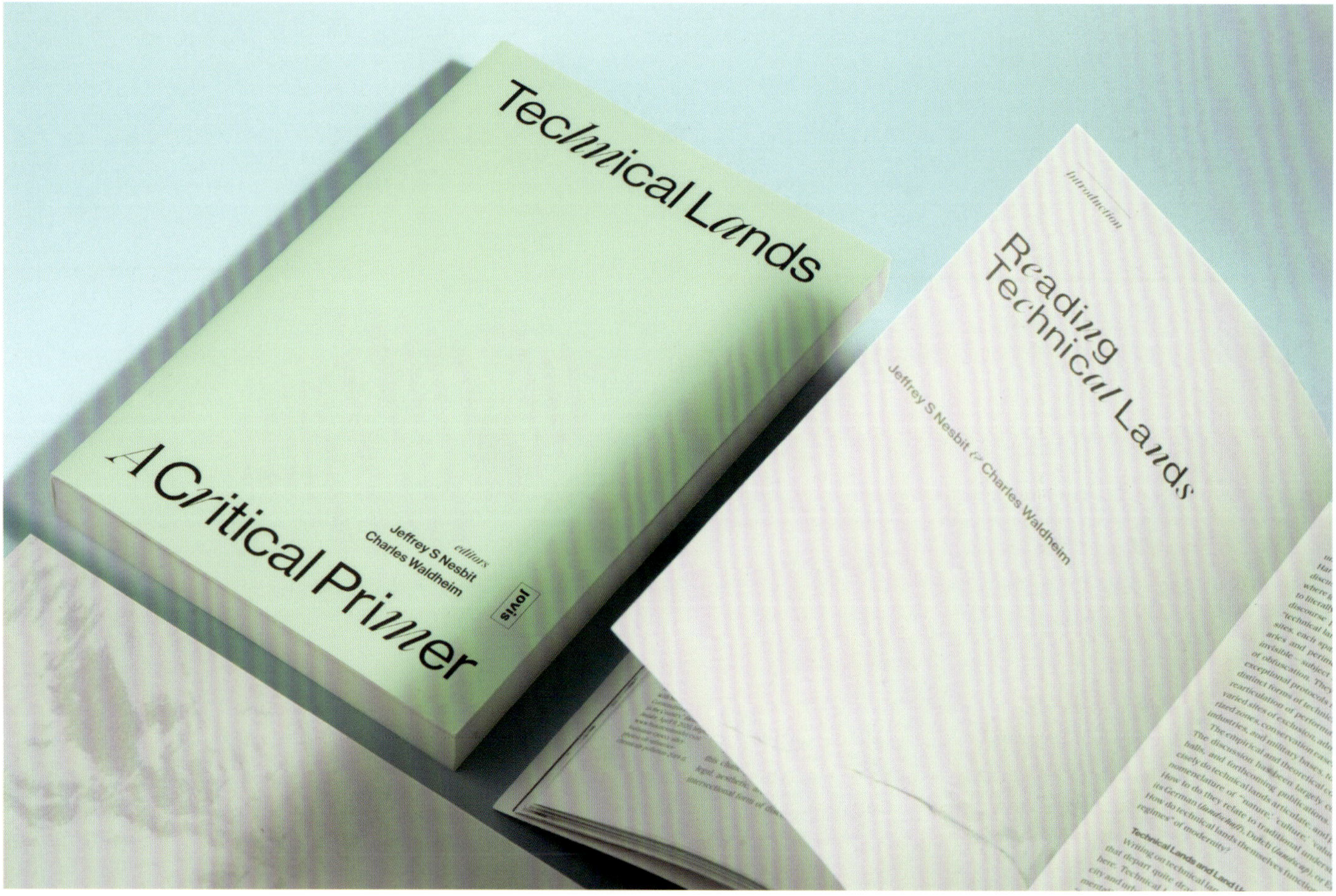

Title: Technical Lands: A Critical Primer | **Clients:** Jeffrey S. Nesbit, Charles Waldheim, Jovis | **Design Firm:** Siena Scarff Design

CARLOS CAICEDO

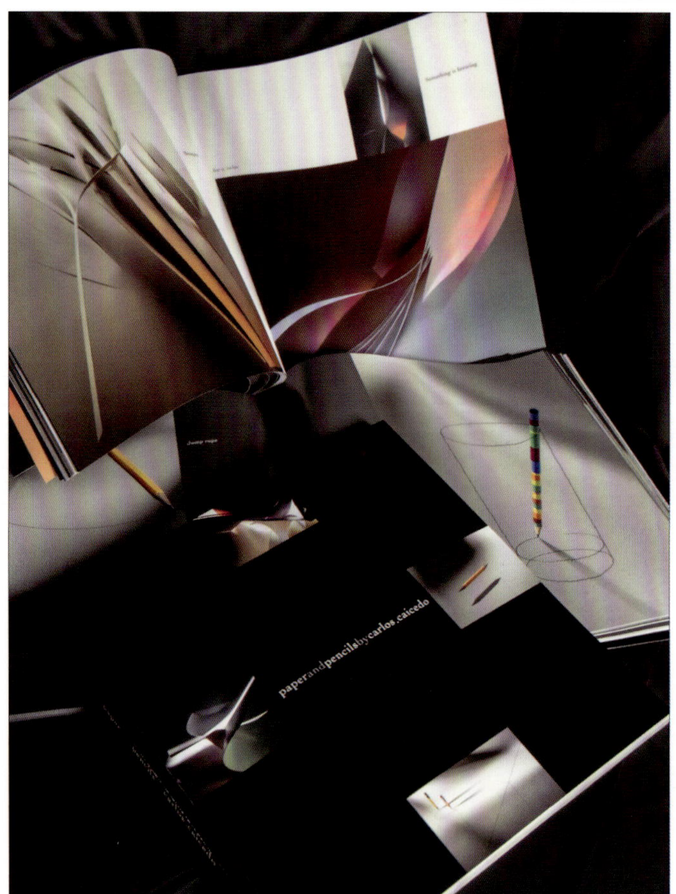

Title: Paper and Pencil By Carlos Caicedo
Client: Self-initiated | **Design Firm:** Carlos Caicedo

JAN ŠABACH

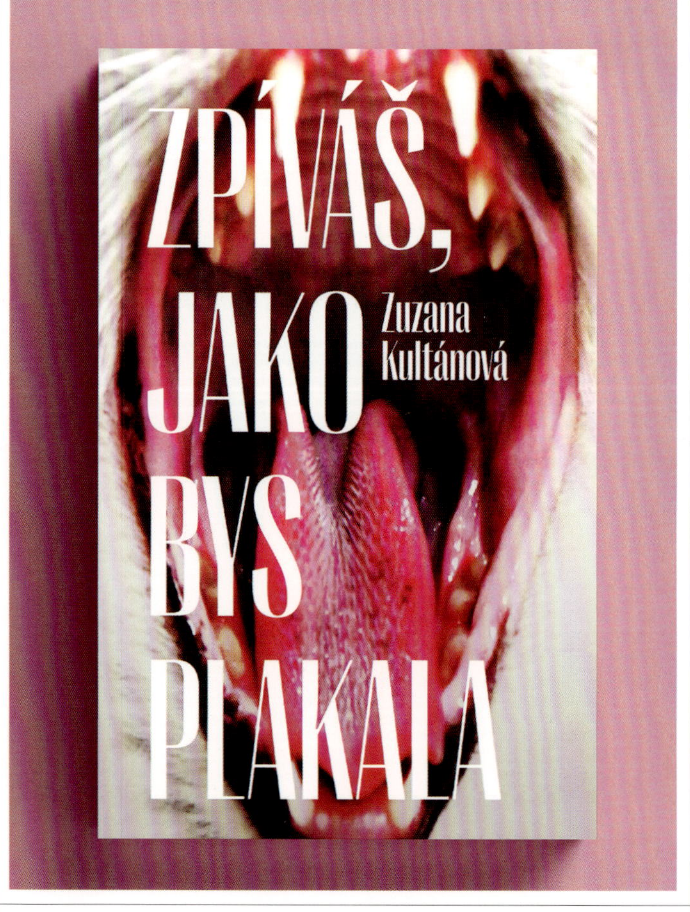

Title: Zpíváš, Jako bys Plakala ("You Sing as if You Were Crying")
Client: Paseka Publishing House | **Design Firm:** Code Switch

ODDSENSE, E. BOWSTEAD, J. VEGA, R. YE PARK

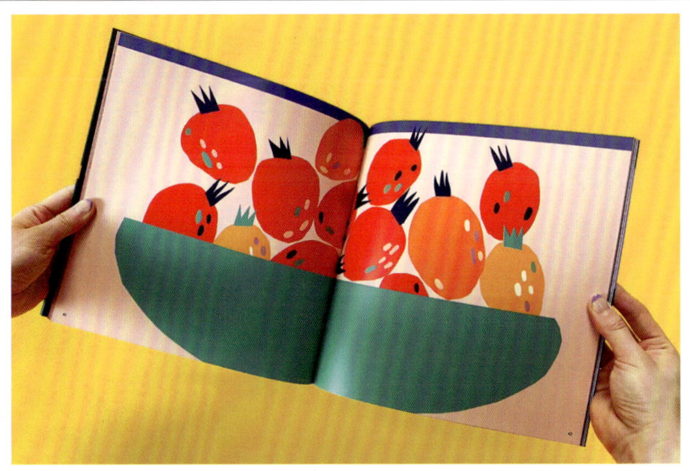

Title: "Memories by Murphy" | **Client:** Murphy's String Figures
Design Firm: ODDSENSE

BRAD HOLLAND

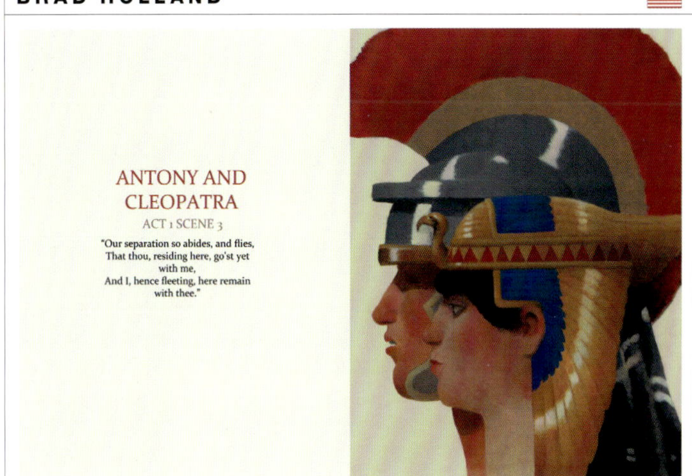

Title: Such Stuff As Dreams | **Client:** Nuage Editions
Design Firm: Brad Holland

JOHN SLEMP PHOTOGRAPHY

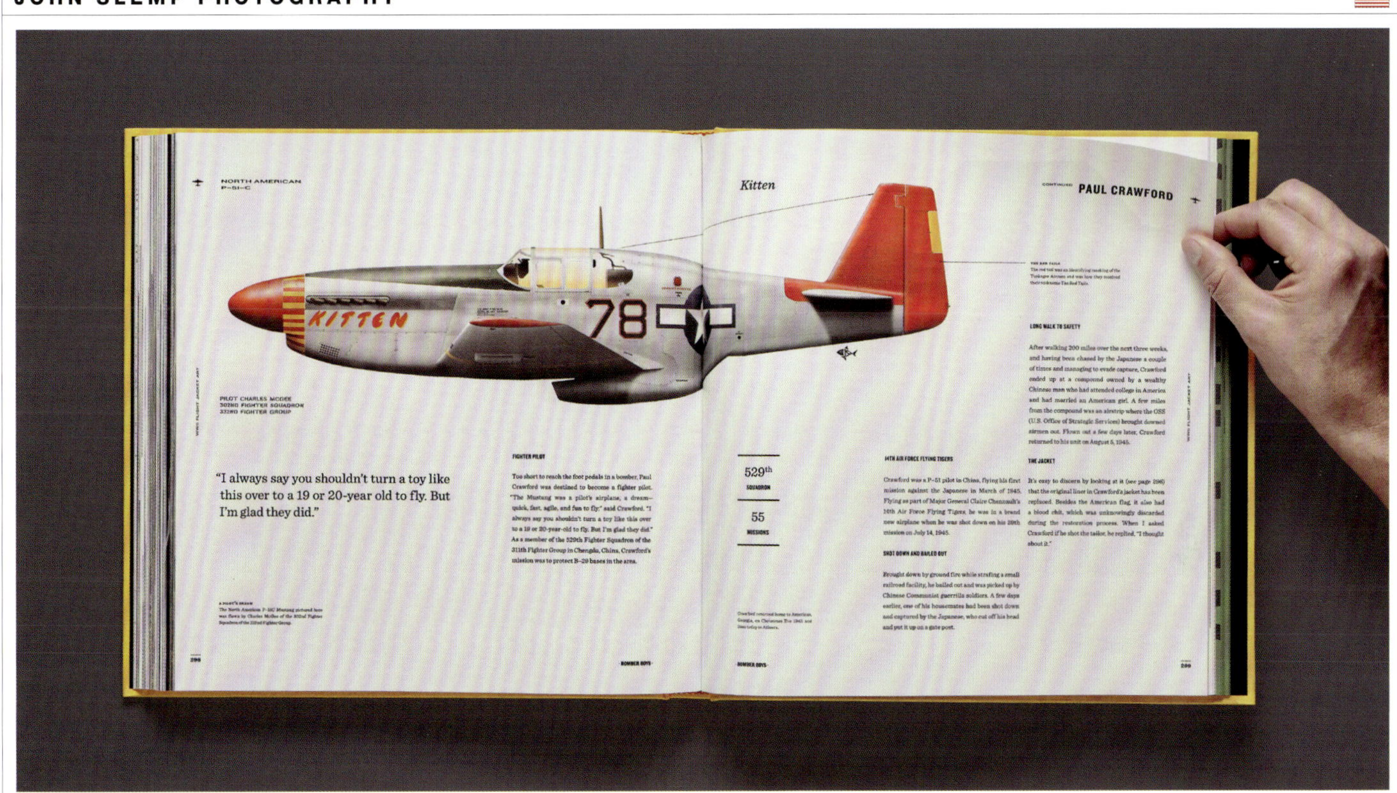

Title: Bomber Boys WWII Flight Jacket Art | **Client:** John Slemp | **Design Firm:** Fournir

J. MOCKRIN, A. CAMPBELL, S. CARTIER LUCY, N. BRYSON

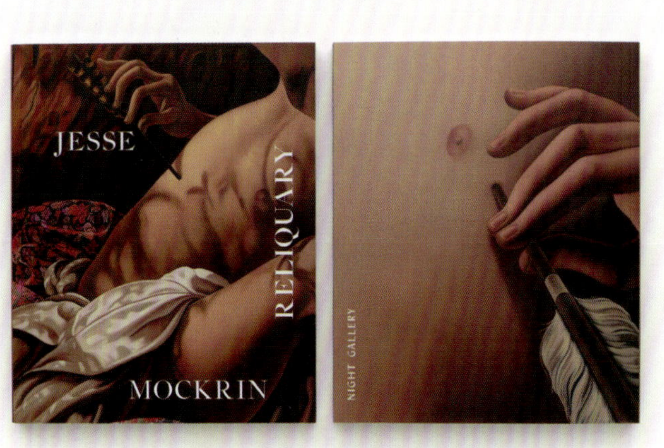

Title: Jesse Mockrin, Reliquary | **Client:** Night Gallery
Design Firm: Still Room

UNDERLINE STUDIO

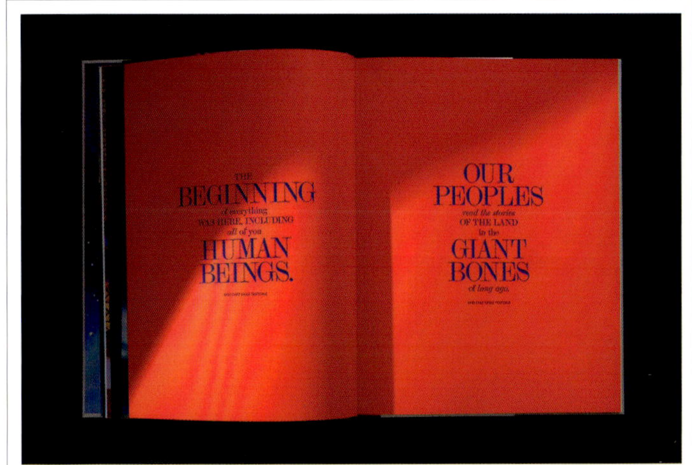

Title: Kent Monkman: Being Legendary | **Client:** Art Canada Institute
Design Firm: Underline Studio

JEFF MILLER

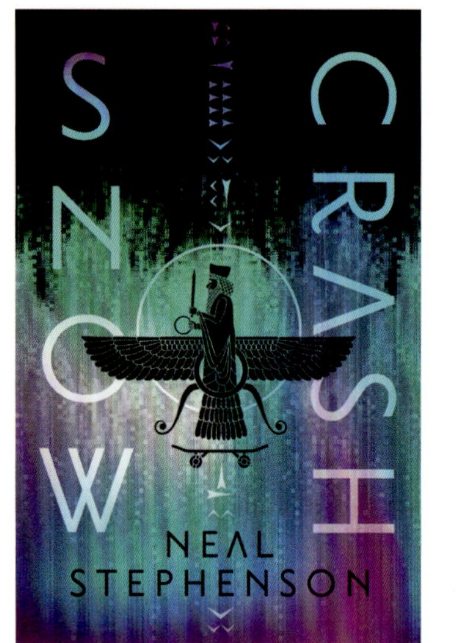

Title: Snow Crash
Client: Penguin Random House
Design Firm: Faceout Studio

CHASE QUARTERMAN

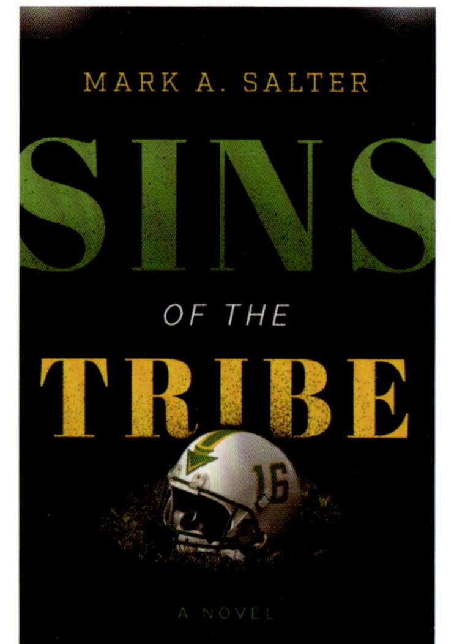

Title: Sins of the Tribe
Client: Mark A. Salter
Design Firm: Greenleaf Book Group

AMANDA HUDSON

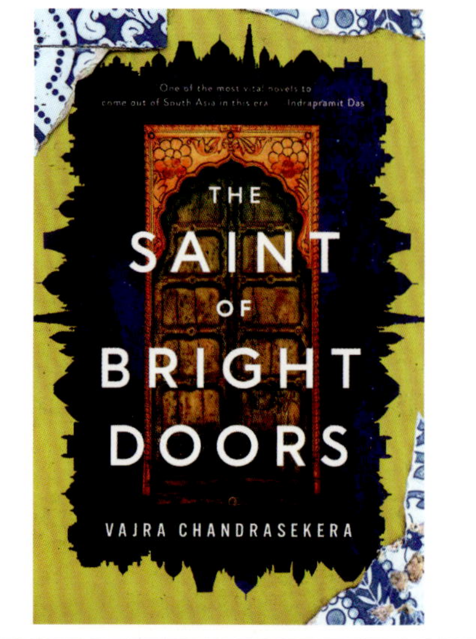

Title: The Saint of Bright Doors
Clients: Tor/Forge Books, Christine Foltzer
Design Firm: Faceout Studio

BRIAN PHILLIPS

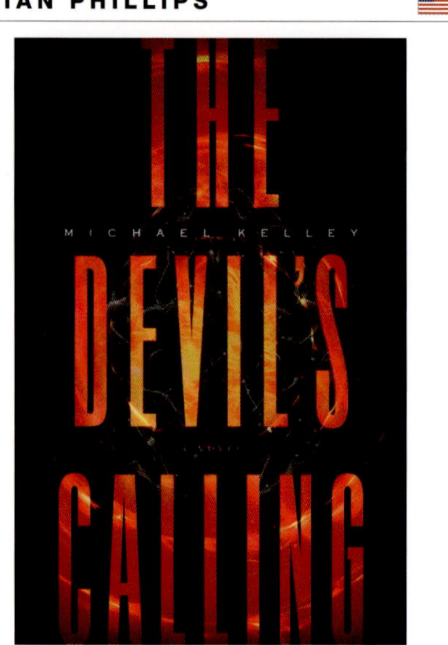

Title: The Devil's Calling
Client: Michael Kelley
Design Firm: Greenleaf Book Group

MOLLY VON BORSTEL

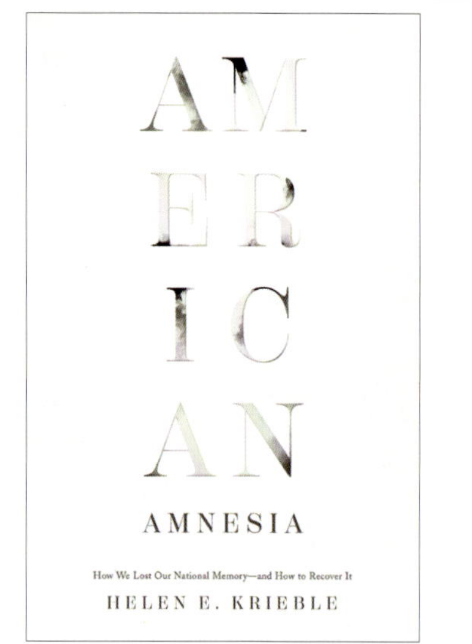

Title: American Amnesia
Client: Simon & Schuster
Design Firm: Faceout Studio

TIM GREEN

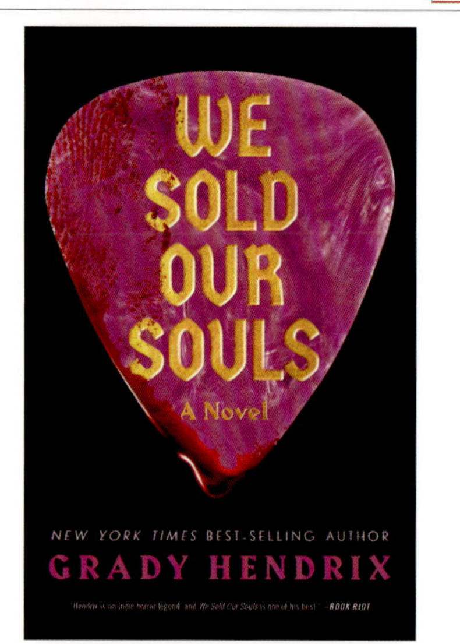

Title: We Sold Our Souls
Clients: Quirk Books, Andie Reid
Design Firm: Faceout Studio

TIM GREEN

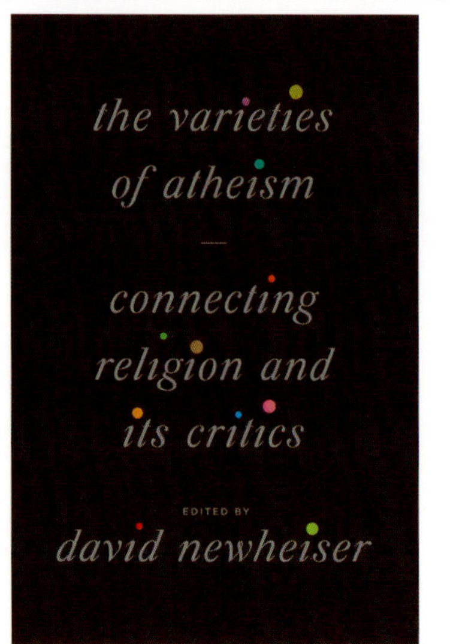

Title: The Varieties of Atheism
Client: University of Chicago Press
Design Firm: Faceout Studio

ANNA JORDAN

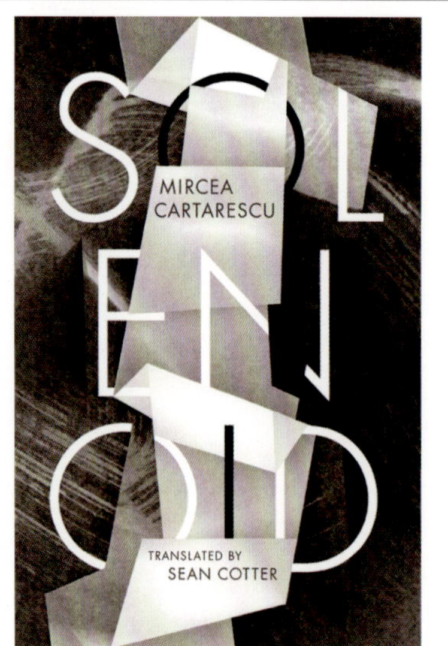

Title: Solenoid
Client: Deep Vellum
Design Firm: Anna Jordan

AMANDA HUDSON

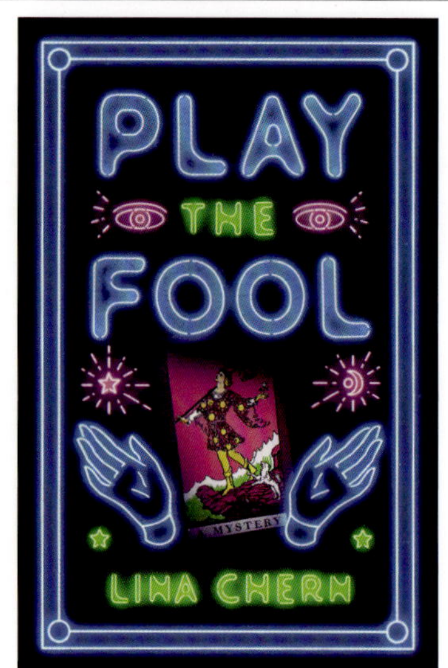

Title: Play the Fool
Clients: Penguin Random House, Sarah Horgan
Design Firm: Faceout Studio

HANNAH GASKAMP

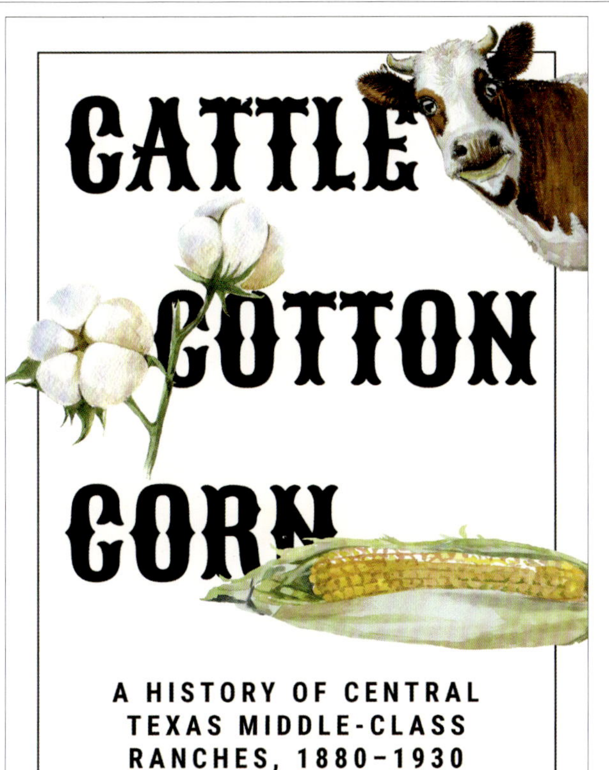

Title: Cattle Cotton Corn | **Client:** Self-initiated
Design Firm: Texas Tech University Press

PAUL NIELSEN

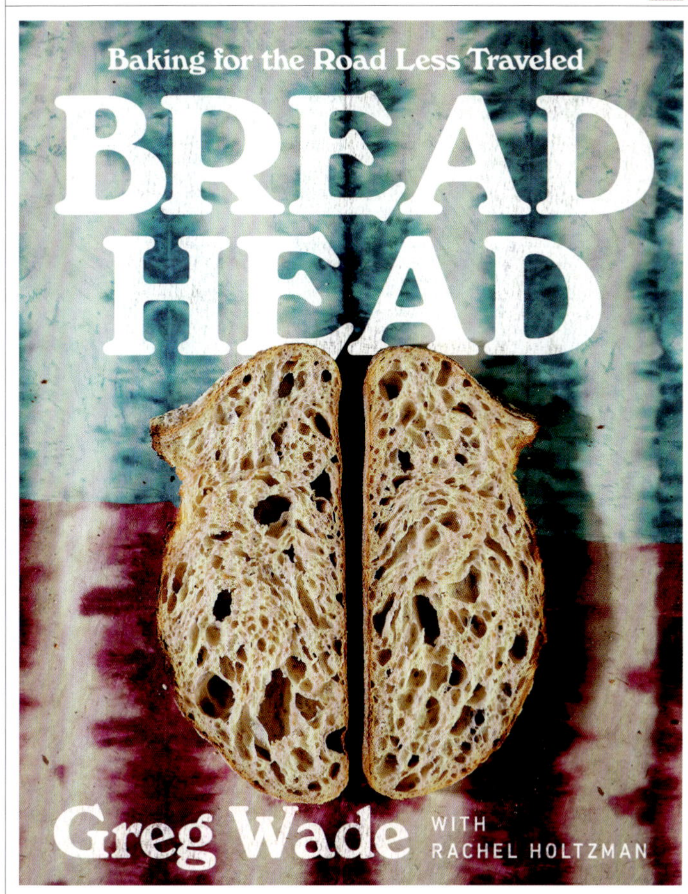

Title: Bread Head | **Client:** W.W. Norton
Design Firm: Faceout Studio

AMANDA HUDSON

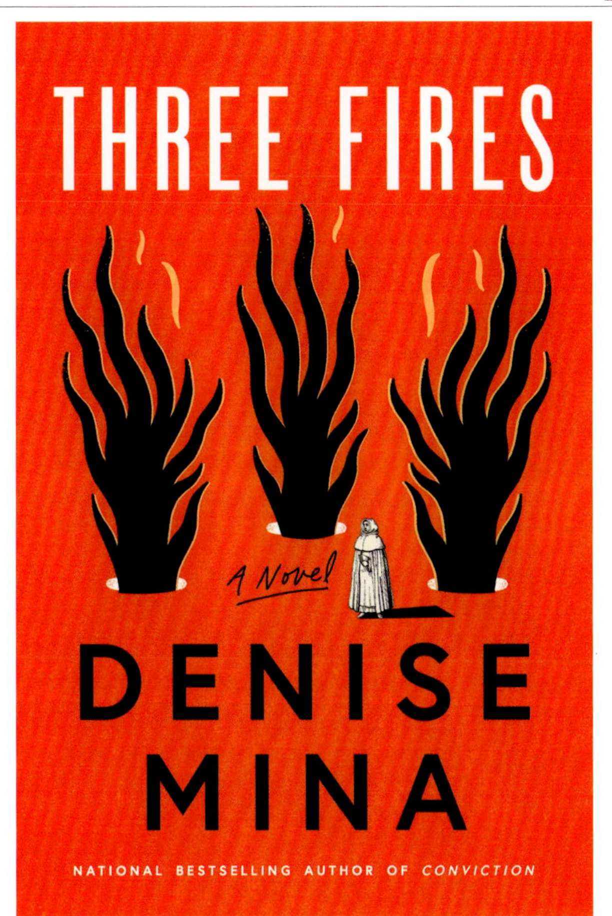

Title: Three Fires | **Clients:** Pegasus Books, Claiborne Hancock
Design Firm: Faceout Studio

DELFIN

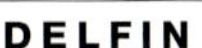

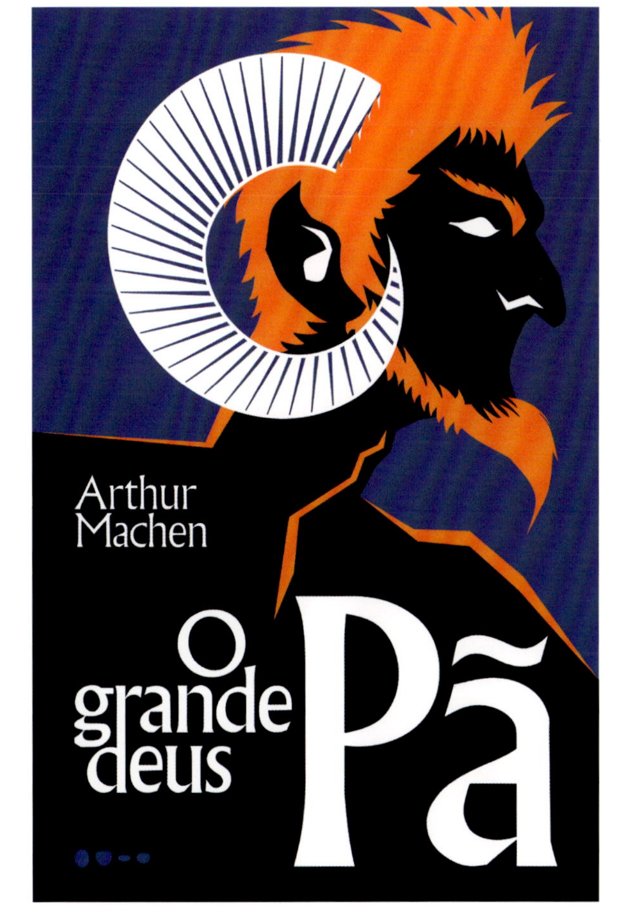

Title: O Grande Deus Pã (The Great God Pan)
Client: Editora Todavia (Brazil) | **Design Firm:** Studio DelRey

SJI ASSOCIATES

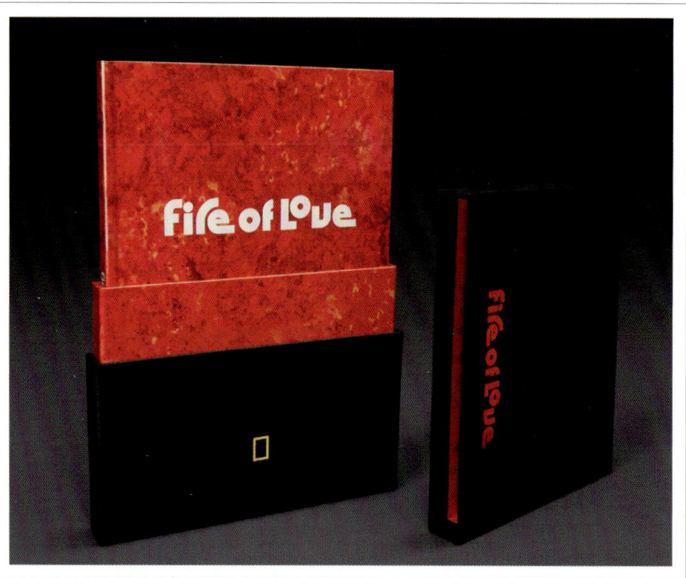

Title: FIRE OF LOVE | **Clients:** Chris Albert, National Geographic
Design Firm: SJI Associates

R. GEE, D. ALDRIDGE, J. HITE, Y. WHEELER

A tribute to
America's heroes
vizient

Title: A Tribute to America's Heroes | **Client:** Self-initiated
Design Firm: Vizient Inc.

MIRA NAKASHIMA

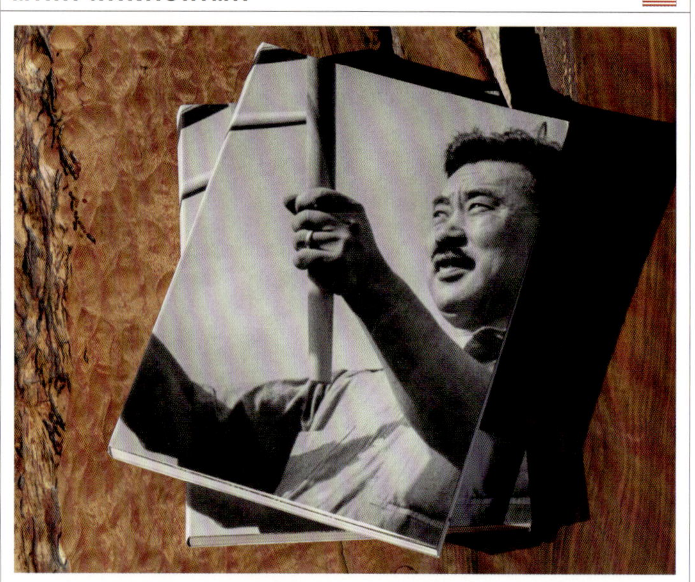

Title: Process Book | **Client:** George Nakashima Woodworkers
Design Firm: Asad Pervaiz

SHANTANU SUMAN

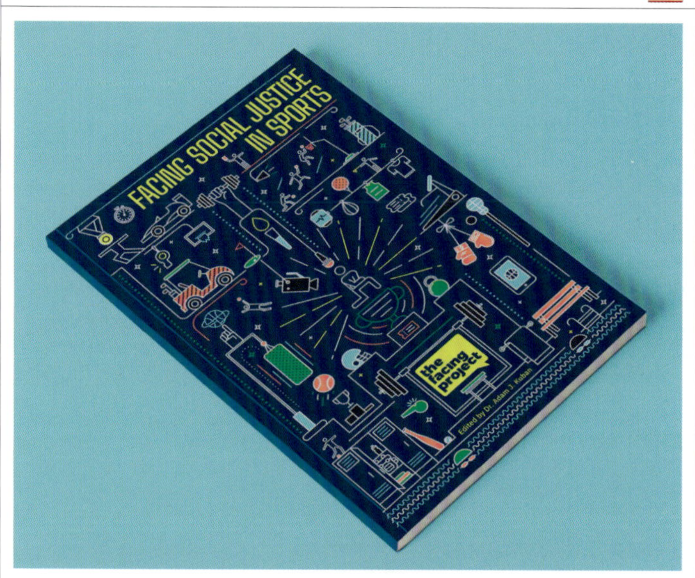

Title: Facing Social Justice in Sports Book Cover Design
Client: The Facing Project | **Design Firm:** Open Door Design Studio

CONTE IVANO BAJAMONTI

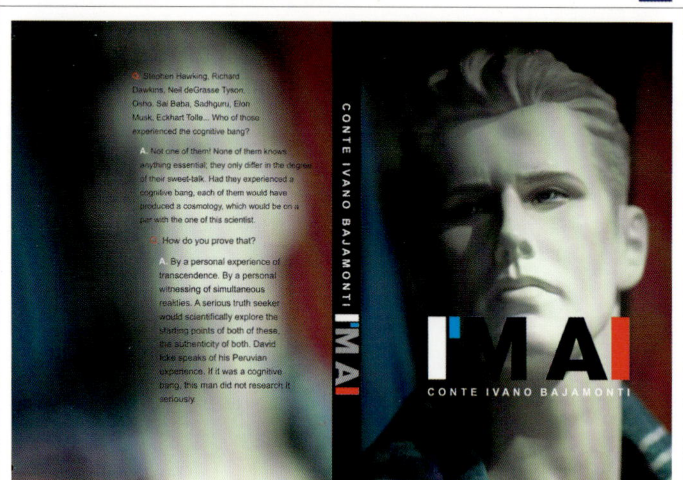

Title: Two Covers: "I'M AI" and "The Witness New York"
Client: Conte Ivano Bajamonti | **Design Firm:** STUDIO INTERNATIONAL

PATTI JUDD, JUDD BRAND MEDIA

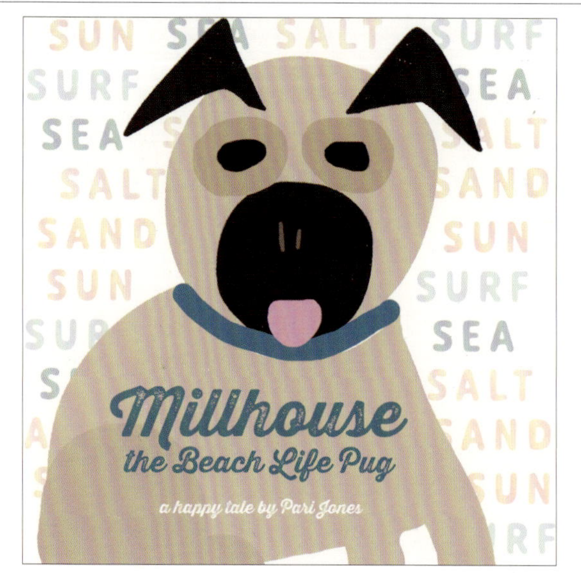

Title: Millhouse the Beach Life Pug - Book Cover
Client: Beach Town Studio | **Design Firm:** Judd Brand Media

MIRKO ILIC

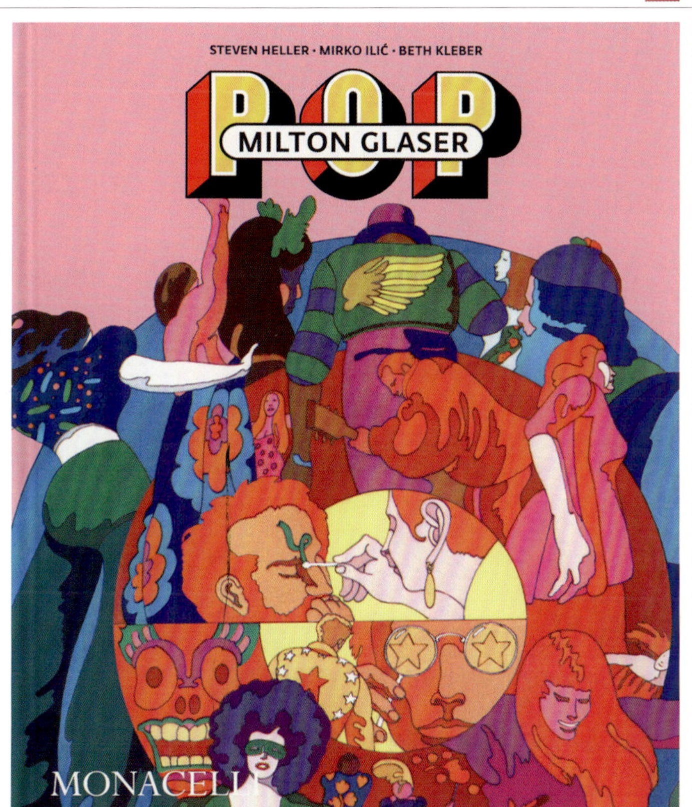

Title: Milton Glaser: Pop | **Client:** The Monacelli Press
Design Firm: Mirko Ilic Corp.

ANNA JORDAN

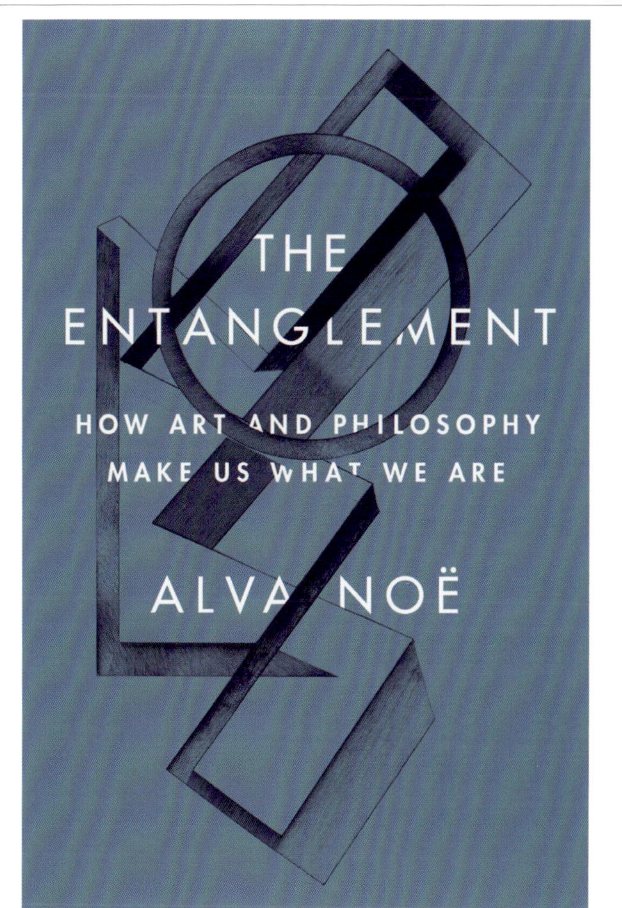

Title: The Entanglement | **Client:** Princeton University Press
Design Firm: Anna Jordan

DAVID LEAL, FILIPA OLIVEIRA

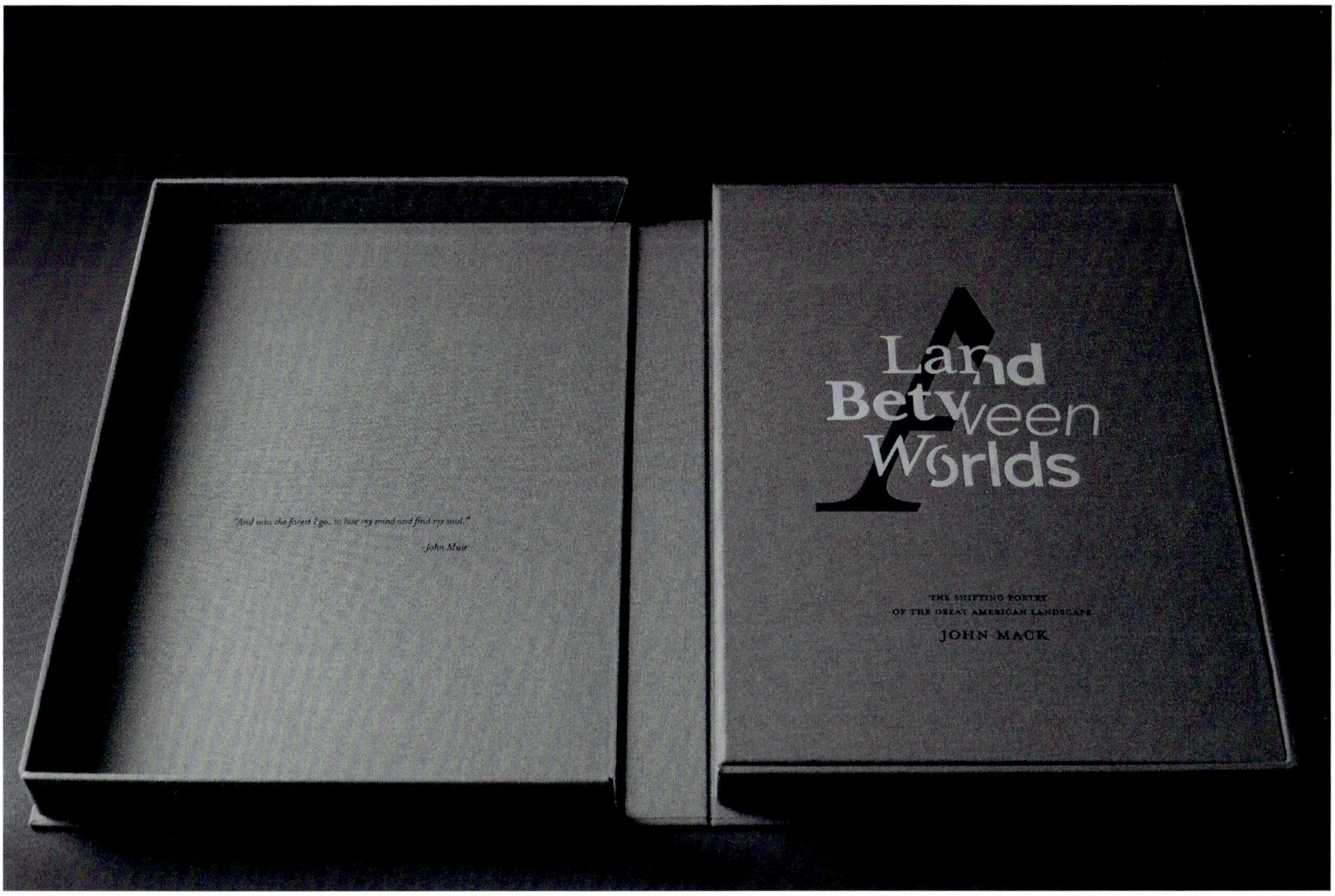

Title: A Land Between Worlds - The Shifting Poetry of the Great American Landscape | **Client:** Life Calling | **Design Firm:** Yup, It's a Hub

LISA SIRBAUGH CREATIVE

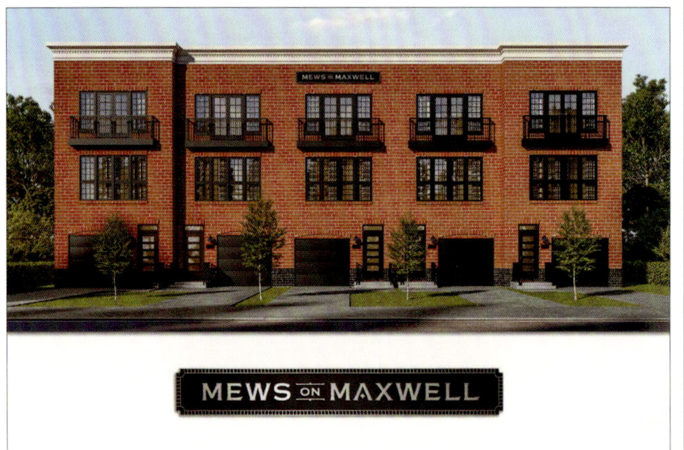

Title: Mews on Maxwell Branding | **Client:** JR Capital Build
Design Firm: Lisa Sirbaugh Creative

DANYANG MA

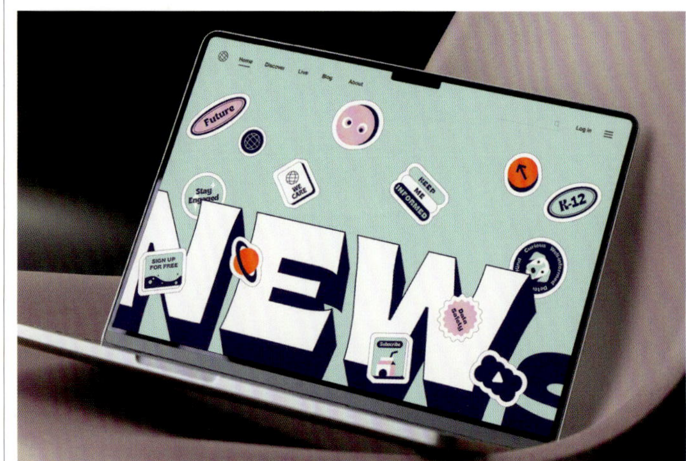

Title: New News Branding | **Client:** Youth Media International
Design Firm: Danyang Ma

WOLFF OLINS

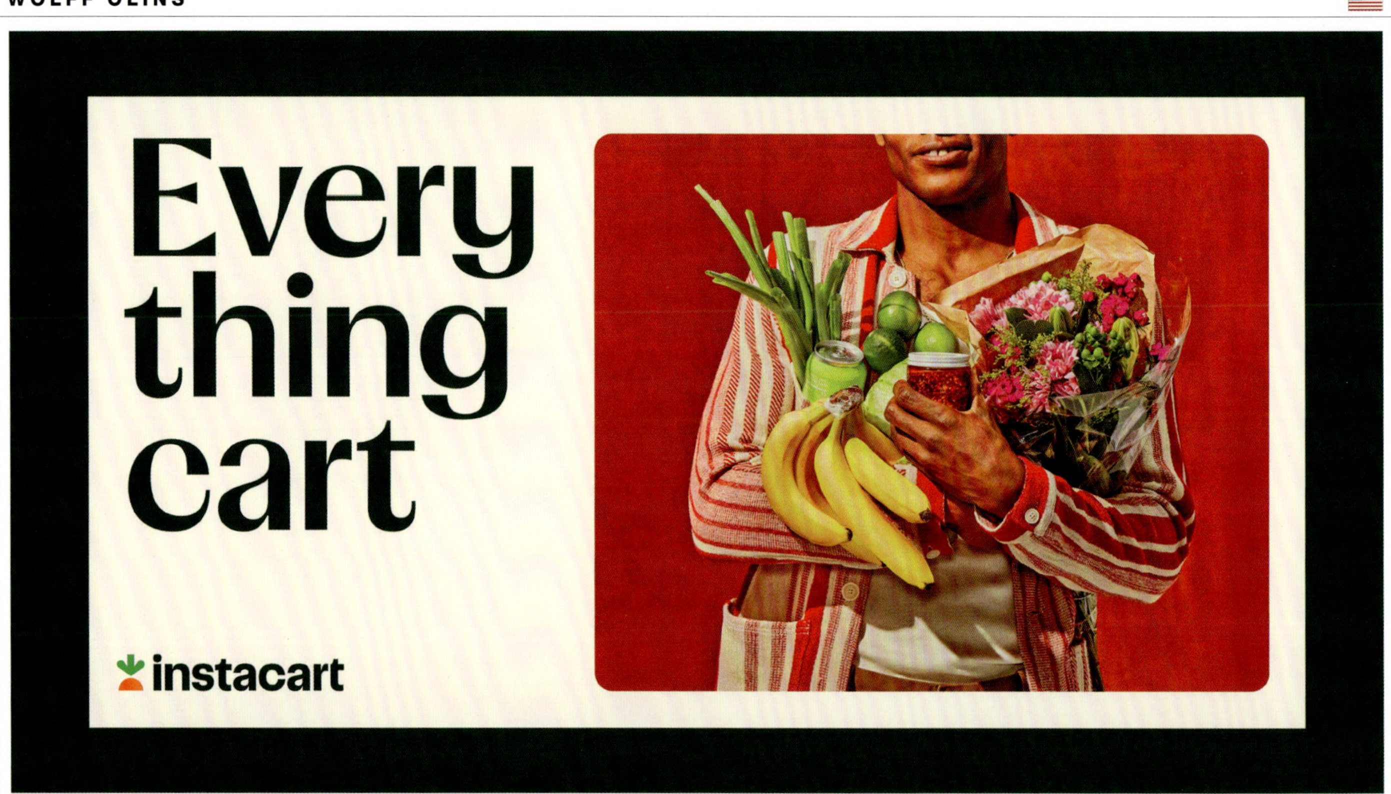

Title: Grounded in Their Roots, Growing Into the Future | **Client:** Instacart | **Design Firm:** Wolff Olins

ABBY GUIDO, BRYAN SATALINO

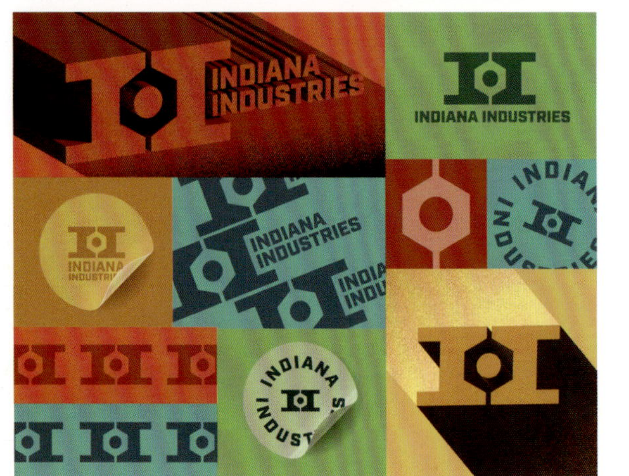

Title: Indiana Industries Branding | **Client:** Indiana Industries
Design Firm: Abby Ryan Design

AIMEE BABCOCK, NICK BONDURA (+11)

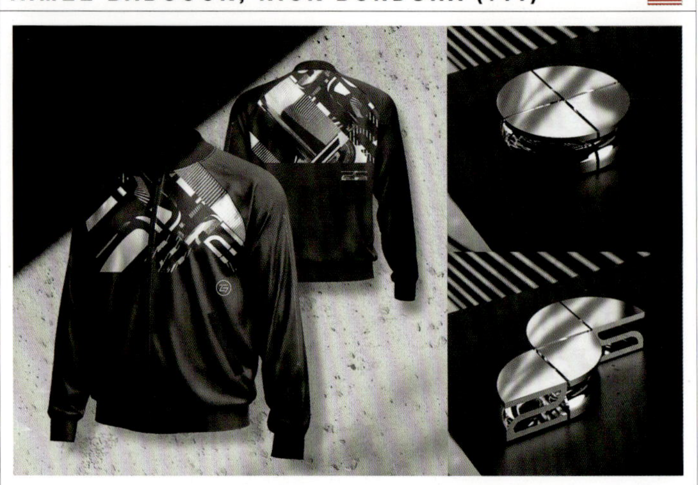

Title: TGD 25th Anniversary | **Client:** Self-initiated
Design Firm: TGD

TOBEN

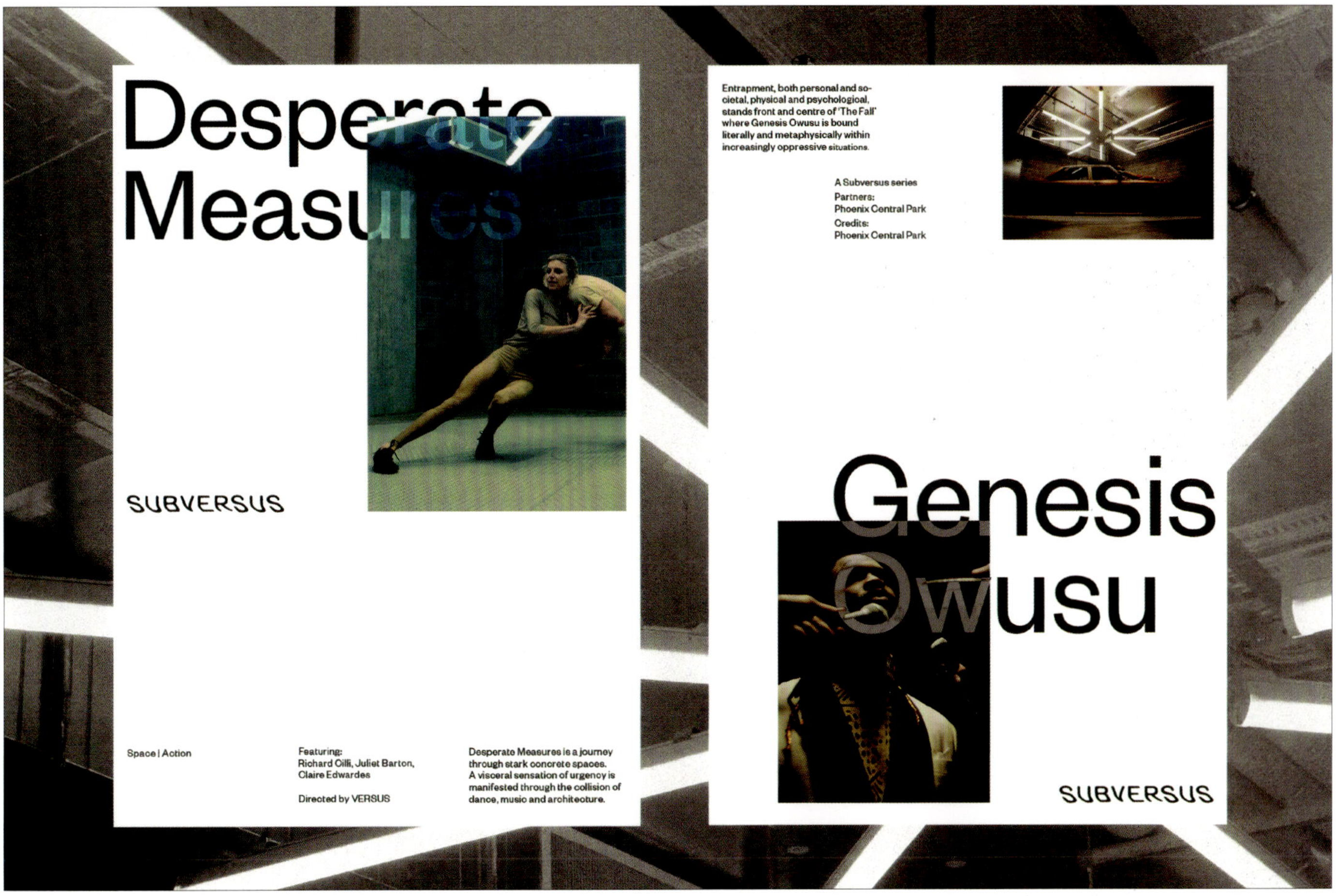

Title: Subversus | Client: Subversus | Design Firm: Toben

TSUYOSHI OMORI

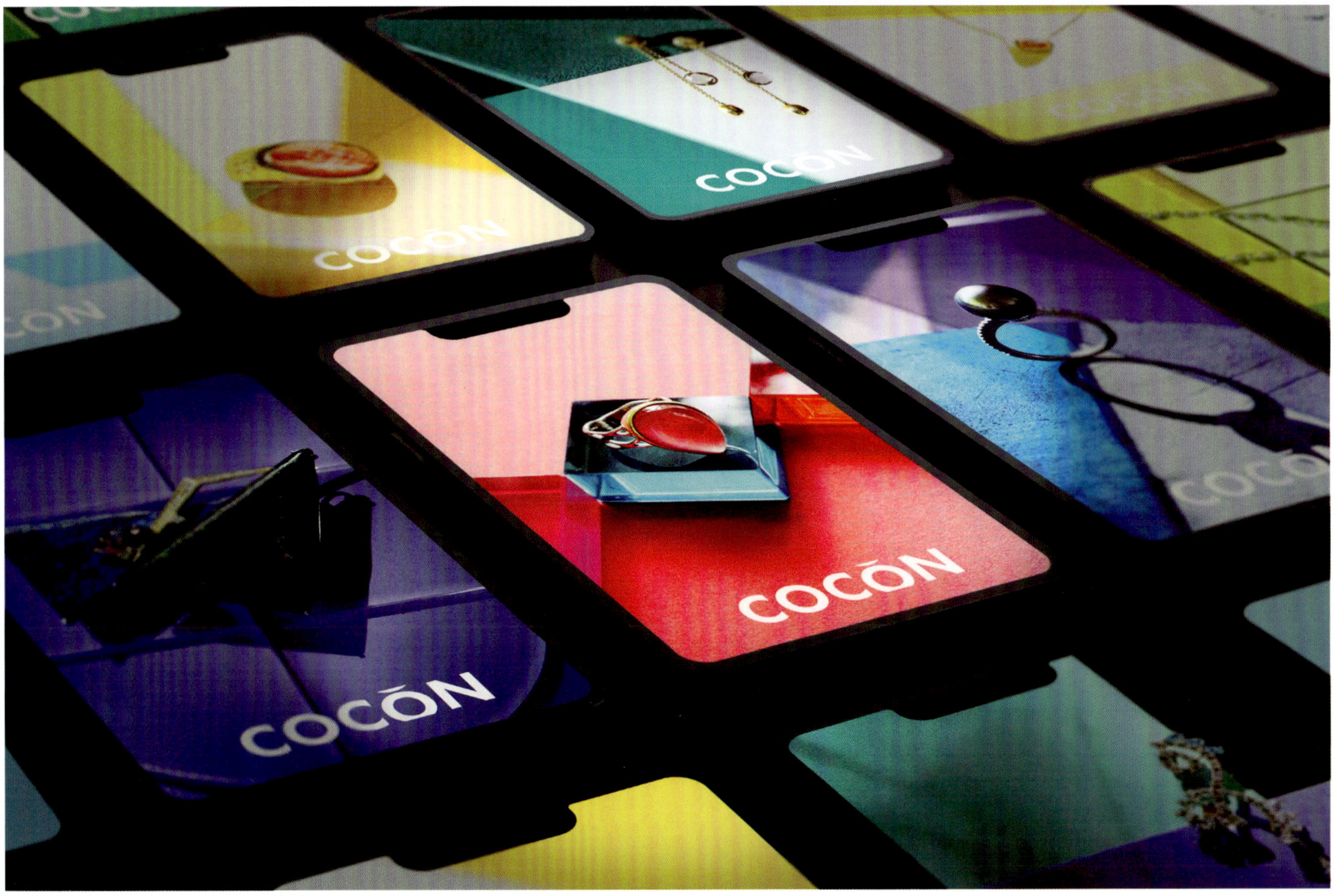

Title: COCON -THE NEW LIFE OF JEWELRY- | Client: WAKO Inc. | Design Firm: Triplet Design Inc.

BYRON DOWLER

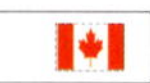

Title: Branding
Client: Rimex Supply
Design Firm: Coastlines Creative Group

BRAND BAR COMMUNICATIONS

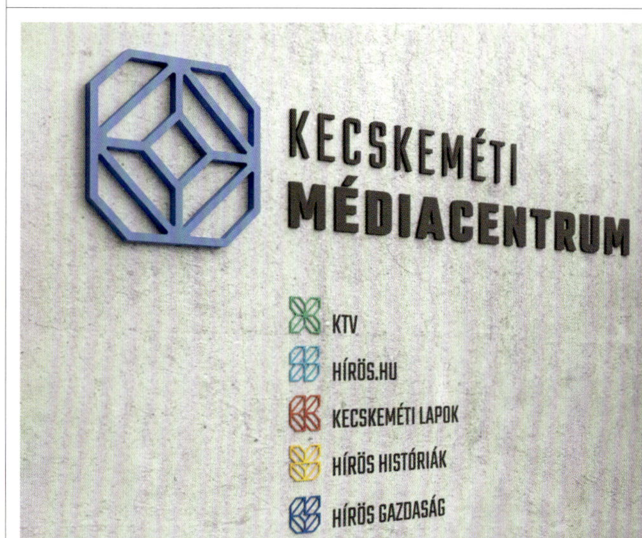

Title: Stained Glass with a Spin - Logo System
Client: Media Center of Kecskemet
Design Firm: Brand Bar Communications

XIAOXIAO MA, ZILI MA

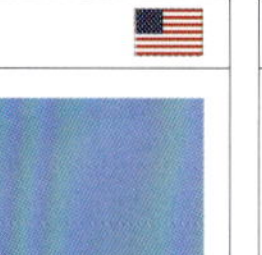

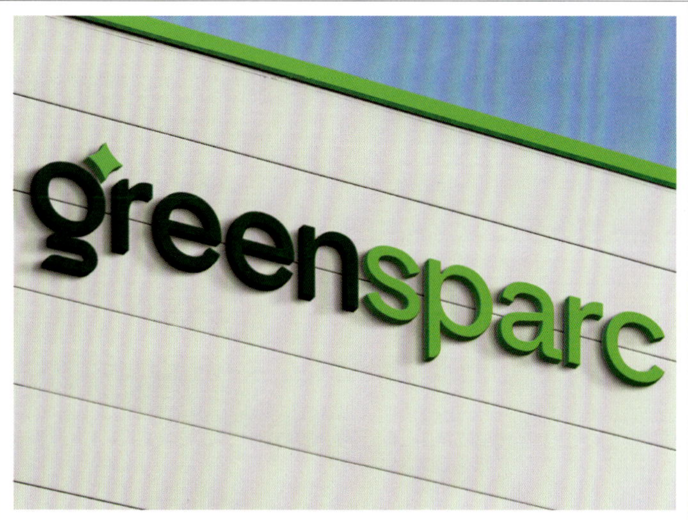

Title: Greensparc
Client: Greensparc
Design Firm: Noise 13

KOREAN CULTURAL CENTER OSAKA

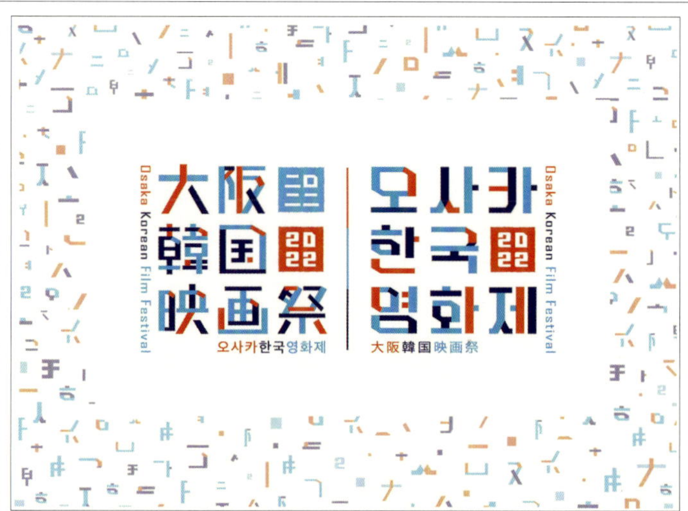

Title: Osaka Korean Film Festival Logo Design
Client: Korean Cultural Center OSAKA
Design Firm: KINDAI Graphic Art Course Laboratory

TRACTION FACTORY

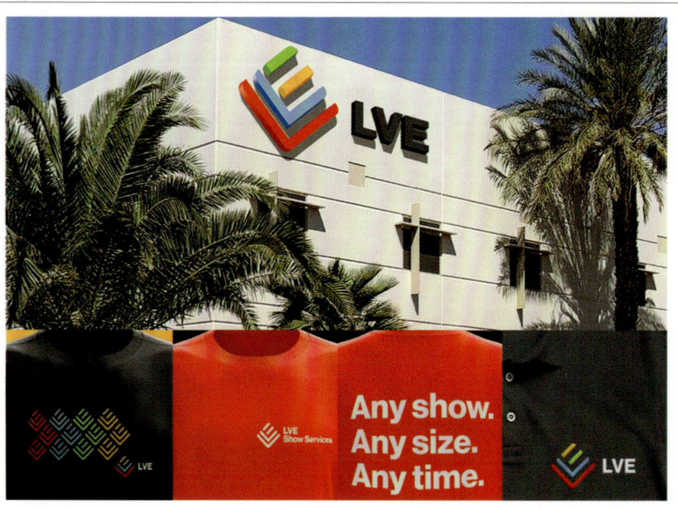

Title: LVE Identity System
Client: Las Vegas Expo
Design Firm: Traction Factory

TEIGA, STUDIO.

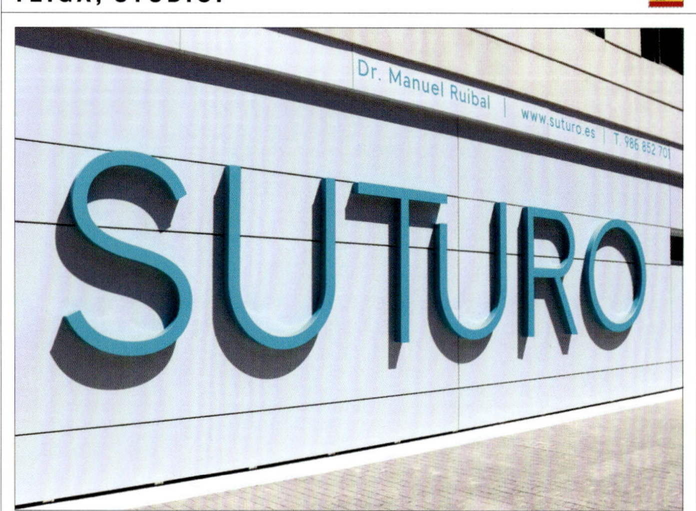

Title: Suturo
Client: Suturo
Design Firm: Teiga, Studio.

COLEY PORTER BELL, MARTIN GUITAR

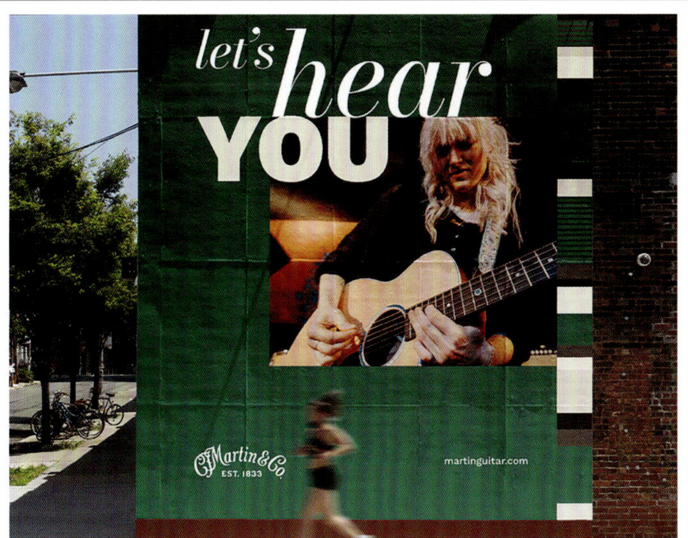

Title: Martin Guitar Rebrand
Client: Martin Guitar
Design Firm: Coley Porter Bell

STUDIO EDUARDO AIRES

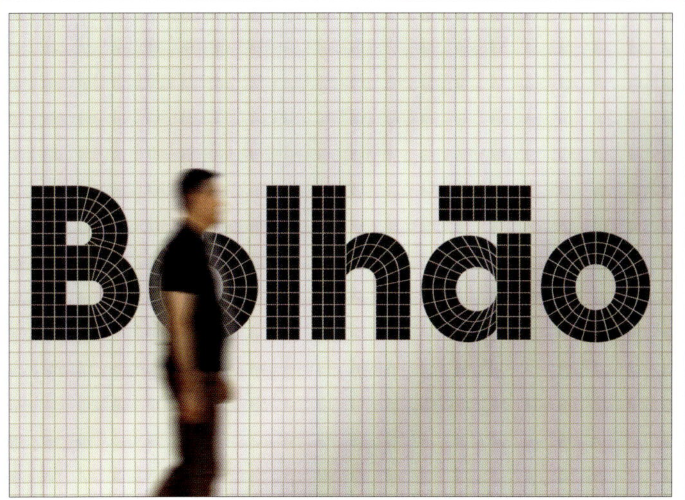

Title: Bolhão, Porto's Historic Market
Client: GO Porto - Porto City Hall
Design Firm: Studio Eduardo Aires

SHARON LLOYD MCLAUGHLIN

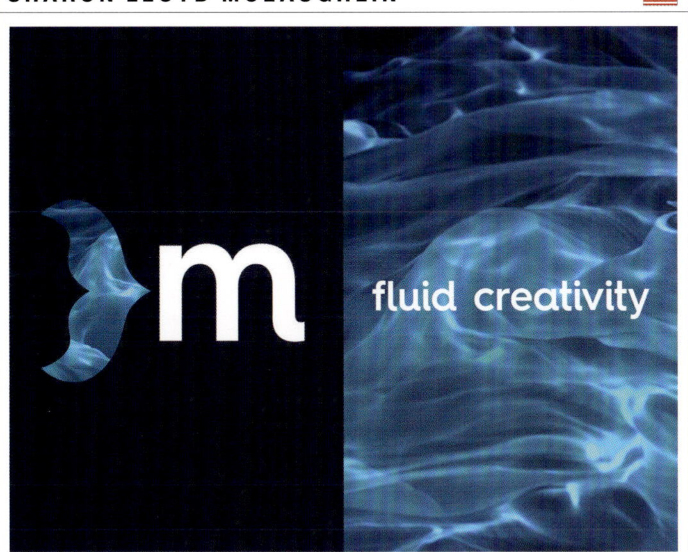

Title: Mermaid, Inc. | Fluid Creativity Branding
Client: Self-initiated
Design Firm: Mermaid, Inc.

ARIEL FREANER

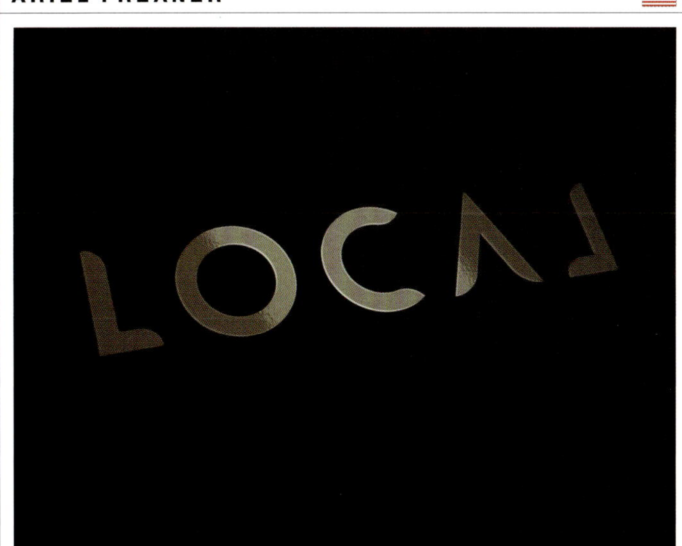

Title: LOCAL Architects Branding
Client: LOCAL Architects
Design Firm: Freaner Creative & Design

ARIEL FREANER

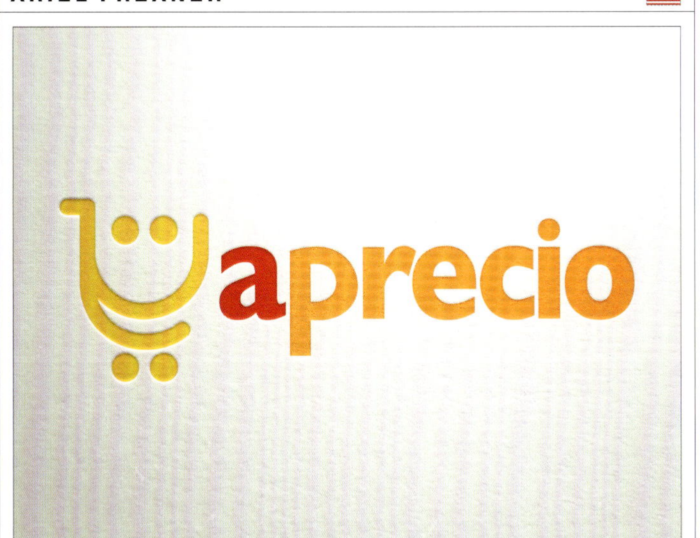

Title: Aprecio Supermarket Stores
Clients: Aprecio, Rosella Fimbres
Design Firm: Freaner Creative & Design

CLINTON CARLSON

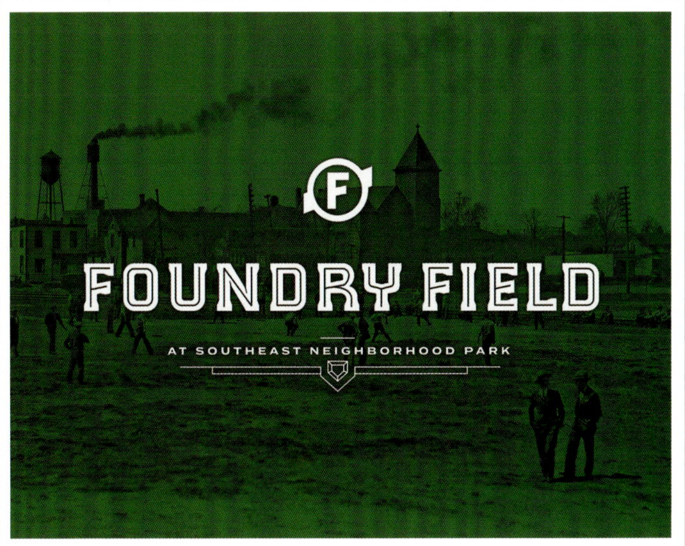

Title: Foundry Field: The Story of Race, Representation, Access, and Baseball in South Bend, Indiana | **Client:** Foundry Field
Design Firm: Clinton Carlson Design | University of Notre Dame

GAETANO GRIZZANTI, GIANCARLO TOSONI

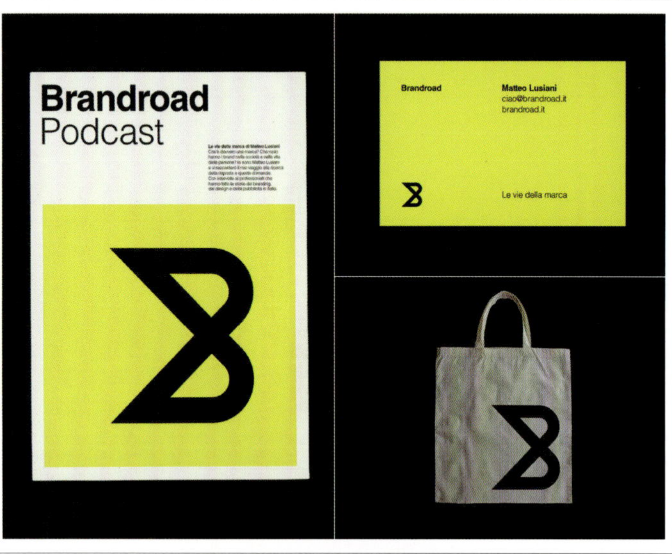

Title: Brandroad: An Italian Podcast
Client: Matteo Lusiani
Design Firm: Univisual SRL

HISA IDE, TOSHIAKI IDE

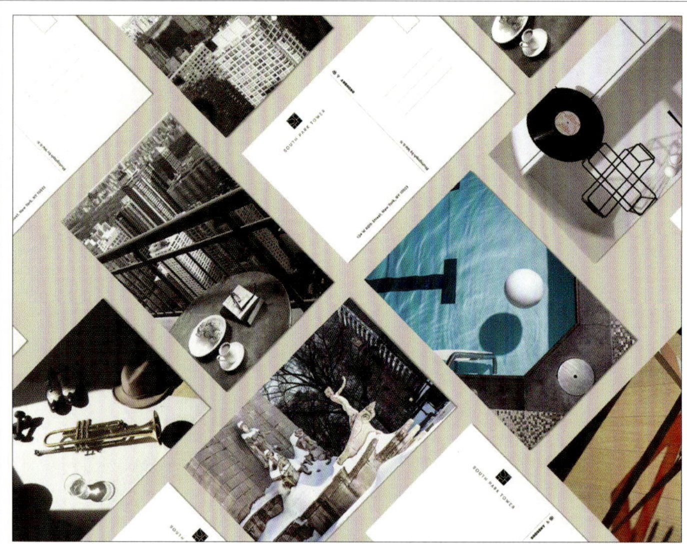

Title: South Park Tower Postcards
Client: Brodsky
Design Firm: IF Studio

LISA SIRBAUGH CREATIVE

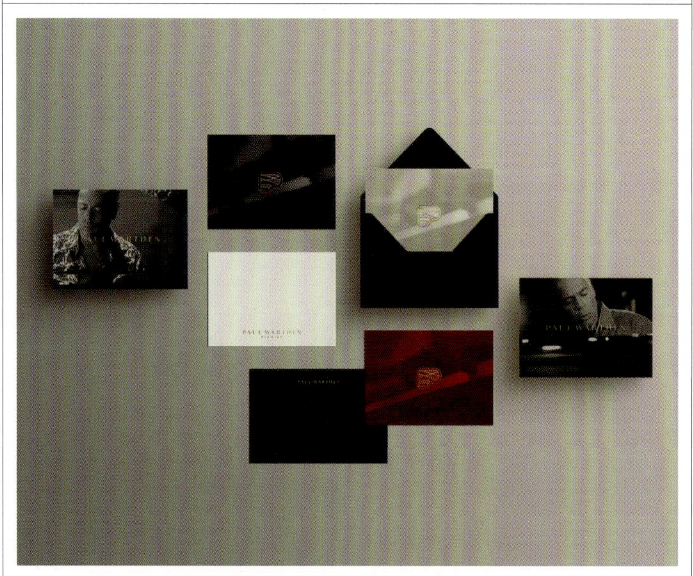

Title: Pianist Paul Warthen Branding | **Client:** Paul Warthen
Design Firm: Lisa Sirbaugh Creative

JEFF ANDERSON, AIMEE BABCOCK(+13)

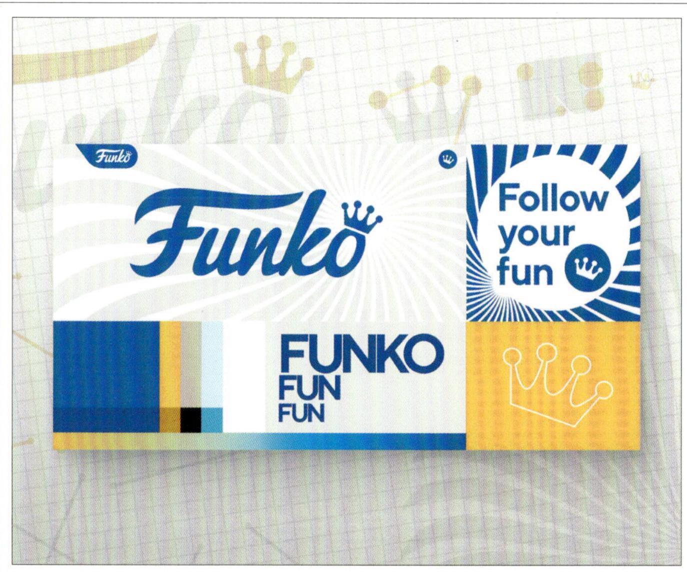

Title: Funko Brand Refresh | **Clients:** Funko, Dave Bere, Hillary Gray
Design Firm: TGD

MAYA KOPYTMAN

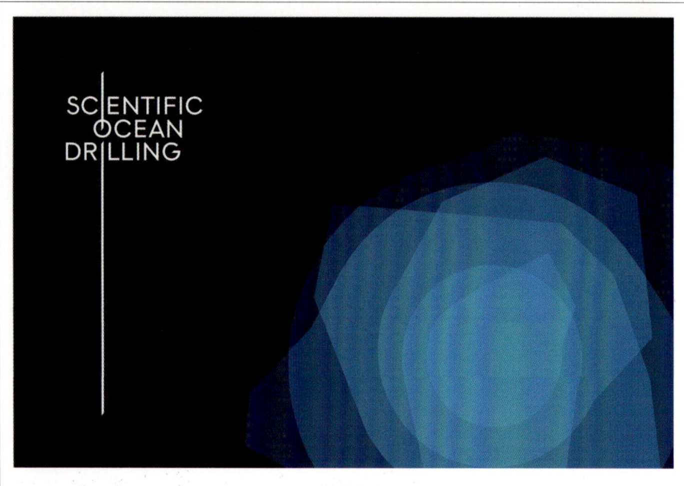

Title: US Science Support Program Branding
Client: US Science Support Program
Design Firm: C&G Partners

SHARON LLOYD MCLAUGHLIN

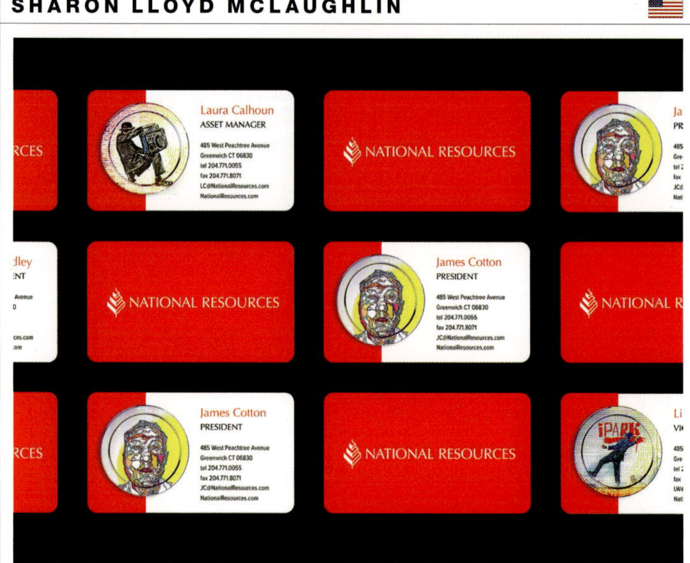

Title: National Resources Branding
Client: National Resources
Design Firm: Mermaid, Inc.

JOÃO NUNES, ANA MENEZES, SUSANA NUNES, MARIANA MELO

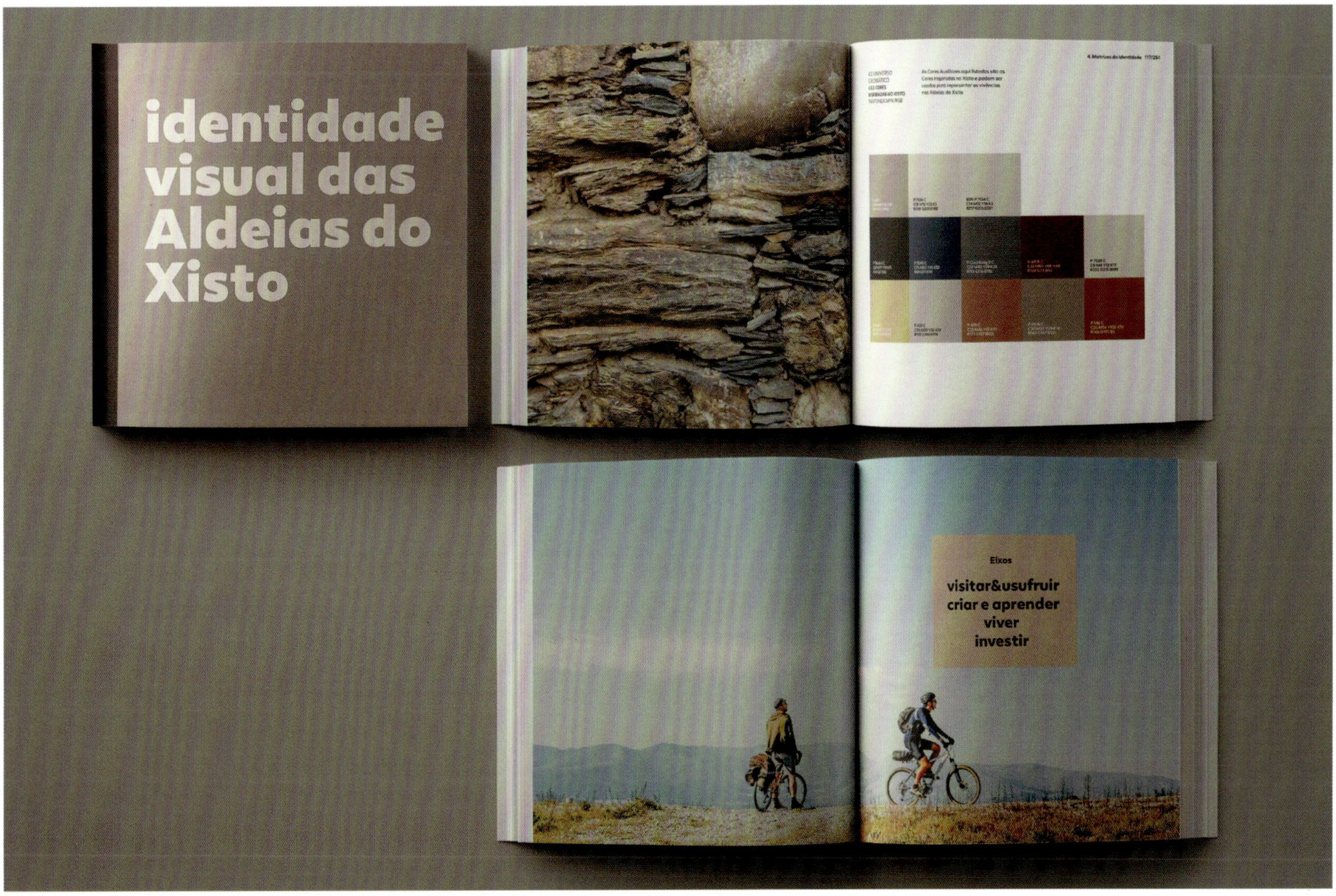

Title: Rebranding ADXTUR | **Client:** ADXTUR – Schist Villages Tourism Development Agency | **Design Firm:** Atelier Nunes e Pã, lda

STUDIO EDUARDO AIRES

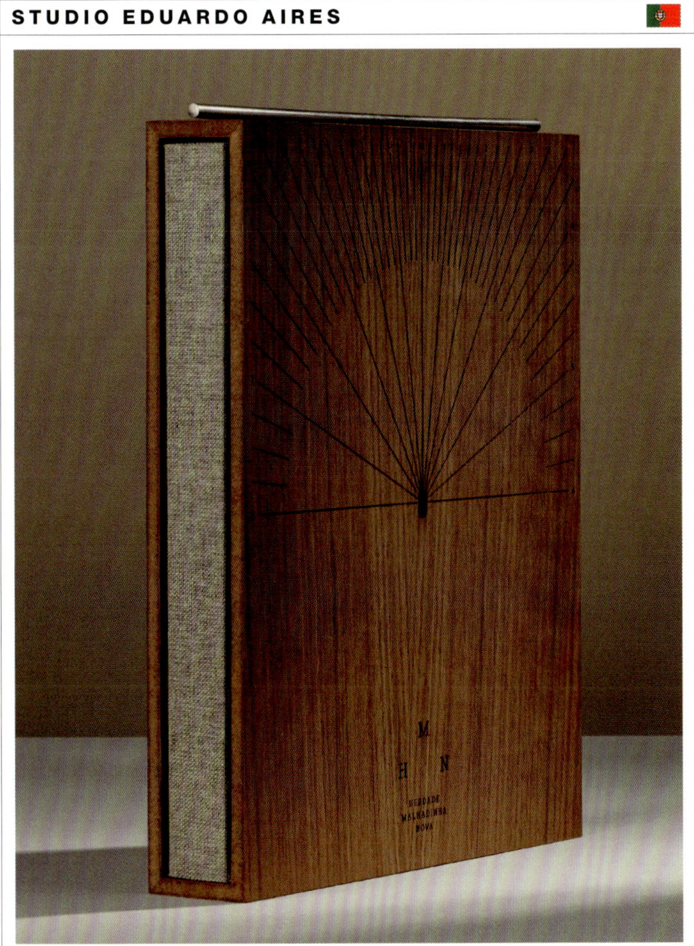

Title: Herdade da Malhadinha Nova | **Client:** Herdade da Malhadinha Nova
Design Firm: Studio Eduardo Aires

MATT ELLIS

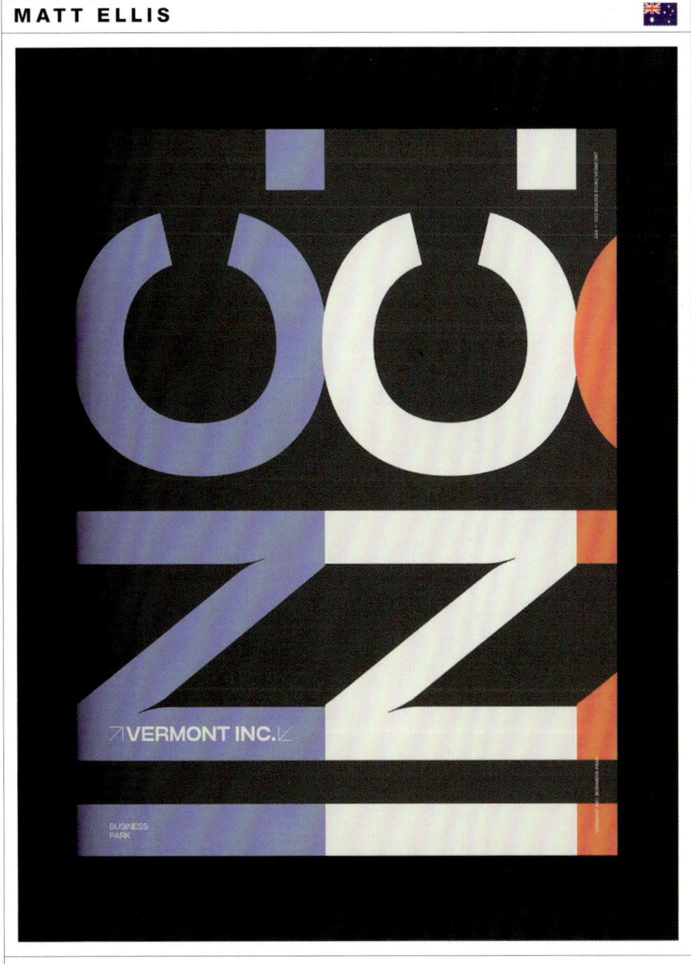

Title: Vermont Inc. | **Client:** Ledlin Develop
Design Firm: Hoyne

ROSE

Title: The Royal Parks – Brand Identity | Client: The Royal Parks
Design Firm: Rose

TOBEN

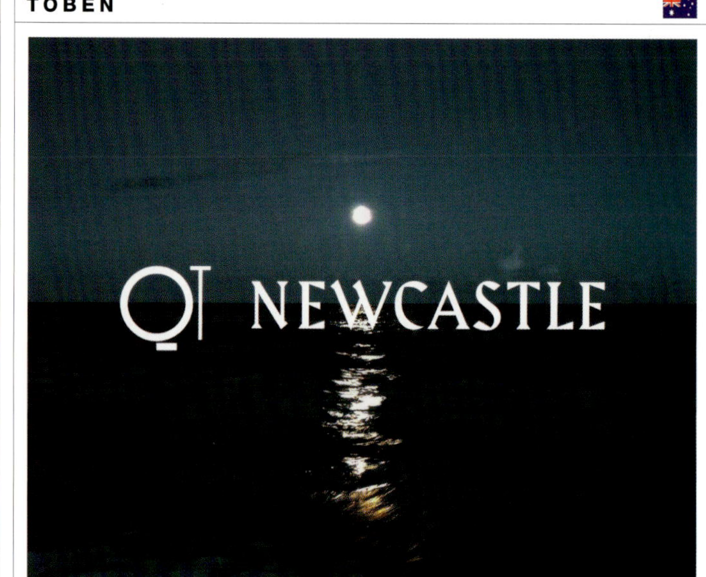

Title: QT Newcastle | Client: QT Hotels & Resorts
Design Firm: Toben

TOTAL DESIGN

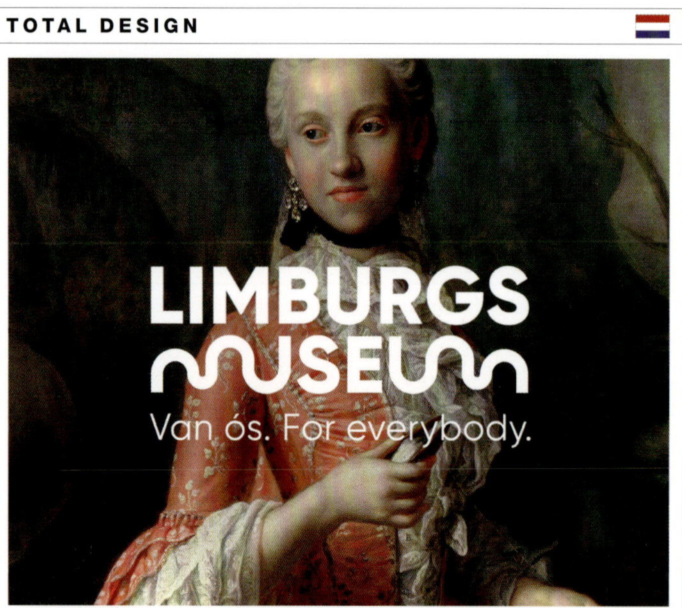

Title: Limburgs Museum – Van ós. For Everybody.
Client: Limburgs Museum | Design Firm: Total Design

LAFAYETTE AMERICAN

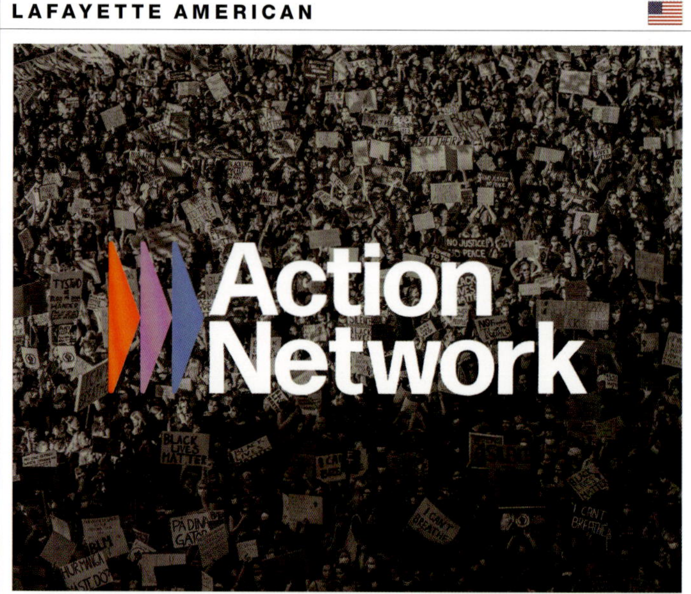

Title: Action Network Branding
Client: Action Network | Design Firm: Lafayette American

KEN MCVEAGH

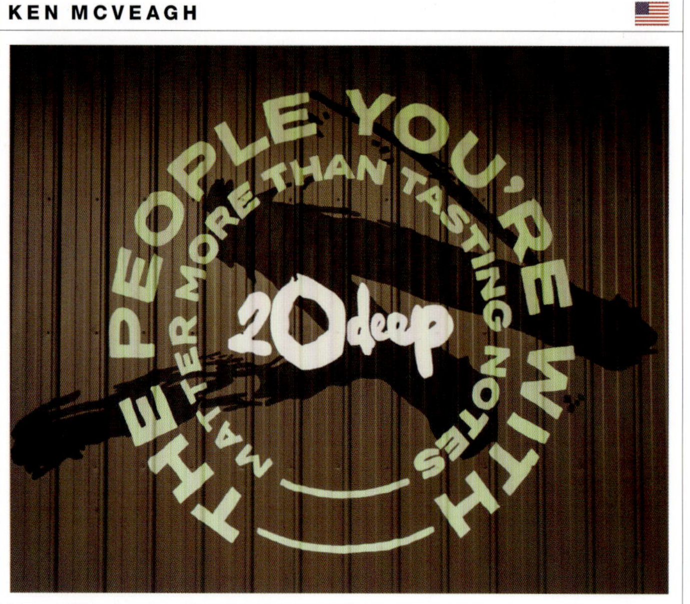

Title: 20 Deep Winery Brand Identity | Client: 20 Deep Winery
Design Firm: Truth Collective

NICHOLE TRIONFI

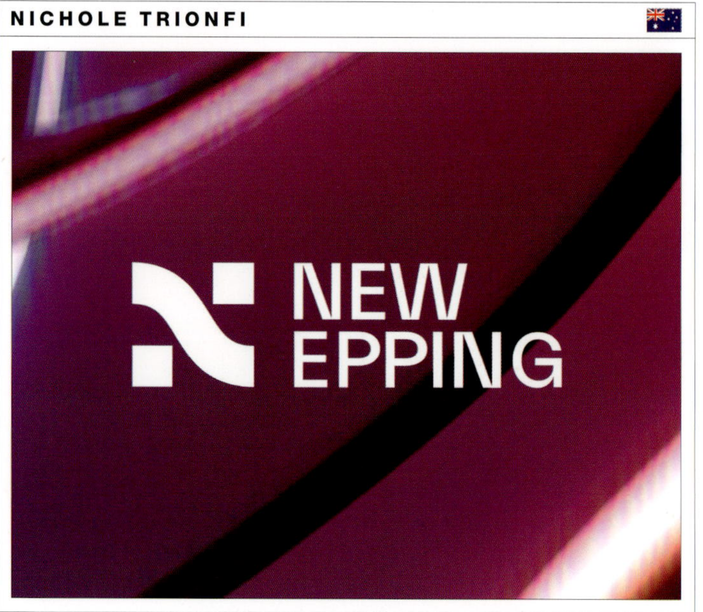

Title: New Epping | Client: Riverlee
Design Firm: Hoyne

JOHN BALL, LAUREN LAMB, ANIQUE MAUTNER

Title: San Diego Foundation Brand Identity
Client: San Diego Foundation | **Design Firm:** MiresBall

BOTOND VÖRÖS

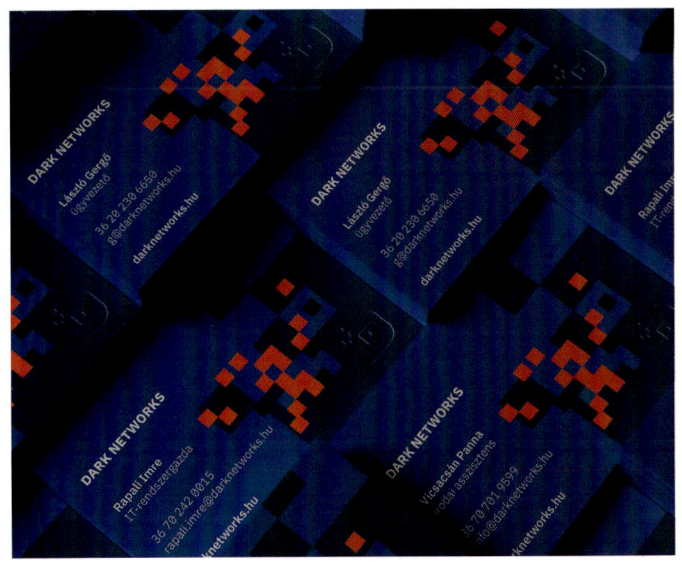

Title: Dark Networks
Client: Dark Networks | **Design Firm:** Botond Vörös

ASHA & CO.

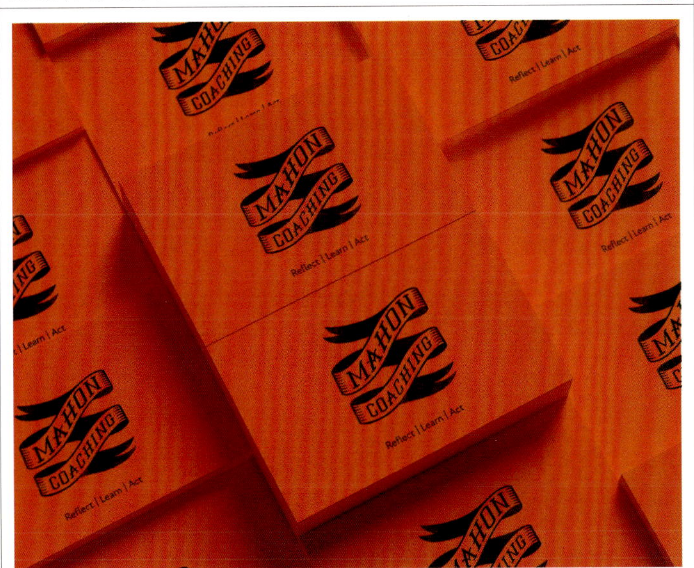

Title: Mahon Coaching | **Client:** Rose Mahon
Design Firm: ASHA & Co.

ENTRO

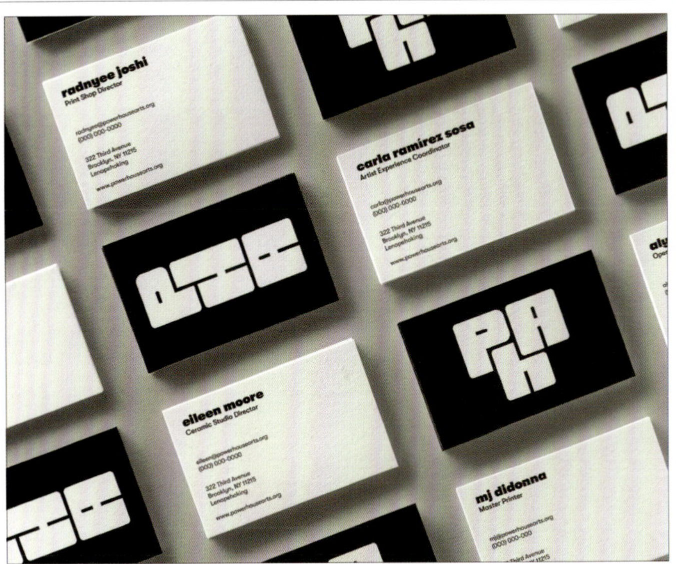

Title: Powerhouse Arts Rebrand | **Client:** Powerhouse Arts
Design Firm: Entro

LISA SIRBAUGH CREATIVE

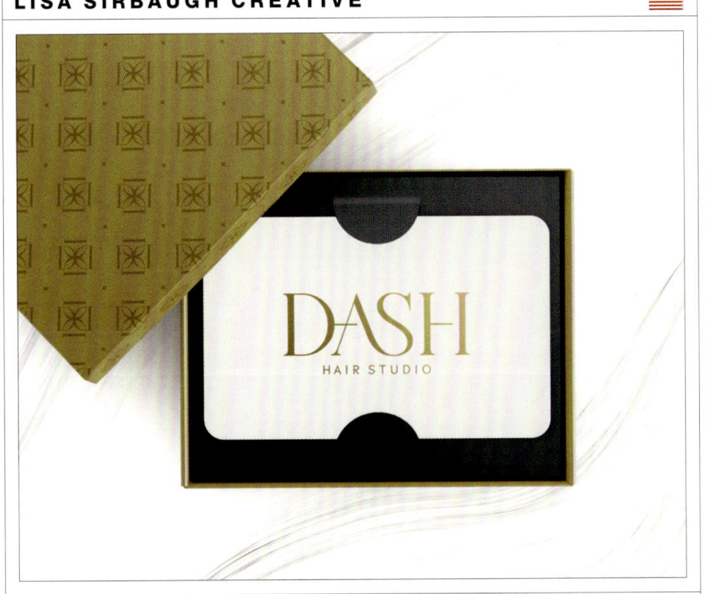

Title: Dash Hair Studio Branding
Client: Dash Hair Studio | **Design Firm:** Lisa Sirbaugh Creative

NATHAN PLAISTED

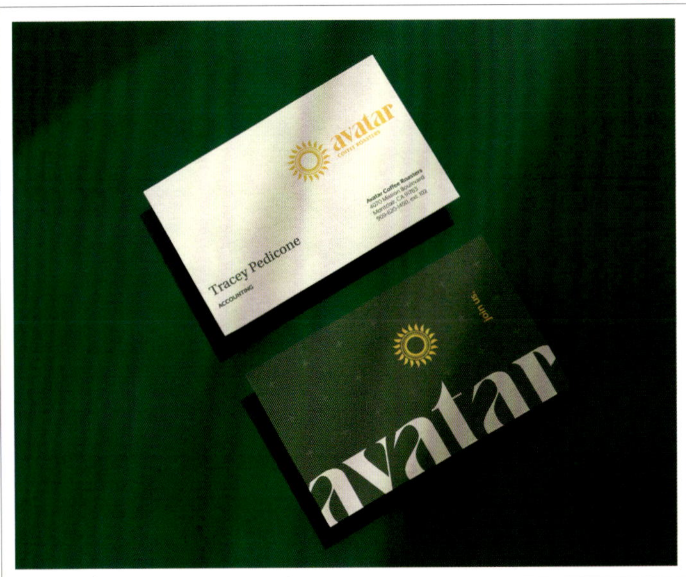

Title: Renewing Rituals to Uplift Communities Locally and at Origin
Client: Avatar Coffee Roasters | **Design Firm:** Playstead

ELMWOOD

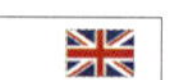

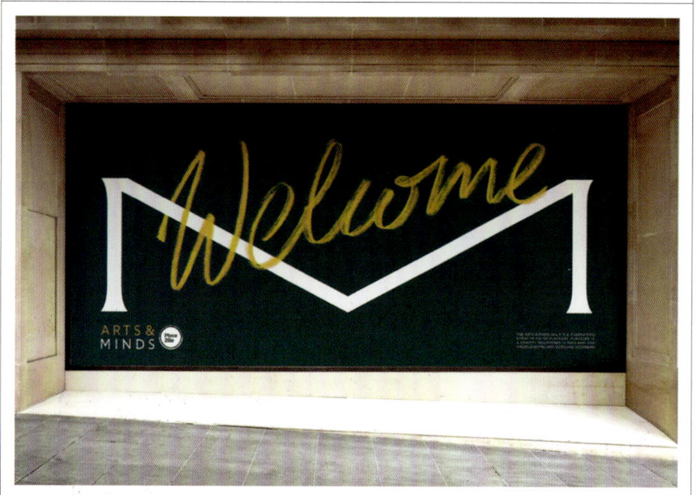

Title: Place2Be | **Client:** Place2Be | **Design Firm:** Elmwood

MEGHAN MURRAY

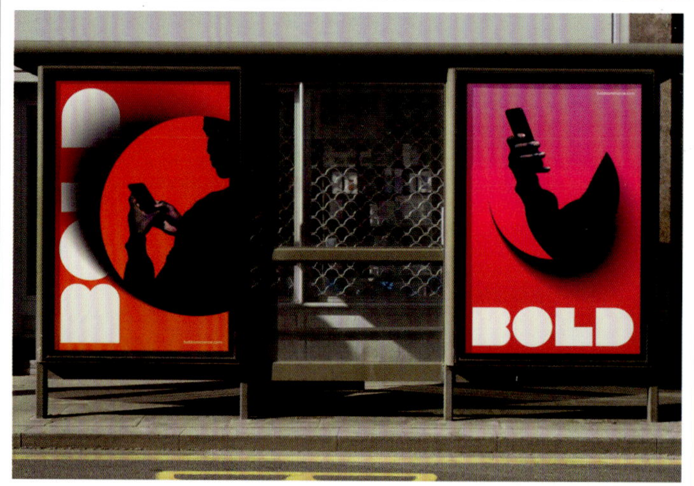

Title: Bold Rebrand | **Client:** Bold | **Design Firm:** Matchstic

CHRIS GARVEY

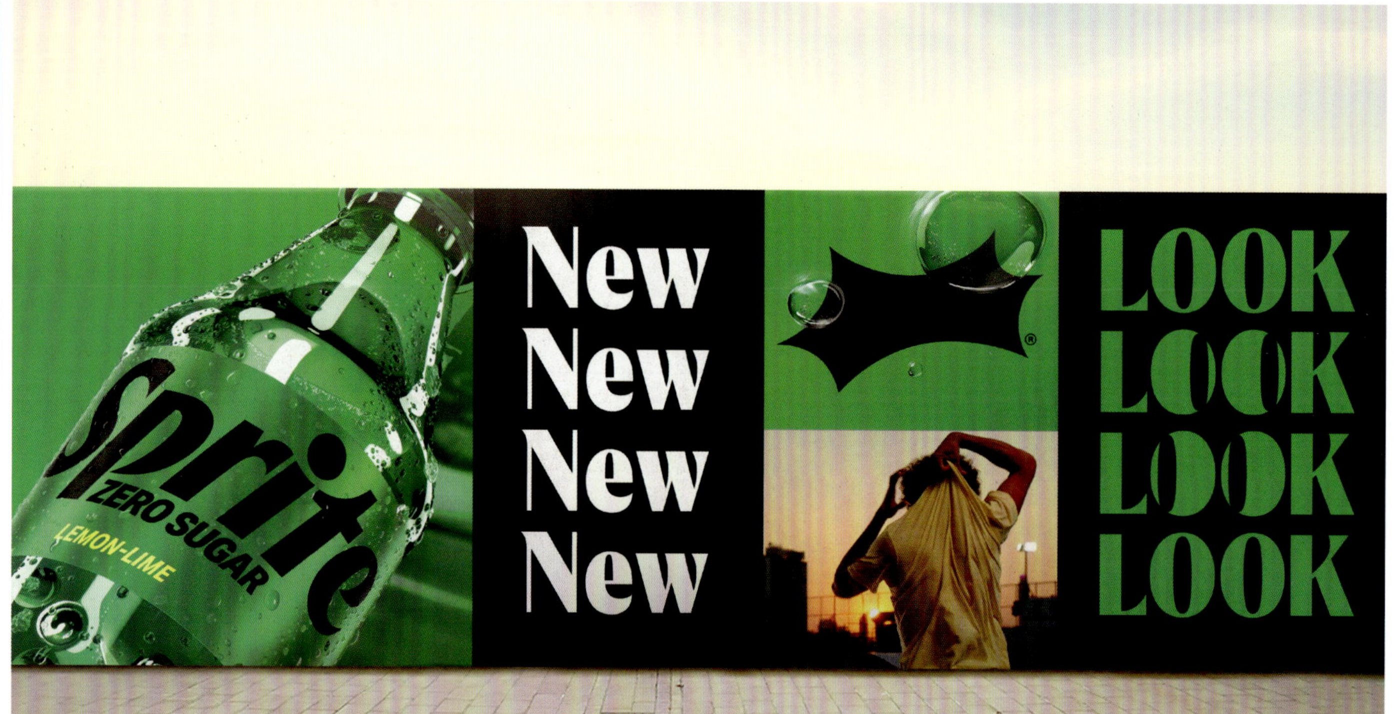

Title: Sprite VIS | **Client:** Coca Cola | **Design Firm:** Turner Duckworth: London, San Francisco & New York

RESOURCE BRANDING

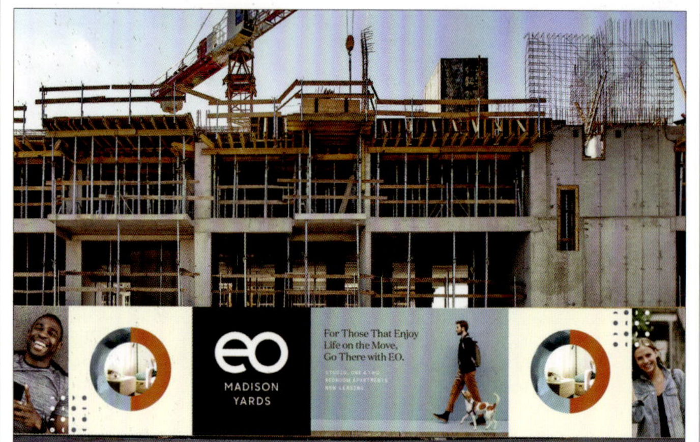

Title: EO Madison Yards Brand Identity
Client: Gilbane Development Company
Design Firm: Resource Branding

ELAINE CHAW, JEROME HARRIS

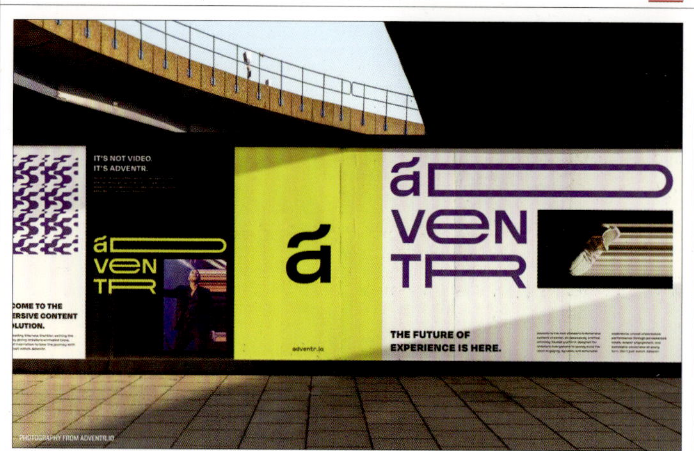

Title: Adventr
Client: Adventr
Design Firm: Noise 13

JOE ROSS

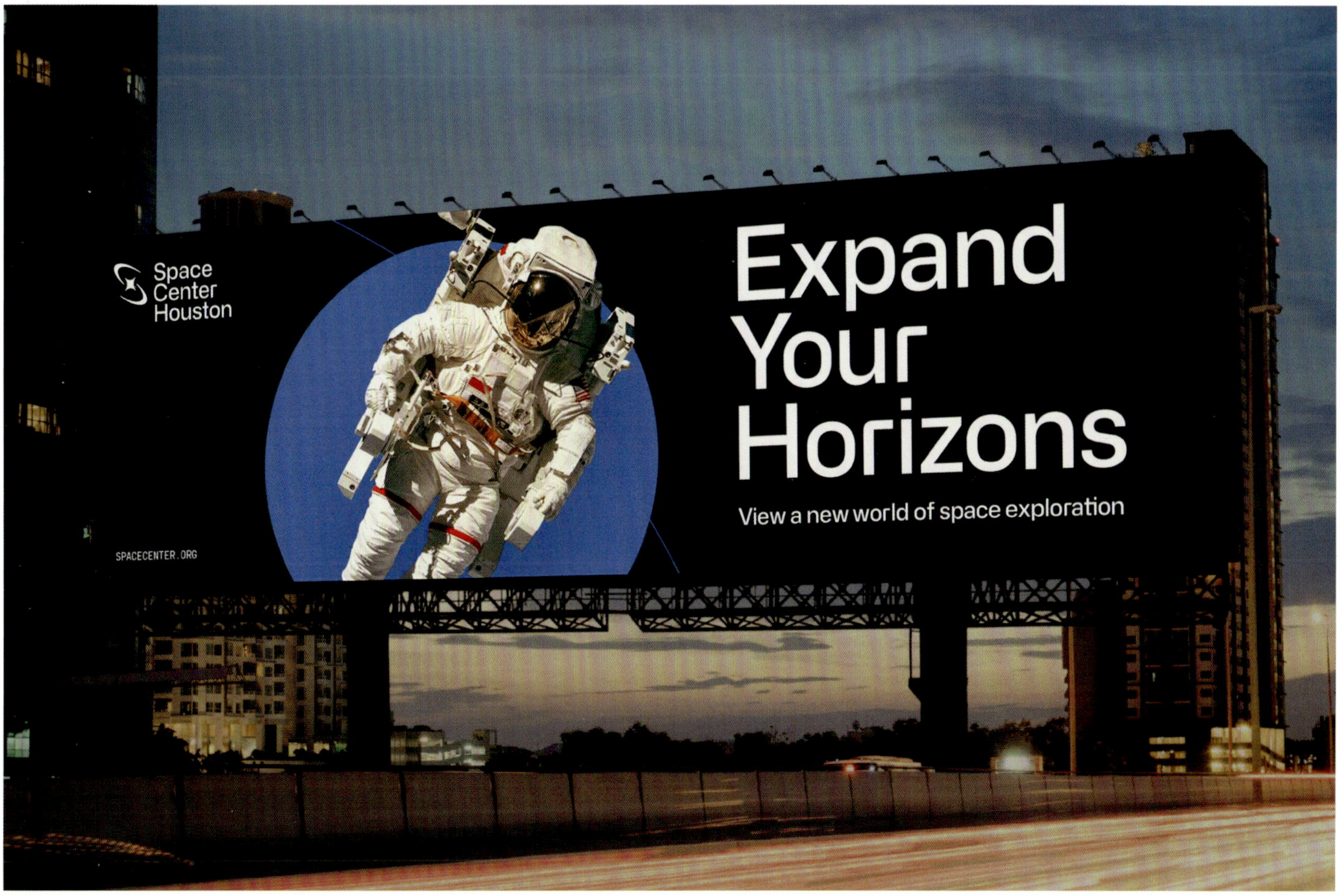

Title: Space Center Houston Rebrand | **Client:** Space Center Houston | **Design Firm:** Traina

S. YU, C. CHUNG, T. YUAN CHIOU, C. CHUN FENG, S. YU, Y. CHEN, K. HSUEH, M. NEGRI, R. HUANG, L. CHIEN

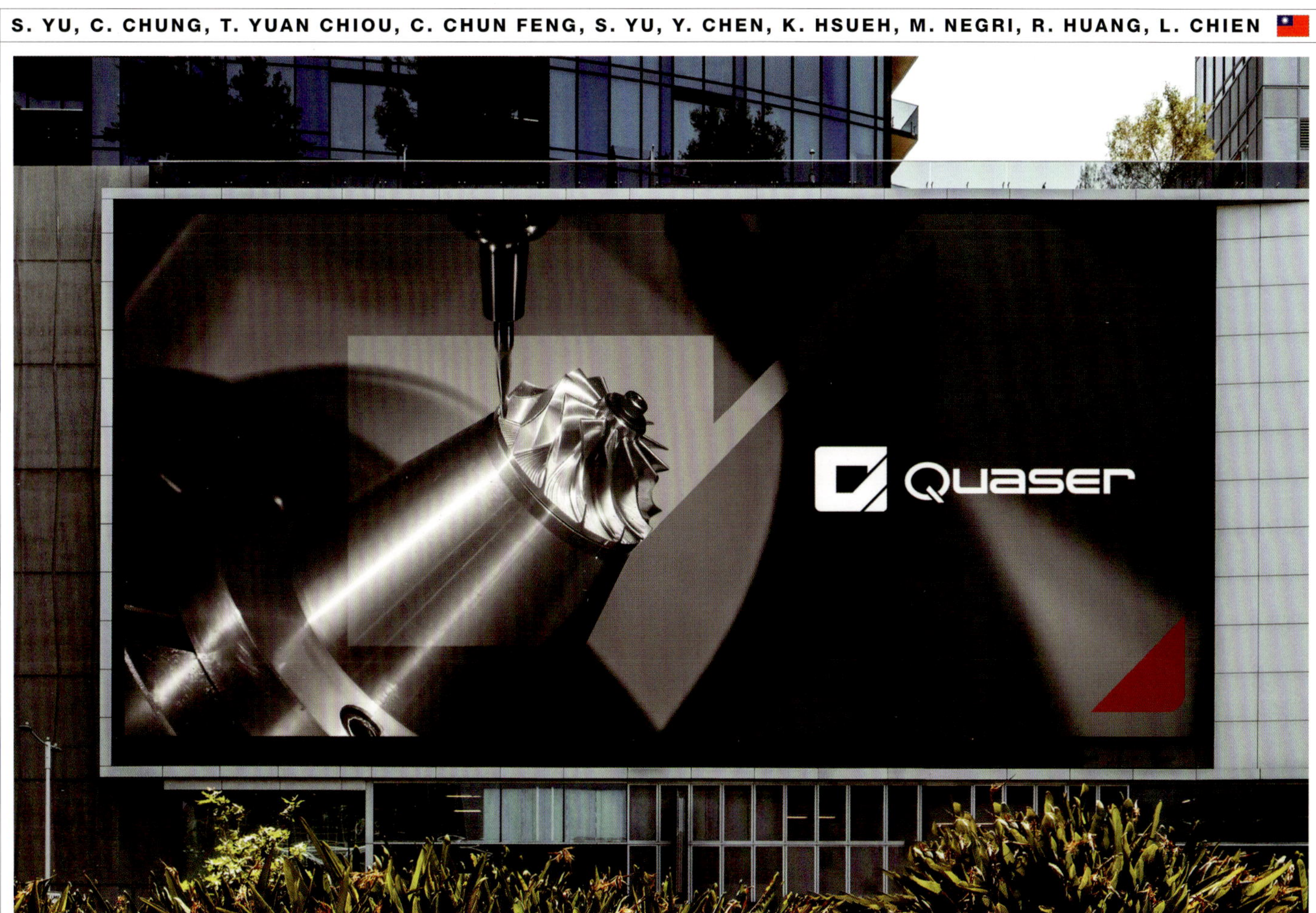

Title: Quaser Group | **Client:** Quaser Machine Tools | **Design Firm:** RedPeak Global

TOBEN

Title: KomplyAi | Client: KomplyAi
Design Firm: Toben

COLEY PORTER BELL, HALLIBURTON

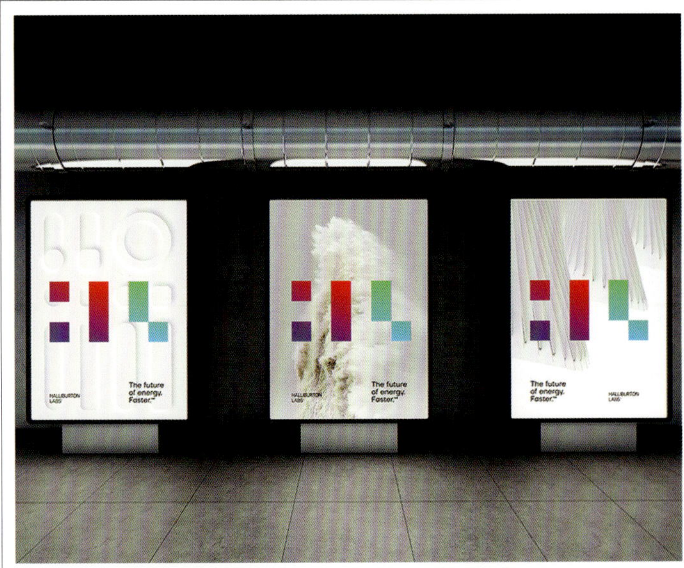

Title: Halliburton Labs Rebrand | Client: Halliburton
Design Firm: Coley Porter Bell

TOBEN

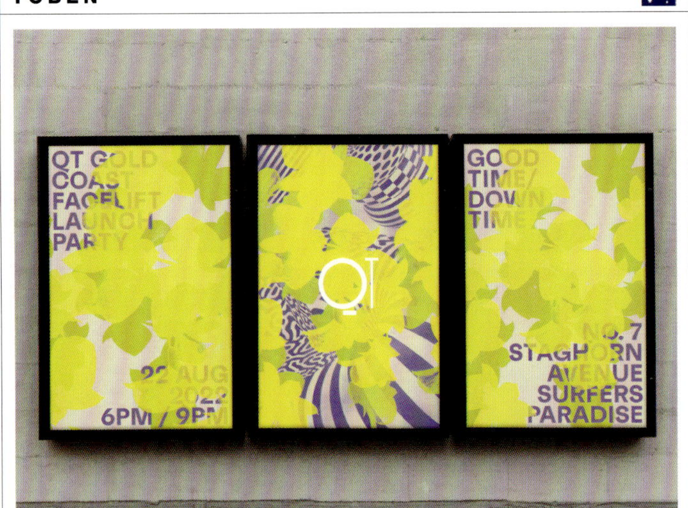

Title: QT Gold Coast | Client: QT Hotels & Resorts
Design Firm: Toben

CHRIS CACCI

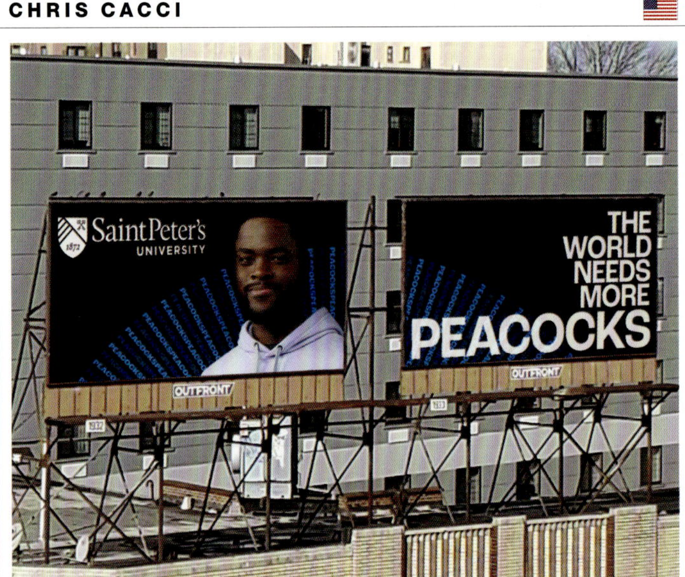

Title: A Rebranding Takes Flight | Client: St. Peter's University
Design Firm: Yes& Lipman Hearne

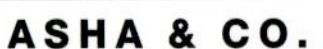

ASHA & CO.

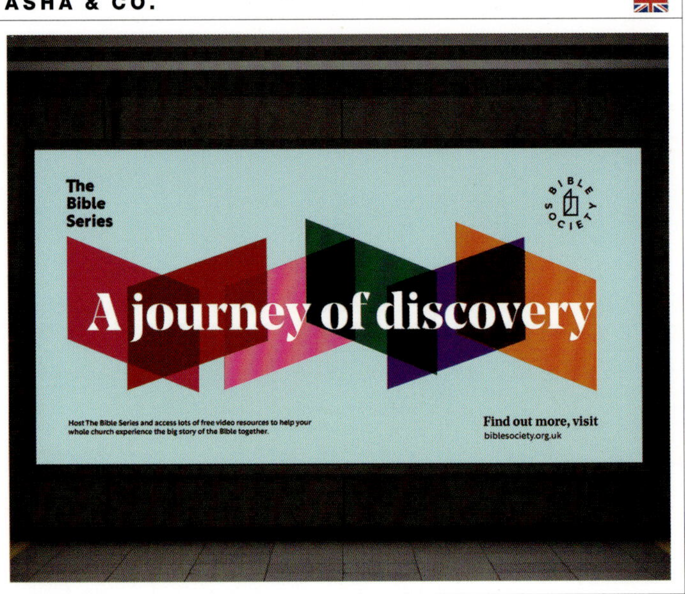

Title: Bible Society | Client: Bible Society
Design Firm: ASHA & Co.

ONREPEAT STUDIO

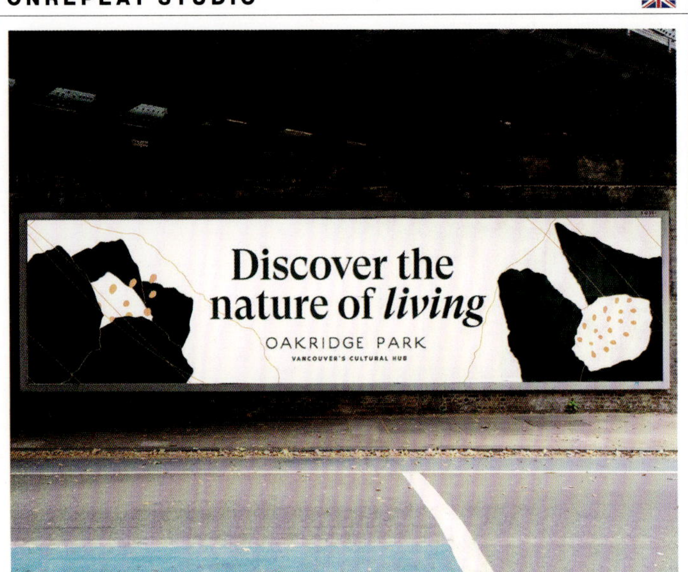

Title: Oakridge Park | Clients: Westbank, QuadReal
Design Firm: OnRepeat Studio

BRIT BLANKENSHIP

Title: Brightwild Rebrand | Client: Brightwild | Design Firm: Matchstic

UNDERLINE STUDIO

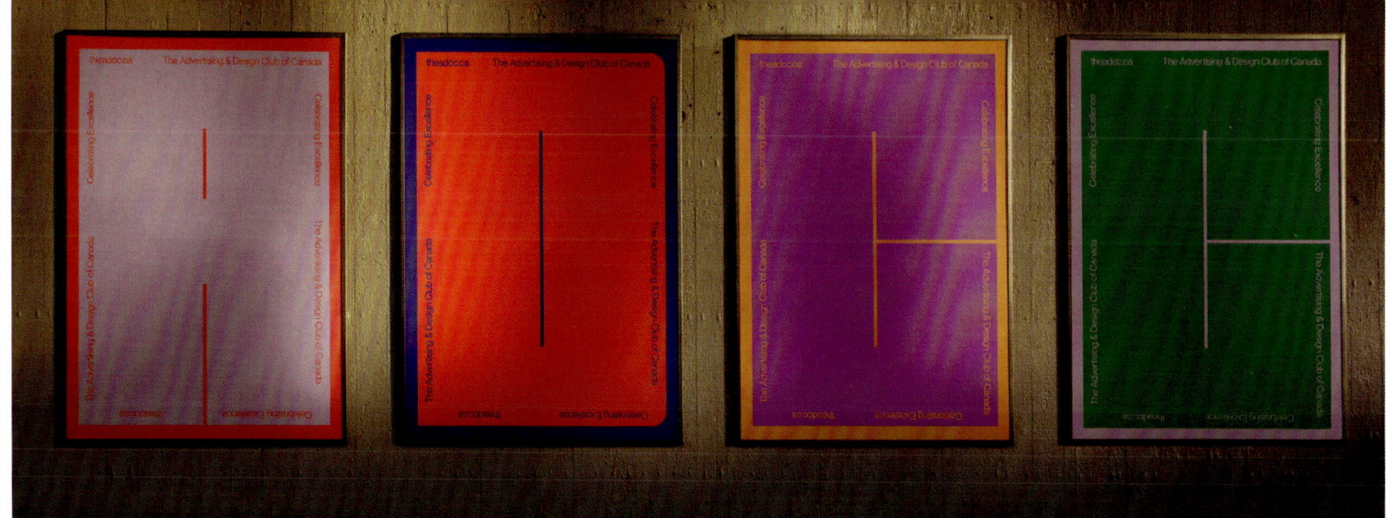

Title: ADCC Identity | Client: Advertising and Design Club of Canada | Design Firm: Underline Studio

AARON TRAVIS, JESSAH HOFKER, NICK BONDURA, RYAN BURLINSON, JOHANN A. GÓMEZ, MAT MCINELLY (+6)

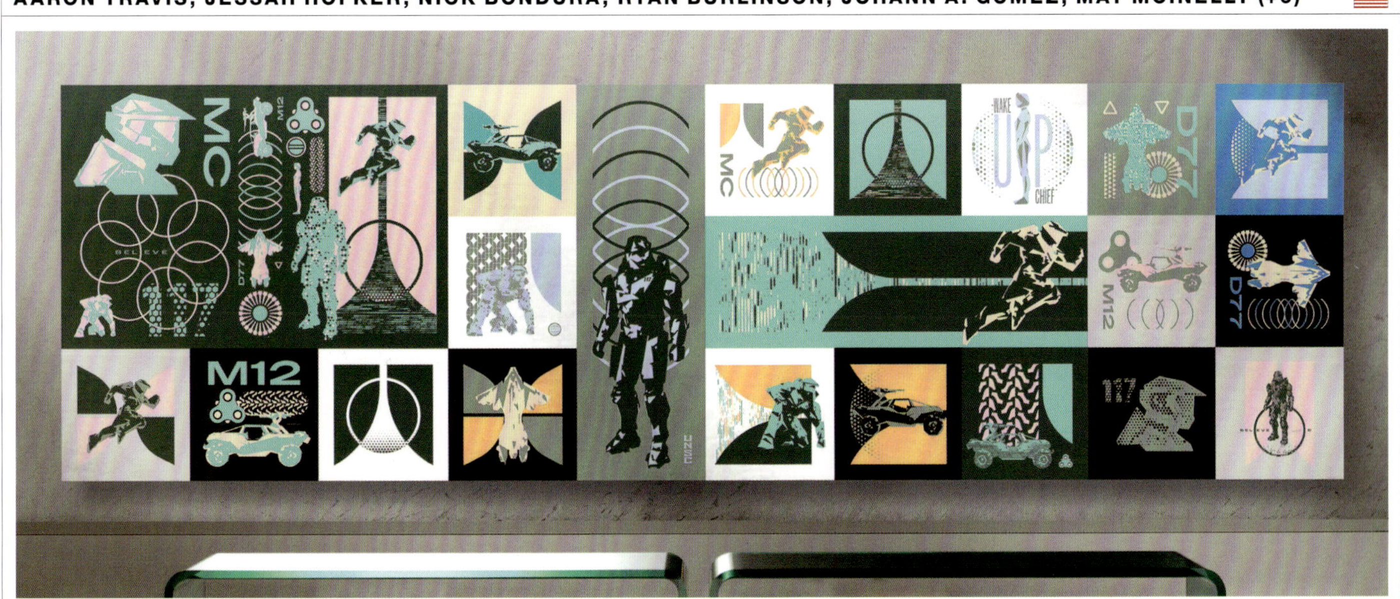

Title: Halo Infinite Styleguide | Clients: 343 Industries, Tiffany O'Brien, Rick Blanco | Design Firm: TGD

JOOHYUN PARK

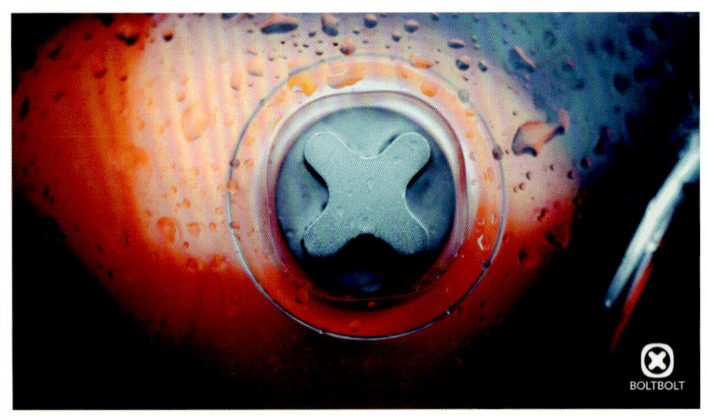

Title: BOLTBOLT
Client: Self-initiated
Design Firm: BOLTBOLT

TEST MONKI

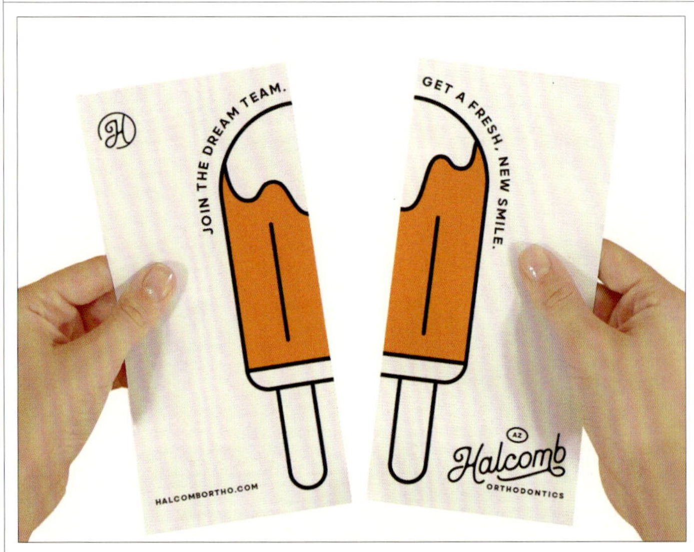

Title: Halcomb Ortho Brand Identity
Client: Halcomb Orthodontics
Design Firm: Test Monki

SHAO-WEI CHUANG

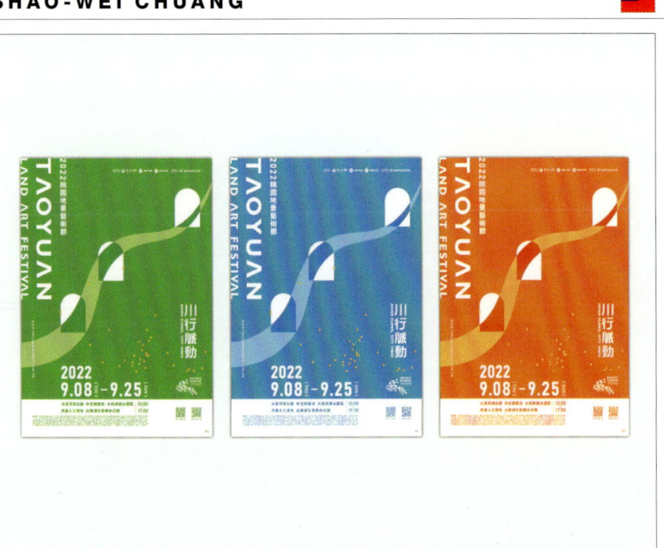

Title: 2022 Taoyuan Land Art Festival “RIVER FLOWS, CITY VIBES”
Client: Taoyuan City Government, Department of Cultural Affairs
Design Firm: VANGUARD Visual Design Ltd.

QICHAO AN

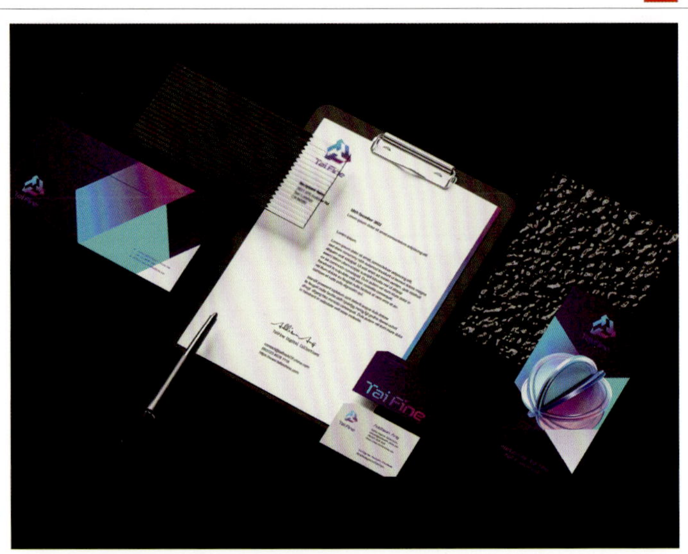

Title: TaiFine Branding
Client: TaiFine
Design Firm: Wuhan Mornice Brand Design Co., Ltd.

ARIEL FREANER

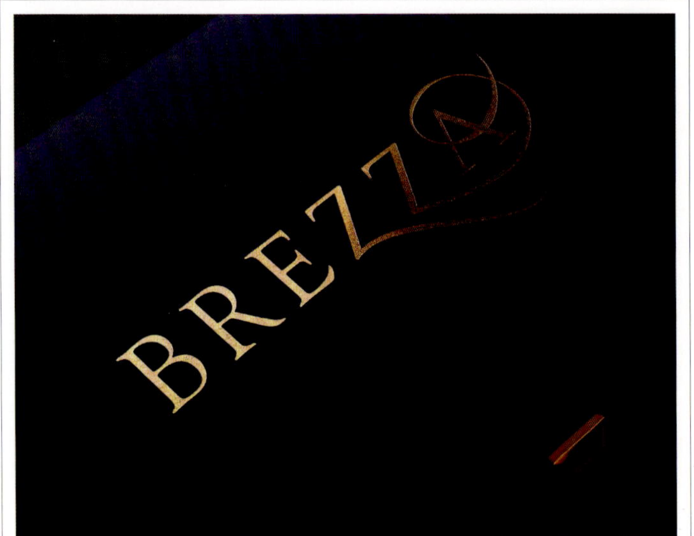

Title: Brezza Hotel Branding
Client: Brezza Hotel
Design Firm: Freaner Creative & Design

SUSANNE PINTER

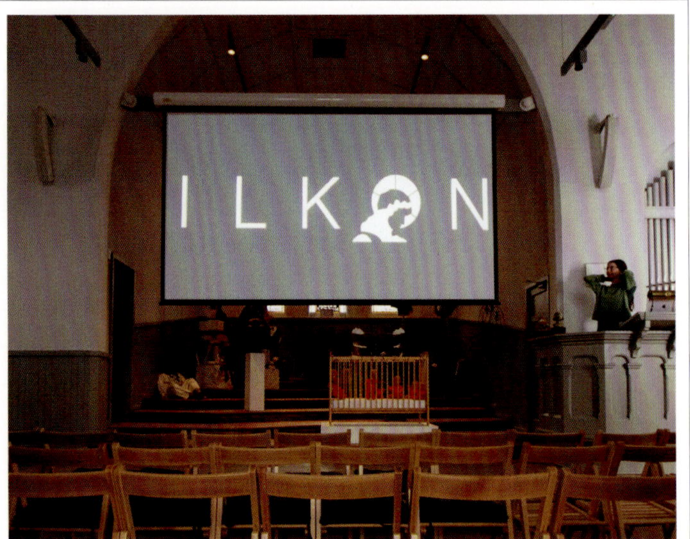

Title: ILKON: Ilkeston Contemporary Arts
Client: ILKON: Ilkeston Contemporary Arts
Design Firm: Pinter-Parrott

RESOURCE BRANDING

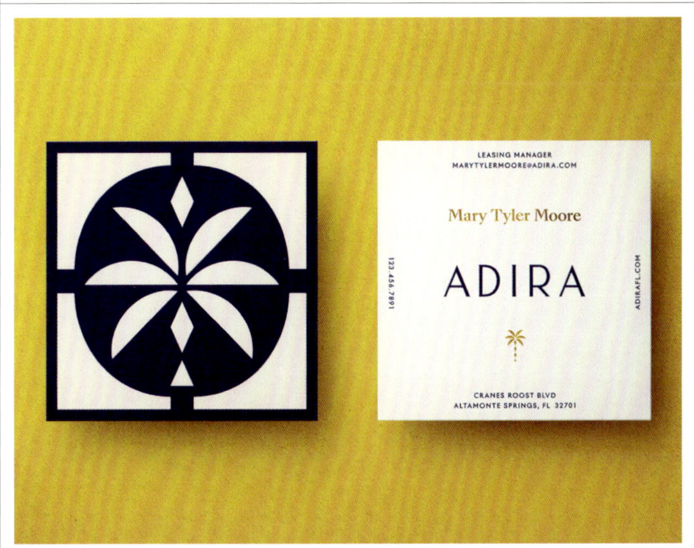

Title: Adira Altamonte Springs Brand Identity
Client: Gilbane Development Company
Design Firm: Resource Branding

STUDIO EDUARDO AIRES

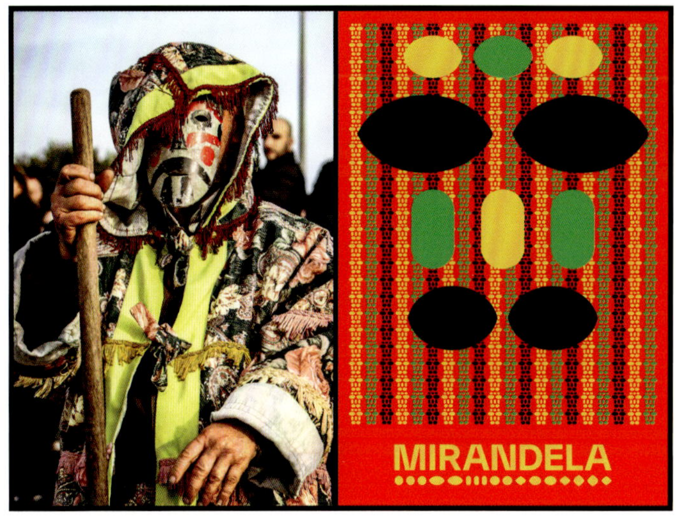

Title: Mirandela
Client: Mirandela City Hall
Design Firm: Studio Eduardo Aires

TIERNEY CUNNINGHAM

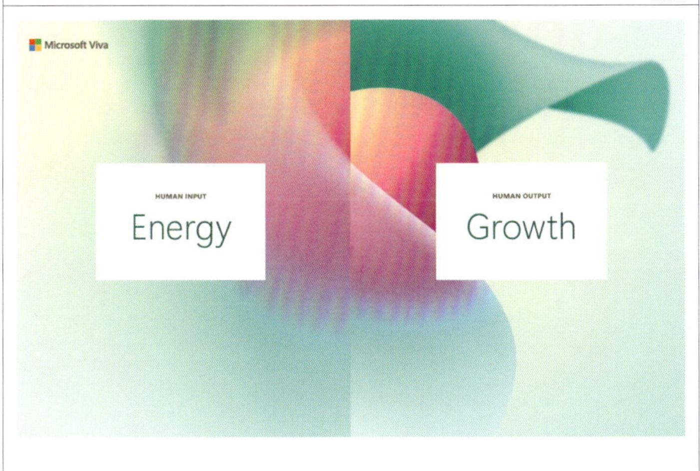

Title: Microsoft Viva Brand Expression
Client: Microsoft Viva
Design Firm: Microsoft Cloud Marketing Brand Studio

PAULO MARCELO

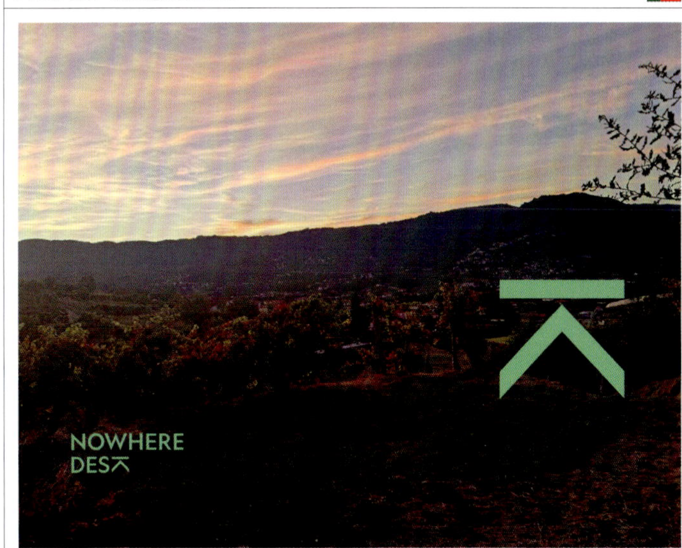

Title: Nowhere Desk
Client: Nowhere Desk
Design Firm: PMDESIGN

LEGIS DESIGN

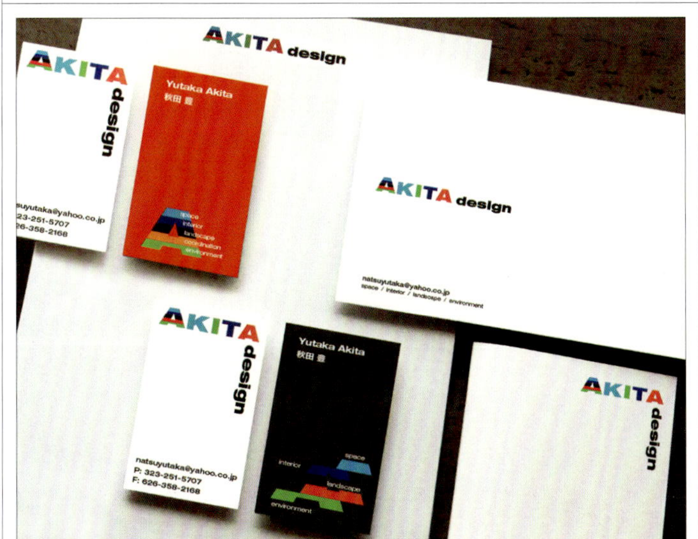

Title: AKITA Design Branding
Client: AKITA Design
Design Firm: Legis Design

ALAN COLVIN

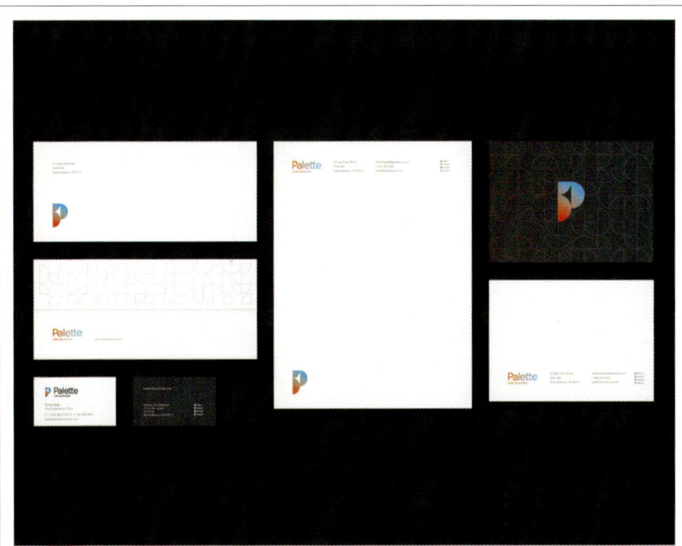

Title: Palette Life Sciences
Client: Palette Life Sciences
Design Firm: Cue

PEPSICO DESIGN & INNOVATION

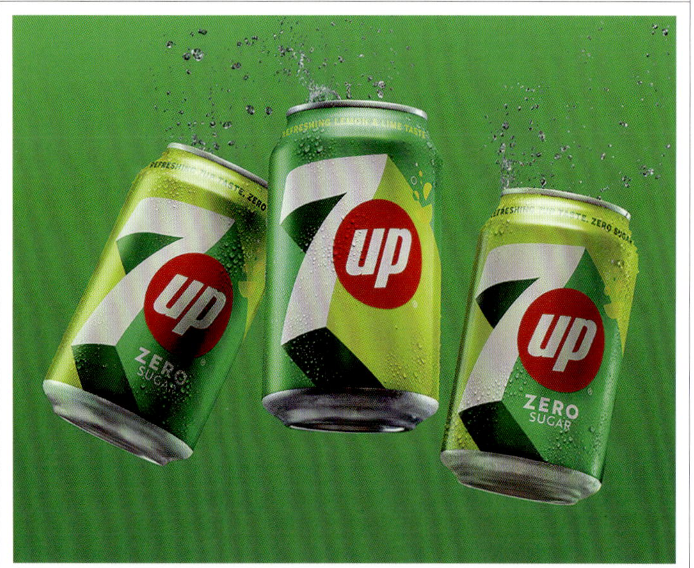

Title: 7UP Global Brand Restage | **Client:** Self-initated
Design Firm: PepsiCo Design & Innovation

PEPSICO DESIGN & INNOVATION

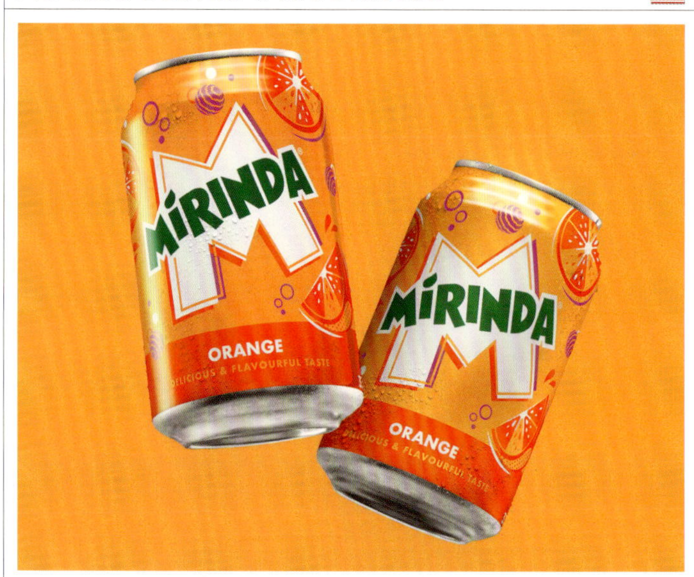

Title: Mirinda Global Restage | **Client:** Self-initated
Design Firm: PepsiCo Design & Innovation

RONN LEE

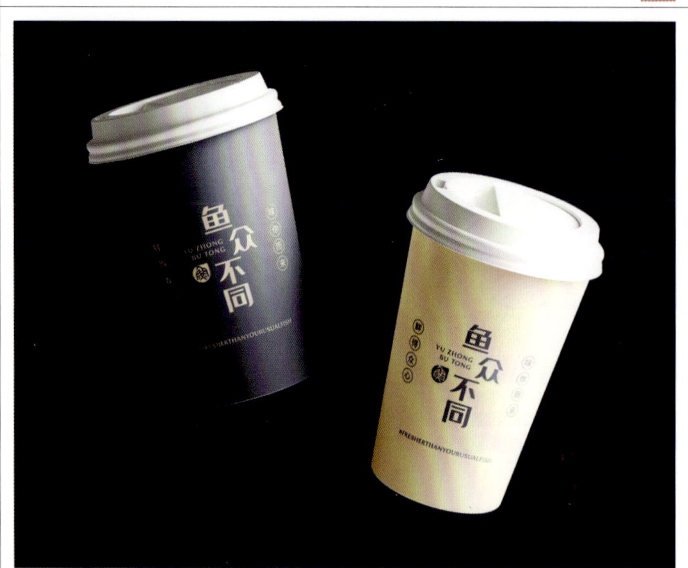

Title: Yu Zhong Bu Tong Brand Identity | **Client:** Yu Zhong Bu Tong
Design Firm: BEAMY

CHRIS ZAWADA

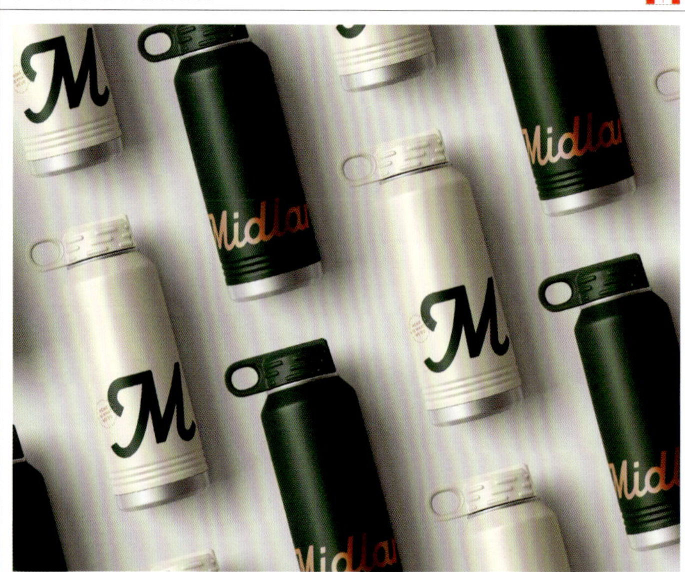

Title: A Beautiful Fit | **Client:** Nick Brouard
Design Firm: Full Punch

ELAINE CHAW, ZILI MA

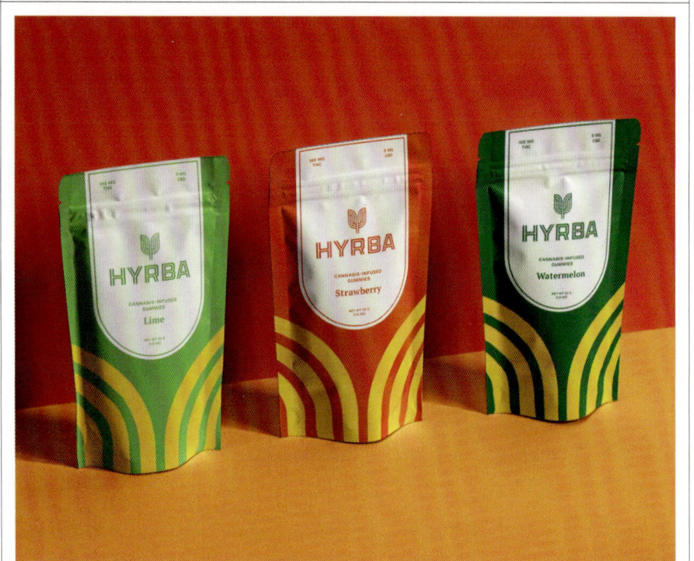

Title: Hyrba | **Client:** Hyrba
Design Firm: Noise 13

ALAN COLVIN

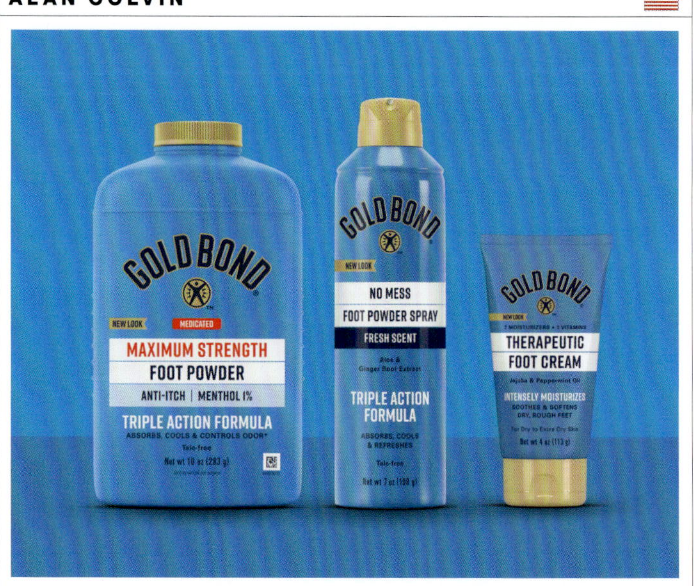

Title: Gold Bond | **Client:** Gold Bond
Design Firm: Cue

UNDERLINE STUDIO

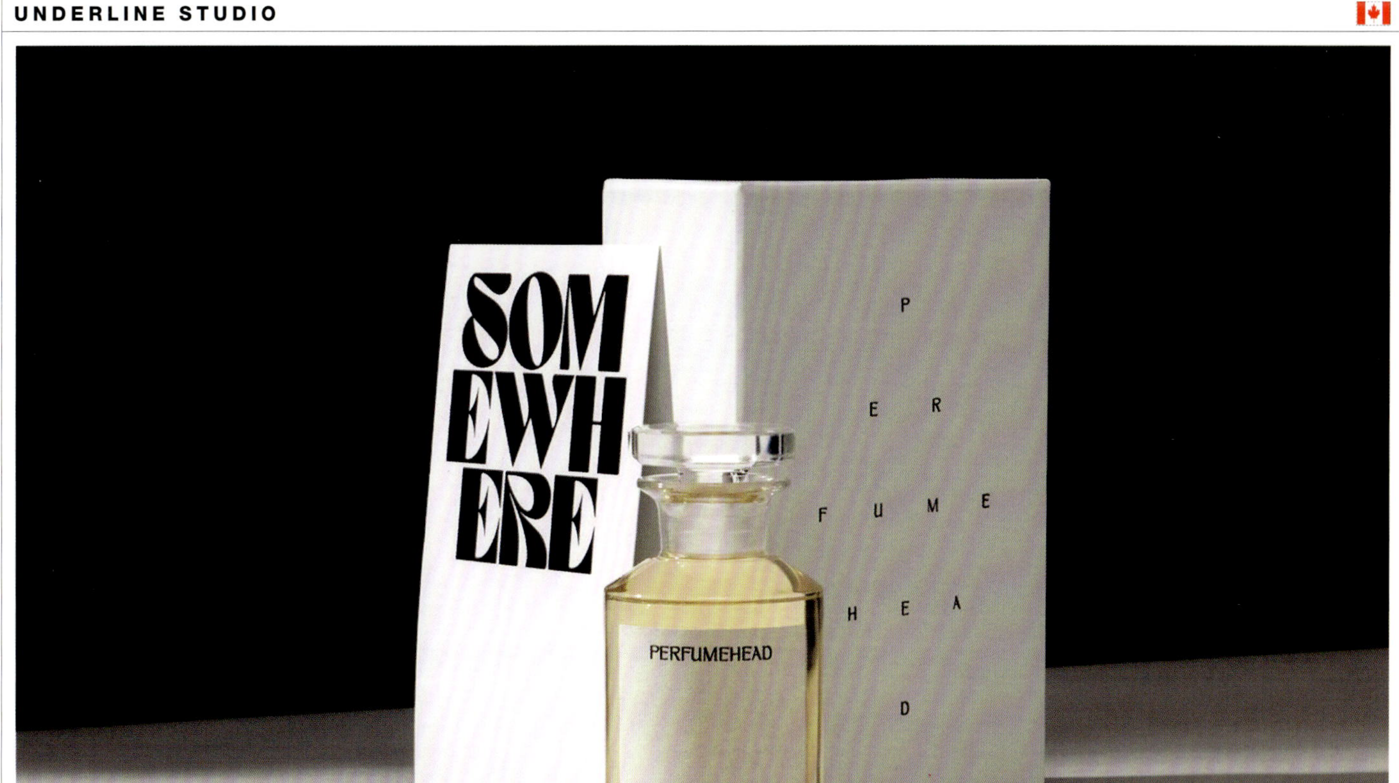

Title: Perfumehead Brand | **Client:** Perfumehead | **Design Firm:** Underline Studio

BULLETPROOF

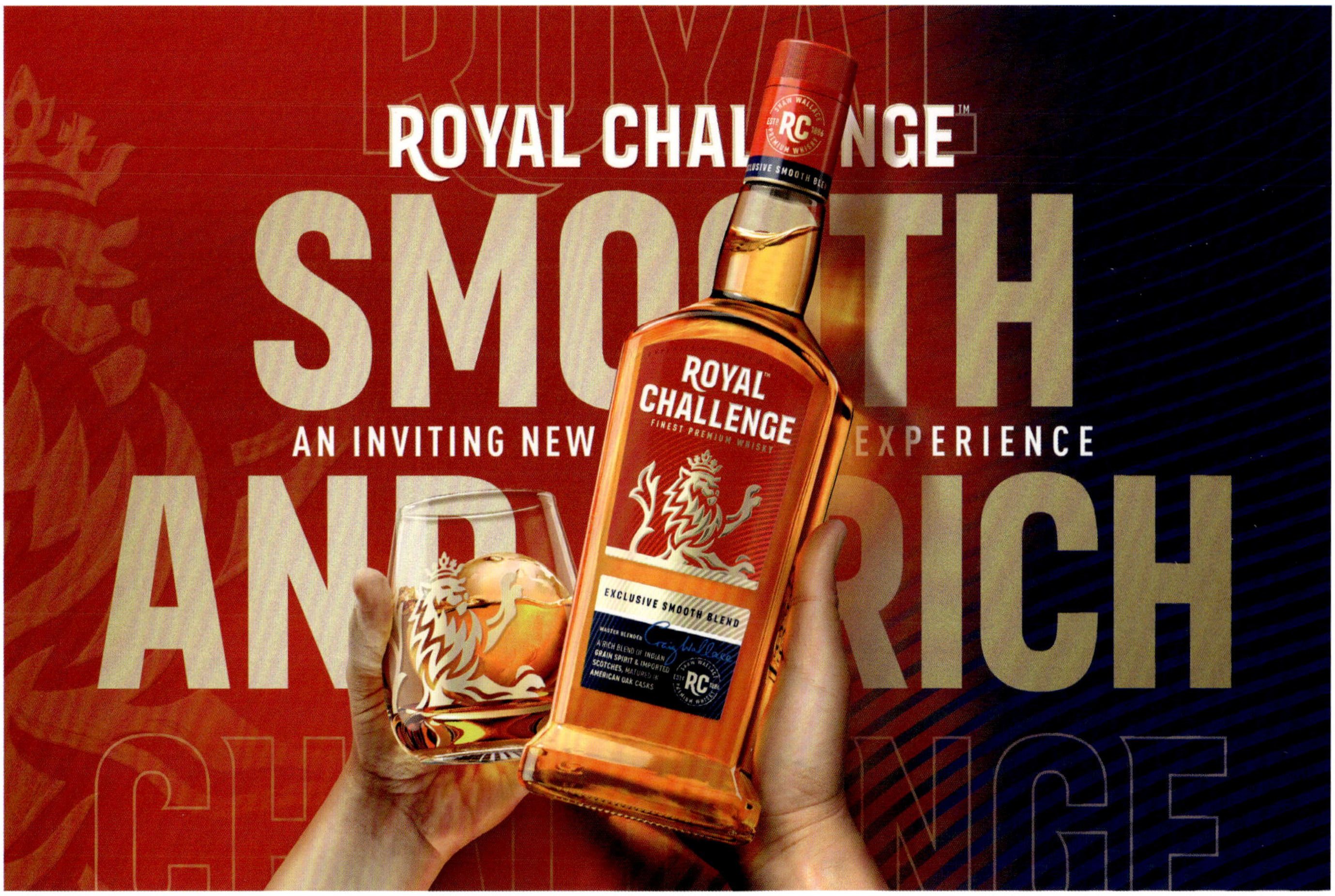

ROYAL CHALLENGE™
SMOOTH
AN INVITING NEW EXPERIENCE
AND RICH
ROYAL CHALLENGE
FINEST PREMIUM WHISKY
EXCLUSIVE SMOOTH BLEND

Title: Royal Challenge Brand Redesign 2022 | **Clients:** Diageo India, Hiren Dedhia | **Design Firm:** Bulletproof

ASHA & CO.

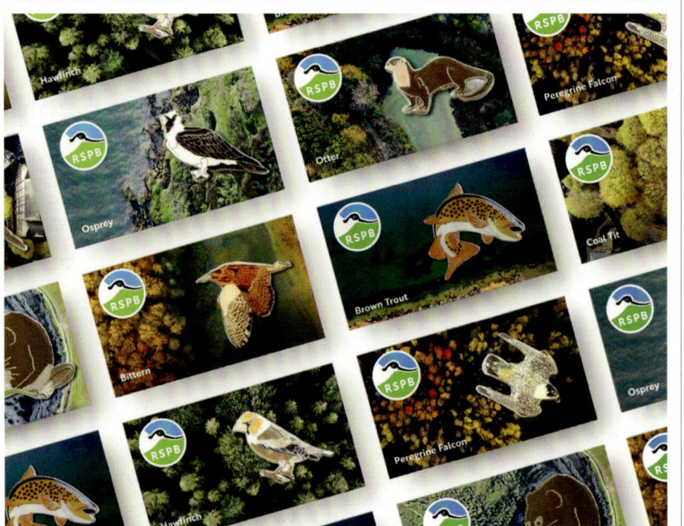

Title: The RSPB
Client: The RSPB
Design Firm: ASHA & Co.

M. MAZZA, M. MANNING, S. LAVALAIS, A. WOOD

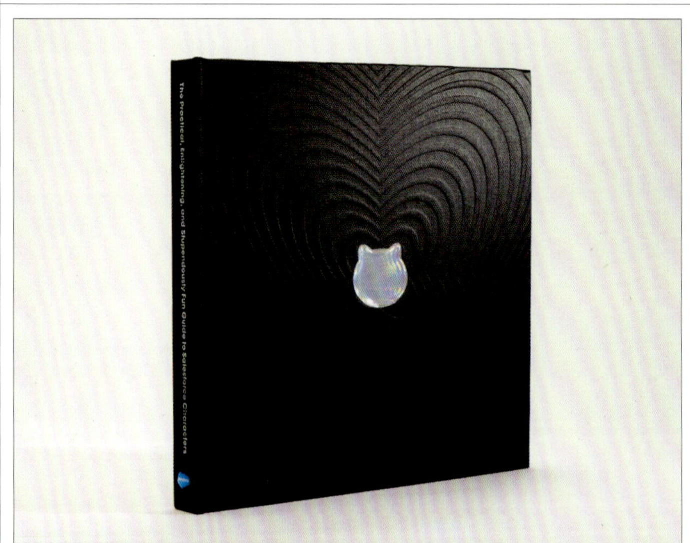

Title: The Practical, Enlightening, and Stupendously Fun Guide to Salesforce Characters
Client: Self-initiated | **Design Firm:** Salesforce

ARIEL FREANER

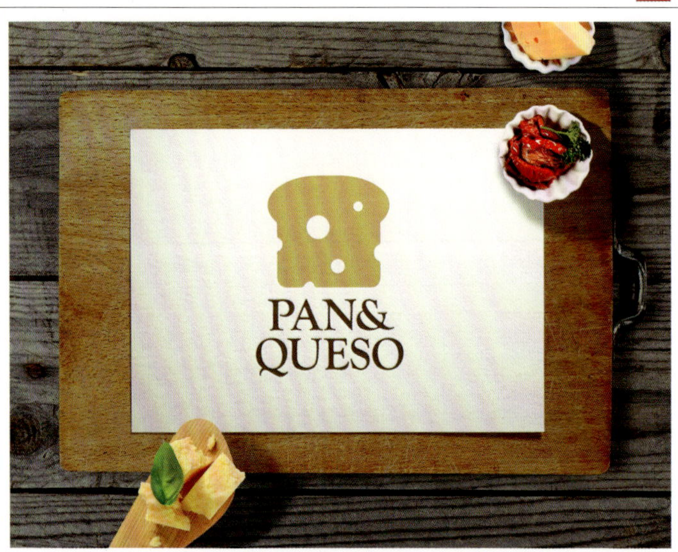

Title: Pan & Queso (Bread and Cheese) Branding
Client: Pan & Queso (Bread and Cheese)
Design Firm: Freaner Creative & Design

COURTNEY SPENCER

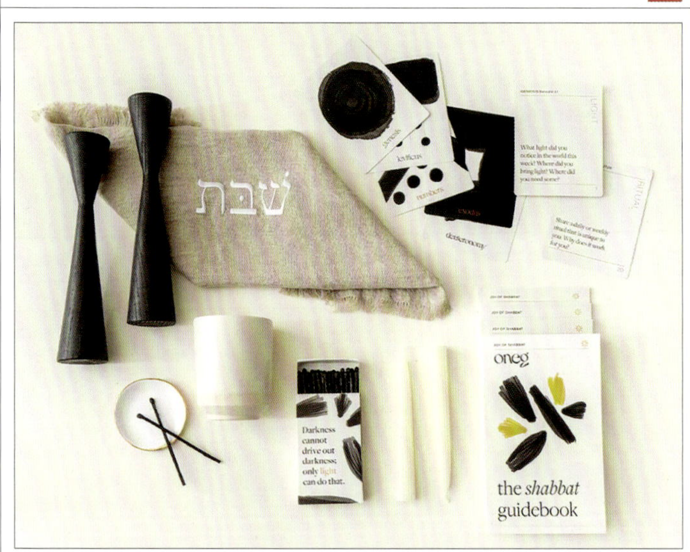

Title: Oneg Branding
Clients: Oneg, Jeanie Milbauer
Design Firm: Dear Fellow Design Studio

ARIEL FREANER

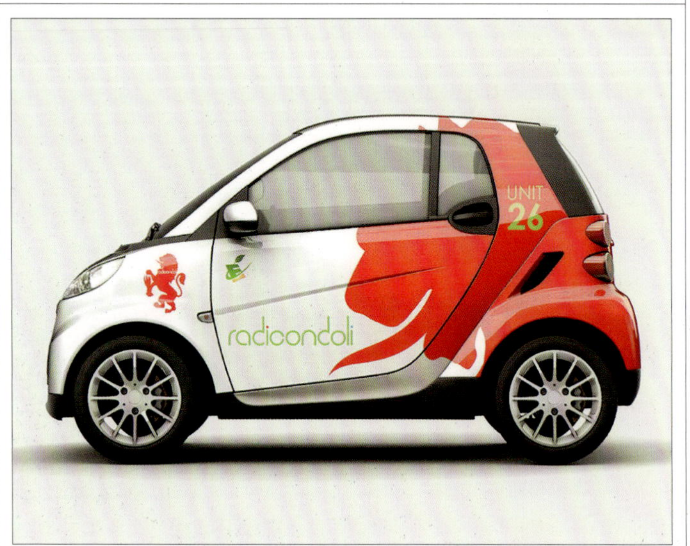

Title: Radicondoli City Brand (Italy)
Client: Radicondoli City Council, Italy
Design Firm: Freaner Creative & Design

JOHN BALL

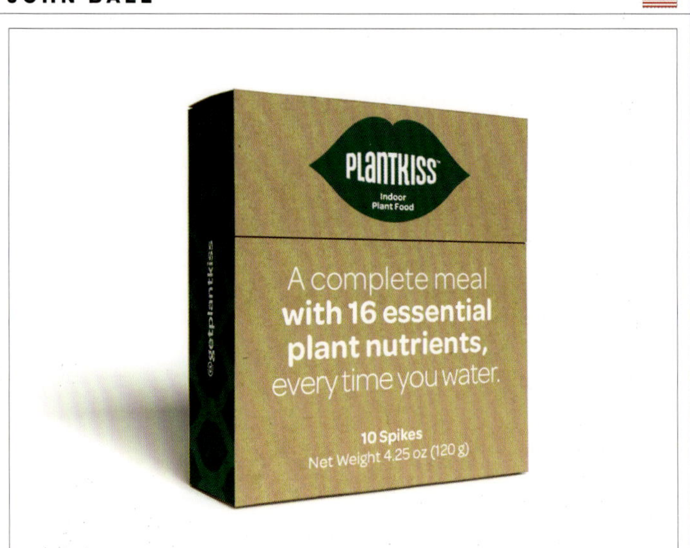

Title: PlantKiss Brand Identity System
Client: PlantKiss
Design Firm: MiresBall

YIHUANG ZHOU, YIXUAN CAO

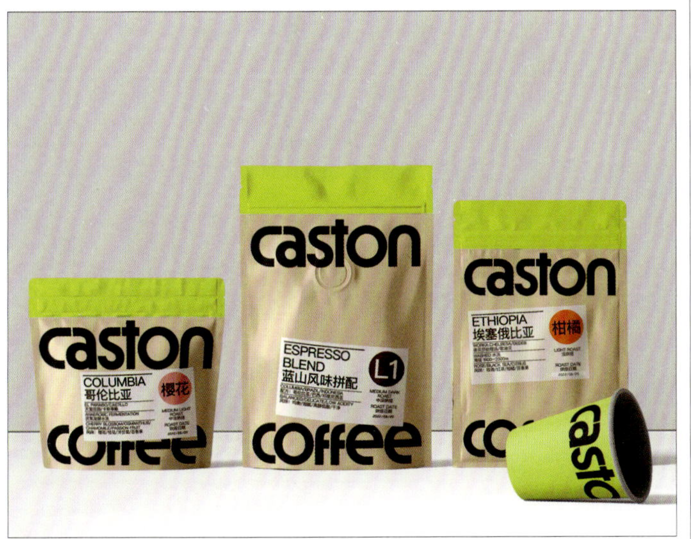

Title: Caston Coffee Roasters Branding
Client: Caston Coffee Roasters
Design Firm: YSFT Inc.

PEPSICO DESIGN & INNOVATION

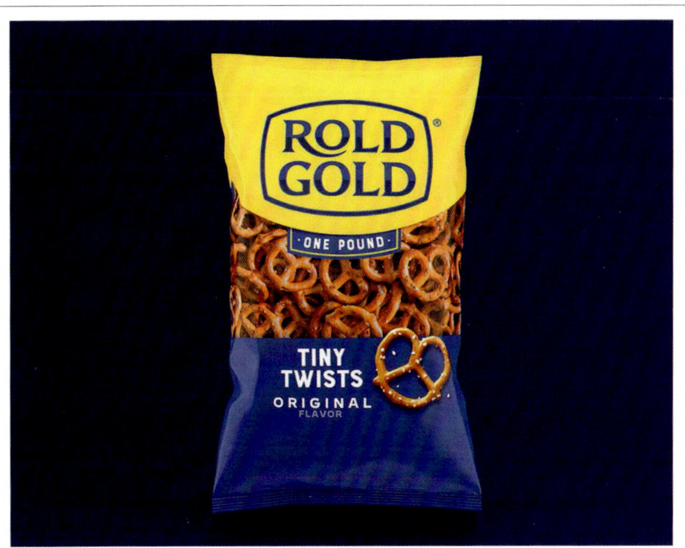

Title: Rold Gold Redesign
Client: Self-initated
Design Firm: PepsiCo Design & Innovation

ELLEN BRUSS DESIGN

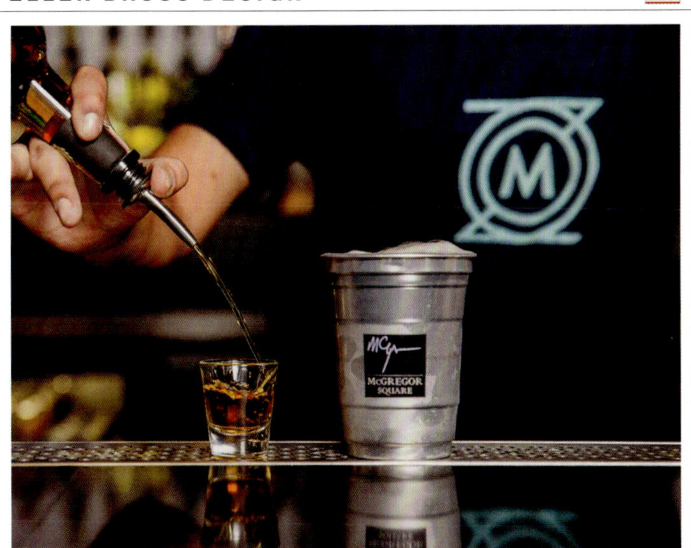

Title: Milepost Zero
Client: Continuum Partners
Design Firm: Ellen Bruss Design

ALAN COLVIN

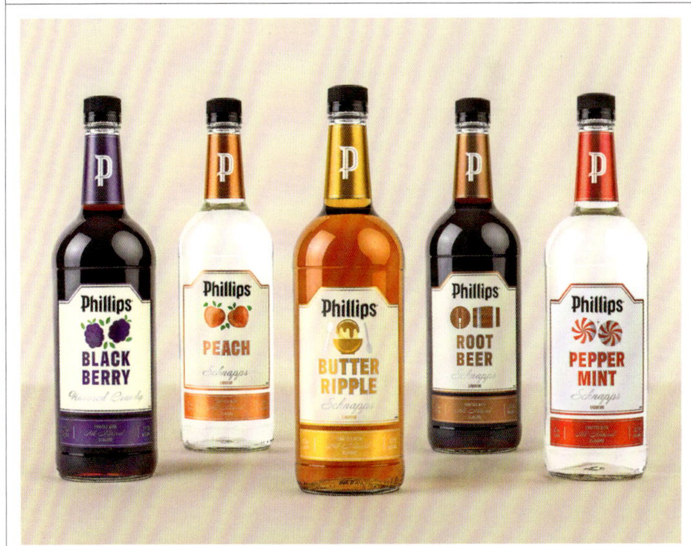

Title: Phillips Redesign
Client: Phillips Distilling Co.
Design Firm: Cue

TOSHIHIRO ONIMARU

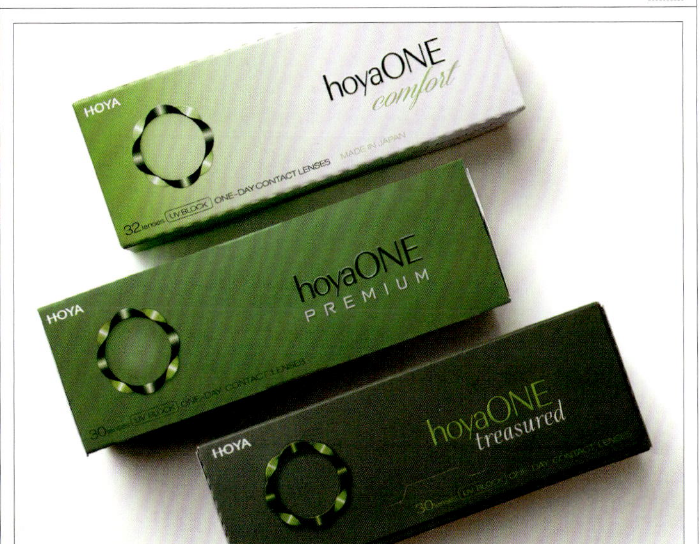

Title: HoyaONE Contact Lens
Client: Hoya Corporation
Design Firm: GRAPHICS & DESIGNING INC.

SUKLE ADVERTISING & DESIGN

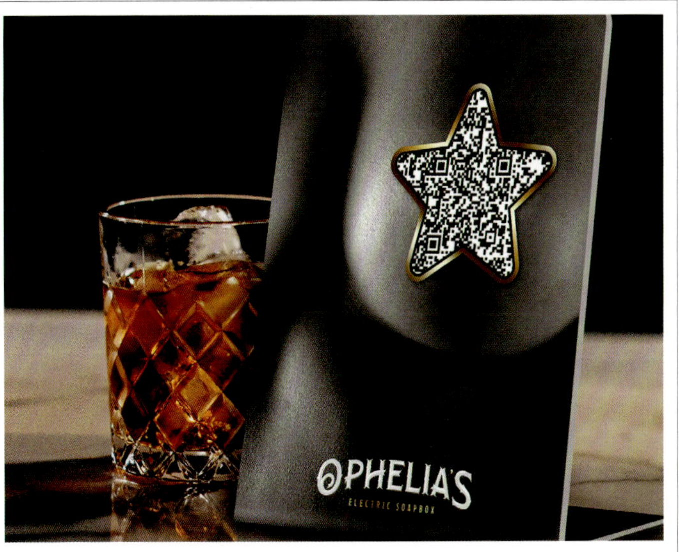

Title: Ophelia's Electric Soapbox Branding
Client: Ophelia's Electric Soapbox
Design Firm: Sukle Advertising & Design

DAVID JONES, ANDEE MAZZOCCO

Title: Kouvenda Media | **Clients:** Stephanie Marudas, Emily Previti
Design Firm: SAYGRID

VINCENZO PERRI

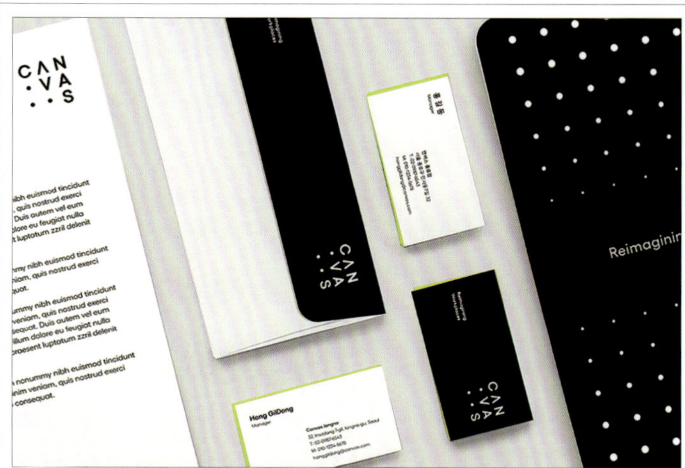

Title: Reimagining Workplaces with Canvas | **Client:** Canvas
Design Firm: Lippincott

CRAIG BYERS

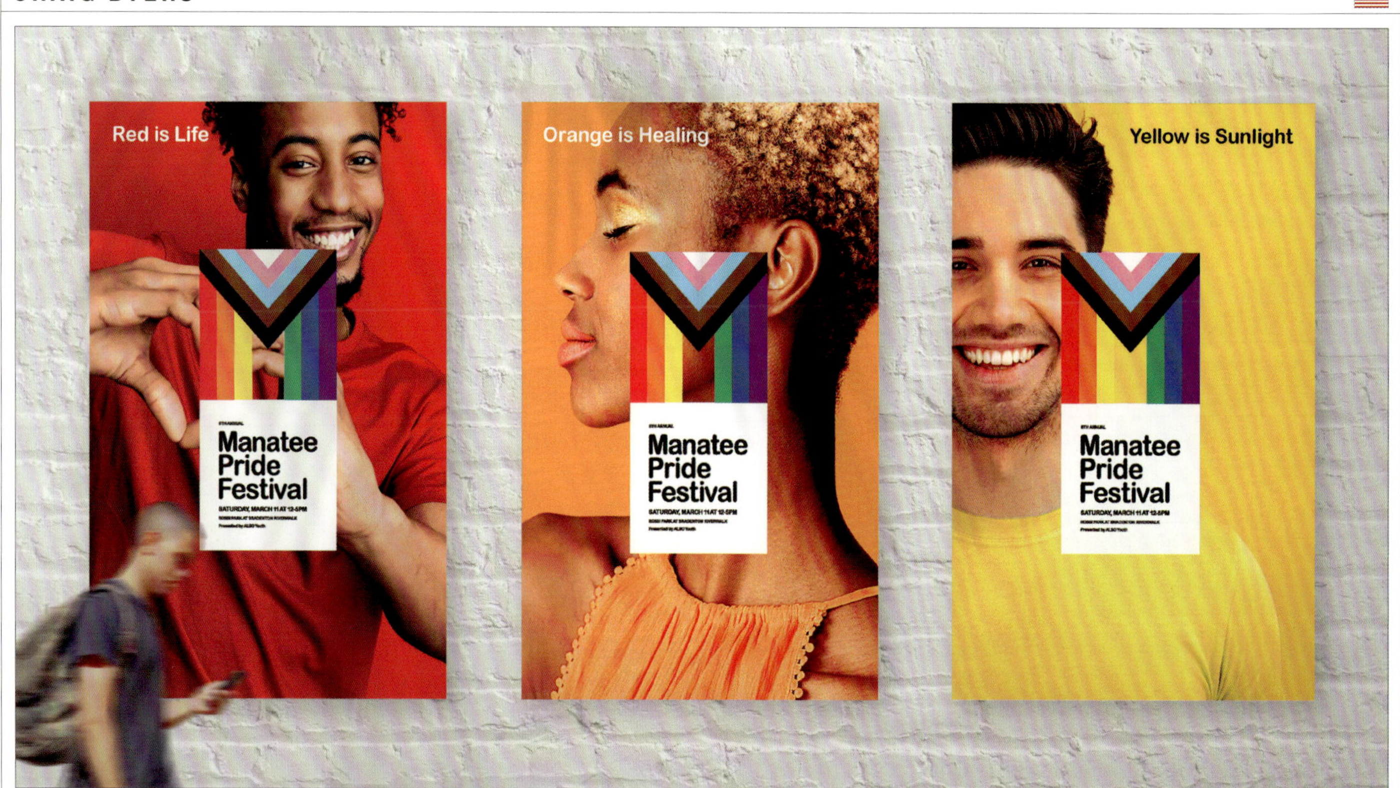

Title: Joining Together to Celebrate Our Community | **Client:** ALSOYouth | **Design Firm:** Studio Craig Byers

STUDIO EDUARDO AIRES

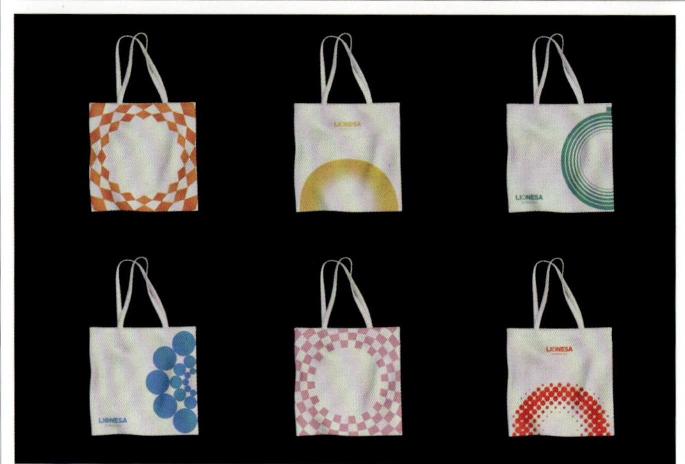

Title: Lionesa Business Hub | **Client:** Lionesa Business Hub
Design Firm: Studio Eduardo Aires

JOHN BOWLES

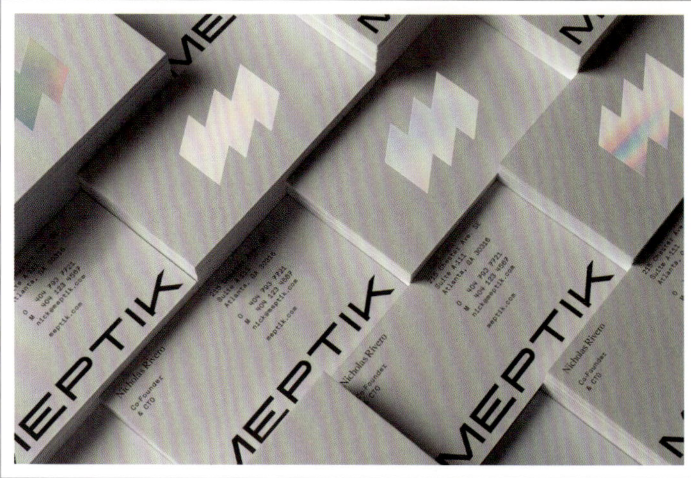

Title: Meptik Rebrand | **Client:** Meptik
Design Firm: Matchstic

HISA IDE, TOSHIAKI IDE

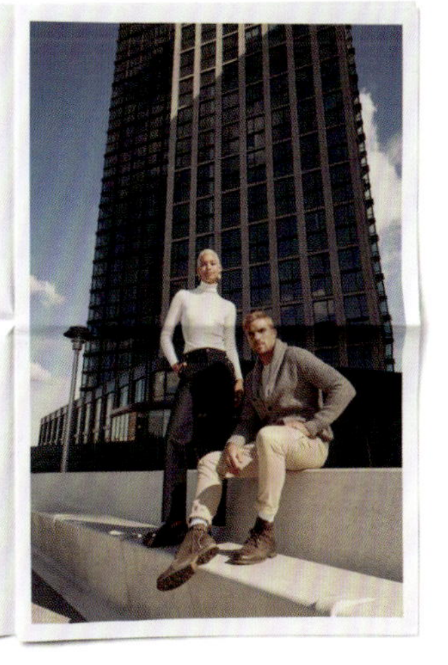

Title: The Bellslip Brochure | **Client:** Brookfield Properties
Design Firm: IF Studio

CLAUDIA NERI

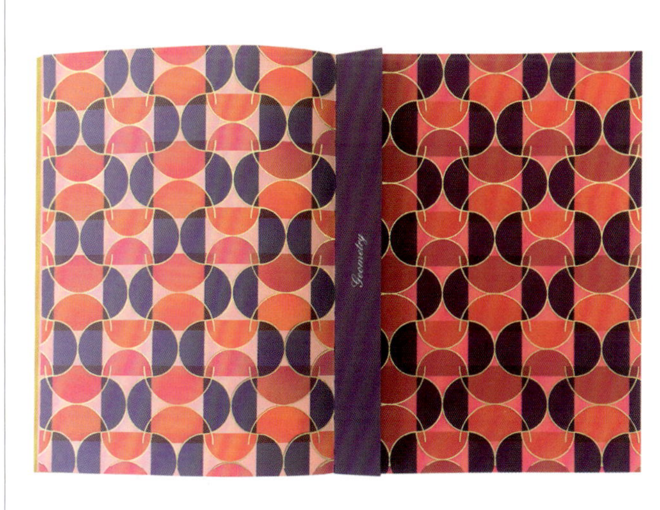

Title: Sartoriale | **Client:** Arjowiggins Creative Papers
Design Firm: Teikna Design

HISA IDE, TOSHIAKI IDE

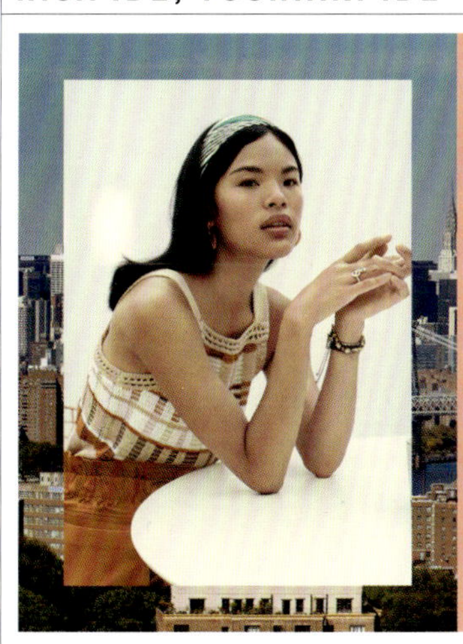
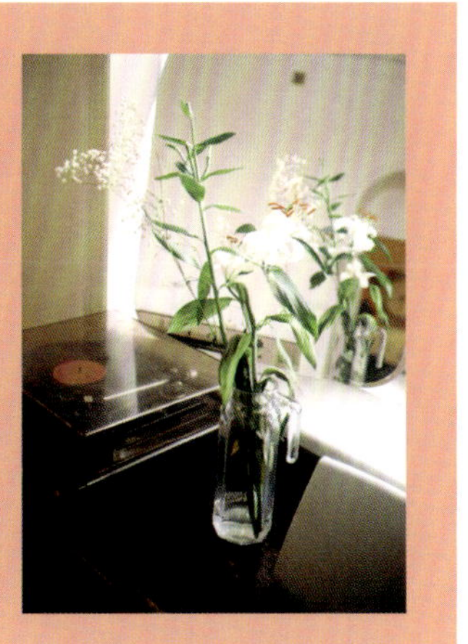

Title: Plank Road Brochure | **Client:** Brodsky
Design Firm: IF Studio

LEE BRADLEY, SCOTT COCKERHAM

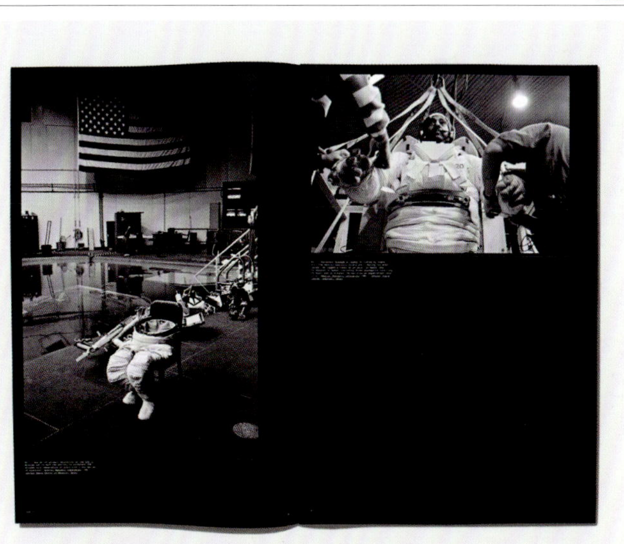

Title: STS-72 | **Client:** John Angerson
Design Firm: B&W Studio

LISA SIRBAUGH CREATIVE

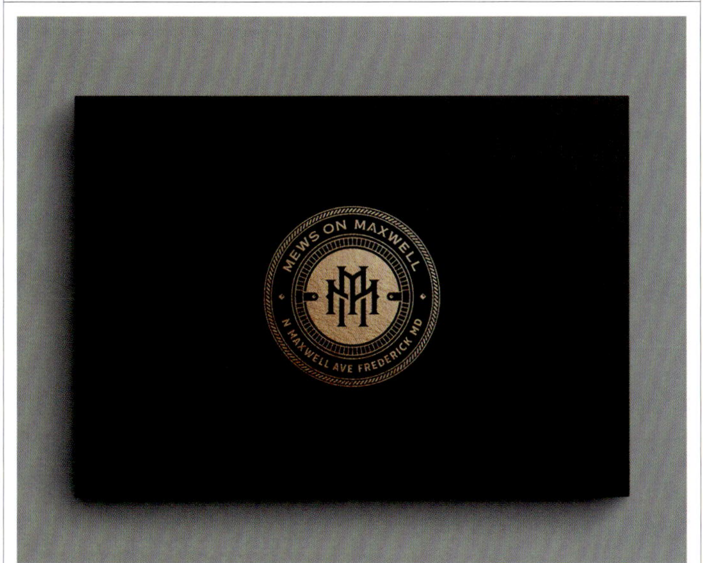

Title: Mews on Maxwell Viewbook
Client: JR Capital Build | **Design Firm:** Lisa Sirbaugh Creative

JAMIE MAHONEY

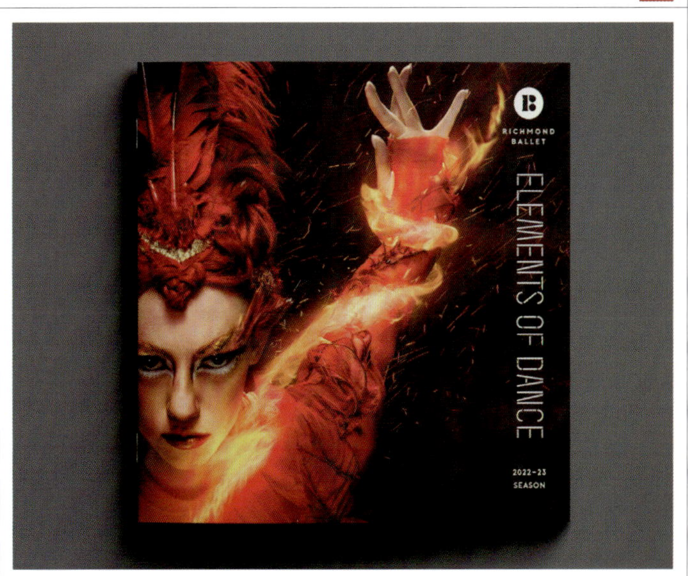

Title: Richmond Ballet's Elements of Dance Campaign
Client: Richmond Ballet | **Design Firm:** Karnes Coffey Design

STEVEN TAYLOR

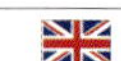

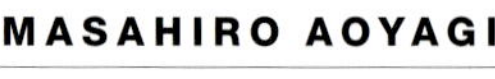

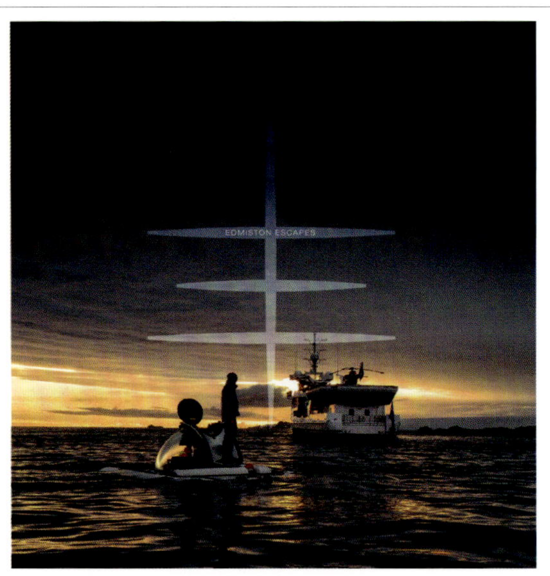

Title: Edmiston Escapes | **Client:** Edmiston
Design Firm: TAYLOR

MASAHIRO AOYAGI

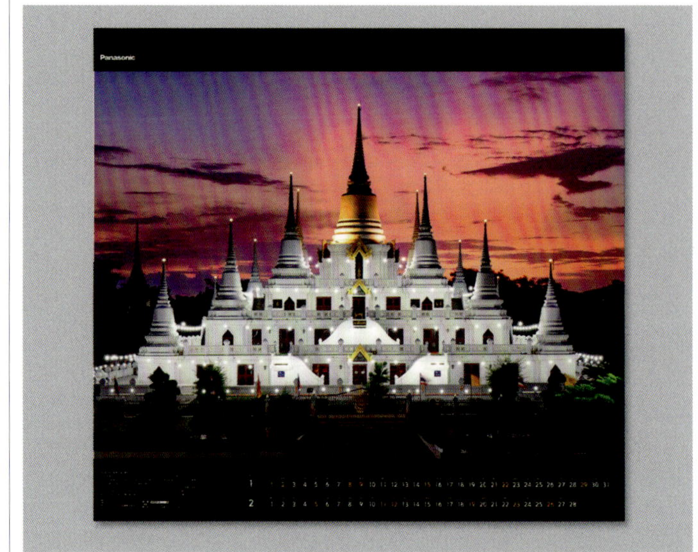

Title: CONNECT WITH CITY LIGHTS | **Client:** Panasonic Homes Co., Ltd.
Design Firm: Toppan Inc.

MASAHIRO AOYAGI

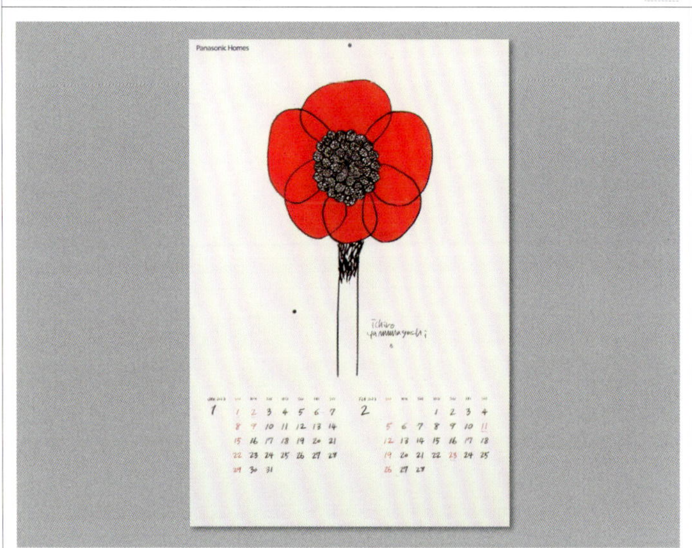

Title: 2023 Panasonic Homes CALENDAR "PEACE"
Client: Panasonic Homes Co., Ltd.
Design Firm: Toppan Inc.

STUDIO 5 DESIGNS INC.

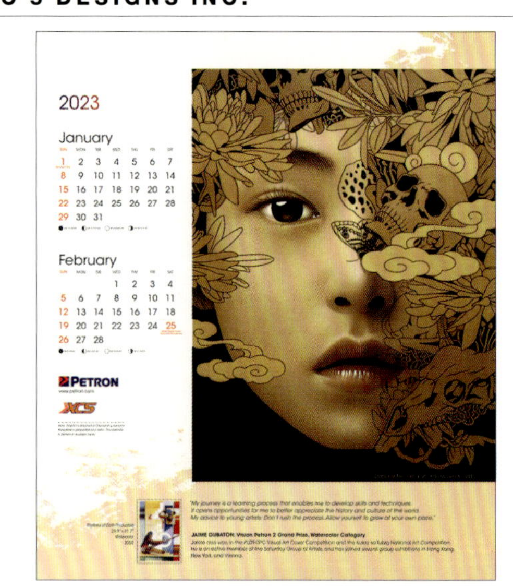

Title: Petron Calendar: Celebrating Ninety Years of Excellence
Clients: Petron Corporation, Ramon Cruz
Design Firm: Studio 5 Designs Inc.

MASAHIRO AOYAGI

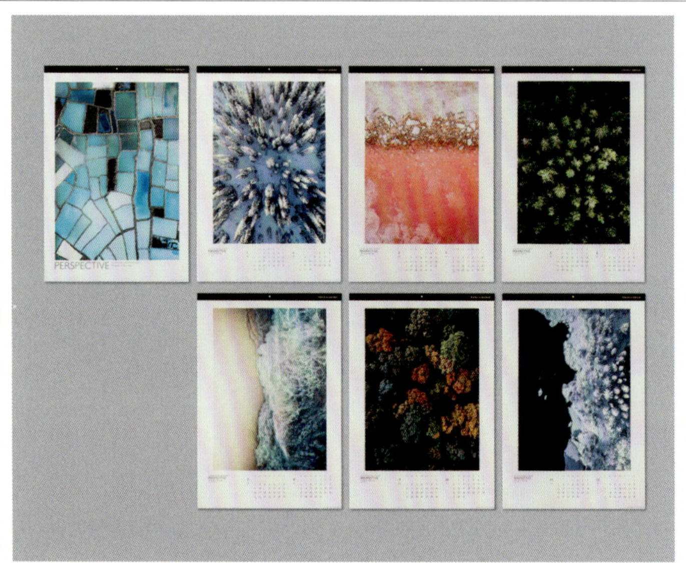

Title: 2023 Toyo Ink Group Calendar "Perspective"
Client: Toyo Ink SC Holdings Co., Ltd. | **Design Firm:** Toppan Inc.

MASAHIRO AOYAGI

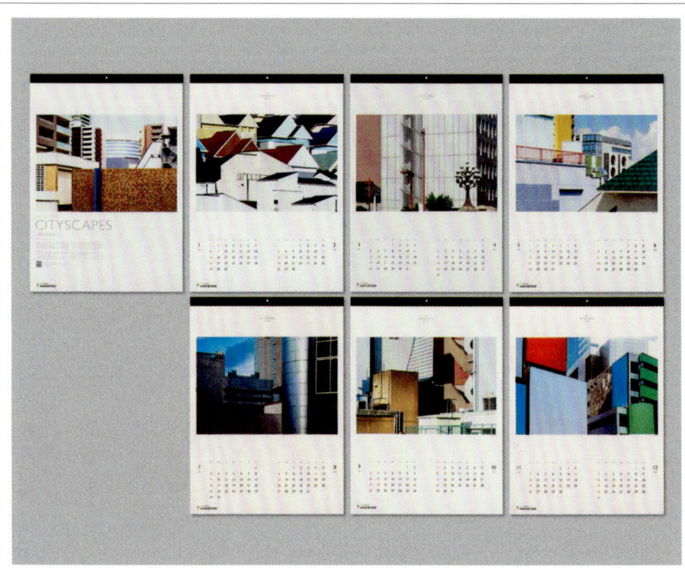

Title: 2023 Calendar "Cityscapes -Discovery-"
Client: Obayashi Corporation | **Design Firm:** Toppan Inc.

ROGER SAWHILL

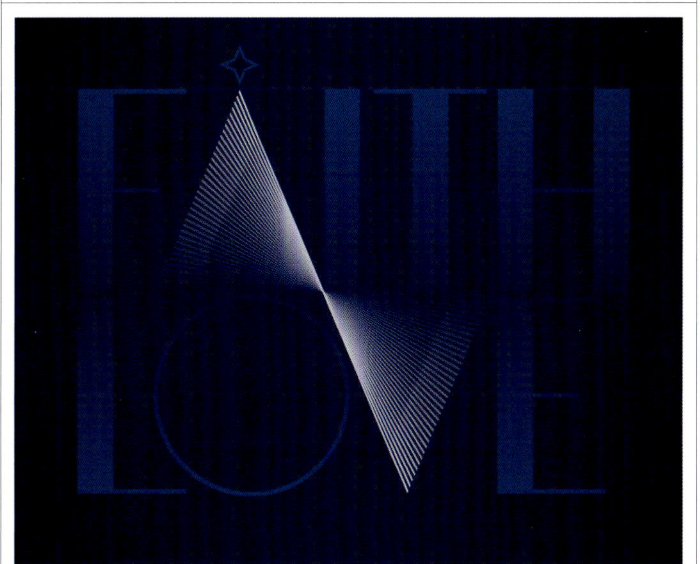

Title: Faith, Love, Hope Christmas Card | **Client:** UP-Fun
Design Firm: UP-Ideas

LISA VEIGEL GARCIA, KATE WATSON, LORI STADIG

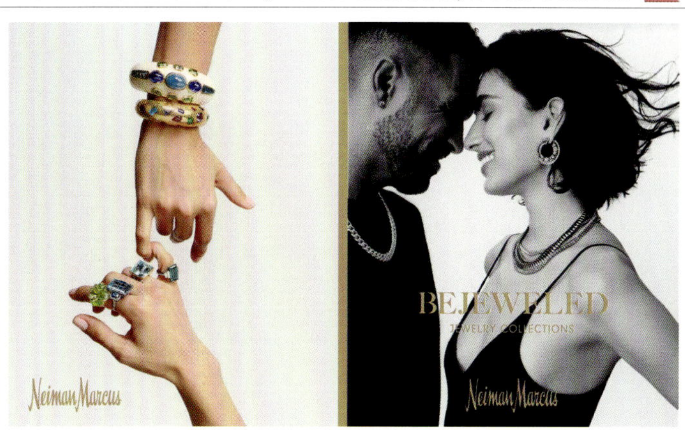

Title: Neiman Marcus Bejeweled Mailer | **Client:** Self-initiated
Design Firm: Neiman Marcus Creative Services

TOM VENTRESS

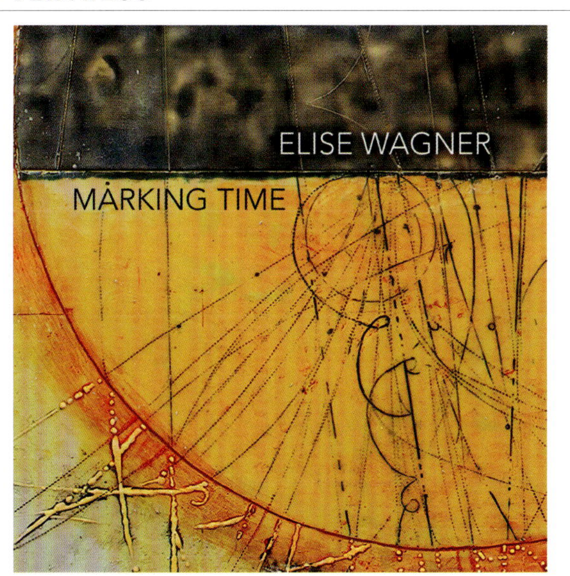

Title: Marking Time Exhibition Catalog | **Client:** Elise Wagner
Design Firm: Ventress Design Works

FERNANDO PALOMINO

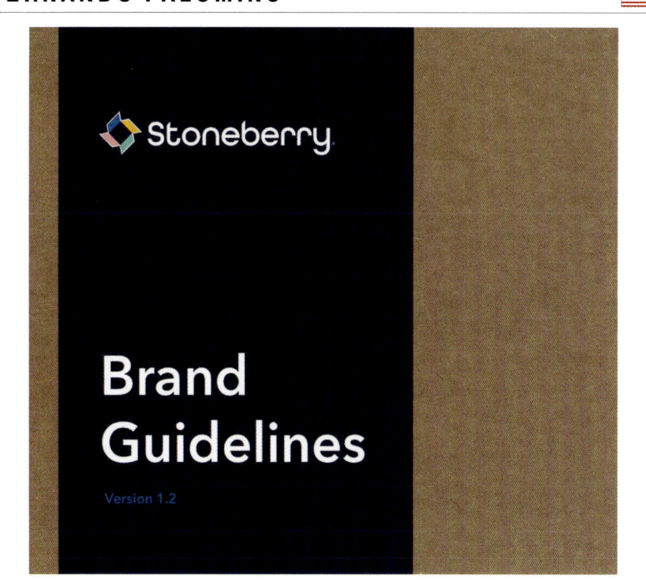

Title: Stoneberry Brand Guidelines | **Client:** Mason Companies
Design Firm: Preston Spire

TIM CRONIN

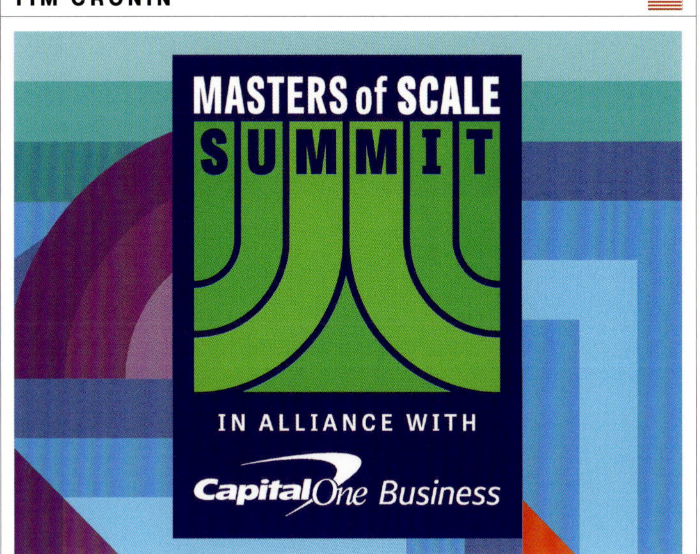

Title: Masters of Scale Inaugural Summit 2022
Client: Masters of Scale
Design Firm: WaitWhat (In-House)

STUDIONORTH

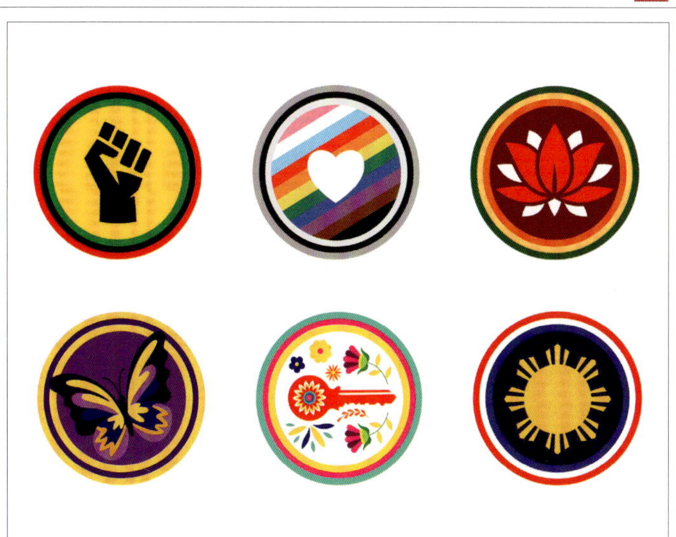

Title: College of American Pathologists: Employee Resource Groups Emblems
Client: College of American Pathologists | **Design Firm:** StudioNorth

GAETANO GRIZZANTI, GIANCARLO TOSONI

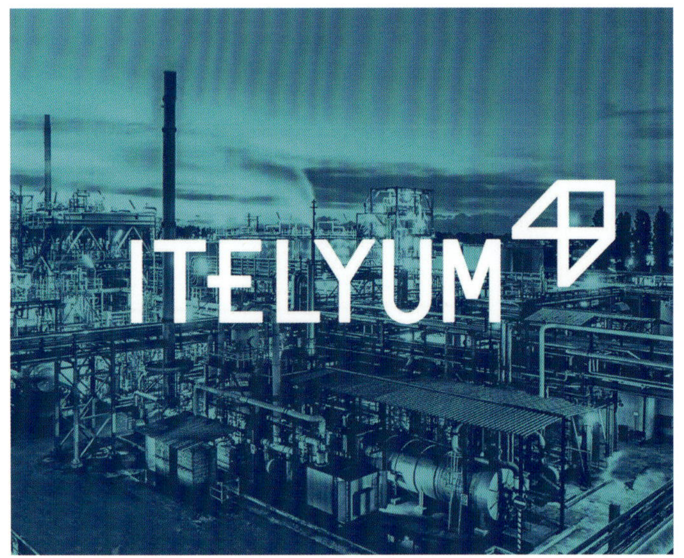

Title: The Icon of Sustainability | **Client:** Itelyum Group
Design Firm: Univisual SRL

MICROSOFT BRAND STUDIO

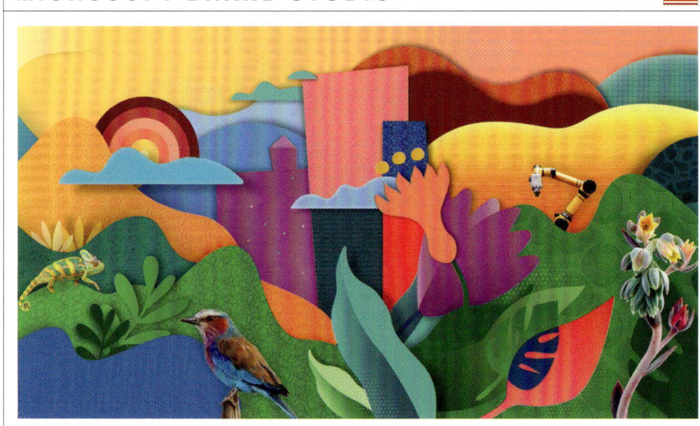

Title: The Future is Wild | **Client:** Self-initiated
Design Firm: Microsoft Brand Studio

ELMWOOD

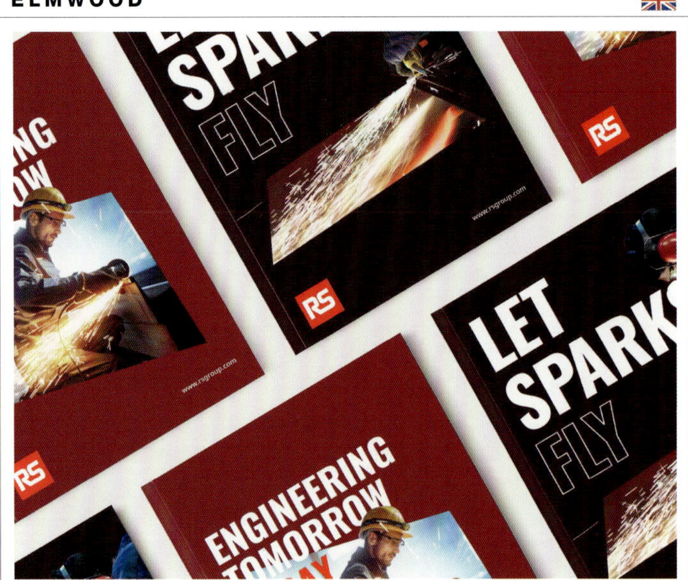

Title: Elmwood | **Client:** RS
Design Firm: Elmwood

ARIEL FREANER

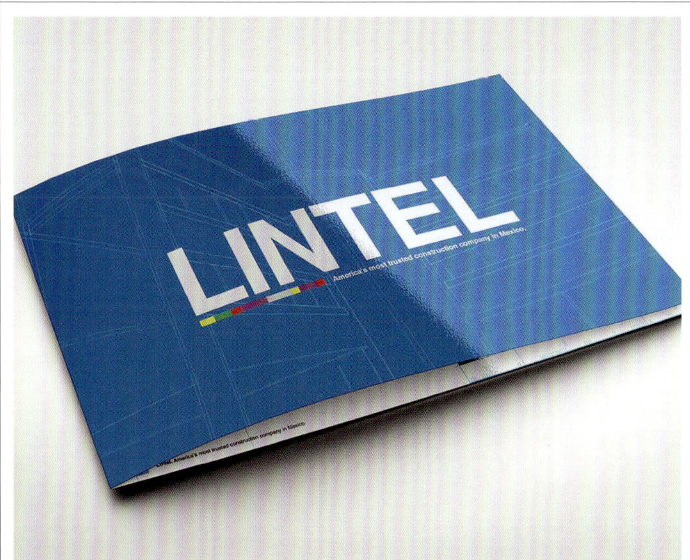

Title: LINTEL Corporate Brochure | **Clients:** LINTEL, Miguel Barreda
Design Firm: Freaner Creative & Design

SCHOOL OF DESIGN STUDENTS & ALUM

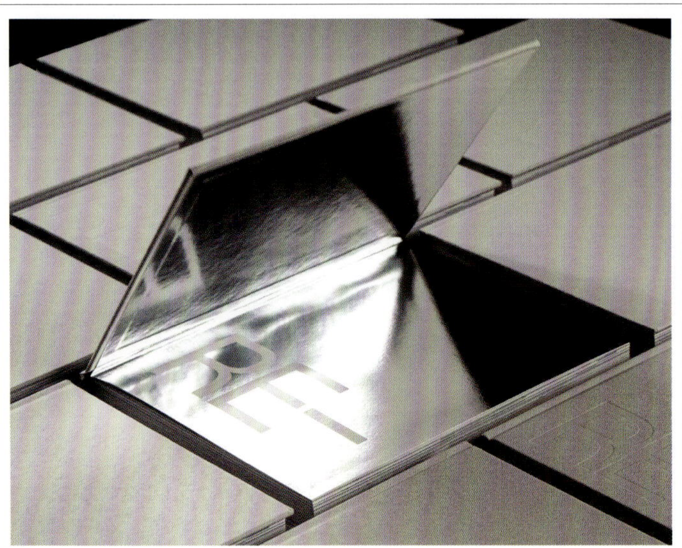

Title: RE: The School of Design 2018-21 Triennial
Clients: Ana Rita Morais, Luigi Ferrara, George Brown College School of Design | **Design Firm:** Jasmine Silang

ANOTHER COLLECTIVE, RAFAEL TONON

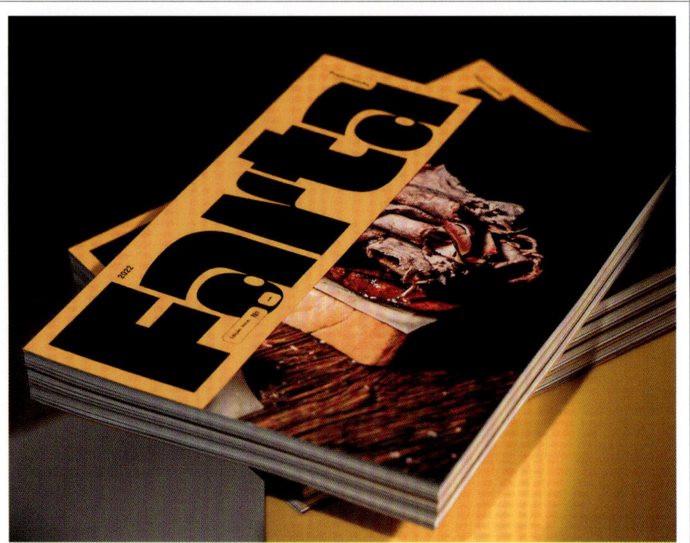

Title: Farta
Clients: Revista Farta, Self-initiated
Design Firm: Another Collective

TREVETT MCCANDLISS, NANCY CAMPBELL

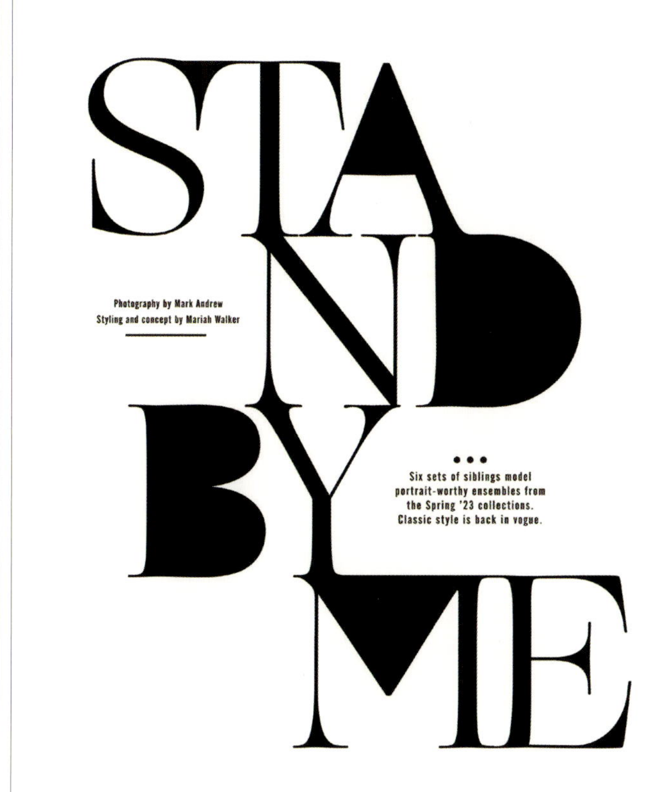

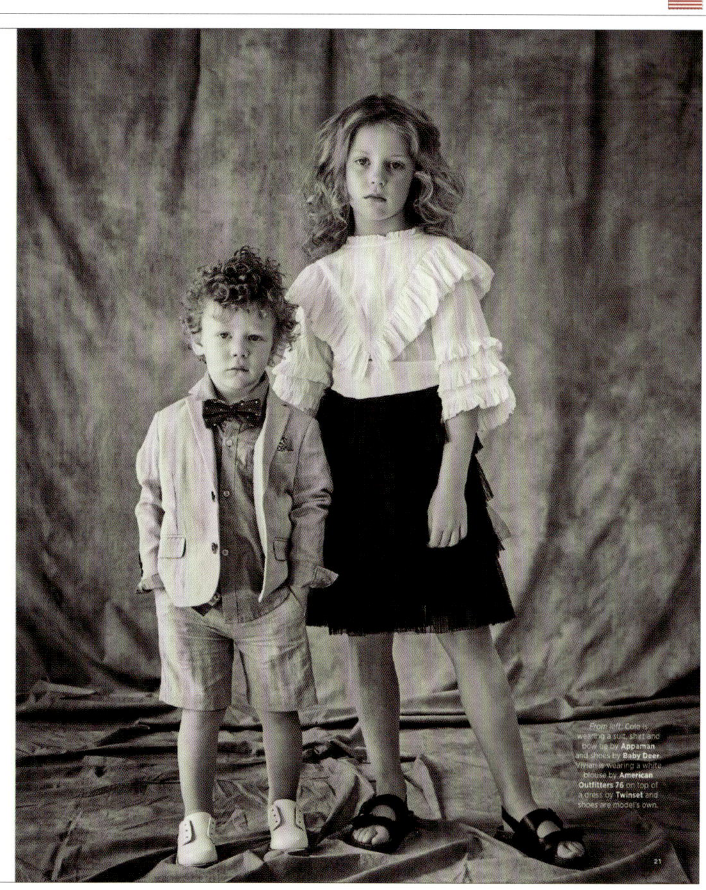

Title: Stand By Me | **Client:** Earnshaw's Magazine | **Design Firm:** Wainscot Media

TREVETT MCCANDLISS, NANCY CAMPBELL

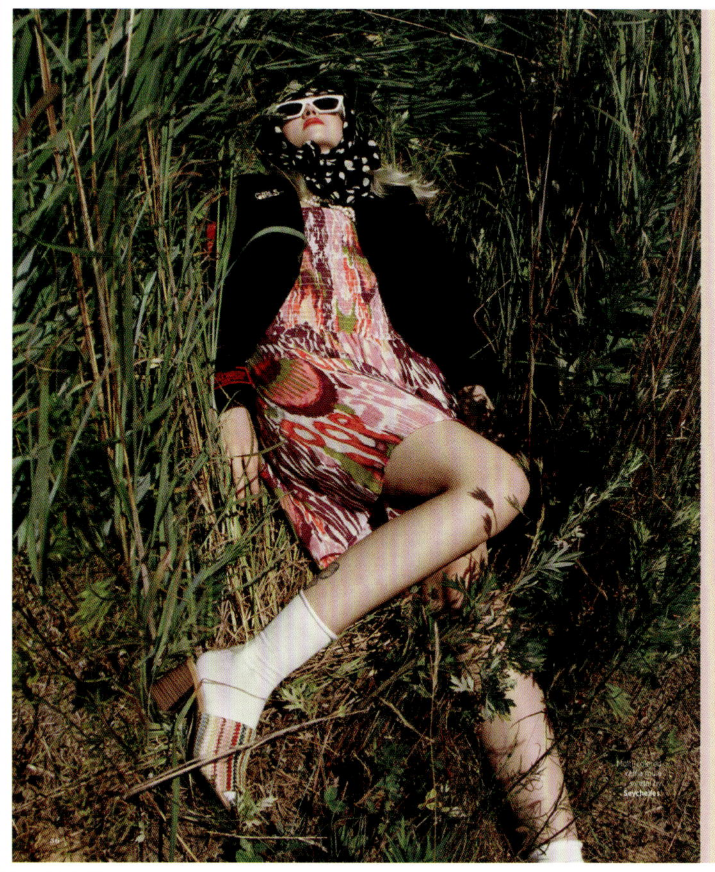

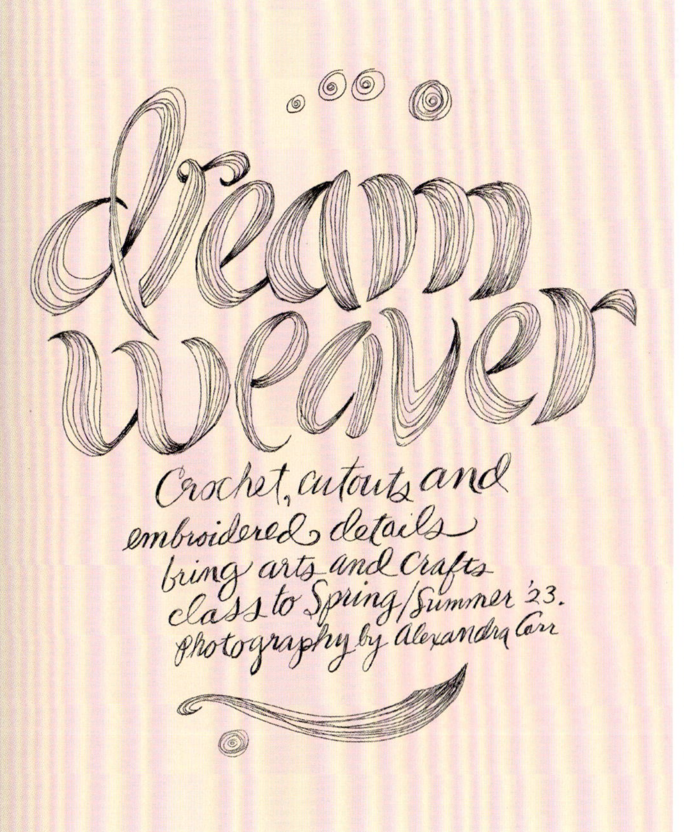

Title: Dream Weaver | **Client:** Footwear Plus Magazine | **Design Firm:** Wainscot Media

TREVETT MCCANDLISS, NANCY CAMPBELL

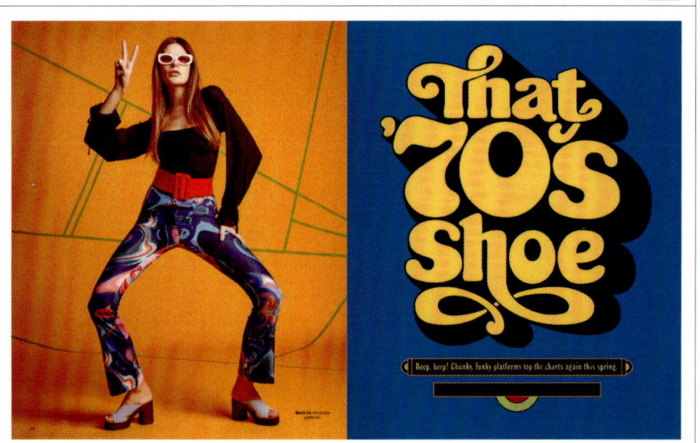

Title: That 70s Shoe | **Client:** Footwear Plus Magazine
Design Firm: Wainscot Media

TREVETT MCCANDLISS, NANCY CAMPBELL

W I L D
W O R L D
the wind calls me
Morning again
Here, a friend
Off to see the day

Title: Wild World | **Client:** Earnshaw's Magazine
Design Firm: Wainscot Media

TREVETT MCCANDLISS, NANCY CAMPBELL

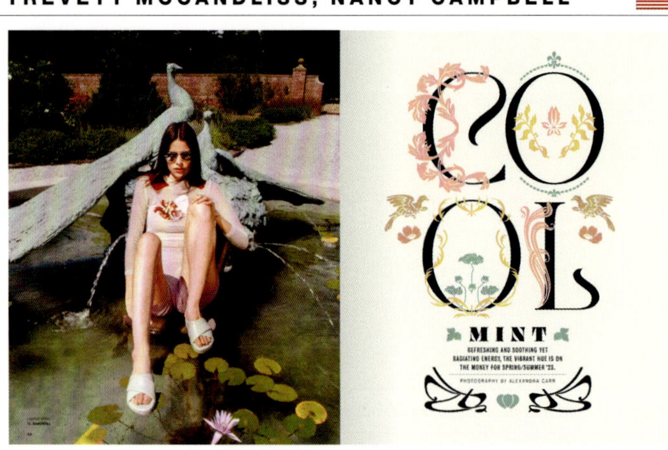

Title: Cool Mint | **Client:** Footwear Plus Magazine
Design Firm: Wainscot Media

TREVETT MCCANDLISS, NANCY CAMPBELL

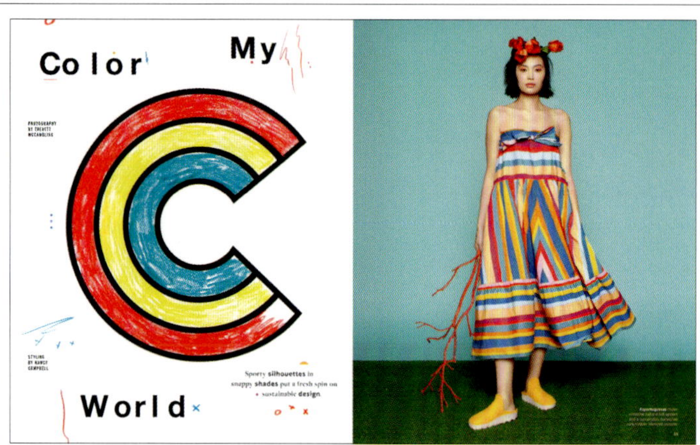

Title: Color My World | **Client:** Footwear Plus Magazine
Design Firm: Wainscot Media

TREVETT MCCANDLISS, NANCY CAMPBELL

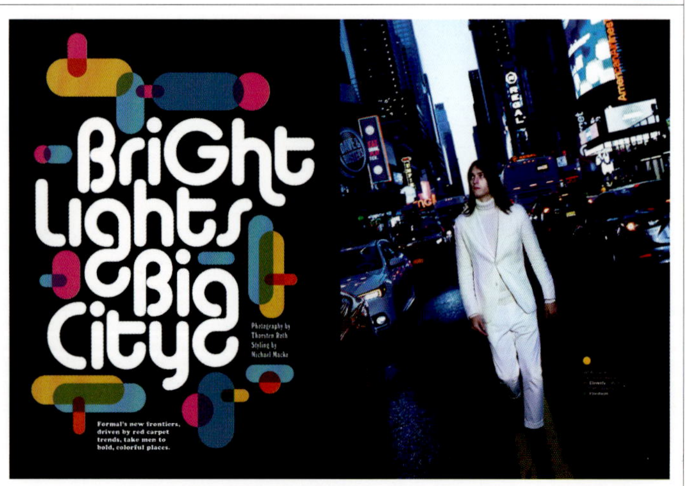

Title: Bright Lights, Big City | **Client:** MR Magazine
Design Firm: Wainscot Media

TREVETT MCCANDLISS, NANCY CAMPBELL

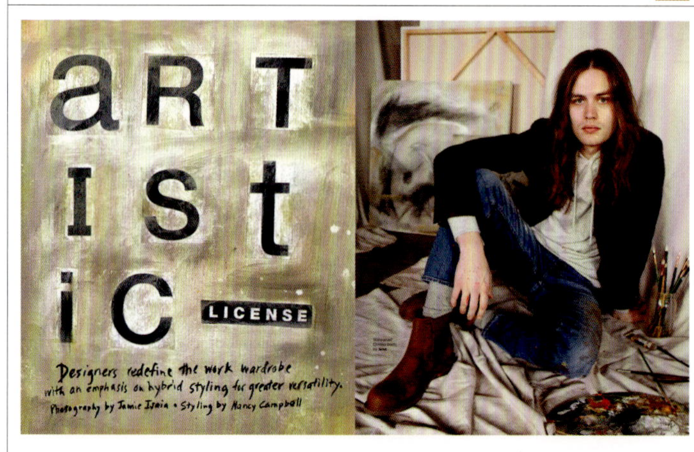

Title: Artistic License | **Client:** Footwear Plus Magazine
Design Firm: Wainscot Media

TREVETT MCCANDLISS, NANCY CAMPBELL

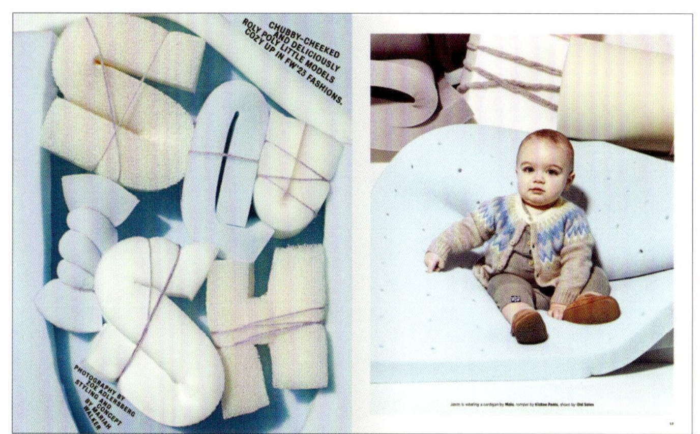

Title: Squish | **Client:** Earnshaw's Magazine
Design Firm: Wainscot Media

TREVETT MCCANDLISS, NANCY CAMPBELL

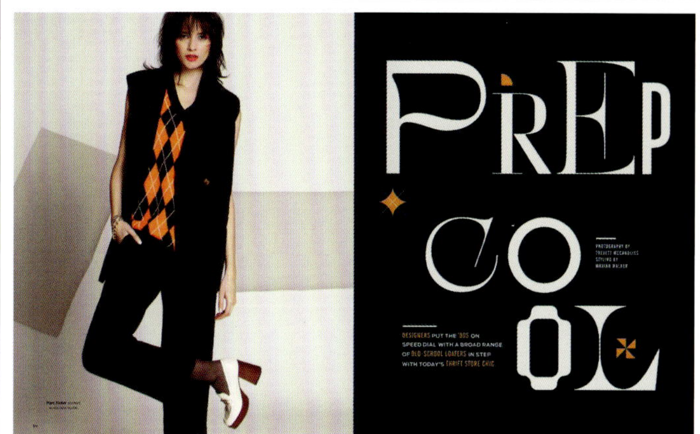

Title: Prep Cool | **Client:** Footwear Plus Magazine
Design Firm: Wainscot Media

TREVETT MCCANDLISS, NANCY CAMPBELL

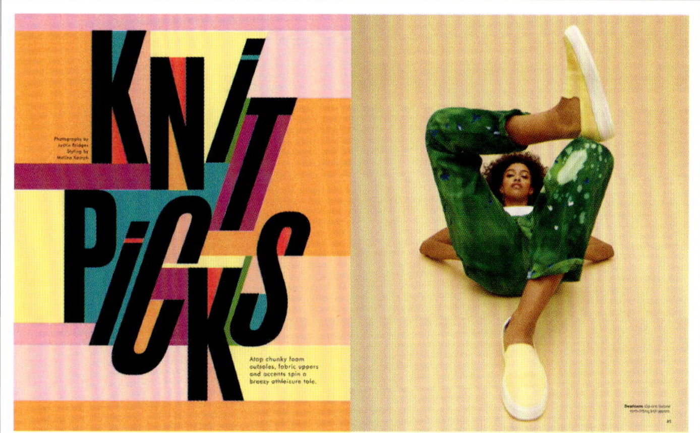

Title: Knit Picks | **Client:** Footwear Plus Magazine
Design Firm: Wainscot Media

TREVETT MCCANDLISS, NANCY CAMPBELL

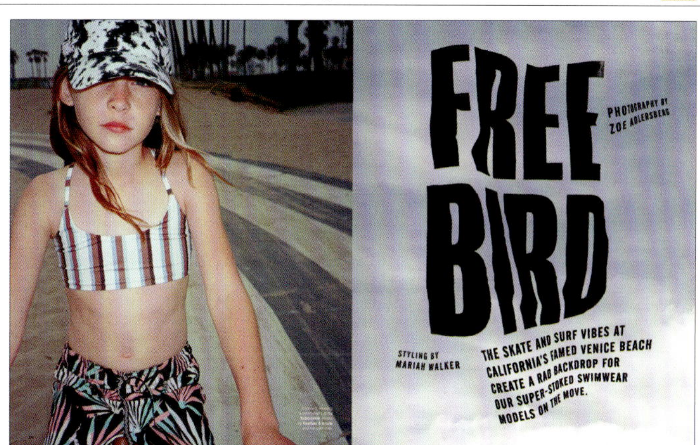

Title: Free Bird | **Client:** Earnshaw's Magazine
Design Firm: Wainscot Media

TREVETT MCCANDLISS, NANCY CAMPBELL

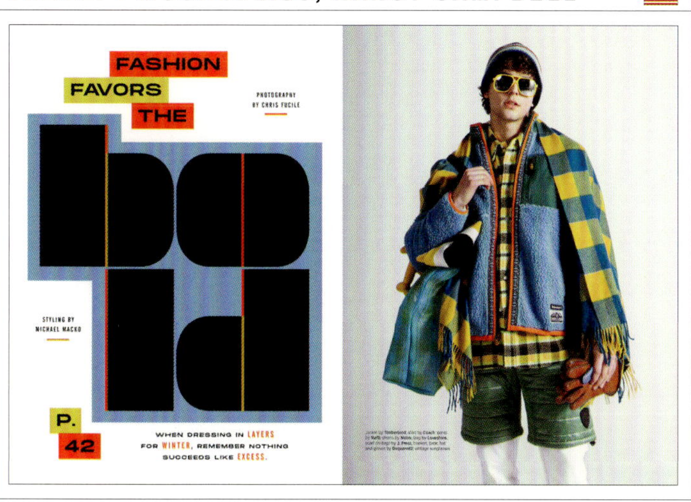

Title: Fashion Favors the Bold | **Client:** MR Magazine
Design Firm: Wainscot Media

TREVETT MCCANDLISS, NANCY CAMPBELL

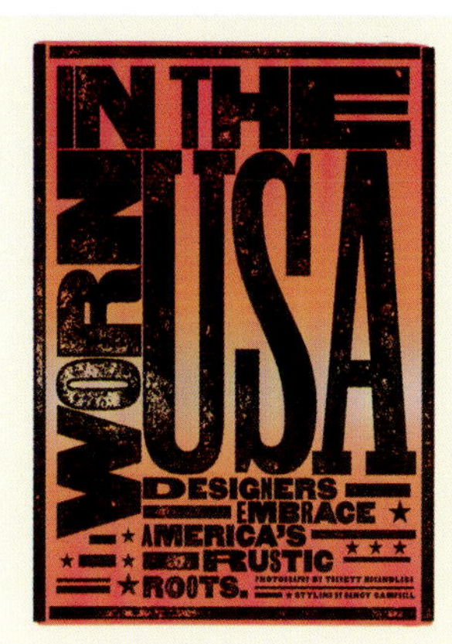

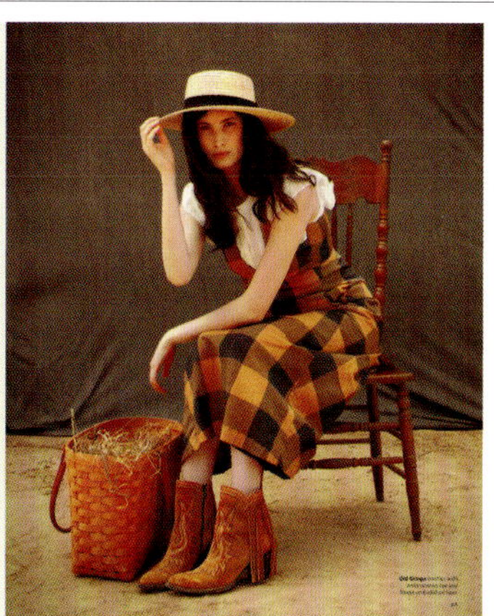

Title: Worn in the USA | **Client:** Footwear Plus Magazine
Design Firm: Wainscot Media

TIM MACKAY

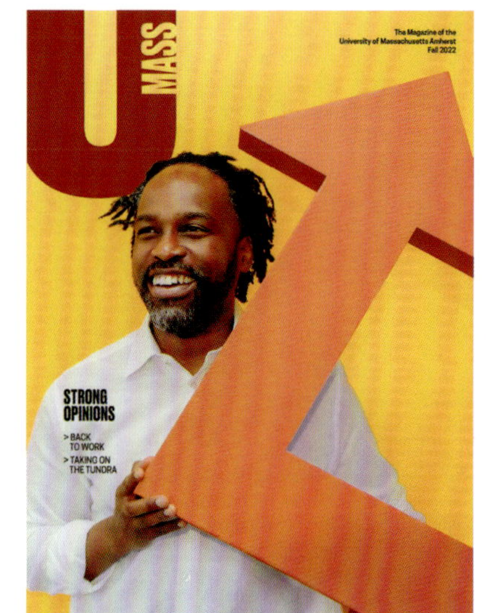

Title: UMass Magazine - Fall 2022
Client: University of Massachusetts Amherst
Design Firm: BRIGADE

DELFIN

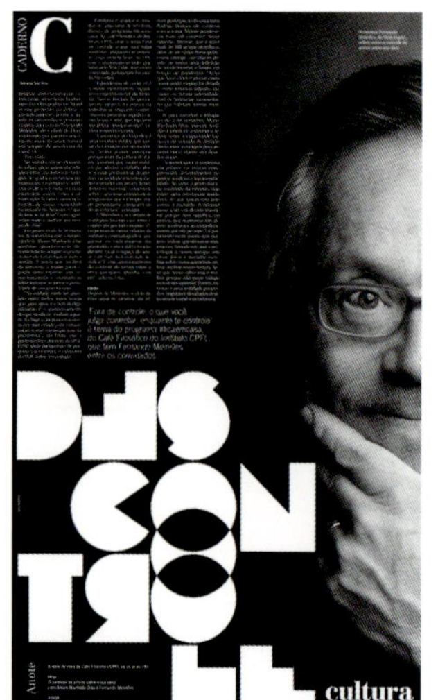

Title: Descontrole (Uncontrolled)
Client: Correio Popular
Design Firm: Studio DelRey

ARNAUD GHELFI

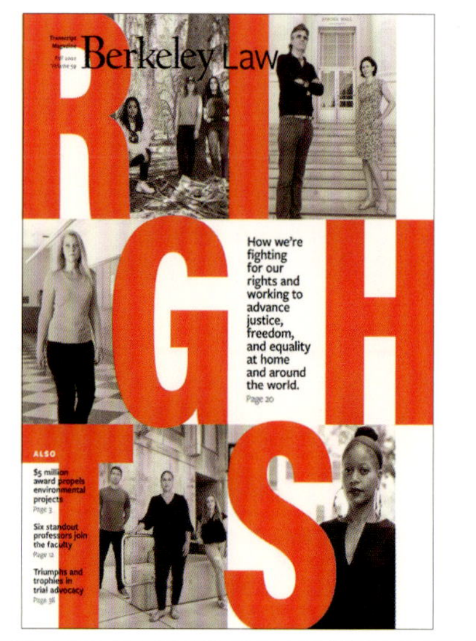

Title: RIGHTS
Clients: UC Berkeley Law, Transcript Magazine
Design Firm: Atelier Starno

KATHY MUELLER

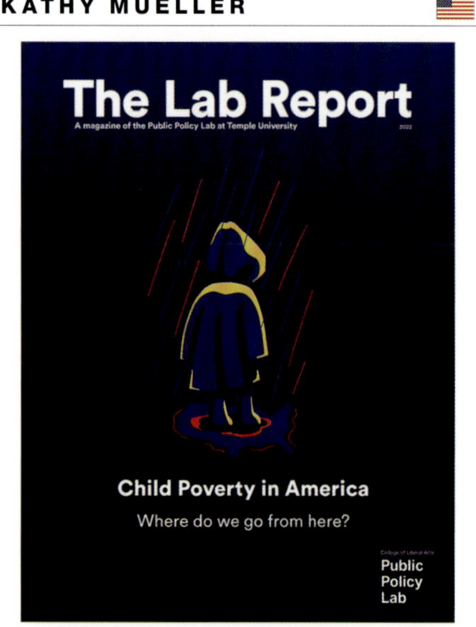

Title: Child Poverty in America
Client: Public Policy Lab at Temple University
Design Firm: Kathy Mueller Design, LLC

MINGXIN CHENG

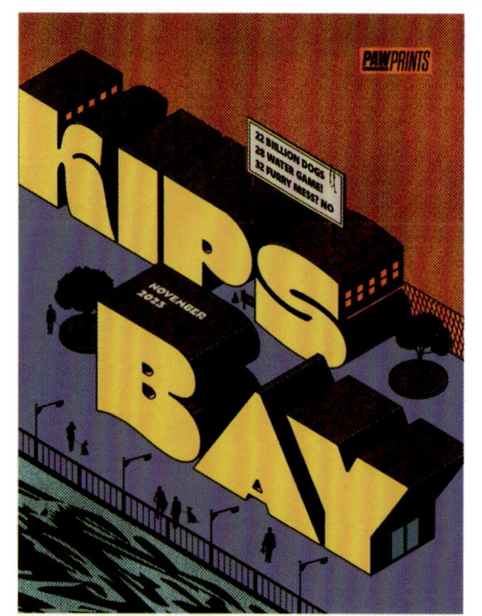

Title: PAWPRINTS Magazine Cover Series
Client: Self-initiated
Design Firm: Mingxin Cheng

MYSTIE DO

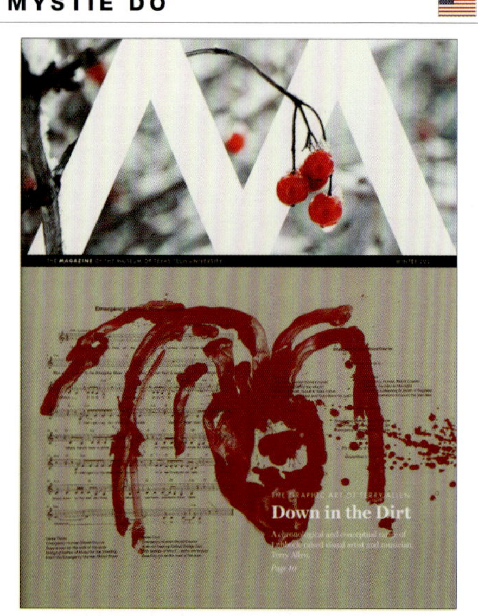

Title: M Magazine | **Client:** Self-initiated
Design Firm: Museum of Texas Tech University, Communications & Marketing

TIM PITTMAN (+6)

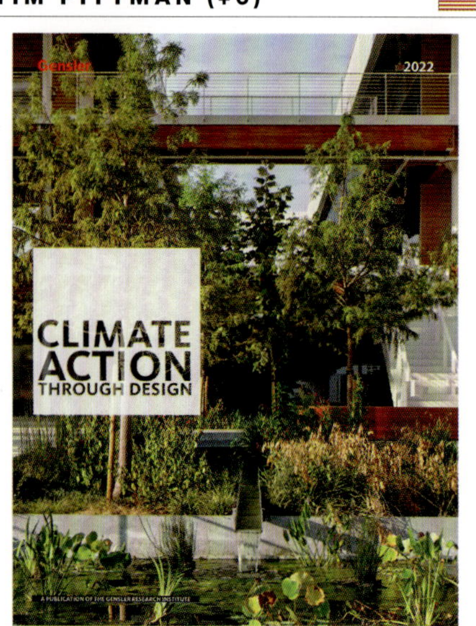

Title: Climate Action Through Design 2022
Client: Self-initiated
Design Firm: Gensler

CHRISTINE BARBER (+5)

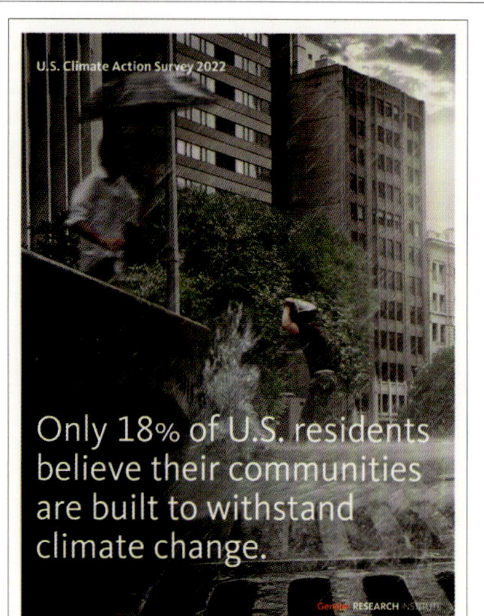

Title: Climate Action Survey 2022
Client: Self-initiated
Design Firm: Gensler

KRISTEN MORABITO

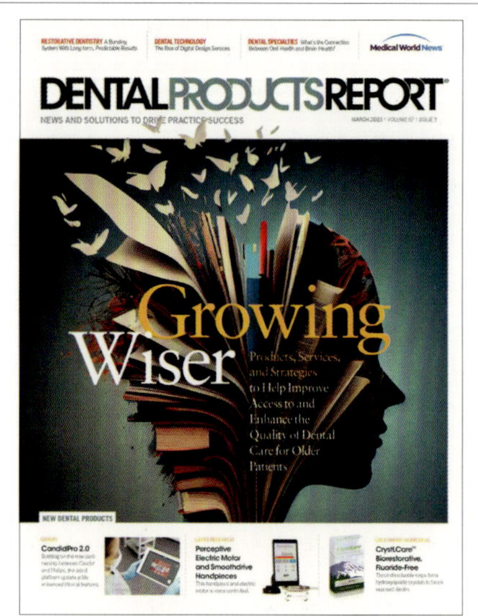

Title: Growing Wiser
Client: Dental Products Report
Design Firm: MJH Life Sciences

MICK ROCK

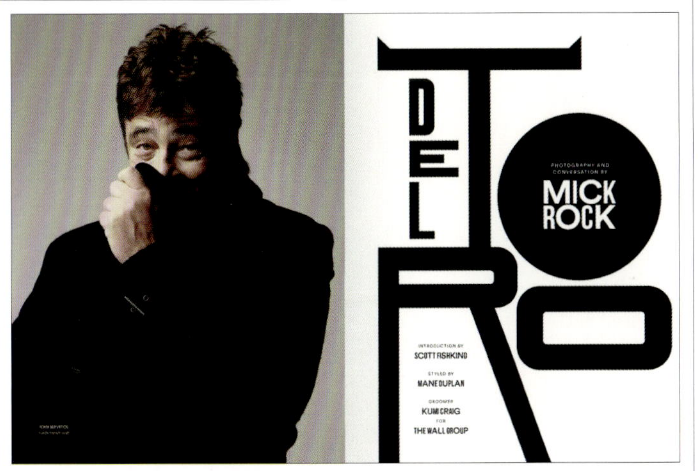

Title: Del Toro by Mick Rock for AS IF Mag | **Client:** Self-initiated
Design Firm: AS IF Media Group

JENNIFER BARLOW

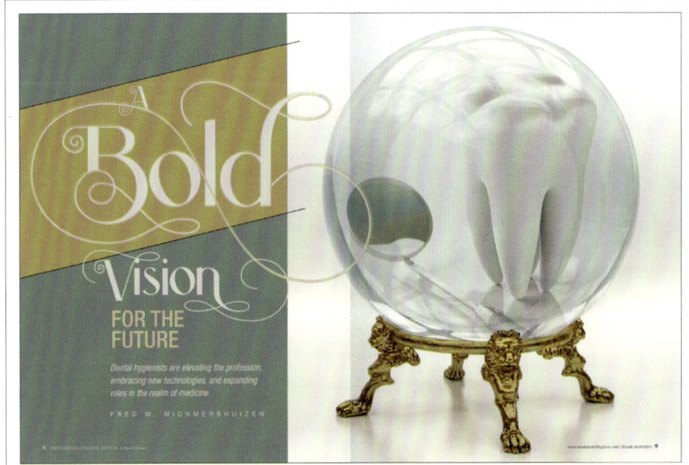

Title: A Bold Vision for the Future | **Client:** Inside Dental Hygiene
Design Firm: BroadcastMed

JUAN CARLOS PAGAN

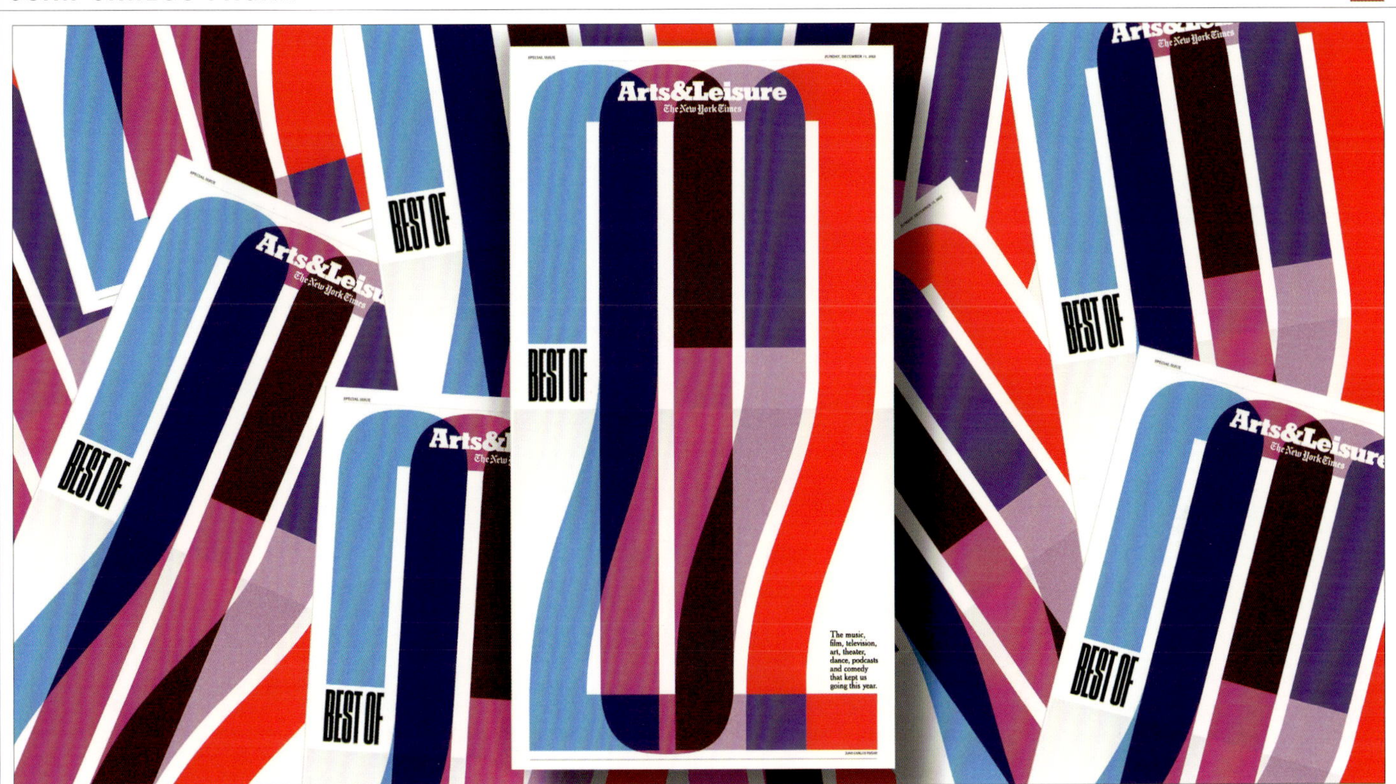

Title: New York Times Cover, Best of 2022 | **Client:** The New York Times | **Design Firm:** Sunday Afternoon

MICROSOFT BRAND STUDIO, O0

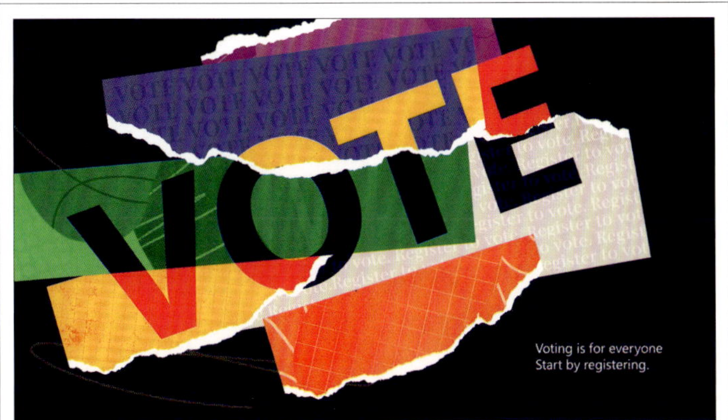

Title: Empowering GenZ to Take Control of Their Future
Client: Microsoft
Design Firms: Microsoft Brand Studio, O0

STERLING, BLK:OPS, BIGROCKXR, MICROSOFT BRAND STU.

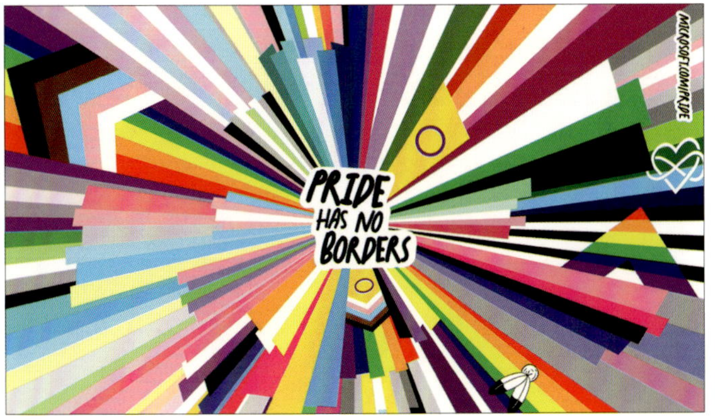

Title: Pride Has No Borders
Client: Microsoft
Design Firms: Sterling, Blk:ops, BigRockXR, Microsoft Brand Studio

RANDY CLARK

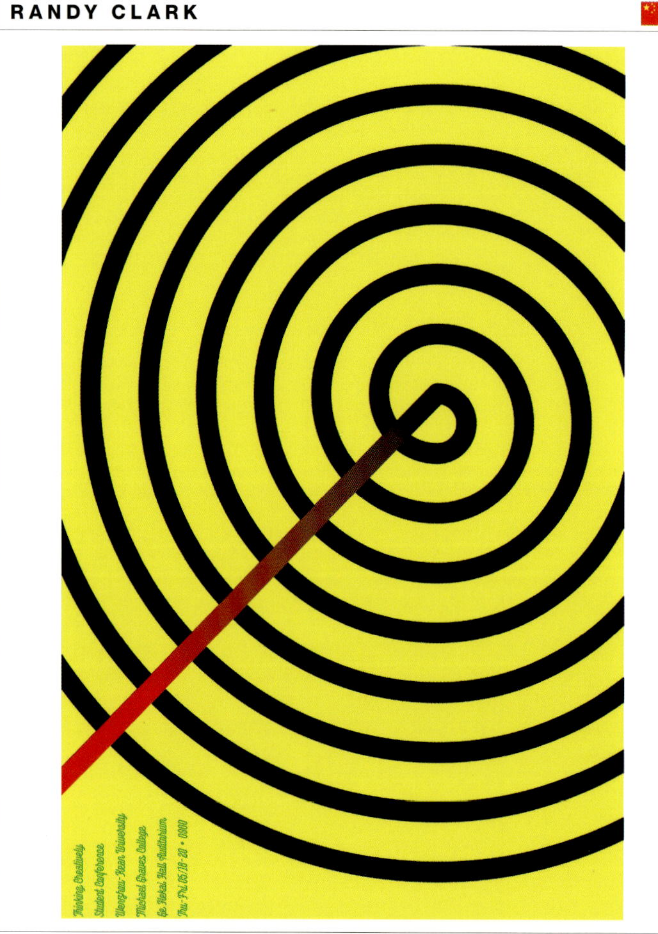

Title: Thinking Creatively Student Conference Poster
Clients: Wenzhou Kean University, Michael Graves College
Design Firm: Randy Clark Graphic Design

MICHAEL BRALEY

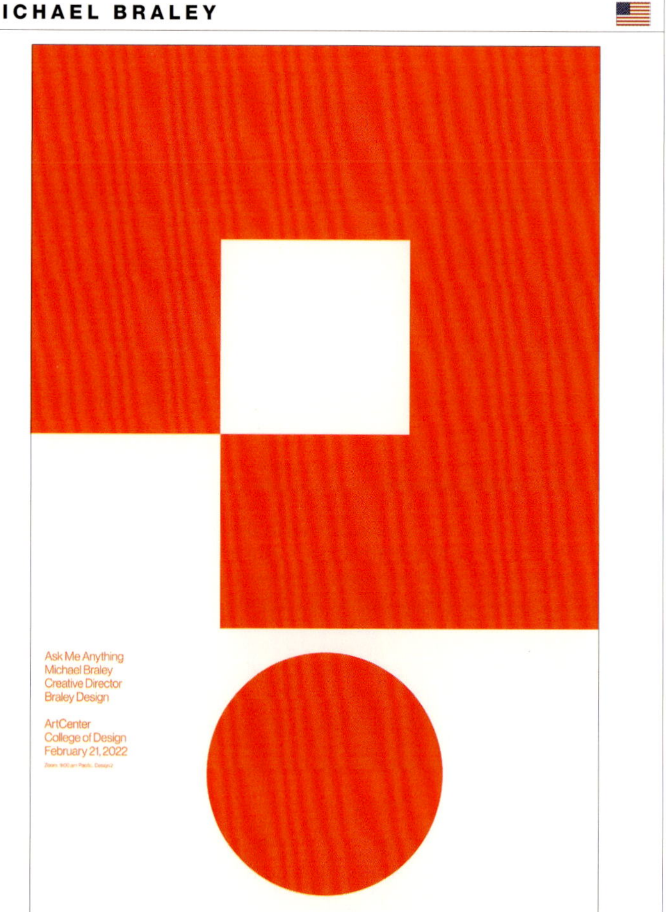

Title: ArtCenter: Ask Me Anything Lecture Poster
Client: ArtCenter College of Design
Design Firm: Braley Design

MARIA VILAVERDE

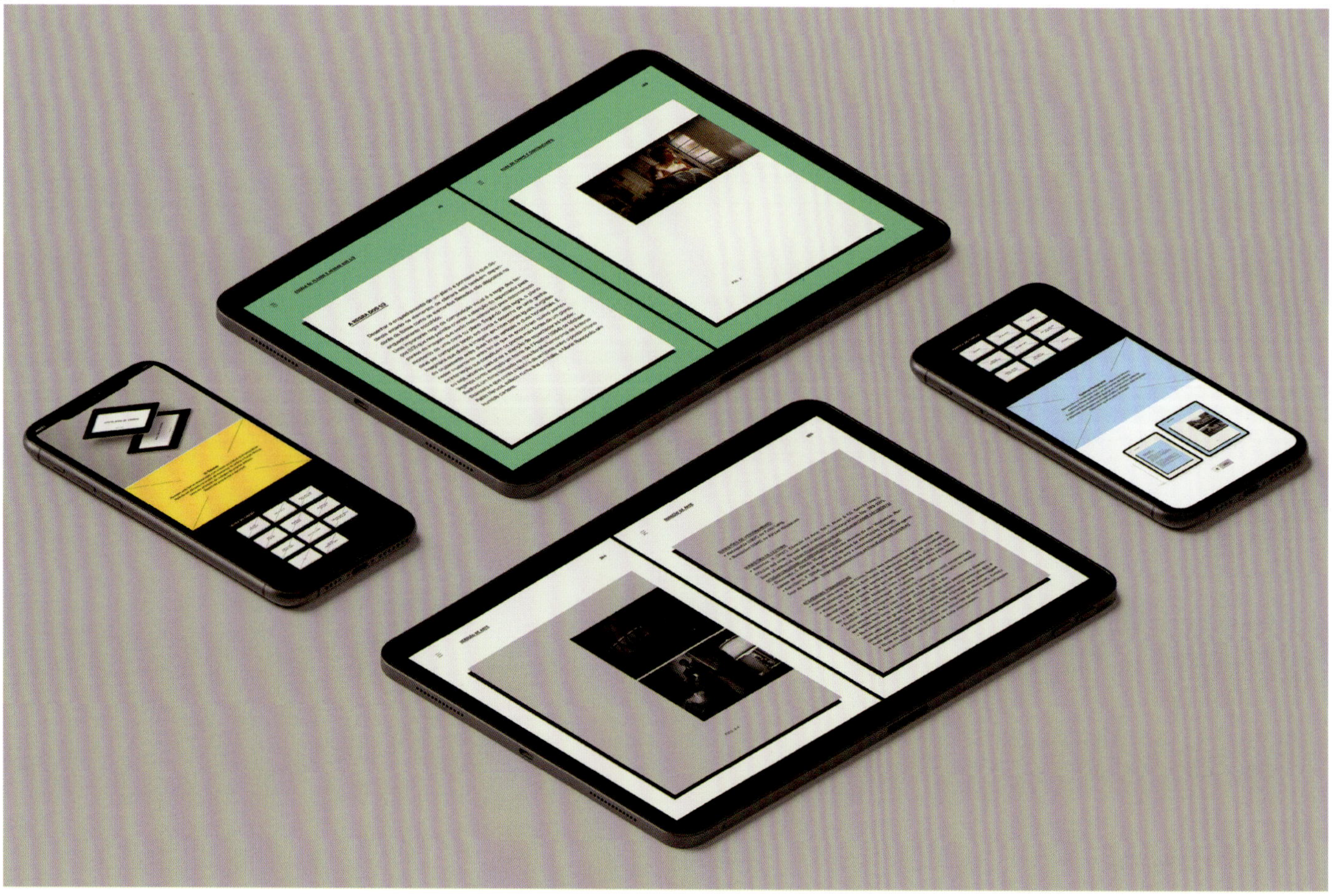

Title: Insert | **Client:** Universidade Católica Portuguesa School of Arts | **Design Firm:** By Scala

ASTERISK

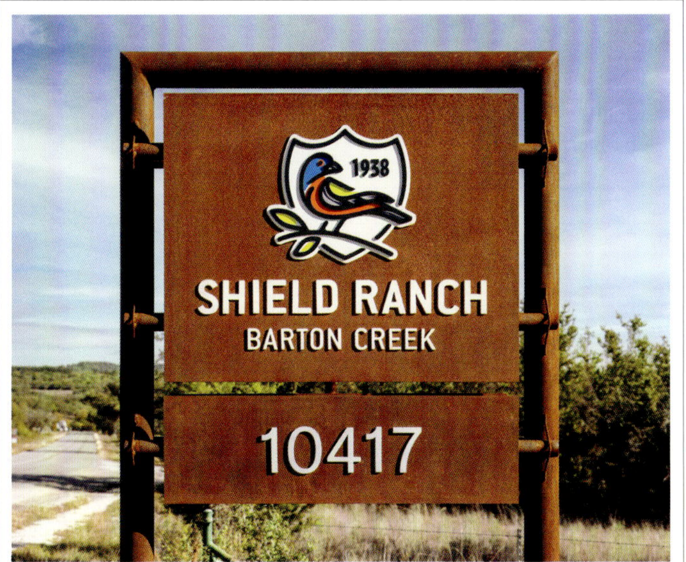

Title: The Campsite at Shield Ranch
Client: Shield Ranch Foundation | **Design Firm:** Asterisk

EMANUEL BARBOSA

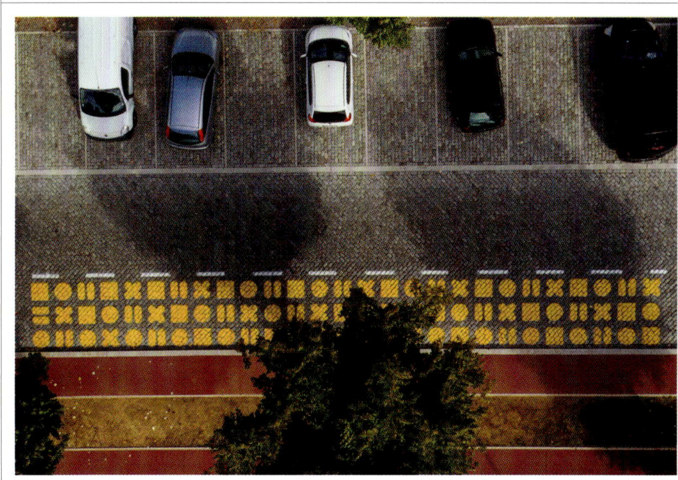

Title: Kiss & Go School Lanes Vila Real
Client: Câmara Municipal de Vila Real | **Design Firm:** Vestígio Design

SIENA SCARFF

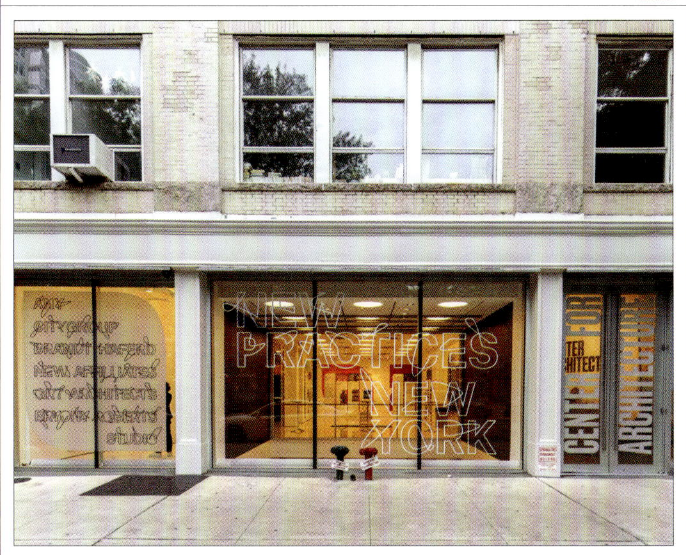

Title: Center for Architecture | New Practices New York Exhibition
Client: Center for Architecture New York
Design Firm: Siena Scarff Design

LEWIS COMMUNICATIONS

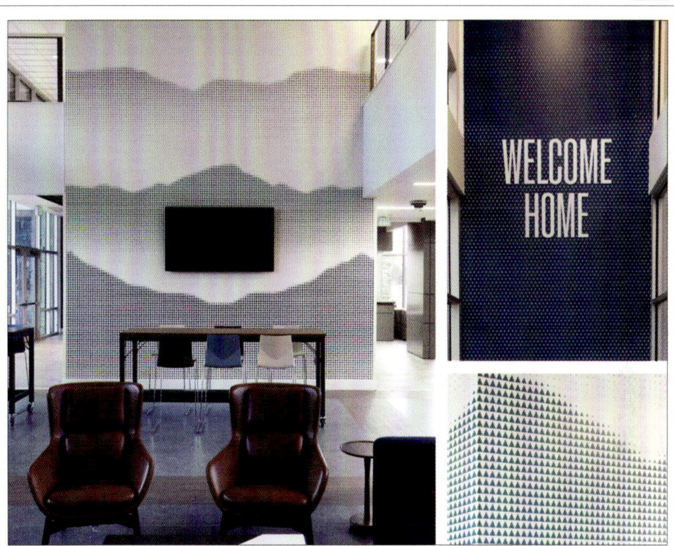

Title: Residence Hall Design
Client: Highlands College
Design Firm: Lewis Communications

ENTRO

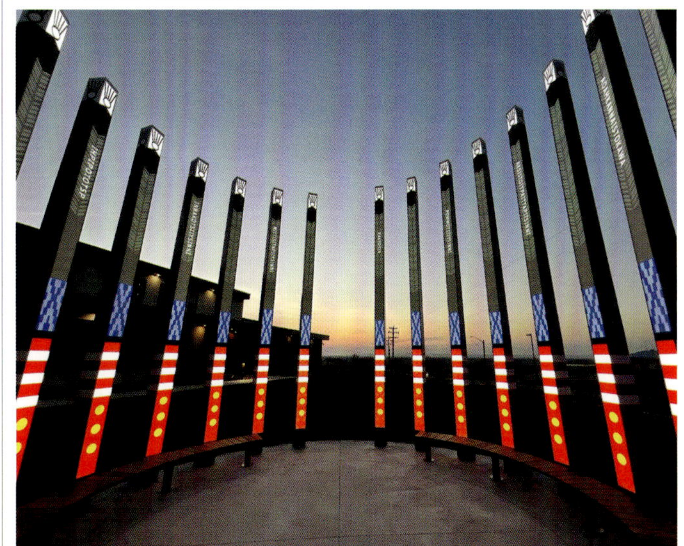

Title: Mi'kai'sto (Red Crow Community College)
Client: Mi'kai'sto (Red Crow Community College) | **Design Firm:** Entro

ENTRO

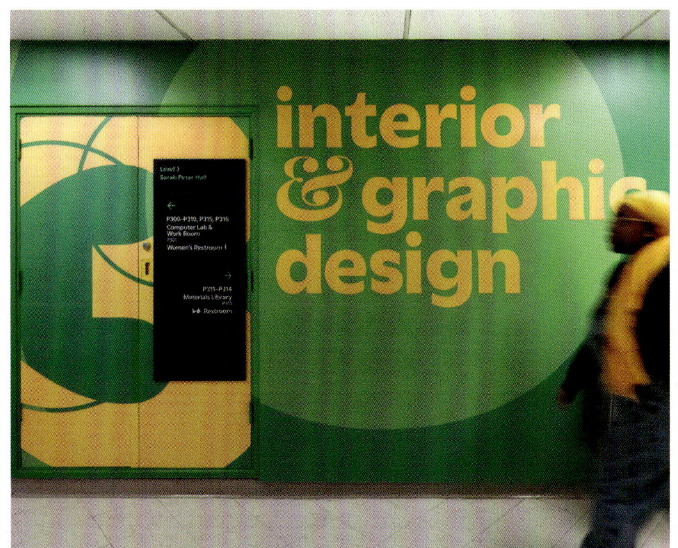

Title: Moore College of Art & Design Experiential Graphics
Client: Moore College of Art & Design | **Design Firm:** Entro

ARTHOUSE DESIGN

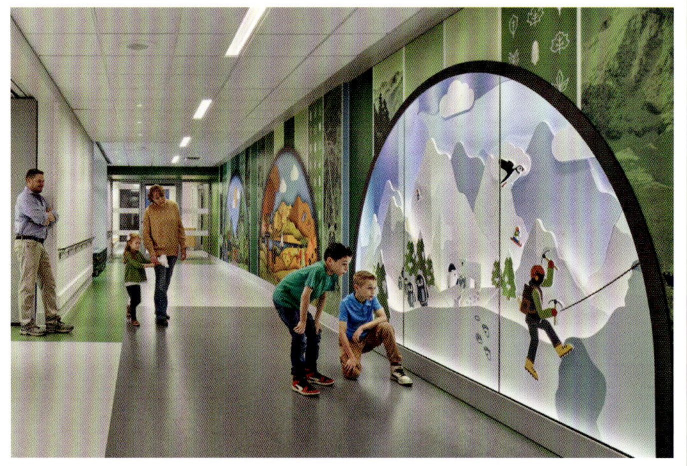

Title: Boston Children's Hospital Hale Family Clinical Building
Client: Boston Children's Hospital | **Design Firm:** ArtHouse Design

3D IDENTITY

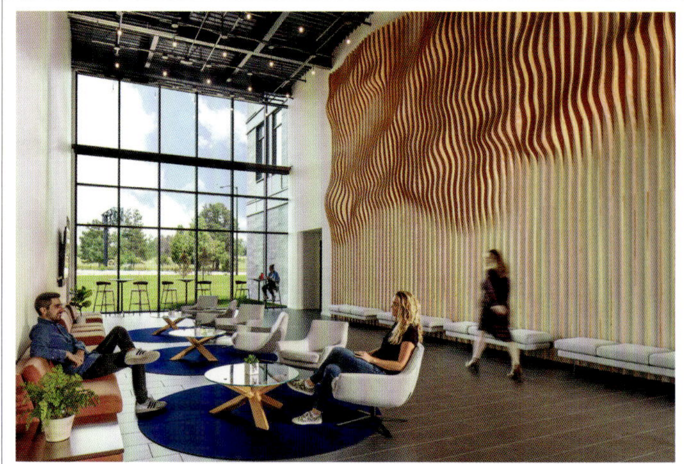

Title: Placemaking + Experiential Branding: Blue Federal Credit Union
Client: Blue Federal Credit Union | **Design Firm:** 3D Identity

AIRSPACE

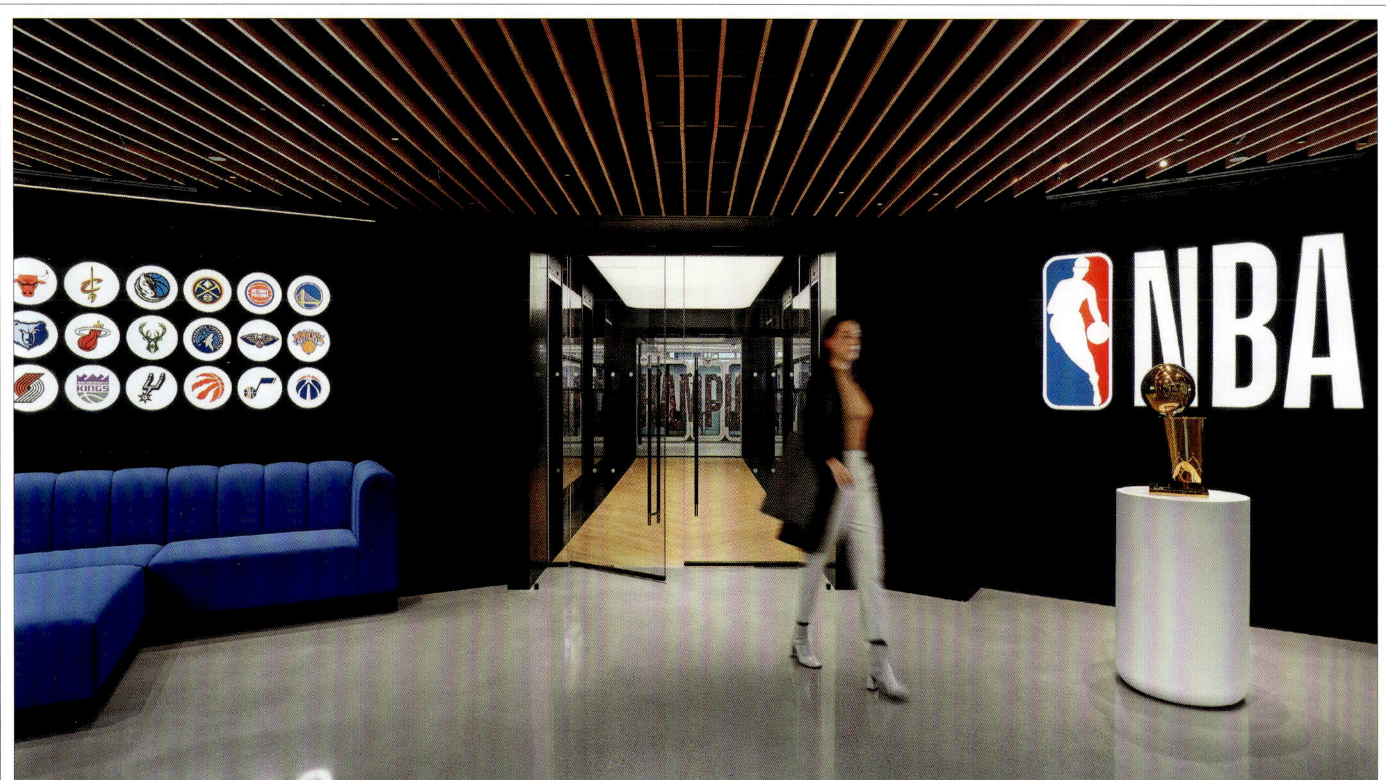

Title: National Basketball Association, NBA | **Client:** National Basketball Association (NBA) | **Design Firm:** Airspace

ENTRO

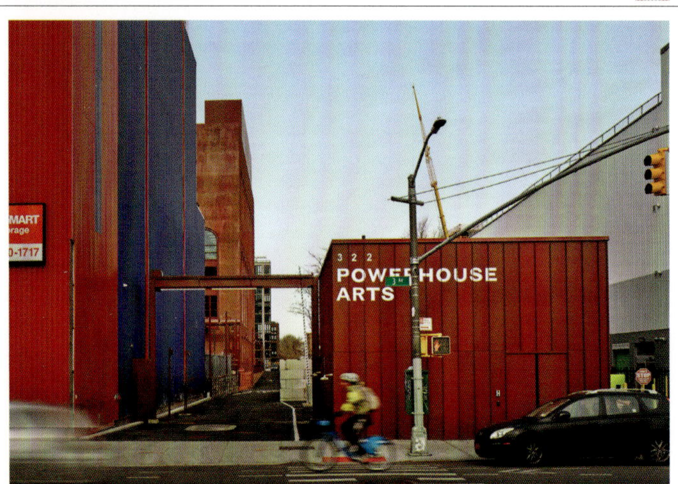

Title: Powerhouse Arts | **Client:** Powerhouse Arts | **Design Firm:** Entro

ASTERISK

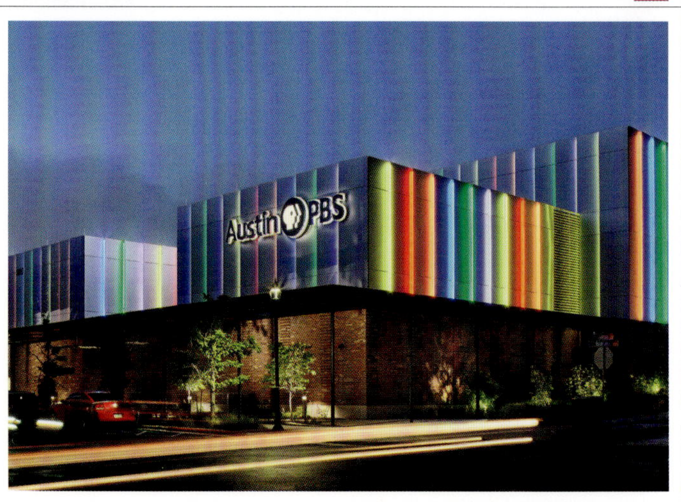

Title: Austin PBS | **Client:** Austin PBS | **Design Firm:** Asterisk

LEE COOMBER, LIPPINCOTT

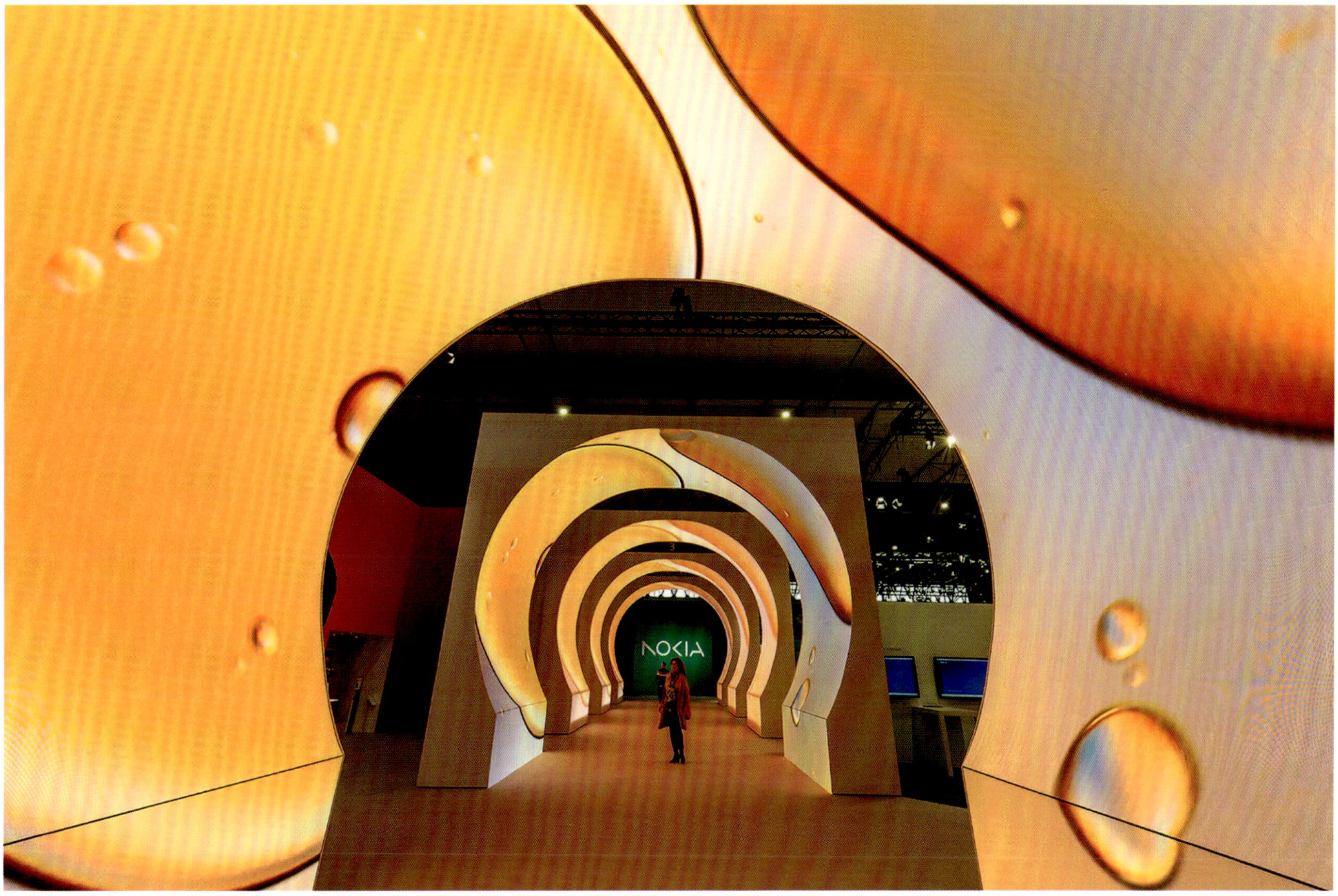

Title: Nokia at Mobile World Congress | **Client:** Nokia | **Design Firm:** Lippincott

DLR GROUP, JOVANEY HOLLINGSWORTH

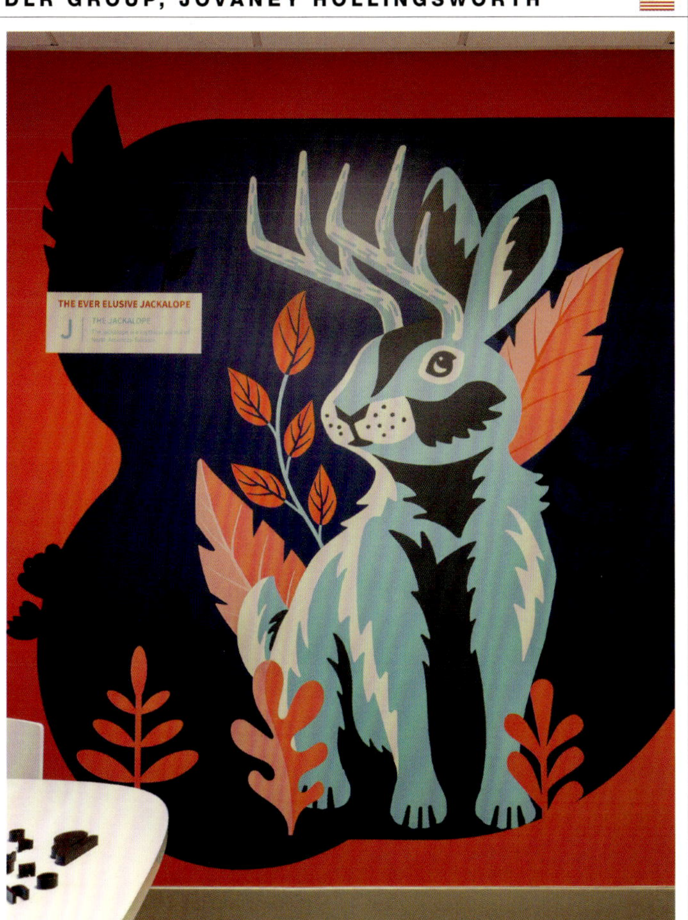

Title: DLR Group - Austin Studio
Client: Self-initiated | **Design Firm:** DLR Group

ARTHOUSE DESIGN

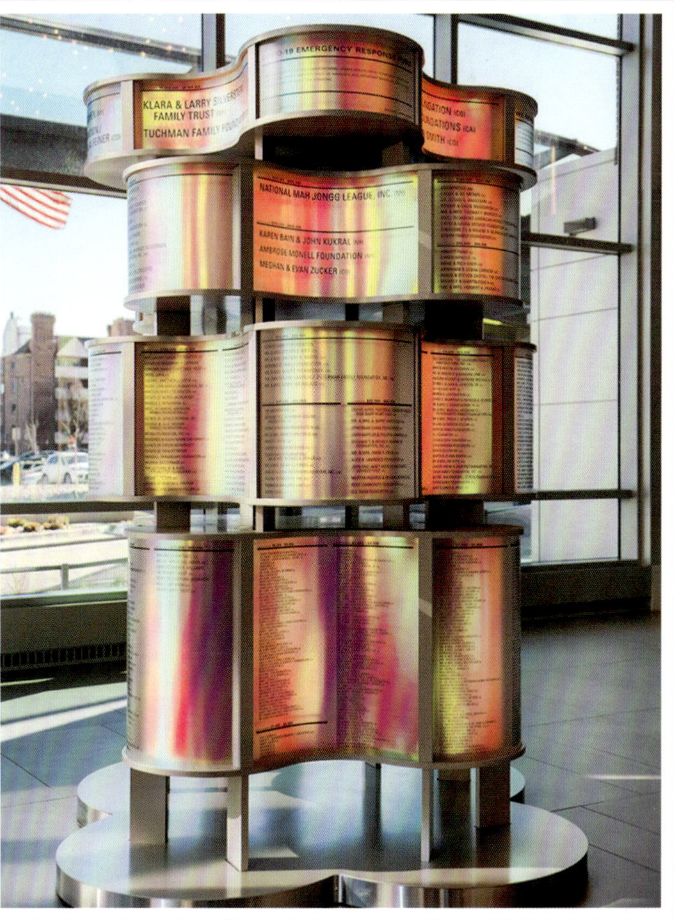

Title: Donor Recognition for the New NJH Outpatient Health Building
Client: National Jewish Health | **Design Firm:** ArtHouse Design

INSIGHT CREATIVE

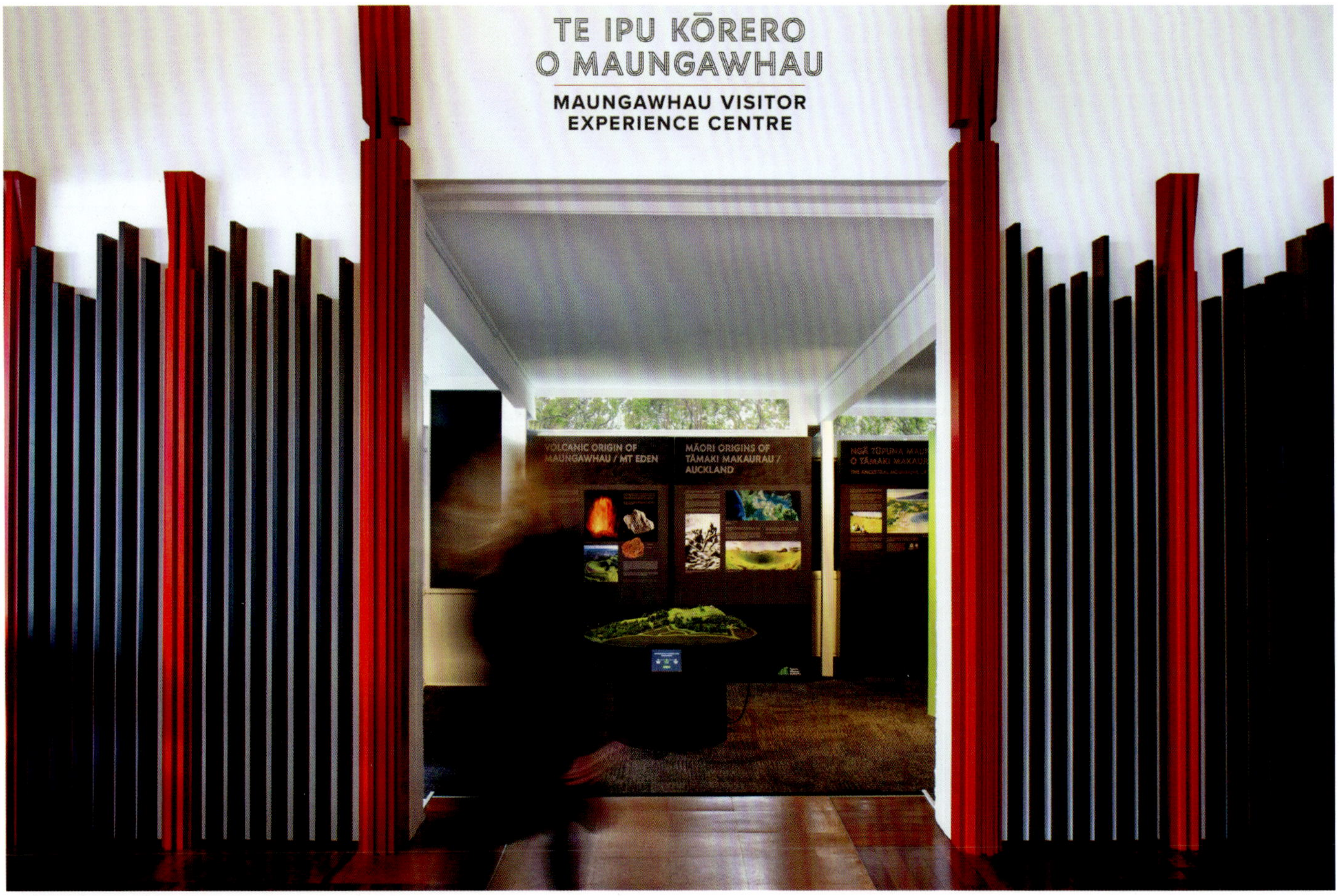

Title: Maungawhau Visitor Information Center Showcase | **Client:** Tupuna Maunga Authority | **Design Firm:** Insight Creative

RALPH APPELBAUM ASSOCIATES

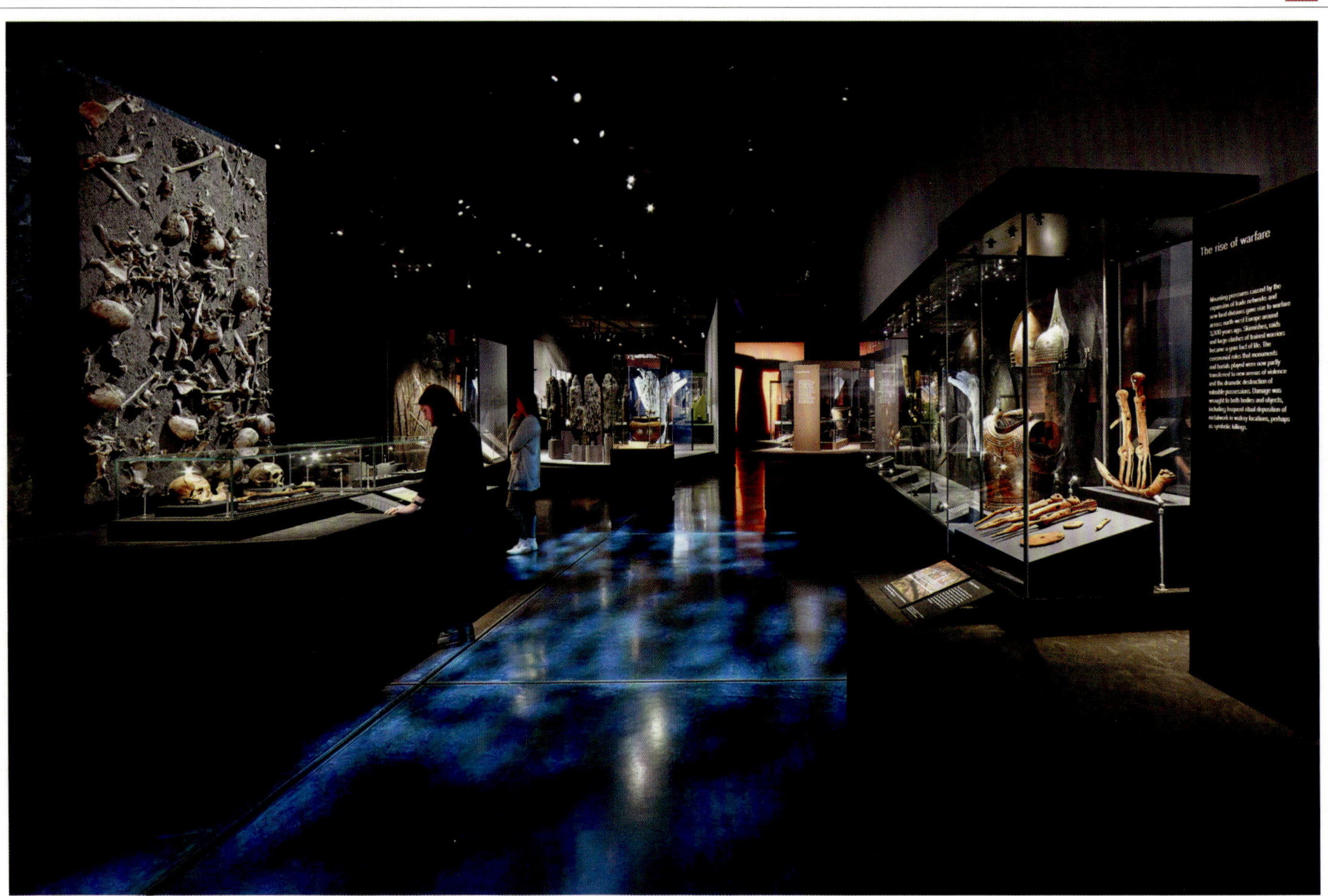

Title: The World of Stonehenge | **Client:** The British Museum | **Design Firm:** Ralph Appelbaum Associates

JONATHAN ALGER

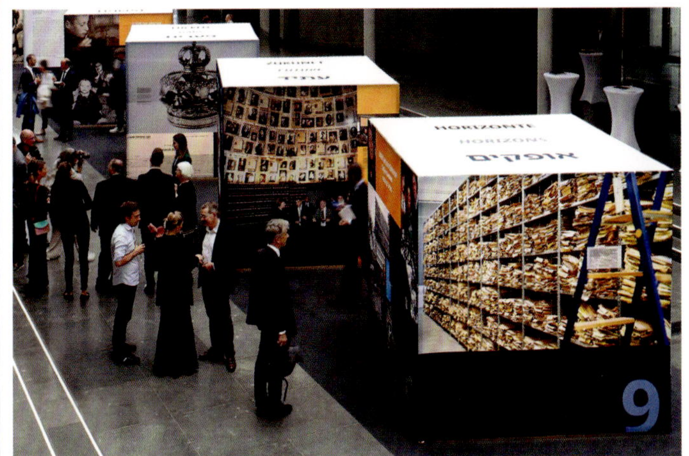

Title: Exhibition on the 70th Anniversary of the Luxembourg Agreements
Client: Claims Conference | **Design Firm:** C&G Partners

RALPH APPELBAUM ASSOCIATES

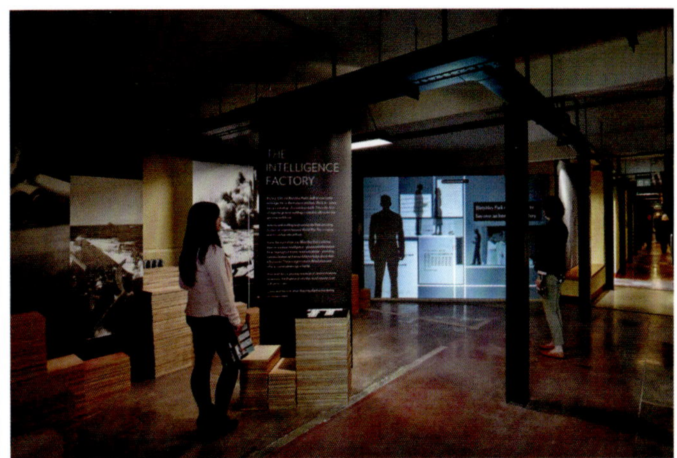

Title: Intelligence Factory
Client: Bletchley Park | **Design Firm:** Ralph Appelbaum Associates

AMERICAN MUSEUM OF NATURAL HISTORY

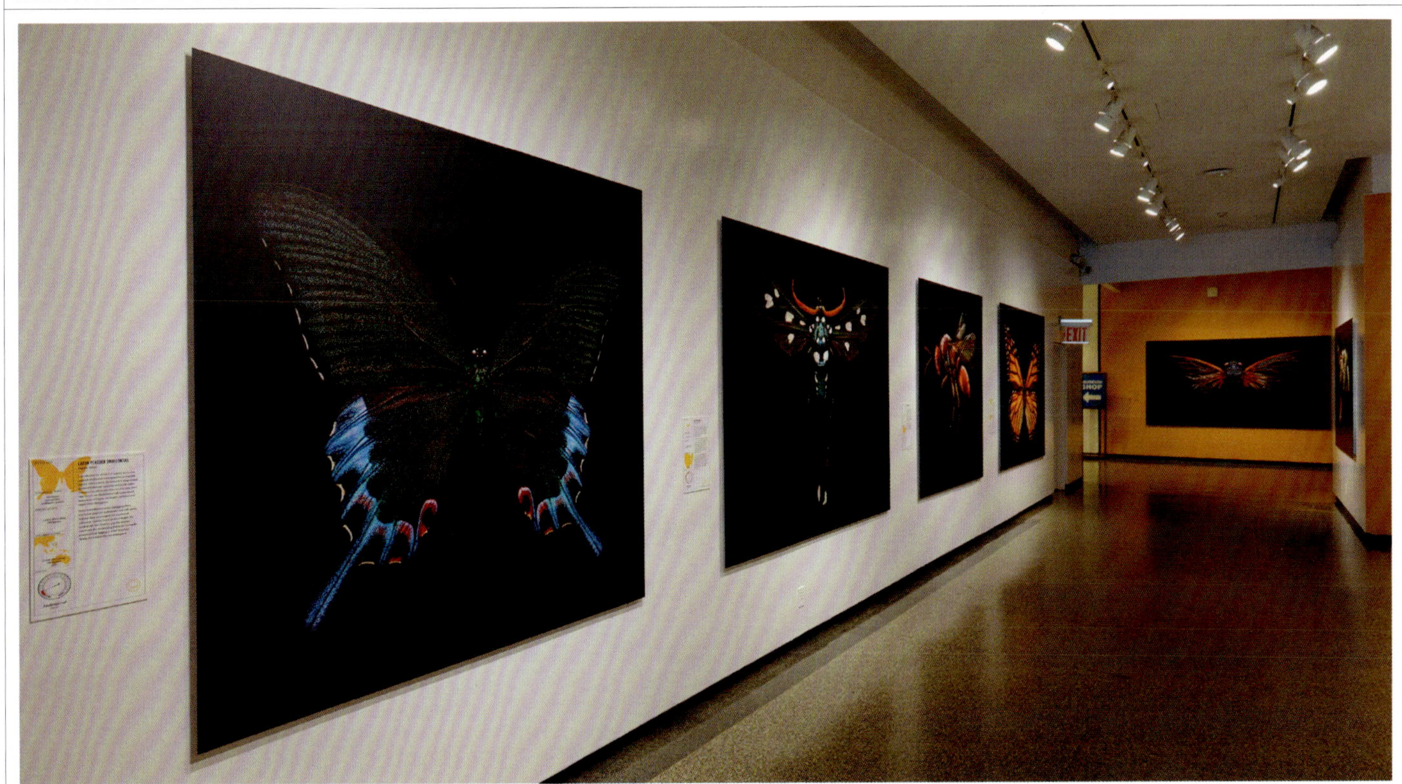

Title: Extinct & Endangered: Insects in Peril | **Client:** Self-initiated | **Design Firm:** American Museum of Natural History (In-House)

ANNA FARKAS

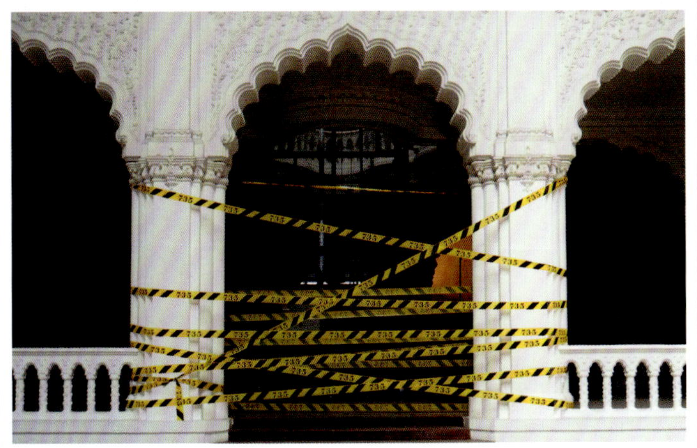

Title: Opus 735 (Traces of War on Artworks from the Treasury of the Princes Esterházy)
Client: Museum of Applied Arts | **Design Firm:** Anagraphic

SIENA SCARFF DESIGN

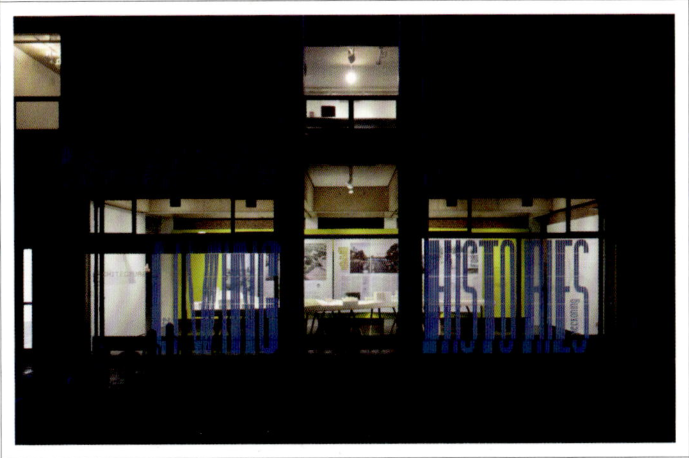

Title: Living Histories Space for Reckoning Exhibition
Client: Princeton University
Design Firm: Siena Scarff Design

HATCH DESIGN

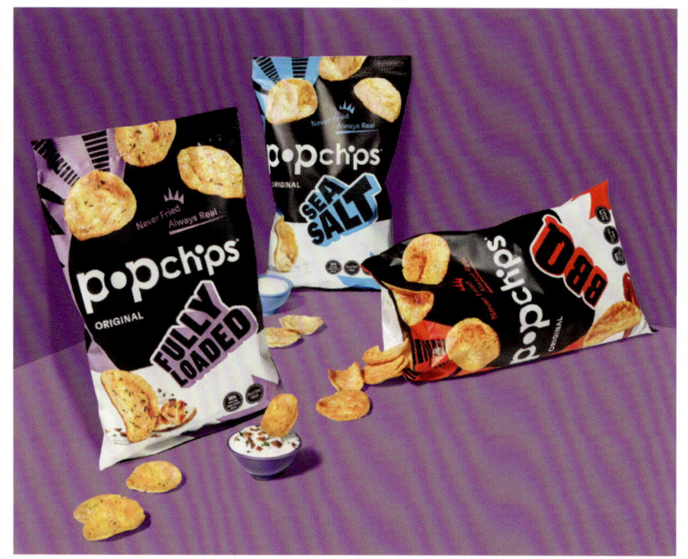

Title: Popchips Redesign | Client: Velocity Snack Brands
Design Firm: Hatch Design

HATCH DESIGN

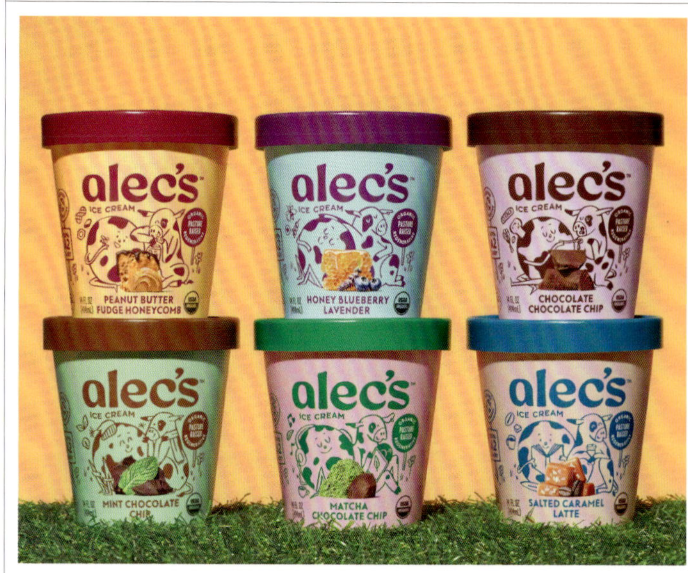

Title: Alec's Ice Cream Redesign | Client: Alec's Ice Cream
Design Firm: Hatch Design

OMDESIGN

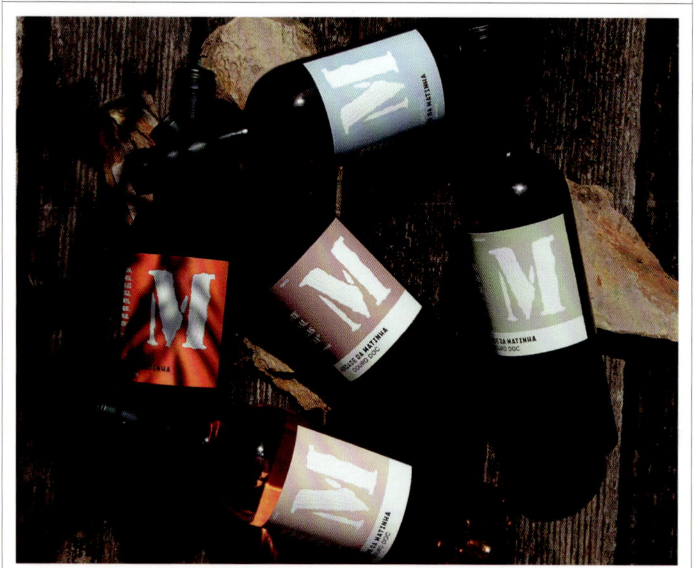

Title: Herdade da Matinha Wine Range | Client: Herdade da Matinha
Design Firm: Omdesign

PEPSICO DESIGN & INNOVATION

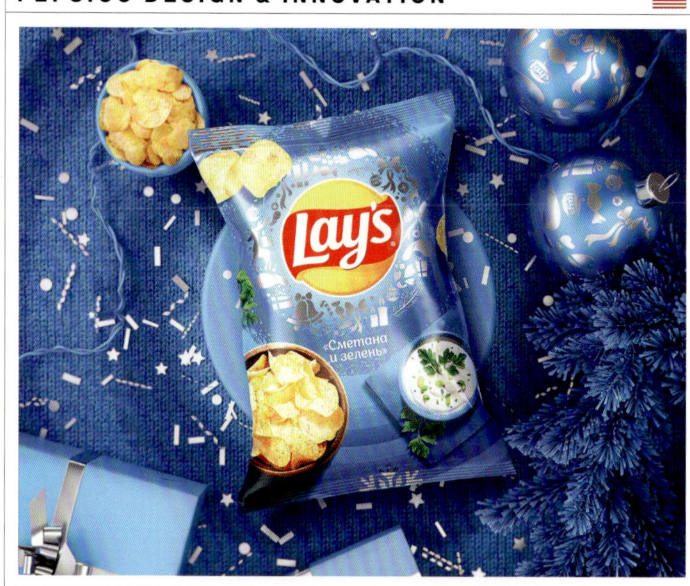

Title: Lay's New Year 2022 | Client: Self-initated
Design Firm: PepsiCo Design & Innovation

HATCH DESIGN

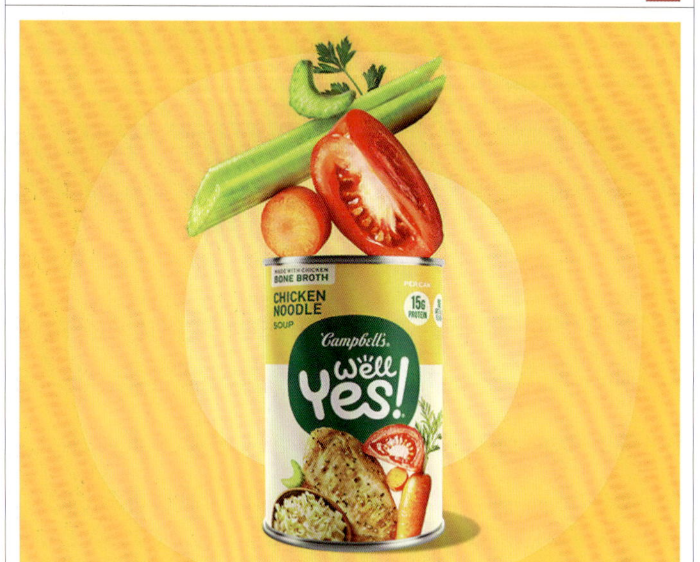

Title: Well, Yes! Refresh | Client: Campbell Soup Company
Design Firm: Hatch Design

HATCH DESIGN

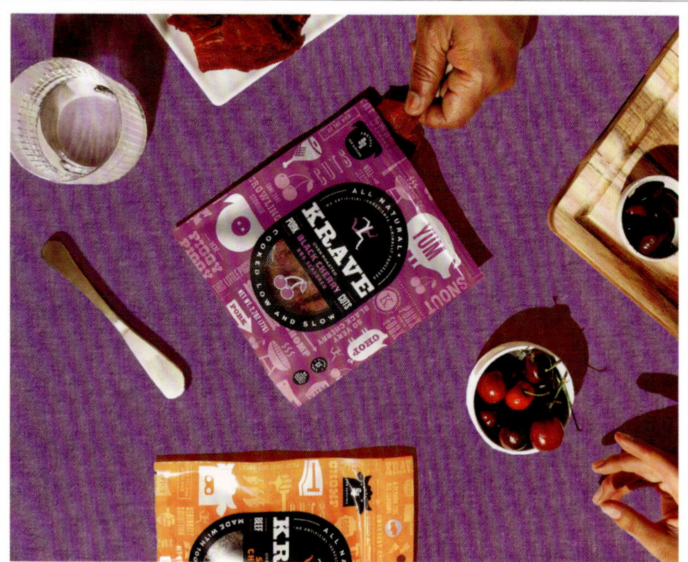

Title: KRAVE Jerky Revitalization | Client: Sonoma Brands Capital
Design Firm: Hatch Design

BUTTERFLY CANNON, ARRON EGAN

Title: Godawan - A Rare Whisky To Save A Rare Species
Clients: Diageo India, Hiren Dedhia | **Design Firm:** Butterfly Cannon

OMDESIGN

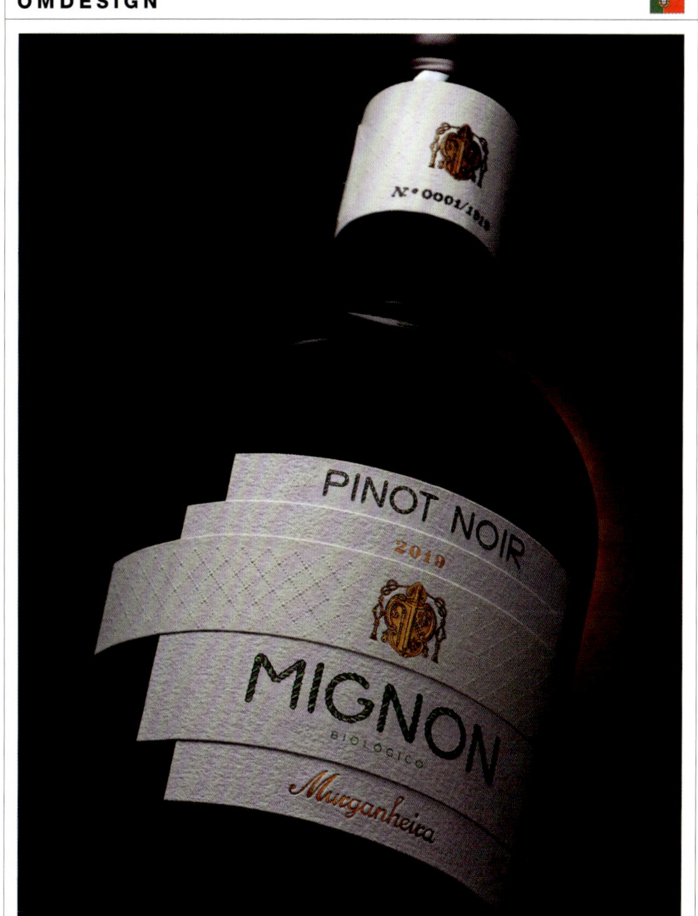

Title: Murganheira Mignon
Client: Murganheira | **Design Firm:** Omdesign

OMDESIGN

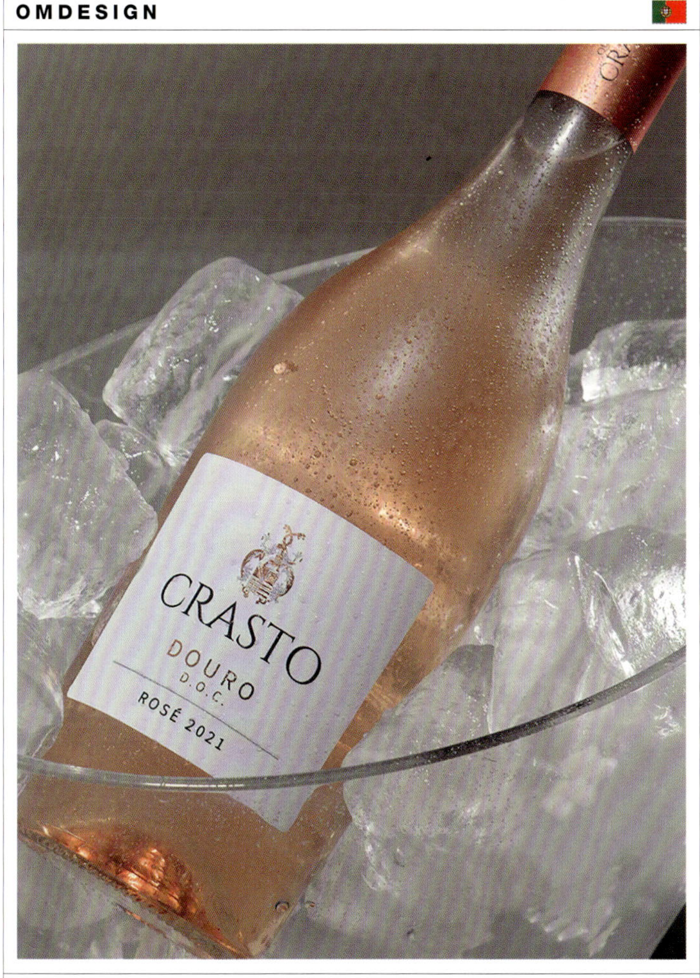

Title: Crasto Rosé | **Client:** Quinta do Crasto | **Design Firm:** Omdesign

LEGIS DESIGN

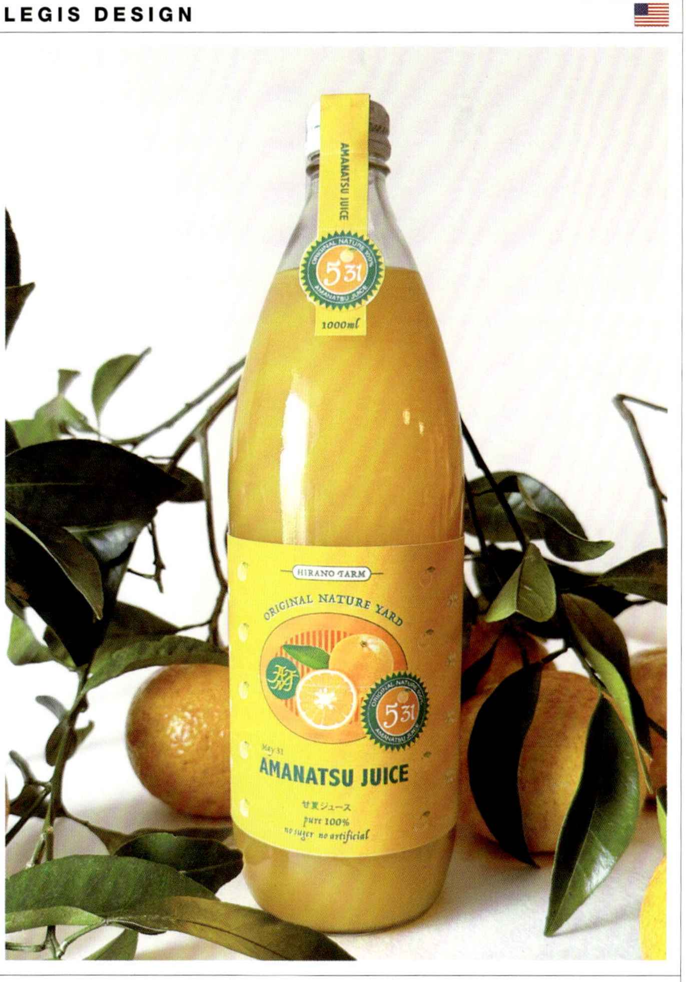

Title: AMANATSU JUICE | **Client:** Hirano Farm | **Design Firm:** Legis Design

LAFAYETTE AMERICAN

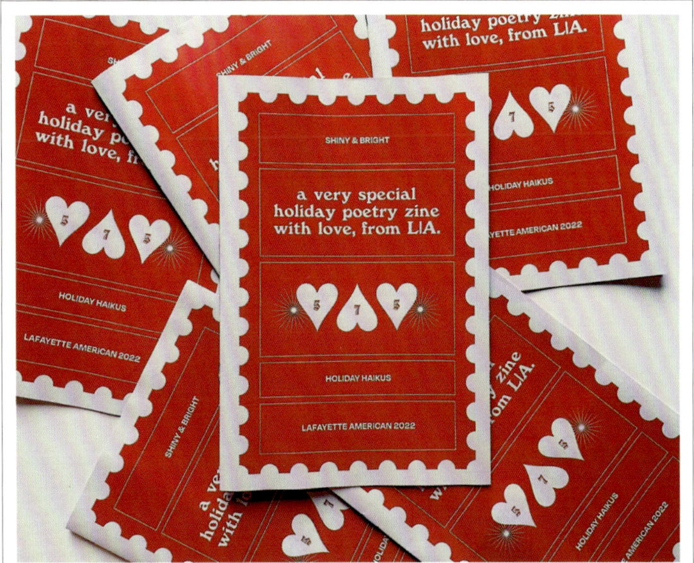

Title: Lafayette American Holiday Haikus Mailer | **Client:** Self-initiated
Design Firm: Lafayette American

ALEX FLORES

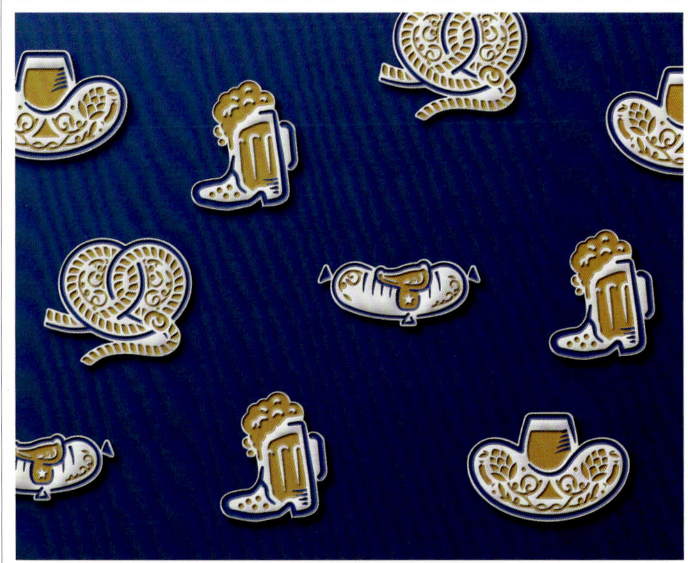

Title: Slacktoberfest Iconography | **Client:** Slack Davis Sanger
Design Firm: Spire Agency

MEDIA.WORK

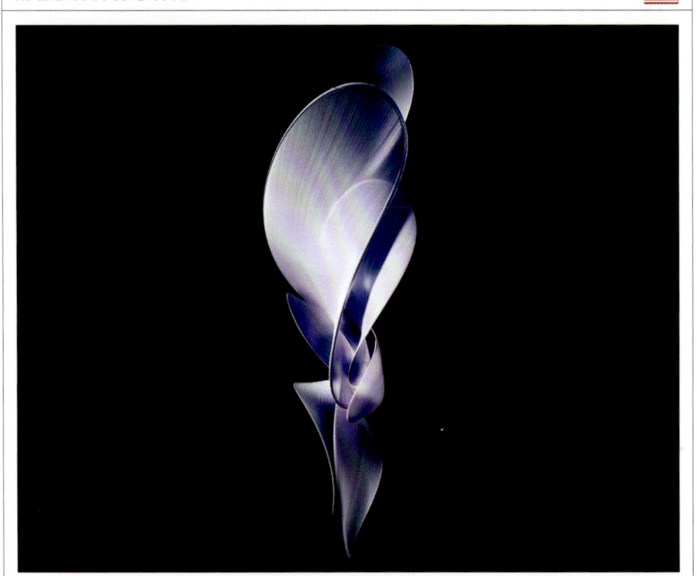

Title: OPPO Dragonfly | **Client:** OPPO
Design Firm: Media.Work

FEIXUE MEI

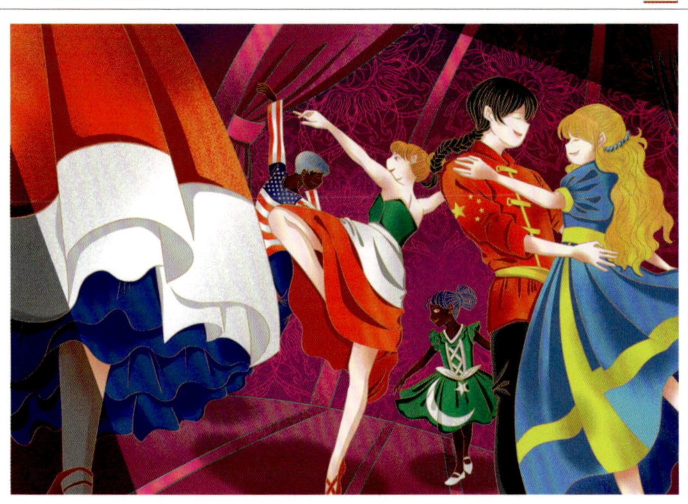

Title: Escape | **Client:** Self-initiated
Design Firm: Northwest Missouri State University

ALLISON INOUYE, RYAN OWENS

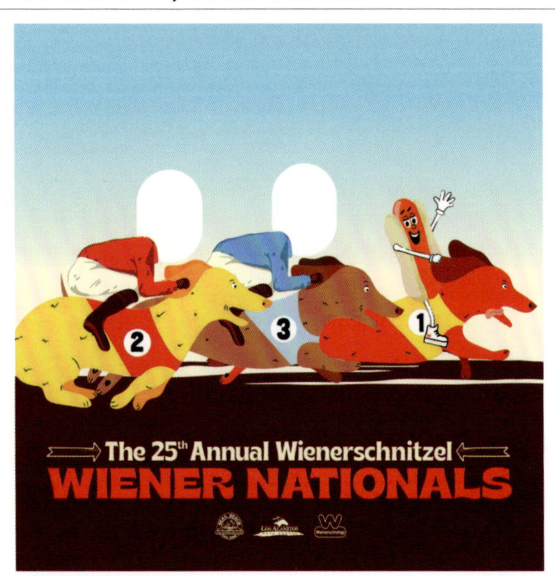

Title: 25th Annual Wienerschnitzel Wiener Nationals
Client: Wienerschnitzel | **Design Firm:** INNOCEAN USA

MARK BRAUGHT

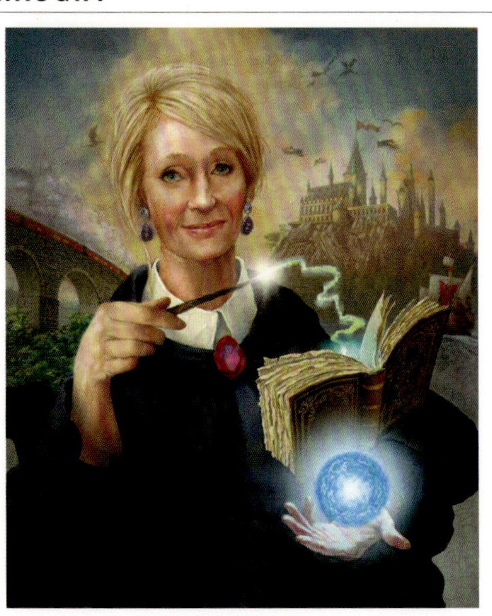

Title: JK Rowling
Client: Self-initiated | **Design Firm:** Mark Braught Studios

C. BARBER, T. PITTMAN, S. SONG, C. COLEMAN, S. DONOVAN, L. LATHAM, M. LEE, L. JOHNSON

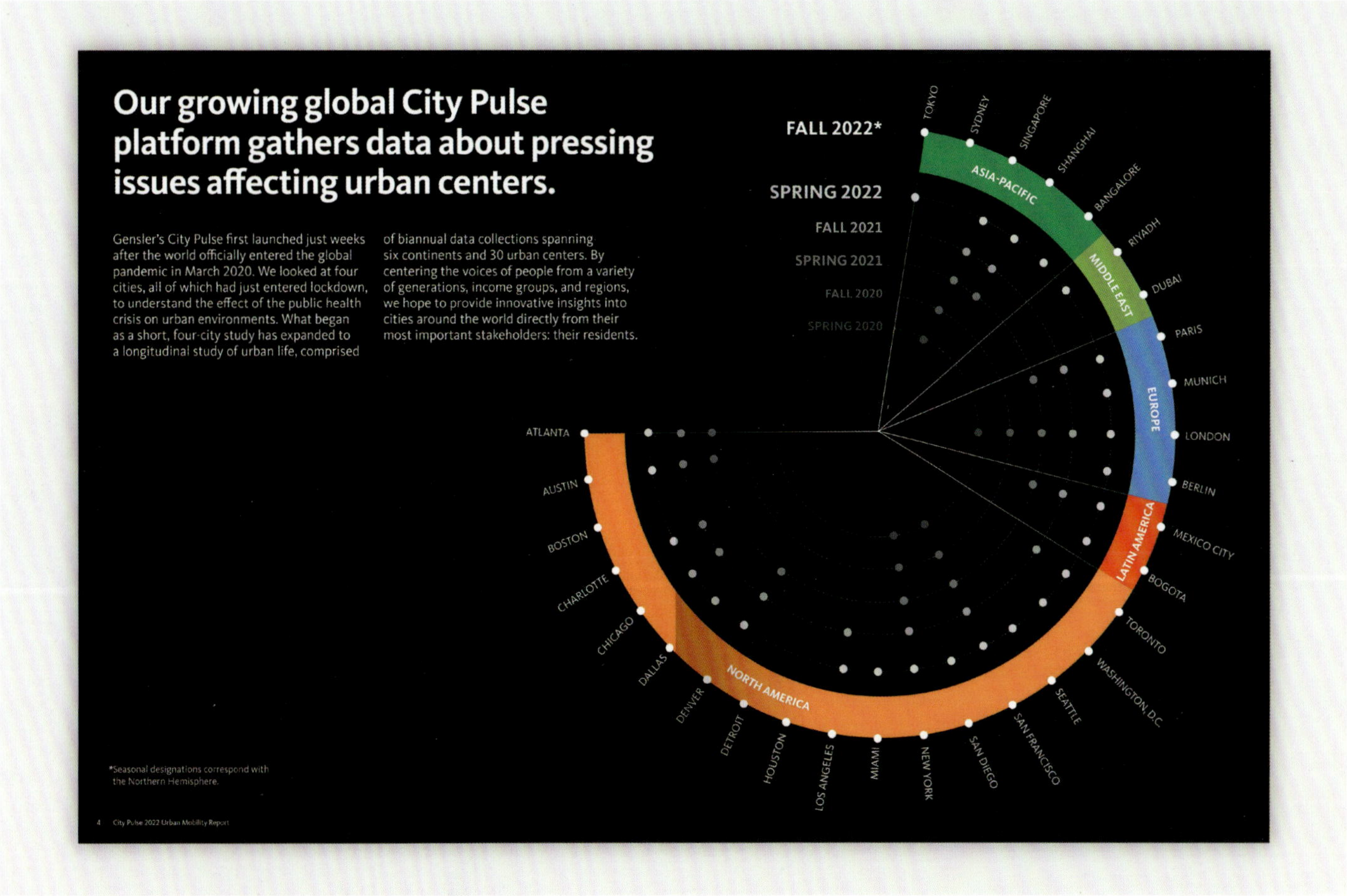

Our growing global City Pulse platform gathers data about pressing issues affecting urban centers.

Gensler's City Pulse first launched just weeks after the world officially entered the global pandemic in March 2020. We looked at four cities, all of which had just entered lockdown, to understand the effect of the public health crisis on urban environments. What began as a short, four-city study has expanded to a longitudinal study of urban life, comprised of biannual data collections spanning six continents and 30 urban centers. By centering the voices of people from a variety of generations, income groups, and regions, we hope to provide innovative insights into cities around the world directly from their most important stakeholders: their residents.

FALL 2022*
SPRING 2022
FALL 2021
SPRING 2021
FALL 2020
SPRING 2020

ASIA-PACIFIC: TOKYO, SYDNEY, SINGAPORE, SHANGHAI, BANGALORE
MIDDLE EAST: RIYADH, DUBAI
EUROPE: PARIS, MUNICH, LONDON, BERLIN
LATIN AMERICA: MEXICO CITY, BOGOTA
NORTH AMERICA: TORONTO, WASHINGTON, D.C., SEATTLE, SAN FRANCISCO, SAN DIEGO, NEW YORK, MIAMI, LOS ANGELES, HOUSTON, DETROIT, DENVER, DALLAS, CHICAGO, CHARLOTTE, BOSTON, AUSTIN, ATLANTA

*Seasonal designations correspond with the Northern Hemisphere.

4 City Pulse 2022 Urban Mobility Report

Title: City Pulse 2022 Urban Mobility Report | **Client:** Self-initiated | **Design Firm:** Gensler

JOHN BIONDI, DREW LINTVEDT (+3)

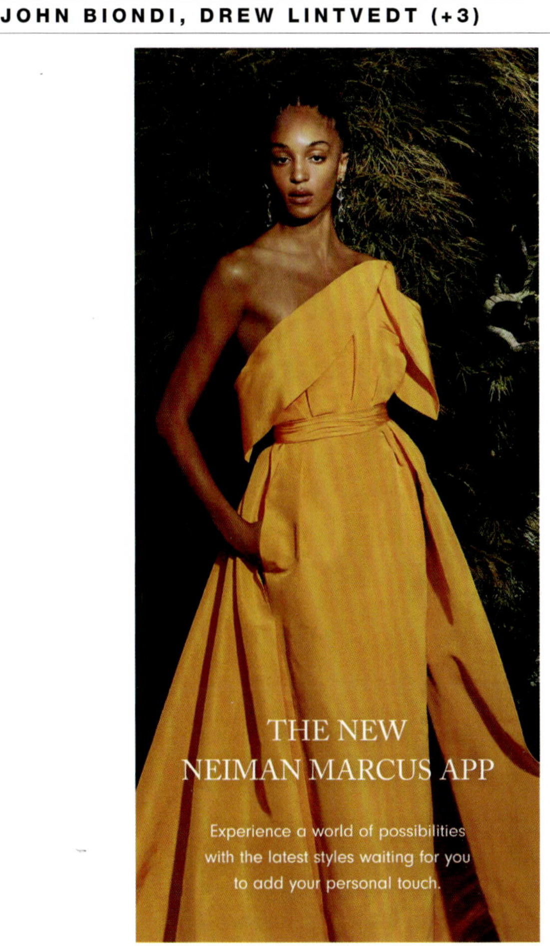

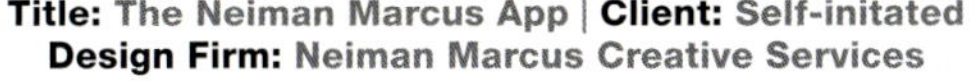

Title: The Neiman Marcus App | **Client:** Self-initated
Design Firm: Neiman Marcus Creative Services

RONG JIA, ROCHELL VAUGHNS, NATALIA BEARD

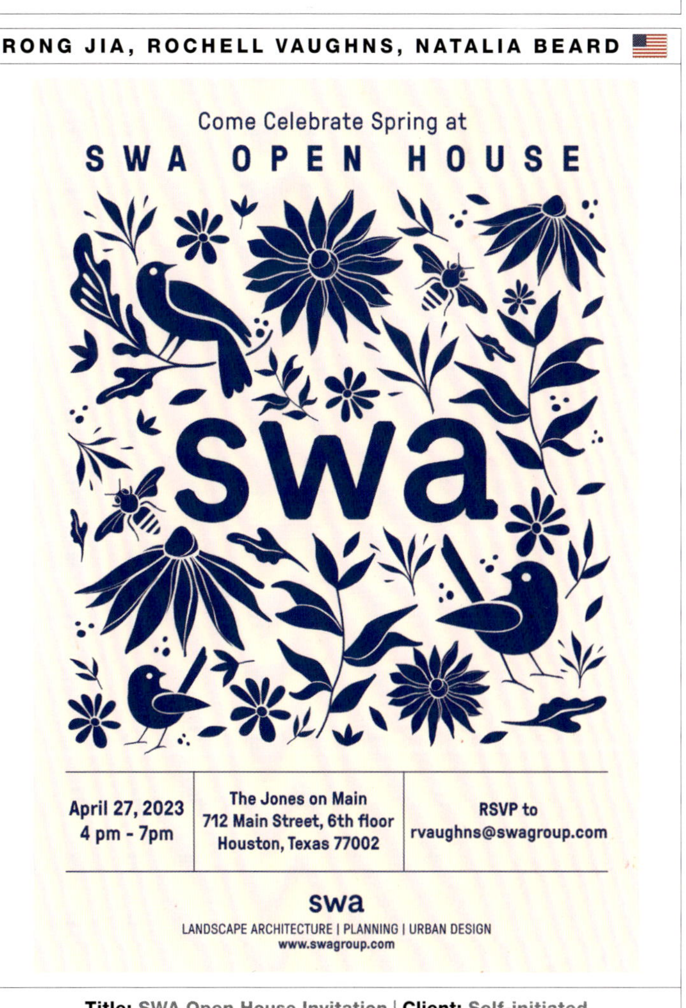

Title: SWA Open House Invitation | **Client:** Self-initiated
Design Firm: SWA Group

ARIEL FREANER

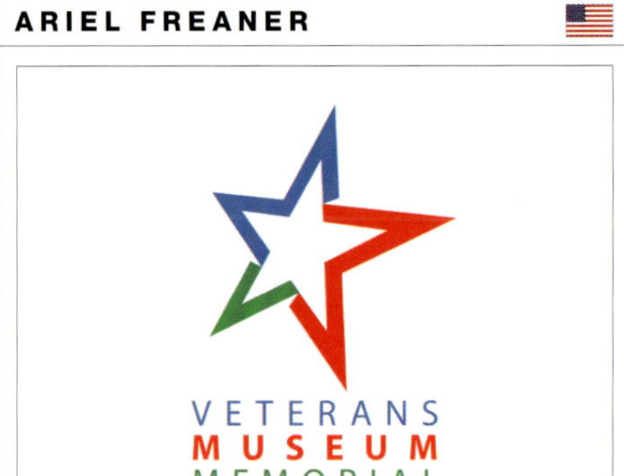

Title: Veterans Museum Memorial Logo
Client: Veterans Museum Memorial
Design Firm: Freaner Creative & Design

DELFIN

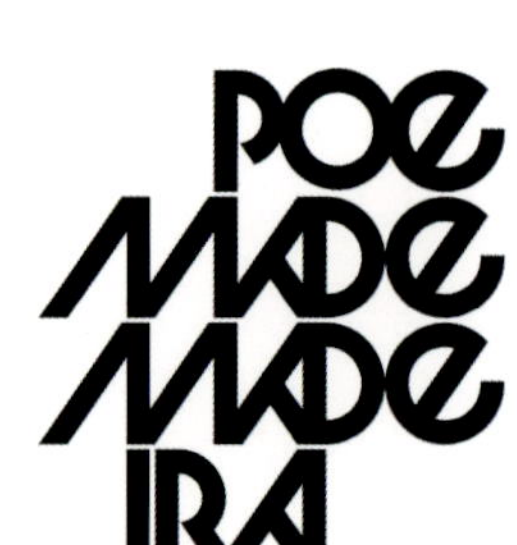

Title: Poema de Madeira (Wooden Poem)
Client: Marília Giesbrecht
Design Firm: Studio DelRey

WOLFF OLINS

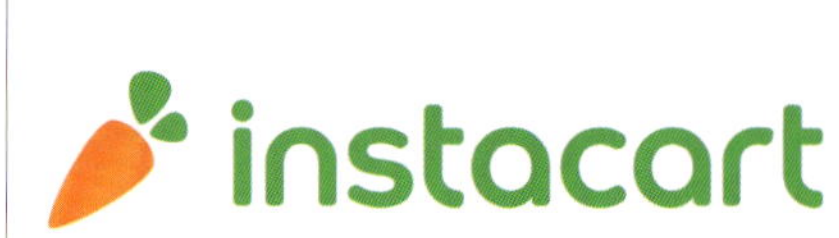

Title: Grounded in Their Roots, Growing Into the Future
Client: Instacart | **Design Firm:** Wolff Olins

HANNAH GASKAMP

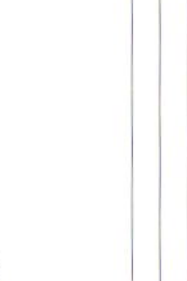

Title: Politics of the Modern Southwest
Client: Self-initiated
Design Firm: Texas Tech University Press

YANIRA JANES PARSONS

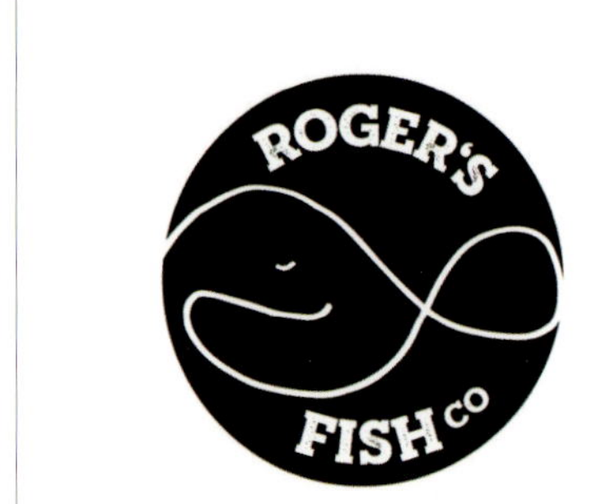

Title: Roger's Fish Co.
Client: Roger's Fish Co.
Design Firm: DeVito/Verdi

HANNAH GASKAMP

Title: Desert Humanities
Client: Self-initiated
Design Firm: Texas Tech University Press

ROGER SAWHILL

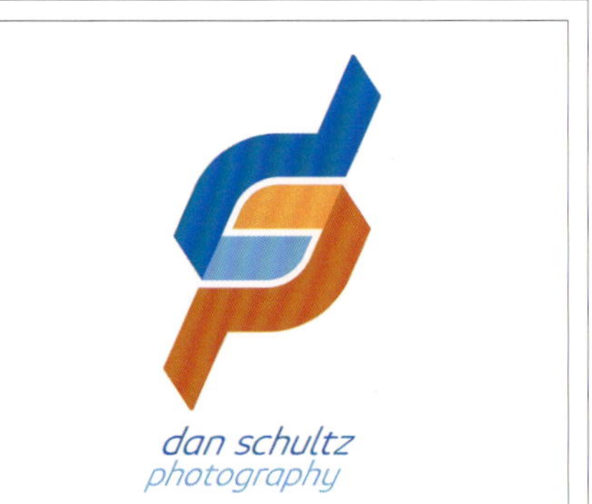

Title: DSP Logo
Client: Dan Shultz Photography (DSP)
Design Firm: UP-Ideas

KATE BORMAN RICHARDSON

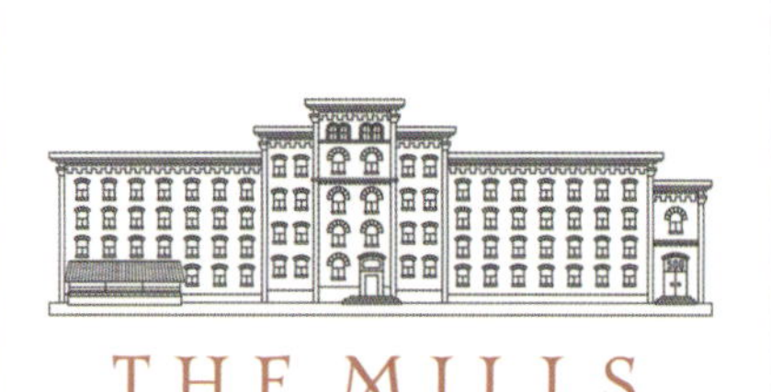

Title: The Mills Yonkers
Client: RJ Rose Realty
Design Firm: Kate Borman Creative Design Co.

LISA SIRBAUGH CREATIVE

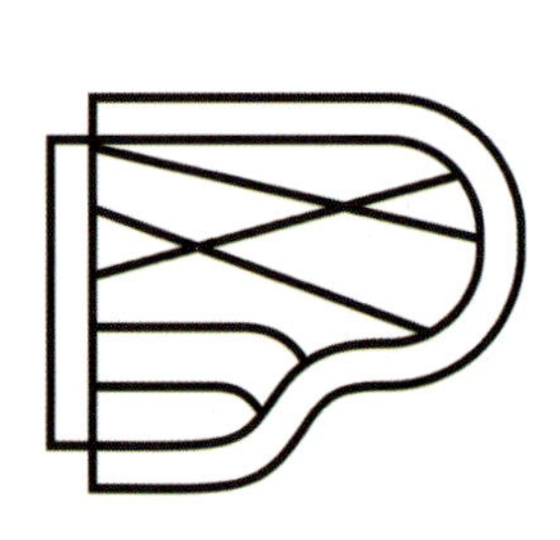

Title: Pianist Paul Warthen Brandmark
Client: Paul Warthen
Design Firm: Lisa Sirbaugh Creative

EL PASO, GALERÍA DE COMUNICACIÓN

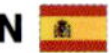

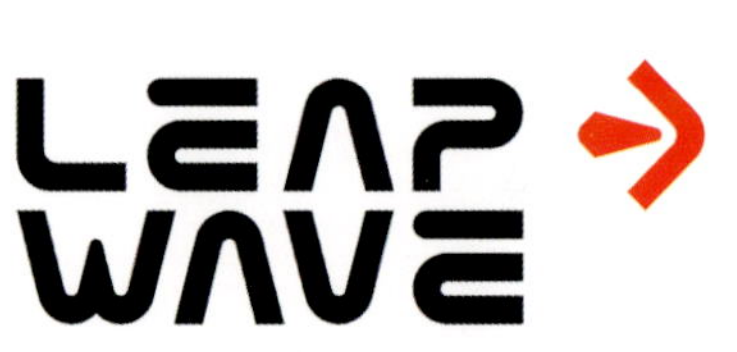

Title: LeapWave
Client: LeapWave Technologies
Design Firm: El Paso, Galería de Comunicación

JOHN BALL, RENEE CHAN

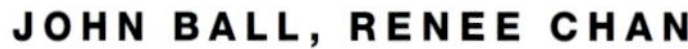

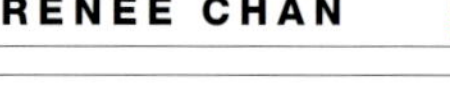

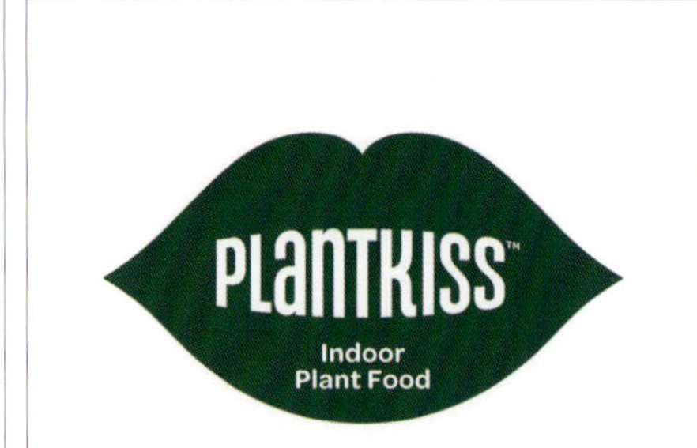

Title: PlantKiss Identity
Client: PlantKiss
Design Firm: MiresBall

ARIEL FREANER

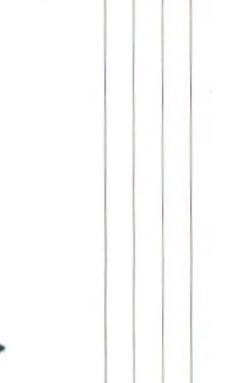

Title: Organics Unlimited Logo
Client: Organics Unlimited
Design Firm: Freaner Creative & Design

STEWART JUNG
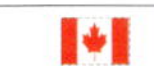

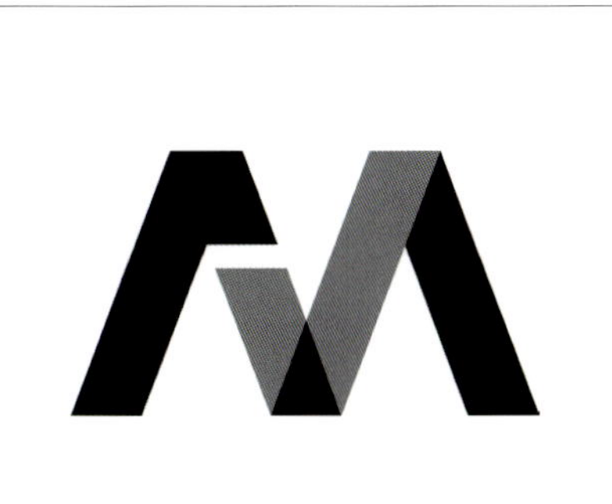

Title: AJ Massullo Logo
Client: AJ Massullo Excavation and Demolition
Design Firm: AG Creative Group

LAUREN LAMB, JOHN BALL
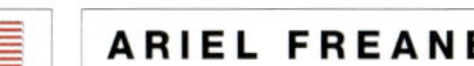

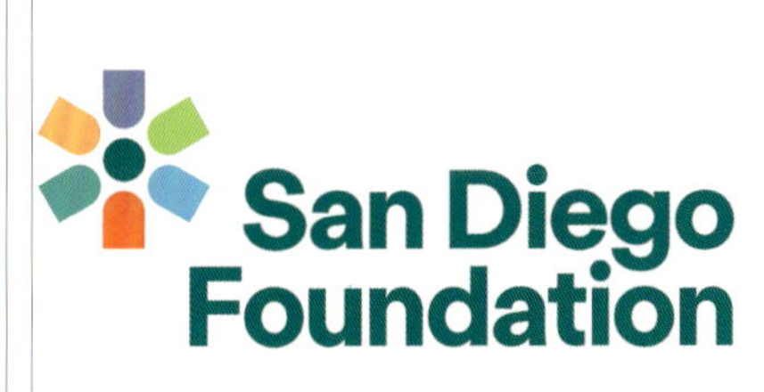

Title: San Diego Foundation Identity
Client: San Diego Foundation
Design Firm: MiresBall

ARIEL FREANER
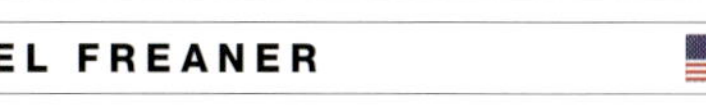

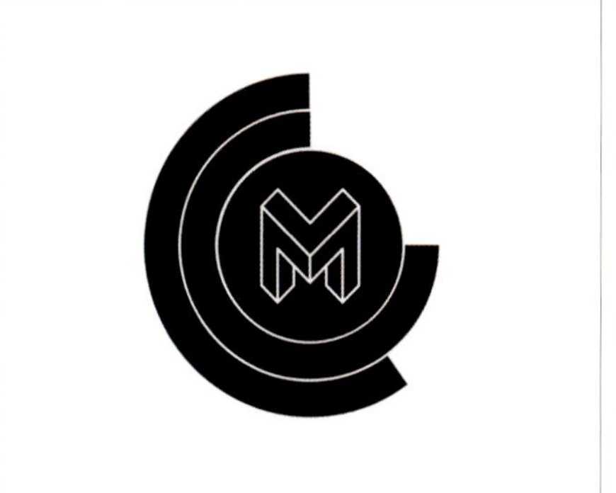

Title: Otay Mesa Chamber of Commerce Logo
Client: Otay Mesa Chamber of Commerce
Design Firm: Freaner Creative & Design

MARK BRAUGHT

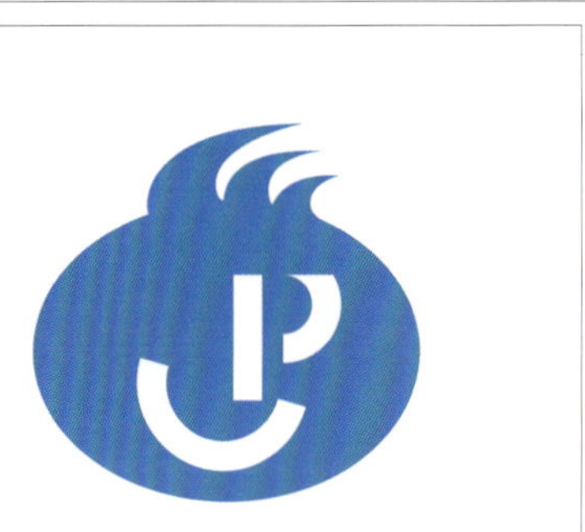

Title: UP-Fun Logo
Client: Self-initiated
Design Firm: UP-Ideas

KEITH HARRIS

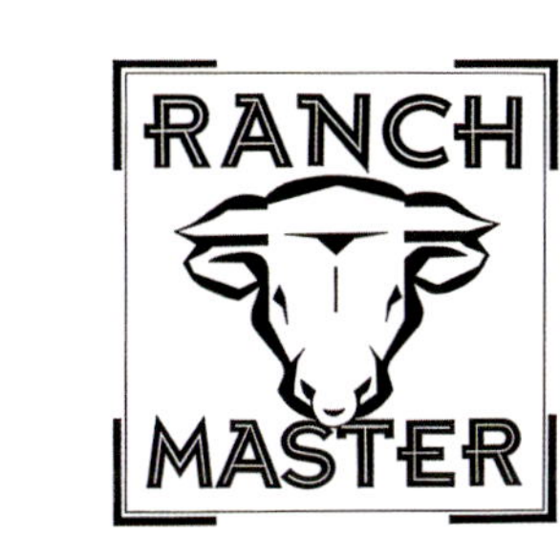

Title: Ranch Master Logo
Client: Ranch Master
Design Firm: Keith Harris Design

VANESSA RYAN

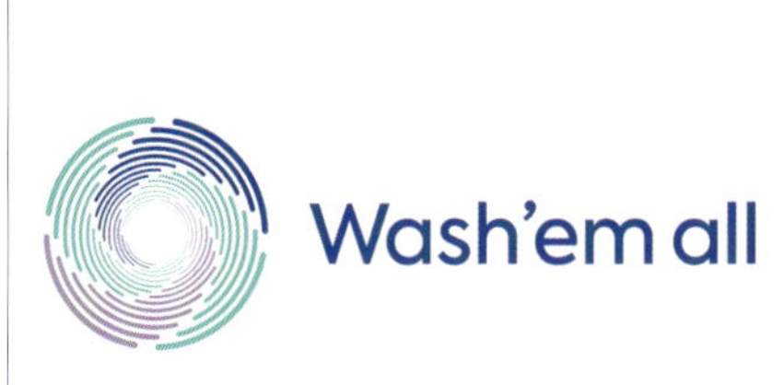

Title: Wash'Em All Identity
Client: AirDay Solution
Design Firm: SML Design

ARRON EGAN, BUTTERFLY CANNON

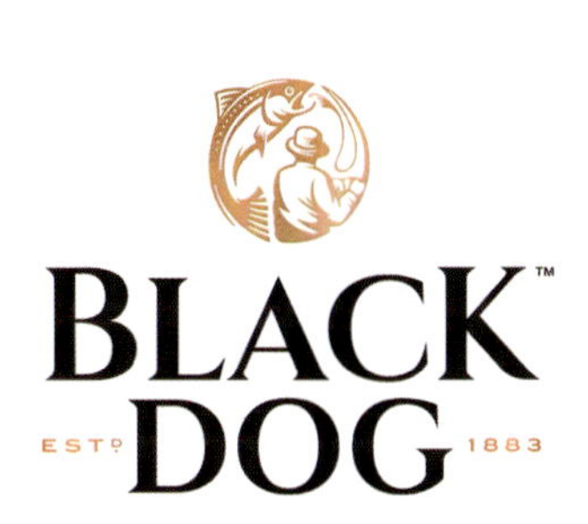

Title: Black Dog - The Scotch Icon Back To No.1
Clients: Hiren Dedhia, Diageo India
Design Firm: Butterfly Cannon

ANTON TIELEMANS

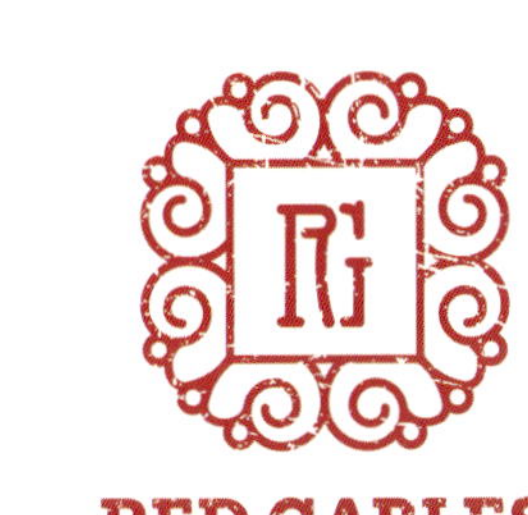

Title: Red Gables Logo
Client: Red Gables
Design Firm: Tielemans Design

ANTON TIELEMANS

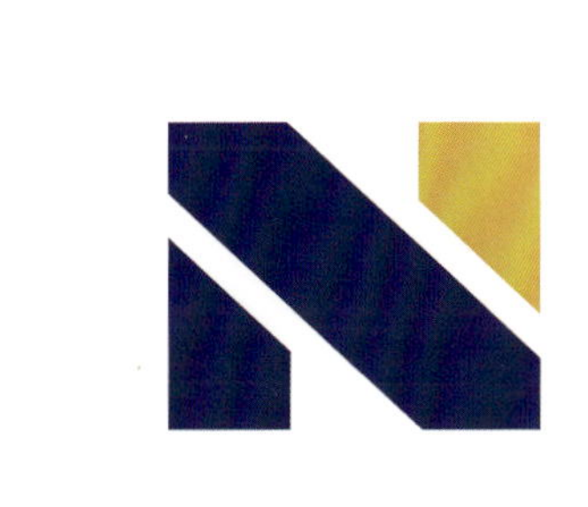

Title: Nevada Bank & Trust Logo
Client: Nevada Bank & Trust
Design Firm: Tielemans Design

SHARON LLOYD MCLAUGHLIN

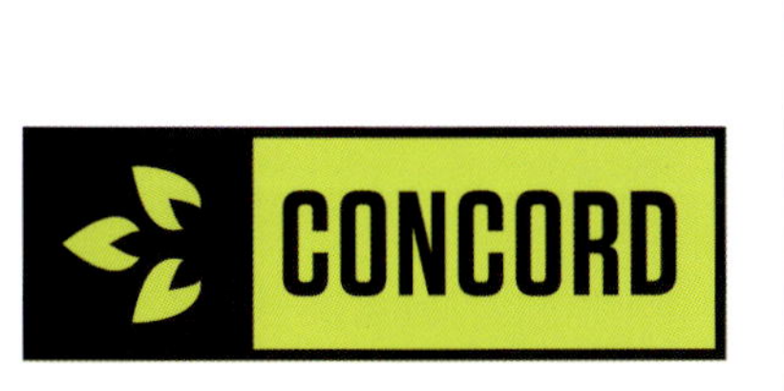

Title: Concord Federal Credit Union Logo
Client: Concord Federal Credit Union
Design Firm: Mermaid, Inc.

QIN LUO

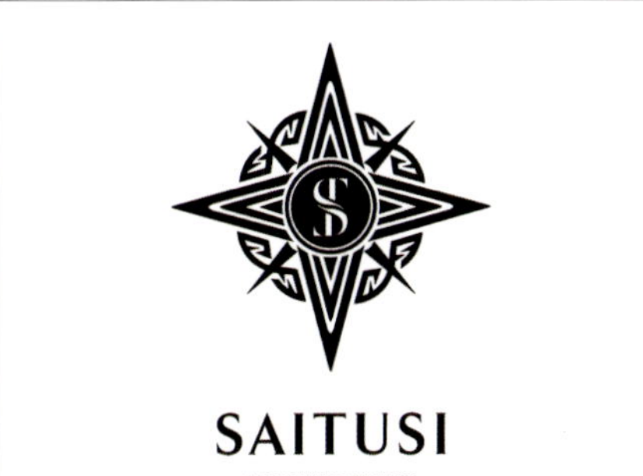

Title: SAITUSI
Client: Shandong Hongyao Trading Co. Ltd.
Design Firm: Roking Art Design

YOSHINORI SHIMOUSA

Title: The Logo of Shimousa Laboratory
Client: Shimousa Laboratory
Design Firm: USADesign

THREADS OF CULTURE PROJECT

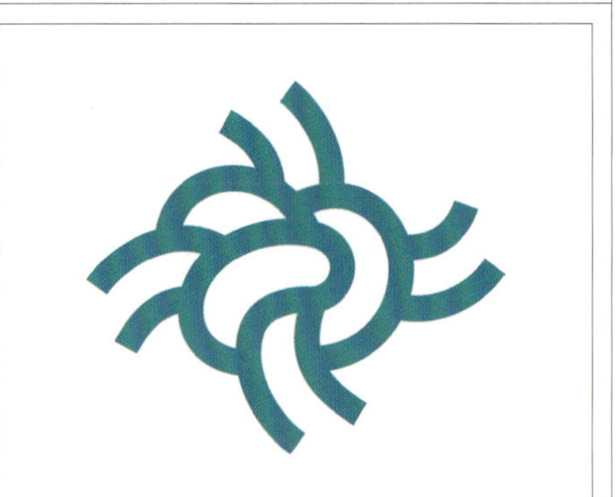

Title: Threads of Culture
Client: Istanbul Foundation for Culture and Arts
Design Firm: BEK Design

BEK DESIGN

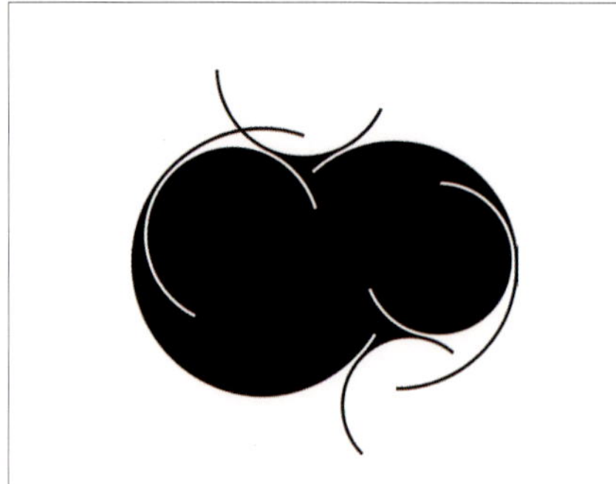

Title: Ozden Architecture Firm
Client: Arif Ozden
Design Firm: BEK Design

ARIEL FREANER

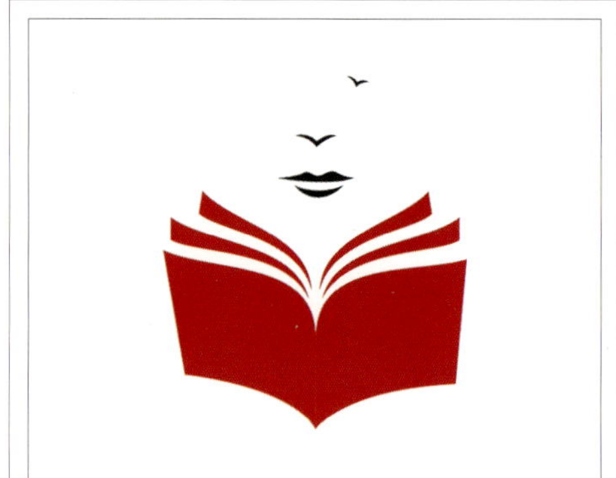

Title: Tres y Contando Logo
Client: Tres y Contando
Design Firm: Freaner Creative & Design

SHARON LLOYD MCLAUGHLIN

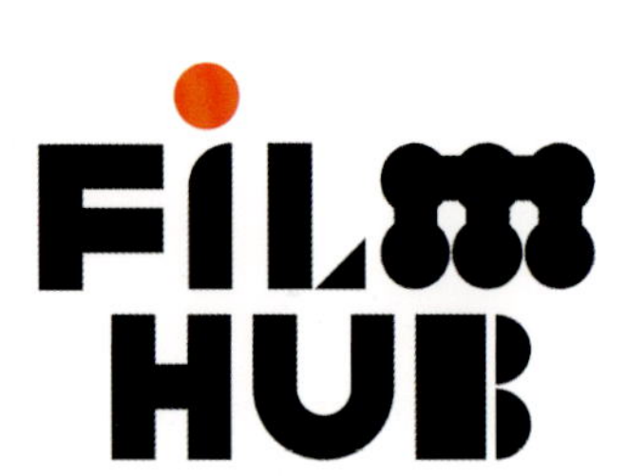

Title: Film Hub Logo
Client: National Resources
Design Firm: Mermaid, Inc.

HANNAH GASKAMP

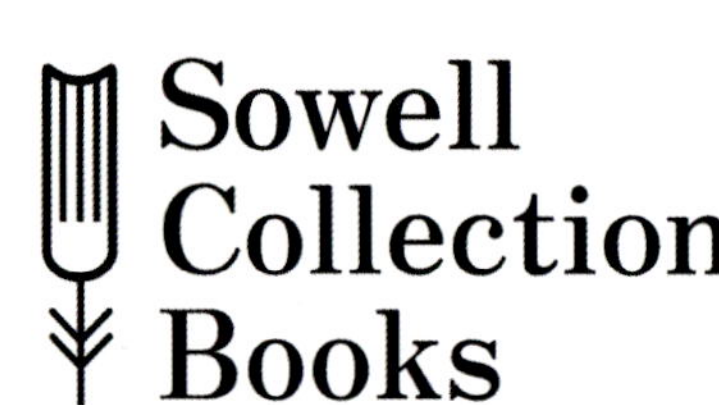

Title: Sowell Collection Books
Client: Self-initiated
Design Firm: Texas Tech University Press

ENRICO SEMPI

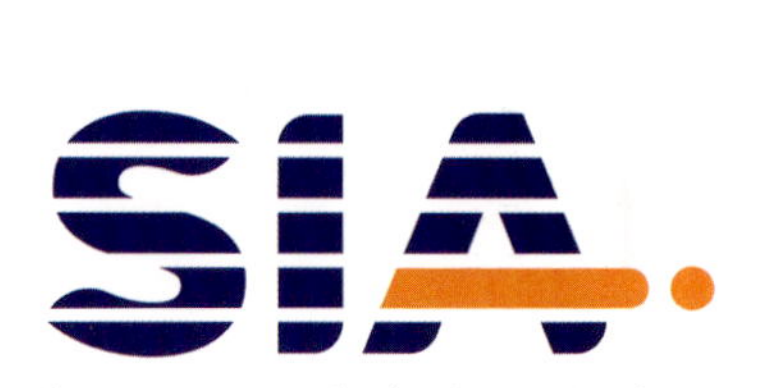

Title: New Corporate Identity SIA
Client: SIA
Design Firm: Tangram Strategic Design

COLEY PORTER BELL, HALLIBURTON

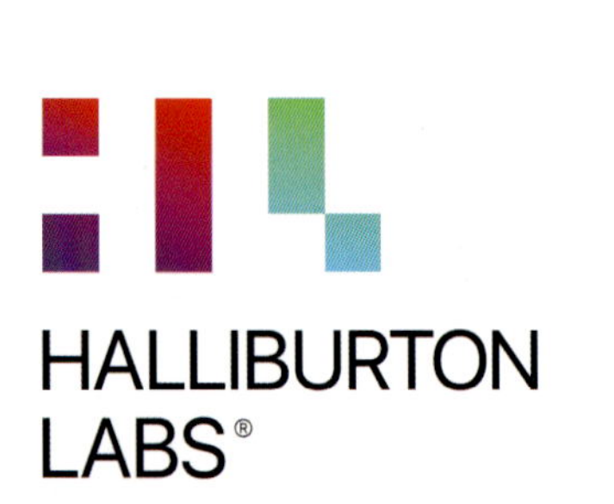

Title: Halliburton Labs Logo
Client: Halliburton
Design Firm: Coley Porter Bell

JORDAN FRETZ

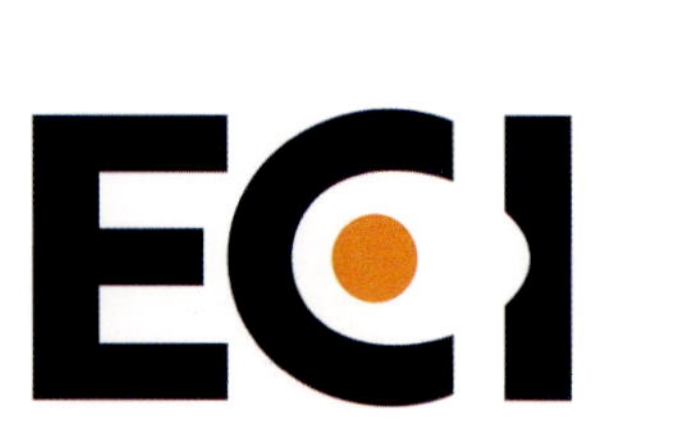

Title: ECI (Egg Clearinghouse Inc.) Logo
Client: ECI (Egg Clearinghouse Inc.)
Design Firm: Jordan Fretz Design

FERNANDO PALOMINO

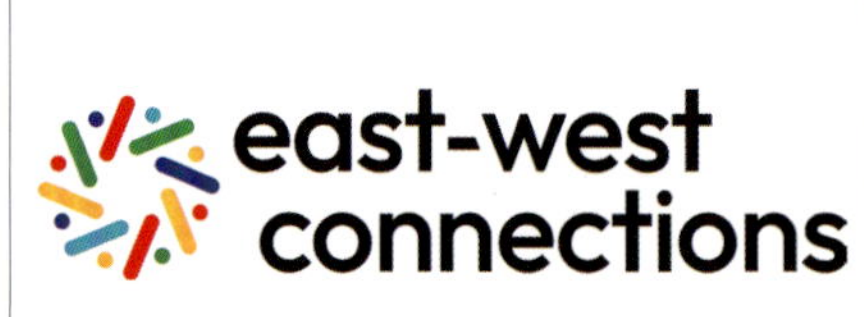

Title: East-West Connections - Brand Identity
Client: East-West Connections
Design Firm: Preston Spire

ROSE

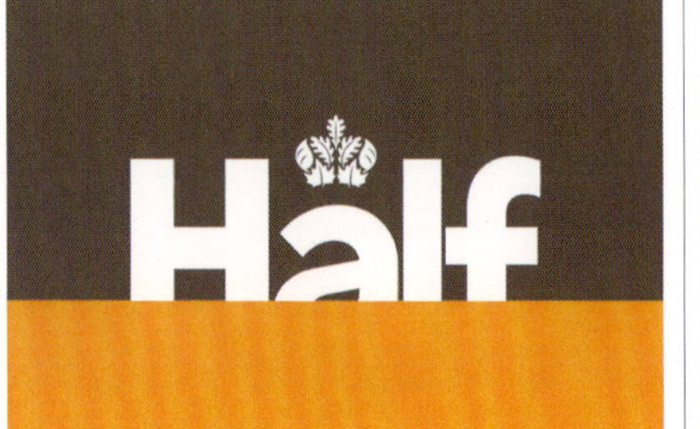

Title: The Royal Parks Half
Client: The Royal Parks
Design Firm: Rose

ROGER ARCHBOLD

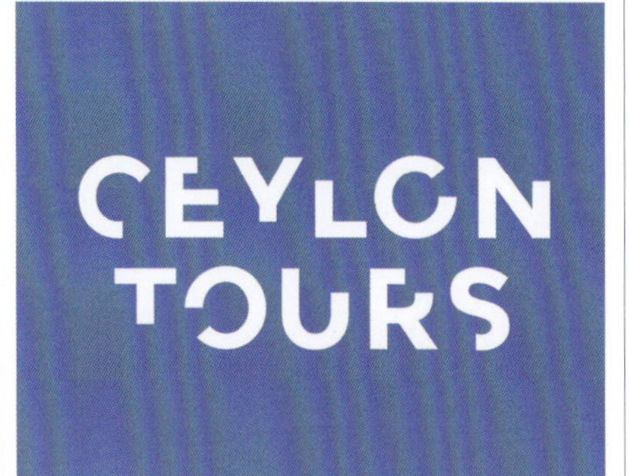

Title: Ceylon Tours Logo
Client: Ceylon Tours
Design Firm: Roger Archbold

PATRICK FINLEY

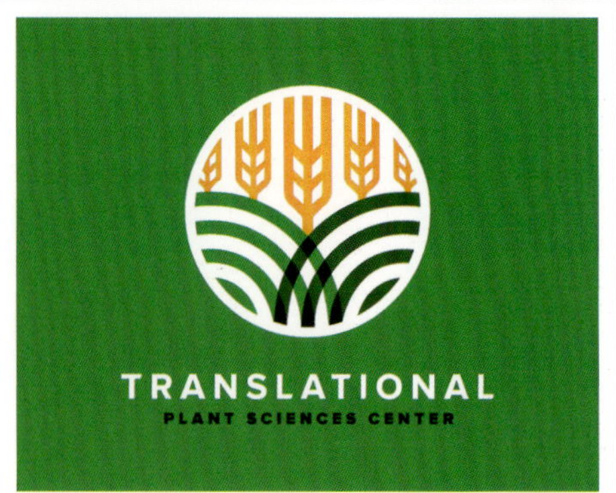

Title: Translational Plant Sciences Center
Client: Virginia Tech's Translational Plant Sciences Center | **Design Firm:** Patrick Finley

JOSH HERMES, JED HIGGERSON (+3)

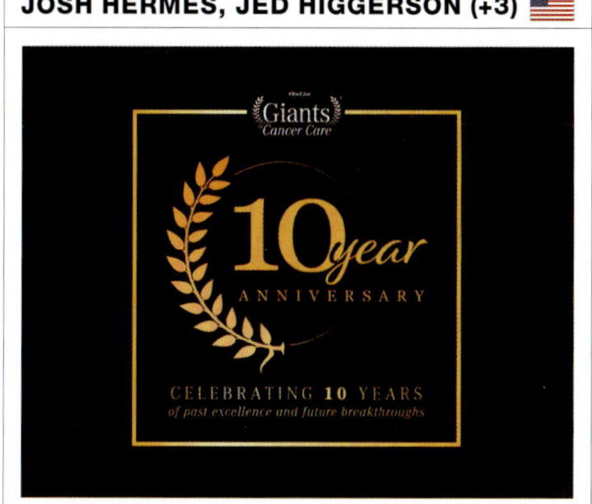

Title: Giants of Cancer Care® 10-Year Anniversary Logo | **Client:** Giants of Cancer Care® | **Design Firm:** MJH Life Sciences

JOE ROSS

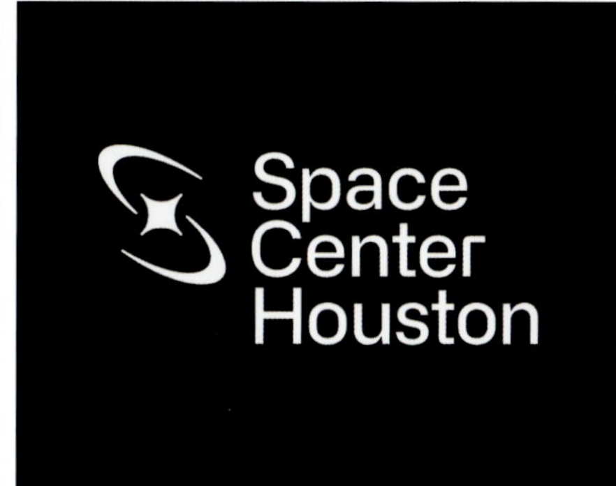

Title: Space Center Houston Logo
Client: Space Center Houston
Design Firm: Traina

PATRICK FINLEY

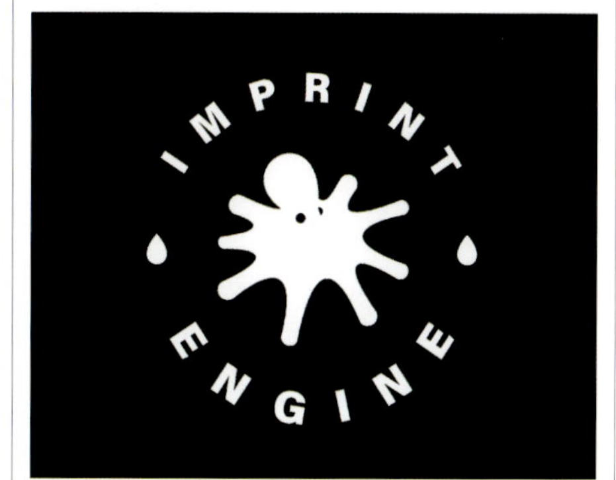

Title: Imprint Engine
Client: Imprint Engine
Design Firm: Joba Studio

TAILFEATHER

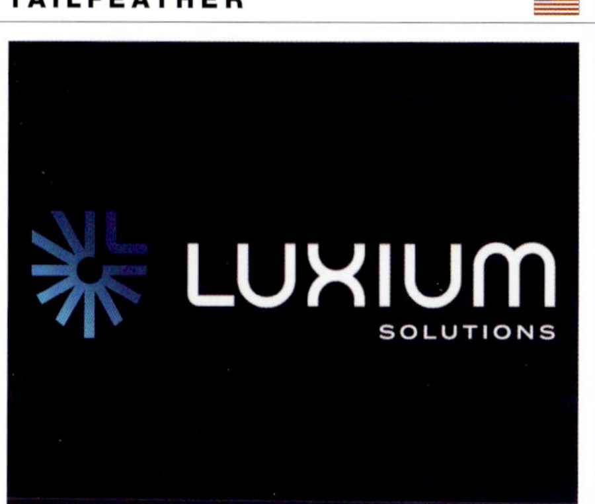

Title: Luxium Solutions | **Client:** Luxium Solutions
Design Firm: Haystack Needle LLC DBA Tailfeather

RESOURCE BRANDING

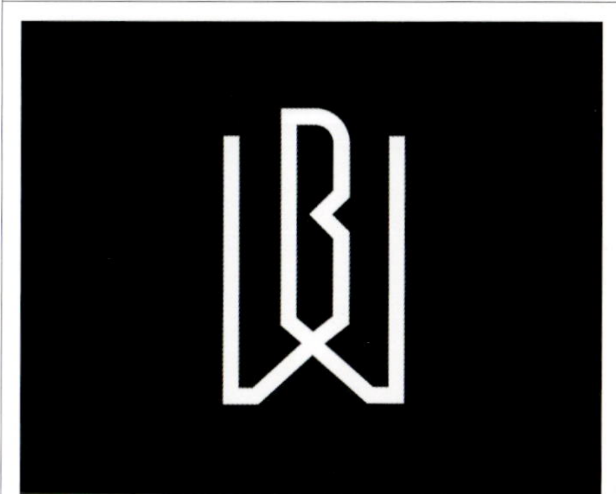

Title: Westbound At The Works Logomark
Client: Selig Enterprises
Design Firm: Resource Branding

SUSANNE PINTER (+1)

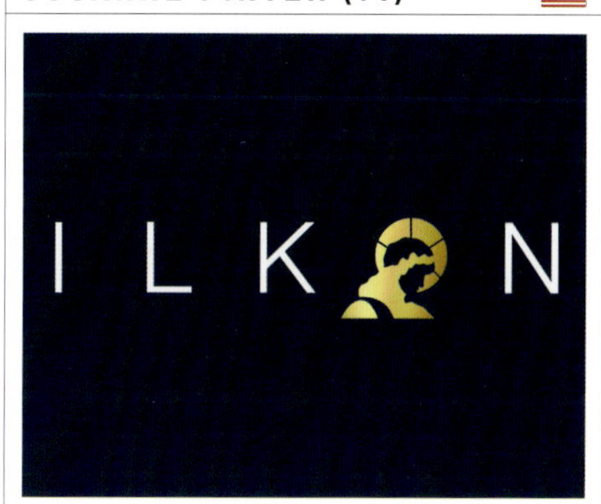

Title: ILKON. Ilkeston Contemporary Arts
Client: ILKON: Ilkeston Contemporary Arts
Design Firm: Susanne Pinter & Francesca Pinter-Parrott

RESOURCE BRANDING

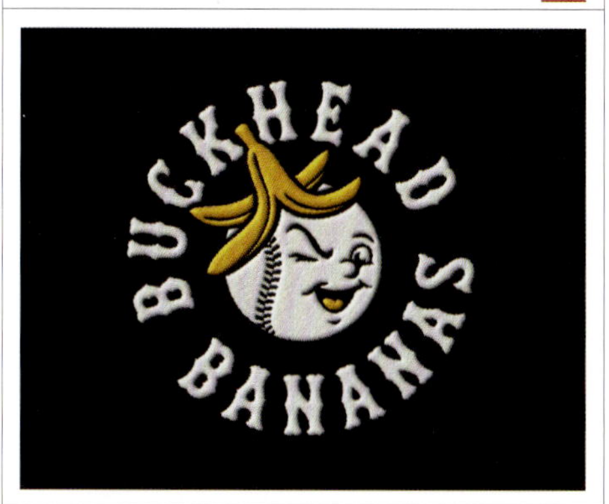

Title: Buckhead Bananas Logomark
Client: Buckhead Bananas U12 Baseball Team
Design Firm: Resource Branding

SILVIA YU, CHRIS CHUNG (+7)

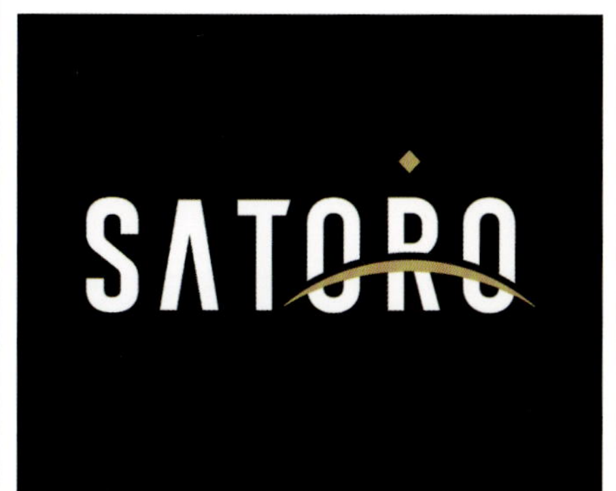

Title: Satoro
Client: Satoro Inc.
Design Firm: RedPeak Global

MICHAEL GRAZIOLO

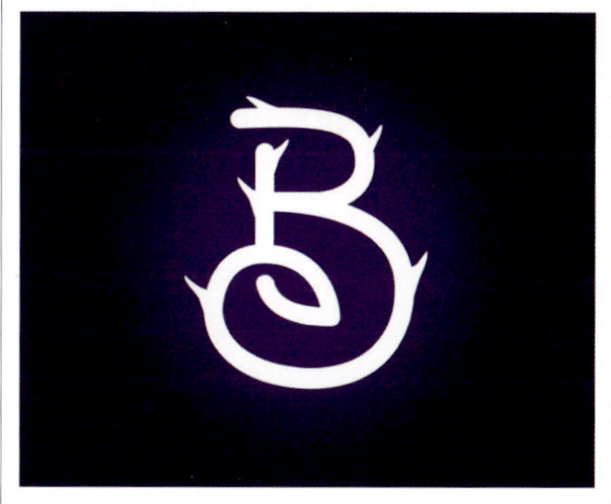

Title: Bramble Logo
Client: Tor Publishing Group
Design Firm: Drive Communications

HOLLY TIENKEN

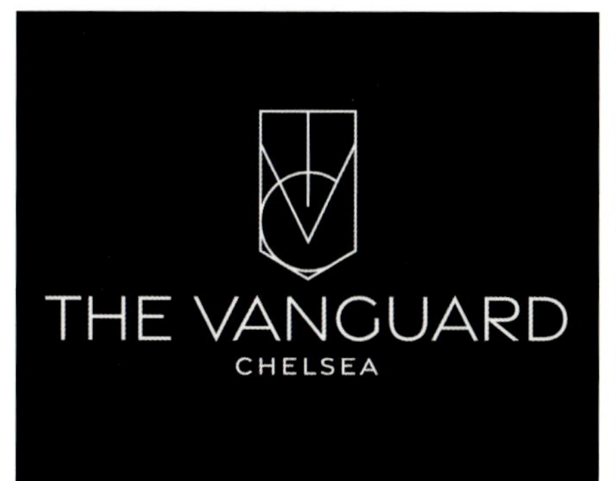

Title: The Vanguard Chelsea Logo
Client: The Albanese Organization
Design Firm: Holly Tienken Design

DAVID JONES

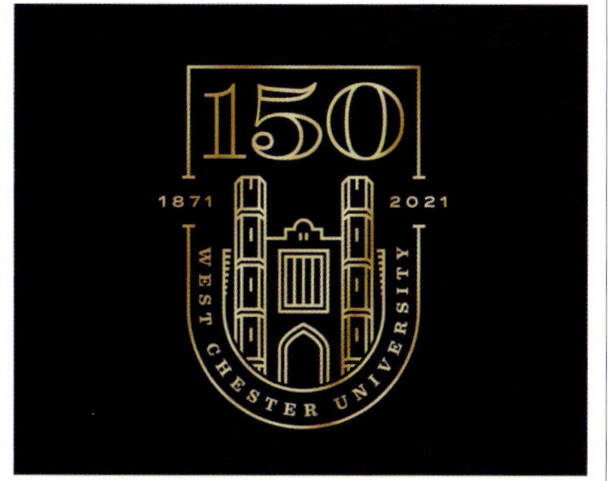

Title: West Chester University 150th Anniversary Brand | **Client:** West Chester University
Design Firm: DPL Jones

G. GRIZZANTI, G. TOSONI

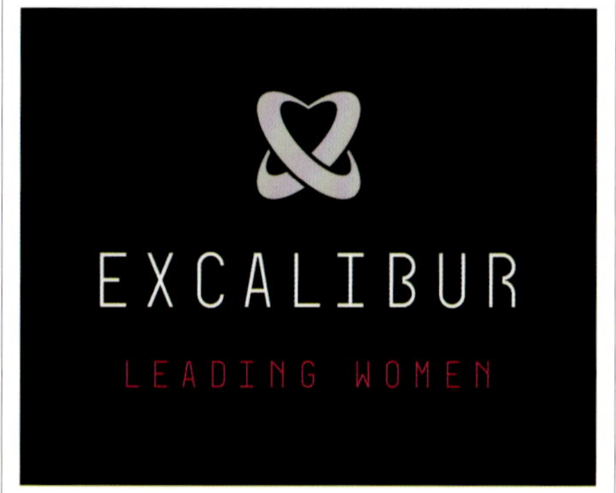

Title: Excalibur: Leading Women
Client: Confederation of Italian Industry
Design Firm: Univisual SRL

DAEKI SHIM, LEEJUN CHANG, MIJI KIM / GIDP

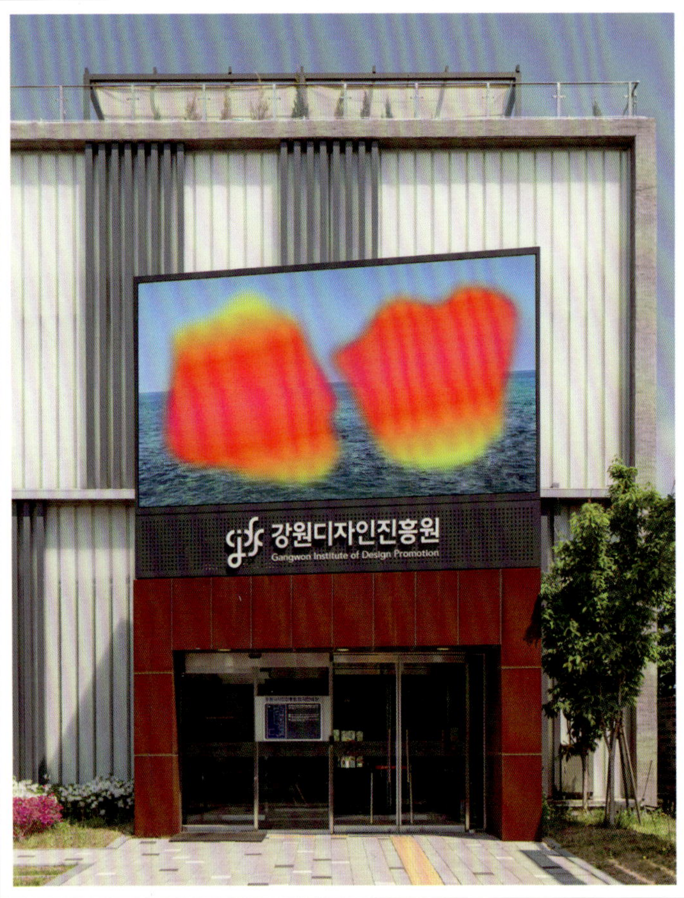

Title: WAVE: East Sea International Art Pre-Biennale (EIAB)
Clients: Gangwon State, Gangwon Institute of Design Promotion (GIDP)
Design Firm: DAEKI and JUN

RALPH APPELBAUM ASSOCIATES

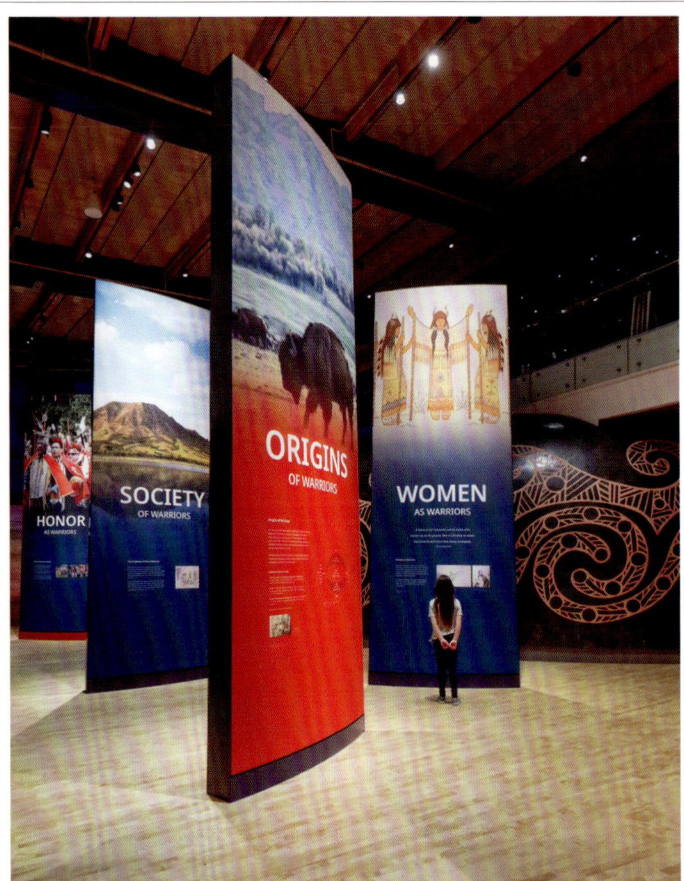

Title: First Americans Museum
Client: First Americans Museum
Design Firm: Ralph Appelbaum Associates

RANDY CLARK

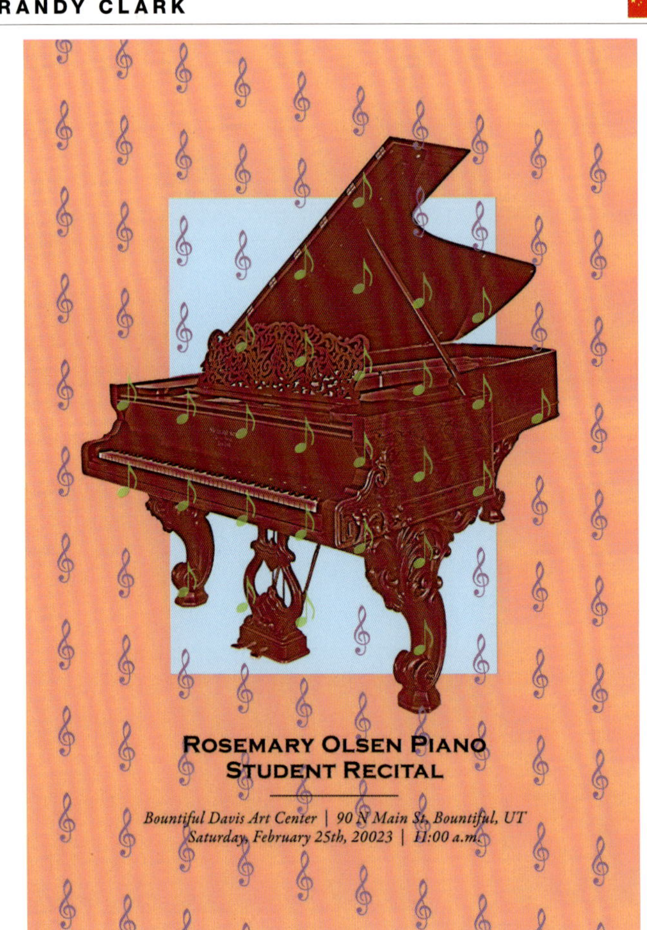

Title: Rosemary Olsen Student Piano Recital
Client: Rosemary Olsen Piano | **Design Firm:** Randy Clark Graphic Design

TE-SIAN SHIH

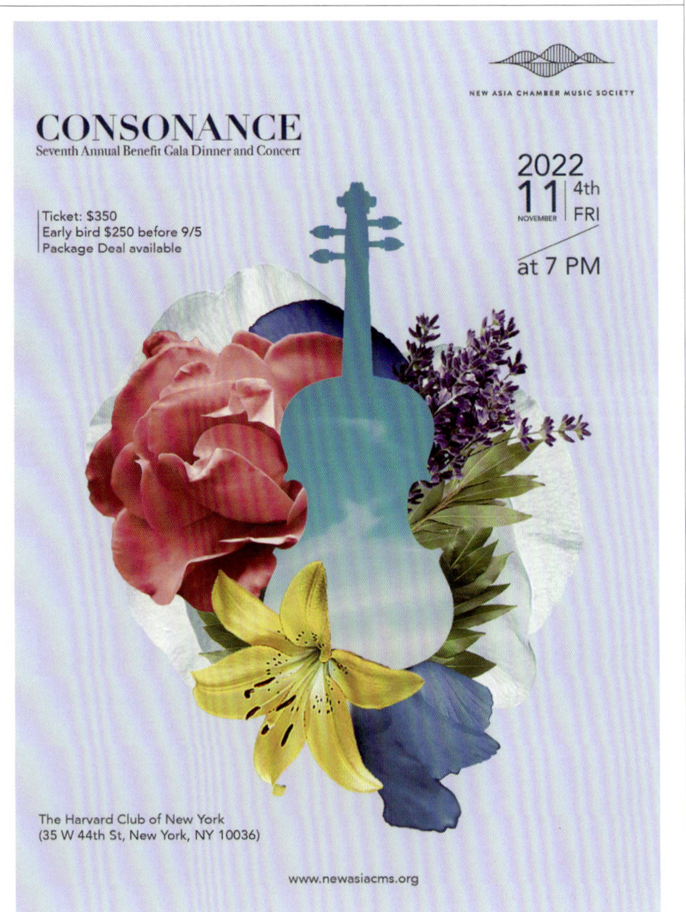

Title: Consonance | **Client:** The New Asia Chamber Music Society
Design Firm: Te-Sian Shih's Design Studio

DOUGLAS THOMAS

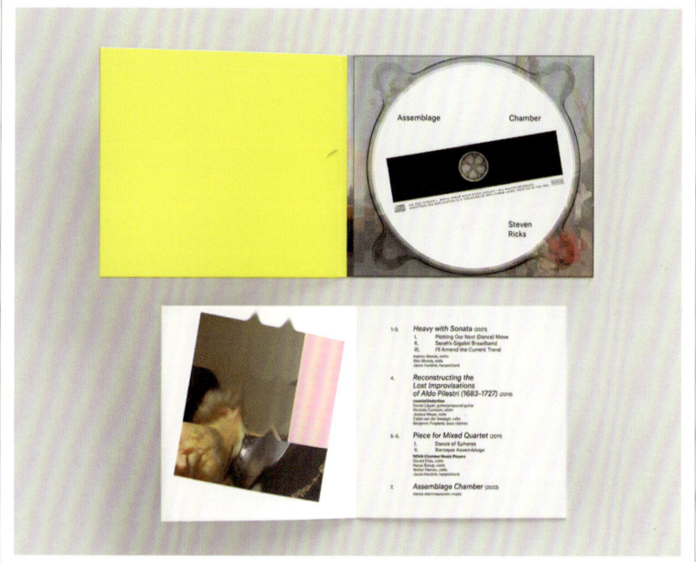

Title: Assemblage Chamber
Clients: Steve Ricks, New Focus Recordings | **Design Firm:** Kunstwerk

THE ROOTS, THE ISLAND DEF JAM MUSIC RECORDS

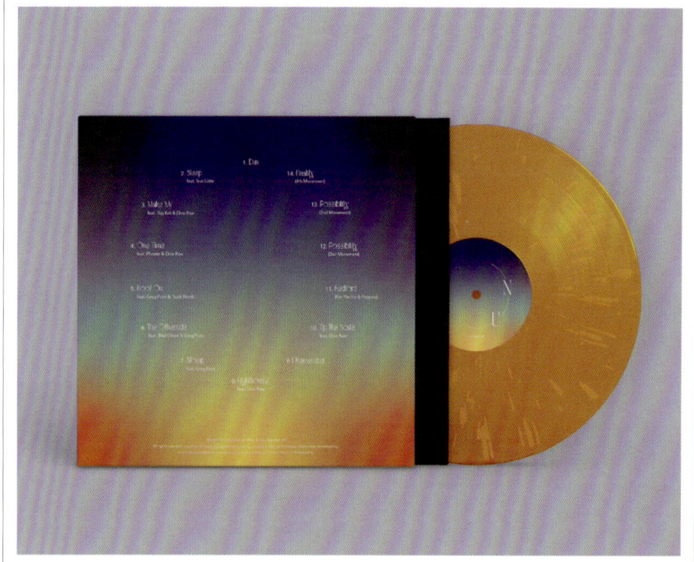

Title: Undun by The Roots: Vinyl Packaging and Lyric Book
Client: Self-initiated | **Design Firm:** Ehmija Design

ARIEL FREANER

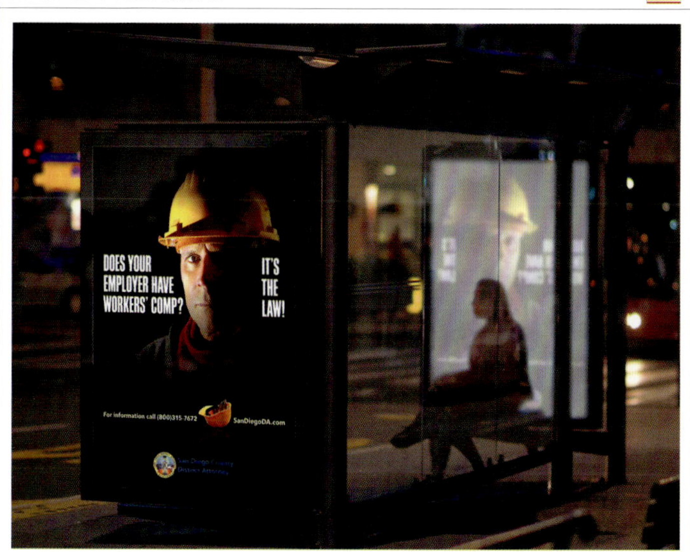

Title: San Diego District Attorney's Office Insurance Fraud Outdoor Campaign | **Client:** San Diego District Attorney's Office
Design Firm: Freaner Creative & Design

SAVANNAH COLLEGE OF ART & DESIGN

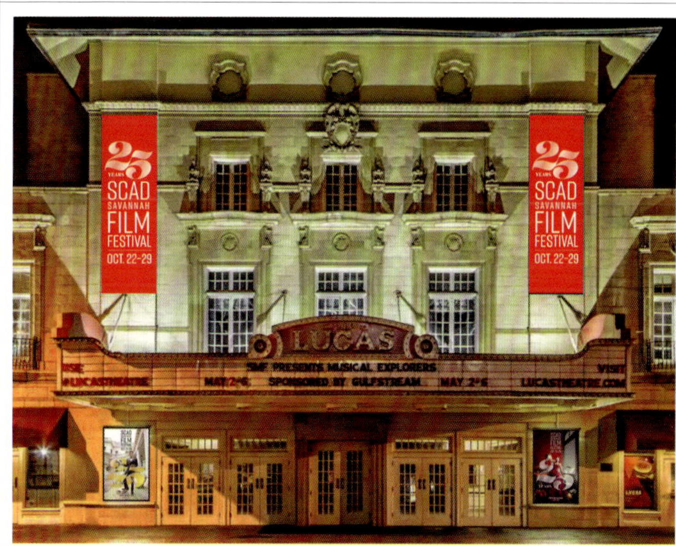

Title: Savannah Film Festival Campaign 2022
Client: Self-initiated
Design Firm: Savannah College of Art & Design

STUDIO DUY

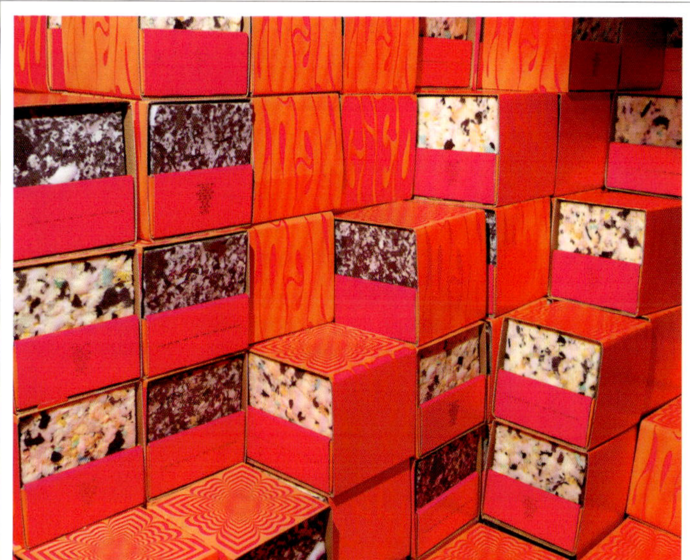

Title: GIEO — Album Package Design
Clients: NGOT, LP Music | **Design Firm:** Studio DUY

XIAOYONG MIAO

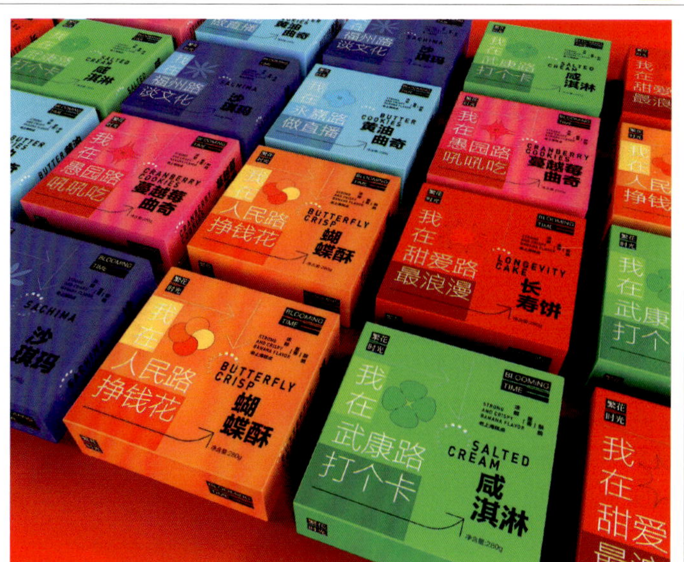

Title: BLOSSOM TIME Product Packaging Design
Client: BLOSSOM TIME | **Design Firm:** Spud Studio

PEPSICO DESIGN & INNOVATION

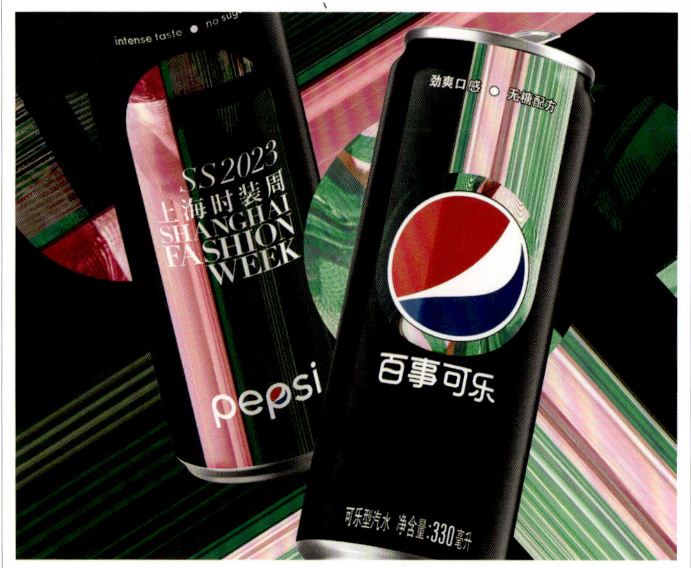

Title: Pepsi Black x DIGITAL SHFW 2023 | **Client:** Self-initated
Design Firm: PepsiCo Design & Innovation

OMDESIGN

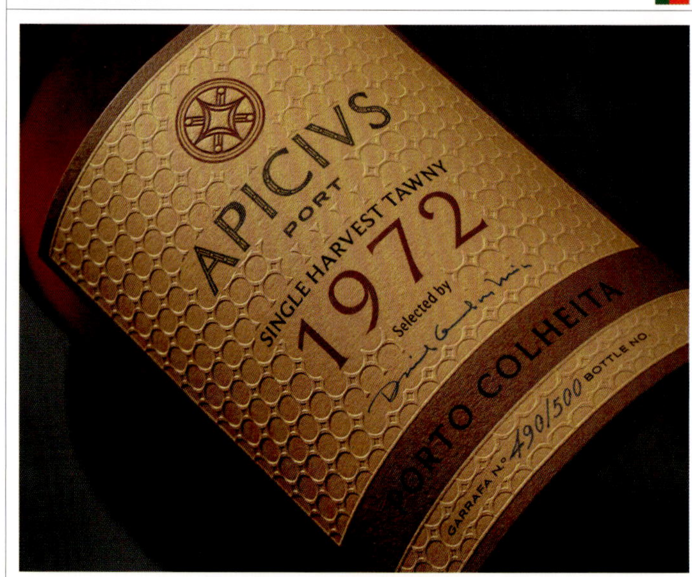

Title: Apicius 1972 | **Client:** Apicius
Design Firm: Omdesign

XIAOYONG MIAO

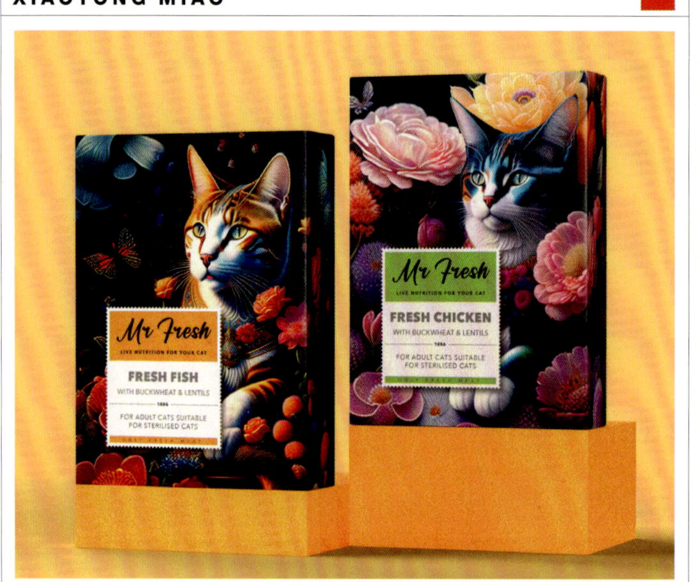

Title: Mr. Fresh Packaging Design | **Client:** Mr. Fresh
Design Firm: Spud Studio

SHAOBIN LIN

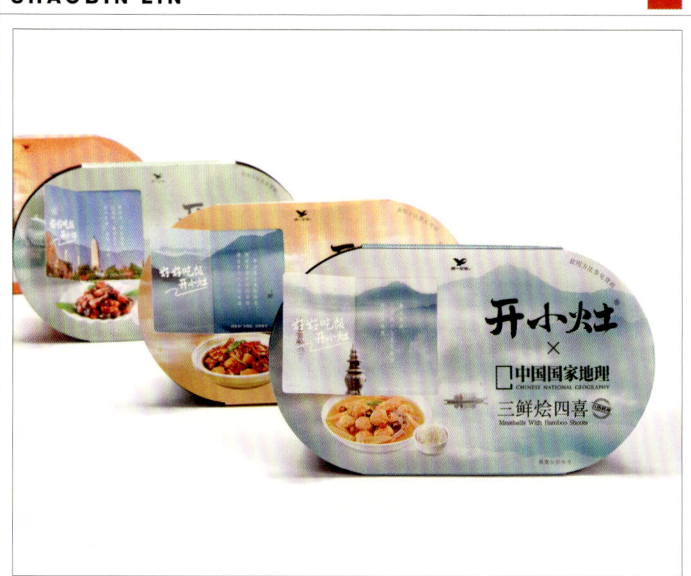

Title: Kaixiaozao Self-Heating Hot Pot | **Client:** Uni-President
Design Firm: Linshaobin Design Shenzhen

LEANNE BALEN

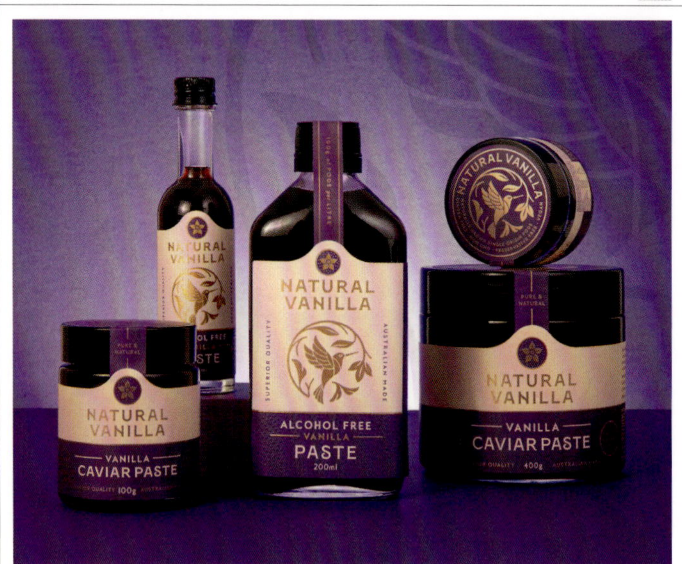

Title: Natural Vanilla
Client: Natural Vanilla | **Design Firm:** Dessein

DAVID JONES

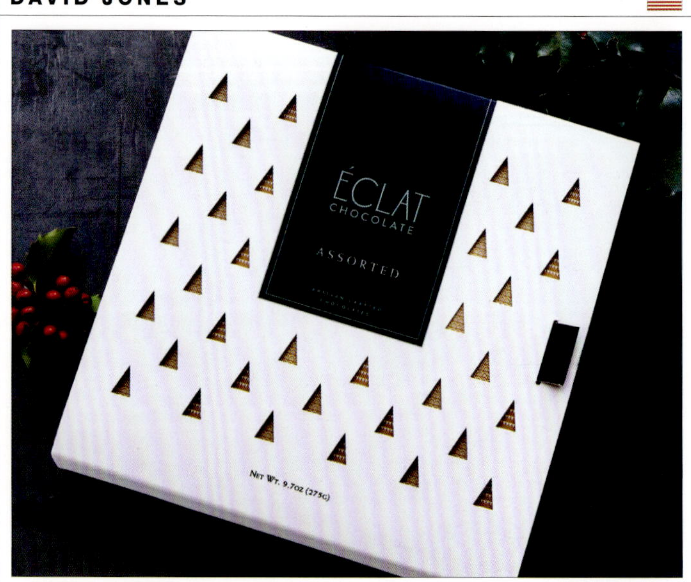

Title: Eclat Chocolate Pull Tab Holiday Packaging
Client: Eclat Chocolate | **Design Firm:** DPL Jones

GRETA RIDER

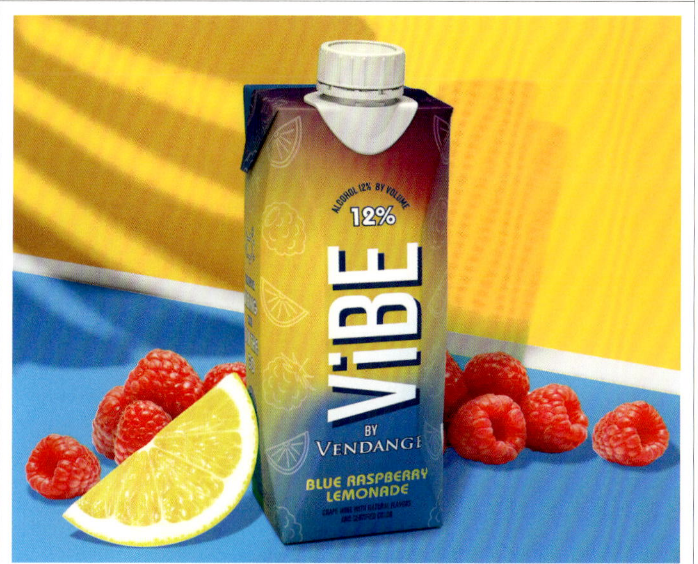

Title: ViBE
Client: Vendange | **Design Firm:** Gallo Creative

J. HISCHE, L. DIBBLE, S. AREVALOS, A. LANIER

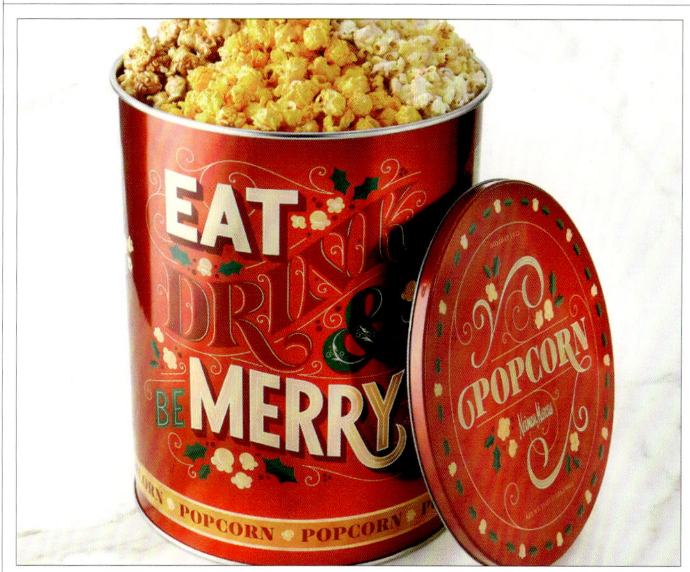

Title: Neiman Marcus Holiday Epicure Packaging
Client: Self-initated | **Design Firm:** Neiman Marcus Creative Services

ECOCHAIN PACKAGING DESIGN TEAM

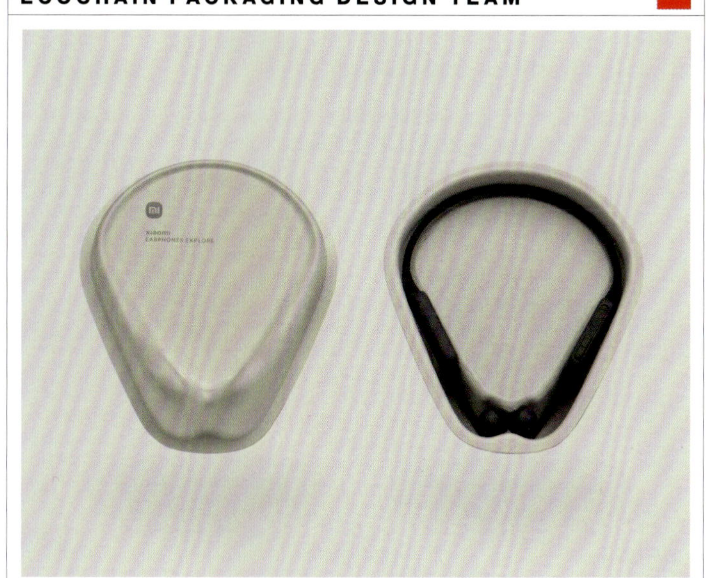

Title: Mi Earphones Explore
Client: Self-initiated | **Design Firm:** Xiaomi

ANOTHER COLLECTIVE

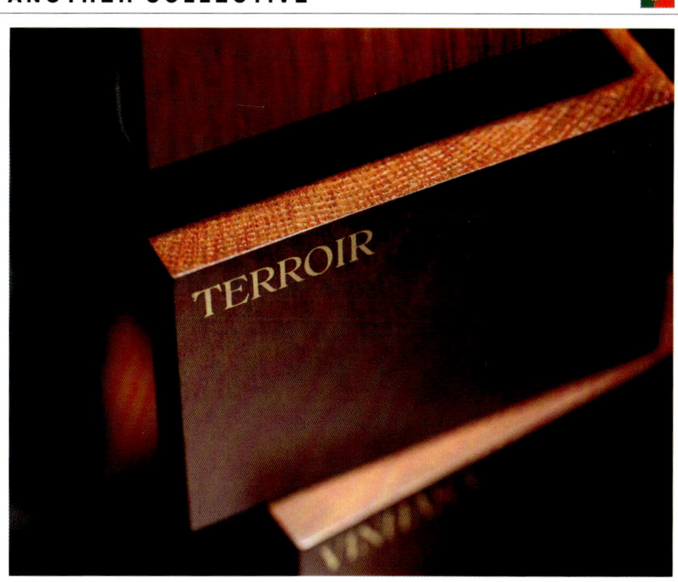

Title: Quinta da Boavista
Client: Quinta da Boavista - Sogevinus | **Design Firm:** Another Collective

PEPSICO DESIGN & INNOVATION

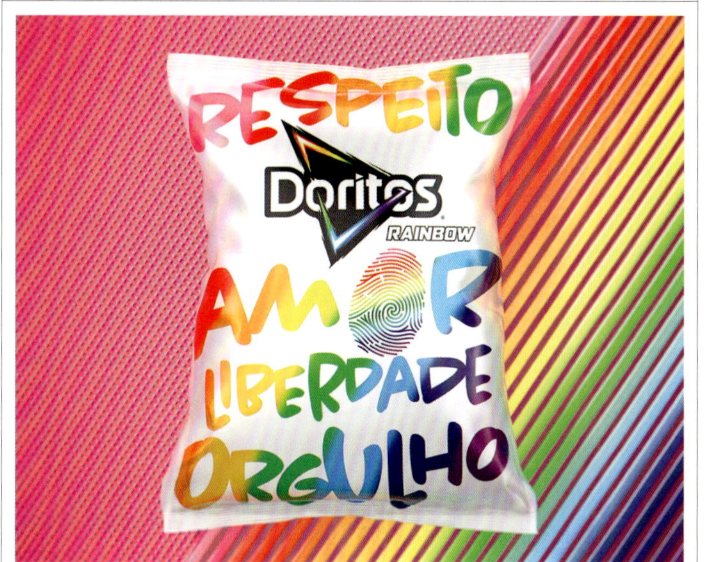

Title: Doritos Rainbow Limited Edition 2022 | **Client:** Self-initated
Design Firm: PepsiCo Design & Innovation

PEPSICO DESIGN & INNOVATION

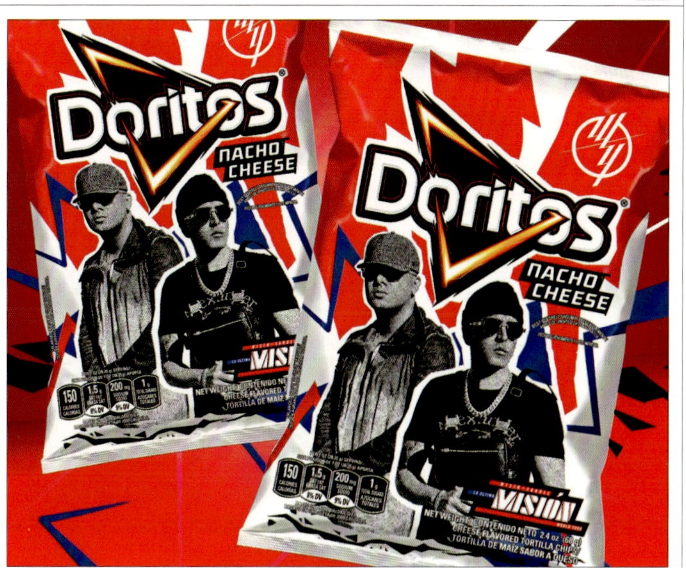

Title: Doritos W&Y | **Client:** Self-initated
Design Firm: PepsiCo Design & Innovation

FORCEMAJEURE DESIGN

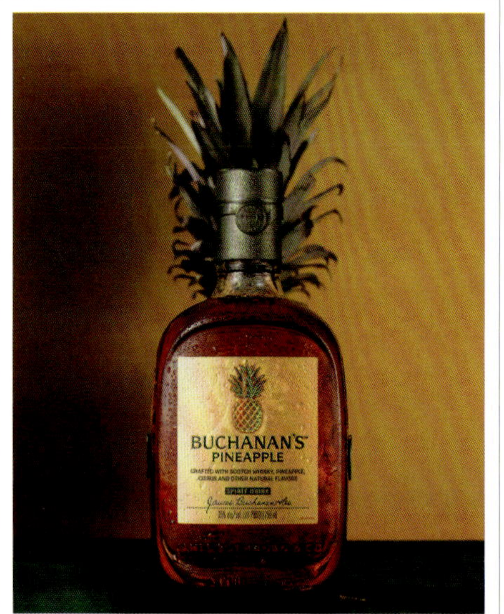

Title: Buchanan's Pineapple | **Client:** Diageo
Design Firm: forceMAJEURE Design

CF NAPA BRAND DESIGN

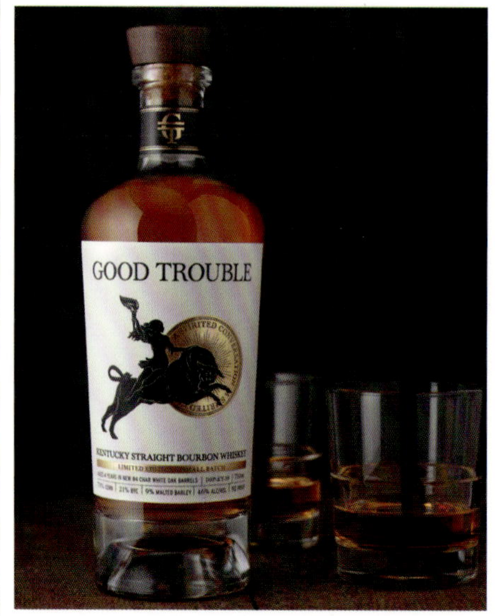

Title: Good Trouble | **Client:** Good Trouble Bourbon
Design Firm: CF Napa Brand Design

KUAN FU WU

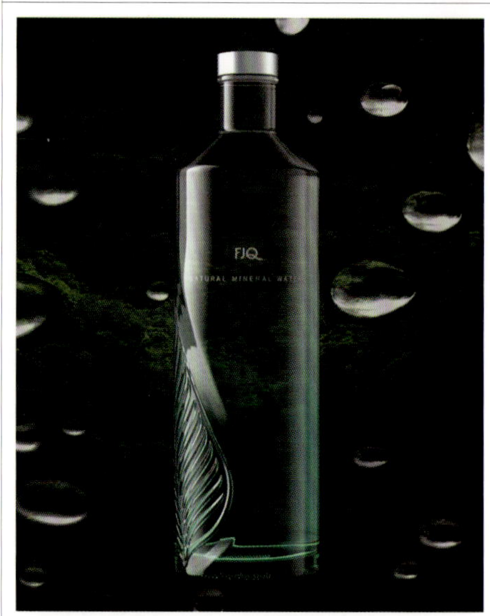

Title: FJQ | **Client:** FJQ | **Design Firm:** Shenzhen Excel Brand Design Consultant Co., Ltd.

CF NAPA BRAND DESIGN

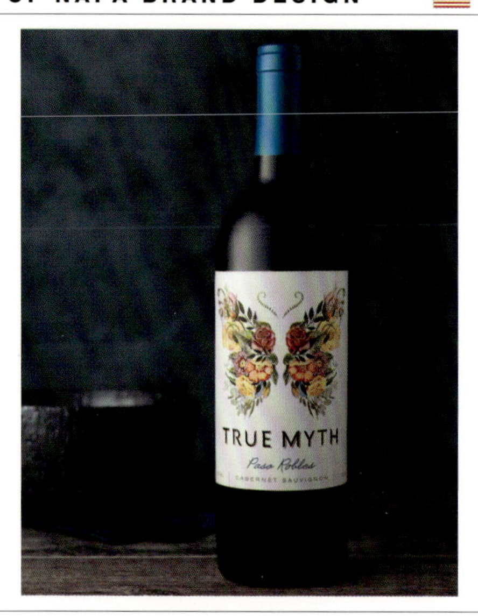

Title: True Myth
Client: WX Brands
Design Firm: CF Napa Brand Design

MUQIANG FU

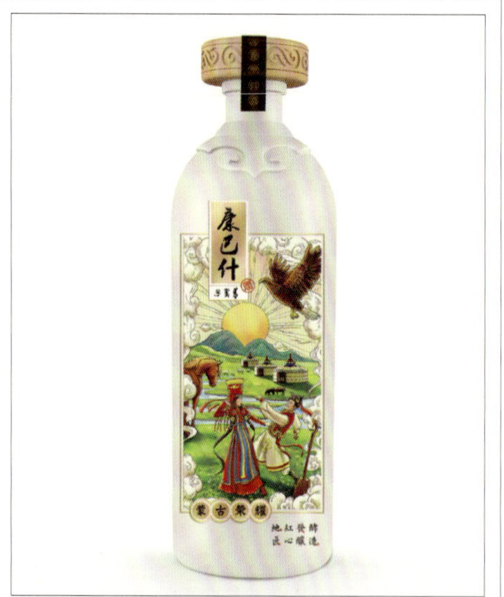

Title: Kangbashi | **Client:** Inner Mongolia Kangbashi Distillery Co., Ltd.
Design Firm: Sungoo Design

ERIC LE

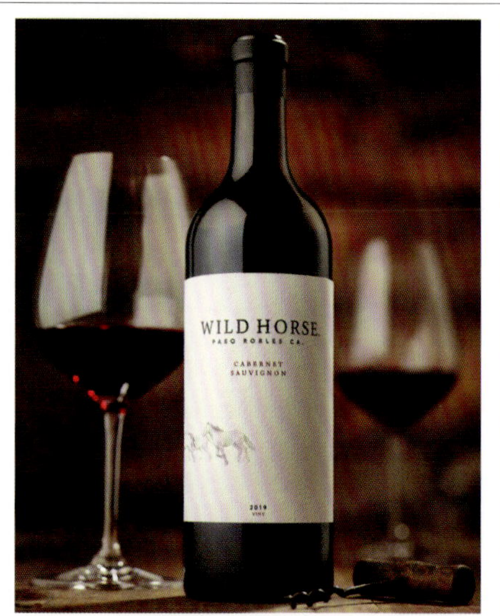

Title: Wild Horse
Client: Wild Horse
Design Firm: Gallo Creative

DAVID SCHUEMANN

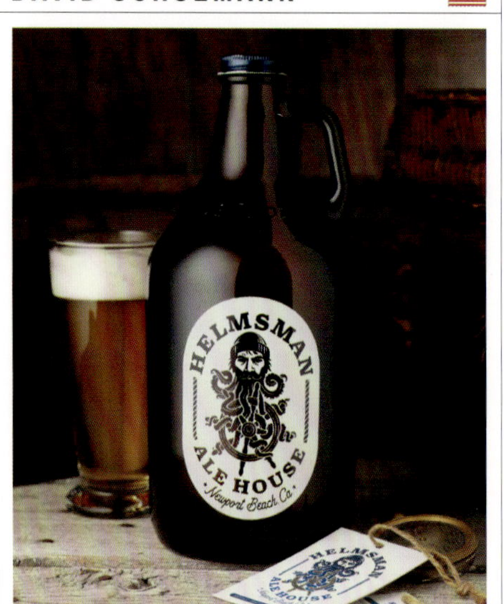

Title: Helmsman Ale House
Client: Helmsman Ale House
Design Firm: CF Napa Brand Design

BULLETPROOF

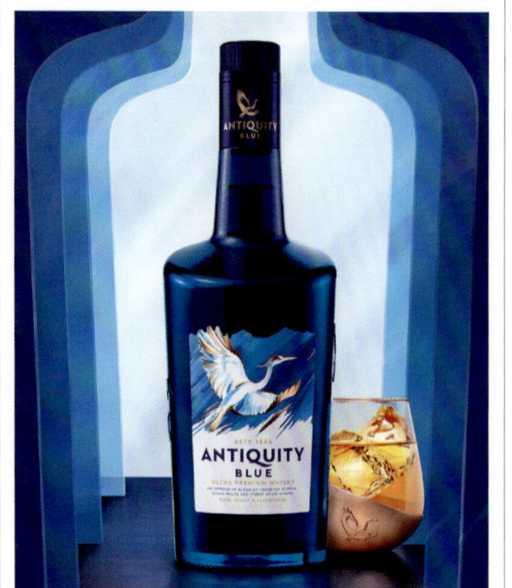

Title: Antiquity Brand Refresh 2023
Clients: Diageo India, Hiren Dedhia
Design Firm: Bulletproof

STRANGER & STRANGER

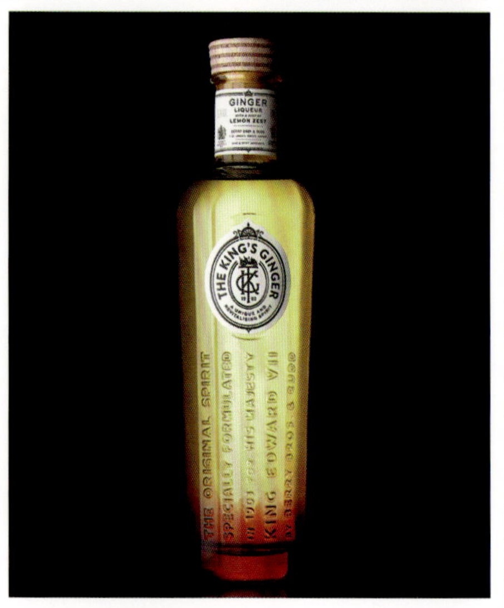

Title: The King's Ginger
Client: Berry Brothers & Rudd
Design Firm: Stranger & Stranger

IGOR POTURIC

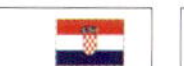

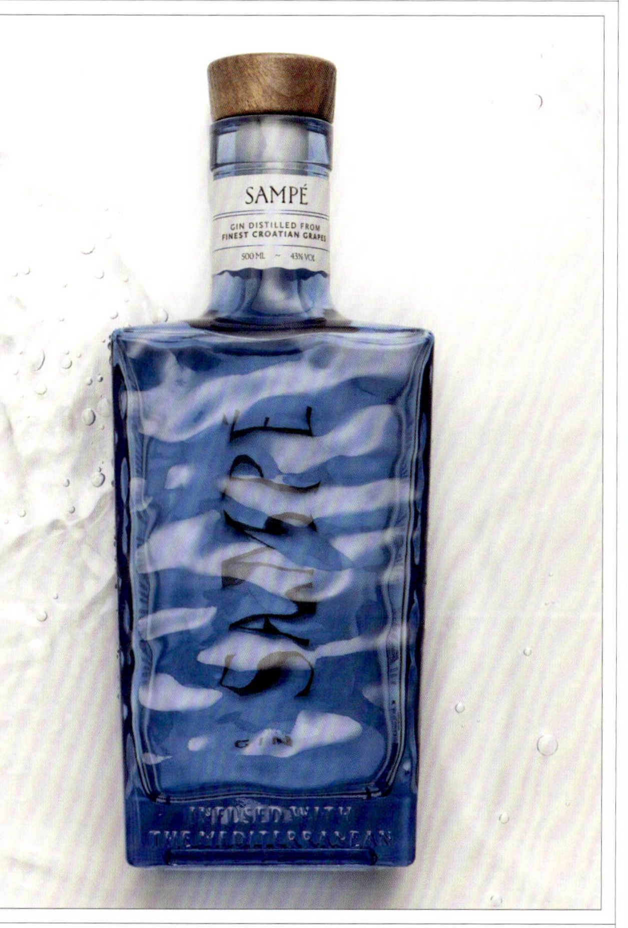

Title: SAMPÉ Gin | **Client:** High Spirits
Design Firm: Design Bureau Izvorka Juric

STRANGER & STRANGER

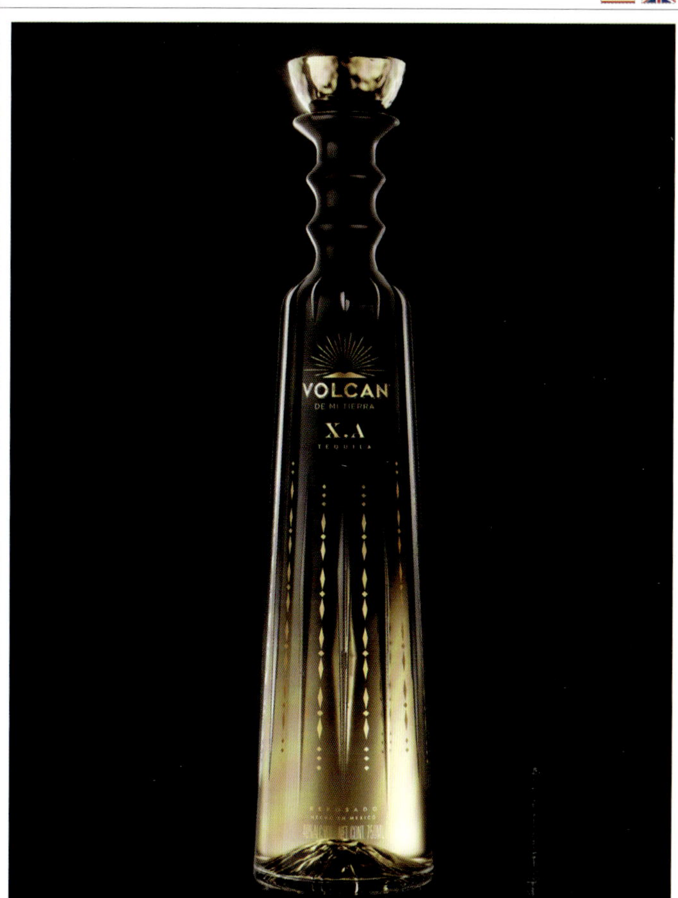

Title: Volcan XA Tequila | **Client:** LVMH
Design Firm: Stranger & Stranger

CF NAPA BRAND DESIGN

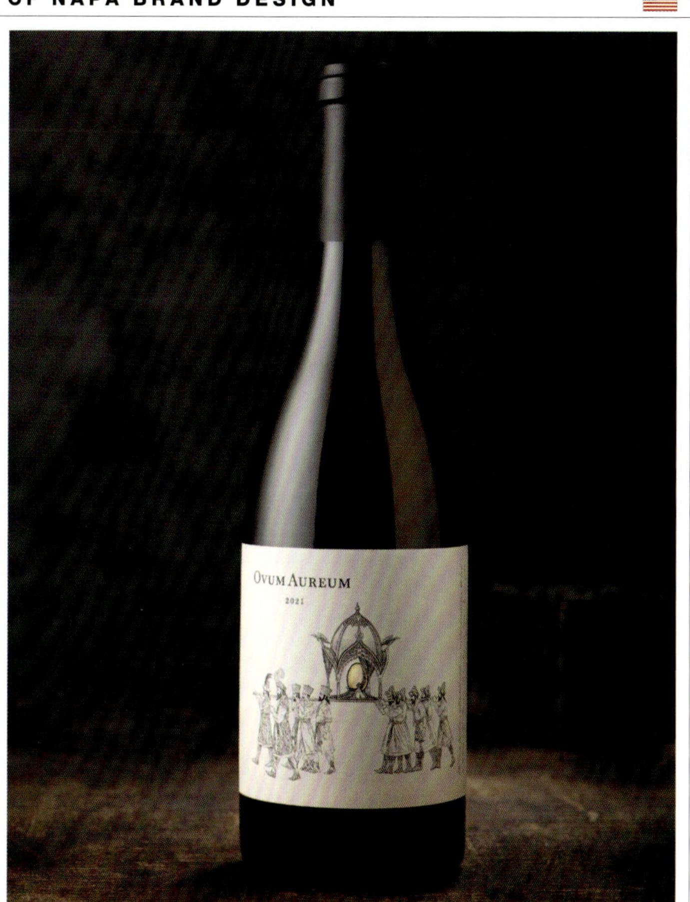

Title: Mira Winery Ovum Aureum
Client: Mira Winery
Design Firm: CF Napa Brand Design

CASEY BRETT

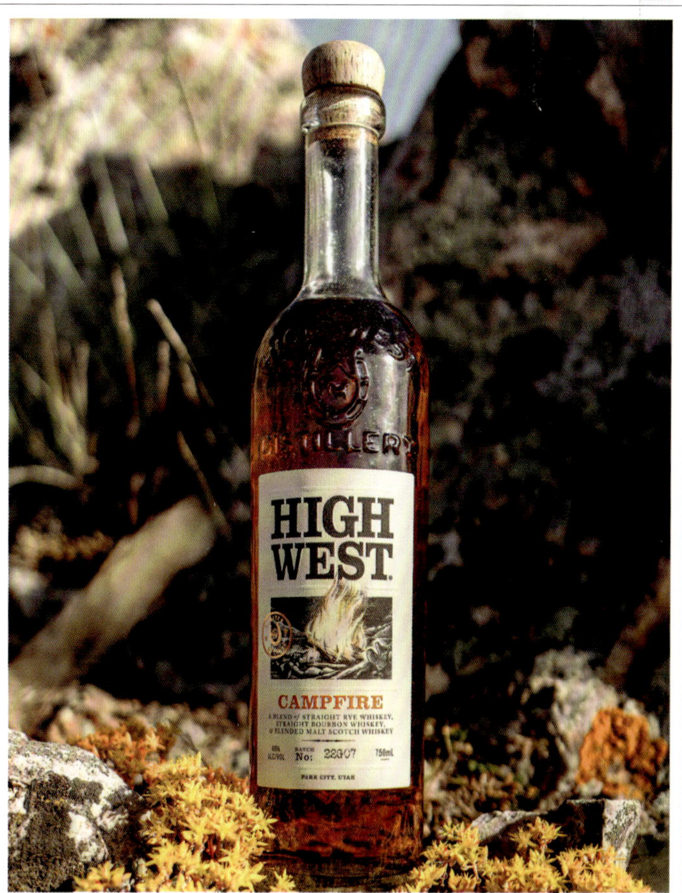

Title: High West Limited Release Whiskey Packaging
Client: Constellation Brands, Inc.
Design Firm: Vine Creative Studios at Partners + Napier

CF NAPA BRAND DESIGN

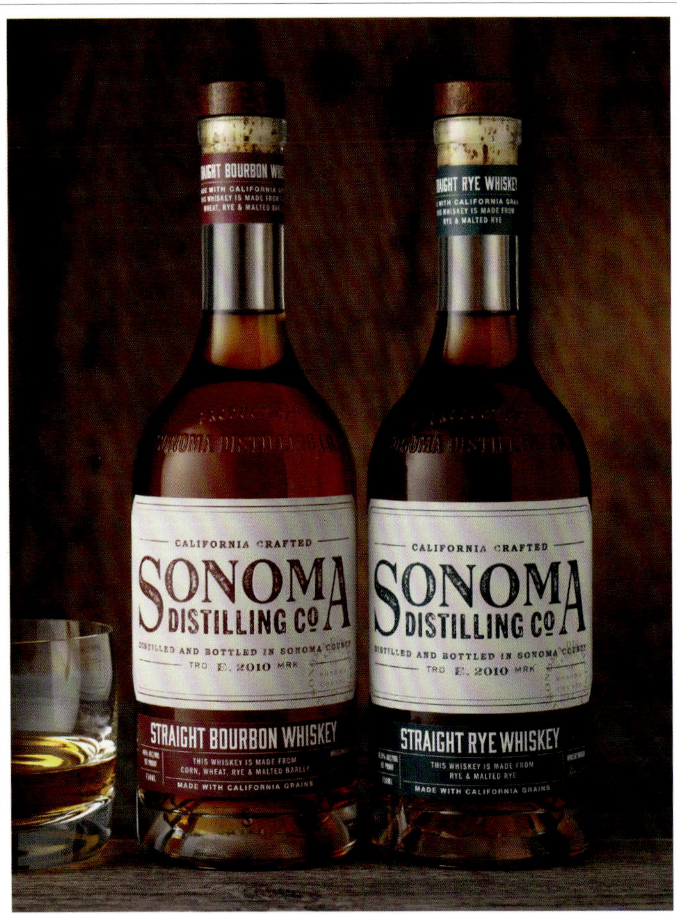

Title: Sonoma Distilling Co. Portfolio
Client: Corning & Company | **Design Firm:** CF Napa Brand Design

CF NAPA BRAND DESIGN

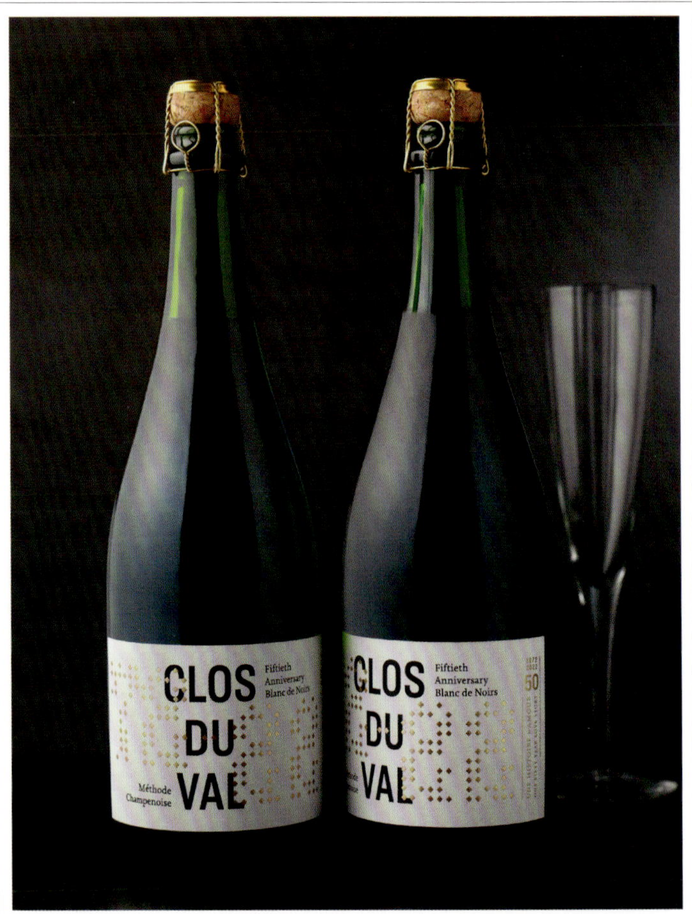

Title: Clos du Val 50th Anniversary Sparkling Blanc de Noirs
Client: Clos du Val | **Design Firm:** CF Napa Brand Design

CF NAPA BRAND DESIGN

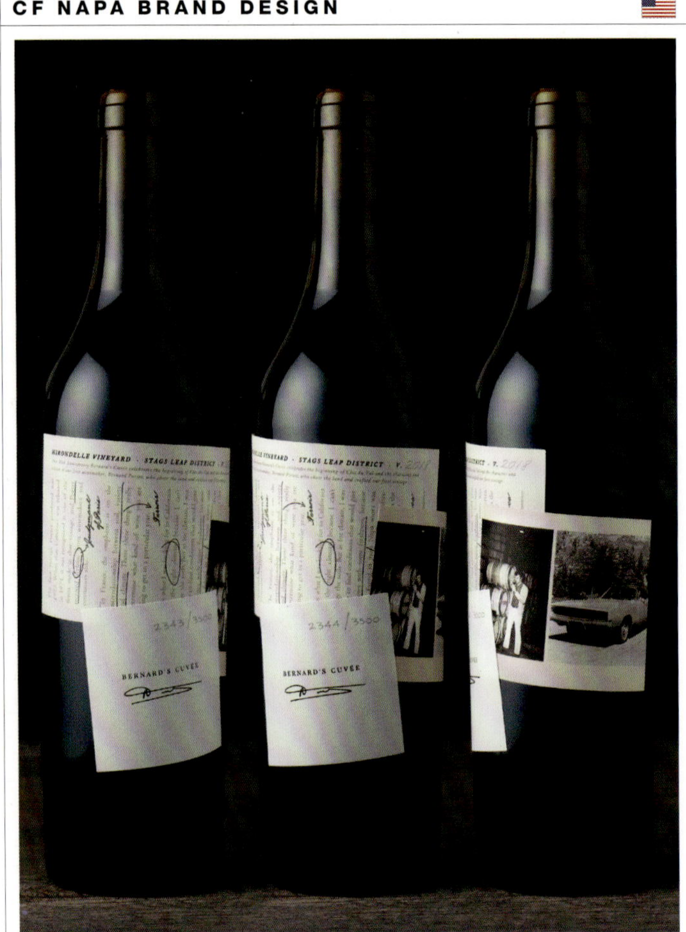

Title: Clos du Val Bernard's Cuvée | **Client:** Clos du Val
Design Firm: CF Napa Brand Design

CF NAPA BRAND DESIGN

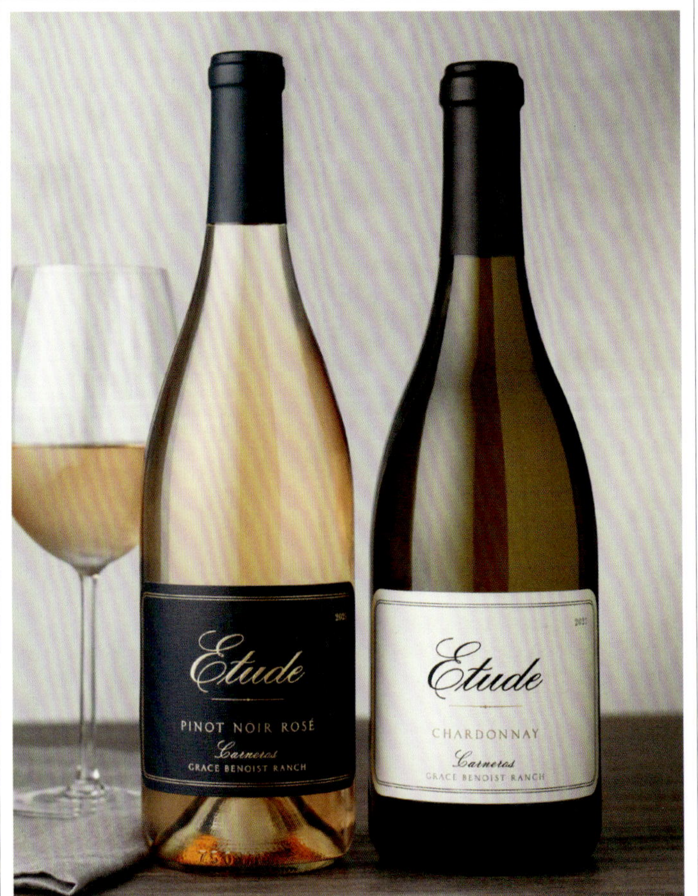

Title: Etude Portfolio | **Client:** Treasury Wine Estates
Design Firm: CF Napa Brand Design

KUAN FU WU

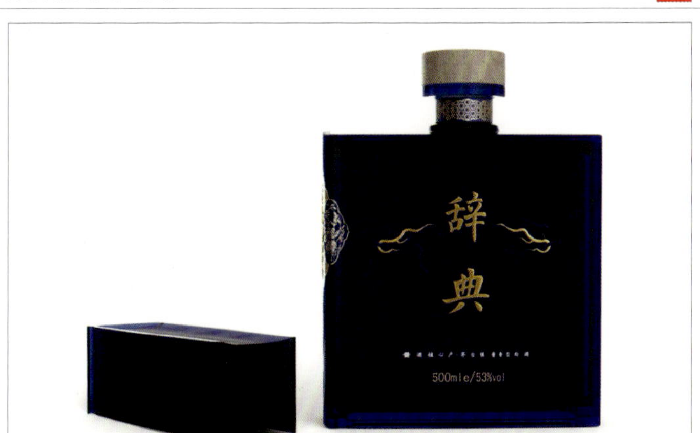

Title: CI DIAN
Client: Ci Dian
Design Firm: Shenzhen Excel Brand Design Consultant Co., Ltd.

JARED BRITTON

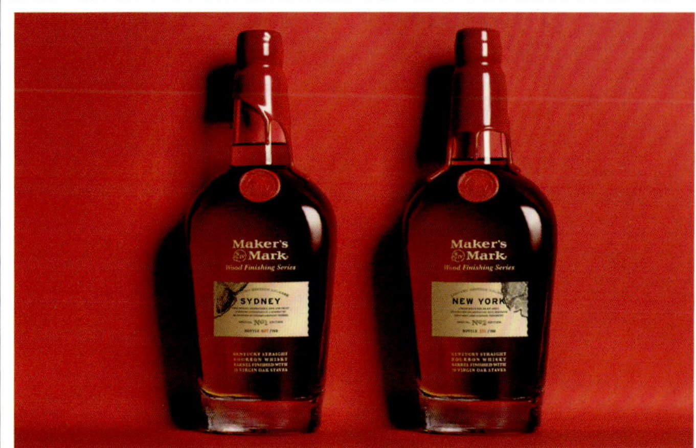

Title: Packaging for Maker's Mark Wood Finishing City Series
Client: Maker's Mark
Design Firm: Turner Duckworth: London, San Francisco & New York

BUTTERFLY CANNON, ARRON EGAN

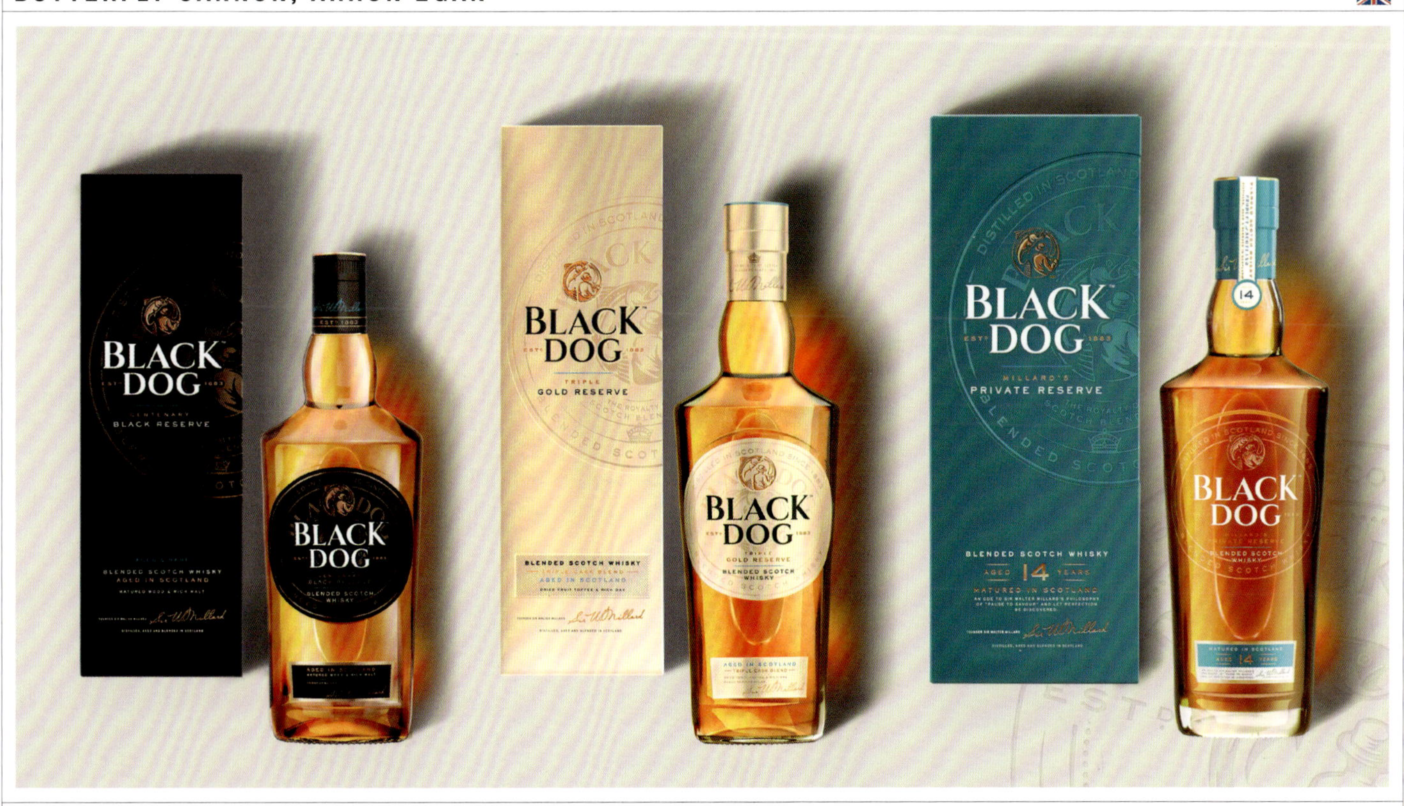

Title: Black Dog - The Scotch Icon Back To No.1 | **Clients:** Hiren Dedhia, Diageo India | **Design Firm:** Butterfly Cannon

BULLETPROOF

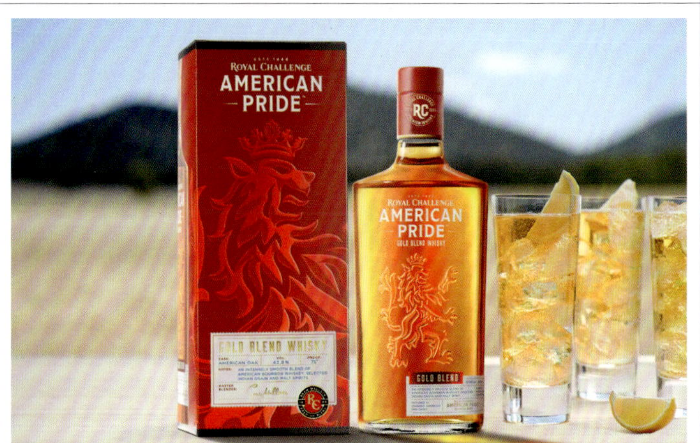

Title: Royal Challenge - American Pride Whisky
Clients: Hiren Dedhia, Diageo India
Design Firm: Bulletproof

LISA SIRBAUGH CREATIVE

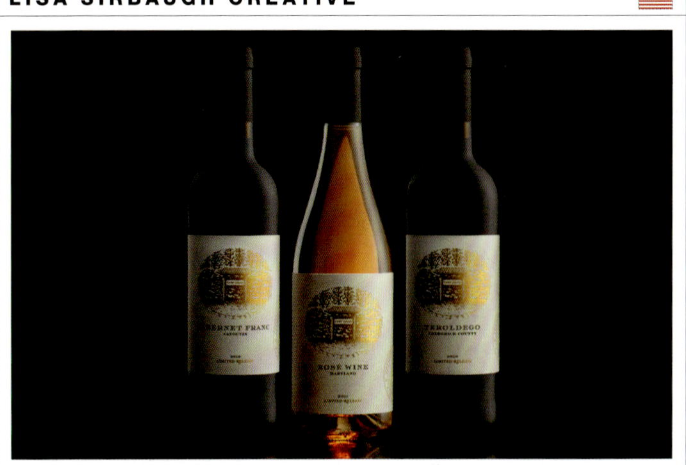

Title: Camp David Presidential Retreat Private Label Wine Series
Client: Camp David Presidential Retreat
Design Firm: Lisa Sirbaugh Creative

STAN CHURCH

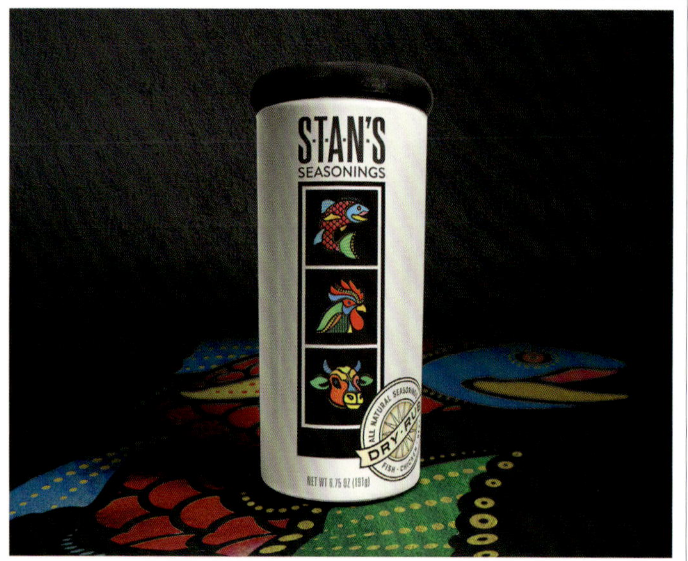

Title: Stan's Seasonings | **Client:** Self-initiated
Design Firm: Stan Church Incorporated

PEPSICO DESIGN & INNOVATION

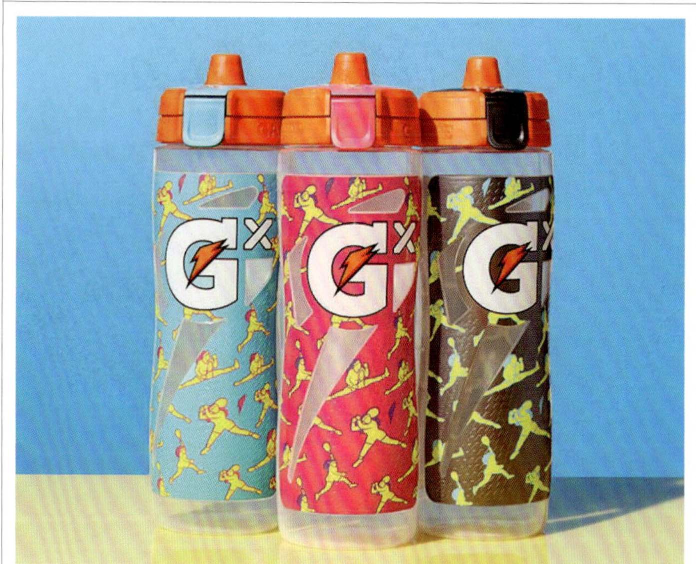

Title: Gatorade x Serena Gx Bottle | **Client:** Self-initated
Design Firm: PepsiCo Design & Innovation

SHERRY KUO, HSINHUI KUO

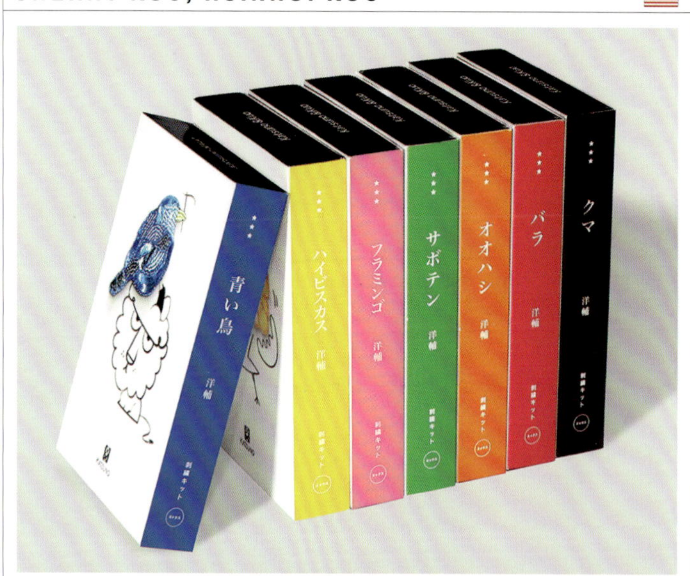

Title: Katsuno Embroidery Starter Kit | **Client:** Katsuno Japan
Design Firm: andKuo

ECOCHAIN PACKAGING DESIGN TEAM

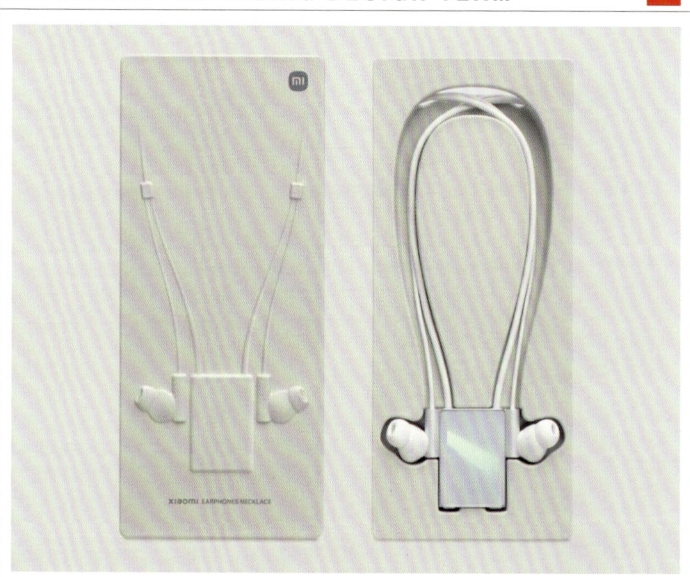

Title: Mi Earphones Necklace | **Client:** Self-initiated
Design Firm: Xiaomi

PEPSICO DESIGN & INNOVATION

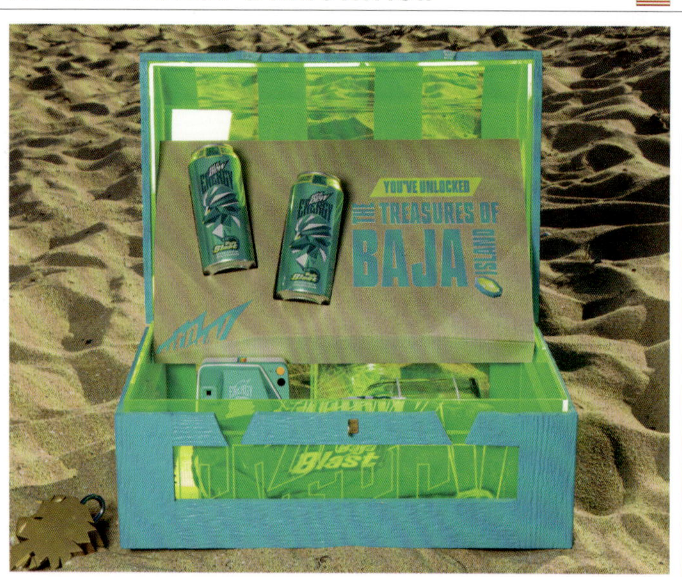

Title: MTN DEW ENERGY BAJA BLAST | **Client:** Self-initated
Design Firm: PepsiCo Design & Innovation

TRACY KENWORTHY

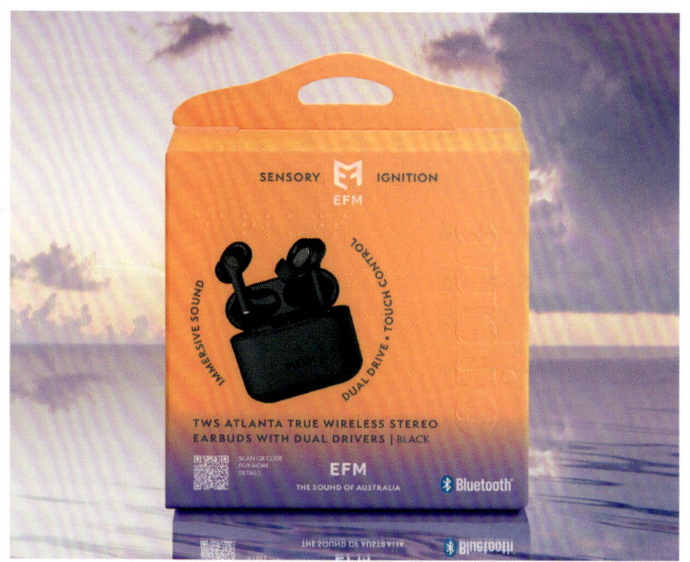

Title: EFM | **Client:** Force Technology
Design Firm: Dessein

IAN DE LEMOS

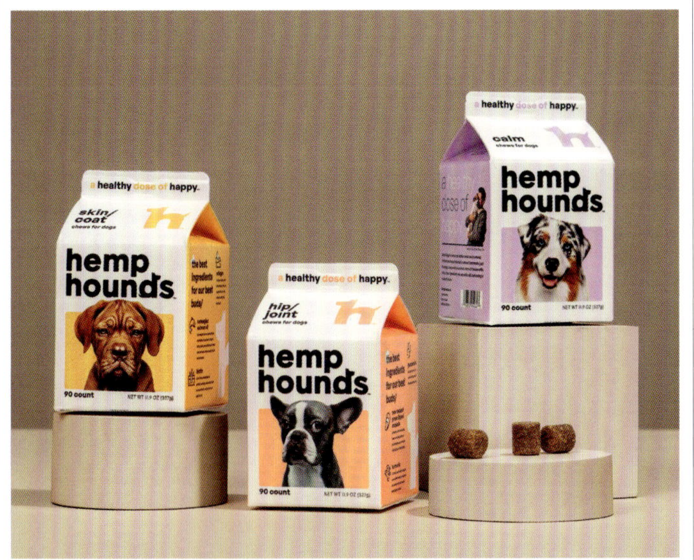

Title: Hemp Hounds Packaging
Clients: Hemp Hounds, Matthew Kennedy | **Design Firm:** BexBands

KUAN FU WU

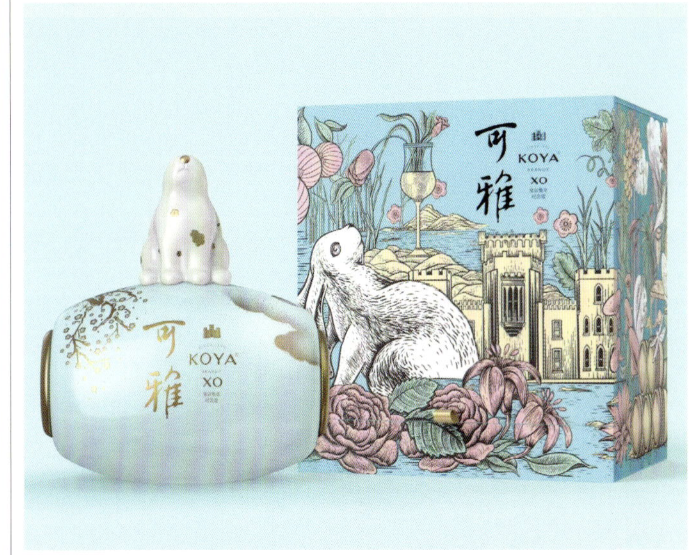

Title: KOYA·THE RABBIT YEAR | **Client:** KOYA
Design Firm: Shenzhen Excel Brand Design Consultant Co., Ltd.

PEPSICO DESIGN & INNOVATION

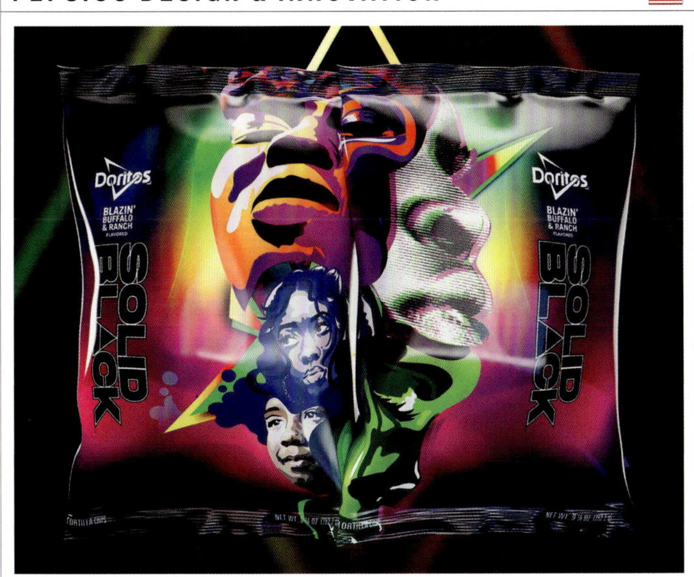

Title: Doritos Solid Black 2022 | **Client:** Self-initated
Design Firm: PepsiCo Design & Innovation

PEPSICO DESIGN & INNOVATION

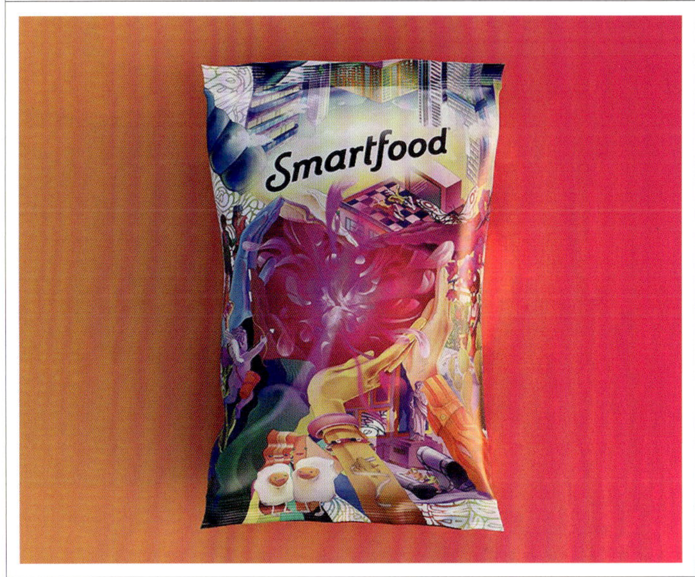

Title: All Love is Smart Love – Smartfood x GLAAD Valentine's Day Influencer Kits | **Client:** Self-initated | **Design Firm:** PepsiCo Design & Innovation

ECOCHAIN PACKAGING DESIGN TEAM

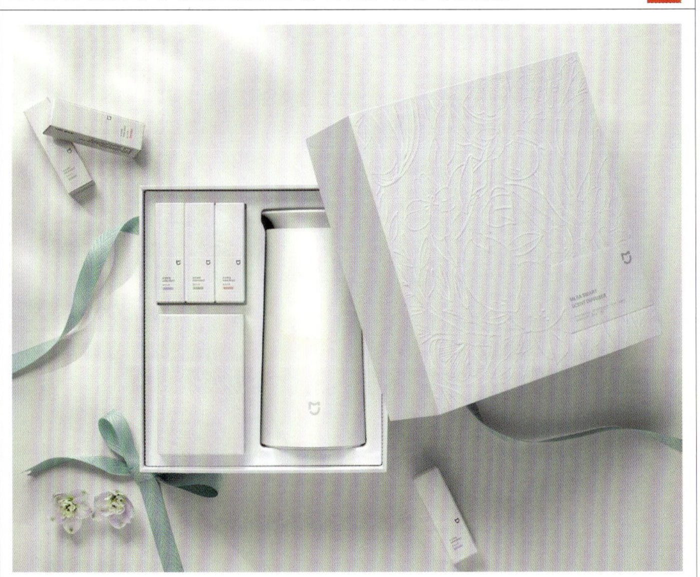

Title: Mijia Smart Scent Diffuser | **Client:** Self-initiated
Design Firm: Xiaomi

BECKY DAHL, JEREMY DAHL

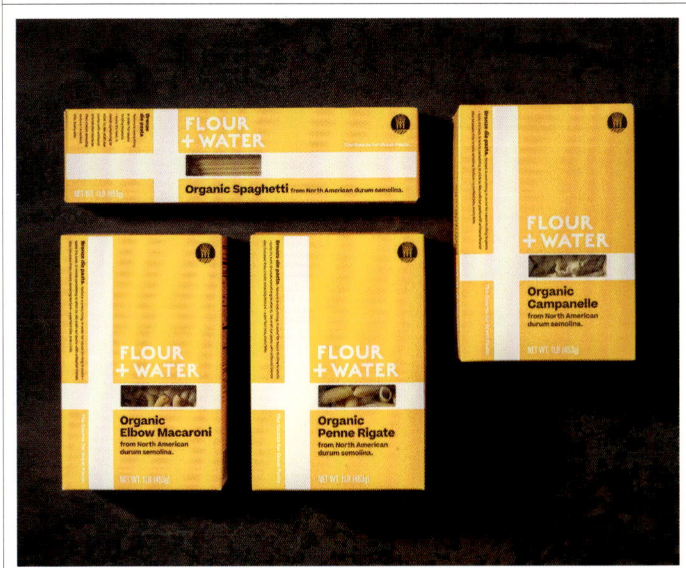

Title: Flour + Water Packaging | **Client:** Flour + Water
Design Firm: BexBrands

ASHFORD STAMPER

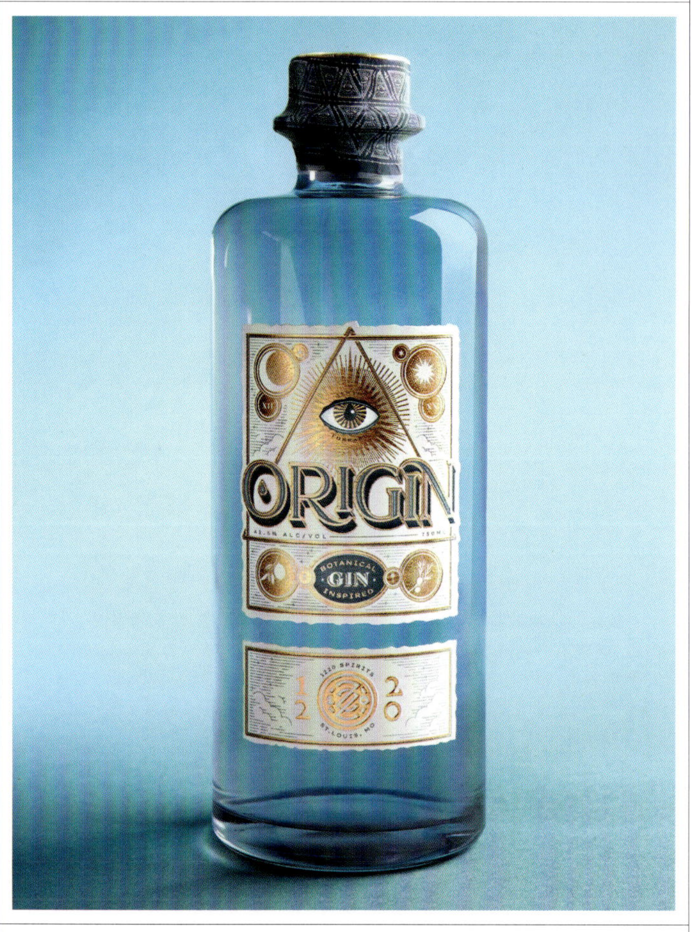

Title: Origin Gin Packaging | **Client:** 1220 Spirits
Design Firm: TOKY Branding + Design

KUAN FU WU

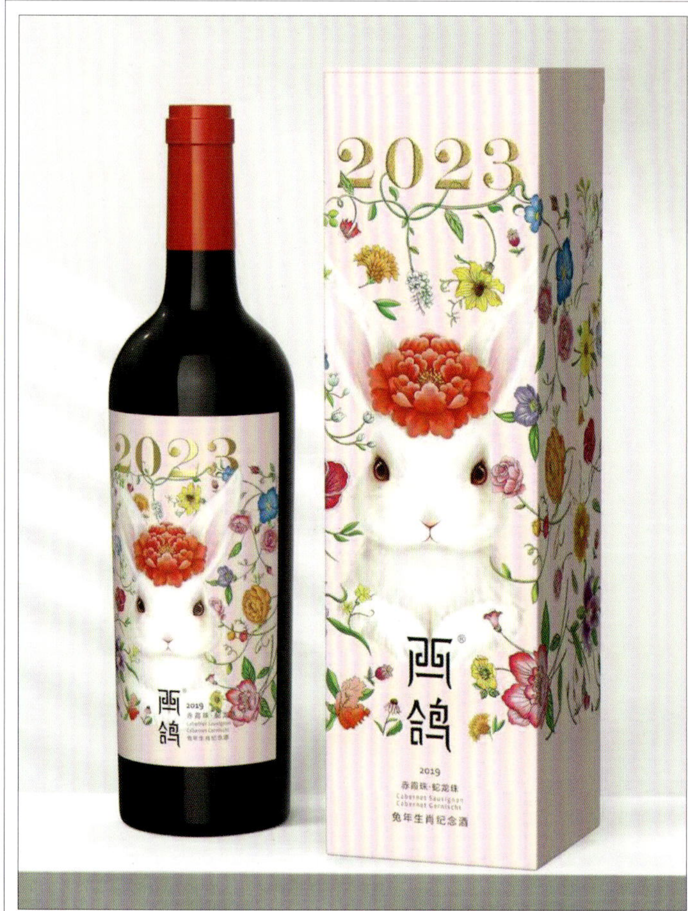

Title: XIGE·THE RABBIT YEAR | **Client:** XIGE
Design Firm: Shenzhen Excel Brand Design Consultant Co., Ltd.

CF NAPA BRAND DESIGN

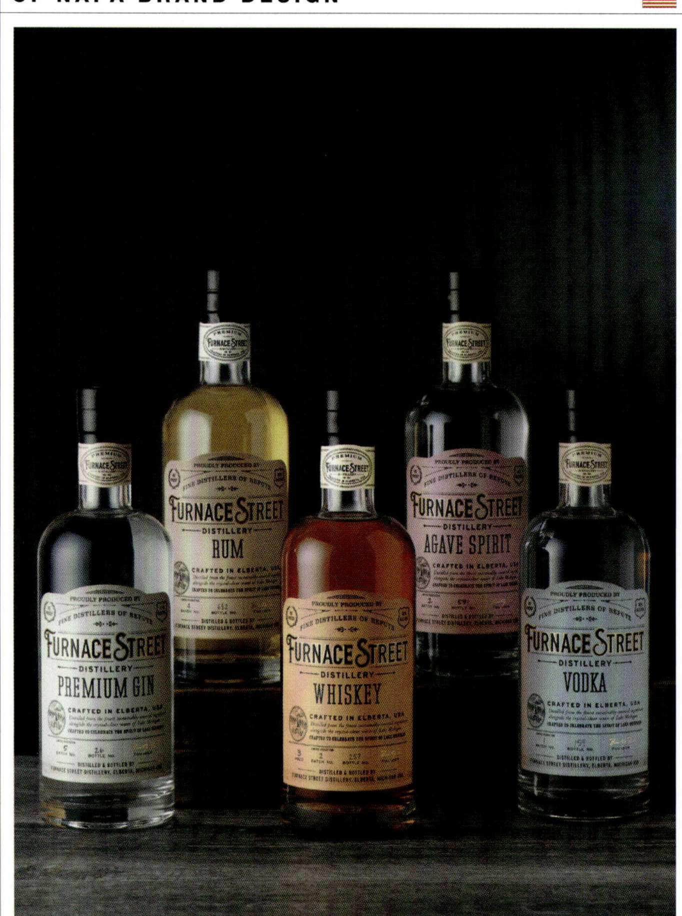

Title: Furnace Street Distillery | **Client:** Furnace Street Distillery
Design Firm: CF Napa Brand Design

CF NAPA BRAND DESIGN

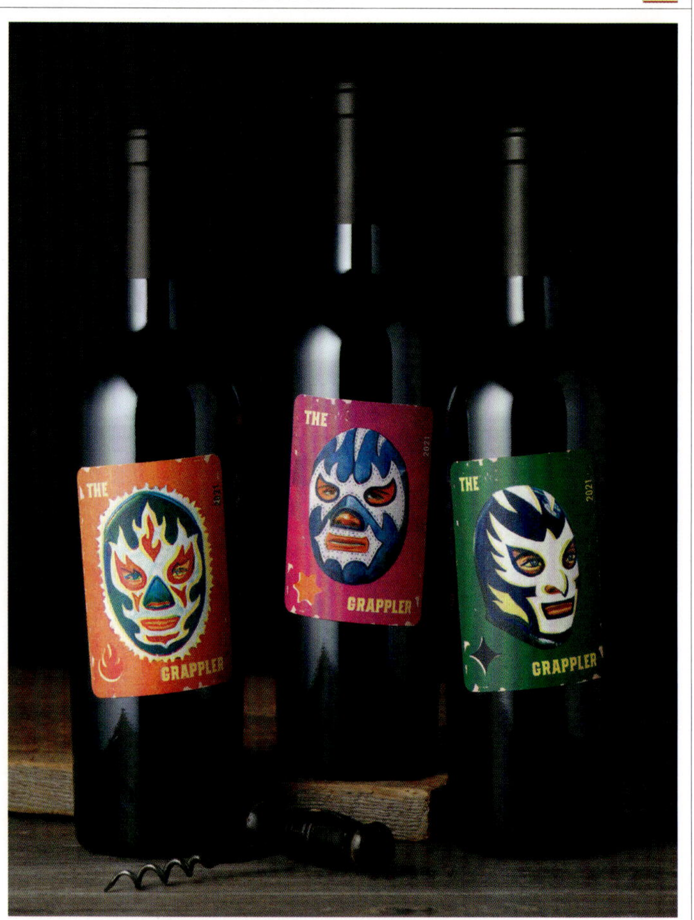

Title: The Grappler | **Client:** Vinoce Vineyards
Design Firm: CF Napa Brand Design

STRANGER & STRANGER

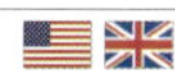

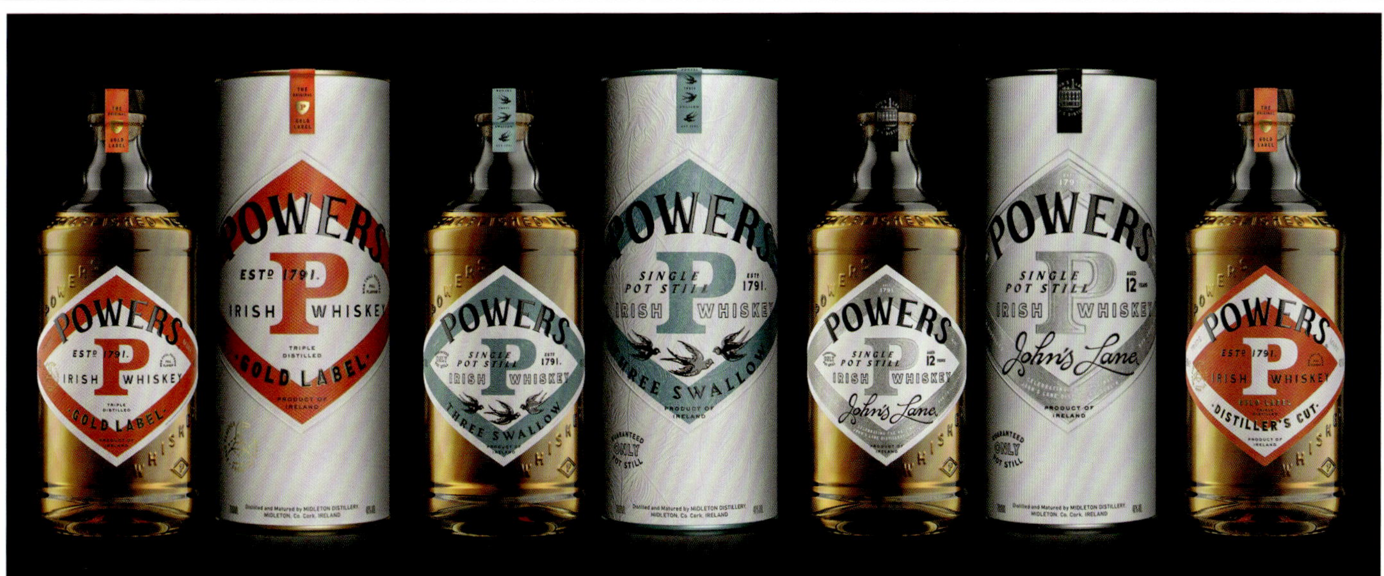

Title: Powers Irish Whiskey | **Client:** Irish Distillers Ltd. | **Design Firm:** Stranger & Stranger

QIN LUO

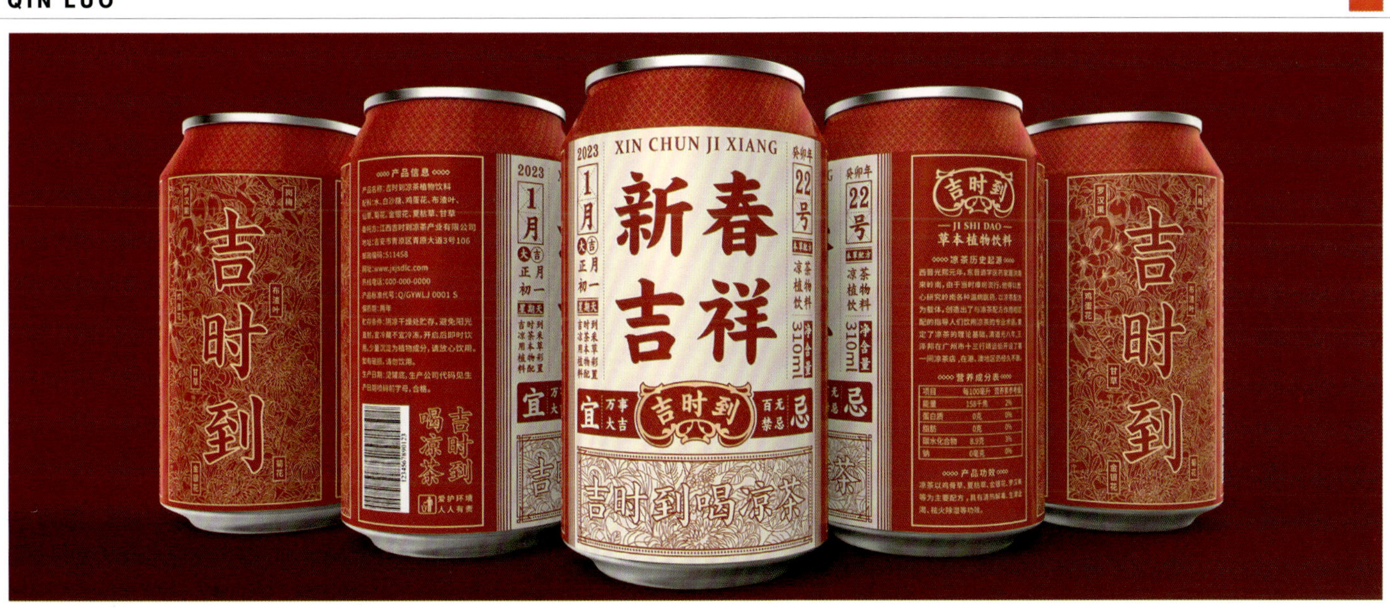

Title: Ji Shi Dao Herbal Tea Packaging Design | **Client:** Jiangxi Jishidao Herbal Tea Industry Co., Ltd. | **Design Firm:** Roking Art Design

PEPSICO DESIGN & INNOVATION

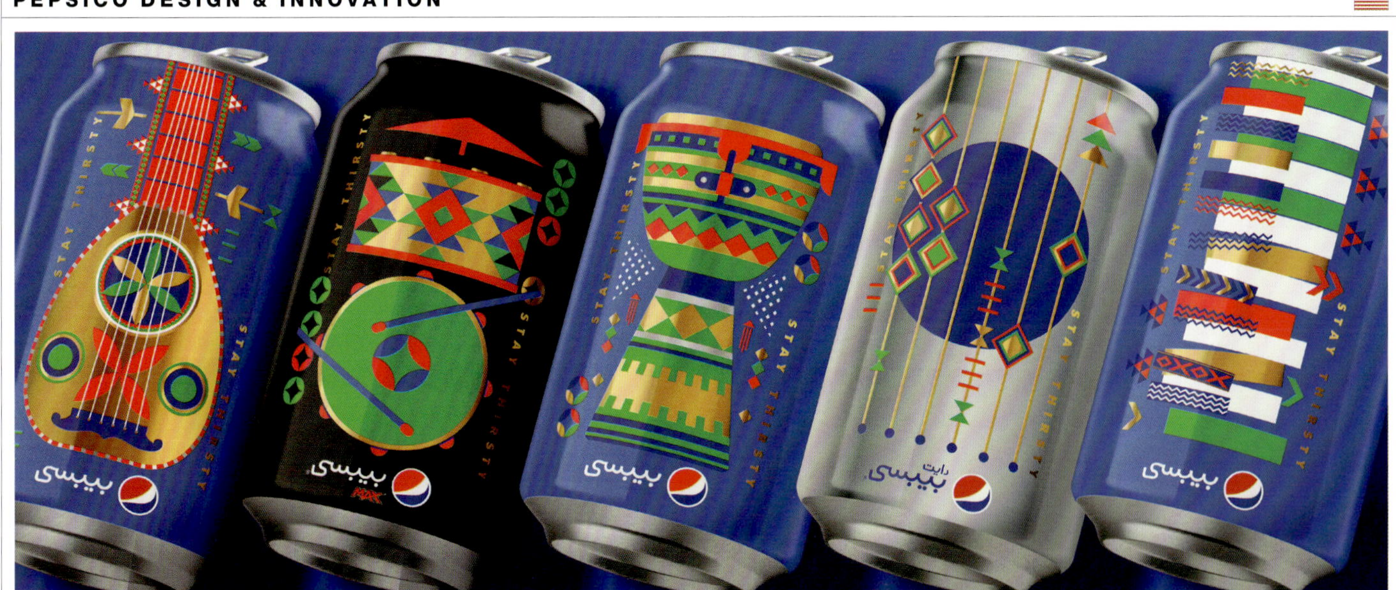

Title: Pepsi x Music | **Client:** Self-initated | **Design Firm:** PepsiCo Design & Innovation

LEWIS COMMUNICATIONS

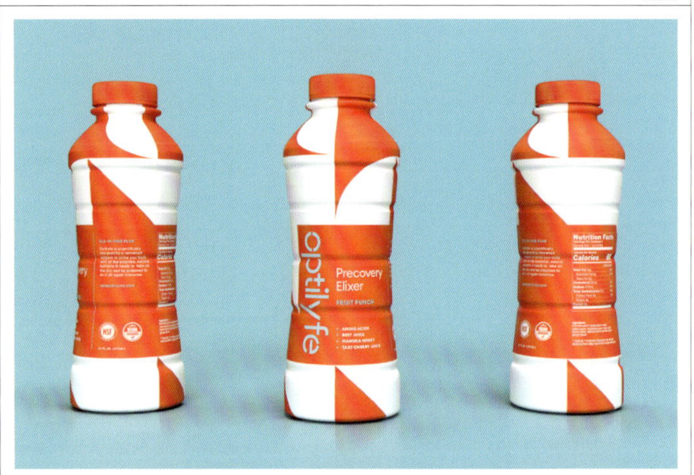

Title: Optilyfe Branding | **Client:** Optilyfe
Design Firm: Lewis Communications

STAN CHURCH

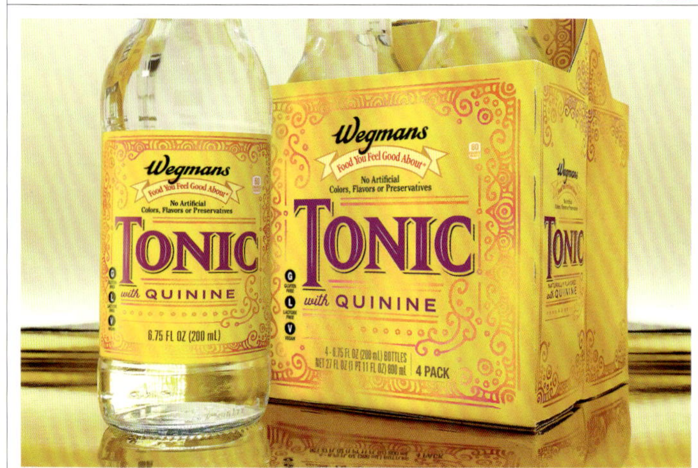

Title: Wegmans Tonic Water | **Client:** Wegmans
Design Firm: Wallace Church & Co.

ERIC LE

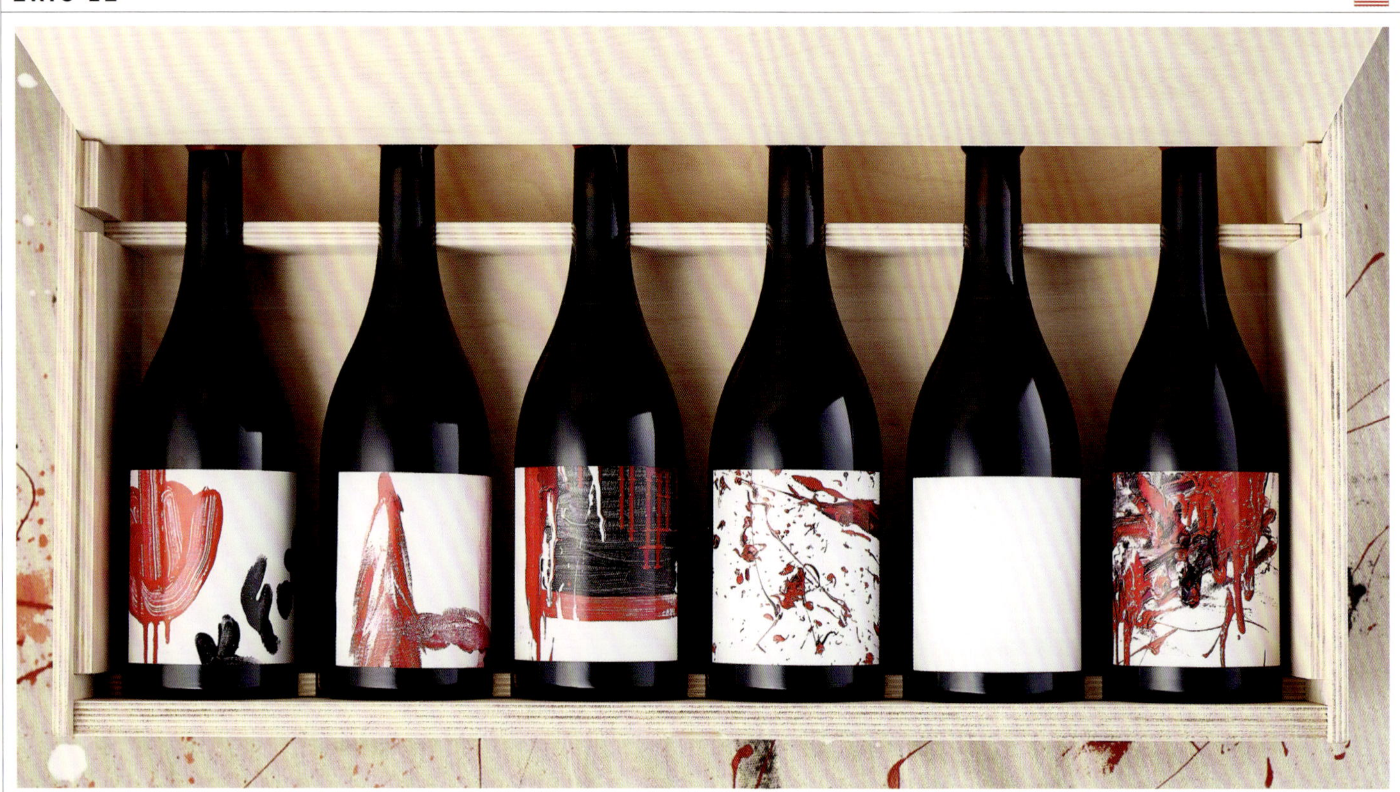

Title: Orin Swift Cellars Equinox 17 | **Client:** Orin Swift Cellars | **Design Firm:** Gallo Creative

PEPSICO DESIGN & INNOVATION

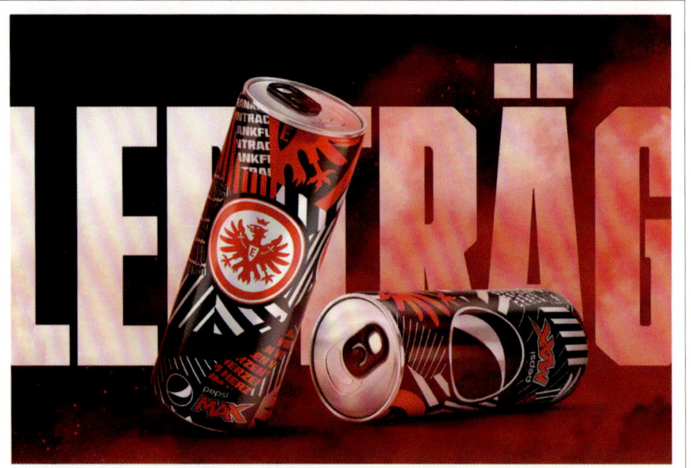

Title: Pepsi Max x Eintracht Frankfurt Collaboration
Client: Self-initated | **Design Firm:** PepsiCo Design & Innovation

PEPSICO DESIGN & INNOVATION

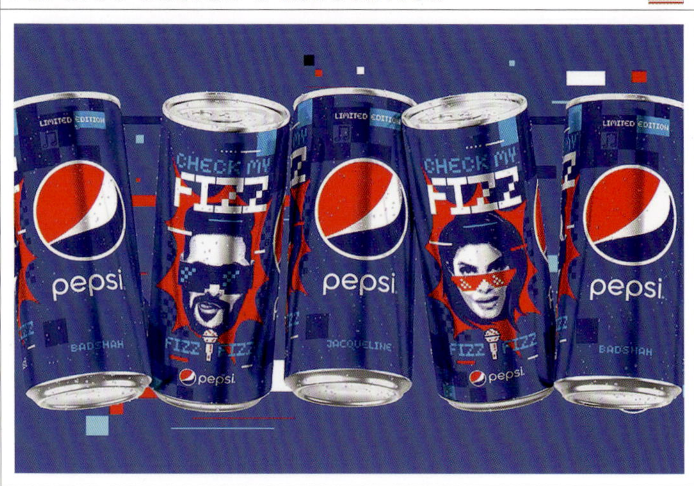

Title: Pepsi Music & Dance LTO
Client: Self-initated | **Design Firm:** PepsiCo Design & Innovation

SAVANNAH COLL. OF ART & DESIGN

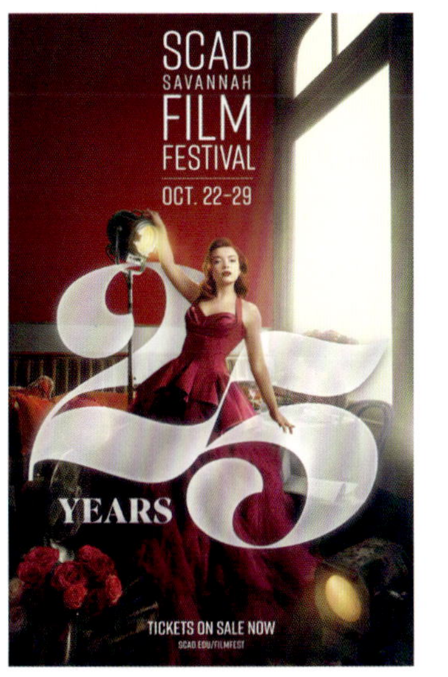

Title: Savannah Film Festival Campaign 2022
Client: Self-initiated
Design Firm: Savannah College of Art & Design

ADONIS DURADO

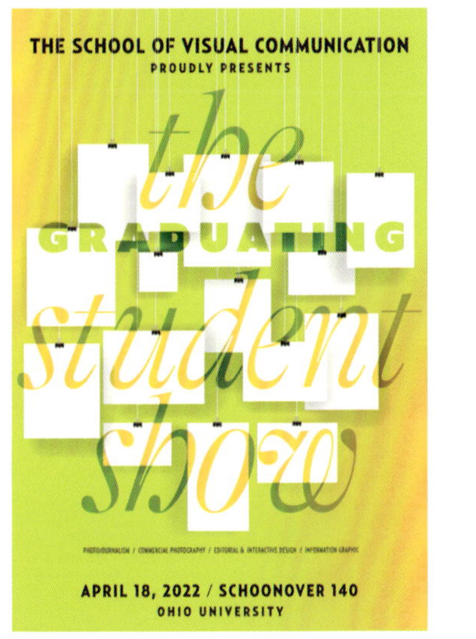

Title: The Graduating Students Show 2022
Client: Self-initiated | **Design Firm:** Ohio University's School of Visual Communication

MICHAEL BRALEY

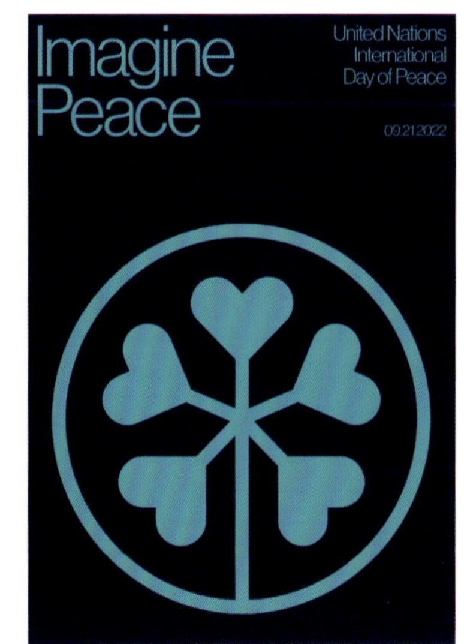

Title: Imagine Peace
Clients: US State Department, US Embassy Moscow | **Design Firm:** Braley Design

HAJIME TSUSHIMA

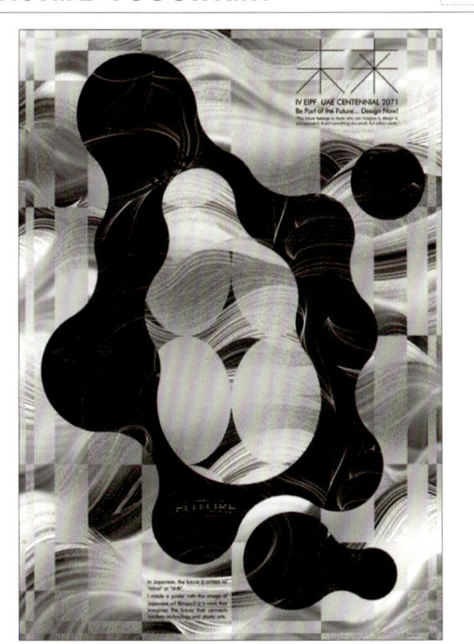

Title: FUTURE | **Client:** The Culture & SciеInternational Committee of the 4th Emirates International Poster Festival | **Design Firm:** Tsushima Design

DERWYN GOODALL

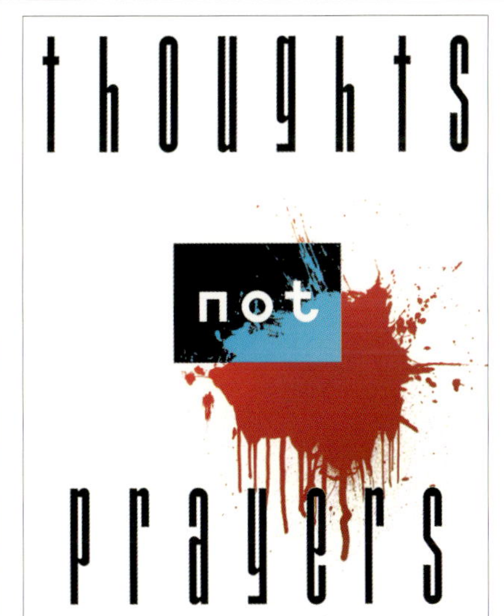

Title: Thoughts Not Prayers
Client: Self-initiated
Design Firm: Goodall Integrated Design

RANDY CLARK

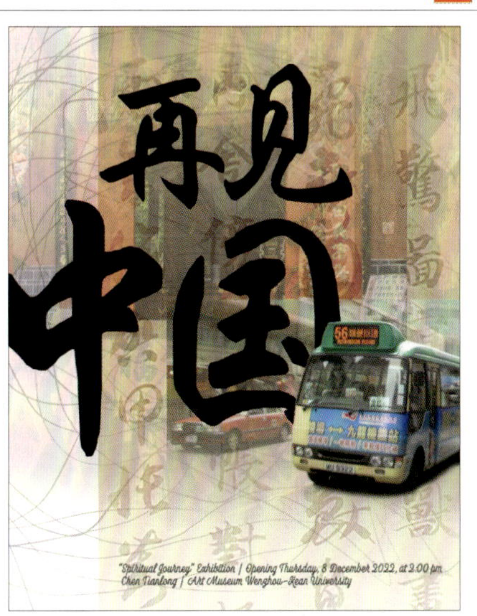

Title: Bye Bye China | **Clients:** Wenzhou Kean University, Michael Graves College
Design Firm: Randy Clark Graphic Design

SJI ASSOCIATES

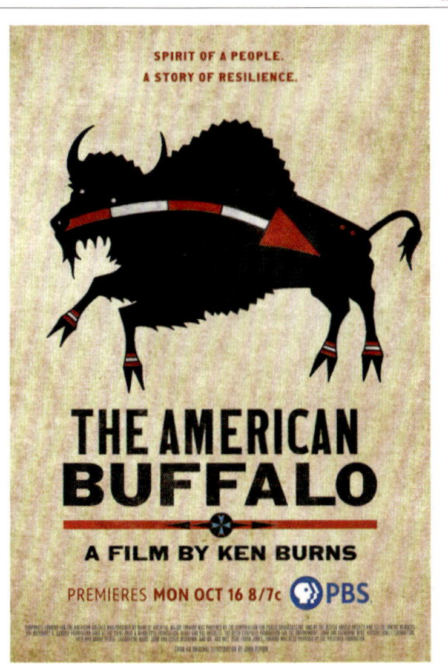

Title: THE AMERICAN BUFFALO
Client: PBS Creative Services
Design Firm: SJI Associates

BAILEY LAUERMAN

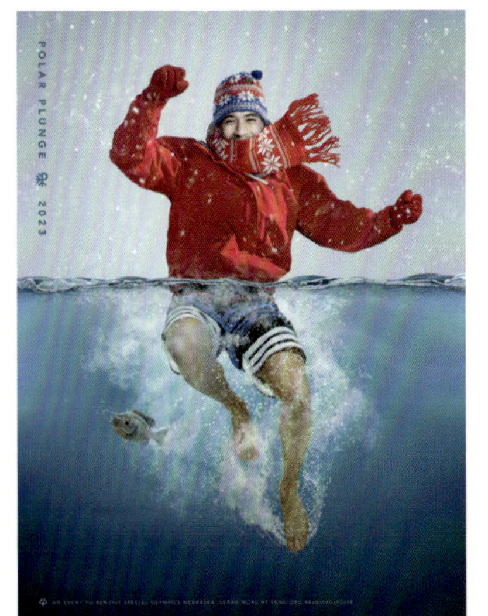

Title: Under The Surface
Client: Special Olympics Nebraska
Design Firm: Bailey Lauerman

ROZINA VAVETSI

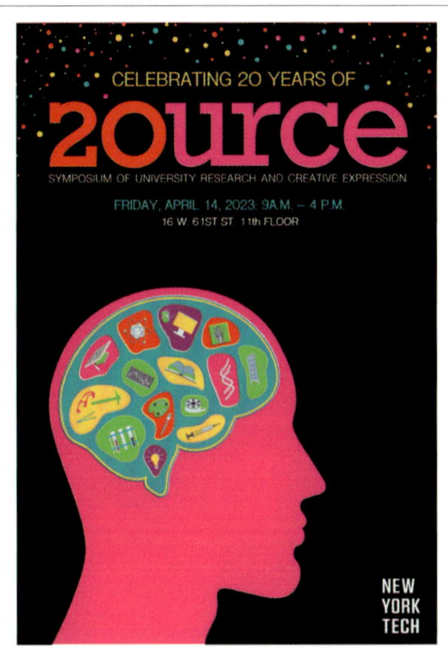

Title: Celebrating 20 Years of SOURCE
Client: New York Tech
Design Firm: Rozina Design

DLR GROUP, JOVANEY HOLLINGSWORTH

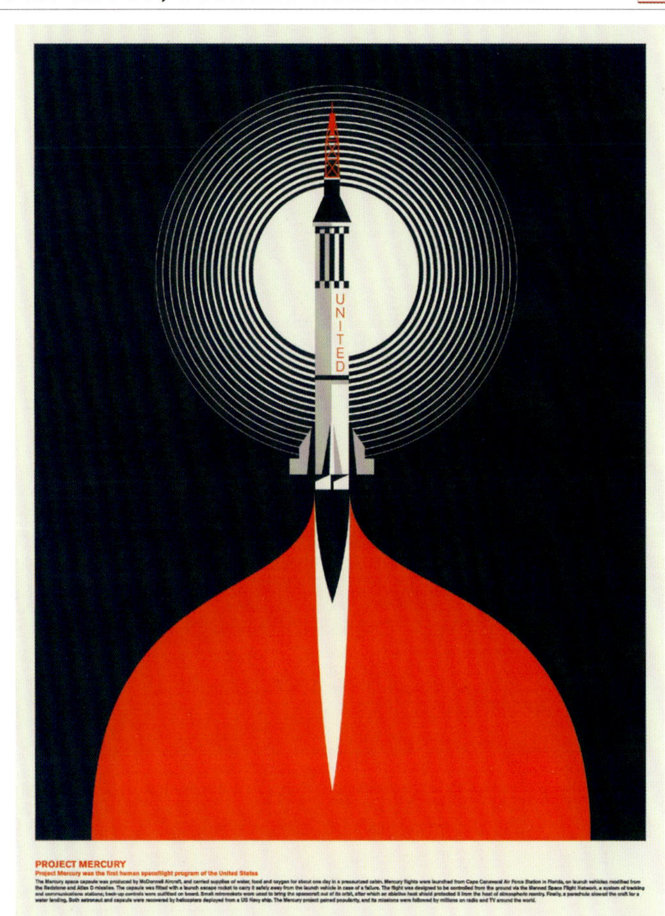

Title: Space Program History | **Client:** Confidential Technology Company
Design Firm: DLR Group

SJI ASSOCIATES

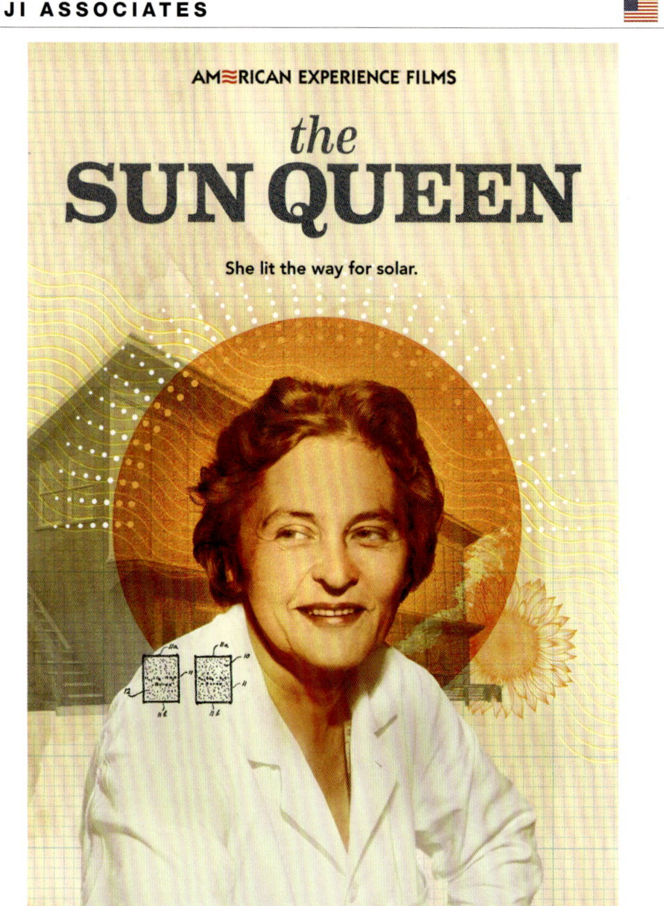

Title: THE SUN QUEEN | **Clients:** Chika Offurum, American Experience Films | **Design Firm:** SJI Associates

HOON-DONG CHUNG

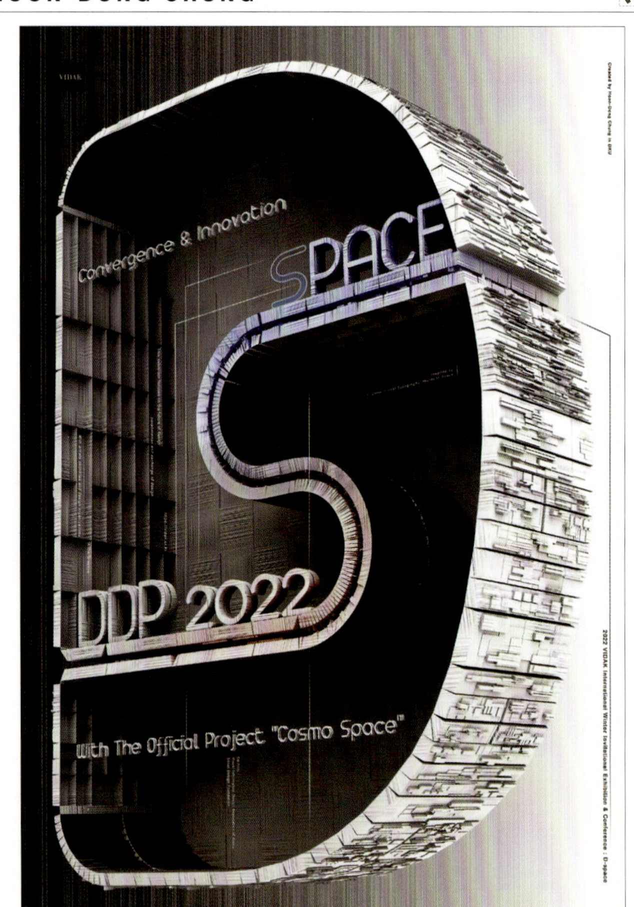

Title: D-Space | **Client:** Visual Information Design Association of Korea
Design Firm: Dankook University

DERWYN GOODALL

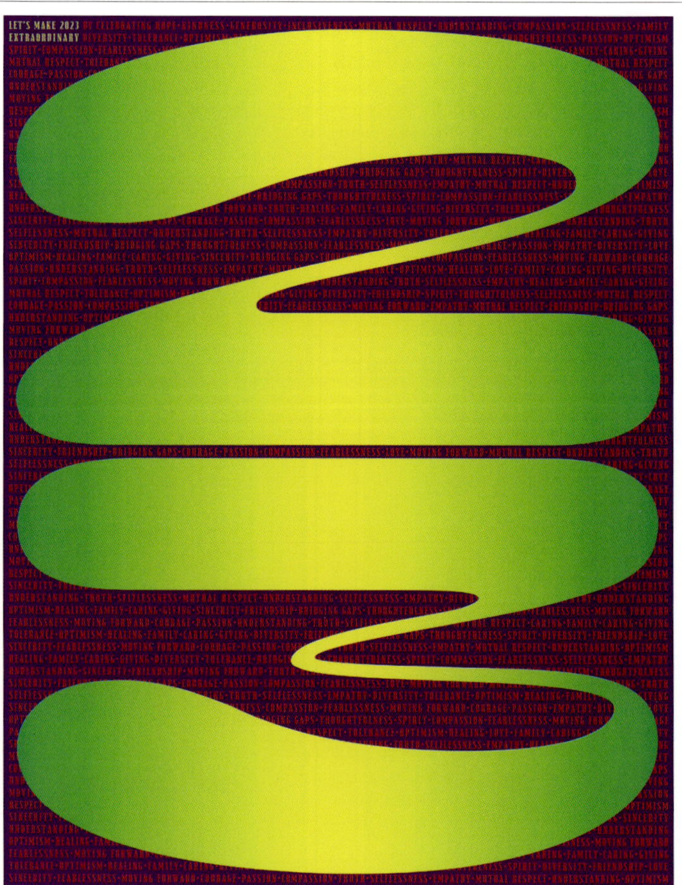

Title: Let's Make 2023 Extraordinary! | **Client:** Self-initiated
Design Firm: Goodall Integrated Design

ARSONAL(+2)

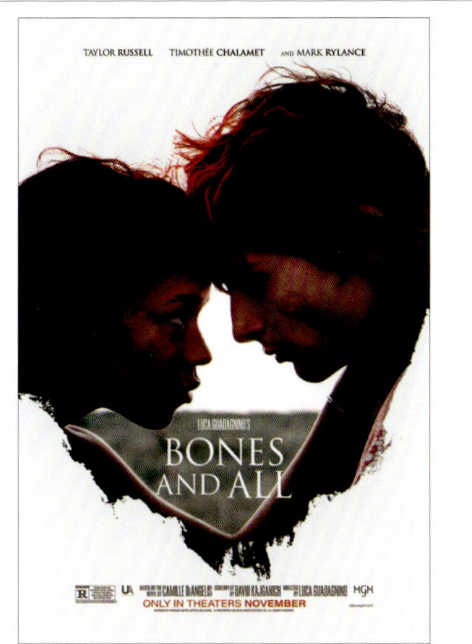

Title: Bones And All | **Clients:** Metro Goldwyn Mayer Pictures, United Artists Releasing
Design Firm: ARSONAL

FX NETWORKS

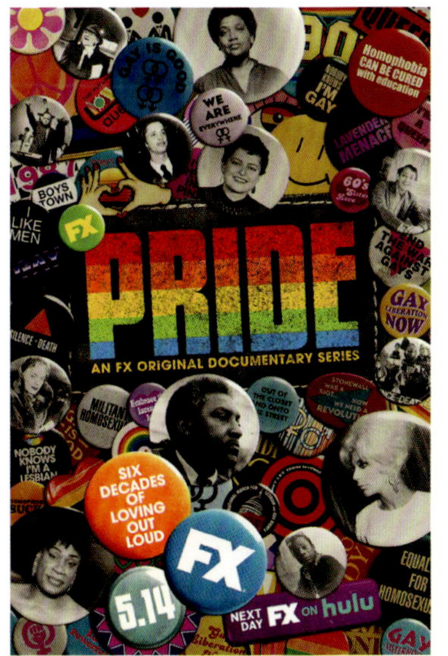

Title: Pride - Payoff and Decades Campaign
Client: FX Networks
Design Firm: AV Print

ARSONAL, AMC

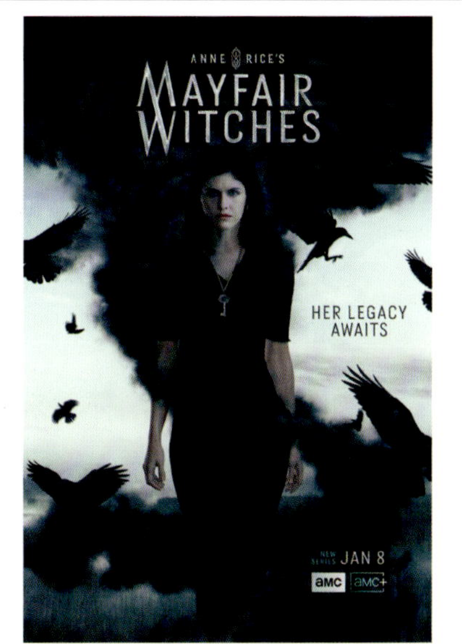

Title: Mayfair Witches S1
Client: AMC
Design Firm: ARSONAL

CINTHIA WEN

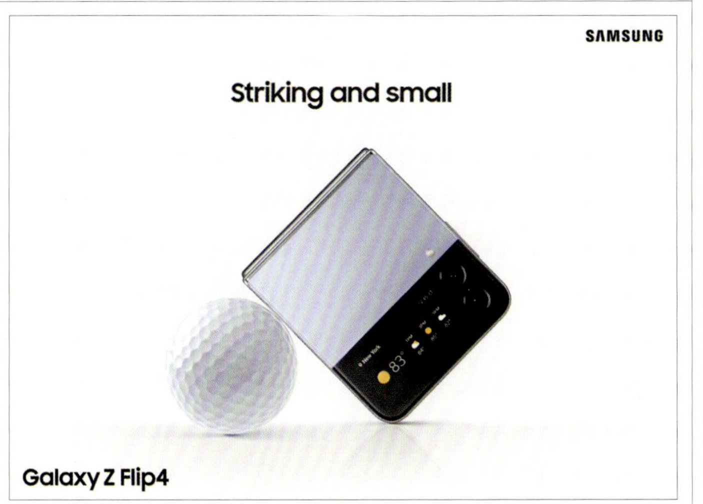

Title: Samsung Galaxy Z Flip4 Launch Posters
Client: Samsung
Design Firm: Turner Duckworth: London, San Francisco & New York

JIM MA

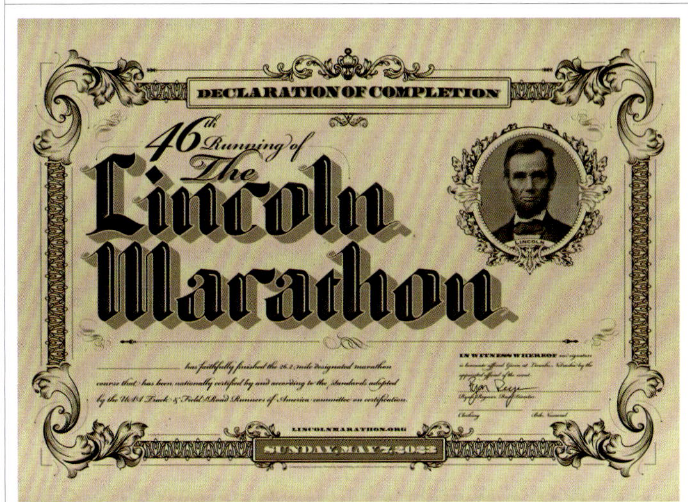

Title: Lincoln Marathon Declaration of Completion
Client: Lincoln Track Club
Design Firm: Bailey Lauerman

SCOTT RAY

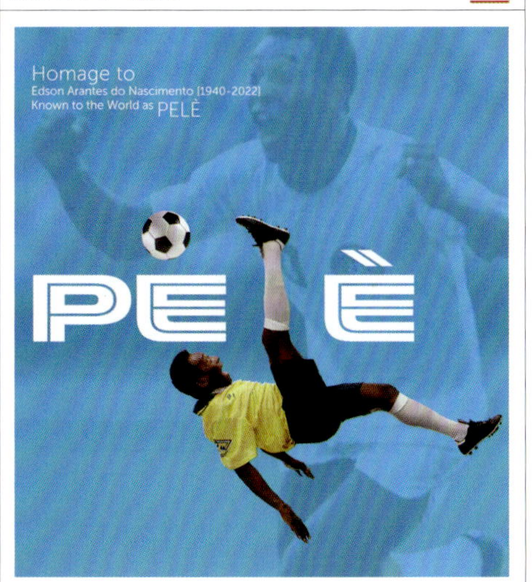

Title: Homage to PELE Poster
Client: Self-initiated
Design Firm: Peterson Ray & Company

PAUL HUBER

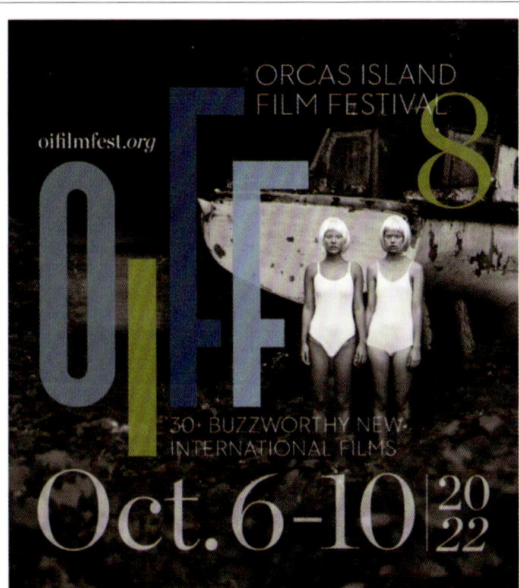

Title: Orcas Island Film Festival 2022 Poster
Client: Orcas Island Film Festival
Design Firm: Huber Design Werks

DERWYN GOODALL

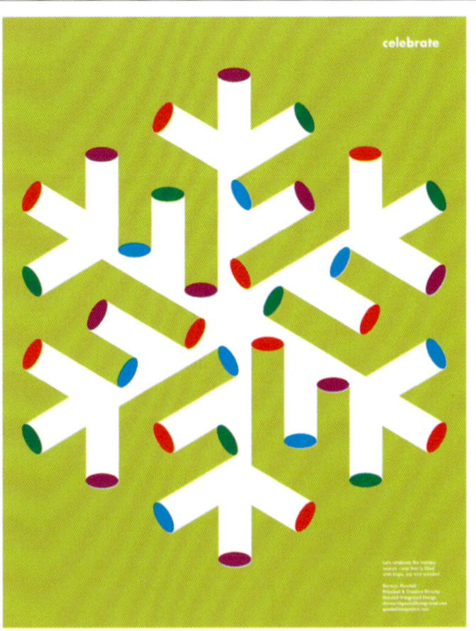

Title: Goodall Integrated Design 2022 Holiday Poster | **Client:** Self-initiated
Design Firm: Goodall Integrated Design

MICHAEL GRAZIOLO

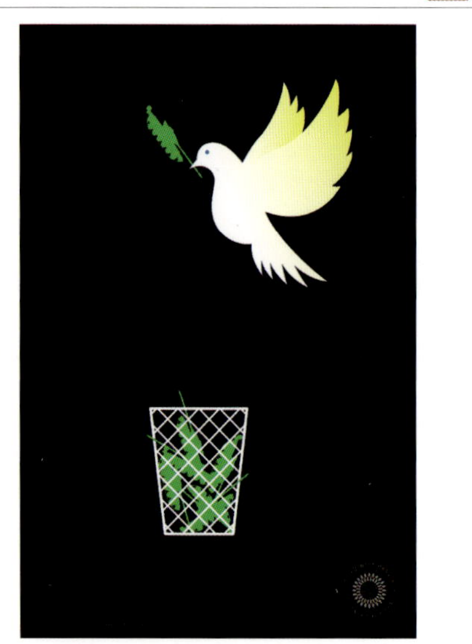

Title: Peace in Ukraine | **Client:** Graphis Designers for Peace Poster Competition
Design Firm: Drive Communications

WU QIXIN

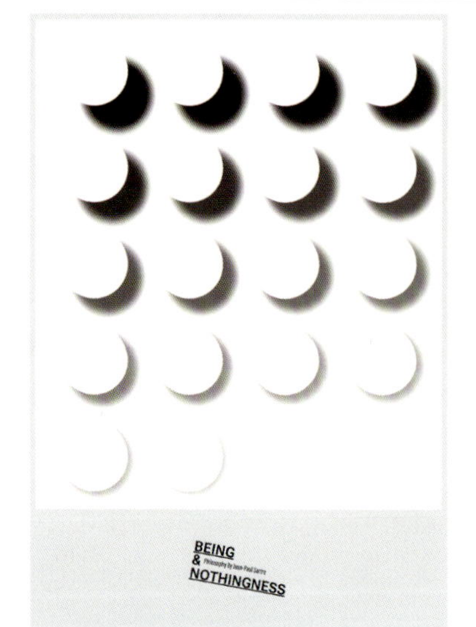

Title: Being&Nothingness
Client: Jean-Paul Sartre
Design Firm: Cul-box

HISA IDE

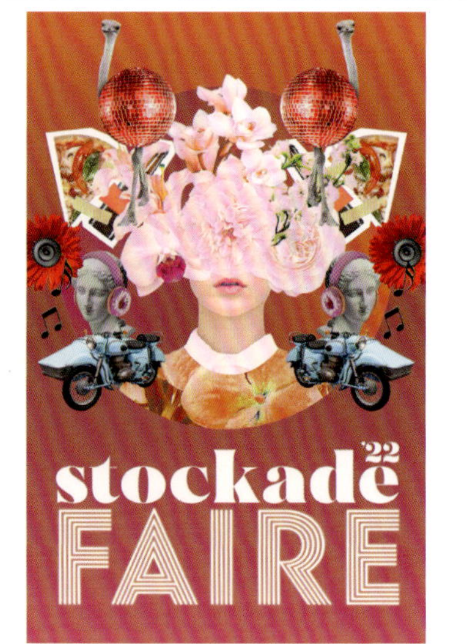

Title: Stockade Faire '22
Client: Stockade Faire
Design Firm: IF Studio

PATRICK FINLEY

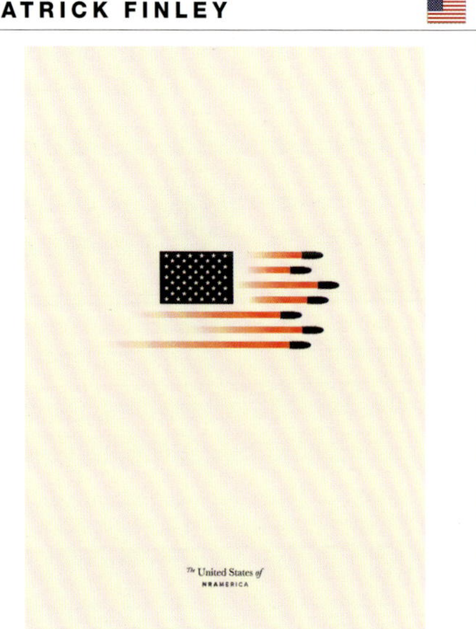

Title: The United States of NRAmerica
Client: Self-initiated
Design Firm: Patrick Finley

DERWYN GOODALL

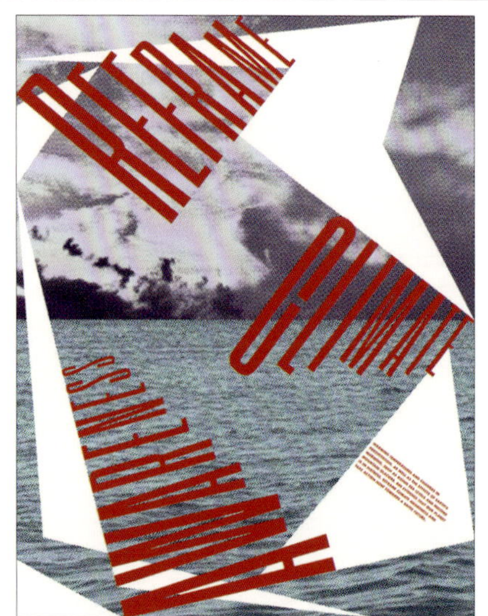

Title: Reframe Climate Awareness
Client: Self-initiated
Design Firm: Goodall Integrated Design

DERWYN GOODALL

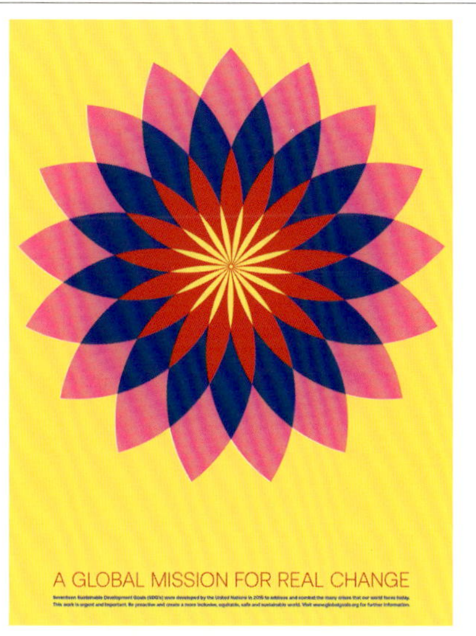

Title: A Global Mission for Real Change
Client: Taiwan International Image Design Invitational Exhibit | **Design Firm:** Goodall Integrated Design

DOUGLAS THOMAS

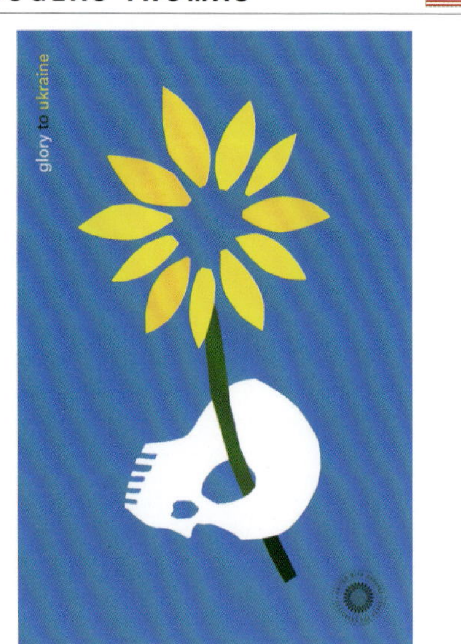

Title: Glory to Ukraine
Client: Graphis Designers for Peace Poster Competition | **Design Firm:** Kunstwerk

UNDERLINE STUDIO

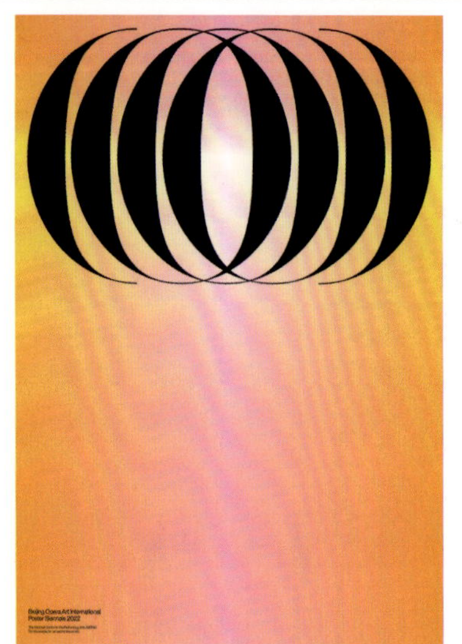

Title: Beijing Opera International Biennale Poster
Client: Beijing Opera International Poster Biennale 2022 | **Design Firm:** Underline Studio

WU QIXIN

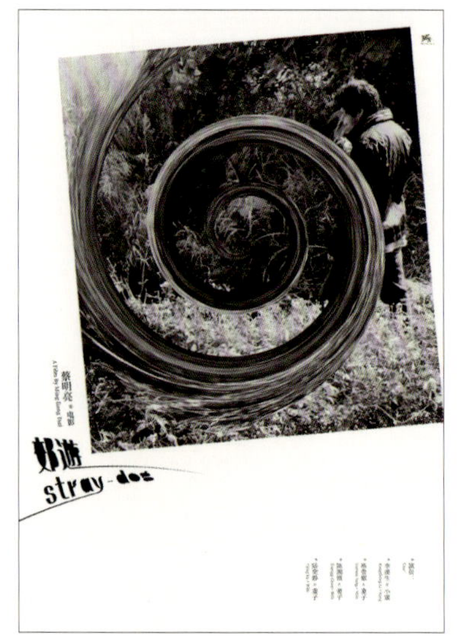

Title: Stray Dog
Client: Stray Dog
Design Firm: Cul-box

MICHAEL BRALEY

woman.
life.
freedom.
Support Iranian Women

Title: Woman. Life. Freedom. Support Iranian Women.
Client: Self-initiated
Design Firm: Braley Design

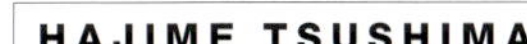

HAJIME TSUSHIMA

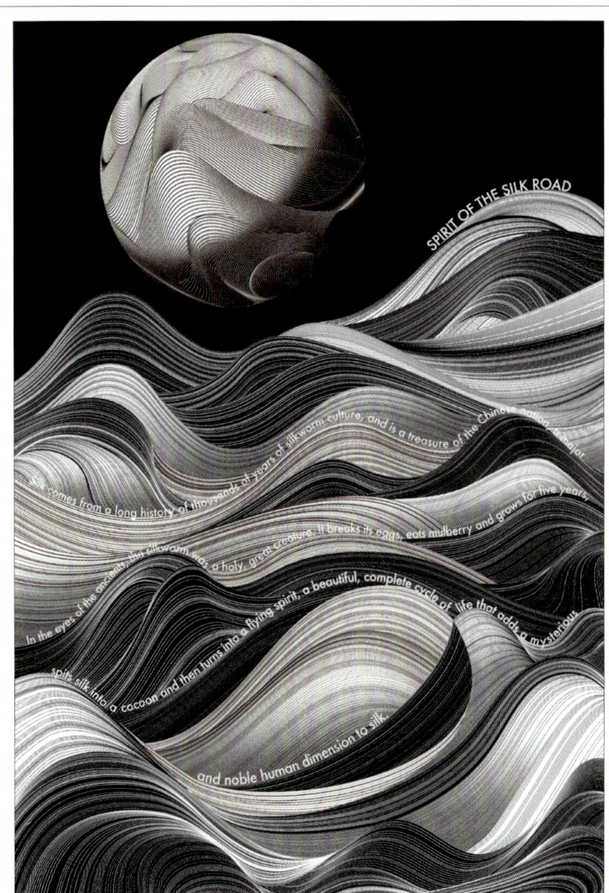

Title: SPIRIT OF THE SILK ROAD | **Client:** International Poster Design Exhibition of Silkworm Culture Organizing Committee
Design Firm: Tsushima Design

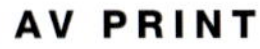

AV PRINT

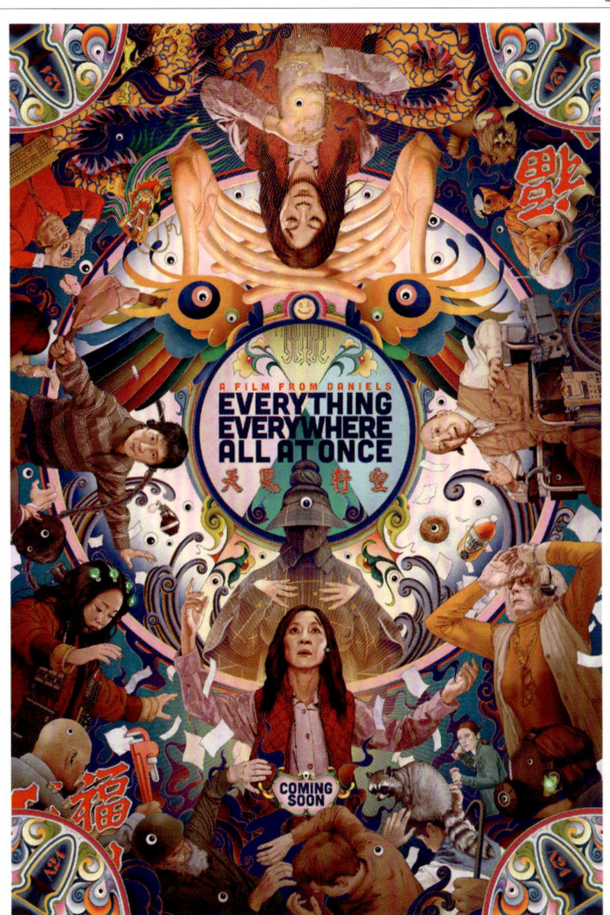

Title: Everything Everywhere All At Once Campaign | **Client:** A24
Design Firm: AV Print

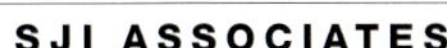

SJI ASSOCIATES

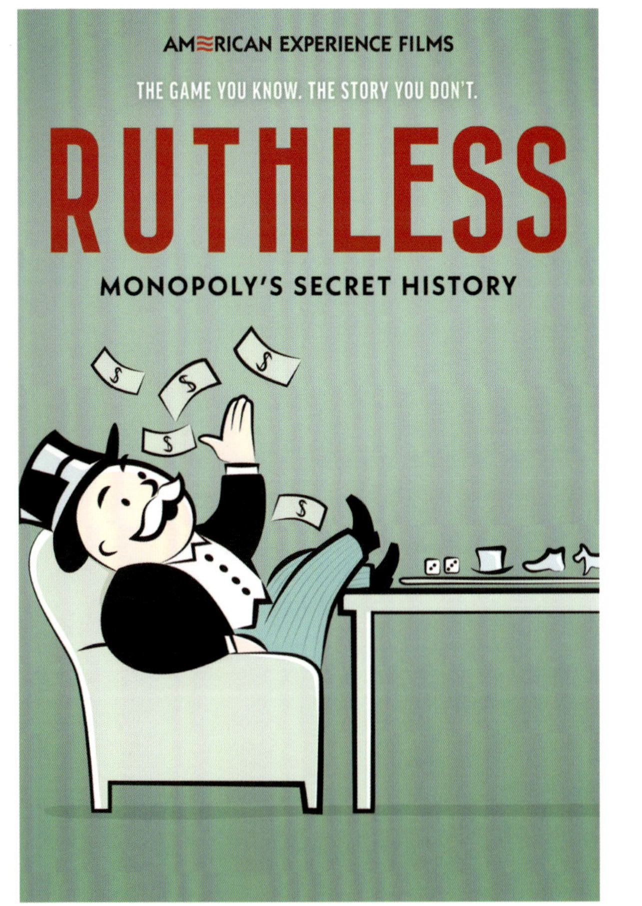

Title: RUTHLESS | **Clients:** Chika Offurum, American Experience Films
Design Firm: SJI Associates

SJI ASSOCIATES

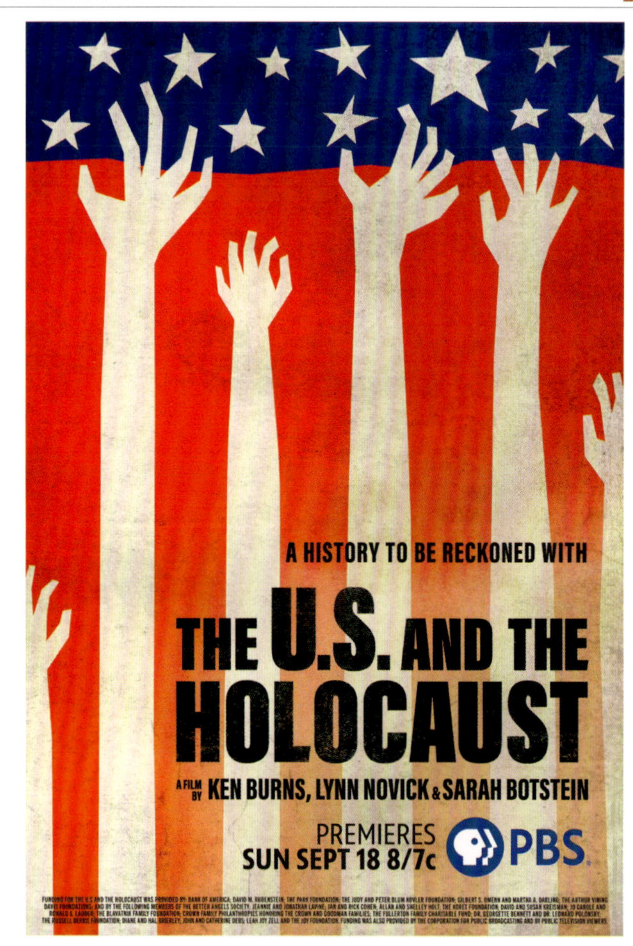

Title: THE US AND THE HOLOCAUST | **Client:** PBS Creative Services
Design Firm: SJI Associates

ARSONAL, AMC, AMC+

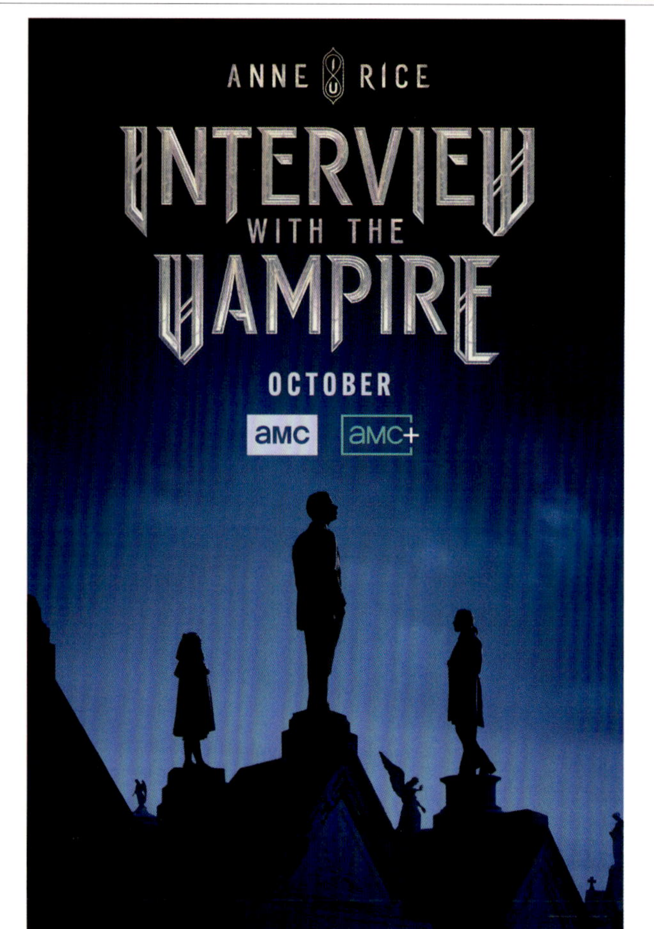

Title: Interview With The Vampire | **Clients:** AMC, AMC+
Design Firm: ARSONAL

CINTHIA WEN

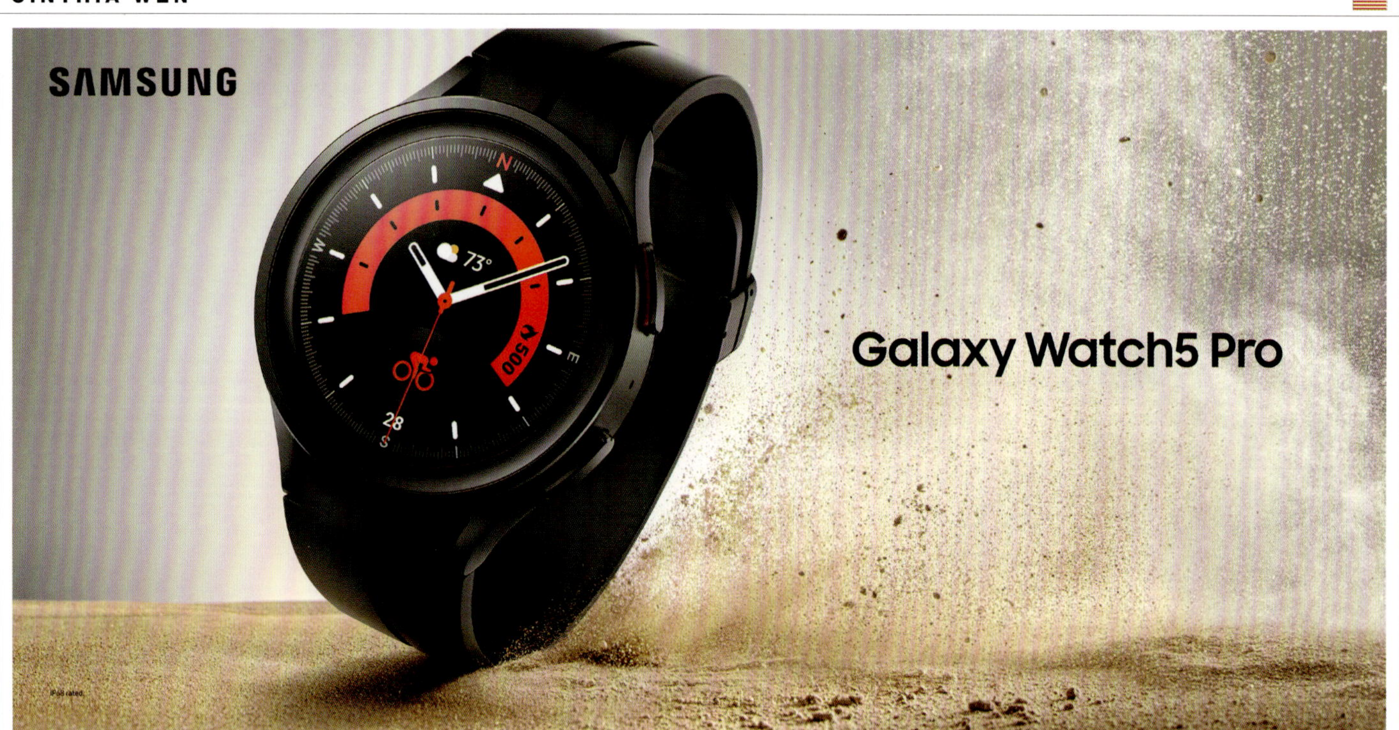

Title: Samsung Galaxy Watch5 Pro Launch Poster | **Client:** Samsung | **Design Firm:** Turner Duckworth: London, San Francisco & New York

HYUNGJOO A. KIM

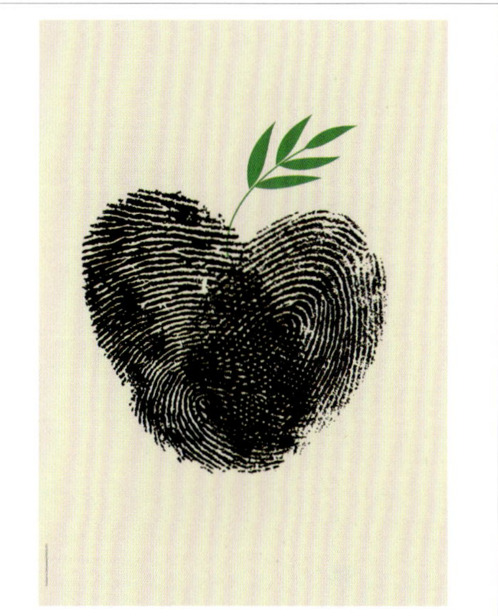

Title: Creating PEACE | **Client:** Nanjing International Poster Biennial for Peace
Design Firm: Hyungjoo Kim Design Lab

FERNANDO PALOMINO

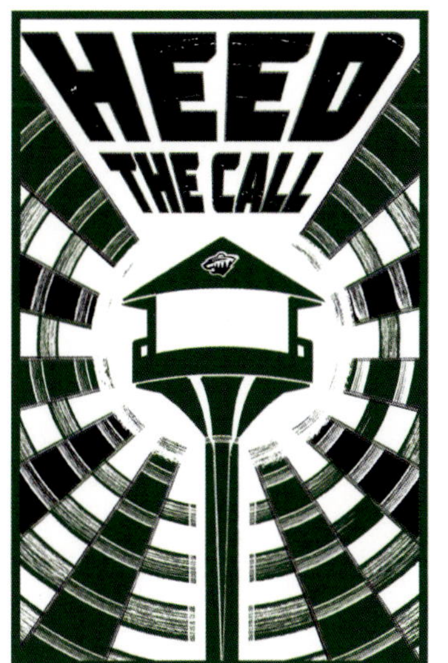

Title: Heed the Call
Client: Minnesota Wild
Design Firm: Preston Spire

HISA IDE, TOSHIAKI IDE

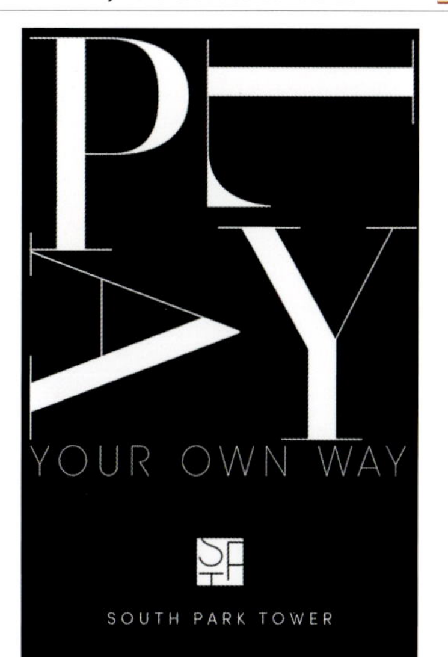

Title: South Park Tower Posters
Client: Brodsky
Design Firm: IF Studio

KOESTER DESIGN

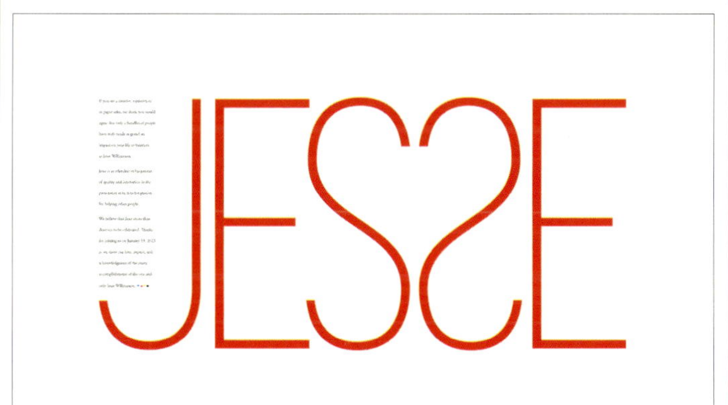

Title: Jesse Williamson Celebration Poster | **Client:** Clampitt Paper
Design Firm: Koester Design

ADONIS DURADO

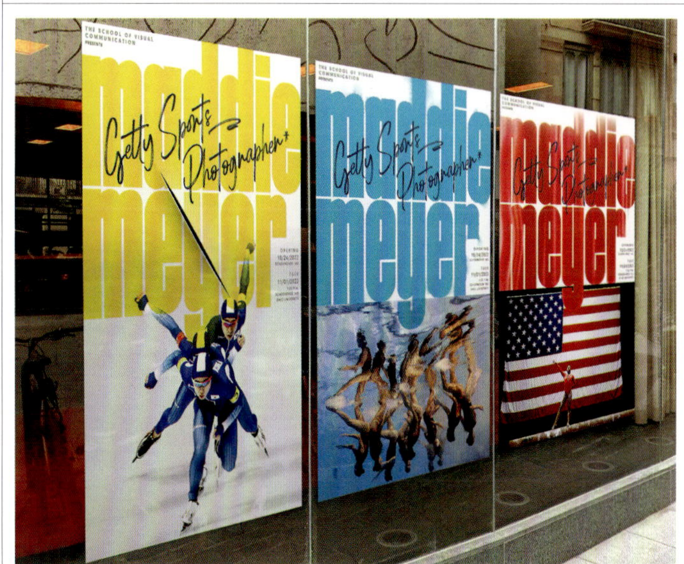

Title: Maddie Meyer Exhibit Poster Series | **Client:** Self-initiated
Design Firm: Ohio University's School of Visual Communication

SUKLE ADVERTISING & DESIGN

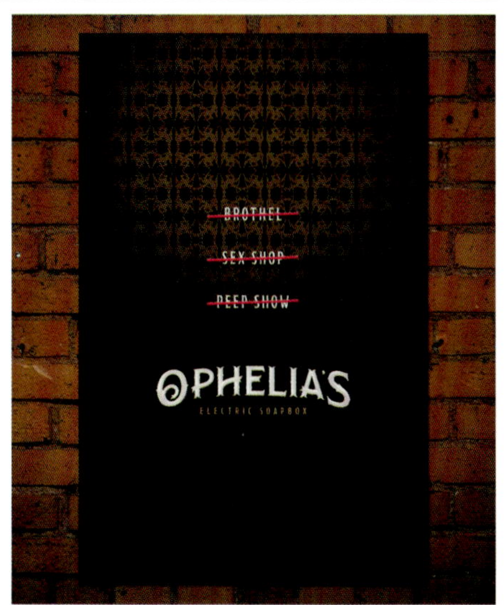

Title: Ophelia's Electric Soapbox Posters
Client: Ophelia's Electric Soapbox
Design Firm: Sukle Advertising & Design

TE-SIAN SHIH

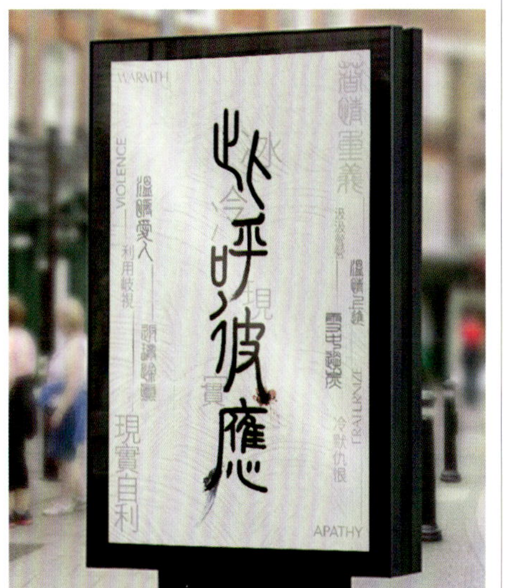

Title: Rat Race and In People's Hour of Need
Clients: Taiwanese American Arts Council, NYSMHO
Design Firm: Te-Sian Shih's Design Studio

MITCH FEICKERT

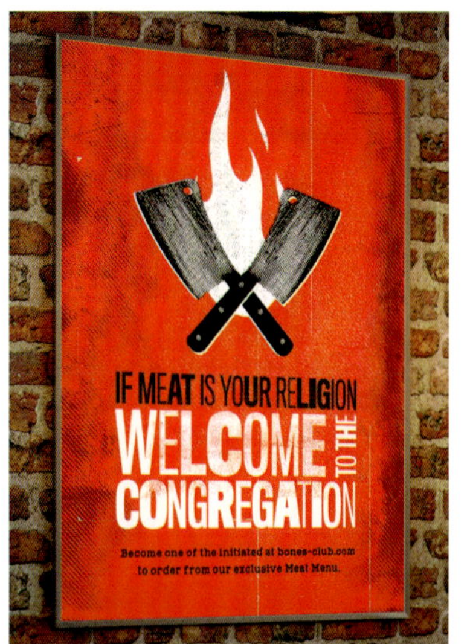

Title: Meat Menu Campaign Posters
Client: Smokey Bones
Design Firm: Dunn&Co.

SO DSGN, MAKESHIFT STUDIOS, NOT REAL, O0, TWISTED POLY, MICROSOFT BRAND STUDIO

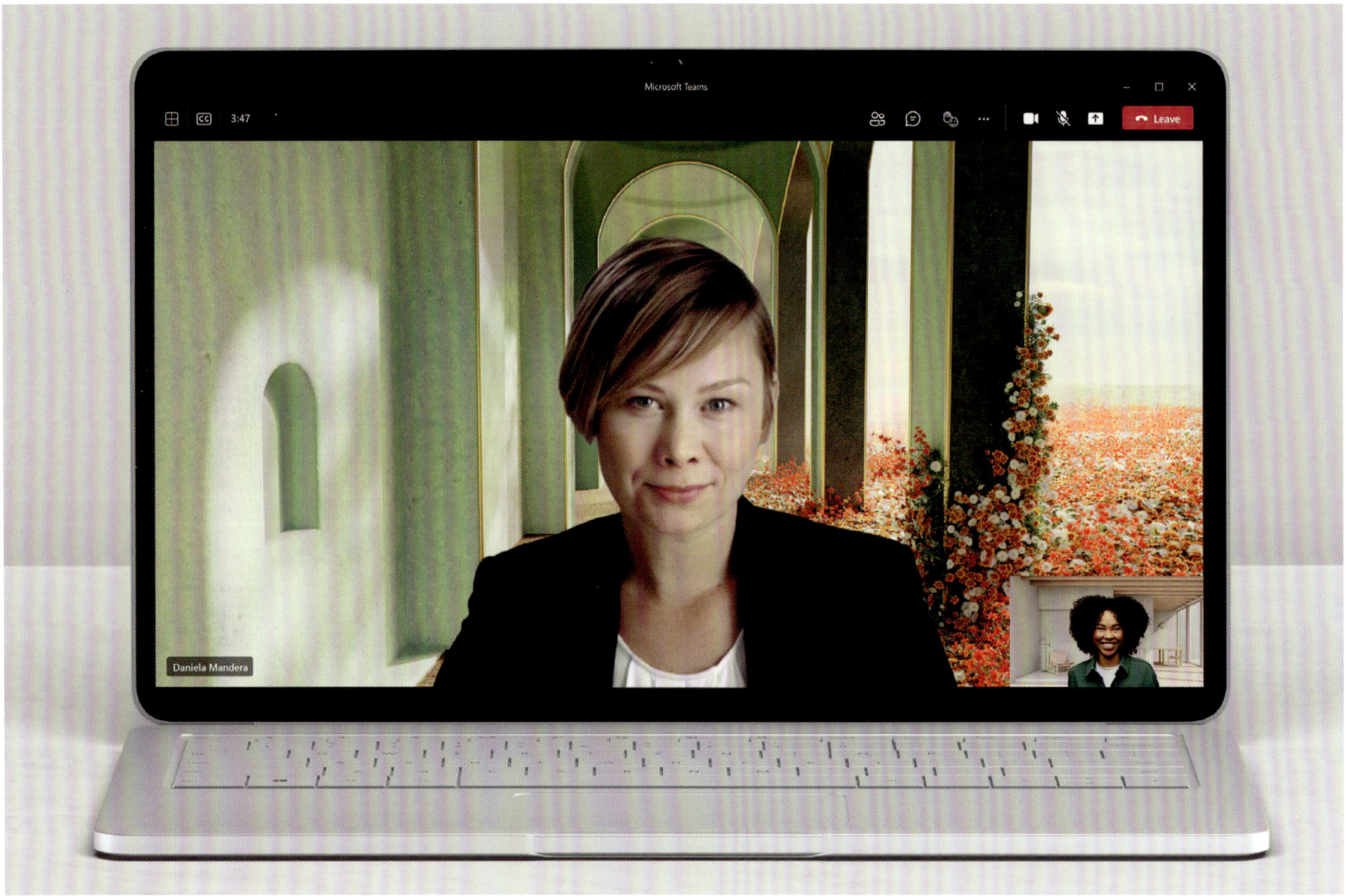

Title: From the Background to the Foreground | **Client:** Microsoft | **Design Firms:** SO DSGN, Makeshift Studios, Not Real, O0, Twisted Poly, Microsoft Brand Studio

RYAN BREESER

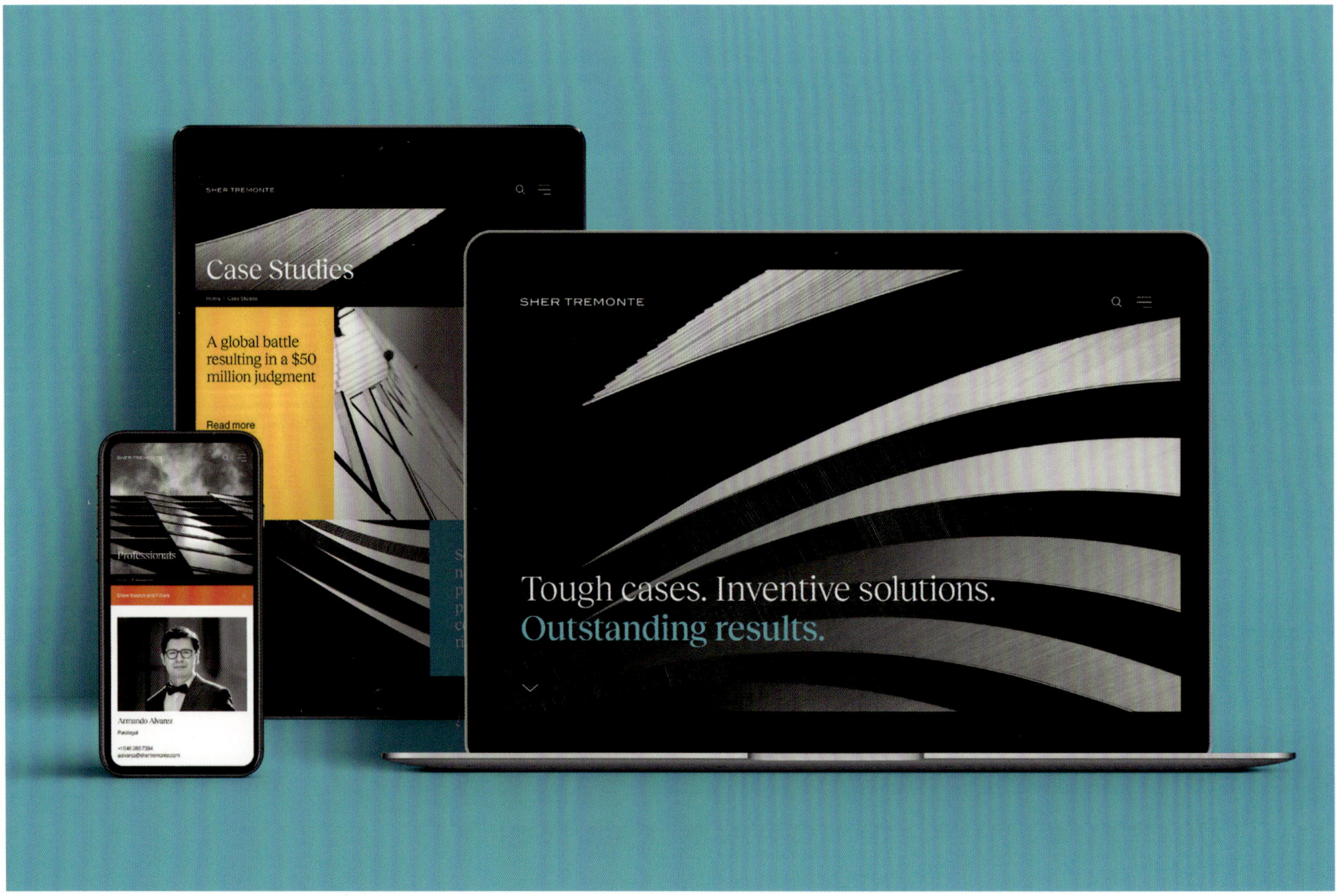

Title: Sher Tremonte Website | **Client:** Sher Tremonte | **Design Firm:** Decker Design

INSIGHT CREATIVE

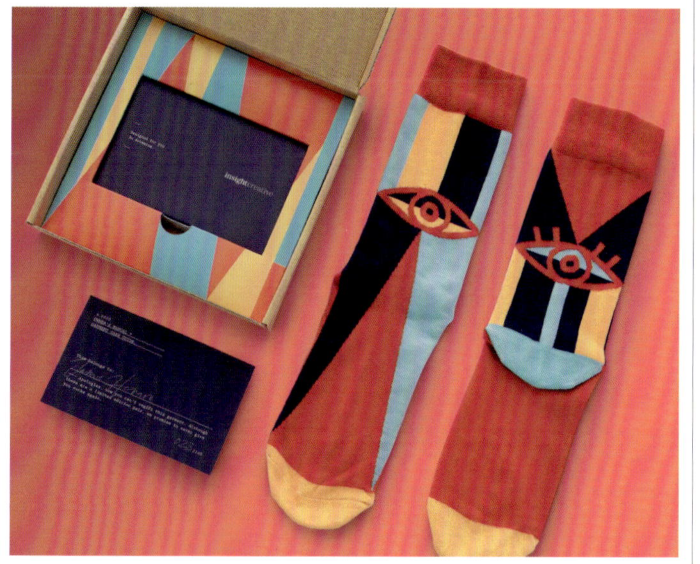

Title: Insight Christmas Socks | **Client:** Self-initiated
Design Firm: Insight Creative

MEAGHAN BARRY, LILIAN CRUM

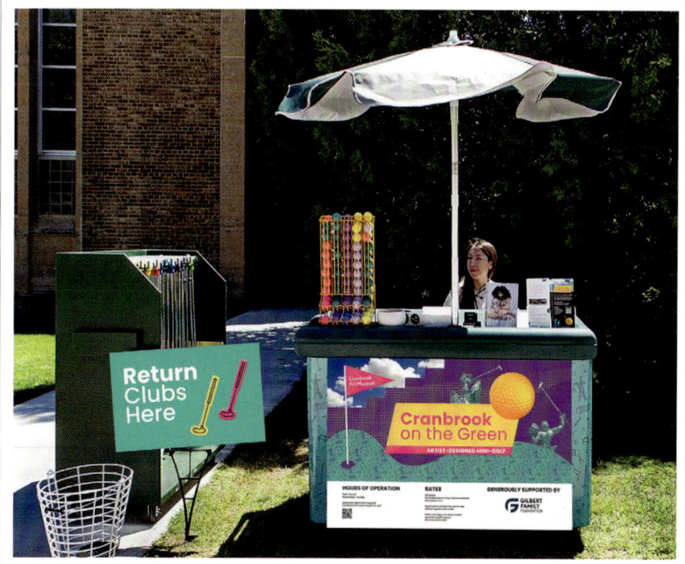

Title: Cranbrook on the Green: Artist-Designed Mini-Golf
Client: Cranbrook Art Museum | **Design Firm:** Unsold Studio

ANTON TIELEMANS

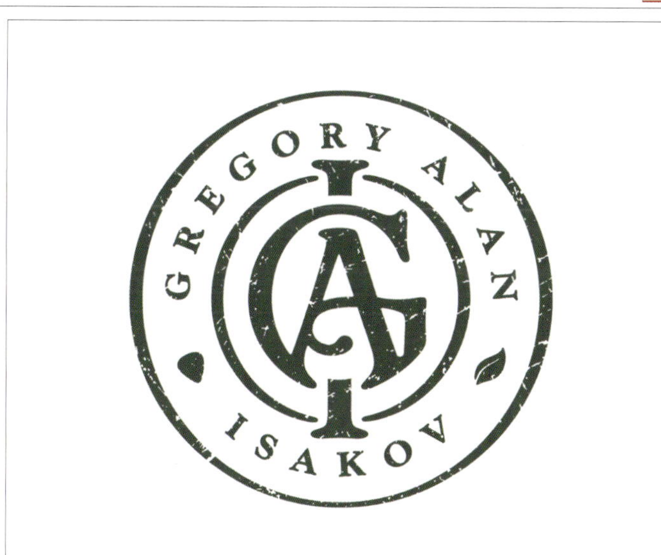

Title: Gregory Isakov Merchandise
Client: Gregory Alan Isakov | **Design Firm:** Tielemans Design

JANG WON LEE

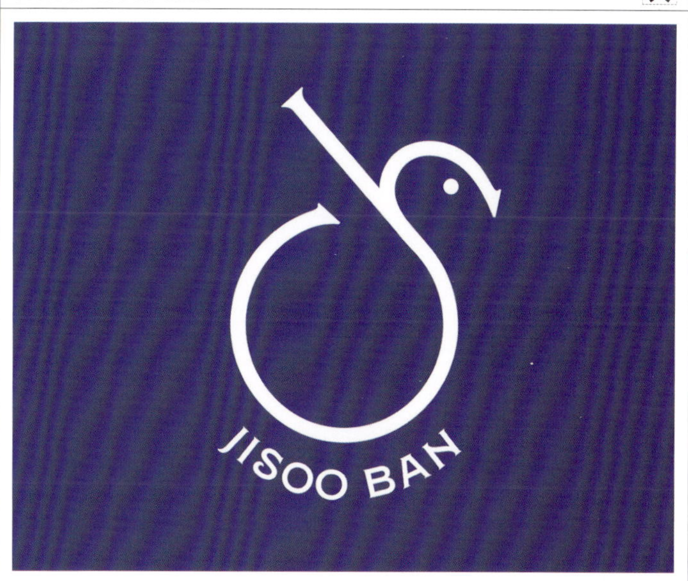

Title: Jisoo Ban: Personal Brand Identity & Merchandise Design
Client: Jisoo Ban | **Design Firm:** Whimsical Studio

SARAH BILLS

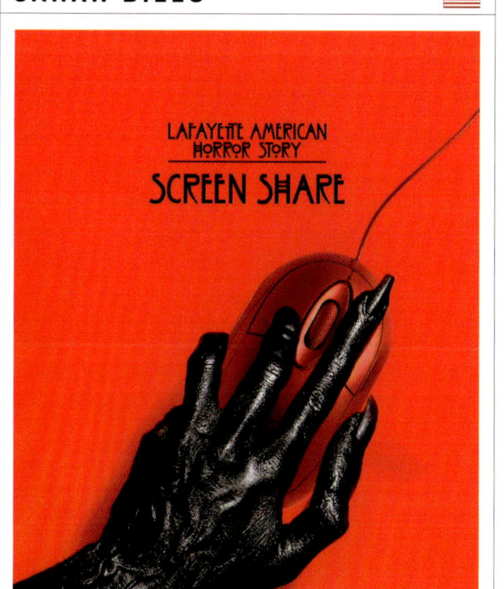

Title: Lafayette American Horror Story
Client: Self-initiated
Design Firm: Lafayette American

INSIGHT CREATIVE

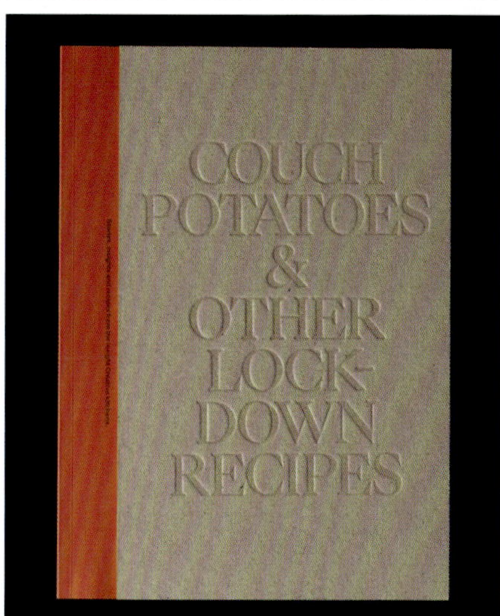

Title: Couch Potatoes & Other Lockdown Recipes
Client: Self-initiated
Design Firm: Insight Creative

CLAUDIA NERI

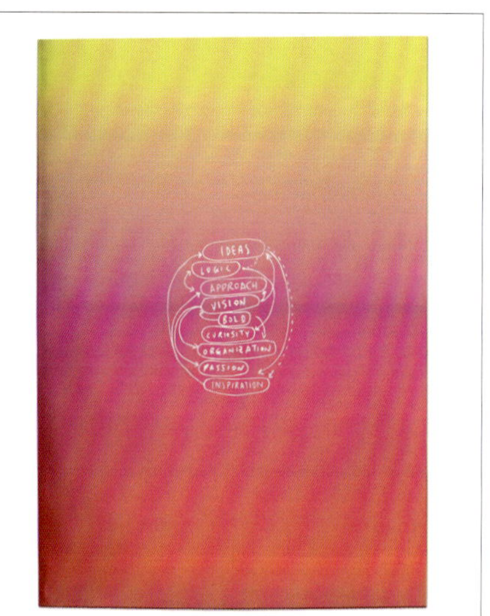

Title: Teikna Design Look Book
Client: Self-initiated
Design Firm: Teikna Design

LAFAYETTE AMERICAN

Title: Lafayette American Puzzle 2022 | **Client:** Self-initiated
Design Firm: Lafayette American

ARIEL FREANER

Title: ZETA Lithograph | **Client:** ZETA Weekly
Design Firm: Freaner Creative & Design

YIFEI HU

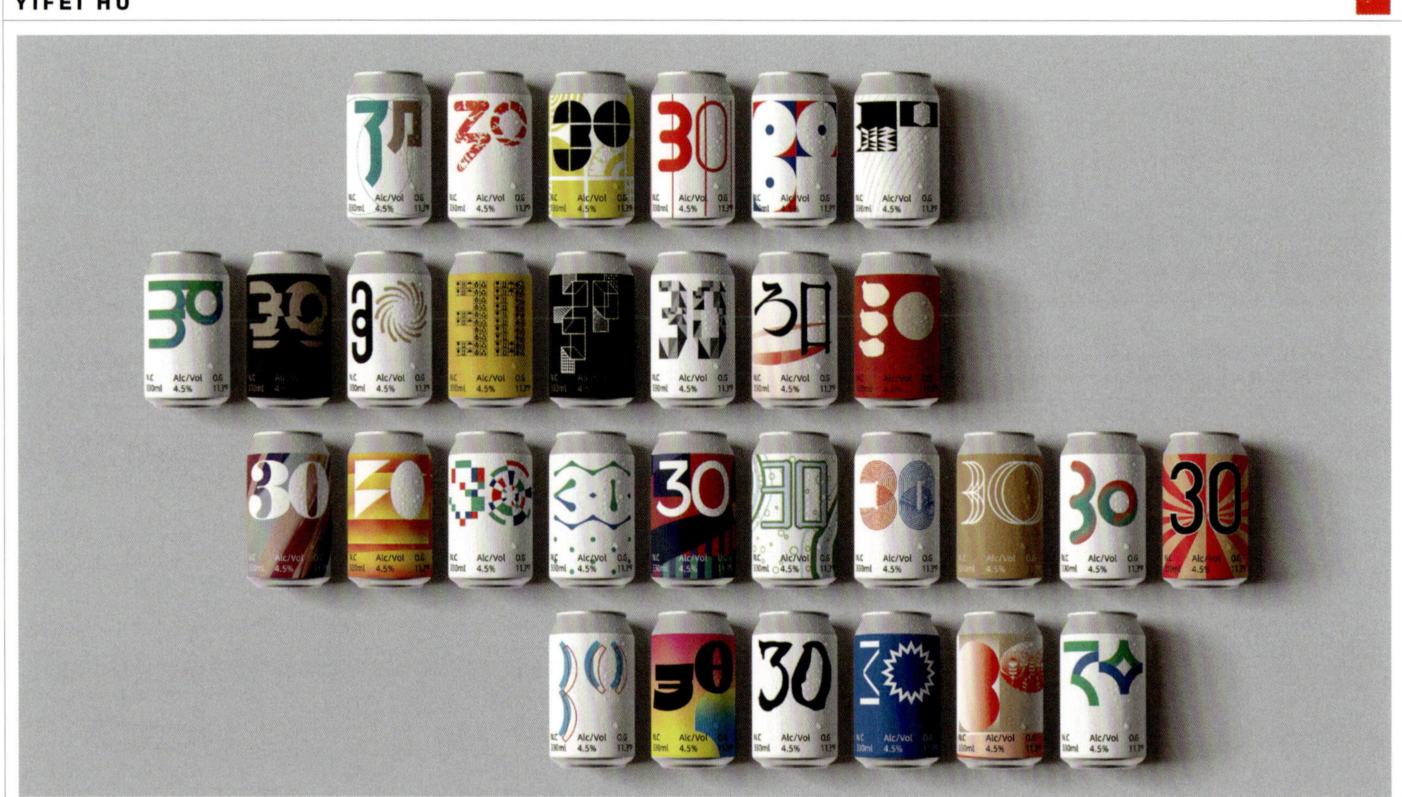

Title: Happy Birthday | **Client:** Self-initiated | **Design Firm:** DesignOut Lab.

CHRIS TAYLOR, MOE HUNG, TY JEPPESEN

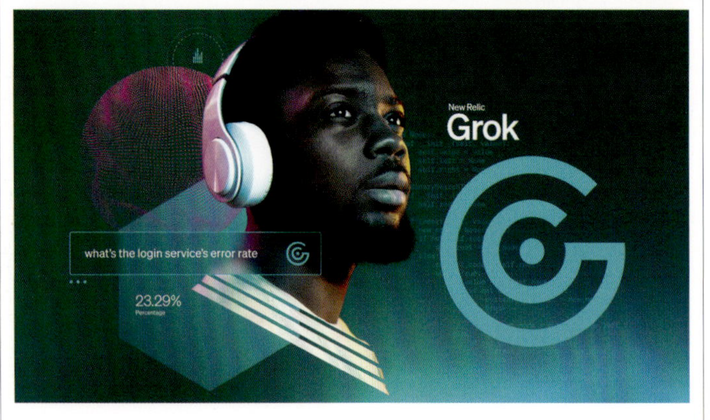

Title: New Relic Grok—Generative AI | **Client:** Self-initiated
Design Firms: New Relic, The Design Farm

DORIS PALMEROS

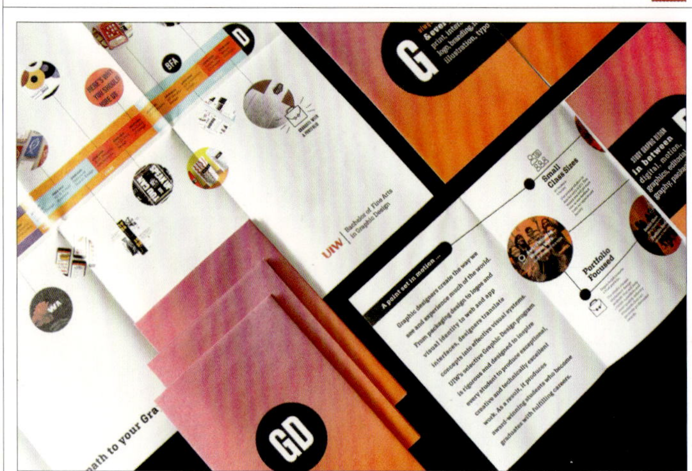

Title: GD Promotion: A Point Set in Motion | **Client:** Self-initiated
Design Firm: UIW Graphic Design Department

JOHN SPOSATO

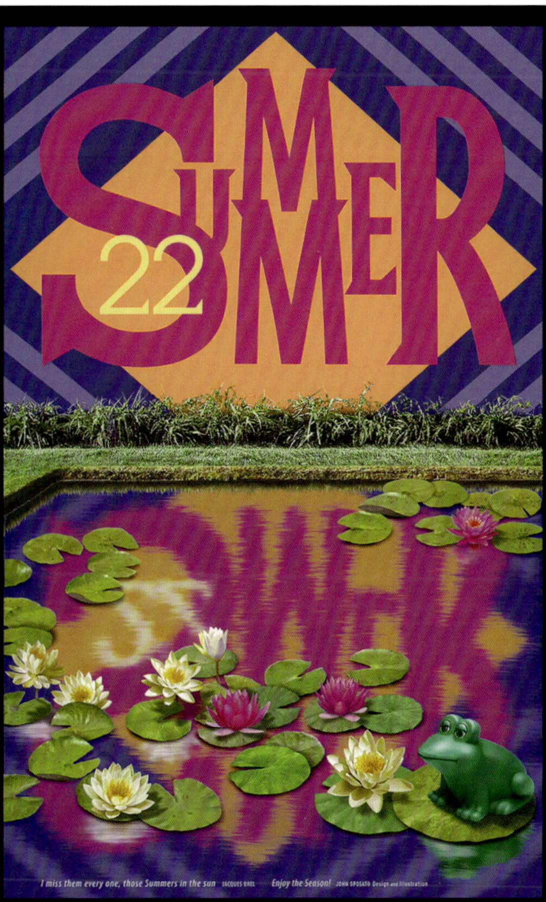

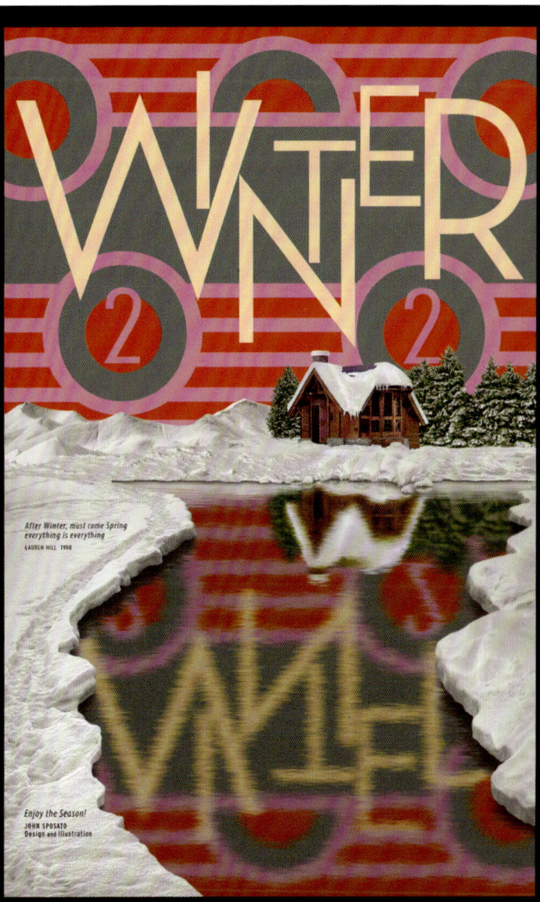

Title: Summer/Winter 2022 | **Client:** Self-initiated | **Design Firm:** John Sposato Design & Illustration

TRACTION FACTORY

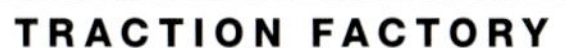

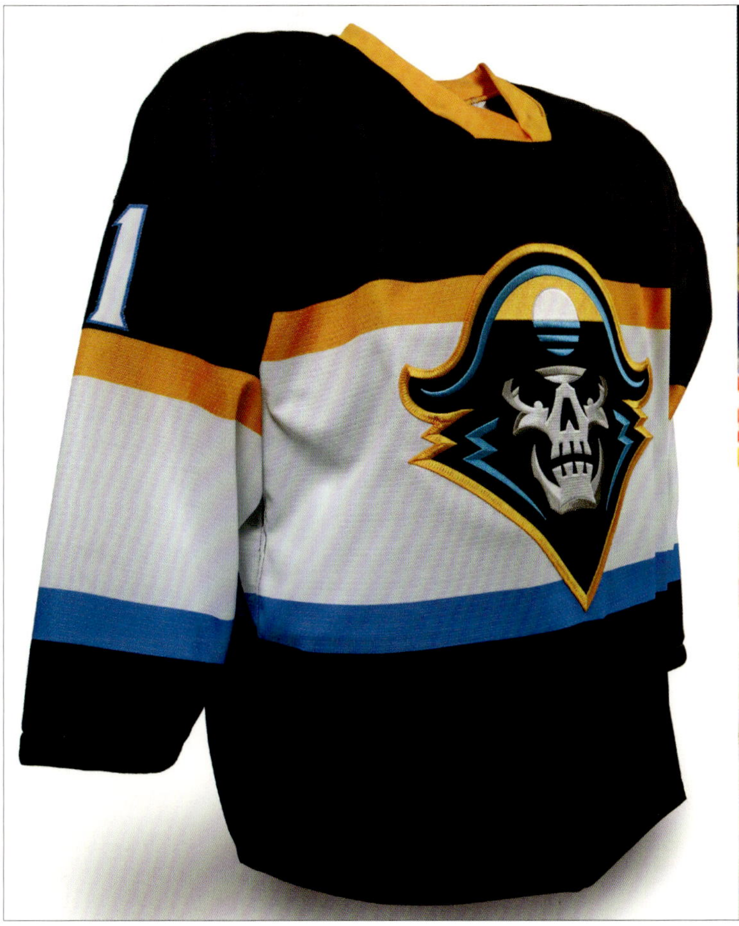

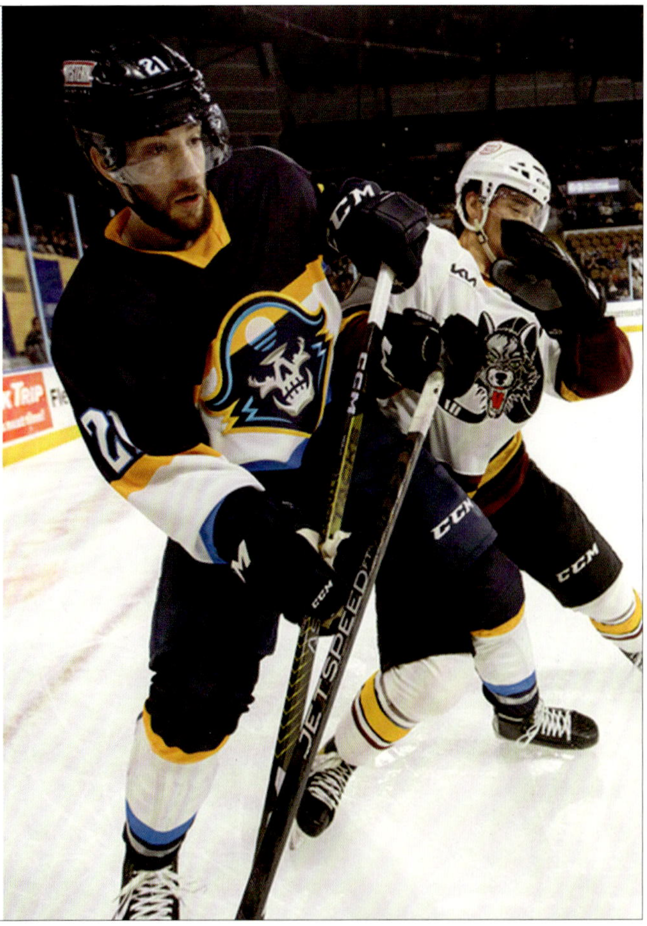

Title: 414 Day Jersey | **Client:** Milwaukee Admirals | **Design Firm:** Traction Factory

SHANTANU SUMAN

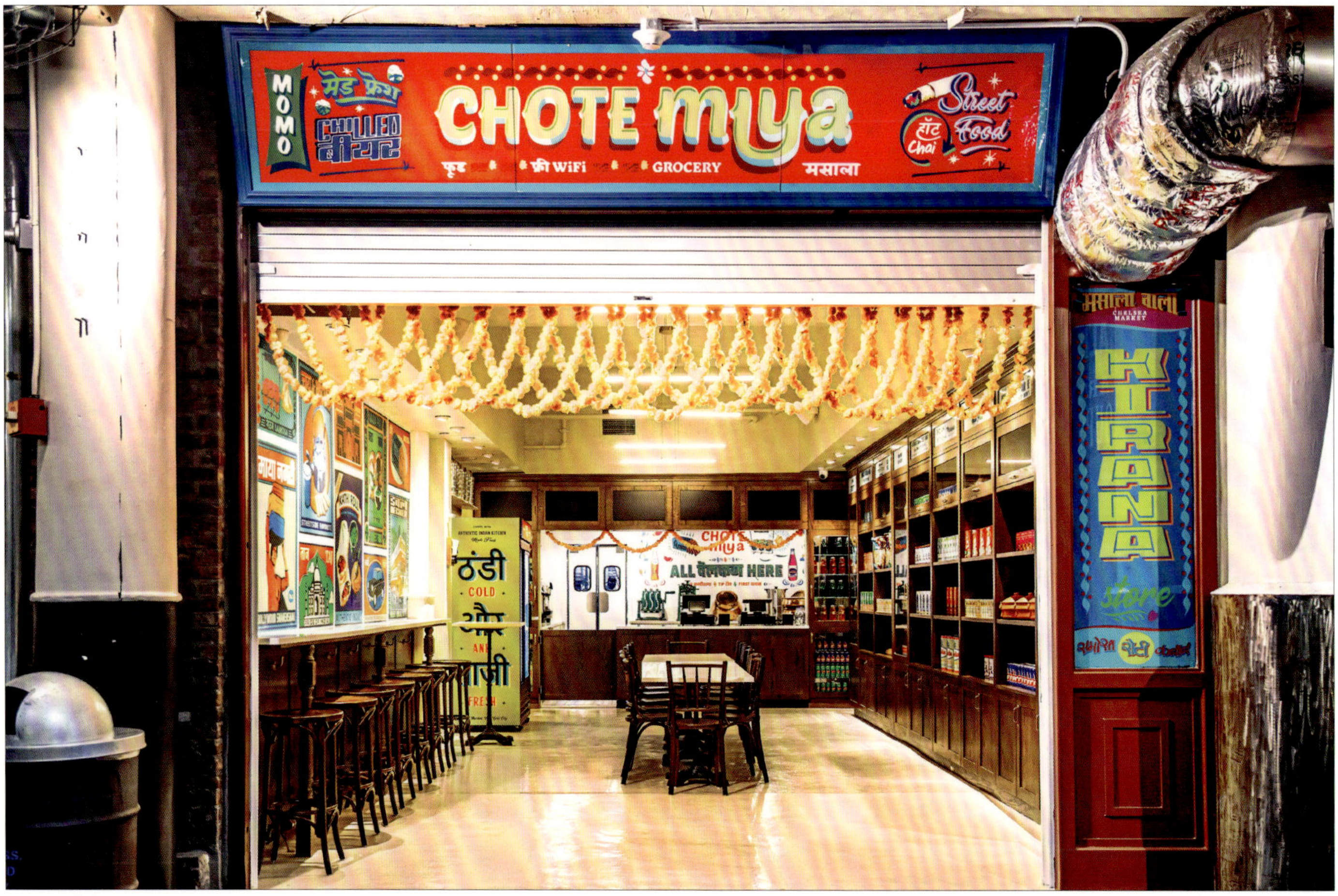

Title: Chote Miya Restaurant Signage and Mural Design | **Clients:** Jimmy Rizvi, Chote Miya | **Design Firm:** Open Door Design Studio (ODDS)

ELLEN BRUSS DESIGN

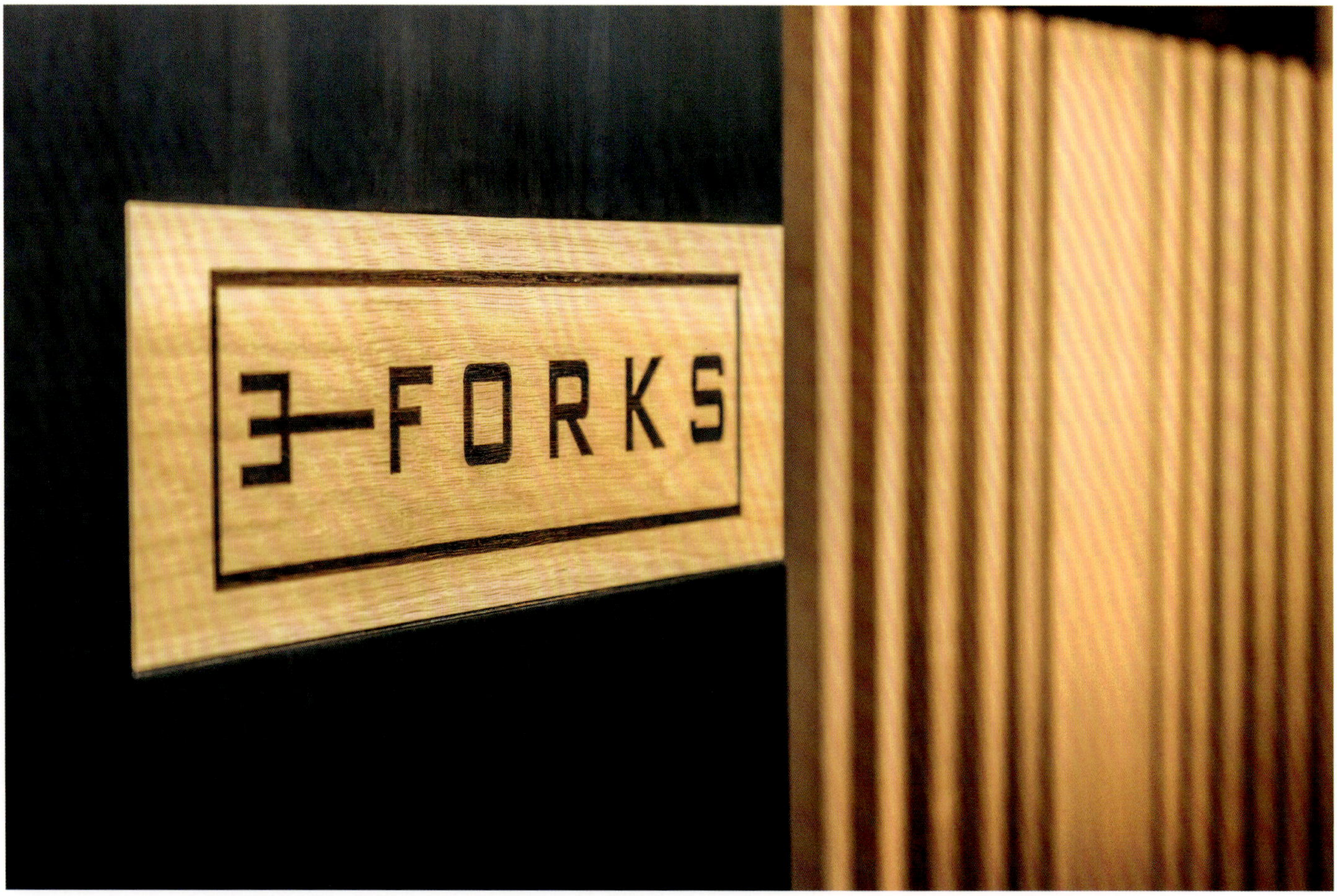

Title: 3 Forks Bar and Restaurant | **Client:** Lone Mountain Land Company | **Design Firm:** Ellen Bruss Design

LORI DIBBLE, STEPHEN AREVALOS

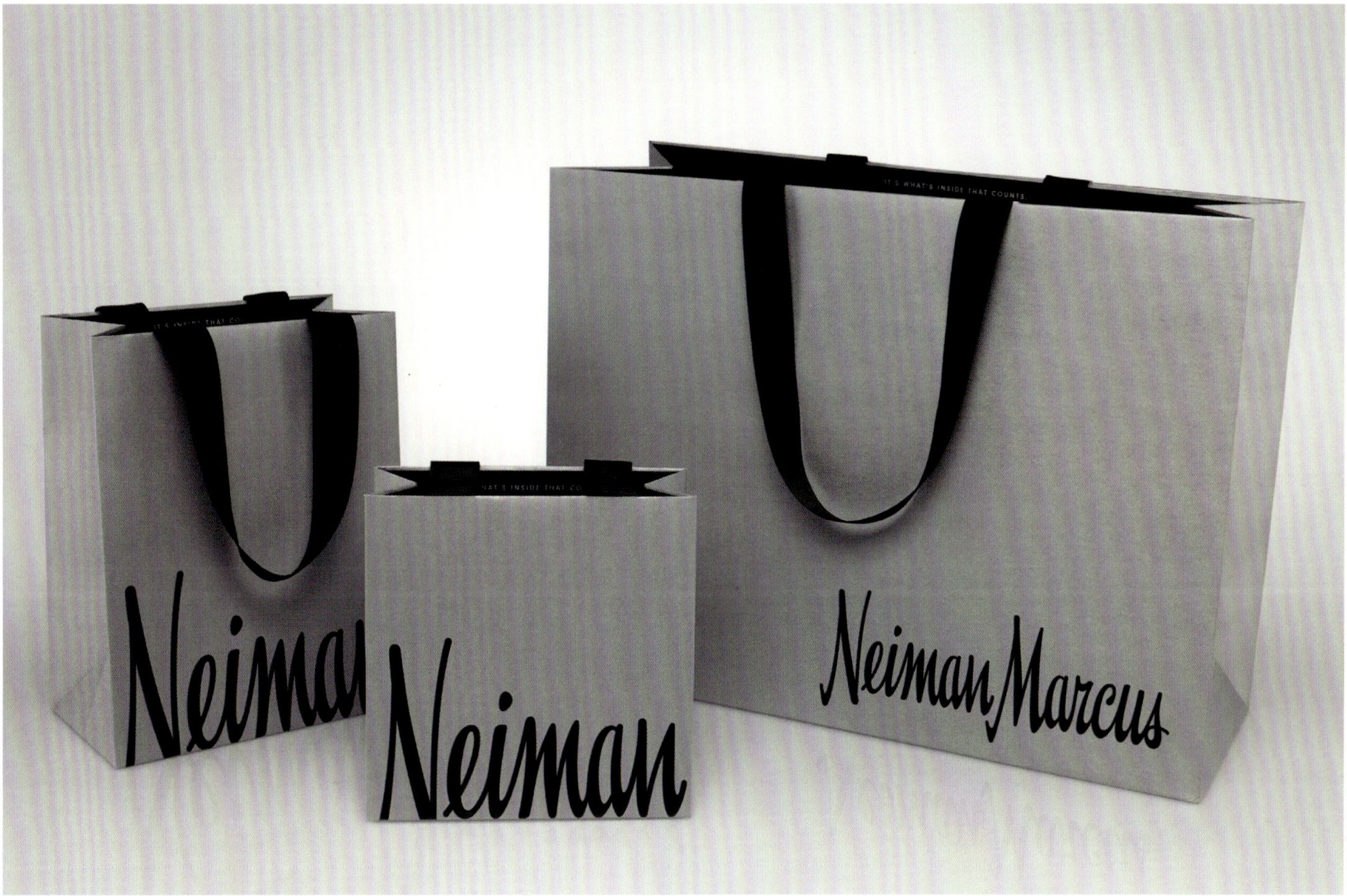

Title: Neiman Marcus Shopping Bag | **Client:** Self-initiated | **Design Firm:** Neiman Marcus Creative Services

PAULINA SHOWALTER

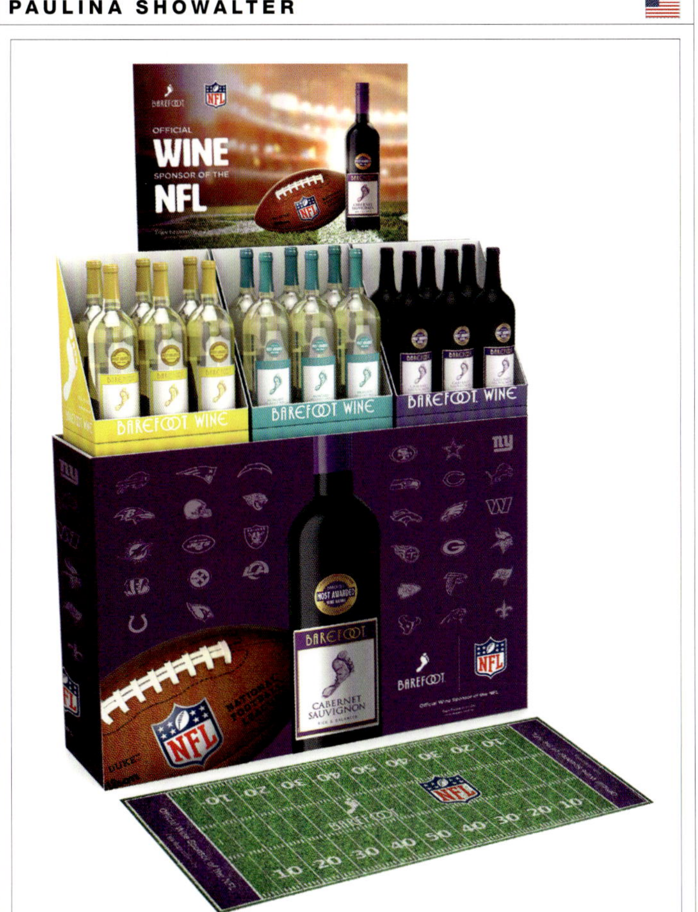

Title: Barefoot + NFL Partnership | **Client:** Barefoot Cellars
Design Firm: Gallo Creative

WENDY LOWDEN

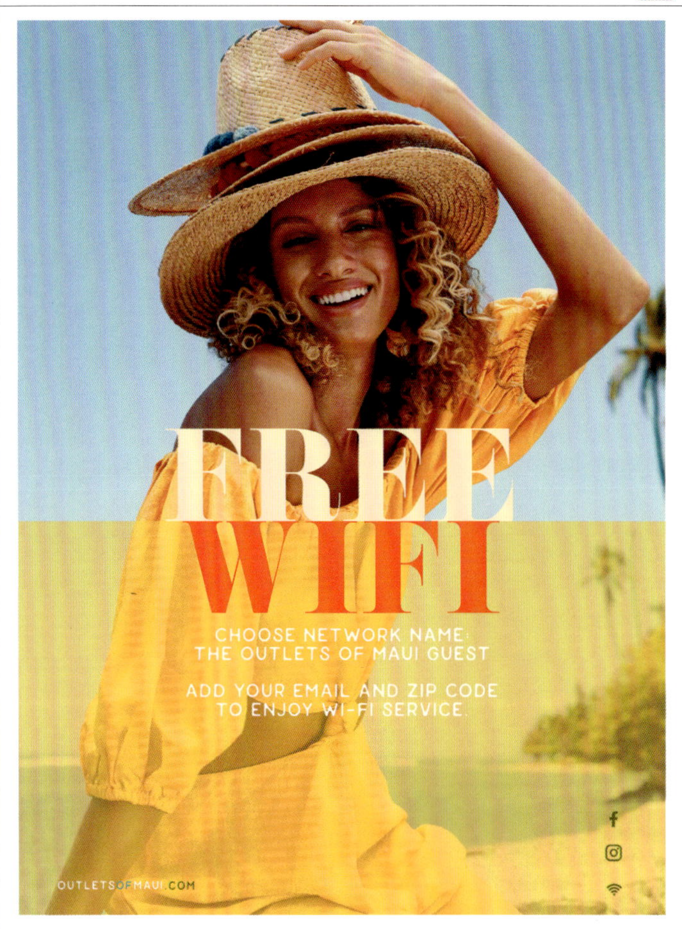

Title: The Outlets of Maui Campaign | **Client:** M&J Wilkow
Design Firm: House of Current

BAUB MERCURIO

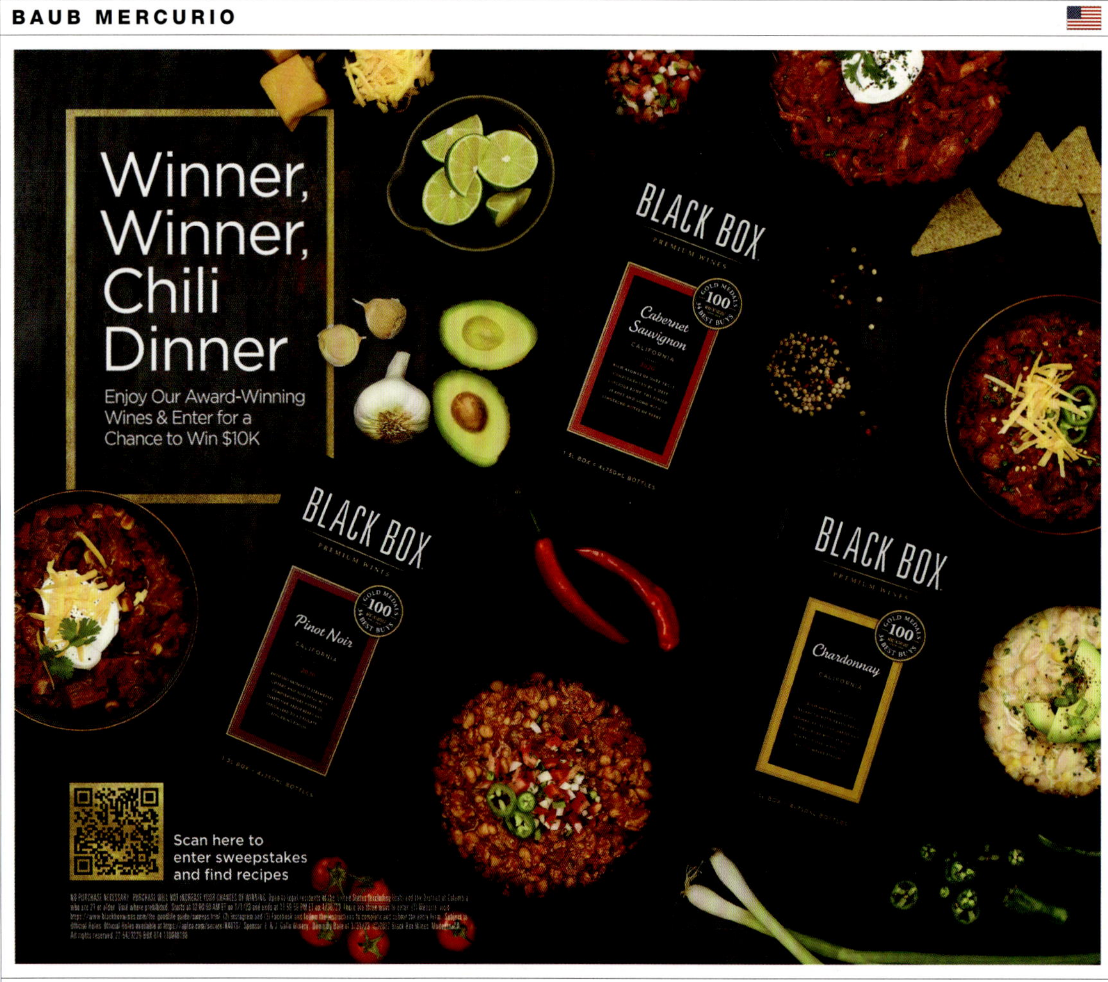

Title: Black Box Chili Program | **Client:** Black Box | **Design Firm:** Gallo Creative

NANCY STAHL

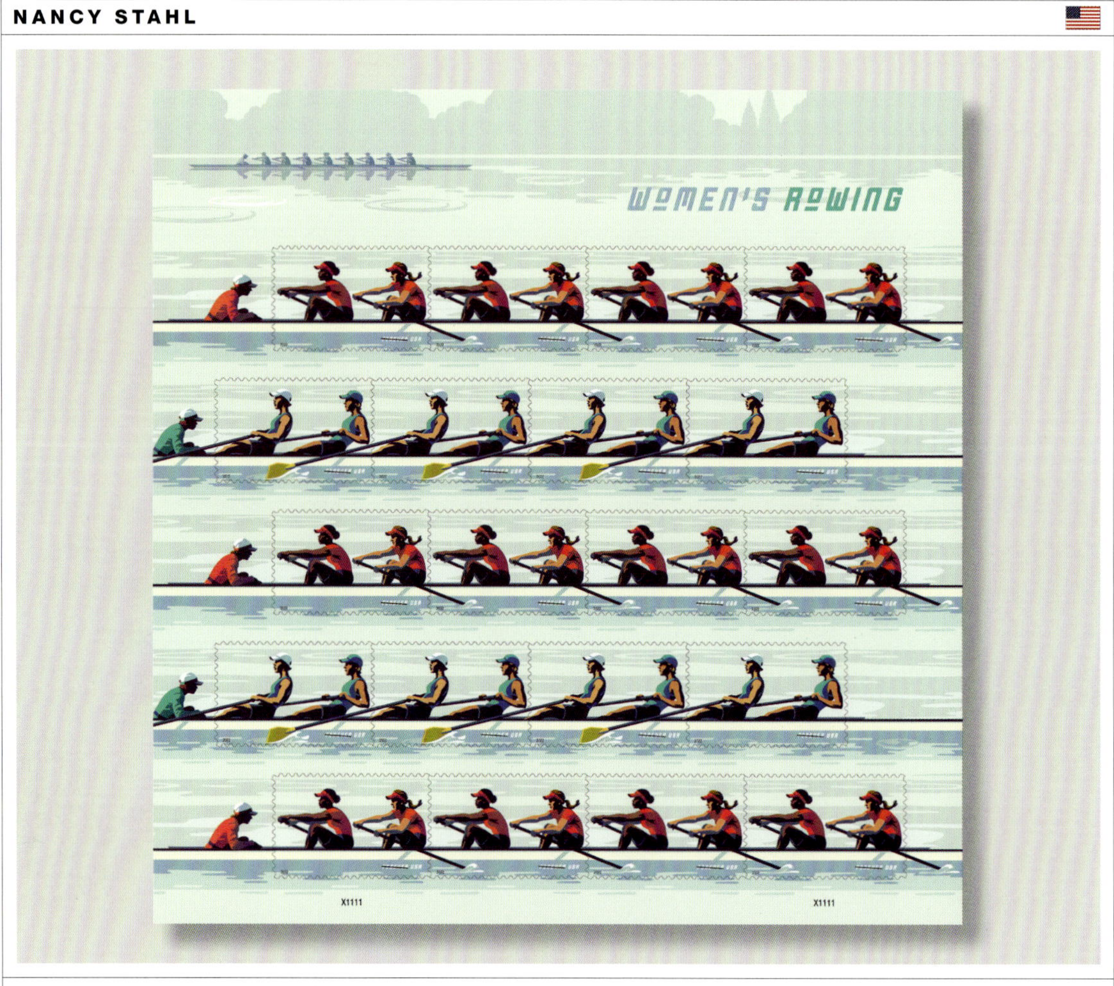

Title: Women's Rowing | **Client:** United States Postal Service | **Design Firm:** Nancy Stahl

ERIN ROBINSON

KWANZAA
FOREVER/USA
2022

Title: Kwanzaa | **Client:** United States Postal Service
Design Firm: Studio A

MELINDA BECK

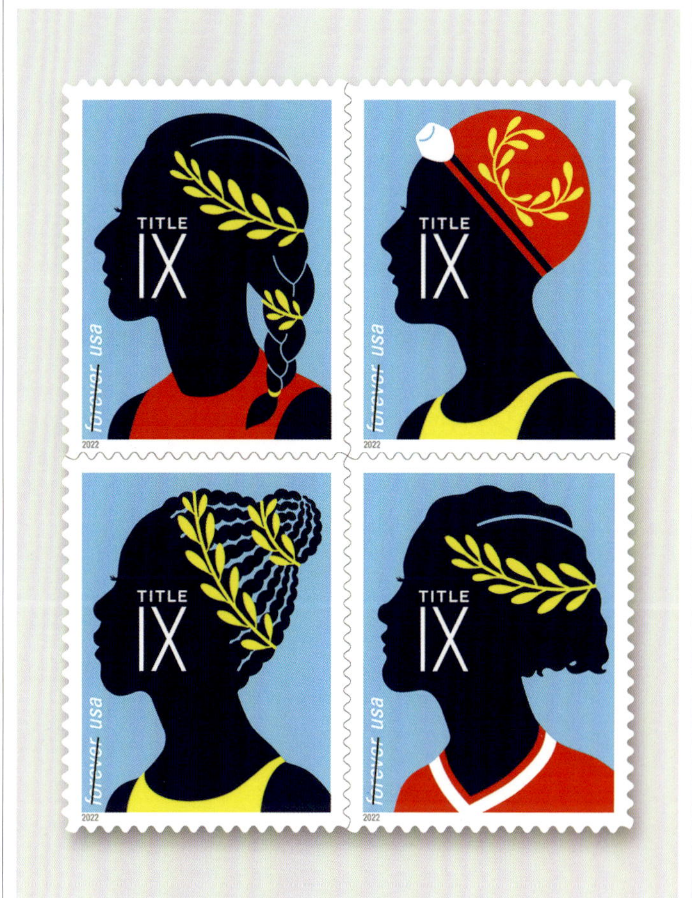

Title: Title IX | **Client:** United States Postal Service
Design Firm: Melinda Beck Illustration & Design

JEANETTE KUVIN OREN

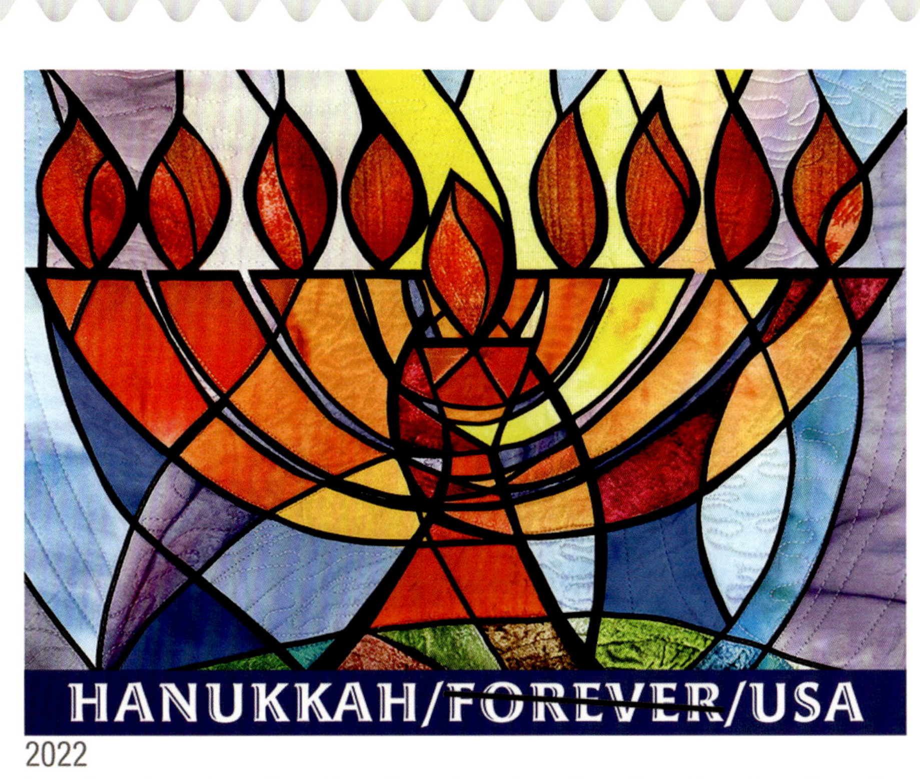

Title: Hanukkah | **Client:** United States Postal Service | **Design Firm:** Jeanette Kuvin Oren

LILI ARNOLD

Title: Mountain Flora | Client: United States Postal Service | Design Firm: Kessler Design Group

AMANDA PHINGBODHIPAKKIYA

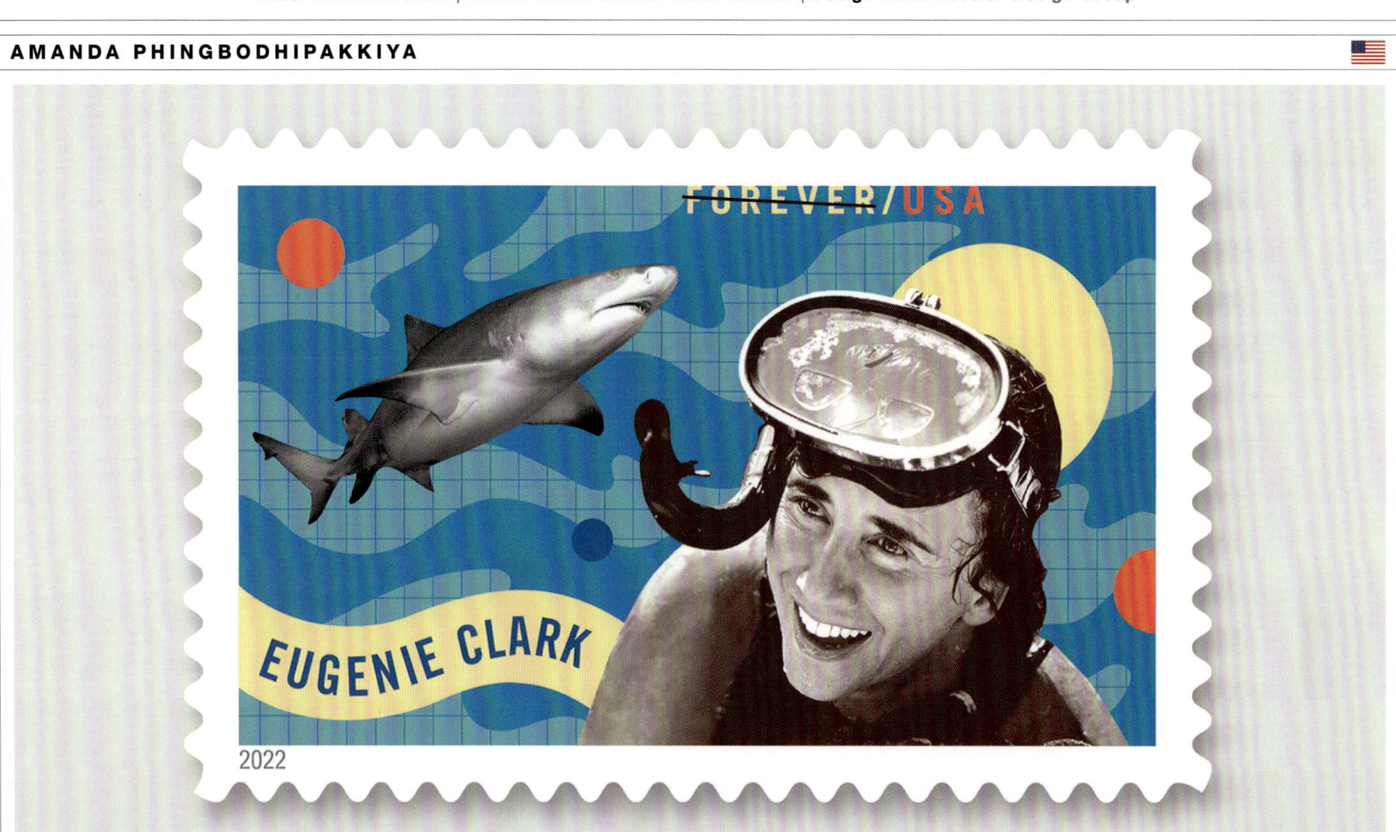

Title: Eugenie Clark | Client: United States Postal Service | Design Firm: Amanda Phingbodhipakkiya

RAFAEL LÓPEZ

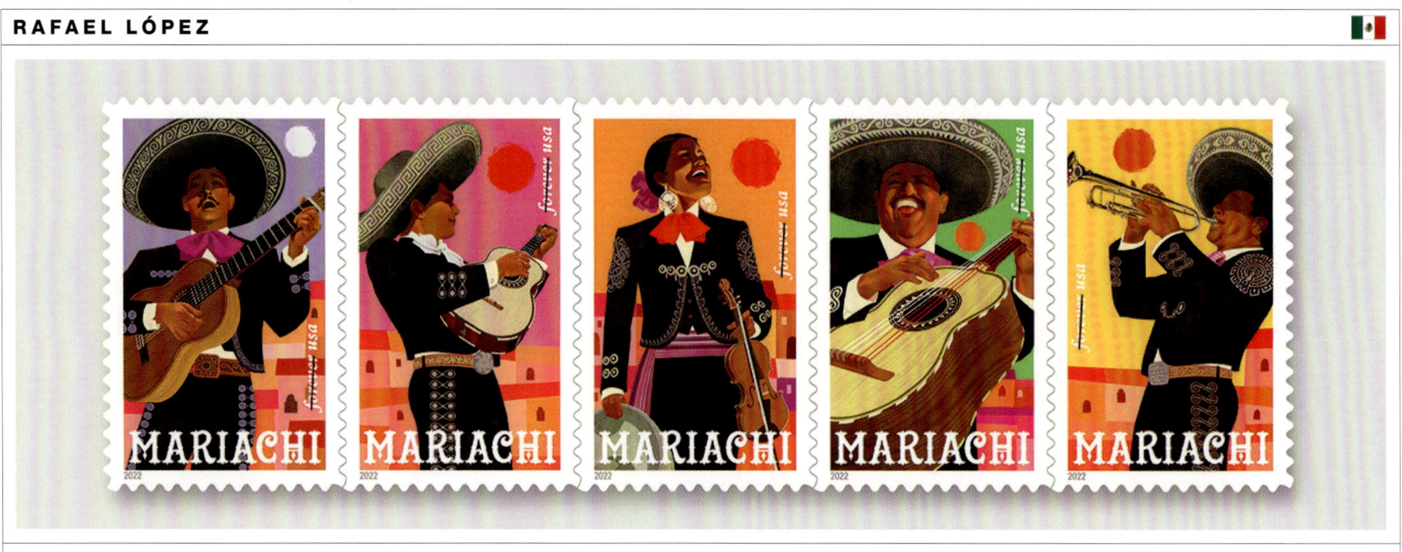

Title: Mariachi | Client: United States Postal Service | Design Firm: Rafael López

FILIPPOS FRAGKOGIANNIS

AaBbCcDdEe
FfGgHhIiJjKk
LlMmNnOoPp
QqRrSsTtUu
VvWwXxYyZz
1234567890

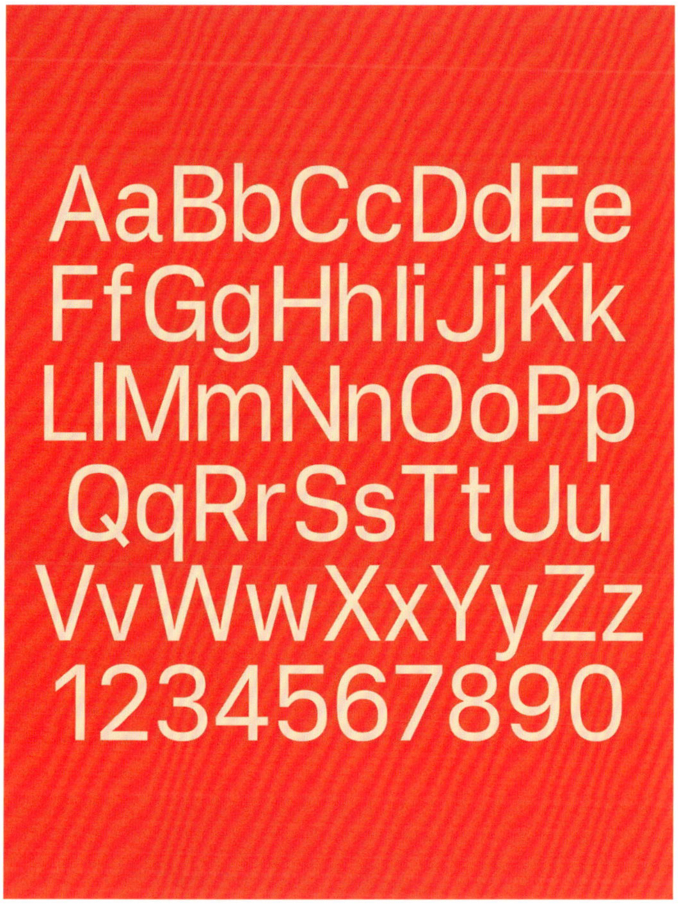

Title: Vercetti Regular | **Client:** Self-initiated
Design Firm: Filippos Fragkogiannis

ERICA HOLEMAN

Title: Upside | **Client:** Self-initiated
Design Firm: Erica Holeman

FILIPPOS FRAGKOGIANNIS 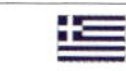

LONG
TERM

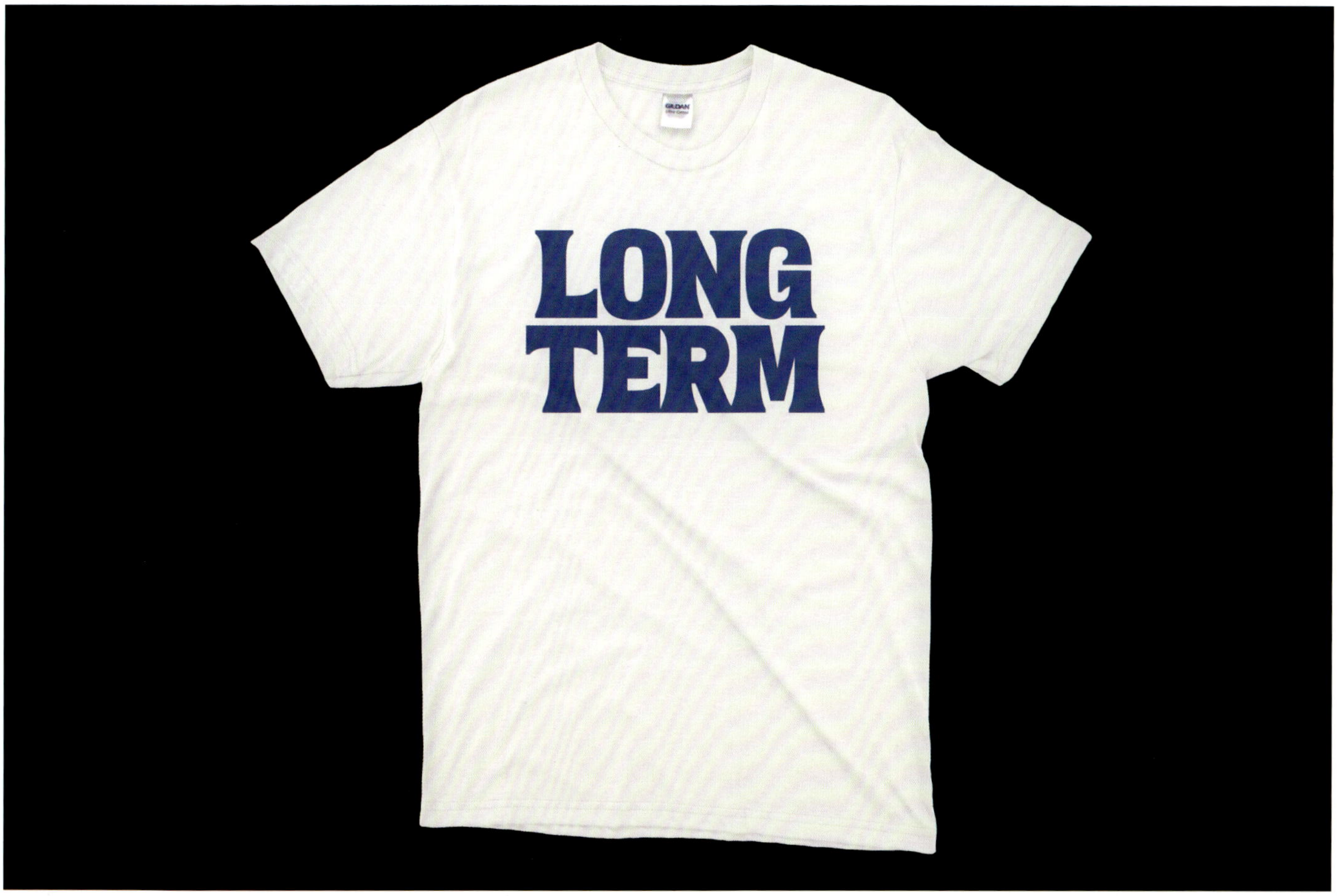

Title: Long Term T-shirt | **Client:** Self-initiated | **Design Firm:** Filippos Fragkogiannis

WOLFF OLINS

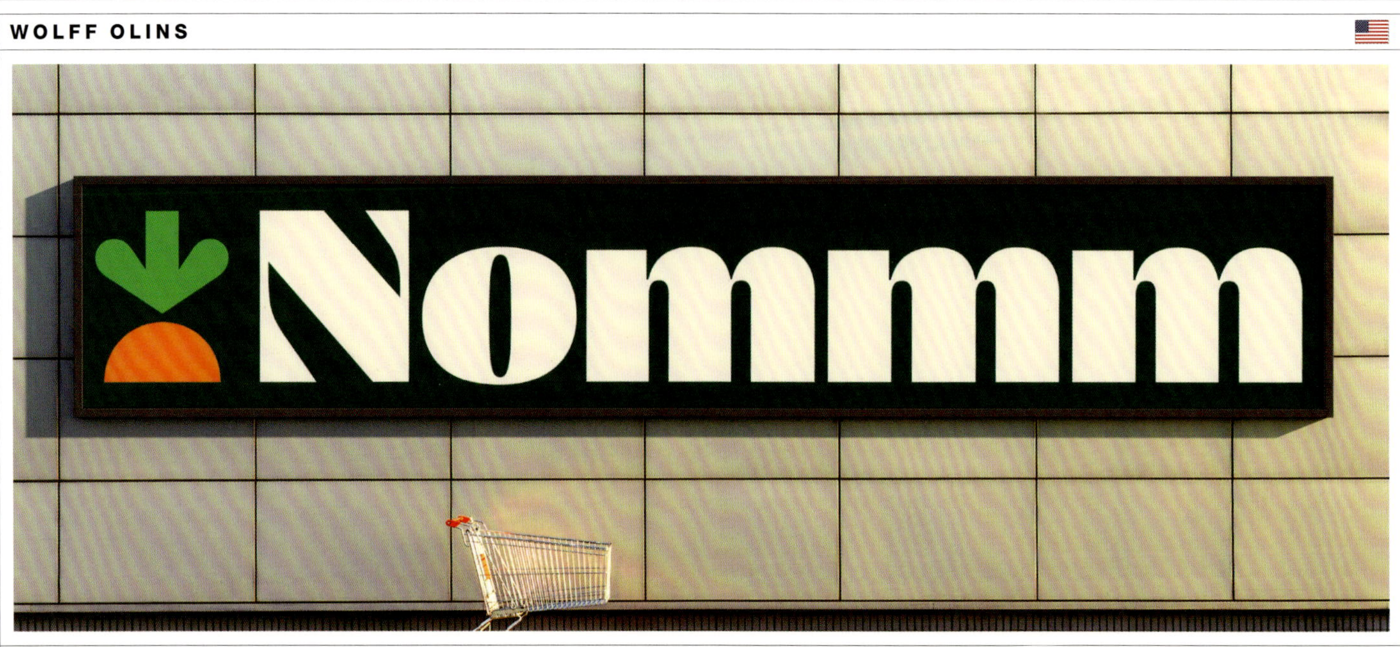

Title: Grounded in Their Roots, Growing Into the Future | **Client:** Instacart | **Design Firm:** Wolff Olins

ARIEL FREANER

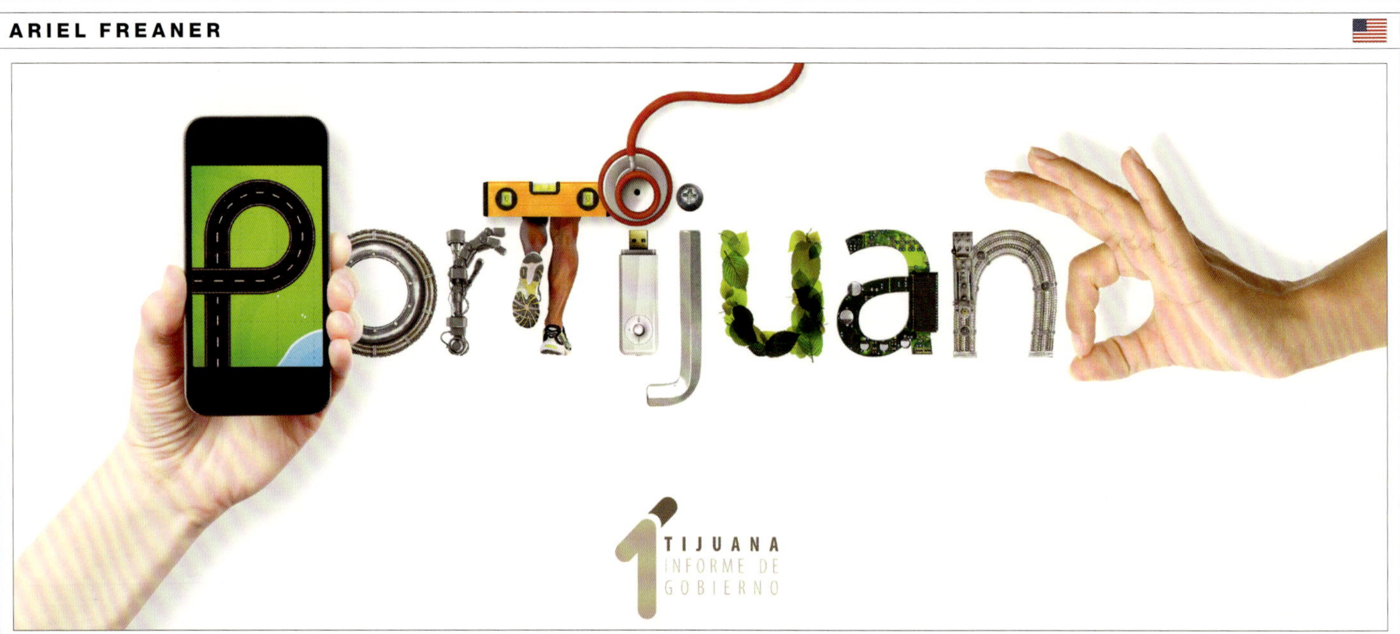

Title: Por Tijuana - 1st State of the Union Announcement | **Clients:** City of Tijuana, Jorge Astiazaran | **Design Firm:** Freaner Creative & Design

INSIGHT CREATIVE

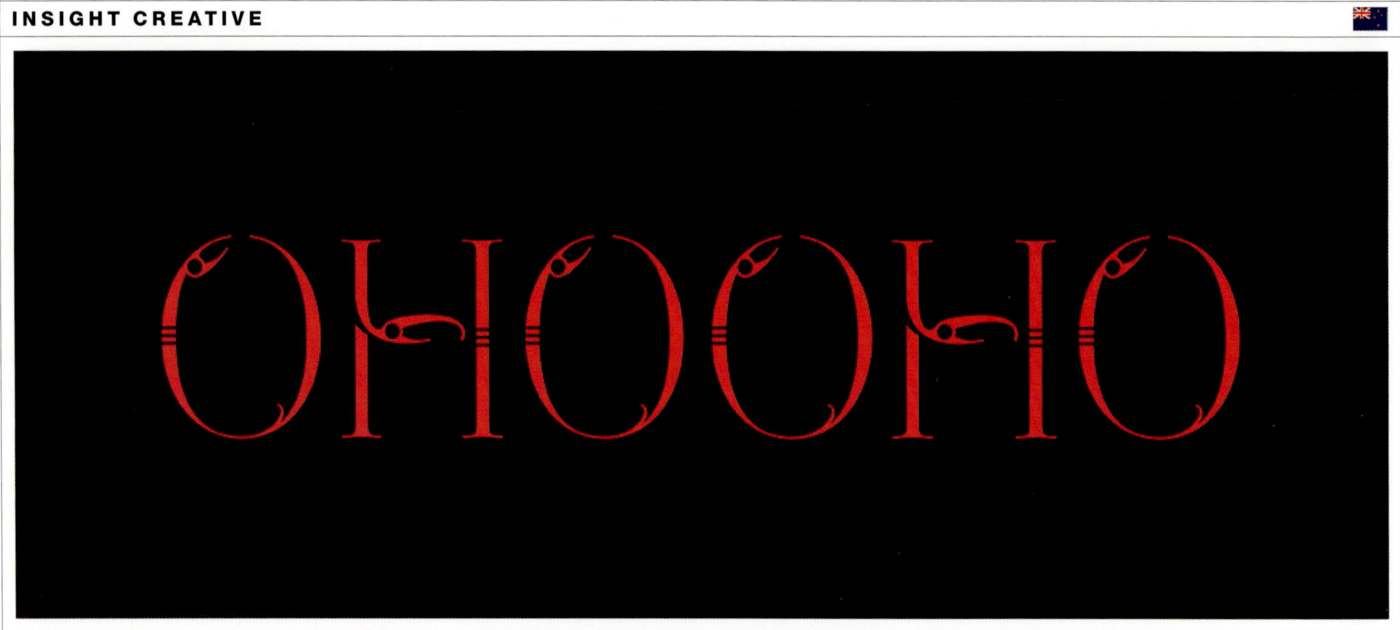

Title: Manaia Typography | **Client:** Self-initiated | **Design Firm:** Insight Creative

MAYA KOPYTMAN

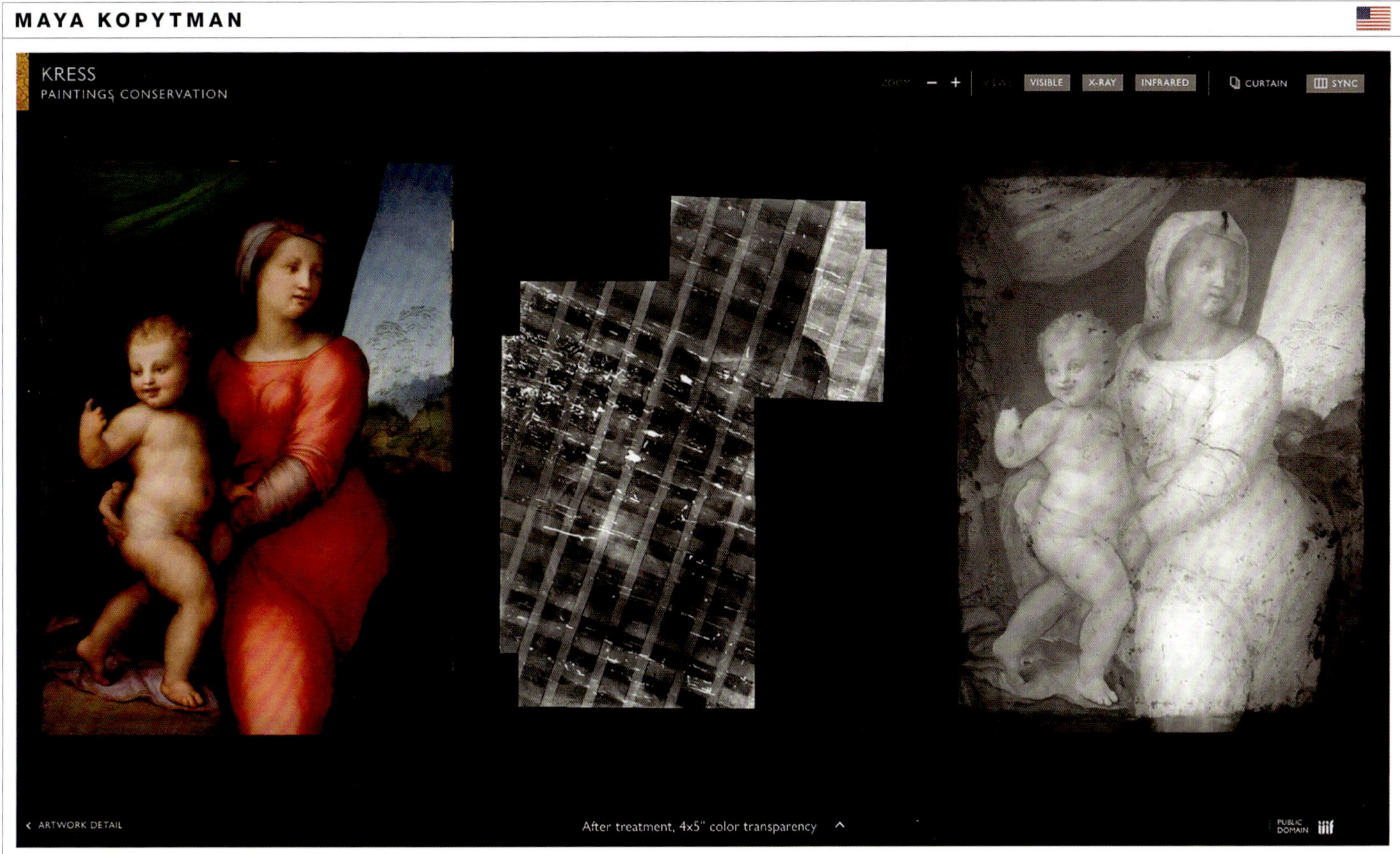

Title: Kress Program in Paintings Conservation Website | **Client:** Kress Program in Paintings Conservation | **Design Firm:** C&G Partners

HISA IDE, TOSHIAKI IDE

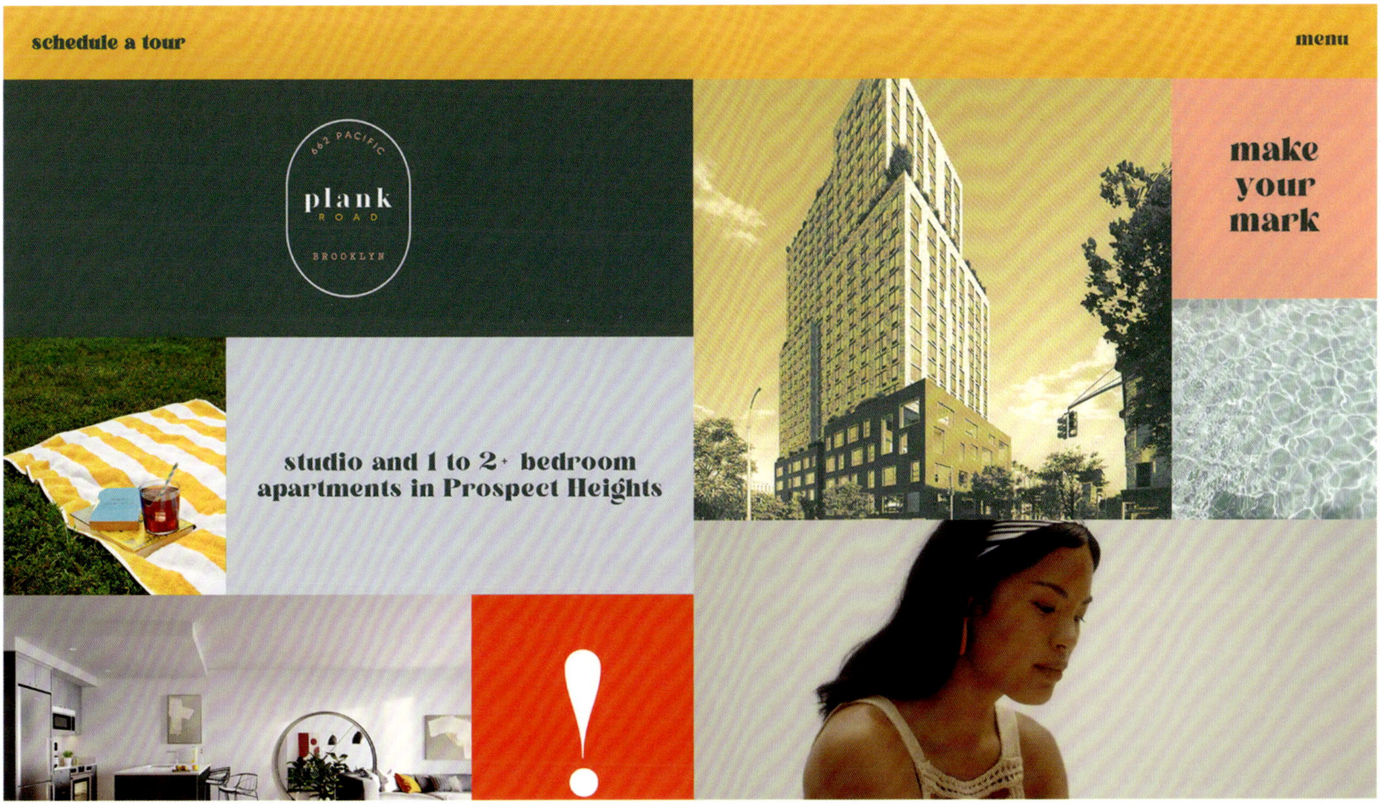

schedule a tour

menu

662 PACIFIC plank ROAD BROOKLYN

make your mark

studio and 1 to 2+ bedroom apartments in Prospect Heights

Title: Plank Road Website | **Client:** Brodsky | **Design Firm:** IF Studio

ARIEL FREANER

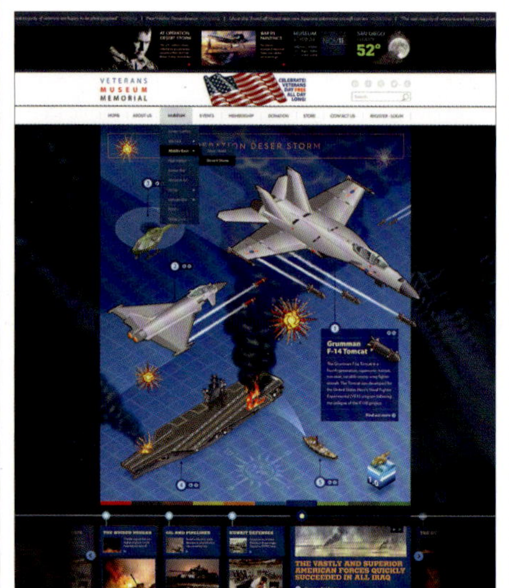

Title: Veterans Museum Memorial Website
Client: Veterans Museum Memorial
Design Firm: Freaner Creative & Design

ARIEL FREANER

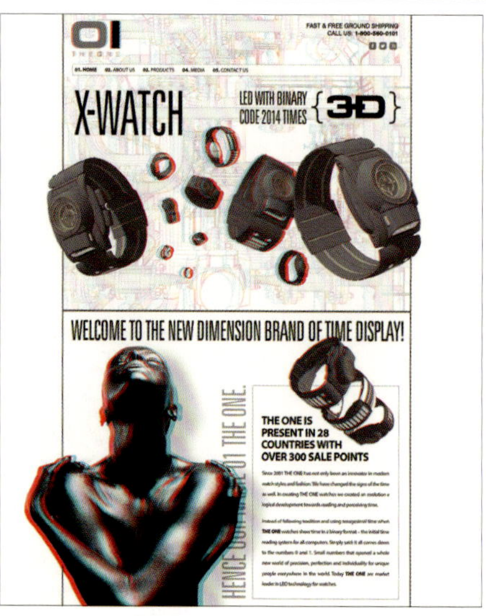

Title: OI One Watches 3-D Micro Website
Client: Self-initiated
Design Firm: Freaner Creative & Design

ARIEL FREANER

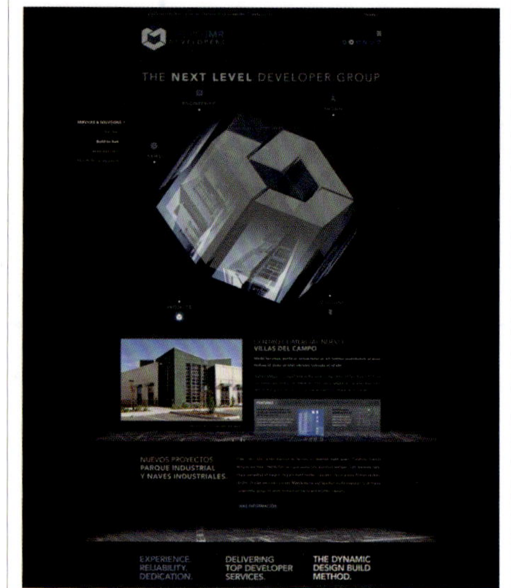

Title: JMR Developers and Construction Landing Page | **Client:** JMR Developers
Design Firm: Freaner Creative & Design

SHARON LLOYD MCLAUGHLIN

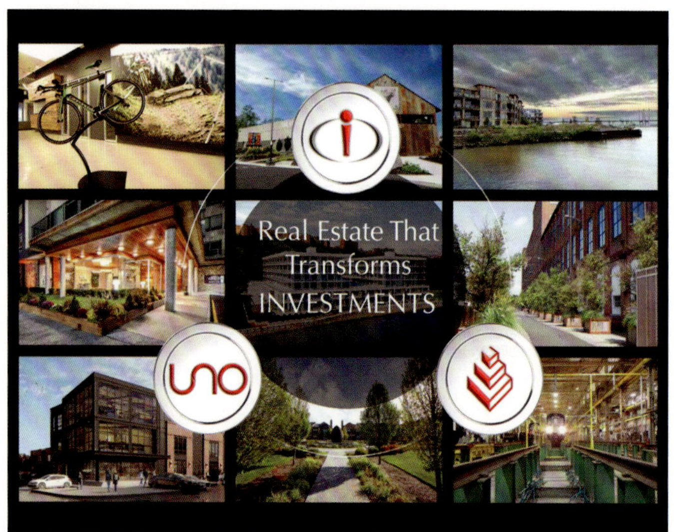

Title: National Resources Website
Client: National Resources
Design Firm: Mermaid, Inc.

ARIEL FREANER

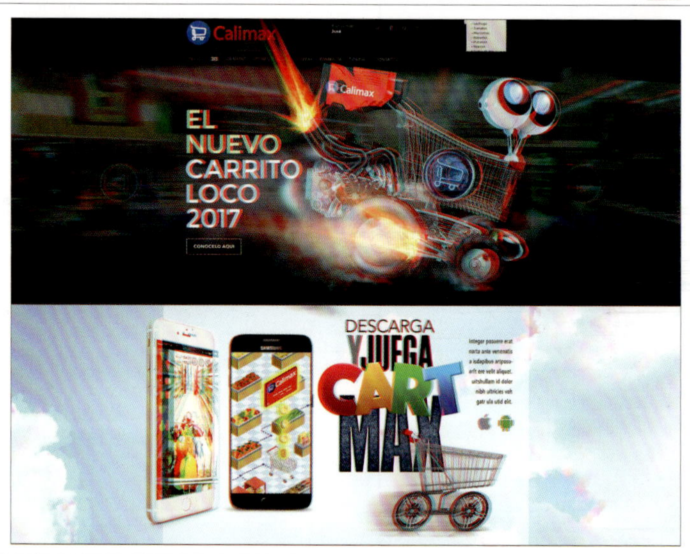

Title: Calimax Website Special Advertising Landing Pages
Clients: Calimax, Ignacio Fimbres, Jose Fimbres
Design Firm: Freaner Creative & Design

ARIEL FREANER

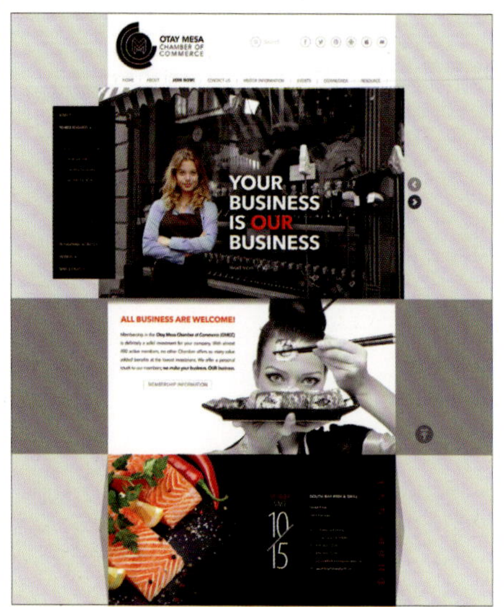

Title: Otay Mesa Chamber of Commerce Special Landing Pages | **Client:** Otay Mesa Chamber of Commerce | **Design Firm:** Freaner Creative & Design

ARIEL FREANER

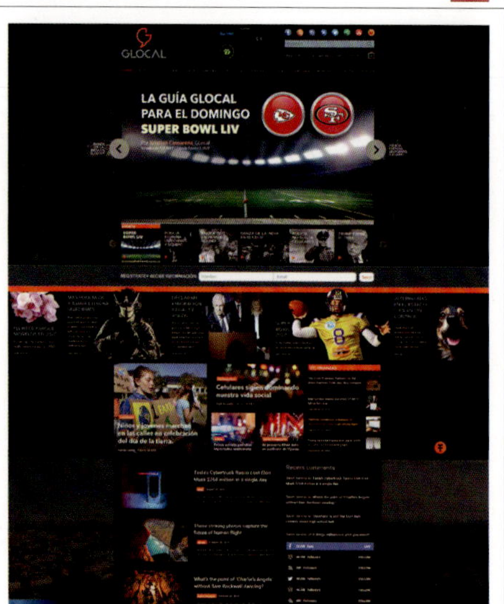

Title: Glocal Media News Website Landing Pages
Client: Glocal Media News
Design Firm: Freaner Creative & Design

ARIEL FREANER

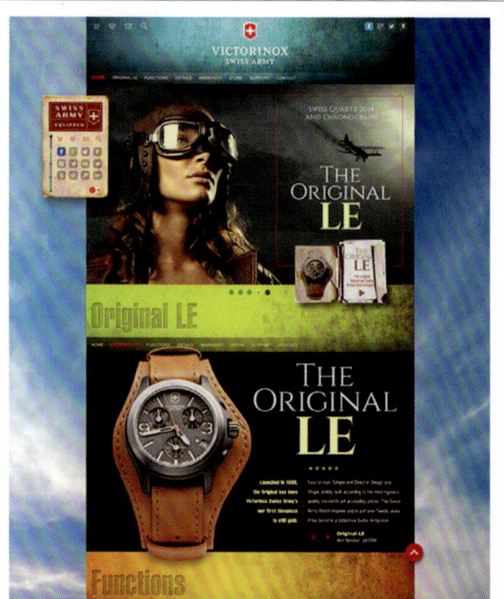

Title: Victorinox Original LF Watches Local Microsite | **Client:** Victorinox
Design Firm: Freaner Creative & Design

Graphis Honorable Mentions

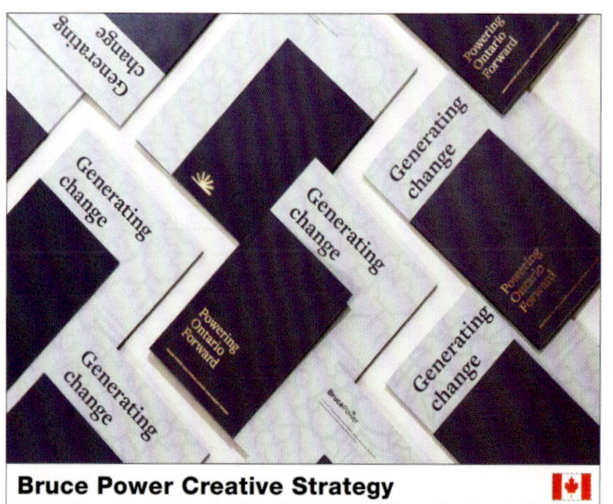

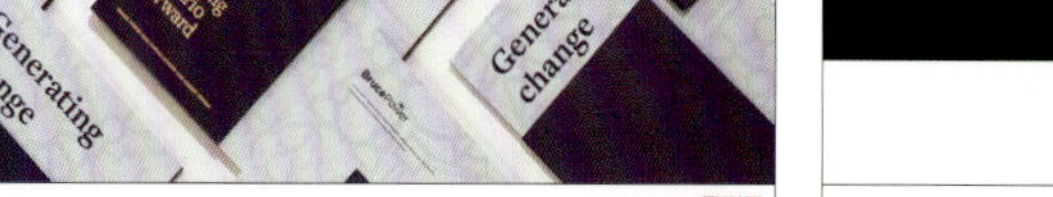

Bruce Power Creative Strategy

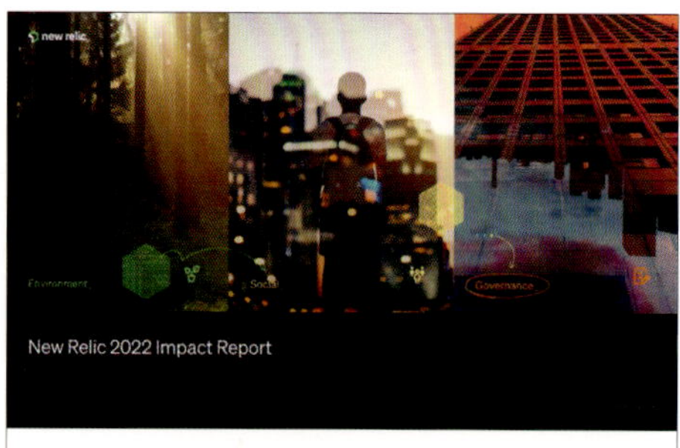

New Relic, The Design Farm

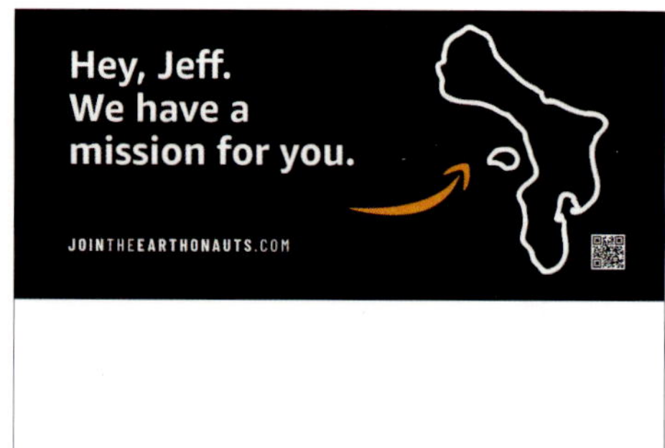

Dunn&Co.

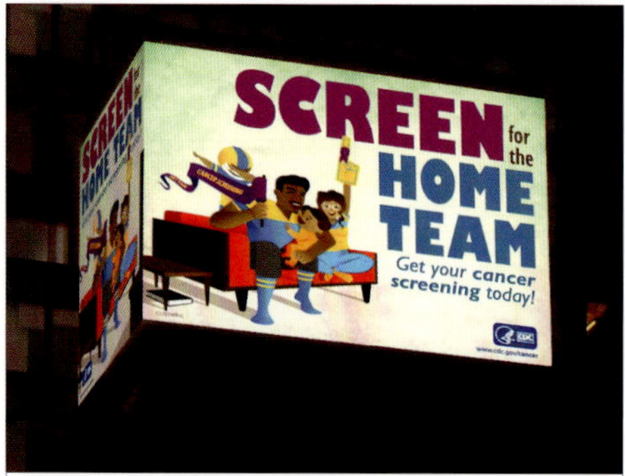

Centers for Disease Control & Prevention

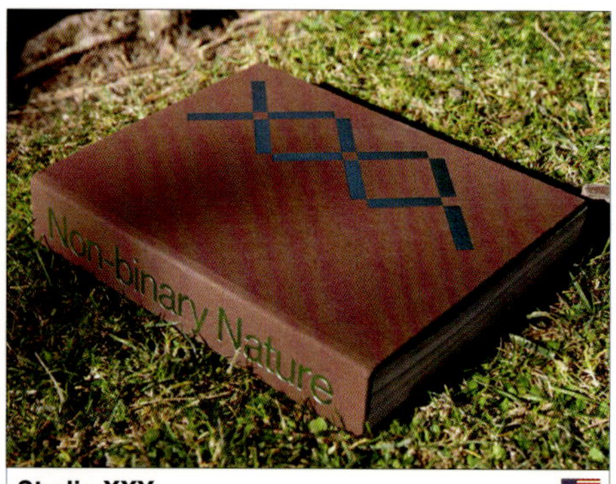

Studio XXY

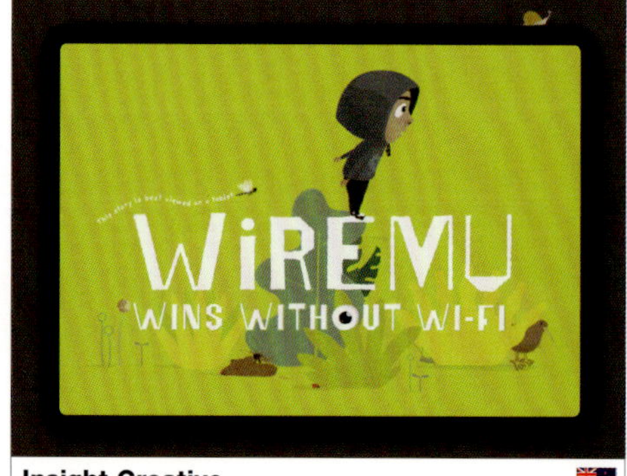

Insight Creative

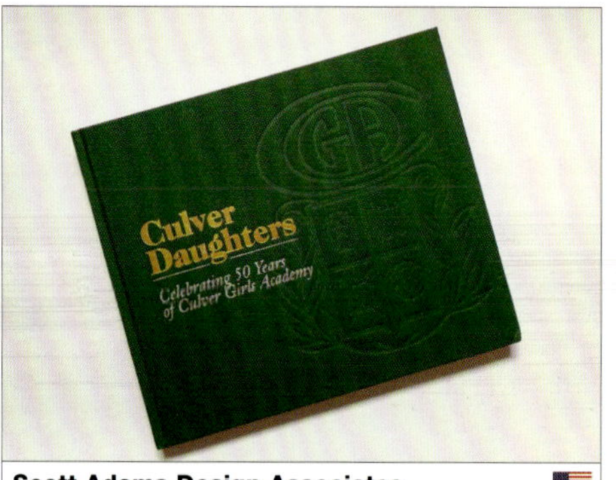

Scott Adams Design Associates

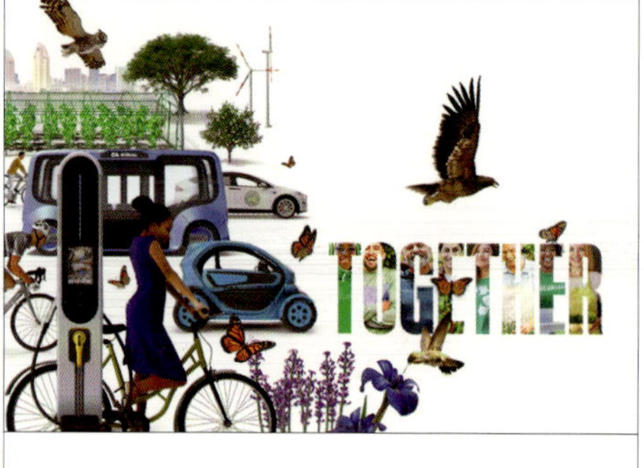

Freaner Creative & Design

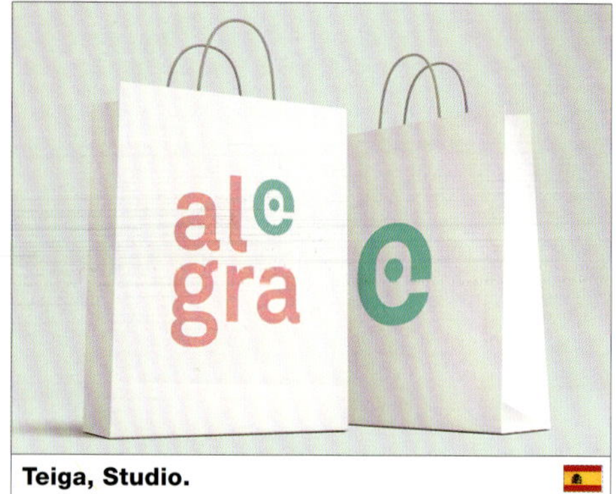

Teiga, Studio.

Hoyne

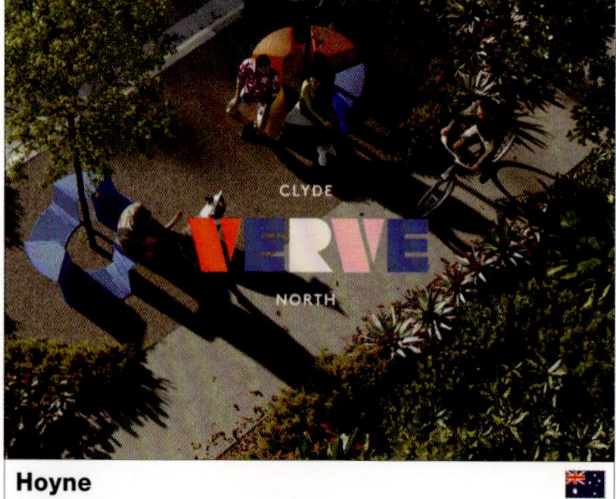

Hoyne

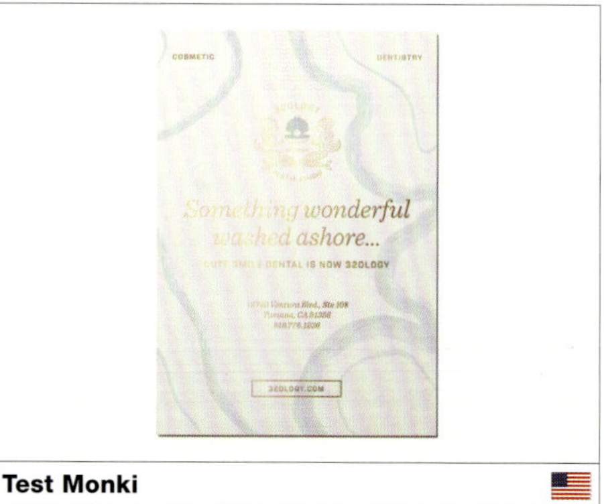

Test Monki

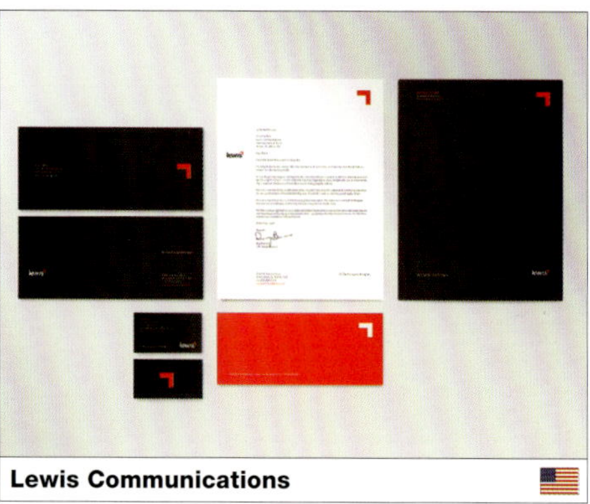

Lewis Communications

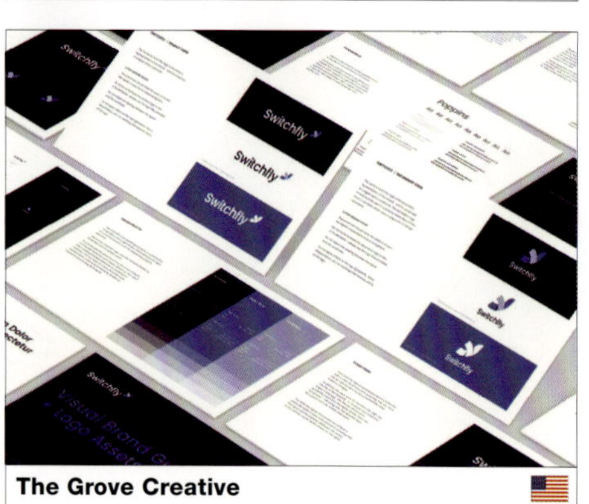

The Grove Creative

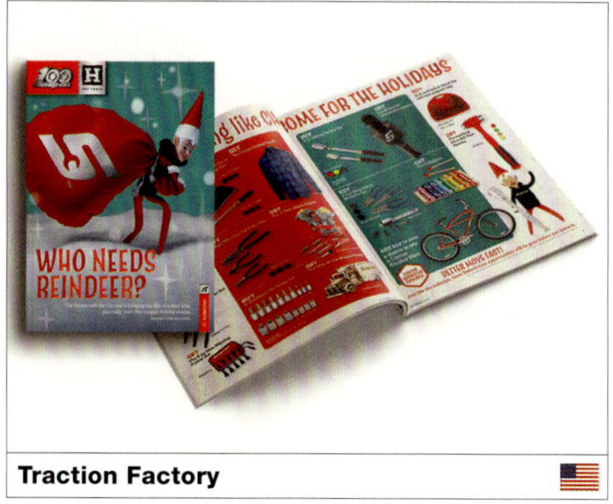

Traction Factory

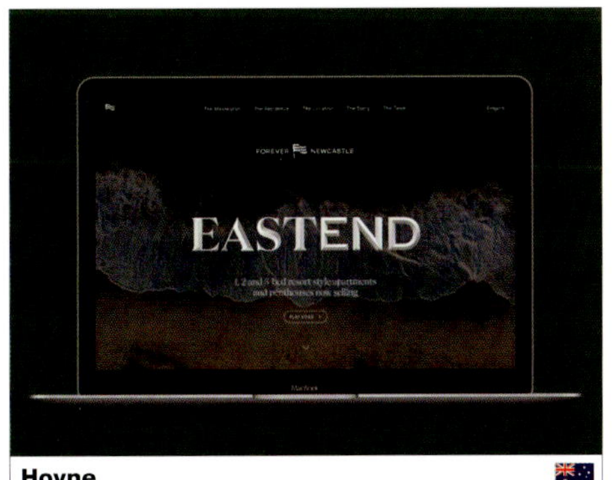

Hoyne

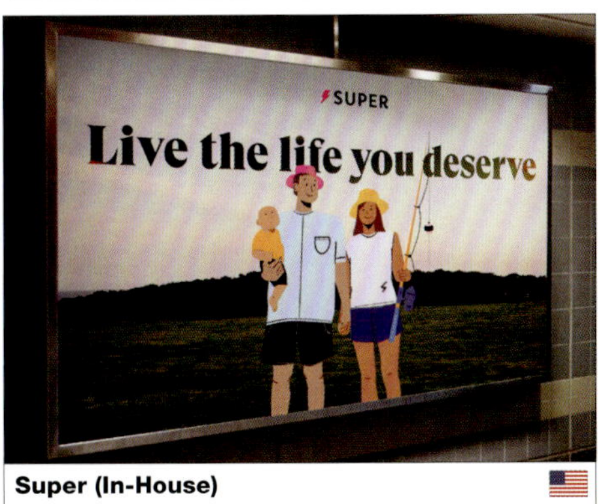

Super (In-House)

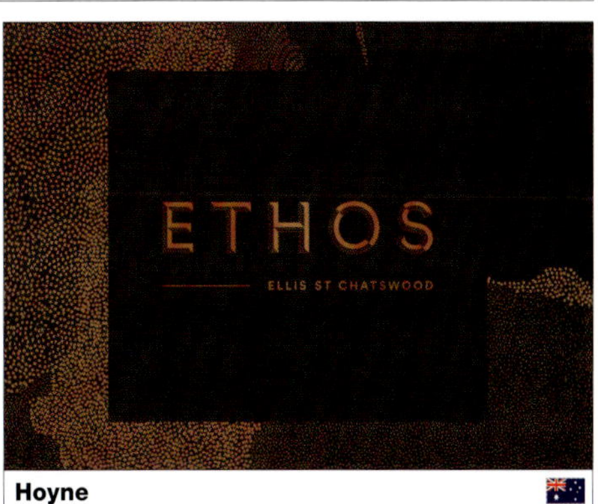

Hoyne

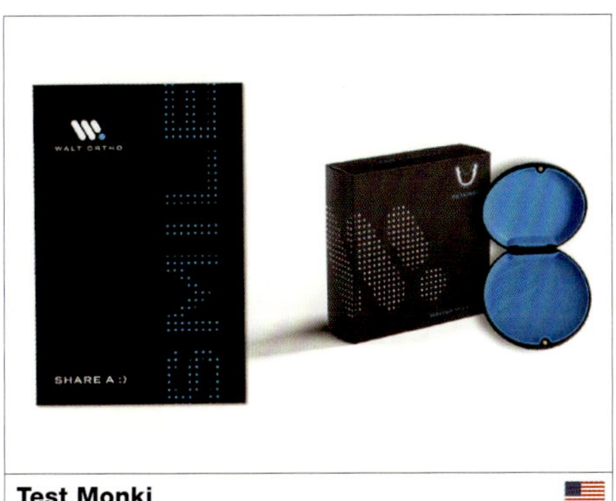

Test Monki

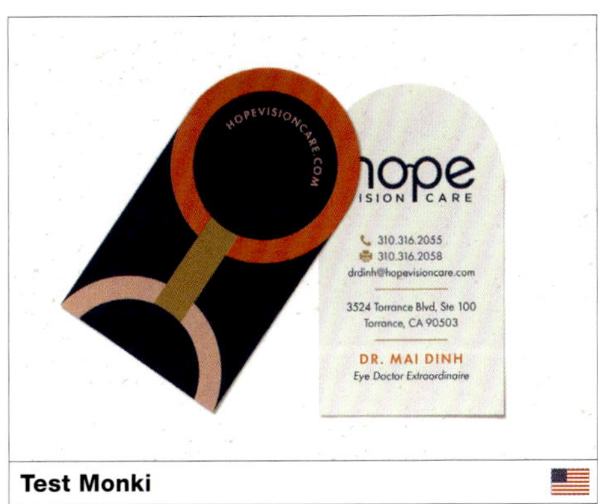

Test Monki

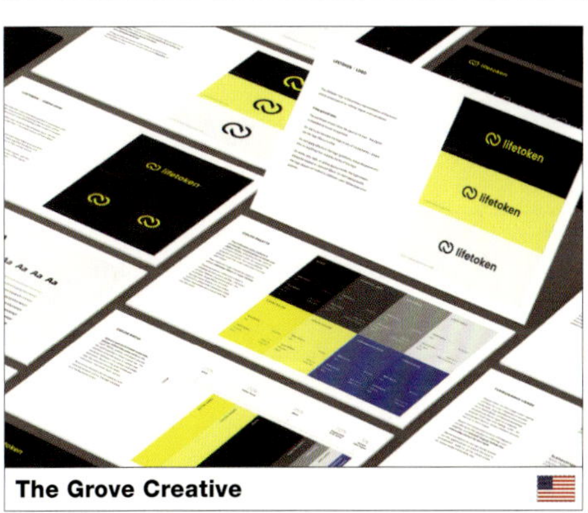

The Grove Creative

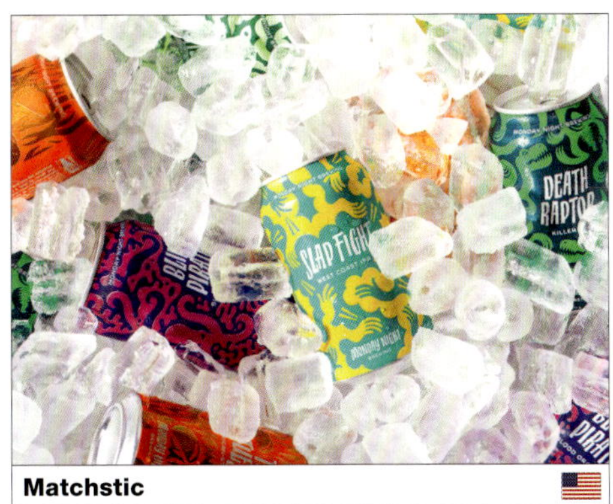
Matchstic

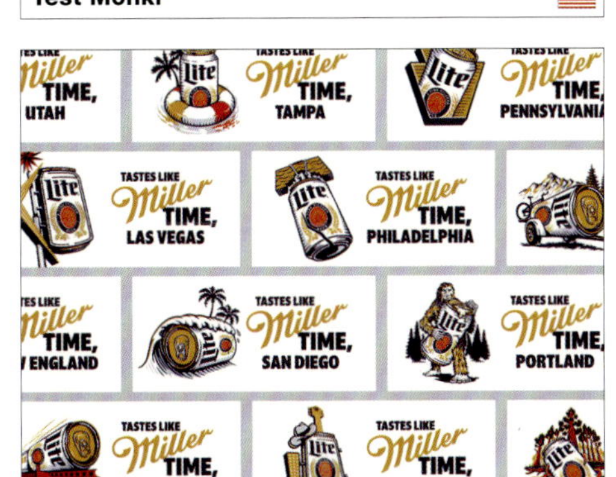

Turner Duckworth: London, SF & NY

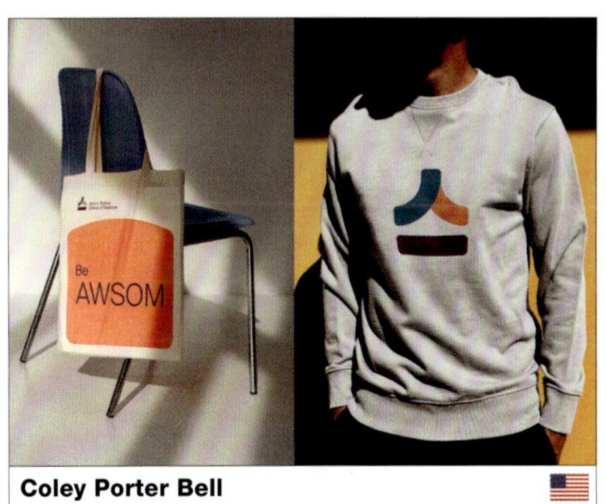

Coley Porter Bell

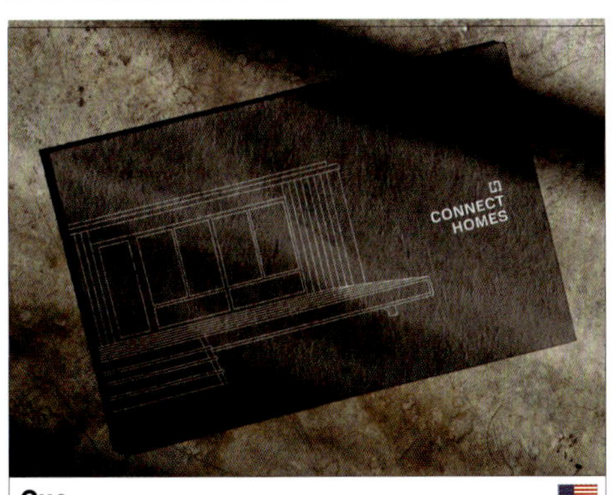

Cue

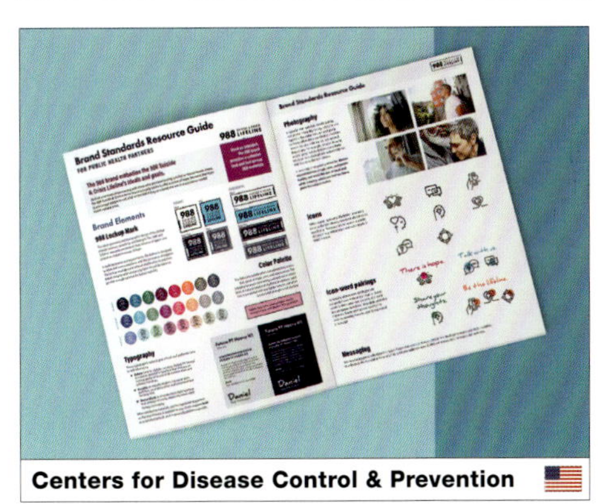

Centers for Disease Control & Prevention

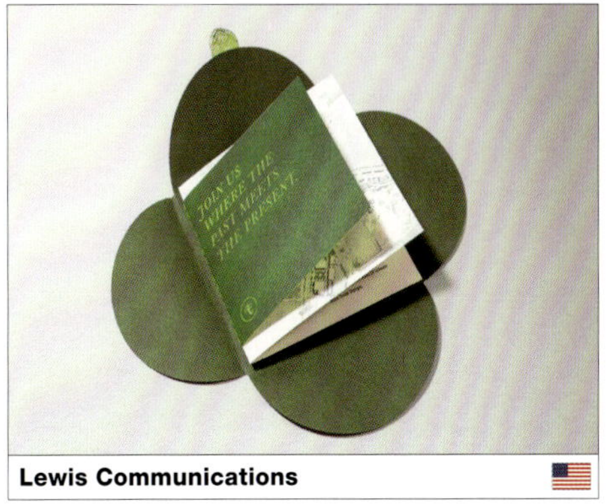
Lewis Communications

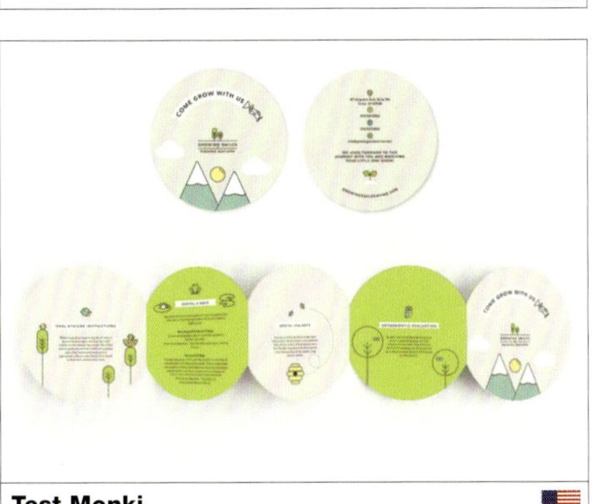
Test Monki

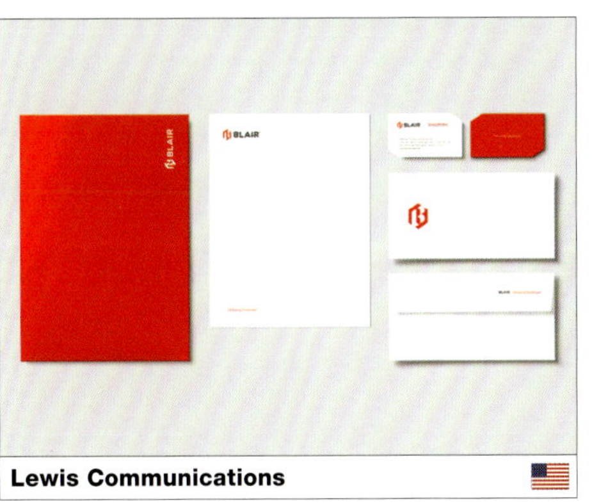
Lewis Communications

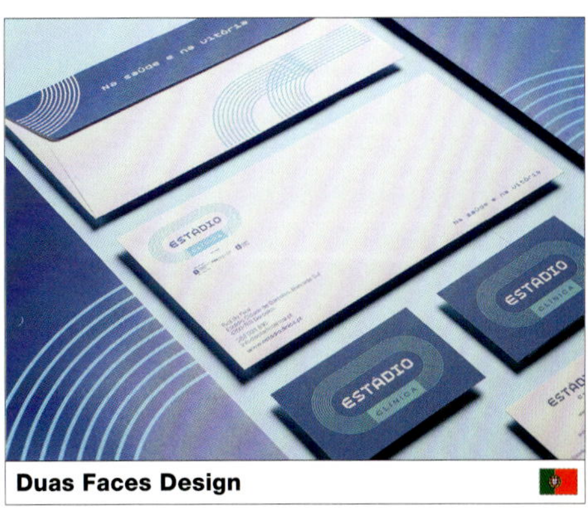

Duas Faces Design

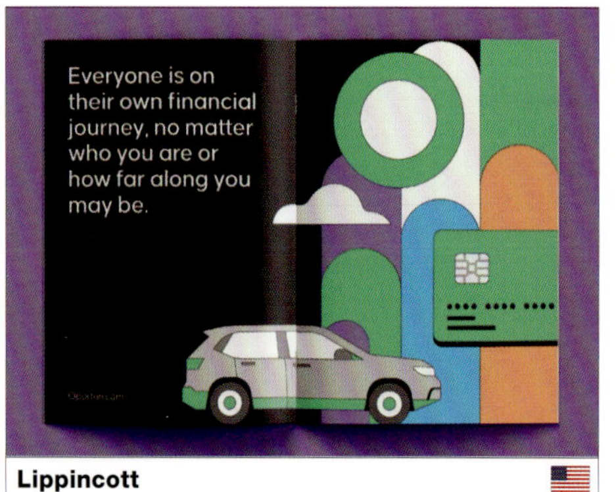

Lippincott

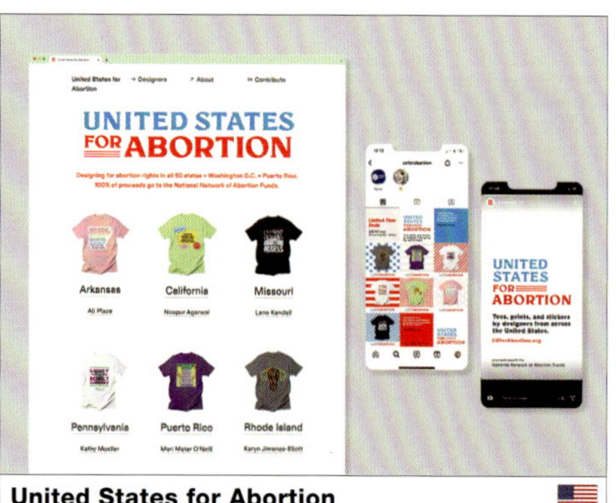

United States for Abortion

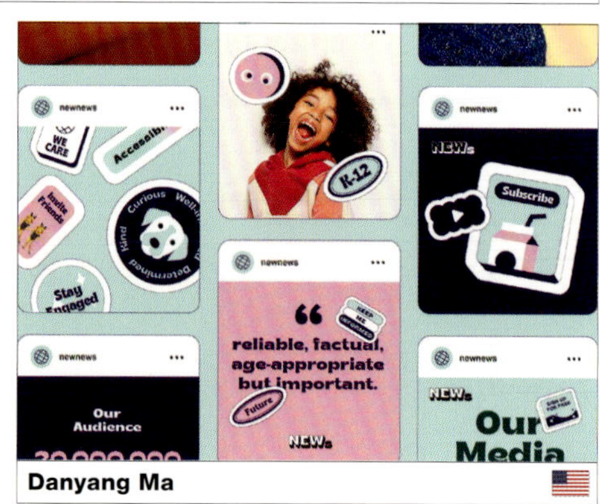

Danyang Ma

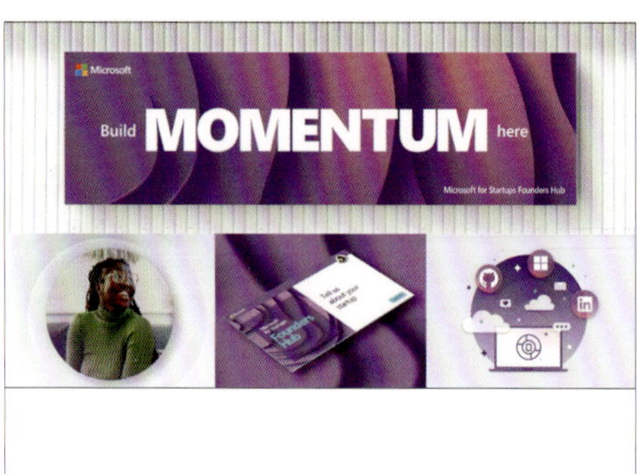

TGD

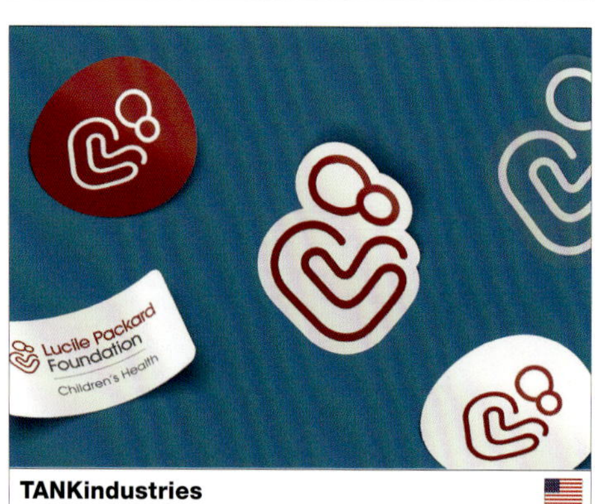

TANKindustries

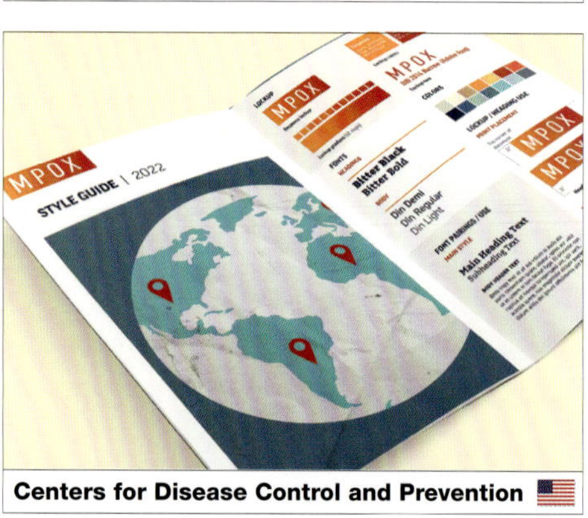

Centers for Disease Control and Prevention

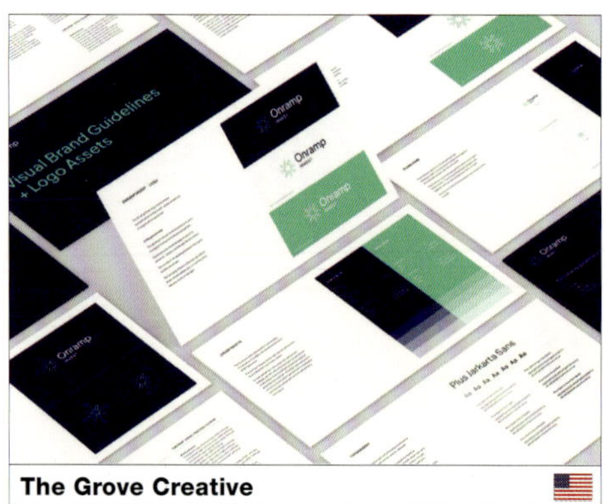

The Grove Creative

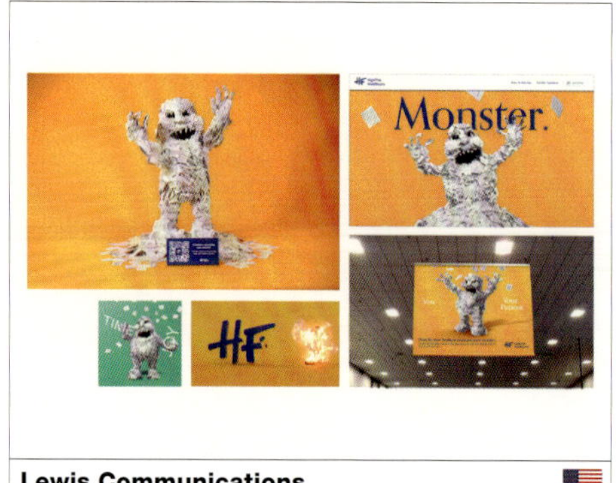

Lewis Communications

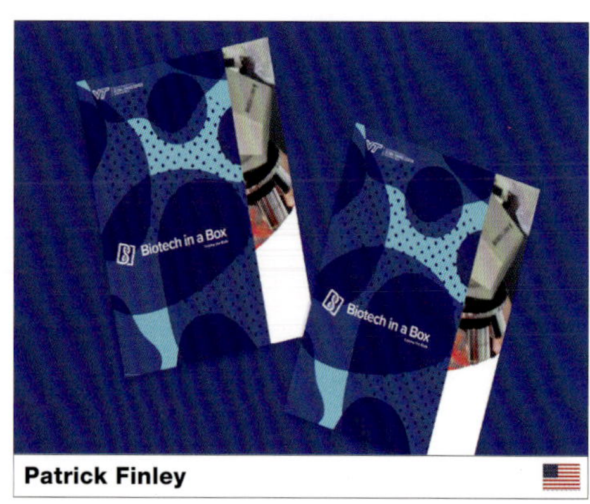

Patrick Finley

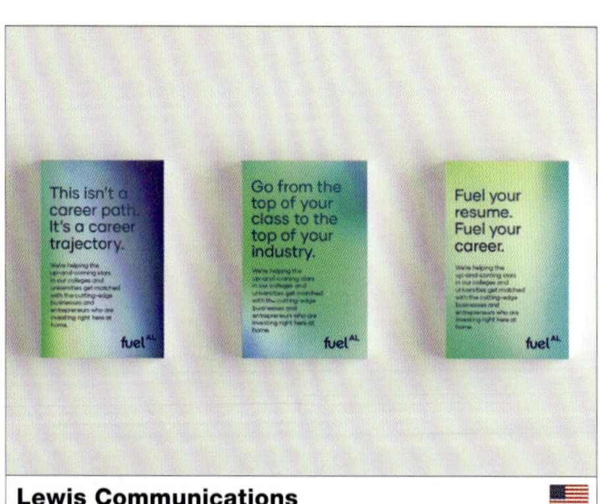

Lewis Communications

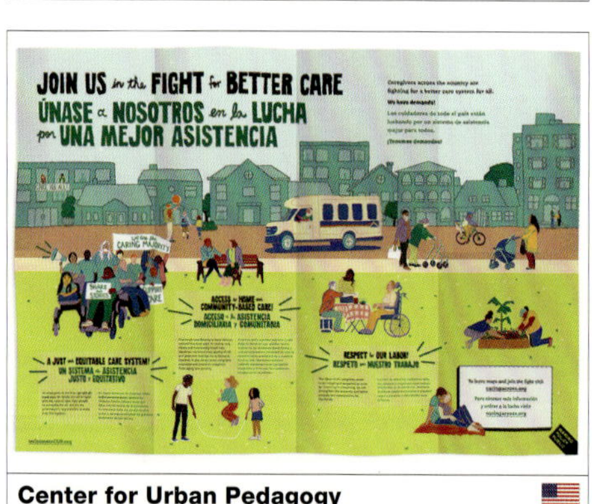

Center for Urban Pedagogy

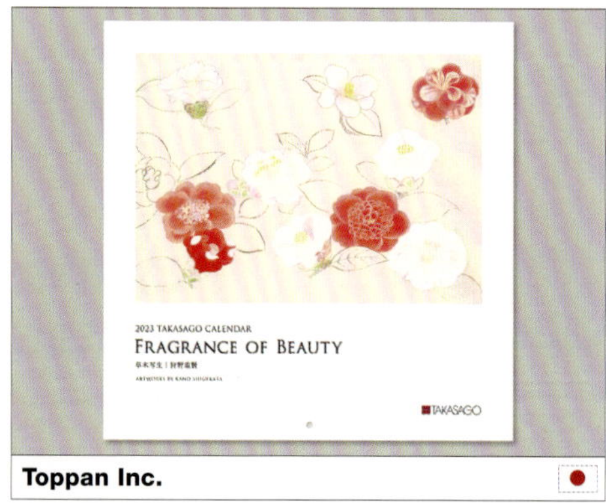

Toppan Inc.

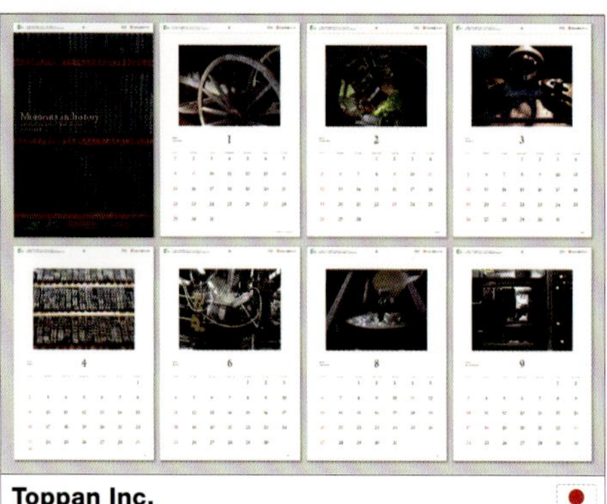

Toppan Inc.

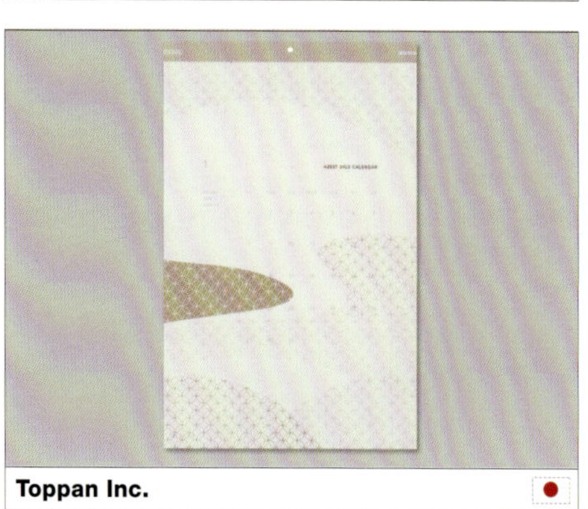

Toppan Inc.

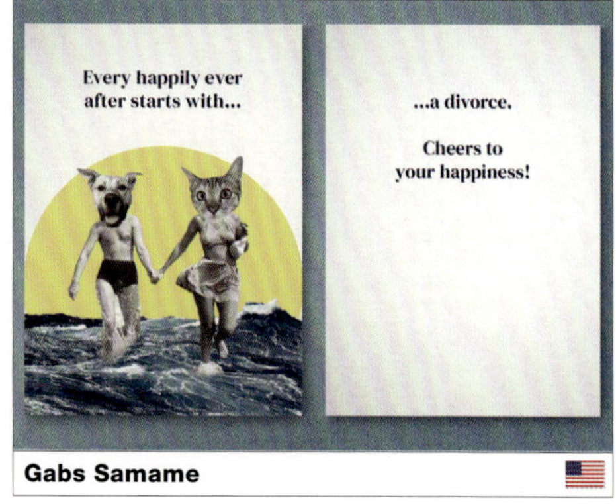

Gabs Samame

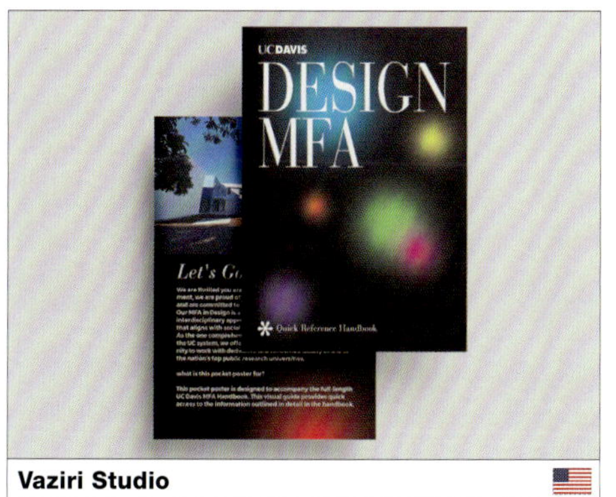

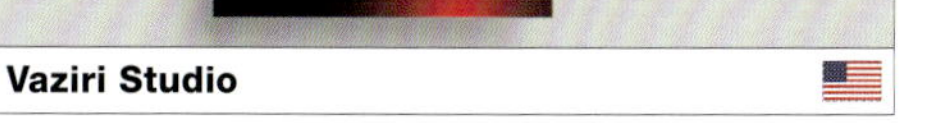

Vaziri Studio

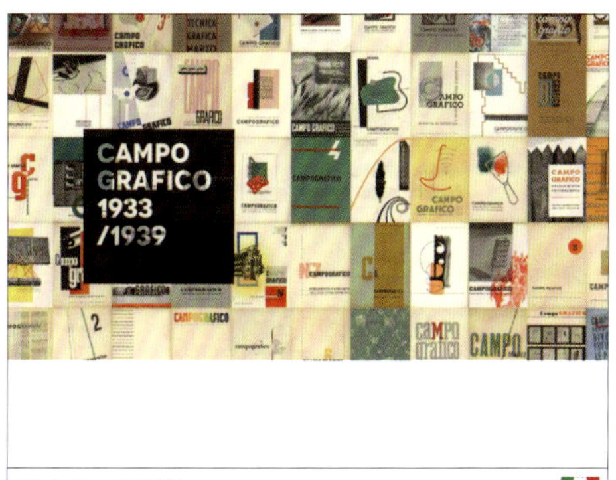

Univisual SRL

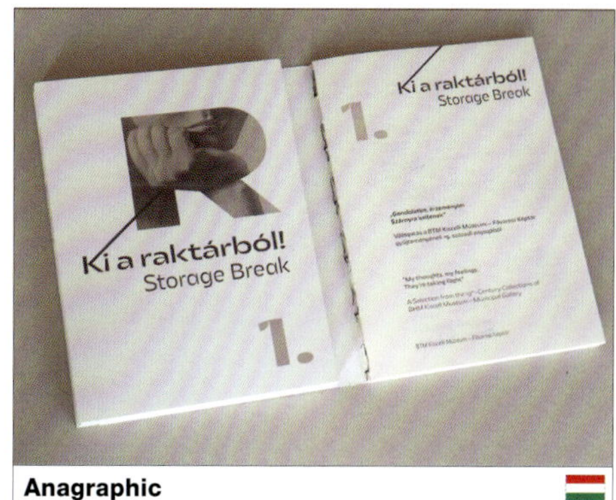

Anagraphic

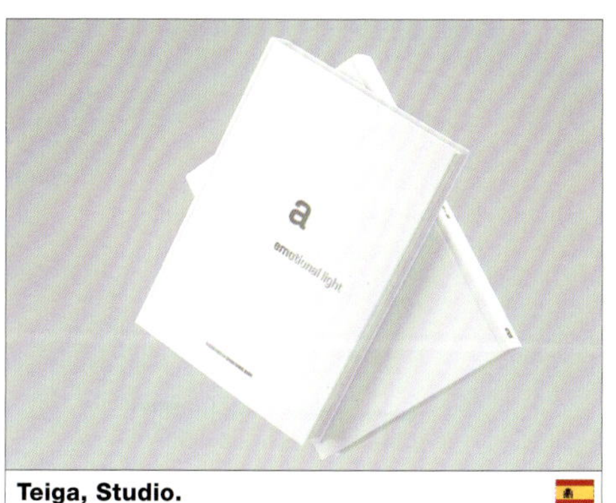

Teiga, Studio.

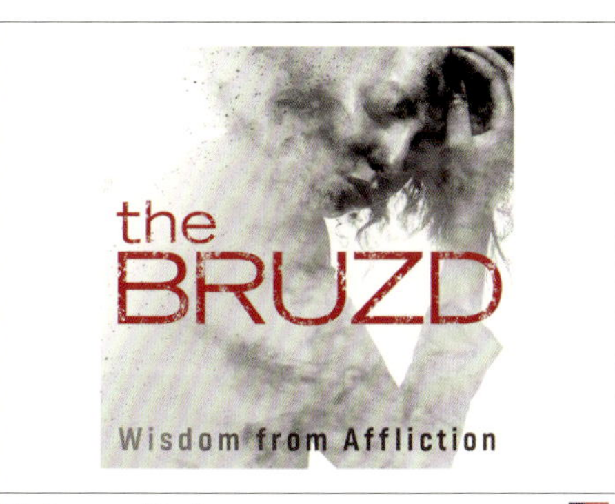

Tielemans Design

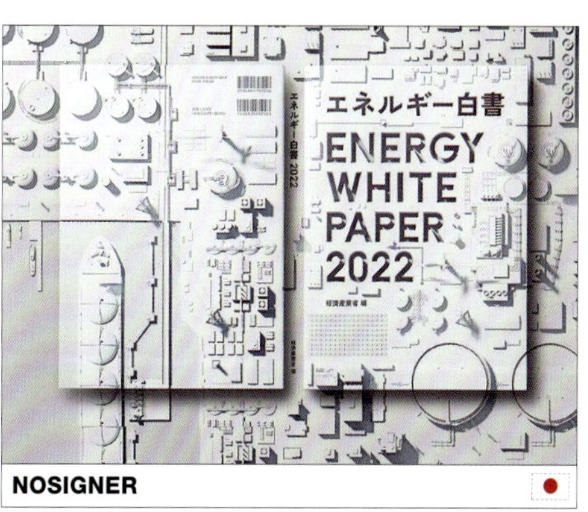

NOSIGNER

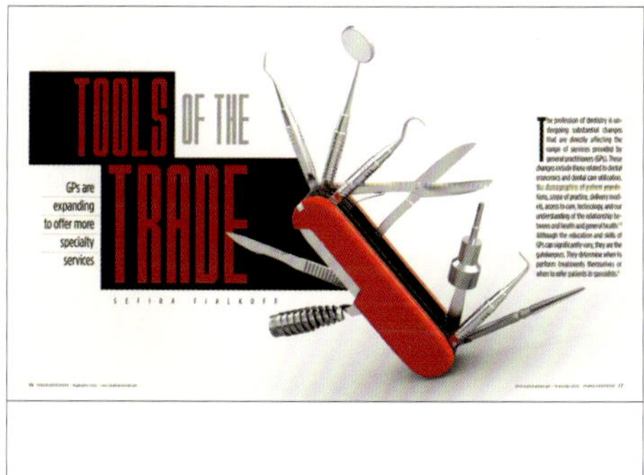

BroadcastMed

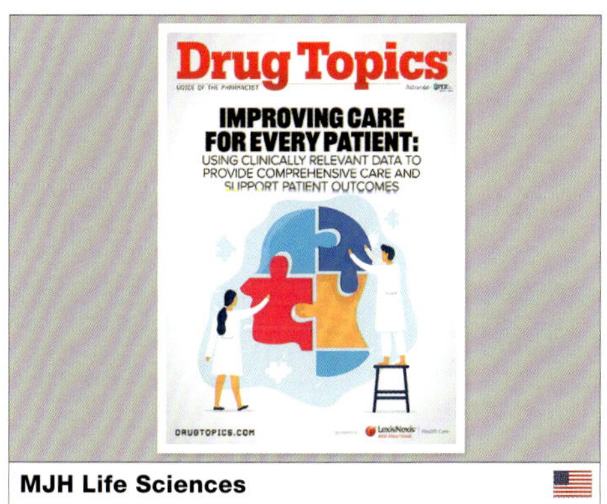

MJH Life Sciences

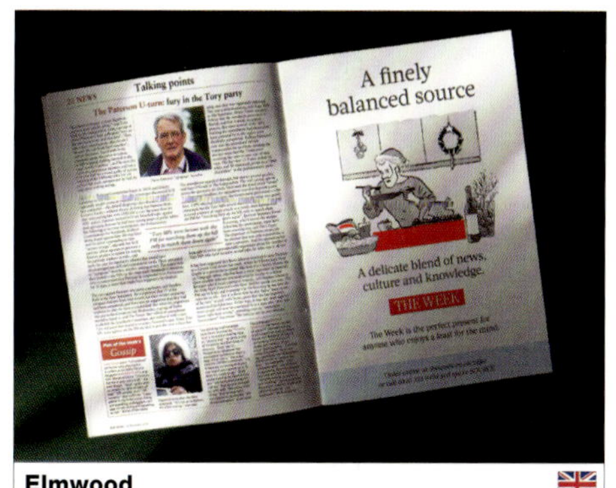

Elmwood

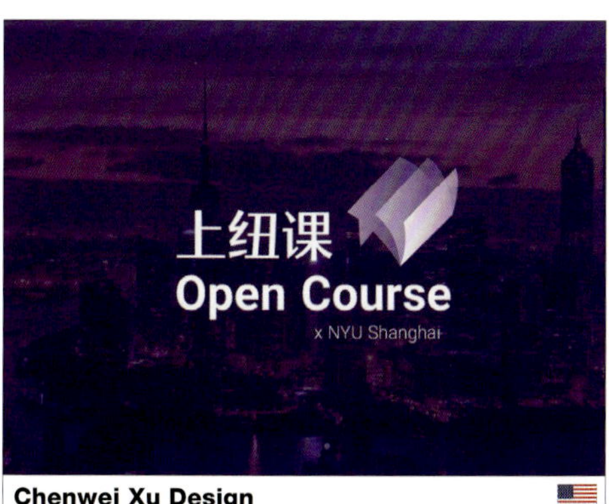

Chenwei Xu Design

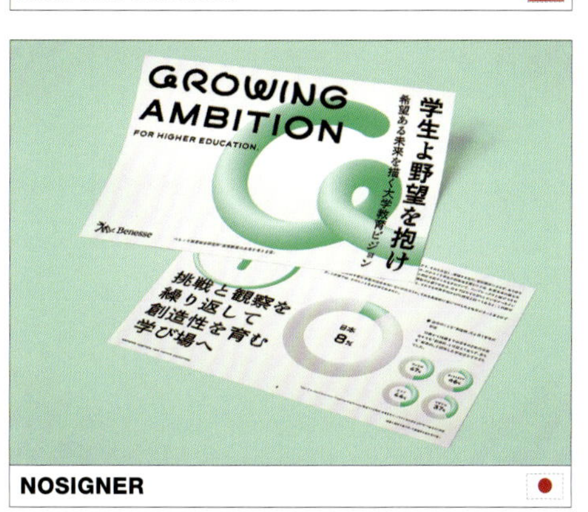

NOSIGNER

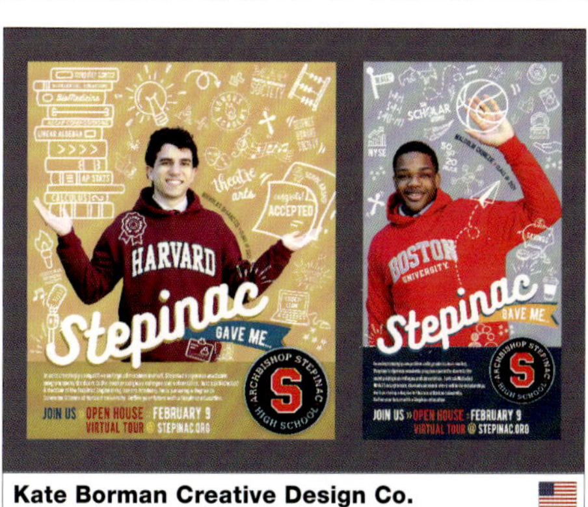

Kate Borman Creative Design Co.

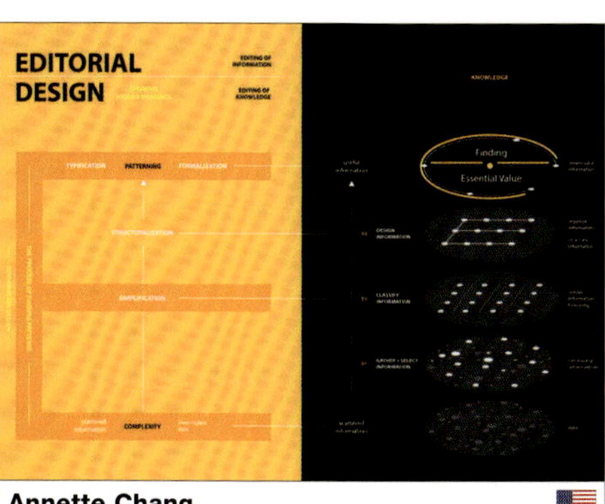

Annette Chang

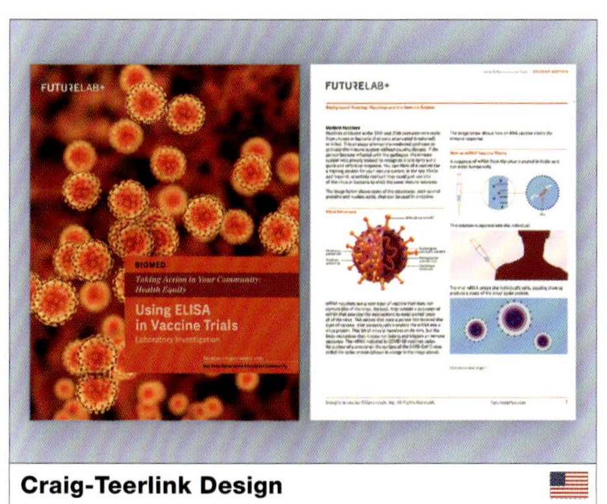

Craig-Teerlink Design

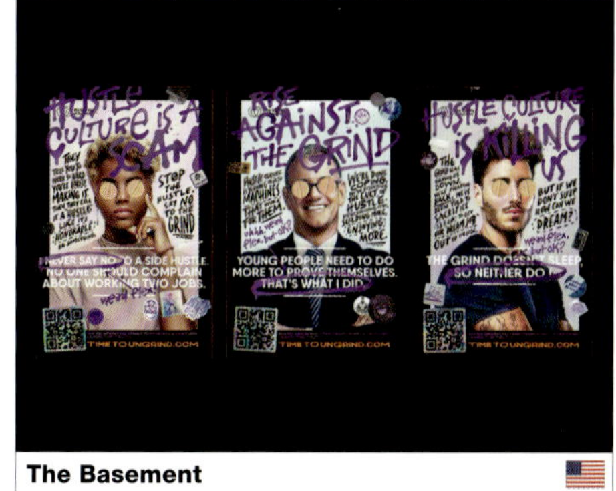

The Basement

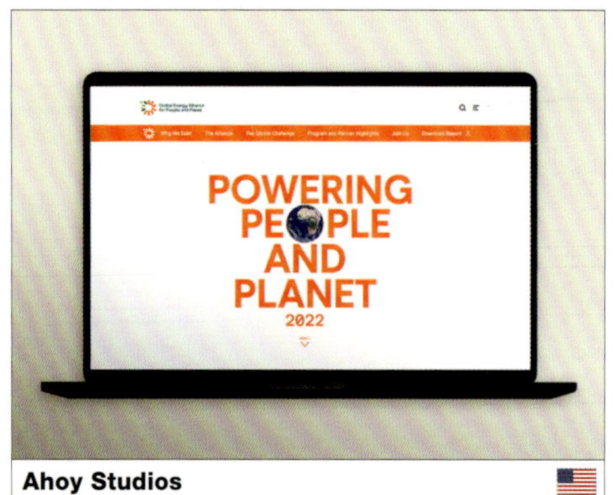

Ahoy Studios

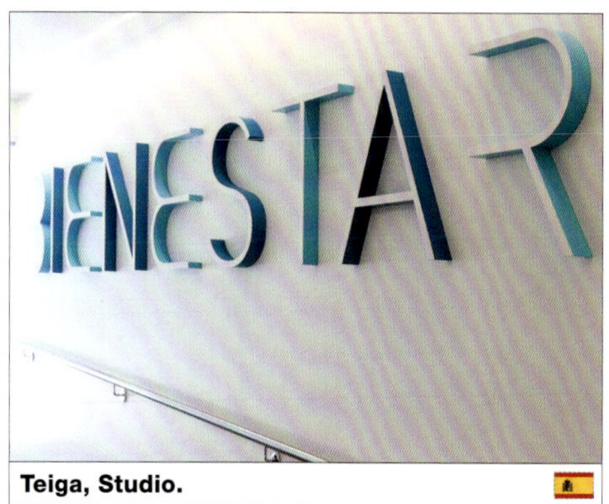

Teiga, Studio.

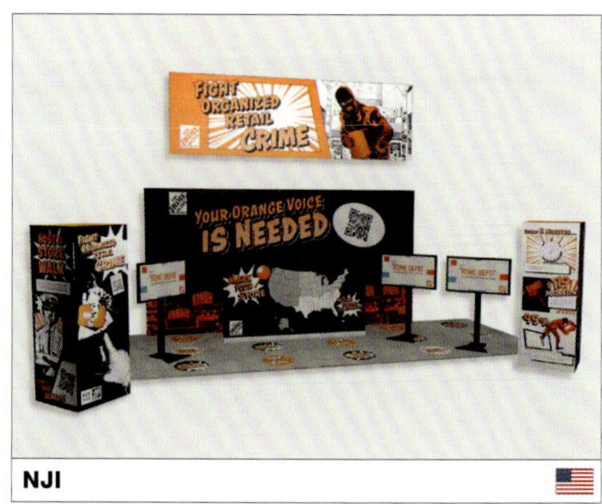

NJI

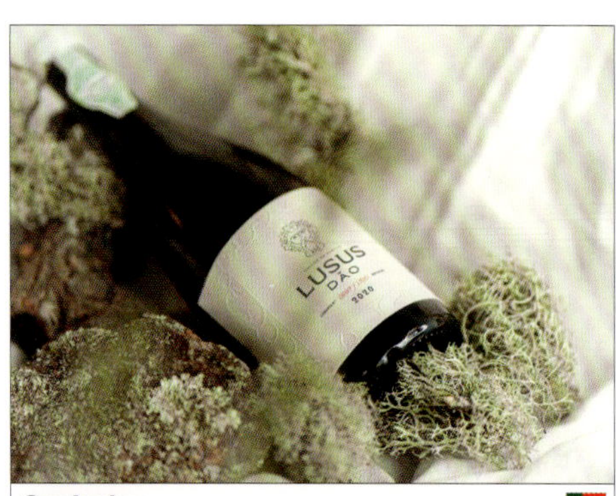

Omdesign

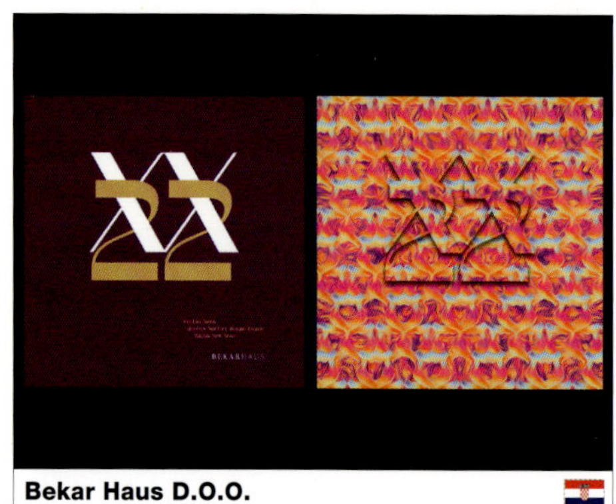

Bekar Haus D.O.O.

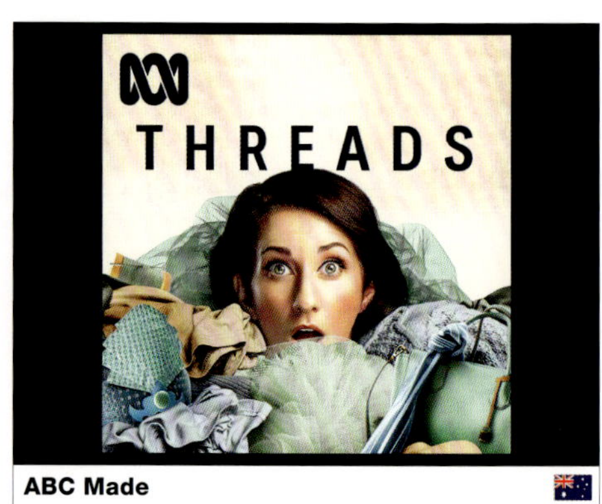

ABC Made

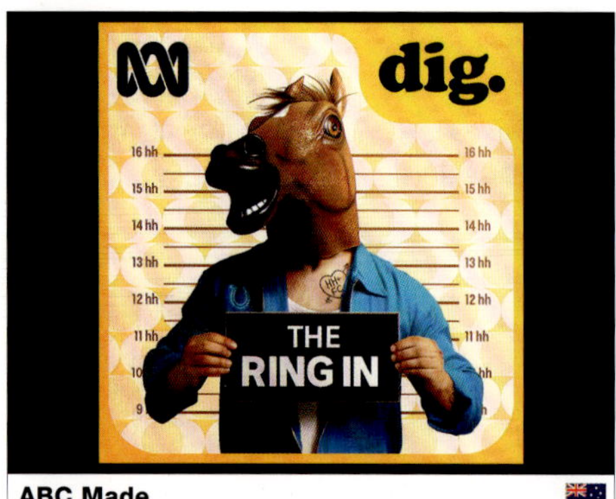

ABC Made

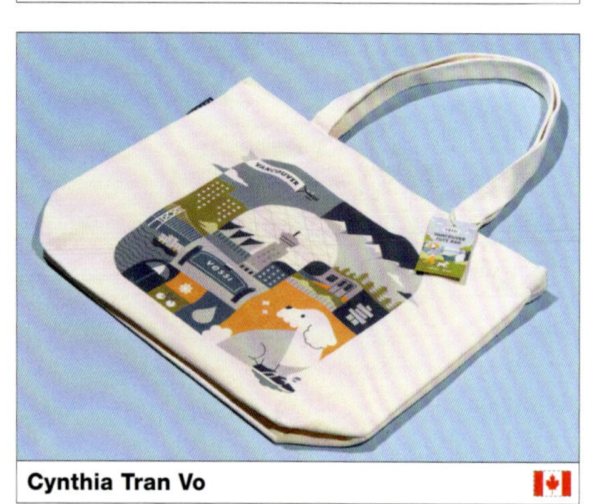

Cynthia Tran Vo

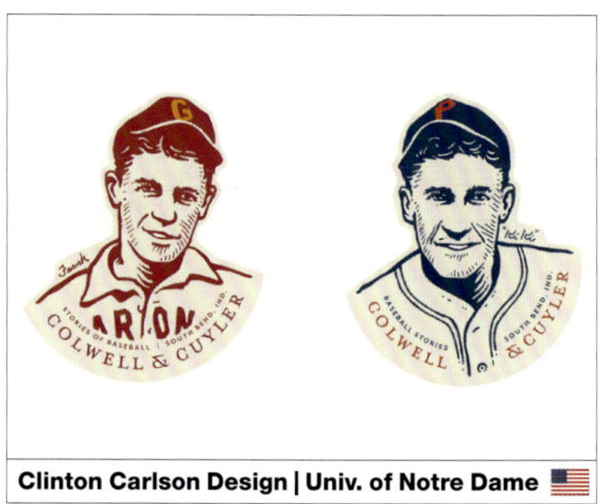

Clinton Carlson Design | Univ. of Notre Dame

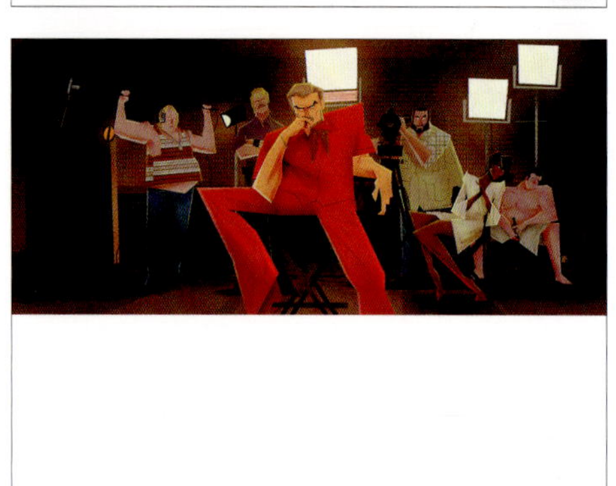

HandMade Monsters

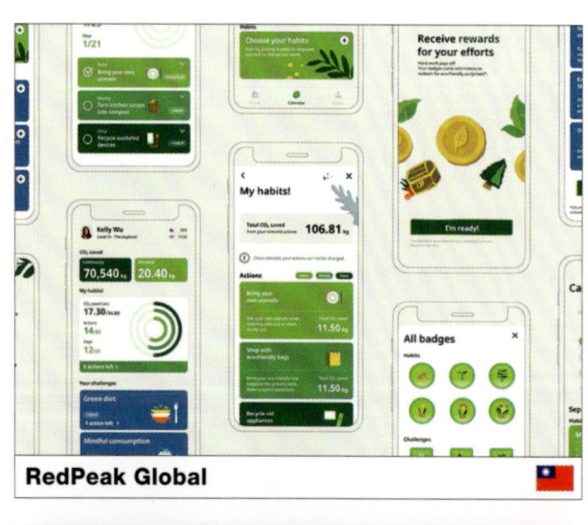

RedPeak Global

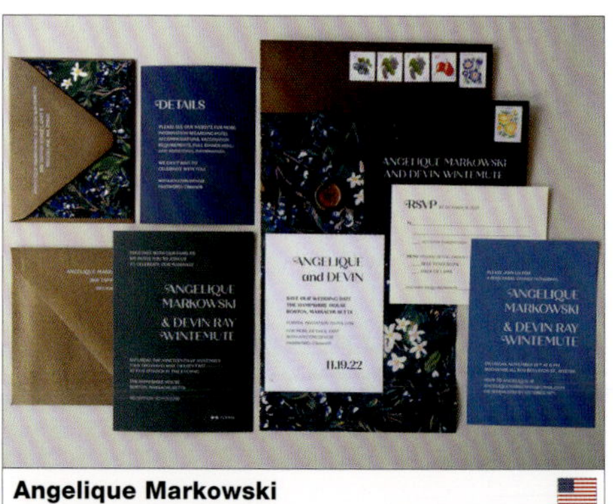

Angelique Markowski

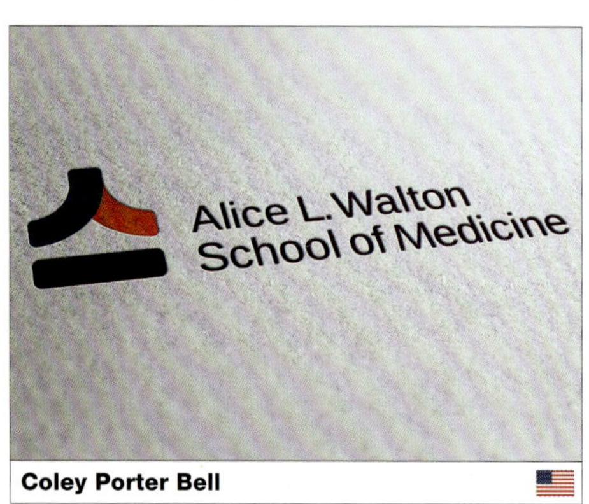

Coley Porter Bell

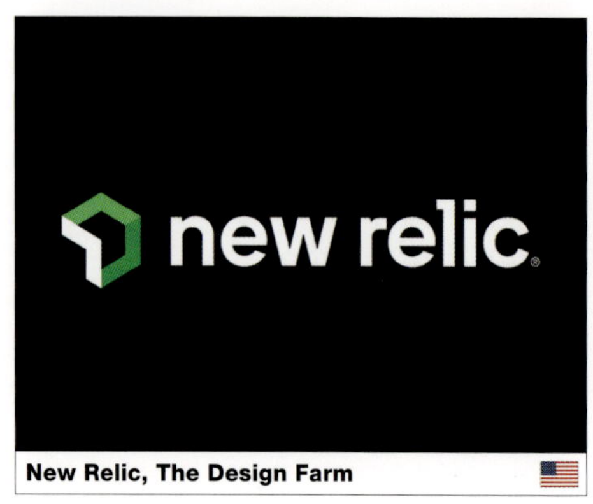

New Relic, The Design Farm

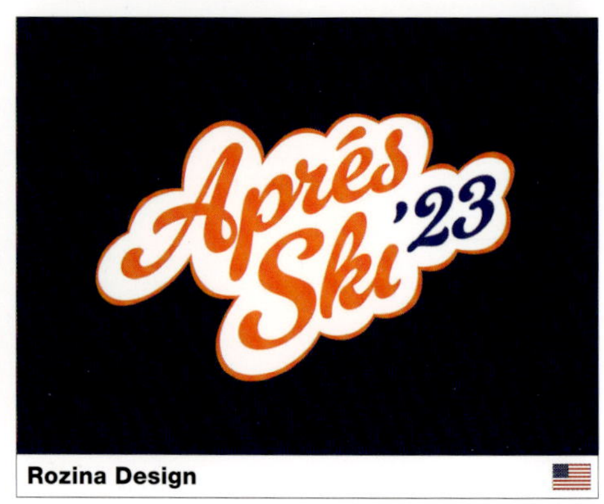

Rozina Design

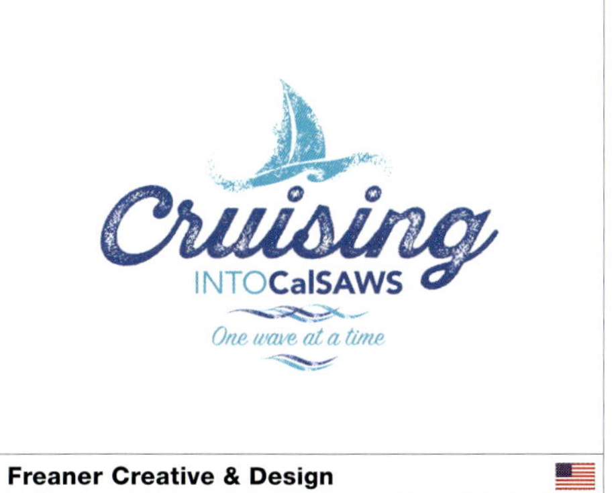

Freaner Creative & Design

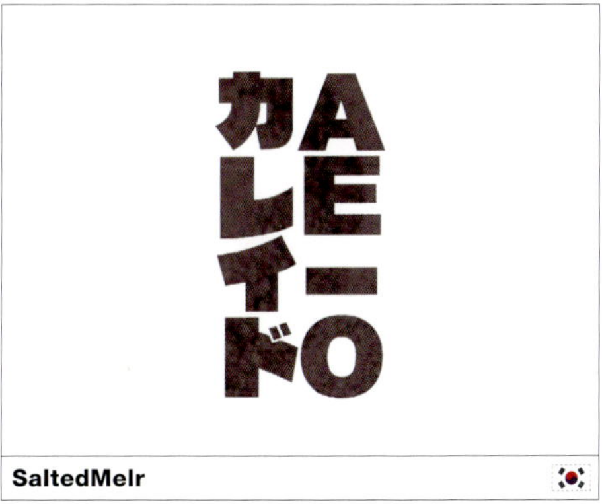

SaltedMelr

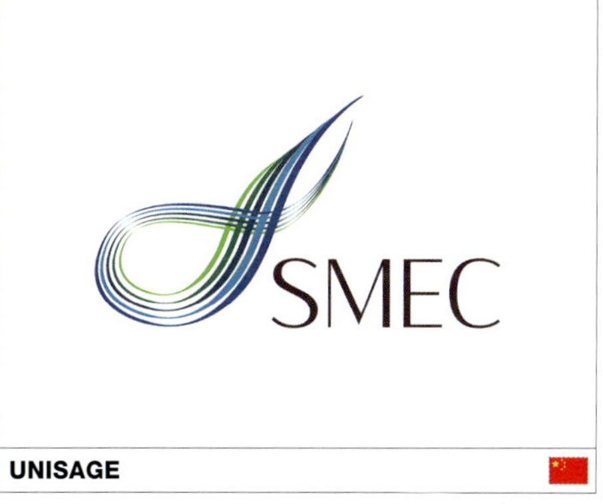

UNISAGE

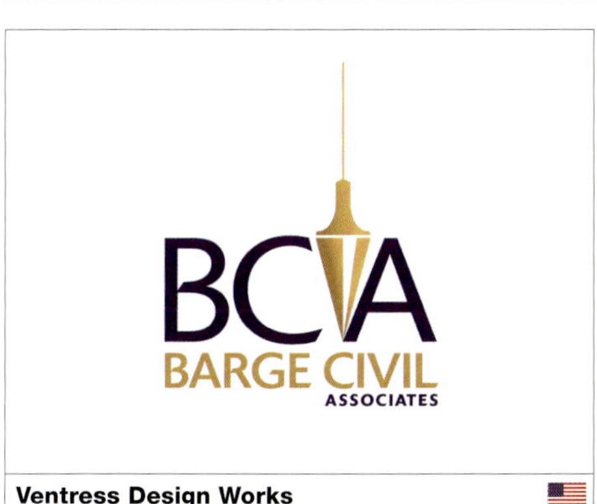

Ventress Design Works

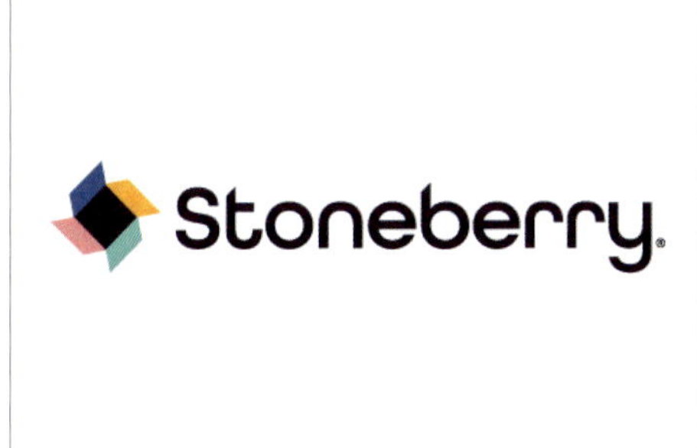

Preston Spire

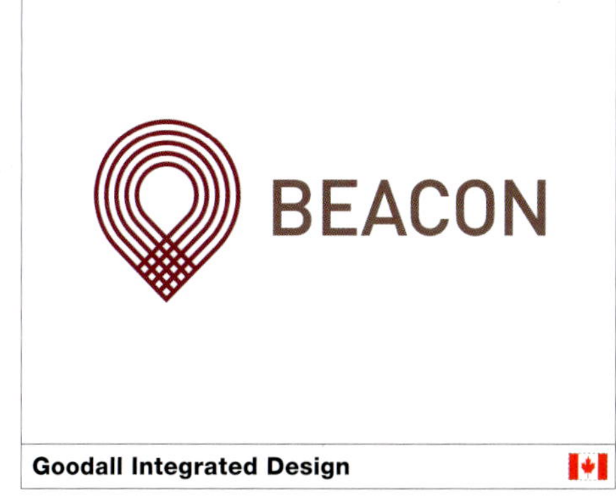

Goodall Integrated Design

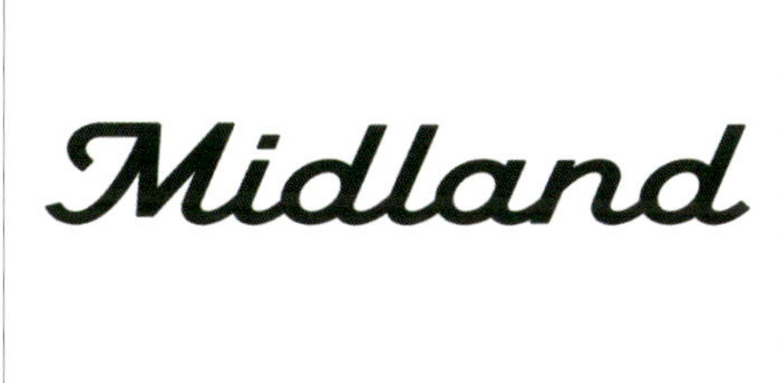

Full Punch

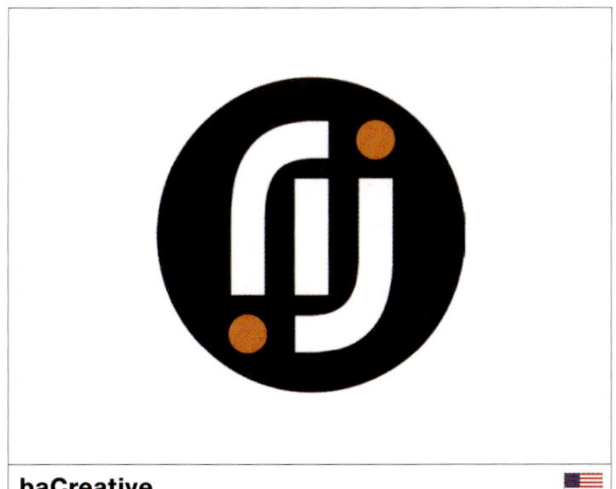

baCreative

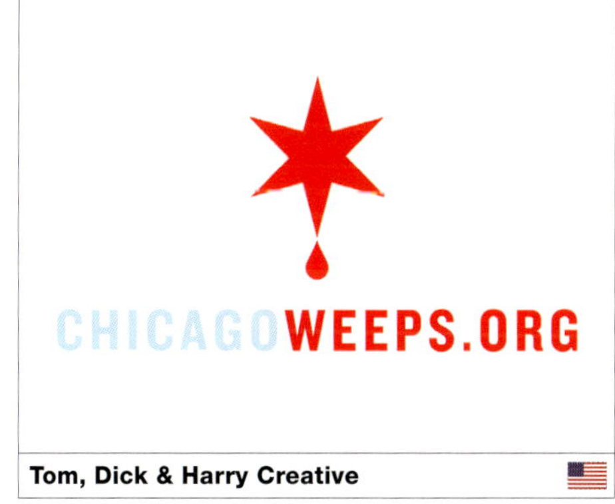

Tom, Dick & Harry Creative

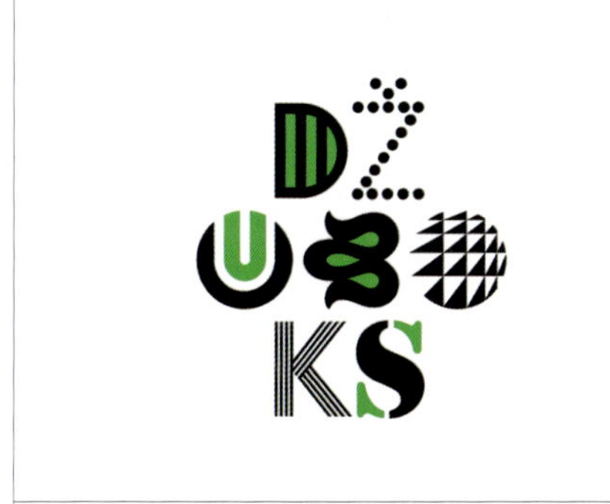

Radovan Jenko Atelier

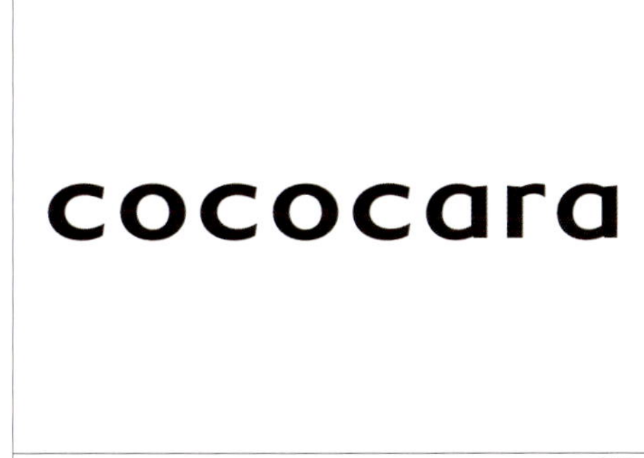

USADesign

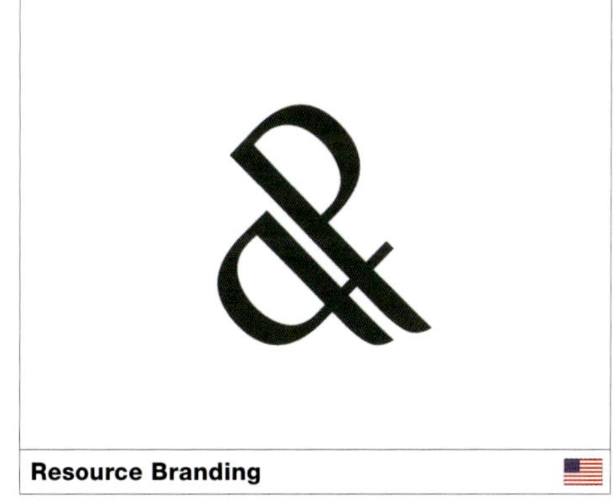

Resource Branding

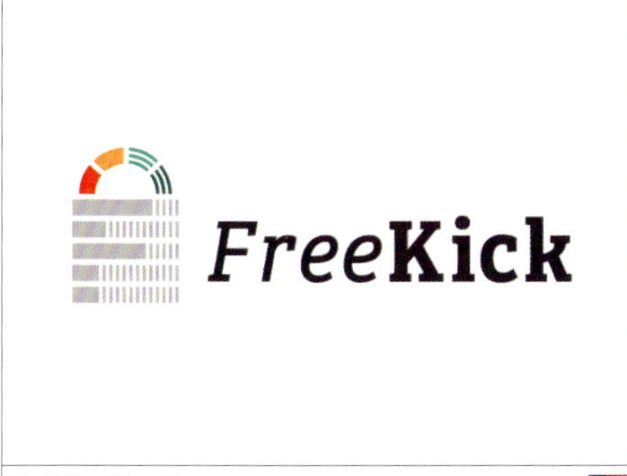

DeVito/Verdi

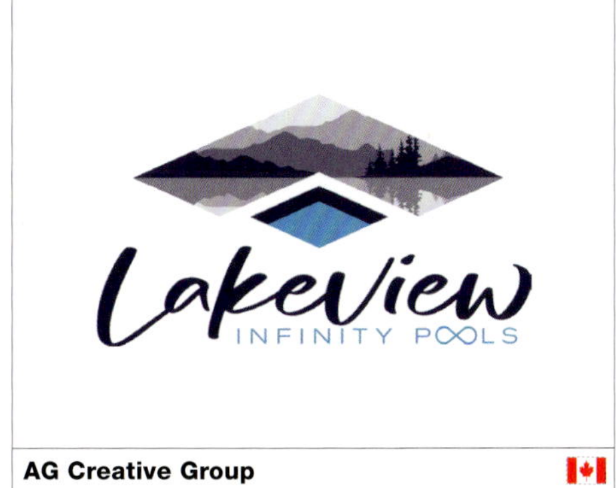

AG Creative Group

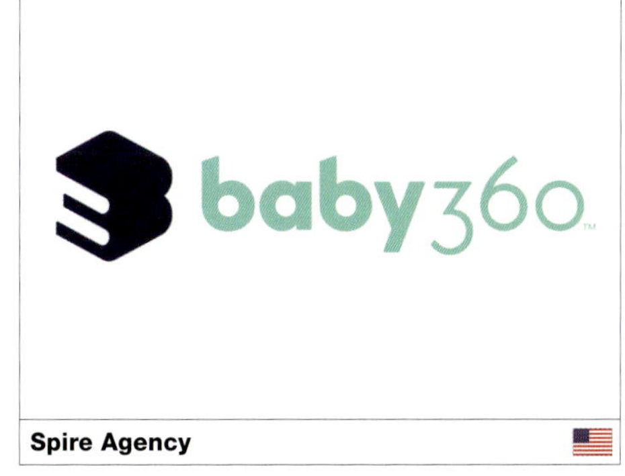

Spire Agency

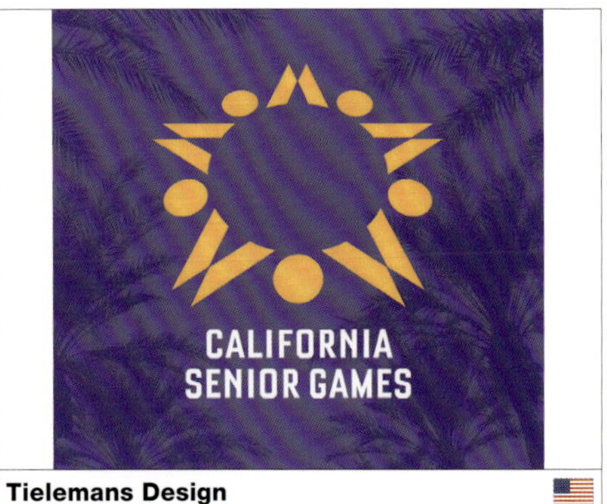

Tielemans Design

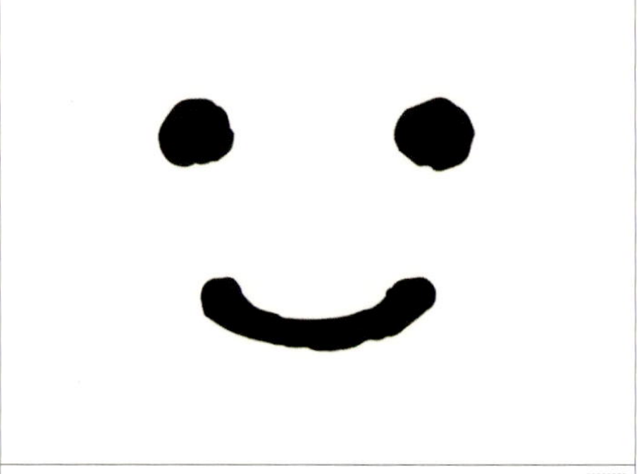

USADesign

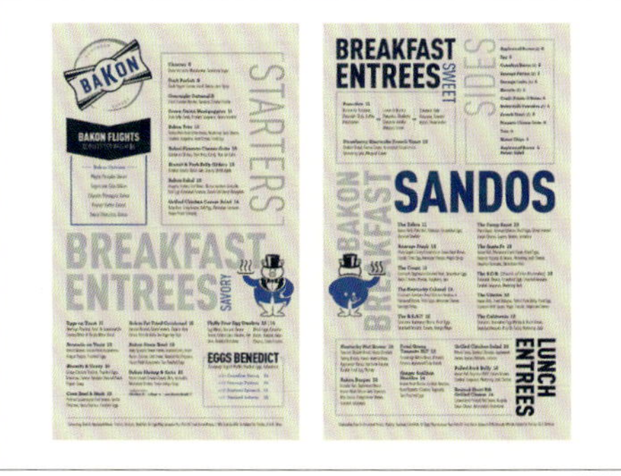

Nate Gulledge

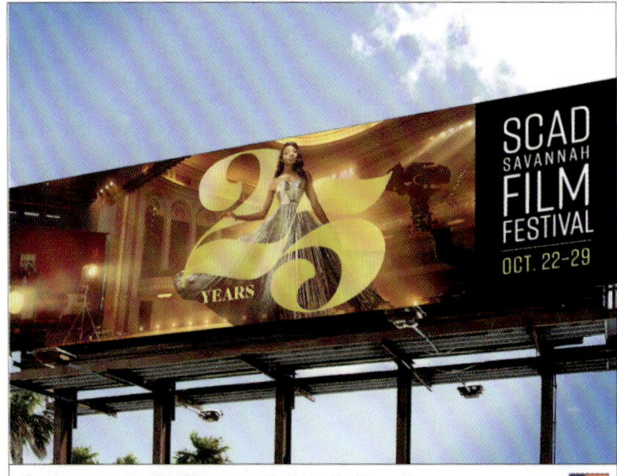

Savannah College of Art & Design

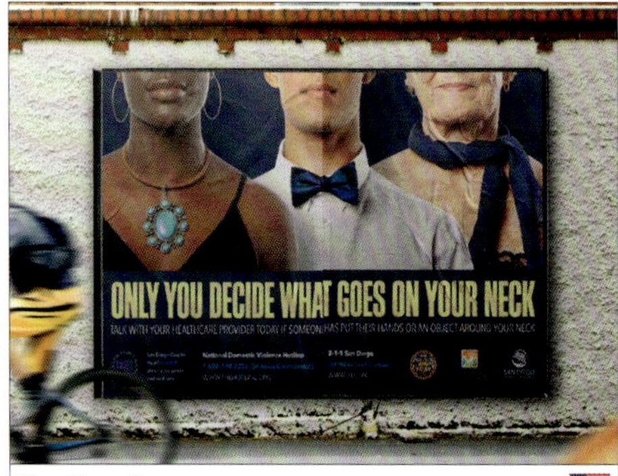

BexBrands

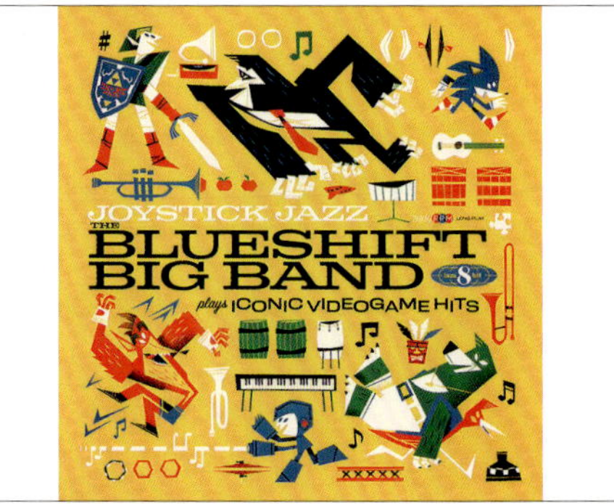

HandMade Monsters

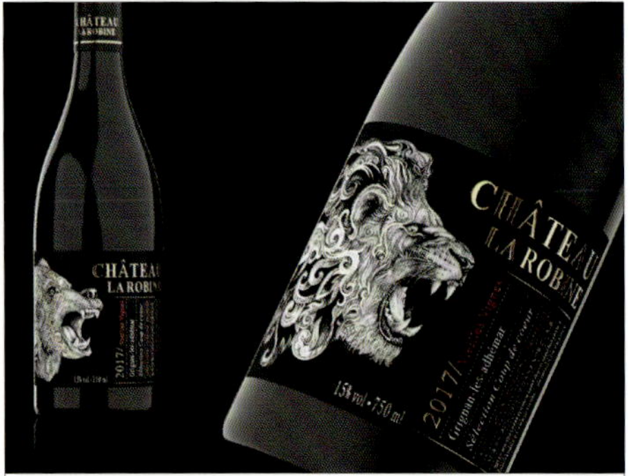

Roking Art Design

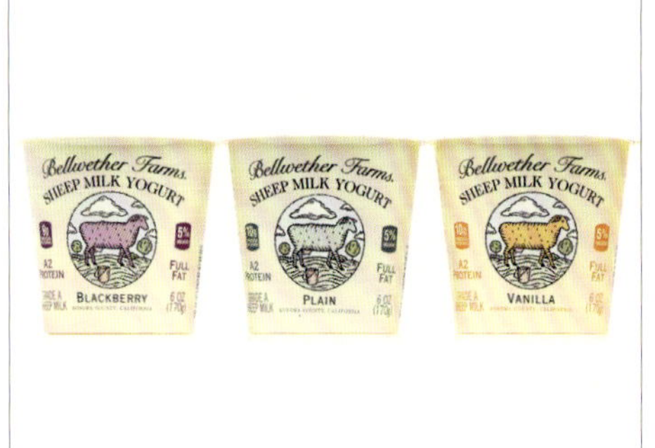

Mark Oliver, Inc.

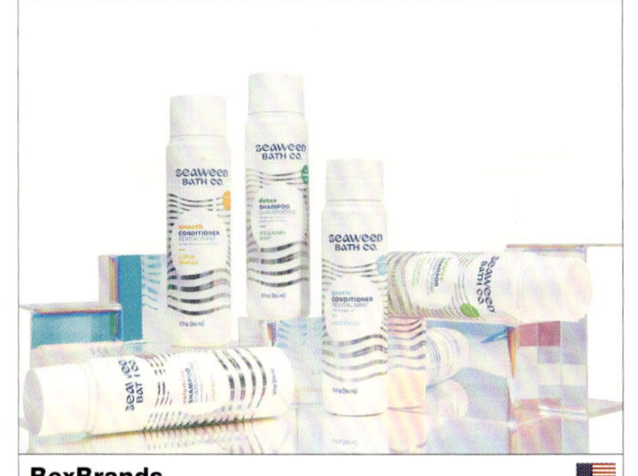

BexBrands

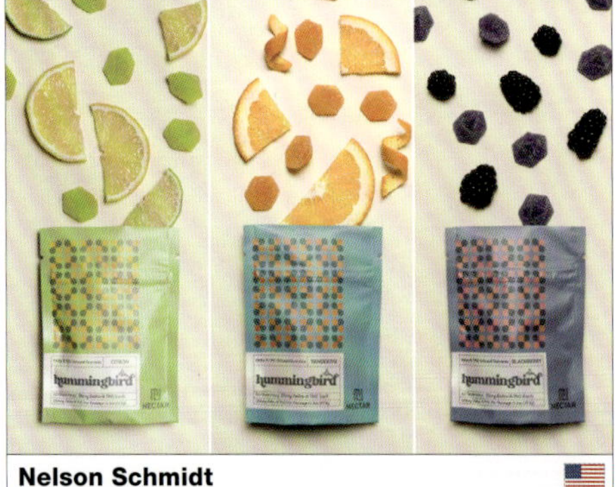

Nelson Schmidt

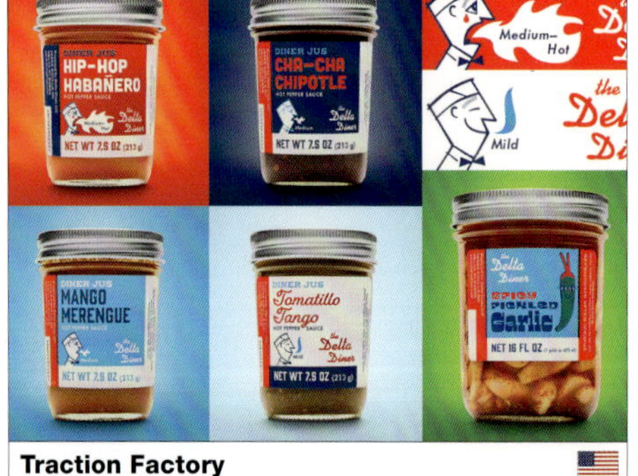

Traction Factory

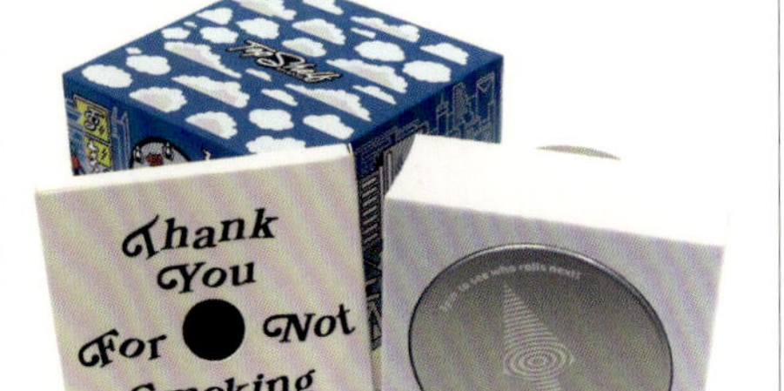

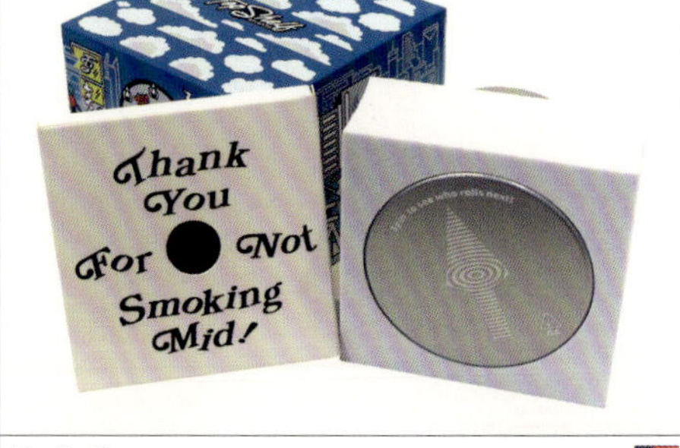

Broly Su

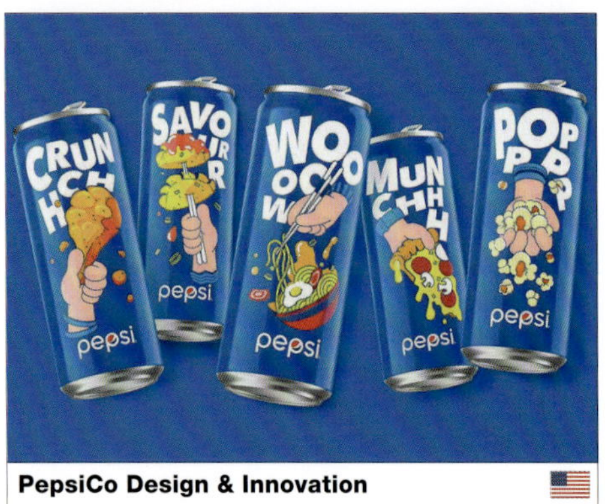

PepsiCo Design & Innovation

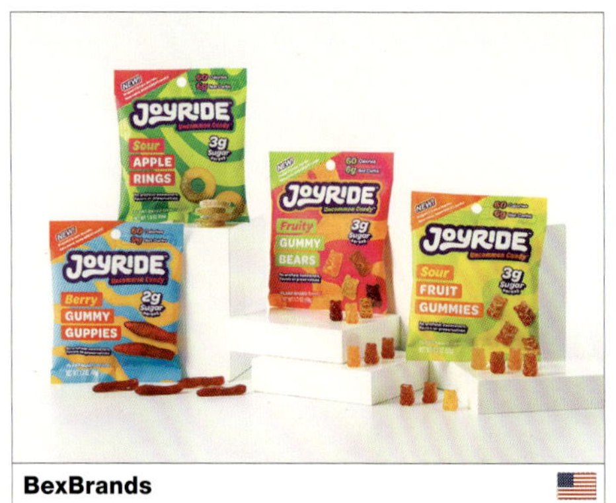

BexBrands

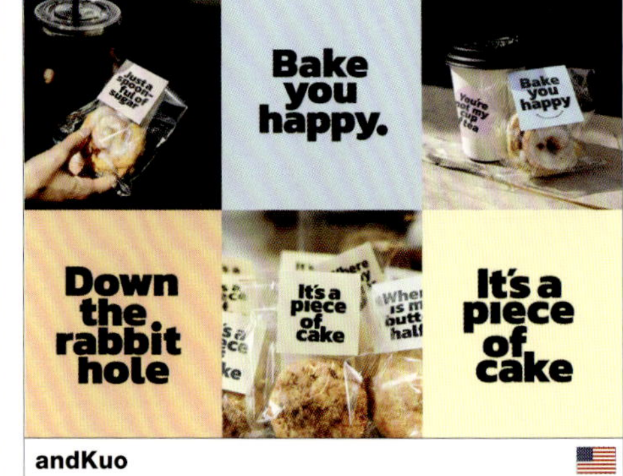

andKuo

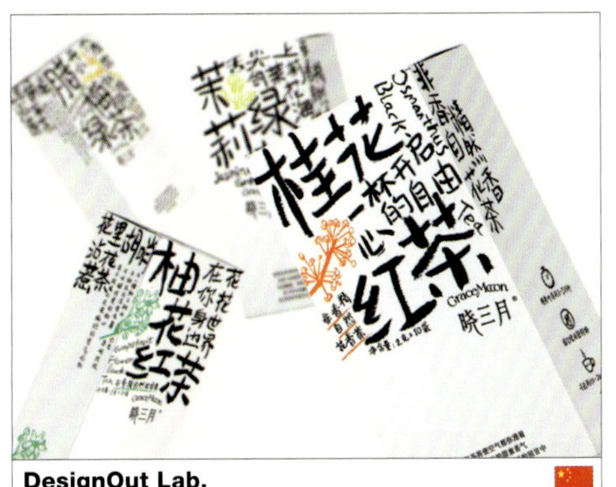

DesignOut Lab.

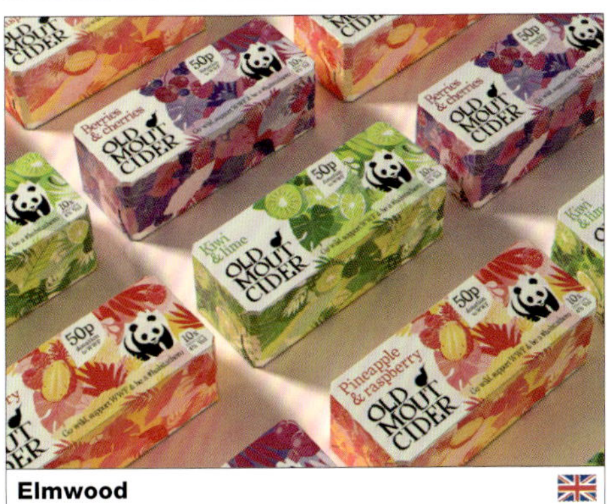

Elmwood

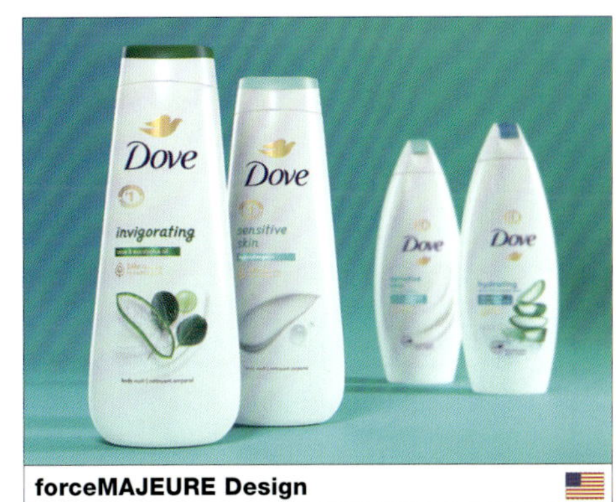

forceMAJEURE Design

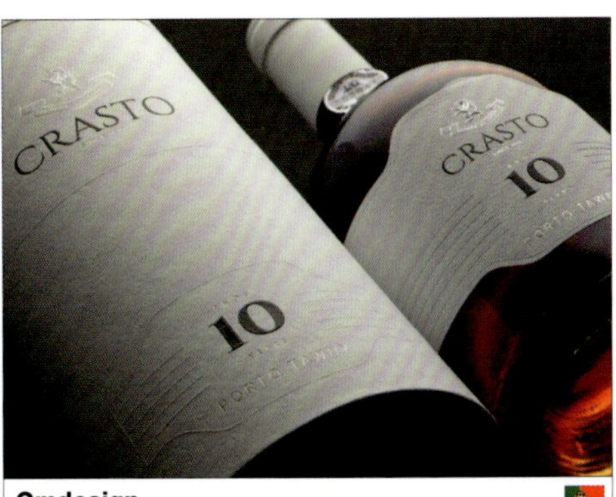

Omdesign

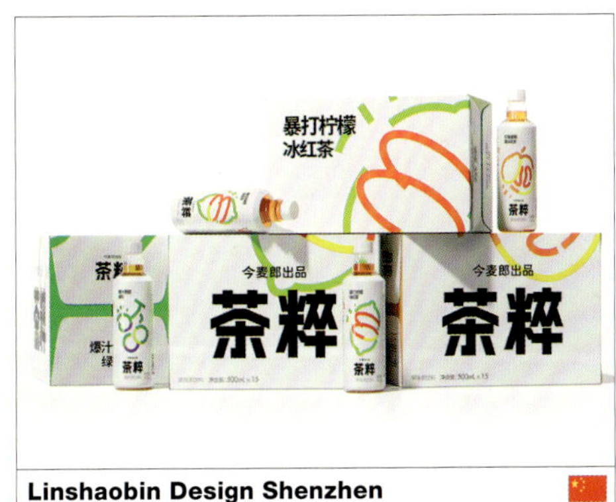

Linshaobin Design Shenzhen

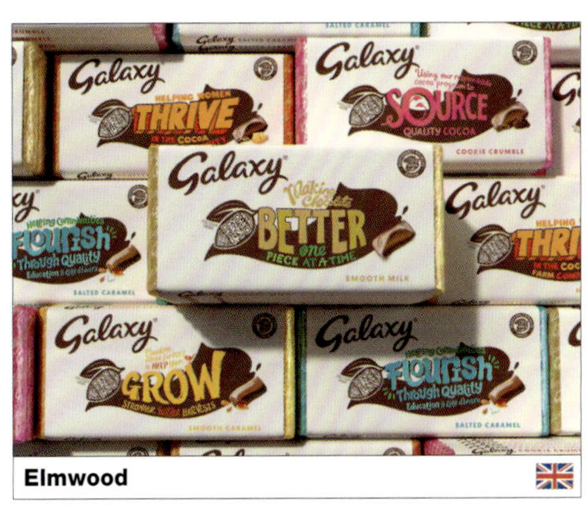

Elmwood

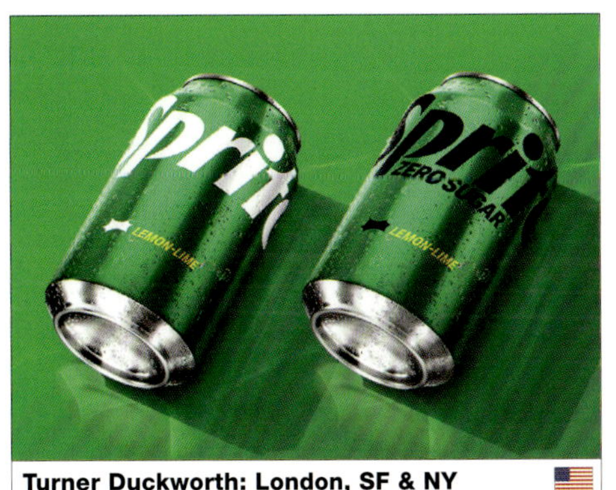

Turner Duckworth: London, SF & NY

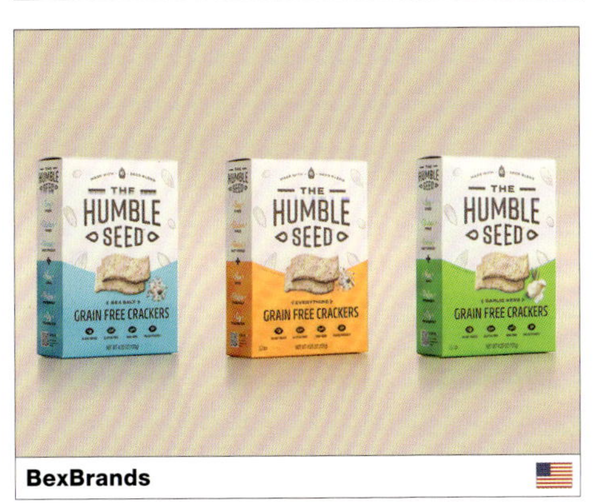

BexBrands

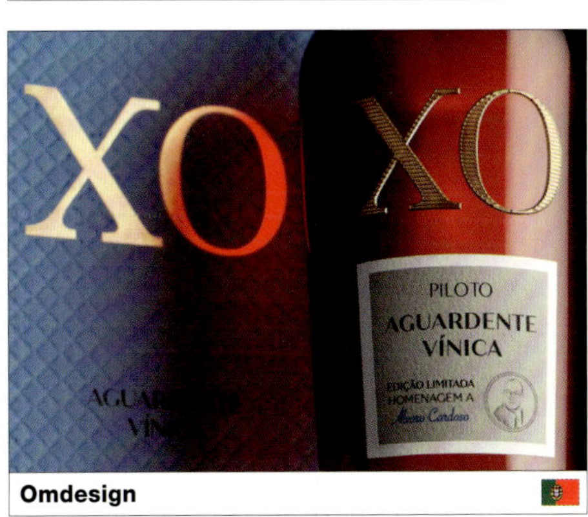

Omdesign

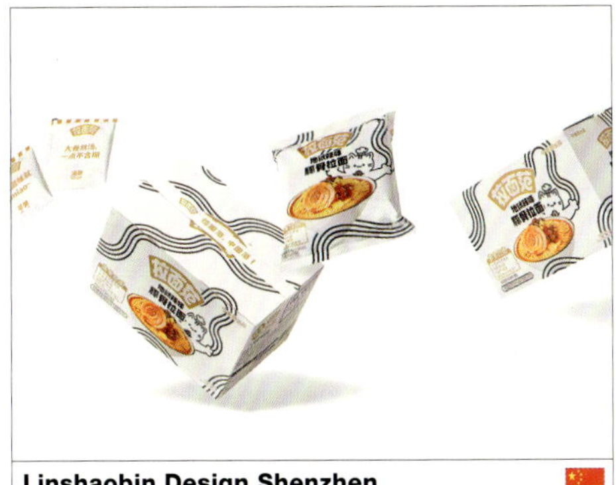

Linshaobin Design Shenzhen

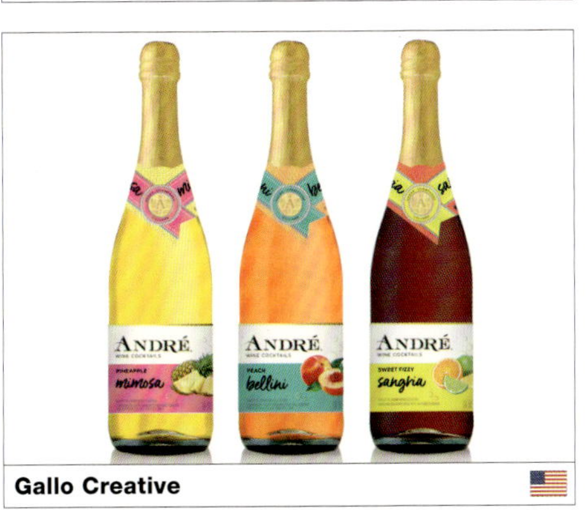

Gallo Creative

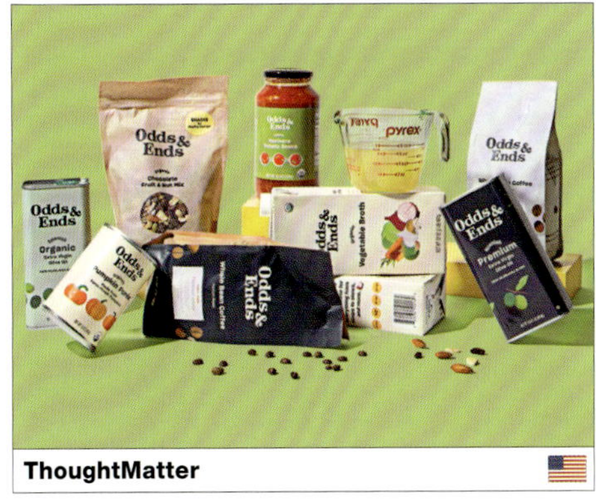

ThoughtMatter

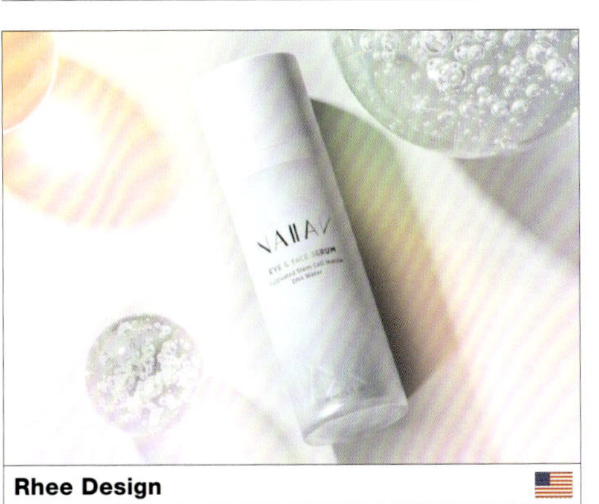

Rhee Design

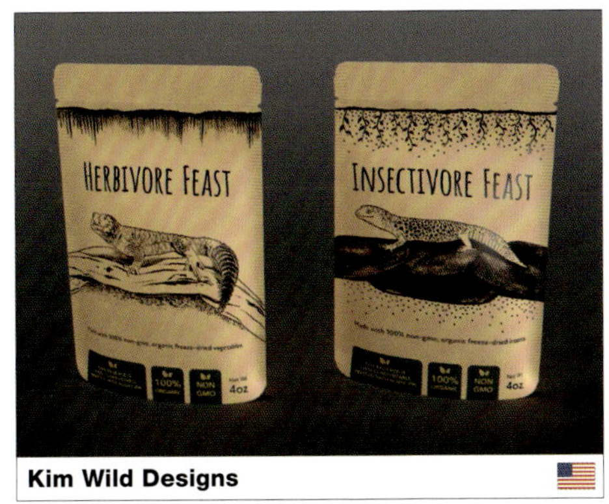

Kim Wild Designs

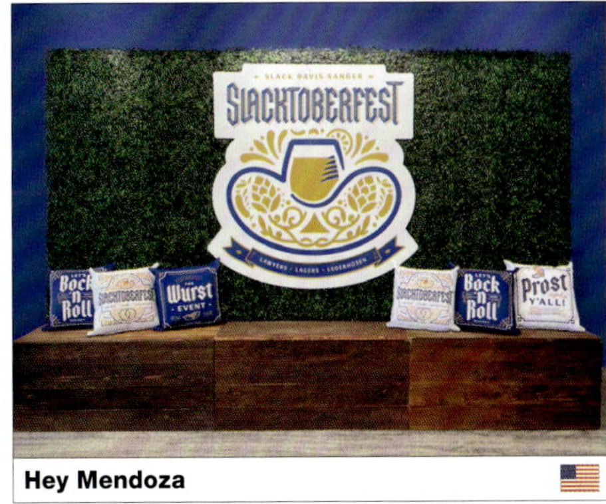

Hey Mendoza

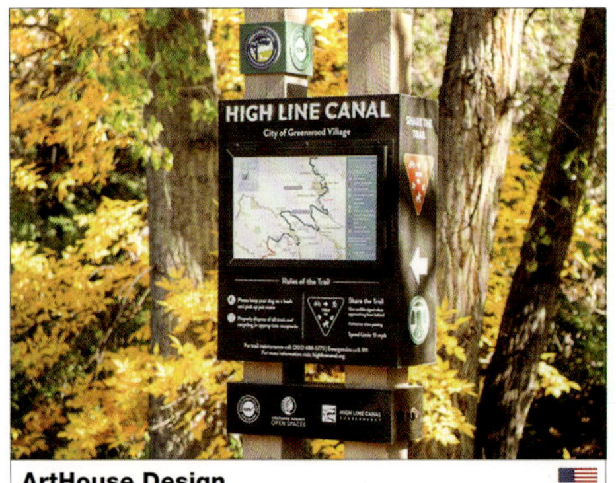

ArtHouse Design

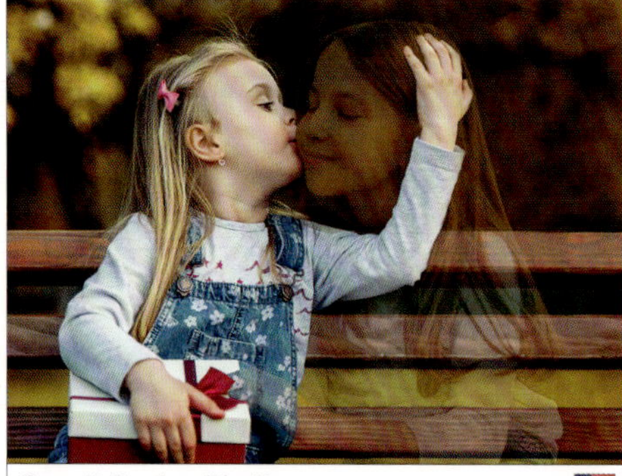
Carmit Design Studio

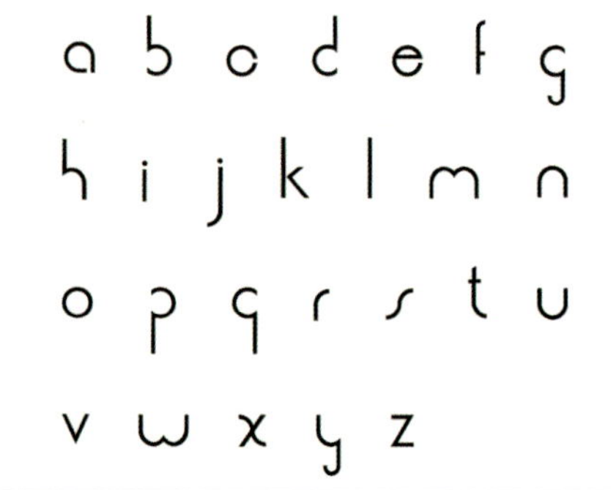

Freaner Creative & Design

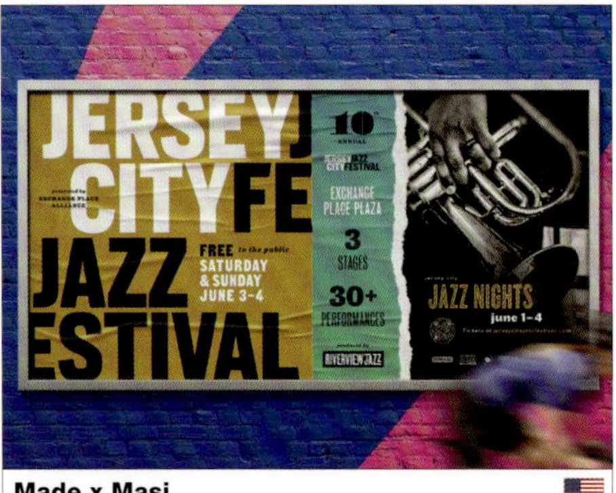

Made x Masi

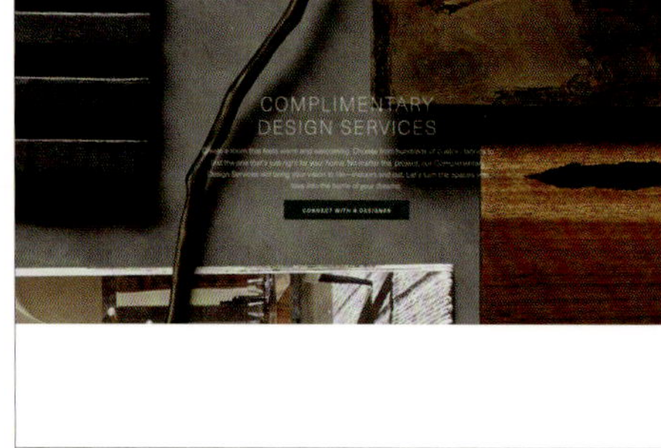

Tomorrow Agency

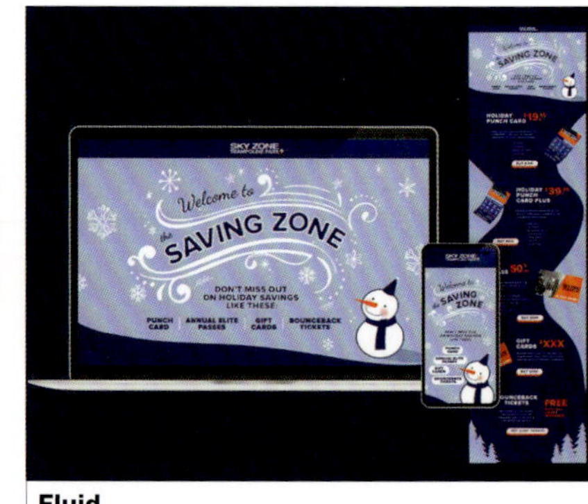

Fluid

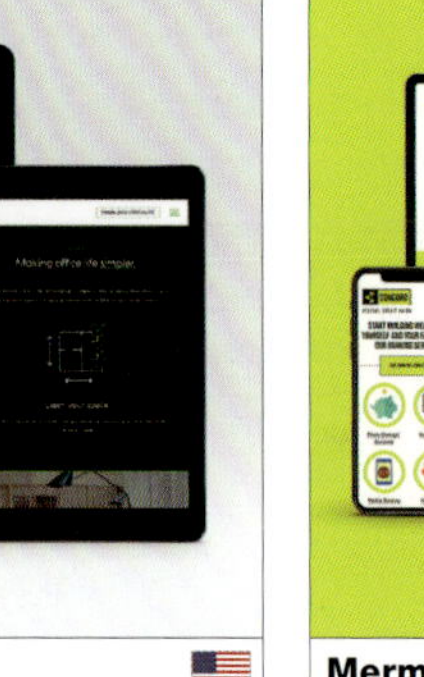
Resource Branding

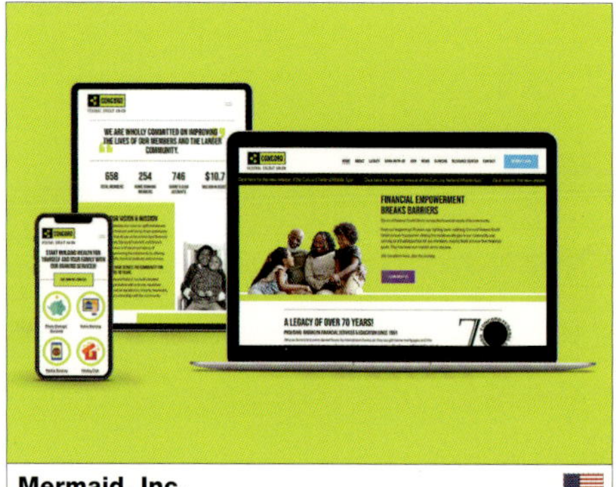

Mermaid, Inc.

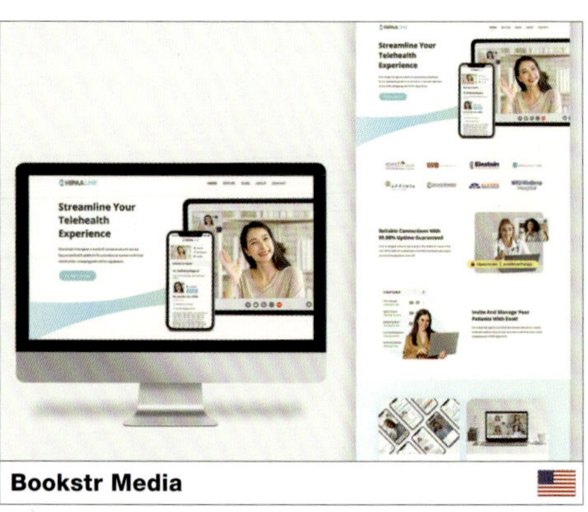

Bookstr Media

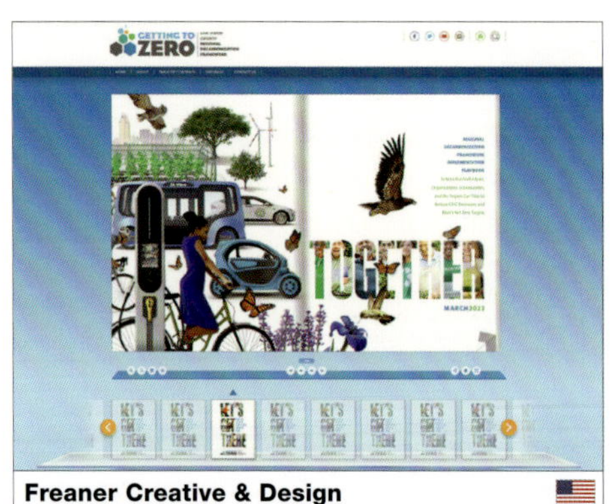

Freaner Creative & Design

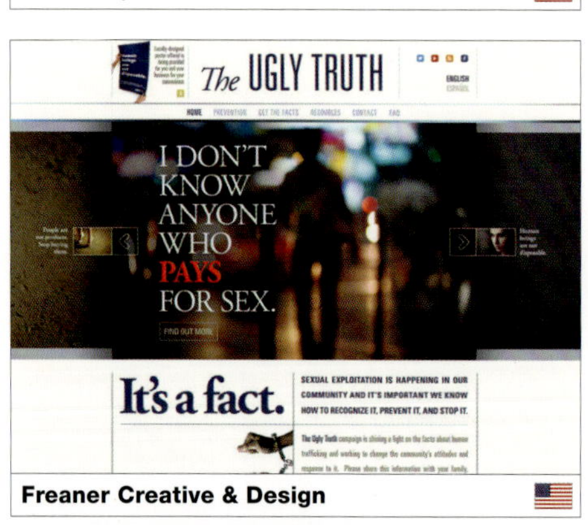

Freaner Creative & Design

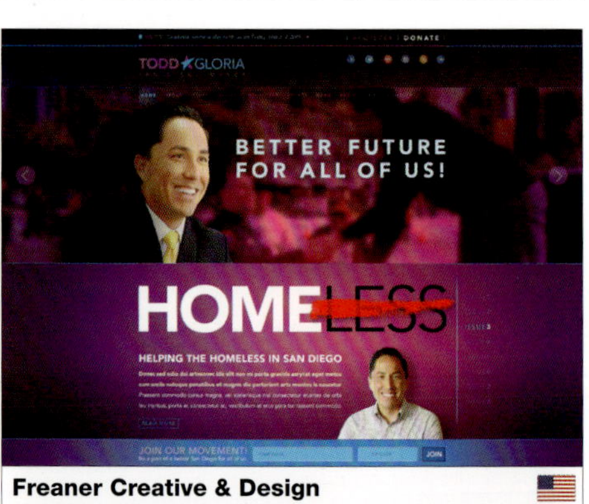

Freaner Creative & Design

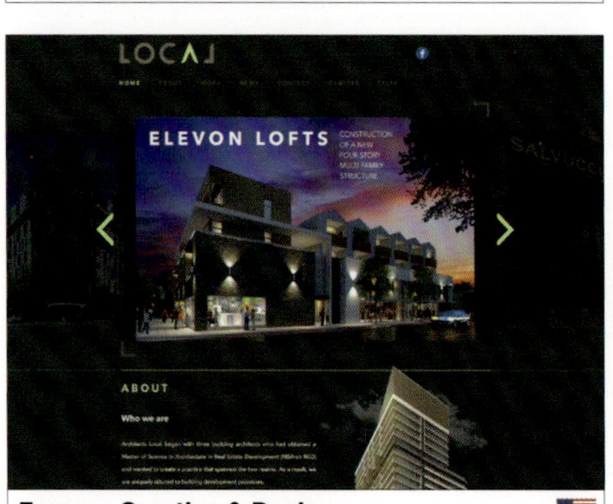

Freaner Creative & Design

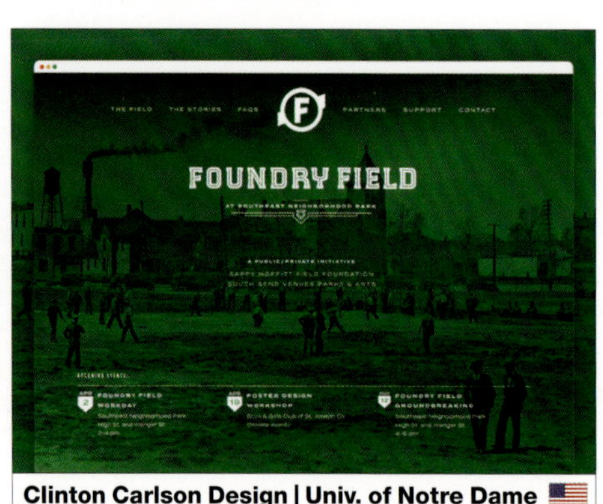

Clinton Carlson Design | Univ. of Notre Dame

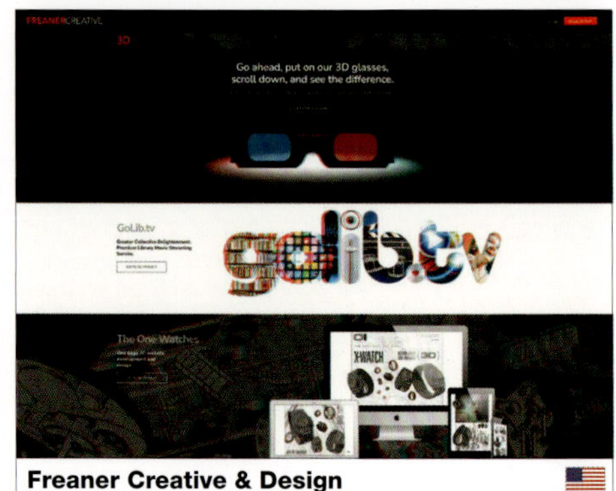

Freaner Creative & Design

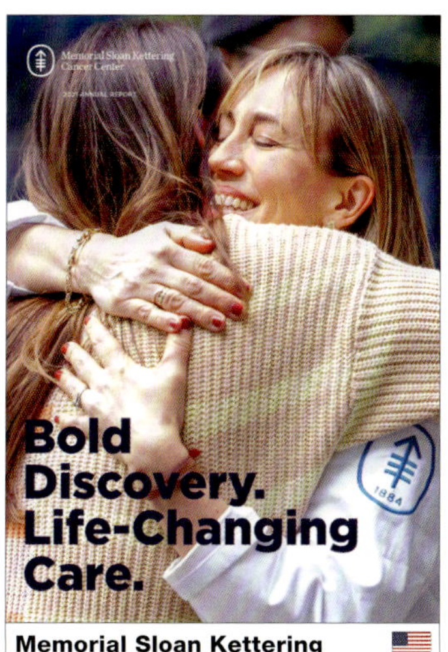

Memorial Sloan Kettering

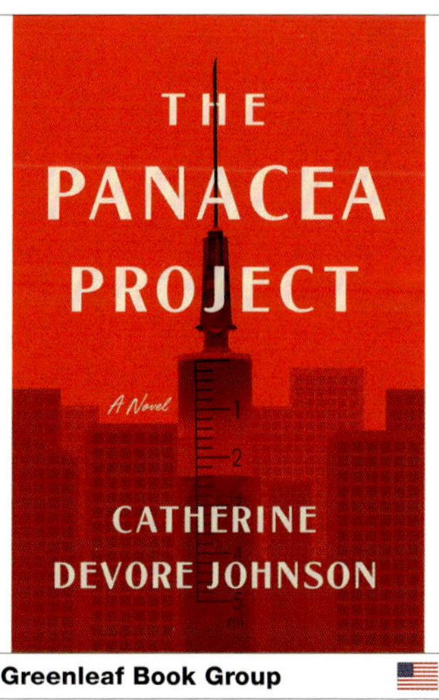

Greenleaf Book Group

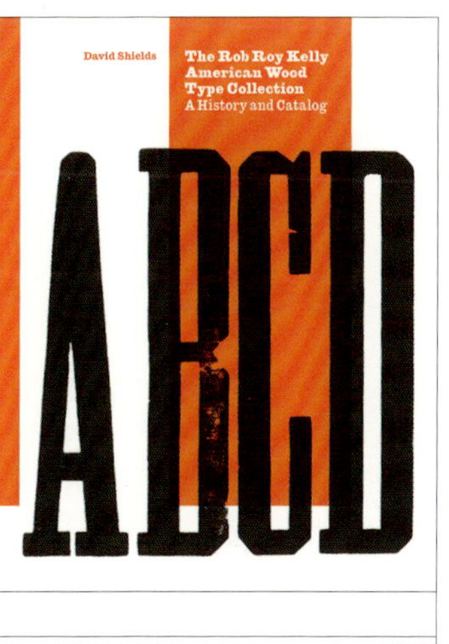

David Shields

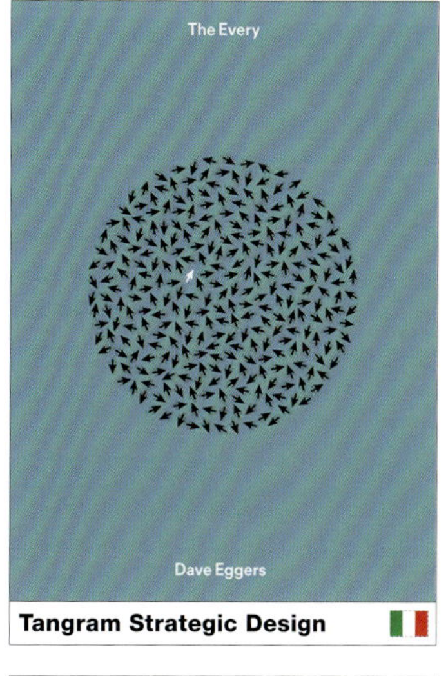

Tangram Strategic Design

Faceout Studio

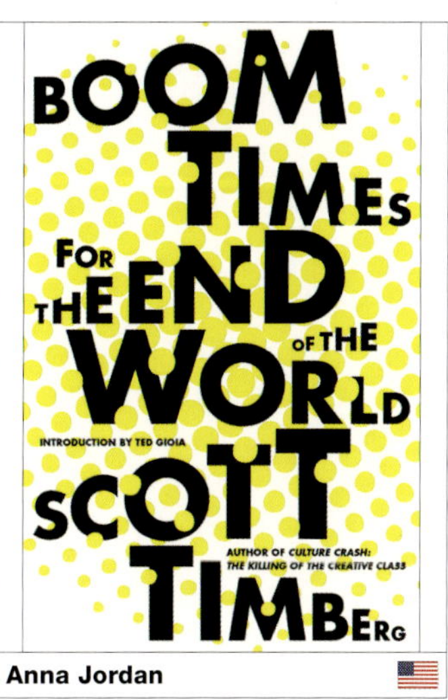

Anna Jordan

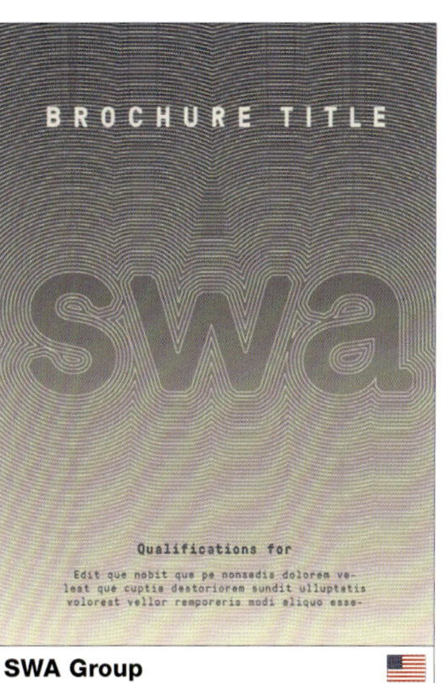

SWA Group

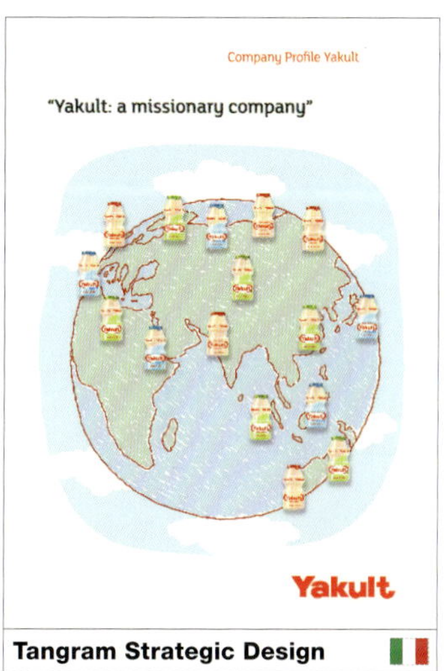

Tangram Strategic Design

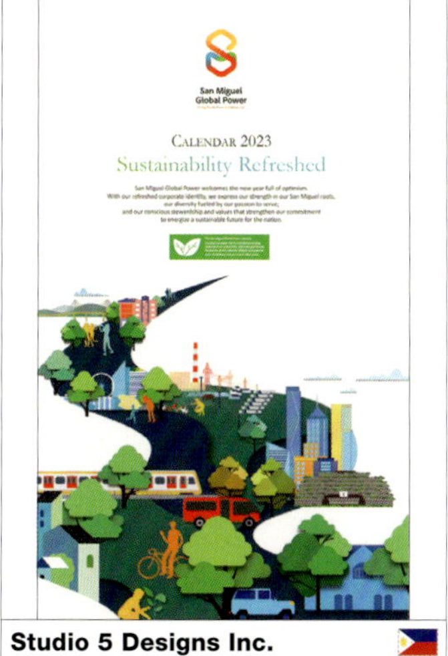

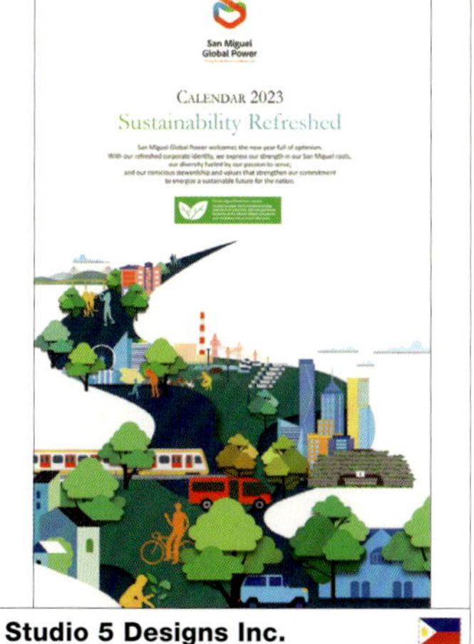
Studio 5 Designs Inc.

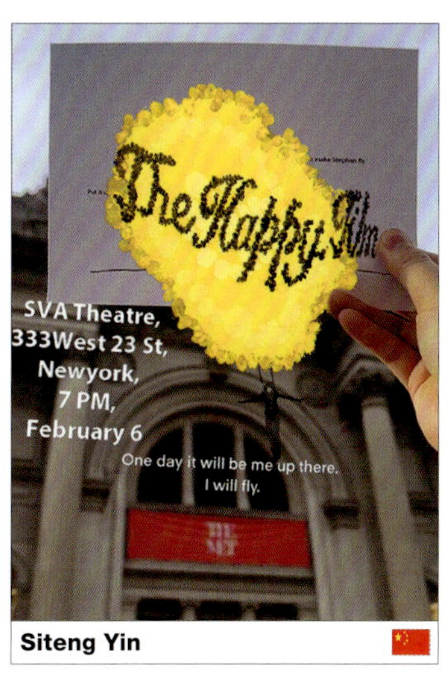

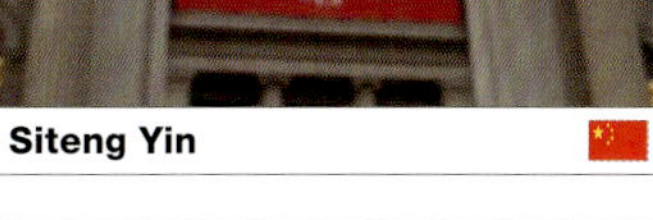
Siteng Yin

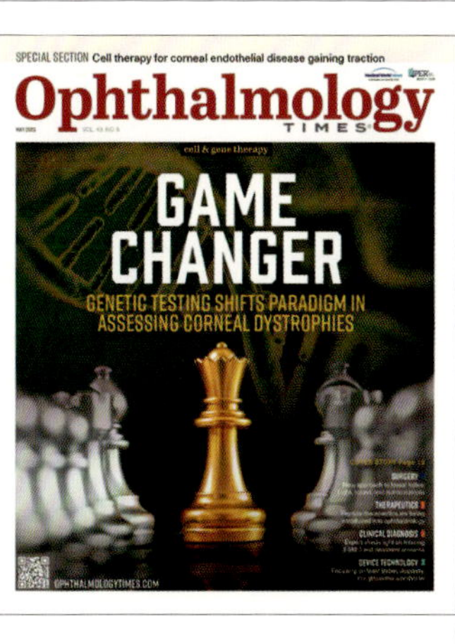

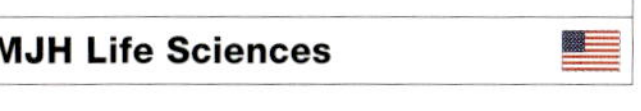
MJH Life Sciences

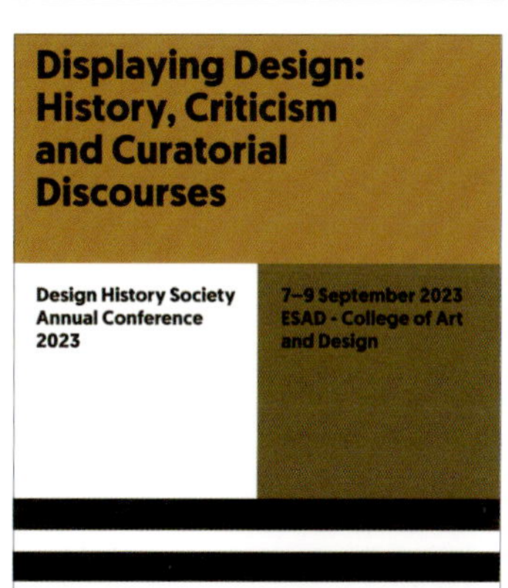

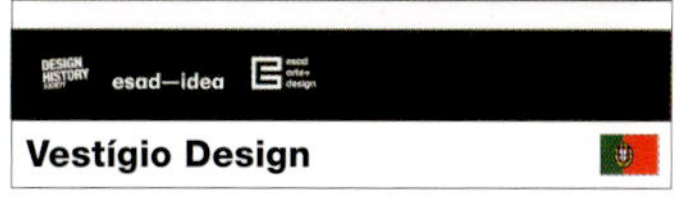

Vestígio Design

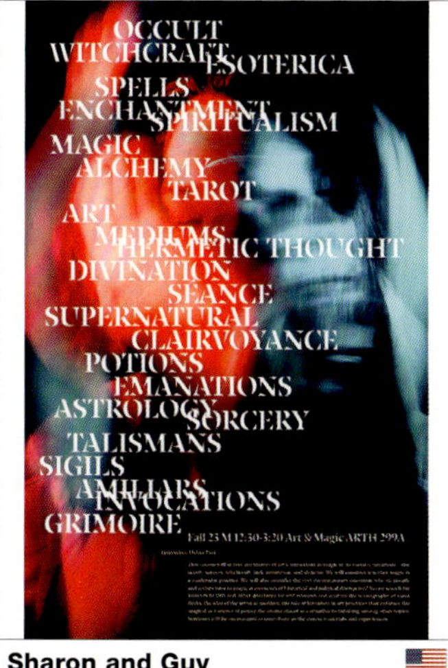

Sharon and Guy

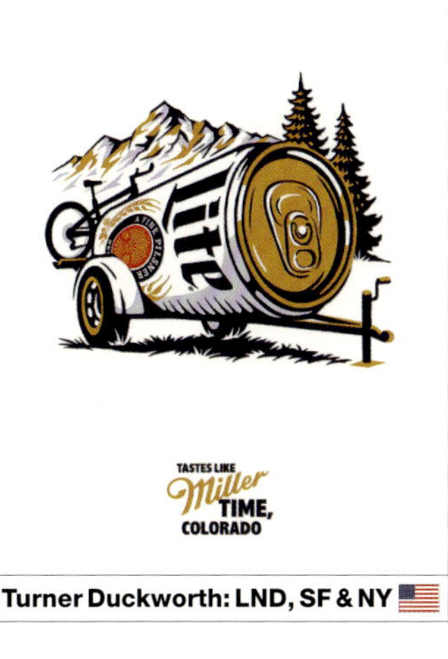

Turner Duckworth: LND, SF & NY

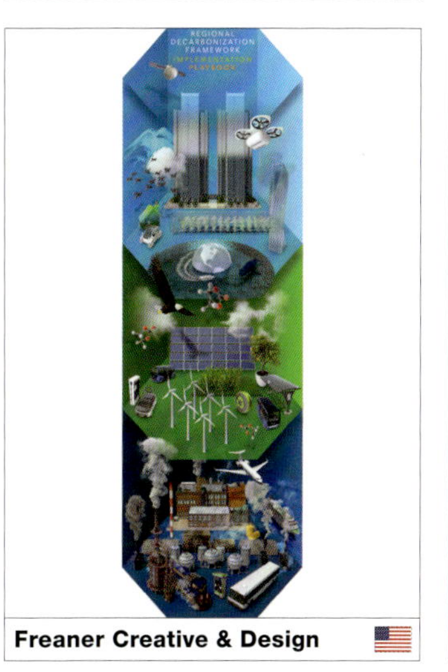
Freaner Creative & Design

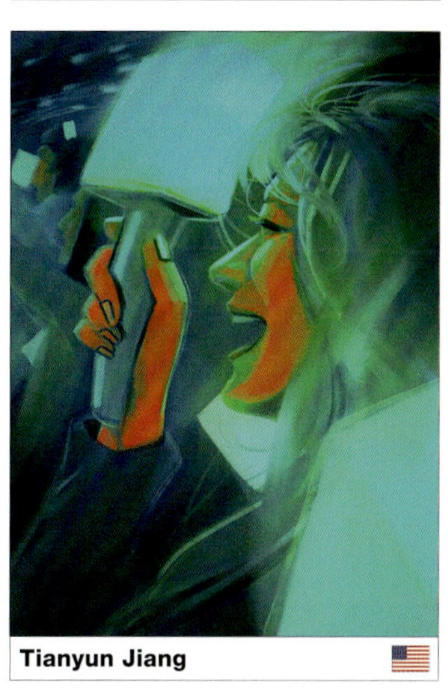
Tianyun Jiang

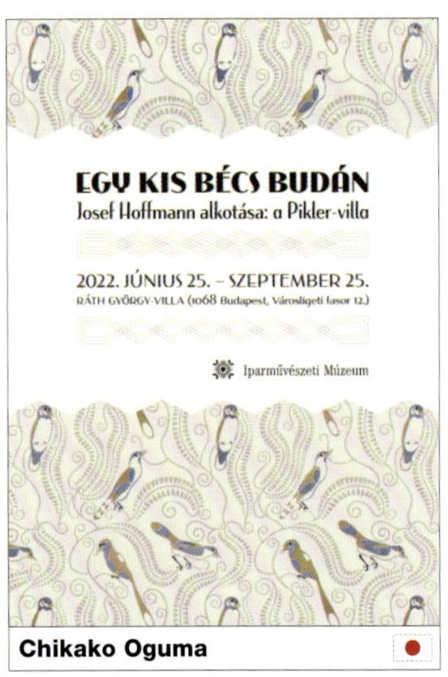

Chikako Oguma

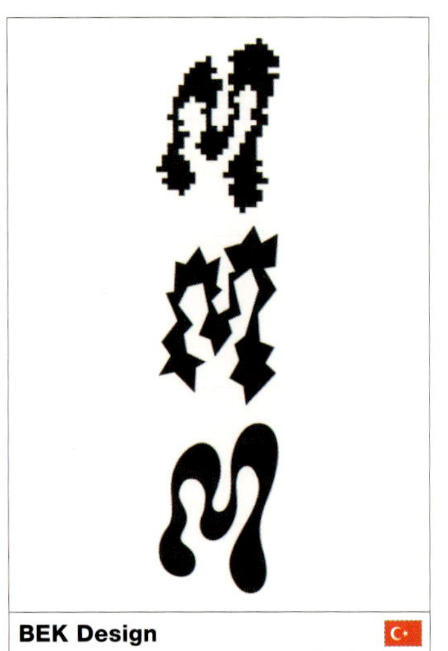
BEK Design

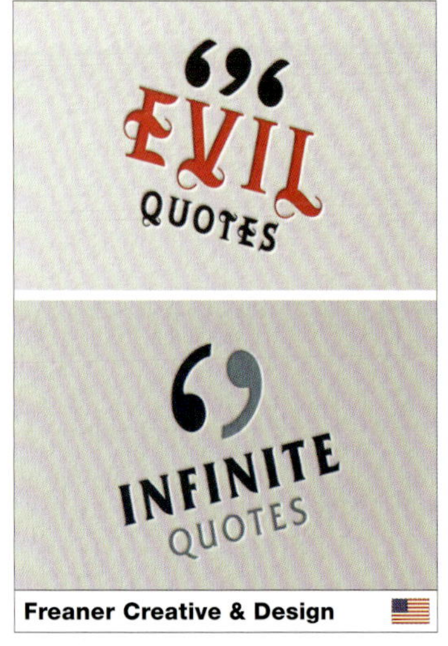

Freaner Creative & Design

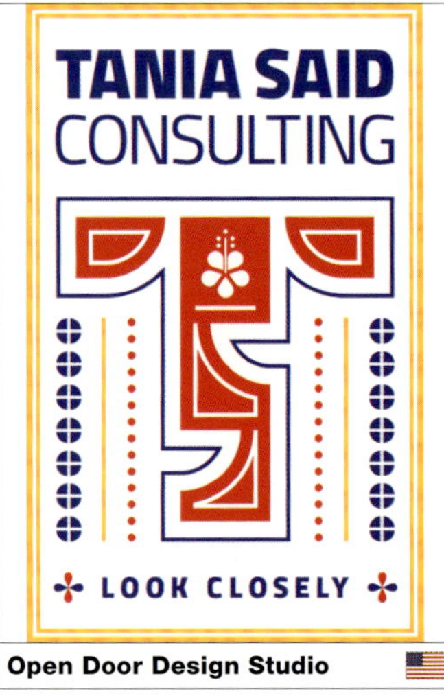

Open Door Design Studio

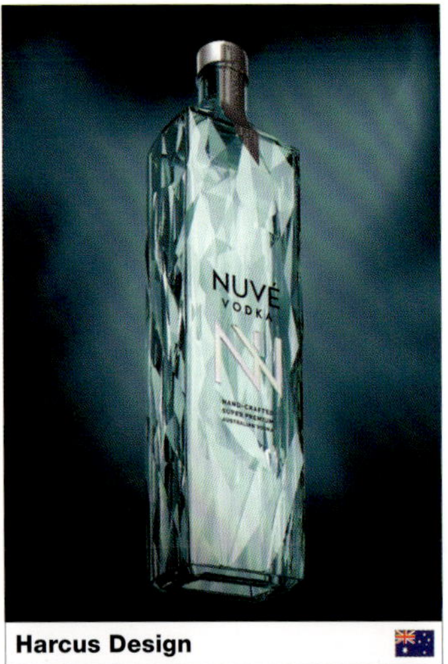

Harcus Design

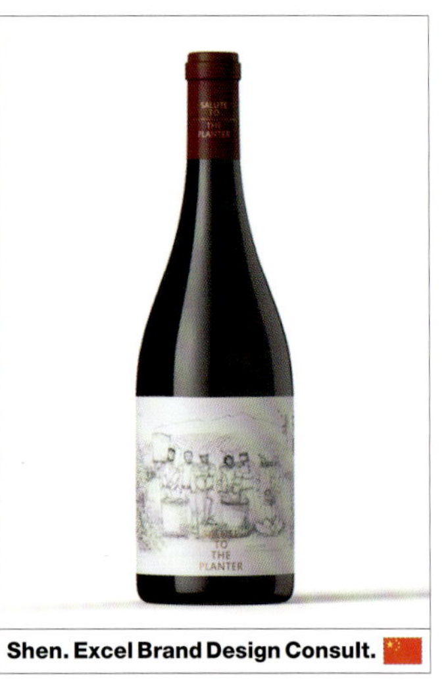
Shen. Excel Brand Design Consult.

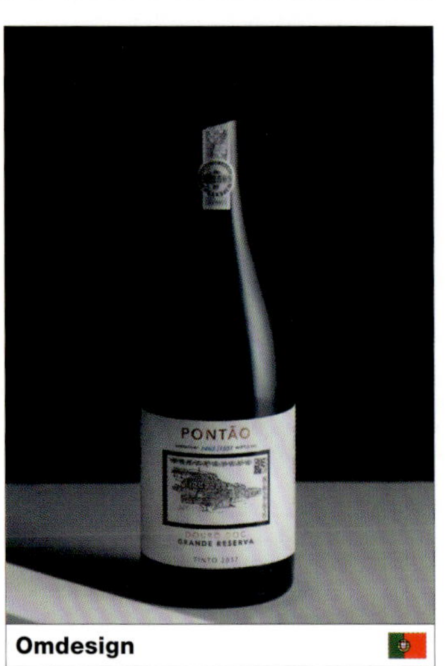

Omdesign

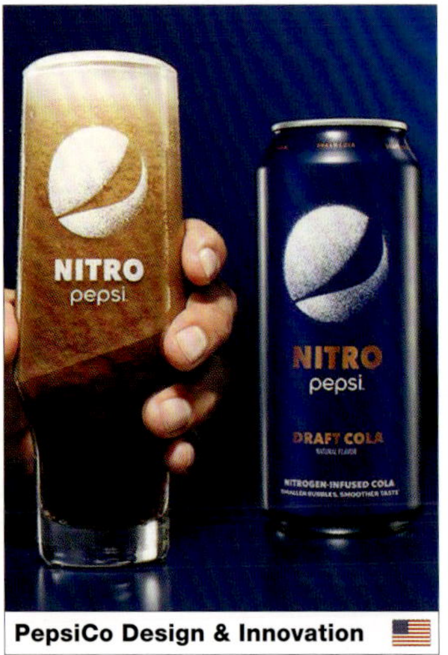

PepsiCo Design & Innovation

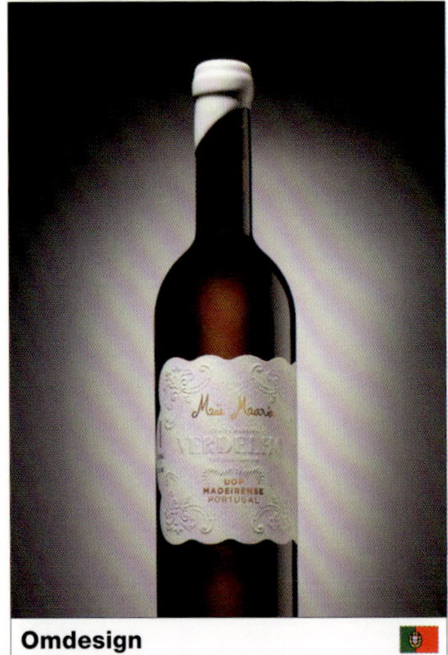
Omdesign

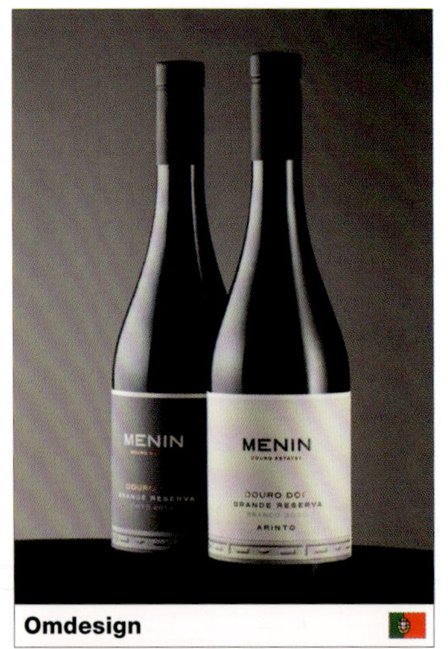

Omdesign

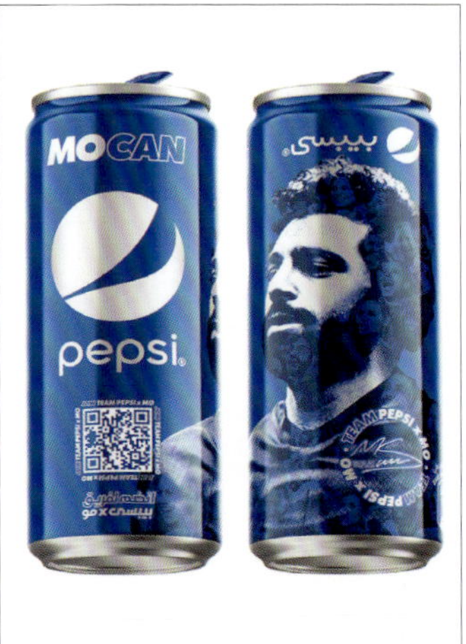

PepsiCo Design & Innovation

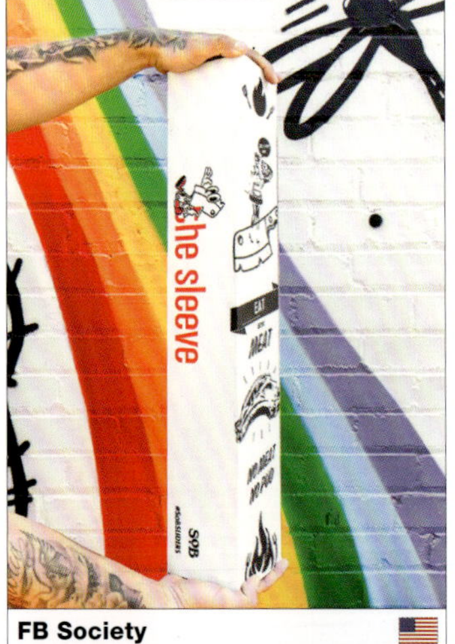

FB Society

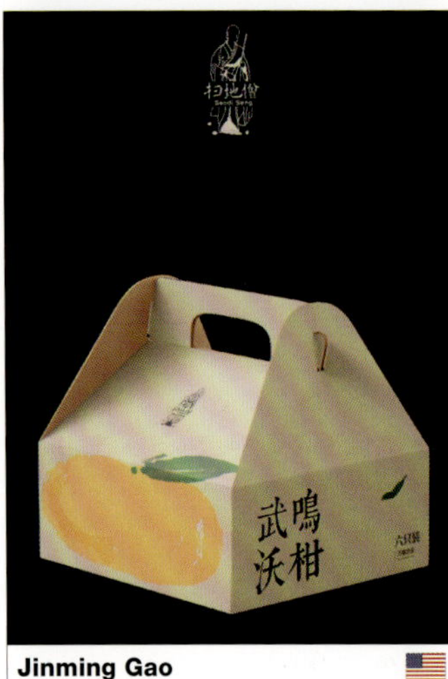

Jinming Gao

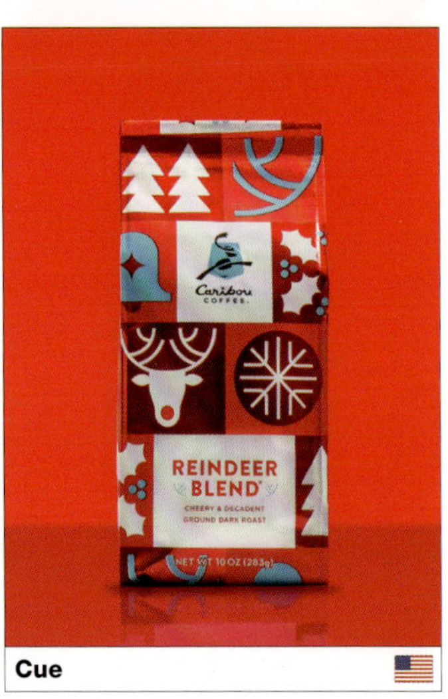

Cue

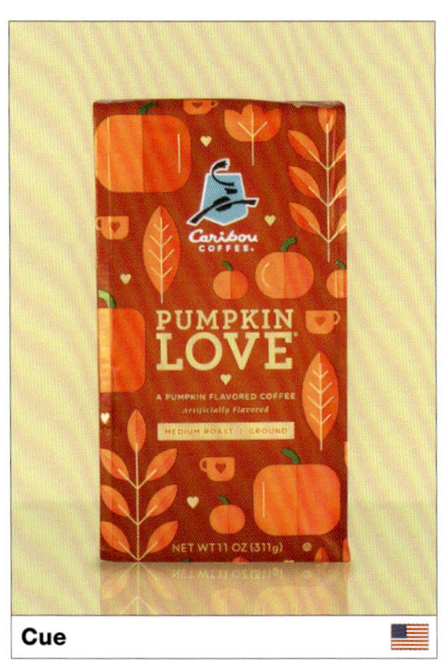

Cue

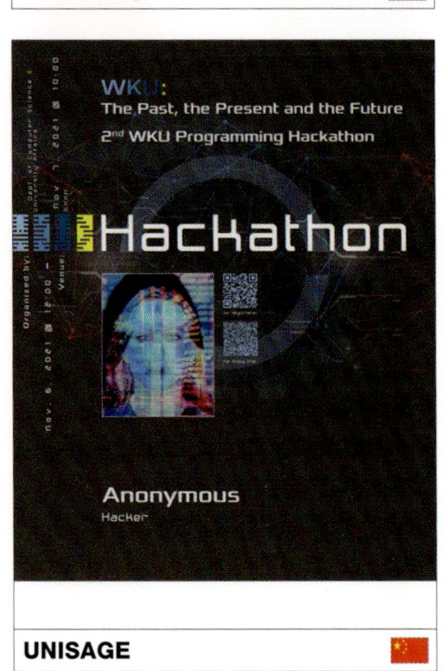

UNISAGE

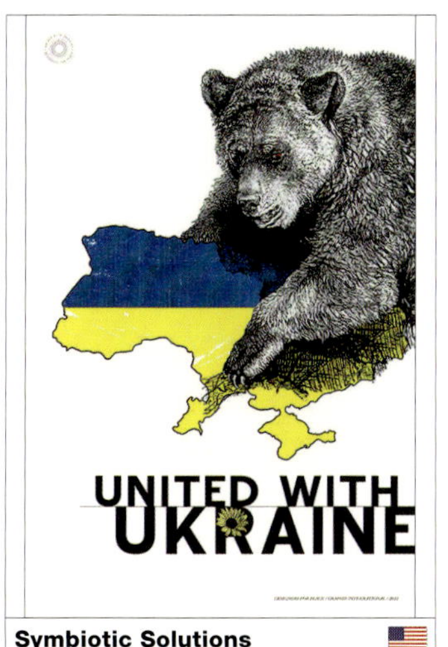

Symbiotic Solutions

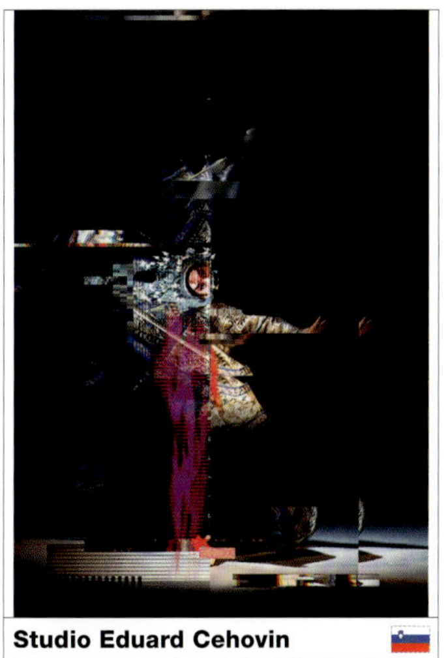

Studio Eduard Cehovin

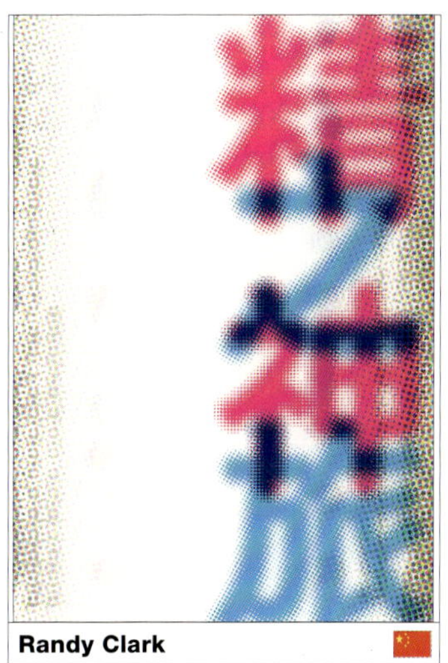

Randy Clark

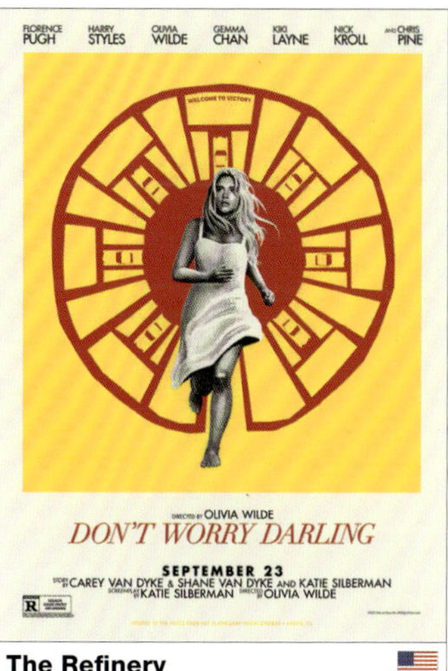

The Refinery

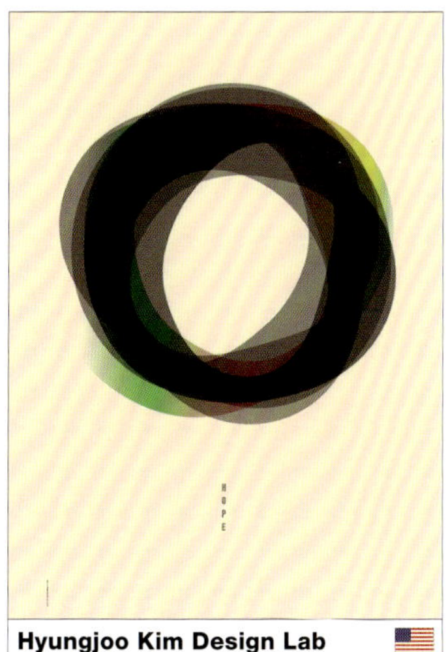

Hyungjoo Kim Design Lab

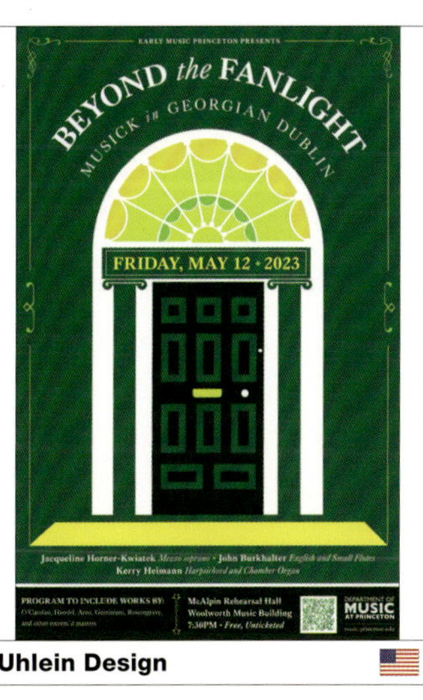

Uhlein Design

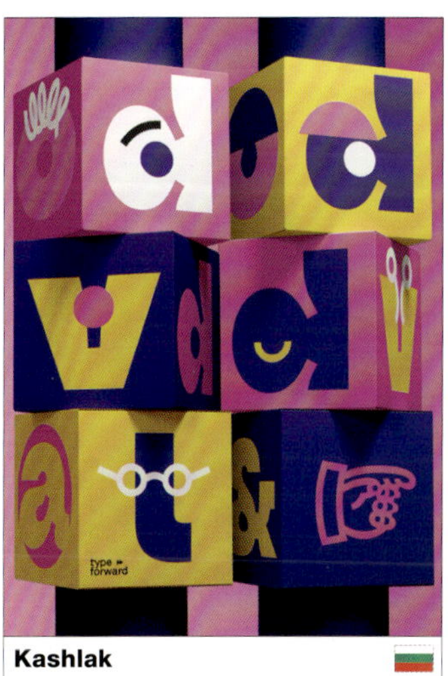

Kashlak

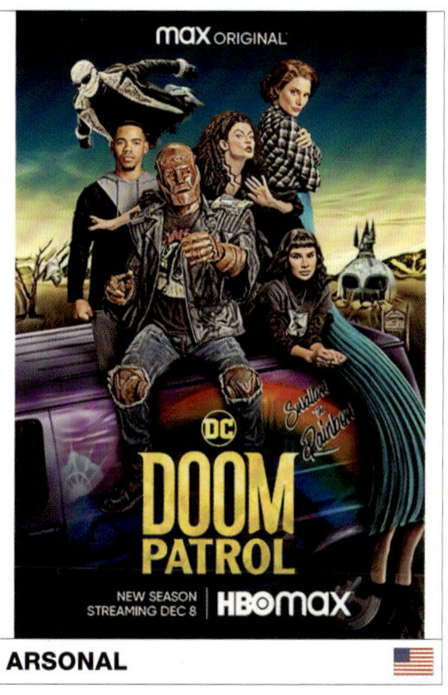

ARSONAL

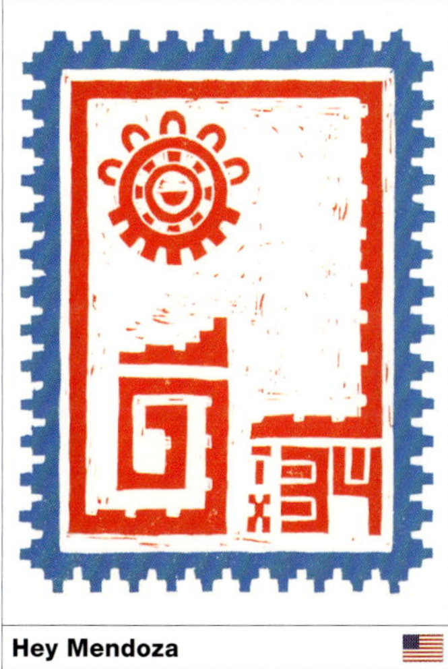

Hey Mendoza

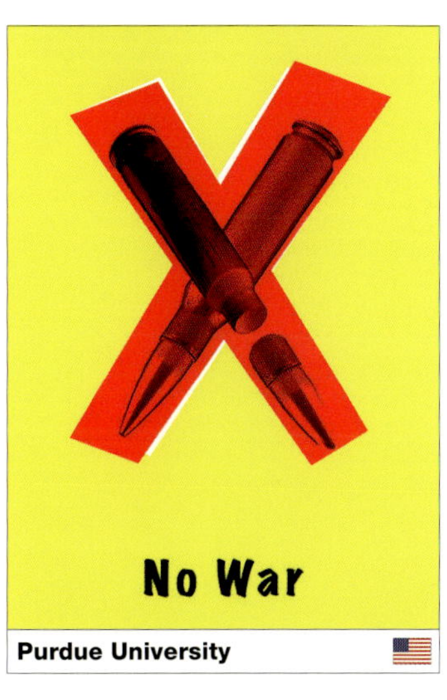

Purdue University

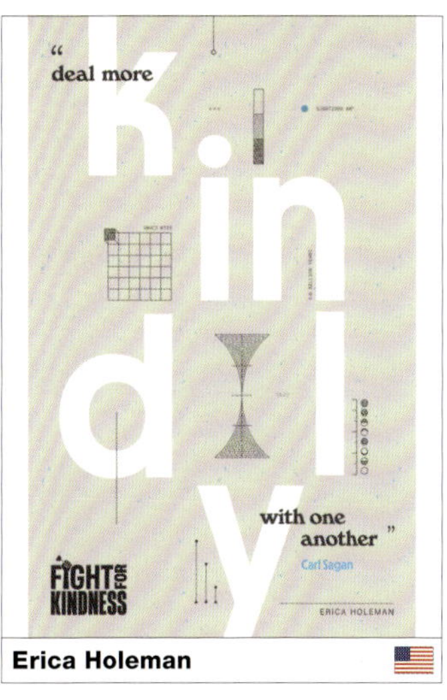

Erica Holeman

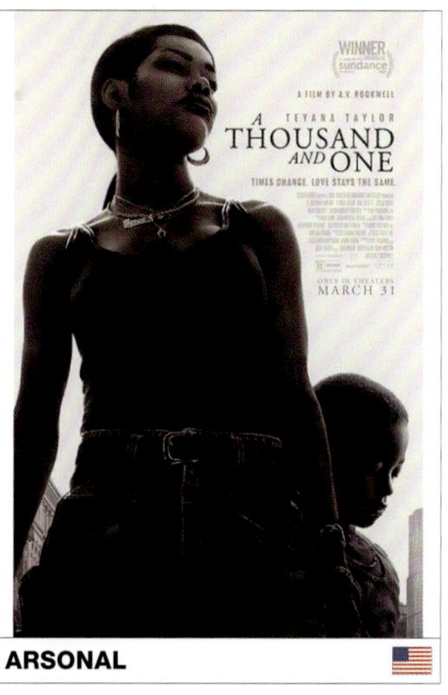

ARSONAL

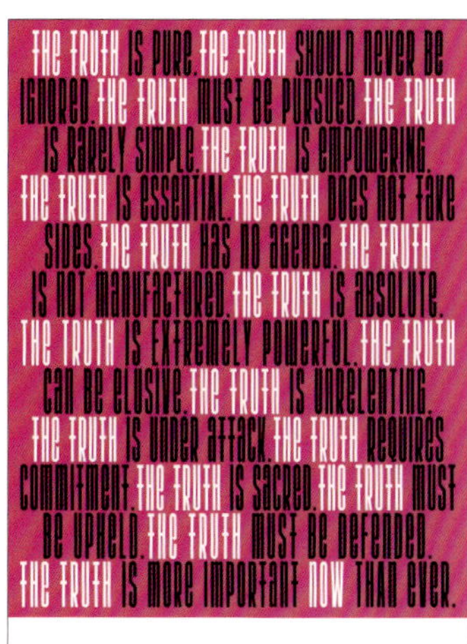

Goodall Integrated Design

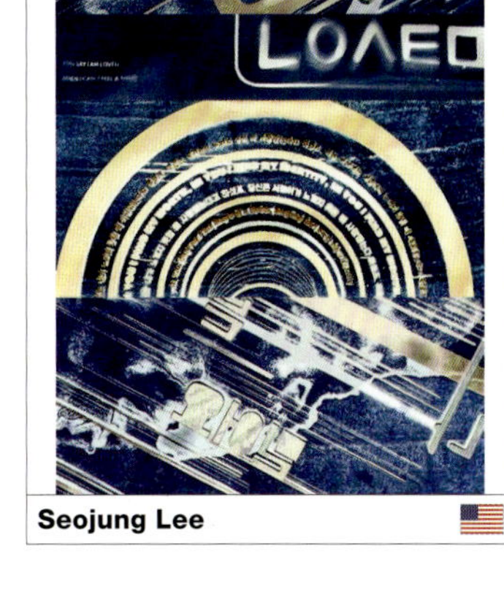

Seojung Lee

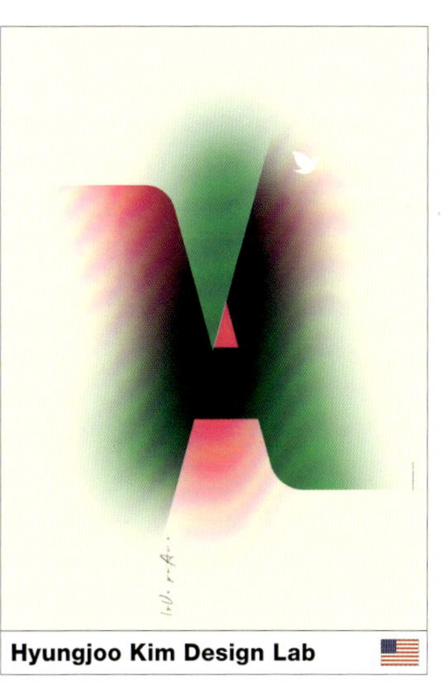

Hyungjoo Kim Design Lab

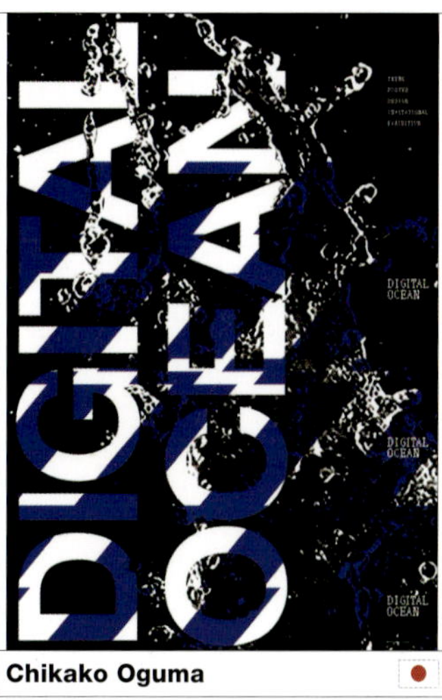

Chikako Oguma

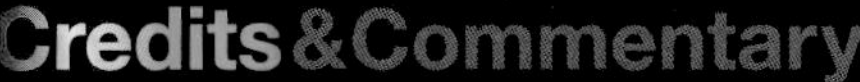

PLATINUM WINNERS:

22 THE SAMBURU | Design Firm: Wonderlust Industries, Inc.
Designer: Mark Sagato | Client: The Thorntree Project | Chief Creative Director: Lyle Owerko
Photographer: Lyle Owerko | Main Contributor: Lyle Owerko

Assignment: The Samburu portrait series was shot as a document of the people The Thorntree Project supports through educational infrastructure and scholarship programs in northern Kenya. These portraits were released in a book project in June 2022 to commemorate 20 years of Thorntree's work in the Samburu community.
Approach: Working in conditions with no electricity, limited resources, and ample sunshine a rudimentary portrait studio was set up using tree branches and scrims made by a local tailor to create a unique environment to photograph in.
Results: As a part of The Thorntree Project's endeavors literally hundreds of students have been sent to higher education and college and in turn bringing prosperity back to their families and community. This book project documented the soul of the community and their reach for a higher self in a changing world.

23 THE POP COLLECTION | Design Firm: Studio Eduardo Aires
Designer: Eduardo Aires | Client: Livraria Lello | Art Director: Eduardo Aires
Graphic Designers: Pedro Mata Nogueira, Vasco Castro, Miguel Almeida
Photographer: Jorge Almeida | Main Contributor: Studio Eduardo Aires

Assignment: Livraria Lello is a cultural and artistic reference in the city of Porto that has often been called the world's most beautiful bookshop. As part of the rebranding process that took place in 2022, the bookshop's pocket collection of literary classics, published in four languages, was extended from 29 to 43 titles.
Approach: In order to meet and match the new visual identity, their covers were redesigned exploring bold contrasts and finishing details. Exclusively typographical, they explore the glyphs created by the custom typeface designed by Dino dos Santos, with its distinctive ligatures. Starting from the primary and secondary colors of the bookshop's visual identity, the wider color palette allows for a continuous expansion of combinations. The book's finishings and details were carefully selected, from the dustjacket printed with the bookshop's signature monogram pattern to the matching bookmark ribbon. Classical yet contemporary, bold yet elegant, Livraria Lello's "The Pop Collection" aim's to bring together literature's finest over a vibrant, very graphical shelf.

24 "THE GREAT GATSBY" BY F. SCOTT FITZGERALD LUXURY EDITION
Design Firm: Anna and Elena Balbusso (Balbusso Twins Artist Duo)
Designers: Anna Balbusso, Elena Balbusso | Editor: Josh O'Neill
Client: Beehive Books | Art Director: Maëlle Doliveux | Artists: Anna Balbusso, Elena Balbusso
Publisher: Beehive Books | Main Contributors: Anna Balbusso, Elena Balbusso

Assignment: We created the design of the slipcase, the cover art, and the interior illustrations for the luxury signed and numbered edition of The Great Gatsby by F. Scott Fitzgerald published by Beehive Books and part of the Illuminated Editions 2022. The book is an oversized 9x12" hardcover edition, cloth-bound in sewn signatures, and enclosed in an elaborately embossed and debossed die-cut slipcase, which creates a topographical map of the interior artwork in foil blocking. The 1925 Fitzgerald story is set in the Jazz Age on Long Island, near New York City. It depicts first-person narrator Nick Carraway's interactions with mysterious millionaire Jay Gatsby and Gatsby's obsession to reunite with his former lover, Daisy Buchanan.
Approach: In regard to the painting techniques, we used traditional and digital tools: gouache, pen, pencil, and digital. We kept a perceptible pictorial material: coarse grains, brush strokes, rough textures, and collage. The story gave us the opportunity to look at artists and artistic movements of the Modernist era that have long inspired us: the painters of the historical avant-gardes (futurism, expressionism), including Giacomo Balla, Mario Sironi, and Lyonel Feininger. We wanted our images to conjure the energy of the Roaring Twenties but with a contemporary interpretation. We chose to mix abstract, geometric shapes with figurative elements to create an elegant and sophisticated feel inspired by Art Deco and Bauhaus. The style with which we rendered the characters draws influence from Tamara de Lempicka's paintings, early twentieth-century fashion illustration, and Classical Hollywood's black-and-white films.
Results: The edition was funded by a hugely successful Kickstarter Campaign. The Illustrations for The Great Gatsby edition have received important recognition and appreciation such as the 2023 WIA World Illustration Awards 2023 Longlisted and the 2022 Merit Award 3x3 Show No.19.

25 CHELSEA BEE | Design Firm: Michael Pantuso Design
Designer: Michael Pantuso | Client: Self-initiated | Main Contributor: Michael Pantuso

Assignment: "Chelsea Bee" is a digital artwork that I created as a variation of my mechanical bee design from 2015. I designed this artwork specifically for an art talk event in late 2023. The new version is more intricate than the original, and it incorporates elements and techniques that have evolved since the beginning of the series. By utilizing digital drawing tools and techniques, I was able to bring a modern twist to the design, which allowed me to express the true essence of my idea. Through the use of digital drawing tools and techniques, I was able to create an artwork that truly captures the essence of my idea. The result is a more intricate and detailed piece that showcases the evolution of my design process since the original mechanical bee in 2015. I am excited to present "Chelsea Bee" at the upcoming art talk event and share with others the intricacies of its design.
Approach: Hand-drawn digital.

26 PEPSI LABEL-FREE MULTIPACK | Design Firm: PepsiCo Design & Innovation
Designer: PepsiCo Design & Innovation | Client: Self-initiated
Main Contributor: PepsiCo Design & Innovation

Assignment: As part of our pep+ (PepsiCo Positive) transformation, PepsiCo is committed to having a positive impact on the planet and people. Creating innovative and sustainable packaging solutions plays a huge role in achieving that. To celebrate Earth Day, Pepsi launched the brand's first label-free PET bottle available for purchase in multipack format in China.
Approach: With this bold product created with the Design Team, Pepsi removed the plastic label of a traditional PET bottle and the ink printing at the bottle cap, reducing the carbon footprint throughout the entire product life cycle. Pepsi Label-free Multipack reduces packaging materials, manufacturing energy, and recycling energy needed. Instead, the Pepsi logo and labeling are printed directly on the bottle, making it an intrinsic part of the 8ujm PET design. Since the body of the bottle is a single material, there is no need for separation during the recycling process, meaning more bottles are recycled. The label-free bottles are packaged in a multipack format, with the bold Pepsi blue outer wrap made using 24% recycled plastic. Pepsi also included an innovative icon on the outer wrap reading "widely recycled" to help inform consumers. The icon includes an encouraging thumbs-up gesture that recognizes the two-way interaction of shared positive recycling behavior and sustainable practices made by both Pepsi and the consumer.
Results: Since the launch, it has received a positive response from consumers, the industry, and sales channels. The product launch was covered by 5,000+ media and received over 170 million exposures.

27 OMEL | Design Firm: Omdesign | Designer: Diogo Gama Rocha
Client: Self-initiated | Main Contributor: Omdesign

Assignment: Since 1998, we believe that true luxury lies in simplicity and details. Year after year, we raise awareness for the importance of preserving nature and the urgency of preparing for the future. In 2023, we want to continue to be part of the solution, and drew inspiration from a small, great being, with a huge impact on our planet. We interpreted the way of life of solitary bees, true pollinating nomads and synonymous with hard work, to create this original piece and thus inaugurate a network of 150 hotels! Each Bee Om Hotel is special and will help to instill a sustainable, united, and purposeful mindset. We tasted the bees' honey ("Mel", in Portuguese) and gave life to OMel, a pack that seeks to return to the environment a refuge for solitary bees to make it home and continue to protect the biodiversity of ecosystems. History has written that only in perfect harmony and integration of all parts it is possible for us to cohabit with the glimpse of a future.
Approach: We have chosen an elegant jar to carry our bee's honey, we covered it with a natural cork stopper (specifically designed for this pack), representing the usual raw material that welcomes them, and we gave life to this pack. Built with reused and surplus production of wooden wine boxes, the external structure of OMel counts with six layers that form our project, creating a hive shape. Each wooden layer presents holes made between 7 and 10mm in diameter, showing the perfect fit for bees not allowing the entrance of other bigger and invasive species. On top is the spoon-shaped pencil, made from excesses of Viarco's pencil production, the starting point to continue writing the rest of the story. With it, we also collect the nectar delivered by the bees and we invite you to reuse the jar afterwards.
Results: We created OMel as a self-promotion giftpack in order to promote eco-friendly measures on their daily projects and to raise awareness for the importance of bees. We want to help change the packaging paradigm, focusing on sustainability as a central point. OMel gathers all the ecological strategies in a singular piece, so it should also represent our mindset, namely to recycle and reuse, in conjunction with an educational purpose. This set won't only decorate our gardens, houses, or public spaces. It will function as a home for solitary bees, and at the same time will inspire us to continue working for the greater and common good.

28 DON'T | Design Firm: Sun Design Production
Designers: Xian Liyun, Liang Gang | Client: Shanghai Municipal Government
Main Contributor: Shanghai Municipal Department of Environmental Protection

Assignment: The message is that reducing the use of paper cups will save trees and improve our natural environment.
Approach: Intuitive persuasion and understanding were aimed. Therefore, images taken by crumpling paper cups and trees were drawn to express them, and the method of not using paper cups was emphasized to save the environment.
Results: I believe that this campaign will bring a lot of public interest in the environment and an understanding of future life.

29 DOWNTON ABBEY: A NEW ERA - ILLUSTRATED TRAVEL POSTER SERIES
Design Firm: AV Print | Designer: AV Print | Clients: Focus Features, Blair Green, SVP Creative Advertising and Head of Brand Design, Marcus Kaye, VP Creative Advertising & Marketing
Main Contributor: AV Print

Assignment: Working on the campaign for the second Downton Abbey movie with Focus Features presented a very fun creative challenge. While we were tied to including an overwhelming amount of people in the main posters, we were given more freedom to fill out the larger campaign.
Approach: Coming from the incredibly successful show and following up the first film with such beloved and well-established characters, we really needed to celebrate what makes A New Era, new. One of the defining elements of this sequel is the fact that we leave the Abbey. With this illustrated travel poster homage, we were able to show these characters and this film in a fun and adventurous new light.
Results: By sharing these pieces on social media, we were able to reach audiences far and wide to share this wistful reminder of luxury travel in a bygone era.

30 PEACE | Design Firm: Namseoul University | Designer: Mi-Jung Lee
Client: Ministry of Unification | Main Contributor: Mi-Jung Lee

Assignment: A large number of birds symbolizing peace and wishing for peace gather together to form partly a person, and the shape is a poster composed and expressed as another large person. The message is that if people work for peace, they will also find peace.
Approach: It is a campaign poster that embodies that peace is life and life.
Results: It has fully conveyed its function as a poster that informs many people of the value and importance of peace and induces interest.

31 FIXED | Design Firm: Carmit Design Studio
Designer: Carmit Makler Haller | Client: Self-initiated
Photographer: Adobe Stock | Digital Artists: Jorge Gamboa, Mal De Ojo
Main Contributor: Carmit Makler Haller, Carmit Design Studio

Assignment: I decided to develop a series of broken, aloof, and dependent women who underwent a "fixed" procedure. It conveys the female's obsession with her body; an obsession that ranged from anorexia to body disfiguration and plastic surgery. However, the reason for their operation still remained unclear: were they

pursuing the perfect figure according to the cruel fashion industry? Or was it a deeper, more violent trauma they were convalescing from?
Approach: The red thread, symbolizing life and energy, stitches together the broken and distorted body, but at what cost? Type was threaded into the bodies, as if they were tattooed, or branded. The actual thread was photographed separately, and was digitally edited into the image, giving it a realistic feel.

32 WORLD CUP 2022 POSTERS | Design Firm: Underline Studio
Designer: Fidel Peña | Client: George Brown College School of Design
Creative Directors: Fidel Peña, Claire Dawson | Printer: Flash Reproductions
Main Contributor: Underline Studio
Assignment: A series of posters created for a series of viewing parties during the World Cup at George Brown College's School of Design in support of the United Way. We created a series of simple, graphic posters each designed in a different typeface to reflect the team represented in each of the posters. The exhibition was held in support of the work of United Way, in Toronto.
Approach: Be a United Way champion throughout the World Cup. Loose change for cheers. If you are able, kindly contribute any change or small donations to the United Way. We recognize that there have been several human rights violations in Qatar and while we are unable to work to dismantle those, we can certainly raise awareness and support local UW charities who help support organizations that advocate for workers, women, and LGBTQ2+ folks.

33 PONY CARS | Design Firm: Journey Group
Designer: Zack Bryant | Client: United States Postal Service | Artist: Tom Fritz
Art Director: Greg Breeding | Main Contributor: Tom Fritz
Assignment: The Pony Car stamps were initially commissioned as a follow-up to the popular Muscle Car series. The stamps were intended to show how car design evolved into something fast and fun. These stamps celebrate the performance coupes and convertibles that brought a youthful spirit to the automotive world.
Approach: The artist, one of the preeminent motorsports artists of his time, worked with the art director, and designer to capture the energy and mystique of pony cars. The Pony Cars Forever stamps celebrate five iconic U.S. automobiles—the 1969 Ford Mustang Boss 302, the 1970 Dodge Challenger R/T, the 1969 Chevrolet Camaro Z/28, the 1967 Mercury Cougar XR-7 GT, and the 1969 AMC Javelin SST. The artist based his artwork on photographs of the cars, painting each car using oil paint on panels. With bold colors and dramatic lighting, the artist and the design team captured the energy and mystique of each pony car.
Results: Designed to be on sale for two years, the stamps are now 70% sold.

GOLD WINNERS:
35 COMVITA ANNUAL REPORT | Design Firm: Insight Creative | Designer: Brian Slade
Client: Comvita | Writer: Mark Di Somma | Strategy Directors: Mike Tisdall, Steven Giannoulis
Production: Chrissy Saw | Account Director: Mason Smith | Main Contributor: Insight Creative
Assignment: Comvita is the global market leader in Manuka honey and a leading global consumer brand. A series of challenges in recent years saw a reduced focus on core business and this was reflected in their results. A new CEO and a new strategic plan was the start of transforming the business. Following a few runs quick wins, it was time to convince long-patient stakeholders that the new strategy was already delivering a strong turnaround. The annual report provided the perfect opportunity to share Comvita's transformation journey.
Approach: We quickly got our head around where Comvita was, their three-phased strategy and the results it would deliver. We resolved that this needed to be a message driven report that was open, direct and accessible in its language and design. Disarming and honest headlines such as 'This may sting a little' set the narrative up to deal with key issues in a very direct way. We recommended a frank long-form Q&A for the CEO and Chair's sections. We then used the report's opening spreads to clearly and succinctly present the three phases of the turnaround strategy and to build belief in Comvita's ability to deliver transformation. The visual treatment of this section was deliberately differentiated from the rest of the report, providing the engaging storytelling layer and the wayfinding to more details later in the report. The three-phased strategy also informed the visual execution with each hero image utilising a three layered treatment to reflect the strategy and to reinforce an overall message of focus. A serious colour palette and fine key line infographics and icons offer a sense of structure, consideration and planning. The typographic treatment is bold, clear and accessible, using a balance of serif and sans serif to create a quality feel aligned with Comvita's premium positioning. Layering the content with engaging headlines, callouts, top-line numbers, break-out panels and infographics allows a highly scannable experience, letting users jump in and out as it suits them. These features, along with clear hierarchy and navigation allows the pace of the report to be varied within different pages and sections, further enhancing the reading experience.
Results: Comvita received strong and positive feedback from the team, investors and wider stakeholders. One of the Board members described it as "a huge turnaround on previous reports and the best report Comvita's ever produced." As year one of a three year plan, the report set the design platform and theme for the annual reports that followed. One example is the print approach. This year's report was printed in uncoated A4 stock. Over the next two year, both size and stock quality was upweighted to reflect the results and the impact of the strategy. Over the three years, Comvita has seen both a significant rise in share price and number of shareholders – a testament to the power of well-designed communications.

36 AGRICULTURAL WEIGHTS AND MEASURES 2021 CROP REPORT
Design Firm: Freaner Creative & Design | Designer: Ariel Freaner
Clients: San Diego County Agricultural Weights and Measures, Bosko Celic, Porfirio Mancillas, Megan Moore, Ha Dang | Digital Artist: Ariel Freaner | Creative Director: Ariel Freaner
Illustrator: Ariel Freaner | Main Contributor: Ariel Freaner
Assignment: The County of San Diego Department of Agriculture, Weights and Measures' 2021 Crop Statistics Report promote and informs the public of the agriculture status of the county.
Approach: We designed and developed The County of San Diego Department of Agriculture, Weights and Measures' 202 Crop Statistics and Annual Report. The report contains the acreage, yield, and value of agricultural production for San Diego County. This report details crop information and highlights the many diverse programs to support the County's Strategic Initiatives of Building Better Health, Living Safely, Sustainable Environments/Thriving, and Operational Excellence. Our approach was to bring the Crop report to life by adding color, images, and a theme. This year our theme was Nursery. The information is displayed with Infographics in different styles, colorful designs, and a clean and neat layout.
Results: This report succeeded for the public as they could understand and digest the information much better due to the graphics, layout, and presentation. We even received an online compliment via Twitter and Facebook from Jason Mraz about the content and presentation of the 2021 Crop Report.

37 THE WORLD AMONG FLOWERS - A RESEARCH EXHIBITION OF KU SHULAN'S WORKS COLLECTED BY THE SHAANXI PROVINCE ART MUSEUM | Design Firm: HILLS
Designer: Liu Jun Tao | Client: Shaanxi Province Art Museum | Art Director: Liu Jun Tao
Assignment: The research exhibition of Ku Shulan's works is the largest comprehensive exhibition of Ku Shulan's paper-cut art in history. The exhibition combines rich physical and documentary materials, as well as contemporary art and design works that have been specially invited and collected, presenting a research exhibition of Ku Shulan's works with multiple perspectives, rich content and fascinating.
Approach: The book design combines the traditional folk five-color paper, environment-friendly recycled paper and other art papers with modern design techniques, and presents the artistic path of folk arts and crafts master Ku Shulan and the artistic beauty of his paper-cut works in a multi-level and multi-dimensional way through a variety of book binding forms and languages, forming a time-space dialogue between traditional art and contemporary design.
Results: The exhibition has a strong social response, and has been postponed twice, with nearly 40000 people attending the exhibition.

38 OVERLAP/DISSOLVE | Design Firm: Skolos-Wedell | Designer: Nancy Skolos
Client: Self-initiated | Publisher: ORO Editions | Photographer: Thomas Wedell
Authors: Nancy Skolos, Thomas Wedell | Main Contributors: Nancy Skolos, Thomas Wedell
Assignment: This autobiographical monograph presents a retrospective of the 40-year innovative graphic design practice of husband-and-wife team, Nancy Skolos and Thomas Wedell. The two have seamlessly merged the boundaries between graphic design, photography, and typography, fusing two-and three-dimensional space through overlapping type and image.
Approach: The book's grid subdivides the pages into two vertical halves and two horizontal areas with a square lower section. Enlarged poster details occupy the half-pages to create the illusion of overlap by eclipsing images that appear in-full representation on an adjacent spread reinforcing the progression of projects as one dissolves into the next. Prototypes, iterations, and studio set-ups shed light on the process behind the finished work which unfolds in chronological order, subdivided in decades: 80s, 90s, 00s, 10s, 20s. Tom and Nancy interview each other to describe their collaborative design process, share personal inspiration, and reflect on how their work progressed. The foreword, written by Andrew Blauvelt, Director of the Cranbrook Art Museum in Bloomfield Hills, Michigan, contextualizes Skolos-Wedell within the history of photography and graphic design.
Results: Trim: 7.5" x 10.5" Portrait. Extent: 288pp. Binding: Hardbound + vellum jacket. ISBN: 978-1-957183-31-2. Released: Spring 2023. 588 color images

39 RATIONAL SIMPLICITY: RUDOLPH DE HARAK, GRAPHIC DESIGNER
Design Firm: Poulin + Morris Inc. | Designers: Richard Poulin, Derek Koch, Tyler Cheli
Client: Thames & Hudson Ltd. | Main Contributor: Cary Graphic Design Archive @RIT
Assignment: Rudolph de Harak (1924-2002) was one of the most influential graphic designers of the mid-twentieth century. Inspired by early modernist masters as well as by the rigor, simplicity, and rationalism of the International Typographic Style, European Modernism, Abstract Expressionism, and Op Art, de Harak developed and refined his timeless and pioneering work from his early years in Los Angeles to his success as a design consultant and educator in New York City. Throughout his illustrious career, he was continuously exploring the potential of abstraction, geometry and color, as well as experimenting with photography and various photographic techniques in new and exciting ways. De Harak brought his pioneering inventiveness to everything he created, from album covers, book jackets, and branding to furniture, exhibitions, and museums. Organized chronologically, "Rational Simplicity" is the first publication to document de Harak's pioneering and prolific work for a wide range of clients, including The Metropolitan Museum of Art, Columbia Records, Esquire magazine, McGraw-Hill Publishing, and the Cummins Engine Company, among many others. With over 500 illustrations, including reproductions of de Harak's seldom-seen paintings and collages, and remembrances from friends, colleagues, former students, artists, and family members, this comprehensive monograph provides an in-depth and definitive account of the influential designer's life and work.

40 SING WITH ME AT THE EDGE OF PARADISE | Design Firm: Texas Tech University Press
Designer: Hannah Gaskamp | Client: Self-initated | Main Contributor: Hannah Gaskamp
Assignment: Sing With Me at the Edge of Paradise is a collection of sixteen short stories surrounding queer men of various ages trying to temper their expectations of the world with their lived experience.
Approach: Because the titular story has to do with Adam and Eve The Rebuke of Adam and Eve by Charles-Joseph Natoire was chosen. I was interested in playing with the idea of "edge" mentioned in the title, hence the margin-less title text and interaction with Adam's fist.
Results: Author was thrilled.

41 THE DAUGHTER OF DOCTOR MOREAU | Design Firm: Faceout Studio
Designer: Tim Green | Clients: Penguin Random House, Cassie Gonzales
Main Contributor: Tim Green
Assignment: Book cover assignment.
Approach: A retelling of H.G. Wells' Island of Dr. Moreau from the point of view of the doctor's daughter and set in the Yucatan in the 19th century, a beautiful young woman who has grown up in his ranch/secret laboratory in the jungle.

42 WATERMARK | Design Firm: Texas Tech University Press
Designer: Hannah Gaskamp | Client: Self-initiated | Main Contributor: Hannah Gaskamp
Assignment: Watermark is a landmark 25th anniversary edition of the quintessential anthology of Vietnamese American literature. The artwork, by Trinh Mai, was provided by the editors.
Approach: The text was aligned vertically to reflect and interact with the artwork. As a book of poetry there is lots of unusual formatting within, which also aided in this choice. As part of our Diasporic Vietnamese Artist Network series a more angular font vaguely similar to Vietnamese characters was chosen.
Results: Editors were elated.

43 THE CATBIRD SEAT | Design Firm: Greenleaf Book Group | Designer: Kim Lance
Client: Rebecca Hollingsworth | Art Director: Neil Gonzalez | Main Contributor: Kim Lance
Assignment: The Catbird Seat follows two intertwined narratives. One is set in the present, where Gillian Culkin, inconvenienced by demonstrators debating the presence of the Confederate flag at the South Carolina State House, begins to realize the flag's presence represents important and entrenched issues of race and inequality. Meanwhile, she studies the 1857 diary of a dirt farmer who buys a slave at auction for a quick profit. In a subsequent journey, the man's view of enslavement changes.
Approach: This was truly a collaborative approach with the author. She provided inspirational artwork from favorite paintings and vintage posters along with important historical details about the book's location and characters.
Results: Since I took care to apply the author's input to the final artwork, she was thrilled with the results. It's grounded in a historically accurate rendering of a civil war diary but adds just the right amount of playful, visual interest (in color and other story elements) to attract readers.

44 DOODLEBUGS AND DOWSERS | Design Firm: Texas Tech University Press
Designer: Hannah Gaskamp | Client: Self-initiated | Main Contributor: Hannah Gaskamp
Assignment: Doodlebugs and Dowsers is a popular history of the eccentric and nonscientific methods used in oil exploration.
Approach: This book details all of the strange and sometimes mystical methods used to seek out oil throughout history. An iteration of a Ouija board was used to represent the kind of magical and unusual approaches taken. While most of the imagery is related to the classic board, some was replaced to instead reference the oil industry, namely a drop of oil and a barrel spilling it out.
Results: Author was pleased.

45 TABLE FOR TEN (ASEAN SHARED FOOD TRADITIONS)
Design Firm: Studio 5 Designs Inc. | Designer: Rogel Vidallo | Clients: Asean Ladies Foundation, Department of Foreign Affairs, Ma. Luisa Locsin, Cecille Wenceslao | Illustrator: Dante Divina
Creative Director: BG Hernandez | Writers: Micky Fenix, Datu Shariff, Bryan Koh
Account Executive: Marily Orosa | Main Contributor: Studio 5 Designs Inc.
Assignment: The ASEAN Ladies Foundation of the Department of Foreign Affairs aimed to create a book that would showcase the commonalities and shared food traditions of the ten member nations of the ASEAN (Association of Southeast Asian Nations) of which the Philippines was a founding member in 1967. The ten member states of this political and economic union are Brunei, Cambodia, Indonesia, Laos, Malaysia, Myanmar, Philippines, Singapore, Thailand, and Vietnam. Thus, the book title TABLE FOR TEN.
Approach: The book chapters feature select recipes that are common to the ten member states. Watercolor illustrations of each of the recipes add a romantic flavor to the book that differentiates it from existing photographic- style food books. The font chosen, a script-like alphabet, evokes memories of happy times in an Asian kitchen, and memorable meals with the family, the nucleus of every Asian Family. The nostalgic feel is kept throughout the book to elicit warmth, joy city and camaraderie, qualities present in Asian homes.
Results: TABLE FOR TEN was launched in a colorful food event attended by the ASEAN Ladies Foundation and the diplomatic corps. The buffet featured many of the recipes in the book. The proponent, Mrs Luisa Locsin, wife of the Philippine Secretary of Foreign Affairs and head of the ASEAN Ladies Foundation, proudly distributed the books to guests. The book was also the Christmas giveaway of the Philippine embassy to the embassies of the ten ASEAN nations featured in the book. It will be entered in the International Business Awards, a global search engine for the best in publication designs, and Gourmand Awards in Paris.

46 LIVRARIA LELLO BRANDING | Design Firm: Studio Eduardo Aires
Designers: Pedro Mata Nogueira, Vasco Castro, Joana Teixeira, Raquel Piteira, Rita Palha Lopes, Guillermo Zetek, Miguel Almeida, Anastasiia Potapenko | Client: Livraria Lello
Art Director: Eduardo Aires | Writer: Helena Sofia Silva | Content Developer: Helena Sofia Silva
Photographer: Oscar Almeida | Main Contributor: Studio Eduardo Aires
Assignment: It's the world's most beautiful bookshop. Jaw-droping since 1906, Livraria Lello is a cultural and artistic reference in the city of Porto, admired all over the world. Since 2015, a new administration is driving it further. The building underwent an extensive renovation and there's a new space – Sala Gemma – dedicated to rare and antique books, among other initiatives. Commited to the promotion of books, their stories, their writers and literary heritage, Livraria Lello is looking ahead. The new visual identity is another step down this new path. It aims to be bolder, more contemporary and aligned with the next chapters.
Approach: In the ceiling of the bookshop there is a stained glass window. Its motif is a blacksmith and the latin sentence "Decus in Labore", which is used as the bookshop's brand. The development of the new shape started there, trying to preserve recognizable elements from the previous visual identity. Gradually, the blacksmith came into the foreground and into the middle of Livraria Lello. Besides that placement, he can also stand alone, grow or adopt different expressions. The font is Livraria Lello Logo, a variation within a more complex system designed by Dino dos Santos (DSType Foundry). The stained glass, woodwork and iconic crimson staircase provide the colour palette. The secondary colours were chosen to favour bolder contrasts in the development of applications. One of the ligatures in the font is a double LL, corresponding to 'Livraria Lello'. This ligature is also the monogram of the bookshop, to be used alone or as a module in the development of patterns. The main version of the pattern, used in wrapping paper and gift bags is constructed through a rotation of 180 degrees, followed by successive reflections in the horizontal and vertical axes. The colour schemes vary between a more institutional approach, and the vibrant contrasts provided by the secondary colours.

47 CASALEX | Design Firm: Haotian Dong | Designer: Haotian Dong
Client: Alex Beaufort | Main Contributor: Haotian Dong
Assignment: Design a whole branding kit for new-established design studio by graphic designer Alex Beaufort based in NYC.
Approach: CASALEX is a new-established design studio by graphic designer Alex Beaufort based in NYC. It strives to elevate communication through tailored, functional, and aesthetic messages. The naming and branding design of CASALEX revolves around Alex's monogram, designed by the same designer. CASALEX combines "CASA" and "Alex," meaning everyone can find their best design here, just like at home.
Results: It's been really successful, client is really satisfied with it. It has been featured on multiple platforms and magazines.

48 THE CAPITOL FOLDER | Design Firm: IF Studio | Designer: Hisa Ide
Client: Madison Group | Artist: Magnus Gjoen | Design Director: Hisa Ide
Creative Strategist: Sarah Tan | Creative Director: Toshiaki Ide
Photographer: Athena Azevedo | Managing Partner: Amy Frankel
Account Director: Anya LaLonde | Main Contributors: Hisa Ide, Toshiaki Ide

49 ROCCO UP FILM BRAND STRATEGY & DESIGN | Design Firm: Decker Design
Designer: Lynda Decker | Client: Ditch Plains Productions
Photographer: John Madere | Main Contributor: Kevin Lamb
Assignment: Rocco Up, a documentary filmed & directed by John Madere, captures the heartfelt story of a severely autistic boy whose father taught him to surf as a non-verbal means of connecting with him. Along their journey, the surf community of Montauk, NY, was instrumental in cheering him to stand "up" on the surfboard. Our challenge was to create a brand strategy and to promote the film to support the production's fundraising effort.
Approach: The Decker Design team curated still images from the film to engage the audience in the emotional story while highlighting the natural beauty of Montauk—the backdrop to this tale. We designed the film's brand identity to provide visual consistency across all communication channels. We created the strategy and design for the website, all promotional print and digital collateral for events, and a social media campaign to drive awareness and funding.
Results: As of October, Rocco Up was accepted into the Hamptons International Film Festival, Portland Film Festival, Toronto Film Festival, Korean International Short Film Festival and Surfalorus Film Festival. The film's director, John Madere, won the award for Best Documentary at the Korean International Short Film Festival and the editor and writer, Ruth Mamaril, won the award for Best Editing at the Surfalorus Film Festival. Social media has been meeting donor acquisition goals.

50 DRIVING RECOGNITION FOR NOKIA AS A B2B TECH POWERHOUSE
Design Firm: Lippincott | Designers: Carl Baldwin, Vimmi Sveinsson, Lee Coomber, Louise Cantrill, Timothy Stewart, Ariel Chan, Kannie Lam, Josh Grazier | Client: Nokia
Strategy: Greg Handrick, Simon Glynn, Helen MacVicar, Tamara Belair, George Bigden
Main Contributor: Lee Coomber
Assignment: Nokia was once in the pockets of over a billion people worldwide. However, over the past decade, the brand has evolved, transforming into a leader in B2B networking technology. Despite this evolution, most people continue to see Nokia as a mobile phone company. Lippincott partnered with the brand on a full-scale transformation, fusing the brand's rich heritage with a bold, digital-first identity fit for the future. The goal? Unlock the brand's next stage of growth while demanding reappraisal of Nokia's as a leader in B2B technology innovation.
Approach: Lippincott got to work by distilling the company's ambition into a brand positioning that reflects the valuable role Nokia plays: pioneering the future where networks meet cloud to accelerate the impact of digital in every industry. We further articulated Nokia as a strategic collaborator and a distinctly human brand with a new purpose: "At Nokia, we create technology that helps the world act together." This purpose comes alive in a fresh new logo and visual identity. We built the identity to echo Nokia's rich heritage as the inventor of essential technologies, while giving it a fresh, contemporary, dynamic feel. This meant simplifying the geometry of the original logo and striking the right degree of visual evolution so the iconic logo was still instantly recognizable. To visually represent Nokia's purpose, the logo's individual letters were abstracted so they only read as 'Nokia' when they act together. The new digital-first identity goes further with a kaleidoscopic color palette and bold imagery. The logo's N, O and K letterforms have been repurposed as bold graphics to use across all content, so every communication from the brand is distinctively Nokia.
Results: The new Nokia was revealed to the world on February 26, 2023 through the brand's exhibition at Mobile World Congress in Barcelona. Nokia's presence proved to be a hit, with Forbes referring to it as "the most flash-worthy news at MWC," setting the stage for an uber-successful launch week, with the new Nokia receiving 1.7 billion impressions and 500k engagements globally across social media channels.

51 SIP CITY SPIRITS, WINE, & BEER IDENTITY PROGRAM
Design Firm: Ventress Design Works | Designer: Tom Ventress
Client: Randall Family Enterprises Inc. | Illustrator: Tom Ventress
Interior Designer: Shelley Prael, le Nest Design | Main Contributor: Tom Ventress
Assignment: Uptown Liquor was a typical small liquor store in Portland, Oregon. The owners had a dream of making something bigger and better and had the opportunity to move into a retail space four times larger. Originally they just asked for our help with a simple update to their existing logo. They had wisely retained retail designer, Shelley Prael, to design the store and she realized that more than a simple logo was needed to make it the store the Randalls hoped for. By the end of the project, the work comprised a new logo, exterior signage, window artwork, a graphic treatment for the entrance and exit doors, wayfinding signage, interior wall graphics, as well as other needs that pop up during a rebranding effort—van

design, coming soon graphics, and design work for the billboard above the store.
Approach: In addition to the logo update, the owners wanted to tell a story with the 70-foot run of windows that faces one of Portlands's busiest streets. We presented three concepts. The clients were especially keen on the photorealistic, multi-scene montages we offered: four windows for each product category to fill twelve windows with a logo display on the remaining window. Shortly after we finished the window art, the client was thrown a curve ball and told they couldn't use the name "Uptown" at the new store. So, in a town known as "Rip City" since the 1970s, "Sip City" became the name of the new location. All visual ties to the old store were jettisoned and we worked towards an interpretation of Shelley's fun take on modern industrial design. We tried several typographic approaches. In working with University Light Ultra Condensed, the "Y"in "City"suggested a sherry glass. Once we capped it and raised the baseline so it tucked up under the "P"in "Sip" we knew we had it. Shelley and the Randalls saw it and jumped right on it.
Results: The employees and customers have enthusiastically embraced Sip City's visual branding. Sales have been extremely strong and Sip City has solidified their place as Oregon's top retailer of spirits.

52 SLIP JOINT PLIERS PRODUCT LAUNCH | Design Firm: Traction Factory
Designer: Mike Basse | Client: Snap-on Tools | Project Manager: Pam Sallis
Design Director: David Brown | Art Director: Mike Basse | Copywriter: Tom Dixon
Production Artist: Jenni Wierzba | Account Director: Shannon Egan
Main Contributor: Traction Factory
Assignment: Our challenge was to assist Snap-on® franchisees in bringing the new Long Nose Slip Joint Pliers to the technician market. Materials needed to emphasize the unique design combination of the long, tapered nose design and three-position joint that make the new pliers a must-have for any automotive technician. Our promise: The new Snap-on Long Nose Slip Joint Pliers is the only pliers that provide extreme gripping strength and versatility in jaw spread, providing control in tight spaces with limited gripping surface space.
Approach: In addition to disruptive van materials, we provided franchisees with engaging tote-and-promote support that was portable off the van too. Finally, the product was supported in print advertising in the monthly Hot Tools sales flyer distributed by franchisees to every customer and prospect.
Results: The disruptive communications illustrated the unique design of the new product in an unexpected and visual way. In a sales environment where being the highlight of a customer's day is the key driver of success, we were able to build sales momentum leading to a successful product launch.

53 TIJUANA CITY BRAND | Design Firm: Freaner Creative & Design | Designer: Ariel Freaner
Client: City of Tijuana | Digital Artist: Ariel Freaner | Main Contributor: Ariel Freaner
Assignment: Tijuana needed a presence in areas of the United States to promote their industrial parks capabilities and services with a limited budget.
Approach: We created the word TIJUANA formed of all the industry services Tijuana can provide. The brand was used for a full international campaign including print, outdoor, video, and other digital applications.
Results: Increased awareness of the city of Tijuana to potential foreign investors.

54 THE REP REBRAND | Design Firm: Rose
Designers: Rose, Yafet Bisrat, Ryan Peart-Donaldson | Client: Birmingham Repertory Theater
Web Designer: Substrakt | Creative Directors: Simon Elliott, Garry Blackburn
Copywriter: Andy Ridgen | Strategy: Rob Macpherson
Project Manager: Joanna Waclawski | Main Contributor: Rose
Assignment: The Birmingham Repertory Theatre (The Rep) is Birmingham's world-class producing theatre that creates inclusive, exciting and exceptional theatrical experiences. The Rep has become renowned for nurturing talent, connecting communities, sharing stories and imaginatively creating theatre. Our brief was to create a strong and flexible visual identity to compliment their new values, mission and ambition. The identity needed to reflect the quality and diversity of artistic programming and their local community, to capture the imagination of new audiences post pandemic, and deliver a revitalised and cohesive experience across all three performance spaces in their central Birmingham venue, whilst retaining the loyalty of their existing customer base. Another key part of their brief was to ensure touring productions can deliver an equally consistent experience to local audiences, when they inherit third party artwork from partners.
Approach: At the heart of the new brand strategy is the ambition to deliver experiences that are created by, with and for the people of Birmingham. So we adopted this commitment and used it to inspire the brand assets and creative direction for the new brand identity. We started with the name. Everyone in Birmingham knows the theatre as 'The Rep'. So we recommended dropping their full name and replaced it with their more familiar and memorable nickname. We then crafted their new logo, using the world renowned typeface, Baskerville. We also took inspiration from the rounded front windows of The Rep's listed building for the secondary typeface family, and in doing so provided a modern visual expression to the identity to compliment the craft and heritage of Baskerville. As an entertainment brand, we also wanted to challenge preconceptions from people who might have decided theatre wasn't for them, and highlight to the Netflix generation that there is a fundamental difference when experiencing theatre – that performances are 'live'. So our new approach to Rep imagery (whether new productions or the back of their tickets) captures live moments in time, placing audiences in the thick of the action, as they would if experiencing it live.
Results: Our marketing framework enables them to amplify home grown productions, whilst also providing a consistent way of delivering the eclectic artwork they receive and need to use from touring partners and third party productions. We have been responsible for creating the primary applications for the brand including their core marketing principles, signage, master artworks and guidelines which are being used internally to roll out the identity, alongside third party agencies and partners.

55 GDF BRANDING | Design Firm: DAEKI and JUN | Designers: Daeki Shim, Hyojun Shim
Clients: Gangwon State, Gangwon Institute of Design Promotion (GIDP), Insuk Choi, Kyoungcheol Shin, Yongsun Choi, Mikyung Lee, Aeri Jang, Seongyeong Shin, Kyuseong Shim
Creative Directors: Daeki Shim, Hyojun Shim | Art Directors: Daeki Shim, Hyojun Shim
Assistant Designers: Hyunjin Cho (Intern), Hangyeol Park (Intern)
Main Contributors: Daeki Shim, Hyojun Shim
Assignment: The 2022 Gangwon Design Festa (GDF) is an exhibition and event showcasing design project achievements conducted by the Gangwon Institute of Design Promotion (GIDP) over the past three years (2019-2022) aimed at strengthening the competitiveness of regional industrial design in Gangwon State. During the 2022 GDF period, various achievements were presented to revitalize the design industry in Gangwon State. These include "Reinforcement of State's design capacity through education," "Reinforcement of SME product competitiveness through design development support," "Exhibition for citizens' design culture enjoyment," "Design culture diffusion through design awards," and "Establishment of design networking between industry-academia-research." Since its establishment in 2019, the Gangwon Institute of Design Promotion(GIDP) has laid the foundation for leading the design industry and culture in Gangwon State through various design projects over the past three years, preparing (Ready) and setting (Set) the groundwork. Now, to make a more special start (Start!) for Gangwon State, they have held the 2022 Gangwon Design Festa (GDF). *GIDP is a government design institution established for Gangwon State.
Approach: Starting with GDF (Gangwon Design Festa) in 2022, it is a new flexible identity for an annual event and exhibition held at the end of each year. The GDF flexible identity embodies the meaning of new "changes", dynamic "progress", and "growth" in Gangwon State's design industry and culture. For the branding of GDF, the following items have been designed:, Basic System, Application System, Series of Moving Images, and Identity Manual Book.

56 THE CAPITOL BROCHURE | Design Firm: IF Studio | Designer: Hisa Ide
Client: Madison Group | Artist: Magnus Gjoen | Design Director: Hisa Ide
Creative Strategist: Sarah Tan | Creative Director: Toshiaki Ide
Photographers: Yi Hsuan, Athena Azevedo | Managing Partner: Amy Frankel
Account Director: Anya LaLonde | Main Contributors: Hisa Ide, Toshiaki Ide

57 ALIAS BROCHURE | Design Firm: IF Studio | Designer: Hisa Ide | Client: Madison Group
Design Director: Hisa Ide | Creative Strategist: Sarah Tan | Creative Director: Toshiaki Ide
Photographers: Alexander Hankoff, Athena Azevedo | Managing Partner: Amy Frankel
Account Director: Anya LaLonde | Main Contributors: Hisa Ide, Toshiaki Ide

58 CHARM OF FINANCIAL MATRICES
Design Firm: Bekar Haus D.O.O. | Designers: Alira Hrabar Bekar, Dušan Bekar
Client: HRVATSKA POŠTANSKA BANKA | Creative Team: Alira Hrabar Bekar, Dušan Bekar
Main Contributors: Alira Hrabar Bekar, Dušan Bekar
Assignment: Created for the Croatian market as a gift to the clients, calendar was designed as part of New Year's program for HPB — Croatian Postal Bank — bank with relevant market influence in Croatia.
Approach: Client's requirements were that product has to have an original artistic value, that does not conflict with the practical value and that the production does not exceed the costs of making a classic 12 leaf wall calendar. Conditions generated idea for a solution shaped into a 'composite' calendar constitute of calendar cover and artistic graphic, that is made to last much longer than one year. Unique design has been devised that crosses the boundaries of utilitarian value — it moves from the sphere of information to the sphere of art.
Results: Elegant and attractive visual is solved by a combination of color and typographic elements directly relying on the visual code of the Bank's identity. Content-wise, it relies on a computer lexicon that results from mathematical operations, playing with the mathematical concept of a matrix which undoubtedly reflects the nature of the client's business. At the core of solution lies the concept of discovery. It enables the unification of two paradigms — time-limited and permanent value. During the year, the user tears off the "wrapper" month by month, which gradually reveals the graphic. He is not limited to the order of disclosure, but can do so at his discretion. Concept requires constant interaction with the user and affects the dynamics of the physics of the visual. It arouses interest in creation, as well as in observing of the created changes. User stops being just an observer but feels like an active participant in those changes — as a cocreator.

59 100TH ANNIVERSARY KOMORI 2023 CALENDAR | Design Firm: Toppan Inc.
Designer: Masahiro Aoyagi | Client: Komori Corporation | Art Director: Masahiro Aoyagi
Print Designer: Riichi Yamaguchi | Photographers: Kate Scott, Jirawat Plekhongthu, joSon
Main Contributor: Masahiro Aoyagi
Approach: The calendar celebrates its 100th anniversary with floral motifs by three photographers based in Europe, Asia, and the United States. Using high-value-added printing on an eight-color press, the calendar expresses vivid colors and a variety of textures through the combination of multiple varnishes to match the motifs. This calendar has been well received at exhibitions around the world as a sample of printing technology using Komori Corporation's printing presses.

60 MR MAGAZINE AWARDS COVER | Design Firm: Wainscot Media
Designers: Trevett McCandliss, Nancy Campbell | Client: MR Magazine
Editor-in-Chief: Karen Alberg Goldberg | Editor: John Russel Jones
Main Contributors: Trevett McCandliss, Nancy Campbell
Assignment: We needed to create a cover for MR magazine, which featured the winners of the MR Awards, which are given to people in the menswear industry.
Approach: We created a colorful customized type design for the cover.
Results: People loved the cover design.

61 RAIN PEACE IN UKRAINE | Design Firm: Randy Clark Graphic Design
Designer: Randy Clark | Client: Self-initiated | Main Contributor: Randy Clark
Assignment: We all feel immense pain for the war in Ukraine. People are dying needlessly, Ukrainians and Russians alike. I just can't sit by and not have a voice.
Approach: It was a simple approach. Simply urge an end to the fighting and bless the people of Ukraine. Wars rarely solve problems.

62 PROJECT ECHO | Design Firm: Lisa Winstanley Design
Designers: Lisa Winstanley, Iffah Qistina Binte Irwan | Client: Project Echo
Photographer: Lisa JiaXian Peh | Assistant: Mari Carpio | Main Contributor: Lisa Winstanley

Assignment: Project Echo was created to support art & design educators in addressing visual plagiarism in the creative classroom. Beginning by examining the definition of visual plagiarism from an art & design education perspective and moving to explore the challenges that artists and designers face from a moral and ethical standpoint. It is intended to guide educators who want to introduce creative integrity into their educational spaces. The Project Echo Toolkit was designed to be a modular resource, partitioning complex moral and ethical issues into bite-sized topics. Each topic is presented in an easy-to-use lesson booklet, explicitly designed with students in mind; these lessons are also supported by an accompanying activity booklet that engages students in discussion, critical thinking, and creative practice.
Approach: An echo can be described as a close parallel to an idea, and this notion is what Project Echo branding was inspired by. Its use of concentric circles visually represents the repetition and reverberation of an echo. Project Echo brand was also designed to be friendly and approachable, given that the topic of visual plagiarism often tends not to be. The word-mark utilises a legible, rounded sans serif typeface with a customised circular icon substituting the letter O. The primary monochromatic colour palette provides a bold backdrop for a contrasting rainbow gradient. These contrasting elements have been selected to appeal to a youthful and creative audience. Each Modular Toolkit Contains: Custom Designed Outer Folder, A6 Teacher's Guidebook, 2 Custom Bookmarks, Custom Sized Lesson Booklet (Student), A3 folded to A5 Activity (Student).
Results: Project Echo is part of a larger research study on addressing visual plagiarism in the creative classroom. The creative work has gone on to win the Asia Design Prize and C IDEA Design Awards and has been nominated for several more. The project toolkit will be leveraged to inform design education at Nanyang Technological University in Singapore and the research has led to international collaborations with Mississippi University in the USA and future research projects with the Royal College of Art, UK. A competitive MOE fund for over half a million dollars has been applied for based on the research findings of this project and if successful will be the first research of its kind into faculty and industry perspectives on addressing visual plagiarism.

63 NORTHWEST COAST HALL | Design Firm: American Museum of Natural History (In-House)
Designer: American Museum of Natural History | Client: Self-initiated
Creative Director: Lauri Halderman | Directors: Michael Meister, Sasha Nemecek
Art Director: Catharine Weese | Graphic Designers: Eleanor Kung, Nicole Fox, Ron Demetrio
Environmental Designers: Lydia Romero, Cine Ostrow | Project Coordinator: Ron Demetrio
Production Manager: Antonia Gabor | Senior Producer: Peter Whitely | Producer: Ḥaayuups
Photo Editor: José Ramos | Writers: Willow Lawson, Margaret Dornfeld
Main Contributor: American Museum of Natural History
Assignment: Opened in 1899, the Northwest Coast Hall is the oldest gallery within the Museum of Natural History. Continuing with a long tradition of collaborating with the Northwest Coast peoples, the museum's goal was to create a modern exhibition which showcases the unique history and current way of life for these individuals. The new interpretation was developed with Consulting Curators from all 10 Native nations represented throughout the hall, and features names and terms in both English and Native languages.
Approach: Organized as a series of permeable alcoves, the redesign of this historic hall showcases more than 1,000 restored cultural treasures of ten Native Nations of the Pacific Northwest. The revitalized hall highlights the vitality and persistence of these communities, with new interpretation, storytelling, and dynamic media developed with Native scholars, artists, historians, filmmakers, and language experts. The new design opens up the hall, emphasizing the interconnectedness of Northwest Coast communities, and provides multiple vantage points on the treasures. The background shades of blue-green evoke the cedar forests and dark water of the region; and large photographic murals provide a window into the natural environment. The interpretive design brings the living communities into focus, featuring current voices and people, while contextualizing the important historical work. Several alcoves are devoted to the work of contemporary Northwest Coast artists, demonstrating both continuity and reinvention in the art forms.
Results: This fresh, collaborative way of presenting these stories has been carefully curated to balance the preservation of cultural heritage with a modern, accessible approach, making it a valuable resource for both visitors and researchers.

64 QUINTA DE ADORIGO | Design Firm: Studio Eduardo Aires
Designer: Eduardo Aires | Client: Quinta de Adorigo | Art Director: Eduardo Aires
Graphic Designers: Dário Cannatà, Guillermo Zetek, Joana Teixeira
Photographers: Óscar Almeida (Product), Mir AS (Landscape)
Main Contributor: Studio Eduardo Aires
Assignment: In Douro's monumental landscape there is a new project underway. A new winery and hotel designed by architect Sérgio Rebelo merges into Douro's natural scenario, framing nature as it creates spaces for contemplation. A recipient of an Architizer Award and a World Architecture Festival Award in 2021, the project's winery evokes the confluent terraces that characterize the landscape.
Approach: Quinta de Adorigo's new wine labels refer to the rows of terraces that are part and parcel of Douro's landscape and are reflected in the architecture project. Terraces that have long shaped the territory with their metrics, monumental walls and sun oriented slopes, representing the harmonious adaptation of nature to human activities. In the new labels we drew their geometry in a graphical synthesis to match the project's contemporary orientation.

65 LAUDA REGINA | Design Firm: Mark Braught Studios | Designer: Mark Braught
Client: Strange Duck Brewery | Studio: Mark Braught Studios | Art Director: Kristan Robertson
Illustrator: Mark Braught | Main Contributor: Mark Braught
Assignment: Created for small IPA brewery, Strange Duck in Commerce, Georgia, promoting the unique aspect of their products, for in-store promotion, merchandising, online and print advertising.
Approach: Developed as a pencil sketch to fully rendered digital expression.
Results: This illustration was used widely across various media: direct mail, web/social, fliers, business cards, packaging, apparel, merchandise, limited print advertising, and in-store display. The client was pleased with the illustrations and more "strange ducks" are in the works.

66, 67 CALIFORNIA CONDOR | Design Firm: Michael Pantuso Design
Designer: Michael Pantuso | Client: AOFA Gallery | Art Buyer: Acquisitions of Fine Art
Main Contributor: Michael Pantuso
Assignment: "California Condor: These Broken Wings" is part of an ongoing digital art series that explore the intricate connections between nature and humanity, and build upon ideas of integration and intervention.
Approach: Pencil sketch to digital expression.
Results: First edition was acquired by a private collector. The remaining limited edition is available at the Acquisitions of Fine Art Gallery in Hinsdale, Illinois and West Palm Beach, Florida.

68 2022 PUBLIC ART FUND SPRING PARTY INVITATION
Design Firm: Ahoy Studios | Designers: Connie Koch, Lucia del Zotto, Denise Sommer
Client: Public Art Fund | Main Contributor: Public Art Fund
Assignment: Design in full bloom: We proudly showcase our invitation package for the Public Art Fund Spring Party! The invitation Ahoy designed "blossoms" open to reveal neon petals and holographic accents to emphasize the bold creative spirit of the Public Art Fund. As the leader in its field, Public Art Fund brings dynamic contemporary art to a broad audience in New York City and beyond by mounting ambitious free exhibitions of international scope and impact that offer powerful public experiences with art and the urban environment. Ahoy has designed the materials for the renowned annual fundraising gala for many years, including the visual identity, invitation, advertising, and on-site signage. After a two-year hiatus following the pandemic, we were asked to visualize New York City's spring awakening and the transformational nature of the Public Art Fund.
Approach: The flower graphic did just that. The custom envelope was a bright splash in everyone's mailboxes. As recipients unfolded the custom-shaped envelope, the flower graphic was revealed. The invitation itself was adorned with a holographic foil and a bright pink gilded edge.
Results: The intriguing invitation suite excited the New York art world to attend the party and raise funds for the institution. Attendance was higher than ever!

69 SLACKTOBERFEST INVITATION | Design Firm: Spire Agency
Designer: Alex Flores | Client: Slack Davis Sanger | Chief Creative Officer: Kimberly Tyner
Associate Creative Director: Jason James | Printing: Colormark
Copywriter: Mike Stopper | Senior Account Executive: Caitlyn Pobee
Account Supervisor: Julia Cardali | Main Contributor: Alex Flores
Assignment: Slack Davis Sanger (SDS) is a Texas-based law group that specializes in navigating and winning the challenging personal injury cases that few firms have the in-house resources or niche expertise to take on. Every year, SDS throws an Oktoberfest event. The purpose of this event is to gather local politicians, judges, and attorneys to network and thank them for case referrals and to keep SDS top of mind so that the referrals keep coming.
Approach: The 2022 18th annual Oktoberfest was different than in previous years, most notably by formally branding the name of the event to "Slacktoberfest." The creative inspiration was a "Bat City meets Bavaria" approach that put an Austin, Texas twist on ol' Oktoberfest. An oversized postcard was created to serve as an invitation to the event for the majority of invitees, while a custom gift box was created and delivered as the invitation for the firm's top 75 referral attorneys. The gift box was a custom-designed metallic gold box with blue and gold foil stamps and magnetic snap. The gift item included a high-end German beer stein and messaging about the event details.
Results: The custom gift box was a huge success—a 27% response rate—compared to the 2.7% – 4.4% average response rate for direct mail (Newswires, 2022).

70 ALTA WEST MOREHEAD LOGOMARK | Design Firm: Resource Branding
Designer: Brian Burkey | Client: Wood Partners | Design Director: Rick Grimsley
Account Managers: Cate Pilliod, Cat Touliatous, Lindsey Lane
Main Contributor: Resource Branding
Assignment: Create a logomark for a new residential development located in the old industrial West Morehead neighborhood in Charlotte, NC. The neighborhood is an emerging area featuring a number of trendy developments, restaurants, and breweries, many of which are housed within adaptive reuse spaces. The brand should fit in with and reflect the history of the area.
Approach: Create an integrated AWM icon that speaks to project's location at the highest point in the city next to the radio station. The mark is designed to give a nod to the structural look of the radio tower and use a typographic aesthetic that reflects much of the industrial adaptive reuse in the area. It also incorporates a wavelength shape to pay off the tagline, "Live at a Higher Frequency".
Results: Tours and pre-leasing for this luxury community are going well - the client has been pleased with the brand and the buzz in the market.

70 SMGP LOGO | Design Firm: Studio 5 Designs Inc.
Designer: Rogel Vidallo | Clients: San Miguel Global Power, Kim de Leon-Morgan
Creative Director: BG Hernandez | Account Supervisor: Marily Orosa
Account Director: Raffy Ortega | Main Contributor: Studio 5 Designs Inc.
Assignment: Design of a new corporate identity that symbolisez the unification of 16 energy subsidiaries into one energy company.
Approach: The company's initials—SMGP— was used as the inspiration for the design of the logo. It conveys the company's ability to keep pace with the modern times. The logo is a synergy of shapes, smooth curves, and vibrant colors to deliver the message of unity, harmony and uniqueness that represents the interconnection of the company's businesses. The use of six colors represent svarious meanings which begin with a tribute to their roots (Sunset Gold and Manila Red) to a commitment to sustainability and preservation of its environment (I Chartreuse) to a commitment to heartelt service to their stakeholders.The sustainability agenda is in the form of a heart embedded within the symbol.
Results: The passion with which the company embraced the new logo is seen in its immediate and loving application in all corporate collaterals throughout the breath and length of the company. A brand manual was created to safeguard the new logo at all times.

70 DARKHORSE DESIGN LOGO | Design Firm: Darkhorse Design, LLC
Designer: Robert Talarczyk | Client: Self-initiated | Executive Creative Director: Robert Talarczyk
Art Director: Robert Talarczyk | Main Contributor: Robert Talarczyk

70 85TH ANNIVERSARY Design Firm: Paco Macias Velasco Studio
Designers: Kristofer Macías, Paco Macias Velasco | Client: Laboratorios Liomont
Main Contributor: Kristofer Macías
Assignment: Logo proposal for the Mexican pharmaceutical laboratory Liomont on the occasion of its 85th Anniversary 1938-2023
Approach: This logo is based on the double helix of DNA (deoxyribonucleic acid) that forms the number 8 and 5 is formed by RNA (ribonucleic acid) the DNA helix is represented by Nucleotides, Thymine, Adenine, Cytosine, Guanine in 4 colors, green, yellow, blue and pink in the case of RNA, the nucleotides are the same except Uracil that replaces Thymine. In the context of the decoding of the human genome, pharmacogenetics and pharmacogenomics constitute two emerging disciplines that integrate pharmacology and molecular genetics. From these will emerge a new generation of drugs, more effective and safe, based on the genetic peculiarities of individuals.
Results: The objective when designing this logo was to situate this 85th anniversary of Liomont Laboratories within this current of the design of new medicines. This logo would be used for the year of celebration only.

70 CAT DEFENSE SYSTEM LOGOS | Design Firm: UP-Ideas
Designer: Roger Sawhill | Client: Joanna Sawhill | Main Contributor: Roger Sawhill
Assignment: Faced with a feral cat torturing our indoor cat every night, to the point our cat was throwing himself at a solid glass door, the client engaged UP-Ideas to thwart this invader. We started with a simple, but cleverly designed, box trap — the QUB3. But alas, the feral cat was too smart for this. Undaunted, and with a very sleep deprived client, we sought a different approach — something no cat could withstand — loud noises. With a combination of 9 volt batteries, Estes rocket ignitors, and Black Cat firecrackers, the Sonic Cat Repulsor (sCATr) was born.
Approach: A project that took such effort was worthy of its own logos. Inspired by the hexagon's ability to represent a 3D cube, a shape that could hold all the thinking required to outsmart a cat, each logo is based on this amazing polygon.
Results: With remote switches on 2 levels of the house, the sCATr can be triggered at a moments notice, and with a payload of 3 fire crackers, it be triggered multiple times if needed. Within a month our nemesis ceased to return (apologies to our neighbors for the early morning detonations). Product introduction into the wider commercial market is pending a full legal review.

71 ABYSSINIAN BAPTIST CHURCH FEDERAL CREDIT UNION LOGOMARK
Design Firm: Mermaid, Inc. | Designer: Sharon McLaughlin
Client: Abyssinian Baptist Church Federal Credit Union | Creative Team: Bart McLaughlin
Main Contributor: Sharon Lloyd McLaughlin
Assignment: We were asked to create a logo for Abyssinian Baptist Church Federal Credit Union, a Black federal credit union affiliated with the historic Abyssinian Baptist Church located in Harlem.
Approach: Our approach to creating this logo was deeply rooted in the love and care they have for their members. We wanted to visually communicate this affectionate connection, which led us to incorporate an intertwined heart as a central element in the logo. The intertwined heart symbolizes the strong bond between the credit union and its members, reflecting the genuine care and support provided by Abyssinian FCU. In addition, the style of the heart was deliberately designed as a visual tie to the cross in the Abyssinian Baptist Church's logo.
Results: Our approach successfully captured the essence of the love and connection Abyssinian Federal Credit Union shares with its members. The logo serves as a powerful representation of the credit union's commitment to nurturing relationships and providing financial support within their community. The client was pleased with the result, finding the logo to be a perfect embodiment of the credit union's values and their dedication to fostering strong and caring relationships with their members.

72 FORZA MOTORSPORT REBRAND | Design Firm: TGD | Designer: Johann A. Gómez
Clients: 343 Industries, Ryann Merritt | Main Contributors: Ryan Burlinson, Johann A. Gómez, Mat McInelly, Jessica Larkin, Jessah Hofker
Assignment: The Forza franchise has been a mainstay in gaming since 2006, seeing only slight shifts and changes to its branding since its inception. However, to prepare the franchise for the omnichannel reality of both the gaming marketplace and pop culture today, Forza needed a cohesive brand system to rely on.
Approach: To support a continued legacy of best-selling titles, we collaborated with the Forza team to create a brand and logo system that could flex to the needs of the franchise, but also to individual games. Beyond a system, we also developed a new logo for Forza Motorsport, the franchise's mainline racing series.
Results: Our brand alignment efforts provided the Forza team with technical guidance, creative inspiration, and more. With it, Forza is now equipped with the design system—and the creative fuel—required for a long line of award-winning experiences to come.

72 PTS CONTRACTING | Design Firm: Kate Borman Creative Design Co.
Designer: Kate Borman Richardson | Client: Harrison Edwards Integrated Marketing
Vice President: Lisa Buchman | Main Contributor: Julia Emrick
Assignment: Based in Armonk, NY, PTS Contracting is a specialized expert in healthcare and life sciences construction, providing services for all size projects for clients throughout the Tri-State region - working closely with clients through the design, estimating, pre-construction, and construction. In need of a refresh, PTS Contracting was looking for a new professional logo that was bright, clean, bold and strong. Making use of their "PTS" lettering and representative of a construction hat element as used in their original logo, they were looking for a solid icon that would stand out among others in their field, and boldly lend itself well to truck wraps, uniformed jackets, and a suite of promotional items.
Approach: The meaning & symbolism behind the logo mark: Hexagon (Strength) + Bolt Shape (Connect / Build) + Yellow (Stylized Construction Helmet) + PTS Lettering = PTS lettering created in a structural cube shape, with all lettering connected - symbolizing interior space and a strong build.
Results: Proud that their company presence had been brought to life, PTS contracting was excited to move forward with a website overhaul, update their collateral and present their clients and crew with a collection of newly printed swag.

72 ALFISTI AM SEE LOGO | Design Firm: Keith Harris Design | Designer: Keith Harris
Client: Alfisti am See | Account Manager: Jochen Lang | Main Contributor: Keith Harris
Assignment: Logo for the Alfisti am See, the Club for Alfa Romeo owners centered around Lake Constance.
Approach: The Visconti Serpent gives the club its clear identity.
Results: It was later decided to broaden the membership area, and with that happening, the design was no longer relevant.

73 KERNOVA | Design Firm: El Paso, Galería de Comunicación
Designer: Álvaro Pérez | Client: Kernova | Creative Team: Álvaro Pérez, Curra Medina
Main Contributor: El Paso, Galería de Comunicación
Assignment: Kernova is an engineering company that works in Innovation, from the kern of each challenge. Innovation will thrust the greatest technological, social, human and environmental breakthroughs in the incoming years.
Approach: To name the project and design its logo, we first create the brand. We worked on strategy by defining values, vision and objective. With this, we reached a conclusion that we embodied in the logo: the spark of innovation is at the kern of every Kernova project.

73 GLOCAL MEDIA NEWS LOGO | Design Firm: Freaner Creative & Design
Designer: Ariel Freaner | Client: Glocal Media News | Creative Director: Ariel Freaner
Main Contributor: Ariel Freaner

73 TU HERRERO DE CARAMELO | Design Firm: El Paso, Galería de Comunicación
Designer: Álvaro Pérez | Client: Iván Domene | Creative Team: Álvaro Pérez, Curra Medina
Main Contributor: El Paso, Galería de Comunicación
Assignment: Iván Domene is the entrepreneur behind "Tu Herrero de Caramelo" brand. A young craftsman with plenty of talent and passion for medieval forging and steel. A passion that has led him to start a digital project of informative and entertainment content from a fresh, fun and very personal perspective.
Approach: To design his logo, we first created his brand by defining his values and his vision. With them we were able to focus his goal, work his tone, build his story and finally create his public face with a Candy Helm.

74 BRAND IDENTITY FOR ANNIVERSARY EXHIBITION "SIXTY YEARS OF COLLECTING" | Design Firm: Code Switch | Designer: Jan Šabach
Client: University Museum of Contemporary Art at University of Massachusetts, Amherst
Main Contributor: Jan Šabach
Assignment: Identity for an anniversary exhibition Sixty Years of Collecting at the University Museum of Contemporary Art, University of Massachusetts Amherst.
Approach: The variety of exhibited art is illustrated by the variety of typefaces.
Results: The client loved their identity.

75 QUINTA DA BOAVISTA - MICHELIN GUIDE | Design Firm: Another Collective
Designers: Bruno Soares, Eduardo Rodrigues | Client: Quinta da Boavista - Sogevinus
Art Directors: Bruno Soares, Eduardo Rodrigues | Photographer: Álvaro Martino
Main Contributor: Another Collective
Assignment: The challenge consisted of creating an object with the function of honoring the chefs who carry the flag of Portuguese gastronomy the highest, through the recognition obtained in the Michelin Guide. The intention was to develop an object capable of reflecting the essence of Quinta da Boavista and carrying on its legacy. The object has the mission of honoring the one who's gifted but also of giving meaning to what it holds within itself, since, in addition to carrying the wine, it serves as a communication piece, where the range of wines from Quinta da Boavista.
Approach: The concept is based on the premise of associating the box with the Quinta's historical past that must be preserved. The connection to The Baron of Forrester, an unavoidable figure in the history of the Douro and Port wine, with a strong connection to Quinta da Boavista, a scholar of his time and creator of an important publication of 1848: a remarkable map of the Douro river, from the Spanish border to the mouth of the Douro.
Thus, we designed the box in order to convey an idea of a case/box, almost like an object that carries something worthy of study, a sample to be explored and evaluated - a legacy of a centuries-old farm.

76 "THE THREAD" MOONCAKE PACKAGING DESIGN | Design Firm: Tianyun Jiang
Designer: Tianyun Jiang | Client: Self-initiated | Main Contributor: Tianyun Jiang
Assignment: This packaging is designed as a 2022 Hongkong Maxim Mooncake gift box for consumers who want to send a gift to families and friends during Mid-Autumn Festival. The general design is inspired by the Chinese emperor style back in Qing Dynasty. The outside dark and golden color code set a high-end tone for the product. Meanwhile, the inside creates a surprising moment with flaming and exuberant colors, telling a touching love story.
Approach: The illustration in the box was created by procreate. The rendering of the whole brand was created in Cinema4D with Octane Plug-in.

77 PEPSI BLACK EDC MEXICO 2023 | Design Firm: PepsiCo Design & Innovation
Designer: PepsiCo Design & Innovation | Client: Self-initiated
Assignment: Pepsi is a brand that is always in line with what's new and now in pop culture, and has a long history and partnership with music. The Electric Daisy Carnival (EDC) is the premiere electronic music festival in Latin America. In February 2023, Pepsi Black launched limited edition packaging for EDC Mexico, along with a full communications and digital campaign to bring more relevance and distinction to the brand. Music festivals offer a unique atmosphere for discovery and connection and creates a shared experience exclusive to the event-goers. Today more than ever, centennial audiences are in search of emotionally-resonant shared experiences to bring them together with likeminded people. The festival landscape is becoming more specialized, offering niche events with

distinct philosophies and proposals. Today, these themed events belong to specific communities that endure over time.
Approach: To create the limited edition packaging, the Design Team brought together the main EDC visual assets and elements from the Pepsi Black brand toolkit. Inspired by the rhythm of EDC, the look and feel of the packaging reflects the intense flavor of Pepsi Black and the idea of turning up the music to the next level. The color palette is represented with a sleek black substrate overlaid with metallic silver graphics, contrasting hues of bright and light blue reminiscent of neon lights, and pops of red accent color. The EDC logo pops with a silver moon that appears floating amidst a field of electric daisies, swaying to the beat.
Results: With this limited edition can, Pepsi Black spreads brand love throughout the EDC community, represents its brand essence and positioning on a large scale, and contributes to Pepsi Non-Sugar portfolio growth.

78 XUN MI HONEY PACKAGING DESIGN | Design Firm: Roking Art Design
Designer: Qin Luo | Client: Ji An Xun Bee Industry Co., Ltd. | Main Contributor: Qin Luo
Assignment: Combined with the consumption habits of the current young people, the purpose is to create a unique category attributes in the market, can make the product stand out in the era of homogenization honey packaging design.
Approach: The packaging shape creates a unique visual symbol of the product through the bee tail and the color matching of yellow and black. The packaging design of the small jar for one-time consumption is not only easy to carry, but also solves the problem that the large jar of honey is not eaten for a long time after being opened. Deterioration or affect the taste; bees are a symbol of industriousness. The numbers 1 to 31 on the top cover of the small jar of honey are designed according to the trajectory of the honey bee's flight every day. The calendar-style hollow packaging can intuitively see the production of the product. At the same time, it can urge consumers to remember to drink a cup of honey every day. After the package is opened, the cardboard holding the small jar of honey can also be folded into a small hexagonal calendar. edible.
Results: The packaging design makes the product form very novel, the product category attributes are very strong, leaving a deep impression in the minds of consumers, occupying the minds of consumers, at the same time, the small pot type of consumption, more appropriate to consumers' drinking habits.

79 ASTRAEA GIN | Design Firm: Stranger & Stranger
Designer: Stranger & Stranger | Client: Astraea LLC | Main Contributor: Stranger & Stranger
Assignment: Reimagine the Astraea range of Pacific north west inspired gins to increase shelf presence and perceived quality.
Approach: The first task was to create a strong logotype so the brandname would be seen in a bar. The nature based flavors; mist, meadow, ocean and forest, were expressed through a flexible and color coded illustration system.The tall bottle which is very anticategory, makes sure that the brand stands literally head and shoulders above the competition.
Results: "Same award winning gin, new spectacular packaging."

79 VIA CAROTA CRAFT COCKTAILS | Design Firm: Stranger & Stranger
Designer: Stranger & Stranger | Client: Via Carota | Main Contributor: Stranger & Stranger
Assignment: Via Carota is an iconic Italian restaurant in New York's west village. Our task was to develop a range of premium ready to drink cocktails and Italian aperitifs using the restaurants famous name.
Approach: A unique and evocative glass bottle was essential to highlight the different colored liquids. It can be repurposed for olive oil, vinegar and more.
Results: "I'm excited to share that our early momentum continues to be strong and exceed our expectations." Bart Silvestro, Chief Executive Officer

80 LAY'S - MORE BELGIAN REALLY IMPOSSIBLE!
Design Firm: PepsiCo Design & Innovation
Designer: PepsiCo Design & Innovation | Client: Self-initiated
Assignment: The global snack market has become more competitive than ever, with more local players introducing relevant flavors and product claims. In Belgium, the Lay's brand launched new flavor innovations and a new design approach to both retain current brand loyalists and acquire new consumers. Partnering with Brussels Ketjep, Lay's launched two new iconic and localized flavors: Lay's Fries Mayo and Fries Andalouse along with a campaign, #MoreBelgianImpossible.
Approach: Lay's decided to directly engage Belgian consumers by challenging them to come up with design concepts that they would capture authentic local insights. The two most voted designs would then have the honor of being featured and credited on #MoreBelgianisReallyImpossible limited edition packs. Belgian consumers cast their votes, and the two winning concepts, both Comic Strips, became a creative springboard to change the packaging design of Lay's Frites Mayo and Frietjes Andalouse flavor crisps. One concept was presented in Flemish (stripverhalen) and the other in French (band dessinée), the two main languages in Belgium. It was no surprise that a comic strip concept resonated with local consumers, as Belgium has a long tradition of comic book art. Working in partnership with illustrator Serge Seidlitz, the Design Team created a unique flavor story in a contemporary adult comic book style. With the unmistakable Lay's branding front and center on pack, the comic book frames expanded across the pack, telling the story of the main character Frite/Frietje searching for their friend Mayo/Andalouse. The interchangeable pack designs follow Frites as the character searches, finds, and loses Mayo, and then begins the search again on the next pack.
Results: To date the Lay's #MoreBelgianisReallyImpossible campaign has been positively received, having contributed to positive sales results as of week 45, when the new packs were released on shelf and above-the-line media began. Ultimately, with consumer involvement, what began as a Lay's iconic local flavor launch became so much more - a co-creation and celebration of Belgian flavors and culture.

81 PEPSI BLACK ZERO NFT COLLECTION | Design Firm: PepsiCo Design & Innovation
Designer: PepsiCo Design & Innovation | Client: Self-initiated
Assignment: To authentically connect with younger generations and further the mission of Pepsi to create a culture that promotes innovation, self-expression, and evolution, the brand's design sensibilities have also evolved with the changing cultural landscape. In 2022, the brand relaunched Pepsi® Black™ with a new packaging design and corresponding 360-degree campaign. The launch of the first Pepsi Black Zero Sugar NFT collection is another forward-thinking step in this direction. Looking at the popularity of current metaverse trends, Pepsi® wanted to create a communication touchpoint for metaverse consumers that would be anchored on the key proposition of Zero Sugar for future generations.
Approach: With the Pepsi Black Zero Sugar philosophy at its core, the Design Team created a set of 22 NFTs minted on the Polygon blockchain. The design strategy included representing all seven passion points of the Pepsi brand executed in an appealing aesthetic for NFT collectors. The NFT art collectibles center on alterations of the classic Pepsi Black Zero Sugar visual, portraying poignant nuances of the brand passions, such as sustainability, rhythm, and art. Each piece captures the essence of the represented genres, including detailed elements such as fabric for fashion, sound bars for music, and moving blocks for games.
Results: With three variations of each theme and four variations inspired from music, the Pepsi Black Zero Sugar NFT collection was listed on Open Sea, the world's largest web marketplace for NFTs and crypto collectibles. The NFTs were given away free of cost to the winners of #PepsiBlackeffect challenge conducted on the homegrown Indian social media platform, Moj. Consumers could enter the contest using the quirky Pepsi Black lens and flaunt their "max SWAG" personas for a chance to win. The NFT launch was met with excitement and consumer engagement with the contest was massive, with 1B total views and 317K posts of user-generated content created to win the brand's first-ever NFTs.

82 TEXAS OUTLAW REVENUERS | Design Firm: CF Napa Brand Design
Designer: CF Napa Brand Design | Client: Solenopsis Distilling
Main Contributor: CF Napa Brand Design
Assignment: Solenopsis Distilling came to CF Napa to create the logo and packaging for their Texas Outlaw Revenuers brand.
Approach: Inspired by the Prohibition Era rebel lawmen that refused to enforce the alcohol ban and protested the resulting increase in income tax put in place to recoup money lost on liquor tax, the design needed to harken back to that snapshot in time and embody the bold and brave spirit of the outlaw revenuers.
Results: Drawing inspiration from "wanted" posters of the period, CF Napa created an illustration of 1920s revenuers walking around a classic Cadillac V-16, the style of car owned by the infamous gangster, Al Capone. This artwork is nostalgic, referencing a pivotal time in American history. The double-sided label packs a dynamic punch with the Revenuers illustration on the front and barrels of protected whiskey on the other side, visible through the back of the bottle. The paper was given a burned and aged treatment, mimicking the effects of time on a hidden bottle of forbidden spirits.

83 WANLIZOUDANJI | Design Firm: Sungoo Design | Designer: Muqiang Fu
Client: Drunkard Wine Co., Ltd. | Main Contributor: Muqiang Fu
Assignment: The bottle box design of Jiuguijiu adopts modern methods to interpret cultural traditions. Under the light and luxurious modern style, it adds to the historical and cultural value, which coincides with the watchman spirit of Walking. While continuing the classic brand imprint of Jiugui Liquor, we used original illustrations and crystal bottles to make innovations.
Approach: We have depicted the most distinctive twelve scenes among the twelve world heritage sites on a cultural map. The landscape carvings run through these ancient monuments, which are located in the north and south of the world. The paintings show their respective historical and cultural charms, allowing people to read them carefully and have sufficient cultural commemorative value.
Illustrations are the cultural basis and design focus of this product. We spent two months and repeated scrutiny to trace the spirit of each building from the ground on paper without losing its charm.
Results: As a product with World Heritage as a design element, we have displayed China's twelve design heritage in the form of illustrations on the bottle box, which has been well received by culture lovers and wine lovers alike. We hope that through these twelve bottles of wine, we can awaken everyone's understanding and emotion of culture.

84 BUCK DANCER BOURBON | Design Firm: Chad Michael Studio
Designer: Chad Makerson Michael | Client: La Crosse Distilling Co.
Assignment: To develop the brand name and design from the ground-up that reinforced the presented strategy based on product, origin, and distilling methods. "Buck Dancer is the most premium spirit La Crosse Distillery has produced to date. This Red Corn Bourbon is true to earth and was born by channeling the full spirit of Wisconsin's native lands into each barrel. The farmers and distillers behind Buck Dancer hold to the same values as the Native American tribes that once inhabited the very same lands. It only takes what is needed and returns the favor in kind. Their foot print is light and their foraging is quiet as to not disturb."
Approach: The single phrase that was narrowed down to describe the above was "A Whiskey in Harmony". Harmony in terms of the tasting notes but, more importantly, harmony with the lands from where the whiskey was born. The package design depicts nature's fiddle growing to an exaggerated size from the roots of the land. Even with its' big, beautiful notes it lives in harmony with the environment and wildlife that surrounds it.
Results: The brand launch was a huge success. The client initially released 2000 bottles in a presale strategy and sold out within a week. We plan on continuing the range and releasing different labels using different instruments.

85 HEADY BELLA COFFEE WHISKEY | Design Firm: Chad Michael Studio
Designer: Chad Makerson Michael | Client: La Crosse Distilling Co.
Main Contributor: Red Productions
Assignment: To develop and design the brand and packaging for a new organic, additive-free, Coffee Whiskey. From our strategy presentation to client "It's a non-conformist living free, feet-to-earth, soaking in all nature has to offer. Crafted from a lightly aged organic Rye whiskey, locally farmed coffee beans, and maple syrup tapped from Wisconsin's native terroir this product sets a new standard for a new generation of spirits.

Approach: Design direction pitched: To embrace and balance whiskey's original western roots with that of the green, raw, and individualist aspect of the product itself. We can classify this as "Western Bohemian". The design will be seen as genuine, native, and human. The pack will pair energy and color through pattern and reflect the one-of-a-kind product within through incredibly unique label structuring. Vibrant pops of sunbeaten color will be paired with the rough, rugged character of the West.
Results: The Coffee Whiskey is now the 2nd best-seller at the distillery's public restaurant and bar located in La Crosse, WI.

86 CLOS DU VAL PORTFOLIO | Design Firm: CF Napa Brand Design
Designer: CF Napa Brand Design | Client: Clos du Val
Main Contributor: CF Napa Brand Design
Assignment: As one of the original wineries of the famed Stags Leap District and an American entrant in the historic 1976 Judgment of Paris, Clos du Val is a Napa Valley legend. CF Napa was tasked to consult on the brand's tiering structure and then refresh the brand logo and packaging–returning the brand to its former status and appropriate pedigree.
Approach: We decided to incorporate a more youthful freshness combined with a sophisticated French sensibility to honor the founding family's ties to Bordeaux.
Results: CF Napa refreshed the brand's five tiers; the first to launch was the Red Blend for their international market. The Clos du Val wordmark was refined to be more readable, and their Three Graces icon was redrawn to be more representative of the sculpture on which it was based and with the intention of creating a symbol with the flexibility to be used across diverse mediums while implementing a more contemporary take. Both a positive and reverse version were developed so that the logo could be easily used across a wide range of mediums. The final touch to the label was the use of their historic terracotta color. Following the Red Blend, and the first to launch domestically in the new packaging, was the iconic Napa Valley Cabernet Sauvignon. The new label prominently features the redrawn Three Graces icon. A version of the brand's wordmark with swirls framed the new illustration while harkening back to the brand's historical packaging. The previously dark colored capsules were replaced with a cream to aid in visibility in stores. For the super-premium Estate tier, the Three Graces portrait was accentuated by a debossed frame for a highly tactile design and was accompanied by minimal text to provide the understated elegance of a fine art piece. A handwritten vintage date accentuated the exclusivity of the sophisticated wine. A luxurious icon wine was developed as the highest point of the Clos du Val portfolio – Yettalil. This wine utilized the brand's trademark terracotta. The redrawn Three Graces icon was given its due reverence as the only design element on the front label – a white border framed the label like a piece of fine art. A neck label and a metal cork seal embossed with the Three Graces provided the final touches.

87 MERSEY CRAFT SPIRITS | Design Firm: CF Napa Brand Design
Designer: CF Napa Brand Design | Client: FA Poole & Co. Distillers
Main Contributor: CF Napa Brand Design
Assignment: F.A. Poole & Co. Distillers came to CF Napa to refine their story and create the packaging design for their Mersey Craft Spirits brand.
Approach: The brand owner was inspired by his grandfather, F.A. Poole, whose adventurous spirit led him to brave the open ocean aboard the Queen of the Mersey. The products of Mersey Craft Spirits are curated from a collection of discovered spirits from all over the world, igniting the spirit of exploration in the imbiber.
Results: For the main graphic, CF Napa drew the brand icon as a ship. The label design's usage of type and label shape is a modern take on nostalgic travel tickets. The inclusion of the recipe and bottle numbers emphasizes the brand's unique curation model and limited production.

88 7UP X RAMADAN 2022 | Design Firm: PepsiCo Design & Innovation
Designer: PepsiCo Design & Innovation | Client: Self-initiated
Assignment: To celebrate the spirit of Ramadan in Bangladesh, 7UP® embraced the single largest occasion of the year with its latest limited-edition packaging that fully reflected the themes of this auspicious period. Ramadan is one of the most important cultural occasions in the country, with families and friends coming together to feast each evening at the time of Iftar. 7UP is the CSD leader in Bangladesh, so it was important for the brand to embrace local relevance with Ramadan-specific designs and be a welcome addition to Iftar tables across the country.
Approach: The Design Team drew inspiration from the local motifs surrounding Ramadan. A green substrate reflects the strong association with Ramadan and Bangladeshi culture, while anchoring the 7UP brand. And the design language was influenced by Islamic architecture, utilizing geometric symmetry and expanding to infinite patterns. Luxe gold tone and celestial design elements capture consumers' initial attention. And a crescent moon and stars, which are culturally relevant icons of the Ramadan season, encircle the 7UP logo. Smaller red star accents subtly borrow from the 7UP logo color scheme, lending to brand recognition. And to really help the product shine, gems and stones were added atop these patterns.
Results: The 7UP x Ramadan campaign was well received, reaching 14.46 million people and garnering 22 total media stories (both print and online). Additionally supporting these efforts, 7UP collaborated with Prothom Alo, the leading Bangla language daily newspaper in the nation, to publish 'Summer Cooler' recipes under the campaign #IftaarWith7UP. These refreshing drink recipes were made and presented with the 7UP bottles in tow. This content was aired on TV (Nagorik TV) and shared on social platforms (Prothom Alo) and appreciated by viewers.

89 PEPSI CULTURE CAN - CHINA CITY EDITION
Design Firm: PepsiCo Design & Innovation
Designer: PepsiCo Design & Innovation | Client: Self-initiated
Assignment: Following the success of last year's Culture Can series in China, a campaign in which we utilized new media platforms to empower traditional culture in innovative ways, the Pepsi team decided to continue building its cultural relevance with a new series of cans for 2022. The objective for this series was to win in strategic areas of the Chinese market through the Pepsi brand embracing and reflecting Chinese heritage and therefore increasing desirability with local consumers.
Approach: The Design Team created Pepsi Culture Cans - China City Edition with three different designs tailored to three Chinese cities: Xi'an, Jilin, and Luoyang. Leaning into the use of visual language that carries strong regional relevance allows Pepsi to build local consumer recognition. On each can, iconic landmarks and unique local patterns are illustrated with distinctive colors and metallic accents to capture the attention of consumers and invite them to engage with the product. Each design features bold typography, proudly representing the name of each city. We set the design representing Xi'an on a bold blue Pepsi substrate and illustrated the city's 600+ year old iconic bell tower in central Xi'an, with orange and red accents. In the background, we included beautifully painted Chinese fans, a unique genre of Chinese painting. We also added peonies, known as "the king of flowers", which brings to mind the abundance and lush beauty of eras gone by. Next in the series is a design with symbols from Jilin City, one of the oldest cities in Northeast China. Also set atop a bold blue substrate, the design is accented in green and silver. For this design, we included an illustration of Heaven Lake, a crater lake that lies atop the volcanic Paektu Mountain. In the background, we also included fans used in Northeast Errenzhuan, a popular form of local folk opera and duet that involves storytelling, singing and dancing. Finally, to complete the series, we included icons from the city of Luoyang, the capital of nine ruling dynasties and a Buddhist center. The city was noted for its fine buildings, pleasure parks, and literary culture, especially Confucian scholarship. We depicted the Luoyang Ruins, accenting the black background with pops of gold. We also included Chinese sky lanterns with floral details, which are used as a part of long-established festivities.
Results: Illustrated in a sophisticated yet approachable style, this Pepsi Culture x People's Daily series stays true to the global Pepsi brand while embracing local relevancy and exuding national pride. Ultimately, Pepsi Culture Cans - China City Edition continues to build the Pepsi culture platform, driving brand relevance, and preference with the younger generations of Chinese consumers.

90 LIAN XIANG PERFUME PACKAGING DESIGN | Design Firm: Roking Art Design
Designer: Qin Luo | Client: Xiangxi Lotus Fragrance Perfume Co., Ltd.
Main Contributor: Qin Luo
Assignment: As an Oriental beauty brand, Love Fragrance aims to carry forward and inherit Oriental traditional aesthetics. Love Fragrance perfume is mainly a product packaging design developed for the Miao culture in western Hunan.
Approach: The Miao people are a minority ethnic group with a long history, and the most representative ones are the silver headdress and neck ornaments worn by the Miao people. Silver ornaments have become the most representative symbolic features of the Miao people. Therefore, the symbolic features of silver ornaments and neck ornaments are extracted from the packaging design of the fragrance perfume to carry out the shape design. The chisel above is engraved with Miao ethnic pattern and the pattern of Erlong playing beads. The bottle cap is designed according to the inspiration of bull horn headdress. The blue glass bottle body is matched with silver, showing a modern sense and traditional aesthetic feeling. The box is covered with upper and lower caps, and the lid part hollowed out the perfume bottle body. When the box is covered down, the perfume bottle body in the box will be protruded from the hollowed out place. The neck, bottom of the bottle and the graphic and text information of the lid part adopt the process of convex and scalding silver, which gives people a modern and simple feeling. To achieve the concept of environmental protection.
Results: The packaging design of this product not only integrates the characteristic culture of the Miao minority in it, but also presents traditional things through modern expression techniques. The overall style tone is simple and fashionable, and the design of the outer packaging also reflects the concept of environmental protection.

91 FEATHER & FOLLY | Design Firm: CF Napa Brand Design
Designer: CF Napa Brand Design | Client: Goose Ridge Estate Vineyard & Winery
Main Contributor: CF Napa Brand Design
Assignment: Goose Ridge Estate Vineyard & Winery came to CF Napa to develop the name, logo, and packaging for their new-age gin distilled from wine grapes.
Approach: The gin would initially launch in the Pacific Northwest and was targeted toward Millennials who prefer a lower juniper flavor profile. The goal was for it to be favored by adventurous mixologists and curious cocktail lovers alike.
Results: CF Napa developed the name Feather & Folly to express a free-spirited personality and provide a wink back to Goose Ridge. The tattoo-style illustration makes use of the age-old symbolism of the Garden of Eden and depicts the balance of free will and the folly of human nature through the hidden symbology of the serpent in pursuit of the bird. Key botanical ingredients of the gin along with other flora are woven throughout the illustration. The bright yellow of the label was selected for its optimistic and youthful connotations while providing a fresh fruit-forward flavor cue and an ownable brand color within the competitive landscape of gin.

92 FIADH RUADH | Design Firm: CF Napa Brand Design
Designer: CF Napa Brand Design | Client: Fiadh Ruadh
Main Contributor: CF Napa Brand Design
Assignment: Nova Cadamatre MW, the first female winemaker in the US to achieve the title of Master of Wine, came to CF Napa to bring her latest project to life.
Approach: Fiadh Ruadh (pronounced Fay-ah Roo-ah), Gaelic for "untamed wild red deer," symbolizes her strength, grace, and persistence—which the packaging needed to embody. The label needed to have a high-fashion edginess as well as maintain an ultra-premium Napa Valley sense of luxury.
Results: CF Napa captured Fiadh Ruadh's badass ethos through a modern label design highlighted by sculpture embossed, gold foil deer skulls, and antlers. These iconic skull and antlers also provided a subtle connection to the wine's Stags Leap District AVA. The illustration was duplicated so that one skull and antlers could be viewed straight on when the bottle was turned, but when the brand name faced forward, the two intertwined to frame the brand name and label information.

93 BLACK STEEL BOURBON | Design Firm: Chad Michael Studio
Designer: Chad Makerson Michael | Client: Black Steel Spirit Co.
Main Contributor: Red Productions

Assignment: To create a distinctly different Bourbon brand for renown online personality Guy Beahm, aka "Dr. Disrespect, with the underlining goal of combining the aesthetics and respect of an established Bourbon with an eccentric personality that would cater to a younger demographic. Rebellion meets Respectable.
Approach: Pitched and created a design / direction that bridged the gap between celebrated youthful ridiculousness and sophisticated craftsmanship. Bespoke, demanding, typography paired with an electric pop of color that would contrast with a more traditional image found in old Scotch and Bourbon, the family crest. However, we pushed the typical family crest look by injecting modernity and dipping it in subtle humor hints the lightning breathing panthers! All ties back to the founder "Dr. Disrespect" and his notoriously unconventional personality.
Results: The brand launched online with a limited of run of 5,000 bottles which then sold out in 24 hours.

94 WALKER·BOUNDLESS | Design Firm: Shenzhen Excel Brand Design Consultant Co., Ltd.
Designer: Shenzhen Excel Brand Design Consultant Co., Ltd. | Client: WALKER
Main Contributor: Kuan Fu Wu
Assignment: The ladder design of the bottle body symbolizes continuous climbing and fearlessness of arduous journeys, which forms a strong contrast with the traditional jute bag pottery bottle of Jiugui Liquor, and conforms to the brand vision of "Travelers without Borders" seeking breakthrough and self subversion.

95 XIANQIN | Design Firm: Sungoo Design | Designer: Muqiang Fu
Client: Qin Hanzhang Wine Sales Co., Ltd. | Main Contributor: Muqiang Fu
Assignment: In memory of Mr. Qin Hanzhang, a generation of liquor masters, this Xianqin sauce wine is specially made. Mr. Ji Keliang, the former chairman of Moutai Group and a student of the Chinese liquor master and also a student of Mr. Qin, personally named his teacher and wrote the word "Xianqin" in his own hand, in order to show respect for the pioneer who created the contemporary liquor master. It is also the origin of the name of Xianqin Liquor.
Approach: Song porcelain is the traditional Chinese utensil we seek to recall Qin Lao. In the history of Chinese ceramic craftsmanship, Song porcelain is famous for its high development of monochromatic glaze, and its color tone is unparalleled. In the culture of the Song Dynasty where the stars are full of stars, the Song porcelain green vase has a unique place. We found it to condense the body of the Xianqin wine. Song porcelain presents the charm of Chinese style, with a long history of noble demeanor, and a sense of fashion that will never go out of style. In the product design of Xianqin Liquor, we adopt the "post-classical" expression technique, retro and not into the vulgar, and put the bones of the fairy style that have come over the years to plastic bottles.
Results: The perfect fusion of Song Dynasty celadon and hand-painted crane carvings, coupled with modern color matching, attracted the attention of consumers and became an innovative design model popular in the market.

96 DEVIL'S BOTANY METTLESOME LIBATIONS
Design Firm: Chad Michael Studio | Designer: Chad Makerson Michael
Client: Devil's Botany | Main Contributor: Red Productions
Assignment: To design an "experimental series" label that had a distinct departure visually from the core range but told the story of toiling in the apothecary and connected to the fact that all Devil's Botany recipes are derived from original recipes that date back to early 1800's.
Approach: Illustrated and designed a full label wrap that was inspired by the "Ex Libris" style. A label that felt mystical and full of wonder. It connects the academic side of their distillation with the original recipes of Old London Absinthe.
Results: Devil's Botany is London's first true Absinthe distillery. The reaction to both the core range and the "Mettlesome Libation" series has gone above expectations. The bottle has consistently sold out at trade shows and events.

97 RIMFIRE WHISKEY | Design Firm: CF Napa Brand Design
Designer: CF Napa Brand Design | Client: Lightburn Spirits
Main Contributor: CF Napa Brand Design
Assignment: Lightburn Spirits came to CF Napa to develop a premium whiskey from the ground up.
Approach: This new brand needed to capture the beauty, people, and independent spirit of West Virginia and the crafted care put into every bottle. The name "Rimfire" was developed as an ode to Eli "Rimfire" Hamrick, a mountaineer and one of West Virginia's most iconic figures.
Results: CF Napa developed a flask-style custom bottle with cartouches of the brand name on the sides and back. For the label, CF Napa commissioned an illustration of the adventurous Rimfire exploring the breathtaking West Virginia landscape. Intricate gold foil details light up the drawing, branding, and whiskey information against the bold blue label. A custom wooden T-top with an inset metal coin modeled after a West Virginia coal coin was crafted for the closure. The packaging design captures the spirit of adventure and invites the imbiber to live bold, free, and independent.

98 PEPSIMAX POPFIZZAHH 2022 | Design Firm: PepsiCo Design & Innovation
Designer: PepsiCo Design & Innovation | Client: Self-initiated
Assignment: For cola drinkers, popping open a can of Pepsi MAX® is a ritual that comes with a complete sensory experience. It begins with anticipation and the icy chill of the can in hand, then crack of the seal and satisfying fizz of the release of carbonation under pressure, and finally resolves with that first refreshing sip of cola delighting the taste buds. Consuming a Pepsi MAX is more than just a drink - it offers a distinct moment of pleasure amidst everyday routines. In the United Kingdom, there is steep competition in the cola market, where consumers often default to and stick with their existing cola preference. Pepsi MAX knows it wins on taste, but this alone isn't enough to convert cola drinkers. The brand needed to communicate the emotionally attractive taste experience specific to Pepsi MAX, packed with positivity and uplifting joy.
Approach: Around the world, Pepsi represents popular youth culture and contagious enjoyment, rooted in its American heritage and prime place in the landscape of pop culture. We sought to leverage this brand positioning, funneling it into the creative direction for a new Pepsi MAX PopFizzAhh campaign. So, Pepsi MAX sought to establish a distinctive and universally understood ritual of enjoyment that would allow it to break out of its category bubble to create greater consumer appeal and increase interest for the brand. To create a bold and irreverent visual world for the Pepsi MAX PopFizzAhh campaign, the Design Team was inspired by the visceral feeling of each of the moments of enjoying a Pepsi. We took a graphic, minimal design approach that allowed typography to fully drive the Pepsi MAX story in a bold and impactful way. By focusing each key visual on a single word tied to the drinking ritual, each design was able to express the feeling of the word through crafted letterforms and carefully placed cola splashes. The Design Team carefully crafted the letterforms, arranging them to bring the feeling to life. The POP feels as if it was the actual moment of the Pepsi ring-pull popping open. The FIZZ appears truly fizzy as the delicious cola bubbles. And the AHHH embodies the sigh of pure, refreshing enjoyment after taking that first sip. The graphic shapes and cola splashes were carefully placed around to frame, but not overcomplicate, each visual.
Results: In a sea of product depictions and liquid splashes in beverage advertising, the Pepsi MAX PopFizzAhh campaign truly broke the norm for both the category and for the historical representation of the brand. By focusing on the individual moments of the drinking ritual and allowing typography to express more than just the can and cola, we heightened the overall product experience and created something much more art-forward and modern that really stood out. Across the PopFizzAhh campaign period, Pepsi MAX led on positive buzz when compared with other brands. Mid-campaign, Pepsi MAX beat out leading competitors in recommendation, while also leading on recommendations after the activity ended. Pepsi MAX reported* value share gains of 11.2% PEP Growth, 1.1 PEP Share and volume share gains of 6.4% PEP Growth, 1.9 PEP Share.

99 CHÂTEAU KSARA NEW YEAR 2023 | Design Firm: Mink
Designers: Moe Minkara, Jessy Ghostine, Rua Tohme | Client: Château Ksara
Associate Creative Director: Jessy Ghostine | Executive Creative Director: Moe Minkara
Assignment: We were assigned to create a 2023 New Year greeting for Château Ksara, the biggest and oldest winery in Lebanon.
Approach: We simply used the bottle opener to create the number 3 for 2023 leaving a powerful, elegant and simple visual which needed no tagline or explanation.
Results: The print quickly went viral beyond the brand itself. People were sharing it amongst each other as their NYE greeting. Due to its popularity, the client also asked us to go on outdoor with it in key locations f the city.

100 PRAY FOR PEACE | Design Firm: Jingyi Cai | Designer: Jingyi Cai
Client: Self-initiated | Main Contributor: Jingyi Cai
Assignment: Although I am living in a peaceful enviroment far away from war, my compassion for those currently suffering due to war inspired me to create this poster. Prayer, a timeless practice embraced worldwide, became my chosen theme for its universal significance. Through this poster, I aim to convery a message: pray for peace, stop the war.
Approach: In this poster, I have chosen prayer as the central theme, recognizing its universal significance and power. The silhouette of a man praying is composed using two rifles, symbolizing the transformation from conflict to contemplation. In many cultures, doves symbolize peace. They are flying around the praying person hoping peace will come and stay forever.
Results: This poster has won Graphic Design USA Award and was a selected project to showcase at the Peru Design Biennial.

101 NO WAR | Design Firm: Tsushima Design | Designer: Hajime Tsushima
Client: Peace-Loving Innovators of Nations | Main Contributor: Hajime Tsushima
Assignment: It's been four months since the war between Ukraine and Russia began. I watch the miserable sight of Ukraine on TV every day. I really hurt my heart. Why should we fight? Why do we have to wage a war that involves the general public? I want you to finish it as soon as possible. I think most people in the world are screaming.
Approach: I expressed the cry of people all over the world. So far, various places in Ukraine have been blown up. Every time I want to scream. I want these posters to resonate with me.
Results: I hope the war will end soon and no longer destroy everyone's happiness.

102 SILENT TWINS | Design Firm: ARSONAL | Designers: ARSONAL, Focus Features
Clients: Focus Features, Blair Green, SVP Creative Advertising and Head of Brand Design, Marcus Kaye, VP Creative Advertising & Marketing Deanna Shiverick, Coordinator Creative Advertising, Evie Kennedy, Assistant Creative Advertising | Creative Director: ARSONAL
Copywriter: ARSONAL | Main Contributors: ARSONAL, Focus Features
Assignment: Representing the true story of Silent Twins respectfully and beautifully was the main goal. In order to do so, it was our job to balance realism with whimsy, dark thematic undertones with symbols of light and positivity, all while conveying the severity of the story without turning audiences away.
Approach: Palette, treatment, photography and selection of expressions were our major tools in creating this piece of key art. While many of the color hues are darker, we softened the art overall. It was through balancing techniques such as this we were able to explore the light and darkness of their story. The central device offers a unique approach in uniting and separating the twin's faces simultaneously while the symbols inside integrated with the type hinted at the sometimes chaotic and confusing nature between them.
Results: The client was so pleased with our presentation, it was difficult for them to select just one approach. However, they felt this piece of art was the best overall interpretation of balance across the board to drive viewership.

103 FOR ALL MANKIND S3 | Design Firm: ARSONAL | Designer: ARSONAL
Client: Apple TV+ | Main Contributors: ARSONAL, Apple TV+
Assignment: Season 3 of For All Mankind has the exploration teams landing on Mars, so Apple wanted an iconic piece of art that highlighted where the season was going without giving away any spoilers as to which teams actually made it.
Approach: While competition and advancements in space technology open new

possibilities of discovery, our heroes, and their loved ones, face a new world of unprecedented risk. We knew we needed to not just highlight Mars, but also hint at the danger that comes with it. We used a generic spacesuit in order to avoid any potential spoilers, and added the landscape in the reflection of the mask for a sense of place and scope. The suit then begins to break apart into dust, demonstrating the treachery of the new frontier.
Results: The art conveyed the major plot point of this season, intriguing and exciting fans and the client. It was also developed into a motion piece by our digital team that ran across digital and out-of-home paid media.

104 A SMALL LIGHT | Design Firm: SJI Associates | Designer: David O'Hanlon
Clients: National Geographic, EVP Creative - Chris Spencer, VP Design - Brian Everett, Design Director - Mariano Barreiro, Project Manager - Leah Wojda
President: Suzy Jurist | Main Contributor: SJI Associates
Assignment: Debut the new limited series showcasing the humanity and fearlessness of Miep Gies, who, along with her husband, risked everything to hide Anne Frank, her family, and four other Dutch Jews from the Nazis.
Approach: A series of intimate portraits of the main cast, lit by the glow of a single candle, brings the viewer into the world they inhabited; one of terrifying silence and paranoia as well as boundless courage and hope.
Results: This key art drove interest and awareness for the new series, and was showcased in social, digital, OOH, and on-air graphics, driving views.

105 INSIDE | Design Firm: ARSONAL | Designer: ARSONAL | Clients: Focus Features, Blair Green, SVP Creative Advertising and Head of Brand Design, Marcus Kaye, VP Creative Advertising & Marketing, Deanna Shiverick, Coordinator Creative Advertising, Evie Kennedy, Assistant Creative Advertising | Copywriter: ARSONAL | Creative Director: ARSONAL
Art Director: ARSONAL | Main Contributors: ARSONAL, Focus Features
Assignment: Inside tells the story of a high-end art thief, Nemo (Dafoe), who becomes trapped in a luxury, high-tech penthouse in New York's Times Square after his heist does not go as planned. While this is a story about escape and survival, the client wanted the art to focus more on the heart of the film which taps into much larger themes of isolation, art vs commerce, and relative worth.
Approach: We wanted to capture the tension, isolation and claustrophobia of the film to reflect Nemo's spiral of desperation as he tries to escape from what began as an art lover's heaven, but quickly turns into a living hell. As we follow his trauma, we start to question - is this some sort of forced performance piece? Is he the art? So we wanted the art to also reflect this question living amid the underlying themes of the film.
Results: The art was so well received we ended up finishing six different pieces, three of which have been submitted here. The key art was also well received on our client's social platforms with long lists of comments praising the art and, for ARSONAL, was our highest liked post on Instagram ever.

106 COSMO | Design Firm: Tsushima Design | Designer: Hajime Tsushima
Client: Visual Information Design Association of Korea | Main Contributor: Hajime Tsushima
Assignment: This poster is for the International Winter Invitational Exhibition & its Conference. This exhibition is about design, collaboration, exchange of designs with artists, countries and design associations.
Approach: I expressed the beauty of Cosmo and the infinite breadth
Results: It was held from December 3rd to December 11th, 2022 at Dongdaemun Design Plaza (DDP) Museum - Desian Pathway.

107 FRAMENELLI | Design Firm: BEK Design | Designer: Bulent Erkmen
Clients: Amijai Benderski, Juan Martín Lusiardo, Santiago Ternande
Assignment: "Massimo Vignelli frequently used an interlaced symbol of the letters "M" and "V" to signify his name and surname in his works.
I used Vignelli's sign and combined it with the framing gesture that is often used in cinematography to compose a visual, fusing the word "frame" with Vignelli's "nelli" to make up the word "framenelli".
"Framenelli" to me means looking at design, at all aspects of design, even at life itself, as Massimo Vignelli would have, that is, looking through his framing."

108 FREEDOM | Design Firm: Sun Design Production
Designers: Xian Liyun, Liang Gang | Client: Shanghai Women's Federation
Main Contributor: Shanghai Municipal Government
Assignment: Dialogue for women's rights.
Approach: It is a reality these days that women's human rights are ignored in many parts of the global community. This poster is a message to protect women's human rights through dialogue and harmony. To this end, the conversation was emphasized by overlapping the image of a woman reversed up and down.
Results: I hope this campaign will amplify movement and interest and induce understanding of women's human rights in the global community.

109 STAY STRONG, STAND UP, HAVE A VOICE | Design Firm: Studio Eduard Cehovin
Designer: Eduard Cehovin | Client: The International Reggae Poster Contest
Creative Director: Eduard Cehovin | Main Contributor: Eduard Cehovin
Assignment: The guideline in the design was to visually describe the meaning of reggae using design elements of colour, line, dot, shape, texture, space and form. The latter are directly related to the structure of reggae. Their rhythmic relationships are detected from the counterpoint between the bass and offbeat rhythmic sections and drum downbeat.
Approach: Women, as the theme of the design, are visually expressed in a stylised image and enhanced by the use of a distinctive colour composition. The motto STAY STRONG, STAND UP and HAVE A VOICE is devoted to all reggae music women singers and women authors wherever they are.
Results: Project was very successful from my point of view.

110 WOMAN, LIFE, FREEDOM | Design Firm: BEK Design | Designer: Bülent Erkmen
Client: Movement for Women of Iran | Main Contributor: BEK Design

111 WE STAND FOR PEACE | Design Firm: Purdue University
Designer: Li Zhang | Client: Ogaki Poster Museum in Japan | Main Contributor: Li Zhang
Assignment: With the tragedy of Ukraine caused by the invasion of Russia, can we do anything for them? To raise a voice to appeal "NO WAR", "STOP WAR" with the power of the poster design. It is an activity to send a message to the world with posters design so that peaceful daily life can be returned to Ukraine.
Approach: We Stand for Peace - Ukraine's national flag is embedded in the army helmet to represent their courage to fight for peace. We who believes in peace stand with Ukraine for peace.
Results: The poster was a great success and received a lot of recognition in the exhibition organized by the Ogaki Poster Museum in Japan. As a woman designer, I am invited to another exhibition with Paula Scher and Luba Lukova. It is great honor that my posters have been recognized by "Graphis" since 1999.

112 TOLERANCE | Design Firm: Tsushima Design
Designer: Hajime Tsushima | Client: Tolerance Poster Show
Main Contributor: Hajime Tsushima
Assignment: This is a poster for the Tolerance Poster Show, which travels around the world. Each poster had to include the word "tolerance" in the artist's native language. The typography in the middle depicts the meaning of tolerance using Japanese kana. I also expressed tolerance in the image of the whole poster.
Approach: The country where I live, Japan, has three types of characters: hiragana, katakana, and kanji. I used hiragana in the middle of this poster, and kanji on the left and right sides of the poster. In this way, it is characteristic that there are three types of characters, and different images can be expressed.
Results: The Tolerance Poster Show has been held in many countries and regions so far, and many people have seen it. I think it's a very worthwhile show to be able to see the unique design power of designers from various countries.

113 F FOR FACE | Design Firm: Dankook University
Designer: Hoon-Dong Chung | Client: Osaka Poster Festival 2022
Main Contributor: Hoon-Dong Chung
Assignment: This poster is for the 2nd international Osaka Poster Fest 2022 in Japan. The main theme of the exhibition is 'FACE' in the COVID-19 Pandemic. The COVID-19 pandemic forced us to wear masks, which replaced our 'FACE'. Our ample emotions were covered with masks and 3 years have stolen by. During this time, the hidden faces were covered all over with 'anxiety', the virus. This is why we long for our previously intact 'FACE' more than ever.
Approach: Symbol, Metaphor and 3D Typography
Results: This got good reviews on the design field.

114 CONTACT | Design Firm: Dankook University
Designer: Hoon-Dong Chung | Client: Osaka Poster Festival 2022
Main Contributor: Hoon-Dong Chung
Assignment: This is an unreleased poster for the 1st international Osaka Poster Fest 2021 in Japan.
Approach: In 3D Typography, this poster emphasizes the cyclical and communicative nature for the main theme 'CONTACT'.
Results: This got good reviews on the design field.

115 VOUGA TRAIL NATIONAL CHAMPIONSHIP POSTER | Design Firm: Duas Faces Design
Designer: Patricia Machado | Client: Municipio de Sever do Vouga
Account Manager: Ana Monteiro | Motion Designer: Filipa Esteves
Assignment: The purpose was to bring a fun and eye-catching approach, referring to the elements that are the ex libris of the peculiar Vila de Sever do Vouga, respecting the colors of the pedestrian routes.
Approach: Sever do Vouga offers us different pedestrian routes, routes that are the stage of the trail running race "Vouga Trail" and, to facilitate the intuitive interpretation by the participants and visitors, the representation of each itinerary is made with the use of a distinctive color, uniquely highlighting the vibrant nature of the event. The poster illustrates the main elements of Sever do Vouga, such as the waterfalls and the bridge of Santiago (ex-libris of the region). It also captures the movement of the river's crystal clear water, an element present at various stages of the event, bringing an authentic feel to the whole experience.
Results: The poster stood out from other national events, managing to call the public's attention in a simple and appealing way, generating a buzz that led to the event selling out quickly. The entire graphic environment of the poster was replicated in digital media, and even in the merchandising of the event.

116 WOMEN. LIFE. FREEDOM. | Design Firm: Goodall Integrated Design
Designer: Derwyn Goodall | Client: Self-initiated | Main Contributor: Derwyn Goodall
Assignment: To create a memorable poster on the topic of Women's Rights.
Approach: March 8 2023 was International Women's Day. A global holiday celebrated annually as a focal point in the women's rights movement, bringing attention to issues such as gender equality, and violence and abuse against women. The prosecution of women in Iran really brought this to the fore. Women not heard, struggling to break out of repression. My poster attempts to capture the essence of that struggle.
Results: Very positive results from clients and colleagues.

117 KISS OF THE SPIDER WOMAN | Design Firm: Paco Macias Velasco Studio
Designer: Paco Macías Velasco | Client: Self-initiated | Main Contributor: Danielle Jouanen
Assignment: The Kiss of the Spider Woman is a novel by the Argentine writer Manuel Puig, published in 1976. Based on a part of the life of Luis González de Alba, a political prisoner for the student movement in 1968. Puig changed the sexuality of the protagonists. The book tells the story of two prisoners who live in the same cell, one is a political prisoner and the other is a sexual dissident defined as "crazy" and self-perceived as a woman (registered by the State as a man). It was included in the list of the 100 best novels in Spanish of the 20th century by the Spanish newspaper El Mundo. This story, banned in the 1970s by the Argentine military dictatorship (Manuel Puig's country of origin), was made into a film in 1985 by director Héctor Babenco and starred Sônia Braga, William Hurt and Raúl Juliá.
Approach: I did a photo session with my friend the model Danielle Jouanen. When she made a kissy gesture with her full, sensual lips, I told her to exaggerate the gesture and when she did so I immediately suggested that I was going to name it after

the Broadway musical novel and film "Kiss of the Spider Woman." The result was a powerful image that conveys the essence of the work's title. It was a pleasure for me to do it, let's just say that I took a creative license that I now share in the form of a poster with those who remember the novel, the film or the Broadway musical.
Results: Communication through images is a matter of perception, a visual synthesis that sometimes amuses while it instructs or instructs while it amuses, as Bertold Brecht once said.

118 DESIGNER FOR PEACE: UNITED WITH UKRAINE | Design Firm: BEK Design
Designer: Bülent Erkmen | Client: Graphis Designers for Peace Poster Competition
Main Contributor: BEK Design

119 WAR CRIMINAL | Design Firm: Code Switch | Designer: Jan Šabach
Client: Graphis Designers for Peace Poster Competition | Main Contributor: Jan Šabach
Assignment: Poster for Graphis' Designers for Peace poster competition.

120 WOMAN LIFE FREEDOM | Design Firm: Vanderbyl Design
Designers: Michael Vanderbyl, Tori Koch | Client: Woman, Life, Freedom Movement
Creative Director: Michael Vanderbyl
Assignment: Social movement poster supporting women's rights in Iran.
Approach: The poster shows the duality of Iranian women's lives. Scissors became a major symbol of their voices. Many women cut their hair in public as a protest. This poster celebrates their bravery.

121 FACE TO FACE | Design Firm: Tsushima Design | Designer: Hajime Tsushima
Client: Osaka Poster Festival 2022 | Main Contributor: Hajime Tsushima
Assignment: This is a poster exhibited at OSAKA POSTER FEST2022 Virtual Poster Exhibition. The theme is FACE.
Approach: Due to Covid19, people had to cover their faces with masks. I think that communication can be measured only when we face each other face to face. I represented this graphically.
Results: From November 18, 2022, the virtual exhibition was held. The exhibition was a success with 64 designers from all over the world participating. It's virtual, so anyone can go see it anytime, anywhere.

122 SUGAR ENERGY | Design Firm: Goodall Integrated Design
Designer: Derwyn Goodall | Client: 2023 Sweet & Health International Poster Design Exhibition
Main Contributor: Derwyn Goodall
Assignment: Design a poster around the dangers of excessive sugar consumption.
Approach: For the poster's main image, I wanted to graphically represent the capital S in "sugar" as dynamic, bursting with energy using vivid colours on a dark field. That in combination with text explaining what sugar is and it's potential health risks when used in abundance. Sugar is a carbohydrate that serves as one of the energy sources required by the human body. However, excessive intake of sugar can increase the risk of diabetes and cardiovascular diseases. Consumed in appropriate amounts, sugar helps maintain energy levels and normal physiological function. Controlling sugar intake and promoting healthy lifestyles will ensure good overall health.
Results: Positive results from clients and colleagues.

123 THE OTHER SIDE OF TIJUANA | Design Firm: Freaner Creative & Design
Designer: Ariel Freaner | Clients: City of Tijuana, Jorge Astiazaran
Digital Artist: Ariel Freaner | Main Contributor: Ariel Freaner
Assignment: The City of Tijuana needed to improve its image domestically and across the border with San Diego, California.
Approach: We created a series of posters promoting the image and social acceptance of Tijuana to show the good, bright, and better side of Tijuana, such as arts, folklore, culinary arts, etc.
Results: The City of Tijuana improved tourism traffic and image.

124 JEJU EVENING | Design Firm: May & Co. | Designer: Douglas May
Client: Communication Design Association of Korea | Main Contributor: Douglas May
Assignment: The theme of the poster exhibition is "Seom Tada, Sseom Tada," which is a play on the Korean words "seom (an island)" and "sseom (something going on–as at the start of a romantic relationship)." It may be loosely translated as "Longing for the island. Flirting with the island."
Approach: The island's landscape is transformed into the profile of a beautiful woman floating in the ocean on a moonlit night.
Results: The poster has exhibited at The International Exhibition of Professional Artists exhibition was held at the Seogwipo Arts Center in Korea Jeju-do in 2022. The poster was also included at the International Design Education Expo & Conference held at the Gangwon Institute of Design Promotion in June 2023.

125 REEL TIME | Design Firm: Judd Brand Media | Designer: Patti Judd
Client: Coronado Island Film Festival | Main Contributor: Merridee Book, CIFF Executive Director
Assignment: The Coronado Island Film Festival is an annual event celebrating the best of cinema in a setting that exudes beauty, history, and charm. For the 2022 festival, we wanted to pay tribute to the elegance and nostalgia of classic cinema through a poster design that echoes a stylized retro vibe. The main image features a vibrant woman, representative of the iconic figures of classic Hollywood, holding up a giant film reel while perched on a rock on the Coronado beach.
Approach: Objective: Design a striking, memorable, and aesthetically pleasing poster that encapsulates the spirit of the Coronado Island Film Festival and its unique blend of history, location, and love for cinema. This poster was designed to not only promote the event but also become a sought-after collectible piece for film enthusiasts. The tone of the poster is nostalgic and elegant, capturing the golden era of Hollywood, yet vibrant and exciting to reflect the contemporary atmosphere of the film festival. Retro-inspired with a stylized, modern twist. Think 1950's Hollywood meets contemporary art. Bold colors, sleek lines, and vintage typography coexist with modern design elements to create a balance between the past and the present. The woman is depicted as timeless, elegant, and strong, reflecting the classic Hollywood, while the beach setting and film reel tie in the core elements of the festival. The poster communicates the glamour and playful excitement of the film festival, paying homage to the magic of cinema, and the unique beauty of Coronado Island. The message being "Celebrating the past, present, and future of cinema at the scenic Coronado Island." Deliverables: A high-resolution poster design for print and digital distribution. Variations of the poster for social media promotion and merchandise.
Results: 1. Increase in ticket sales and festival attendance. 2. Positive feedback and engagement on social media. 3. Demand for festival merchandise featuring the poster design. 4. Recognition and appreciation of the poster design within the design and film communities. 5. Increased awareness and reputation of the Coronado Island Film Festival.

126 GAMING IS A MATTER OF PRIDE | Design Firm: Microsoft Brand Studio
Designer: Microsoft Brand Studio | Client: Self-initiated | Main Contributors: Cam Gatta, Carol Hutchinson, Chaya Wilkins, Daniel Ruiz, Eileen Mikloiche, Elliot Hsu, GeriAnn Baptista, iAsia Brown, Jenn Panattoni, Jessica Tsujikawa, Kaity Butcher, Lori Gross, McCann Worldgroup, Phyllis Murphy, Pia Rodriguez, Aleksey Fedorov, Sarah Bender, Steve Wiens, Sven Seger
Assignment: LGBTQIA+ identities are still not widely represented nor welcome in gaming—yet showing up as who you want to be is at the heart of what gaming stands for. Gender expression and identity often evolve faster than their understanding and acceptance. To bridge the gap, we transformed an iconic Xbox controller into a symbol of inclusive gaming with a memorable display of expansive LGBTQIA+ identities. An Xbox controller is not just an object—it's a conduit to the game and extension of the self. It's tactile. It's visceral. It's one of the most considered industrial designs that Microsoft produces. Its form and materiality allow for close identification with the console—a design that's provocative enough to spark a conversation and a movement.
Approach: In 2021, we created a limited run of Xbox Pride controllers that gathered 18 LGBTQIA+ community flags into a one-of-a-kind design. Seeded with top LGBTQIA+ players, the idea went viral. When a Change.org petition was received in 2022 to make the controller publicly available, we welcomed the opportunity. Today, our Xbox Pride controller celebrates 35 unique LGBTQIA+ communities and is available to everyone. Microsoft's industrial design team used the highest quality materials and maximalist graphic design to make this unforgettable product as comfortable and sustainable as possible. The controller can be further customized by players in hundreds of ways to make it even more unique and personal, so it truly represents a wide spectrum of LGBTQIA+ people. The product was paired with a multimedia campaign and web experience—so people could learn more about expansive LGBTQIA+ identities. The stories brought to life the diversity of the LGBTQIA+ communities represented by the flags on the controller's body design.
Results: The Xbox controller ignited provocative conversations on social about LGBTQIA+ identities and their acceptance in gaming that went totally viral. Responses ran the gamut between extremely positive and extremely critical. We received 500,000+ likes and retweets, and 83 media outlets covered the launch with 500M impressions. Over time, people recognized the flag graphic used on the Xbox Pride controller was even more representative of the LGBTQIA+ community than traditional graphics, such as the iconic Pride flag itself. Many appreciated our expansion, noting how they'd never truly seen themselves represented in classic Pride designs. So we open-sourced the Pride graphic as a flag to make it available to all on Figma and GitHub. The Xbox Pride controller has been a top seller since day one. Our design worked because it was a true symbol of LGBTQIA+ communities—layered, nuanced, unique, and interconnected.

127 NATRALIS™ PRODUCT LAUNCH | Design Firm: Nexus Designs
Designers: Sally Evans, Myra Murtagh, Nexus Designs | Client: Armstrong Flooring Australia
Assistant Designer: Georgia Swinbourne | Art Director: Sally Evans
Photographer: Lillie Thompson | Senior Designer: Myra Murtagh
Stylist: Marsha Golemac | Main Contributor: Nexus Designs
Assignment: Our brief was to explore opportunities for repositioning Armstrong Flooring in the Australian commercial architectural and design market through the launch of a new locally manufactured product range. Natralis™ is a homogenous vinyl sheet flooring product used primarily for commercial applications with stringent regulatory needs where specification is often based mainly on function and performance. Our challenge was to stay true to product integrity while championing the potential for creative expression; at once respecting function while capturing the audience imagination. With a goal to raising perception of the brand, the Natralis™ launch campaign was a balancing act between staying true to function while exploring the possibility of creative expression.
Approach: Prior to conceptual design for the campaign collateral, Nexus Designs consulted on the development of the Natralis™ range itself. A product colour palette inspired by the diversity of Australia's flora, fauna and natural landscapes, we advised on range breadth, colour families and product naming, culminating in the formation of a range of 22 colours. Simultaneously we undertook a comprehensive communications review, designing and facilitating an industry survey to learn and validate specifier experience and expectation around product and brand. This knowledge established core strategic thinking and informed the Natralis™ launch creative design direction. With a recent rebrand, executed in the US, for the Armstrong Flooring company, we adapted the new brand architecture for the Australian manufacturing business while exploring a tone of voice and icon graphic suited to the campaign language of Play with Colour Connect with Place. The imagery is distinct in its visual storytelling; centred around a series of creative photographic sets showcasing the Natralis™ product alongside leading complementary Australian furniture and building products, the imagery becomes the central visual language in a rollout of printed collateral, sample packs and digital assets that counteract evocative landscapes and environments. Campaign collateral keeps the specifier in mind, both informative and inspiring, with a product range folder, fan-deck, four direct mail sample packs and custom packaging all using local and sustainable paper stocks where possible.
Results: As a local Australian manufacturer of high-quality and trusted flooring, reinvigorating the Armstrong Flooring brand and products in the creative minds of Australian specifiers was our key challenge. The concept of authenticity is at the heart of the Natralis™ storytelling – staying true to function and values while not

forgoing beauty and the wonder of the imagination. We focused on amplifying the representation of the Natralis™ product, displaying vinyl as it has never been seen before, refreshing the idea of how this humble product can be used and reigniting creative thinking. As an outcome, the Natralis™ product launch has been a confident and honest initiative in the Australian architectural and design market and a highly successful commercial move. Armstrong Flooring have not shied away from engaging with specifiers directly, asking for feedback, integrating new brand guidelines and investing in creative content they have never produced before. They have retained their values of brand authenticity, connection to landscape, sustainability and local manufacturing, while increasing their production output and growing their customer base. Armstrong Flooring have forged new alliances with specifiers, brands, manufacturers and creatives, improving their standing in the industry and stepping up into new conversations.

128 THE STANDARD 7: PACKAGING PERCEPTIONS
Design Firm: Studio Hinrichs | Designer: Kit Hinrichs | Client: Sappi | Printer: Classic Color
Copywriter: Delphine Hirasuna | Main Contributors: Nancy Stahl, Mario Zucca, Mallory Heyer, Daniel Pelavin, John Mattos, Getty Images
Assignment: The Standard is aimed at printers and marketers, offering tips and techniques on packaging design as well as alternatives to plastic packaging.
Approach: The seventh in a series, this volume explores how good design, quality printing, and sensory packaging can heighten a consumer's perception of a brand and increase a company's sales.
Results: Printed with complete production notes, including varnishes and coatings, this educational publication provides information useful for both seasoned professionals and beginners curious about the possibilities of print production.

129 TRIBE-X | Design Firm: Ron Taft Brand Innovation & Media Arts
Designer: Ron Taft | Client: Creative Projects Group | Creative Director: Ron Taft
Photographer: E.S. James | Titles: Ron Taft, Peter Greco | Main Contributor: Ron Taft
Assignment: Create a title design that travels across a variety of episodes that explore tribalistic culture from inner cities to the extreme outer limits.
Approach: The Tribe-X title design will reflect the indigenous culture and art style of each subject explored.
Results: The Chairman/CEO of Creative Projects Group and Executive Producer of the Tribe-X series is thrilled with the branded series icon concept and is currently developing an entire apparel collection celebrating indigenous tribal art emanating from episodic content.

130 TYPO LANTERNS / BEAUTIFUL SEOUL | Design Firm: Simon Peter Bence
Designer: Peter Bence Simon | Client: KECD (Korea Ensemble of Contemporary Design Association) | Main Contributor: Peter Bence Simon
Assignment: The poster was designed for the theme: Beautiful Seoul.
Approach: While looking for visual key that catches Seoul's character, I was caught by the cavalcade of the Seoul Lantern Festival. "In a Buddhist tradition, lanterns are lit and hung on houses, streets and temples in South Korea. The upcoming birthday of the Buddha is celebrated with the lantern parade."
Results: At the lantern event, the curved, spherical body of the lanterns fully cover the field of vision, densely next to and above each other. I processed this cavalcade with my own typographically motivated solution.

131 ART_UNLIMITED (SERIES) | Design Firm: Hufax Arts/FJCU
Designer: Fa-Hsiang Hu | Client: ADLINK Education Foundation
Main Contributors: Fa-Hsiang Hu, Fei Hu, Di Hu
Assignment: The featured program of this Taiwan Traditional Opera Academy performance festival is to travel through time, encounter the past and present, and blend East and West through a dialogue of modern style and cultural inheritance. This extends the audience's sense of time and space, not only by integrating the physical aesthetics, cultural ideas, and skills of the East and West, but also by creating a rare encounter between the two in a seemingly conflicting form.
Approach: The visual design concept is to use the Chinese characters representing Eastern culture to deconstruct and reconstruct the characters for "unlimited drama" as a curtain for young people on the new stage. Using contemporary internationalist design techniques, layers of Chinese character strokes are deconstructed to create a three-dimensional space and relationship between performers and the stage, presenting the artistic trend and momentum of the new generation of Taiwanese performers. The symbolic roles also roam among the stage curtains, showcasing the physical movements of performance art with the aesthetic beauty of calligraphy strokes.

132 YOUTUBE COUNTDOWN | Design Firm: Sunday Afternoon
Designer: Juan Carlos Pagan | Client: YouTube | Main Contributor: Juan Carlos Pagan
Assignment: Every year Youtube commissions artists to create 10 minute countdown clocks across a wide variety of design & animation disciplines. These countdown clocks are used on the YouTube platform as users premiere a video live to their audience. Users can gather 10 minutes before the video goes live. Last year I was asked to create a countdown clock. I wanted the countdown to capture the ephemeral nature of time, and I couldn't think of a better metaphor for the fleetingness of time than bubbles. I have always found the creation and destruction of bubbles to be a beautiful demonstration of time. Weightless objects visually bending everything it's path. Created and destroyed in an instant. In this case the countdown bubbles warp and manipulate the custom drawn letterforms. These two representations of time interacting and distorting each other.

132 LET'S GET THERE CAMPAIGN LOGO | Design Firm: Freaner Creative & Design
Designer: Ariel Freaner | Clients: County of San Diego Land Use & Environment, Donna Durckel
Digital Artist: Ariel Freaner | Main Contributor: Ariel Freaner

133 POST HOUSE WEBSITE | Design Firm: IF Studio
Designers: Toshiaki Ide, Hisa Ide | Client: Sterling Town Equities
Managing Partner: Amy Frankel | Web Designers: Sung Yong Kim, Yingchi Hsu
Design Director: Hisa Ide | Creative Director: Toshiaki Ide
Account Director: Lisa Meyer | Main Contributors: Hisa Ide, Toshiaki Ide

SILVER WINNERS:

135 NEW ZEALAND SUPERFUND ANNUAL REPORT | Design Firm: Insight Creative
Designers: Brian Slade, Alice McKeown | Client: New Zealand Superfund
Creative Director: Brian Slade | Strategy Director: Steven Giannoulis
Project Director: Mason Smith | Production: Kirsty Drummond, Joanne Otto, Rainer Leisky
Account Manager: Emma Thompson | Account Director: Claire Evans
Main Contributor: Insight Creative

135 "RAR SEEN BY" | Design Firm: Atelier Nunes e Pã, Ida | Designer: Atelier Nunes e Pã, Ida
Client: RAR Holding, S.A. | Main Contributor: Atelier Nunes e Pã, Ida

135 VISION WITHOUT LIMITS - TYLER TECHNOLOGIES 2021 ANNUAL REPORT
Design Firm: Spire Agency | Designer: Tyler Fonville | Client: Tyler Technologies
Chief Creative Officer: Kimberly Tyner | Associate Creative Director: Jason James
Copywriter: Nick Reese | Account Supervisor: Julia Cardali
Printing: Blanks | Main Contributor: Tyler Fonville

135 RESILIENCE IN ACTION – NEW YORK PUBLIC RADIO – ANNUAL REPORT – FISCAL YEAR 2021 | Design Firm: Ahoy Studios
Designers: Connie Koch, Denis Kuchta, Giulia Zoavo, Denise Sommer
Client: New York Public Radio | Main Contributor: New York Public Radio

135 TSMC 2020 CSR ANNUAL REPORT | Design Firm: RedPeak Global
Designers: Chien Chun Feng, Yu Shan Huang, Tai Yuan Chiou, Li En Liao, Timothy Fang, I Li Lin
Client: Taiwan Semiconductor Manufacturing Company (TSMC) | Chairman: Silvia Yu
Creative Director: Chris Chung | Account Managers: Kevin Hsueh, E Yu Ren, Lea Chien
Main Contributors: Silvia Yu, Chris Chung, Chien Chun Feng, Yu Shan Huang, Tai Yuan Chiou, Li En Liao, Timothy Fang, I Li Lin, Kevin Hsueh, E Yu Ren, Lea Chien

136 EF IMPACT REPORT | Design Firm: Kathy Mueller Design, LLC
Designers: Robin Goffman, Kathy Mueller, Eva Schenck | Client: Eisenhower Fellowships
Illustrator: Eva Schenck | Main Contributor: Kathy Mueller

136 YSLETA DEL SUR PUEBLO 2021 YEAR-END REPORT
Design Firm: Anne M. Giangiulio Design | Designer: Anne M. Giangiulio
Clients: Ysleta del Sur Pueblo, Helix Solutions | Printer: Tovar Printing, El Paso, TX, USA
Main Contributor: Listed in Book

136 TSL ANNUAL REPORT 2021/22 | Design Firm: TSL Group Creative
Designer: Chan Chi Lung | Client: Tse Sui Luen Jewellery (International) Limited
Main Contributor: Toppan Merrill

136 AWM 2022 CROP REPORT | Design Firm: Freaner Creative & Design
Designer: Ariel Freaner | Clients: San Diego County Agricultural Weights and Measures, Megan Moore, Ha Dang, Bosko Celic, Porfirio Mancillas | Creative Director: Ariel Freaner
Illustrator: Ariel Freaner | Digital Artist: Ariel Freaner | Main Contributor: Ariel Freaner

136 ACNB CORPORATION 2021 ANNUAL REVIEW
Design Firm: Lisa Sirbaugh Creative | Designer: Lisa Sirbaugh
Client: ACNB Corporation | Printer: Graphcom | Copywriter: ACNB Corporation
Main Contributor: Lisa Sirbaugh Creative

137 MAKE YOUR MARK FROM COAST TO COAST | Design Firm: INNOCEAN USA
Designer: INNOCEAN USA | Client: Genesis Motor America | Creative Director: David Mesfin
Copywriter: Nicole Barlow | Photography Studio: M.P. Curtet
Group Creative Director: Cary Ruby | Main Contributor: M.P. Curtet

137 "MIGHTY DREAM FORUM" BILLBOARDS | Design Firm: Chiquitucto Group
Designer: Edward Chiquitucto | Client: I Am Other by Pharrell Williams
Art Director: Jackie Requeima | Creative Director: Anita Patel
Production Managers: Eve Cohen, Kelly Markus | Production Company: Hunters Point
Main Contributor: Edward Chiquitucto

138 TECHNICAL LANDS: A CRITICAL PRIMER | Design Firm: Siena Scarff Design
Designer: Siena Scarff | Clients: Jeffrey S. Nesbit, Charles Waldheim, Jovis
Photographer: Jennifer Holt | Main Contributor: Siena Scarff Design

138 PAPER AND PENCIL BY CARLOS CAICEDO | Design Firm: Carlos Caicedo
Designer: Carlos Caicedo | Client: Self-initiated | Writer: Chris Moore
Printer: DG3 | Main Contributor: Carlos Caicedo

138 ZPÍVÁŠ, JAKO BYS PLAKALA ("YOU SING AS IF YOU WERE CRYING")
Design Firm: Code Switch | Designer: Jan Šabach | Client: Paseka Publishing House
Photographer: Serena Koi/Pexels | Art Director: Vojta Sedláček | Main Contributor: Jan Šabach

139 "MEMORIES BY MURPHY" | Design Firm: ODDSENSE | Designer: Regina Ye Park
Client: Murphy's String Figures | Art Directors: Emerson Bowstead, Justin Vega
Writer: James R. Murphy | Producer: ODDSENSE | Main Contributors: Produced by Oddsense, Art Direction by Emerson Bowstead & Justin Vega, Illustration & Curation by Regina Ye Park

139 SUCH STUFF AS DREAMS | Design Firm: Brad Holland
Designer: Brad Holland | Client: Nuage Editions | Main Contributor: Brad Holland

139 BOMBER BOYS WWII FLIGHT JACKET ART | Design Firm: Fournir
Designer: Daren Guillory | Client: John Slemp | Illustrator: John Mollison
Marketing Manager: Lee Anne Patterson | Main Contributor: John Slemp Photography

139 JESSE MOCKRIN, RELIQUARY | Design Firm: Still Room
Designer: Jessica Fleischmann | Client: Night Gallery | Design Assistant: Taylor Miles-Hopkins
Printer: Ofset Yapimevi | PrePress: Echelon Color | Photographer: Brica Wilcox
Main Contributors: Jesse Mockrin, Andy Campbell, Shannon Cartier Lucy, Norman Bryson

139 KENT MONKMAN: BEING LEGENDARY | Design Firm: Underline Studio
Designers: Fidel Peña, Ritu Kanal | Client: Art Canada Institute
Creative Directors: Claire Dawson, Fidel Peña | Production Manager: Wali Mahmud
Printer: Type A | Photographer: Paul Eekhoff | Editor: Sara Angel
Main Contributor: Underline Studio

140 SNOW CRASH | Design Firm: Faceout Studio | Designer: Jeff Miller
Client: Penguin Random House | Art Director: David Stevenson | Main Contributor: Jeff Miller

140 SINS OF THE TRIBE | Design Firm: Greenleaf Book Group
Designer: Chase Quarterman | Client: Mark A. Salter | Art Director: Neil Gonzalez
Main Contributor: Chase Quarterman

140 THE SAINT OF BRIGHT DOORS | Design Firm: Faceout Studio
Designer: Amanda Hudson | Clients: Tor/Forge Books, Christine Foltzer
Main Contributor: Amanda Hudson

140 THE DEVIL'S CALLING | Design Firm: Greenleaf Book Group | Designer: Brian Phillips
Client: Michael Kelley | Art Director: Neil Gonzalez | Main Contributor: Brian Phillips

140 AMERICAN AMNESIA | Design Firm: Faceout Studio | Designer: Molly von Borstel
Client: Simon & Schuster | Art Director: Jackie Seow | Main Contributor: Molly von Borstel

140 WE SOLD OUR SOULS | Design Firm: Faceout Studio
Designer: Tim Green | Clients: Quirk Books, Andie Reid | Main Contributor: Tim Green

140 THE VARIETIES OF ATHEISM | Design Firm: Faceout Studio | Designer: Tim Green
Client: University of Chicago Press | Art Director: Jill Shimabukuro | Main Contributor: Tim Green

140 SOLENOID | Design Firm: Anna Jordan | Designer: Anna Jordan
Client: Deep Vellum | Main Contributor: Anna Jordan

140 PLAY THE FOOL | Design Firm: Faceout Studio | Designer: Amanda Hudson
Clients: Penguin Random House, Sarah Horgan | Main Contributor: Amanda Hudson

141 CATTLE COTTON CORN | Design Firm: Texas Tech University Press
Designer: Hannah Gaskamp | Client: Self-initiated | Main Contributor: Hannah Gaskamp

141 BREAD HEAD | Design Firm: Faceout Studio
Designers: Spencer Fuller, Paul Nielsen | Client: W.W. Norton
Art Directors: Steve Attardo, Devon Zahn | Main Contributor: Paul Nielsen

141 THREE FIRES | Design Firm: Faceout Studio | Designer: Amanda Hudson
Clients: Pegasus Books, Claiborne Hancock | Main Contributor: Amanda Hudson

141 O GRANDE DEUS PÃ (THE GREAT GOD PAN) | Design Firm: Studio DelRey
Designer: Delfin | Client: Editora Todavia (Brazil) | Main Contributor: Delfin

142 FIRE OF LOVE | Design Firm: SJI Associates | Designer: Shawna Dermer
Clients: Chris Albert, National Geographic | President: Suzy Jurist | Art Director: Jill Vinitsky
Main Contributor: SJI Associates

142 A TRIBUTE TO AMERICA'S HEROES | Design Firm: Vizient Inc.
Designers: Rex Gee, Donna Aldridge, Jessica Hite | Client: Self-initiated
Creative Director: Yvette Wheeler | Copywriter: Individual Stories by Vizient Veterans
Retoucher: David Vaught | Project Manager: Niall Turner | Print Producer: Maressa Currie
Printers: Mark Watson, ColorMark Printing | Marketing: Lionel Carter, Monica Puckett,
Monica Davey, Liz Lombardo, James Tran, Amanda Devers | Illustrator: Rex Gee
Photographers: Personal Images, Getty Images | Production Designer: Jessica Hite
Editor: Kelly Randall | Main Contributor: Rex Gee, Donna Aldridge, Jessica Hite, Yvette Wheeler

142 PROCESS BOOK | Design Firm: Asad Pervaiz | Designer: Asad Pervaiz
Client: George Nakashima Woodworkers | Art Director: Alexis Caldero
Creative Director: Asad Pervaiz | Typeface: Prophet by Dinamo, Sectra by Grilli Type, Freight Big
by Joshua Darden | Printing: Conti Tipocolor | Paper: Munken Print White 20
Photographers: Woong Chul An, Juli Daost, Christian Giannelli, Matthew Johnson, Naho Kubota,
Chris Mottalini, Martien Mulder, Manolo Yllera, Matt Zugale
Photo Retouching: Christian Giannelli, Asad Pervaiz | Writer: Mira Nakashima
Editor: Nate Muscato | Main Contributor: Mira Nakashima

142 FACING SOCIAL JUSTICE IN SPORTS BOOK COVER DESIGN
Design Firm: Open Door Design Studio (ODDS) | Designer: Shantanu Suman
Client: The Facing Project | Publisher: Facing Project Press
Editor: Adam J. Kuban | Main Contributor: Shantanu Suman

142 TWO COVERS: "I'M AI" AND "THE WITNESS NEW YORK"
Design Firm: STUDIO INTERNATIONAL | Designer: Boris Ljubicic | Client: Conte Ivano Bajamonti
Artist: Boris Ljubicic | Typography Design: Vilibald Pečenik
Photographers: Boris Ljubicic, Darko Bavoljak | Main Contributor: Conte Ivano Bajamonti

142 MILLHOUSE THE BEACH LIFE PUG - BOOK COVER
Design Firm: Judd Brand Media | Designer: Patti Judd | Client: Beach Town Studio
Main Contributor: Patti Judd

143 MILTON GLASER: POP | Design Firm: Mirko Ilic Corp.
Designers: Mirko Ilic, Ignacio Serrano | Client: The Monacelli Press
Art Director: Mirko Ilic | Main Contributor: Mirko Ilic

143 THE ENTANGLEMENT | Design Firm: Anna Jordan | Designer: Anna Jordan
Client: Princeton University Press | Main Contributor: Anna Jordan

143 A LAND BETWEEN WORLDS - THE SHIFTING POETRY OF THE GREAT AMERICAN LANDSCAPE | Design Firm: Yup, It's a Hub | Designers: David Leal, Filipa Oliveira
Client: Life Calling | Author: John C. Mack | Illustrator: David Leal
Project Manager: Inês Portugal | Production Manager: Joao Flecha
Production: Gráfica Maiadouro | Developer: Treeline Interactive

144 MEWS ON MAXWELL BRANDING | Design Firm: Lisa Sirbaugh Creative
Designer: Lisa Sirbaugh | Client: JR Capital Build | Sign Fabricator: Frederick Sign & Banner Co.
Printer: The YGS Group | Main Contributor: Lisa Sirbaugh Creative

144 NEW NEWS BRANDING | Design Firm: Danyang Ma | Designer: Danyang Ma
Client: Youth Media International | Main Contributor: Danyang Ma

144 GROUNDED IN THEIR ROOTS, GROWING INTO THE FUTURE
Design Firm: Wolff Olins | Designers: Colin Kinsley, Daniel Renda, Ryan Bugden, Jess Yan,
Vanessa Hopkins, Nicholas Samendinger | Client: Instacart
Associate Creative Director: Jess Yan | Creative Director: Daniel Renda
Typeface Designer: Ryan Bugden | Strategy Director: Michele Kim
Photographer: Stephanie Gonot | Motion Designers: Draeger Gillespie, Jason Chen
Marketing: Tal Ayala Kamin | Account Manager: Ian Carroll
Account Executive: Marina Ammirato | Main Contributor: Wolff Olins

144 INDIANA INDUSTRIES BRANDING | Design Firm: Abby Ryan Design
Designers: Abby Guido, Bryan Satalino | Client: Indiana Industries
Junior Designer: Audrey Lee | Main Contributors: Abby Guido, Bryan Satalino

144 TGD 25TH ANNIVERSARY | Design Firm: TGD | Designer: Johann A. Gómez
Client: Self-initiated | Creative Director: Ryan Burlinson | Writer: Nick Bondura
Main Contributors: Aimee Babcock, Nick Bondura, Ryan Burlinson, Brandon Feely,
Johann A. Gómez, Jesse Gregory, Arthur Hagman, Jessah Hofker, Jessica Larkin, Albert Loo,
Heather Ottmar, Luke Shelley, Dani VonGunten

145 SUBVERSUS | Design Firm: Toben | Designer: Thorsten Kulp
Client: Subversus | Art Director: Thorsten Kulp | Creative Director: Katja Hartung
Web Developer: Brendan Foster | Main Contributor: Toben

145 COCON -THE NEW LIFE OF JEWELRY- | Design Firm: Triplet Design Inc.
Designer: Tsuyoshi Omori | Client: WAKO Inc. | Copywriter: Taro Nakamura
Photographer: Hiroto Hata | Translator: Yukiko Nishikawa | Main Contributor: Tsuyoshi Omori

146 BRANDING | Design Firm: Coastlines Creative Group
Designer: Byron Dowler | Client: Rimex Supply | Main Contributor: Byron Dowler

146 STAINED GLASS WITH A SPIN - LOGO SYSTEM
Design Firm: Brand Bar Communications | Designer: Róbert Válóczi
Client: Media Center of Kecskemet | Creative Director: Attila Simon
Main Contributor: Brand Bar Communications

146 GREENSPARC | Design Firm: Noise 13 | Designers: Xiaoxiao Ma, Zili Ma
Client: Greensparc | Chief Creative Officer: Dava Guthmiller
Associate Creative Director: André Carnevale | Strategy: Sara Leslie, Miriam Stone
Project Manager: Brenna Kilpatrick | Main Contributors: Xiaoxiao Ma, Zili Ma

146 OSAKA KOREAN FILM FESTIVAL LOGO DESIGN
Design Firm: KINDAI Graphic Art Course Laboratory | Designers: Kiyoung An, Rion Nishino
Client: Korean Cultural Center OSAKA | Main Contributor: Korean Cultural Center OSAKA

146 LVE IDENTITY SYSTEM | Design Firm: Traction Factory
Designer: Mark Brautigam | Client: Las Vegas Expo | Art Director: Mark Brautigam
Design Director: David Brown | Creative Director: David Brown | Copywriter: S.J. Barlament
Project Manager: Liz Wilson | Production Artist: Jenni Wierzba
Account Director: Shannon Egan | Main Contributor: Traction Factory

146 SUTURO | Design Firm: Teiga, Studio. | Designer: María Toucedo Cal
Client: Suturo | Art Directors: Xosé Teiga, María Toucedo Cal
Creative Team: María Toucedo, Laura Santos, Xosé Teiga | Creative Director: Xosé Teiga
Copywriters: Xosé Teiga, María Toucedo Cal | Video: Laura Santos
Graphic Designers: Cristina Gónzalez, María Toucedo Cal
Design Manager: María Toucedo Cal | Main Contributor: Teiga, Studio.

147 MARTIN GUITAR REBRAND | Design Firm: Coley Porter Bell
Designers: Linda Becker, Ben Davidson, Alison Dyer, Sam Knott, Steve Ferrier
Client: Martin Guitar | President: Jenn Szekely | Motion Designer: Yukari Schrickel
Strategy Director: John Clark | Strategy: Andy Humphreys
Group Creative Director: John Malozzi | Executive Creative Director: James Ramsden
Account Management: Alice Lee | Main Contributors: Coley Porter Bell, Martin Guitar

147 BOLHÃO, PORTO'S HISTORIC MARKET | Design Firm: Studio Eduardo Aires
Designer: Eduardo Aires | Client: GO Porto - Porto City Hall | Writer: Helena Sofia Silva
Art Director: Eduardo Aires | Content Developer: Helena Sofia Silva
Graphic Designers: Dário Cannatà, Guillermo Zetek, Joana Teixeira, Miguel Almeida
Photographers: Alexandre Delmar, Oscar Almeida, Marta Maria Ferreira, Luís Ferreira Alves
Main Contributor: Studio Eduardo Aires

147 MERMAID, INC. | FLUID CREATIVITY BRANDING | Design Firm: Mermaid, Inc.
Designer: Sharon Lloyd McLaughlin | Client: Self-initiated
Creative Team: Bart McLaughlin | Main Contributor: Sharon Lloyd McLaughlin

147 LOCAL ARCHITECTS BRANDING | Design Firm: Freaner Creative & Design
Designer: Ariel Freaner | Client: LOCAL Architects | Digital Artist: Ariel Freaner
Creative Directors: Ariel Freaner, LOCAL Master Logo | Main Contributor: Ariel Freaner

147 APRECIO SUPERMARKET STORES | Design Firm: Freaner Creative & Design
Designer: Ariel Freaner | Clients: Aprecio, Rosella Fimbres | Creative Director: Ariel Freaner
Illustrator: Ariel Freaner | Main Contributor: Ariel Freaner

147 FOUNDRY FIELD: THE STORY OF RACE, REPRESENTATION, ACCESS, AND BASEBALL IN SOUTH BEND, INDIANA
Design Firm: Clinton Carlson Design | University of Notre Dame | Designer: Clinton Carlson
Client: Foundry Field | Architect: Kevin Buccellato | Typeface: Custom: Foundry Gothic,
Foundry Slab. Also: Solano Gothic, Termina, Luminance | Copywriters: Clinton Carlson,
Michael Hebbeler, Matthew Insley, Sean Kennedy | Research: Greg Bond, Kevin Buccellato,
Clinton Carlson, Michael Hebbeler, Matthew Insley, Sean Kennedy, Nick Mainieri, Katie Walden
Source Credits: Rene Francisco Garza, Sr. photographs and papers — Civil Rights Heritage
Center | Indiana University South Bend Archives; The History Museum; Pokagon Band of
Potawatomi; Studebaker National Museum. | Main Contributor: Clinton Carlson

148 BRANDROAD: AN ITALIAN PODCAST | Design Firm: Univisual SRL
Designers: Gaetano Grizzanti, Giancarlo Tosoni | Client: Matteo Lusiani
Main Contributors: Gaetano Grizzanti, Giancarlo Tosoni

148 SOUTH PARK TOWER POSTCARDS | Design Firm: IF Studio
Designer: Hisa Ide | Client: Brodsky | Design Director: Hisa Ide
Creative Strategist: Sarah Tan | Creative Director: Toshiaki Ide
Photographers: Wei and Xi, Michael Imlay | Managing Partner: Amy Frankel
Account Manager: Mercedes Barba | Main Contributors: Hisa Ide, Toshiaki Ide

148 PIANIST PAUL WARTHEN BRANDING | Design Firm: Lisa Sirbaugh Creative
Designer: Lisa Sirbaugh | Client: Paul Warthen | Copywriter: Hilary O'Brien
Photographer: Jessica Patterson Photography | Video: In Depth Photo & Video
Printers: Mamas Sauce, MOO | Main Contributor: Lisa Sirbaugh Creative

148 FUNKO BRAND REFRESH | Design Firm: TGD
Designers: Johann A. Gómez, Jeff Anderson, Kelsie LeBlanc, Mat McInelly, Luke Shelley, Katherine Wion | Clients: Funko, Dave Bere, Hillary Gray | Creative Director: Ryan Burlinson
Main Contributors: Jeff Anderson, Aimee Babcock, Nick Bondura, Ryan Burlinson, Karrie Gaylord, Jesse Gregory, Johann A. Gómez, Jessah Hofker, Jessica Larkin, Kelsie LeBlanc, Mat McInelly, Heather Ottmar, Luke Shelley, Sam Trimble, Katherine Wion

148 US SCIENCE SUPPORT PROGRAM BRANDING
Design Firm: C&G Partners | Designers: Maya Kopytman, Maya Zimmer, Melinda Sekela
Client: US Science Support Program | Main Contributor: Maya Kopytman

148 NATIONAL RESOURCES BRANDING | Design Firm: Mermaid, Inc.
Designer: Sharon Lloyd McLaughlin | Client: National Resources
Web Developer: Bart McLaughlin | Marketing Manager: Lauren Calabria
Main Contributor: Sharon Lloyd McLaughlin

149 REBRANDING ADXTUR | Design Firm: Atelier Nunes e Pã, Ida
Designers: João Nunes, Ana Menezes, Susana Nunes, Mariana Melo, Paula Simões, Teresa Nascimento, Bárbara Vitoriano, Inês Ferreira, Vânia Oliveira, Margarida Pereira
Client: ADXTUR – Schist Villages Tourism Development Agency
Main Contributors: João Nunes, Ana Menezes, Susana Nunes, Mariana Melo

149 HERDADE DA MALHADINHA NOVA | Design Firm: Studio Eduardo Aires
Designer: Eduardo Aires | Client: Herdade da Malhadinha Nova | Writer: Helena Sofia Silva
Art Director: Eduardo Aires | Photographers: Nuno Moreira, Oscar Almeida
Graphic Designers: Guillermo Zetek, André Pimentel, Luisa Tormenta, Miguel Almeida
Content Developer: Helena Sofia Silva | Illustrator: Iñaki Aires
Main Contributor: Studio Eduardo Aires

149 VERMONT INC. | Design Firm: Hoyne | Designer: Walter Ochoa
Client: Ledlin Develop | Creative Director: Matt Ellis | Account Director: Katrina Legge

150 THE ROYAL PARKS – BRAND IDENTITY | Design Firm: Rose
Designers: Paloma Kaluzinska, Rose, Ethan Major, Yafet Bisrat | Client: The Royal Parks
Creative Directors: Garry Blackburn, Simon Elliott | Illustrators: Rose, Rebecca Sutherland
Copywriter: Jim Davies | Project Managers: Ghislaine Gayyo, Joanna Waclawski
Main Contributor: Rose

150 QT NEWCASTLE | Design Firm: Toben | Designers: Thorsten Kulp, Sam Grainger
Client: QT Hotels & Resorts | Art Director: Thorsten Kulp | Creative Director: Katja Hartung
Copywriter: Language Design (James Harvey) | Print Producer: Lisa McCulloch (EVT)
Main Contributor: Toben

150 LIMBURGS MUSEUM – VAN ÓS. FOR EVERYBODY. | Design Firm: Total Design
Designers: Adam Lane, Alicia Castro, Timon Weerstand, Edwin van Praet
Client: Limburgs Museum | Web Developers: Erwin van Ekeren, Lex van Hees, Rosyl Budike
Strategy Director: Sieds de Boer | Creative Director: Edwin van Praet
Project Managers: Francis Brüggenwirth, Eveline Wiegmans | Motion Designer: Kassahun Villa
Digital Director: Joppe Andriessen | Main Contributor: Total Design

150 ACTION NETWORK BRANDING | Design Firm: Lafayette American
Designer: Lafayette American | Client: Action Network
Web Designer: Action Network | Main Contributor: Lafayette American

150 20 DEEP WINERY BRAND IDENTITY | Design Firm: Truth Collective
Designer: Justyn Iannucci | Client: 20 Deep Winery | Strategy: Ken McVeagh
Copywriter: Suzette Dorrielan | Account Executive: Sydney Aspenleiter
Main Contributor: Ken McVeagh

150 NEW EPPING | Design Firm: Hoyne | Designer: Elliott Pearson | Client: Riverlee
Art Producer: Sylvain Sommacal | Creative Director: Nichole Trionfi
Copywriters: Matt Ellis, Jacquie Byron | Account Director: Katrina Legge

151 SAN DIEGO FOUNDATION BRAND IDENTITY | Design Firm: MiresBall
Designers: Lauren Lamb, John Ball | Client: San Diego Foundation
Design Director: Lauren Lamb | Creative Director: John Ball
Main Contributors: John Ball, Lauren Lamb, Anique Mautner

151 DARK NETWORKS | Design Firm: Botond Vörös
Designer: Botond Vörös | Client: Dark Networks | Main Contributor: Botond Vörös

151 MAHON COACHING | Design Firm: ASHA & Co.
Designers: ASHA & Co., Steven Tatlow, Lizzie Botterill | Client: Rose Mahon
Chief Creative Officer: Marksteen Adamson | Associate Creative Director: Scott McGuffie
Design Director: Simon Dryland | Managing Director: Mike Horne
Account Management: Hannah Mapleston | Main Contributor: ASHA & Co.

151 POWERHOUSE ARTS REBRAND | Design Firm: Entro
Designers: Entro, Radnyee Joshi, Shraddha Bedmutha | Client: Powerhouse Arts
Creative Director: Eileen Moore | Partner: Anna Crider | Creative Director: Anna Crider
Project Manager: Alyssa Weinstein | Main Contributor: Entro

151 DASH HAIR STUDIO BRANDING | Design Firm: Lisa Sirbaugh Creative
Designer: Lisa Sirbaugh | Client: Dash Hair Studio | Copywriter: Dash Hair Studio
Sign Fabricator: Express Signs | Print Producer: Chatterbox | Printer: MOO
Photographer: Kathy White Photography | Main Contributor: Lisa Sirbaugh Creative

151 RENEWING RITUALS TO UPLIFT COMMUNITIES LOCALLY AND AT ORIGIN
Design Firm: Playstead | Designer: Nathan Plaisted
Client: Avatar Coffee Roasters | Main Contributor: Nathan Plaisted

152 PLACE2BE | Design Firm: Elmwood
Designer: Elmwood | Client: Place2Be | Creative Director: Kyle Whybrow
Account Manager: Nicole Segal | Account Director: Eleanor Westwood
Others: Mike Preston: Middleweight Designer, Oli Minchin: Head of Animation
Main Contributor: Elmwood

152 BOLD REBRAND | Design Firm: Matchstic | Designers: Meghan Murray, Sean Jones
Client: Bold | Writer: Pam Henman | Strategy Director: Tracy Clark
Project Manager: Melissa Kruse | Partner: Blake Howard
Creative Director: Blake Howard | Main Contributor: Meghan Murray

152 SPRITE VIS | Design Firm: Turner Duckworth: London, San Francisco & New York
Designers: Jack Powell, Justin Tolentino, Mike Bagnardi, Breehn Sasaki | Client: Coca Cola
Production: Jeff Ensslen | Photographer: Martin Wonnacott
Implementation Manager: Sara Scanlan | Account Manager: Julia Kranzler
Account Director: Kelly Ongpin | Main Contributor: Chris Garvey

152 EO MADISON YARDS BRAND IDENTITY | Design Firm: Resource Branding
Designers: Juliana Hill, Shaina Patel | Client: Gilbane Development Company
Design Director: Rick Grimsley | Copywriters: Jessica Childers, Bertrand Pinneo
Web Developer: Erik Rühling | Account Management: Cate Pilliod, Sarah Krausen
Strategy: Gary Thompson | Main Contributor: Resource Branding

152 ADVENTR | Design Firm: Noise 13 | Designers: Elaine Chaw, Jerome Harris
Client: Adventr | Chief Creative Officer: Dava Guthmiller
Associate Creative Director: André Carnevale | Copywriter: Kimber Bowman
Strategy: Sara Leslie, Miriam Stone | Project Manager: Eugenia Semjonova
Junior Designer: Montana Siddle | Main Contributors: Elaine Chaw, Jerome Harris

153 SPACE CENTER HOUSTON REBRAND | Design Firm: Traina
Designer: Joe Ross | Client: Space Center Houston | Copywriter: Jarrett Haley
President: David Traina | Brand Strategy: Matt Bachmann, Sandra Rivera
Graphic Designers: Erwin Hines, Mark DeRose, Carlo Palazzolo, John Laird
Animator: Chris Hylton | Account Director: Kristi Jones | Main Contributor: Joe Ross

153 QUASER GROUP | Design Firm: RedPeak Global
Designers: Chris Chung, Tai Yuan Chiou, Chien Chun Feng, Stacey Yu, Yu Chen
Client: Quaser Machine Tools | Strategy: Marco Negri, Kevin Hsueh
Chairman: Silvia Yu | Account Manager: Lea Chien | Account Director: Raychard Huang
Main Contributors: Silvia Yu, Chris Chung, Tai Yuan Chiou, Chien Chun Feng, Stacey Yu, Yu Chen, Kevin Hsueh, Marco Negri, Raychard Huang, Lea Chien

154 KOMPLYAI | Design Firm: Toben | Designers: Thorsten Kulp, Sam Grainger
Client: KomplyAi | Art Director: Thorsten Kulp | Creative Director: Katja Hartung
Main Contributor: Toben

154 HALLIBURTON LABS REBRAND | Design Firm: Coley Porter Bell
Designers: Linda Becker, Ollie Williams, Ben Davidson | Client: Halliburton
President: Jenn Szekely | Group Creative Director: John Malozzi
Executive Creative Director: James Ramsden
Account Management: Maggie Thomas, Alice Lee
Main Contributors: Coley Porter Bell, Halliburton

154 QT GOLD COAST | Design Firm: Toben
Designers: Thorsten Kulp, Geoff Courtman | Client: QT Hotels & Resorts
Art Director: Thorsten Kulp | Creative Director: Katja Hartung
Digital Artist: Chris Thompson | Print Producer: Lisa McCulloch (EVT)
Main Contributor: Toben

154 A REBRANDING TAKES FLIGHT | Design Firm: Yes& Lipman Hearne
Designers: Chris Cacci, Raúl Peña | Client: St. Peter's University
Creative Director: Chris Cacci | Senior Art Director: Raúl Peña

154 BIBLE SOCIETY | Design Firm: ASHA & Co.
Designers: ASHA & Co., Lizzie Botterill, Steven Tatlow | Client: Bible Society
Chief Creative Director: Marksteen Adamson | Associate Creative Director: Scott McGuffie
Managing Director: Mike Horne | Design Director: Simon Dryland
Account Management: Hannah Mapleston | Main Contributor: ASHA & Co.

154 OAKRIDGE PARK | Design Firm: OnRepeat Studio
Designer: Joao Oliveira | Clients: Westbank, QuadReal | Copywriter: Axel Van Weel
Creative Directors: Joao Oliveira, Axel Van Weel | Main Contributor: OnRepeat Studio

155 BRIGHTWILD REBRAND | Design Firm: Matchstic | Designer: Brit Blankenship
Client: Brightwild | Writer: Cam Leberecht | Strategy Director: Tracy Clark
Strategy: Kenny Isidoro | Project Manager: Melissa Kruse | Partner: Blake Howard
Creative Director: Blake Howard | Main Contributor: Brit Blankenship

155 ADCC IDENTITY | Design Firm: Underline Studio
Designer: Brittany Waldner | Client: Advertising and Design Club of Canada
Creative Directors: Fidel Peña, Claire Dawson | Main Contributor: Underline Studio

155 HALO INFINITE STYLEGUIDE | Design Firm: TGD | Designer: Johann A. Gómez
Clients: 343 Industries, Tiffany O'Brien, Rick Blanco | Creative Director: Ryan Burlinson
Main Contributors: Aaron Travis, Jessah Hofker, Nick Bondura, Ryan Burlinson, Johann A. Gómez, Mat McInelly, Jeff Anderson, Kelsie LeBlanc, Amy Curtiss, Aaron Jacobo, Liz Fitzwater, Jessica Larkin

156 BOLTBOLT | Design Firm: BOLTBOLT | Designer: Joohyun Park
Client: Self-initiated | General Director: Ken Chen | Main Contributor: Joohyun Park

156 HALCOMB ORTHO BRAND IDENTITY | Design Firm: Test Monki
Designer: Test Monki | Client: Halcomb Orthodontics | Main Contributor: Test Monki

156 2022 TAOYUAN LAND ART FESTIVAL "RIVER FLOWS, CITY VIBES"
Design Firm: VANGUARD Visual Design Ltd. | Designer: Shao-Wei Chuang
Client: Taoyuan City Government, Department of Cultural Affairs
Chief Creative Officer: Ying-Hua Ouyang | Vice Presidents: Kuo-Wei Lu, Chia-Huang Chao
Project Manager: Chia-Huang Chao | Print Producers: Wu-Tse Hsiu, Jia-Ning Lu
Photographer: Shu-fu Yang | Animator: Hung-Ming Chen | Main Contributor: Shao-Wei Chuang

156 TAIFINE BRANDING | Design Firm: Wuhan Mornice Brand Design Co., Ltd.
Designer: Qichao An | Client: TaiFine | Main Contributor: Qichao An

156 BREZZA HOTEL BRANDING | Design Firm: Freaner Creative & Design
Designer: Ariel Freaner | Client: Brezza Hotel | Digital Artist: Ariel Freaner
Creative Director: Ariel Freaner | Main Contributor: Ariel Freaner

156 ILKON: ILKESTON CONTEMPORARY ARTS
Design Firm: Pinter-Parrott | Designers: Susanne Pinter, Francesca Pinter-Parrott
Client: ILKON: Ilkeston Contemporary Arts | Main Contributor: Susanne Pinter

157 ADIRA ALTAMONTE SPRINGS BRAND IDENTITY | Design Firm: Resource Branding
Designers: Hannah West, Mandy Rahiya | Client: Gilbane Development Company
Design Director: Rick Grimsley | Copywriters: Bob Devol, Jessica Childers
Strategy: Jessica Childers | Account Management: Cate Pilliod, Sarah Krausen
Main Contributor: Resource Branding

157 MIRANDELA | Design Firm: Studio Eduardo Aires
Designer: Eduardo Aires | Client: Mirandela City Hall | Art Director: Eduardo Aires
Writer: Helena Sofia Silva | Content Developer: Helena Sofia Silva | Photographer: Hugo Reis
Graphic Designers: Raquel Piteira, Pedro Mata Nogueira, Joana Teixeira, Vasco Castro,
Miguel Almeida | Main Contributor: Studio Eduardo Aires

157 MICROSOFT VIVA BRAND EXPRESSION
Design Firm: Microsoft Cloud Marketing Brand Studio
Designer: Microsoft Cloud Marketing Brand Studio | Client: Microsoft Viva
Brand Strategy: Brandon Larson | Associate Creative Director: Tierney Cunningham
Animator: Thomas Nichols | Agency: Cinco Design | Project Manager: Jeff McInnis
Photo Director: Kelly Anderson | Executive Creative Director: Douglas Montague
Main Contributor: Tierney Cunningham

157 NOWHERE DESK | Design Firm: PMDESIGN | Designer: Paulo Marcelo
Client: Nowhere Desk | Main Contributor: Paulo Marcelo

157 AKITA DESIGN BRANDING | Design Firm: Legis Design
Designer: Mayumi Kato | Client: AKITA Design | Main Contributor: Legis Design

157 PALETTE LIFE SCIENCES | Design Firm: Cue
Designer: Matt Erickson | Client: Palette Life Sciences
Creative Directors: Alan Colvin, Webb Blevins | Main Contributor: Alan Colvin

158 7UP GLOBAL BRAND RESTAGE | Design Firm: PepsiCo Design & Innovation
Designer: PepsiCo Design & Innovation | Client: Self-initated

158 MIRINDA GLOBAL RESTAGE | Design Firm: PepsiCo Design & Innovation
Designer: PepsiCo Design & Innovation | Client: Self-initated

158 YU ZHONG BU TONG BRAND IDENTITY | Design Firm: BEAMY
Designer: BEAMY | Client: Yu Zhong Bu Tong | Design Director: I.V. Toh
Creative Director: Ronn Lee | Main Contributor: Ronn Lee

158 A BEAUTIFUL FIT | Design Firm: Full Punch | Designer: Christian Hanson
Client: Nick Brouard | Chief Strategy Officer: Jack Dayan | Agency Producer: Claire Khan
Copywriter: Nick Brouard | President: Mike Leslie | Typographer: Paul von Excite
Executive Creative Director: Chris Zawada | Account Manager: Ilana Solomons
Main Contributor: Chris Zawada

158 HYRBA | Design Firm: Noise 13
Designers: Elaine Chaw, Zili Ma | Client: Hyrba | Chief Creative Officer: Dava Guthmiller
Associate Creative Director: André Carnevale | Strategy: Jane Johnson
Junior Designer: Shannon Steed | Project Manager: Brenna Kilpatrick
Main Contributors: Elaine Chaw, Zili Ma

158 GOLD BOND | Design Firm: Cue | Designer: Katelyn McVey
Client: Gold Bond | Creative Director: Alan Colvin | Main Contributor: Alan Colvin

159 PERFUMEHEAD BRAND | Design Firm: Underline Studio
Designers: Claire Dawson, Brittany Waldner, Ritu Kanal | Client: Perfumehead
Creative Directors: Claire Dawson, Fidel Peña | Production Manager: Wali Mahmud
Main Contributor: Underline Studio

159 ROYAL CHALLENGE BRAND REDESIGN 2022 | Design Firm: Bulletproof
Designers: Nino Yaputra, Yonglong Zhang, Hieu Trieu | Clients: Diageo India, Hiren Dedhia
Executive Creative Director: Mark Armstrong | Creative Director: David Solzbacher
Strategy: Kaavya Krishnan | Retoucher: Harry Lim | Illustrator: Jason Liw
Production Manager: Jesse Moran | Senior Account Director: Katie Osborn
Account Manager: Samantha Lee | Main Contributor: Bulletproof

160 THE RSPB | Design Firm: ASHA & Co.
Designers: ASHA & Co., Lizzie Botterill, Steven Tatlow | Client: The RSPB
Chief Creative Director: Marksteen Adamson | Associate Creative Director: Scott McGuffie
Design Director: Simon Dryland | Managing Director: Mike Horne
Account Management: Hannah Mapleston | Main Contributor: ASHA & Co.

160 THE PRACTICAL, ENLIGHTENING, AND STUPENDOUSLY FUN GUIDE TO SALESFORCE CHARACTERS | Design Firm: Salesforce
Designers: Mike Mazza, Michael Manning, Shirleen Lavalais, Andy Wood | Client: Self-initiated
SVP Creative Advertising: Scott Larson | Production Manager: Iain Boltin
Copywriters: Daniel Krewson, Mike Mazza | Printer: Colorbar Graphic Construction
Main Contributors: Mike Mazza, Michael Manning, Shirleen Lavalais, Andy Wood

160 PAN & QUESO (BREAD AND CHEESE) BRANDING
Design Firm: Freaner Creative & Design | Designer: Ariel Freaner
Client: Pan & Queso (Bread and Cheese) | Illustrator: Ariel Freaner
Creative Director: Ariel Freaner | Digital Artist: Ariel Freaner | Main Contributor: Ariel Freaner

160 ONEG BRANDING | Design Firm: Dear Fellow Design Studio
Designer: Courtney Spencer | Clients: Oneg, Jeanie Milbauer
Senior Designer: Emily Funck | Product Designer: Olivia Miller
Marketing Manager: Stephanie Kimel | Main Contributor: Courtney Spencer

160 RADICONDOLI CITY BRAND (ITALY) | Design Firm: Freaner Creative & Design
Designer: Ariel Freaner | Client: Radicondoli City Council, Italy | Creative Director: Ariel Freaner
Digital Artist: Ariel Freaner | Typeface Designer: Ariel Freaner | Main Contributor: Ariel Freaner

160 PLANTKISS BRAND IDENTITY SYSTEM | Design Firm: MiresBall
Designers: Lauren Lamb, John Ball, Renee Chan, Luke Meyer
Client: PlantKiss | Creative Director: John Ball | Copywriter: Dylan Speed
Digital Director: Anique Mautner | Main Contributor: John Ball

161 CASTON COFFEE ROASTERS BRANDING | Design Firm: YSFT Inc.
Designers: Yihuang Zhou, Yixuan Cao | Client: Caston Coffee Roasters
Main Contributors: Yihuang Zhou, Yixuan Cao

161 ROLD GOLD REDESIGN | Design Firm: PepsiCo Design & Innovation
Designer: PepsiCo Design & Innovation | Client: Self-initated

161 MILEPOST ZERO | Design Firm: Ellen Bruss Design
Designer: Ken Garcia | Client: Continuum Partners | Creative Director: Ellen Bruss
Art Director: Ken Garcia | Main Contributor: Ellen Bruss Design

161 PHILLIPS REDESIGN | Design Firm: Cue | Designer: Matt Erickson
Client: Phillips Distilling Co. | Creative Director: Alan Colvin | Main Contributor: Alan Colvin

161 HOYAONE CONTACT LENS | Design Firm: GRAPHICS & DESIGNING INC.
Designers: Toshihiro Onimaru | Client: Hoya Corporation | Art Director: Toshihiro Onimaru
Creative Director: Toshihiro Onimaru | Main Contributor: Toshihiro Onimaru

161 OPHELIA'S ELECTRIC SOAPBOX BRANDING
Design Firm: Sukle Advertising & Design | Designer: Greg Jesse
Client: Ophelia's Electric Soapbox | Project Manager: Kathleen Ryan
Creative Director: Mike Sukle | Associate Creative Directors: Curtis Smith, Dan Delli-Colli
Digital Artist: Matt Carpenter | Director of Client Services: Amy Taylor
Senior Account Director: Katie Dondale | Account Services: Alexis Supangan
Main Contributor: Sukle Advertising & Design

162 KOUVENDA MEDIA | Design Firm: SAYGRID | Designer: David Jones
Clients: Stephanie Marudas, Emily Previti | Creative Directors: Stephanie Marudas, Emily Previti
Art Director: Andee Mazzocco | Partners: Stephanie Marudas, Emily Previti
Main Contributors: David Jones, Andee Mazzocco

162 REIMAGINING WORKPLACES WITH CANVAS | Design Firm: Lippincott
Designers: Jessica Ho, Kim Lai, Myung Jin Lee, Vincenzo Perri, Alicia Chiu, Michelle Kwan,
YK Lam | Client: Canvas | Strategy: Jessica Lee, Jamie Lee, Sean Doh
Main Contributor: Vincenzo Perri

162 JOINING TOGETHER TO CELEBRATE OUR COMMUNITY
Design Firm: Studio Craig Byers | Designer: Craig Byers
Client: ALSOYouth | Main Contributor: Craig Byers, Brand Designer

162 LIONESA BUSINESS HUB | Design Firm: Studio Eduardo Aires
Designer: Eduardo Aires | Client: Lionesa Business Hub | Writer: Helena Sofia Silva
Content Developer: Helena Sofia Silva | Art Director: Eduardo Aires
Graphic Designers: Vasco Castro, Pedro Mata Nogueira, Raquel Piteira, Joana Teixeira,
Miguel Almeida, Rita Palha Lopes | Main Contributor: Studio Eduardo Aires

162 MEPTIK REBRAND | Design Firm: Matchstic | Designers: John Bowles, Rachel Jackson
Client: Meptik | Writer: Acree Macam | Strategy: Mitchell Ditto | Project Manager: Patrice Fielder
Partner: Blake Howard | Creative Director: Blake Howard | Main Contributor: John Bowles

163 THE BELLSLIP BROCHURE | Design Firm: IF Studio | Designer: Hisa Ide
Client: Brookfield Properties | Design Director: Hisa Ide | Creative Director: Toshiaki Ide
Creative Strategist: Sarah Tan | Photographers: Marley Rizzuti, Michael Imlay
Managing Partner: Amy Frankel | Illustrator: Olivia Knapp | Account Director: Lisa Meyer
Main Contributors: Hisa Ide, Toshiaki Ide

163 SARTORIALE | Design Firm: Teikna Design | Designers: Claudia Neri, Elisa Stagnoli
Client: Arjowiggins Creative Papers | Printer: Tiburtini SRL | Main Contributor: Claudia Neri

163 PLANK ROAD BROCHURE | Design Firm: IF Studio | Designer: Hisa Ide
Client: Brodsky | Creative Director: Toshiaki Ide | Design Director: Hisa Ide
Creative Strategist: Sarah Tan | Photographer: Blair Getz Mezibov
Managing Partner: Amy Frankel | Account Manager: Mercedes Barba
Main Contributors: Hisa Ide, Toshiaki Ide

163 STS-72 | Design Firm: B&W Studio
Designers: Lee Bradley, Scott Cockerham | Client: John Angerson

163 MEWS ON MAXWELL VIEWBOOK | Design Firm: Lisa Sirbaugh Creative
Designer: Lisa Sirbaugh | Client: JR Capital Build | Printer: The YGS Group
Copywriter: JR Capital Build | Main Contributor: Lisa Sirbaugh Creative

163 RICHMOND BALLET'S ELEMENTS OF DANCE CAMPAIGN
Design Firm: Karnes Coffey Design | Designer: Christine Coffey | Client: Richmond Ballet
Creative Directors: Christine Coffey, Jamie Mahoney | Director: Emily Morgan, Choreographer:
Ma Cong, Post Studio: Alice Blue, Meredith Ott, David Waraksa | Photographer: Eric Lusher
Photo Retouching: Josh Zuercher, Alice Blue | Photographer's Assistant: Ben Corfield
Hair & Makeup: Kim Reyes | Dancers: Eri Nishihara, Naomi Wilson, Joe Seaton,

Naomi Robinson, Garret McNally, Jack Miller, Ira White, Enrico Hipolito, Sabrina Sabino, Celeste Gaiera, Izabella Tokev, Sarah Joan Smith, Colin Jacob, Khaiyom Khojaev
Additional Titles: Fire Artists: Jonathan Sanford, Kierstin Kratzer, Costume
Main Contributor: Jamie Mahoney

164 EDMISTON ESCAPES | Design Firm: TAYLOR | Designers: Steven Taylor, Cos Iacovou
Client: Edmiston | Copywriter: Steven Taylor | Main Contributor: Steven Taylor

164 CONNECT WITH CITY LIGHTS | Design Firm: Toppan Inc.
Designer: Masahiro Ogawa | Client: Panasonic Homes Co., Ltd.
Photographer: Atsushi Malta | Art Director: Masahiro Aoyagi
Main Contributor: Masahiro Aoyagi

164 2023 PANASONIC HOMES CALENDAR "PEACE" | Design Firm: Toppan Inc.
Designers: Kaoru Kasai, Masahiro Ogawa | Client: Panasonic Homes Co., Ltd.
Print Designer: Daijiro Hasegawa | Creative Director: Masako Aizawa
Art Directors: Masahiro Aoyagi, Kaoru Kasai | Main Contributor: Masahiro Aoyagi

164 PETRON CALENDAR: CELEBRATING NINETY YEARS OF EXCELLENCE
Design Firm: Studio 5 Designs Inc. | Designer: Ice de Leon
Clients: Petron Corporation, Ramon Cruz | Creative Director: BG Hernandez
Account Director: Marily Orosa | Main Contributor: Studio 5 Designs Inc.

164 2023 TOYO INK GROUP CALENDAR "PERSPECTIVE"
Design Firm: Toppan Inc. | Designers: Masahiro Aoyagi, Masahiro Ogawa
Client: Toyo Ink SC Holdings Co., Ltd. | Photographer: Tobias Hägg
Art Director: Masahiro Aoyagi | Main Contributor: Masahiro Aoyagi

164 2023 CALENDAR "CITYSCAPES -DISCOVERY-"
Design Firm: Toppan Inc. | Designer: Masahiro Aoyagi | Client: Obayashi Corporation
Photographer: Rumi Ando | Main Contributor: Masahiro Aoyagi

165 FAITH, LOVE, HOPE CHRISTMAS CARD | Design Firm: UP-Ideas
Designer: Roger Sawhill | Client: UP-Fun | Main Contributor: Roger Sawhill

165 NEIMAN MARCUS BEJEWELED MAILER
Design Firm: Neiman Marcus Creative Services | Designer: Lisa Veigel Garcia
Client: Self-initiated | Art Director: Lori Stadig | Editors: JoAnne Crist, Katy Richardson
Senior Designer: Lisa Veigel Garcia | Senior Design Director: Lori Dibble
Project Manager: Katherine Cromwell | Writer: Kate Watson | Stylist: Kim Stanley
Main Contributors: Lisa Veigel Garcia, Kate Watson, Lori Stadig

165 MARKING TIME EXHIBITION CATALOG | Design Firm: Ventress Design Works
Designer: Tom Ventress | Client: Elise Wagner | Artist: Elise Wagner
Printer: Pollock Printing | Main Contributor: Tom Ventress

165 STONEBERRY BRAND GUIDELINES | Design Firm: Preston Spire
Designer: Fernando Palomino | Client: Mason Companies | Chief Creative Officer: Chris Preston
Associate Creative Director: Brett Essman | Senior Designer: Fernando Palomino
Senior Copywriter: Aylâ Larsen | Senior Studio Artist: Mike Fritz | Account Director: Ron Hall
Senior Project Manager: Kelsey Winter | Senior Copywriter: Aylâ Larsen
Main Contributor: Fernando Palomino

165 MASTERS OF SCALE INAUGURAL SUMMIT 2022 | Design Firm: WaitWhat (In-House)
Designers: Kelsie Capitano, Sammie Oputa, Luisa Vélez Henao, Justin Winslow, Tim Cronin
Client: Masters of Scale | Executive Creative Directors: June Cohen, Lori Hoffman, Deron Triff
Creative Director: Tim Cronin | Art Director: Tim Cronin | Production Designer: Julie Wilson
Copywriters: June Cohen, Lori Hoffman, Emily McManus, Deron Triff | Production: CK Circle
Executive Producers: Jodine Dorcé, Carrie Kennedy | Project Manager: DeAngela Napier
Lighting Design: Christopher Wren | Environmental Designer: Christopher Wren
Print Producer: Patrick Brandell | Main Contributor: Tim Cronin

165 COLLEGE OF AMERICAN PATHOLOGISTS: EMPLOYEE RESOURCE GROUPS EMBLEMS | Design Firm: StudioNorth | Designer: Becky Gutsell
Client: College of American Pathologists | Creative Director: Mark Schneider
Others: Opel Aguila, Director, Creative Design Communications, College of American Pathologists, Clemmie Lozano, Senior Manager, Global Marketing Operations, College of American Pathologists | Main Contributor: StudioNorth

166 THE ICON OF SUSTAINABILITY | Design Firm: Univisual SRL
Designers: Gaetano Grizzanti, Giancarlo Tosoni | Client: Itelyum Group
Main Contributors: Gaetano Grizzanti, Giancarlo Tosoni

166 THE FUTURE IS WILD | Design Firm: Microsoft Brand Studio
Designer: Microsoft Brand Studio | Client: Self-initiated
Main Contributors: Cam Gatta, Dave Leichtman, Hailey Geller, Jenn Panattoni, Jooyeon Chae, Jordan Grainger, Josh Stein, Ju Hyun Lee, Kaity Butcher, Kate Fisher, Kelly Parsons, Lori Gross, O0, Phyllis Murphy, Rachel Raisin, Sven Seger, Aleksey Fedorov

166 RS | Design Firm: Elmwood | Designer: Elmwood | Client: RS
Design Director: Paz Martinez Capuz | Creative Director: Kyle Whybrow
Senior Designer: Matt Churchill | Strategy Director: Esther Hastings
Senior Account Director: Paul Waters | Others: Oli Minchin: Head of Animation, Mike Preston: Middleweight Designer, Greg Taylor: Chief Provocation Officer | Main Contributor: Elmwood

166 LINTEL CORPORATE BROCHURE | Design Firm: Freaner Creative & Design
Designer: Ariel Freaner | Clients: LINTEL, Miguel Barreda | Creative Director: Ariel Freaner
Main Contributor: Ariel Freaner

166 RE: THE SCHOOL OF DESIGN 2018-21 TRIENNIAL
Design Firm: Jasmine Silang | Designer: Jasmine Silang
Clients: Ana Rita Morais, Luigi Ferrara, George Brown College School of Design
Creative Director: Jasmine Silang | Graphic Designer: Dave Ho Sang
Writer: Jane Weber | Content Developer: Jane Weber | Printer: Andora Graphics
Photographers: Lee Jong, Jadon Lem | Photographer's Assistant: Marcus Macapinlac
Typeface: Neue Montreal by Pangram Pangram
Main Contributor: School of Design Students & Alum

166 FARTA | Design Firm: Another Collective | Designer: Eduardo Rodrigues
Clients: Revista Farta, Self-initiated | Art Directors: Bruno Soares, Eduardo Rodrigues
Project Manager: Ricardo Barbosa | Illustrator: Min | Editor-in-Chief: Rafael Tonon
Photographers: Álvaro Martino, Pedro Lopes, Tiago Lessa
Text: Diana Barnabé, Inês Matos Andrade, Pedro Tavares, Rafael Tonon, Teresa Castro Viana
Main Contributors: Another Collective, Rafael Tonon

167 STAND BY ME | Design Firm: Wainscot Media
Designers: Trevett McCandliss, Nancy Campbell | Client: Earnshaw's Magazine
Photographer: Mark Andrew | Hair & Makeup: Clelia Bergonzoli
Fashion Director: Mariah Walker | Editor-in-Chief: Michele Silver
Main Contributors: Trevett McCandliss, Nancy Campbell

167 DREAM WEAVER | Design Firm: Wainscot Media
Designers: Trevett McCandliss, Nancy Campbell | Client: Footwear Plus Magazine
Photographer: Alexandra Carr | Editor-in-Chief: Greg Dutter
Model: Mary Ocean / Q Management | Makeup: Maya Ling Feero
Main Contributors: Trevett McCandliss, Nancy Campbell

168 THAT 70S SHOE | Design Firm: Wainscot Media
Designers: Trevett McCandliss, Nancy Campbell | Client: Footwear Plus Magazine
Photographer: Trevett McCandliss | Model: Miglė Gromnickaitė / Q Model Mgmt.
Makeup: Maya Ling Feero | Hair: Vera Koumbiadis | Editor-in-Chief: Greg Dutter
Main Contributors: Trevett McCandliss, Nancy Campbell

168 WILD WORLD | Design Firm: Wainscot Media
Designers: Trevett McCandliss, Nancy Campbell | Client: Earnshaw's Magazine
Fashion Director: Mariah Walker | Editor-in-Chief: Michele Silver | Hair: Brent Lavett
Writer: Katie Belloff | Photographer: Stefano Azario
Main Contributors: Trevett McCandliss, Nancy Campbell

168 COOL MINT | Design Firm: Wainscot Media
Designers: Trevett McCandliss, Nancy Campbell | Client: Footwear Plus Magazine
Photographer: Alexandra Carr | Model: Zaira Gonzalez / Supreme Model Mgmt.
Makeup: Maya Ling Feero | Editor-in-Chief: Greg Dutter
Main Contributors: Trevett McCandliss, Nancy Campbell

168 COLOR MY WORLD | Design Firm: Wainscot Media
Designer: Trevett McCandliss, Nancy Campbell | Client: Footwear Plus Magazine
Photographer: Trevett McCandliss | Hair & Makeup: Clelia Bergonzoli
Editor-in-Chief: Greg Dutter | Model: Mai Karybekova / Major Model Mgmt.
Main Contributors: Trevett McCandliss, Nancy Campbell

168 BRIGHT LIGHTS, BIG CITY | Design Firm: Wainscot Media
Designers: Trevett McCandliss, Nancy Campbell | Client: MR Magazine
Stylist: Michael Macko | Photographer: Thorsten Roth | Hair & Makeup: Robert Bradley
Editor-in-Chief: Karen Alberg Goldberg | Editor: Karen Alberg Goldberg
Model: Aubrey James / Union Model Management
Main Contributors: Trevett McCandliss, Nancy Campbell

168 ARTISTIC LICENSE | Design Firm: Wainscot Media
Designers: Trevett McCandliss, Nancy Campbell | Client: Footwear Plus Magazine
Creative Directors: Trevett McCandliss, Nancy Campbell | Photographer: Jamie Isaia
Hair: Vera Koumbiadis | Editor-in-Chief: Greg Dutter | Model: Noah Hart / One Management
Main Contributors: Trevett McCandliss, Nancy Campbell

169 SQUISH | Design Firm: Wainscot Media
Designers: Trevett McCandliss, Nancy Campbell | Client: Earnshaw's Magazine
Creative Directors: Trevett McCandliss, Nancy Campbell | Set Designer & Props: Mariah Walker
Photographer: Zoe Adlersberg | Editor-in-Chief: Michele Silver | Fashion Director: Mariah Walker
Main Contributors: Trevett McCandliss, Nancy Campbell

169 PREP COOL | Design Firm: Wainscot Media
Designers: Trevett McCandliss, Nancy Campbell | Client: Footwear Plus Magazine
Stylist: Mariah Walker | Photographer: Trevett McCandliss
Model: Leticia Orchanheski / Fenton Models | Makeup: Maya Ling Feero
Hair: Vera Koumbiadis | Fashion Director: Mariah Walker | Editor-in-Chief: Greg Dutter
Main Contributors: Trevett McCandliss, Nancy Campbell

169 KNIT PICKS | Design Firm: Wainscot Media
Designers: Trevett McCandliss, Nancy Campbell | Client: Footwear Plus Magazine
Stylist: Melina Kemph | Set Designer & Props: Diana Bianchi | Photographer: Justin Bridges
Hair & Makeup: Lindsay Cullen | Model: Lauren Forge / The Industry Model Mgmt.
Editor-in-Chief: Greg Dutter | Main Contributors: Trevett McCandliss, Nancy Campbell

169 FREE BIRD | Design Firm: Wainscot Media
Designers: Trevett McCandliss, Nancy Campbell | Client: Earnshaw's Magazine
Photographer: Zoe Adlersberg | Fashion Director: Mariah Walker
Editor-in-Chief: Michele Silver | Main Contributors: Trevett McCandliss, Nancy Campbell

169 FASHION FAVORS THE BOLD | Design Firm: Wainscot Media
Designers: Trevett McCandliss, Nancy Campbell | Client: MR Magazine | Stylist: Michael Macko
Photographer: Chris Fucile | Model: Ryan Winter / New York Model Mgmt.
Hair & Makeup: Robert Bradley | Editor-in-Chief: Karen Alberg Goldberg
Editor: John Russel Jones | Main Contributors: Trevett McCandliss, Nancy Campbell

169 WORN IN THE USA | Design Firm: Wainscot Media
Designers: Trevett McCandliss, Nancy Campbell | Client: Footwear Plus Magazine
Photographer: Trevett McCandliss | Model: Nadine Stracqualursi / Fenton Model Mgmt.
Hair & Makeup: Nevio Ragazzini | Editor-in-Chief: Greg Dutter
Main Contributors: Trevett McCandliss, Nancy Campbell

170 UMASS MAGAZINE - FALL 2022 | Design Firm: BRIGADE
Designers: Tim MacKay, Stephen Oparowski | Client: University of Massachusetts Amherst
Illustrator: Thom Dudley | Executive Creative Director: Kirsten Modestow
Creative Director: Tim MacKay | Account Manager: Alexia Geary
Main Contributor: Tim MacKay

170 DESCONTROLE (UNCONTROLLED) | Design Firm: Studio DelRey
Designer: Delfin | Client: Correio Popular | Text: Adriana Giachini
Photographer: Jario Goldflus | Photo Corrector: Laert Silva
Editor: Suzamara Santos | Main Contributor: Art Direction & Design: Delfin

170 RIGHTS | Design Firm: Atelier Starno | Designer: Arnaud Ghelfi
Clients: UC Berkeley Law, Transcript Magazine | Creative Director: Laurie Frasier
Writer: Gwyneth K. Shaw | Managing Editor: Andrew Cohen | Editor: Alex A.G. Shapiro
Main Contributor: Arnaud Ghelfi

170 CHILD POVERTY IN AMERICA | Design Firm: Kathy Mueller Design, LLC
Designer: Kathy Mueller | Client: Public Policy Lab at Temple University
Main Contributor: Kathy Mueller

170 PAWPRINTS MAGAZINE COVER SERIES | Design Firm: Mingxin Cheng
Designer: Mingxin Cheng | Client: Self-initiated | Main Contributor: Mingxin Cheng

170 M MAGAZINE
Design Firm: Museum of Texas Tech University, Communications & Marketing
Designer: Mystie Do | Client: Self-initiated | Writers: Peter S. Briggs, Jill Hoffman,
Chris Taylor, Lisa C. Bradley, Laura Ray | Editors: Lisa C. Bradley, Aaron Pan, Laura Ray
Main Contributor: Mystie Do

170 CLIMATE ACTION THROUGH DESIGN 2022 | Design Firm: Gensler
Designers: Laura Latham, Minjung Lee, Georgia Wilson | Client: Self-initiated
Main Contributors: Tim Pittman, Rives Taylor, Laura Latham, Cindy Coleman, Stella Donovan,
Minjung Lee, Georgia Wilson

170 CLIMATE ACTION SURVEY 2022 | Design Firm: Gensler | Designers: Laura Latham,
Georgia Wilson | Client: Self-initiated | Main Contributors: Christine Barber, Tim Pittman,
Rives Taylor, Laura Latham, Stella Donovan, Georgia Wilson

170 GROWING WISER | Design Firm: MJH Life Sciences | Designer: Kristen Morabito
Client: Dental Products Report | Main Contributor: Kristen Morabito

171 DEL TORO BY MICK ROCK FOR AS IF MAG | Design Firm: AS IF Media Group
Designer: Diego Pinilla Amaya | Client: Self-initiated | Design Director: Diego Pinilla Amaya
Creative Directors: Scott Fishkind, Tatijana Shoan | Writer: Scott Fishkind | Stylist: Mane Duplan
Photographer: Mick Rock | Hair: Kumi Craig | Main Contributor: Mick Rock

171 A BOLD VISION FOR THE FUTURE | Design Firm: BroadcastMed
Designer: Jennifer Barlow | Client: Inside Dental Hygiene | Main Contributor: Jennifer Barlow

171 NEW YORK TIMES COVER, BEST OF 2022 | Design Firm: Sunday Afternoon
Designer: Juan Carlos Pagan | Client: The New York Times
Art Director: Jennifer Ledbury | Main Contributor: Juan Carlos Pagan

171 EMPOWERING GENZ TO TAKE CONTROL OF THEIR FUTURE
Design Firms: Microsoft Brand Studio, O0 | Designers: Microsoft Brand Studio, O0
Client: Microsoft | Main Contributors: Cam Gatta, Dave Leichtman, Hailey Geller, Jenn Panattoni,
Jooyeon Chae, Jordan Grainger, Josh Stein, Ju Hyun Lee, Kaity Butcher, Kate Fisher,
Kelly Parsons, Lori Gross, O0, Phyllis Murphy, Rachel Raisin, Sven Seger, Aleksey Fedorov

171 PRIDE HAS NO BORDERS
Design Firms: Sterling, Blk:ops, BigRockXR, Microsoft Brand Studio
Designers: Sterling, Blk:ops, BigRockXR, Microsoft Brand Studio | Client: Microsoft
Main Contributors: Andre Bazire, BigRockXR, Blk:ops, Cam Gatta, Carol Hutchinson,
Chaya Wilkins, Daniel Ruiz, Eileen Mikloiche, Elliot Hsu, GeriAnn Baptista, iAsia Brown,
Jenn Panattoni, Jessica Tsujikawa, Kaity Butcher, Lori Gross, Phyllis Murphy, Pia Rodriguez,
Sarah Bender, Sterling, Steve Wiens, Sven Seger, Aleksey Fedorov

172 THINKING CREATIVELY STUDENT CONFERENCE POSTER
Design Firm: Randy Clark Graphic Design | Designer: Randy Clark
Clients: Wenzhou Kean University, Michael Graves College | Main Contributor: Randy Clark

172 ARTCENTER: ASK ME ANYTHING LECTURE POSTER | Design Firm: Braley Design
Designer: Michael Braley | Client: ArtCenter College of Design
Creative Director: Michael Braley | Main Contributor: Michael Braley

172 INSERT | Design Firm: By Scala | Designer: Maria Vilaverde
Client: Universidade Católica Portuguesa School of Arts | Main Contributor: Maria Vilaverde

173 THE CAMPSITE AT SHIELD RANCH | Design Firm: Asterisk
Designers: Shawn Harrington, David Cajolet, Oscar Morris, Callie Gabbert
Client: Shield Ranch Foundation | Creative Director: Susanne Harrington
Main Contributor: Asterisk

173 KISS & GO SCHOOL LANES VILA REAL | Design Firm: Vestígio Design
Designer: Emanuel Barbosa | Client: Câmara Municipal de Vila Real
Main Contributor: Emanuel Barbosa

173 CENTER FOR ARCHITECTURE | NEW PRACTICES NEW YORK EXHIBITION
Design Firm: Siena Scarff Design | Designer: Siena Scarff
Client: Center for Architecture New York | Main Contributor: Siena Scarff

173 RESIDENCE HALL DESIGN | Design Firm: Lewis Communications
Designers: Ben Blackburn, Rachel Carney | Client: Highlands College
Design Director: Geoff Johnson | Creative Director: Ryan Gernenz
Copywriter: Cedrick Bearss | Main Contributor: Lewis Communications

173 MI'KAI'STO (RED CROW COMMUNITY COLLEGE) | Design Firm: Entro
Designers: Entro, Monika Meyer, Shehrbano Aktar, Kevin Cortez, Aleks Bozovic, Colin Burrows,
Sabrina Diehl | Client: Mi'kai'sto (Red Crow Community College)
Design Director: Chris Herringer | Artists: Faye HeavyShield, Apoiskumapi (Little Brown Boy),
Adrian A. Stimson, Api'soomaahka, William Singer III, Ahkoiinnimaki (Pipe Woman), Star Crop
Eared Wolf, Aa Pa Man Ski (Across Singing), Delia Cross Child, Iikaamannistpo (Speaks more
than one language, understand several thought systems), John Chief Calf, Iikaakskitowa
(Wounded Mouth), Cowboy Smith, Iinniiwahkiimah (Buffalo Herder) Terrance Houle, Iniskim Aki,
Janice Elizabeth Tanton (artist deeply connected to the Siksika Nation), Koo Kii (Corner),
Ryan Jason Allen Willert, Ponokaki, Marjie Crop Eared Wolf, Nato'yi'kina'soyi, Hali Heavy Shield,
Naatoiyiki (Holy Whistle), Cheyenne McGinnis, Mano'taanikaapi, Bryce Many Fingers/Singer,
Lauren Crazybull | Other: Independent Art Curator, Mary-Beth Laviolette
Main Contributor: Entro

173 MOORE COLLEGE OF ART & DESIGN EXPERIENTIAL GRAPHICS
Design Firm: Entro | Designers: Entro, Radnyee Joshi | Client: Moore College of Art & Design
Partner: Anna Crider | Creative Director: Anna Crider, Kevin Spencer | Photographer: Kat Kendon
Project Manager: Jessica Schrader | Research: Vedran Dzebic | Main Contributor: Entro

174 BOSTON CHILDREN'S HOSPITAL HALE FAMILY CLINICAL BUILDING
Design Firm: ArtHouse Design | Designers: Abigail Knab, Evan Bethel, Maddie Bonthron,
Aaron Hilst, Mikayla Zancanelli, Anaïs Mares, Daisy Corso, Zach Kotel
Client: Boston Children's Hospital | Creative Directors: Marty Gregg, Beth Rosa | Printer: InPro
Fabricator: Dillonworks | Main Contributor: ArtHouse Design

174 PLACEMAKING + EXPERIENTIAL BRANDING: BLUE FEDERAL CREDIT UNION
Design Firm: 3D Identity | Designer: Kyle Starrett | Client: Blue Federal Credit Union
Art Director: Brandon Bird | Architect: Open Studio Architecture
Account Director: Mike Doody | Main Contributor: 3D Identity

174 NATIONAL BASKETBALL ASSOCIATION, NBA
Design Firm: Airspace | Designers: Jill Ayers, Rachel Einsidler, Daniel Berja
Client: National Basketball Association (NBA) | Creative Director: Jill Ayers
Project Manager: Rachel Einsidler | Main Contributor: Airspace

174 POWERHOUSE ARTS | Design Firm: Entro | Designers: Entro, Radnyee Joshi,
Elliot Langejans | Client: Powerhouse Arts | Partner: Anna Crider
Creative Directors: Anna Crider, Eileen Moore | Main Contributor: Entro

174 AUSTIN PBS | Design Firm: Asterisk | Designers: Shawn Harrington, Pam Caperton,
Oscar Morris, Callie Gabbert | Client: Austin PBS | Creative Director: Susanne Harrington
Main Contributor: Asterisk

175 NOKIA AT MOBILE WORLD CONGRESS | Design Firm: Lippincott
Designers: Louise Cantrill, Vimmi Sveinsson, Timothy Stewart, Friedemann Rimansberger-Vetter,
Carl Baldwin, Lee Coomber, Wenger.One GmbH, Lippincott | Client: Nokia
Account Managers: Maria Wüstefeld, George Andreas, Wenger.One GmbH
Main Contributor: Lee Coomber, Lippincott

175 DLR GROUP - AUSTIN STUDIO | Design Firm: DLR Group
Designers: Adam Ross, Jovaney Hollingsworth | Client: Self-initiated
Managing Director: Adam Wells | Main Contributors: DLR Group, Jovaney Hollingsworth

175 DONOR RECOGNITION FOR THE NEW NJH OUTPATIENT HEALTH BUILDING
Design Firm: ArtHouse Design | Designers: Chuck Desmoineaux, Mikayla Zancanelli
Client: National Jewish Health | Creative Director: Marty Gregg | Fabricator: BSC Signs
Main Contributor: ArtHouse Design

176 MAUNGAWHAU VISITOR INFORMATION CENTER SHOWCASE
Design Firm: Insight Creative | Designer: Christopher Gough Palmer
Client: Tupuna Maunga Authority | Creative Director: Brian Slade | Developer: Mitch Duncan
Digital Director: Jeremy Sweetman | Strategy Director: Steven Giannoulis | Producer: Kylie Rose
Production: Joanne Otto, Kirsty Drummond | Account Director: Monique Wallace
Main Contributor: Insight Creative

176 THE WORLD OF STONEHENGE | Design Firm: Ralph Appelbaum Associates
Designer: Ralph Appelbaum Associates | Client: The British Museum
Project Director: Phillip Tefft | Graphic Designers: Mat Mason, Laurène Ciocco
Content Designer: Helen Schulte | Content Coordinators: Sadie Levy Gale, Charlotte Stevens
Exhibition Designers: Caroline Sjöholm, Bob de Graaf, Cristina Salvi
Main Contributor: Ralph Appelbaum Associates

177 EXHIBITION ON THE 70TH ANNIVERSARY OF THE LUXEMBOURG AGREEMENTS
Design Firm: C&G Partners | Designer: Jonathan Alger | Client: Claims Conference
Production: Conference on Jewish Material Claims Against Germany, Bundesministerium der
Finanzen (German Finance Ministry) | Editor: Suzanne Zuber
Others: Dr. Gabriel Goldstein, Curatorial Consultant, Burkhardt Leitner
Main Contributor: Jonathan Alger, Managing Partner

177 INTELLIGENCE FACTORY | Design Firm: Ralph Appelbaum Associates
Designer: Ralph Appelbaum Associates | Client: Bletchley Park | Art Director: Mat Mason
Graphic Designers: Laurène Ciocco, Eva Köhle | Project Director: Sarah Pollard
Content Designers: Helen Schulte, Sadie Levy Gale, Muriel Bryans
Exhibition Designers: Vassiliki Holeva, Bob De Graaf
Main Contributor: Ralph Appelbaum Associates

177 EXTINCT & ENDANGERED: INSECTS IN PERIL
Design Firm: American Museum of Natural History (In-House)
Designers: Nicole Fox, American Museum of Natural History | Client: Self-initiated
Creative Director: Lauri Halderman | Art Director: Catharine Weese
Editor-in-Chief: Sasha Nemecek | Project Coordinator: Ron Demetrio
Production Manager: Antonia Gabor | Photographer: Levon Biss
Main Contributor: American Museum of Natural History

177 OPUS 735 (TRACES OF WAR ON ARTWORKS FROM THE TREASURY OF THE PRINCES ESTERHÁZY) | Design Firm: Anagraphic | Designer: Anna Farkas
Client: Museum of Applied Arts | Main Contributor: Anna Farkas

177 LIVING HISTORIES SPACE FOR RECKONING EXHIBITION
Design Firm: Siena Scarff Design | Designer: Siena Scarff
Client: Princeton University | Production Manager: Kira McDonald
Photographer: Michael Vahrenwald/Courtesy Princeton University School of Architecture
Models: Sergio Marino, Alexander O'Hagan, Alexander O'Hagan Jr, Isabela Marino,
Julian Zapata, Brett Bradley | Main Contributor: Siena Scarff Design

178 POPCHIPS REDESIGN | Design Firm: Hatch Design | Designer: Kristen McGriff
Client: Velocity Snack Brands | Creative Director: Nicole Flores
Design Director: Bryan Cleghorn | Associate Creative Director: Patrick Smith
Production: Richard Eriksson | Main Contributor: Hatch Design

178 ALEC'S ICE CREAM REDESIGN | Design Firm: Hatch Design
Designer: Ryann Woods | Client: Alec's Ice Cream | Creative Director: Nicole Flores
Design Director: Sean Morse | Production: Richard Eriksson
Main Contributor: Hatch Design

178 HERDADE DA MATINHA WINE RANGE | Design Firm: Omdesign
Designer: Diogo Gama Rocha | Client: Herdade da Matinha | Main Contributor: Omdesign

178 LAY'S NEW YEAR 2022 | Design Firm: PepsiCo Design & Innovation
Designer: PepsiCo Design & Innovation | Client: Self-initated

178 WELL, YES! REFRESH | Design Firm: Hatch Design
Designers: Patrick Smith, Dany Vo | Client: Campbell Soup Company
Creative Director: Nicole Flores | Associate Creative Director: Patrick Smith
Design Director: Jerimy Lumia | Production: Richard Eriksson
Main Contributor: Hatch Design

178 KRAVE JERKY REVITALIZATION | Design Firm: Hatch Design
Designers: Dany Vo, Yijing Yan | Client: Sonoma Brands Capital
Creative Director: Nicole Flores | Design Director: Bryan Cleghorn
Production: Richard Eriksson | Main Contributor: Hatch Design

179 GODAWAN - A RARE WHISKY TO SAVE A RARE SPECIES
Design Firm: Butterfly Cannon | Designer: Simon Gibbs | Clients: Diageo India, Hiren Dedhia
Creative Director: Arron Egan | Design Lead: Simon Gibbs | Strategy Director: Natasha Samek
Account Director: Georgina Jones | Main Contributors: Butterfly Cannon, Arron Egan

179 MURGANHEIRA MIGNON | Design Firm: Omdesign | Designer: Diogo Gama Rocha
Client: Murganheira | Main Contributor: Omdesign

179 CRASTO ROSÉ | Design Firm: Omdesign | Designer: Diogo Gama Rocha
Client: Quinta do Crasto | Main Contributor: Omdesign

179 AMANATSU JUICE | Design Firm: Legis Design | Designer: Mayumi Kato
Client: Hirano Farm | Main Contributor: Legis Design

180 LAFAYETTE AMERICAN HOLIDAY HAIKUS MAILER
Design Firm: Lafayette American | Designer: Lafayette American | Client: Self-initiated
Printer: The Newspaper Club | Main Contributor: Lafayette American

180 SLACKTOBERFEST ICONOGRAPHY | Design Firm: Spire Agency
Designer: Alex Flores | Client: Slack Davis Sanger
Chief Creative Officer: Kimberly Tyner | Associate Creative Director: Jason James
Account Supervisor: Julia Cardali | Main Contributor: Alex Flores

180 OPPO DRAGONFLY | Design Firm: Media.Work
Designers: Sergey Shurupov, Kirill Makhin, Daniil Makhin, Denis Semenov, Dmitry Ponomarev,
Artur Gadzhiev, Aleksei Komarov, Roman Eltsov, Alexandra Vorobeva, Vasily Zinchuk
Client: OPPO | Creative Director: Igor Sordokhonov | Art Director: Dmitry Ponomarev
Producer: Alexandra Kotova | Main Contributor: Media.Work

180 ESCAPE | Design Firm: Northwest Missouri State University
Designer: Feixue Mei | Client: Self-initiated | Main Contributor: Feixue Mei

180 25TH ANNUAL WIENERSCHNITZEL WIENER NATIONALS
Design Firm: INNOCEAN USA | Designers: Allison Inouye, Ryan Owens | Client: Wienerschnitzel

180 JK ROWLING | Design Firm: Mark Braught Studios
Designer: Mark Braught | Client: Self-initiated | Illustrator: Mark Braught
Studio: Mark Braught Studios | Main Contributor: Mark Braught

181 CITY PULSE 2022 URBAN MOBILITY REPORT | Design Firm: Gensler
Designers: Laura Latham, Minjung Lee, Lela Johnson | Client: Self-initiated
Main Contributors: Christine Barber, Tim Pittman, Sofia Song, Cindy Coleman, Stella Donovan,
Laura Latham, Minjung Lee, Lela Johnson

181 THE NEIMAN MARCUS APP | Design Firm: Neiman Marcus Creative Services
Designers: John Biondi, Drew Lintvedt, Sarah Schoonover, Joanna Tiller, Ryan Mayott
Client: Self-initated | Senior Design Director: Lori Dibble
Main Contributors: John Biondi, Drew Lintvedt, Sarah Schoonover, Joanna Tille, Ryan Mayott

181 SWA OPEN HOUSE INVITATION
Design Firm: SWA Group | Designer: Rong Jia | Client: Self-initiated
Main Contributors: Rong Jia, Rochell Vaughns, Natalia Beard

182 VETERANS MUSEUM MEMORIAL LOGO | Design Firm: Freaner Creative & Design
Designer: Ariel Freaner | Client: Veterans Museum Memorial
Creative Director: Ariel Freaner | Main Contributor: Ariel Freaner

182 POEMA DE MADEIRA (WOODEN POEM) | Design Firm: Studio DelRey
Designer: Delfin | Client: Marilia Giesbrecht | Main Contributor: Delfin

182 GROUNDED IN THEIR ROOTS, GROWING INTO THE FUTURE
Design Firm: Wolff Olins | Designers: Vanessa Hopkins, Daniel Renda, Nicholas Samendinger,
Colin Kinsley, Ryan Bugden, Jess Yan | Client: Instacart | Creative Director: Daniel Renda
Associate Creative Director: Jess Yan | Typeface Designer: Ryan Bugden
Strategy Director: Michele Kim | Photographer: Stephanie Gonot | Marketing: Tal Ayala Kamin
Motion Designers: Jason Chen, Draeger Gillespie| Account Manager: Ian Carroll
Account Executive: Marina Ammirato | Main Contributor: Wolff Olins

182 POLITICS OF THE MODERN SOUTHWEST | Design Firm: Texas Tech University Press
Designer: Hannah Gaskamp | Client: Self-initiated | Main Contributor: Hannah Gaskamp

182 ROGER'S FISH CO. | Design Firm: DeVito/Verdi | Designer: Yanira Janes Parsons
Client: Roger's Fish Co. | Main Contributor: Yanira Janes Parsons

182 DESERT HUMANITIES | Design Firm: Texas Tech University Press
Designer: Hannah Gaskamp | Client: Self-initiated | Main Contributor: Hannah Gaskamp

182 DSP LOGO | Design Firm: UP-Ideas | Designer: Roger Sawhill
Client: Dan Shultz Photography (DSP) | Main Contributor: Roger Sawhill

182 THE MILLS YONKERS | Design Firm: Kate Borman Creative Design Co.
Designer: Kate Borman Richardson | Client: RJ Rose Realty
Main Contributor: Kate Borman Richardson

182 PIANIST PAUL WARTHEN BRANDMARK | Design Firm: Lisa Sirbaugh Creative
Designer: Lisa Sirbaugh | Client: Paul Warthen | Main Contributor: Lisa Sirbaugh Creative

182 LEAPWAVE | Design Firm: El Paso, Galería de Comunicación | Designer: Álvaro Pérez
Client: LeapWave Technologies | Creative Team: Álvaro Pérez, Curra Medina
Main Contributor: El Paso, Galería de Comunicación

182 PLANTKISS IDENTITY | Design Firm: MiresBall | Designers: John Ball, Renee Chan
Client: PlantKiss | Creative Director: John Ball | Main Contributors: John Ball, Renee Chan

182 ORGANICS UNLIMITED LOGO | Design Firm: Freaner Creative & Design
Designer: Ariel Freaner | Client: Organics Unlimited | Illustrator: Ariel Freaner
Main Contributor: Ariel Freaner

183 AJ MASSULLO LOGO | Design Firm: AG Creative Group
Designer: Stewart Jung | Client: AJ Massullo Excavation and Demolition
Creative Director: Stewart Jung | Main Contributor: Stewart Jung

183 SAN DIEGO FOUNDATION IDENTITY | Design Firm: MiresBall
Designers: Lauren Lamb, John Ball | Client: San Diego Foundation
Creative Director: John Ball | Main Contributors: Lauren Lamb, John Ball

183 OTAY MESA CHAMBER OF COMMERCE LOGO
Design Firm: Freaner Creative & Design | Designer: Ariel Freaner
Client: Otay Mesa Chamber of Commerce | Creative Director: Ariel Freaner
Main Contributor: Ariel Freaner

183 UP-FUN LOGO | Design Firm: UP-Ideas | Designer: Mark Braught
Client: Self-initiated | Main Contributor: Mark Braught

183 RANCH MASTER LOGO | Design Firm: Keith Harris Design | Designer: Keith Harris
Client: Ranch Master | Main Contributor: Typography and Illustrator - Keith Harris

183 WASH'EM ALL IDENTITY | Design Firm: SML Design
Designer: Wendy Cho | Client: AirDay Solution | Chief Creative Director: Vanessa Ryan
Main Contributor: Vanessa Ryan

183 BLACK DOG - THE SCOTCH ICON BACK TO NO.1 | Design Firm: Butterfly Cannon
Designer: Arron Egan | Clients: Hiren Dedhia, Diageo India | Creative Director: Arron Egan
Design Lead: Arron Egan | Strategy Director: Natasha Samek
Account Director: Georgina Jones | Main Contributors: Arron Egan, Butterfly Cannon

183 RED GABLES LOGO | Design Firm: Tielemans Design
Designer: Anton Tielemans | Client: Red Gables | Main Contributor: Anton Tielemans

183 NEVADA BANK & TRUST LOGO | Design Firm: Tielemans Design
Designer: Anton Tielemans | Client: Nevada Bank & Trust | Main Contributor: Anton Tielemans

183 CONCORD FEDERAL CREDIT UNION LOGO | Design Firm: Mermaid, Inc.
Designer: Sharon McLaughlin | Client: Concord Federal Credit Union
Creative Team: Bart McLaughlin | Marketing Manager: Sheila Greene
Main Contributor: Sharon Lloyd McLaughlin

183 SAITUSI | Design Firm: Roking Art Design | Designer: Qin Luo
Client: Shandong Hongyao Trading Co. Ltd. | Main Contributor: Qin Luo

183 THE LOGO OF SHIMOUSA LABORATORY | Design Firm: USADesign
Designer: Yoshinori Shimousa | Client: Shimousa Laboratory
Art Director: Yoshinori Shimousa | Main Contributor: Yoshinori Shimousa

184 THREADS OF CULTURE | Design Firm: BEK Design | Designer: Bülent Erkmen
Client: Istanbul Foundation for Culture and Arts | Main Contributor: Threads of Culture Project

184 OZDEN ARCHITECTURE FIRM | Design Firm: BEK Design
Designer: Bülent Erkmen | Client: Arif Ozden | Main Contributor: BEK Design

184 TRES Y CONTANDO LOGO | Design Firm: Freaner Creative & Design
Designer: Ariel Freaner | Client: Tres y Contando | Creative Director: Ariel Freaner
Illustrator: Ariel Freaner | Main Contributor: Ariel Freaner

184 FILM HUB LOGO | Design Firm: Mermaid, Inc. | Designer: Sharon McLaughlin
Client: National Resources | Creative Team: Bart McLaughlin
Marketing Manager: Lauren Calabria | Main Contributor: Sharon Lloyd McLaughlin

184 SOWELL COLLECTION BOOKS | Design Firm: Texas Tech University Press
Designer: Hannah Gaskamp | Client: Self-initiated | Main Contributor: Hannah Gaskamp

184 NEW CORPORATE IDENTITY SIA | Design Firm: Tangram Strategic Design
Designer: Pamela Cino | Client: SIA | Main Contributor: Enrico Sempi (Creative Director)

184 HALLIBURTON LABS LOGO | Design Firm: Coley Porter Bell
Designers: Linda Becker, Ollie Williams, Ben Davidson | Client: Halliburton
President: Jenn Szekely | Executive Creative Director: James Ramsden
Group Creative Director: John Malozzi | Account Management: Maggie Thomas, Alice Lee
Main Contributors: Coley Porter Bell, Halliburton

184 ECI (EGG CLEARINGHOUSE INC.) LOGO | Design Firm: Jordan Fretz Design
Designer: Jordan Fretz | Client: ECI (Egg Clearinghouse Inc.) | Main Contributor: Jordan Fretz

184 EAST-WEST CONNECTIONS - BRAND IDENTITY | Design Firm: Preston Spire
Designer: Fernando Palomino | Client: East-West Connections
Senior Designer: Fernando Palomino | Chief Creative Officer: Chris Preston
Senior Project Manager: Kelsey Winter | Senior Studio Artist: Mike Fritz
Account Manager: Emma Vik | Main Contributor: Fernando Palomino

184 THE ROYAL PARKS HALF | Design Firm: Rose | Designers: Rose, Yafet Bisrat
Client: The Royal Parks | Creative Directors: Simon Elliott, Garry Blackburn
Project Manager: Joanna Waclawski | Main Contributor: Rose

184 CEYLON TOURS LOGO | Design Firm: Roger Archbold | Designer: Roger Archbold
Client: Ceylon Tours | Main Contributor: Roger Archbold

184 TRANSLATIONAL PLANT SCIENCES CENTER | Design Firm: Patrick Finley
Designer: Patrick Finley | Client: Virginia Tech's Translational Plant Sciences Center
Main Contributor: Patrick Finley

185 GIANTS OF CANCER CARE® 10-YEAR ANNIVERSARY LOGO
Design Firm: MJH Life Sciences | Designer: Rachel Keatley | Client: Giants of Cancer Care®
Main Contributors: Josh Hermes & Jed Higgerson (landing page), Kellie Ehrmann (publication spread), Kristin Grogg (glamor shot), Ryan J. Brown (print ad)

185 SPACE CENTER HOUSTON LOGO | Design Firm: Traina | Designer: Joe Ross
Client: Space Center Houston | Account Director: Kristi Jones
President: David Traina | Main Contributor: Joe Ross

185 IMPRINT ENGINE | Design Firm: Joba Studio
Designer: Patrick Finley | Client: Imprint Engine | Account Manager: Robyn Jones
Main Contributor: Patrick Finley

185 LUXIUM SOLUTIONS | Design Firm: Haystack Needle LLC DBA Tailfeather
Designer: Dylan Menke | Client: Luxium Solutions | Main Contributor: Tailfeather

185 WESTBOUND AT THE WORKS LOGOMARK | Design Firm: Resource Branding
Designers: Courtney Haddon, Shaina Patel | Client: Selig Enterprises
Design Director: Rick Grimsley | Account Managers: Cate Pilliod, Cat Touliatous
Main Contributor: Resource Branding

185 ILKON. ILKESTON CONTEMPORARY ARTS
Design Firm: Susanne Pinter and Francesca Pinter-Parrott
Designers: Susanne Pinter, Francesca Pinter-Parrott | Client: ILKON: Ilkeston Contemporary Arts
Main Contributors: Susanne Pinter, Francesca Pinter-Parrott

185 BUCKHEAD BANANAS LOGOMARK | Design Firm: Resource Branding
Designer: Brian Burkey | Client: Buckhead Bananas U12 Baseball Team
Design Director: Rick Grimsley | Account Management: Jae Robbins
Main Contributor: Resource Branding

185 SATORO | Design Firm: RedPeak Global
Designer: Lillian Liao | Client: Satoro Inc. | Chairman: Silvia Yu
Creative Director: Chris Chung | Strategies: Nathan Liao, Lucas Willery, Kevin Hsueh
Account Director: Raychard Huang | Account Managers: Peggy Lee, Jasmine Hung
Main Contributors: Silvia Yu, Chris Chung, Lillian Liao, Nathan Liao, Lucas Willery, Kevin Hsueh, Raychard Huang, Peggy Lee, Jasmine Hung

185 BRAMBLE LOGO | Design Firm: Drive Communications | Designer: Michael Graziolo
Client: Tor Publishing Group | Main Contributor: Michael Graziolo

185 THE VANGUARD CHELSEA LOGO | Design Firm: Holly Tienken Design
Designer: Holly Tienken | Client: The Albanese Organization | Main Contributor: Holly Tienken

185 WEST CHESTER UNIVERSITY 150TH ANNIVERSARY BRAND
Design Firm: DPL Jones | Designer: David Jones | Client: West Chester University
Main Contributor: David Jones

185 EXCALIBUR: LEADING WOMEN | Design Firm: Univisual SRL
Designers: Gaetano Grizzanti, Giancarlo Tosoni | Client: Confederation of Italian Industry
Main Contributors: Gaetano Grizzanti, Giancarlo Tosoni

186 WAVE: EAST SEA INTERNATIONAL ART PRE-BIENNALE (EIAB)
Design Firm: DAEKI and JUN | Designers: Daeki Shim, Leejun Chang, Miji Kim (intern)
Clients: Gangwon State / Gangwon Institute of Design Promotion (GIDP): President Insuk Choi / Team Manager Kyoungcheol Shin, Yongsun Choi / Manager Mikyung Lee, Aeri Jang, Yeongshin Seong / Assistant Manager Kyuseong Shim | Art Director: Daeki Shim
Main Contributors: Daeki Shim, Leejun Chang, Miji Kim(intern) / Gangwon Institute of Design Promotion (GIDP)

186 FIRST AMERICANS MUSEUM | Design Firm: Ralph Appelbaum Associates
Designer: Ralph Appelbaum Associates | Client: First Americans Museum
Graphic Designers: Josh Whitehead, Jessica Cooper, Cassidy Lavine
Content Coordinators: Maggie Tomaszewski, Helios Tavio, Lily Remmert
Project Director: Marianne Schuit | Content Designers: Madeline Chinnici, Laura Epstein
Exhibition Designers: Josh Dudley, Michell Cardona, Ni-Tsia Cheong | Media: Molly McBride
Main Contributor: Ralph Appelbaum Associates

186 ROSEMARY OLSEN STUDENT PIANO RECITAL
Design Firm: Randy Clark Graphic Design | Designer: Randy Clark
Client: Rosemary Olsen Piano | Main Contributor: Randy Clark

186 CONSONANCE | Design Firm: Te-Sian Shih's Design Studio | Designer: Te-Sian Shih
Client: The New Asia Chamber Music Society (NACMS) | Main Contributor: Te-Sian Shih

187 ASSEMBLAGE CHAMBER | Design Firm: Kunstwerk
Designer: Douglas Thomas | Clients: Steve Ricks, New Focus Recordings
Main Contributor: Douglas Thomas

187 UNDUN BY THE ROOTS: VINYL PACKAGING AND LYRIC BOOK
Design Firm: Ehmija Design | Designer: Daisy Rodriguez | Client: Self-initiated
Main Contributors: The Roots, The Island Def Jam Music Records

187 SAN DIEGO DISTRICT ATTORNEY'S OFFICE INSURANCE FRAUD OUTDOOR CAMPAIGN | Design Firm: Freaner Creative & Design | Designer: Ariel Freaner
Clients: San Diego District Attorney's Office, Barbara Medina, Tannya Sierra, Steve Walker, Summer Stephan | Digital Artist: Ariel Freaner | Main Contributor: Ariel Freaner

187 SAVANNAH FILM FESTIVAL CAMPAIGN 2022
Design Firm: Savannah College of Art & Design | Designer: Savannah College of Art & Design
Client: Self-initiated | Executive Directors: Eric Breen, Chris Miller
Creative Director: Siobhan Bonnouvrier | Senior Art Director: Jennifer McCarn
Photo Directors: Chris Ambrose, Hadley Stambaugh | Photographer: Colin Gray
Project Manager: Monica Redman | Main Contributor: Savannah College of Art & Design

187 GIEO — ALBUM PACKAGE DESIGN | Design Firm: Studio DUY
Designers: Duy Dao, Hiep Hoang | Clients: NGOT, LP Music | Art Director: Duy Dao
Assistants: Tom Huy, Thuy Nguyen | Client Support: Minh Ha | Illustrator: Khim Dang
Photographers: Duc Viet, Vidua Studio | Production Manager: Colin Tran | Publisher: LP Music
Account Director: Anh Nguyen | Main Contributor: Studio DUY

187 BLOSSOM TIME PRODUCT PACKAGING DESIGN | Design Firm: Spud Studio
Designer: Xiaoyong Miao | Client: BLOSSOM TIME | Main Contributor: Xiaoyong Miao

188 PEPSI BLACK X DIGITAL SHFW 2023 | Design Firm: PepsiCo Design & Innovation
Designer: PepsiCo Design & Innovation | Client: Self-initated

188 APICIUS 1972 | Design Firm: Omdesign | Designer: Diogo Gama Rocha
Client: Apicius | Main Contributor: Omdesign

188 MR. FRESH PACKAGING DESIGN | Design Firm: Spud Studio
Designer: Xiaoyong Miao | Client: Mr. Fresh | Main Contributor: Xiaoyong Miao

188 KAIXIAOZAO SELF-HEATING HOT POT | Design Firm: Linshaobin Design Shenzhen
Designers: Shaobin Lin, Xianqi Cai, Minjia Wu, Xiaoxuan Chen, Jie Zhou, Zhengzhi Zhou, Jiawen Zhang | Client: Uni-President | Main Contributor: Shaobin Lin

188 NATURAL VANILLA | Design Firm: Dessein | Designer: Leanne Balen
Client: Natural Vanilla | Director: Tracy Kenworthy | Photographer: Geoff Bickford
Main Contributor: Leanne Balen

188 ECLAT CHOCOLATE PULL TAB HOLIDAY PACKAGING | Design Firm: DPL Jones
Designer: David Jones | Client: Eclat Chocolate | Creative Director: Christopher Curtin
Associate Creative Director: Jenn Newport | Photographer: Brett Thomas Photography
Main Contributor: David Jones

189 VIBE | Design Firm: Gallo Creative | Designer: Greta Rider | Client: Vendange
Project Manager: Mary Sherwood | Main Contributor: Greta Rider, Creative Director

189 NEIMAN MARCUS HOLIDAY EPICURE PACKAGING
Design Firm: Neiman Marcus Creative Services | Designers: Jessica Hische, Stephen Arevalos, Alyse Lanier | Clients: Russ Patrick, Rebecca Gremillion, Hayley Louden, Madison Rentz, Summer Maccubbin, Self-initiated | Art Directors: Jessica Hische, Stephen Arevalos
Senior Design Director: Lori Dibble | Design Manager: Stephen Arevalos | Printer: Royal Summit (Bret de St. Jeor) | Illustrator: Jessica Hische | Product Designers: Cat Caudillo, Alyse Lanier
Project Manager: Jessica Edwards | Production Manager: Rhoda Gonzales
Main Contributors: Jessica Hische, Lori Dibble, Stephen Arevalos, Alyse Lanier

189 MI EARPHONES EXPLORE | Design Firm: Xiaomi
Designer: EcoChain Packaging Design Team | Client: Self-initiated | Creative Director: Lu Chen
Graphic Designer: Weijing Jiang | Manufacturer: Golden Arrow Printing Technology (KunShan)
Production: 1More Inc. | Structural Engineers: Tong Ge, Zhizhuang Song
Main Contributor: EcoChain Packaging Design Team

189 QUINTA DA BOAVISTA | Design Firm: Another Collective
Designers: Bruno Soares, Eduardo Rodrigues | Client: Quinta da Boavista - Sogevinus
Art Directors: Bruno Soares, Eduardo Rodrigues | Photographer: Álvaro Martino
Main Contributor: Another Collective

189 DORITOS RAINBOW LIMITED EDITION 2022
Design Firm: PepsiCo Design & Innovation
Designer: PepsiCo Design & Innovation | Client: Self-initated

189 DORITOS W&Y | Design Firm: PepsiCo Design & Innovation
Designer: PepsiCo Design & Innovation | Client: Self-initated

190 BUCHANAN'S PINEAPPLE | Design Firm: forceMAJEURE Design
Designers: Pierre Delebois, Tim Devereaux | Client: Diageo
Main Contributor: forceMAJEURE Design

190 GOOD TROUBLE | Design Firm: CF Napa Brand Design
Designer: CF Napa Brand Design | Client: Good Trouble Bourbon
Main Contributor: CF Napa Brand Design

190 FJQ | Design Firm: Shenzhen Excel Brand Design Consultant Co., Ltd.
Designer: Shenzhen Excel Brand Design Consultant Co., Ltd. | Client: FJQ
Main Contributor: Kuan Fu Wu

190 TRUE MYTH | Design Firm: CF Napa Brand Design | Designer: CF Napa Brand Design
Client: WX Brands | Main Contributor: CF Napa Brand Design

190 KANGBASHI | Design Firm: Sungoo Design | Designer: Muqiang Fu
Client: Inner Mongolia Kangbashi Distillery Co., Ltd. | Main Contributor: Muqiang Fu

190 WILD HORSE | Design Firm: Gallo Creative | Designer: Eric Le
Client: Wild Horse | Creative Director: Emil Sandman
Project Manager: Kristen Wilkinson | Main Contributor: Eric Le

190 HELMSMAN ALE HOUSE | Design Firm: CF Napa Brand Design
Designer: Antonio Rivera | Client: Helmsman Ale House | Illustrator: Antonio Rivera
Chief Creative Director: David Schuemann | Art Director: Antonio Rivera

190 ANTIQUITY BRAND REFRESH 2023 | Design Firm: Bulletproof
Designers: Nino Yaputra, Dominic Tan, Nattanisha Tanudsintum, Yonglong Zhang
Clients: Diageo India, Hiren Dedhia | Executive Creative Director: Mark Armstrong
Design Director: Fiona Lim | Production Manager: Jesse Moran
Strategy: Kaavya Krishnan | Senior Account Director: Katie Osborn
Account Manager: Samantha Lee | Main Contributor: Bulletproof

190 THE KING'S GINGER | Design Firm: Stranger & Stranger
Designer: Stranger & Stranger | Client: Berry Brothers & Rudd
Main Contributor: Stranger & Stranger

191 SAMPÉ GIN | Design Firm: Design Bureau Izvorka Juric
Designers: Izvorka Juric, Jurica Kos | Client: High Spirits
Production Manager: Natalija Najjar | Main Contributor: Igor Poturic

191 VOLCAN XA TEQUILA | Design Firm: Stranger & Stranger
Designer: Stranger & Stranger | Client: LVMH | Main Contributor: Stranger & Stranger

191 MIRA WINERY OVUM AUREUM | Design Firm: CF Napa Brand Design
Designer: CF Napa Brand Design | Client: Mira Winery
Main Contributor: CF Napa Brand Design

191 HIGH WEST LIMITED RELEASE WHISKEY PACKAGING
Design Firms: Design Firm: Vine Creative Studios at Partners + Napier | Designer: Casey Brett
Client: Constellation Brands, Inc. | Copywriter: Justin Lahue | Illustrator: Matt Bielewicz
Project Manager: Mike LaTona | Proofreaders: Erin Dwyer, Bess Johnson, Sarah Terry

192 SONOMA DISTILLING CO. PORTFOLIO | Design Firm: CF Napa Brand Design
Designer: CF Napa Brand Design | Client: Corning & Company
Main Contributor: CF Napa Brand Design

192 CLOS DU VAL 50TH ANNIVERSARY SPARKLING BLANC DE NOIRS
Design Firm: CF Napa Brand Design | Designer: CF Napa Brand Design
Client: Clos du Val | Main Contributor: CF Napa Brand Design

192 CLOS DU VAL BERNARD'S CUVÉE | Design Firm: CF Napa Brand Design
Designer: CF Napa Brand Design | Client: Clos du Val | Main Contributor: CF Napa Brand Design

192 ETUDE PORTFOLIO | Design Firm: CF Napa Brand Design
Designer: CF Napa Brand Design | Client: Treasury Wine Estates
Main Contributor: CF Napa Brand Design

193 CI DIAN | Design Firm: Shenzhen Excel Brand Design Consultant Co., Ltd.
Designer: Shenzhen Excel Brand Design Consultant Co., Ltd. | Client: Ci Dian
Main Contributor: Kuan Fu Wu

193 PACKAGING FOR MAKER'S MARK WOOD FINISHING CITY SERIES
Design Firm: Turner Duckworth: London, San Francisco & New York
Designers: Janice Bonner, Kristina Valiunas | Client: Maker's Mark
Executive Creative Director: Jamie McCathie | Map Creation: Lovell Jones
Wood Print Artist: Erik Linton | Photographer: Camille Stewart
Production: Giovanna Giordano | Account Manager: Michael Green
Account Director: Wyeth Whiting | Main Contributor: Jared Britton

193 BLACK DOG - THE SCOTCH ICON BACK TO NO.1 | Design Firm: Butterfly Cannon
Designer: Arron Egan | Clients: Hiren Dedhia, Diageo India | Creative Director: Arron Egan
Design Lead: Arron Egan | Strategy Director: Natasha Samek | Account Director: Georgina Jones
Main Contributors: Butterfly Cannon, Arron Egan

193 ROYAL CHALLENGE - AMERICAN PRIDE WHISKY | Design Firm: Bulletproof
Designers: Nino Yaputra, Eric Liang, Yonglong Zhang | Clients: Hiren Dedhia, Diageo India
Executive Creative Director: Mark Armstrong | Creative Director: Chris Jenkins
Strategy: Kaavya Krishnan | Art Producer: Yein Yee | Senior Account Director: Katie Osborn
Account Manager: Samantha Lee | Main Contributor: Bulletproof

193 CAMP DAVID PRESIDENTIAL RETREAT PRIVATE LABEL WINE SERIES
Design Firm: Lisa Sirbaugh Creative | Designer: Lisa Sirbaugh
Client: Camp David Presidential Retreat | Printer: KSidrane
Production: Golden State Box Factory, Lafitte Cork & Capsule
Main Contributor: Lisa Sirbaugh Creative

194 STAN'S SEASONINGS | Design Firm: Stan Church Incorporated | Designer: Stan Church
Client: Self-initiated | Illustrators: Frank Castaldi, Final Art, Niki Giokas, Original Sketches
Main Contributor: Stan Church

194 GATORADE X SERENA GX BOTTLE | Design Firm: PepsiCo Design & Innovation
Designer: PepsiCo Design & Innovation | Client: Self-initated

194 KATSUNO EMBROIDERY STARTER KIT | Design Firm: andKuo
Designers: Sherry Kuo, Hsinhui Kuo | Client: Katsuno Japan
Main Contributors: Sherry Kuo, Hsinhui Kuo

194 MI EARPHONES NECKLACE | Design Firm: Xiaomi
Designer: EcoChain Packaging Design Team | Client: Self-initiated | Creative Director: Lu Chen
Structural Engineering: Tong Ge, Zhizhuang Song | Graphis Designer: Weijing Jiang
Production: 1More Inc. | Manufacturer: Golden Arrow Printing Technology (KunShan)
Main Contributor: EcoChain Packaging Design Team

194 MTN DEW ENERGY BAJA BLAST | Design Firm: PepsiCo Design & Innovation
Designer: PepsiCo Design & Innovation | Client: Self-initated

194 EFM | Design Firm: Dessein | Designer: Tracy Kenworthy | Client: Force Technology
Structural Engineering: Geoff Bickford | Main Contributor: Tracy Kenworthy

195 HEMP HOUNDS PACKAGING | Design Firm: BexBands | Designer: Ian de Lemos
Clients: Hemp Hounds, Matthew Kennedy | Creative Directors: Becky Dahl, Jeremy Dahl
Project Manager: Michael Thompson | Main Contributor: Ian de Lemos

195 KOYA·THE RABBIT YEAR
Design Firm: Shenzhen Excel Brand Design Consultant Co., Ltd.
Designer: Shenzhen Excel Brand Design Consultant Co., Ltd. | Client: KOYA
Main Contributor: Kuan Fu Wu

195 DORITOS SOLID BLACK 2022 | Design Firm: PepsiCo Design & Innovation
Designer: PepsiCo Design & Innovation | Client: Self-initated

195 ALL LOVE IS SMART LOVE – SMARTFOOD X GLAAD VALENTINE'S DAY INFLUENCER KITS | Design Firm: PepsiCo Design & Innovation
Designer: PepsiCo Design & Innovation | Client: Self-initated

195 MIJIA SMART SCENT DIFFUSER | Design Firm: Xiaomi
Designer: EcoChain Packaging Design Team | Client: Self-initiated | Creative Director: Lu Chen
Graphic Designer: Dijing Wang | Illustrator: Yan Ni | Structural Engineering: Zhizhuang Song
Main Contributor: EcoChain Packaging Design Team

195 FLOUR + WATER PACKAGING | Design Firm: BexBrands
Designers: Becky Dahl, Jeremy Dahl, Jacqueline Swanson | Client: Flour + Water
Project Manager: Michael Thompson | Main Contributors: Becky Dahl, Jeremy Dahl

196 ORIGIN GIN PACKAGING | Design Firm: TOKY Branding + Design
Designer: Ashford Stamper | Client: 1220 Spirits

196 XIGE·THE RABBIT YEAR
Design Firm: Shenzhen Excel Brand Design Consultant Co., Ltd.
Designer: Shenzhen Excel Brand Design Consultant Co., Ltd. | Client: XIGE
Main Contributor: Kuan Fu Wu

196 FURNACE STREET DISTILLERY | Design Firm: CF Napa Brand Design
Designer: CF Napa Brand Design | Client: Furnace Street Distillery
Main Contributor: CF Napa Brand Design

196 THE GRAPPLER | Design Firm: CF Napa Brand Design | Designer: CF Napa Brand Design
Client: Vinoce Vineyards | Main Contributor: CF Napa Brand Design

197 POWERS IRISH WHISKEY | Design Firm: Stranger & Stranger
Designer: Stranger & Stranger | Client: Irish Distillers Ltd. | Main Contributor: Stranger & Stranger

197 JI SHI DAO HERBAL TEA PACKAGING DESIGN | Design Firm: Roking Art Design
Designer: Qin Luo | Client: Jiangxi Jishidao Herbal Tea Industry Co., Ltd.
Main Contributor: Qin Luo

197 PEPSI X MUSIC | Design Firm: PepsiCo Design & Innovation
Designer: PepsiCo Design & Innovation | Client: Self-initated

198 OPTILYFE BRANDING | Design Firm: Lewis Communications | Designer: Geoff Johnson
Client: Optilyfe | Creative Director: Ryan Gernenz | Senior Designer: Geoff Johnson
Copywriter: Cedrick Bearss | Main Contributor: Lewis Communications

198 WEGMANS TONIC WATER | Design Firm: Wallace Church & Co.
Designer: Madeline Simon | Client: Wegmans | Illustrator: Frank Castaldi
Executive Creative Director: John Bruno | Account Director: Maureen McKenna
Main Contributor: Stan Church, Chief Creative Officer

198 ORIN SWIFT CELLARS EQUINOX 17 | Design Firm: Gallo Creative
Designer: Eric Le | Client: Orin Swift Cellars | Creative Director: Kiran Mann
Project Manager: April Joseph | Photo Director: Joel Tucker | Main Contributor: Eric Le

198 PEPSI MAX X EINTRACHT FRANKFURT COLLABORATION
Design Firm: PepsiCo Design & Innovation
Designer: PepsiCo Design & Innovation | Client: Self-initated

198 PEPSI MUSIC & DANCE LTO | Design Firm: PepsiCo Design & Innovation
Designer: PepsiCo Design & Innovation | Client: Self-initated

199 SAVANNAH FILM FESTIVAL CAMPAIGN 2022
Design Firm: Savannah College of Art & Design | Designer: Savannah College of Art & Design
Client: Self-initiated | Executive Creative Director: Chris Miller | Executive Director: Eric Breen
Creative Director: Siobhan Bonnouvrier | Senior Art Director: Jennifer McCarn
Project Manager: Monica Redman | Photographer: Colin Gray
Photo Director: Chris Ambrose | Main Contributor: Savannah College of Art & Design

199 THE GRADUATING STUDENTS SHOW 2022
Design Firm: Ohio University's School of Visual Communication | Designer: Adonis Durado
Client: Self-initiated | Main Contributor: Adonis Durado

199 IMAGINE PEACE | Design Firm: Braley Design | Designer: Michael Braley
Clients: US State Department, US Embassy Moscow | Creative Director: Michael Braley
Main Contributor: Michael Braley

199 FUTURE | Design Firm: Tsushima Design | Designer: Hajime Tsushima
Client: The Culture and ScieInternational Committee of the 4th Emirates International Poster Festival | Main Contributor: Hajime Tsushima

199 THOUGHTS NOT PRAYERS | Design Firm: Goodall Integrated Design
Designer: Derwyn Goodall | Client: Self-initiated | Main Contributor: Derwyn Goodall

199 BYE BYE CHINA | Design Firm: Randy Clark Graphic Design | Designer: Randy Clark
Clients: Wenzhou Kean University, Michael Graves College | Main Contributor: Randy Clark

199 THE AMERICAN BUFFALO | Design Firm: SJI Associates | Designer: David O'Hanlon
Clients: PBS Creative Services: Ira Rubenstein–Chief Digital and Marketing Officer,
Stacey Libbrecht–Vice President/Creative Services, John Ruppenthal–Creative Director,

Jared Traver–Sr. Director of Production, Claire Quin–Sr. Print & Digital Producer
President: Suzy Jurist | Art Director: David O'Hanlon | Illustrator: John Isaiah Pepion
Main Contributor: SJI Associates

199 UNDER THE SURFACE | Design Firm: Bailey Lauerman | Designer: Caitlin Viar
Client: Special Olympics Nebraska | Chief Creative Officer: Carter Weitz
Copywriter: Sophia Messineo | Production Manager: Gayle Adams | Printer: Firespring
Photo Retouching: Joe McDermott | Account Director: Jessica Jarosh
Main Contributor: Bailey Lauerman

199 CELEBRATING 20 YEARS OF SOURCE | Design Firm: Rozina Design
Designer: Rozina Vavetsi | Client: New York Tech | Main Contributor: Rozina Vavetsi

200 SPACE PROGRAM HISTORY | Design Firm: DLR Group
Designer: Jovaney Hollingsworth | Client: Confidential Technology Company
Main Contributors: DLR Group, Jovaney Hollingsworth

200 THE SUN QUEEN | Design Firm: SJI Associates | Designer: Adam Selbst
Clients: Chika Offurum, American Experience Films | Copywriter: David O'Hanlon
Art Director: David O'Hanlon | President: Suzy Jurist | Main Contributor: SJI Associates

200 D-SPACE | Design Firm: Dankook University | Designer: Hoon-Dong Chung
Client: Visual Information Design Association of Korea | Main Contributor: Hoon-Dong Chung

200 LET'S MAKE 2023 EXTRAORDINARY! | Design Firm: Goodall Integrated Design
Designer: Derwyn Goodall | Client: Self-initiated | Main Contributor: Derwyn Goodall

201 BONES AND ALL | Design Firm: ARSONAL
Designer: ARSONAL | Clients: Metro Goldwyn Mayer Pictures, United Artists Releasing,
Amy Mastriona, EVP Creative Advertising | Art Director: ARSONAL
Main Contributors: ARSONAL, Metro Goldwyn Mayer Pictures, United Artists Releasing

201 PRIDE - PAYOFF AND DECADES CAMPAIGN | Design Firm: AV Print
Designers: FX Networks, AV Print | Client: FX Networks | President: Stephanie Gibbons,
FX Networks, Creative Director/President, Creative, Strategy & Digital, Multi-Platform Marketing
Senior Vice Presidents: Michael Brittain, FX Networks, SVP Print Design, Todd Heughens, FX
Networks, Creative Director/SVP Print Design | Vice President: Todd Russell, FX Networks, VP,
Print Design | Project Director: Laura Handy, FX Networks, Project Director, Print Design
Director: Lisa Lejeune, FX Networks, Production Director, Print Design
Main Contributor: FX Networks

201 MAYFAIR WITCHES S1 | Design Firm: ARSONAL | Designer: ARSONAL
Clients: AMC, Ed Sherman, VP Brand & Design Mark Williams SVP Creative & Campaign
Marketing Nancy Hennings, VP Production Brand & Design | Art Director: ARSONAL
Creative Director: ARSONAL | Main Contributors: ARSONAL, AMC

201 SAMSUNG GALAXY Z FLIP4 LAUNCH POSTERS
Design Firm: Turner Duckworth: London, San Francisco & New York
Designers: Janice Bonner, Yar Kukhtin | Client: Samsung | Creative Director: Alice Koswara
Implementation Manager: Josh Michels | Account Services: Gabriela Lovelace, Mallari Batlaw
Account Director: Marco Vaschetto | Main Contributor: Cinthia Wen, Head of Creative

201 LINCOLN MARATHON DECLARATION OF COMPLETION
Design Firm: Bailey Lauerman | Designer: Jim Ma | Client: Lincoln Track Club
Production Manager: Gayle Adams | Chief Creative Officer: Carter Weitz
Printer: Regal Printing | Account Supervisor: Abbie Perry | Main Contributor: Jim Ma

201 HOMAGE TO PELE POSTER | Design Firm: Peterson Ray & Company
Designer: Scott Ray | Client: Self-initiated | Main Contributor: Scott Ray

201 ORCAS ISLAND FILM FESTIVAL 2022 POSTER | Design Firm: Huber Design Werks
Designer: Paul Huber | Client: Orcas Island Film Festival | Photographer: Jovana Rikalo
Creative Directors: Carl Spence, Donna Laslo, Paul Huber | Art Director: Paul Huber
Main Contributor: Paul Huber

201 GOODALL INTEGRATED DESIGN 2022 HOLIDAY POSTER
Design Firm: Goodall Integrated Design | Designer: Derwyn Goodall
Client: Self-initiated | Main Contributor: Derwyn Goodall

202 PEACE IN UKRAINE | Design Firm: Drive Communications | Designer: Michael Graziolo
Client: Graphis Designers for Peace Poster Competition | Main Contributor: Michael Graziolo

202 BEING&NOTHINGNESS | Design Firm: Cul-box | Designer: Wu Qixin
Client: Jean-Paul Sartre | Main Contributor: Wu Qixin

202 STOCKADE FAIRE '22 | Design Firm: IF Studio | Designer: Hisa Ide
Client: Stockade Faire | Creative Director: Toshiaki Ide | Design Director: Hisa Ide
Project Manager: Christine Beattie | Managing Partner: Amy Frankel | Main Contributor: Hisa Ide

202 THE UNITED STATES OF NRAMERICA | Design Firm: Patrick Finley
Designer: Patrick Finley | Client: Self-initiated | Main Contributor: Patrick Finley

202 REFRAME CLIMATE AWARENESS | Design Firm: Goodall Integrated Design
Designer: Derwyn Goodall | Client: Self-initiated | Main Contributor: Derwyn Goodall

202 A GLOBAL MISSION FOR REAL CHANGE | Design Firm: Goodall Integrated Design
Designer: Derwyn Goodall | Client: Taiwan International Image Design Invitational Exhibit
Main Contributor: Derwyn Goodall

202 GLORY TO UKRAINE | Design Firm: Kunstwerk | Designer: Douglas Thomas
Client: Graphis Designers for Peace Poster Competition | Design Associate: Henry Becker
Main Contributor: Douglas Thomas

202 BEIJING OPERA INTERNATIONAL BIENNALE POSTER
Design Firm: Underline Studio | Designer: Fidel Peña | Client: Beijing Opera International Poster
Biennale 2022 | Creative Directors: Fidel Peña, Claire Dawson | Printer: Flash Reproductions
Main Contributor: Underline Studio

202 STRAY DOG | Design Firm: Cul-box | Designer: Wu Qixin | Client: Stray Dog

203 WOMAN. LIFE. FREEDOM. SUPPORT IRANIAN WOMEN. | Design Firm: Braley Design
Designer: Michael Braley | Client: Self-initiated | Creative Director: Michael Braley
Main Contributor: Michael Braley

203 SPIRIT OF THE SILK ROAD | Design Firm: Tsushima Design
Designer: Hajime Tsushima | Client: International Poster Design Exhibition of Silkworm Culture
Organizing Committee | Main Contributor: Hajime Tsushima

203 EVERYTHING EVERYWHERE ALL AT ONCE CAMPAIGN | Design Firm: AV Print
Designers: AV Print, James Jean | Client: A24 | Main Contributor: AV Print

203 RUTHLESS | Design Firm: SJI Associates | Designer: Christian Luis
Clients: Chika Offurum, American Experience Films | President: Suzy Jurist
Art Director: David O'Hanlon | Copywriter: David O'Hanlon | Main Contributor: SJI Associates

204 THE US AND THE HOLOCAUST | Design Firm: SJI Associates
Designer: SJI Associates | Client: PBS Creative Services | President: Suzy Jurist
Art Director: David O'Hanlon | Copywriter: Carole Mayer | Main Contributor: SJI Associates

204 INTERVIEW WITH THE VAMPIRE | Design Firm: ARSONAL | Designer: ARSONAL
Clients: AMC, AMC+, Ed Sherman, VP Brand & Design Kevin Vitale, SVP Creative,
Nancy Hennings, VP Production Brand & Design | Art Director: ARSONAL
Creative Director: ARSONAL | Copywriter: ARSONAL
Main Contributors: ARSONAL, AMC, AMC+

204 SAMSUNG GALAXY WATCH5 PRO LAUNCH POSTER
Design Firm: Turner Duckworth: London, San Francisco & New York | Designer: Jack Powell
Client: Samsung | Design Director: Glenn Chan | Creative Director: Carolyn Ashburn
Implementation Manager: Josh Michels | Account Services: Christy Kim
Account Director: Marco Vaschetto | Main Contributor: Cinthia Wen, Head of Creative

205 CREATING PEACE | Design Firm: Hyungjoo Kim Design Lab
Designer: Hyungjoo A. Kim | Client: Nanjing International Poster Biennial for Peace
Main Contributor: Hyungjoo A. Kim

205 HEED THE CALL | Design Firm: Preston Spire | Designer: Fernando Palomino
Client: Minnesota Wild | Chief Creative Officer: Chris Preston
Creative Director: Charlie Tournat | Associate Creative Director: Brett Essman
Senior Designer: Fernando Palomino | Senior Studio Artist: Mike Fritz
Senior Project Manager: Kelsey Winter | Account Director: Ron Hall
Main Contributor: Fernando Palomino

205 SOUTH PARK TOWER POSTERS | Design Firm: IF Studio | Designer: Hisa Ide
Client: Brodsky | Creative Director: Toshiaki Ide | Design Director: Hisa Ide
Creative Strategist: Sarah Tan | Photographers: Michael Imlay, Wei and Xi
Managing Partner: Amy Frankel | Account Manager: Mercedes Barba
Main Contributors: Hisa Ide, Toshiaki Ide

205 JESSE WILLIAMSON CELEBRATION POSTER | Design Firm: Koester Design
Designer: Ken Koester | Client: Clampitt Paper | Copywriters: Don Clampitt, Ken Koester
Printers: Dave Carpenter, Jarvis Press | Paper: Clampitt Paper Company
Main Contributor: Koester Design

205 MADDIE MEYER EXHIBIT POSTER SERIES
Design Firm: Ohio University's School of Visual Communication
Designer: Adonis Durado | Client: Self-initiated | Photographer: Maddie Meyer
Main Contributor: Adonis Durado, Designer & Art Director

205 OPHELIA'S ELECTRIC SOAPBOX POSTERS | Design Firm: Sukle Advertising & Design
Designer: Katie Dondale | Client: Ophelia's Electric Soapbox | Creative Director: Mike Sukle
Associate Creative Director: Curtis Smith | Art Director: Katie Dondale
Project Manager: Kathleen Ryan | Agency Producer: Michon Schmidt
Agency: Sukle Advertising & Design | Digital Artist: Matt Carpenter
Director of Client Services: Amy Taylor | Account Services: Alexis Supangan
Main Contributor: Sukle Advertising & Design

205 RAT RACE AND IN PEOPLE'S HOUR OF NEED
Design Firm: Te-Sian Shih's Design Studio | Designer: Te-Sian Shih
Clients: Taiwanese American Arts Council, New York Student Mental Health Organization
(NYSMHO) | Main Contributor: Te-Sian Shih

205 MEAT MENU CAMPAIGN POSTERS | Design Firm: Dunn&Co.
Designer: Mitch Feickert | Client: Smokey Bones | Chief Creative Officer: Troy Dunn
Associate Creative Director: Max Dempster | Art Director: Mitchell Goodrich
Copywriter: Michala Jackson | Strategy: Nicole Sullivan, Rylie Nightengale
Senior Designer: Matt Mewis | Executive Creative Director: Chris Corley
Director of Client Services: Melissa Ebanks | Senior Account Executive: Jessica Hall
Main Contributor: Mitch Feickert

206 FROM THE BACKGROUND TO THE FOREGROUND
Design Firms: SO DSGN, Makeshift Studios, Not Real, O0, Twisted Poly, Microsoft Brand Studio
Designers: SO DSGN, Makeshift Studios, Not Real, O0, Twisted Poly, Microsoft Brand Studio
Client: Microsoft | Main Contributors: Andrew Spiziri, Bruna Darini, Colin Day, Harin Lee,
Jooyeon Chae, Kaity Butcher, Lori Gross, Makeshift Studios, Not Real, O0, Phyllis Murphy,
Pia Rodriguez, SO DSGN, Sven Seger, Twisted Poly, Aleksey Fedorov

206 SHER TREMONTE WEBSITE | Design Firm: Decker Design | Designer: Lynda Decker
Client: Sher Tremonte | Photographer: John Madere | Project Manager: Shannon Hughes
Developer: MANYFOLD | Main Contributor: Interactive Designer: Ryan Breeser

207 INSIGHT CHRISTMAS SOCKS | Design Firm: Insight Creative
Designer: Christopher Gough Palmer | Client: Self-initiated | Creative Director: Brian Slade
Writer: Steven Giannoulis | Strategy: Steven Giannoulis | Project Director: Mason Smith
Production: Kirsty Drummond, Rainer Leisky | Account Directors: Paul Saris, Mason Smith
Main Contributor: Insight Creative

207 CRANBROOK ON THE GREEN: ARTIST-DESIGNED MINI-GOLF
Design Firm: Unsold Studio | Designers: Meaghan Barry, Lilian Crum
Client: Cranbrook Art Museum | Main Contributors: Meaghan Barry, Lilian Crum

207 GREGORY ISAKOV MERCHANDISE | Design Firm: Tielemans Design
Designer: Anton Tielemans | Client: Gregory Alan Isakov | Hand Lettering: Peter Horridge
Main Contributor: Anton Tielemans

207 JISOO BAN: PERSONAL BRAND IDENTITY & MERCHANDISE DESIGN
Design Firm: Whimsical Studio | Designer: Jang Won Lee | Client: Jisoo Ban
Photographer: Jang Won Lee | Main Contributor: Jang Won Lee

207 LAFAYETTE AMERICAN HORROR STORY | Design Firm: Lafayette American
Designer: Sarah Bills | Client: Self-initiated | Creative Director: Sarah Bills
Associate Creative Director: Philip Bator | Main Contributor: Sarah Bills

207 COUCH POTATOES & OTHER LOCKDOWN RECIPES | Design Firm: Insight Creative
Designers: Brian Slade, Kellie Pruden, Josephine Ross, Ella Cross, Ying Chu
Client: Self-initiated | Design Directors: Edwin Hooper, Christopher Gough Palmer
Creative Director: Brian Slade | Strategy Directors: Steven Giannoulis, Mike Tisdall
Production Manager: Rainer Leisky | Production: Joanne Otto, Kirsty Drummond, Chrissy Saw
Producers: Kylie Rose, Ravenne Jariol | Digital Director: Jeremy Sweetman
Account Manager: Emma Thompson | Account Directors: Claire Evans, Paul Saris,
Gabe Graham, Mason Smith, Monique Wallace, Tanya Smith | Additional Title: Anna Spreys
Main Contributor: Insight Creative

207 TEIKNA DESIGN LOOK BOOK | Design Firm: Teikna Design
Designers: Claudia Neri, Elisa Stagnoli | Client: Self-initiated | Printer: Tiburtini SRL
Main Contributor: Claudia Neri

208 LAFAYETTE AMERICAN PUZZLE 2022 | Design Firm: Lafayette American
Designer: Lafayette American | Client: Self-initiated | Main Contributor: Lafayette American

208 ZETA LITHOGRAPH | Design Firm: Freaner Creative & Design
Designer: Ariel Freaner | Client: ZETA Weekly | Creative Director: Ariel Freaner
Illustrator: Ariel Freaner | Digital Artist: Ariel Freaner | Main Contributor: Ariel Freaner

208 HAPPY BIRTHDAY | Design Firm: DesignOut Lab. | Designer: YiFei Hu
Client: Self-initiated | Creative Director: YiFei Hu | Typography Design: YiFei Hu
Main Contributor: YiFei Hu

208 NEW RELIC GROK—GENERATIVE AI | Design Firms: New Relic, The Design Farm
Designers: New Relic, The Design Farm | Client: Self-initiated
Chief Creative Director: Chris Taylor | Creative Directors: Ty Jeppesen, Moe Hung
Main Contributors: Chris Taylor, Moe Hung, Ty Jeppesen

208 GD PROMOTION: A POINT SET IN MOTION
Design Firm: UIW Graphic Design Department | Designers: Doris Palmeros, Teresa Treviño
Client: Self-initiated | Main Contributor: Doris Palmeros

209 SUMMER/WINTER 2022 | Design Firm: John Sposato Design & Illustration
Designer: John Sposato | Client: Self-initiated | Main Contributor: John Sposato

209 414 DAY JERSEY | Design Firm: Traction Factory | Designer: Eric Taggart
Client: Milwaukee Admirals | Art Director: Eric Taggart | Design Director: David Brown
Copywriter: Tom Dixon | Production Artist: Jenni Wierzba | Project Manager: Liz Wilson
Account Director: Shannon Egan | Main Contributor: Traction Factory

210 CHOTE MIYA RESTAURANT SIGNAGE AND MURAL DESIGN
Design Firm: Open Door Design Studio (ODDS) | Designer: Shantanu Suman
Clients: Jimmy Rizvi, Chote Miya | Photographer: Katrine Moite
Interior Designer: Shaila Rizvi | Main Contributor: Shantanu Suman

210 3 FORKS BAR AND RESTAURANT | Design Firm: Ellen Bruss Design
Designer: Ken Garcia | Client: Lone Mountain Land Company | Art Director: Ken Garcia
Creative Director: Ellen Bruss | Main Contributor: Ellen Bruss Design

211 NEIMAN MARCUS SHOPPING BAG | Design Firm: Neiman Marcus Creative Services
Designers: Lori Dibble, Stephen Arevalos | Client: Self-initiated
Writers: Stacey Yervasi, Meredith Frazier | Design Manager: Stephen Arevalos
Senior Design Director: Lori Dibble | Photographer: J Gonzalez Photography
Main Contributors: Lori Dibble, Stephen Arevalos

211 BAREFOOT + NFL PARTNERSHIP | Design Firm: Gallo Creative
Designer: Paulina Showalter | Client: Barefoot Cellars | Creative Director: Kristina Hinton
Design Manager: Lisa Toth | Main Contributor: Paulina Showalter, Design Manager

211 THE OUTLETS OF MAUI CAMPAIGN | Design Firm: House of Current
Designer: Wendy Lowden | Client: M&J Wilkow | Art Director: Sarah Wiggins
Creative Director: Wendy Lowden | Production Manager: Scott Brannon
Photographer: Scott Lowden | Account Manager: Stefanie Demoff
Account Director: Lisa Maloof | Main Contributor: Wendy Lowden

212 BLACK BOX CHILI PROGRAM | Design Firm: Gallo Creative
Designers: Baub Mercurio, Chris Heron | Client: Black Box
Creative Director: Kristina Hinton | Main Contributor: Baub Mercurio, Senior Designer

212 WOMEN'S ROWING | Design Firm: Nancy Stahl | Designer: Nancy Stahl
Client: United States Postal Service | Illustrator: Nancy Stahl
Art Director: Ethel Kessler | Main Contributor: Nancy Stahl

213 KWANZAA | Design Firm: Studio A | Designer: Antonio Alcalá
Client: United States Postal Service | Artist: Erin Robinson
Art Director: Antonio Alcalá | Main Contributor: Erin Robinson

213 TITLE IX | Design Firm: Melinda Beck Illustration & Design | Designer: Melinda Beck
Client: United States Postal Service | Typographer: Melinda Beck
Artist: Melinda Beck | Art Director: Derry Noyes | Main Contributor: Melinda Beck

213 HANUKKAH | Design Firm: Jeanette Kuvin Oren | Designer: Jeanette Kuvin Oren
Client: United States Postal Service | Artist: Jeanette Kuvin Oren | Art Director: Ethel Kessler
Main Contributor: Jeanette Kuvin Oren

214 MOUNTAIN FLORA | Design Firm: Kessler Design Group
Designer: Ethel Kessler | Client: United States Postal Service
Artist: Lili Arnold | Art Director: Ethel Kessler | Main Contributor: Lili Arnold

214 EUGENIE CLARK | Design Firm: Amanda Phingbodhipakkiya
Designer: Amanda Phingbodhipakkiya | Client: United States Postal Service
Artist: Amanda Phingbodhipakkiya | Art Director: Antonio Alcalá
Main Contributor: Amanda Phingbodhipakkiya

214 MARIACHI | Design Firm: Rafael López | Designer: Rafael López
Client: United States Postal Service | Artist: Rafael López
Art Director: Derry Noyes | Main Contributor: Rafael López

215 VERCETTI REGULAR | Design Firm: Filippos Fragkogiannis
Designer: Richard Mandona | Client: Self-initiated | Creative Director: Filippos Fragkogiannis
Category: Sans-Serif | Styles: Regular | Realease Date: 8 September 2022
Contributors: Matthieu Salvaggio, David Súid, Adrien Midzic, Valerio Monopoli, Christian Gruber
Country: Greece | Language: Latin | Website: https://filipposfragkogiannis.com
Link: https://filipposfragkogiannis.com/fonts/vercetti-regular
Main Contributor: Filippos Fragkogiannis

215 UPSIDE | Design Firm: Erica Holeman | Designer: Erica Holeman
Client: Self-initiated | Main Contributor: Erica Holeman

215 LONG TERM T-SHIRT | Design Firm: Filippos Fragkogiannis
Designer: Filippos Fragkogiannis | Client: Self-initiated
Production Company: Print Social | Typeface: BBBouquet Bold by Lobbby24
Release Date: June 2022 | Category: Typography | Country: Greece | Language: English
Link: https://www.weareprintsocial.com/campaigns/long-term
Website: https://filipposfragkogiannis.com | Main Contributor: Filippos Fragkogiannis

216 GROUNDED IN THEIR ROOTS, GROWING INTO THE FUTURE
Design Firm: Wolff Olins | Designers: Ryan Bugden, Jess Yan, Daniel Renda, Colin Kinsley
Client: Instacart | Creative Director: Daniel Renda | Associate Creative Director: Jess Yan
Typeface Designer: Ryan Bugden | Strategy Director: Michele Kim | Marketing: Tal Ayala Kamin
Motion Designers: Jason Chen, Draeger Gillespie | Account Manager: Ian Carroll
Account Executive: Marina Ammirato | Main Contributor: Wolff Olins

216 POR TIJUANA - 1ST STATE OF THE UNION ANNOUNCEMENT
Design Firm: Freaner Creative & Design | Designer: Ariel Freaner
Clients: City of Tijuana, Jorge Astiazaran | Digital Artist: Ariel Freaner
Creative Director: Ariel Freaner | Main Contributor: Ariel Freaner

216 MANAIA TYPOGRAPHY | Design Firm: Insight Creative
Designer: Christopher Gough Palmer | Client: Self-initiated | Creative Director: Brian Slade
Artist: James Molnar | Strategy Director: Steven Giannoulis | Main Contributor: Insight Creative

217 KRESS PROGRAM IN PAINTINGS CONSERVATION WEBSITE
Design Firm: C&G Partners | Designers: Glenn Jeon, Maya Kopytman, Bartek Lewandowski
Client: Kress Program in Paintings Conservation | Producer: Shuyler Nazareth
Other: Red de Leon, Technical Director
Main Contributor: Maya Kopytman, Partner / Creative Director

217 PLANK ROAD WEBSITE | Design Firm: IF Studio | Designer: Hisa Ide
Client: Brodsky | Design Director: Hisa Ide | Creative Strategist: Sarah Tan
Creative Director: Toshiaki Ide | Web Designers: Sung Yong Kim, Yingchi Hsu
Photographer: Blair Getz Mezibov | Managing Partner: Amy Frankel
Account Manager: Mercedes Barba | Main Contributors: Hisa Ide, Toshiaki Ide

218 VETERANS MUSEUM MEMORIAL WEBSITE | Design Firm: Freaner Creative & Design
Designer: Ariel Freaner | Client: Veterans Museum Memorial | Creative Director: Ariel Freaner
Digital Artist: Ariel Freaner | Main Contributor: Ariel Freaner

218 OI ONE WATCHES 3-D MICRO WEBSITE
Design Firm: Freaner Creative & Design | Designer: Ariel Freaner | Client: Self-initiated
Digital Artist: Ariel Freaner | Creative Director: Ariel Freaner | Main Contributor: Ariel Freaner

218 JMR DEVELOPERS AND CONSTRUCTION LANDING PAGE
Design Firm: Freaner Creative & Design | Designer: Ariel Freaner | Client: JMR Developers
Digital Artist: Ariel Freaner | Creative Director: Ariel Freaner | Main Contributor: Ariel Freaner

218 NATIONAL RESOURCES WEBSITE | Design Firm: Mermaid, Inc.
Designer: Sharon Lloyd McLaughlin | Client: National Resources
Web Developer: Bart McLaughlin | Marketing Manager: Lauren Calabria
Main Contributor: Sharon Lloyd McLaughlin

218 CALIMAX WEBSITE SPECIAL ADVERTISING LANDING PAGES
Design Firm: Freaner Creative & Design | Designer: Ariel Freaner
Clients: Calimax, Ignacio Fimbres, Jose Fimbres | Creative Director: Ariel Freaner
Digital Artist: Ariel Freaner | Main Contributor: Ariel Freaner

218 OTAY MESA CHAMBER OF COMMERCE SPECIAL LANDING PAGES
Design Firm: Freaner Creative & Design | Designer: Ariel Freaner
Client: Otay Mesa Chamber of Commerce | Creative Director: Ariel Freaner
Digital Artist: Ariel Freaner | Illustrator: Ariel Freaner | Main Contributor: Ariel Freaner

218 GLOCAL NEWS MEDIA WEBSITE LANDING PAGES
Design Firm: Freaner Creative & Design | Designer: Ariel Freaner | Client: Glocal Media News
Web Designer: Ariel Freaner | Creative Director: Ariel Freaner | Illustrator: Ariel Freaner
Digital Artist: Ariel Freaner | Main Contributor: Ariel Freaner

218 VICTORINOX ORIGINAL LF WATCHES LOCAL MICROSITE
Design Firm: Freaner Creative & Design | Designer: Ariel Freaner | Client: Victorinox
Creative Director: Ariel Freaner | Digital Artist: Ariel Freaner | Main Contributor: Ariel Freaner

Index

DESIGN FIRMS

CLIENTS

CHIEF CREATIVE DIRECTORS/CHIEF CREATIVE OFFICERS

EXECUTIVE CREATIVE DIRECTORS

CREATIVE DIRECTORS/ASSOCIATE CREATIVE DIRECTORS

DESIGN DIRECTORS/SENIOR DESIGN DIRECTORS/DESIGN MANAGERS/DESIGN LEADS/DESIGN ASSOCIATES

ART DIRECTORS/SENIOR ART DIRECTORS

DIRECTORS/GENERAL DIRECTORS/EXECUTIVE DIRECTORS/DIGITAL DIRECTORS/MANAGING DIRECTORS

SENIOR DESIGNERS/ASSISTANT DESIGNERS/JUNIOR DESIGNERS/DESIGN ASSISTANTS

DESIGNERS

GRAPHIC DESIGNERS

ARTISTS/DIGITAL ARTISTS/ART BUYERS/SENIOR STUDIO ARTISTS/WOOD PRINT ARTISTS

TYPOGRAPHERS/TYPOGRAPHY DESIGNERS/TYPEFACES/TITLES/HAND LETTERING

ILLUSTRATORS/ANIMATORS

MOTION DESIGNERS/WEB DESIGNERS/PRINT DESIGNERS

CONTENT DESIGNERS/CONTENT COORDINATORS/PRODUCTION DESIGNERS/PRODUCT DESIGNERS

EDITOR-IN-CHIEFS/EDITORS/MANAGING EDITORS

WRITERS/AUTHORS

COPYWRITERS/SENIOR COPYWRITERS

PHOTOGRAPHERS/PHOTO EDITORS

RETOUCHERS/PHOTO CORRECTORS/PHOTOGRAPHY STUDIOS/PHOTO DIRECTORS/PHOTOGRAPHER'S ASSISTANTS

DEVELOPERS/CONTENT DEVELOPERS/WEB DEVELOPERS

ARCHITECTS/STRUCTURAL ENGINEERING/SIGN FABRICATORS/FABRICATORS/IMPLEMENTATION MANAGERS

PRINTERS/PRINT PRODUCERS/PREPRESS/PAPERS

PRESIDENTS/VICE PRESIDENTS/SENIOR VICE PRESIDENTS/CHAIRMEN

PRODUCERS/EXECUTIVE PRODUCERS/PRODUCTION COMPANIES/SENIOR PRODUCERS/ART PRODUCERS/AGENCY PRODUCERS

PROJECT MANAGERS/SENIOR PROJECT MANAGERS/PROJECT DIRECTORS/PROJECT COORDINATORS

PRODUCTION MANAGERS

PRODUCTION/PRODUCTION COMPANIES/PRODUCTION ARTISTS/MANUFACTURERS

ACCOUNT DIRECTORS, EXECUTIVES, MANAGERS, SUPERVISORS/SENIOR ACCOUNT EXECUTIVES, DIRECTORS

PLATINUM

Anna and Elena Balbusso (Balbusso Twins Artist Duo)
www.balbussotwins.myportfolio.com
Milan, Lombardy
Italy
Tel +1 212 333 2551
balbusso.twins@gmail.com

AV Print
www.avsquad.com
101 S. La Brea Ave., 2nd Floor
Los Angeles, CA 90036
United States
Tel +1 323 790 8888
printaccountteam@avsquad.com

Carmit Design Studio
www.carmitdesign.com
2208 Bettina Ave.
Belmont, CA 94002
United States
Tel +1 650 283 1308
carmit@carmitdesign.com

Journey Group
www.journeygroup.com
418 4th St. NE
Charlottesville, VA 22902
United States
Tel +1 434 961 2500
gregb@journeygroup.com

Michael Pantuso Design
www.pantusodesign.com
820 S. Thurlow St.
Hinsdale, IL 60521
United States
Tel +1 312 318 1800
michaelpantuso@me.com

Namseoul University
www.nsu.ac.kr
91 Daehak-ro, Seonghwan-eup, Seobuk-gu
Cheonan-si,
Chungcheongnam-do
South Korea
Tel +82 41 580 2000
mijung6@nate.com

Omdesign
www.omdesign.pt
Rua de Vila Franca,
54 - Leça da Palmeira
Matosinhos 4450-802
Portugal
Tel +351 229 982 960
comunicacao@omdesign.pt

PepsiCo Design & Innovation
www.design.pepsico.com
350 Hudson St., 2nd Floor
New York, NY10014
United States
Tel +1 646 681 5095
emily.ford.contractor@pepsico.com

Studio Eduardo Aires
www.eduardoaires.com
Alexandre Braga, N94-1E
Porto 4000-049
Portugal
Tel +351 226 169 080
mail@eduardoaires.com

Sun Design Production
China
1023484137@qq.com

Underline Studio
www.underlinestudio.com
247 Wallace Ave., 2nd Floor
Toronto, ON M6H 1V5
Canada
Tel +1 416 341 0475
studiomanager@underlinestudio.com

Wonderlust Industries, Inc.
www.lyleowerko.com
958 N. Western Ave., #507
Los Angeles, CA 90068
United States
Tel +1 917 319 0715
lyle@owerko.com

GOLD

Ahoy Studios
www.ahoystudios.com
456 Broadway, 3rd Floor
New York, NY 10013
United States
Tel +1 212 645 0565
denise@ahoystudios.com

American Museum of Natural History (In-House)
www.amnh.org
200 Central Park West
New York, NY 10024
United States
Tel +1 212 769 5100
rdemetrio@amnh.org

Another Collective
www.anothercollective.pt
Rua França Júnior,
Mercado Municipal
Espaço 6 Matosinhos 4450-137
Portugal
Tel +35 191 322 8450
mgmt@anothercollective.pt

ARSONAL
www.arsonal.com
3524 Hayden Ave.
Culver City, CA 90232
United States
Tel +1 310 815 8824
info@arsonal.com

BEK Design
www.bek.com.tr
Tesvikiye Caddesi 49/9 Nisantasi
Istanbul N/A 34365
Turkey
Tel +212 343 9910
kagan@bek.com.tr

Bekar Haus D.O.O.
www.bekar.haus
Fra Andrije Kačića Miošića 12
Zagreb 10000
Croatia
Tel +38 591 984 1739
dizajn.net@icloud.com

CF Napa Brand Design
www.cfnapa.com
2787 Napa Valley Corporate Drive
Napa, CA 94558
United States
Tel +1 707 265 1891
cfnapa@cfnapa.com

Chad Michael Studio
www.chadmichaelstudio.com
Dallas, TX
United States
chad@chadmichaelstudio.com

Code Switch
www.codeswitchdesign.com
262 Crescent St.
Northampton, MA 01060
United States
jansabach@mac.com

DAEKI and JUN
www.b-d-b.xyz
Hannamdong Yongsan-gu
Seoul 04418
South Korea
win.daekiandjun@gmail.com

Dankook University
www.dankook.ac.kr
Room 317, College of Arts, 126
Jukjeon, Suji Yongin Gyeonggi
448-701
South Korea
Tel +82 10 9117 0517
finvox3@naver.com

Darkhorse Design, LLC
www.darkhorsedesign-usa.com
8 Whitefield Lane
Lancaster, PA 17602
United States
Tel +1 717 844 2888
roberttalarczyk@mac.com

Decker Design
www.deckerdesign.com
14 W. 23rd St., 3rd Floor
New York, NY 10010
United States
Tel +1 212 633 8588
shannonh@deckerdesign.com

Duas Faces Design
www.duasfaces.net
Rua Barata Feyo, 140 - 2°
Andar - Escritório 2.5
Porto Porto 4250-076
Portugal
Tel +35 191 245 2123
duasfaces.design@gmail.com

El Paso, Galería de Comunicación
www.elpasocomunicacion.com
c. Sagunto, 13 Madrid
Madrid 28010
Spain
Tel +34 91 594 2248
elpaso@elpasocomunicacion.com

Faceout Studio
www.faceoutstudio.com
414 W. Washington Ave.,
Suite B
Sisters, OR 97759
United States
Tel +1 541 323 3220
torrey@faceoutstudio.com

Freaner Creative & Design
www.freaner.com
113 W. G St., No. 650
San Diego, CA 92101
United States
Tel +1 619 870 4699
arielfreaner@freaner.com

Goodall Integrated Design
www.goodallintegrated.com
35 Tyrrel Ave.
Toronto, ON M6G 2G1
Canada
Tel +1 416 435 3653
derwyn@goodallintegrated.com

Greenleaf Book Group
www.greenleafbookgroup.com
PO Box 91869
Austin, TX 78709
United States
Tel +1 512 891 6100
lmacqueen@greenleafbookgroup.com

Haotian Dong
www.howteeann.com
New York, NY
United States
Tel +1 929 393 1997
hocheon01@gmail.com

HILLS
China
jianshan816@126.com

Hufax Arts/FJCU
www.facebook.com/HufaxArts
No. 17, 13F., Lane 47, Sec. 1,
Baofu Road
Yonghe Dist., New Taipei City
23444
Taiwan
Tel +88 693 399 1520
hufa@ms12.hinet.net

IF Studio
www.ifstudiony.com
306 W. 48th St., Apt 40C
New York, NY 10036
United States
Tel +1 203 550 1432
toshi@ifstudiony.com

Insight Creative
www.insightcreative.co.nz
L1 21 Allen St.
Te Aro, Wellington 6037
New Zealand
Tel +644 801 6644
mason@insightcreative.co.nz

Jingyi Cai
Virginia
United States
jingyi.cai.99@gmail.com

Judd Brand Media
www.juddbrandmedia.com
249 S. Highway 101, #322
Solana Beach, CA 92075
United States
pjudd7@gmail.com

Kate Borman Creative Design Co.
www.kbcdco.com
United States
Tel +1 914 980 9651
kate@kbcdco.com

Keith Harris Design
www.gmx.de
Markgrafenstrasse 17 Konstanz
Baden
Württemberg 78467
Germany
Tel +171 873 4894
keith.harris@gmx.de

Lippincott
www.lippincott.com
499 Park Ave.
New York, NY 10022
United States
Tel +1 212 521 0000
christina.clemente@lippincott.com

Lisa Winstanley Design
www.lisawinstanley.com
52J Nanyang View 02-17
639668
Singapore
Tel +83 437 608
lwinstanley@ntu.edu.sg

Mark Braught Studios
www.markbraught.com
740 Ashley Laine Walk
Lawrenceville, GA 30043
United States
Tel +1 770 912 3120
markbraught@markbraught.com

May & Co.
www.mayandco.com
6316 Berwyn Lane
Dallas, TX 75214
United States
Tel +1 214 536 0599
dougm@mayandco.com

Mermaid, Inc.
www.mermaidnyc.com
479 W. 152nd St., Studio 1B
New York. NY 10031
United States
Tel +1 212 337 0707
sharon@mermaidnyc.com

Michael Pantuso Design
www.pantusodesign.com
820 S. Thurlow St.
Hinsdale, IL 60521
United States
Tel +1 312 318 1800
michaelpantuso@me.com

Microsoft Brand Studio
www.microsoft.com
One Microsoft Way
Redmond, WA 98052
United States
Tel +1 425 638 7777
kaitlin.butcher@microsoft.com

Mink
www.mink.agency
Sidra Tower, Office 1005,
Sufouh Gardens
Dubai 922202
United Arab Emirates
Tel +97 15 0250 4177
moe@mink.agency

Nexus Designs
www.nexusdesigns.com.au
260 Park St.
South Melbourne, VIC 3146
Australia
Tel +61 3 9690 2277
sallye@nexusdesigns.com.au

Paco Macias Velasco Studio
www.pacomaciasvelasco.mx
Leopoldo Romano 6-1
Adolfo López Mateos Cuajimalpa
Distrito Federal 05280
Mexico
Tel +1 52 55 1498 5864
pacomaciasvelasco@yahoo.
com.mx

PepsiCo Design & Innovation
www.design.pepsico.com
350 Hudson St., 2nd Floor
New York, NY10014
United States
Tel +1 646 681 5095
emily.ford.contractor@pepsico.
com

Poulin + Morris Inc.
www.poulinmorris.com
919 Bernardi Lane
Palm Springs, CA 92262
United States
Tel +1 917 750 1009
richard@poulinmorris.com

Purdue University
www.purdue.edu
552 W. Wood St.
West Lafayette, IN 47907
United States
lzhang3@purdue.edu

Randy Clark Graphic Design
www.randyclark.myportfolio.com
88 Daxue Road, Ouhai District
Wenzhou, Zhejiang
China
Tel +86 5775 5870 000
randyclarkmfa@icloud.com

Resource Branding
www.resourceatlanta.com
3453 Pierce Dr., No.140
Chamblee, GA 30341
United States
Tel +1 404 625 8856
rick@resourceatlanta.com

Roking Art Design
China
1632001733@qq.com

Ron Taft Brand Innovation & Media Arts
www.rontaft.com
2934 Beverly Glen Circle, #372
Los Angeles, CA 90077
United States
Tel +1 310 339 2442
ron@rontaft.com

Rose
www.rosedesign.co.uk
The Old School, 70 St.
Marychurch St.
London, SE16 4HZ
United Kingdom
Tel +44 020 7394 2800
hello@rosedesign.co.uk

Shenzhen Excel Brand Design Consultant Co., Ltd.
3rd Floor, Yidasheng Building,
Wuhe Ave. South 5th,
Longgang District,
518129 Shenzhen
China
Tel +86 755 8282 1024
695938757@qq.com

Simon Peter Bence
www.spx.hu
Cinege ut 1-3., A.
Budapest 1121
Hungary
simonpeterbence@gmail.com

SJI Associates
www.sjiassociates.com
127 W. 24th St., 2nd Floor
New York, NY 10011
United States
Tel +1 212 391 4140
david@sjiassociates.com

Skolos-Wedell
www.skolos-wedell.com
177 Everett Ave.
Providence, RI 02906
United States
Tel +1 617 291 8888
nancy@skolos-wedell.com

Spire Agency
www.spireagency.com
5055 Keller Springs Road,
Suite 510
Dallas, TX 75001
United States
Tel +1 214 477 2097
awards@spireagency.com

Stranger & Stranger
www.strangerandstranger.com
68 Greenpoint Ave.
Brooklyn, NY 11222
United States
Tel +1 212 625 2441
nyc@strangerandstranger.com

Studio 5 Designs Inc.
www.studio5designsph.net
Unit 3022,
Beacon Residences-Tower 3
Chino Roces Ave., Legaspi
Village
Makati City 1229
The Philippines
Tel +63 917 885 5507
marilyo@yahoo.com

Studio Eduard Cehovin
www.designresearch.si
Ul. Milana Majcna 35
Ljubljana SI-1000
Slovenia
Tel +386 40 458 657
eduard.cehovin@siol.net

Studio Eduardo Aires
www.eduardoaires.com
Alexandre Braga, N94-1E
Porto 4000-049
Portugal
Tel +351 226 169 080
mail@eduardoaires.com

Studio Hinrichs
www.studio-hinrichs.com
2064 Powell St.
San Francisco, CA 94133
United States
Tel +1 415 543 1776
reception@studio-hinrichs.com

Sun Design Production
China
1023484137@qq.com

Sunday Afternoon
www.sundayafternoon.us
343 Canal St., 5th Floor
New York, NY 10013
United States
Tel +1 845 206 1383
juancarlos@sundayafternoon.us

Sungoo Design
Furong Pavilion, Phase 2,
Hepingli, Heping Road
Longhua District,
518000 Shenzhen
China
Tel +86 151 2397 9553
384158339@qq.com

Texas Tech University Press
www.ttupress.org
2310 70th St., Apt 244
Lubbock, TX 79412
United States
Tel +1 512 470 6235
hdgaskamp@gmail.com

TGD
www.tengundesign.com
120 3rd Ave.
South Edmonds, WA 98020
United States
Tel +1 425 361 7284
johanng@tengundesign.com

Tianyun Jiang
New York, NY
United States
jty.19971019@gmail.com

Toppan Inc.
www.toppan.com/en
9F, 1-3-3, Suido Bunkyo-ku
Tokyo 112-8531
Japan
Tel +81 3 5840 2192
mescal@mac.com

Traction Factory
www.tractionfactory.com
247 S. Water St.
Milwaukee, WI 53204
United States
Tel +1 414 944 0900
tf_awards@tractionfactory.com

Tsushima Design
www.tsushima-design.com
1-17-204, 1-17, Matsukawa-cho,
Minami-ku
Hiroshima 7320826
Japan
Tel +81 82 567 5586
info@tsushima-design.com

UP-Ideas
www.up-ideas.com
740 Ashley Laine Walk
Lawrenceville, GA 30043
United States
Tel +1 770 912 3120
roger.sawhill@gmail.com

Vanderbyl Design
www.vanderbyl.com
511 Tokay Lane
St. Helena, CA 94574
United States
Tel +1 415 543 8447
michael@vanderbyl.com

Ventress Design Works
www.ventress.com
1565 N. Shaver St.
Portland, OR 97227
United States
Tel +1 615 833 2108
tom@ventress.com

Wainscot Media
www.mccandlissandcampbell.
com
433 N. Windsor Ave.
Brightwaters, NY 11718
United States
Tel +1 631 252 3527
mcandcstudio@gmail.com

SILVER

3D Identity
www.3d-identity.com
2501 Blake St.
Denver, CO 80202
United States
Tel +1 303 471 4334
lduits@workplaceelements.com

Abby Ryan Design
www.abbyryandesign.com
2164 E. Cumberland St.
Philadelphia, PA 19125
United States
Tel +1 917 523 2817
abby@abbyryandesign.com

AG Creative Group
www.agcreative.ca
100-2250 Boundary Road
Burnaby, BC V5M 3Z3
Canada
Tel +1 604 559 1411
stew@agcreative.ca

Ahoy Studios
www.ahoystudios.com
456 Broadway, 3rd Floor
New York, NY 10013
United States
Tel +1 212 645 0565
denise@ahoystudios.com

Airspace
www.airspace.nyc
41 Flatbush Ave.
Brooklyn, NY 11217
United States
Tel +1 917 593 5200
jill@airspace.nyc

Amanda Phingbodhipakkiya
www.alonglastname.com
Brooklyn, NY
United States
amanda@alonglastname.com

American Museum of Natural History (In-House)
www.amnh.org
200 Central Park West
New York, NY 10024
United States
Tel +1 212 769 5100
rdemetrio@amnh.org

Anagraphic
www.anagraphic.hu
Attila út 105.
Budapest 1012
Hungary
Tel +36 1 202 0555
anagraphic@anagraphic.hu

andKuo
www.andkuo.com
United States
sherry@andkuo.com

Anna Jordan
www.annatype.com
55 Lomb Memorial Drive
Rochester, NY 14623
United States
Tel +1 401 688 0123
annatype@gmail.com

Anne M. Giangiulio Design
www.annegiangiulio.com
500 W. University Avenue
El Paso, TX 79968
United States
Tel +1 915 222 1134
annegiangiulio@gmail.com

Another Collective
www.anothercollective.pt
Rua França Júnior, Mercado
Municipal
Espaço 6 Matosinhos 4450-137
Portugal
Tel +35 191 322 8450
mgmt@anothercollective.pt

ARSONAL
www.arsonal.com
3524 Hayden Ave.
Culver City, CA 90232
United States
Tel +1 310 815 8824
info@arsonal.com

ArtHouse Design
www.arthousedenver.com
2373 Central Park Blvd., #204
Denver, CO 80238
United States
Tel +1 303 892 9816
mikayla@arthousedenver.com

AS IF Media Group
www.behance.net/DiegoPinil
laAmaya
1438 28th Ave., Apt. 2R
New York, NY 11102
United States
Tel +1 929 319 2259
dpamaya17@gmail.com

Asad Pervaiz
www.workbyindex.com
500 Grand St., Apt. A9A
New York, NY 10002
United States
Tel +1 347 743 8935
asad@workbyindex.com

ASHA & Co.
www.ashaandco.uk
Formal House, 60 St.
George's Place
Cheltenham, Gloucestershire
GL50 3PN
United Kingdom
Tel +44 01242 574111
kerry@ashaandco.uk

Asterisk
www.asteriskdesign.com
1710 Houston St.
Austin, TX 78756
United States
Tel +1 512 371 1618
pam@asteriskdesign.com

Atelier Nunes e Pã, lda
www.ateliernunesepa.pt
Rua de Fez
143 Oporto 4150-329
Portugal
Tel +35 122 619 8310
administracao@ateliernunese
pa.pt

Atelier Starno
www.starno.com
9 Endeavor Cove
Corte Madera, CA 94925
United States
Tel +1 415 279 7301
ag@starno.com

AV Print
www.avsquad.com
101 S. La Brea Ave., 2nd Floor
Los Angeles, CA 90036
United States
Tel +1 323 790 8888
printaccountteam@avsquad.com

B&W Studio
www.bandwstudio.co.uk
Unit 7 - Carlton Mills
Pickering Mount, Leeds LS12
2QG
United Kingdom
Tel +44 0113 263 6600
lee@bandwstudio.co.uk

Bailey Lauerman
www.baileylauerman.com
1299 Farnam St., 9th Floor
Omaha, NE, 68102
United States
Tel +1 402 514 9400
sfaden@baileylauerman.com

BEAMY
www.wearebeamy.com
1375 Huaihai Middle Road, 18A
Shanghai 200031
China
Tel +86 215 423 3675
hello@wearebeamy.com

BEK Design
www.bek.com.tr
Tesvikiye Caddesi 49/9 Nisantasi
Istanbul N/A 34365
Turkey
Tel +212 343 9910
kagan@bek.com.tr

BexBands
www.bexbrands.com
4411 Park Blvd., #201
San Diego, CA 92116
United States
Tel +1 619 298 1932
becky@bexbrands.com

BigRockXR
www.bigrockxr.com
Los Angeles, CA
United States
info@bigrockxr.com

Blk:ops
www.blkops.co
4434 Mariota Ave.
Toluca Lake, CA 91602
United States
Tel +1 818 452 9340
info@blk-ops.com

BOLTBOLT
www.joopark.info
California
United States
hello@joopark.info

Botond Vörös
www.botondvoros.com
Hungary
Tel +36 70 228 5187
iambotondvoros@gmail.com

Brad Holland
www.bradholland.net
96 Greene St.
New York, NY 10012
United States
brad-holland@rcn.com

Braley Design
www.braleydesign.com
750 Shaker Drive, #202
Lexington, KY 40504
United States
Tel +1 415 706 2700
braley@braleydesign.com

Brand Bar Communications
www.brandbar.eu
Naphegy Utca 21.
Budapest Pest 1016
Hungary
Tel +36 70 380 9419
kapcsolat@brandbar.hu

BRIGADE
www.weareBRIGADE.com
296 Nonotuck St.
Florence, MA 01062
United States
Tel +1 413 387 0307
kirsten@weareBRIGADE.com

BroadcastMed
www.broadcastmed.com
195 Farmington Ave.
Farmington, CT 06032
United States
Tel +1 800 880 8618
jennifer.barlow@broadcastmed.
com

Bulletproof
www.wearebulletproof.com
Singapore
Tel +65 906 05 420
hannah.ganesh@wearebullet
proof.com

Butterfly Cannon
www.butterflycannon.com
Holborn Tower, 137-144 High
Holborn
London, WC1V 6PL
United Kingdom
chris.joscelyne@butterflycannon.
com

By Scala
www.byscala.com
Portugal
vilaverde@byscala.com

C&G Partners
www.cgpartnersllc.com
116 E. 16th St., Floor 10
New York, NY 10003
United States
Tel +1 212 532 4460
sehba@cgpartnersllc.com

Carlos Caicedo
31 Ormont Road
Chatham, NJ 07928
United States
Tel +1 917 445 5923
carloscedo@yahoo.com

CF Napa Brand Design
www.cfnapa.com
2787 Napa Valley Corporate Drive
Napa, CA 94558
United States
Tel +1 707 265 1891
cfnapa@cfnapa.com

Chiquitucto Group
www.chiquitucto.com
New York, NY
United States
ednewyork@gmail.com

Clinton Carlson Design | University of Notre Dame
www.clintoncarlson.com
1244 Garland Road
South Bend, IN 46614
United States
Tel +1 970 402 2599
ccarlso6@nd.edu

Coastlines Creative Group
www.coastlinescreative.com
77 Walter Hardwick Ave., Ste. 412
Vancouver, BC V5Y 0C6
Canada
Tel +1 604 785 1017
byron@coastlinescreative.com

Code Switch
www.codeswitchdesign.com
262 Crescent St.
Northampton, MA 01060
United States
jansabach@mac.com

Coley Porter Bell
www.coleyporterbell.com
636 11th Ave.
New York, NY 10036
United States
Tel +1 212 237 4628
jenn.szekely@coleyporterbell.
com

Cue
www.designcue.com
520 Nicollet Mall, Suite 500
Minneapolis, MN 55402
United States
Tel +1 612 465 0030
info@designcue.com

Cul-box
China
art008.hi@163.com

DAEKI and JUN
www.b-d-b.xyz
Hannamdong Yongsan-gu
Seoul 04418
South Korea
win.daekiandjun@gmail.com

Dankook University
www.dankook.ac.kr
Room 317, College of Arts, 126
Jukjeon, Suji Yongin Gyeonggi
448-701
South Korea
Tel +82 10 9117 0517
finvox3@naver.com

Danyang Ma
www.danyangma.com
2840 Jackson Ave., Apt. 4E
Long Island City, NY 11101
United States
danyangm0717@gmail.com

Dear Fellow Design Studio
www.dearfellow.co
United States
courtney-spencer@dearfellow.co

Decker Design
www.deckerdesign.com
14 W. 23rd St., 3rd Floor
New York, NY 10010
United States
Tel +1 212 633 8588
shannonh@deckerdesign.com

Design Bureau Izvorka Juric
www.designbureauizvorkajuric.
com
Jaruščica 21
CRO – 10020 Zagreb
Croatia
izvorka@designbureauizvorka-
juric.com

DesignOut Lab.
www.designout.cargo.site
A-Z Town, No. 500, East Section
2, Ring Road 2
Chenghua District, Chengdu City,
Sichuan Province 610051
China
649579994@qq.com

Dessein
www.dessein.com.au
130 Aberdeen St.
Northbridge Perth, WA 6003
Australia
Tel +61 892 280 661
geoff@dessein.com.au

DeVito/Verdi
www.devitoverdi.com
330 Hudson St., 16th Floor
New York, NY 10013
United States
Tel +1 212 431 4694
nryan@devitoverdi.com

DLR Group
www.dlrgroup.com
7290 W. 133rd Street
Overland Park, KS 66213
United States
Tel +1 402 975 9510
awells@dlrgroup.com

DPL Jones
www.dpljones.com
901 Sheridan Drive
West Chester, PA 19382
United States
Tel +1 484 716 0909
djones2@wcupa.edu

Drive Communications
www.drivecom.com
237 W. 16th St., 2nd Floor
New York, NY 10011
United States
Tel +1 212 989 5103
mail@drivecom.com

Dunn&Co.
www.dunn-co.com
202 S. 22nd St.
Tampa, FL 33605
United States
Tel +1 813 350 7990
dunn@dunn-co.com

Ehmija Design
www.ehmija.com
Bakersfield, CA
United States
daisy.n.rodriguez@gmail.com

El Paso, Galería de Comunicación
www.elpasocomunicacion.com
c. Sagunto, 13 Madrid
Madrid 28010
Spain
Tel +34 91 594 2248
elpaso@elpasocomunicacion.
com

Ellen Bruss Design
www.ebd.com
2500 Walnut St., #401
Denver, CO 80205
United States
Tel +1 303 830 8323
competitions@ebd.com

Elmwood
www.elmwood.com
7 Gee St.
London, EC1V 3RD
United Kingdom
Tel +44 (0)20 7637 0884
alex.ehrensperger@elmwood.
com

Entro
www.entro.com
33 Harbour Square, Suite 202
Toronto, ON M5J 2G2
Canada
Tel +44 020 7637 0884
valerie@entro.com

Erica Holeman
www.ericaholeman.com
Dallas, TX
United States
erica.holeman@unt.edu

Faceout Studio
www.faceoutstudio.com
414 W. Washington Ave.,
Suite B
Sisters, OR 97759
United States
Tel +1 541 323 3220
torrey@faceoutstudio.com

Filippos Fragkogiannis
www.filipposfragkogiannis.com
Dimitrakopoulou 129
Kallithea Attica 17676
Greece
Tel +69 432 27 559
studio@filipposfragkogiannis.com

forceMAJEURE Design
www.forcemajeure.design
219 36th St.
Brooklyn, NY 11232
United States
Tel +1 212 625 0708
rmahieu@forcemajeure.design

Fournir
www.fournir.co
16642 Lake Prince Lane
Houston, TX 77044
United States
Tel +1 832 465 4498
dguillory@fournir.co

Freaner Creative & Design
www.freaner.com
113 W. G St., No. 650
San Diego, CA 92101
United States
Tel +1 619 870 4699
arielfreaner@freaner.com

Full Punch
www.fullpunch.com
770-1199 W. Pender St.
Vancouver, BC V6E 2R1
Canada
Tel +1 604 910 0744
chris.zawada@fullpunch.com

Gallo Creative
www.gallo.com
Modesto, CA
United States
Tel +1 877 687 9463
greta.rider@ejgallo.com

Gensler
www.gensler.com
San Francisco, CA
United States
minjung_lee@gensler.com

Goodall Integrated Design
www.goodallintegrated.com
35 Tyrrel Ave.
Toronto, ON M6G 2G1
Canada
Tel +1 416 435 3653
derwyn@goodallintegrated.com

GRAPHICS & DESIGNING INC.
www.gandd.co.jp/profile-onimaru
3-3-1 Shirokanedai
Minato-ku Tokyo 108-0071
Japan
gd_onimaru@mac.com

Greenleaf Book Group
www.greenleafbookgroup.com
PO Box 91869
Austin, TX 78709
United States
Tel +1 512 891 6100
lmacqueen@greenleafbookgroup.com

Hatch Design
www.hatchsf.com
1600 Bryant St., #411633
San Francisco, CA 94141
United States
Tel +1 628 895 0067
inquiries@hatchsf.com

Haystack Needle LLC DBA Tailfeather
www.haystackneedle.com
2280 8th Ave.
New York, NY 10027
United States
Tel +1 917 971 7979
hello@haystackneedle.com

Holly Tienken Design
www.hollytienken.design
Jersey City, NJ
United States
tienken@kutztown.edu

House of Current
www.houseofcurrent.com
154 Krog St., Suite 160
Atlanta GA 30307
United States
Tel +1 404 816 0094
sbrannon@houseofcurrent.com

Hoyne
www.hoyne.com.au
99 Elizabeth St., Level 5
Sydney, NSW 2000
Australia
Tel +1 419 290 768
hello@hoyne.com.au

Huber Design Werks
www.huberdesignwerks.com
239 Bromley Drive
Eastsound, Orcas Island, WA 98245
United States
Tel +1 415 412 8690
paulhuber26@gmail.com

Hyungjoo Kim Design Lab
www.cla.purdue.edu/academic/rueffschool/ad/vcd/Faculty.html
Rueff School of Design, Art, and Performance
552 W. Wood St.
West Lafayette, IN 47907
United States
Tel +1 765 494 3071
hakim@purdue.edu

IF Studio
www.ifstudiony.com
306 W. 48th St., Apt 40C
New York, NY 10036
United States
Tel +1 203 550 1432
toshi@ifstudiony.com

INNOCEAN USA
www.innoceanusa.com
180 5th St., Suite 200
Huntington Beach, CA 92648
United States
Tel +1 714 861 5371
awardshows@innoceanusa.com

Insight Creative
www.insightcreative.co.nz
L1 21 Allen St.
Te Aro, Wellington 6037
New Zealand
Tel +644 801 6644
mason@insightcreative.co.nz

Jasmine Silang
www.jasminesilang.com
Toronto, ON
Canada
jasminenicolesilang@gmail.com

Jeanette Kuvin Oren
www.kuvinoren.com
Woodbridge, CT
United States
jeanette@kuvinoren.com

Joba Studio
www.jobastudio.com
2200 Kraft Drive, Suite 1050
Blacksburg, VA, 24060
United States
Tel +1 540 553 8143
hello@jobastudio.com

John Sposato Design & Illustration
www.johnsposato.carbonmade.com
179 Hudson Terrace
Piermont, NY 10968
United States
Tel +1 845 300 7591
johnsposatodesign@gmail.com

Jordan Fretz Design
www.jordanfretzdesign.com
5 Monpetit Place
Simpsonville, SC 29680
United States
jordanfretzdesign@gmail.com

Judd Brand Media
www.juddbrandmedia.com
249 S. Highway 101, #322
Solana Beach, CA 92075
United States
pjudd7@gmail.com

Karnes Coffey Design
www.karnescoffey.com
4908 Darrowby Road
Glen Allen, VA 23060
United States
Tel +1 804 424 0850
christine@karnescoffey.com

Kate Borman Creative Design Co.
www.kbcdco.com
Connecticut
United States
Tel +1 914 980 9651
kate@kbcdco.com

Kathy Mueller Design, LLC
www.kmuellerdesign.com/home
Philadelphia, PA
United States
kmueller@temple.edu

Keith Harris Design
www.gmx.de
Markgrafenstrasse 17 Konstanz
Baden
Württemberg 78467
Germany
Tel +171 873 4894
keith.harris@gmx.de

Kessler Design Group
www.kesslerdesigngroup.com
5225 Pooks Hill Road, Apt. 619 North
Bethesda, MD 20814
United States
Tel +1 301 907 3233
info@kesslerdesigngroup.com

KINDAI Graphic Art Course Laboratory
www.facebook.com/ANkiyoung
KINDAI University,
E-Campus, A-2F
Sinkamikosaka 228-3,
Higashi-osaka Osaka 577-0813
Japan
Tel +81 90 9319 9396
aky6815@hotmail.com

Koester Design
www.koesterdesign.com
756 Kilbridge Lane
Coppell, TX 75019
United States
Tel +1 972 571 7843
ken@koesterdesign.com

Kunstwerk
883 N. 1200 East
Provo, UT 84604
United States
Tel +1 810 369 7854
dougthomas31@gmail.com

Lafayette American
www.lafayetteamerican.com
5000 Grand River Ave.
Detroit, MI 48208
United States
Tel +1 313 757 2720
doug.patterson@mac.com

Legis Design
273 Ramona Ave.
Sierra Madre, CA 91024
United States
legis@pa2.so-net.ne.jp

Lewis Communications
www.lewiscommunications.com
2030 1st Ave. N
Birmingham, AL 35203
United States
Tel +1 205 980 0774
ryan@lewiscommunications.com

Linshaobin Design Shenzhen
SOHO Building, Room 1705
Suning Plaza, No. 90
Changping Road,
Longhu District,
Shantou Guangdong 515000
China
Tel +86 135 5644 7610
write000@sina.com

Lippincott
www.lippincott.com
499 Park Ave.
New York, NY 10022
United States
Tel +1 212 521 0000
christina.clemente@lippincott.com

Lisa Sirbaugh Creative
www.lisasirbaughcreative.com
31 W. Patrick St., Suite 209
Frederick, MD 21701
United States
Tel +1 301 788 6455
lisa@lisasirbaugh.com

Makeshift Studios
www.makeshiftstudios.com
Issaquah, WA
United States
hello@makeshiftstudios.com

Mark Braught Studios
www.markbraught.com
740 Ashley Laine Walk
Lawrenceville, GA 30043
United States
Tel +1 770 912 3120
markbraught@markbraught.com

Matchstic
www.matchstic.com
437 Memorial Drive SE,
Unit A7
Atlanta, GA 30312
United States
Tel +1 770 203 1236
marketing@matchstic.com

Media.Work
www.media.work
453 S. Spring St., Ste 400 PMB 102
Los Angeles, CA 90013
United States
Tel +1 813 502 7416
alexandra@media.work

Melinda Beck Illustration & Design
www.melindabeck.com
Brooklyn, NY
United States
Tel +1 347 463 2306
studio@melindabeck.com

Mermaid, Inc.
www.mermaidnyc.com
479 W. 152nd St., Studio 1B
New York. NY 10031
United States
Tel +1 212 337 0707
sharon@mermaidnyc.com

Microsoft Brand Studio
www.microsoft.com
3900 148th Ave.
Redmond, WA 98052
United States
Tel +1 425 638 7777
kaitlin.butcher@microsoft.com

Microsoft Cloud Marketing Brand Studio
www.microsoft.com
One Microsoft Way
Redmond, WA 98052
United States
Tel +1 425 638 7777
kaitlin.butcher@microsoft.com

Mingxin Cheng
www.mingxin-cheng.com/design
New York, NY
United States
dullahan174@yahoo.com

MiresBall
www.miresball.com
2605 State St.
San Diego CA 92103
United States
Tel +1 619 234 6631
marketing@miresball.com

Mirko Ilic Corp.
www.mirkoilic.com
41 Union Square West,
Room 824
New York, NY 10003
United States
Tel +1 917 957 6040
studio@mirkoilic.com

MJH Life Sciences
www.mjhlifesciences.com
2 Clarke Drive, Suite 101
Cranbury, NJ 08512
United States
Tel +1 609 716 7777
kbaron@mjhlifesciences.com

Museum of Texas Tech University, Communications & Marketing
www.mysticity.net
2500 Broadway W
Lubbock, TX 79409
United States
mystie.do@gmail.com

Nancy Stahl
www.nancystahl.com
New York, NY
United States
Tel +1 212 362 8779
nancy@nancystahl.com

Neiman Marcus Creative Services
www.neimanmarcus.com
Dallas, TX 75209
United States
Tel +1 512 466 0092
stephenarevalos@gmail.com

New Relic
www.newrelic.com
188 Spear St., Suite 1000
San Francisco, CA 94105
United States
Tel +1 415 539 3008
mhung@newrelic.com

Noise 13
www.noise13.com
1616 16th St., Suite 370
San Francisco, CA 94103
United States
Tel +1 415 957 1313
info@noise13.com

Northwest Missouri State University
www.feixuemei.info
800 University Dr.
Maryville, MO 64468
United States
Tel +1 660 562 1212
feixuefeixuemei@gmail.com

Not Real
www.notreal.tv
Buenos Aires
Argentina
hello@notreal.tv

O0
www.ozero.design
Kyiv
Ukraine
krupa@ozero.design

ODDSENSE
www.oddsensenyc.com
119 8th St., #100
Brooklyn, NY 11215
United States
Tel +1 646 584 8157
emerson@oddsensenyc.com

Ohio University's School of Visual Communication
www.ohio.edu/scripps-college/viscom
Schoonover Center
1 Ohio University
Athens, OH 45701
United States
Tel +1 740 593 4883
durado@ohio.edu

Omdesign
www.omdesign.pt
Rua de Vila Franca,
54 - Leça da Palmeira
Matosinhos 4450-802
Portugal
Tel +351 229 982 960
comunicacao@omdesign.pt

OnRepeat Studio
www.onrepeat.studio
Copenhagen Court Pell St.,
Flat 105
London, SE8 5ES
United Kingdom
joao@onrepeat.net

Open Door Design Studio (ODDS)
www.shantanusuman.com
Art & Journalism Building
3401 N. Tillotson Ave., AJ 401
Muncie, IN 47306
United States
Tel +1 352 792 5100
sumanshantanu@gmail.com

Patrick Finley
www.behance.net/pfinley
2385 Lake Vista Drive
Christiansburg, VA 24073
United States
Tel +1 608 235 9273
pfinley05@gmail.com

PepsiCo Design & Innovation
www.design.pepsico.com
350 Hudson St., 2nd Floor
New York, NY10014
United States
Tel +1 646 681 5095
emily.ford.contractor@pepsico.com

Peterson Ray & Company
www.peterson.com
230 Snowden Road
Seagoville, TX 75159
United States
Tel +1 972 809 0153
scott@peterson.com

Pinter-Parrott
www.pinterparrott.com
Los Angeles, CA
United States
fran@pinterparrott.com

Playstead
www.playstead.design
San Diego, CA
United States
nathan@playstead.design

PMDESIGN
www.pmdesign.pt
R. Travanca Cima
570 Santa Maria da Feira
4520-819
Portugal
Tel +351 914 066 898
mail@pmdesign.pt

Preston Spire
www.prestonspire.com
105 S. 5th Ave., Suite 200
Minneapolis, MN 55401
United States
Tel +1 612 843 4000
invoices@prestonspire.com

Rafael López
www.rafaellopez.com
Mexico
rafaellopezstudio@gmail.com

Ralph Appelbaum Associates
www.raai.com
88 Pine St.
New York, NY 10005
United States
Tel +1 212 334 8200
caseylynn@raai.com

Randy Clark Graphic Design
www.randyclark.myportfolio.com
88 Daxue Road, Ouhai District
Wenzhou, Zhejiang
China
Tel +86 5775 5870 000
randyclarkmfa@icloud.com

RedPeak Global
www.red-peak.com
Level 21, Suite C, No.7, Xinyi
Road, Section 5
Taipei 110
Taiwan
Tel +88 628 101 6216
hello@red-peak.com

Resource Branding
www.resourceatlanta.com
3453 Pierce Dr., No.140
Chamblee, GA 30341
United States
Tel +1 404 625 8856
rick@resourceatlanta.com

Roger Archbold
www.rogerarchbold.com
PO Box 327
Chewton, VIC 3451
Australia
roger@rogerarchbold.com

Roking Art Design
China
1632001733@qq.com

Rose
www.rosedesign.co.uk
The Old School,
70 St. Marychurch St.
London, SE16 4HZ
United Kingdom
Tel +44 020 7394 2800
hello@rosedesign.co.uk

Rozina Design
www.rozinavavetsi.crevado.com
1855 Broadway
New York, NY 10023
United States
Tel +1 516 686 1254
rvavetsi@nyit.edu

Salesforce
www.salesforce.com
1 Market St.
San Francisco, CA 94105
United States
Tel +1 800 664 9073
slavalais@salesforce.com

Savannah College of Art & Design
www.scad.edu
P.O. Box 3146
Savannah, GA 31402
United States
Tel +1 912 525 6830
awards@scad.edu

SAYGRID
www.saygrid.com
Philadelphia, PA
United States
Tel +1 215 880 4406
andee@saygrid.com

Shenzhen Excel Brand Design Consultant Co., Ltd.
3rd Floor, Yidasheng Building,
Wuhe Ave. South 5th,
Longgang District,
518129 Shenzhen
China
Tel +86 755 8282 1024
695938757@qq.com

Siena Scarff Design
www.sienascarff.com
302 Harvard St.
Cambridge, MA 02139
United States
Tel +1 857 756 8372
siena@sienascarff.com

SJI Associates
www.sjiassociates.com
127 W. 24th St., 2nd Floor
New York, NY 10011
United States
Tel +1 212 391 4140
david@sjiassociates.com

SML Design
www.smldesign.com.au
1 Kent Lane
Prahran, VIC 3181
Australia
Tel +40 381 4001
vanessa@smldesign.com.au

SO DSGN
www.so-design.co
1719 S. Clinton St.
Chicago, IL 60616
United States
info@so-design.co

Spire Agency
www.spireagency.com
5055 Keller Springs Road,
Suite 510
Dallas, TX 75001
United States
Tel +1 214 477 2097
awards@spireagency.com

Spud Studio
Jinping Road, Lane 788,
Room 401, No. 204
Shanghai 200240 PRC
China
Tel +1 376 424 4466
miaoxiao@126.com

Stan Church Incorporated
www.wallacechurch.com
330 E. 48th St., 3rd Floor
New York, NY 10017
United States
Tel +1 212 755 2903
rich@wallacechurch.com

Sterling
www.sterlingbrands.com
720 California St.,
2nd Floor
San Francisco, CA 94108
United States
Tel +1 415 427 1200
hello@sterlingbrands.com

Still Room
www.still-room.com
2169 Lemoyne St.
Los Angeles CA 90026
United States
Tel +1 213 453 0370
studio@still-room.com

Stranger & Stranger
www.strangerandstranger.com
68 Greenpoint Ave.
Brooklyn, NY 11222
United States
Tel +1 212 625 2441
nyc@strangerandstranger.com

Studio 5 Designs Inc.
www.studio5designsph.net
Unit 3022,
Beacon Residences-Tower 3
Chino Roces Ave.,
Legaspi Village
Makati City 1229
The Philippines
Tel +63 917 885 5507
marilyo@yahoo.com

Studio A
www.studioa.com
1019 Queen St.
Alexandria, VA 22314
United States
Tel +1 703 684 7729
info@studioa.com

Studio Craig Byers
www.studiocraigbyers.com
4609 Del Sol Blvd.
Sarasota, FL 34243
United States
Tel +1 917 597 4388
byers.craig@gmail.com

Studio DelRey
www.studiodelrey.com.br
Brazil
studiodelrey@gmail.com

Studio DUY
www.studioduy.com
Vietnam
duydao95@gmail.com

Studio Eduardo Aires
www.eduardoaires.com
Alexandre Braga, N94-1E
Porto 4000-049
Portugal
Tel +351 226 169 080
mail@eduardoaires.com

STUDIO INTERNATIONAL
www.studio-international.com
Buconjiceva 43/III
Zagreb HR-10 000
Croatia
Tel +385 98 276 932
boris@studio-international.com

StudioNorth
www.studionorth.com
1616 Green Bay Road
Chicago, IL 60064
United States
Tel +1 847 785 2146
marks@studionorth.com

Sukle Advertising & Design
www.sukle.com
2430 W. 32nd Ave.
Denver, CO 80211
United States
Tel +1 303 964 9100
info@sukle.com

Sunday Afternoon
www.sundayafternoon.us
343 Canal St., 5th Floor
New York, NY 10013
United States
Tel +1 845 206 1383
juancarlos@sundayafternoon.us

Sungoo Design
Furong Pavilion, Phase 2,
Hepingli, Heping Road
Longhua District,
518000 Shenzhen
China
Tel +86 151 2397 9553
384158339@qq.com

Susanne Pinter and Francesca Pinter-Parrott
www.pinterparrott.com
Los Angeles, CA
United States
fran@pinterparrott.com

SWA Group
www.swagroup.com
530 Bush St., 6th Floor
San Francisco, CA 94108
United States
Tel +1 415 836 8770
ronjia20@gmail.com

Tangram Strategic Design
www.tangramsd.it
Viale Michelangelo Buonarroti, 10/C
Novara 28100
Italy
Tel +39 0321 35 662
esempi@tangramsd.it

TAYLOR
www.taylor.agency
535 Kings Road,
The Plaza - Unit 3-17
London, SW10 0SZ
United Kingdom
Tel +44 207 351 2345
steven@taylor.agency

Te-Sian Shih's Design Studio
www.lera-shih.squarespace.com
New York, NY
United States
tesian0816@gmail.com

Teiga, Studio.
www.xoseteiga.com
Avd. da Barca 18
Bajo Poio Pontevedra 36163
Spain
Tel +60 715 5211
xoseteiga@gmail.com

Teikna Design
www.teikna.com
Via San Vito
6 Milan 20123
Italy
Tel +39 02 3651 5524
claudia@teikna.com

Test Monki
www.testmonki.com
10800 Gosling Road, #131898
Spring, TX 77393
United States
Tel +1 281 323 4903
suzy@testmonki.com

Texas Tech University Press
www.ttupress.org
2310 70th St., Apt. 244
Lubbock, TX 79412
United States
Tel +1 512 470 6235
hdgaskamp@gmail.com

TGD
www.tengundesign
120 3rd Ave.
South Edmonds, WA 98020
United States
Tel +1 425 361 7284
johanng@tengundesign.com

The Design Farm
www.thedesignfarm.com
United States
mhung@newrelic.com

Tielemans Design
www.tielemansdesign.com
1535 Roughrider Circle
Henderson, NV 89014
United States
Tel +1 702 946 5511
anton@tielemansdesign.com

Toben
www.toben.com.au
1 Danks St., Unit 8
Waterloo, NSW 2017
Australia
Tel +61 280 601 136
thorsten@toben.com.au

TOKY Branding + Design
www.toky.com
3001 Locust St.
St. Louis, MO 63103
United States
Tel +1 314 534 2000
eric@toky.com

Toppan Inc.
www.toppan.com/en
9F, 1-3-3, Suido Bunkyo-ku
Tokyo 112-8531
Japan
Tel +81 3 5840 2192
mescal@mac.com

Total Design
www.totaldesign.com
Pedro de Medinalaan 9
Amsterdam Noord Holland 1086 XK
The Netherlands
Tel +31 20 750 95 00
edwin@totaldesign.com

Traction Factory
www.tractionfactory.com
247 S. Water St.
Milwaukee, WI 53204
United States
Tel +1 414 944 0900
tf_awards@tractionfactory.com

Traina
www.wearetraina.com
10680 Treena St., Suite 520
San Diego, CA 92131
United States
Tel +1 619 567 7100
awards@wearetraina.com

Triplet Design Inc.
www.tsuyoshiomori.com
06 Haneginomori, 1-21-23
Hanegi Setagaya,
Tokyo 156-0042
Japan
Tel +81 3 6265 7273
tsuyoshi@triplet.jp

Truth Collective
www.truthcollective.com
25 Russell St.
Rochester, NY 14607
United States
Tel +1 585 690 0844
awards@truthcollective.com

TSL Group Creative
G/F, Summit Building,
30 Man Yue St.
Hung Hom, Kowloon, 000
Hong Kong
Tel +852 6886 5828
c.chan@ymail.com

Tsushima Design
www.tsushima-design.com
1-17-204, 1-17, Matsukawa-cho, Minami-ku
Hiroshima 7320826
Japan
Tel +81 82 567 5586
info@tsushima-design.com

Turner Duckworth: London, San Francisco & New York
www.turnerduckworth.com
375 Hudson St., Lvl 8
New York, NY 10014
United States
Tel +1 212 463 2400
xavier.drudge@turnerduckworth.com

Twisted Poly
www.twistedpoly.com
Slovenia
nejc@twistedpoly.com

UIW Graphic Design Department
www.uiw.edu/smd/academics/departments/graphic-design/
1001 W. Mulberry Ave.
San Antonio, TX 78201
United States
Tel +1 210 865 0988
kdmlmc@gmail.com

Underline Studio
www.underlinestudio.com
247 Wallace Ave., 2nd Floor
Toronto, ON M6H 1V5
Canada
Tel +1 416 341 0475
studiomanager@underlinestudio.com

Univisual SRL
www.identitymarks.it
Via Lepanto 1
Milano 20125
Italy
Tel +39 335 836 7976
info@identitymarks.it

Unsold Studio
www.unsoldstudio.com
Detroit, MI
United States
Tel +1 978 257 4450
hello@unsoldstudio.com

UP-Ideas
www.up-ideas.com
740 Ashley Laine Walk
Lawrenceville, GA 30043
United States
Tel +1 770 912 3120
roger.sawhill@gmail.com

USADesign
www.fdcommit.tohtech.ac.jp/Profiles/8/0000795/profile.htm l?lang=en
Tohoku Institute of Technology, Shimousa Lab, 6
Futatsusawa, Taihaku-ku,
Sendai-shi Miyagi-ken 9828588
Japan
shimousa@usadesign.jp

VANGUARD Visual Design Ltd.
www.behance.net/a3332565m12649
No. 6, Lane 174, Sec. 2,
Bade Road, Zhongshan Dist.
9F.-2, No. 57, Sec. 3,
Minsheng E. Road, Taipei City
104 104080
Taiwan
Tel +88 691 754 6161
a3332565m1@gmail.com

Ventress Design Works
www.ventress.com
1565 N. Shaver St.
Portland, OR 97227
United States
Tel +1 615 833 2108
tom@ventress.com

Vestígio Design
www.vestigio.com
Rua Chaby Pinheiro, 191 - R/C
Senhora da Hora Matosinhos
4460-278
Portugal
Tel +35 191 879 4080
barbosa@vestigio.com

Vine Creative Studios at Partners + Napier
www.partnersandnapier.com/vine-creative-studios
1 South Clinton Ave., Suite 400
Rochester, NY
United States
Tel +1 585 454 1010
katy.collar@partnersandnapier.com

Vizient Inc.
www.vizientinc.com
290 E. John Carpenter Freeway
Irving, TX 75062
United States
Tel +1 972 830 0000
brand@vizientinc.com

Wainscot Media
www.mccandlissandcampbell.com
433 N. Windsor Ave.
Brightwaters, NY 11718
United States
Tel +1 631 252 3527
mcandcstudio@gmail.com

WaitWhat (In-House)
www.waitwhat.com
393 Canal St., #229
New York, NY 10013
United States
Tel +1 347 469 7370
luisa@waitwhat.com

Wallace Church & Co.
www.wallacechurch.com
330 E. 48th St., 3rd Floor
New York, NY 10017
United States
Tel +1 212 755 2903
rich@wallacechurch.com

Whimsical Studio
www.whimsical-studio.com
E-3/6-ho, 12th Floor,
20 Jangchungdan-ro
13-gil Jung-gu Seoul 04563
South Korea
Tel +82 50 6759 5801
hello@whimsical-studio.com

Wolff Olins
www.wolffolins.com
195 Broadway, Floor 17
New York, NY 10007
United States
Tel +1 212 505 7337
tal.kamin@wolffolins.com

Wuhan Mornice Brand Design Co., Ltd.
China
zhiansheji@qq.com

Xiaomi
www.mi.com
Xiaomi Campus,
Anningzhuang Road,
Haidian District
Beijing 100085
China
Tel +86 130 5109 1837
chenlu@xiaomi.com

Yes& Lipman Hearne
www.yesandlipmanhearne.com
227 W. Monroe St., 21st Floor
Chicago, IL 60606
United States
Tel +1 312 356 8000
ebraithwaite@lipmanhearne.com

YSFT Inc.
www.yihvang.com
New York, NY
United States
yihvang@gmail.com

Yup, It's a Hub
www.sudsud.pt
Rua Nova da Trindade nº1,
2º ESQ.
1200-301 Lisboa
Portugal
Tel +351 968 396 472
joao@sudsud.pt

It's clear there is strong, thoughtful, and beautiful work being produced around the globe.

Antonio Alcalá, *Designer, Art Director, Founder, & Co-owner, Studio A*

BEST IN THE AMERICAS

ARGENTINA

BRAZIL

CANADA

MEXICO

UNITED STATES

BEST IN EUROPE/AFRICA

CROATIA

GERMANY

GREECE

HUNGARY

ITALY

NETHERLANDS

PORTUGAL

SPAIN

SLOVENIA

UNITED KINGDOM

UKRAINE

BEST IN ASIA/OCEANIA

AUSTRALIA

CHINA

HONG KONG

JAPAN

NEW ZEALAND

PHILIPPINES

SINGAPORE

SOUTH KOREA

TAIWAN

TURKEY

UNITED ARAB EMIRATES

VIETNAM

Graphis Titles

Poster Annual 2024

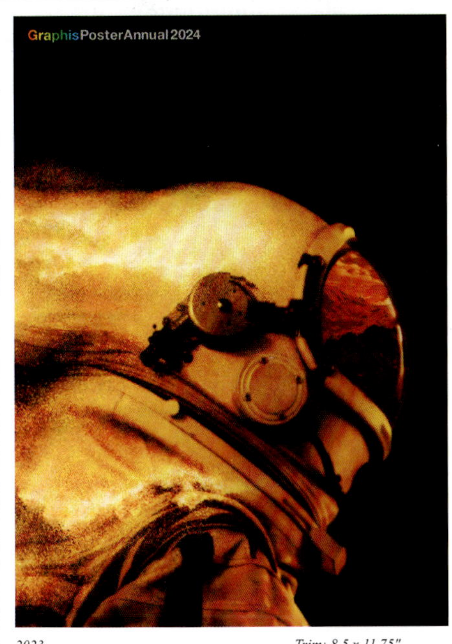

2023
Hardcover: 256 pages
200-plus color illustrations
Trim: 8.5 x 11.75"
ISBN: 978-1-954632-23-3
US $75

Awards: Graphis presents 14 Platinum, 100 Gold, and 266 Silver awards, along with 211 Honorable Mentions.
Platinum Winners: This year's group of international designers include Antonio Castro Design, Atelier Radovan Jenko, Chemi Montes, Holger Matthies, Kashlak, Kiyoung An Graphic Art Course Laboratory, Mirko Ilic Corp., MOCEAN, Peter Diamond Illustration, Šesnić&Turković, Supremat, The Refinery, and Underline Studio.
Content: This book features international Platinum, Gold, and Silver-winning work. Honorable Mentions are also presented. Award-winning work from the judges and a section of Platinum-winning works from 2014 are also included. Platinum and Gold-winning designers discuss their posters and explain the approach they took that resulted in their winning work.

New Talent Annual 2023

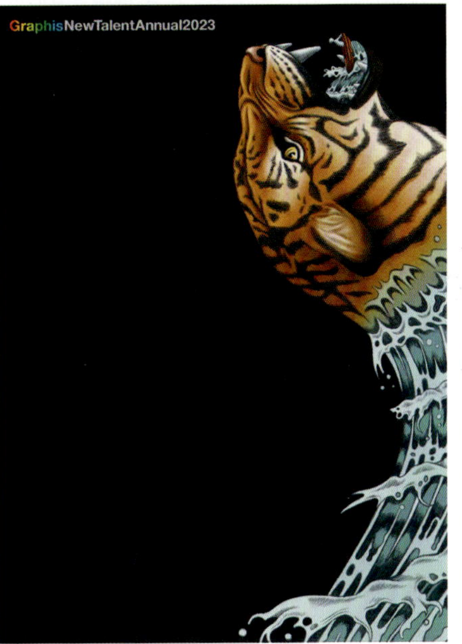

2023
Hardcover: 272 pages
200-plus color illustrations
Trim: 8.5 x 11.75"
ISBN: 978-1-954632-16-5
US $75

Awards: Graphis presents 12 Platinum, 169 Gold, and 344 Silver awards, along with 638 Honorable Mentions.
Platinum-winning Instructors: Advertising: Mark Allen. Design: Elaine Alderette, Brad Bartlett, Brian Boyd, Gayle Donahue, Mads Greve, Seung-Min Han, Réka Holló-Szabó, Miguel Lee, Douglas May, Miles Mazzie, Dong-Joo Park, Søren Patger, Brian Rea, Paul Rogers, Carlos Roncajolo, Simon Sticker, Carter Tindall, Judit Tóth, and Cardon Webb. Photography: Manolo Garcia.
Content: This book contains award-winning entries in Advertising, Design, Photography, and Film/Video. We also present A Decade of New Talent, featuring Platinum-winning works from 2013. All entries are organized by discipline like our professional annuals.

Photography Annual 2023

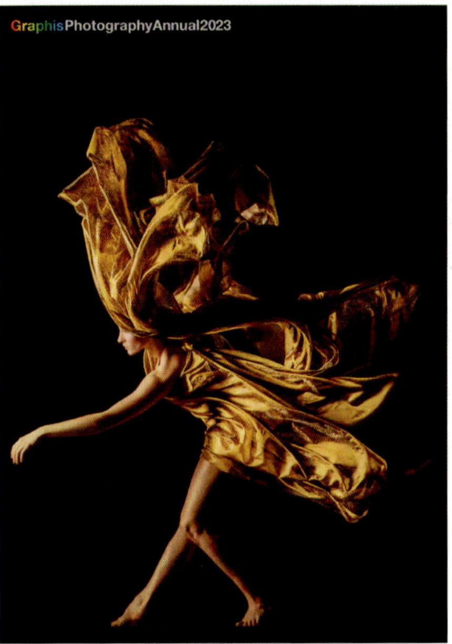

2023
Hardcover: 256 pages
200-plus color illustrations
Trim: 8.5 x 11.75"
ISBN: 978-1-954632-18-9
US $75

Awards: Graphis presents 12 Platinum, 101 Gold, and 218 Silver awards, along with 53 Honorable Mentions.
Platinum Winners: Per Breiehagen, Ross Brown, Alexandra Carr, Andreas Franke, Terry Heffernan, Takahiro Igarashi, John Madere, Eric Melzer, R.J. Muna, Howard Schatz, and Tatijana Shoan.
Content: This book is full of exceptional work by our masterful judges, our Platinum, Gold, and Silver award winners, and our Honorable Mentions. It also includes a retrospective on our Platinum 2013 Photography winners, a list of international photography museums and galleries, and an In Memoriam list of photographers that have passed away this year.

Advertising Annual 2023

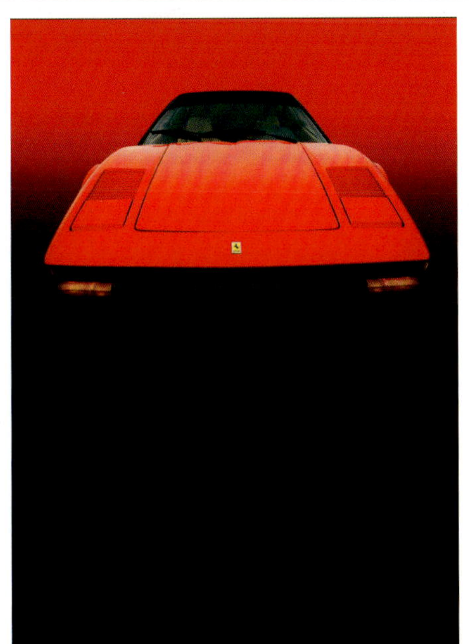

2022
Hardcover: 224 pages
200-plus color illustrations
Trim: 8.5 x 11.75"
ISBN: 978-1-954632-15-8
US $75

Awards: Graphis presents 12 Platinum, 104 Gold, and 72 Silver awards, along with 31 Honorable Mentions.
Platinum Winners: ARSONAL, Centre for Design Research, Dalian RYCX Advertising, Eversana Intouch, Hufax Arts, Ken-Tsai Lee Design Lab, Partners + Napier, PETROL Advertising, Ron Taft Design, and VSA Partners.
Content: This book includes amazing Platinum, Gold, and Silver Award-winning print and video advertisements, as well as Honorable Mentions. Also featured is a selection of award-winning judge's work and our annual In Memoriam for the advertising talent we've lost over the last year.

Packaging 10

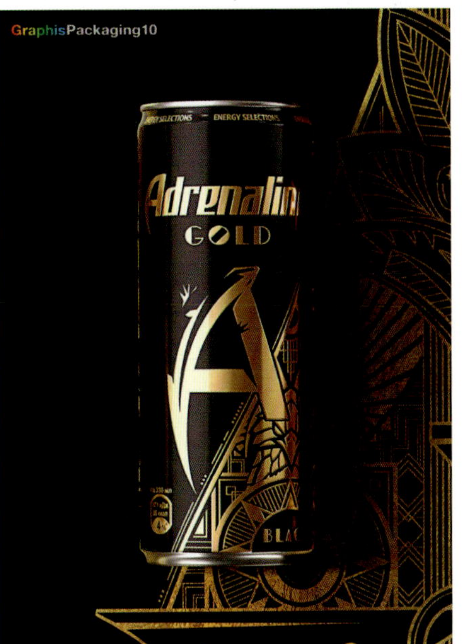

2022
Hardcover: 240 pages
200-plus color illustrations
Trim: 8.5 x 11.75"
ISBN: 978-1-954632-12-7
US $75

Awards: Graphis presents 12 Platinum, 100 Gold, 204 Silver, and 249 Honorable Mentions for innovative work in product packaging.
Platinum Winners: Michele Gomes Bush (Next), Chad Roberts (Chad Roberts Design Ltd.), XiongBo Deng (Shenzhen Lingyun Creative Packaging Design Co., Ltd.) and Lu Chen (Xiaomi), Vishal Vora (Sol Benito), Mattia Conconi (Gottschalk+Ash Int'l), and Frank Anselmo (New York Mets), Ivan Bell (Stranger & Stranger), Brian Steele (SLATE), and the team at PepsiCo Design & Innovation.
Content: This book contains award-winning packaging from the judges, as well as international Platinum, Gold, and Silver-winning packaging designs from designers and design firms from around the world. Honorable Mentions are presented, and a feature of award-winning work from our Packaging 9 Annual is also included.

Protest Posters 2

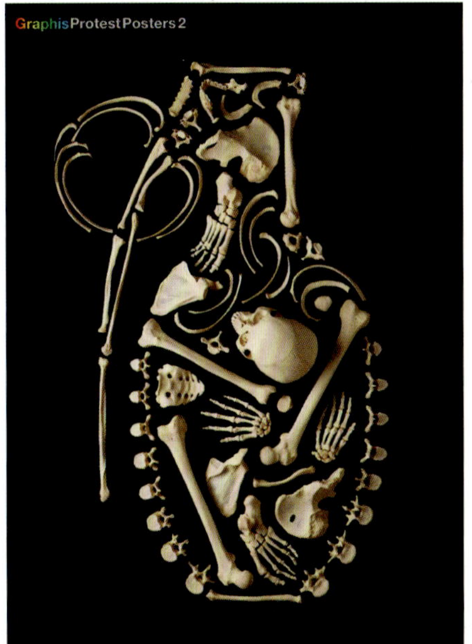

2021
Hardcover: 256 pages
200-plus color illustrations
Trim: 8.5 x 11.75"
ISBN: 978-1-954632-04-2
US $75

Awards: Graphis presents 12 Platinum, 137 Gold, 176 Silver awards, and 94 Honorable Mentions for outstanding talent in photography.
Platinum Winners: Presenting Platinum winners Alireza Nosrati Studio, Andrew Sloan, Dogan Arslan Design, IF Studio, Katarzyna Zapart, Marlena Buczek Smith, Randy Clark, Scott Laserow Posters, Wesam Haddad, and Yossi Lemel.
Judges: Andrea Castelletti, Paul Garbett, Wesam Mazhar Haddad, Woody Pirtle, and Marlena Buczek Smith, and Chikako Oguma.
Content: This book is a source of inspiration with work from talented poster designers that addresses a diverse series of international issues going on in the world today.

Books are available at store.graphis.com